msdn training

2373B: Programming with Microsoft® Visual Basic® .NET

Microsoft®

Course Number: 2373B
Part Number: X09-90418
Released: 02/2002

END-USER LICENSE AGREEMENT FOR MICROSOFT OFFICIAL CURRICULUM COURSEWARE -STUDENT EDITION

PLEASE READ THIS END-USER LICENSE AGREEMENT ("EULA") CAREFULLY. BY USING THE MATERIALS AND/OR USING OR INSTALLING THE SOFTWARE THAT ACCOMPANIES THIS EULA (COLLECTIVELY, THE "LICENSED CONTENT"), YOU AGREE TO THE TERMS OF THIS EULA. IF YOU DO NOT AGREE, DO NOT USE THE LICENSED CONTENT.

1. GENERAL. This EULA is a legal agreement between you (either an individual or a single entity) and Microsoft Corporation ("Microsoft"). This EULA governs the Licensed Content, which includes computer software (including online and electronic documentation), training materials, and any other associated media and printed materials. This EULA applies to updates, supplements, add-on components, and Internet-based services components of the Licensed Content that Microsoft may provide or make available to you unless Microsoft provides other terms with the update, supplement, add-on component, or Internet-based services component. Microsoft reserves the right to discontinue any Internet-based services provided to you or made available to you through the use of the Licensed Content. This EULA also governs any product support services relating to the Licensed Content except as may be included in another agreement between you and Microsoft. An amendment or addendum to this EULA may accompany the Licensed Content.

2. **GENERAL GRANT OF LICENSE.** Microsoft grants you the following rights, conditioned on your compliance with all the terms and conditions of this EULA. Microsoft grants you a limited, non-exclusive, royalty-free license to install and use the Licensed Content solely in conjunction with your participation as a student in an Authorized Training Session (as defined below). You may install and use one copy of the software on a single computer, device, workstation, terminal, or other digital electronic or analog device ("Device"). You may make a second copy of the software and install it on a portable Device for the exclusive use of the person who is the primary user of the first copy of the software. A license for the software may not be shared for use by multiple end users. An "Authorized Training Session" means a training session conducted at a Microsoft Certified Technical Education Center, an IT Academy, via a Microsoft Certified Partner, or such other entity as Microsoft may designate from time to time in writing, by a Microsoft Certified Trainer (for more information on these entities, please visit www.microsoft.com). WITHOUT LIMITING THE FOREGOING, COPYING OR REPRODUCTION OF THE LICENSED CONTENT TO ANY SERVER OR LOCATION FOR FURTHER REPRODUCTION OR REDISTRIBUTION IS EXPRESSLY PROHIBITED.

3. DESCRIPTION OF OTHER RIGHTS AND LICENSE LIMITATIONS

3.1 *Use of Documentation and Printed Training Materials.*

3.1.1 The documents and related graphics included in the Licensed Content may include technical inaccuracies or typographical errors. Changes are periodically made to the content. Microsoft may make improvements and/or changes in any of the components of the Licensed Content at any time without notice. The names of companies, products, people, characters and/or data mentioned in the Licensed Content may be fictitious and are in no way intended to represent any real individual, company, product or event, unless otherwise noted.

3.1.2 Microsoft grants you the right to reproduce portions of documents (such as student workbooks, white papers, press releases, datasheets and FAQs) (the "Documents") provided with the Licensed Content. You may not print any book (either electronic or print version) in its entirety. If you choose to reproduce Documents, you agree that: (a) use of such printed Documents will be solely in conjunction with your personal training use; (b) the Documents will not republished or posted on any network computer or broadcast in any media; (c) any reproduction will include either the Document's original copyright notice or a copyright notice to Microsoft's benefit substantially in the format provided below; and (d) to comply with all terms and conditions of this EULA. In addition, no modifications may made to any Document.

Form of Notice:

© 2002. Reprinted with permission by Microsoft Corporation. All rights reserved.

Microsoft and Windows are either registered trademarks or trademarks of Microsoft Corporation in the US and/or other countries. Other product and company names mentioned herein may be the trademarks of their respective owners.

3.2 *Use of Media Elements.* The Licensed Content may include certain photographs, clip art, animations, sounds, music, and video clips (together "Media Elements"). You may not modify these Media Elements.

3.3 *Use of Sample Code.* In the event that the Licensed Content includes sample code in source or object format ("Sample Code"), Microsoft grants you a limited, non-exclusive, royalty-free license to use, copy and modify the Sample Code; if you elect to exercise the foregoing rights, you agree to comply with all other terms and conditions of this EULA, including without limitation Sections 3.4, 3.5, and 6.

3.4 *Permitted Modifications.* In the event that you exercise any rights provided under this EULA to create modifications of the Licensed Content, you agree that any such modifications: (a) will not be used for providing training where a fee is charged in public or private classes; (b) indemnify, hold harmless, and defend Microsoft from and against any claims or lawsuits, including attorneys' fees, which arise from or result from your use of any modified version of the Licensed Content; and (c) not to transfer or assign any rights to any modified version of the Licensed Content to any third party without the express written permission of Microsoft.

3.5 *Reproduction/Redistribution Licensed Content.* Except as expressly provided in this EULA, you may not reproduce or distribute the Licensed Content or any portion thereof (including any permitted modifications) to any third parties without the express written permission of Microsoft.

4. **RESERVATION OF RIGHTS AND OWNERSHIP.** Microsoft reserves all rights not expressly granted to you in this EULA. The Licensed Content is protected by copyright and other intellectual property laws and treaties. Microsoft or its suppliers own the title, copyright, and other intellectual property rights in the Licensed Content. You may not remove or obscure any copyright, trademark or patent notices that appear on the Licensed Content, or any components thereof, as delivered to you. **The Licensed Content is licensed, not sold.**

5. **LIMITATIONS ON REVERSE ENGINEERING, DECOMPILATION, AND DISASSEMBLY.** You may not reverse engineer, decompile, or disassemble the Software or Media Elements, except and only to the extent that such activity is expressly permitted by applicable law notwithstanding this limitation.

6. **LIMITATIONS ON SALE, RENTAL, ETC. AND CERTAIN ASSIGNMENTS.** You may not provide commercial hosting services with, sell, rent, lease, lend, sublicense, or assign copies of the Licensed Content, or any portion thereof (including any permitted modifications thereof) on a stand-alone basis or as part of any collection, product or service.

7. **CONSENT TO USE OF DATA.** You agree that Microsoft and its affiliates may collect and use technical information gathered as part of the product support services provided to you, if any, related to the Licensed Content. Microsoft may use this information solely to improve our products or to provide customized services or technologies to you and will not disclose this information in a form that personally identifies you.

8. **LINKS TO THIRD PARTY SITES.** You may link to third party sites through the use of the Licensed Content. The third party sites are not under the control of Microsoft, and Microsoft is not responsible for the contents of any third party sites, any links contained in third party sites, or any changes or updates to third party sites. Microsoft is not responsible for webcasting or any other form of transmission received from any third party sites. Microsoft is providing these links to third party sites to you only as a convenience, and the inclusion of any link does not imply an endorsement by Microsoft of the third party site.

9. **ADDITIONAL LICENSED CONTENT/SERVICES.** This EULA applies to updates, supplements, add-on components, or Internet-based services components, of the Licensed Content that Microsoft may provide to you or make available to you after the date you obtain your initial copy of the Licensed Content, unless we provide other terms along with the update, supplement, add-on component, or Internet-based services component. Microsoft reserves the right to discontinue any Internet-based services provided to you or made available to you through the use of the Licensed Content.

10. **U.S. GOVERNMENT LICENSE RIGHTS**. All software provided to the U.S. Government pursuant to solicitations issued on or after December 1, 1995 is provided with the commercial license rights and restrictions described elsewhere herein. All software provided to the U.S. Government pursuant to solicitations issued prior to December 1, 1995 is provided with "Restricted Rights" as provided for in FAR, 48 CFR 52.227-14 (JUNE 1987) or DFAR, 48 CFR 252.227-7013 (OCT 1988), as applicable.

11. **EXPORT RESTRICTIONS**. You acknowledge that the Licensed Content is subject to U.S. export jurisdiction. You agree to comply with all applicable international and national laws that apply to the Licensed Content, including the U.S. Export Administration Regulations, as well as end-user, end-use, and destination restrictions issued by U.S. and other governments. For additional information see <http://www.microsoft.com/exporting/>.

12. **TRANSFER.** The initial user of the Licensed Content may make a one-time permanent transfer of this EULA and Licensed Content to another end user, provided the initial user retains no copies of the Licensed Content. The transfer may not be an indirect transfer, such as a consignment. Prior to the transfer, the end user receiving the Licensed Content must agree to all the EULA terms.

13. **"NOT FOR RESALE" LICENSED CONTENT.** Licensed Content identified as "Not For Resale" or "NFR," may not be sold or otherwise transferred for value, or used for any purpose other than demonstration, test or evaluation.

14. **TERMINATION.** Without prejudice to any other rights, Microsoft may terminate this EULA if you fail to comply with the terms and conditions of this EULA. In such event, you must destroy all copies of the Licensed Content and all of its component parts.

15. **<u>DISCLAIMER OF WARRANTIES</u>. TO THE MAXIMUM EXTENT PERMITTED BY APPLICABLE LAW, MICROSOFT AND ITS SUPPLIERS PROVIDE THE LICENSED CONTENT AND SUPPORT SERVICES (IF ANY) *AS IS AND WITH ALL FAULTS,* AND MICROSOFT AND ITS SUPPLIERS HEREBY DISCLAIM ALL OTHER WARRANTIES AND CONDITIONS, WHETHER EXPRESS, IMPLIED OR STATUTORY, INCLUDING, BUT NOT LIMITED TO, ANY (IF ANY) IMPLIED WARRANTIES, DUTIES OR CONDITIONS OF MERCHANTABILITY, OF FITNESS FOR A PARTICULAR PURPOSE, OF RELIABILITY OR AVAILABILITY, OF ACCURACY OR COMPLETENESS OF RESPONSES, OF RESULTS, OF WORKMANLIKE EFFORT, OF LACK OF VIRUSES, AND OF LACK OF NEGLIGENCE, ALL WITH REGARD TO THE LICENSED CONTENT, AND THE PROVISION OF OR FAILURE TO PROVIDE SUPPORT OR OTHER SERVICES, INFORMATION, SOFTWARE, AND RELATED CONTENT THROUGH THE LICENSED CONTENT, OR OTHERWISE ARISING OUT OF THE USE OF THE LICENSED CONTENT. ALSO, THERE IS NO WARRANTY OR CONDITION OF TITLE, QUIET ENJOYMENT, QUIET POSSESSION, CORRESPONDENCE TO DESCRIPTION OR NON-INFRINGEMENT WITH REGARD TO THE LICENSED CONTENT. THE ENTIRE RISK AS TO THE QUALITY, OR ARISING OUT OF THE USE OR PERFORMANCE OF THE LICENSED CONTENT, AND ANY SUPPORT SERVICES, REMAINS WITH YOU.**

16. **<u>EXCLUSION OF INCIDENTAL, CONSEQUENTIAL AND CERTAIN OTHER DAMAGES</u>. TO THE MAXIMUM EXTENT PERMITTED BY APPLICABLE LAW, IN NO EVENT SHALL MICROSOFT OR ITS SUPPLIERS BE LIABLE FOR ANY SPECIAL, INCIDENTAL, PUNITIVE, INDIRECT, OR CONSEQUENTIAL DAMAGES WHATSOEVER (INCLUDING, BUT NOT**

LIMITED TO, DAMAGES FOR LOSS OF PROFITS OR CONFIDENTIAL OR OTHER INFORMATION, FOR BUSINESS INTERRUPTION, FOR PERSONAL INJURY, FOR LOSS OF PRIVACY, FOR FAILURE TO MEET ANY DUTY INCLUDING OF GOOD FAITH OR OF REASONABLE CARE, FOR NEGLIGENCE, AND FOR ANY OTHER PECUNIARY OR OTHER LOSS WHATSOEVER) ARISING OUT OF OR IN ANY WAY RELATED TO THE USE OF OR INABILITY TO USE THE LICENSED CONTENT, THE PROVISION OF OR FAILURE TO PROVIDE SUPPORT OR OTHER SERVICES, INFORMATION, SOFTWARE, AND RELATED CONTENT THROUGH THE LICENSED CONTENT, OR OTHERWISE ARISING OUT OF THE USE OF THE LICENSED CONTENT, OR OTHERWISE UNDER OR IN CONNECTION WITH ANY PROVISION OF THIS EULA, EVEN IN THE EVENT OF THE FAULT, TORT (INCLUDING NEGLIGENCE), MISREPRESENTATION, STRICT LIABILITY, BREACH OF CONTRACT OR BREACH OF WARRANTY OF MICROSOFT OR ANY SUPPLIER, AND EVEN IF MICROSOFT OR ANY SUPPLIER HAS BEEN ADVISED OF THE POSSIBILITY OF SUCH DAMAGES. BECAUSE SOME STATES/JURISDICTIONS DO NOT ALLOW THE EXCLUSION OR LIMITATION OF LIABILITY FOR CONSEQUENTIAL OR INCIDENTAL DAMAGES, THE ABOVE LIMITATION MAY NOT APPLY TO YOU.

17. **LIMITATION OF LIABILITY AND REMEDIES. NOTWITHSTANDING ANY DAMAGES THAT YOU MIGHT INCUR FOR ANY REASON WHATSOEVER (INCLUDING, WITHOUT LIMITATION, ALL DAMAGES REFERENCED HEREIN AND ALL DIRECT OR GENERAL DAMAGES IN CONTRACT OR ANYTHING ELSE), THE ENTIRE LIABILITY OF MICROSOFT AND ANY OF ITS SUPPLIERS UNDER ANY PROVISION OF THIS EULA AND YOUR EXCLUSIVE REMEDY HEREUNDER SHALL BE LIMITED TO THE GREATER OF THE ACTUAL DAMAGES YOU INCUR IN REASONABLE RELIANCE ON THE LICENSED CONTENT UP TO THE AMOUNT ACTUALLY PAID BY YOU FOR THE LICENSED CONTENT OR US$5.00. THE FOREGOING LIMITATIONS, EXCLUSIONS AND DISCLAIMERS SHALL APPLY TO THE MAXIMUM EXTENT PERMITTED BY APPLICABLE LAW, EVEN IF ANY REMEDY FAILS ITS ESSENTIAL PURPOSE.**

18. **APPLICABLE LAW.** If you acquired this Licensed Content in the United States, this EULA is governed by the laws of the State of Washington. If you acquired this Licensed Content in Canada, unless expressly prohibited by local law, this EULA is governed by the laws in force in the Province of Ontario, Canada; and, in respect of any dispute which may arise hereunder, you consent to the jurisdiction of the federal and provincial courts sitting in Toronto, Ontario. If you acquired this Licensed Content in the European Union, Iceland, Norway, or Switzerland, then local law applies. If you acquired this Licensed Content in any other country, then local law may apply.

19. **ENTIRE AGREEMENT; SEVERABILITY.** This EULA (including any addendum or amendment to this EULA which is included with the Licensed Content) are the entire agreement between you and Microsoft relating to the Licensed Content and the support services (if any) and they supersede all prior or contemporaneous oral or written communications, proposals and representations with respect to the Licensed Content or any other subject matter covered by this EULA. To the extent the terms of any Microsoft policies or programs for support services conflict with the terms of this EULA, the terms of this EULA shall control. If any provision of this EULA is held to be void, invalid, unenforceable or illegal, the other provisions shall continue in full force and effect.

Should you have any questions concerning this EULA, or if you desire to contact Microsoft for any reason, please use the address information enclosed in this Licensed Content to contact the Microsoft subsidiary serving your country or visit Microsoft on the World Wide Web at http://www.microsoft.com.

Si vous avez acquis votre Contenu Sous Licence Microsoft au CANADA :

DÉNI DE GARANTIES. Dans la mesure maximale permise par les lois applicables, le Contenu Sous Licence et les services de soutien technique (le cas échéant) sont fournis *TELS QUELS ET AVEC TOUS LES DÉFAUTS* par Microsoft et ses fournisseurs, lesquels par les présentes dénient toutes autres garanties et conditions expresses, implicites ou en vertu de la loi, notamment, mais sans limitation, (le cas échéant) les garanties, devoirs ou conditions implicites de qualité marchande, d'adaptation à une fin usage particulière, de fiabilité ou de disponibilité, d'exactitude ou d'exhaustivité des réponses, des résultats, des efforts déployés selon les règles de l'art, d'absence de virus et d'absence de négligence, le tout à l'égard du Contenu Sous Licence et de la prestation des services de soutien technique ou de l'omission de la 'une telle prestation des services de soutien technique ou à l'égard de la fourniture ou de l'omission de la fourniture de tous autres services, renseignements, Contenus Sous Licence, et contenu qui s'y rapporte grâce au Contenu Sous Licence ou provenant autrement de l'utilisation du Contenu Sous Licence. PAR AILLEURS, IL N'Y A AUCUNE GARANTIE OU CONDITION QUANT AU TITRE DE PROPRIÉTÉ, À LA JOUISSANCE OU LA POSSESSION PAISIBLE, À LA CONCORDANCE À UNE DESCRIPTION NI QUANT À UNE ABSENCE DE CONTREFAÇON CONCERNANT LE CONTENU SOUS LICENCE.

EXCLUSION DES DOMMAGES ACCESSOIRES, INDIRECTS ET DE CERTAINS AUTRES DOMMAGES. DANS LA MESURE MAXIMALE PERMISE PAR LES LOIS APPLICABLES, EN AUCUN CAS MICROSOFT OU SES FOURNISSEURS NE SERONT RESPONSABLES DES DOMMAGES SPÉCIAUX, CONSÉCUTIFS, ACCESSOIRES OU INDIRECTS DE QUELQUE NATURE QUE CE SOIT (NOTAMMENT, LES DOMMAGES À L'ÉGARD DU MANQUE À GAGNER OU DE LA DIVULGATION DE RENSEIGNEMENTS CONFIDENTIELS OU AUTRES, DE LA PERTE D'EXPLOITATION, DE BLESSURES CORPORELLES, DE LA VIOLATION DE LA VIE PRIVÉE, DE L'OMISSION DE REMPLIR TOUT DEVOIR, Y COMPRIS D'AGIR DE BONNE FOI OU D'EXERCER UN SOIN RAISONNABLE, DE LA NÉGLIGENCE ET DE TOUTE AUTRE PERTE PÉCUNIAIRE OU AUTRE PERTE

DE QUELQUE NATURE QUE CE SOIT) SE RAPPORTANT DE QUELQUE MANIÈRE QUE CE SOIT À L'UTILISATION DU CONTENU SOUS LICENCE OU À L'INCAPACITÉ DE S'EN SERVIR, À LA PRESTATION OU À L'OMISSION DE LA 'UNE TELLE PRESTATION DE SERVICES DE SOUTIEN TECHNIQUE OU À LA FOURNITURE OU À L'OMISSION DE LA FOURNITURE DE TOUS AUTRES SERVICES, RENSEIGNEMENTS, CONTENUS SOUS LICENCE, ET CONTENU QUI S'Y RAPPORTE GRÂCE AU CONTENU SOUS LICENCE OU PROVENANT AUTREMENT DE L'UTILISATION DU CONTENU SOUS LICENCE OU AUTREMENT AUX TERMES DE TOUTE DISPOSITION DE LA U PRÉSENTE CONVENTION EULA OU RELATIVEMENT À UNE TELLE DISPOSITION, MÊME EN CAS DE FAUTE, DE DÉLIT CIVIL (Y COMPRIS LA NÉGLIGENCE), DE RESPONSABILITÉ STRICTE, DE VIOLATION DE CONTRAT OU DE VIOLATION DE GARANTIE DE MICROSOFT OU DE TOUT FOURNISSEUR ET MÊME SI MICROSOFT OU TOUT FOURNISSEUR A ÉTÉ AVISÉ DE LA POSSIBILITÉ DE TELS DOMMAGES.

LIMITATION DE RESPONSABILITÉ ET RECOURS. MALGRÉ LES DOMMAGES QUE VOUS PUISSIEZ SUBIR POUR QUELQUE MOTIF QUE CE SOIT (NOTAMMENT, MAIS SANS LIMITATION, TOUS LES DOMMAGES SUSMENTIONNÉS ET TOUS LES DOMMAGES DIRECTS OU GÉNÉRAUX OU AUTRES), LA SEULE RESPONSABILITÉ 'OBLIGATION INTÉGRALE DE MICROSOFT ET DE L'UN OU L'AUTRE DE SES FOURNISSEURS AUX TERMES DE TOUTE DISPOSITION DEU LA PRÉSENTE CONVENTION EULA ET VOTRE RECOURS EXCLUSIF À L'ÉGARD DE TOUT CE QUI PRÉCÈDE SE LIMITE AU PLUS ÉLEVÉ ENTRE LES MONTANTS SUIVANTS : LE MONTANT QUE VOUS AVEZ RÉELLEMENT PAYÉ POUR LE CONTENU SOUS LICENCE OU 5,00 $US. LES LIMITES, EXCLUSIONS ET DÉNIS QUI PRÉCÈDENT (Y COMPRIS LES CLAUSES CI-DESSUS), S'APPLIQUENT DANS LA MESURE MAXIMALE PERMISE PAR LES LOIS APPLICABLES, MÊME SI TOUT RECOURS N'ATTEINT PAS SON BUT ESSENTIEL.

À moins que cela ne soit prohibé par le droit local applicable, la présente Convention est régie par les lois de la province d'Ontario, Canada. Vous consentez Chacune des parties à la présente reconnaît irrévocablement à la compétence des tribunaux fédéraux et provinciaux siégeant à Toronto, dans de la province d'Ontario et consent à instituer tout litige qui pourrait découler de la présente auprès des tribunaux situés dans le district judiciaire de York, province d'Ontario.

Au cas où vous auriez des questions concernant cette licence ou que vous désiriez vous mettre en rapport avec Microsoft pour quelque raison que ce soit, veuillez utiliser l'information contenue dans le Contenu Sous Licence pour contacter la filiale de succursale Microsoft desservant votre pays, dont l'adresse est fournie dans ce produit, ou visitez écrivez à : Microsoft sur le World Wide Web à http://www.microsoft.com

Contents

Module 5: Object-Oriented Programming in Visual Basic .NET

Module 6: Using Windows Forms

Module 7: Building Web Applications

Module 8: Using ADO.NET

Module 9: Developing Components in Visual Basic .NET

Module 10: Deploying Applications

Module 11: Upgrading to Visual Basic .NET

About This Course

This section provides you with a brief description of the course, audience, suggested prerequisites, and course objectives.

Description

This five day instructor-led course provides students with the knowledge and skills needed to develop Microsoft® .NET–based applications by using Microsoft Visual Basic® .NET. The course focuses on the new features and enhancements to Visual Basic.

Audience

This course is intended for experienced Visual Basic developers who want to upgrade to Visual Basic .NET.

Student Prerequisites

This course requires that students meet the following prerequisites:

- Experience developing applications using Microsoft Visual Basic 4.0 or later
- Successful completion of Course 1013A, *Mastering Microsoft Visual Basic 6 Development,* or equivalent knowledge

  – Or –
- Successful completion of Course 1016A, *Mastering Enterprise Development Using Microsoft Visual Basic 6,* or equivalent knowledge
- Familiarity with basic concepts of object-oriented programming
- Familiarity with the Extensible Markup Language (XML)
- Familiarity with Microsoft's .NET strategy as described on Microsoft's .NET Web site at http://www.microsoft.com/net/
- Familiarity with the .NET Framework as described on the following Web sites:

  http://msdn.microsoft.com/msdnmag/issues/0900/Framework/Framework.asp

  and

  http://msdn.microsoft.com/msdnmag/issues/1000/Framework2/Framework2.asp

Course Objectives

After completing this course, the student will be able to:

- List the major elements of the .NET Framework and describe some of the major enhancements to the new version of Visual Basic.
- Describe the basic structure of a Visual Basic .NET project and use the main features of the integrated development environment (IDE).
- Use the new language features and syntax in Visual Basic .NET.
- Explain the basic concepts and terminology of object-oriented design specifically for Visual Basic .NET.
- Explain and use the basic concepts and terminology of object-oriented programming in Visual Basic .NET.
- Create applications by using Microsoft Windows® Forms.
- Create Internet applications that use Web Forms and Web Services.
- Create applications that use ADO.NET.
- Create components in Visual Basic .NET.
- Set up and deploy various types of Visual Basic .NET–based applications.
- Prepare existing Visual Basic–based applications for upgrade to Visual Basic .NET.

Student Materials Compact Disc Contents

The Student Materials compact disc contains the following files and folders:

- *Autorun.exe.* When the compact disc is inserted into the CD-ROM drive, or when you double-click the **Autorun.exe** file, this file opens the compact disc and allows you to browse the Student Materials compact disc or install Internet Explorer.
- *Default.htm.* This file opens the Student Materials Web page. It provides you with resources pertaining to this course, including additional reading, review and lab answers, lab files, multimedia presentations, and course-related Web sites.
- *Readme.txt.* This file explains how to install the software for viewing the Student Materials compact disc and its contents and how to open the Student Materials Web page.
- *2373B_ms.doc.* This file is the Manual Classroom Setup Guide. It contains a description of classroom requirements, classroom setup instructions, and the classroom configuration.
- *Addread.* This folder contains additional reading pertaining to this course. If there are no additional reading files, this folder does not appear.
- *Appendix.* This folder contains appendix files for this course. If there are no appendix files, this folder does not appear.
- *DemoCode.* This folder contains demonstration code. If there is no demonstration code, this folder does not appear.
- *Flash.* This folder contains the installer for the Macromedia Flash 5.0 browser plug-in. If there are no Flash animations in the course, this folder does not appear.
- *Fonts.* This folder contains fonts that are required to view the PowerPoint presentation and Web-based materials.
- *Labs.* This folder contains files that are used in the hands-on labs. These files may be used to prepare the student computers for the hands-on labs.
- *Media.* This folder contains files that are used in multimedia presentations for this course. If this course does not include any multimedia presentations, this folder does not appear.
- *Menu.* This folder contains elements for Autorun.exe.
- *Mplayer.* This folder contains files that are required to install Windows Media Player.
- *Practices.* This folder contains files that are used in the hands-on practices. If there are no practices, this folder does not appear.
- *Sampapps.* This folder contains the sample applications associated with this course. If there are no associated sample applications, this folder does not appear.

- *Sampcode*. This folder contains sample code that is accessible through the Web pages on the Student Materials compact disc. If there is no sample code, this folder does not appear.
- *Sampsite*. This folder contains files that create the sample site associated with this course. If there is no sample site, this folder does not appear.
- *Webfiles*. This folder contains the files that are required to view the course Web page. To open the Web page, open Windows Explorer, and in the root directory of the compact disc, double-click **Default.htm** or **Autorun.exe**.
- *Wordview*. This folder contains the Word Viewer that is used to view any Word document (.doc) files that are included on the compact disc.

Document Conventions

The following conventions are used in course materials to distinguish elements of the text.

Convention	Use
◆	Indicates an introductory page. This symbol appears next to a topic heading when additional information on the topic is covered on the page or pages that follow it.
bold	Represents commands, command options, and syntax that must be typed exactly as shown. It also indicates commands on menus and buttons, dialog box titles and options, and icon and menu names.
italic	In syntax statements or descriptive text, indicates argument names or placeholders for variable information. Italic is also used for introducing new terms, for book titles, and for emphasis in the text.
Title Capitals	Indicate domain names, user names, computer names, directory names, and folder and file names, except when specifically referring to case-sensitive names. Unless otherwise indicated, you can use lowercase letters when you type a directory name or file name in a dialog box or at a command prompt.
ALL CAPITALS	Indicate the names of keys, key sequences, and key combinations—for example, ALT+SPACEBAR.
`monospace`	Represents code samples or examples of screen text.
[ ]	In syntax statements, enclose optional items. For example, [*filename*] in command syntax indicates that you can choose to type a file name with the command. Type only the information within the brackets, not the brackets themselves.
{ }	In syntax statements, enclose required items. Type only the information within the braces, not the braces themselves.
|	In syntax statements, separates an either/or choice.
▶	Indicates a procedure with sequential steps.
...	In syntax statements, specifies that the preceding item may be repeated.
. . .	Represents an omitted portion of a code sample.

msdn® training

Introduction

Contents

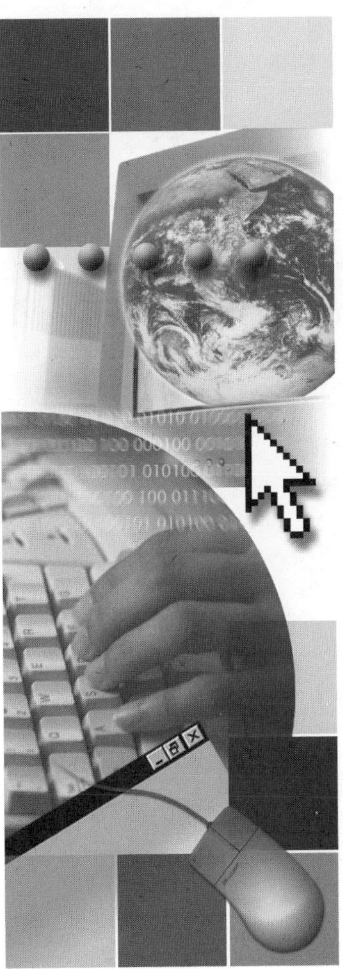

Introduction

- Name
- Company Affiliation
- Title/Function
- Job Responsibility
- Visual Basic Programming Experience
- Expectations for the Course

Course Materials

- Name Card
- Student Workbook
- Student Materials Compact Disc
- Course Evaluation

The following materials are included with your kit:

- *Name card.* Write your name on both sides of the name card.
- *Student workbook.* The student workbook contains the material covered in class, in addition to the hands-on lab exercises.
- *Student Materials compact disc.* The Student Materials compact disc contains the Web page that provides you with links to resources pertaining to this course, including additional readings, review and lab answers, lab files, multimedia presentations, and course-related Web sites.

Note To open the Web page, insert the Student Materials compact disc into the CD-ROM drive, and then in the root directory of the compact disc, double-click **Autorun.exe** or **Default.htm**.

- *Course evaluation.* To provide feedback on the course, training facility, and instructor, you will have the opportunity to complete an online evaluation near the end of the course.

  To provide additional comments or inquire about the Microsoft Certified Professional program, send e-mail to mcphelp@microsoft.com.

Prerequisites

- Experience developing applications in Visual Basic 4.0 or later
- Familiarity with the Microsoft .NET strategy
- Familiarity with the Microsoft .NET Framework

This course requires that you meet the following prerequisites:

- Experience developing applications in Microsoft Visual Basic® 4.0 or later
- Successful completion of Course 1013A, *Mastering Microsoft Visual Basic 6 Development,* or equivalent knowledge

  – Or –
- Successful completion of course 1016A, *Mastering Enterprise Development Using Microsoft Visual Basic 6*, or equivalent knowledge
- Familiarity with basic object-oriented concepts
- Familiarity with Extensible Markup Language (XML)
- Familiarity with Microsoft's .NET strategy as described on Microsoft's .NET Web site (http://www.microsoft.com/net/)
- Familiarity with the .NET Framework as described on the following Web sites:

  http://msdn.microsoft.com/msdnmag/issues/0900/Framework/Framework.asp

  and

  http://msdn.microsoft.com/msdnmag/issues/1000/Framework2/Framework2.asp

Course Outline

- Module 1: Overview of the Microsoft .NET Platform
- Module 2: Development Environment Features
- Module 3: Language and Syntax Enhancements
- Module 4: Object-Oriented Design for Visual Basic .NET
- Module 5: Object-Oriented Programming in Visual Basic .NET

Module 1, "Overview of the Microsoft .NET Platform," describes the rationale and features that provide the foundation for the .NET platform, including the .NET components. The purpose of this module is to build an understanding of the .NET platform for which you will be developing Visual Basic .NET version 7.0 code. After completing this module, you will be able to describe the components of the .NET platform.

Module 2, "Development Environment Features," describes the major benefits of the new integrated development environment (IDE) and the basic structure of a Visual Basic .NET–based application. You will learn how to create projects in Visual Basic .NET, and will try some of the tools that make the IDE powerful for application development. Finally, you will learn how to debug your projects and how to compile them.

Module 3, "Language and Syntax Enhancements," describes the many language and syntax enhancements available in Visual Basic .NET. You will learn how these enhancements help make it an excellent development tool for the .NET platform.

Module 4, "Object-Oriented Design for Visual Basic .NET," describes how to begin the class design process by using use cases. You will then learn about some common object-oriented programming concepts, including inheritance, interfaces, and polymorphism. Finally, you will see how to document your system design.

Module 5, "Object-Oriented Programming in Visual Basic .NET," provides information on how to implement object-oriented programming in Visual Basic .NET–based applications. You will learn how to define classes, their properties, and their methods. You will learn about the life cycle of an object, from creation to destruction. You will also learn how to work with classes by using inheritance, interfaces, polymorphism, shared members, events, and delegates.

Course Outline *(continued)*

- Module 6: Using Windows Forms
- Module 7: Building Web Applications
- Module 8: Using ADO.NET
- Module 9: Developing Components in Visual Basic .NET
- Module 10: Deploying Applications
- Module 11: Upgrading to Visual Basic .NET

Module 6, "Using Windows Forms," describes how to use the new features available in Microsoft Windows® Forms and how to make changes to forms and controls, and to their properties, methods, and events. You will also learn how to create some of the standard Windows dialog boxes. Finally, you will learn about visual inheritance, which allows you to use object-oriented techniques within your forms.

Module 7, "Building Web Applications," explains how to create dynamic, powerful Web applications by using the ASP.NET framework. You will learn how to use Web Services from a browser or from another client application.

Module 8, "Using ADO.NET," explains how to use ADO.NET. You will learn about the Microsoft .NET providers included in the .NET Framework and about how to use the **DataSet** object. You will also learn how to use the Microsoft Visual Studio .NET data designers and how to bind data to Microsoft Windows® Forms and Web Forms. Finally, you will learn about the integration of Extensible Markup Language (XML) with ADO.NET.

Module 9, "Developing Components in Visual Basic .NET," describes the different types of components that can be created in Visual Basic .NET, including component classes and serviced components. This module also explains how to enhance your applications by using threading.

Module 10, "Deploying Applications," explains how to deploy assemblies for use by client applications, how to decide what type of distribution strategy to implement, and how to deploy Windows-based and Web-based applications.

Module 11, "Upgrading to Visual Basic .NET," explains the factors you must consider when deciding whether to upgrade an existing application, the options you have for upgrading, and how to use the Upgrade Wizard.

Microsoft Certified Professional Program

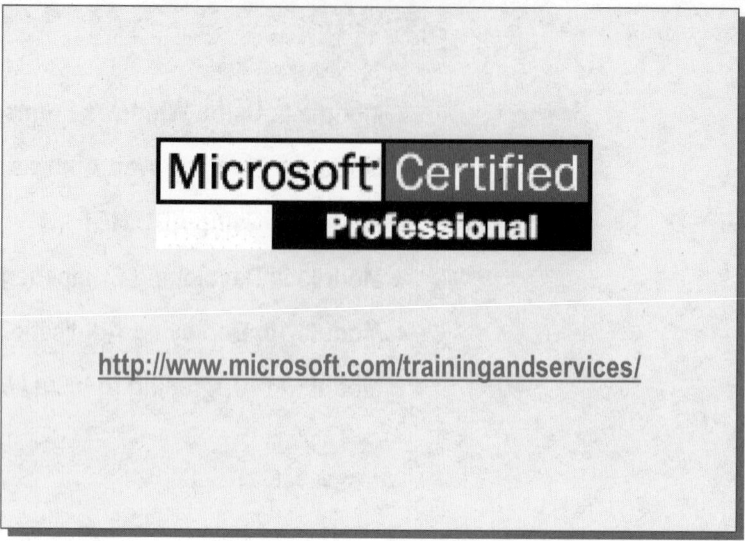

The Microsoft Certified Professional program is a leading certification program that validates your experience and skills to keep you competitive in today's changing business environment. The following table describes each certification in more detail.

Certification	Description
MCSA on Microsoft Windows 2000	The Microsoft Certified Systems Administrator (MCSA) certification is designed for professionals who implement, manage, and troubleshoot existing network and system environments based on Microsoft Windows 2000 platforms, including the Windows .NET Server family. Implementation responsibilities include installing and configuring parts of the systems. Management responsibilities include administering and supporting the systems.
MCSE on Microsoft Windows 2000	The Microsoft Certified Systems Engineer (MCSE) credential is the premier certification for professionals who analyze the business requirements and design and implement the infrastructure for business solutions based on the Microsoft Windows 2000 platform and Microsoft server software, including the Windows .NET Server family. Implementation responsibilities include installing, configuring, and troubleshooting network systems.
MCSD	The Microsoft Certified Solution Developer (MCSD) credential is the premier certification for professionals who design and develop leading-edge business solutions with Microsoft development tools, technologies, platforms, and the Microsoft Windows DNA architecture. The types of applications that MCSDs can develop include desktop applications and multi-user, Web-based, N-tier, and transaction-based applications. The credential covers job tasks ranging from analyzing business requirements to maintaining solutions.

(continued)

Certification	Description
MCDBA on Microsoft SQL Server 2000	The Microsoft Certified Database Administrator (MCDBA) credential is the premier certification for professionals who implement and administer Microsoft SQL Server™ databases. The certification is appropriate for individuals who derive physical database designs, develop logical data models, create physical databases, create data services by using Transact-SQL, manage and maintain databases, configure and manage security, monitor and optimize databases, and install and configure SQL Server.
MCP	The Microsoft Certified Professional (MCP) credential is for individuals who have the skills to successfully implement a Microsoft product or technology as part of a business solution in an organization. Hands-on experience with the product is necessary to successfully achieve certification.
MCT	Microsoft Certified Trainers (MCTs) demonstrate the instructional and technical skills that qualify them to deliver Microsoft Official Curriculum through Microsoft Certified Technical Education Centers (Microsoft CTECs).

Certification Requirements

The certification requirements differ for each certification category and are specific to the products and job functions addressed by the certification. To become a Microsoft Certified Professional, you must pass rigorous certification exams that provide a valid and reliable measure of technical proficiency and expertise.

For More Information See the Microsoft Training and Certification Web site at http://www.microsoft.com/traincert/.

You can also send e-mail to mcphelp@microsoft.com if you have specific certification questions.

Acquiring the Skills Tested by an MCP Exam

Microsoft Official Curriculum (MOC) and MSDN® Training Curriculum can help you develop the skills that you need to do your job. They also complement the experience that you gain while working with Microsoft products and technologies. However, no one-to-one correlation exists between MOC and MSDN Training courses and MCP exams. Microsoft does not expect or intend for the courses to be the sole preparation method for passing MCP exams. Practical product knowledge and experience is also necessary to pass the MCP exams.

To help prepare for the MCP exams, use the preparation guides that are available for each exam. Each Exam Preparation Guide contains exam-specific information, such as a list of the topics on which you will be tested. These guides are available on the Microsoft Training and Certification Web site at http://www.microsoft.com/traincert/

Facilities

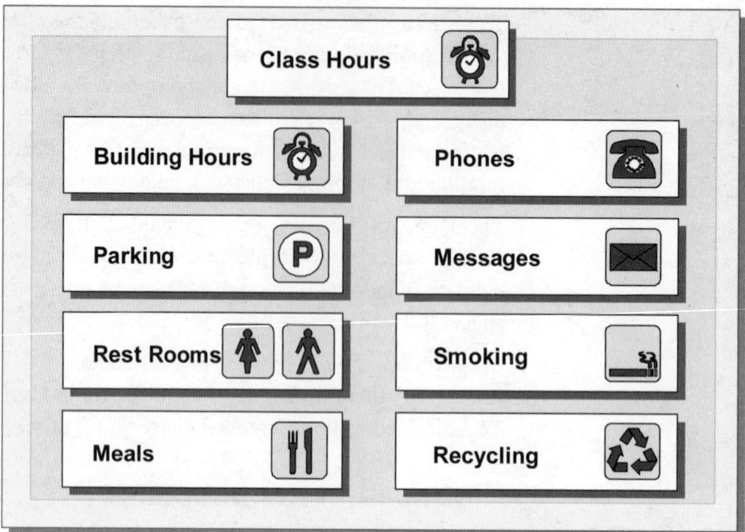
Class Hours
Building Hours
Phones
Parking
P
Messages
Rest Rooms
Smoking
Meals
Recycling

msdn® training

Module 1: Overview of the Microsoft .NET Platform

Contents

Microsoft®

Overview

- What Is the Microsoft .NET Platform?
- What Is the .NET Framework?
- What Are the .NET Framework Components?
- What Are the Visual Basic .NET Enhancements?

Microsoft® Visual Basic® .NET version 7.0 is a major enhancement to the Visual Basic product line. As a Visual Basic developer, you will find it useful to understand the rationale and features that provide the foundation for the Microsoft .NET Platform before you look at Visual Basic .NET in detail.

After completing this module, you will be able to:

- List the main elements of the .NET Platform.
- Describe the .NET Framework and its components.
- List the major enhancements to Visual Basic .NET.

What Is the Microsoft .NET Platform?

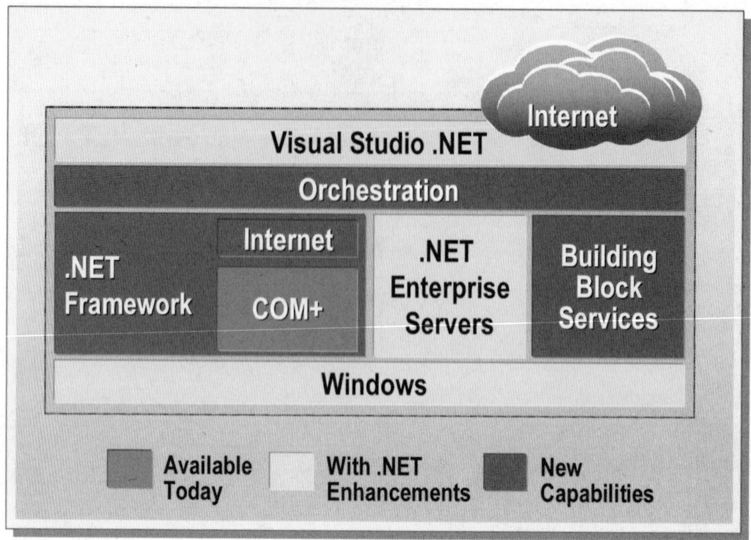

This topic describes the components of the .NET Platform, including the .NET Framework, the .NET Building Block Services, .NET Enterprise Servers, and Microsoft Visual Studio® .NET. The .NET Platform is important to you because the goal of the .NET Platform is to simplify Web development by providing all of the tools and technologies that you need to build distributed Web applications.

The .NET Platform provides:

- A language-independent, consistent programming model across all tiers of an application.
- Seamless interoperability between technologies.
- Easy migration from existing technologies.
- Full support for the Internet's platform-neutral, standards-based technologies, including Hypertext Transfer Protocol (HTTP), Extensible Markup Language (XML), and Simple Object Access Protocol (SOAP).

The .NET Platform

The .NET Platform is a set of technologies designed to transform the Internet into a full-scale distributed computing platform. It provides new ways to build applications from collections of Web Services. The .NET Platform fully supports the existing Internet infrastructure, including HTTP, XML, and SOAP.

Core Technologies in the .NET Platform

The core technologies that make up the .NET Platform include:

- .NET Framework

  The .NET Framework is based on a new common language runtime. This runtime provides a common set of services for projects built in Visual Studio .NET, regardless of the language. These services provide key building blocks for applications of any type, across all application tiers.

  Microsoft Visual Basic, Microsoft Visual C++®, and other Microsoft programming languages have been enhanced to take advantage of these services. Third-party languages that are written for the .NET Platform also have access to the same services.

  Note Because of the common language runtime, all .NET languages will use the same run-time files. This means that there is no need to distribute Visual Basic–specific run-time libraries because .NET run-time files will be installed automatically in future versions of Microsoft Windows®.

- .NET Building Block Services

  The .NET Building Block Services are distributed programmable services that are available both online and offline. A service can be invoked on a stand-alone computer not connected to the Internet, provided by a local server running inside a company, or accessed by means of the Internet. The .NET Building Block Services can be used from any platform that supports SOAP. Services include identity, notification and messaging, personalization, schematized storage, calendar, directory, search, and software delivery.

- Visual Studio .NET

  Visual Studio .NET provides a high-level development environment for building applications on the .NET Framework. It provides key enabling technologies to simplify the creation, deployment, and ongoing evolution of secure, scalable, highly available Web applications and Web Services. It also enables a new generation of Windows-based applications with many new features available through the .NET Framework.

- .NET Enterprise Servers

  The .NET Enterprise Servers provide scalability, reliability, management, and integration within and across organizations, and many other features as described in the following table.

Server	Description
Microsoft SQL Server™ 2000	Includes rich XML functionality, support for Worldwide Web Consortium (W3C) standards, the ability to manipulate XML data by using Transact SQL (T-SQL), flexible and powerful Web-based analysis, and secure access to your data over the Web by using HTTP.
Microsoft BizTalk™ Server 2000	Provides enterprise application integration (EAI), business-to-business integration, and the advanced BizTalk Orchestration technology to build dynamic business processes that span applications, platforms, and organizations over the Internet.
Microsoft Host Integration Server 2000	Provides the best way to embrace Internet, intranet, and client/server technologies while preserving investments in existing systems. Microsoft Host Integration Server 2000 is the replacement for SNA Server.
Microsoft Exchange 2000 Enterprise Server	Builds on the powerful Exchange messaging and collaboration technology by introducing several important new features and further increasing the reliability, scalability, and performance of its core architecture. Other features enhance the integration of Exchange 2000 with Microsoft Windows 2000, Microsoft Office 2000, and the Internet.
Microsoft Application Center 2000	Provides a deployment and management tool for high-availability Web applications.
Microsoft Internet Security and Acceleration Server 2000	Provides secure, fast, and manageable Internet connectivity. Internet Security and Acceleration Server integrates an extensible, multilayer enterprise firewall and a scalable, high-performance Web cache. It builds on Windows 2000 security and directory for policy-based security, acceleration, and management of internetworking.
Microsoft Commerce Server 2000	Provides an application framework, sophisticated feedback mechanisms, and analytical capabilities.

◆ What Is the .NET Framework?

- Overview of the .NET Framework
- Benefits of the .NET Framework
- Languages in the .NET Framework

In this lesson, you will learn how the .NET Framework provides all common services required for your applications to run. You will learn how services are available in any .NET-compatible language through the common language specification (CLS). You will also learn what languages are supported in the .NET Framework.

Overview of the .NET Framework

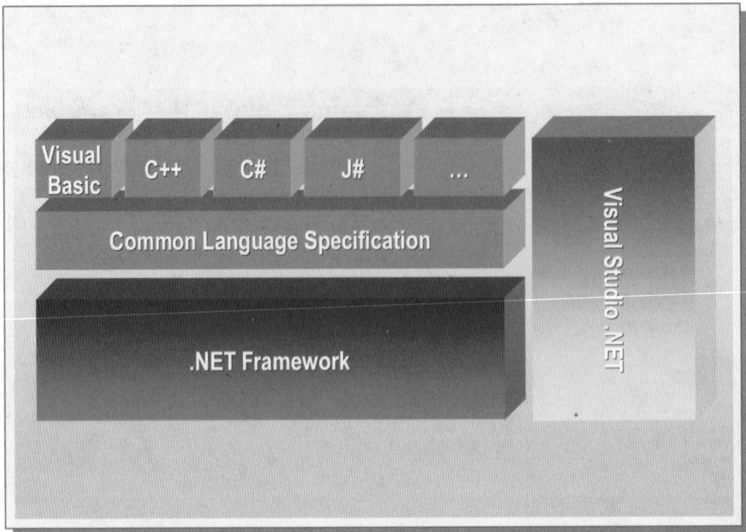

The .NET Framework provides all the common services required to run your Visual Basic .NET applications.

Building Components in the .NET Framework

Before COM, applications were completely separate entities with little or no integration. Using COM, you can integrate components within and across applications by exposing common interfaces. However, as a developer, you must still write the code to wrap, manage, and clean up after components and objects.

In the .NET Framework, components are built on a common foundation. You no longer need to write the code to allow objects to interact directly with each other. In the .NET environment, you no longer need to write component wrappers because components do not use wrappers. The .NET Framework can interpret the constructs that developers are accustomed to using in object-oriented languages. The .NET Framework fully supports class, inheritance, methods, properties, events, polymorphism, constructors, and other object-oriented constructs.

The Common Language Specification

The Common Language Specification (CLS) defines the common standards to which languages and developers must adhere if they want their components and applications to be widely useable by other .NET-compatible languages. The CLS allows Visual Basic .NET developers to create applications as part of a multiple-language team with the knowledge that there will be no problems integrating the different languages. The CLS even allows Visual Basic .NET developers to inherit from classes defined in different languages.

Visual Studio .NET

In the .NET Framework, Visual Studio .NET provides the tools you can use for rapid application development.

Benefits of the .NET Framework

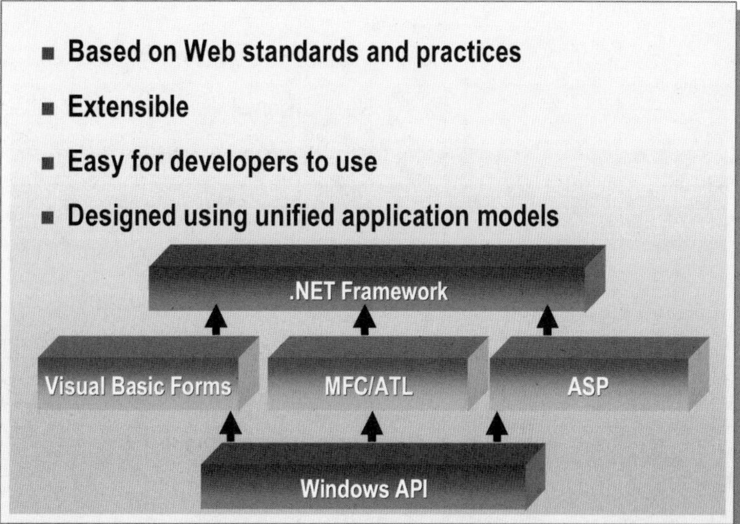

In this topic, you will learn about some of the benefits of the .NET Framework.

Goals of the .NET Framework

The .NET Framework was designed to meet the following goals:

- Based on Web standards and practices

  The .NET Framework fully supports the existing Internet technologies, including Hypertext Markup Language (HTML), XML, SOAP, Extensible Stylesheet Language for Transformations (XSLT), XPath, and other Web standards. The .NET Framework favors loosely connected, stateless Web services.

- Extensible

  The hierarchy of the .NET Framework is not hidden from the developer. You can access and extend .NET classes (unless they are sealed) by using inheritance. You can also implement cross-language inheritance.

- Easy for developers to use

  In the .NET Framework, code is organized into hierarchical namespaces and classes. The Framework provides a common type system, referred to as the unified type system, that is used by any .NET-compatible language. In the unified type system, everything is an object. There are no variant types, there is only one string type, and all string data is Unicode.

- Designed using unified application models

  A .NET class' functionality is available from any .NET-compatible language or programming model.

Languages in the .NET Framework

- **Visual Basic .NET**

  New version of Visual Basic with substantial language innovations
- **C# – designed for .NET**

  New component-oriented language
- **Managed Extensions to Visual C++**

  Provides more power and control
- **J# .NET**

  Takes full advantage of the .NET Framework
- **Third-party languages**

The .NET Platform is language neutral—all common services needed to enable programs to run are provided by the .NET Framework. The .NET Framework provides support for numerous programming languages, including Microsoft and third-party languages.

Language	Description
Microsoft Visual Basic .NET	Visual Basic .NET provides substantial language innovations over previous versions of Visual Basic. Visual Basic .NET supports inheritance, constructors, polymorphism, overloading, structured exceptions, stricter type checking, free threading, and many other features. With this release, Visual Basic Scripting Edition provides full Visual Basic functionality.
Microsoft Visual C#™	C# was designed for the .NET Platform and is the first modern component-oriented language in the C and C++ family. It can be embedded in ASP.NET pages. Some of the key features of this language include classes, interfaces, delegates, boxing and unboxing, namespaces, properties, indexers, events, operator overloading, versioning, attributes, unsafe code, and XML documentation generation. No header or Interface Definition Language (IDL) files are needed.
Managed Extensions C++	The Visual C++ upgrade is a managed, minimal extension to the C++ language. This extension provides access to the .NET Framework that includes garbage collection, single-implementation inheritance, and multiple-interface inheritance. This upgrade also eliminates the need to write plumbing code for components. It offers low-level access where useful.
Microsoft Visual J#™ .NET	J# .NET is a language for Java-language developers who want to build applications and services for the .NET Framework. J# .NET is fully integrated with the Visual Studio .NET IDE, and is designed to take full advantage of the .NET Framework.
Third-party languages	Various third-party languages are supporting the .NET Platform. These languages include APL, COBOL, Pascal, Eiffel, Haskell, ML, Oberon, Perl, Python, Scheme, and SmallTalk.

◆ What Are the .NET Framework Components?

- The .NET Framework Components
- Common Language Runtime
- .NET Framework Class Library
- ADO .NET: Data and XML
- ASP .NET: Web Forms and Services
- User Interface

In this lesson, you will learn about the Microsoft .NET Framework components. The .NET Framework is a set of technologies that are an integral part of the .NET Platform. The .NET Framework provides the basic building blocks to develop Web applications and Web Services by using ASP.NET.

The .NET Framework Components

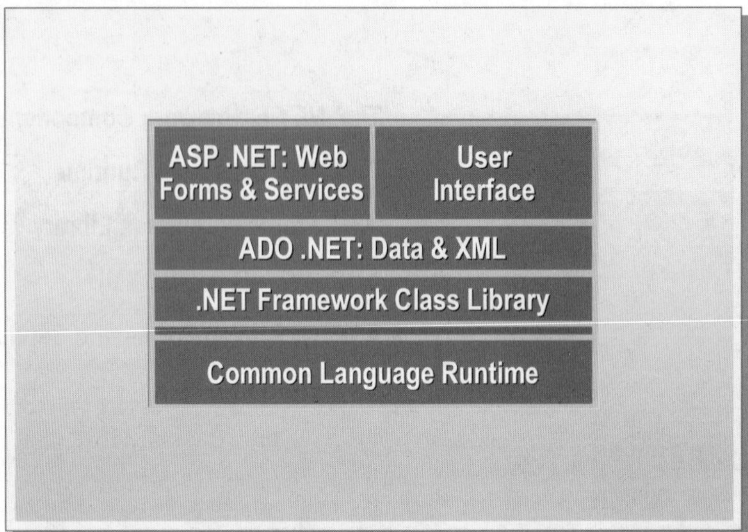

The components of the .NET Framework are as follows:

- Common language runtime
- .NET Framework Class Library
- ADO.NET: data and XML
- ASP.NET: Web Forms and Services
- User interface

Common Language Runtime

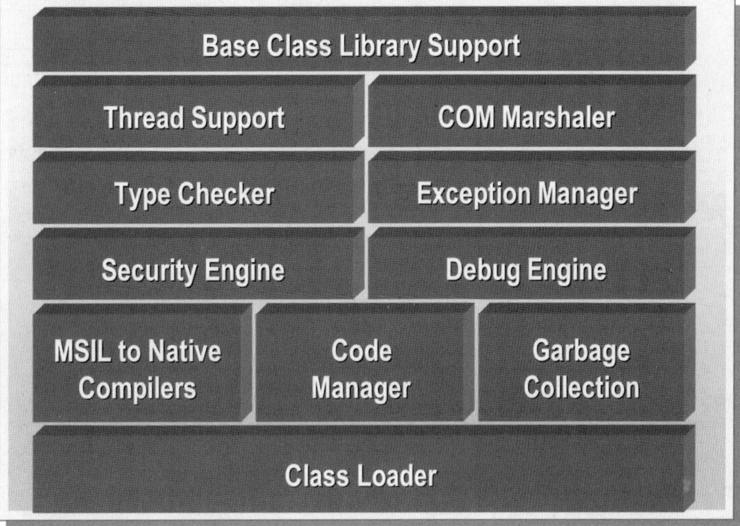

The Common Language Runtime simplifies application development, provides a robust and secure execution environment, supports multiple languages, simplifies application deployment and management, and provides a managed environment.

What Is a Managed Environment?

A managed environment is one in which the environment provides common services automatically. Examples of the types of services a managed environment provides are garbage collection and security.

Common Language Runtime Components

The Common Language Runtime features are described in the following table.

Component	Description
Class loader	Loads the implementation of a loadable type into memory and prepares it for execution.
Microsoft intermediate language (MSIL) to native compiler	Converts MSIL to native code (just-in-time).
Code manager	Manages code execution.
Garbage collection	Provides automatic lifetime management of all of your objects. This is a multiprocessor, scalable garbage collector.
Security engine	Provides evidence-based security based on the origin of the code as well as the user.
Debug engine	Allows you to debug your application and trace the execution of code.
Type checker	Will not allow unsafe casts or uninitialized variables. IL can be verified to guarantee type safety.
Exception manager	Provides structured exception handling, which is integrated with Windows Structured Exception Handling (SEH). Error reporting has been improved.
Thread support	Provides classes and interfaces that enable multithreaded programming.
COM marshaler	Provides marshaling to and from COM.
.NET Framework Class Library support	Integrates code with the runtime that supports the .NET Framework Class Library. The .NET Framework Class Library is covered in the following lesson.

.NET Framework Class Library

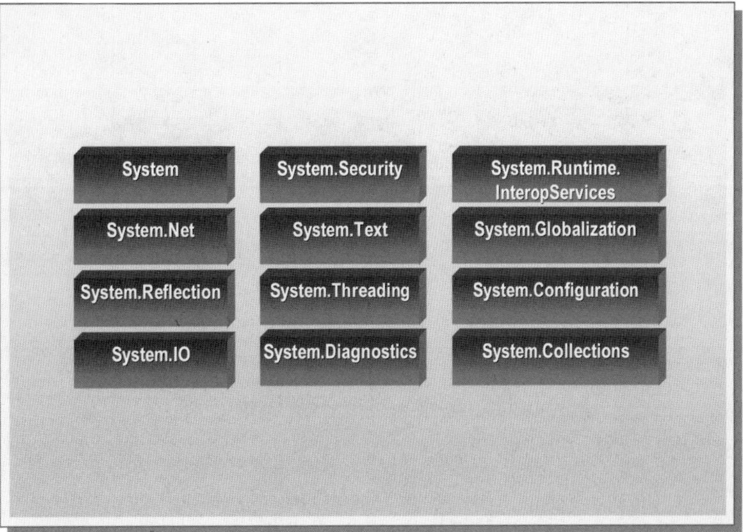

The .NET Framework Class Library exposes features of the runtime and provides other high-level services that every programmer needs through an object hierarchy. This object hierarchy is known as a namespace.

System Namespaces

The **System** namespace contains fundamental classes and base classes that define commonly-used value and reference data types, events and event handlers, interfaces, attributes, and processing exceptions. Other classes provide services supporting data type conversion, method parameter manipulation, mathematics, remote and local program invocation, application environment management, and supervision of managed and unmanaged applications.

The **System.Collections** namespace provides sorted lists, hash tables, and other ways to group data. The **System.IO** namespace provides file I/O, streams, and so on. The **System.NET** namespace provides Transmission Control Protocol/Internet Protocol (TCP/IP) and sockets support.

For more information about namespaces, search for "namespaces" in the .NET Framework SDK documentation. Namespaces will also be covered in Module 2, "Development Environment Features," in Course 2373B, *Programming with Microsoft Visual Basic .NET.*

ADO.NET: Data and XML

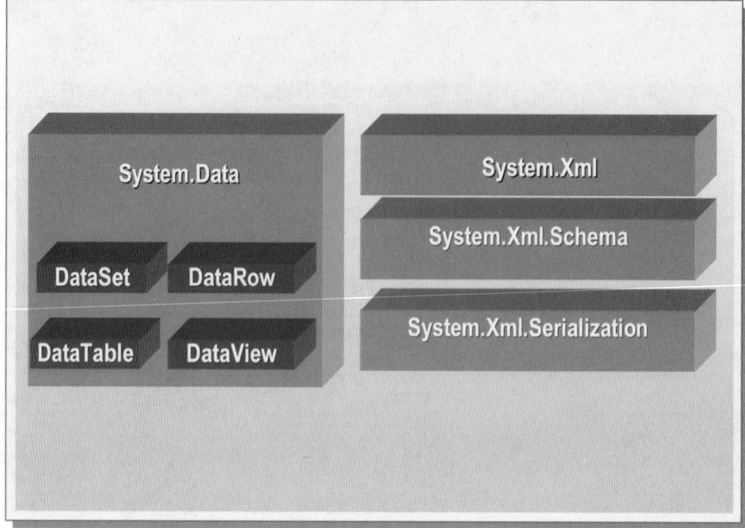

ADO.NET is the next generation of ActiveX® Data Object (ADO) technology. ADO.NET provides improved support for the disconnected programming model. It also provides rich XML support.

System.Data Namespace

The **System.Data** namespace consists of classes that constitute the ADO.NET object model. At a high level, the ADO.NET object model is divided into two layers: the connected layer and the disconnected layer.

The **System.Data** namespace includes the **DataSet** class, which represents multiple tables and their relations. These data sets are completely self-contained data structures that can be populated from a variety of data sources. One data source could be XML, another could be OLE DB, and a third data source could be the direct adapter for SQL Server.

System.Xml Namespace

The **System.Xml** namespace provides support for XML. It includes an XML parser and a writer, which are both W3C compliant. Transformations are provided by the **System.Xml.Xsl** namespace and the implementation of XPath that allows data graph navigation in XML. The **System.XML.Serialization** namespace provides the entire core infrastructure for Web Services, including features such as moving back and forth between objects and an XML representation.

ASP.NET: Web Forms and Services

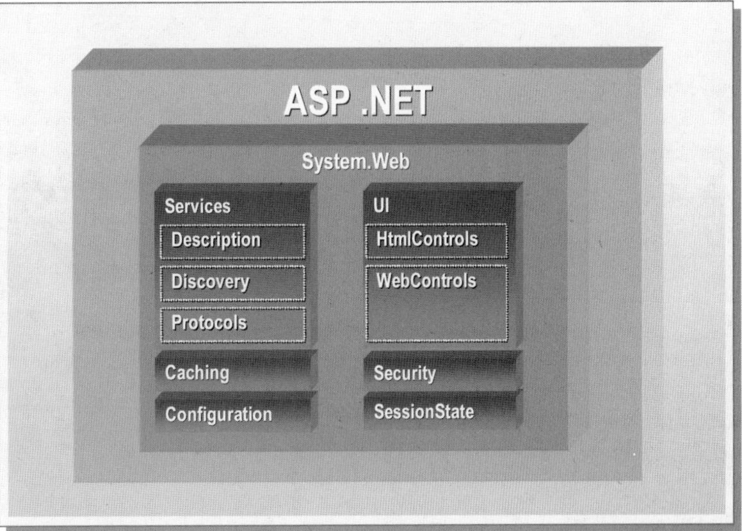

ASP.NET is a programming framework that is built on the common language runtime and that can be used on a server to build powerful Web applications. ASP.NET Web Forms provide an easy and powerful way to build dynamic Web user interfaces (UIs). ASP.NET Web Services provide the building blocks for constructing distributed Web-based applications. Web Services are based on open Internet standards, such as HTTP and XML. You can think of a Web Service as a reusable component that is accessible across the Internet, rather than being limited to Windows clients on a local area network.

The common language runtime provides built-in support for creating and exposing Web Services by using a programming abstraction that is consistent and familiar to both Active Server Pages (ASP) and Visual Basic developers. The resulting model is both scalable and extensible. This model is based on open Internet standards (HTTP, XML, SOAP, and SDL) so that it can be accessed and interpreted from any client or Internet-enabled device. Some of the more common ASP.NET classes are described in the following paragraphs.

System.Web Namespace

In the **System.Web** namespace, there are services such as caching, security, configuration, and others that are shared between Web Services and Web user interface (UI).

System.Web.Services Namespace

The **System.Web.Services** namespace handles Web Service requirements such as transportation protocols and service discovery.

System.Web.UI Namespace

The **System.Web.UI** namespace provides two classes of controls: HTML controls and Web controls. The **HTMLControl**s provide direct mapping of HTML tags, such as <INPUT>. There are also **WebControl**s that are richer and allow you to structure controls with templates (for example, a grid control).

User Interface

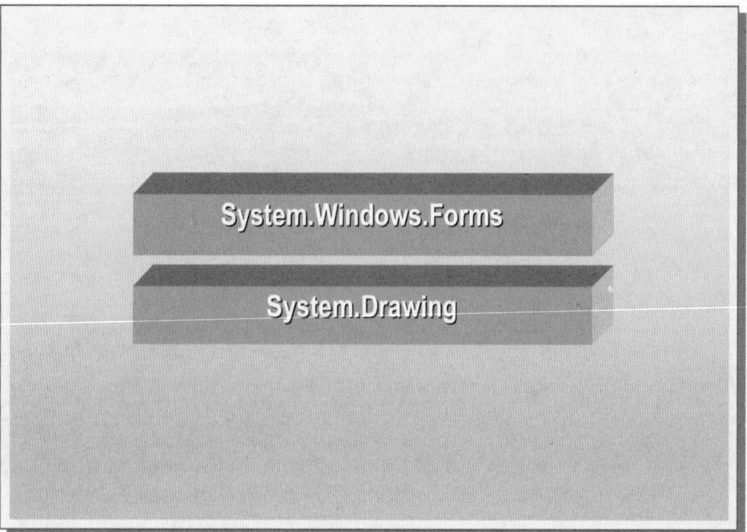

Windows applications can provide more powerful user interfaces than ever by using the .NET Framework's **System.Windows.Forms** and **System.Drawing** namespaces. The new .NET Windows Forms will look very familiar to Visual Basic developers.

System.Windows.Forms Namespace

You can use the **System.Windows.Forms** namespace classes to build the client UI. This class lets you implement the standard Windows UI in your .NET applications. Many functions that were previously only accessible by means of application programming interface (API) calls are now available as part of the forms themselves, making development much easier and more powerful.

System.Drawing Namespace

The **System.Drawing** namespace provides access to GDI+ basic graphics functionality. More advanced functionality is provided in the **System.Drawing.Drawing2D**, **System.Drawing.Imaging**, and **System.Drawing.Text** namespaces.

What Are the Visual Basic .NET Enhancements?

- **Major language enhancements**
  - Enhanced object-oriented support
  - Structured exception handling
- **Full access to the .NET Framework**
  - New threading options
  - Garbage collection
- **Enhanced Web development**
  - Create Web Forms as easily as Windows Forms
  - Create Web Services quickly

Visual Basic .NET provides major language enhancements, full access to the .NET Framework, and enhanced Web development.

Major Language Enhancements

In Visual Basic .NET, Visual Basic has undergone some significant changes to allow Visual Basic developers to create powerful, robust, and scalable enterprise applications.

- Enhanced object-oriented support

  Allows Visual Basic .NET developers to use class inheritance, constructors, destructors, overloading, interfaces, and polymorphism. This gives Visual Basic .NET as much object-oriented power as any other .NET language, such as C# or Visual C++ with managed extensions.

- Structured exception handling

  Simplifies exception handling, and allows you to use powerful features such as nested exceptions. This greatly improves the previous Visual Basic error handler.

Full Access to the .NET Framework

Visual Basic .NET developers have full access to the .NET Framework, including the entire .NET Framework Class Library.

- New threading options

  Allow you to create applications that use multithreaded capabilities. For the first time, Visual Basic developers will be able to create applications that are capable of rivaling Visual C++–based applications in this area.

- Garbage collection

  Ensures that applications created in Visual Basic .NET do not hold on to unreferenced memory. This background process addresses memory-related issues such as memory leaks and circular references that existed in previous versions of Visual Basic and other languages.

Enhanced Web Development

Visual Basic .NET enables developers to quickly create powerful Web applications.

- Create Web Forms easily

  You can do this as easily as Windows Forms by using the familiar technique of writing code behind the event of a control. No longer do developers need to use one integrated development environment (IDE) for Web page development (such as Microsoft Visual InterDev®) and another for component development. All aspects of a Web application are now simply created in a single environment in a way that will be easy for Visual Basic developers to understand.

- Create Web Services quickly

  You can do this quickly in a fashion similar to creating components in previous versions of Visual Basic. Web Services is a powerful technology that allows you to access your components (or other people's components) across the Internet by means of HTTP. Any Visual Basic developer who has created components will easily make the transition to Web Services.

Review

- **What Is the Microsoft .NET Platform?**
- **What Is the .NET Framework?**
- **What Are the .NET Framework Components?**
- **What Are the Visual Basic .NET Enhancements?**

1. What is the .NET Platform?

2. What are the core technologies in the .NET Platform?

3. List the components of the .NET Framework.

4. What is the purpose of common language runtime?

5. What is the purpose of common language specification?

6. What is a Web Service?

7. What is a managed environment?

msdn® training

Module 2: Development Environment Features

Contents

Overview

- Describing the Integrated Development Environment
- Creating Visual Basic .NET Projects
- Using Development Environment Features
- Debugging Applications
- Compiling in Visual Basic .NET

The Microsoft® Visual Studio® .NET version 7.0 integrated development environment (IDE) provides you with enhancements to many tools found in previous versions of Microsoft Visual Basic®, combined with features found in other environments, such as Microsoft Visual C++®.

In this module, you will learn the overall benefits of using this new IDE. You will learn how to create Visual Basic .NET projects, and will try some tools of the new IDE. Finally, you will learn how to debug your projects and how to compile them.

After completing this module, you will be able to:

- Describe the overall benefits of the new IDE.
- Describe the different types of Visual Basic .NET projects and their structures, including their file structures.
- Reference external applications from your project.
- View and set the properties of a project.
- Use the various windows in the IDE, including Server Explorer, the Object Browser, and the Task List.
- Debug a simple application.
- Build and compile a simple application.

Describing the Integrated Development Environment

- **There is one IDE for all .NET projects**
- **Solutions can contain multiple programming languages**
  - Example: Visual Basic .NET and C# in the same solution
- **The IDE is customizable through "My Profile"**
- **The IDE has a built-in Internet browser**

The Visual Studio .NET IDE provides some significant enhancements to previous IDEs for Visual Basic.

- There is one IDE for all Microsoft .NET projects

  The Visual Studio .NET IDE provides a single environment where you can develop all types of .NET applications, from simple applications based on Microsoft Windows®, to complex *n*-tier component systems and complete Internet applications. For example, you no longer need to create your components in a separate environment from your Internet pages and scripts.

- Solutions can contain multiple programming languages

  You can incorporate multiple programming languages within one solution and edit all your code within the same IDE. This can aid team development of a system where parts of the solution are written in Visual Basic .NET, and other parts are written in C# or other .NET-compatible languages.

- The IDE is customizable through My Profile

  The IDE is fully customizable through the My Profile configuration section on the Visual Studio .NET Start Page.

  - You can select a preexisting profile such as the Visual Basic Developer, or you can modify each section manually.
  - You can specify how you want your IDE screen to look and how the keyboard behaves. This is particularly useful if you are used to Visual Basic version 6.0 keyboard shortcuts for various actions.
  - You can choose to filter help files based on your preferences.

- The IDE has a built-in Internet browser

  You can browse the Internet within the IDE, enabling you to look up online resources without moving between multiple application windows. This built-in browser can also display the Visual Studio .NET Help files for easy access to the relevant documentation.

◆ Creating Visual Basic .NET Projects

- Choosing a Project Template
- Analyzing Project Structures
- What Are Assemblies?
- Setting Project References
- What Are Namespaces?
- Creating Namespaces
- Importing Namespaces
- Setting Project Properties

Many aspects of project development in Visual Basic .NET are similar to those in previous versions of Visual Basic. You still have a range of project templates to choose from, you still need to reference other projects and applications, and you still need to set project properties. Visual Basic .NET provides enhancements to these and other aspects of project development.

In this lesson, you will become familiar with the project templates provided by Visual Basic .NET. After completing this lesson, you will be able to:

- Choose the correct template for your project.
- Explain how various Visual Basic .NET projects are structured.
- Explain what assemblies are and how to create them.
- Reference other code from your project.
- Create and use namespaces in your projects.
- Use the **Imports** statement to access objects.
- Set various project properties that affect how your application behaves.

Choosing a Project Template

- Windows Application
- Class Library
- Windows Control Library
- ASP .NET Web Application / Service / Control Library
- Console Application
- Windows Service
- Others

Visual Basic developers are used to having multiple project templates to choose from when starting a new project. Visual Basic .NET provides many familiar templates along with a range of new ones.

Template	Use this template to create:
Windows Application	Standard Windows-based applications.
Class Library	Class libraries that provide similar functionality to Microsoft ActiveX® dynamic-link libraries (DLLs) by creating classes accessible to other applications.
Windows Control Library	User-defined Windows control projects, which are similar to ActiveX Control projects in previous versions of Visual Basic.
ASP.NET Web Application	Web applications that will run from an Internet Information Services (IIS) server and can include Web pages and XML Web services.
ASP.NET Web Service	Web applications that provide XML Web Services to client applications.
Web Control Library	User-defined Web controls that can be reused on Web pages in the same way that Windows controls can be reused in Windows applications.
Console Application	Console applications that will run from a command line.
Windows Service	Windows services that will run continuously regardless of whether a user is logged on or not. Previous versions of Visual Basic require you to use third-party products or low-level application programming interface (API) calls to create these types of applications.
Other	Other templates exist for creating enterprise applications, deployment projects, and database projects.

Analyzing Project Structures

- **Solution files (.sln, .suo)**
- **Project files (.vbproj)**
- **Local project items**
  - Classes, forms, modules, etc. (.vb)
- **Web project items**
  - XML Web services (.asmx)
  - Web forms (.aspx)
  - Global application classes (.asax)

Each project contains a variety of files unique to the type of project. To simplify management, the project files are usually stored within the same project directory.

- Solution files (.sln, .suo)

  The .sln extension is used for solution files that link one or more projects together, and are also used for storing certain global information. These files are similar to Visual Basic groups (.vbg files) in previous versions of Visual Basic. Solution files are automatically created within your Visual Basic .NET projects, even if you are only using one project in the solution.

  The .suo file extension is used for Solution User Options files that accompany any solution records and any customizations you make to your solution. This file saves your settings, such as breakpoints and task items, so that they are retrieved each time you open the solution.

- Project files (.vbproj)

  The project file is an Extensible Markup Language (XML) document that contains references to all project items, such as forms and classes, in addition to project references and compilation options. Visual Basic .NET project files use a .vbproj extension, which allows you to differentiate between files written in other .NET-compatible languages (Microsoft Visual C#™ uses .csproj). This makes it easy to include multiple projects that are based on different languages within the same solution.

- Local project items (.vb)

  Previous versions of Visual Basic use different file extensions to distinguish between classes (.cls), forms (.frm), modules (.bas), and user controls (.ctl). Visual Basic .NET enables you to mix multiple types within a single .vb file. For example, you can create more than one item in the same file. You can have a class and some modules, a form and a class, or multiple classes all within the same file. This allows you to keep any strongly related items together in the same file; for example, the **Customer** and **Address** classes.

  Any files that are not based on a programming language have their own extension; for example, a Crystal Report file (.rpt) or text file (.txt).

- Web project items (.aspx., .asmx, .asax)

  Web projects store their items in a Web server virtual directory and in an offline cache. Like local project items, Web project items also use the .vb file extension for classes and modules. However, Web project items include Web-specific files, such as .aspx for Web Forms, .asmx for XML Web Services, and .asax for global application classes.

Note For more information about Web projects, see Module 7, "Building Web Applications," in Course 2373B, *Programming with Microsoft Visual Basic .NET.*

What Are Assemblies?

- **An assembly is an .exe or .dll file with other supporting files that make up a Visual Studio .NET application**
- **The .NET Framework provides predefined assemblies**
- **Assemblies are created automatically when you compile source files**
  - Click **Build** on the Build menu
  - Use the command-line command **vbc.exe**

An assembly is one or more files that make up a Visual Studio .NET application. These files include an .exe or .dll, and resource files such as manifest files or graphics files. Assemblies are a key concept in .NET development; they serve as a building block for all .NET applications. The .NET Framework provides many predefined assemblies for you to reference within your projects. These assemblies provide the classes and functionality of the common language runtime that enables your applications to work.

Assemblies are created automatically when you compile Visual Studio .NET source files. To create an assembly, compile your application by clicking **Build *<projectname>*** on the **Build** menu. You can also use the command-line command **vbc.exe** to compile an assembly. Your assembly can then be referenced by other applications, in much the same way that ActiveX components can be referenced in previous versions of Visual Basic.

Note For more information about assemblies, see Module 10, "Deploying Applications," in Course 2373B, *Programming with Microsoft Visual Basic .NET*.

Setting Project References

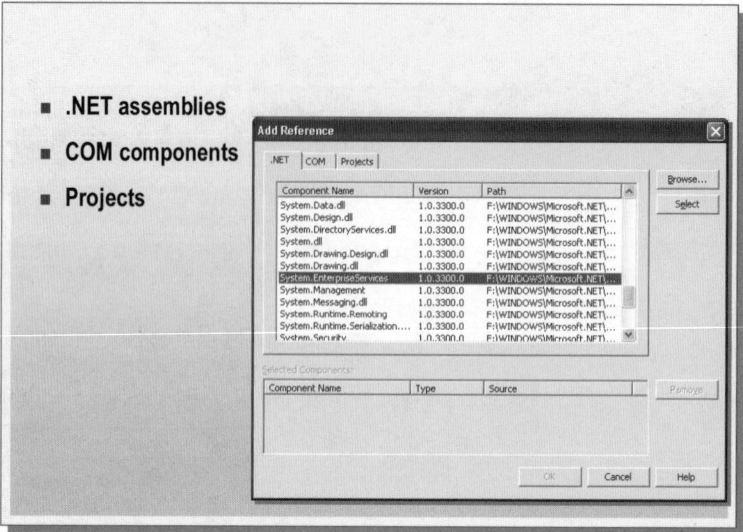

You can set project references to other applications or code libraries in order to use the functionality these applications provide. You can set project references to other .NET assemblies, existing COM components, or other .NET projects within the same .NET solution.

► **To add a reference**

1. Select the current project in Solution Explorer. On the **Project** menu, click **Add Reference**.
2. In the **Add Reference** dialog box, select the appropriate type of reference by clicking the **.NET**, **COM**, or **Projects** tab. Only projects within the same solution are displayed in the **Projects** tab.
3. Locate the required component in the list, or if item is not displayed in the list use the **Browse** button to locate the file. Click the item in the list, and then click **Select**.
4. Repeat step 3 for all the components you require, and then click **OK**.

After you set a reference, you can use it in the same way that you use COM components in previous versions of Visual Basic. You can view information about the reference in the Object Browser and create code that uses the functionality of the reference.

What Are Namespaces?

- **Namespaces organize objects defined in an assembly**
  - Group logically related objects together
- **Namespaces create fully qualified names for objects**
  - Prevent ambiguity
  - Prevent naming conflicts in classes

Namespaces are used in .NET Framework assemblies to organize the objects of an assembly (classes, interfaces, and modules) into a structure that is easy to understand.

Namespaces group logically related objects together so that you can easily access them in your Visual Basic .NET code. For example, the **SQLClient** namespace defined within the **System.Data** assembly provides the relevant objects required to use a Microsoft SQL Server™ database.

When you prefix an object with the namespace it belongs to, the object is considered to be fully qualified. Using unique, fully qualified names for objects in your code prevents ambiguity. You can declare two classes with the same name in different namespaces without conflict.

Creating Namespaces

- **Use Namespace ... End Namespace syntax**
- **Use the root namespace defined in Assembly Properties**

```
Namespace Top              'Fully qualified as MyAssembly.Top
 Public Class Inside       'Fully qualified as MyAssembly.Top.Inside
     ...
 End Class
 Namespace InsideTop       'Fully qualified as MyAssembly.Top.InsideTop
   Public Class Inside
   'Fully qualified as MyAssembly.Top.InsideTop.Inside
     ...
   End Class
 End Namespace
End Namespace
```

You can create your own namespaces in an assembly by creating a block of code that uses the **Namespace...End Namespace** syntax. The following example shows how to create a namespace named **Customers**:

```
Namespace Customers
  'Create classes, modules, and interfaces
  'Related to Customer information
End Namespace
```

The assembly usually defines a root namespace for the project that is set in the **Project Properties** dialog box. You can modify or delete this root namespace if you choose. The following example shows code in an assembly that has a root namespace named **MyAssembly**:

```
Namespace Top
'Fully qualified as MyAssembly.Top

    Public Class Inside
    'Fully qualified as MyAssembly.Top.Inside
         ...
    End Class

    Namespace InsideTop
    'Fully qualified as MyAssembly.Top.InsideTop

        Public Class Inside
        'Fully qualified as MyAssembly.Top.InsideTop.Inside
            ...
        End Class
    End Namespace
End Namespace
```

The following example shows how code from the same assembly, when outside of the **Top** namespace, calls classes. Notice that the **MyAssembly** namespace is not required as part of the fully qualified name, because this code also resides in the **MyAssembly** namespace.

```
Public Sub Perform( )
    Dim x As New Top.Inside( )
    Dim y As New Top.InsideTop.Inside( )
    ...
End Sub
```

Note You can also create nested namespaces without nesting the definitions, by using the fully qualified name. For example, you can declare the **InsideTop** namespace anywhere by using the following code:

```
Namespace MyAssembly.Top.InsideTop
```

Importing Namespaces

- **Fully qualified names can make code hard to read**

```
Dim x as MyAssembly.Top.InsideTop.Inside
```

- **Using the Imports statement results in simpler code by providing scope**

```
Imports MyAssembly.Top.InsideTop
...
Dim x as Inside
```

- **Import aliases create aliases for a namespace or type**

```
Imports IT = MyAssembly.Top.InsideTop
...
Dim x as IT.Inside
```

You can access any object in an assembly by using a fully qualified name. The problem with this approach is that it makes your code difficult to read, because variable declarations must include the entire namespace hierarchy for you to access the desired class or interface.

Using the Imports Statement

You can simplify your code by using the **Imports** statement. The **Imports** statement allows you to access objects without using the fully qualified name. The **Imports** statement does not just point to namespaces in other assemblies. You can also use it to point to namespaces in the current assembly.

The following examples compare two methods for accessing the **InsideTop.Inside** class from an external assembly:

- Example using the fully qualified name:

```
Module ModMain
    Sub Perform( )
        'Fully qualified needed
        Dim x as New MyAssembly.Top.InsideTop.Inside( )
        ...
    End Sub
End Module
```

- Example using the **Imports** statement:

```
Imports MyAssembly.Top.InsideTop

Module ModMain
    Sub Perform( )
        Dim x As New Inside( )  'Fully qualified not needed
        ...
    End Sub
End Module
```

Import Aliases

You can use the **Imports** statement to create import aliases for parts of namespaces. Import aliases provide a convenient way to access items in a namespace. They prevent naming conflicts but still make code easy to write and understand.

The following example creates an import alias called **IT** for the **MyAssembly.Top.InsideTop** namespace. You can reference any item belonging to the namespace by using the **IT** import alias.

```
Imports IT = MyAssembly.Top.InsideTop

Module ModMain
    Sub Perform( )
        Dim x As New IT.Inside( )  'Alias used
        ...
    End Sub
End Module
```

Setting Project Properties

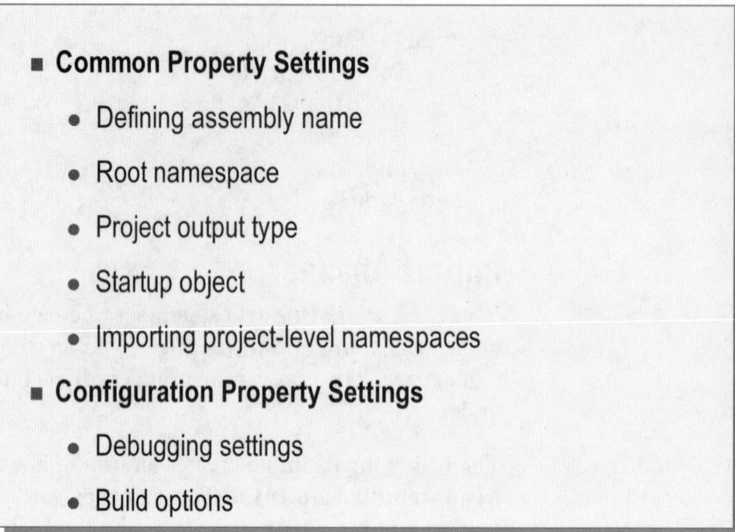

Common Property Settings
Defining assembly name
Root namespace
Project output type
Startup object
Importing project-level namespaces
Configuration Property Settings
Debugging settings
Build options

You can specify many project properties in the project **Property Pages** dialog box. These properties affect how the project behaves both in the IDE and after it is compiled.

The following screen shot shows the project **Property Pages** dialog box for an application named SimpleApp:

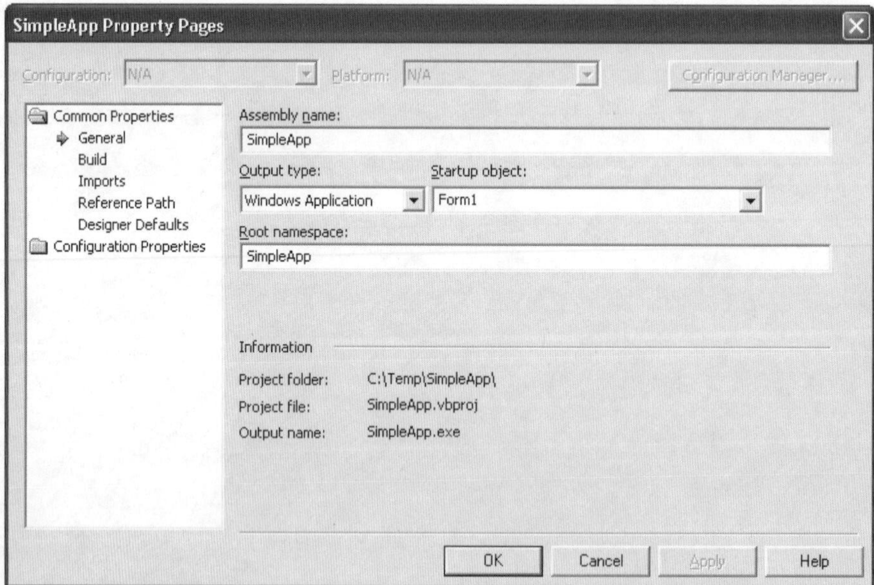

Some of the **Common Property** settings are listed below.

Property	Use this property to:
Assembly name	Specify the name of the assembly when compiled into an .exe or .dll file.
Root namespace	Change the root namespace without affecting the name of the assembly. (A default root namespace is created when you create the project.) This property affects any fully qualified names used for variable declaration.
Project output type	Choose what type of assembly is generated when your project is compiled. You can select Windows Application (.exe), Console Application (.exe), or Class Library (.dll).
Startup object	Select an entry point for your application. This is usually the main form of your application or a **Sub Main** procedure. Class libraries cannot have a startup object.
Importing project-level namespaces	Import multiple namespaces. They are then automatically accessible without forcing you to use the **Imports** statement in each file within the project.

Some of the frequently used **Configuration Property** settings are listed below.

Property	Purpose
Debugging settings	These properties allow you to set debugging options, like for previous versions of Visual Basic. You can choose how your application starts up when debugging by starting the project, starting an external program that calls your code, or displaying a Web page from a URL that calls your code. You can also specify any command-line arguments your application needs for testing purposes.
Build options	You can specify an output directory for your compiled code (\bin is the default). You can also enable or disable the generation of debugging information contained in the .pdb file.

Demonstration: Creating a Visual Basic .NET Project

In this demonstration, you will learn how to create a Visual Basic .NET project based on the project templates. You will also learn about the files that comprise the project structure and how to create a reference to another assembly.

◆ Using Development Environment Features

- Using Solution Explorer
- Using Server Explorer
- Using the Object Browser
- Using the Task List
- Using Dynamic Help
- Using XML Features
- Recording and Using Macros

The Visual Studio .NET IDE contains several features that enable more efficient development of projects. Some of these features are enhancements of existing Visual Basic features. Others are amalgamated from other sources, such as Microsoft Visual InterDev®.

After completing this lesson, you will be able to:

- Use IDE tools such as Solution Explorer, Server Explorer, Object Browser, and Task List.
- Use Dynamic Help while developing your Visual Basic .NET applications.
- Edit XML documents in the IDE.
- Record and use macros for repetitive tasks in your projects.

Using Solution Explorer

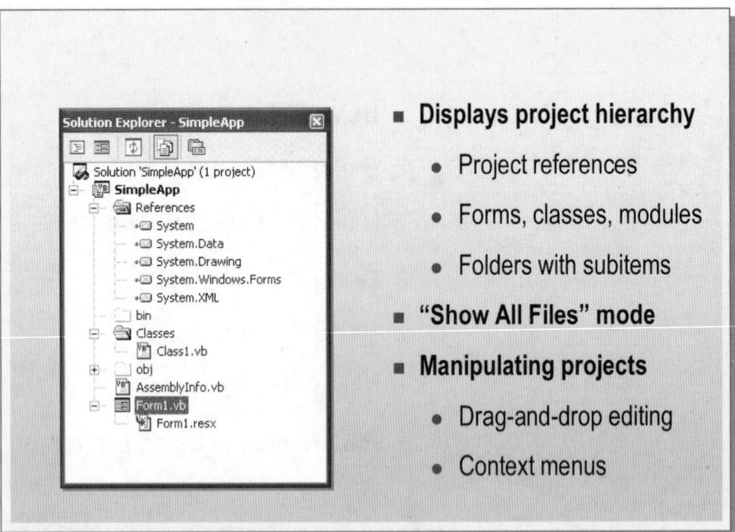

Solution Explorer displays your project hierarchy, including all project references; project items such as forms, classes, modules, and so on; and any subfolders that contain project items. If your solution contains more than one project, you will see the same sort of hierarchy used in previous versions of Visual Basic when a project group exists.

"Show All Files" Mode

By default, Solution Explorer only shows some of the files stored in the project hierarchy. Certain files, which do not form an integral part of the solution, may be hidden or marked as excluded from the project, such as the files in the bin and obj folders on the slides. These files become visible when you click the **Show All Files** toolbar button. This option allows you to see items that are copied manually to the project folders. The slide associated with this topic shows a screen shot of this view of Solution Explorer.

Manipulating Projects

The following features allow you to manipulate your projects with Solution Explorer:

- Drag-and-drop editing

  You can use drag-and-drop editing to move existing project items between folders.

- Context menus

  Most items provide context menus that allow you to perform standard actions, such as adding items to the project, deleting items from the project, and excluding items from the project, which removes the file from the project but does not delete the file. If you use Microsoft Visual SourceSafe®, you can add items to Visual SourceSafe from Solution Explorer.

Using Server Explorer

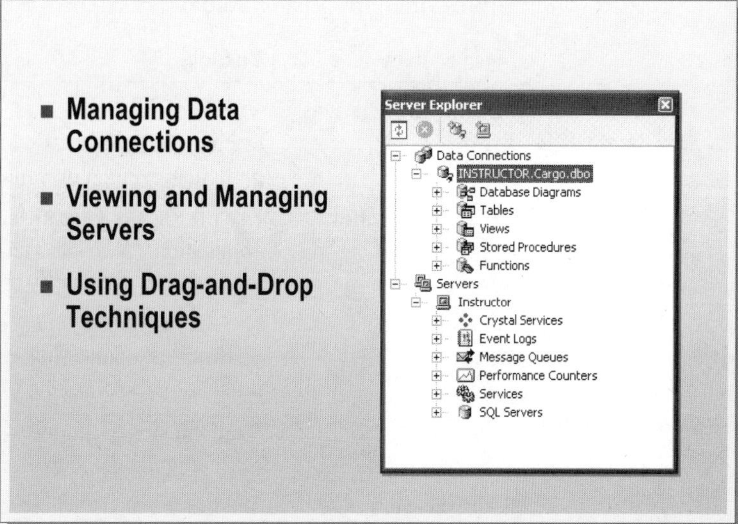

In previous versions of Visual Basic, you can manipulate databases by using the Data View window. Server Explorer provides the same functionality and additional functionality for managing and using server components.

Managing Data Connections

To use Server Explorer to manipulate a database, add a connection to the server by clicking **Connect to Database** on the Server Explorer toolbar. This action brings up the **Data Link Properties** dialog box. After a connection is established, you can view and manipulate the database diagrams, tables, views, stored procedures, and functions.

Viewing and Managing Servers

You can also use Server Explorer to view and manage various server items from within the Visual Studio .NET IDE.

Server item	Purpose
Event Logs	View system event logs for application, security, and system events. The Properties window displays information about each particular event. You can use the context menu to clear the log.
Message Queues	Use message queues to send messages asynchronously between applications. You can view and manipulate any message queues located on the server by using the context menu for the item.
Performance Counters	Use the many performance counters provided by the Windows platform to monitor system-level and application-level interactions, such as the total number of logons to the server.
Services	Start and stop Windows services from Server Explorer by using context menus.
SQL Servers	View and manage Microsoft SQL Server™ databases directly from Server Explorer in the same way that you view and manage data connections.

Using Drag-and-Drop Techniques

You do not use Server Explorer just for viewing and managing server items. You can use drag-and-drop techniques to place items (such as fields from a database) on your forms, or to manipulate server items (such as starting or stopping a Windows service) from within your Visual Basic .NET code.

Using the Object Browser

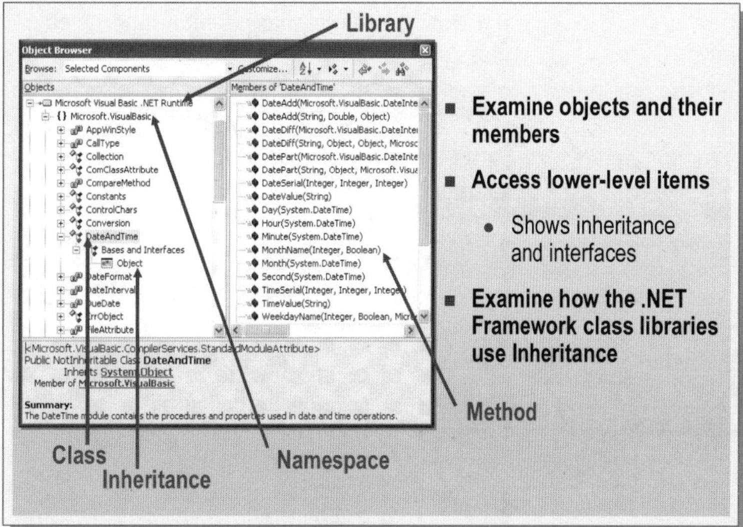
Library
Examine objects and their members
Access lower-level items
Shows inheritance and interfaces
Examine how the .NET Framework class libraries use Inheritance
Method
Class
Inheritance
Namespace

Visual Basic .NET enhances the Object Browser found in previous versions of Visual Basic. Previous versions of the Object Browser show only a high-level view of objects and their methods. Using the Visual Basic .NET Object Browser, you can:

- Examine objects and their members within a library, exploring the object hierarchy to find details about a particular method or item.
- Access lower-level items, such as interfaces and object inheritance details.
- Examine how the .NET Framework class libraries use inheritance in their object hierarchies.

The following screen shot shows the Microsoft Visual Basic .NET Runtime library and its various namespaces. This screen shot highlights the **Microsoft.VisualBasic** namespace and shows the classes it contains, including the **DateAndTime** class, which inherits characteristics from the **System.Object** class.

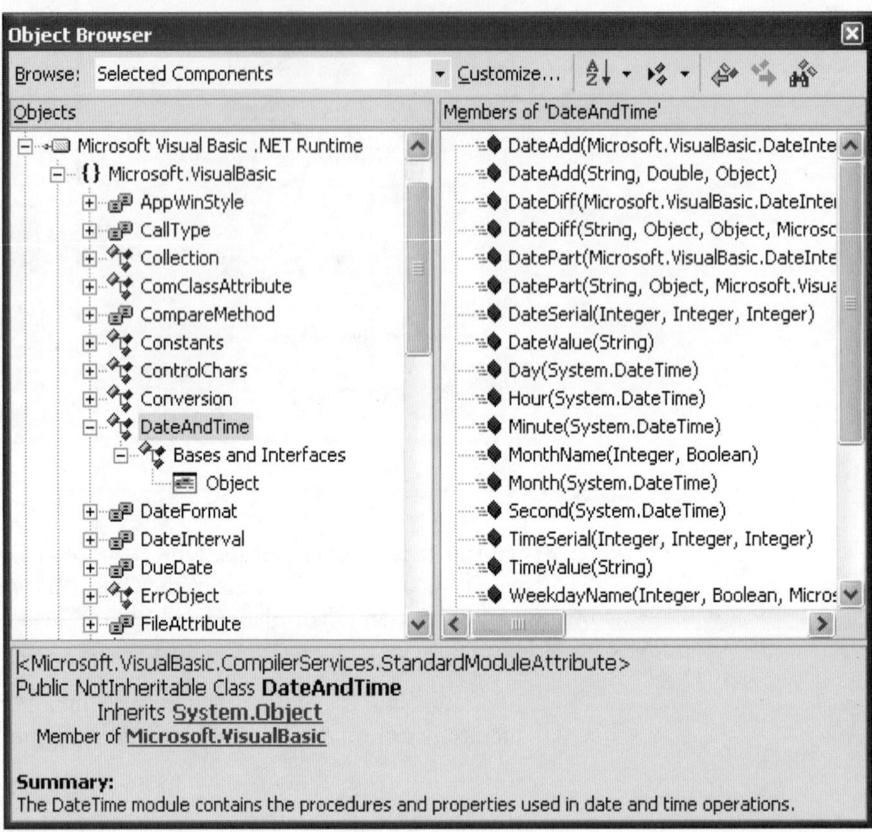

Using the Task List

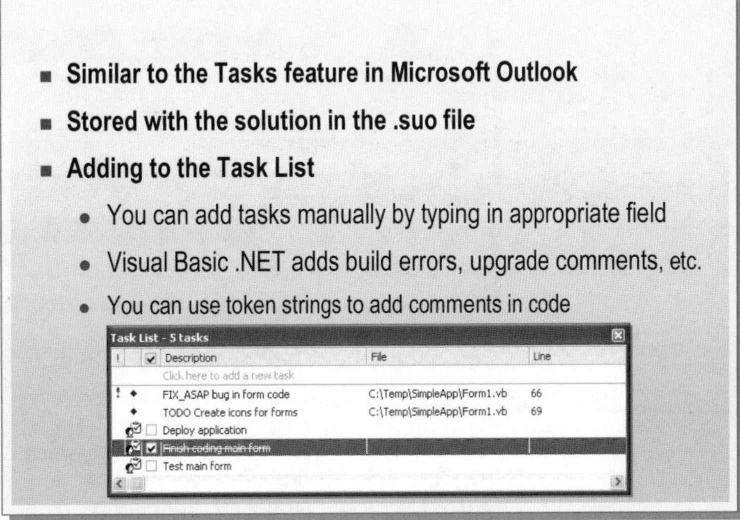

Similar to the Tasks feature in Microsoft Outlook
Stored with the solution in the .suo file
Adding to the Task List
You can add tasks manually by typing in appropriate field
Visual Basic .NET adds build errors, upgrade comments, etc.
You can use token strings to add comments in code
Task List - 5 tasks
Description
File
Line
Click here to add a new task
FIX_ASAP bug in form code
C:\Temp\SimpleApp\Form1.vb
66
TODO Create icons for forms
C:\Temp\SimpleApp\Form1.vb
69
Deploy application
Finish coding main form
Test main form

If you use Microsoft Outlook®, you may be familiar with the Tasks feature. You can use this feature to maintain a list of tasks that you are working on or tracking, and you can clear tasks when you complete them. Visual Studio .NET provides the same functionality through a Task List window, which keeps track of solution-level tasks that you must complete.

Tasks are kept in the .suo project file so that you do not lose information when you close your Visual Studio .NET session. Any stored tasks are available to all developers that use the same .suo project files.

Tasks can be added to your Task List in three ways:

- You can manually add tasks to the task list by typing in the top row that is always visible in the Task List window.
- Visual Studio .NET automatically adds tasks to the list when you attempt to build your application, when you upgrade from a Visual Basic 6.0 project, or at various other stages during the project. This allows you to keep track of what you must do to successfully complete your project.
- You can add tasks by creating comments in your code that use specific token strings defined in the **Options** dialog box, which is accessible from the **Tools** menu. The TODO, HACK, and UNDONE tokens have been created for you, but you can define your own.

The following example shows a code section that uses the **TODO** token and a custom token named **FIX_ASAP**:

```
'TODO create icons for form
'FIX_ASAP bug in form code
```

The following screen shot shows how the Task List window displays information based on this example, with three extra items that have been added to the list manually:

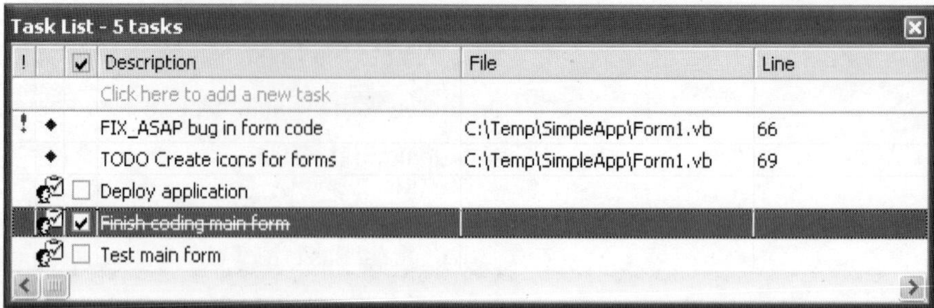

You can use the **View** menu to specify which types of tasks to display in the Task List.

The following screen shot shows how to use the **Options** dialog box to create the **FIX_ASAP** token. Notice that the token has been created so that the items in the Task List display a High priority icon.

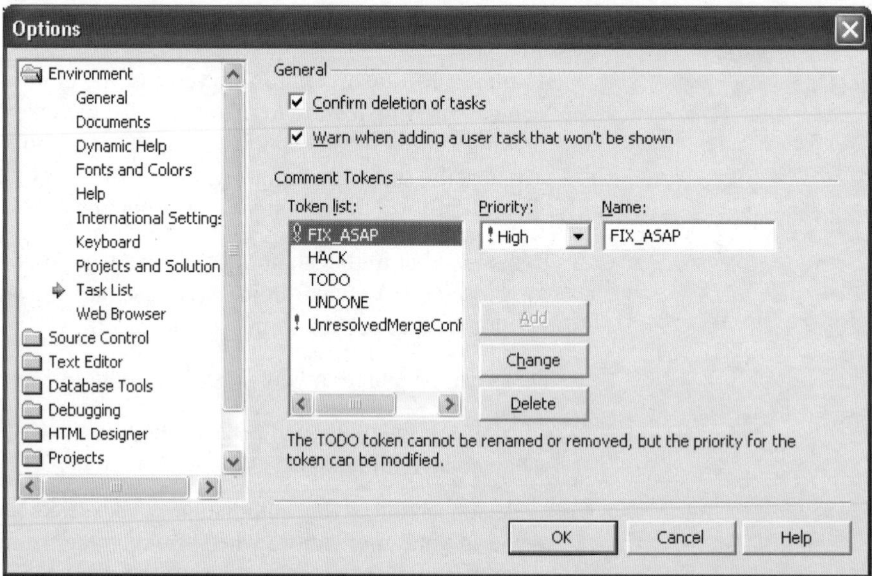

Using Dynamic Help

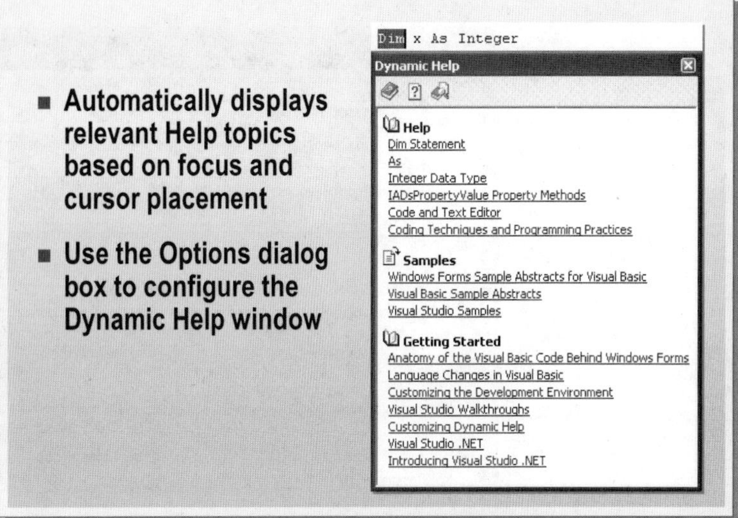

The Dynamic Help window automatically displays appropriate Help links to the .NET Help files, depending on where the cursor is and what text is highlighted. As you move from one window to another within the IDE, information displayed in the Dynamic Help window changes. If you are typing Visual Basic syntax, you see the appropriate Help topic for the syntax you are typing.

For example, the results that the Dynamic Help displays for the following statement vary depending on where the cursor is positioned:

```
Dim x As Integer
```

- If the cursor is positioned within the **Dim** keyword, the Dynamic Help window displays links relevant to the **Dim** keyword at the top of the list.
- If the cursor is positioned within the **Integer** keyword, the Dynamic Help window displays links relevant to integer types at the top of the list.

You can use the **Options** dialog box on the **Tools** menu to configure the items that the Dynamic Help window displays. The following screen shot shows how to use the **Options** dialog box to configure the Dynamic Help window:

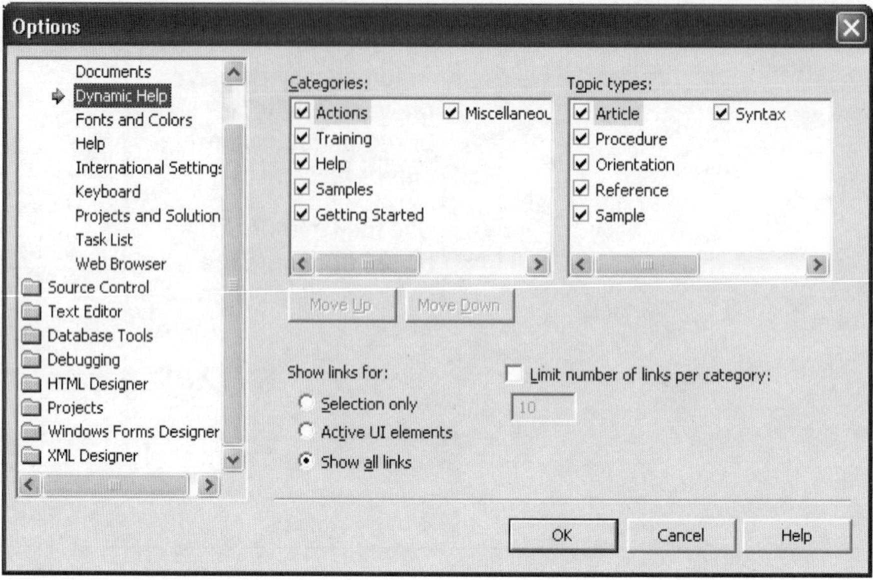

Using XML Features

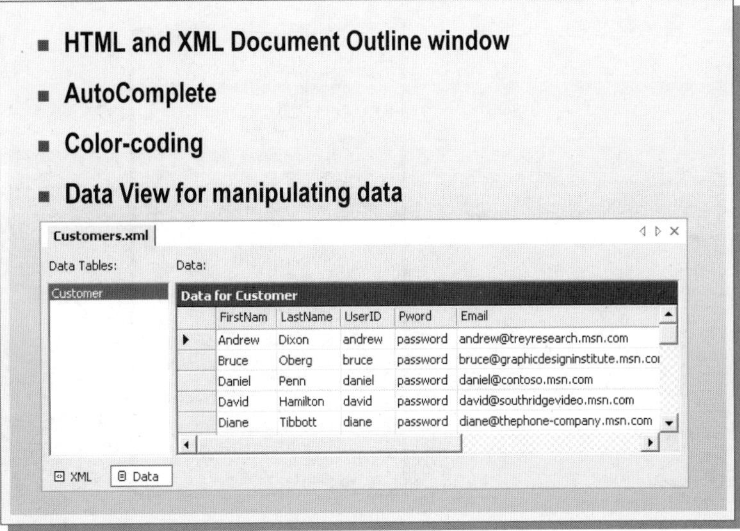

Enterprise applications often use XML documents to specify information as part of the application architecture.

The Visual Studio .NET IDE provides several useful features for creating and editing XML documents, as described in the following table.

XML feature	Description
Hypertext Markup Language (HTML) and XML Document Outline window	Provides a view of the hierarchy of HTML and XML documents within the application.
AutoComplete	Automatically creates the closing tags when you create either HTML or XML starting tags. This feature can be switched off in the **Options** dialog box.
Color-coding	Assists in distinguishing tags from data.
Data View for manipulating data	Allows you to add items to your XML data hierarchy and edit existing information. Provides hyperlinks for navigation to lower-level items in the XML hierarchy.

Recording and Using Macros

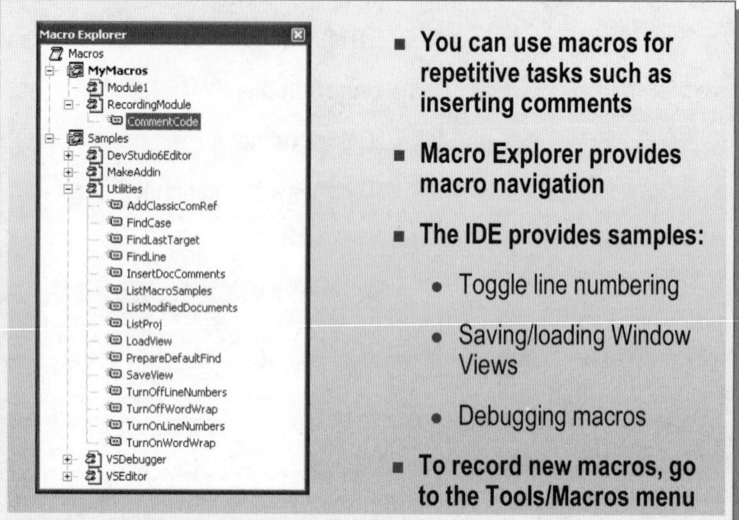

Macros allow users to perform repetitive tasks with the click of a button or menu item. The Visual Studio .NET IDE provides macros, so you can automate tasks that require tedious work, such as inserting standard comments into your code.

The Macro Explorer allows you to edit, rename, delete, or run your macros within the IDE.

Several sample macros are included in the IDE, including the following:

- Toggle line numbering macros
- Saving or loading Window Views macros
- Debugging macros

You can use any of the sample macros in your projects by executing them in the Command window or placing them on menus or toolbars.

► **To record your own macros**

1. On the **Tools** menu, point to **Macros**, and then click **Record TemporaryMacro**.
2. Perform the actions that you wish to record, such as inserting comments in the current module.
3. Click **Stop Recording** on the **Recorder** toolbar to stop recording your macro.
4. Your macro is saved with a temporary name visible in the Macro Explorer. You can rename the temporary macro to save your macro with an appropriate name.

Any macros you create are stored in a subdirectory of the Visual Studio Projects folder in My Documents.

Demonstration: Using the Visual Studio .NET IDE

In this demonstration, you will learn how to use several features of the Visual Studio .NET IDE, including Solution Explorer, Server Explorer, and XML editing tools.

◆ Debugging Applications

- Setting Breakpoints
- Debugging Code
- Using the Command Window

The Visual Studio .NET IDE provides enhanced versions of many of the debugging features found in previous versions of Visual Basic, along with several powerful features found in Visual C++.

After completing this lesson, you will be able to:

- Set breakpoints.
- Debug code in a Visual Basic .NET project.
- Use the Command window while designing and debugging applications.

Setting Breakpoints

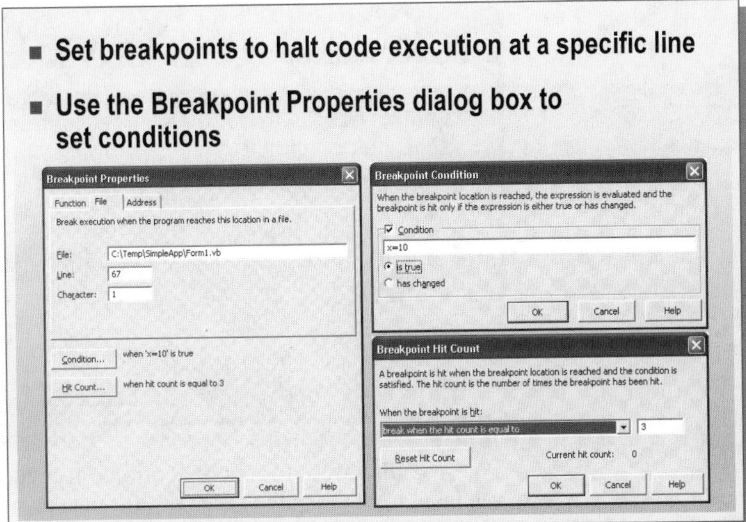

Breakpoints halt execution of code at a specific line. You can set breakpoints at design time or during a debugging session.

There are several ways you can set a breakpoint:

- Click the margin to the left of the code window on the line containing the statement where you want the debugger to halt.
- On the **Debug** menu, click **New Breakpoint**, and choose from the various options.
- Place the cursor on the line where you want the debugger to halt. Press **F9** to switch the breakpoint on or off.

You can use the **Breakpoint Properties** dialog box to make a conditional breakpoint. This feature works in a way similar to watch expressions in previous versions of Visual Basic. You set a breakpoint condition that only halts execution when a particular condition is true or when a variable has changed.

The following screen shot shows a breakpoint condition that only halts when a variable *x* has a value of *10*.

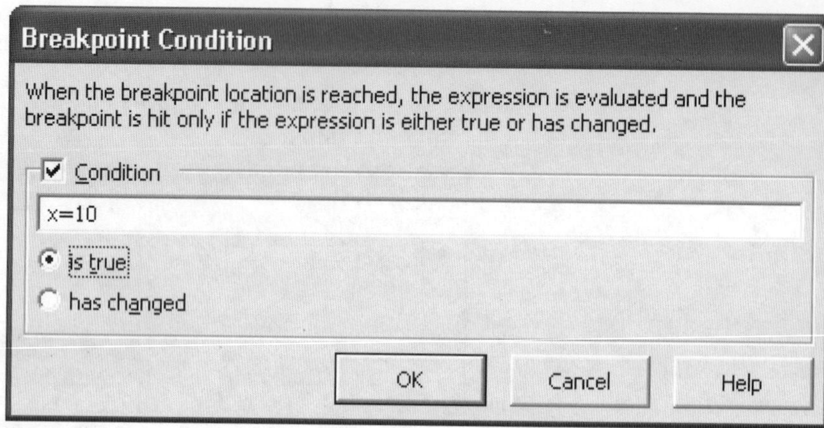

You may also want to halt execution only when the breakpoint has been reached and the breakpoint condition has been satisfied a specific number of times. This number is called the *hit count*.

► **To set a breakpoint hit count**

1. In the **Breakpoint Properties** dialog box, click **Hit Count**.
2. In the **Breakpoint Hit Count** dialog box, choose the type of hit count test that you want to perform from the drop-down combo box, enter the appropriate hit count value, and then click **OK**.

The following screen shot shows how you specify that you want execution to stop the third time that the breakpoint is reached and the breakpoint condition is satisfied:

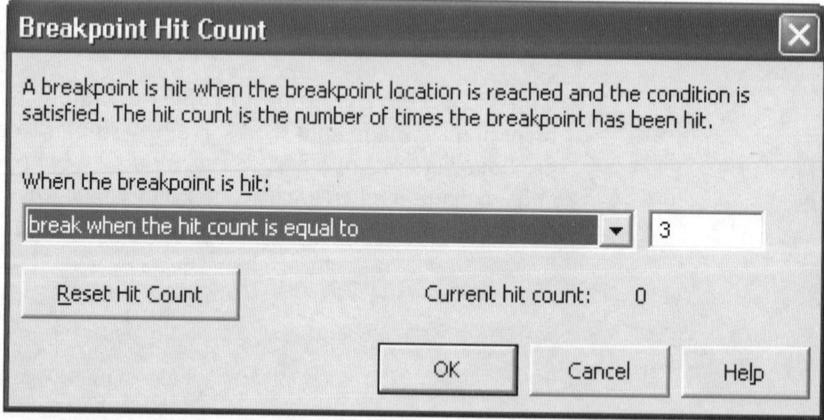

Debugging Code

- **Use the Debug menu or toolbar to step through code**
- **Use the debugging windows:**
  - Locals: to view and modify local variables
  - Output: to view output from the compiler
  - Watch: to view watch expressions
  - Call Stack: to view call history, including parameter information
  - Breakpoints: to view, add, or temporarily disable breakpoints

Debugging your code in Visual Basic .NET is similar to debugging code in previous versions of Visual Basic. When code execution stops at the breakpoint, you can step through the code by using the **Debug** menu or toolbar.

All of the debugging windows found in previous versions of Visual Basic are available in Visual Basic .NET, but with some enhancements.

Debug window	Use this window to:
Locals	View and modify variables. This window provides explicit details about objects, such as inheritance information. The tree view of this window is particularly useful for viewing values in an object hierarchy.
Output	View output information from the compiler, such as the number of compilation errors that occurred and what libraries were loaded. You can use the **Debug.Writeline** statement to print information to the Output window. This statement replaces the **Debug.Print** statement in previous versions of Visual Basic.
Watch	View and manipulate any watch expressions. To add values to the Watch window, type in the **Name** column of an empty row, or click **Quick Watch** on the **Debug** menu. This allows you to quickly add watch expressions during your debugging session. Unlike in previous versions of Visual Basic, you cannot set watch conditions. These have been replaced by breakpoints conditions in Visual Basic .NET.

(continued)

Debug window	Use this window to:
Call Stack	View the history of calls to the line of code being debugged. This window displays the history of the call, including any parameters to procedures and their values.
Breakpoints	View a list of current breakpoints, including information such as how many times the breakpoint has been called, and the conditions the breakpoint has met. You can also add new breakpoints and temporarily disable breakpoints in this window.

Using the Command Window

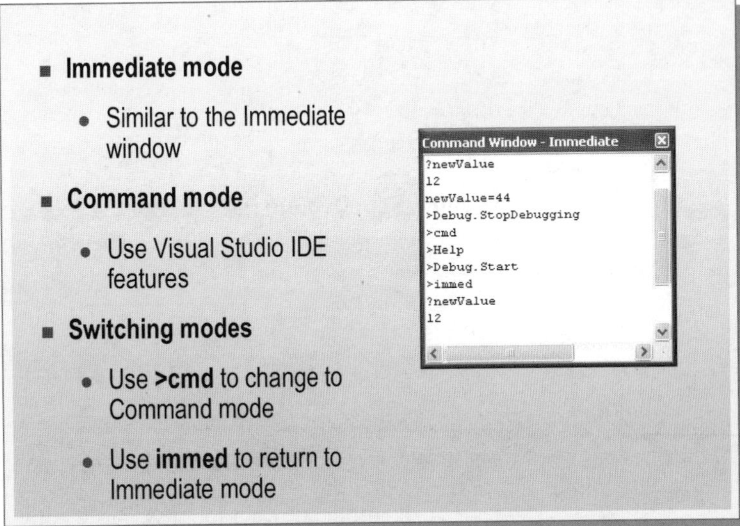
Immediate mode
Similar to the Immediate window
Command mode
Use Visual Studio IDE features
Switching modes
Use >cmd to change to Command mode
Use immed to return to Immediate mode
Command Window - Immediate
?newValue
12
newValue=44
>Debug.StopDebugging
>cmd
>Help
>Debug.Start
>immed
?newValue
12

In Immediate mode, the Command window in Visual Basic .NET provides functionality similar to that found in the Immediate window in previous versions of Visual Basic. You can query local variables while debugging and change their values under certain conditions. You can also run procedures in your code or other .NET Framework class libraries while you are in Immediate mode.

The Command window also has a second purpose. In Command mode, you can use features of the Visual Studio .NET IDE. The features you can use while in Command mode include the following:

- The **Debug.Start** command, to start debugging
- The **Help** command, to display the Visual Studio .NET documentation
- The **Exit** command, to quit the Visual Studio .NET IDE
- Any macros that you recorded
- Any macros that the IDE provides as samples

To switch between the two modes of the Command window:

- Use the **>cmd** command to switch from Immediate mode to Command mode.

  You can issue single commands in Immediate mode by prefixing your command with the > symbol.

- Use the **immed** command to switch from Command mode to Immediate mode.

The following example shows various commands in both Immediate and Command mode. The window is initially in Immediate mode during a debugging session.

```
?newValue
12
newValue=44
?newValue
44
>Debug.StopDebugging
>cmd
>help
>Debug.Start
>immed
?newValue
12
```

The following steps are executed in this code:

1. The example shows a local variable named *newValue* with a value of 12.
2. In Immediate mode, this value is changed to 44.
3. The variable is queried again to confirm the change.
4. A single command is issued to stop debugging.
5. The **cmd** command is used to switch to Command mode.
6. The **help** command is used to display the Visual Studio .NET documentation.
7. The **Debug.Start** command is used to start debugging.
8. The **immed** command is used to switch back to Immediate mode.
9. The *newValue* variable is tested again.

Demonstration: Debugging a Project

In this demonstration, you will learn how to use the debugging features of the Visual Studio .NET IDE to debug a simple Visual Basic .NET project.

◆ Compiling in Visual Basic .NET

- Locating Syntax Errors
- Compilation Options

After completing this lesson, you will be able to:

- Locate syntax errors when you attempt to build your application.
- Select the best compilation option for building your Visual Basic .NET projects.

Locating Syntax Errors

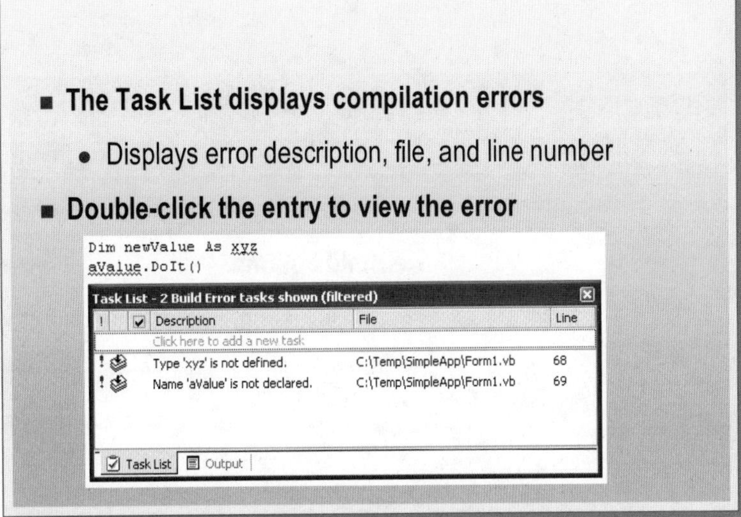

Visual Basic .NET displays compilation errors as you type each statement in your application code. If you ignore these warnings and attempt to build your application, the Task List is displayed, with all build errors included on the list.

Information about the error includes the error description, the file in which the error occurred, and the line number. The error description is the same information that you see if you position the cursor over the highlighted part of your code in the code window.

You can edit the errors by double-clicking the appropriate entry in the Task List. This positions the cursor in the correct file and exact line where the error is located, so you can make the required modifications. As soon as you complete your changes and you move off the modified line, the Task List entries are updated.

Compilation Options

- **Build configurations**
  - Debug – provides debug information
  - Release – optimizes code and executable size
- **Build options**
  - Build – only builds changed projects
  - Rebuild – rebuilds project regardless of changes

The Visual Studio .NET IDE provides several compilation options for building your Visual Basic .NET projects.

Build Configurations

There are two types of build configurations for Visual Basic .NET projects:

- Debug

  During the development phase, you may want to build and test your applications by using compiled assemblies. The Debug configuration produces a .pdb file that contains debugging information. Other applications can use this file to debug your code. To assist these other applications, no optimizations are made to your code. Other applications have access to your complete and original code.

- Release

  After testing is completed, you will want to deploy your application to client computers. The Release configuration performs various code optimizations and attempts to minimize the size of the executable file. No debugging information is generated for a Release configuration build.

Build Options

You can choose what to build by selecting the appropriate **Build** menu options.

- **Build**

  The **Build** option only builds project items whose code has changed since they were last compiled.

- **Rebuild**

  The **Rebuild** option compiles all project items even if they have not been modified since they were last compiled. Use this option when you want to be sure your application contains the latest code and resources.

Lab 2.1: Exploring the Development Environment

Objectives

After completing this lab, you will be able to:

- Use the Visual Studio .NET IDE.
- Create a simple Visual Basic .NET project.
- Set conditional breakpoints.
- Debug an application.
- Use the Task List and Command windows.

Prerequisites

Before working on this lab, you must have experience with developing applications in an earlier version of Visual Basic.

Scenario

In this lab, you will explore the Visual Studio .NET IDE and use its features to create a data connection and view event log information. You will create a simple Windows-based application and add a prewritten form to the project. Finally, you will debug the application by using the various debugging features of the IDE.

Starter and Solution Files

There are starter and solution files associated with this lab. The starter files are in the *install folder*\Labs\Lab021\Ex02\Starter folder, and the solution files are in the *install folder*\Labs\Lab021\Ex02\Solution folder.

Estimated time to complete this lab: 45 minutes

Exercise 1
Becoming Familiar with the Visual Studio .NET IDE

In this exercise, you will use Server Explorer to create a data connection for the Northwind SQL Server database. You will investigate Server Explorer, and the event logs in particular. You will then view the **Options** dialog box to become familiar with the default IDE settings.

The purpose of this exercise is for you to become familiar with the IDE, so take time to explore any parts of the IDE that are interesting to you.

▶ To add a data connection by using Server Explorer

1. Click **start**, point to **All Programs**, point to **Microsoft Visual Studio .NET**, and then click **Microsoft Visual Studio .NET**.
2. On the **View** menu, click **Server Explorer**.
3. On the **Server Explorer** toolbar, click **Connect to Database**. Use the following values to complete the **Data Link Properties** dialog box:

Property	Value
Server name	**localhost**
Logon information	**Use Windows NT Integrated security**
Database	**Northwind**

4. Click **Test Connection** to verify that you have successfully made the connection, and then click **OK**.
5. Click **OK** on the **Data Link Properties** dialog box.
6. If you are not familiar with the Data View window from previous versions of Visual Basic or Microsoft Visual InterDev®, explore the list of tables, views, and stored procedures by expanding the newly created ***servername*.Northwind.dbo** data connection.

▶ To explore the Application event log

1. Under the **Servers** node of Server Explorer, expand the name of your computer.
2. Expand the **Event Logs** node, expand the **Application** node, and then expand the **MSSQLSERVER** node.
3. Select an **EventLogEntry** node and view the application entry information in the Properties window. If the Properties window is not visible, click **Properties Window** on the **View** menu.

▶ To explore the default IDE configuration options

1. On the **Tools** menu, click **Options**.
2. Spend several minutes becoming familiar with the default Environment settings.
3. When you are finished exploring, click **Cancel**.

Exercise 2
Creating a Visual Basic .NET Project

In this exercise, you will create a simple Visual Basic .NET project and remove the default form from the project. You will then add a prewritten form to the project and change the **Startup object** property of the project.

The prewritten form displays a text box and a command button. When you press the button, the value in the text box is sent to a subroutine. This subroutine verifies that the value is not empty and displays a message based on the value. If the value is empty, an error message appears.

▶ To create a new project

1. On the **File** menu, point to **New**, and then click **Project**.
2. In the **Project Types** box, click the **Visual Basic Projects** folder.
3. In the **Templates** box, click **Windows Application**.
4. Change the name of the project to **FirstApp**, set the location to *install folder*\Labs\Lab021\Ex02, and then click **OK**.

▶ To add the test form

1. In Solution Explorer, right-click **Form1.vb**, click **Delete**, and then confirm the deletion warning.
2. On the **Project** menu, click **Add Existing Item**.
3. Set the location to *install folder*\Labs\Lab021\Ex02\Starter, click **frmDebugging.vb**, and then click **Open**.
4. Using Solution Explorer, click **frmDebugging.vb**, and then click the **View Code** button.
5. Examine the code in the **btnDebug_Click** and **PerformValidation** procedures, and ensure that you understand the purpose of the code.

▶ To set the project startup property

1. In Solution Explorer, right-click **FirstApp**, and then click **Properties**.
2. In the **Startup object** list, click **frmDebugging**, and then click **OK**.
3. On the **File** menu, click **Save All** to save the project.

Exercise 3
Using the Debugger

In this exercise, you will use the Visual Studio .NET debugger to debug the simple application that you created in the previous exercise.

You will set a breakpoint to halt execution in the **btnDebug_Click** event handler and use the debugger to step through the subroutine. You will examine the parameter passed to the **PerformValidation** procedure and change the value by using the Locals window. You will then step through the rest of the code and verify that the correct message appears. Finally, you will modify the breakpoint so that it is conditional, and use the Command window to perform various IDE functions.

► To set a breakpoint

1. On the **View** menu, point to **Other Windows**, and then click **Task List**.
2. Right-click anywhere within the Task List window, point to **Show Tasks**, and then click **All**.
3. Double-click the single **TODO** task to navigate to the comment in the code.
4. Place the pointer on the line immediately after the TODO comment and press F9, the breakpoint shortcut key.

► To debug the project

1. On the **Debug** menu, click **Start**.
2. Enter any value into the text box and then click **Debug**.
3. When the program execution halts, on the **Debug** menu, click **Step Into**.
4. Continue to click **Step Into** until the **PerformValidation** procedure begins execution.
5. Examine the contents of each of the following windows: Locals, Breakpoints, and Call Stack.
6. In the Locals window, change the value of the **strValue** variable to a new value. Do not forget to include the quotation marks around the new value. Press ENTER.
7. Step through the remaining lines of code, closing any message boxes, until the form appears again.

► To modify the breakpoint

1. While the form is displayed, move to the Breakpoints window in the IDE.
2. Right-click the breakpoint, and then click **Properties**.
3. Click **Condition**, and then set the following condition value:

Condition	Break When
txtValue.Text	has changed

4. Click **OK** in the **Breakpoint Condition** dialog box, and then click **OK** in the **Breakpoint Properties** dialog box.
5. On the form, click **Debug**. This time your code should execute without debugging.
6. Change the value in the text box and click **Debug**. This will cause execution to halt because you have met the condition of the breakpoint.
7. On the **Debug** menu, click **Continue** to allow the execution to complete.
8. In the Breakpoints window, clear the breakpoint check box to disable the breakpoint. Verify that execution no longer halts, even if you change the value in the text box.

► To use the Command Window

1. Display the **Command Window** and enter the following command: **>Debug.StopDebugging**. The debugging session will end and the IDE will return to the design state.
2. If the Command Window is no longer displayed, on the **View** menu, point to **Other Windows**, and then click **Command Window**.
3. In the Command Window, enter the **Exit** command to quit Visual Studio .NET.

Review

- Describing the Integrated Development Environment
- Creating Visual Basic .NET Projects
- Using Development Environment Features
- Debugging Applications
- Compiling in Visual Basic .NET

1. List the file extensions for the following Visual Basic .NET files: Visual Basic .NET project files, classes, and modules.

2. Describe the purpose of namespaces and the **Imports** keyword.

3. Describe the purpose of Server Explorer.

4. The Object Browser is exactly the same as in previous versions of Visual Basic. True or false? If false, explain why.

5. Describe the purpose of a conditional breakpoint and how to create one.

msdn® training

Module 3: Language and Syntax Enhancements

Contents

Overview

- **Data Types**
- **Using Variables**
- **Functions, Subroutines, and Properties**
- **Exception Handling**

Microsoft® Visual Basic® .NET version 7.0 introduces many language and syntax enhancements that help make it an excellent development tool for the Microsoft .NET platform. Some of these enhancements include:

- Incorporation of the .NET Framework type system, making Visual Basic .NET compatible with other languages in the .NET Framework.
- Enhancements to syntax for working with variables, thereby increasing the clarity and performance of code.
- Changes to functions, subroutines, and properties, making code easier to read and maintain.
- Structured exception handling, making Visual Basic .NET a more robust development language.

After completing this module, you will be able to:

- Describe the changes to data types in Visual Basic .NET.
- Declare and initialize variables and arrays.
- Use shorthand syntax to assign values to variables.
- Implement functions and subroutines.
- Call the default properties of an object.
- Use the new **Try...Catch...Finally** statement to implement structured exception handling.

◆ Data Types

- Common Type System
- Comparing Value-Type and Reference-Type Variables
- New Data Types
- Changes to Existing Data Types
- Using CType to Convert Data Types

In this lesson, you will learn about the data types available in Visual Basic .NET. After you complete this lesson, you will be able to:

- Explain the .NET Framework common type system and how it affects Visual Basic .NET development.
- Explain the difference between value-type variables and reference-type variables.
- Describe and use the data types available in Visual Basic .NET.
- Use the **CType** function to convert values from one data type to another.

Common Type System

- Integrated in the common language runtime
- Shared by the runtime, compilers, and tools
- Controls how the runtime declares, uses, and manages types
- Includes a set of predefined data types
- Common type system objects are based on the System.Object class

The .NET Framework is based on a new common language runtime. The runtime provides a common set of services for projects built in Microsoft Visual Studio® .NET, regardless of the language. The common type system is an integral part of the runtime. The compilers, tools, and the runtime itself share the common type system. It is the model that defines the rules that the runtime follows when declaring, using, and managing types. The common type system establishes a framework that enables cross-language integration, type safety, and high-performance code execution.

All objects in the common type system are based on the **System.Object** class, and all data types declared in Visual Basic .NET code correspond directly to a common type system data-type. For example, when you declare a variable of type **Integer** in Visual Basic .NET, it is the same as declaring a **System.Int32** common type system data type. The keyword **Integer** is an alias for the Int32 data type, and it provides familiar syntax to Visual Basic developers.

Comparing Value-Type and Reference-Type Variables

- **Value-Type Variables**
  - Directly contain their data
  - Each has its own copy of data
  - Operations on one cannot affect another
  - Assignment creates a copy of the data
- **Reference-Type Variables**
  - Store references to their data (known as objects)
  - Two reference variables can reference the same object
  - Operations on one can affect another

When you define a variable, you need to choose the right data type for your variable. The data type determines the allowable values for that variable, which, in turn, determine the operations that can be performed on that variable. The common type system supports both value-type and reference-type variables.

Value-Type Variables

Value-type variables directly contain their data. Each value-type variable has its own copy of data, so operations on one value-type variable cannot affect another variable.

Examples of value-type variables include integers, doubles, floats, and structures.

Reference-Type Variables

Reference-type variables contain references to their data. The data is stored in an instance. Two reference-type variables can reference the same object, so operations on one reference-type variable can affect the object referenced by another reference-type variable.

Examples of reference-type variables include strings, arrays, and classes.

New Data Types

Visual Basic .NET data type	Storage size	Value range
Char	2 bytes	0 to 65535 (unsigned)
Short	2 bytes	-32,768 to 32,767
Decimal	12 bytes	Up to 28 digits on either side of decimal (signed)

There are three new data types available in Visual Basic .NET: **Char**, **Short,** and **Decimal**.

Char

This data type stores a single Unicode character in a two-byte variable.

Short

In Visual Basic 6.0, a 16-bit integer is an **Integer** data type. In Visual Basic .NET, a 16-bit integer is designated as a **Short**.

Decimal

A **Decimal** data type is stored as a 96-bit (12-byte) fixed-point signed integer, scaled by a variable power of 10. The power of 10 specifies the precision of the digits to the right of the decimal point, and ranges from 0 to 28. This data type should be used when calculations are required that cannot tolerate rounding errors; for example, in financial applications.

If no decimal places are required, the **Decimal** data type can store up to positive or negative 79,228,162,514,264,337,593,543,950,335.

Using the full 28 places for precision, the largest value that can be stored is 7.9228162514264337593543950335 and the smallest non-zero value is positive or negative 0.0000000000000000000000000001.

Changes to Existing Data Types

Visual Basic 6.0	Visual Basic .NET
Integer	**Short**
Long (32 bits, signed)	**Integer**
(none)	**Long** (64 bits, signed)
Variant	Not supported: use **Object**
Currency	Not supported: use **Decimal**
Date	No longer stored as a **Double**
String (fixed length)	Not supported

Several data types from Visual Basic 6.0 have changed or are no longer supported in Visual Basic .NET. These changes make data types in Visual Basic .NET more consistent with data types used by other programming languages in the .NET Framework and in the runtime.

Integer

The **Integer** and **Long** data types in Visual Basic 6.0 have a different meaning in Visual Basic .NET, as described in the following table.

Integer size	Visual Basic 6.0 data type	Visual Basic .NET data type	.NET Framework and runtime type
16 bits, signed	Integer	Short	System.Int16
32 bits, signed	Long	Integer	System.Int32
64 bits, signed	(None)	Long	System.Int64

Variant

Visual Basic .NET updates the universal data type to **Object** for compatibility with the common language runtime.

Visual Basic 6.0

You can assign to the **Variant** data type any primitive type (except fixed-length strings) and **Empty**, **Error**, **Nothing**, and **Null**.

Visual Basic .NET

The **Variant** type is not supported, but the **Object** data type supplies its functionality. **Object** can be assigned to primitive data types, **Nothing**, and as a pointer to an object.

Currency

The **Currency** data type is not supported in Visual Basic .NET. You can use the **Decimal** data type as a replacement. The **Decimal** data type uses 12 bytes of memory, and allows more digits on both sides of the decimal point.

Date

The **Date** data type is available in Visual Basic .NET but is not stored in the same format as it was in Visual Basic 6.0.

Visual Basic 6.0

The **Date** data type is stored in a **Double** format.

Visual Basic .NET

Date variables are stored internally as 64-bit integer. Because of this change, there is no implicit conversion between **Date** and **Double** as there is in previous versions of Visual Basic. Representing dates as integers simplifies and speeds up the manipulation of dates.

String

Fixed-length strings are no longer supported, but you can simulate this behavior by padding a string to the desired length with spaces, as shown in the following example:

```
'Create a string containing spaces
Dim s As String = Space(10)
```

The type name **String** is an alias for the **System.String** class. Therefore, **String** and **System.String** can be used interchangeably. The **String** class represents a string of characters that cannot be modified after the text has been created. Methods that appear to modify a string value actually return a new instance of the string containing the modification.

This can impact performance in applications performing a large number of repeated modifications to a string, so the **System.Text.StringBuilder** object is provided. This object allows you to modify a string without creating a new object, and is therefore a better choice if you are performing a large number of string manipulations. The following example shows how to create a **StringBuilder** variable and how to append values to it:

```
Dim s As New System.Text.StringBuilder()
s.Append("This")
s.Append(" is")
s.Append(" my")
s.Append(" text!")
MsgBox(s.ToString)   'generates "This is my text!"
```

Visual Basic 6.0 provides many string manipulation methods that are still available in Visual Basic .NET. The **System.String** class also has many predefined properties and methods that simulate this behavior by using an object-oriented approach. These properties and methods include **Insert**, **Length**, **Copy**, **Concat**, **Replace**, **Trim**, **ToLower**, and **ToUpper**. For more information, search for “string methods” in the Visual Studio .NET documentation.

Using CType to Convert Data Types

- **Use CType to convert values from one data type to another data type**
- **Similar to CStr and CInt in Visual Basic 6.0**
- **Syntax:**
  - CType (*expression, typename*)

You can use the **CType** function to convert any value from one data type to another data type. If the value is outside the range allowed by the type, an error will occur. The **CType** function is similar to the **CStr** and **CInt** conversion functions in Visual Basic 6.0, but it can be used for composite data type conversion in addition to elementary types.

Syntax

Use the following syntax to convert data types:

```
CType(expression, typename)
```

- *expression*

  The expression argument can be any valid expression, such as a variable, a result of a function, or a constant value.

- *typename*

  The typename argument can be any expression that is valid within an **As** clause in a **Dim** statement, such as the name of any data type, object, structure, class, or interface.

Example

The following examples show how to convert a **String** value to an **Integer**, and how to convert to a data structure type:

```
Dim x As String, y As Integer
x = "34"
y = CType(x, Integer)

Dim custNew as Customer 'Predefined structure type
custNew = CType(data, Customer)
```

◆ Using Variables

- **Declaring and Initializing Variables and Arrays**
- **Declaring Multiple Variables**
- **Variable Scope**
- **Creating Data Structures**
- **Compiler Options**
- **Assignment Operators**

After you complete this lesson, you will be able to:

- Declare and initialize variables.
- Explain changes to variable scope in Visual Basic .NET.
- Create data structures.
- Use compiler options effectively.
- Use a new shorthand syntax for assignment operators.

Declaring and Initializing Variables and Arrays

- **You can initialize variables when you declare them**
- **You can initialize arrays with a size, but they are no longer fixed**
  - You can dimension arrays before using **ReDim**

```
Dim i As Integer = 21
Dim dToday As Date = Today( )

'Array declarations
Dim Month(12) As Integer  'Creates array with 13 elements
'Initialize the array with 12 elements
Dim aMonth( ) As Integer = {1,2,3,4,5,6,7,8,9,10,11,12}
```

In Visual Basic .NET, you can use a different process to declare some types of variables, including arrays and strings. For example, you can declare and initialize variables in a single statement.

Declaring and Initializing Variables

In Visual Basic .NET, you can initialize a variable when you declare it by using the following syntax:

```
Dim [WithEvents] varname[([subscripts])] [As [New] type]
[= initexpr]
```

Most of this syntax is familiar to Visual Basic developers. However, there is a new optional **initexpr** argument that allows you to assign an initial value to a variable as long as the argument is not used in conjunction with the **New** keyword.

Examples

The following code shows how to declare and initialize variables in a single statement:

```
Dim i As Integer = 21
Dim dToday As Date = Today( )
Dim dblFloat As Double = 1232.23312
Dim dBirthday As Date = #1/1/1995#
Dim iCalculate As Integer = i * 5
```

Declaring and Initializing Arrays

You use a slightly different syntax to declare and initialize arrays. This syntax allows you to specify not only the size of the array but also the initial values for it.

In Visual Basic .NET, all arrays must have a lower bound value of zero. You cannot declare an array by using the *lower bound* `To` *upper bound* syntax as you do in Visual Basic 6.0. In the following example, the *Month* variable is created with 13 elements, as it is in previous versions of Visual Basic. The *aMonth* variable, however, creates and initializes an array of precisely 12 elements.

```
Dim Month(12) As Integer
Dim aMonth( ) As Integer = {1,2,3,4,5,6,7,8,9,10,11,12}
```

Redimensioning Arrays

In Visual Basic 6.0, you can only redimension an array if it is not dimensioned when it is declared. In Visual Basic .NET, you can redimension an array if it is dimensioned when it is declared.

Visual Basic 6.0

The following code shows how to redimension an array in Visual Basic 6.0:

```
Dim x( ) As String
ReDim x(5) As String     'Correct in Visual Basic 6.0

Dim y(2) As String
ReDim y(5) As String     'Error in Visual Basic 6.0 because you
                         'cannot redim a dimensioned array
```

Visual Basic .NET

The following code shows how to redimension an array in Visual Basic .NET:

```
Dim x( ) As String
ReDim x(5)               'Correct in Visual Basic .NET
Dim y(2) As String
ReDim Preserve y(5)      'Allowed in Visual Basic .NET
```

Using the **Preserve** keyword will copy the original array into a new array, which can result in inefficient code. If you need to do this often, consider using the **ArrayList** class for a more efficient approach.

Declaring Multiple Variables

- **Declaring multiple variables in Visual Basic 6.0**

```
Dim I, J, X As Integer
'Results in I and J As Variant, X As Integer
```

- **Declaring multiple variables in Visual Basic .NET**

```
Dim I, J, X As Integer
'Results in I, J, and X As Integer
```

In Visual Basic 6.0, you can use a single line of code to declare multiple variables, but you may get unexpected results. Consider the following example:

```
Dim I, J, X As Integer
```

Visual Basic 6.0

In Visual Basic 6.0, I and J are created as **Variants**, and X is created as an **Integer** data type.

Visual Basic .NET

In Visual Basic .NET, all three variables are created as **Integers**. This is consistent with how many other programming languages create multiple variables and is more intuitive.

Variable Scope

- **Procedure scope**
  - Variables accessible to entire procedure
- **Block scope**
  - Variables only accessible within that block
  - Lifetime of block variable is entire procedure

```
Dim iLooper As Integer   'Procedure level variable

For iLooper = 1 to 10
    Dim iMax As Integer  'Block level variable
    iMax = iLooper
Next
MsgBox (iMax)     'This line generates a compiler error
```

In Visual Basic 6.0, if you declare variables inside a block of code, they are accessible to the entire procedure that contains the block. This level of accessibility is referred to as *procedure scope*. In Visual Basic .NET, variables inside a block of code are only accessible to that block of code. This level of accessibility is referred to as *block scope*.

Example

Consider an example in which you need procedure scope for your variables.

Visual Basic 6.0

The following code executes successfully in Visual Basic 6.0, because the *iMax* variable has procedure scope. In Visual Basic .NET, the last line of code generates a compile error because the *iMax* variable has block scope and is only accessible in the **For … Next** loop.

```
Dim iLooper As Integer
For iLooper = 1 to 10
    Dim iMax As Integer
    iMax = iLooper
Next
MsgBox (iMax)

'The last line generates a compiler error in Visual Basic .NET
```

Visual Basic .NET

If you rewrite the code as follows, it will execute successfully in Visual Basic .NET.

```
Dim iLooper As Integer
Dim iMax As Integer
For iLooper = 1 to 10
    iMax = iLooper
Next
MsgBox (iMax)
```

Lifetime of Block Variables

Even though the scope of the variable is limited to the block, the lifetime of the variable is the entire procedure. If you reenter that block, the variable will retain its previous value.

The following example shows how on the first run of the loop, True is displayed, but because y retains its value, the second run displays False.

```
Dim iCounter As Integer
For iCounter = 1 To 2
  Dim y As Boolean
  y = Not y
  MsgBox(y)
Next
```

To avoid unexpected results, it is recommended that you initialize the variable within the block. In the following example, True is displayed both times, as y is initialized within the block.

```
Dim iCounter As Integer
For iCounter = 1 To 2
  Dim y As Boolean = False
  y = Not y
  MsgBox(y)
Next
```

Creating Data Structures

- **Structures replace user-defined types**
- **Structures support many features of classes**
- **Use Structure...End Structure to declare structures**
- **Declare structure members with an access modifier**

```
Structure Customer
  Public CustID As Integer
  Dim CustDayPhone As String               'Defaults to public
  Private CustNightPhone As String         'Private allowed
End Structure
```

In Visual Basic 6.0, you create user-defined types (UDTs) by using **Type… End Type** syntax. In Visual Basic .NET, you create your own data types by creating data structures. To create a data structure, you use the **Structure… End Structure** syntax.

The members of UDTs can only contain **Public** data types. Internal members of a data structure can contain **Public**, **Friend**, or **Private** data types. Therefore, you must declare internal members of a structure with one of these access modifiers, as shown in the following code:

```
Structure Customer
  Public CustID As Integer
  Dim CustDayPhone As String               'Defaults to public
  Private CustNightPhone As String         'Private allowed
End Structure
```

The syntax for using structures and classes in Visual Basic .NET is very similar. In fact, structures support most features of classes, including methods.

Note For more information about data structures and access modifiers, see Module 5, "Object-Oriented Programming in Visual Basic .NET," in Course 2373B, *Programming with Microsoft Visual Basic .NET*.

Compiler Options

- **Option Explicit**
  - Default option
- **Option Strict**
  - Enforces strict type semantics and restricts implicit type conversion
  - Late binding by means of the **Object** data type is not allowed
- **Option Base 1 Not Supported**
  - Arrays must start at zero

The compiler options that you select affect many parts of your application. Two options directly influence how your data types will behave and how you should use them: **Option Explicit** and **Option Strict**. You set these options as **On** or **Off** at the beginning of a module by using the following code:

```
Option Explicit On
Option Strict Off
```

Option Explicit

This option is on by default in Visual Basic .NET. When **Option Explicit** is enabled, you must explicitly declare all variables before using them. Undeclared variables generate a compiler error.

Without this option, you may accidentally create unwanted variables as a result of spelling mistakes or other errors.

Option Strict

Option Strict is a new compiler option in Visual Basic .NET that controls whether variable type conversions are implicit or explicit. This option prevents the data inaccuracies that may result from implicit narrowing conversions.

If you select this option, implicit widening type conversion, such as converting an **Integer** to a **Long,** is allowed. However, implicit narrowing type conversions, such as converting a numeric **String** to an **Integer**, or a **Long** to an **Integer**, cause a compiler error.

The following example shows that assigning a **Double** value to an **Integer** variable causes a compiler error with **Option Strict** enabled, because of implicit narrowing. However, assigning an **Integer** value to a **Long** variable will not cause an error because this is implicit widening.

```
Dim i As Integer, i1 As Double, lng As Long
i1 = 12.3122
i = i1        'Causes a compiler error
i = 256
lng = i       'No error because widening is acceptable
```

The following example shows a subroutine that takes an **Integer** argument but is passed a **String** value, resulting in a compiler error:

```
Sub TestLong(ByRef lng As Long)
    ...
End Sub
TestLong("1234")
'Causes a compiler error because narrowing is unacceptable
```

Late binding is not allowed under **Option Strict**. This means that any variable declared `As Object` can only use the methods provided by the **Object** class. Any attempt to use methods or properties belonging to the data type stored in the variable will result in a compiler error.

The following example shows what will happen if you use late binding when **Option Strict** is enabled. A **String** value in an **Object** variable is allowed, but calling a method from the **String** class is not allowed.

```
Dim x As Object
x = "MyStringData"

'Attempt to retrieve a character fails
MsgBox(x.Chars(4))
```

Option Base 1

In Visual Basic .NET, all arrays must start with a lower bound of 0. Therefore, **Option Base 0|1** is not a compiler option in Visual Basic .NET. This is consistent with all programming languages using the .NET Framework.

Assignment Operators

- **Simplified variable assignment operators**

* =	Multiplication
/ =	Division
+ =	Addition
- =	Subtraction
& =	String concatenation

- **Example:** iResult += 25
  - iResult equals the existing value for iResult, plus 25

Visual Basic .NET provides a shorthand syntax that you can use to assign values to variables. The standard assignment operators are still valid; the new syntax is optional.

Syntax

The original syntax and the shorthand version are shown below:

Original: `{variable} = {variable} {operator} {expression}`
Shorthand: `{variable} {operator} = {expression}`

For example:

Original: `iResult = iResult + 25`
Shorthand: `iResult += 25`

Shorthand Operators

The following table shows how the compiler will interpret the new shorthand operators.

Assignment operator	Purpose
*=	Multiplies the value of a variable by the value of an expression and assigns the result to the variable.
/=	Divides the value of a variable by the value of an expression and assigns the result to the variable.
+=	Adds the value of a variable to the value of an expression and assigns the result to the variable. Can also be used for string concatenation.
-=	Subtracts the value of a variable from the value of an expression and assigns the result to the variable.
&=	Concatenates a string variable with the value of an expression and assigns the result to the variable.
^=	Raises the value of a variable to the power of an exponent and assigns the result to the variable.
\=	Divides the value of a variable by the value of an expression and assigns the integer result to the variable.

Example

The following example shows how to use the new assignment operators to concatenate character strings and provides the resulting string:

```
Dim myString As String = "First part of string; "
myString &= "Second part of string"

MsgBox (myString)
'Displays "First part of string; Second part of string"
```

Demonstration: Using Variables and Data Structures

In this demonstration, you will learn how to declare and initialize different data types, including some basic data types, arrays, and data structures. You will also learn how to use block-scoped variables.

◆ Functions, Subroutines, and Properties

- Calling Functions and Subroutines
- Passing Arguments ByRef and ByVal
- Optional Arguments
- Static Function and Static Sub
- Returning Values from Functions
- Using Default Properties

After you complete this lesson, you will be able to work with functions, subroutines, and default properties in Visual Basic .NET.

Calling Functions and Subroutines

- **Visual Basic 6.0**
  - You must follow complex rules regarding use of parentheses
  - You must use parentheses when using a return value from a function
- **Visual Basic .NET**
  - You must use parentheses to enclose the parameters of any function or subroutine
  - You must include empty parentheses for procedures without parameters

In Visual Basic .NET, the syntax that you use to call a procedure is different from the syntax used in Visual Basic 6.0.

Visual Basic 6.0

When calling a procedure, you must follow a complex set of rules regarding the use of parentheses. You must use them when you are using a return value from a function. In other circumstances, use of parentheses will change the passing mechanism being used.

Visual Basic .NET

You must use parentheses to enclose the parameters of any function or subroutine. If you are calling a procedure without supplying any parameters, you must include empty parentheses. The following statements show how to call a subroutine that has parameters:

```
DisplayData(1, 21)   'Subroutine
Call DisplayData(1, 21)
```

Passing Arguments ByRef and ByVal

- Visual Basic 6.0
  - **ByRef** is the default passing mechanism
- Visual Basic .NET
  - **ByVal** is the default passing mechanism

When you define a procedure, you can choose to pass arguments to it either by reference (**ByRef**) or by value (**ByVal**).

If you choose **ByRef**, Visual Basic passes the variable's address in memory to the procedure, and the procedure can modify the variable directly. When execution returns to the calling procedure, the variable contains the modified value.

If you choose **ByVal,** Visual Basic passes a copy of the variable to the procedure. If the procedure modifies the copy, the original value of the variable remains intact. When execution returns to the calling procedure, the variable contains the same value that it had before it was passed.

There are some important differences between the Visual Basic 6.0 and Visual Basic .NET mechanisms for passing parameters.

Visual Basic 6.0

- **ByRef** is the default passing mechanism.

Visual Basic .NET

- **ByVal** is the default passing mechanism, and is automatically added to parameter definitions if you do not specify either ByVal or ByRef.

Optional Arguments

- **Visual Basic 6.0**
  - You do not need to specify default values for optional parameters
  - You can use the **IsMissing** function
- **Visual Basic .NET**
  - You must include default values for optional parameters
  - The **IsMissing** function is not supported

```
Function Add(Value1 As Integer, Value2 As Integer,
Optional Value3 As Integer = 0) As Integer
```

Optional arguments allow you to choose whether or not to pass all parameters to a function or subroutine. There are some changes to how you use optional arguments in Visual Basic .NET.

Visual Basic 6.0

- You do not need to specify default values for optional parameters.
- You can use the **IsMissing** function to verify that the parameters have been passed to the procedure, if arguments are declared as **Variant**.

Visual Basic .NET

- You must include default values for optional parameters.
- The **IsMissing** function is not supported.

The following example shows how to declare an argument as optional in Visual Basic .NET.

```
Function Add(Value1 As Integer, Value2 As Integer, Optional
Value3 As Integer = 0) As Integer
```

Note You can use overloaded functions to provide the same functionality as optional arguments. For more information about overloading, see Module 5, "Object-Oriented Programming in Visual Basic .NET," in Course 2373B, *Programming with Microsoft Visual Basic .NET*.

Static Function and Static Sub

- **Visual Basic 6.0**
  - You can place **Static** in front of any **Function** or **Sub** procedure heading
  - Local variables in a static function or static subroutine retain their values between multiple calls
- **Visual Basic .NET**
  - Static functions and static subroutines are not supported
  - You must explicitly declare all static variables

Static variables are declared differently in Visual Basic .NET.

Visual Basic 6.0

- You can place **Static** before any **Sub** or **Function** procedure heading. This makes all the local variables in the procedure static, regardless of whether they are declared with **Static**, **Dim**, or **Private**, or are declared implicitly.
- Local variables in a static function or static subroutine retain their values between multiple calls to the function or subroutine.

Visual Basic .NET

- Static functions and static subroutines are not supported.
- You must explicitly declare all static variables.

The following example shows how to use a static variable:

```
Dim iLooper As Integer
Static iMax As Integer
For iLooper = 1 To 10
iMax += 1
Next
MsgBox(iMax)
```

Returning Values from Functions

- **Visual Basic 6.0**
  - Use the function name to return the value
- **Visual Basic .NET**
  - You can use the function name
  - You can also use the **Return** statement

Visual Basic .NET provides flexibility in how you can return values from functions.

Visual Basic 6.0

Use the function name to return the value.

Visual Basic .NET

You can use the function name to return the value. The following example shows how to use the function name to return the value:

```
Function GetData( ) As String
    ...
    GetData = "My data"
End Function
```

You can also use the **Return** statement to return the value. This avoids linking the return of the function to the function name, allowing for easier renaming of functions. The following example shows how to use the **Return** statement to return the value:

```
Function GetData( ) As String
    ...
    Return "My data"
End Function
```

Note The **Return** statement exits the function immediately and returns the value to the calling procedure.

Using Default Properties

- **Visual Basic 6.0**
  - Supports default properties on most objects
  - Use **Set** to determine whether assignment is referring to the object or the default property
- **Visual Basic .NET**
  - Supports default properties only for parameterized properties
  - Do not need to differentiate between object and default property assignments
  - Default properties are commonly used to index into collections

---

Visual Basic .NET updates default property support for simplification and improved readability.

Visual Basic 6.0

- Default properties are supported on most objects. For example, the **Text** property of a **TextBox** control is defined as the default property, meaning you can call the property without having to specify the property name.
- To allow this feature, the **Set** keyword is provided to distinguish between using the object itself for assignment and using the object's default property for assignment.

Visual Basic .NET

- You can only mark a property as default if it takes parameters.
- You specify a property as the default property by starting its declaration with the **Default** keyword.
- Default properties are commonly used to index into collections, such as the ADO Recordset's **Fields.Item** collection.

Note **Let** is still a reserved word in Visual Basic .NET, even though it has no syntactical use. This helps avoid confusion with its former meanings. **Set** is used in Visual Basic .NET for property procedures that set the value of a property.

Using Default Properties *(continued)*

- **You can call default properties only if the property takes parameters**

```
Dim rs As ADODB.Recordset, Lab1 As Label
'…initialization

rs.Fields.Item(1).Value = Lab1.Text     'Valid
rs.Fields(1).Value = Lab1.Text          'Valid

rs.Fields(1) = Lab1.Text                'Not valid
Lab1 = "Data Saved"                     'Not valid
```

The following examples show valid and invalid syntax for using default properties:

```
Dim rs As ADODB.Recordset, Lab1 As Label
'…initialization

rs.Fields.Item(1).Value = Lab1.Text
'Valid because no defaults used
rs.Fields(1).Value = Lab1.Text
'Valid because Item is parameterized

rs.Fields(1) = Lab1.Text
'Not valid because Value is not parameterized
Lab1 = "Data Saved"
'Not valid because Text is not parameterized
```

Lab 3.1: Working with Variables and Procedures

Objectives

After completing this lab, you will be able to:

- Declare and initialize variables.
- Create and call functions and subroutines.

Prerequisites

Before working on this lab, you must be familiar with using variables, arrays, and procedures.

Scenario

In this lab, you will create a simple Microsoft Windows® Forms application in which you can enter customer information into an array and then retrieve it. The application will consist of a single form that you use to input this information.

Solution Files

There are solution files associated with this lab. The solution files are in the *install folder*\Labs\Lab031\Solution folder.

Estimated time to complete this lab: 45 minutes

Exercise 1
Creating the Customer Form

In this exercise, you will create the customer entry form.

► **To create a new project**

1. Open Microsoft Visual Studio .NET.
2. On the **File** menu, point to **New**, and then click **Project**.
3. In the **Project Types** box, click the **Visual Basic Projects** folder.
4. In the **Templates** box, click **Windows Application**.
5. Name the project Lab031 in the *install folder*\Labs\Lab031 folder, and then click **OK**.

► **To create the customer form**

1. Using the Solution Explorer, open the design window for Form1.vb.
2. In the Properties window, set the **Text** property of the form to **Customer**.
3. On the **View** menu, click **Toolbox**. Add controls to the form, as shown in the following screen shot:

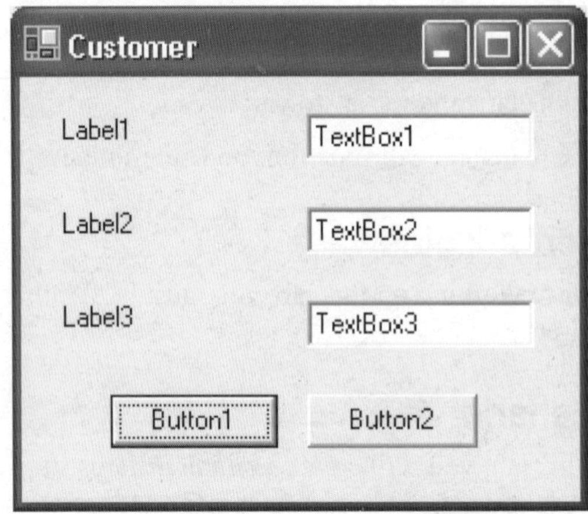

4. Set the properties of the controls as shown in the following table.

Control	Property name	Property value
Label1	**Text**	**First Name:**
	Name	**lblFirstName**
Label2	**Text**	**Last Name:**
	Name	**lblLastName**
Label3	**Text**	**Date of Birth:**
	Name	**lblDOB**
TextBox1	**Text**	**<empty>**
	Name	**txtFirstName**
TextBox2	**Text**	**<empty>**
	Name	**txtLastName**
TextBox3	**Text**	**<empty>**
	Name	**txtDOB**
Button1	**Text**	**Add Customer**
	Name	**btnAddCustomer**
Button2	**Text**	**Retrieve**
	Name	**btnRetrieve**

5. Save the project.

Exercise 2
Adding a Customer

In this exercise, you will write code to add a new customer to an array of customers when the user clicks **Add Customer**.

▶ To create the module-level variables

1. Using the Solution Explorer, open the code window for Form1.vb.
2. Create a private structure called **Customer** after the **Inherits System.Windows.Forms.Form** statement within the **Public Class** code block by using the information in the following table.

Customer member	Data type
Id	**Integer**
FirstName	**String**
LastName	**String**
DateOfBirth	**Date**

3. Declare a private array called **aCustomers** to hold **Customer** elements with an initial size of one.

▶ To add a customer

1. Create the **btnAddCustomer_Click** event handler.
2. In the **btnAddCustomer_Click** event handler, create a local variable named *cCustomer* based on the information in the following table.

Variable name	Data type
cCustomer	**Customer**

3. Assign the upper bound limit of the **aCustomers** array to the Id member of the **cCustomer** object.
4. Assign the **Text** properties of the text boxes to the corresponding members of the *cCustomer* variable as defined in the following table.

   Use the **CDate** function to convert the text property of **txtDOB** to the **Date** data type for use by the **cCustomer.DateOfBirth** member.

cCustomer member	Text box
FirstName	txtFirstName
LastName	txtLastName
DateOfBirth	txtDOB

5. Using the **UBound** function for the array index, add the *cCustomer* variable to the **aCustomers** array.

6. Use the **ReDim Preserve** syntax and the **UBound** function to increase the size of the **aCustomers** array by one.

   This creates one more array element than is required. However, this is acceptable for this exercise.

Important When you use the **UBound** function to increase the size of the array, you must add the integer value of 1 to the result of the **UBound** function.

---

7. Use the **MsgBox** function to display a message box that confirms that the customer has been added.
8. Clear the **txtFirstName**, **txtLastName**, and **txtDOB** text boxes.
9. Save the project.

► **To test your application**

1. On the first line of the **btnAddCustomer_Click** event handler, set a breakpoint.
2. On the **Debug** menu, click **Start**.
3. Enter customer details into the text boxes, and then click **Add Customer**.
4. When the code enters break mode, click **Step Into** on the **Debug** menu.
5. On the **Debug** menu, point to **Windows**, and then click **Locals**. In the Locals window, expand **cCustomer** and view the values of the variables as you step through the code.
6. Close the Customer application.

Exercise 3
Retrieving a Customer

In this exercise, you will write code to retrieve a customer from an array when the user clicks **Retrieve**.

▶ To create the RetrieveCustomer function

1. At the end of the form definition, add a new private function named **RetrieveCustomer**.

   This function takes one argument by value, as defined in the following table. It returns a **Customer** structure.

Argument name	Data type
iIndex	**Integer**

2. Return the **Customer** object stored in the **iIndex** position of the **aCustomers** array as the result of the function.

▶ To call the RetrieveCustomer function

1. In the **btnRetrieve_Click** event handler, declare three local variables as defined in the following table.

Variable name	Data type
aCustomer	**Customer**
sInput	**String**
sMessage	**String**

2. Use the **InputBox** function to ask the user to enter a customer identification number, and then store the response in the *sInput* variable.
3. Use an **If** statement and the **IsNumeric** function to test whether the entered data is numeric.
4. If the data is numeric, call the **RetrieveCustomer** function, and then pass it the value of the *sInput* variable converted to an integer.
5. Store the return value of the **RetrieveCustomer** function in the *aCustomer* variable.
6. To create a message to be displayed to the user, concatenate the values of each of the *aCustomer* elements into the *sMessage* variable, and then display the string in a message box.
7. Save the project.

► To test your application

1. On the **Debug** menu, click **Clear All Breakpoints**.
2. On the first line of the **btnRetrieve_Click** event handler, set a breakpoint.
3. Start the application, and then add three customers of your choice.
4. Click **Retrieve**.
5. On the **Debug** menu, click **Step Into** to step through the code until the InputBox displays.
6. In the InputBox, type **1** and click **OK**. Step through the code and confirm that the correct customer information is displayed.

   You should see details for the second customer that you entered.
7. Quit the application.
8. On the **Debug** menu, click **Clear All Breakpoints**, and then save your project.
9. Quit Visual Studio .NET.

◆ Exception Handling

- Structured Exception Handling
- Try...Catch...Finally
- Using Try...Catch...Finally
- The System.Exception Class
- Filtering Exceptions
- Throwing Exceptions

In this lesson, you will learn about the extensions to error handling (or exception handling) in Visual Basic .NET. After completing this lesson, you will be able to:

- Explain the advantages of the new exception handling system by comparing unstructured handling to structured handling.
- Use the **Try…Catch…Finally** statement in conjunction with the **System.Exception** class to implement structured exception handling.
- Create your own exceptions by using the **Throw** statement.

Structured Exception Handling

- **Disadvantages of unstructured error handling**
  - Code is difficult to read, debug, and maintain
  - Easy to overlook errors
- **Advantages of structured exception handling**
  - Supported by multiple languages
  - Allows you to create protected blocks of code
  - Allows filtering of exceptions similar to **Select Case** statement
  - Allows nested handling
  - Code is easier to read, debug, and maintain

Visual Basic developers are familiar with unstructured exception handling in the form of the **On Error** statement. With **On Error**, developers can check for and handle exceptions in several different ways by using exception labels, **GoTo** statements, and **Resume** statements.

Disadvantages of Unstructured Exception Handling

Unstructured exception handling can make your code difficult to read, maintain, and debug, and may lead you to unintentionally ignore an error. For example, when you use the **On Error Resume Next** statement, you must remember to check the **Err** object after each action that can cause an error. If you do not check the value after each action, you may miss an initial error when a subsequent action also fails. This means you may handle an error incorrectly or unintentionally ignore an error.

The Visual Basic language has been criticized because it lacks structured exception handling. Visual Basic .NET addresses this criticism by supporting structured exception handling, using the syntax **Try...Catch...Finally**.

Advantages of Structured Exception Handling

Structured exception handling is used in many programming languages, such as Microsoft Visual C++® and Microsoft Visual C#™, and combines protected blocks of code with a control structure (similar to a **Select Case** statement) to filter exceptions. Structured exception handling allows you to protect certain areas of code. Any exceptions in code that you leave unprotected are raised to the calling procedure, as in Visual Basic 6.0.

You can filter exceptions by using the **Catch** block, which provides functionality similar to a **Select Case** statement in Visual Basic 6.0. This allows you to filter multiple exceptions in the same way that a **Select Case** can handle outcomes from a comparison.

You can also nest exception handlers within other handlers as needed (in the same procedure or in a calling procedure), and variables declared within each block will have block-level scope.

It is easier to create and maintain programs with structured exception handling. The flow of execution is easy to follow and does not require jumps to non-sequential code.

The old style of error handling is still supported in Visual Basic. NET. The only restriction is that you can't mix both styles of error handling in the same procedure.

Try...Catch...Finally

```
...
Try
' Include code to be tried here
' Can use Exit Try to exit block and resume after End Try

Catch
' Define exception type and action to be taken
' Can use series of statements (multiple error handling)

Finally
' Optional block
' Define actions that need to take place

End Try
...
```

You can implement structured exception handling in Visual Basic .NET by using the **Try...Catch...Finally** statement.

Syntax

The following code shows the structure of a simple **Try...Catch...Finally** statement:

```
Try
' Include code to be tried here
' You can use Exit Try to exit the code & resume after End Try
Catch
' Define the exception type and the action to be taken
' You can use a series of statements (multiple error handling)
Finally
' This block is optional
' Define actions that need to take place
End Try
```

Try Block

Note the following as you examine this code:

- The **Try...End Try** block surrounds an area of code that might contain an error.
- Code placed in this block is considered protected.
- If an exception occurs, processing is transferred to the nested **Catch** blocks.
- You can use the **Exit Try** keyword to instantly exit the **Try...End Try** block. Execution will resume immediately after the **End Try** statement.

Catch Block

If an exception occurs in the **Try** block, execution will continue at the beginning of the nested **Catch** block. The **Catch** block is a series of statements beginning with the keyword **Catch** followed by an exception type and an action to be taken. The following are some guidelines for using the **Catch** block:

- You can choose to handle all exceptions in one **Catch** block. You can also declare multiple **Catch** blocks to filter the exception and handle particular errors, similar to how you might use **Select Case** in previous versions of Visual Basic.
- You can filter using the different exception classes defined by the .NET Framework and runtime, or by using your own exception classes.
- You can use a **When** statement to compare the exception to a particular exception number.
- If you use filtering for the exceptions but do not handle the actual exception that occurred, the exception is automatically raised up to the calling procedure (or to the user if no calling procedure exists). However, by using a **Catch** filter with the **Exception** class, you will catch all of the other exceptions that you have not included in your filters. This is the equivalent of a **Case Else** statement in a **Select Case** structure.

Finally Block

The **Finally** block is optional. If you include this block, it is executed after the **Try** block if no errors occurred, or after the appropriate **Catch** block has been processed.

- The **Finally** block is always executed.
- In this block, you can define actions that need to take place regardless of whether an exception occurs. This may include actions such as closing files or releasing objects.
- The **Finally** block is most often used to clean up operations when a method fails.

Using Try...Catch...Finally

```
Sub TrySimpleException
  Dim i1, i2, iResult As Decimal
  i1 = 22
  i2 = 0
  Try
    iResult = i1 / i2       ' Cause divide-by-zero error
    MsgBox (iResult)        ' Will not execute

  Catch eException As Exception  ' Catch the exception
    MsgBox (eException.Message)  ' Show message to user

  Finally
    Beep
  End Try
End Sub
```

The following example shows how to implement structured exception handling in Visual Basic .NET by using the **Try...Catch...Finally** syntax:

```
Sub TrySimpleException
  Dim i1, i2, iResult As Decimal
  i1 = 22
  i2 = 0
  Try
    iResult = i1 / i2    ' Cause divide by zero exception
    MsgBox (iResult)     ' Will not execute

  Catch eException As Exception  ' Catch the exception

    MsgBox (eException.Message)  ' Show message to user
  Finally
    Beep
  End Try
End Sub
```

The compiler processes this code as follows:

1. Processing begins by attempting the code in the **Try** block.
2. The code creates a divide-by-zero exception.
3. Execution passes to the **Catch** block, where a variable *eException* of type **Exception** class is declared. This variable will display information about the exception to the user.
4. The **Finally** code is executed after all processing in the **Catch** block is complete. The **Finally** code causes a beep to sound, signifying that processing is complete.

Note Any variables declared in any of the three blocks are scoped as block-level variables. They cannot be accessed from outside of the block.

The System.Exception Class

- Provides information about the exception

Property or method	Information provided
Message property	Why the exception was thrown
Source property	The name of the application or object that generated the exception
StackTrace property	Exception history
InnerException property	For nested exceptions
HelpLink property	The appropriate Help file, URN, or URL
ToString method	The name of the exception, the exception message, the name of the inner exception, and the stack

The **System.Exception** class in Visual Basic .NET, similar to the **Err** object in Visual Basic 6.0, provides information about a particular exception. When you use this class in your **Catch** blocks, you can determine what the exception is, where it is coming from, and whether there is any help available.

Some of the most useful properties and methods of the **System.Exception** class are described in the following table.

Property or method	Description
Message property	Use the **Message** property to retrieve information about why an exception was thrown. A generic message is returned if the exception was created without a particular message.
Source property	Use the **Source** property to retrieve the name of the application or object that generated the exception.
StackTrace property	Use the **StackTrace** property to retrieve the stack trace of the exception as a string.
InnerException property	Use the **InnerException** property to navigate to multiple nested exceptions. Nesting exceptions may be useful if a more specific (or general) exception needs to be generated while maintaining the information from the original exception. If only the original exception is required, use the **GetBaseException** method.
HelpLink property	Use the **HelpLink** property to retrieve the appropriate Help file, URN, or URL for the exception. (See the note following this table.)
ToString method	Use the **ToString** method to return the fully qualified name of the exception, the exception message (if there is one), the name of the inner exception, and the stack trace.

Note Uniform Resource Locators (URLs) and Uniform Resource Names (URNs) are both examples of Uniform Resource Identifiers (URIs). A URN is a unique identifier that is not necessarily (but can be) in the form of a URL. They can be any combination of characters that is unique. Large organizations are more likely than individuals to use URNs because the guarantee of uniqueness is more difficult to achieve.

Filtering Exceptions

```
Dim x, y, z As Integer, bSucceeded As Boolean = True
Try
    'Perform various operations on variables
    ...
Catch eException As DivideByZeroException
    MsgBox("You have attempted to divide by zero.")
    bSucceeded = False
Catch eException As OverflowException
    MsgBox("You have encountered an overflow.")
    bSucceeded = False
...
Catch When Err.Number = 11
    MsgBox("Error occurred.")
    bSucceeded = False
Finally
    If bSucceeded Then
        ...
    End If
End Try
```

To learn more about structured exception handling in Visual Basic .NET, consider a more advanced example. In this example, errors are filtered based on the class of the exception.

Example

The following example shows how to use filtering to handle several different exceptions in one **Try...Catch...Finally** statement:

```
Sub TryComplexException( )
  Dim x, y, z As Integer, bSucceeded As Boolean = True

  Try
      'Perform various operations on variables
      ...
  Catch eException As DivideByZeroException
     MsgBox("You have attempted to divide by zero!")
     bSucceeded = False
  Catch eException As OverflowException
     MsgBox("You have encountered an overflow.")
     bSucceeded = False
  Catch eException As ConstraintException
     MsgBox(eException.ToString)
     bSucceeded = False
  Catch When Err.Number = 11
     MsgBox("Error occurred")
     bSucceeded = False
  Finally
     If bSucceeded Then
        MsgBox("Success!")
     Else
        MsgBox("Failure")
     End If
  End Try
End Sub
```

As you examine this code, note the following:

- For demonstration purposes, a test is made against various exception classes such as **DividebyZeroException**, **OverflowException**, and **ConstraintException**. These classes are all derived from the **System.Exception** class.
- One of the **Catch** blocks checks the exception number, **Err.Number**, by using the **When** statement.
- The last **Catch** block uses the **ToString** method of the **Exception** class.
- Note that if the exception does not meet any of the filter expressions, it will be passed up to the calling procedure. Using **System.Exception** as a Catch type would catch other unexpected exceptions.

Throwing Exceptions

- **Use Throw keyword instead of Err.Raise**

```
Try
  If x = 0 Then
      Throw New Exception("x equals zero")
  Else
      Throw New Exception("x does not equal zero")
  End If
Catch eException As Exception
  MsgBox("Error: " & eException.Message)
Finally
  MsgBox("Executing finally block")
End Try
```

In Visual Basic 6.0, you can use the **Raise** method of the **Err** object to raise your own exceptions. You can use this method to create a business logic error or to propagate an error after previously trapping it.

Visual Basic .NET introduces the **Throw** statement, which allows you to create your own exceptions. The **Throw** statement provides similar functionality to the **Err.Raise** method.

Example

The following example shows how to throw an exception in Visual Basic .NET:

```
Try
  If x = 0 Then
      Throw New Exception("x equals zero")
  End If
Catch eException As Exception
  MsgBox("Error: " & eException.Message)

End Try
```

This example will throw an exception if the value of the variable *x* is zero. The **If** statement creates a new **Exception** object and passes a string containing an exception description to the object constructor. This means that the **Catch** block can handle the exception as it would deal with a normal system exception.

If a **Throw** statement is not executed within a **Try** block, the exception will be raised to the calling procedure.

Note For more information about object constructors, see Module 5, "Object-Oriented Programming in Visual Basic .NET," in Course 2373B, *Programming with Microsoft Visual Basic .NET*.

Demonstration: Structured Exception Handling

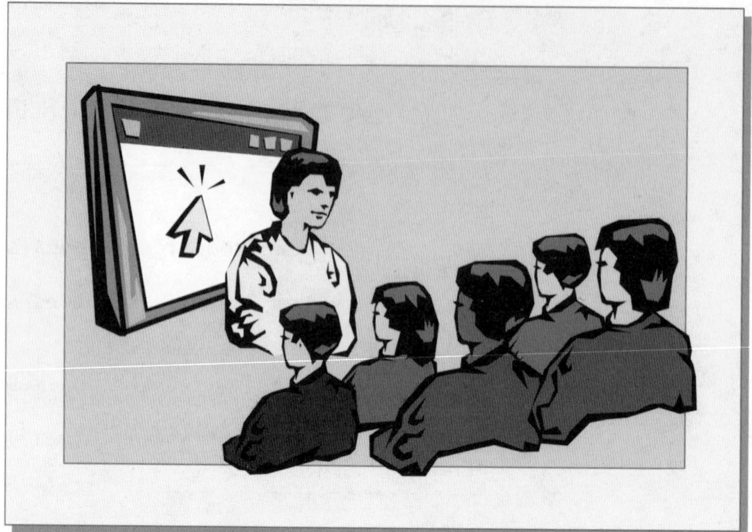

In this demonstration, you will learn how to use the **Try…Catch…Finally** statement to implement structured exception handling. You will also learn how to check values of the **System.Exception** class and how to throw your own exceptions.

Lab 3.2: Implementing Structured Exception Handling

Objectives

After completing this lab, you will be able to:

- Create structured exception handling.
- Throw your own exceptions.

Prerequisites

Before working on this lab, you must:

- Complete Lab 3.1.
- Be familiar with using the **Try...Catch...Finally** statement for structured exception handling.

Scenario

In this lab, you will add structured exception handling to the application that you created in Lab 3.1.

Starter and Solution Files

There are starter and solution files associated with this lab. The starter files are in the *install folder*\Labs\Lab032\Starter folder, and the solution files are in the *install folder*\Labs\Lab032\Solution folder.

Estimated time to complete this lab: 30 minutes

Exercise 1
Adding Exception Handling to Customer Retrieval

In this exercise, you will add structured exception handling to the **RetrieveCustomer** function that you created in Lab 3.1.

▶ To open the previous project

1. Open Microsoft Visual Studio .NET.
2. Open the project from Lab 3.1. If you did not complete Lab 3.1, use the project in the *install folder*\Labs\Lab032\Starter folder.

▶ To add exception handling to the btnRetrieve_Click event handler

1. In the **btnRetrieve_Click** event handler, add a **Try…Catch…Finally** code block around the code that calls the **RetrieveCustomer** function, excluding the variable declarations.
2. Create a new procedure-level **Boolean** variable named *bSuccess*, and then initialize it to the value of **True** on the same line.
3. In the **Catch** block, create a variable named *eException* of the data type **Exception**.

   This catches an exception when a user tries to access an array element that does not exist.
4. In a message box inside the **Catch** block, display the **Message** property from the *eException* variable, and then set the *bSuccess* variable to **False**.
5. In the **Finally** block, create an **If** statement to test the *bSuccess* variable for a value of **True**.
6. Locate the code that concatenates the *sMessage* variable and the **MsgBox** function, and then perform a cut-and-paste operation to place this code inside the **If** block.
7. Save the project.

▶ To test your application

1. On the first line of the **btnRetrieve_Click** event handler, set a breakpoint.
2. Run the application, and add only one customer.
3. Click **Retrieve**. When you enter break mode, step through the code.
4. When asked for the customer identification number, enter the value **20** in the InputBox, and then click **OK**.
5. Step through the code and confirm that this generates an exception in the **RetrieveCustomer** function that is caught by the exception handling in the **btnRetrieve_Click** event handler.
6. Quit the application.

► To add exception handling to the RetrieveCustomer function

1. In the **RetrieveCustomer** function, add a **Try...Catch...Finally** code block around the existing code.
2. In the **Catch** block, create a variable named *eOutOfRange* of type **IndexOutOfRangeException**.

   This catches an exception when a user tries to access an array that does not exist.
3. Add the following line to the **Catch** block:

   ```
   Throw New Exception ("Invalid Customer Id", eOutOfRange)
   ```

   This throws a new exception that includes a specific message, while keeping the original exception as an inner exception. The **Try...Catch...Finally** block in the **btnRetrieve_Click** event handler catches this exception.
4. Delete the **Finally** block.

   It serves no purpose in this procedure.

► To display the inner exception in the btnRetrieve_Click event handler

1. In the **btnRetrieve_Click** event handler, modify the **Catch** block to display additional information about the exception, including the **Message**, the **ToString**, and the **GetBaseException.Message** members of the *eException* variable.
2. Save your project.

► To test your application

1. Start the application, and add only one customer.
2. Click **Retrieve**. When you enter break mode, step through the code.
3. When asked for the customer identification number, enter the value **20** in the InputBox, and then click **OK**.
4. Step through the code and confirm that this generates an exception in the **RetrieveCustomer** function and that it is handled inside the function, but then is raised to the **btnRetrieve_Click** event handler.
5. Quit the application.
6. Close Visual Studio .NET.

Review

- Data Types
- Using Variables
- Functions, Subroutines, and Properties
- Exception Handling

1. Declare and initialize an array that contains the following strings: "one", "two", "three", "four".

2. What types of variables are created by the following declaration if **Option Strict** is off?

```
Dim a, b As Integer, c
```

3. What is the value of *c* after the following code executes:

```
Dim c As Integer
c = 1
CheckValue(c)
...
Sub CheckValue(ByVal iValue As Integer)
   ...
   iValue = 13
End Sub
```

4. Assuming you have an open **Recordset** called rs and a **TextBox** control called txtData, which of the following statements will create a compiler or run-time error with **Option Strict** off? Why?

   a. `txtData.Text = rs(0)`

   b. `txtData.Text = rs.Fields.Item(0)`

   c. `txtData.Text = rs.Fields(0).Value`

5. What is the method or property of the **System.Exception** class that retrieves the most information about an exception?

msdn training

Module 4: Object-Oriented Design for Visual Basic .NET

Contents

Overview

- Designing Classes
- Object-Oriented Programming Concepts
- Advanced Object-Oriented Programming Concepts
- Using Microsoft Visio

Developers using Microsoft® Visual Basic® version 4.0 and later have had some exposure to the benefits of an object-oriented approach to programming, but it is only now that you can take full advantage of an object-oriented paradigm if you so choose. To use these new capabilities, you must be familiar with object-oriented programming concepts. This module explains the areas that you must understand to create object-oriented solutions in Visual Basic .NET.

In this module, you will learn how to begin the class design process by using use cases. You will then learn about some common object-oriented programming concepts, including inheritance, interfaces, and polymorphism. Finally, you will learn how to document your system design by using Microsoft Visio® to build use cases and class diagrams.

After completing this module, you will be able to:

- Describe the basics of object-oriented design.
- Explain the concepts of encapsulation, inheritance, interfaces, and polymorphism.
- Create classes based on use cases.
- Model classes for use in Visual Basic .NET by using Visio.

Note Visio is part of the Enterprise Architect edition of Visual Studio .NET.

Designing Classes

- Use Case Diagrams
- Use Case Diagram Example
- Use Case Descriptions
- Extending Use Cases
- Converting Use Cases into Classes

You can use the Unified Modeling Language (UML) to help you analyze requirements by graphically showing interactions within the system.

After completing this lesson, you will be able to:

- Design classes for use in applications created in Visual Basic .NET.
- Begin the process of designing classes by using use cases.
- Derive classes based on an existing use case.

Use Case Diagrams

- **Use cases**
  - Provide a functional description of major processes
  - Use a non-technical language to describe the process
  - Show a boundary around the problem to be solved
- **Actors**
  - Graphically describe who or what will use the processes

A *use case* is a collection of possible sequences of interactions in a system. Use case diagrams are an integral part of designing a modern software application. You can use the Unified Modeling Language (UML) to help you analyze requirements by graphically showing interactions within the system. Use case diagrams consist of individual use cases and actors.

What Are Use Cases?

You can employ use cases to:

- Provide a functional description of major processes.

  Use cases usually represent common interactions between a user and a computer system. A use case describes a process that is needed in order for a system to fulfill its requirements.

- Use a non-technical language to describe the process.

  Each individual use case will describe a particular process in a non-technical language that can be understood by the intended application user.

  The use case description should concentrate on the sequence of events and decisions that must be made in the process rather than on an overly detailed look at how things will be implemented.

- Show a boundary around the problem to be solved.

  This boundary helps the designers and developers to concentrate on individual processes without getting lost in the detail of the communications between actors and the processes at this stage.

Creating Use Cases

When you create a use case, you will often focus on the people or actors who will be using the system. If you are working with an existing system, you will typically meet with users to discuss how they use the existing system to complete their tasks. You might also observe intended users of your system to record their processes. Each of these approaches leads to the creation of large descriptions that you can then distill into smaller individual use cases.

Actors

An actor graphically represents who or what will use the system. An actor is often a role that a person plays when interacting with a particular process of the system. Actors request functionality of the system by way of a use case and can use many different use cases. Multiple actors can also use the same use case.

Four categories of actors include:

- Principal actors

  People who use the main system functions.

- Secondary actors

  People who perform administration or maintenance tasks.

- External hardware

  Hardware peripheral devices that are part of the application domain and must be used.

- Other systems

  Other systems with which the system must interact.

Identifying actors can help you understand what the system should do and who can use each section of the system. Actors provide a starting point for designing security permissions for the different roles that interact with the system. An actor can also represent another software application or even a hardware device that interacts with the new system.

Use Case Diagram Example

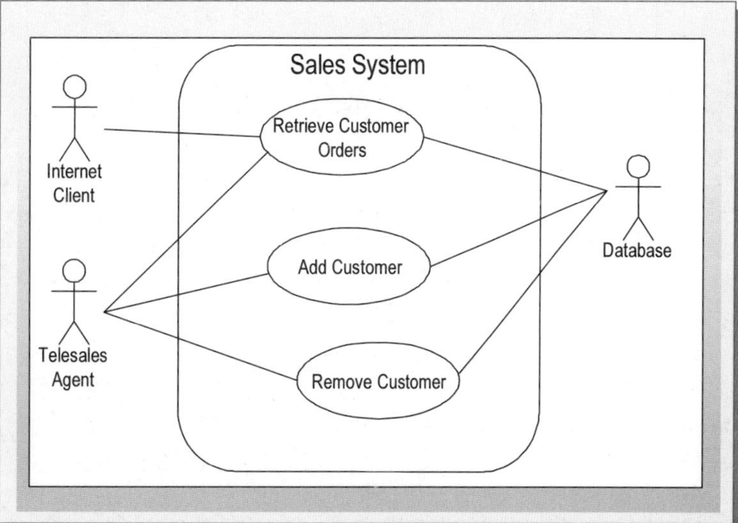

A simple use case diagram is made up of one or more use cases, actors, and the communications between them.

Use Case Example

The example on the slide shows a sales system use case diagram that represents three different processes (or use cases) and the three actors that interact with them.

The illustration shows the system boundary that encapsulates the use cases within its walls. It also shows external parts of the system, such as a database, as external to the system boundary, or outside the walls.

Each actor communicates with one or more of the use cases. These actors help to establish the roles in the system and where security boundaries will need to be set later in lifetime of the application. In the example, you can see that two of the actors are people and that one is a database that is considered another part of the system. The Internet Client actor will only interact with the Retrieve Customer Orders use case, while the Telesales Agent will interact with all three use cases.

Use Case Descriptions

- **"Retrieve Customer Orders" use case description**

A user requests the orders for a customer by using a particular customer ID. The ID is validated by the database, and an error message is displayed if the customer does not exist. If the ID matches a customer, the customer's name, address, and date of birth are retrieved, in addition to any outstanding orders for the customer. Details about each order are retrieved, including the ID, the date, and the individual order items that make up an order.

Use case descriptions provide information about a particular scenario. Here is an example of a scenario from the use case diagram in the preceding topic .The Retrieve Customer Orders use case description reads as follows:

"A user requests the orders for a customer by using a particular customer ID. The ID is validated by the database, and an error message is displayed if the customer does not exist. If the ID matches a customer, the customer's name, address, and date of birth are retrieved, in addition to any outstanding orders for the customer. Details about each order are retrieved, including the ID, the date, and the individual order items that make up an order."

By working through this use case description, you can see that it starts with a request from a user to perform a certain action. Some validation then takes place, and an error message is displayed if appropriate. If the validation succeeds, information about the customer, the customer's orders, and the order items for an order are retrieved and displayed to the user.

Notice that the precise details of how information is retrieved and displayed are not mentioned. The point of a use case description is simply to describe the business process, not provide all information for the developer. From this use case description, various classes can be derived that will become the first version of the detailed design for the system solution.

Extending Use Cases

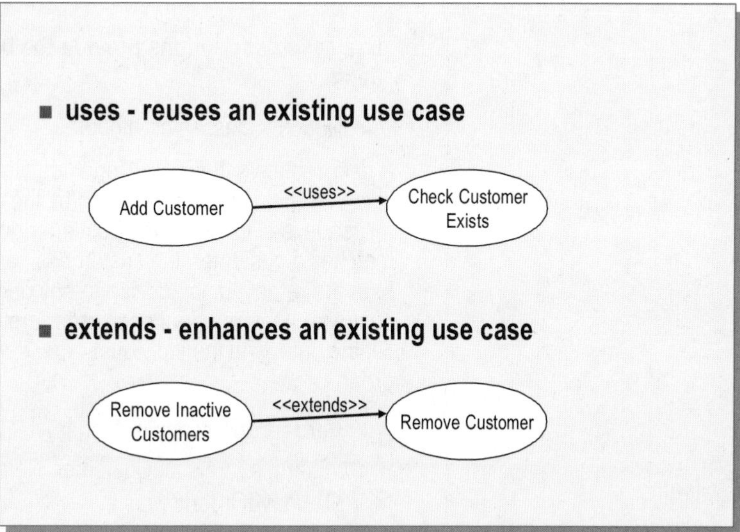

Instead of developing a separate use case for every process, you can reuse use cases. This is a less repetitive approach and can save you a lot of time.

Two keywords that you can use to extend use cases are as follows:

- **uses**

  The **uses** keyword allows an existing use case to be reused by other use cases. This means that if a use case needs to perform some sort of action that has been created elsewhere, there is no need to duplicate the effort. The slide shows how the Add Customer use case might use the Check Customer Exists use case that has been defined for reuse. This means that the Check Customer Exists use case can be called directly from an actor or reused from other use cases.

- **extends**

  The **extends** keyword allows a use case to describe a variation on normal behavior in an existing use case. In other words, it allows a new use case to perform a similar action to an existing use case, except that the new use case builds on the existing one, performing a more complex action. The illustration shows how the Remove Customer use case can be extended to remove the inactive customers who have not placed orders within two months.

Converting Use Cases into Classes

- **Use case descriptions provide the basis for initial class design**
  - Nouns = classes or attributes

A user requests the orders for a customer by using a particular customer ID. The ID is validated by the database, and an error message is displayed if the customer does not exist. If the ID matches a customer, the customer's name, address, and date of birth are retrieved, in addition to any outstanding orders for the customer. Details about each order are retrieved, including the ID, the date, and the individual order items that make up an order.

  - Verbs = operations (methods)

    Example: ValidateCustomer, RetrieveOrders, RetrieveOrderItems

You can create initial class designs by finding the nouns and verbs in use case descriptions. You can begin to identify classes or attributes for classes by finding the nouns in the use case description. You can begin to identify processes that can become operations or methods in a class by finding the verbs in the use case description.

Identifying Classes and Attributes

Using the Retrieve Customer Orders use case description as an example, you can identify several nouns that may lead to classes or attributes of those classes.

"A **user** requests the **orders** for a **customer** by using a particular **customer ID**. The ID is validated by the database, and an error message is displayed if the customer does not exist. If the ID matches a customer, the customer's **name**, **address**, and **date of birth** are retrieved, in addition to any outstanding orders for the customer. Details about each **order** are retrieved, including the **ID**, the **date**, and the individual **order items** that make up an order."

Based on the use case description, you might conclude that the following classes and attributes are possible.

Class	Attributes
User	<Unknown at this stage>
Customer	CustomerID
	Name
	Address
	Date of Birth
	Orders
Order	ID
	Date
	Order Items
Order Items	<Unknown at this stage>

These are only possible classes and attributes based on the use case description, and they may be removed or modified in later design stages.

Identifying Operations and Methods

The name of the use case—Retrieve Customer Orders—gives you an idea for an initial operation or method that begins the business process. The operation ValidateCustomer can be derived from the statement "the id is validated." The purpose of this operation is to check the validity of a customer ID. The verb "Retrieve" can also be used to derive an operation called RetrieveOrders on the **Customer** class.

Although there may not be any other specific verbs in this use case description example, you can see how verbs can be used to produce method names.

Note Using use case descriptions for initial class design is a subjective process. You may have identified classes, attributes, or operations that differ from those that the example shows. This is not unusual because this is only a first stage in the class design process, and the differences will often disappear with further design. However, there is generally more than one correct answer.

Practice: Deriving Classes from Use Cases

In this practice, you will work in pairs to select classes and some attributes or operations based on the following use case descriptions. When you have finished, the instructor and class will discuss the results as a group.

Customer Log On Use Case Description

"A customer logs on to the system by using an e-mail address and password. If the e-mail address or password is not valid, a message stating that information was incorrectly entered is displayed to the customer. If the e-mail address and password are valid, a welcome screen is displayed, showing the customer's full name, date of birth, gender, and address."

Place Order Use Case Description

"The customer selects the product to add to the order by using a product name. To confirm that the customer has selected the correct product, an image, a full description, a manufacturer, and a price is displayed to the customer. The customer must enter a quantity value for the order and press a confirmation button to continue the order process. A delivery date for the order must also be entered by the customer."

◆ Object-Oriented Programming Concepts

- Comparing Classes to Objects
- Encapsulation
- Abstraction
- Association
- Aggregation
- Attributes and Operations

This lesson introduces several important concepts of object-oriented design that will improve the way you design your Visual Basic .NET solutions.

After completing this lesson, you will be able to:

- Distinguish between objects and classes.
- Describe encapsulation, association, and aggregation.
- Explain how properties and methods are used to define a class and the different levels of scope that make them accessible or inaccessible.
- Explain how classes are represented in class diagrams along with their relationships to each other.

Comparing Classes to Objects

Class

- A class is a template or blueprint that defines an object's attributes and operations and that is created at design time

Object

- An object is a running instance of a class that consumes memory and has a finite lifespan

The object-oriented terms *class* and *object* often create some confusion because they can be easily misused by developers when describing a system.

Class

A class is an abstract data type containing data, a set of functions to access and manipulate the data, and a set of access restrictions on the data and on the functions.

You can think of a class as a template or a blueprint for an object. This blueprint defines attributes for storing data and defines operations for manipulating that data. A class also defines a set of restrictions to allow or deny access to its attributes and operations.

A car is an example of a class. We know that a car has attributes, such as the number of wheels, the color, the make, the model, and so on. We know that it also has operations, including unlock door, open door, and start engine.

Object

Objects are instances of classes. A single blueprint or class can be used as a basis for creating many individual and unique objects.

If you consider classes and objects in Visual Basic terms, a class is created at design time and will exist forever, whereas an object is instantiated at run time and will only exist as long as required during the application execution.

For example, an instance of a car would contain specific information for each attribute, such as number or wheels equals four, color equals blue, and so on.

Objects exhibit three characteristics:

- Identity
- Behavior
- State

Identity

One object must be distinguishable from another object of the same class. Without this characteristic, it would be impossible to tell the difference between the two objects, and this would cause great difficulties for developers. This difference could be a simple identifier such as a unique ID number assigned to each object, or several of each object's attributes could be different from those of the other objects.

Note You do not have to generate these unique identifiers yourself, as when you create an object, Visual Basic maintains identity for you.

Behavior

Objects exist to provide a specific behavior that is useful. If they did not exhibit this characteristic, we would have no reason to use them.

The main behavior or purpose of a car is to transport people from one location to another. If the car did not provide this behavior, it would not perform a useful function.

State

State refers to the attributes or information that an object stores. These attributes are often manipulated by an object's operations. The object's state can change by direct manipulation of an attribute, or as the result of an operation. A well-designed object often only allows access to its state by means of operations because this limits incorrect setting of the data.

A car keeps track of how far it has traveled since it was created in the factory. This data is stored internally and can be viewed by the driver. The only way to alter this data is to drive the car, which is an operation that acts upon the internal state.

Encapsulation

- **How an object performs its duties is hidden from the outside world, simplifying client development**
  - Clients can call a method of an object without understanding the inner workings or complexity
  - Any changes made to the inner workings are hidden from clients

Encapsulation is the process of hiding the details about how an object performs its duties when asked to perform those duties by a client. This has some major benefits for designing client applications:

- Client development is simplified because the clients can call a method or attribute of an object without understanding the inner workings of the object.
- Any changes made to the inner workings of the object will be invisible to the client.
- Because private information is hidden from the client, access is only available by means of appropriate operations that ensure correct modification of data.

Example

Driving a car is an example of encapsulation. You know that when you press the accelerator the car will move faster. You do not need to know that the pedal increases the amount of fuel being fed into the engine, producing more fuel ignition and thereby speeding up the output to the axle, which in turn speeds up the car's wheels, which has the final effect of increasing your speed. You simply need to know which pedal to press to have the desired effect.

Likewise, if the car manufacturer changes the amount of fuel being mixed with oxygen to alter the combustion, or creates a drive-by-wire accelerator pedal, you do not need to know this in order to increase your speed. However, if the manufacturer replaces the accelerator pedal with a sliding throttle device, similar to what you would find in an aircraft, you may need to know about it!

Abstraction

- **Abstraction is selective ignorance**
  - Decide what is important and what is not
  - Focus on and depend on what is important
  - Ignore and do not depend on what is unimportant
  - Use encapsulation to enforce an abstraction

Abstraction is the practice of focusing only on the essential aspects of an object. It allows you to selectively ignore aspects that you deem unimportant to the functionality provided by the object. A good abstraction only provides as many operations and attributes as are required to get the job done. The more operations and attributes provided, the more difficult to use the object becomes. If an object is simple to use because it includes only the essential operations, there is a greater possibility that it can be reused by other applications.

A good abstract design will also limit a client's dependency on a particular class. If a client is too dependent on the way an operation is performed by an object, any modification to the internal aspects of that operation may impact the client, requiring that additional work be completed. This is often known as the *principle of minimal dependency*.

Association

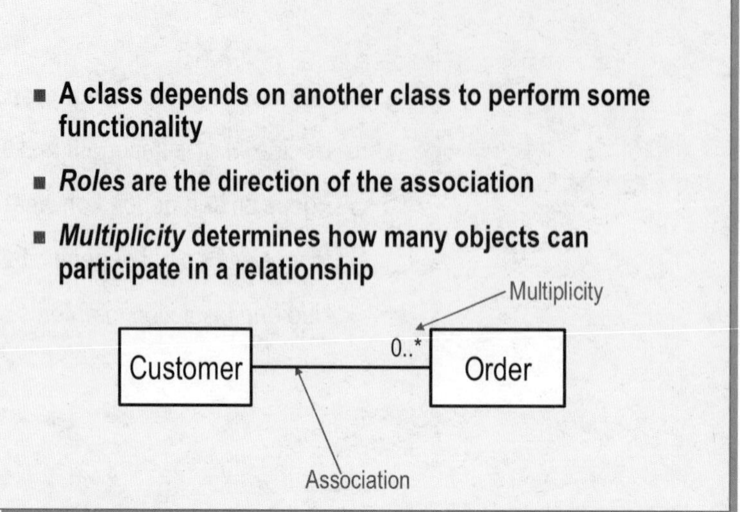

A class depends on another class to perform some functionality
Roles are the direction of the association
Multiplicity determines how many objects can participate in a relationship
Multiplicity
0..*
Customer
Order
Association

An *association* is a relationship between two classes. It represents a dependency, in that one class needs another class to accomplish a specific function.

The slide shows an example of an association between a **Customer** class and an **Order** class. In this relationship, it does not make sense to be able to create an order that does not belong to a particular customer, so we would specify that the **Order** class is dependent on the **Customer** class. The association shows this relationship.

Roles

A *role* is the direction of an association between two classes. The illustrated association between **Customer** and **Order** contains two inherent roles: one from **Customer** to **Order**, and another from **Order** to **Customer**. Roles can be explicitly named by using a label, or implied if not included on a diagram like that of the class name.

Multiplicity

Multiplicity is used to define a numeric constraint on an association that restricts how many objects exist within the relationship. If no multiplicity values are specified, there is an implicit one-to-one relationship between the classes.

In the illustration on the slide, a customer can place many orders. This relationship is signified by the 0..* multiplicity range on the **Order** end. As no multiplicity value is specified at the **Customer** end, an implicit value of one is assumed, signifying that an order can only have one customer.

The following table lists the other possibilities for multiplicity.

Symbol	Meaning
*	Many (zero or more)
0..1	Optional (zero or one)
1..*	One or more
2-3, 6	Specific possibilities
{constraint}	Rules including well-known constraints like Order or Mandatory, or other unique business rules specific to your solution.

Aggregation

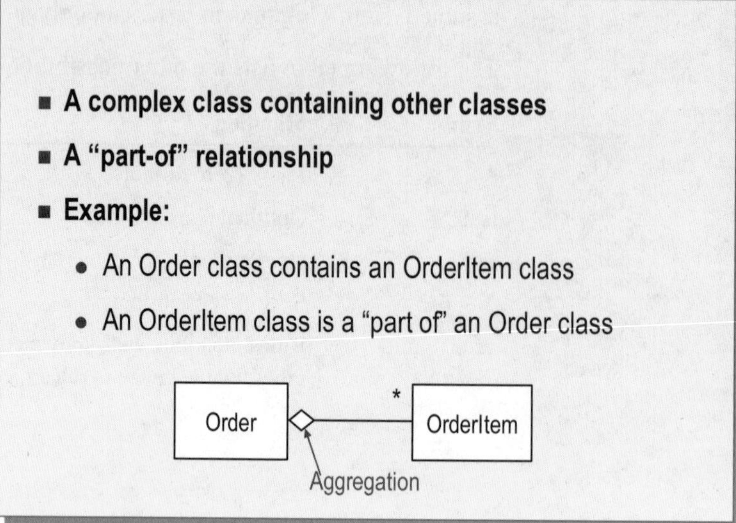

Aggregation represents a relationship where simple objects form parts of a more complex whole object.

This type of relationship is often used when an object does not make any sense in its own right, such as **Order Item** in the example on the slide. An **Order Item** needs to exist as part of a more complex object, such as an **Order**. The **Order** itself is only useful as a complete object that includes individual **Order Items**. The **Order Item** class can be referred to as the *part classifier* and the **Order** class as the *aggregate classifier*.

You can also specify the number of parts that make up the whole by using multiplicity on an aggregation relationship. The slide shows that an **Order** can be made up of one or more **Order Items**.

The words *aggregation* and *composition* are sometimes used as though they are synonyms. In UML, composition has a more restrictive meaning than aggregation:

- Aggregation

  Use aggregation to specify a whole/part relationship in which the lifetimes of the whole and the parts are not necessarily bound together, the parts can be traded for new parts, and parts can be shared. Aggregation in this sense is also known as *aggregation by reference*.

- Composition

  Use composition to specify a whole/part relationship in which the lifetimes of the whole and the parts are bound together, the parts cannot be traded for new parts, and the parts cannot be shared. Composition is also known as *aggregation by value*.

Attributes and Operations

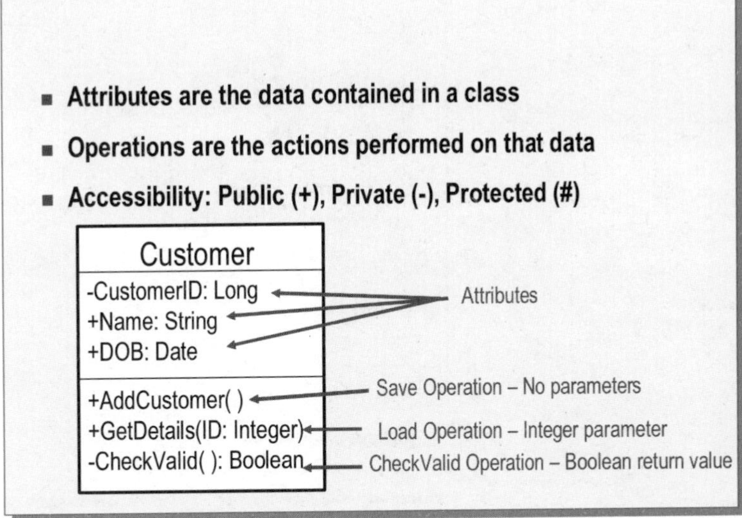

Classes are usually made up of data and actions performed on this data. These are known as *attributes* and *operations* respectively, but developers also call them *properties* and *methods*. These attributes and operations are also defined with an accessibility setting.

Attributes

Attributes are the data members of the class. They can be of any data type, including String, Decimal, or even another class. Each attribute will also have an accessibility option specified, as shown in the following table. In Visual Basic .NET, public attributes will be implemented as either class-level variables or, more appropriately, as class properties that encapsulate internal variables.

Operations

Operations are the actions performed on internal data within the class. They can take parameters, return values, and have different accessibility options specified in the same way that attributes can. In Visual Basic .NET, these are implemented as either functions or subroutines.

Accessibility

Attributes and operations can be defined with one of the access modifiers in the following table.

Value	Meaning
Public (+)	Accessible to the class itself and to any client of the class.
Protected (#)	Only accessible to a child class when used for inheritance. (Inheritance will be covered later in this module.)
Private (-)	Only accessible by code within the class that defines the private attribute or operation.

◆ Advanced Object-Oriented Programming Concepts

- Inheritance
- Interfaces
- Polymorphism

This lesson introduces some advanced concepts of object-oriented design: inheritance, interfaces, and polymorphism.

After completing this lesson, you will be able to:

- Explain inheritance
- Define interfaces
- Define polymorphism

Inheritance

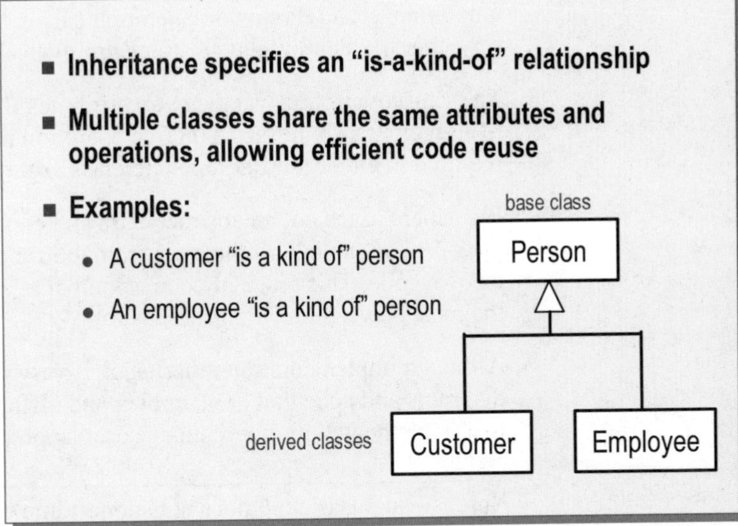

Inheritance is the concept of reusing common attributes and operations from a base class in a derived class. If the base class does not contain implementation code and will never be instantiated as an object, it is known as an abstract class.

The example below shows an inheritance relationship between the **Customer**, **Employee**, and **Person** classes. The **Person** superclass has attributes defined as **Name**, **Gender**, and **Date of Birth** and contains the operations **Create**, **Remove**, and **Validate**. These are all attributes and operations that could equally be applied to a **Customer** or **Employee** subclass, providing a good deal of reuse.

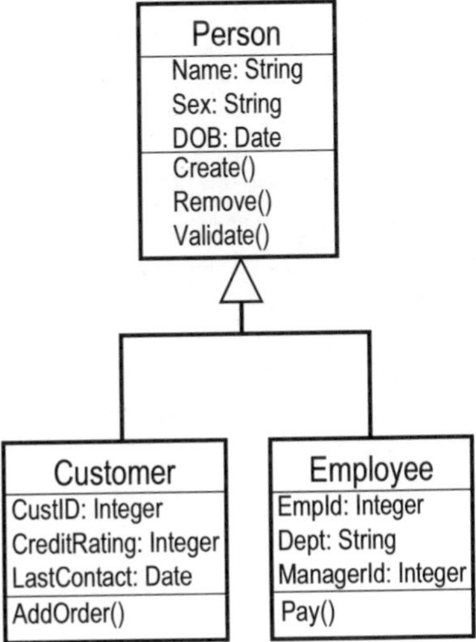

Specialization occurs when a subclass is created and includes attributes or operations specific to that class.

The **Customer** class has the extra attributes **CustomerID**, **CreditRating**, and **LastContacted** in addition to the inherited ones from the **Person** superclass. It also defines its own operation named **AddOrder** that is specific to the **Customer** class. Having an operation called **AddOrder** would not make sense for either the **Person** class or the **Employee** class.

The **Employee** class has the extra attributes **EmployeeID**, **Department**, and **Manager**. It also defines a unique operation named **Pay** that would not be required in either the **Person** superclass or the **Customer** subclass.

If a superclass is not an abstract class and contains some implementation code, the subclass can inherit the code from the superclass or override it by providing its own code. This reuse of code is known as *implementation inheritance* and is the most powerful form of reuse.

Although implementation inheritance is very useful, it can lead to class diagrams and code that are complex and difficult to read. You should ensure that implementation inheritance is used appropriately and not overused.

Note Visual Basic 6.0 does not support implementation inheritance, but Visual Basic .NET does. For more information, see Module 5, "Object-Oriented Programming in Visual Basic .NET," in Course 2373B, *Programming with Microsoft Visual Basic .NET.*

Interfaces

- Interfaces only define the method signatures
- Classes define the implementation of the code for the Interface methods
- *Interface inheritance* means only the Interface is inherited, not the implementation code

Person {abstract}	Employee
Public Sub Create( ) Public Sub Remove( )	Public Sub Create( ) 'implementation code ... End Sub ...

Interfaces are similar to abstract classes. They define the method signatures used by other classes but do not implement any code themselves.

Interface inheritance means that only the method signatures are inherited and that any implementation code is not. You would need to create separate code in the appropriate inherited method of each derived class to achieve any required functionality. Reuse is therefore more limited in interface inheritance as compared to implementation inheritance because you must write code in multiple locations.

Polymorphism

- **The same operation behaves differently when applied to objects based on different classes**
- **Often based on Interface inheritance**
  - Classes inherit from interface base class
  - Each derived class implements its own version of code
  - Clients can treat all objects as if they are instances of the base class, without knowledge of the derived classes

Polymorphism is the ability to call the same method on multiple objects that have been instantiated from different subclasses and generate differing behavior. This is often achieved by using interface inheritance. If two subclasses inherit the same interface, each of them will contain the same method signatures as the superclass. Each one will implement the code in an individual way, allowing different behavior to be created from the same method.

Customer
Inherited Sub Create() 'do specific customer 'code ... End Sub

Employee
Inherited Sub Create() 'do specific employee 'code ... End Sub

In the above example, the **Customer** and **Employee** classes have inherited from the **Person** superclass. Each class implements its own version of the **Create** method differently, but, because they both inherit the same interface, a client could treat both classes the same.

◆ Using Microsoft Visio

- Visio Overview
- Use Case Diagrams
- Class Diagrams
- Creating Class Diagrams

This lesson introduces the Visual Studio .NET modeling tool: Visio.

After completing this lesson, you will be able to:

- Use Visio to help you design your system solution.

Visio Overview

- **Supports:**
  - Use case diagrams
  - Class or static structure diagrams
  - Activity diagrams
  - Component diagrams
  - Deployment diagrams
  - Freeform modeling

Visio allows you to design and document your solution from the initial analysis and design stages all the way to the final deployment of your enterprise system.

It supports many different models, including the following.

Use Case Diagrams

As you have seen previously in this module, use cases are created to document the interactions that take place between the actors and the processes in the system. Visio allows you to model these diagrams and document the use case descriptions within these diagrams.

Class or Static Structure Diagrams

This UML diagram provides a view of some or all of the classes that make up the system. It includes their attributes, their operations, and their relationships. Visio supports all aspects of class diagrams, including attribute visibility, association roles, and interfaces.

Activity Diagrams

This UML diagram provides a view of the system's workflow between activities in a process. They can be used to model the dynamic aspects of the system, usually based on one or more use case descriptions. You can use initial states, transitions, decisions, and final states to model this view.

Component Diagrams

This UML diagram allows you to model physical aspects of a system, such as the source code, executables, files, and database tables. You can use interfaces, components, packages, and dependencies to model this view.

Deployment Diagrams

This UML diagram gives a view of the physical nodes (computational devices) on which the system executes. This type of diagram is especially useful when the system will involve more than one computer, such as in an enterprise solution. Nodes, component instances, and objects are the main shapes used in this diagram.

Freeform Modeling

Visio allows you the flexibility to create freeform models that do not need to adhere to the UML standards. This allows you to create a diagram that incorporates common UML shapes such as classes and components in addition to non-UML shapes such as COM and flowchart shapes. You have the option to validate all or part of your model to see whether it conforms to UML semantics.

Use Case Diagrams

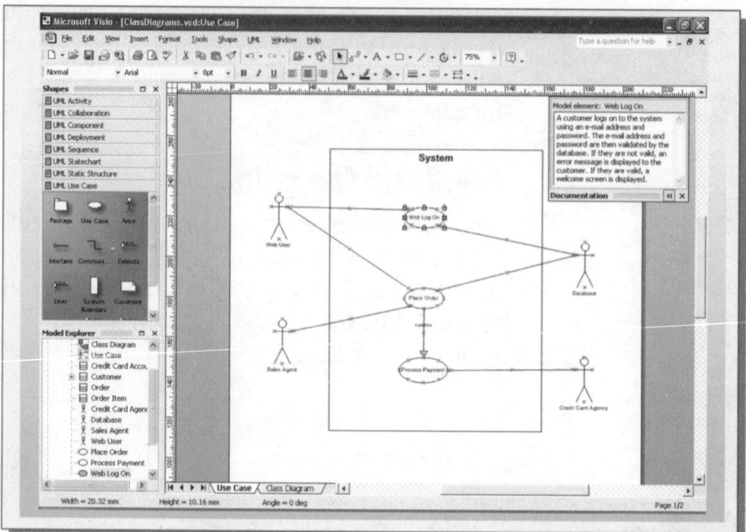

Visio allows you to create fully featured use case diagrams that include:

- Actors.
- Use cases.
- Relationships, including association, dependency, and inheritance. These relationships include attributes such as multiplicity, navigability, and stereotype.
- Notes to help store additional information.

You can add descriptions to all of the objects listed above to fully document your model. You can also add any non-UML shapes from the various stencil tabs to create a freeform model.

Demonstration: Creating Use Case Diagrams

In this demonstration, you will learn how to create a use case diagram in Visio. Note that the use cases created in the demonstration do not represent a completed model; this exercise is for demonstration purposes only.

Class Diagrams

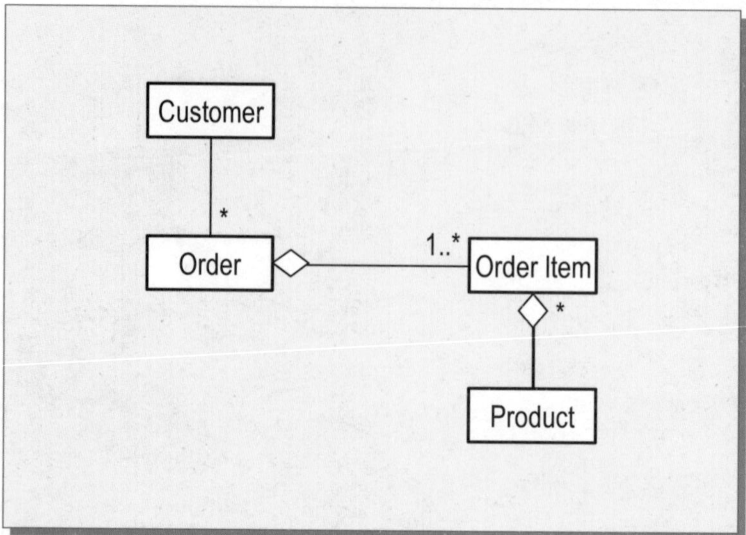

Class diagrams allow you to graphically put all of these relationships together in a single place. With some refinement, class diagrams will help a designer or developer model the system in enough detail to enable code to be generated and development to begin.

The ability to interpret a class diagram is vital in modern software development. The slide shows that a single **Customer** class is associated with between zero and many **Order** classes. An **Order** class is made up of (or aggregated with) **Order Item** classes. The multiplicity for this relationship shows that there must be at least one **Order Item** for an **Order** to be valid, but that there can be an unlimited number of **Order Items** on the **Order**. Finally, each **Order Item** is associated with a single **Product**, but a **Product** can be associated with many **Order Items**.

Note Class diagrams are also known as *static structure diagrams* in Visio and in some other UML modeling tools.

Creating Class Diagrams

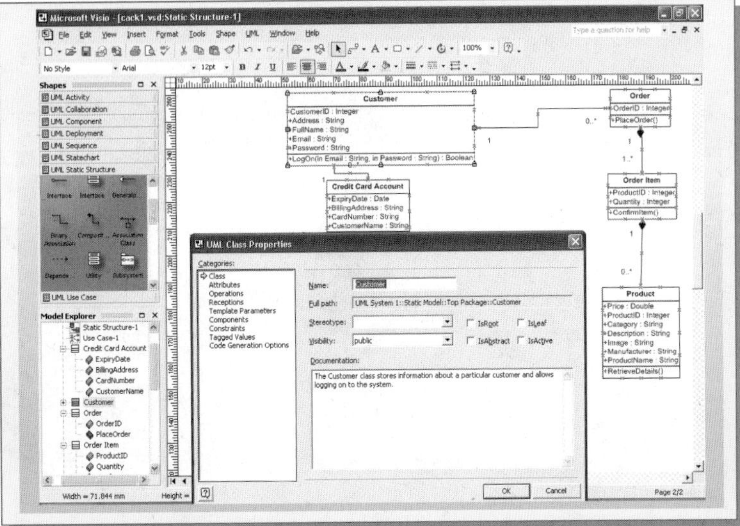

Visio allows you to create extensive class diagrams that include the following elements:

- Classes.
- Abstract classes or interfaces.
- Class attributes with accessibility (private, protected, and public), initial value, and stereotype (data type).
- Class operations with accessibility and parameters (detailed in the following text).
- Operation parameters with direction (in, out, inout, and return) and stereotype (data type).
- Relationships between objects, including association, dependency, aggregation, composition, and inheritance. These relationships include attributes such as multiplicity, navigability, and stereotype.
- Notes to help store additional information.

You can add descriptions to all of the objects listed above to fully document your model. You can also add any non-UML shapes from the various Toolbox tabs to create a freeform model.

Demonstration: Creating Class Diagrams

In this demonstration, you will learn how to create a class diagram in Visio. Note that the classes created in the demonstration do not represent a completed model. This exercise is for demonstration purposes only.

Lab 4.1: Creating Class Diagrams from Use Cases

Objectives

After completing this lab, you will be able to:

- Create classes based on use cases.
- Use Visio to create class diagrams.

Prerequisites

Before working on this lab, you must have:

- Knowledge of use cases and class diagrams.
- Familiarity with modeling tools.

Scenario

The Cargo system will provide the basis for many of the remaining lab exercises in this course. It is based on a simple Internet system for collecting and delivering customer packages. Web customers can log on to the system and create a delivery. Customers can also contact the company by means of a telephone sales operator who can process the order in a similar fashion. More information about the system is detailed in the use case diagram provided to you. However, while the labs are based on this scenario, you will not create a completed system during this course.

In this lab, you will view the descriptions of existing use cases to help you understand the system. You will then create classes based on those descriptions.

Starter and Solution Files

There are starter and solution files associated with this lab. The starter files are in the *install_folder*\Labs\Lab041\Ex0*x*\Starter folders, and the solution files are in the *install_folder*\Labs\Lab041\Ex0*x*\Solution folders (where *x* is the number of the exercise).

Estimated time to complete this lab: 45 minutes

Exercise 1
Viewing the Cargo Use Case Diagram

In this exercise, you will investigate the use case diagram for the Cargo system, the individual actors, and the use case descriptions.

▶ To open the CargoModeler drawing

1. Click **start**, point to **All Programs**, and then click **Microsoft Visio**.
2. On the **File** menu, click **Open**. In the *install_folder*\Labs\Lab041\Ex01 folder, click the **CargoModeler.vsd** drawing, and then click **Open**.

▶ To view the diagram documentation

1. Double-click each actor individually, and read the associated documentation in the **UML Actor Properties** dialog box.
2. Double-click each use case individually, and read the associated documentation in the **UML Use Case Properties** dialog box.

Exercise 2
Creating the Cargo Classes and Relationships

In this exercise, you will create the Cargo system's classes and relationships, based on the use case descriptions from the previous exercise.

▶ To create the Cargo classes

1. On the **File** menu, click **Open**. Browse to the *install_folder*\Labs\Lab041\Ex02\Starter folder, click the **CargoModeler.vsd** drawing, and then click **Open**.
2. In Model Explorer, right-click **Top Package**, point to **New**, and then click **Static Structure Diagram**. Rename the diagram **Classes** in the Model Explorer.
3. On the **UML** menu, click **Options**, and then click **UML Document**. Clear all of the listed data types except **Cargo::VB Data Types** and then click **OK**.
4. In the **Shapes** toolbox, click the **UML Static Structure** tab. Click the **Class** tool and drag it to the drawing. Double-click the new class to display the properties, and rename the class **Customer** and then click **OK**.
5. Repeat step 4 to create the following classes: **Delivery**, **Package**, **Special Package**, **Invoice**, and **Payment**.

▶ To create the class relationships

1. In the **Shapes** toolbox, click the **Binary Association** tool, and drag it to create an association from the **Customer** class to the **Delivery** class.
2. Double-click the new association to display the **UML Association Properties** dialog box. In the **Association Ends** list, change the **Multiplicity** value in the first line to **1**. Change the **Multiplicity** value in the second line to **0..***. (Note that the order of association ends is related to the order in which you created the associations.) Click **OK**.
3. Repeat steps 1 and 2 to create the following relationships and multiplicity values.

From class	To class	Multiplicity value
Customer	**Invoice**	First line: **1**
		Second line: **0..***
Delivery	**Invoice**	First line: **1**
		Second line: **1**
Invoice	**Payment**	First line: **1**
		Second line: **1**
Delivery	**Package**	First line: **1**
		Second line: **1..***

4. Create a generalization relationship from the **Special Package** class to the **Package** class by using the **Generalization** tool.

► To hide the association end names

1. Select all the binary associations, right-click any of the selected associations, and then click **Shape Display Options**. Clear the **First end name** and **Second end name** check boxes, select **Apply to the same selected UML shapes in the current drawing window page**, and click **OK**. This will remove the end names from the diagram.
2. Save the drawing.

Exercise 3
Creating the Customer Class

In this exercise, you will create the **Customer** class attributes and operations.

► To create the Customer class attributes

1. If you have not completed the previous exercise, use the starter code found in the *install_folder*\Labs\Lab041\Ex03\Starter folder.
2. Double-click the **Customer** class to display the **UML Class Properties** dialog box.
3. In the **Attributes** category, click the first line in the list of attributes. Use the information in the following table to add the class attributes.

Attribute	Type	Visibility
CustomerID	VB::Integer	private
Email	VB::String	public
Password	VB::String	public
FirstName	VB::String	public
LastName	VB::String	public
Address	VB::String	public
Company	VB::String	public

► To create the LogOn operation

1. In the **Operations** category, click the first line in the list of operations. Add an operation called **LogOn** with a return type of VB::Boolean.
2. Click **Properties**, and then add the following description in the **Documentation** box:
   "Attempts to log on a customer and retrieve his or her details based on e-mail address and password."
3. In the **Parameters** category, create new parameters based on the following values.

Parameter	Type	Kind
Email	VB::String	in
Password	VB::String	in

4. Click **OK** to return to the **UML Class Properties** dialog box.

▶ To create the AddCustomer operation

1. Create the **AddCustomer** operation with a return type of VB::Integer.
2. Click **Properties**, and then add the following description in the **Documentation** box:
   "Adds a new customer to the database based on the input parameters."
3. In the **Parameters** category, create new parameters based on the following values.

Parameter	Type	Kind
Email	VB::String	in
Password	VB::String	in
FirstName	VB::String	in
LastName	VB::String	in
Company	VB::String	in
Address	VB::String	in

4. Click **OK** to return to the **UML Class Properties** dialog box.

▶ To create the GetDetails operation

1. Create the **GetDetails** operation with a return type of <None>.
2. Click **Properties**, and then add the following description in the **Documentation** box:
   "Returns the customer details based on the CustomerID received."
3. In the **Parameters** category, create new parameters based on the following values.

Parameter	Type	Kind
CustomerID	VB::Integer	in

4. Click **OK** to return to the **UML Class Properties** dialog box, and then click **OK** to return to the drawing.

► **To generate Visual Basic .NET source code**

1. On the **UML** menu, point to **Code**, and then click **Generate**.
2. Select **Visual Basic** as the **Target language**. Select **Add Classes to Visual Studio Project**, and then in the **Template** list, click **Class Library**. Rename both the Project and the Solution as **Cargo**.
3. Click **Browse**, locate the *install_folder*\Labs\Lab041\Ex03\Starter folder, and then click **OK**.
4. Select the **Customer** class only for code generation, and click **OK**.
5. Save the drawing and quit Visio.

► **To view the code**

1. Open Microsoft Visual Studio .NET.
2. On the **File** menu, point to **Open**, and then click **Project**. Set the folder location to *install_folder*\Labs\Lab041\Ex03\Starter, click **Cargo.sln**, and then click **Open**.
3. View the code for Customer.vb.
4. Quit Visual Studio .NET.

If Time Permits
Viewing the Cargo Design Solution

In this optional exercise, you will investigate the class diagram for the completed Cargo system.

► **To open the CargoModeler drawing**

1. Open Visio.
2. On the **File** menu, click **Open**. Browse for the *install_folder*\Labs\Lab041\Ex04 folder, click the **CargoModeler.vsd** drawing, and then click **Open**.

► **To view the classes**

- Investigate each attribute and operation, including the parameters, for each class on the diagram.

Review

- Designing Classes
- Object-Oriented Programming Concepts
- Advanced Object-Oriented Programming Concepts
- Using Microsoft Visio

1. An actor must be a person that interacts with the system. True or false?

2. Define the object-oriented term *encapsulation*.

3. Define the object-oriented term *inheritance*.

4. Describe freeform modeling.

5. In the following use case description, what are the likely classes and attributes?

   A user requests a listing of grades from a school based on a particular student ID. The ID is validated by the database, and an error message appears if the student ID does not exist. If the ID matches a student, the student's name, address, and date of birth are retrieved, in addition to the grades. The user is prompted to verify the information, and the grades are displayed if the verification succeeds. An error message is displayed if the user is unable to verify the information. Three verification attempts are allowed before the user is automatically logged off. The user is automatically logged off after five minutes of inactivity.

Class	Attributes

msdn training

Module 5: Object-Oriented Programming in Visual Basic .NET

Contents

Overview

- Defining Classes
- Creating and Destroying Objects
- Inheritance
- Interfaces
- Working with Classes

In this module, you will learn how to implement object-oriented programming in Microsoft® Visual Basic® .NET version 7.0. You will learn how to define classes, their properties, and their methods. You will learn about the life cycle of an object, from creation to destruction. You will also learn how to work with classes by using inheritance, interfaces, polymorphism, shared members, events, and delegates.

After completing this module, you will be able to:

- Define classes.
- Instantiate and use objects in client code.
- Create classes that use inheritance.
- Define interfaces and use polymorphism.
- Create shared members.
- Create class events and handle them from a client application.

◆ Defining Classes

- **Procedure for Defining a Class**
- **Using Access Modifiers**
- **Declaring Methods**
- **Declaring Properties**
- **Using Attributes**
- **Overloading Methods**
- **Using Constructors**
- **Using Destructors**

In this lesson, you will learn how to define classes in Visual Basic .NET. After completing this lesson, you will be able to:

- Specify access modifiers (scope) for classes and their procedures.
- Declare methods and properties within a class.
- Use attributes to provide metadata about your code.
- Pass different parameters to one method by using overloading.
- Create and destroy objects.

Procedure for Defining a Class

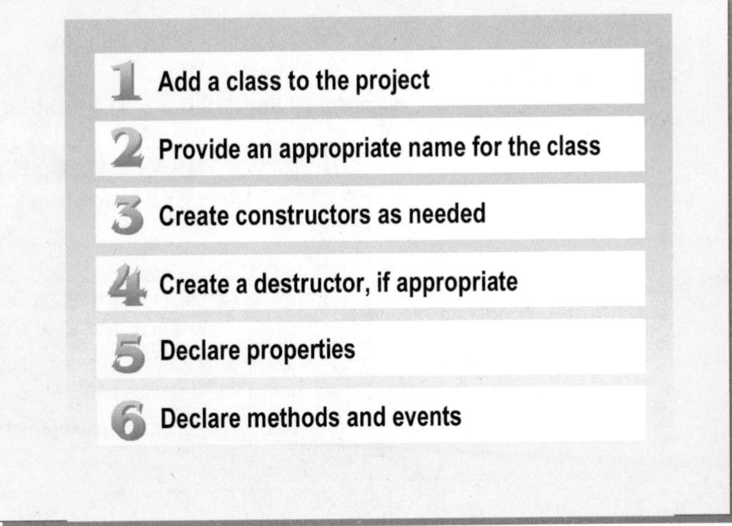
1 Add a class to the project
2 Provide an appropriate name for the class
3 Create constructors as needed
4 Create a destructor, if appropriate
5 Declare properties
6 Declare methods and events

To define a class in Visual Basic .NET, you can follow this general procedure:

1. Add a class to the project.
2. Provide an appropriate file name for the class when you add it. This will name both the file and the class itself. If you do not change the file name when you add it, you can change the class name at any time by changing the class definition in the code window.
3. Create constructors as needed.
4. Create a destructor if appropriate.
5. Declare properties.
6. Declare methods and events.

Note In Visual Basic .NET, you can define more than one class in a single file. You are not limited to one class per file, as you are in previous versions of Visual Basic, because classes are a block level construct.

Using Access Modifiers

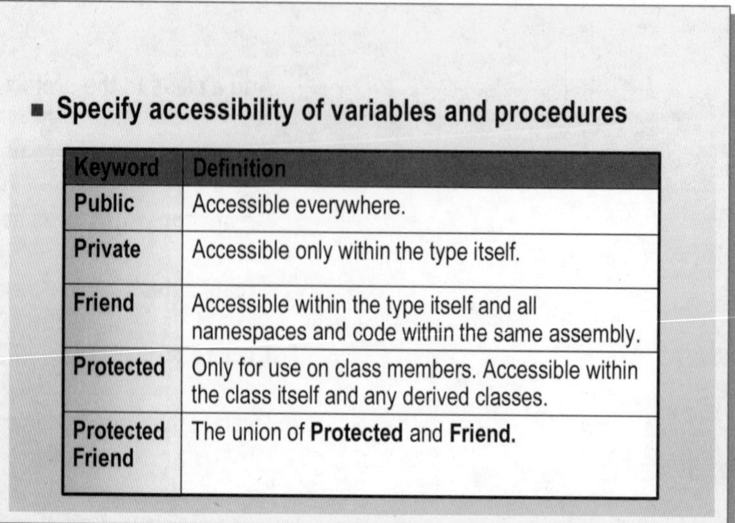
Specify accessibility of variables and procedures
Keyword | Definition
Public | Accessible everywhere.
Private | Accessible only within the type itself.
Friend | Accessible within the type itself and all namespaces and code within the same assembly.
Protected | Only for use on class members. Accessible within the class itself and any derived classes.
Protected Friend | The union of Protected and Friend.

You can use access modifiers to specify the scope of the variables and procedures in the class that you define. Visual Basic .NET retains three access modifiers that are used in previous versions of Visual Basic and adds two more: **Protected** and **Protected Friend**. The following table defines the five access modifiers available in Visual Basic .NET.

Access modifier	Definition
Public	Accessible everywhere.
Private	Accessible only within the type itself.
Friend	Accessible within the type itself and all namespaces and code within the same assembly.
Protected	Accessible within the class itself and, if other classes are inheriting from the class, within any derived classes. Protected members are available outside of an assembly when inherited by derived classes.
Protected Friend	The union of **Protected** and **Friend**. Accessible to code within the same assembly and to any derived classes regardless of the assembly to which they belong.

Note Inheritance in Visual Basic .NET is described in detail in the Inheritance lesson of this module.

Declaring Methods

- Same syntax as in Visual Basic 6.0

```
Public Sub TestIt(ByVal x As Integer)
...
End Sub

Public Function GetIt( ) As Integer
...
End Function
```

You use the same syntax to declare a method in Visual Basic .NET that you used in Visual Basic 6.0, as shown in the following example:

```
Public Class TestClass

    Public Sub TestIt(ByVal x As Integer)
        ...
    End Sub

    Public Function GetIt( ) As Integer
        ...
    End Function

End Class
```

Declaring Properties

- **Syntax differs from that of Visual Basic 6.0**

```
Public Property MyData( ) As Integer
    Get
      Return intMyData        'Return local variable value
    End Get
    Set (ByVal Value As Integer)
      intMyData = Value       'Store Value in local variable
    End Set
End Property
```

- **ReadOnly, WriteOnly, and Default keywords**

```
Public ReadOnly Property MyData( ) As Integer
    Get
      Return intMyData
    End Get
End Property
```

The syntax for declaring class properties has changed significantly in Visual Basic .NET.

Syntax for Declaring Properties

In Visual Basic 6.0, you create properties by declaring two separate procedures: one for the **Get** and one for the **Let** or**Set**. In Visual Basic .NET, you declare your properties by using two code blocks in a single procedure, as follows:

```
[Default|ReadOnly|WriteOnly] Property varname ([parameter
list]) [As typename]
   Get
      [block]
   End Get
   Set (ByVal Value As typename)
      [block]
   End Set
End Property
```

When you create a property declaration, the Visual Basic .NET Code Editor inserts a template for the remainder of the property body.

Example

The following example shows how to declare a property called **MyData** of type **Integer**. The **Get** block returns an unseen local variable called *intMyData* by using a **Return** statement. The **Set** block uses the **Value** parameter to store the passed-in property value to the *intMyData* local variable.

```
Private intMyData As Integer

Public Property MyData( ) As Integer
    Get
        Return intMyData
    End Get
    Set (ByVal Value As Integer)
        intMyData = Value
    End Set
End Property
```

Using Read-Only Properties

You can create read-only properties by using the **ReadOnly** keyword when you declare the property. Read-only properties cannot be used in an assignment statement. The following example shows how to specify a read-only property:

```
Public ReadOnly Property MyData( ) As Integer
    Get
        Return intMyData
    End Get
End Property
```

You cannot use the **Set** block when defining read-only properties because the property cannot be updated. The compiler will generate an error if you attempt to do this.

Using Write-Only Properties

You can create write-only properties by using the **WriteOnly** keyword when you declare the property. Write-only properties cannot be used to retrieve the value of the property. The following example shows how to create a write-only property:

```
Public WriteOnly Property MyData( ) As Integer
    Set (ByVal Value As Integer)
        intMyData = Value
    End Set
End Property
```

You cannot use the **Get** block when defining write-only properties because the property is not readable. The compiler will generate an error if you attempt to do this.

Using Default Properties

You can create a default property for a class by using the **Default** keyword when you declare the property. You must code the property to take at least one argument, and you must specify **Public**, **Protected**, or **Friend** access.

The following example shows how to declare a default property that takes an index as an argument and returns a **Boolean** value:

```
Default Public Property Item(ByVal index As Integer) _
                               As Boolean
  Get
    Return myArray(index) 'Uses a private module-level array
  End Get
  Set(ByVal Value As Boolean)
    myArray(index) = Value
  End Set
End Property
```

Using Attributes

- **Extra metadata supplied by using "< >" brackets**
- **Supported for:**
  - Assemblies, classes, methods, properties, and more
- **Common uses:**
  - Assembly versioning, Web Services, components, security, and custom

```
<Obsolete("Please use method M2")> Public Sub M1( )
  'Results in warning in IDE when used by client code
End Sub
```

You can use attributes to provide extra information or metadata to the developers who read your code. In Visual Basic .NET, you use angular brackets (< and >) to specify an attribute.

You can apply attributes to many items within your application, including assemblies, modules, classes, methods, properties, parameters, and fields in modules, classes, and structures.

Here are some examples of how to use attributes:

- In assemblies, you can specify metadata including the title, description, and version information of the assembly.
- When creating a Web Service, you can define which methods are accessible as part of the service, in addition to adding descriptions to the methods.
- When designing Windows Forms controls, you can specify information to display in the property browser, or you can set the Toolbox icon.
- For components that use enterprise services, you can set transaction and security settings.

Functionality is provided by the Microsoft .NET Framework to allow you to create your own custom attributes and use them as you want in your applications.

Note For more information about creating custom attributes, see "Writing Custom Attributes" in the Microsoft Visual Studio® .NET documentation.

Example

The following example shows how to use the **Obsolete** attribute to warn developers that a method can no longer be used. An optional message is displayed in the Task List window if a developer attempts to use this method. Using the **Obsolete** method will not create an error when the application is compiled, but will generate a warning as follows:

```
<Obsolete("Please use method M2")> Public Sub M1( )
  'Results in warning in IDE when used by client code
End Sub
```

Note All attributes are simply classes that inherit from the **Attribute** class and provide constructors. The **Obsolete** class provides a single constructor that takes a string as the parameter.

Overloading Methods

- Methods with the same name can accept different parameters

```
Public Function Display(s As String) As String
    MsgBox("String: " & s)
    Return "String"
End Sub
Public Function Display(i As Integer) As Integer
    MsgBox("Integer: " & i)
    Return 1
End Function
```

- Specified parameters determine which method to call
- The Overloads keyword is optional unless overloading inherited methods

---

Overloading is a powerful object-oriented feature that allows multiple methods to have the same name but accept different parameters. Overloading allows calling code to execute one method name but achieve different actions, depending on the parameters you pass in.

For overloading to occur, the method signature must be unique. You can achieve this by changing the number of parameters in the signature or by changing the data types of the parameters. Changing the way a parameter is passed (that is, by value or by reference) does not make a signature unique, nor does changing a function return data type.

You can optionally specify a method as overloaded with the **Overloads** keyword. If you do not use the keyword, the compiler assumes it by default when you declare multiple methods that have the same name. However, when overloading a method from an inherited class, you must use the **Overloads** keyword.

Note Overloading a method from an inherited class will be discussed in the Inheritance lesson of this module.

The following example shows how to overload a method. This code allows different types of information (string, integers, and so on) to be displayed by calling the **Display** method of a class and passing in different parameters.

```
Public Function Display(s As String) As String
    MsgBox("String: " & s)
    Return "String"
End Sub

Public Function Display(i As Integer) As Integer
    MsgBox("Integer: " & i)
    Return 1
End Function
```

When you call the **Display** method, the parameters you specify determine which overloaded method will be called.

Without using overloading, you need two different methods, such as **DisplayString** and **DisplayInteger**, to accept the different types of parameters in the preceding example.

Note If the **Option Strict** compiler option is on, you must explicitly declare values as specific types when passing them to the overloaded methods as parameters, and the compiler can identify which instance of the method to call. If **Option Strict** is off and a generic variable (such as **Object**) is passed as a parameter, the decision of which instance of the method to call is left until run time. For more information about overload resolution, see "Procedure Overloading" in the Visual Studio .NET documentation.

Using Constructors

- **Sub New replaces Class_Initialize**
- **Executes code when object is instantiated**

```
Public Sub New( )
    'Perform simple initialization
    intValue = 1
End Sub
```

- **Can overload, but does not use Overloads keyword**

```
Public Sub New(ByVal i As Integer) 'Overloaded without Overloads
    'Perform more complex initialization
    intValue = i
End Sub
```

In Visual Basic 6.0, you place initialization code in the **Class_Initialize** event of your class. This code is executed when the object is instantiated, and you can use it to set initial values of local variables, to open resources, or to instantiate other objects.

In Visual Basic .NET, you control the initialization of new objects by using procedures called *constructors*. The **Sub New** constructor replaces the **Class_Initialize** event and has the following features:

- The code in the **Sub New** block will always run before any other code in a class.
- Unlike **Class_Initialize**, the **Sub New** constructor will only run once: when an object is created.
- **Sub New** can only be called explicitly in the first line of code of another constructor, from either the same class or a derived class using the **MyBase** keyword.

Using Sub New

The following example shows how to use the **Sub New** constructor:

```
Public Sub New( )
    'Perform simple initialization
    intValue = 1
End Sub
```

The change in Visual Basic .NET from the **Class_Initialize** event to the **Sub New** constructor means you can overload the **New** subroutine and create as many class constructors as you require. This is useful if you want to initialize your object when you instantiate it. To do this in Visual Basic 6.0, you must call methods or properties after the object is created.

Overloading Constructors

You can overload constructors just as you can overload any other method in a class. However, you cannot use the **Overloads** keyword when overloading constructors. The following example shows how to overload the **New** subroutine and create multiple class constructors:

```
Public Sub New( )     'Perform simple initialization
    intValue = 1
End Sub

Public Sub New(ByVal i As Integer)
    'Perform more complex initialization
    intValue = i
End Sub

Public Sub New(ByVal i As Integer, _
      ByVal s As String)
    intValue = i
    strValue = s
End Sub
```

Using Destructors

- **Sub Finalize replaces Class_Terminate event**
- **Use to clean up resources**
- **Code executed when destroyed by garbage collection**
  - Important: destruction may not happen immediately

```
Protected Overrides Sub Finalize( )
    'Can close connections or other resources
    conn.Close
End Sub
```

In Visual Basic .NET, you can control what happens during the destruction of objects by using procedures called *destructors*.

The new **Finalize** destructor replaces the **Class_Terminate** event found in previous versions of Visual Basic. This subroutine is executed when your object is destroyed, and you can use it to clean up open resources, such as database connections, or to release other objects in an object model hierarchy.

The following example shows how to use the **Finalize** destructor:

```
Protected Overrides Sub Finalize( )
    'Can close connections of other resources
    conn.Close
End Sub
```

Note You will learn about the **Overrides** keyword in the Inheritance lesson in this module.

In Visual Basic 6.0, the **Class_Terminate** event runs when an object is no longer being referenced by any variables. You use the **Set x = Nothing** statement to release a particular reference. When all the references are gone, the event executes and resources can be cleaned up.

In Visual Basic .NET, when you set an object reference to **Nothing**, you still release variables. However, the object may not be destroyed until a later stage due to the introduction of garbage collection.

◆ Creating and Destroying Objects

- Instantiating and Initializing Objects
- Garbage Collection
- Using the Dispose Method

In this lesson, you will learn about creating and destroying objects. After completing this lesson, you will be able to:

- Instantiate and initialize objects.
- Explain the role that garbage collection plays in the object life cycle.
- Use the **Dispose** method to destroy an object and safely clean up its resources.

Instantiating and Initializing Objects

- **Instantiate and initialize objects in one line of code**

```
'Declare but do not instantiate yet
Dim c1 As TestClass
'Other code
c1 = New TestClass( )        'Instantiate now

'Declare, instantiate & initialize using default constructor
Dim c2 As TestClass = New TestClass( )

'Declare, instantiate & initialize using default constructor
Dim c3 As New TestClass( )

'Declare, instantiate & initialize using alternative constructor
Dim c4 As New TestClass(10)
Dim c5 As TestClass = New TestClass(10)
```

You can now instantiate and initialize objects in one line of code. This means you can write simpler and clearer code that can call different class constructors for multiple variables.

Example 1

The following example shows how to declare a variable in one line and instantiate it in a following line. Remember that the **Set** keyword is no longer needed.

```
'Declare but do not instantiate yet
Dim c1 As TestClass
'Other code
c1 = New TestClass( )        'Instantiate now
```

Example 2

The following example shows how to declare, instantiate, and initialize an object in one statement. The default constructor for the class will be executed.

```
'Declare, instantiate & initialize using default constructor
Dim c2 As TestClass = New TestClass( )
```

Example 3

The following example performs the same functionality as Example 2. It looks similar to code from previous versions of Visual Basic, but behaves quite differently.

```
'Declare, instantiate & initialize using default constructor
Dim c3 As New TestClass
```

Visual Basic 6.0

In Visual Basic 6.0, the preceding code creates the object when the object is first used. If you destroy the variable by assigning the **Nothing** keyword, it will automatically be recreated when it is next referenced.

Visual Basic .NET

In Visual Basic .NET, the preceding code declares and instantiates the object variables immediately. If you destroy the variable by assigning the **Nothing** keyword, it will not automatically be recreated when it is next referenced.

Example 4

The following examples show how to declare, instantiate, and initialize objects in single statements. Both statements call alternative constructors for the class.

```
'Declare, instantiate & initialize using alternate constructor
Dim c4 As New TestClass(10)
Dim c5 As TestClass = New TestClass(10)
```

Garbage Collection

- **Background process that cleans up unused variables**
- **Use *x* = *Nothing* to enable garbage collection**
- **Detects objects or other memory that cannot be reached by any code (even circular references!)**
- **Allows destruction of object**
  - No guarantee of *when* this will happen
  - Potential for resources to be tied up for long periods of time (database connections, files, and so on)
  - You can force collection by using the GC system class

In previous versions of Visual Basic, object destruction is based on a reference count. References are removed when you set the object to **Nothing** or when the variable goes out of scope. When all references to an object have been removed, the object is destroyed. This is effective in most situations, but some objects, such as those left orphaned in a circular reference relationship, may not be destroyed.

In Visual Studio .NET, setting an object reference to **Nothing** or allowing it to go out of scope removes the link from the variable to the object and allows garbage collection to take place. This background process traces object references and destroys those that cannot be reached by executing code, including objects that are not referenced. Some time after the garbage collection has run, the object destructor code will run (the **Finalize** method discussed earlier in this module.)

Garbage collection provides several performance advantages:

- It cleans up circular references and improves code performance because objects do not need to keep a reference count.
- Because reference counting is no longer required, the time taken to instantiate an object is reduced.
- The time taken to release an object variable reference is reduced.
- No storage is required for the reference count, which means that the amount of memory that an object uses is also reduced.

It is important to note that garbage collection introduces a time delay between when the last reference to an object is removed and when the collector destroys the object and reclaims the memory. This time delay can be quite significant if the object is holding open resources that may affect the scalability or performance of the application, such as database connections.

You can force the collection of unused objects by using the **GC** (Garbage Collector) system class's **Collect** method as follows:

```
GC.Collect( )
```

However, using the **Collect** method is not generally recommended because forcing garbage collection may result in poor performance due to the unnecessary collection of other unused objects. Occasionally it is appropriate to use the **Collect** method when you know that you have created garbage, but this should be done with caution.

Using the Dispose Method

- **Create a Dispose method to manually release resources**

```
'Class code
Public Sub Dispose( )
    'Check that the connection is still open
    conn.Close          'Close a database connection
End Sub
```

- **Call the Dispose method from client code**

```
'Client code
    Dim x as TestClass = New TestClass( )
    ...
    x.Dispose( )        'Call the object's dispose method
```

Because of the potential time delay created by finalization, you may want to create a standard method called **Dispose** for your class. Many Visual Studio .NET objects use this method to clean up resources.

When client code has no further need for an object's resources, it can directly call code placed in the **Dispose** method of the object. If the client code does not call the **Dispose** method explicitly before garbage collection occurs, the **Finalize** method of the class can also call the **Dispose** method. For this reason you should write your **Dispose** method to be safely callable multiple times without throwing an exception.

Example

The following simple example shows how to create a **Dispose** method to manually release resources:

```
'Class code
Public Sub Dispose( )
    'Check that the connection is still open
    ...
    conn.Close   'Close a database connection
End Sub

Protected Overrides Sub Finalize( )
    Dispose( )   'Optional call to Dispose
End Sub

'Client code
Dim x as TestClass = New TestClass( )
...
x.Dispose( )     'Call the object's dispose method
```

The IDisposable Interface

The .NET Framework provides an interface called **IDisposable** to improve accuracy and consistency among objects. This interface provides one method, **Dispose**, which does not take any arguments. By implementing this interface in all of your classes, you will consistently provide a **Dispose** method that can be easily called by client code.

Note You will learn how to implement interfaces in the Interfaces lesson of this module.

If you completely clean up your object in a **Dispose** method (whether you use **IDisposable** or not), garbage collection does not need to execute the object's **Finalize** method. You can disable the execution of the **Finalize** method by calling the **SuppressFinalize** method on the **GC** object, as shown in the following example. This method accepts a single argument that is a reference to the object that should not have its **Finalize** method called. In Visual Basic .NET, this is done with the **Me** keyword.

The following example shows a design pattern for using **SuppressFinalize**.

```
' Design pattern for the base class.
' By implementing IDisposable, you are announcing that
' instances of this type allocate scarce resources.
Public Class BaseResource
  Implements IDisposable
  ' Pointer to an external unmanaged resource.
  Private handle As IntPtr
  ' Other managed resource this class uses.
  Private Components As Component
  ' Track whether Dispose has been called.
  Private disposed As Boolean = False

  ' Constructor for the BaseResource Object.
  Public Sub New()
      ' Insert appropriate constructor code here.
  End Sub

  ' Implement Idisposable.
  ' Do not make this method Overridable.
  ' A derived class should not be able to override this.
  Overloads Public Sub Dispose()Implements _
  IDisposable.Dispose
      Dispose(true)
      ' Take yourself off of the finalization queue
      ' to prevent finalization code for this object
      ' from executing a second time.
      GC.SuppressFinalize(Me)
  End Sub

' Dispose(disposing As Boolean) executes in two distinct
' scenarios. If disposing is true, the method has been called
' directly or indirectly by a user's code. Managed and
' unmanaged resources can be disposed.
' If disposing equals false, the method has been called by the
' runtime from inside the finalizer and you should not
' reference other objects. Only unmanaged resources can be
' disposed.
Overloads Protected Overridable Sub Dispose(disposing As _
Boolean)
  ' Check to see if Dispose has already been called.
  If Not (Me.disposed) Then
      ' If disposing equals true, dispose all managed
      ' and unmanaged resources.
      If (disposing) Then
          ' Dispose managed resources.
          Components.Dispose()
      End If
      ' Release unmanaged resources. If disposing is false,
      ' only the following code is executed.
      CloseHandle(handle)
      handle = IntPtr.Zero
      ' Note that this is not thread safe.
      ' Another thread could start disposing the object
      ' after the managed resources are disposed,
```

Code continued on the following page

```
        ' but before the disposed flag is set to true.
    End If
    Me.disposed = true
  End Sub

    ' This Finalize method will run only if the
    ' Dispose method does not get called.
    ' By default, methods are NotOverridable.
    ' This prevents a derived class from overriding this method.
    Overrides Protected Sub Finalize()
        ' Do not re-create Dispose clean-up code here.
        ' Calling Dispose(false) is optimal in terms of
        ' readability and maintainability.
        Dispose(false)
    End Sub

    ' Allow your Dispose method to be called multiple times,
    ' but throw an exception if the object has been disposed.
    ' Whenever you do something with this class,
    ' check to see if it has been disposed.
    Public Sub DoSomething()
        If Me.disposed Then
            Throw New ObjectDisposedException()
        End If
    End Sub
End Class

' Design pattern for a derived class.
' Note that this derived class inherently implements the
' IDisposable interface because it is implemented in the base
' class.
Public Class MyResourceWrapper
    Inherits BaseResource

    ' A managed resource that you add in this derived class.
    Private addedManaged As ManagedResource
        ' A native unmanaged resource that you add in this
        ' derived class.
    Private addedNative As NativeResource
    ' Track whether Dispose has been called.
    Private disposed As Boolean = False

    ' Constructor for the MyResourceWrapper Object.
    Public Sub New()
        MyBase.New()
        ' Insert appropriate constructor code here for the
        ' added resources.
    End Sub

    Protected Overloads Overrides Sub Dispose(disposing As _
    Boolean)
        If Not (Me.disposed) Then
            Try
```

Code continued on the following page

```
                If disposing Then
                    ' Release the managed resources you added in
                    ' this derived class here.
                    addedManaged.Dispose()
                End If
                ' Release the native unmanaged resources you
                ' added in this derived class here.
                CloseHandle(addedNative)
                Me.disposed = true
            Finally
                ' Call Dispose on your base class.
                MyBase.Dispose(disposing)
            End Try
        End If
    End Sub
End Class
' This derived class does not have a Finalize method
' or a Dispose method without parameters because it
' inherits them from the base class.
```

Demonstration: Creating Classes

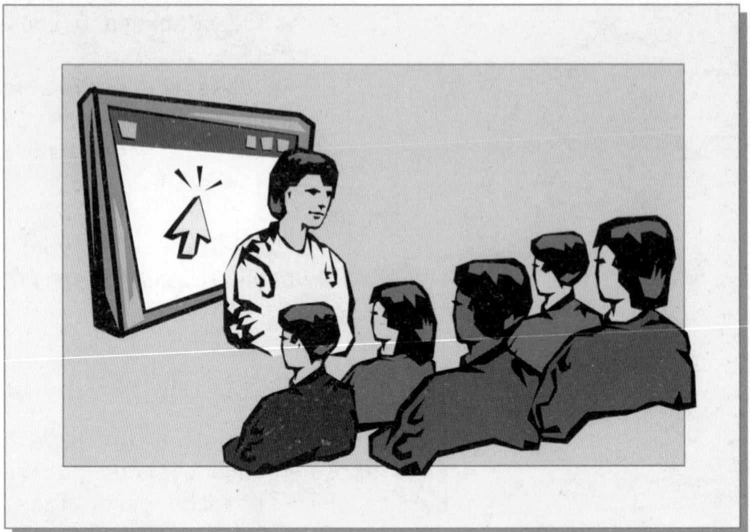

In this demonstration, you will learn how to define a simple class that uses multiple constructors. You will also learn how to instantiate and use the class from within client code.

Lab 5.1: Creating the Customer Class

Objectives

After completing this lab, you will be able to:

- Create classes.
- Instantiate, initialize, and use classes from calling code.

Prerequisites

Before working on this lab, you should be familiar with creating classes in Visual Basic .NET.

Scenario

In this lab, you will begin creating the Cargo system. You will create the **Customer** class and a test application to instantiate, initialize, and test the class.

Starter and Solution Files

There are starter and solution files associated with this lab. The starter files are in the *install folder*\Labs\Lab051\Starter folder, and the solution files are in the *install folder*\Labs\Lab051\Solution folder.

Estimated time to complete this lab: 45 minutes

Exercise 1
Defining the Customer Class

In this exercise, you will define the **Customer** class. The starter project contains several forms that you will use to test your **Customer** class.

► To open the starter project

1. Open Microsoft Visual Studio .NET.
2. On the **File** menu, point to **Open**, and then click **Project**. Set the folder location to *install folder*\Labs\Lab051\Starter, click **Lab051.sln**, and then click **Open**.

► To create the Customer class

1. On the **Project** menu, click **Add Class**.
2. In the **Add New Item** dialog box, change the name of the class file to **Customer.vb**, and click **Open**.

► To define the class properties

1. Add the following private variables to the class definition.

Variable name	Data type
intCustomerID	**Integer**
strFName	**String**
strLName	**String**
strEmail	**String**
strPassword	**String**
strAddress	**String**
strCompany	**String**

2. Add the following public properties, and use these to access the private variables created in the previous step.

Property name	Read/Write access	Data type
CustomerID	Read-only	**Integer**
FirstName	Read-write	**String**
LastName	Read-write	**String**
Email	Read-write	**String**
Password	Read-write	**String**
Address	Read-write	**String**
Company	Read-write	**String**

3. Save the project.

▶ To define the class methods

1. Add the following methods to the class definition.

Method name	Type	Parameters
LogOn	Public Sub	`ByVal strEmail As String` `ByVal strPassword As String`

AddCustomer	Public Function	`ByVal strEmail As String`
		`ByVal strPassword As String`
		`ByVal strFName As String`
		`ByVal strLName As String`
		`ByVal strCompany As String`
		`ByVal strAddress As String`
		`<RETURN VALUE> As Integer`

New	Public Sub	<None>
New	Public Sub	`ByVal intID As Integer`

2. On the **File** menu, point to **Open**, and then click **File**. In the **Files of type** list, click **Text Files**. Click **Code.txt**, and then click **Open**.
3. Locate the LogOn code in Code.txt. Copy the procedure code to the **LogOn** method of the **Customer** class.
4. Locate the AddCustomer code in Code.txt. Copy the procedure code to the **AddCustomer** method of the **Customer** class.

▶ To complete the class constructors

1. In the **Customer** class, locate the default constructor definition (the `Sub New` without parameters), and initialize the *intCustomerID* variable to **-1**.
2. Locate the alternative constructor code in Code.txt. Copy the procedure code to the parameterized constructor of the **Customer** class.
3. Save the project.

Exercise 2
Testing the LogOn Procedure

In this exercise, you will test the **LogOn** procedure from a simple form.

► **To create the Logon button code**

1. Open frmLogOn in the Code Editor and locate the **btnLogOn_Click** event procedure.
2. Declare and instantiate a **Customer** variable called *cusCustomer*.
3. Call the **LogOn** method of the **cusCustomer** object, passing in the text properties of txtEmail and txtPassword as parameters.
4. Display the properties of the **cusCustomer** object in the appropriate text boxes. Use the information in the following table:

Text box	Property of cusCustomer
txtID	**CStr(CustomerID)**
txtFName	**FirstName**
txtLName	**LastName**
txtAddress	**Address**
txtCompany	**Company**

5. Set cusCustomer to **Nothing**.
6. Save the project.

► To test the LogOn code

1. Set a breakpoint on the first line of the **btnLogOn_Click** procedure.
2. On the **Debug** menu, click **Start**. On the menu form, click **Test 'Logon'** to display the test form, and then type the following values in the appropriate text boxes.

Text box	Value
E-mail	**karen@wingtiptoys.msn.com**
Password	**password**

3. Click the **Logon** button, and step through the procedure.
4. Confirm that your code retrieves the customer information and displays it correctly in the text boxes. Close the logon form.
5. Click **Test 'Logon'** and enter the following incorrect values in the appropriate text boxes.

Textbox	Value
E-mail	**john@tailspintoys.msn.com**
Password	**john**

6. Click the **Logon** button, and step through the procedure.
7. Confirm that your code causes an exception to be generated and handled by the form.
8. Close the logon form and then quit the application. Remove the breakpoint on **btnLogOn_Click**.

Exercise 3
Testing Customer Retrieval

In this exercise, you will test the parameterized constructor that retrieves the customer details from a simple form. A sales agent who needs full access to the customer's information could use this type of form.

► **To create the Retrieve button code**

1. Open frmRetrieve in the Code Editor, and locate the **btnRetrieve_Click** event procedure.
2. Declare and instantiate a **Customer** variable called *cusCustomer*. Use the parameterized constructor to pass in the existing customer ID from the txtID text box. (Use the **CInt** function to convert it to an integer value.)
3. Display the properties of the **cusCustomer** object in the appropriate text boxes. Use the information in the following table:

Textbox	Property of cusCustomer
txtEmail	**Email**
txtPassword	**Password**
txtFName	**FirstName**
txtLName	**LastName**
txtAddress	**Address**
txtCompany	**Company**

4. Save the project.

► **To test the Retrieve code**

1. Set a breakpoint on the first line of the **btnRetrieve_Click** procedure.
2. On the **Debug** menu, click **Start**. On the menu form, click **Test 'Get Details'** to display the test form, and then type the value **1119** in the **CustomerID** text box.
3. Click the **Retrieve** button, and step through the procedure.
4. Confirm that your code retrieves the customer information and displays it correctly in the text boxes.
5. Click the **Clear Data** button to reset the information, and then type the value **1100** in the **CustomerID** text box.
6. Click the **Retrieve** button, and step through the procedure.
7. Confirm that your code causes an exception to be generated and handled by the form.
8. Click the **Close** button and then quit the application. Remove the breakpoint on **btnRetrieve_Click**.

Exercise 4
Testing the AddCustomer Procedure

In this exercise, you will test the **AddCustomer** procedure from a simple form.

▶ To create the Add Customer button code

1. Open frmNew in the Code Editor, and locate the **btnNew_Click** event procedure.
2. Declare and instantiate a **Customer** variable called *cusCustomer*.
3. Call the **AddCustomer** function of the **cusCustomer** object, passing in the appropriate values and displaying the return value in a message box. Use the **CStr** function to convert the integer value to a string. Use the information in the following table:

Parameter name	Value
strEmail	**txtEmail.Text**
strPassword	**txtPassword.Text**
strFName	**txtFName.Text**
strLName	**txtLName.Text**
strCompany	**txtCompany.Text**
strAddress	**txtAddress.Text**

4. Save the project.

▶ To test the Add Customer code

1. Set a breakpoint on the first line of the **btnNew_Click** procedure.
2. On the **Debug** menu, click **Start**. On the menu form, click **Test 'New Customer'** to display the test form.
3. Enter values in all text boxes.
4. Click the **New Customer** button, and step through the procedure.
5. Confirm that your code passes the information to the procedure correctly, and that a new ID is returned.
6. Click the **Close** button and quit the application. Remove the breakpoint on **btnNew_Click**.
7. Close Visual Studio .NET.

◆ Inheritance

- What Is Inheritance?
- Overriding and Overloading
- Inheritance Example
- Shadowing
- Using the MyBase Keyword
- Using the MyClass Keyword

In this lesson, you will learn how to implement class inheritance. After completing this lesson, you will be able to:

- Inherit from an existing class.
- Override and overload some base class methods in a derived class.
- Use the **MyBase** keyword to access the base class from a derived class.
- Use the **MyClass** keyword to ensure that you call the correct class.

What Is Inheritance?

- **Derived class inherits from a base class**
- **Properties, methods, data members, events, and event handlers can be inherited (dependent on scope)**
- **Keywords**
  - **Inherits** – inherits from a base class
  - **NotInheritable** – cannot be inherited from
  - **MustInherit** – instances of the class cannot be created; must be inherited from as a base class
  - **Protected** – member scope that allows use only by deriving classes

In Visual Basic .NET, you can use inheritance to derive a class from an existing base class. The derived class can inherit all the base class properties, methods, data members, events, and event handlers, making it easy to reuse the base class code throughout an application.

The Inherits Keyword

The following example shows how to use the **Inherits** keyword to define a derived class that will inherit from an existing base class:

```
Public Class DerivedClass
    Inherits BaseClass
...
End Class
```

The NotInheritable Keyword

The following example shows how to use the **NotInheritable** keyword to define a class that cannot be used as a base class for inheritance. A compiler error is generated if another class attempts to inherit from this class.

```
Public NotInheritable Class TestClass
...
End Class
Public Class DerivedClass
    Inherits TestClass  'Generates a compiler error
...
End Class
```

The MustInherit Keyword

You use the **MustInherit** keyword to define classes that are not intended to be used directly as instantiated objects. The resulting class must be inherited as a base class for use in an instantiated derived class object. If the client code attempts to instantiate an object based on this type of class, a compiler error is generated, as shown in the following example:

```
Public MustInherit Class BaseClass
...
End Class
...
'Client code
Dim x As New BaseClass( ) 'Generates a compiler error
```

The Protected Keyword

You use **Protected** access to limit the scope of a property, method, data member, event, or event handler to the defining class and any derived class based on that base class. Following is an example:

```
Public Class BaseClass
    Public intCounter As Integer   'Accessible anywhere

   'Accessible only in this class or a derived class
    Protected strName As String
...
End Class
```

Note The derived class is also known as a *subclass*, and the base class is known as a *superclass* in Unified Modeling Language (UML) terminology.

Overriding and Overloading

- **Derived class can override an inherited property or method**
  - **Overridable** – can be overridden
  - **MustOverride** – must be overridden in derived class
  - **Overrides** – replaces method from inherited class
  - **NotOverridable** – cannot be overridden (default)
- **Use Overload keyword to overload inherited property or method**

When a derived class inherits from a base class, it inherits all the functions, subroutines, and properties of the base class, including any implementation in the methods. Occasionally you may want to create implementation code specific to your derived class rather than using the inherited methods. This is known as *overriding*. You can also overload methods defined in the base class with the **Overloads** keyword.

Overriding

Use the following keywords to create your own implementation code within a derived class:

- **Overridable**

  To create your own special implementation of the derived class, specify the **Overridable** keyword in a base class member definition for a function, subroutine, or property, as shown in the following example:

  ```
  Public Overridable Sub OverrideMethod( )
      MsgBox("Base Class OverrideMethod")
  End Sub
  ```

- **MustOverride**

  To create a base class member that must be overridden in all derived classes, define the member with the **MustOverride** keyword. Only the member prototype can be created in the base class, with no implementation code. You can only use this keyword in a base class that is marked as **MustInherit**. The following example shows how to define a method that must be overridden:

  ```
  Public MustOverride Sub PerformAction( )
  ```

  MustOverride methods are useful in base classes because they allow you to define baseline functionality without locking in implementation details that can make them difficult to extend.

- **Overrides**

  To specify that a derived class method overrides the implementation of the base class method, use the **Overrides** keyword. If the base class method that is being overridden is not marked as **Overridable**, a compile-time error will occur. The method signature must exactly match the method being overridden, except for the parameter names. The following example shows how to declare a derived class method that overrides the base class implementation:

```
Public Overrides Sub OverrideMethod( )
    MsgBox("Derived Class OverrideMethod")
End Sub
```

Note You can override methods by selecting (Overrides) in the Class Name drop-down list in the IDE, and then selecting the method you want to override.

- **NotOverridable**

  Base class members without the **Overridable** keyword are, by default, not overridable. However, if a base class member is marked as overridable, then the member will be overridable in any derived classes based on the immediate deriving class. To prevent this behavior, mark the overridden method in the derived class as **NotOverridable**. This will stop subsequent inheritance from overriding the method.

  The following example shows how to declare a derived class method that overrides the base class implementation but does not allow any further overriding:

```
Public NotOverridable Overrides Sub OverrideMethod( )
    MsgBox("Derived Class OverrideMethod")
End Sub
```

Overloading

You can create a method in a derived class that overloads a method defined in a base class by using the **Overloads** keyword. Just as for overloading methods within the same class, the method signatures must include different parameters or parameter types. The following example shows how to overload a method from a base class:

```
Public Overloads Sub Other(ByVal i As Integer)
    MsgBox("Overloaded CannotOverride")
End Sub
```

Note that the base class method does not need to be marked as **Overridable** to be overloaded.

Inheritance Example

```
Public Class BaseClass
    Public Overridable Sub OverrideMethod( )
        MsgBox("Base OverrideMethod")
    End Sub
    Public Sub Other( )
        MsgBox("Base Other method - not overridable")
    End Sub
End Class
```

```
Public Class DerivedClass
    Inherits BaseClass
    Public Overrides Sub OverrideMethod( )
        MsgBox("Derived OverrideMethod")
    End Sub
End Class
```

```
Dim x As DerivedClass = New DerivedClass( )
x.Other( )           'Displays "Base Other method - not overridable"
x.OverrideMethod( )  'Displays "Derived OverrideMethod"
```

There are three parts to this inheritance example:

- Code for the base class
- Code for the derived class
- Code for the calling client

Base Class Code

The base class in the following example is specified as **MustInherit**. This means that the class must be inherited from because it cannot be instantiated directly.

```
Public MustInherit Class BaseClass
    Public MustOverride Sub PerformAction( )

    Public Overridable Sub OverrideMethod( )
        MsgBox("Base OverrideMethod")
    End Sub

    Public Sub Other( )
        MsgBox("Base Other method - not overridable")
    End Sub
End Class
```

The following table explains the methods used in the preceding code.

Method	Declared as	Description
PerformAction	**MustOverride**	Any implementation for this method must be created in the deriving class.
OverrideMethod	**Overridable**	Any implementation for this method can be overridden as a derived class.
Other	**NotOverridable** (by default)	Any implementation for this method cannot be overridden in a derived class. **NotOverridable** is the default for any method.

Derived Class Code

The derived class in the following example inherits from the base class. This means that the class inherits all of the methods and properties of the base class.

```
Public Class DerivedClass
    Inherits BaseClass

    Public NotOverridable Overrides Sub PerformAction( )
        MsgBox("Derived PerformAction")
    End Sub

    Public Overrides Sub OverrideMethod( )
        MsgBox("Derived OverrideMethod")
    End Sub

    Public Overloads Sub Other(ByVal i As Integer)
        MsgBox("Overloaded Other")
    End Sub
End Class
```

Because the **PerformAction** method was marked as **MustOverride** in the base class, it must be overridden in this derived class. This derived class also marks the method as **NotOverridable** so that no other class can override this method if **DerivedClass** is used as a base class for inheritance.

The method **OverrideMethod** is overridden in this derived class. Any calls to **OverrideMethod** will result in the derived class implementation being executed rather than the base class implementation.

The **Other** method cannot be overridden, but can be overloaded by the derived class using the **Overloads** keyword.

Calling Code

The preceding example defines and instantiates a **DerivedClass** variable. The following example shows how to call all the individual methods for the derived class. The results are shown as comments in the code.

```
Dim x As DerivedClass = New DerivedClass( )
x.Other( )      'Displays "Base Other method - not overridable"
x.Other(20)           'Displays "Overloaded Other"
x.OverrideMethod( )  'Displays "Derived OverrideMethod"
x.PerformAction( )   'Displays "Derived PerformAction"
```

Shadowing

- **Hides base class members, even if overloaded**

```
Class aBase
    Public Sub M1( )    'Non-overridable by default
    ...
    End Sub
End Class
Class aShadowed
    Inherits aBase
    Public Shadows Sub M1(ByVal i As Integer)
        'Clients can only see this method
    ...
    End Sub
End Class
```

```
Dim x As New aShadowed( )
x.M1( )        'Generates an error
x.M1(20)       'No error
```

When a derived class inherits from a base class, it can either override a method on the base class or shadow it. Overriding replaces the existing method based on the method name and signature. Shadowing effectively hides the method in the base class, based solely on the method name. This means shadowing a method also hides any overloaded methods within the base class. You can shadow a method regardless of whether the base method is specified as overridable.

To learn how shadowing works, consider an example of a derived class that shadows a method from the base class. The method in the base class has not been specified as overridable.

The following example shows a base class that defines a single method called **M1**. The derived class declares an **M1** method that automatically shadows the base class method and accepts a single argument. The client code can only access the shadowed method that accepts the argument, and an error will be generated if it attempts to access the base class method.

```
Class aBase
    Public Sub M1( ) 'Non-overridable by default
    ...
    End Sub
End Class

Class aShadowed
    Inherits aBase
    Public Shadows Sub M1(ByVal i As Integer)
        'Clients can only see this method
    ...
    End Sub
End Class

'Client Code
Dim x As New aShadowed( )
x.M1( )  'Generates an error because method is hidden
x.M1(20) 'No error
```

Using the MyBase Keyword

- **Refers to the immediate base class**
- **Can only access public, protected, or friend members of base class**
- **Is not a real object (cannot be stored in a variable)**

```
Public Class DerivedClass
    Inherits BaseClass

    Public Overrides Sub OverrideMethod( )
        MsgBox("Derived OverrideMethod")
        MyBase.OverrideMethod( )
    End Sub
End Class
```

You can use the **MyBase** keyword to access the immediate base class from which a derived class is inheriting. When using **MyBase**, you should be aware of some limitations:

- It refers only to the immediate base class in the hierarchy. You cannot use **MyBase** to gain access to classes higher in the hierarchy.
- It allows access to all of the public, protected, or friend members of the base class.
- It is not a real object, so you cannot assign **MyBase** to a variable.

If a derived class is overriding a method from a base class but you still want to execute the code in the overridden method, you can use **MyBase**. This is a common practice for constructors and destructors. The following example shows how to use the **MyBase** keyword to execute a method as implemented in the base class:

```
Public Class DerivedClass
    Inherits BaseClass
    Public Sub New()
        MyBase.New() 'Call the constructor of the base class
        intValue = 1
    End Sub
    Public Overrides Sub OverrideMethod()
        MsgBox("Derived OverrideMethod")
        MyBase.OverrideMethod() 'Call the original method
    End Sub
End Class
```

Using the MyClass Keyword

- Ensures that base class gets called, not derived class

```
Public Class BaseClass
    Public Overridable Sub OverrideMethod( )
        MsgBox("Base OverrideMethod")
    End Sub
    Public Sub Other( )
        MyClass.OverrideMethod( )'Will call above method
        OverrideMethod( )        'Will call derived method
    End Sub
End Class
```

```
Dim x As DerivedClass = New DerivedClass( )
x.Other( )
```

You can use the **MyClass** keyword to ensure that a base class implementation of an overridable method is called, rather than that of a derived class. **MyClass** always refers to the class within which the current code is running. When using **MyClass**, you should be aware of the following limitations:

- It allows access to all of the public, protected, or friend members of the deriving class.
- It is not a real object, so you cannot assign **MyClass** to a variable.

Example

The following example shows how to call a base class method from a derived class by using the **MyClass** keyword:

```
Public Class BaseClass
    Public Overridable Sub OverrideMethod( )
        MsgBox("Base OverrideMethod")
    End Sub

    Public Sub Other( )
        MyClass.OverrideMethod( )  'Will call above method
    End Sub
End Class

Public Class DerivedClass
    Inherits BaseClass
    Public Overrides Sub OverrideMethod( )
        MsgBox("Derived OverrideMethod")
    End Sub
End Class

Dim x As DerivedClass = New DerivedClass( )
x.Other( )
```

Output

The output from the execution of the preceding code is as follows:

```
Base OverrideMethod
```

Flow of Execution

The code in the example is executed as follows:

1. The **Other** method is called on the **DerivedClass** object, but because there is no implemented code in the derived class, the base class code is executed.
2. When the **MyClass.OverrideMethod** call is executed, the **OverrideMethod** subroutine is implemented in the base class.
3. Execution returns to the client code.

Important The **Me** keyword in previous versions of Visual Basic is not the same as the **MyClass** keyword. The **Me** keyword has the same effect as if no keyword were used. In the example in this topic, the derived class implementation would be executed even if **Me** were used within the base class.

Demonstration: Inheritance

In this demonstration, you will see how to define a base class with a mixture of overridable and non-overridable methods. You will see how to derive a class that inherits from the base class, and how to use the **MyBase** keyword.

◆ Interfaces

- Defining Interfaces
- Achieving Polymorphism

In this lesson, you will learn how to use interfaces to achieve polymorphism. After completing this lesson, you will be able to:

- Define an interface by using the **Interface** keyword.
- Add member signatures that define the properties, methods, and events that your interface supports.
- Implement an interface by using the **Implements** keyword.

Defining Interfaces

- **Interfaces define public procedure, property, and event signatures**
- **Use the Interface keyword to define an interface module**
- **Overload members as for classes**

```
Interface IMyInterface
    Function Method1(ByRef s As String) As Boolean
    Sub Method2( )
    Sub Method2(ByVal i As Integer)
End Interface
```

- **Use the Inherits keyword in an interface to inherit from other interfaces**

An interface defines signatures for procedures, properties, and events but contains no implementation code. These signatures define the names of the members, the parameter details, and the return values. Interfaces form a binding contract between clients and a server. This contract enables a client application to ensure that a class will always support particular member signatures or functionality, and this aids in the versioning of components.

In Visual Basic 6.0, interfaces are created automatically whenever a public class is compiled as part of a COM component. This functionality works fine in most situations; however, you need to create a class in order to define an interface, which is not always necessary from a developer's perspective.

Visual Basic .NET introduces the **Interface** keyword, which allows you to explicitly create an interface without creating a class. Interfaces can be defined in the **Declarations** section of any module. This new approach creates a visible distinction between a class and an interface, and this makes the concept clearer for the developer.

You can use overloading when you define interfaces—just as you use it to define classes—to create multiple versions of a member signature with different parameters.

Example

The following example shows how to define an interface that includes three method signatures, two of which are overloaded:

```
Interface IMyInterface
    Function Method1(ByRef s As String) As Boolean
    Sub Method2( )
    Sub Method2(ByVal i As Integer)
End Interface
```

An interface can also inherit another interface if you use the **Inherits** keyword before any member signatures are defined. If an interface is inherited from the above example, it will contain all of the base interface signatures, in addition to those defined in the new interface definition.

Achieving Polymorphism

- **Polymorphism**
  - Many classes provide the same property or method
  - A caller does not need to know the type of class the object is based on
- **Two approaches**
  - Interfaces
    Class implements members of interface
    Same approach as in Visual Basic 6.0
  - Inheritance
    Derived class overrides members of base class

Polymorphism is achieved when multiple classes provide the same properties or methods and the calling code does not need to know what type of class the object is based on. This creates a form of reuse because you can write generic client code to handle multiple types of classes without knowing about the methods of each individual class. You can use two different approaches to achieve polymorphism in Visual Basic .NET: interfaces and inheritance.

Interfaces

In Visual Basic 6.0, you can achieve polymorphism by creating an abstract class—with the sole purpose of defining an interface—and then implementing that interface in other classes by using the **Implements** keyword. This approach allows multiple classes to share the same interface and allows classes to have multiple interfaces.

In Visual Basic .NET, you do not need abstract classes to achieve polymorphism. You can create interfaces explicitly by using a combination of the **Interface** and **Implements** keywords.

Example

The following example shows how to implement polymorphism in Visual Basic .NET. As you examine this code, note the following:

- The **IPerson** interface defines two member signatures: **LastName** and **Display**.
- The **Employee** class implements the **IPerson** interface and both of its members.
- By using the **Implements** keyword for each individual method, you can specify your own name for the method and it will still be executed if a client application requests the original name of the interface.

```
Interface IPerson            'IPerson interface definition
    Property LastName( ) As String
    Sub Display( )
End Interface

Class Employee               'Employee class definition
    Implements IPerson       'Implements IPerson interface
    Private strName As String
    Private strCompany As String

    'This method is public but also implements IPerson.Display
    Public Sub Display( ) Implements IPerson.Display
        MsgBox(LastName & " " & Company,, "Employee")
    End Sub

    'This property is private but implements IPerson.LastName
    Private Property LastName( ) As String _
      Implements IPerson.LastName
        Get
            Return strName
        End Get
        Set (ByVal Value As String)
        ...
        End Set
    End Property

    Public Property Company( ) As String
    ...
    End Property
End Class
```

Client Code Example

The following code shows how the **Employee** class and **IPerson** interface could be used in a client application or within the same assembly as the class and interface definitions.

- An **Employee** object is instantiated and details specific to the employee, such as the **Company** property, are assigned.
- An **IPerson** interface variable is then assigned to the **Employee** object to access methods that can only be accessed through the **IPerson** interface, such as the **LastName** property.
- Both calls to the **Display** methods actually call the same code within the **Employee** class, as shown in the previous example.

```
Dim perPerson As IPerson, empEmployee As New Employee( )
empEmployee.Company = "Microsoft"
perPerson = empEmployee
perPerson.LastName = "Jones"
perPerson.Display( ) 'Call the display method on the interface
empEmployee.Display( ) 'Display method is defined as public
```

Inheritance

Another way to achieve polymorphism with Visual Basic .NET is to use class inheritance. A base class can be created that contains member signatures and that optionally contains implementation code that can be inherited in a derived class. The derived class must then override the individual methods with its own implementation code, achieving unique functionality while retaining a common method signature.

Note For more information about polymorphism, search for "Polymorphism" in the Visual Studio .NET documentation.

Demonstration: Interfaces and Polymorphism

In this demonstration, you will learn how to create an interface and implement it to achieve polymorphism in two separate classes.

◆ Working with Classes

- Using Shared Data Members
- Using Shared Procedure Members
- Event Handling
- What Are Delegates?
- Using Delegates
- Comparing Classes to Structures

In this lesson, you will learn how to work with classes. After completing this lesson, you will be able to:

- Use shared data members to share data across class instances.
- Use shared procedure members.
- Define and handle class events.
- Use delegates in event handling.
- Describe how structures differ from classes.

Using Shared Data Members

- **Allow multiple class instances to refer to a single class-level variable instance**

```
Class SavingsAccount
    Public Shared InterestRate As Double
    Public Name As String, Balance As Double
    Sub New(ByVal strName As String, ByVal dblAmount As Double)
        Name = strName
        Balance = dblAmount
    End Sub
    Public Function CalculateInterest( ) As Double
        Return Balance * InterestRate
    End Function
End Class
```

```
SavingsAccount.InterestRate = 0.003
Dim acct1 As New SavingsAccount("Joe Howard", 10000)
MsgBox(acct1.CalculateInterest, , "Interest for " & acct1.Name)
```

In Visual Basic 6.0, you can share data among objects by using a module file and a global variable. This approach works, but there is no direct link between the objects and the data in the module file, and the data is available for anyone to access.

In Visual Basic .NET, you can use shared data members to allow multiple instances of a class to refer to a single instance of a class-level variable. You can use shared members for counters or for any common data that is required by all instances of a class.

An advantage of shared data members is that they are directly linked to the class and can be declared as public or private. If you declare data members as public, they are accessible to any code that can access the class. If you declare the data members as private, provide public shared properties to access the private shared property.

The following example shows how you can use a shared data member to maintain interest rates for a savings account. The **InterestRate** data member of the **SavingsAccount** class can be set globally regardless of how many instances of the class are in use. This value is then used to calculate the interest on the current balance.

```
Class SavingsAccount
    Public Shared InterestRate As Double

    Public Name As String, Balance As Double

    Sub New(ByVal strName As String, _
            ByVal dblAmount As Double)
        Name = strName
        Balance = dblAmount
    End Sub

    Public Function CalculateInterest( ) As Double
        Return Balance * InterestRate
    End Function
End Class
```

The following code shows how a client application can use the **SavingsAccount** class in the previous example. As you examine this code, note the following:

- The **InterestRate** can be set before and after any instances of the **SavingsAccount** object are created.
- Any changes to the **InterestRate** will be seen by all instances of the **SavingsAccount** class.

```
Sub Test( )
    SavingsAccount.InterestRate = 0.003

    Dim acct1 As New SavingsAccount("Joe Howard", 10000)
    Dim acct2 As New SavingsAccount("Arlene Huff", 5000)

    MsgBox(acct1.CalculateInterest, , "Interest for " & _
          acct1.Name)
    MsgBox(acct2.CalculateInterest, , "Interest for " & _
          acct2.Name)
End Sub
```

The following example shows how to implement a public shared property for a private shared data member:

```
Class SavingsAccount
    Private Shared InterestRate As Double

    Shared Property Rate( )
        Get
            Return InterestRate
        End Get
        Set(ByVal Value)
            InterestRate = Value
        End Set
    End Property
End Class
```

The following code shows how a client application can use the shared property in the previous example:

```
SavingsAccount.Rate = 0.003
```

Using Shared Procedure Members

- Share procedures without declaring a class instance
- Similar functionality to Visual Basic 6.0 "global" classes
- Can only access shared data

```
'TestClass code
Public Shared Function GetComputerName( ) As String
    ...
End Function
```

```
'Client code
MsgBox(TestClass.GetComputerName( ))
```

You can use shared procedure members to design functions that can be called without creating an instance of the class. Shared procedures are particularly useful for creating library routines that other applications can easily access. This concept is similar to the **GlobalMultiUse** and **GlobalSingleUse** classes used in Visual Basic 6.0.

As described in the previous topic, shared members can only access data that is marked as **Shared**. For example, a shared method cannot access a module level variable that is marked as **Dim**, **Private**, or **Public**.

Example

The following example shows how a commonly used function, such as **GetComputerName**, can be created as a shared procedure member so that a client application can easily use it. The client only needs to reference the method prefixed by the class name because no instance of the class is required.

```
'TestClass code
Public Shared Function GetComputerName( ) As String
...
End Function

'Client code
MsgBox(TestClass.GetComputerName( ))
```

Event Handling

- **Defining and raising events: same as Visual Basic 6.0**
- **WithEvents keyword: handles events as in Visual Basic 6.0**
  - In Visual Basic .NET, works with **Handles** keyword to specify method used to handle event
- **AddHandler keyword: allows dynamic connection to events**

```
Dim x As New TestClass( ), y As New TestClass( )
AddHandler x.anEvent, AddressOf HandleEvent
AddHandler y.anEvent, AddressOf HandleEvent
...

Sub HandleEvent(ByVal i As Integer)
    ...
End Sub
```

- **RemoveHandler keyword: disconnects from event source**

As a Visual Basic developer, you are familiar with creating events. However, Visual Basic .NET provides powerful new event handling features with the addition of the **Handles**, **AddHandler** and **RemoveHandler** keywords.

Defining and Raising Events

In Visual Basic .NET, you can define and raise events in the same way you do in Visual Basic 6.0, by using the **Event** and **RaiseEvent** keywords.

Example

The following example shows how to define and raise an event:

```
'TestClass code
Public Event anEvent(ByVal i As Integer)

Public Sub DoAction( )
    RaiseEvent anEvent(10)
End Sub
```

The WithEvents Keyword

You can use the **WithEvents** keyword in the same way that you used it in Visual Basic 6.0. However, in Visual Basic .NET you also use the **Handles** keyword to specify which method will be used to handle an event. You can link an event to any handler, whether it is the default handler or your own method. This approach allows you to link multiple events with a single method handler, as long as the parameters match those of the events.

Example

The following example shows how you can use **WithEvents** in conjunction with the new **Handles** keyword to link an event with a handler.

```
'Client code
Dim WithEvents x As TestClass
Dim WithEvents y As TestClass

Private Sub Button1_Click(...) Handles Button1.Click
    x = New TestClass( )
    y = New TestClass( )
    x.DoAction( )
    y.DoAction( )
End Sub

Private Sub HandleEvent(ByVal x As Integer) _
  Handles x.anEvent, y.anEvent
...
End Sub
```

The AddHandler Keyword

The new **AddHandler** keyword allows you to dynamically connect to the events of an object and handle them in any chosen method. This has some advantages over the **WithEvents** keyword: the variable does not need to be declared at the module level, and you can point multiple events from the same object to a single handler method. You can also point events from multiple objects to the same handler method by using the **AddHandler** keyword.

Syntax

The syntax for **AddHandler** is shown below.

```
AddHandler object.EventName, AddressOf methodName
```

Example

The following example shows a single method handler called **HandleEvent** being used for two instances of **TestClass**:

```
Dim x As New TestClass( ), y As New TestClass( )

AddHandler x.anEvent, AddressOf HandleEvent
AddHandler y.anEvent, AddressOf HandleEvent
```

The RemoveHandler Keyword

The new **RemoveHandler** keyword disconnects your event handler from the object's events.

Syntax

The syntax for **RemoveHandler** is shown below.

```
RemoveHandler object.EventName, AddressOf methodName
```

Note **AddressOf** creates a reference to a procedure that can be passed to appropriate methods. It was introduced in previous versions of Visual Basic. For more information about **AddressOf**, search for "AddressOf" in the Visual Studio .NET documentation.

Demonstration: Handling Events

In this demonstration, you will learn how to define and raise events in a class and how to handle them in client code.

What Are Delegates?

- **Objects that call the methods of other objects**
- **Similar to function pointers in Visual C++**
- **Reference type based on the System.Delegate class**
- **Type-safe, secure, managed objects**
- **Example:**
  - Useful as an intermediary between a calling procedure and the procedure being called

The common language runtime supports objects called *delegates* that can call the methods of other objects dynamically. Delegates are sometimes described as *type-safe function pointers* because they are similar to the function pointers used in other programming languages. Unlike function pointers, Visual Basic .NET delegates are a reference type based on the class **System.Delegate** and can reference both shared methods (methods that can be called without a specific instance of a class) and instance methods. Delegates provide the same flexibility as function pointers in Microsoft Visual C++® without the risk of corrupted memory because they are type-safe, secure, managed objects.

Delegates are useful when you need an intermediary between a calling procedure and the procedure being called. For example, you might want an object that raises events to be able to call different event handlers under different circumstances. Unfortunately, the object raising events cannot know ahead of time which event handler is handling a specific event. Visual Basic .NET allows you to dynamically associate event handlers with events by creating a delegate for you when you use the **AddHandler** statement. At run time, the delegate forwards calls to the appropriate event handler.

Using Delegates

- **Delegate keyword declares a delegate and defines parameter and return types**

```
Delegate Function CompareFunc( _
        ByVal x As Integer, ByVal y As Integer) As Boolean
```

- **Methods must have the same function parameter and return types**
- **Use Invoke method of delegate to call methods**

You use the **Delegate** keyword to declare a delegate function signature that defines the parameter and return types. Only methods that have the same function parameter and return types can be used with a particular delegate object.

Example

To learn how delegates work, consider an example that shows how to declare a delegate function signature, create methods to accept the parameter types you have defined, and call the functions by using the delegate object. The final part of this example shows how to use the delegate to perform a bubble sort.

Declaring a Delegate Function Signature

The following code shows how to create a delegate function called **CompareFunc**, which takes two **Integer** parameters and returns a **Boolean** value.

```
Delegate Function CompareFunc( _
        ByVal x As Integer, ByVal y As Integer) As Boolean
```

Creating Methods

After you create a delegate, you can then create methods that accept the same parameter types, as follows:

```
Function CompareAscending( _
        ByVal x As Integer, ByVal y As Integer) As Boolean
    Return (y > x)
End Function
Function CompareDescending( _
        ByVal x As Integer, ByVal y As Integer) As Boolean
    Return (x > y)
End Function
```

Calling Methods

After you create the necessary functions, you can write a procedure to call these two functions by using a delegate object as follows:

```
Sub SimpleTest( )
    Dim delDelegate As CompareFunc

    delDelegate = New CompareFunc(AddressOf CompareAscending)
    MsgBox(delDelegate.Invoke(1, 2))

    delDelegate = New CompareFunc(AddressOf CompareDescending)
    MsgBox(delDelegate.Invoke(1, 2))
End Sub
```

Performing a Bubble Sort by Using Delegates

Now that you have created a delegate and defined its methods, you can start using the delegate. A bubble sort routine is a good example of how you might use delegates. This type of sort routine starts at the top of a list and compares each item, moving it up the list if appropriate (bubbling it up), until the complete list is sorted. The following method takes a *sortType* parameter that will specify whether the sort should be ascending or descending. It also takes an array of **Integer** values to be sorted. The appropriate delegate object is created, depending on the order of the sort.

```
Sub BubbleSort(ByVal sortType As Integer, _
                      ByVal intArray( ) As Integer)
   Dim I, J, Value, Temp As Integer
   Dim delDelegate As CompareFunc

   If sortType = 1 Then    'Create the appropriate delegate
     delDelegate = New CompareFunc(AddressOf CompareAscending)
   Else
     delDelegate = New CompareFunc(AddressOf _
                                  CompareDescending)
   End If

   For I = 0 To Ubound(intArray)
       Value = intArray(I)
       For J = I + 1 To Ubound(intArray)
           If delDelegate.Invoke(intArray(J), Value) Then
               intArray(I) = intArray(J)
               intArray(J) = Value
               Value = intArray(I)
           End If
       Next J
   Next I
End Sub
```

The following code shows how to call the bubble sort procedure:

```
Sub TestSort( )
    Dim a( ) As Integer = {4, 2, 5, 1, 3}

    BubbleSort(1, a)    'Sort using 1 as ascending order
    MsgBox(a(0) & a(1) & a(2) & a(3) & a(4), , "Ascending")

    BubbleSort(2, a)    'Sort using 2 as descending order
    MsgBox(a(0) & a(1) & a(2) & a(3) & a(4), , "Descending")
End Sub
```

Comparing Classes to Structures

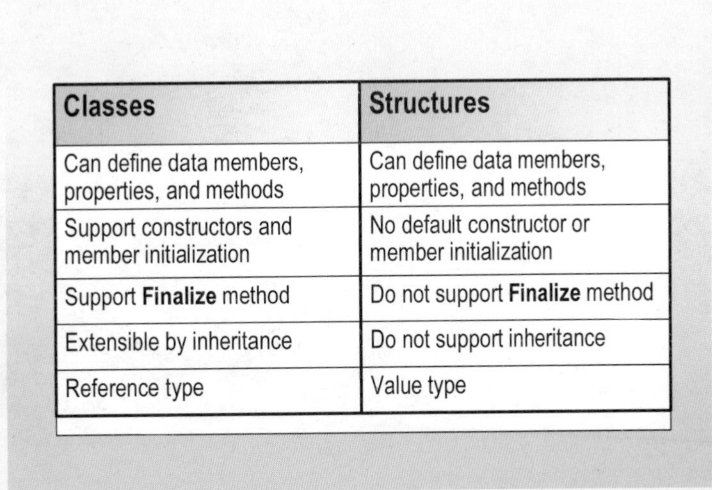

Classes	Structures
Can define data members, properties, and methods	Can define data members, properties, and methods
Support constructors and member initialization	No default constructor or member initialization
Support **Finalize** method	Do not support **Finalize** method
Extensible by inheritance	Do not support inheritance
Reference type	Value type

Classes and structures are similar in several ways: both can define data members, properties, and methods. However, classes provide some advanced features that developers can use.

	Classes	Structures
Initialization	Supports constructors and member initialization.	No default constructor and no initialization of members.
Finalize method	Support **Finalize** method.	Do not support **Finalize** method. You must manually release resources.
Inheritance	Extensible by inheritance.	Do not support inheritance.
Data type	Reference data type.	Value data type.
	When an object variable is passed to a function, the address reference of the data is passed rather than the data itself.	When a structure variable is passed to a function, the actual data must be copied to the function.
	Assigning one class variable to another points both variables to the same object. Any updates to either variable will therefore affect the other.	Assigning one structure variable to another creates an actual copy of the structure. Updates to one of the variables will therefore not affect the other.

Lab 5.2: Inheriting the Package Class

Objectives

After completing this lab, you will be able to:

- Create base classes.
- Create derived classes that use inheritance.
- Use inherited classes from calling code.

Prerequisites

Before working on this lab, you should be familiar with inheritance in Visual Basic .NET.

Scenario

In this lab, you will continue creating the Cargo system. You will create the **Package** base class, the **SpecialPackage** derived class, and the test application. Some of the code has been created for you.

Starter and Solution Files

There are starter and solution files associated with this lab. The starter files are in the *install folder*\Labs\Lab052\Starter folder, and the solution files are in the *install folder*\Labs\Lab052\Solution folder.

Estimated time to complete this lab: 60 minutes

Exercise 1
Completing the SpecialPackage Class

In this exercise, you will examine the pre-written **Package** class and complete the partially written **SpecialPackage** class. You will inherit from the **Package** class, and override some of its methods.

▶ To open the starter project

1. Open Visual Studio .NET.
2. On the **File** menu, point to **Open**, and click **Project**. Set the folder location to *install folder*\Labs\Lab052\Starter, click **Lab052.sln**, and then click **Open**.

▶ To examine the Package class

1. Open the Package.vb class.
2. Examine the existing properties and methods.

   The **Package** class retrieves and stores information about a single package that will be delivered to a customer. It contains information about the package, including a description, size dimensions, instructions, weight, and value. These properties have been created for you.

   The **Package** class provides methods to simulate the creation, retrieval, and deletion of package information. These methods are marked as overridable for inheriting classes. Note that the **IsSpecialPackage** method is marked as shared so that it can be accessed without instantiating object variables. These methods have been created for you.

▶ To examine the SpecialPackage class

1. Open the SpecialPackage.vb class.
2. Examine the existing properties.

▶ To inherit from the Package class

1. At the top of the **SpecialPackage** class, locate the list of private variables. Insert the following line immediately before the variable declarations:

```
Inherits Package
```

   This will create the relationship between the **Package** base class and the derived class **SpecialPackage**.

2. Add the following methods to the **SpecialPackage** class definition:

Method name	Type	Parameters
GetDetails	`Public Overrides Sub`	`ByVal intID As Integer`

CreatePackage	`Public Overloads Function`	`ByVal intDeliveryID As Integer`
		`ByVal strDescription As String`
		`ByVal strDimensions As String`
		`ByVal strInstructions As String`
		`ByVal strWeight As String`
		`ByVal dblValue As Double`
		`ByVal blnOxygen As Boolean`
		`ByVal strTemperature As String`
		`ByVal strTimeLimit As String`
		`ByVal strExtra As String`
		`<RETURN VALUE> As Integer`

DeletePackage	`Public Overrides Sub`	`ByVal intID As Integer`

▶ To implement the GetDetails method

1. Locate the **GetDetails** method declaration and add code to call the **MyBase.GetDetails** method, passing the *intID* as the parameter to retrieve the simulated **Package** details.

2. After the call to **MyBase.GetDetails**, assign the following values to the **SpecialPackage** properties to simulate a returned record from the database:

Property	Value
OxygenRequired	**True**
Temperature	**80**
TimeLimit	**5 hours**
ExtraInstructions	**Feed if time limit exceeded**

▶ To implement the CreatePackage method

1. Locate the **CreatePackage** method declaration, and add code to call the **MyBase.CreatePackage** method, passing in the following values as the parameters to create the simulated **Package** record.

Parameter Name	Value
intDeliveryID	*intDeliveryID*
strDescription	*strDescription*
strDimensions	*strDimensions*
strInstructions	*strInstructions*
strWeight	*strWeight*
dblValue	*dblValue*

2. After the call to **MyBase.CreatePackage**, assign the following values to the **SpecialPackage** properties to simulate the update to the database.

Property	Value
OxygenRequired	**blnOxygen**
Temperature	**strTemperature**
TimeLimit	**strTimeLimit**
ExtraInstructions	**strExtra**

3. After the property value assignments, use the **MsgBox** function to display the message "Special instructions added".
4. Return the PackageID as the return value of the **CreatePackage** method.

▶ To implement the DeletePackage method

1. Locate the **DeletePackage** method declaration, and insert code to use the **MsgBox** function to display the message "Deleting special package details" to simulate the deletion of the **SpecialPackage** database record.
2. After the displaying the message, call the **MyBase.DeletePackage** method, passing *intID* as the parameter, to simulate the deletion of the **Package** record.
3. Save the project.

Exercise 2
Retrieving Packages

In this exercise, you will write the calling code for the **Retrieve** button that calls either a **Package** or a **SpecialPackage** object. You will then test your code by entering some values into the Package form.

▶ To create the Retrieve button code

1. Open frmPackage in the Code Editor, and locate the **btnRetrieve_Click** event procedure.
2. Create an **If** statement that calls the **Package.IsSpecialPackage** shared function, passing in the **Text** property of txtID as the parameter. (Use the **CInt** function to convert the text value into an **Integer**.)

▶ To use a SpecialPackage object

1. In the true part of the **If** statement, declare and instantiate a **SpecialPackage** variable called **aSpecial**.
2. Set the **Checked** property of chkSpecial to **True**.
3. Call the **GetDetails** method of the **aSpecial** object, passing in the **Text** property of txtID as the parameter. (Use the **CInt** function to convert the text value into an **Integer**.)
4. Display the properties of the **aSpecial** object in the appropriate text boxes. Use the information in the following table to assign the text box values to the properties of the **aSpecial** object.

Control	Property of aSpecial
txtDeliveryID.Text	**DeliveryID**
txtDescription.Text	**Description**
txtDimensions.Text	**Dimensions**
txtInstructions.Text	**Instructions**
txtValue.Text	**Value**
txtWeight.Text	**Weight**
txtExtra.Text	**ExtraInstructions**
txtTemperature.Text	**Temperature**
txtTimeLimit.Text	**TimeLimit**
chkOxygen.Checked	**OxygenRequired**

▶ To use the Package object

1. In the false block of the **If** statement, set the **Checked** property of chkSpecial to **False**, and declare and instantiate a **Package** variable called **aPackage**.
2. Call the **GetDetails** method of the **aPackage** object, passing in the **Text** property of txtID as the parameter. (Use the **CInt** function to convert the text value into an **Integer**.)
3. Display the properties of the **aPackage** object in the appropriate textboxes. Use the information in the following table to assign the text box values to the properties of the **aPackage** object.

Control	Property of aPackage
txtDeliveryID.Text	**DeliveryID**
txtDescription.Text	**Description**
txtDimensions.Text	**Dimensions**
txtInstructions.Text	**Instructions**
txtValue.Text	**Value**
txtWeight.Text	**Weight**
txtExtra.Text	""
txtTemperature.Text	""
txtTimeLimit.Text	""
chkOxygen.Checked	**False**

4. Save the project.

▶ To test the Retrieve button code

1. Set a breakpoint on the first line of the **btnRetrieve_Click** procedure. On the **Debug** menu, click **Start**.
2. Enter the value **18** in the **Package ID** box, click the **Retrieve** button, and then step through the procedure.
3. Confirm that your code retrieves the package information and displays it correctly in the text boxes.
4. Click the **Clear Data** button to reset the information.
5. Enter the value **33** in the **Package ID** box, click the **Retrieve** button, and step through the procedure.
6. Confirm that your code retrieves the special package information and displays it correctly in the text boxes.
7. Click the **Close** button to quit the application. Remove the breakpoint on **btnRetrieve_Click**.

Exercise 3
Creating Packages

In this exercise, you will write the calling code for the **New** button that creates either a **Package** or **SpecialPackage** object. You will then test your code by entering some values into the Package form.

▶ To create the New Package button code

1. Locate the **btnNew_Click** event procedure.
2. Create an **If** statement that checks the **Checked** property of the chkSpecial check box.

▶ To create a Package object

1. In the false part of the **If** statement, declare and instantiate a **Package** variable called **aPackage**.
2. Call the **CreatePackage** method of the **aPackage** object and store the return value in the **Text** property of the **txtID** box. (Use the **CStr** function to convert the **Integer** to a **String**.) Pass the following values as parameters to the method.

Parameter	TextBox
intDeliveryID	CInt(txtDeliveryID.Text)
strDescription	txtDescription.Text
strDimensions	txtDimensions.Text
strInstructions	txtInstructions.Text
strWeight	txtWeight.Text
dblValue	CDbl(txtValue.Text)

► To create a SpecialPackage object

1. In the true part of the **If** statement, declare and instantiate a **SpecialPackage** variable called **aPackage**.
2. Call the overloaded **CreatePackage** method of the **aPackage** object and store the return value in the **Text** property of the **txtID** box. (Use the **CStr** function to convert the **Integer** to a **String**.) Pass the following values as parameters to the method.

Parameter	Value
intDeliveryID	CInt(txtDeliveryID.Text)
strDescription	txtDescription.Text
strDimensions	txtDimensions.Text
strInstructions	txtInstructions.Text
strWeight	txtWeight.Text
dblValue	CDbl(txtValue.Text)
blnOxygen	chkOxygen.Checked
strTemperature	txtTemperature.Text
strTimeLimit	txtTimeLimit.Text
strExtra	txtExtra.Text

3. Save the project.

► To test the standard Package code

1. Set a breakpoint on the first line of the **btnNew_Click** procedure.
2. On the **Debug** menu, click **Start**.
3. Enter the following values.

Control	Value
DeliveryID	**11**
Description	**Software**
Instructions	**None**
Dimensions	**NA**
Weight	**NA**
Value	**50**

4. Click the **New** button, and step through the procedure.
5. Confirm that the code correctly passes the values to the package class.
6. Click the **Clear Data** button.

► To test the SpecialPackage code

1. Enter the following values.

Control	Value
DeliveryID	**43**
Description	**Heart Transplant**
Instructions	**Deliver to Joe Howard**
Dimensions	**NA**
Weight	**NA**
Value	**0**
Special Package	**Checked**
Extra Instructions	**Speed is essential**
Oxygen Required	**Unchecked**
Temperature	**20**
Time Limit	**2 hours**

2. Click the **New** button, and step through the procedure.
3. Confirm that the code passes the values to the **SpecialPackage** class correctly.
4. Click the **Close** button to quit the application, and remove the breakpoint on **btnNew_Click**.

Exercise 4
Deleting Packages

In this exercise, you will write the calling code for the **Delete** button that deletes either a **Package** or **SpecialPackage** object. You will then test your code by entering some values into the Package form.

▶ To create the Delete button code

1. Locate the **btnDelete_Click** event procedure.
2. Create an **If** statement that calls the **Package.IsSpecialPackage** shared function, passing in the **Text** property of txtID as the parameter. (Use the **CInt** function to convert the text value into an **Integer**.)

▶ To delete a SpecialPackage object

1. In the true part of the **If** statement, declare and instantiate a **SpecialPackage** variable called **aSpecial**.
2. Call the **DeletePackage** method of the **aSpecial** object, passing in the **Text** property of txtID as the parameter. (Use the **CInt** function to convert the text value into an **Integer**.)

▶ To delete a Package object

1. In the false part of the **If** statement, declare and instantiate a **Package** variable called **aPackage**.
2. Call the **DeletePackage** method of the **aPackage** object, passing in the **Text** property of txtID as the parameter. (Use the **CInt** function to convert the text value into an **Integer**.)
3. Save the project.

▶ To test the Delete button code

1. Set a breakpoint on the first line of the **btnDelete_Click** procedure, and on the **Debug** menu, click **Start**.
2. Enter the value **18** in the **Package ID** text box, click the **Delete** button, and step through the procedure.
3. Confirm that your code simulates the deletion of the **Package** object.
4. Click the **Clear Data** button to reset the information.
5. Enter the value **33** in the **Package ID** text box, click the **Delete** button, and step through the procedure.
6. Confirm that your code simulates the deletion of the **SpecialPackage** object.
7. Click the **Close** button to quit the application, and remove the breakpoint on **btnDelete_Click**.
8. Close Visual Studio .NET.

Review

- Defining Classes
- Creating and Destroying Objects
- Inheritance
- Interfaces
- Working with Classes

1. Create code that defines multiple constructors for a **Person** class. The first constructor will not take any arguments. The second will take two string values: **FirstName** and **LastName**.

2. Garbage collection occurs immediately after all references to an object are removed. True or false? If false, explain why.

3. Describe the functionality of the **MyBase** keyword.

4. What is a potential problem that may result from the following class code sample? How can you rewrite the code to resolve the problem?

```
Class Person
    Private Sub Save( )
        'Save the local data in a database
    End Sub

    Sub Dispose( )
        Save( )
    End Sub

    Protected Overrides Sub Finalize( )
        Dispose( )
        MyBase.Finalize( )
    End Sub
End Class
```

5. You can create an interface explicitly in Visual Basic .NET. True or false? If false, explain why.

6. Will the following code compile correctly? If not, why?

```
Class Person
    Event NameChanged( )
    Private strName As String

    Sub ChangeName(ByVal strNewName As String)
        strName = strNewName
        RaiseEvent NameChanged( )
    End Sub
End Class

Module TestCode
 Sub Main( )
    Dim x As New Person( )
    AddHandler x.NameChanged, AddressOf HandleIt
    x.ChangeName("Jeff")
 End Sub

 Sub HandleIt(ByVal strValue As String)
    MsgBox(strValue)
 End Sub
End Module
```

msdn® training

Module 6: Using Windows Forms

Contents

Overview

- Why Use Windows Forms?
- Structure of Windows Forms
- Using Windows Forms
- Using Controls
- Windows Forms Inheritance

This module describes the new Microsoft® Windows® Forms that are provided by the Microsoft .NET Framework. Windows Forms are the Microsoft Visual Basic® .NET version 7.0 equivalent to Visual Basic forms.

You will learn about the new features available in Windows Forms and how to make changes to forms and controls, and their properties, methods, and events. You will also learn how to create some of the standard Windows dialog boxes. Finally, you will learn about visual inheritance, which allows you to use object-oriented techniques within your forms.

After completing this module, you will be able to:

- Describe the benefits of Windows Forms.
- Use the new properties and methods of Windows Forms.
- Write event-handling code.
- Use the new controls and control enhancements.
- Add and edit menus.
- Create a form that inherits from another form.

Why Use Windows Forms?

- Rich set of controls
- Flat look style
- Advanced printing support
- Advanced graphics support – GDI+
- Accessibility support
- Visual inheritance
- Extensible object model
- Advanced forms design

Windows Forms provide many enhancements over standard Visual Basic forms, including:

- Rich set of controls

  By using classes in the **System.Windows.Forms** namespace, you can create Visual Basic .NET applications that take full advantage of the rich user interface features available in the Microsoft Windows operating system. This namespace provides the **Form** class and many other controls that can be added to forms to create user interfaces. Many additional controls are included that were previously only available through external libraries (.ocx's) or third-party products. Some existing controls now allow simple access to properties and methods from the object model instead of requiring complex application programming interfaces (APIs) to perform extended functionality.

- Flat look style

  Windows Forms allow you to create applications that use the new flat look style as seen previously in Microsoft Money 2000.

- Advanced printing support

  Windows Forms provide advanced printing support through the **PageSetupDialog**, **PrintPreviewControl**, **PrintPreviewDialog**, and **PrintDialog** controls.

- Advanced graphics support—GDI+

  The **System.Drawing** namespace provides access to GDI+ basic graphics functionality. GDI+ provides the functionality for graphics in Windows Forms that are accessible in the .NET Framework. More advanced functionality is provided in the **System.Drawing.Drawing2D**, **System.Drawing.Imaging**, and **System.Drawing.Text** namespaces.

  You can take full advantage of these system classes to create applications that provide the user with a richer graphical environment.

- Accessibility support

  Windows Forms provide accessibility properties for controls so that you can develop applications that people with disabilities can use.

- Visual inheritance

  Windows Forms are classes and can benefit from inheritance. Windows Forms can be inherited in derived forms that automatically inherit the controls and code defined by the base form. This adds powerful reuse possibilities to your applications.

- Extensible object model

  The Windows Forms class library is extensible, so you can enhance existing classes and controls with your own functionality.

  You can also create your own designers, similar to the docking or anchoring designers, that will work in the Microsoft Visual Studio® .NET integrated development environment (IDE).

- Advanced forms design

  Developers have traditionally spent much time writing code to handle form resizing, font changes, and scrolling. Windows Forms provide much of this functionality with built-in properties for docking, anchoring, automatic sizing, and automatic scrolling. These new features allow you to concentrate on the functions of your applications.

◆ Structure of Windows Forms

- Windows Forms Class Hierarchy
- Using the Windows.Forms.Application Class
- Examining the Code Behind Windows Forms

Windows Forms appear similar to Visual Basic 6.0 forms, but the structure of the Windows Form code is different from previous Visual Basic forms. This is because the Windows Forms library in the .NET Framework is object oriented.

After completing this lesson, you will be able to:

- Describe several of the classes in the Windows Forms class hierarchy.
- Use the **Windows.Forms.Application** class to manage your application at run time.
- Interpret the code generated by Windows Forms.

Windows Forms Class Hierarchy

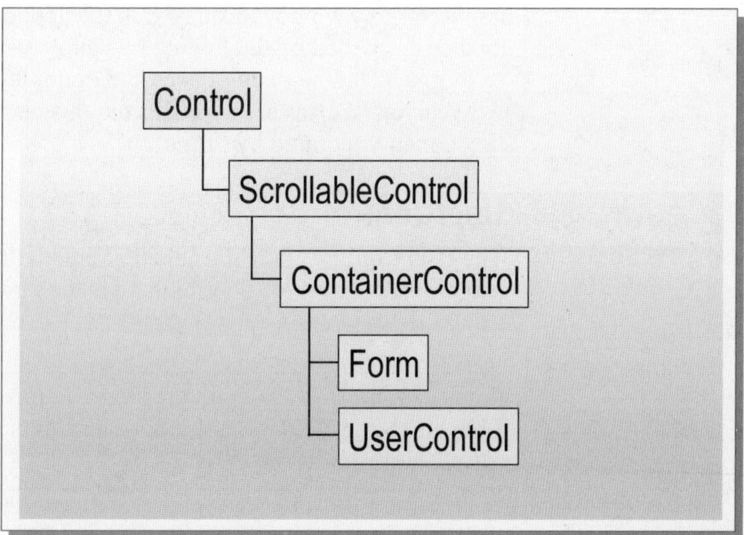

The .NET Framework provides all of the classes that make up Windows Forms–based applications through the **System.Windows.Forms** namespace. The inheritance hierarchy provides many common features across the .NET Windows Forms classes, providing a consistent set of properties and methods for many controls and forms. Some of the classes are examined below.

Control

The **Control** class is the fundamental base class for other controls. It provides the basic functionality for a control, such as sizing, visibility, and tab order.

ScrollableControl

The **ScrollableControl** class inherits directly from the **Control** class and provides automatic scrolling capabilities for any control that requires scroll bars.

ContainerControl

The **ContainerControl** class inherits directly from the **ScrollableControl** class and adds tabbing and focus management functionality for controls that can host other controls.

Form

The **Form** class inherits directly from the **ContainerControl** class and represents any window displayed in the application. The properties and methods provided by the **Form** class allow you to display many different types of forms, including dialog boxes and multiple-document interface (MDI) forms. All Windows Forms are derived from this class because it provides the basic functionality required by forms.

UserControl

The **UserControl** class also inherits directly from the **ContainerControl** class and provides an empty control that you can use to create your own controls by using the Windows Forms Designer.

Note For information about creating controls, see Module 9, "Developing Components in Visual Basic .NET," in Course 2373B, *Programming with Microsoft Visual Basic .NET.*

Using the Windows.Forms.Application Class

- **Starting and ending applications**

```
Sub Main( )
    Dim frmFirst as New Form1( )
    frmFirst.Show( )            'Displays the first form
    Application.Run( )
'Allows the application to continue after the form is closed
End Sub
```

- **Using DoEvents**
- **Setting and retrieving application information**

```
Dim strAppPath As String
strAppPath = Application.StartupPath
'use this path to access other files installed there
```

You can use the **Windows.Forms.Application** class for managing your application at run time, in a similar way to using the **App** object in Visual Basic 6.0. You cannot instantiate this class in your code because a single instance exists for the duration of your application at run time.

Starting and Ending Applications

The **Application** object provides methods that you use to start and end your applications. Use the **Run** method to start an application and the **Exit** method to terminate an application.

The **Run** method has an optional parameter that specifies the form to be displayed. If you specify this parameter, the application will end when that form is closed. To enable your application to continue running after the initial form has closed, use the **Show** method of the form before calling the **Run** method of the **Application**. When you use the **Show** method before calling the **Run** method, you must use the **Exit** method to explicitly end your application. Calling this does not run the Close event on your forms, but simply ends the application.

The following example shows how to use the **Application** class to start your application, keep it running after the first form is closed, and end the application. You must remember to change the **Startup Object** property of the project from the name of a form to **Sub Main** for this to work.

```
Sub Main( )
    Dim frmFirst as New Form1( )
    frmFirst.Show( )     ' Displays the first form
    Application.Run( )
' Allows the application to continue after the form is closed
End Sub

Private Sub LastForm_Closing (ByVal sender As Object, ByVal e
As System.ComponentModel.CancelEventArgs) Handles
MyBase.Closing
   ' Any cleanup code for the application
  Application.Exit
End Sub
```

Using DoEvents

The **Application** class also provides the **DoEvents** method. This method is similar to the **DoEvents** function in Visual Basic 6.0, but it is now implemented as a method of the **Application** object.

You use this method to allow other messages in the message queue to be processed during the handling of a single event in your code. By default, when your form handles an event, it processes all code in that event handler and will not respond to other events that may be occurring. If you call the **DoEvents** method in that code, your application will have a chance to handle these other events, such as the repainting of a form that has had another window dragged over it. You will typically use this method within loops to ensure that other messages are processed.

Warning When you use the **DoEvents** method, be careful not to re-enter the same code. This will cause your application to stop responding.

Setting and Retrieving Application Information

The **Application** class contains many useful properties that you can use to set and retrieve application-level information.

You can use the **CommonAppDataRegistry** and **UserAppDataRegistry** properties to set the keys to which shared and user-specific registry information for your application will be written when you are installing an application. After your application is installed, both of these properties are read-only.

The **StartUpPath** property specifies where the running executable file is stored, just like the **App.Path** property in Visual Basic 6.0. You can use this information to access other files that will be installed into the same folder.

The following example shows how you can use the **StartUpPath** property to provide the installation path of the application:

```
Dim strAppPath As String
strAppPath = Application.StartupPath
'Use this path to access other files installed there
```

Examining the Code Behind Windows Forms

- **Imports**
  - To alias namespaces in external assemblies

```
Imports Winforms = System.Windows.Forms
```

- **Class**
  - Inherits from **System.Windows.Forms.Form**
  - Constructor – **Sub New( )**
  - Initializer – **Sub InitializeComponent( )**
  - Destructor – **Sub Dispose( )**

The structure of the code behind a Windows Form differs from the structure of the code behind a Visual Basic 6.0 form because of the object-orientation of the .NET Framework.

Imports

At the top of the code, you may find a list of **Imports** statements, which you can use to provide access to functionality contained within namespaces in referenced external assemblies. If you do not use an **Imports** statement, then all references to classes in external assemblies must use fully qualified names. Using **Imports** allows you to specify an alias to be used for the namespace.

The following example shows how to use the **Imports** statement to declare an alias of *Winforms* for the **System.Windows.Forms** namespace. This statement allows you to use the alias in place of the full name for the rest of the form's code.

```
Imports Winforms = System.Windows.Forms
```

Class

A form is an instance of a class in Visual Basic .NET, so all the code belonging to the form is enclosed within a **Public Class** definition. This structure allows you to implement visual inheritance by creating forms that inherit from other forms.

Inherits System.Windows.Forms.Form

Forms inherit from the **System.Windows.Forms.Form** class. If you create a form in Visual Studio .NET, this inheritance is automatic, but if you create forms elsewhere, you must manually add the **Inherits** statement. This gives you the standard functionality of a form but allows you to override methods or properties as required.

Constructor

In Visual Basic 6.0, you use the **Form_Initialize** and **Form_Load** events to initialize your forms. In Visual Basic .NET, the **Form_Initialize** event has been replaced with the class constructor **Public Sub New**.

Initializer

As in previous versions of Visual Basic, you can assign many property values at design time. These design-time values are used by the run-time system to provide initial values. In Visual Basic 6.0, properties are initialized through the run-time system, and the code is not visible to the developer. In Visual Basic .NET, the Windows Form Designer creates a subroutine called **InitializeComponent** that contains the settings you define in the properties window at design time. This subroutine is called from the class constructor code.

Destructor

In previous versions of Visual Basic, you use the **Form_Terminate** and **Form_Unload** events to provide finalization code. In Visual Basic .NET, these events have been replaced with the class destructor **Public Sub Dispose** and the **Form_Closed** event. When a form is shown non-modally, Dispose is called when the form is closed. When you show forms modally, you must call the Dispose method yourself.

◆ Using Windows Forms

- Using Form Properties
- Using Form Methods
- Using Form Events
- Handling Events
- Creating MDI Forms
- Using Standard Dialog Boxes

Using Windows Forms is similar to using Visual Basic 6.0 forms, but there are a number of new properties, methods, and events.

In this lesson, you will learn how to use the new form properties, methods, and events. You will also learn how to use MDI forms and standard Windows dialog boxes.

Using Form Properties

- DialogResult
- Font
- Opacity
- MaximumSize and MinimumSize
- TopMost
- AcceptButton and CancelButton

Windows Forms have many new powerful properties that previously would have required API calls to achieve a similar functionality. Many properties are inherited from classes such as the **Control**, **ScrollableControl**, and **ContainerControl** classes, and some properties are defined by the **Form** class itself.

DialogResult

Windows Forms allow you to easily create your own customized dialog boxes. You can create customized dialog boxes by setting the **DialogResult** property for buttons on your form and displaying the form as a dialog box. Once the form is closed, you can use the **DialogResult** property of the form to determine which button was clicked.

The following example shows how to use the **DialogResult** property of a Windows Form:

```
Form1.ShowDialog( )
'The DialogResult property is updated when a button is pressed
and the form closed
If Form1.DialogResult = DialogResult.Yes Then
   'Do something
End If
Form1.Dispose( )
```

Font

The **Font** property of a Windows Form behaves slightly differently than that of a Visual Basic 6.0 form. Controls inherit **Font.BackColor** and **Font.ForeColor** from their parent control. If the font is not set on a control, then the control inherits the font from the parent. This allows you to change the font on the form, and have all controls on the form automatically pick up that new font.

Opacity

By default, all Windows Forms are 100 percent opaque. In Windows 2000 and Windows XP, it is possible to create forms that are transparent or translucent. You can do this by changing the **Opacity** property of a form. This holds a double value between 0 and 1, with 1 being opaque and 0 being transparent.

The following example shows how to make a form 50% opaque:

```
Me.Opacity = 0.5
```

MaximumSize and MinimumSize

These two properties allow you to define maximum and minimum sizes of a form at run time. Their data type is **Size**, which has a **Height** property and a **Width** property to define a total size of the form.

The following example shows how to use these properties:

```
Dim MaxSize As New Size( )
Dim MinSize As New Size( )
MaxSize.Height = 500
MaxSize.Width = 500
MinSize.Height = 200
MinSize.Width = 200
Me.MaximumSize = MaxSize
Me.MinimumSize = MinSize
```

TopMost

The **TopMost** property allows your form to remain on top of all other windows, even when it does not have the focus. This is what the Windows Task Manager does by default. In previous versions of Visual Basic, this frequently used feature can be achieved only by using API calls. In Visual Basic .NET, you simply assign a **Boolean** property of a Windows Form.

The following example shows how to toggle the **TopMost** property:

```
Me.TopMost = Not Me.TopMost
```

AcceptButton and CancelButton

The **AcceptButton** and **CancelButton** properties of a Windows Form allow you to specify which buttons should be activated when the ENTER and ESC keys are pressed, like setting the **Default** and **Cancel** properties of **CommandButtons** in Visual Basic 6.0. The following example shows how to specify your **OK** and **Cancel** buttons as the **AcceptButton** and **CancelButton**:

```
Me.AcceptButton = btnOK
Me.CancelButton = btnCancel
```

Using Form Methods

- **Close**

```
If blnEndApp = True Then
       Me.Close( )
End If
```

- **Show and ShowDialog**

```
Dim frm2 As New Form2( )
frm2.ShowDialog( )
If frm2.DialogResult = DialogResult.OK Then
    MessageBox.Show("Processing request")
ElseIf frm2.DialogResult = DialogResult.Cancel Then
    MessageBox.Show("Cancelling request")
End If
frm2.Dispose( )
```

Windows Forms provide several new methods in addition to supporting some existing methods from previous versions of Visual Basic, such as **Hide** and **Refresh**.

Close

This method is similar to the **Unload** method in Visual Basic 6.0. You can use it to close the current form and release any resources it is holding. The following example shows how to use the **Close** method of a Windows Form:

```
If blnEndApp = True Then
  Me.Close( )
End If
```

Show and ShowDialog

You can use these methods to display a form on the screen. The **Show** method simply displays the form by setting its **Visible** property to **True**. The **ShowDialog** method displays the form as a modal dialog box.

The following example shows how to display a form as a modal dialog box and how to use the **DialogResult** property of the form to determine the action to be taken:

```
Dim frm2 As New Form2( )
frm2.ShowDialog( )
If frm2.DialogResult = DialogResult.OK Then
    MessageBox.Show("Processing request")
ElseIf frm2.DialogResult = DialogResult.Cancel Then
    MessageBox.Show("Cancelling request")
End If
frm2.Dispose( )
```

Using Form Events

- Activated and Deactivate
- Closing
- Closed
- MenuStart and MenuComplete

Many events from previous versions of Visual Basic are unchanged in Visual Basic .NET, such as mouse and focus events (although these events do have different parameters). Several events have been replaced with slightly different events from the .NET Framework to become standard across the .NET-compatible languages. A number of new events have also been added to allow further flexibility when designing Windows Forms–based applications. In this topic, you will take a closer look at these changes.

Activated and Deactivate

The **Activated** event is raised when the form is activated by code or by user interaction, and the **Deactivate** event is raised when the form loses focus. In Visual Basic 6.0, the **Activate** event was raised only when the form was activated from within the same application. In Visual Basic .NET, it is raised whenever the form is activated, regardless of where it is activated from. You can use this event to ensure that a particular control is always selected when you activate a form.

The following example shows how to use the **Activated** event to select the text in a text box:

```
Private Sub Form2_Activated(ByVal sender As System.Object,
ByVal e As System.EventArgs) Handles MyBase.Activated
  TextBox1.Focus( )
  TextBox1.SelectAll( )
End Sub
```

Closing

This event is similar to the Visual Basic 6.0 **Unload** event. It occurs when the form is being closed and allows you to cancel the closure through the use of the **CancelEventArgs** argument.

The following example shows how to use the **Closing** event to query whether the user wants to end the application:

```
Private Sub Form1_Closing(ByVal sender As Object, ByVal e As
System.ComponentModel.CancelEventArgs) Handles MyBase.Closing
  If MessageBox.Show("Do you really want to close this form?",
  "Closing", MessageBoxButtons.YesNo) = DialogResult.No Then
      e.Cancel = True
  End If
End Sub
```

Closed

The **Closed** event occurs after the **Closing** event but before the **Dispose** method of a form. You can use it to perform tasks such as saving information from the form.

The following example shows how to use the **Closed** event to store information in a global variable:

```
Private Sub Form2_Closed(ByVal sender As System.Object, ByVal
e As System.EventArgs) Handles MyBase.Closed
  strName = "Charlie"
End Sub
```

MenuStart and MenuComplete

These two events are raised when a menu receives and loses focus. You can use these events to set properties of the menu items, such as the **Checked** or **Enabled** property.

The following example shows how to enable and disable menu items based on the type of control on the form that currently has the focus:

```
If TypeOf (ActiveControl) Is TextBox Then
  mnuCut.Enabled = True
  mnuCopy.Enabled = True
Else
  mnuCut.Enabled = False
  mnuCopy.Enabled = False
End If
```

Handling Events

- **Handling multiple events with one procedure**

```
Private Sub AddOrEditButtonClick(ByVal sender As Object,
ByVal e As System.EventArgs)
Handles btnAdd.Click, btnEdit.Click
```

- **Using AddHandler**

```
AddHandler btnNext.Click, AddressOf NavigateBtnClick
```

In previous versions of Visual Basic, you create event handlers by selecting the object and event from the **Object** and **Procedure** boxes in the Code Editor. You can create event handlers in Visual Basic .NET the same way, although to create some of the common event handlers for forms, you need to access the (Base Class Events) group in the **Object** box. You can also add event handlers programmatically by using the **AddHandler** keyword.

Handling Multiple Events with One Procedure

Events can also be handled by any procedure that matches the argument list of the event, also referred to as its *signature*. This allows you to handle events from multiple controls within one procedure, reducing code duplication in a similar way that control arrays do in previous versions of Visual Basic.

You can achieve this functionality by using the **Handles** keyword in conjunction with controls that are declared using the **WithEvents** keyword.

The following example shows how to handle multiple events programmatically with one procedure:

```
Private Sub AddOrEditButtonClick(ByVal sender As
System.Object, ByVal e As System.EventArgs) Handles
btnAdd.Click, btnEdit.Click
  btnFirst.Enabled = False
  btnLast.Enabled = False
  btnNext.Enabled = False
  btnPrevious.Enabled = False
  btnSave.Enabled = True
  btnCancel.Enabled = True
End Sub
```

Note The *signature* of an event is the list of variables passed to an event-handling procedure. For a procedure to handle multiple events, or to handle events from multiple controls, the argument list must be identical for each event or else a compilation error will occur.

Using AddHandler

The **AddHandler** keyword allows you to add event handling to your form or control at run time by using one of two techniques, as is described for classes in Module 5, "Object-Oriented Programming in Visual Basic .NET," in Course 2373B, *Programming with Microsoft Visual Basic .NET.* It is similar to the **Handles** keyword in that it also allows you to use one event-handling procedure for multiple events or multiple controls. With **AddHandler**, however, you do not need to declare the control variable by using the **WithEvents** modifier. This allows a more dynamic attaching of events to handlers.

The following example shows how to use the **AddHandler** keyword to assign control events to procedure:

```
Private Sub NavigateBtnClick(ByVal sender As System.Object,
ByVal e As System.EventArgs)
  MessageBox.Show("Moving record")
End Sub

Private Sub Form1_Load(ByVal sender As System.Object, ByVal e
As System.EventArgs) Handles MyBase.Load
  AddHandler btnNext.Click, AddressOf NavigateBtnClick
  AddHandler btnPrevious.Click, AddressOf NavigateBtnClick
End Sub
```

Note The **RemoveHandler** keyword removes an event handler from a form or control's event. For more information about **RemoveHandler**, see Module 5, "Object-Oriented Programming in Visual Basic .NET," in Course 2373B, *Programming with Microsoft Visual Basic .NET.*

Practice: Using Form Events

In this practice, you will create a Windows-based application containing a single form that displays event information in the Debug Output window.

► **To create the application**

1. Open Microsoft Visual Studio .NET.
2. On the **File** menu, point to **New**, and then click **Project**. Set the location to *install folder*\Practices\Mod06, and rename the solution FormEvents.
3. Create event handlers for the following form events, and enter the specified code in the code window.

Event	Code
Form1_Activated	`Debug.WriteLine("Activated")`
Form1_Closed	`Debug.WriteLine("Closed")`
Form1_Deactivate	`Debug.WriteLine("Deactivated")`
Form1_SizeChanged	`Debug.WriteLine("Size changed")`

► **To test the application**

1. On the **Debug** menu, click **Start**.
2. On the **View** menu, point to **Other Windows**, and then click **Output** to display the Debug Output window.
3. Perform the following actions on the form: **Resize**, **Minimize**, **Restore**, and **Close**. (Ensure that you can view the activity in the Debug Output window as you perform each action.)
4. Close Visual Studio .NET.

Creating MDI Forms

- Creating the parent form

```
Me.IsMdiContainer = True
Me.WindowState = FormWindowState.Maximized
```

- Creating child forms

```
Dim doc As Form2 = New Form2( )
doc.MdiParent = Me
doc.Show( )
```

- Accessing child forms
- Arranging child forms

Creating multiple-document interface (MDI) applications is a common task for Visual Basic developers. There have been a number of changes to this process in Visual Basic .NET, although the basic concepts of parent forms and child forms remain the same.

Creating the Parent Form

You can use the **IsMdiContainer** property of a form to make it an MDI parent form. This property holds a **Boolean** value and can be set at design time or run time.

The following example shows how to specify a form as an MDI parent and maximize it for easy use.

```
Private Sub Form1_Load(ByVal sender As System.Object, ByVal e
As System.EventArgs) Handles MyBase.Load
  Me.IsMdiContainer = True
  Me.WindowState = FormWindowState.Maximized
End Sub
```

Creating Child Forms

You can create child forms by setting the **MdiParent** property of a form to the name of the already-created MDI parent.

The following example shows how to create an MDI child form. This procedure could be called from the **Form_Load** procedure, and a New Document menu item. It uses a global variable to store the number of child windows for use in the caption of each window.

```
Private Sub AddDoc( )
  WindowCount = WindowCount + 1
  Dim doc As Form2 = New Form2( )
  doc.MdiParent = Me
  doc.Text = "Form" & WindowCount
  doc.Show( )
End Sub
```

Accessing Child Forms

It is common to use menus on the MDI parent form to manipulate parts of the MDI child forms. When you use this approach, you need to be able to determine which is the active child form at any point in time. The **ActiveMdiChild** property of the parent form identifies this for you.

The following example shows how to close the active child form:

```
Private Sub mnuFileClose_Click(ByVal sender As Object, ByVal e
As System.EventArgs) Handles mnuFileClose.Click
  Me.ActiveMdiChild.Close( )
End Sub
```

Arranging Child Forms

You can use the **LayoutMdi** method of the parent form to arrange the child forms in the main window. This method takes one parameter that can be one of the following:

- **MdiLayout.Cascade**
- **MdiLayout.ArrangeIcons**
- **MdiLayout.TileHorizontal**
- **MdiLayout.TileVertical**

The following examples show how to use these settings:

```
Private Sub mnuWindowCascade_Click(ByVal sender As
System.Object, ByVal e As System.EventArgs) Handles
mnuWindowCascade.Click
  Me.LayoutMdi(MdiLayout.Cascade)
End Sub

Private Sub mnuWinArrIcons_Click(ByVal sender As
System.Object, ByVal e As System.EventArgs) Handles
mnuWinArrIcons.Click
  Me.LayoutMdi(MdiLayout.ArrangeIcons)
End Sub

Private Sub mnuWinTileHoriz_Click(ByVal sender As
System.Object, ByVal e As System.EventArgs) Handles
mnuWinTileHoriz.Click
  Me.LayoutMdi(MdiLayout.TileHorizontal)
End Sub

Private Sub mnuWinTileVert_Click(ByVal sender As
System.Object, ByVal e As System.EventArgs) Handles
mnuWinTileVert.Click
  Me.LayoutMdi(MdiLayout.TileVertical)
End Sub
```

Creating a Window List

In previous versions of Visual Basic, you can set the **WindowList** property of a menu to create a list of child forms at the bottom of that menu. In Visual Basic .NET, you can achieve this functionality by setting the **MdiList** property of a menu.

Using Standard Dialog Boxes

- **MsgBox**

```
If MsgBox("Continue?", MsgBoxStyle.YesNo +
MsgBoxStyle.Question, "Question") = MsgBoxResult.Yes Then
    ...
End If
```

- **MessageBox Class**

```
If MessageBox.Show("Continue?", "Question",
MessageBoxButtons.YesNo, MessageBoxIcon.Question)
= DialogResult.Yes Then
    ...
End If
```

- **InputBox**

Modal forms or dialog boxes require that users close the window before they can continue interacting with other windows in the application. You can create them in any of three different ways.

MsgBox

The traditional **MsgBox** function used by Visual Basic developers is still provided in the .NET Framework. You use the same syntax that you used in previous versions, except you define the display style by the **MsgBoxStyle** enumeration and the resulting user decision by the **MsgBoxResult** enumeration. The following example shows how to use the **MsgBox** function:

```
If MsgBox("Continue?", _
        MsgBoxStyle.YesNo + MsgBoxStyle.Question, _
        "Question") _
      = MsgBoxResult.Yes Then
    ...
End If
```

MessageBox Class

In the .NET Framework, you use the **MessageBox** class for displaying a simple message in a dialog box. It provides a **Show** method and integer constants for controlling the display style of the message box. You can compare the resulting user decision to the **System.Windows.Forms.DialogResult** enumeration, as shown in the following example:

```
If MessageBox.Show("Continue?", "Question", _
     MessageBoxButtons.YesNo, MessageBoxIcon.Question) _
     = DialogResult.Yes Then
   ...
End If
```

The **Show** method allows extra flexibility by allowing you to optionally specify a different form as the owner of the dialog box.

InputBox

The **InputBox** function is still supported in Visual Basic .NET and has not changed from previous versions of Visual Basic.

Demonstration: Manipulating Windows Forms

In this demonstration, you will learn how to use the properties and methods of a Windows Form, including owner forms and automatic scrolling.

◆ Using Controls

- New Controls
- Using Control Properties
- Using Control Methods
- Creating Menus
- Providing User Help
- Implementing Drag-and-Drop Functionality

Visual Basic .NET introduces several new controls and many enhancements to the way you use existing controls.

After completing this lesson, you will be able to:

- Describe the new controls in the developer's Toolbox.
- Apply new properties and methods to existing controls.
- Use menus to improve user interaction with your application.
- Implement a Help system for your application.
- Create drag-and-drop operations.

New Controls

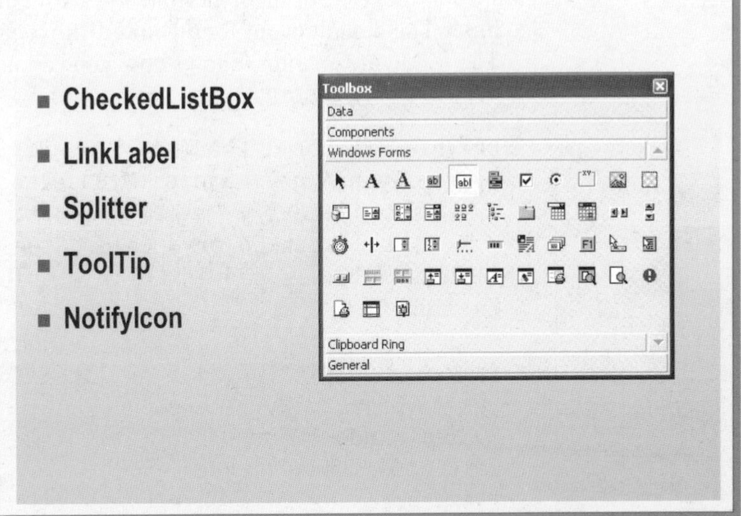

Visual Basic .NET provides many controls that will be familiar to Visual Basic developers, in addition to some new controls to help you create your Windows Forms–based applications. There are also some controls provided in the default Toolbox that are only available by using ActiveX® controls in Visual Basic 6.0, such as the **CommonDialog** controls and the Windows common controls library.

CheckedListBox

The **CheckedListBox** control allows you to use a list box with check boxes beside each item. This is a commonly used control in Windows and was previously available through the **Style** property of a standard **ListBox**.

The following example shows how you can use the **CheckedItems** property to access the selected items in the list:

```
Dim intTotalChecked As Integer
For intTotalChecked = 0 To _
  CheckedListBox1.CheckedItems.Count - 1
  Messagebox.Show(CheckedListBox1.CheckedItems _
      (intTotalChecked).ToString)
Next
```

LinkLabel

Using the **LinkLabel** control, you can display hyperlinks on a form. You can specify the **Text** of the hyperlink and the **VisitedLinkColor** and **LinkColor** of links. The default event for a **LinkedLabel** control is the **LinkClicked** event. The following example shows how you can use this to display a Web page in a **WebBrowser** control:

```
Private Sub Form1_Load(ByVal sender As Object, ByVal e As
System.EventArgs) Handles MyBase.Load
  LinkLabel1.Text = "www.microsoft.com"
  LinkLabel1.LinkColor = Color.Blue
  LinkLabel1.VisitedLinkColor = Color.Purple
End Sub

Private Sub LinkLabel1_LinkClicked(ByVal sender As
System.Object, ByVal e As
System.Windows.Forms.LinkLabelLinkClickedEventArgs) Handles
LinkLabel1.LinkClicked
  AxWebBrowser1.Navigate(LinkLabel1.Text)
End Sub
```

Splitter

Splitter controls have become a common feature of Microsoft applications over the last few years. Visual Basic .NET provides a built-in control to allow the user to resize the different sections of your form without any need for resizing code.

To use the **Splitter** control, you must perform the following steps:

1. Add the control to be resized to a container.
2. Dock the control to one side of the container.
3. Add the **Splitter** to the container.
4. Dock the **Splitter** to the side of the control to be resized.

After completing these steps, when you rest the mouse pointer on the edge of the control, the pointer will change shape and the control can be resized.

ToolTip

In Visual Basic 6.0, most built-in controls have a **ToolTip** property that allows you to attach textual Help to a control. This is implemented by means of the **ToolTip** control in Visual Basic .NET. You can use one **ToolTip** control to implement ToolTips on many controls on your form. The following example shows how to link the ToolTip text to be used with a particular control in the **Form_Load** event:

```
Private Sub Form1_Load(ByVal sender As Object, ByVal e As
System.EventArgs) Handles MyBase.Load
  ToolTip1.SetToolTip(Button1, "Click to confirm")
  ToolTip1.SetToolTip(Button2, "Click to cancel")
End Sub
```

NotifyIcon

The **NotifyIcon** control is a component that displays an icon in the notification area of the Windows taskbar, like the Windows Volume Control icon. The component is placed in the component tray of the Windows Forms Designer for a particular form. When that form is displayed at run time, the icon will display automatically in the notification area and will be removed when the **Dispose** method of the **NotifyIcon** component is called. A **ContextMenu** can be associated with the component so that users can right-click on the icon and select options from the menu.

Note For more information about other new controls, search for "Controls" in the Visual Basic .NET documentation.

Using Control Properties

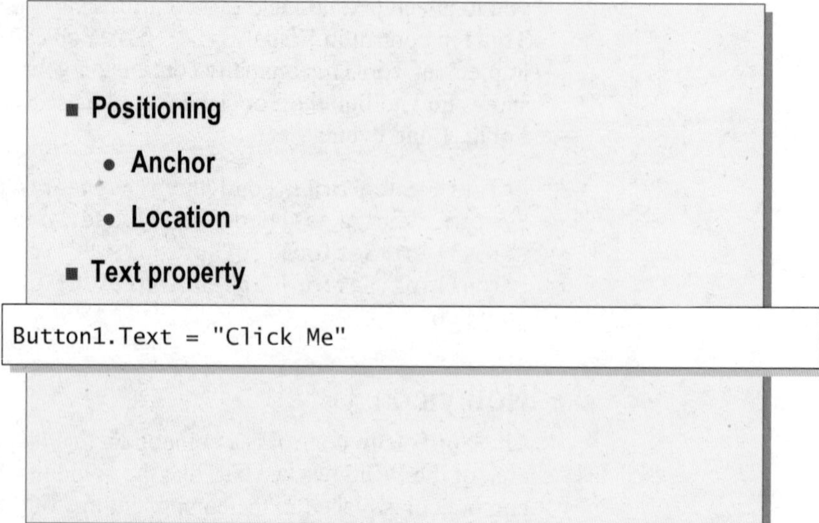

Many of the Windows Forms controls share some new common properties because they inherit from the same base classes.

Positioning

In Visual Basic 6.0, you regularly have to write code to cope with the resizing of a form. If a user maximizes a form at run time, the controls will stay in their original position relative to the top left corner of a form. This means that if you have a set of command buttons—for example, **OK** and **Cancel**—positioned either in the top right corner of a form or across the bottom of a form, you need to write your own code to reposition these controls. In Visual Basic .NET, this type of functionality is built into the controls and form classes.

- **Anchor** property

  In Visual Basic .NET, you can anchor a control to the top, bottom, left, or right side of a form (or any combination). This means that at design time you can use the Properties window to anchor a control, and you no longer need to write repositioning code in the **Resize** event of a form.

- Resizing

  Because you can anchor any or all of the sides of a control, you can effectively resize a control to correspond to the resizing of a form. If you have a form containing a picture box that you want to fill the form, you can anchor it to all sides, and it will remain the same distance from the edges of the form at all times. This feature cannot override the size restrictions applied to some of the Visual Basic .NET controls, such as the height of a combo box.

- **Location** property

  This property allows you to specify the location of a control with respect to the top left corner of its container. The property takes a **Point** data type, which represents an x and y coordinate pair. This property replaces the Top and Left properties used in Visual Basic 6.

Text Property

In earlier versions of Visual Basic, you used different methods to set the text displayed in the various controls. For instance, **Forms** and **Label** controls have a **Caption** property, whereas **TextBox** controls have a **Text** property. In Visual Basic .NET, any textual property of a control is determined by the **Text** property. This provides consistency within Visual Basic, and with the other .NET-compatible languages.

The following example shows how to initialize a **Button** control in the **Form_Load** or **InitializeComponent** procedures.

```
Button1.Top = 20
Button1.Height = 50
Button1.Left = 20
Button1.Width = 120
Button1.Text = "Click Me"
```

Using Control Methods

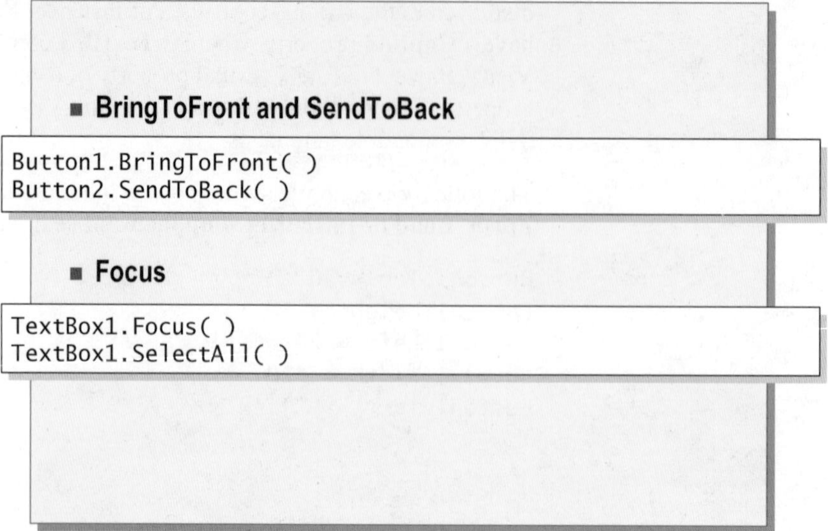
BringToFront and SendToBack
Button1.BringToFront( )
Button2.SendToBack( )
Focus
TextBox1.Focus( )
TextBox1.SelectAll( )

Many of the Windows Forms controls share some new common methods because they inherit from the same base classes.

BringToFront and SendToBack

You can use the **BringToFront** method of a control to place it in front of other controls, and the **SendToBack** method to place it behind all other controls. In earlier versions of Visual Basic, you can achieve this functionality by setting the **ZOrder** property of a control. The following example shows how to rearrange the order of controls at run time:

```
Button1.BringToFront( )
Button2.SendToBack( )
```

Focus

You can use this method to set the focus to a specific control. It is similar to the **SetFocus** method used in Visual Basic 6.0. The following example shows how to check the **Text** property of a **TextBox** control and return focus to the control if the text is not valid:

```
If TextBox1.Text <> "password" Then
  MessageBox.Show("Incorrect password")
  TextBox1.Focus( )
  TextBox1.SelectAll( )
End If
```

When trapping focus events, you should use the Enter and Leave events, rather than the GotFocus and LostFocus events.

Creating Menus

- **Menu classes**
- **Creating menus at design time**
  - Use the Menu Designer
- **Creating menus at run time**

```
Dim mnuMain As New MainMenu( )
Dim mnuItem1 As New MenuItem, mnuItem2 As New MenuItem( )
mnuItem1.Text = "File"
mnuMain.MenuItems.Add(mnuItem1)
mnuItem2.Text = "Exit"
mnuMain.MenuItems(0).MenuItems.Add(mnuItem2)
AddHandler mnuItem2.Click, AddressOf NewExitHandler
Menu = mnuMain
```

In Visual Basic .NET, the process of creating menus is very different from that of Visual Basic 6.0. You can have more than one menu system per form, which reduces the complexity of creating dynamic menus, and you can create **ContextMenus** directly without designing them as top-level menus first.

Menu Classes

There are three main classes that you will use when creating menus:

- **MainMenu**

  You use the **MainMenu** class to create a standard Windows menu bar at the top of a form.

- **ContextMenu**

  You use the **ContextMenu** class to define pop-up menus associated with particular controls.

- **MenuItem**

  You use the **MenuItem** class to define menu items within a **MainMenu** or a **ContextMenu**.

Creating Menus at Design Time

You can use the Menu Designer to create your menus at design time, which is something you cannot do in Visual Basic 6.0. You can also design and edit your menus in-place, rather than in a separate dialog box.

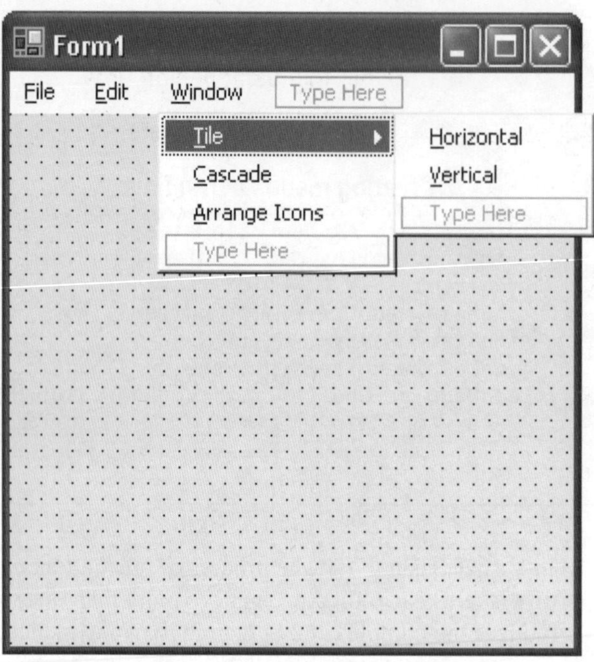

Creating Menus at Run Time

You can add or edit menus at run time by using the **MainMenu**, **ContextMenu**, and **MenuItem** classes. Each of these classes contains a **MenuItems** collection that has **Add** and **Remove** methods. The following example shows how to dynamically create menus:

```
Dim mnuMain As New MainMenu( )
Dim mnuItem1 As New MenuItem( )
Dim mnuItem2 As New MenuItem( )

mnuItem1.Text = "File"
mnuMain.MenuItems.Add(mnuItem1)

mnuItem2.Text = "Exit"
mnuMain.MenuItems(0).MenuItems.Add(mnuItem2)
AddHandler mnuItem2.Click, AddressOf NewExitHandler

Menu = mnuMain
```

Providing User Help

- **ErrorProvider control**
  - Error icon appears next to control, and message appears like a ToolTip when mouse pauses over icon
  - Used mainly for data binding
- **HelpProvider control**
  - Points to .chm, .hlp, or .html Help file
  - Controls provide Help information by means of **HelpString** or **HelpTopic** properties

Visual Basic .NET allows you to create user Help in a number of ways by using controls. Each of these controls is placed in the component tray for an individual form.

ErrorProvider Control

The **ErrorProvider** control indicates to the user that a control has an error associated with it by displaying a small icon near the control. When the user pauses the mouse over the icon, a ToolTip showing the error message appears. **ErrorProvider** can also be used with bound data.

You can set your own error messages manually, as shown in the following example, or when working with bound data, you set the **DataSource** property of the **ErrorProvider** to automatically pick error messages up from the database.

```
Public Sub TextBox1_Validating(ByVal sender As Object, _
  ByVal e As System.ComponentModel.CancelEventArgs) Handles
TextBox1.Validating

    If TextBox1.Text = "" Then
        ErrorProvider1.SetError(TextBox1, _
          "Please enter a value for the text box")
    Else
        ErrorProvider1.SetError(TextBox1, "")
    End If
End Sub
```

The **Validating** event is raised whenever the next control receives focus, providing that the next control has **CausesValidation** property set to **True**, allowing the **Text** property of the control to be tested. If this property contains an empty string, the **ErrorProvider** will display an exclamation icon next to the control and update the ToolTip for the error. If the error message is an empty string, the icon does not appear.

HelpProvider Control

You can use the **HelpProvider** control to display a simple pop-up Help window or online Help from a Help file specified by the **HelpProvider.HelpNamespace** property. This Help is automatically activated when the user presses the F1 Help key while a control has focus.

Implementing Pop-up Help

You can specify pop-up Help at design time by using the **HelpString** property in the Properties window for each control. Each control can have more than one **HelpString** property if the form has more than one **HelpProvider** control, if you use the format *HelpString on HelpProviderControlName*. You can also set the Help string programmatically by using the **SetHelpString** method of the **HelpProvider** control, passing in the control reference and the Help string.

Implementing Online Help

If you specify a Help file, each control can specify the relevant Help topic with the **HelpTopic** property. As for the **HelpString** property, each control can have more than one **HelpTopic** property if the form has more than one **HelpProvider** control, if you use the format *HelpTopic on HelpProviderControlName*. The Help topic can also be set programmatically by using the **SetTopicString** method of the **HelpProvider** control, passing in the control reference and the Help topic string.

Using SetShowHelp

You can also turn Help on or off for an individual control by using the **SetShowHelp** method of the **HelpProvider** control as shown in this example:

```
Sub SetTextboxHelp( )
    HelpProvider1.SetHelpString(TextBox1, "This is my help")
    HelpProvider1.SetShowHelp(TextBox1, True) 'True = On
End Sub
```

Demonstration: Using Controls

In this demonstration, you will learn how to use the layout properties of a **Button** control. You will also learn how to handle control events from multiple controls in one event handler. Finally, you will learn how to provide simple user assistance with the **HelpProvider** and **ToolTip** controls, and how to programmatically create a context menu.

Implementing Drag-and-Drop Functionality

- **Starting the process**
  - Use the **DoDragDrop** method in the **MouseDown** event of the originating control
- **Changing the drag icon**
  - Set the **AllowDrop** property of the receiving control to **True**
  - Set the **Effect** property of the **DragEventsArg** in the **DragOver** event of the receiving control
- **Dropping the data**
  - Use the **Data.GetData** method to access the data

Drag-and-drop techniques in Visual Basic .NET are significantly different from those of previous versions of Visual Basic.

Starting the Process

You can use the **DoDragDrop** method of a control to initiate the dragging and to halt the execution of code until the item is dropped. This method takes two parameters: *data*, which defines the information that is to be dropped, and *allowedEffects* which defines which operations are valid, such as Copy, Move, Link and so on.

The following example shows how to use the **DoDragDrop** method to begin the dragging process:

```
Private Sub TextBox1_MouseDown(ByVal sender As System.Object,
ByVal e As MouseEventArgs) Handles TextBox1.MouseDown
  Dim DragDropResult As DragDropEffects
  If e.Button = MouseButtons.Left Then
      DragDropResult = TextBox1.DoDragDrop(TextBox1.Text, _
      DragDropEffects.All)
      If DragDropResult = DragDropEffects.Move Then
          TextBox1.Text = ""
      End If
  End If
End Sub
```

Changing the Drag Icon

For a control to receive drag-drop notifications, you must set its **AllowDrop** property to **True**. Without this setting, the **DragDrop**, **DragOver**, **DragEnter**, and **DragLeave** events will not execute.

You can use the **KeyState** property of the **DragEventsArg** argument passed to controls in the **DragOver** event of a control to change the drag icon to an appropriate symbol. This helps the user to know what action they are about to perform. This property is an integer property that specifies which keys (such as SHIFT and CONTROL) are being held down during the drag process.

The following example shows how to set the appropriate icon:

```
Private Sub TextBox2_DragOver(ByVal sender As Object, ByVal e
As DragEventArgs) Handles TextBox2.DragOver
  Select Case e.KeyState
      Case 1
          'No key pressed
          e.Effect = DragDropEffects.Move
      Case 9
          'CONTROL key pressed
          e.Effect = DragDropEffects.Copy
      Case Else
          e.Effect = DragDropEffects.None
  End Select
End Sub
```

Dropping the Data

You can drop the data in the **DragDrop** event of the receiving control. The following example shows how to write code to accept textual data from another **TextBox** control:

```
Public Sub TextBox2_DragDrop(ByVal sender As Object, ByVal e
As DragEventArgs) Handles TextBox2.DragDrop
  TextBox2.Text = e.Data.GetData(DataFormats.Text).ToString
End Sub
```

Demonstration: Implementing Drag-and-Drop Functionality

In this demonstration, you will learn how to use drag-and-drop operations within a simple application.

◆ Windows Forms Inheritance

- Why Inherit from a Form?
- Creating the Base Form
- Creating the Inherited Form
- Modifying the Base Form

Visual Basic .NET introduces the concept of visual inheritance to Visual Basic developers. This type of inheritance can improve code reuse in your applications and provide them with a standard appearance and behavior.

After you complete this lesson, you will be able to use visual inheritance to:

- Create a form that inherits from a given base form.
- Modify a base form from which other forms have inherited.

Why Inherit from a Form?

- A form is a class, so it can use inheritance
- Applications will have a standard appearance and behavior
- Changes to the base form will be applied to derived forms
- Common examples:
  - Wizard forms
  - Logon forms

You will likely need to create forms that are similar to forms you have created before. In previous versions of Visual Basic, you can create templates on which to base your forms. In Visual Basic .NET, you can inherit from existing forms.

Inheriting from a form is as simple as deriving one class from another, because a form is simply a class with an extra visual component. This technique allows you to define a base form that can be derived from in order to create a standard appearance and behavior of your applications. It also shares the same benefits as class inheritance, in that code can be reused from the base form in all of the derived forms.

Any changes that you make to the base form can be applied to any of the derived forms, making simple updates to multiple forms easy.

You can use visual inheritance whenever forms behave in a similar way or need to have a standard appearance. Common examples of these types of forms are wizards and logon forms.

Creating the Base Form

1. **Carefully plan the base form**
2. **Create the base form as for a normal form**
3. **Set the access modifiers property of controls**
   - Private – Control can only be modified in the base form
   - Protected – Control can be modified by deriving form
   - Public – Control can be modified by any code module
   - Friend – Control can be modified within the base form project
4. **Add the Overridable keyword to appropriate methods**
5. **Build the solution for the base form**

The base form serves as the template for your standard form. You design and code the form in the usual way, to perform whatever functionality you want to be inherited. After you have created the base form, you can build your solution to make the form accessible, and then inherit from it.

When creating a base form, use the following process:

1. Carefully plan the base form.

   Changes are easier to make before any forms inherit from your base form because making changes afterwards will require extra retesting.

2. Create the base form as you would a normal form.

   Create the base form using the same techniques you would use to create a normal form.

3. Set the access modifiers property of controls.

   - Private controls cannot have their properties modified outside of the base form.
   - Public controls can have their properties modified by any form or code module without restriction.
   - Protected controls can have their properties modified by the deriving form.
   - Friend controls can have their properties modified within the base form project.

4. Add the **Overridable** keyword to appropriate methods.

   Any method that can be overridden in a derived form must be marked as overridable in the base form.

5. Build the solution for the base form.

   You cannot create a form that inherits from a base form until the base form has been built.

Creating the Inherited Form

- Ensure that the base form is as complete as possible
- Reference the assembly
- Create a new Inherited Form item
- Change control properties where necessary
- Override methods or events as required

After you have designed your base form and built the solution, you are ready to begin deriving forms. To do this, you simply add a new item to the project by clicking **Inherited Form** in the **Add New Item** window. This will run the Inheritance Picker for you.

When inheriting from a base Windows Form, consider the following guidelines carefully:

- Ensure that the base form is as complete as possible.

  Make any last minute changes to the base form before inheriting from it.
- Reference the assembly.

  If the base form is not in the same project, you must make a reference to the appropriate assembly.
- Create a new Inherited Form item.

  Add a new Inherited Form item to your project, selecting the base form in the **Inheritance Picker** dialog box. A list of available base forms is shown, and you can browse for other assemblies.
- Change control properties where necessary.

  You can programmatically change public and protected controls, and you can use the Properties window of the Windows Forms Designer for a derived form. Private and Friend controls cannot be altered outside of the base form project.
- Override methods or events as required.

  If methods or event handlers have been marked as overridable, you can implement your own code in the derived form.

Modifying the Base Form

- **Changing the base form**
  - Changes affect derived forms when rebuilt
- **Checking derived forms**
  - Verify changes before rebuilding application
  - Retest after rebuilding application

The derived form is linked directly to the base form; it is not a copy of the base form. This means that changes you make to the base form will be reflected in the derived form when the project is rebuilt. You can quickly update a series of forms that contain the same code or visual elements by making the changes in the base form. However, you may find that changes that are valid in the base form can introduce errors into the derived forms.

For example, any overridden method that calls a method on the **MyBase** object may expect a certain behavior, and careful retesting is needed to validate this expectation. This is true of all types of inheritance, not just visual inheritance.

Demonstration: Using Windows Forms Inheritance

In this demonstration, you will learn how to create a base form specifically for inheritance purposes. You will learn how to inherit from the form and how to override properties and methods of the base form controls. Finally, you will learn how to modify the base form after it has been used for inheritance and learn the effects the base form modifications have on the derived form.

Lab 6.1: Creating the Customer Form

Objectives

After completing this lab, you will be able to:

- Use Windows Forms in an application.
- Use the layout properties of controls.
- Create menus.
- Provide user assistance by means of ToolTips.

Prerequisites

Before working on this lab, you must have designed forms in previous versions of Visual Basic.

Scenario

In this lab, you will continue working with the Cargo system. The **Customer** class from Lab 5.1 of Course 2373B, *Programming with Microsoft Visual Basic .NET,* has been enhanced for you, and a **CustomerList** class has been provided so you can iterate through the customers. The basic Customer form has been provided for you, but it requires further development.

Starter and Solution Files

There are starter and solution files associated with this lab. The starter files are in the *install folder*\Labs\Lab061\Starter folder, and the solution files are in the *install folder*\Labs\Lab061\Solution folder.

Estimated time to complete this lab: 45 minutes

Exercise 1
Extending the Customer Form

In this exercise, you will enhance the existing Customer form by using the layout properties of the controls and form. The form is currently only intended to retrieve customer information.

▶ To open the starter project

1. Open Microsoft Visual Studio .NET.
2. On the **File** menu, point to **Open**, and click **Project**. Set the folder location to *install folder*\Labs\Lab061\Starter, click **Lab061.sln**, and then click **Open**.

▶ To view the frmCustomer form

1. Open the frmCustomer.vb design window, and examine the layout of the controls.
2. Open the frmCustomer.vb code window, and examine the existing code.

▶ To test the application

1. Locate the **Sub New** procedure in frmCustomer.vb, and set a breakpoint on the following line by using the F9 key:

   ```
   custList = New CustomersList( )
   ```

2. On the **Debug** menu, click **Start**.
3. Step through the code by using the F11 key (to step into procedures) and the F10 key (to step over procedures) until you understand how the application loads the customer information into the list. Press F5 to resume execution.
4. Click different customers in the list, and observe the resulting behavior.
5. Click **Close** to quit the application, and remove the breakpoint from the **Sub New** procedure.

▶ To set the layout properties of the controls

1. Open the frmCustomer.vb design window, and set the **Anchor** properties of the following controls to the following values in the Properties window.

Control	Anchor value
lstCustomers	**Top, Bottom, Left**
txtID	**Top, Left, Right**
txtEmail	**Top, Left, Right**
txtTitle	**Top, Left, Right**
txtFName	**Top, Left, Right**
txtLName	**Top, Left, Right**
txtAddress	**Top, Left, Right**
txtCompany	**Top, Left, Right**
btnClose	**Bottom, Right**

2. Set the following properties for the form and controls in the Properties window.

Object	Property	Value
txtAddress	**Multiline**	**True**
txtAddress	**AcceptsReturn**	**True**
txtAddress	**Size.Height**	**60**
frmCustomer	**CancelButton**	**btnClose**

3. Open the frmCustomer.vb code window.
4. Add the following line immediately before the end of the **Sub New** procedure:

```
Me.MinimumSize = Me.Size
```

▶ To test the project

1. Run the project.
2. Resize the form to confirm that all controls are anchored correctly and that the **MinimumSize** property limits the form size so that all controls are visible.
3. Click the **Close** button to quit the application.

Exercise 2
Adding a Menu and ToolTips

In this exercise, you will add a menu and ToolTips to the frmCustomer form.

▶ **To add a menu**

1. Open the frmCustomer.vb design window.
2. Using the Toolbox, add a **MainMenu** control, renaming it **mnuMain**.
3. Using the Menu Designer, add menu items as shown in the following illustration.

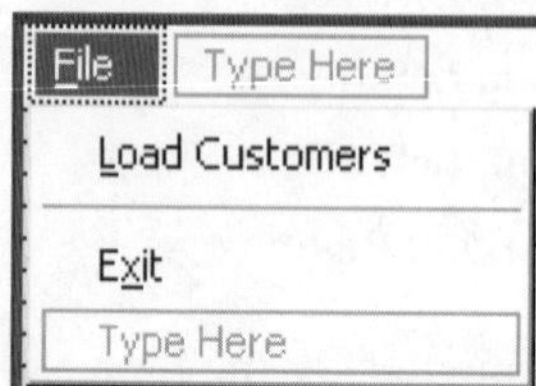

4. Use the following table to name the menu items.

Caption	Name
&File	**mnuFile**
&Load Customers	**mnuFileLoad**
-	**mnuFileSeparator**
E&xit	**mnuFileExit**

5. Create the **Click** event handler for the mnuFileLoad menu item.

6. From the **Sub New** procedure, cut the existing code for loading customers, and paste it into the new event handler (making sure to leave the **MinimumSize** code that was added in the previous exercise as it is). Your code should now look as follows:

```
Public Sub New( )
    MyBase.New( )

    'This call is required by the Windows Forms Designer.
    InitializeComponent( )

    'Add any initialization after the InitializeComponent()
call

    Me.MinimumSize = Me.Size
End Sub

Private Sub mnuFileLoad_Click(ByVal sender As _
System.Object, ByVal e As System.EventArgs) Handles _
mnuFileLoad.Click
   'create the customerlist object
   custList = New CustomersList( )

   'load the customers
   custList.LoadCustomers( )

   'populate the list box with customers
   PopulateListBox( )
   LoadCustomer(0)
End Sub
```

7. Locate the existing **btnClose_Click** event handler, and rename the procedure **CloseForm**, leaving the arguments unchanged, and adding the following statement after the existing **Handles** clause. This allows both events to be handled by the same procedure.

```
, mnuFileExit.Click
```

8. Save the project.

▶ To add ToolTip user assistance

1. Open the frmCustomer.vb design window.
2. Using the Toolbox, add a **ToolTip** control, renaming it **ttCustomerList**.
3. Using the Properties window, set the **ToolTip** property for lstCustomers to "Select a customer to display the full details."

▶ To test the application

1. On the **Debug** menu, click **Start**.
2. On the **File** menu, click **Load Customers**.
3. Rest the mouse pointer on the **Customer** list to confirm that the ToolTip appears.
4. On the **File** menu, click **Exit** to quit the application.

Exercise 3
Adding a Shortcut Menu

In this exercise, you will programmatically add a shortcut menu for the customer **ListBox** control.

▶ To create the context menu

1. Open the frmCustomer.vb code window, and locate the **Sub New** procedure.
2. After the call to the **InitializeComponent** procedure, declare a **ContextMenu** variable called *cmListBox*, and a **MenuItem** variable called *mItem*.
3. Instantiate the *cmListBox* context menu object by using the default **New** constructor.
4. Add a menu item to the context menu, as shown in the following code:
   ```
   mItem = cmListBox.MenuItems.Add("&Delete")
   ```
5. Disable this menu item until there are entries in the list box, as shown in the following code:
   ```
   mItem.Enabled = False
   ```
6. Add an event handler for the new *mItem* object by using the **AddHandler** function, as shown in the following code:
   ```
   AddHandler mItem.Click, AddressOf onDeleteClick
   ```
7. Assign the new context menu to the **ContextMenu** property of the lstCustomers control, as shown in the following code:
   ```
   lstCustomers.ContextMenu = cmListBox
   ```
8. Before the **Catch** statement in the **LoadCustomer** procedure, enable the context menu as shown in the following code:
   ```
   lstCustomers.ContextMenu.MenuItems(0).Enabled = True
   ```

▶ To create the event handler for the context menu item

1. At the end of the form definition, create a new private subroutine called **onDeleteClick** that accepts the following arguments:
   ```
   ByVal sender As Object, ByVal e As System.EventArgs
   ```
2. Display a message box with the following options specified.

Argument	Value
Text	"Are you sure you want to delete " & lstCustomers.SelectedItem
Caption	Confirm
Buttons	MessageBoxButtons.YesNo
Icon	MessageBoxIcon.Question

3. Use an **If** statement to test the result of the **MessageBox.Show** method against the value **DialogResult.Yes**. In the **True** section, enter the following code:

```
custList.RemoveAt(lstCustomers.SelectedIndex)
PopulateListBox( )
```

4. Insert an **If** statement into the procedure to test to see whether the number of items in lstCustomers is zero. (Hint: Use the **lstCustomers.Items.Count** property).
5. In the **True** section, disable the **Delete** menu item.
6. Save the project.

▶ To test the application

1. On the **Debug** menu, click **Start**.
2. On the **File** menu, click **Load Customers**.
3. Select, and then right-click a customer, and click **Delete**.
4. When the confirmation message appears, click **Yes**.
5. On the **File** menu, click **Exit** to quit the application.
6. Close and exit Visual Studio .NET.

If Time Permits
Creating an About Box Form Using Visual Inheritance

In this optional exercise, you will create an About box form by inheriting from an existing base form.

► **To review and build the base form project**

1. Open Visual Studio .NET.
2. On the **File** menu, point to **Open**, and then click **Project**. Set the folder location to *install folder*\Labs\Lab061\Starter\AboutForm, click **AboutForm.sln**, and then click **Open**.
3. Open the frmBase.vb design window, and examine the controls and their properties, taking particular note of the **Modifiers** property of the controls.
4. Open the frmBase.vb code window, and examine the existing code.
5. On the **Build** menu, click **Build Solution**.
6. On the **File** menu, click **Close Solution**.

► **To inherit the base form**

1. Open your solution to the previous exercise.
2. On the **Project** menu, click **Add Inherited Form**, rename the file **frmAbout.vb**, and then click **Open**.
3. In the **Inheritance Picker** dialog box, click **Browse**. Navigate to *install folder*\Labs\Lab061\Starter\AboutForm\bin, click **AboutForm.dll**, and then click **Open**. Click **frmBase**, and then click **OK**.
4. Open the frmAbout.vb design window.
5. Change the **Text** property of the lblProductName control to **Cargo**.

   Note that you cannot change the properties of the other controls because their **Modifiers** property is set to **Friend**.

► **To display the About box form**

1. Open the frmCustomer.vb design window.
2. Add the following menus to the mnuMain control.

Caption	Name
&Help	**mnuHelp**
&About…	**mnuHelpAbout**

3. Create the **Click** event handler for the mnuHelpAbout menu item, and add the following code:

   ```
   Dim aboutForm As New frmAbout( )
   aboutForm.ShowDialog( )
   ```

4. Save the project.

► **To test the About box form**

1. On the **Debug** menu, click **Start**.
2. On the **Help** menu, click **About**.
3. Click **OK** to close the **About Form** dialog box.
4. Click **Close** to quit the application.
5. Close Visual Studio .NET.

Review

- Why Use Windows Forms?
- Structure of Windows Forms
- Using Windows Forms
- Using Controls
- Windows Forms Inheritance

1. Identify some of the benefits of Windows Forms.

2. The **ContainerControl** class is the fundamental base class for all other controls. True or false?

3. Write the code to access the path from which an executable is running.

4. Describe an owned form.

5. Write code to make the code behind a button called btnOK execute when a user presses RETURN.

6. List two ways to provide Help to the user.

7. Write code to create a Help menu with one menu item—**About**— at run time.

msdn® training

Module 7: Building Web Applications

Contents

Overview

- Introduction to ASP.NET
- Creating Web Form Applications
- Building Web Services
- Using Web Services

Using Microsoft® Visual Basic® .NET and ASP.NET, you can create a new generation of dynamic, powerful Web applications.

After completing this module, you will be able to:

- Explain and take advantage of the benefits of ASP.NET and its various libraries in application development.
- Create Web Form applications.
- Use HTML server controls and Web server controls.
- Create Web Services.
- Use Web Services from a browser or from another client application.

◆ Introduction to ASP.NET

- Overview of ASP.NET
- Using Response and Request Objects
- Maintaining Client-Side State
- Maintaining Server-Side State
- Managing an ASP.NET Application
- Overview of ASP.NET Security
- Using Global Events with Global.asax

ASP.NET introduces many improvements upon traditional approaches to Web development. Its extensive framework of classes enables you to rapidly create powerful, scalable, manageable, and secure Internet applications.

After you complete this lesson, you will be able to:

- Describe the advantages that ASP.NET provides over its predecessor, Active Server Pages (ASP).
- Use two important ASP.NET objects: **Request** and **Response**.
- Use the various client-side and server-side state facilities that are available in ASP.NET applications.
- Explain basic concepts in managing and securing ASP.NET applications.
- Use the Global.asax application file for global events.

Overview of ASP.NET

- **Code behind development**
  - Intuitive approach to development similar to Windows Forms
- **Code can be compiled using any .NET-compatible language**
  - Significant performance improvement
- **ASP.NET pages run side-by-side with ASP pages**
  - Files with the .aspx extension run side-by-side with current ASP applications on IIS
- **Automatic support for multiple browsers**
  - Rich DHTML, HTML 3.2, and small devices
- **ASP.NET namespaces provide rich functionality**
- **Built-in support for Web Services**

For several years, Web developers have used ASP to produce Internet applications containing dynamic content. ASP.NET is the evolution of this technology, and it provides many benefits to Web developers:

- Code-behind support

  ASP.NET uses an event-driven programming model familiar to Visual Basic and ASP developers. Web Forms use the drag-and-drop style of page creation. You can modify code behind the controls on Web Forms in the same way that you do on Visual Basic forms. This code resides in a separate file to separate the content from the code.

- Code can be compiled from any Microsoft .NET-compatible language

  You can create your ASP.NET applications by using any of the .NET compatible languages, including Visual Basic .NET, C#, and Microsoft JScript®. While ASP contains scripts that are interpreted when you execute a page, ASP.NET code is compiled rather than interpreted. This allows early binding, strong typing, and just-in-time (JIT) compilation to native code. These factors greatly improve the performance of ASP.NET applications, particularly when you have an increased number of clients.

- ASP.NET pages run side-by-side with ASP pages

  ASP.NET uses the .aspx file extension to allow ASP.NET pages to run side-by-side with existing ASP pages on Internet Information Services (IIS). The ASP.NET runtime will only process files with .aspx extensions; .asp files will be processed with the original ASP engine. You can easily migrate existing .asp files to .aspx files without making many changes to the code.

- Automatic support for multiple browsers

  ASP.NET applications have the ability to render information differently to suit the capabilities of different browsers. You can create your application in the same way for both a simple browser that only supports HTML 3.2 and for an enhanced browser that supports dynamic HTML (DHTML), such as Microsoft Internet Explorer 4.0. You can even use Visual Basic .NET to create Web applications that will run on small devices such as Handheld PCs because of the ability of the ASP.NET Web server controls to render themselves appropriately for each client browser.

- ASP.NET namespaces provide rich functionality

  The ASP.NET framework provides several namespaces that allow you to use powerful built-in features, such as the ability to communicate between browser and server, to increase application performance by caching information, and to fully secure a Web site. The framework provides Web Service capabilities to allow access to your system services, and provides many predefined controls for use on Web Forms.

- Built-in support for Web Services

  ASP.NET includes built-in support for Web Services, enabling developers to build loosely coupled applications that use Simple Object Access Protocol (SOAP) for application-to-application communication.

Using Response and Request Objects

- The System.Web namespace provides common Web functionality
- Requesting information from the client
  - **Request** object

```
Dim strValue As String = Request.Form("txtInput")
```

- Sending information to the client
  - **Response** object

```
Response.Write("<H2>The date is: " & Now.Date & "</H2>")
```

You can use the **System.Web** namespace to access many of the classes that provide the base functionality of ASP.NET applications. Many of these classes are similar to those used by developers in ASP applications and have been enhanced in ASP.NET.

You can use the **Response** and **Request** objects, provided by the **System.Web** namespace, to communicate between the client browser and the server computer. Both of these objects provide new properties and methods for their equivalent objects in ASP.

Requesting Information from the Client Browser

You can request information such as query string, cookie, and form values from a client browser by using the **HttpRequest** class. An instance of this class is available by means of the **Request** property of the current Web Form.

The following example shows how to request the value currently stored in a text box on a Web Form:

```
Dim strValue As String = Request.Form("txtInput")
```

Sending Information to the Client Browser

You can send information such as cookie values, HTML output, and browser redirection to the client browser by using the **HttpResponse** class. An instance of this class is available by means of the **Response** property of the current Web Form.

The following example uses the **Response** object to display the current date:

```
Response.Write("<H2>The date is: " & Now.Date & "</H2>")
```

Maintaining Client-Side State

- **Maintaining control state across multiple requests**
  - Set **EnableViewState** property of control
  - Use the **StateBag** class to store extra data

```
ViewState("TempData") = 25
```

  - Send data to client as hidden string

```
<input type="hidden" name="__VIEWSTATE" value="dO…NnU=" />
```

- **Using cookies for enhanced client-side state**

```
Response.Cookies("User_FullName").Value = strFullName
…
strFullName = Request.Cookies("User_FullName").Value
```

Web pages are generally regarded as *stateless* devices, meaning that they do not remember any values between being displayed, destroyed, and displayed again. However, in ASP.NET you can choose to maintain state for a Web page when you need to. You can do this by using view state at the page and control level.

Maintaining Control State

Web pages are re-created each time a client browser makes a request. Normally this means that all control state is reset with each request. However, you can save the state of a page and its content by using the view state property or the **StateBag** class. Both approaches use a hidden variable to store the information as part of the page that is sent to the browser. This information is then retrieved when the page is posted back to the server.

Using View State

The **System.Web.UI.Control** class implements a property named **EnableViewState**. You can set this property to achieve the following functionality:

- **True**

  If you set this property to **True** (the default), any control that inherits from this base class will maintain its view state and the view state of any constituent control, through multiple requests by a single client browser.

- **False**

  If a page does not post back to itself, you can set this property to **False** to increase performance by reducing the size of the page.

Using State Bags

You can use the **StateBag** class to maintain additional cross-request information. An instance called **ViewState** is accessible from each Web Form and allows you to store and retrieve extra information.

The following example shows how to create a stateful property (a value that is maintained for multiple requests) called **TempData** and assign a value of 25. You can then retrieve this data from the **StateBag** instance and display it to the user by using the **Response.Write** method.

```
ViewState("TempData") = 25

Response.Write(ViewState("TempData"))
```

When the page is sent to the browser, a hidden variable is included, as shown in the following example:

```
<input type="hidden" name="__VIEWSTATE" value="dO...NnU=" />
```

Using Cookies for Enhanced Client-Side State

A *cookie* is a simple mechanism for storing information in a text file on a client computer. You can use the **HttpCookie** class to provide a type-safe way to access cookies and manipulate cookie properties such as **Expires**, **Value**, and **Name**. Read and write access to a cookie is provided by means of the **Cookies** collection property for the **Request** and **Response** objects, respectively.

The following example stores a cookie with an expiration date on the client computer before reading the data back from the client:

```
Response.Cookies("User_FullName").Value = strFullName
Response.Cookies("User_FullName").Expires = _
                                Now.AddMonths(1)
...
If Not (Request.Cookies("User_FullName") Is Nothing) Then
    strFullName = Request.Cookies("User_FullName").Value
End If
```

Maintaining Server-Side State

- **Application object maintains application-level state**
  - Data for use by all users

```
Application("App_StartTime") = Now
```

- **Session object maintains session-level state**
  - Data for use by a single client browser
  - Data recoverable by means of Windows Service or SQL Server database

```
Session("Session_StartTime") = Now
```

Some parts of your Web application may need to maintain cross-request state. For example, a shopping cart application may need to maintain information about a customer order through multiple visits to a page before the items are purchased. You can maintain state at either the application or session level.

Maintaining Application State

You can use the **HttpApplicationState** class to store application-level information. You can use the intrinsic **Application** object during a Web request to share global data across the application. The default **Item** property of this object stores and retrieves a collection of objects, allowing anything from a string to a user-defined object to be maintained for the lifespan of the application. Application state is not shared across a Web farm or a Web garden.

Note A *Web farm* is an application that is hosted across multiple computers. A *Web garden* is an application that is hosted on a single computer with multiple processors.

Example

The following example shows how to store the start time of the application and then displays the information at a later stage:

```
Application("App_StartTime") = Now
...
Response.Write("Application Started: " & _
  Application("App_StartTime"))
```

About Application State

Note the following information when using application state:

- The **Contents** collection property of the **HttpApplicationState** class provides backward compatibility with ASP.
- Multiple-user sessions within an ASP.NET application can potentially modify data, resulting in values that differ from those expected by a single user. The following example shows how you can use the **Lock** and **Unlock** methods to avoid this problem:

  ```
  Application.Lock
  Application("aCounter") = Application("aCounter") + 1
  Application.Unlock
  ```

Maintaining Session State

The server maintains session state information for each browser client as a logical "session" until the session ends. The session ends when a time out occurs or when the user moves away from the ASP.NET application.

Example

You can use the intrinsic **Session** object to access this state information. The following example shows how to use session state to store a start time that can be retrieved at a later stage during the user's session:

```
Session("Session_StartTime") = Now
...
Response.Write("Session started: " & _
  Session("Session_StartTime"))
```

About Session State

Note the following facts and guidelines when using session state in ASP.NET applications:

- ASP.NET session state maintains backward compatibility with ASP session state.
- You can store session state in three ways:
  - As part of the application process
  - As an external Microsoft Windows® Service, allowing for ASP.NET application restarts and data sharing across multiple processors (Web gardens)
  - As data in a Microsoft SQL Server™ database, allowing the session data to be available across multiple computers (Web farms)
- While ASP applications require a cookie to store a unique SessionID value that links a user to a particular session, ASP.NET does not require cookies in order to store session state. In the Web.config file, you can choose the option to automatically encode the SessionID value in the Uniform Resource Locator (URL). This means that all browsers can use session information even if the user has disabled cookie support.

Note For more information about configuring session state, search for "web.config" in the Microsoft Visual Studio® .NET documentation.

Managing an ASP.NET Application

- **Configuring ASP.NET applications**
  - XML configuration file – Web.config
  - Human-readable and writeable
  - Stored with the application
- **Deploying ASP.NET applications**
  - XCOPY the pages, components, and configuration
  - No registration required
- **Updating ASP.NET applications**
  - Copy new files over old files
  - No update utility, restart, or reboot required
  - Live update keeps applications running

ASP.NET applications are simple to configure, deploy, and maintain.

Configuring ASP.NET Applications

An ASP.NET application can contain web.config configuration files. These files store information about the application, including application settings, custom browser capabilities, custom errors, security, and more. The document format is Extensible Markup Language (XML), so you can use any text or XML editor to read or edit the file.

You deploy the configuration file to the same virtual directory as the application it configures. The file also configures any applications in subdirectories of that virtual directory, unless those applications have their own configuration file.

Note For more information about configuring ASP.NET applications, search for "ASP.NET configuration" in the Visual Studio .NET documentation.

Deploying ASP.NET Applications

You deploy an ASP.NET application by copying the required files to a virtual directory on an IIS computer. No component registration is required because the components contain their own self-describing metadata. This also solves registry problems previously associated with deploying components.

Note For more information about deployment of Visual Basic .NET-based applications, see Module 10, "Deploying Applications," in Course 2373B, *Programming with Microsoft Visual Basic .NET*.

Updating ASP.NET Applications

You can update an ASP.NET application at any time without needing to restart the application or IIS, because no components are locked at any stage. No update utility is required because you can simply copy new files over the old ones. The ASP.NET framework detects the update, and it upgrades the live application.

Overview of ASP.NET Security

- **Security settings stored in web.config file**
- **Out-of-box authentication support**
  - Windows authentication – Basic, Digest, or Integrated
  - Microsoft Passport authentication
  - Forms (Cookie) authentication
- **Role-based security architecture**

Most companies need to secure their Web applications so that users can only perform actions they are authorized to perform. The required levels of security can include simple public access to Web pages, secure validation of credit card information, and secure access for trading partners. The **System.Web.Security** namespace provides all aspects of ASP.NET security.

Security Settings Stored in web.config File

You can specify security settings in the web.config configuration file that is then deployed with the application. This allows you to define which security options your applications use and, optionally, which users can use the system.

Out-of-Box Authentication Support

ASP.NET works closely with IIS 5.0 to accept and validate user credentials by using the following authentication methods.

- Windows authentication.

  Windows authentication does not require any specific coding in your ASP.NET application, but it does require extra administration when the application is deployed. IIS provides three ways to perform Windows authentication: Basic, Digest, and Integrated.

Authentication	Definition
Basic	Before information without encryption is posted to IIS, a Windows dialog box appears in which users enter their user name and password.
Digest	Performs the same action as Basic authentication; however, the information is encrypted when sent to the server.
Integrated	Uses the user's logged-on Windows domain account details. This option is more suitable for an intranet application than for an Internet application because it cannot be used through firewalls or proxy servers.

The following example shows how to specify Windows authentication in the Web.config file:

```
<authentication mode="Windows" />
```

Note For more information about the different types of authentication, see *Designing Secure Web-Based Applications for Microsoft Windows 2000,* by Michael Howard, Microsoft Press®.

- Microsoft Passport authentication.

  Passport authentication requires the user to have a Microsoft Passport that can be created on the Internet. This approach benefits users because they use the same sign-in name and password for any Web site that uses this type of authentication.

  Note For more information about passports, go to http://www.passport.com/Business.

- Forms (Cookie) authentication.

  Web sites that require users to logon to the system from an HTML form usually store a cookie on the client computer. The cookie is used for subsequent visits to the site and the information can then be used for whatever purpose the site requires. This type of authentication is ideal for querying user details against a database in an e-commerce situation.

Role-Based Security Architecture

ASP.NET allows you to selectively allow or deny requests from specific users or groups of users known as *roles*. You can store the list of users and roles as part of the Web.config file or as a separate XML document.

The following example shows code to use in the Web.config file to allow access for two particular users and the Admins role but deny access to all others using Windows authentication:

```
<authentication mode="Windows" />
<authorization>
  <allow users="Doug,Denise" />
  <deny users="*" />
  <allow roles="Admins" />
  <deny roles="*" />
</authorization>
```

Note For more information about role-based security, see ASP.NET Authorization in the Visual Studio .NET documentation.

Using Global Events with Global.asax

- **Useful for initializing data for application or session state**

```
Sub Application_Start(ByVal Sender As Object, ByVal e As EventArgs)
  Application("SessionCounter") = 0
End Sub
Sub Session_Start(ByVal Sender As Object, ByVal e As EventArgs)
  Application("SessionCounter") = Application("SessionCounter") + 1
  Session("StartTime") = Now
End Sub
Sub Session_End(ByVal Sender As Object, ByVal e As EventArgs)
  Application("SessionCounter") = Application("SessionCounter") - 1
End Sub
```

You can initialize state for application-level or session-level data by using the Global.asax application file. This application file enhances the Global.asa application file used in ASP.

Avoid using local variables to store information, because ASP.NET may create multiple instances of the global class. If you need to store information, use application-state or session-state.

Application-Level Events

ASP.NET provides several events to initialize state at the application level, including the following:

- **Application_Start**

  This event is activated when the first user attempts to gain access to access your Web application. Any subsequent requests will not activate this event even if multiple instances of the Global class have been instantiated. This event is particularly useful for initializing application-state information.

- **Application_BeginRequest**

  This event is activated whenever a request for a URL is received from a client application.

- **Application_EndRequest**

  This event is activated whenever a request for a URL has been completed.

- **Application_End**

  This event is activated when the last instance of the Global class is destroyed so that any final resources can be cleaned up.

Session-Level Events

ASP.NET also provides session-level events, including the following:

- **Session_Start**

  This event is activated at the beginning of a new client session and is useful for initializing session-state information.

- **Session_End**

  This event is activated when a client session ends after a period of inactivity or if the **Session.Abandon** method is explicitly called as part of your application code.

Example

The following example shows how you could use these events in conjunction with state management objects to initialize stateful data:

```
Sub Application_Start(ByVal sender As Object, _
                              ByVal e As EventArgs)
    'Initialize the application-level counter
    Application("SessionCounter") = 0
End Sub

Sub Session_Start(ByVal sender As Object, _
                              ByVal e As EventArgs)
    'Increment the application-level counter
    Application("SessionCounter") = _
             Application("SessionCounter") + 1

    'Assign new value to session-level data
    Session("StartTime") = Now
End Sub

Sub Session_End(ByVal sender As Object, ByVal e As EventArgs)
    'Decrement the application-level counter
    Application("SessionCounter") = _
                    Application("SessionCounter") - 1
End Sub
```

◆ Creating Web Form Applications

- Structure of Web Forms
- Using HTML Controls
- Advantages of Web Server Controls
- Using Web Server Controls
- Handling Events

Traditionally, you create Web applications by using a combination of static HTML pages and dynamic content provided by client-side and server-side script. ASP.NET provides Web Forms to improve and enhance Web applications.

After you complete this lesson, you will be able to:

- Describe the files that constitute a Web Form.
- Use the different types of controls available on a Web Form, including HTML and Web server controls.
- Write code in event handlers that will execute on the server.

Structure of Web Forms

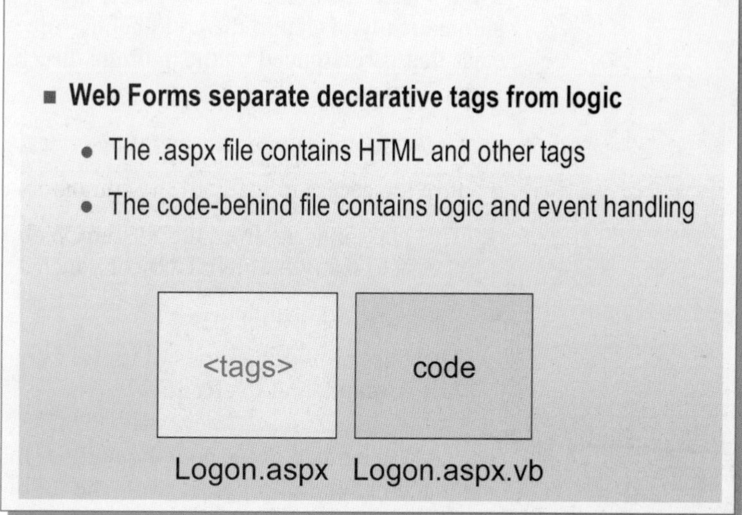

Web Forms separate declarative tags from logic
The .aspx file contains HTML and other tags
The code-behind file contains logic and event handling
<tags>
code
Logon.aspx
Logon.aspx.vb

Because ASP pages often contain HTML tags mixed with user interface event-handling script, they can be difficult to maintain. When developing applications with the Visual Studio .NET Integrated Development Environment (IDE), ASP.NET Web Forms consist of two separate files: the .aspx file for HTML and other tags, and the code-behind file for the code that executes as a result of user interaction. Because the tags and the code are separated in ASP.NET, you can more easily locate bugs and maintain code.

The .aspx File

The .aspx file contains definitions for the visual elements of the Web Form, such as the HTML tags, Web controls, client-side script, and static text. This file also includes any ASP.NET directives, such as links to the code-behind module that contains the logic and event-handling code of the Web Form.

You can use the Web Forms Designer in Design view to create a page by using drag-and-drop techniques. You can use the HTML view to edit the HTML tags. Microsoft IntelliSense® is provided in this view to increase the efficiency and accuracy of creating HTML tag expressions.

The Code-Behind File

The *code-behind file* is a file with an .aspx.vb extension in an ASP.NET project using Visual Basic.NET. Your server-side and event-handling code is automatically placed in the code-behind file of a Web Form. This file defines a class that is referenced by the @ **Page** directive within the .aspx file of the Web Form. You can use this class to:

- Create methods or event-handling code.
- Provide access to many of the commonly used ASP.NET objects.

  This class inherits from the **System.Web.UI.Page** class to provide direct access to many ASP.NET objects, such as **Request** and **Response**.
- Provide event handlers.

  The class provides a series of useful event handlers, such as the page **Load**, **Init**, **Unload**, and **PreRender** events.

The code generated in the code-behind file looks very similar to the code generated in Windows Forms. Note the following when using the code-behind file:

- It contains variable declarations.

  The code contains variable declarations for the visible controls so they can be accessed programmatically within your procedures.
- It contains variable events.

  As the control variables are declared using the **WithEvents** modifier, you can use the control events to execute user interface code to handle events like submitting information to a database or linking to another page.
- It automatically compiles with your application.

  The code in this file is automatically compiled into your dynamic-link library (DLL) when you build the application.

Using HTML Controls

- **Direct relationship to preexisting HTML tags**
  - Client side by default
  - Server side with `runat=server` directive
  - Properties correspond one-to-one with HTML, weakly typed
  - Defined with HTML tag

```
<input type=text id="text1" value="some text" runat="server">
```

- **ASP.NET includes HTML controls for commonly used HTML elements**

HTML controls have a direct relationship to preexisting HTML tags. The controls are defined by classes in the **System.Web.UI.HtmlControls** namespace supplied by the .NET Framework. These controls correspond very closely to the HTML elements that they render.

Specifying Client-Side or Server-Side HTML Controls

By default, HTML controls are run on the client. They are treated as opaque text by the server and passed straight through to the browser for interpreting as HTML elements. You can also write client-side script to process control events on the client.

To run controls on the server, set the **runat** directive to the value of **server** to convert the HTML elements to HTML server controls. You can do this manually by editing the HTML tag of the control, or you can select the option on the context menu of the control.

Manipulating HTML Controls

You define all HTML by using an HTML tag. For example, the following code declares a text input field to run on the server:

```
<input type=text id="text1" value="some text" runat="server">
```

You can manipulate control properties programmatically from server-side code when the control is marked to run on the server. These properties correspond directly to their equivalent HTML tag predecessors. For example, the HTML tag <INPUT> supports an attribute called *Value*, and the **HTMLInputText** class supports an equivalent **Value** property.

You can set other properties of the HTML control by using the **Attributes** collection property of the control. This type of property setting is considered weakly typed because the collection only stores and retrieves **String** values, as shown in the following example:

```
HTMLTable1.Attributes("bgColor") = "Green" 'Weakly typed
```

To specify the programmatic accessor that identifies the control in the server code, use the *ID* attribute. To set the initial display value of the text field, use the *VALUE* attribute.

HTML Elements and HTML Server Controls

ASP.NET includes HTML controls for commonly used HTML elements such as forms, input elements, tables, and so on. The following list matches the client-side HTML elements with their corresponding HTML server controls.

HTML element	HTML server control
<A>	**HTMLAnchor**
<IMG>	**HTMLImage**
<FORM>	**HTMLForm**
<TABLE>	**HTMLTable**
<TR>	**HTMLTableRow**
<TD>	**HTMLTableCell**
<SELECT>	**HTMLSelect**
<TEXTAREA>	**HTMLTextArea**
<BUTTON>	**HTMLButton**
<INPUT TYPE=TEXT>	**HTMLInputText**
< INPUT TYPE=FILE>	**HTMLInputFile**
< INPUT TYPE=SUBMIT>	**HTMLInputButton**
< INPUT TYPE=BUTTON>	**HTMLInputButton**
< INPUT TYPE=RESET>	**HTMLInputButton**
< INPUT TYPE=HIDDEN>	**HTMLInputHidden**

Advantages of Web Server Controls

- **Automatic browser detection**
  - Detect capabilities of client and render accordingly
- **Strongly typed, consistent object model**
  - Enables compile-time type checking
- **Declared with XML tags**
  - Server side only using `runat=server` directive

```
<asp:textbox id="text2" text="some text" runat="server">
</asp:textbox>
```

- **Rich functionality**
  - Example: **Calendar** or **RadioButtonList** control

In addition to HTML controls, ASP.NET Web Forms also provide Web server controls. Web server controls run exclusively on the server, and provide the following advantages:

- Automatic browser detection

  Web server controls can render themselves differently to suit the capabilities of different browsers. For example, a control may send dynamic HTML (DHTML) to a rich browser (HTML 4.0 and later), and send HTML and script to a more basic client browser. This is known as creating uplevel and downlevel capability.

- Strongly typed, consistent object model

  Web server controls are strongly typed, so compile-time checking of code provides you with accurate error messages before the application is built. With Web controls, you can use a consistent object model, which is similar to Windows Forms controls. For example, you can set the **BackColor** property of a **Button** control explicitly by using a strongly typed constant, as shown in the following example.

  ```
  Button.BackColor = Color.Green              'Strongly typed
  ```

- Declared with XML tags

  You declare Web server controls by using an XML tag. This tag references the **asp** namespace and specifies information regarding the type of Web control, a programmatic identifier through use of the *ID* attribute, and any initial values.

  The following example shows the syntax for creating a simple **TextBox** Web control whose *ID* is "text2" and whose initial *TEXT* value is "some text."

  ```
  <asp:TextBox id="text2" text="some text" runat="server">
  </asp:TextBox>
  ```

- Rich functionality

  Web server controls include enhanced versions of traditional HTML form controls such as **Button** and **TextBox**, as well as complex controls such as **Calendar**, **DataGrid**, and **AdRotator** (advertisement rotator). These controls do not correspond directly to HTML elements or attributes.

Using Web Server Controls

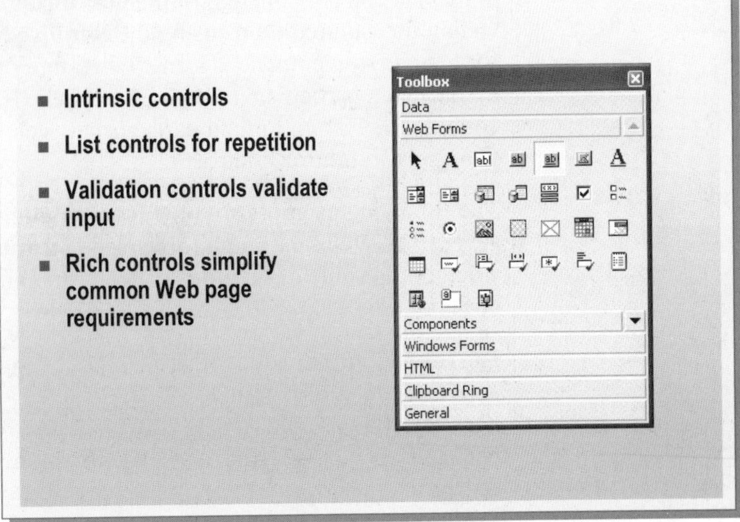
Intrinsic controls
List controls for repetition
Validation controls validate input
Rich controls simplify common Web page requirements
Toolbox
Data
Web Forms
Components
Windows Forms
HTML
Clipboard Ring
General

ASP.NET Web server controls can be separated into four main categories: intrinsic, list, validation, and rich controls. The table below explains each of these categories.

Category	Definition	Examples
Intrinsic controls	Provides the basic functionality for user interaction with the browser. Many of these controls are similar to the corresponding HTML controls, but their enhanced properties and methods allow a more powerful and consistent programming style.	**Button**, **TextBox**, **CheckBox**
List controls	Used for repetition when displaying any type of list.	**DropDownList, ListBox, Repeater**, **DataGrid**
Validation controls	Provides simple control validation that displays a message to the user without making a return trip to the server.	**RequiredFieldValidator, RangeValidator, RegularExpressionValidator**, **CompareValidator**
Rich controls	Simplifies common Web page requirements.	**AdRotator, Calendar**

Using Validation Controls

You can link a validation control to another control at design time or run time to make a comparison against the linked control. This validation can include testing for required fields using the **RequiredFieldValidator** control, testing for a range of input values using the **RangeValidator** control, testing for values that match a particular expression using the **RegularExpressionValidator** control, and testing for comparisons between multiple controls using the **CompareValidator** control.

The following example shows a **RangeValidation** control named **rngTest** and a **TextBox** Web server control named **txtInput**. The validation control checks whether the value in **txtInput** matches the range and displays a message if it does not.

```
rngTest.ControlToValidate = "txtInput"
rngTest.MinimumValue = "10"
rngTest.MaximumValue = "20"
rngTest.ErrorMessage = "Please enter a value between 10 and
20."
```

This validation control is rendered in client-side script when the page is displayed so that return trips to the server are not required simply for control validation.

Using Rich Controls

Using the **AdRotator** control, you can display advertisement banners on a page that automatically changes the displayed advertisement whenever the page is refreshed or revisited. The information is stored in an XML file that includes details about what image to use, where to redirect the browser when the advertisement is clicked, and how frequently the advertisement should appear.

The following example shows how you can use the **AdRotator** control on a page:

```
<body>
  <form id="WebForm2" method="post" runat="server">
    <asp:AdRotator id="AdRotator1" runat="server"
      Width="401px" Height="45px"
      AdvertisementFile="ads.xml">
    </asp:AdRotator>
  </form>
</body>
```

The following example shows the information required in the XML file to rotate the advertisements:

```
<Advertisements>
  <Ad>
    <ImageUrl>images/graphic1.gif</ImageUrl>
  <NavigateUrl>http://www.example1.microsoft.com</NavigateUrl>
    <AlternateText>
      Click here for products page 1
    </AlternateText>
    <Keyword>Products 1</Keyword>
    <Impressions>80</Impressions>
  </Ad>
  <Ad>
    <ImageUrl>images/graphic2.gif</ImageUrl>
<NavigateUrl>http://www.example2.microsoft.com</NavigateUrl>
    <AlternateText>
      Click here for products page 2
    </AlternateText>
    <Keyword>Products 2</Keyword>
    <Impressions>80</Impressions>
  </Ad>
</Advertisements>
```

The HTML produced by these controls when rendered may be substantially different from the object model that developers code against.

The following segment of a Web Form shows how the HTML syntax looks when viewed in the HTML design window for a Web Form containing a **RadioButtonList**.

```
<form id="WebForm1" method="post" runat="server">
  <asp:RadioButtonList id="RadioButtonList1" runat="server">
    <asp:ListItem Value="One">One</asp:ListItem>
    <asp:ListItem Value="Two">Two</asp:ListItem>
  </asp:RadioButtonList>
</form>
```

The following HTML is generated when the Web Form is rendered in Internet Explorer version 6.0. It shows that the **RadioButtonList** control is rendered in a table with HTML input tags and labels.

Example

```
<form name="WebForm1" method="post" action="WebForm1.aspx"
id="WebForm1">
<table id="RadioButtonList1" border="0">
 <tr><td>
    <input type="radio" id="RadioButtonList1_0" value="One"
           name="RadioButtonList1" />
    <label for="RadioButtonList1_0">One</label>
  </td></tr>
 <tr><td>
    <input type="radio" id="RadioButtonList1_1" value="Two"
           name="RadioButtonList1" />
    <label for="RadioButtonList1_1">Two</label>
  </td></tr>
</table>
</form>
```

Note For information about creating Web Form controls, see Module 9, "Developing Components in Visual Basic .NET," in Course 2373B, *Programming with Microsoft Visual Basic .NET*.

Handling Events

- Event handlers contain code for user interactions
- Page events: Init, Load, PreRender, UnLoad

```
Private Sub Page_Load(ByVal Sender As System.Object, _
        ByVal e As System.EventArgs) Handles MyBase.Load
  If Not IsPostBack Then 'IsPostBack is also available via 'Me'
      'Perform action first time page is displayed
  End If
End Sub
```

- Control events: Click, Changed, PreRender

```
Private Sub btn_Click(ByVal sender As System.Object, _
        ByVal e As System.EventArgs) Handles btn.Click
    btn.Text = "clicked"
End Sub
```

Interacting with users is one of the primary reasons for creating ASP.NET Web Forms. You program various events to handle these interactions as you do in traditional Visual Basic development. The Web page itself can execute code, and so can the many events raised by different objects, including all of the server controls.

Page Events

Every Web Form inherits from the **Page** class, which provides several useful events indirectly from other inherited classes such as the **Control** and **TemplateControl** classes. Several of these events are included in the following list, in the order in which they occur when a user accesses a page:

- **Init**

  This event occurs as the first step in the page lifecycle, when the page is initialized. You use this event to initialize local variables. Do not use this event to access view state information or controls on the page, because they may not be created or accessible at this point.

- **Load**

  This event occurs after the **Init** event and before the **PreRender** events are raised. You can use this event to view state information or access controls.

- **PreRender**

  This event occurs when the page is about to render its contents to the Web browser. Use it to perform any pre-rendering steps before the view state is saved.

- **Unload**

  This event occurs when the page is unloaded, after rending has occurred. Use it for removing any resources created throughout the request.

Using the Load Event

The **Load** event is commonly used to test the **IsPostBack** property of the Web Form to see whether the page is being loaded and displayed for the first time or whether it is being displayed in response to a client postback.

The following example shows this common usage:

```
Private Sub Page_Load(ByVal sender As System.Object, _
  ByVal e As System.EventArgs) Handles MyBase.Load
    'IsPostBack is also available by means of 'Me'
    If Not IsPostBack Then
        'Perform action first time page is displayed
    End If
End Sub
```

Control Events

Server controls are based on the **WebControl** class, which is based on the **System.Web.UI.Control** class. The **Page** class is also based indirectly on the **System.Web.UI.Control** class, through the **TemplateControl** class. Therefore, server controls share the events described in the preceding Page Events section.

Individual controls also add their own events to the object model to allow easier interaction with the user. Examples include the simple **Click** event for the **Button** class, the **TextChanged** event for the **TextBox** class, and the **SelectedIndexChanged** event for the **ListControl** class.

Some controls post their events to the server immediately, such as the **Click** event of the **Button** class. Other controls, such as the **TextChanged** event of the **TextBox** class, may only register their events when other means are used to post events to the server. These events are stored and then raised sequentially to the server code when the post event is triggered. You can alter this behavior by setting the **AutoPostBack** property of the control to **True**. In this way, you can raise events immediately regardless of the default behavior. In the case of a **TextBox** control, this means the event will be posted every time the text value is modified and the control loses focus.

Using Control Events

The following example shows how to add to events to individual controls, **TextBox** and **Button**, to facilitate user interaction on a Web Form:

```
Private Sub btnPost_Click(ByVal sender As System.Object, _
  ByVal e As System.EventArgs) Handles btnPost.Click
    Response.Write("Button Pressed")
    txtInput.AutoPostBack = True
End Sub

Public Sub txtInput_TextChanged(ByVal sender As Object, _
  ByVal e As System.EventArgs) Handles txtInput.TextChanged
    Response.Write("Text Changed")
End Sub
```

The preceding code is processed as follows:

1. When the user types a value into the **txtInput** control and tabs to the **btnPost** control, the **TextChanged** event is held back until the button is clicked.
2. This posts to the Web Form and executes first the **txtInput_TextChanged** handler and then the **btnPost_Click** handler.
3. The page is then displayed again with the event order written as part of the page, using the **Response.Write** method.
4. The post will now occur as soon as the user changes the value and tabs out of the **txtInput** control because the **txtInput.AutoPostBack** property has been set to **True**.

Important Using the **AutoPostBack** property for multiple controls on the same form will slow down the performance of the application because of the need for multiple trips to the server.

Demonstration: Creating Web Forms

In this demonstration, you will learn how to create a simple Web Form application that uses Web server controls for posting data to the server.

Lab 7.1: Creating the Customer Logon Web Forms

Objectives

After completing this lab, you will be able to:

- Create a Web Forms application.
- Create Web Forms.
- Use Web controls, such as the validation controls.
- Use the **Session** state object.

Prerequisites

Before working on this lab, you must be familiar with creating Web Forms in Visual Basic .NET.

Scenario

In this lab, you will create Web Forms that register and logon customers for the Cargo system.

The **WebCustomer** class is provided for you to use as a basis for your Web application. It provides some existing customer details to test your application and allows you to add new customers. Any customer details added are only valid for a single test session because they are not persisted to disk at this time.

Starter and Solution Files

There are starter and solution files associated with this lab. The starter files are in the *install folder*\Labs\Lab071\Starter folder, and the solution files are in the *install folder*\Labs\Lab071\Solution folder.

Estimated time to complete this lab: 60 minutes

Exercise 1
Creating the DefaultPage Web Form

In this exercise, you will create a Web Application and its default menu page.

► To create the Web application project

1. Open Microsoft Visual Studio .NET.
2. On the **File** menu, point to **New**, and then click **Project**.
3. From the **Visual Basic Projects** folder, click **ASP.NET Web Application**.
4. Change the **Location** to the following Web directory: http://localhost/2373/Labs/Lab071 and then click **OK**.

► To add the WebCustomer class

1. On the **Project** menu, click **Add Existing Item**.
2. Go to *install folder*\Labs\Lab071\Starter, click **WebCustomer.vb**, and then click **Open**.

► To create the DefaultPage Web Form

1. In Solution Explorer, right-click **WebForm1.aspx**, and then click **Delete**, confirming the deletion when prompted.
2. On the **Project** menu, click **Add Web Form**. Rename the item **DefaultPage**, and then click **Open**.
3. Click in the design window for DefaultPage.aspx to display the Properties window for the Web form. Change the **pageLayout** property for the **DOCUMENT** object to **FlowLayout**.
4. In the design window for DefaultPage.aspx, type the following text on separate lines.

Text	Format
Welcome to the Cargo Online System	Heading 1
Please select from the following options:	Normal

5. From the Web Forms toolbox, insert the following controls, separated by line breaks.

Control	Property	Value
Hyperlink	**(ID)**	**lnkExisting**
	Text	**I am an existing customer**
	NavigateUrl	**LogOn.aspx**
Hyperlink	**(ID)**	**lnkNewCustomer**
	Text	**I am a new customer**
	NavigateUrl	**NewCustomer.aspx**

6. Save your project.

Exercise 2
Creating the NewCustomer Web Form

In this exercise, you will create a Web Form to allow new customers to register.

► To create the NewCustomer Web Form

1. On the **Project** menu, click **Add Web Form**. Rename the item **NewCustomer**, and then click **Open**.
2. Click in the design window for NewCustomer.aspx to display the Properties window for the Web form. Change the **pageLayout** property for the **DOCUMENT** object to **FlowLayout**.
3. In the design window for NewCustomer.aspx, type the following text on separate lines.

Text	Format
Please enter your details	Heading 1
Full name:	Normal
E-mail:	Normal
Password:	Normal
Confirm password:	Normal

4. From the Web Forms toolbox, insert the following controls, and set their properties as shown in the following table.

Control	Property	Value
TextBox	**(ID)**	**txtFullName**
RequiredFieldValidator	**(ID)**	**rfvName**
	ErrorMessage	**Please enter your full name**
	ControlToValidate	**txtFullName**
TextBox	**(ID)**	**txtEmail**
RegularExpressionValidator	**(ID)**	**revEmail**
	ErrorMessage	**Your e-mail address is invalid**
	ControlToValidate	**txtEmail**
	ValidationExpression	**Click the browse button and select Internet E-mail Address**
	Display	**Dynamic**
RequiredFieldValidator	**(ID)**	**rfvEmail**
	ErrorMessage	**Please enter an e-mail address**
	ControlToValidate	**txtEmail**
	Display	**Dynamic**
TextBox	**(ID)**	**txtPassword**

(*continued*)

Control	Property	Value
	TextMode	Password
RegularExpressionValidator	(ID)	revPassword
	ErrorMessage	Your password must be at least 4 characters long
	ControlToValidate	txtPassword
	ValidationExpression	Click the browse button and select (Custom) from the list, entering the following value \w{4,}
	Display	Dynamic
RequiredFieldValidator	(ID)	rfvPassword
	ErrorMessage	Please enter a password
	ControlToValidate	txtPassword
	Display	Dynamic
TextBox	(ID)	txtConfirm
	TextMode	Password
CompareValidator	(ID)	cvConfirm
	ErrorMessage	Passwords do not match
	ControlToValidate	txtConfirm
	ControlToCompare	txtPassword
	Display	Dynamic
RequiredFieldValidator	(ID)	rfvConfirm
	ErrorMessage	Please confirm the password
	ControlToValidate	txtConfirm
	Display	Dynamic
Button	(ID)	btnSubmit
	Text	Submit

5. Create your Web Form so that it looks like the following illustration.

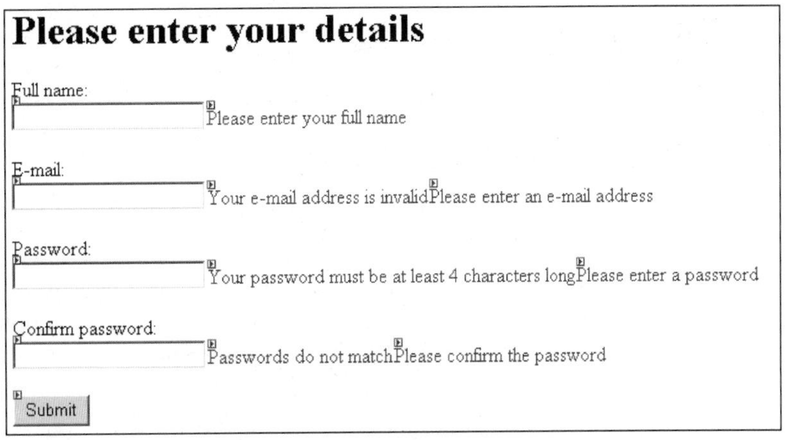

Please enter your details

Full name:

Please enter your full name

E-mail:

Your e-mail address is invalidPlease enter an e-mail address

Password:

Your password must be at least 4 characters longPlease enter a password

Confirm password:

Passwords do not matchPlease confirm the password

Submit

6. Double-click **btnSubmit**, and add the following code to the **btnSubmit_Click** event handler:

```
Dim newCust As New WebCustomer( )
newCust.AddCustomer(txtEmail.Text, txtPassword.Text, _
                    txtFullName.Text)
Session("User_FullName") = newCust.FullName

Response.Redirect("Welcome.aspx")
```

7. Save your project.

Exercise 3
Creating the LogOn Web Form

In this exercise, you will create the LogOn Web Form for existing customers.

► To create the LogOn Web Form

1. On the **Project** menu, click **Add Web Form**. Rename the item **LogOn**, and then click **Open**.
2. Click in the design window for LogOn.aspx to display the Properties window for the Web form. Change the **pageLayout** property for the **DOCUMENT** object to **FlowLayout**.
3. Open the design window for LogOn.aspx, and type the following text on separate lines.

Text	Format
Please enter your details	Heading 1
E-mail:	Normal
Password:	Normal

4. From the Web Forms toolbox, insert the following controls, separated by line breaks, arranging them with their related text values.

Control	Property	Value
TextBox	**(ID)**	**txtEmail**
RegularExpressionValidator	**(ID)**	**revEmail**
	ErrorMessage	**Your e-mail address is invalid**
	ControlToValidate	**txtEmail**
	ValidationExpression	**Click the browse button and select Internet E-mail Address**
	Display	**Dynamic**
RequiredFieldValidator	**(ID)**	**rfvEmail**
	ErrorMessage	**Please enter an e-mail address**
	ControlToValidate	**txtEmail**
	Display	**Dynamic**
TextBox	**(ID)**	**txtPassword**
	TextMode	**Password**
RequiredFieldValidator	**(ID)**	**rfvPassword**
	ErrorMessage	**Please enter a password**
	ControlToValidate	**txtPassword**
	Display	**Dynamic**

(continued)

Control	Property	Value
Label	**(ID)**	**lblNotFound**
	Text	**Not found message**
	ForeColor	**Red**
	Visible	**False**
Button	**(ID)**	**btnSubmit**
	Text	**Submit**

5. Your Web Form should look like the following illustration.

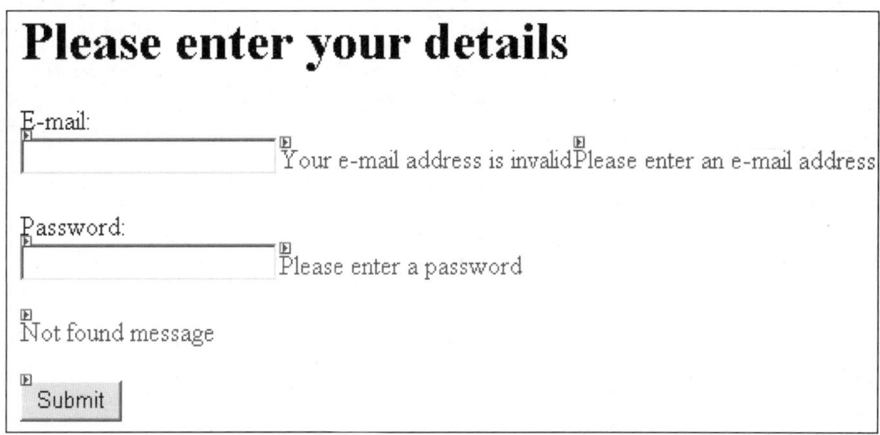

6. Double-click the **btnSubmit** button, and add the following code to the **btnSubmit_Click** event handler:

```
Dim existingCustomer As New WebCustomer( )
lblNotFound.Visible = False

Try
    existingCustomer.LogOn(txtEmail.Text, txtPassword.Text)

    Session("User_FullName") = existingCustomer.FullName
    Response.Redirect("Welcome.aspx")
Catch ex As Exception
    lblNotFound.Text = ex.Message
    lblNotFound.Visible = True
Finally
    existingCustomer = Nothing
End Try
```

7. Save your project.

Exercise 4
Creating the Welcome Web Form

In this exercise, you will create the Welcome Web Form that customers see after they are logged on to the system.

► **To create the Welcome Web Form**

1. From the **Project** menu, click **Add Web Form**. Rename the item **Welcome**, and then click **Open**.
2. Click in the design window for Welcome.aspx to display the Properties window for the Web form. Change the **pageLayout** property for the **DOCUMENT** object to **FlowLayout**.
3. Open the Welcome.aspx file in the design window. In the **Block Format** box on the **Formatting** toolbar, click **Heading 1**. Insert the following control within the **Heading 1** block, and set the property values as shown.

Control	Property	Value
Label	**(ID)**	**lblWelcome**
	Text	**Welcome…**

4. Open the Code Editor for Welcome.aspx.vb, and locate the **Page_Load** event handler. Enter the following code:

```
lblWelcome.Text = "Welcome " & _
                  Session("User_FullName")
```

5. Save your project.

► **To test existing customers**

1. In Solution Explorer, right-click **DefaultPage.aspx**, and click **Set As Start Page**.
2. On the **Debug** menu, click **Start**.
3. Click the **I am an existing customer** hyperlink.
4. Click **Submit** to view the validation messages.
5. Enter the following values.

Text box	Value
E-mail	**karen@wingtiptoys.msn.com**
Password	**password**

6. Click **Submit** to view the welcome message.
7. Use the **Back** button of the browser to return to the first page.

► **To test new customers**

1. Click the **I am a new customer** hyperlink.
2. Enter your full name, e-mail address and the password **TRY**. Use the TAB key to exit the field. The error message will appear.
3. Type a valid password and confirm it.
4. Click **Submit** to view the welcome message.
5. Close the browser.

If Time Permits
Using Cookies

In this optional exercise, you will use cookies to store and retrieve information about a customer.

▶ To persist the cookie for a customer

1. Open the design window for LogOn.aspx.
2. Add a **CheckBox** control before the btnSubmit control, and set the following properties.

Property	Value
(ID)	**chkSave**
Checked	**True**
Text	**Save details**

3. Open the Code Editor for LogOn.aspx.vb, and locate the **btnSubmit_Click** event handler. Add the following code after the call to the **existingCustomer.LogOn** method:

```
If chkSave.Checked = True Then
  Response.Cookies("User_FullName").Value = _
        existingCustomer.FullName
  Response.Cookies("User_FullName").Expires = _
        Now.AddMonths(1)
End If
```

▶ To retrieve the cookie for a customer

- Open the code window for DefaultPage.aspx.vb, and locate the **Page_Load** event handler. Add the following code.

```
If Not (Request.Cookies("User_FullName") Is Nothing) Then
   Session("User_FullName") = _
                    Request.Cookies("User_FullName").Value
   Response.Redirect("Welcome.aspx")
End If
```

► **To test the application**

1. On the **Debug** menu, click **Start**.
2. Click the **I am an existing customer** hyperlink.
3. Enter the following values.

Control	Value
E-mail	**karen@wingtiptoys.msn.com**
Password	**password**
Save details	**Checked**

4. Click **Submit** to view the welcome message.
5. Close the browser.
6. On the **Debug** menu, click **Start**.
7. Confirm that the **Welcome** page is the first page displayed and that it displays the correct user details.
8. Close Internet Explorer and close Visual Studio .NET.

◆ Building Web Services

- What Are Web Services?
- Creating a Web Service
- Enabling Web Service Discovery
- Deploying and Publishing a Web Service

Internal client applications have been able to access shared components for many years, but allowing external client applications access has been a difficult challenge for both developers and administrators. Web Services allow you to easily provide access to your application logic across the Internet without any special configuration of firewalls or corporate networks by using the HTTP protocol.

After you complete this lesson, you will be able to:

- Describe how the Internet and open standards such as XML and Hypertext Transfer Protocol (HTTP) enable Web Services to be used by any client application, regardless of its location or operating system.
- Create a Web Service by using Visual Basic .NET.
- Enable discovery of Web services.
- Deploy and publish your Web Services.

What Are Web Services?

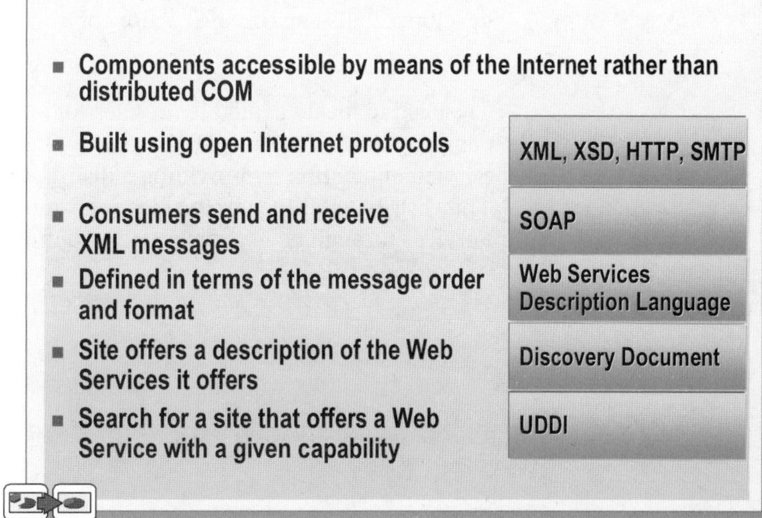

Components have traditionally been accessible only through local area networks by means of object-model specific protocols such as DCOM. This limitation is partly due to the complexity involved in allowing external access through ports to the internal network, as well as the dependence on both parties using a particular protocol.

Web Services remove this limitation by allowing access to components by means of the Internet and HTTP while still maintaining security. The supporting framework for Web Services provides the following:

- Open Internet protocols

  Web Services use open Internet protocols such as XML, XML Schema Definition (XSD), HTTP, and Simple Mail Transfer Protocol (SMTP) to transmit messages. This allows any client application to use a Web Service regardless of the operating system it is running on or the language it is written in.

- XML messages and SOAP

  SOAP is an industry standard for using XML to represent data and commands in an extensible way. Web Services do not have to use SOAP to specify the message formats; HTTP GET and HTTP POST mechanisms can also be used. These mechanisms are not as powerful as SOAP, but they can be used by all HTTP clients. SOAP supports extra functionality, including passing classes, datasets, and by-reference parameters to a Web Service.

- Messages defined by Web Services Description Language (WSDL)

  Web Services must provide a contract that client applications can rely upon to accurately describe the service's methods and their arguments. WSDL is an XML-based way to describe the contract information that can be read by all client applications that can work with XML.

- Service descriptions available through discovery

  The discovery specification describes a standard way for service providers to publish Web Service contracts. It also describes how developers and developer tools can discover these contract documents.

- Universal Discovery Description and Integration (UDDI)

  The need to locate available services for an entire industry or individual company has led to the UDDI project, which creates a framework for Web Service integration by providing a distributed directory of Web Services. This distributed directory enables registration and discovery of Web Services through an assortment of predefined SOAP messages.

Creating a Web Service

1. **Add a Web Service module to the project**
   - The .asmx file contains **WebService** directive

```
<%@ WebService Language="vb" Codebehind="User.asmx.vb"
Class="WebApp.User"%>
```

2. **Create a Web Service description**
3. **Add public subroutines or functions to .asmx.vb file**
   - Add WebMethod attribute to procedure definitions

```
<WebMethod()> Public Function AddUser(…) As String
    'Functionality to add a user and return new ID
    Return strNewId
End Function
```

To create a Web Service in Visual Basic .NET, use the following process:

1. Add a Web Service module to your project.
2. Create a Web Service description.
3. Add public subroutines and functions to the module, and add the **WebMethod** attribute to the procedure definitions.
4. Create the remaining code as usual.

What Is a Web Service Module?

A Web Service module uses the .asmx file extension and is made up of two files—the .asmx file and the .asmx.vb file—similar to the composition of a Web Form.

- The .asmx file

  The .asmx file simply contains the **WebService** directive that specifies the language in which the developer wrote the code, the name of the code file, and the name of the class that you use when referencing the service.

  The following example declares a service named User written in Visual Basic .NET, using the User.asmx.vb module for the code, in the **WebApp** namespace.

```
<%@ WebService Language="vb" Codebehind="User.asmx.vb"
   Class="WebApp.User" %>
```

- The .asmx.vb file

  The .asmx.vb file contains the code that executes when you invoke a Web Service method as if it were a regular class definition. The class inherits from the **System.Web.Services.WebService** class and provides direct access to common ASP.NET objects such as **Application**, **Server**, **Session**, and **User**.

Creating a Web Service Description

You can create a description for your Web Service by using the **WebService** attribute in the class definition and specifying the **Description** parameter, as shown in the following example. This information will be visible when the Web Service URL is entered in a browser.

```
<WebService(Namespace:="http://tempuri.org/", _
Description:="Provides user details.")> _
Public Class User
    Inherits System.Web.Services.WebService
    ...
End Class
```

Note Inheriting from **System.Web.Services.WebService** is not a requirement for a Web Service to work.

Adding Public Subroutines or Functions

You can create procedures for the Web Service class by using standard method syntax for either subroutines or functions. In order for these methods to be used as Web Services, you must mark them as public and use the **WebMethod** class attribute. The following example shows how to create a function that can be accessed through a Web Service:

```
<WebMethod( )> Public Function AddUser(ByVal strName As _
String) As String
    'Functionality to add a user and return new ID
    ...
    Return strNewId
End Function

<WebMethod( )> Public Sub DeleteUser(ByVal strId As String)
    'Functionality to delete a user based on ID
    ...
End Sub
```

You can add a description for each method by specifying the **Description** argument of the **WebMethod** attribute, as shown in the following example:

```
<WebMethod(Description:="This method performs an action")> _
Public Sub PerformAction( )
    ...
End Function
```

Tip If you already have components that you want to convert to Web Services, you can simply create a wrapper Web Service module that calls your preexisting components and returns any results.

Enabling Web Service Discovery

- **Discovery document**
  - Enables location and interrogation of Web Service descriptions
  - Contains links to resources that describe services
  - Stores information in XML format
  - Created manually or dynamically

```
<?xml version="1.0" ?>
<discovery xmlns="http://schemas.xmlsoap.org/disco/" ...>
<contractRef ref="http://www.nwtraders.msft/Shopping/User.asmx?wsdl"
   docRef="http://www.nwtraders.msft/Shopping/User.asmx"
   xmlns="http://schemas.xmlsoap.org/disco/wsdl/" />
...
</discovery>
```

A Web Service is not very useful if other developers do not know that the service exists. Locating and interrogating Web Services is known as *discovery*. It is through the discovery process that client applications learn that a Web Service exists, what its capabilities are, and how to properly interact with it.

What Is a Discovery Document?

You can programmatically discover a Web Service if it publishes a discovery document. This file contains links to other resources that describe each Web Service, such as WSDL documents. The discovery document uses XML format, so any client application can read this document.

Manually Creating a Discovery Document

You can create a discovery document by using any XML editor, as is shown in the following example:

```
<?xml version="1.0" ?>
<disco:discovery
  xmlns:disco="http://schemas.xmlsoap.org/disco"
  xmlns:WSDL="http://schemas.xmlsoap.org/disco/WSDL">
   <WSDL:contractRef
     ref="http://WebServerName/User.asmx?WSDL"/>
   <disco:discoveryRef ref="SomeFolder/default.disco" />
</disco:discovery>
```

Using this type of discovery document, you can explicitly expose only those Web Services that you want to be publicly available. This type of discovery document uses the .disco file extension.

Creating a Dynamic Discovery Document

Alternatively, you can create a dynamic discovery document that will look up the Web Services under a given virtual directory when queried by a client application. This is the type of discovery document that Visual Studio .NET creates automatically and that uses the .vsdisco file extension, as shown in the following example:

```
<?xml version="1.0" encoding="utf-8" ?>
<dynamicDiscovery
  xmlns="urn:schemas-dynamicdiscovery:disco.2000-03-17">
<exclude path="_vti_cnf" />
<exclude path="_vti_pvt" />
<exclude path="_vti_log" />
<exclude path="_vti_script" />
<exclude path="_vti_txt" />
<exclude path="Web References" />
</dynamicDiscovery>
```

You can use this type of discovery document to exclude particular folders from the dynamic discovery process. The folders excluded in the previous example are those used for Microsoft FrontPage® Extensions and any Web references used by the project, but you can manually list as many folders as you want.

The preceding dynamic discovery document will produce the following results when queried by a client application:

```
<?xml version="1.0" encoding="utf-8"?>
<discovery xmlns:xsd="http://www.w3.org/2001/XMLSchema"
xmlns:xsi="http://www.w3.org/2001/XMLSchema-instance"
xmlns="http://schemas.xmlsoap.org/disco/">
  <contractRef ref="http://www.nwtraders.msft
/Shopping/User.asmx?WSDL"
   docRef="http://www.nwtraders.msft/Shopping/User.asmx"
   xmlns="http://schemas.xmlsoap.org/disco/scl/" />
  <soap address="http://www.nwtraders.msft/Shopping/User.asmx"
   xmlns:q1="http://tempuri.org/ binding="q1:Service1Soap"
   xmlns="http://schemas.xmlsoap.org/disco/soap/" />
</discovery>
```

Note A discovery document is not required for creating a Web Service. Another site could be used to describe the service, or there may not be a publicly available means of finding the service if it is only intended for private use.

Deploying and Publishing a Web Service

- **Deploying a Web Service**
  - Copy .asmx, Web.config, and any components to an IIS virtual directory
- **Publishing a Web Service**
  - The discovery document is copied to IIS virtual directory
  - Dynamic discovery document produced by ASP.NET generates information for all services in all subfolders
  - Manually created discovery document returns only explicitly defined information

Once you create your Web Service, you can deploy it to a Web server and then publish it.

Deploying a Web Service

You can deploy a Web Service by copying the various files to an IIS virtual directory. These files should include:

- Web Service files

  Copy only the .asmx files because the .asmx.vb files are included in your compiled assembly.
- Configuration file

  Copy the Web.config configuration file.
- Internal assemblies

  Include all .dll files required to perform the services.
- External assemblies

  Include any external assemblies not supplied by the .NET Framework.

Publishing a Web Service

If you want to publish your Web Service, you can copy the discovery document to the root of the IIS virtual directory. If you are using the dynamic discovery file produced by ASP.NET, this will return the details of all Web Services contained in the root directory and any subdirectories. If you manually create the discovery document, it will return only the information explicitly contained in the file.

You can then choose how to direct your users to your discovery document. You could do this by adding a link from your home page or by making the discovery document the default page. However, you may not want to make your discovery document publicly available, in which case you can implement alternate ways of providing access to this file.

Demonstration: Creating a Web Service

In this demonstration, you will learn how to create a simple Web Service and add descriptions to the service and its methods.

◆ Using Web Services

- Exploring Web Services
- Invoking a Web Service from a Browser
- Invoking a Web Service from a Client

Web Services are an important component of the .NET Framework. Visual Basic .NET–based client applications enable you to easily discover and use Web Services.

After you complete this lesson, you will be able to:

- Discover and interrogate a Web Service by using discovery and WSDL documents.
- Call a Web Service from an Internet browser.
- Pass the service parameters to a Web Service.
- Reference a discovery document from Visual Basic .NET.
- Create client code that interacts with the Web Service.

Exploring Web Services

- **HTML description page**
  - Describes Web Service methods and arguments
  - Provides simple test utility for methods
  - Displays additional descriptions from attributes
  - Appears when you enter Web Service URL

```
http://webservername/virtualdirectory/webservice.asmx
```

- **WSDL describes methods, arguments, and responses**
  - Generated by using Web Service URL with ?WSDL switch

Exploring Web Services involves looking at two parts of the system: the HTML description page and the WSDL document.

What Is the HTML Description Page?

The HTML description page is automatically generated when you call a Web Service without specifying a particular method to execute. The HTML description page provides the following:

- Web Service methods and arguments

  The page contains links that describe the methods and arguments that make up the Web Service.

- Simple test utility for methods

  The links include test facilities for each method, in which you can input each parameter through a text input field. When you enter values in the text input fields and click the **Invoke** button, the Web Service executes and displays any results in XML format. This facility is only provided for methods that do not include any by-reference parameters because **HTTPGet** and **HTTPPost** are the protocols used to process this page's requests.

- Additional descriptions from attributes

  Additional information about each method can be displayed if the developer has specified the **Description** parameter for the **WebMethod** attribute of a method, or for the **WebService** attribute of the class.

You can view the description page by entering the Web Service URL in a browser by using the following syntax:

```
http://webservername/virtualdirectory/webservice.asmx
```

You can also view the description page within Visual Studio .NET by right-clicking the .asmx file in Solution Explorer, and then clicking **View In Browser**.

Near the top of the HTML description page, there is also a "Service Description" hyperlink to the WSDL document.

What Is a WSDL Document?

A WSDL document uses XML to define the syntax and parameters of the available methods of a Web Service. This document is created automatically when you add the ?WSDL switch to the Web Service URL, as shown in the following example:

```
http://webservername/virtualdirectory/webservice.asmx?WSDL
```

It is possible to read and interpret the WSDL document, but it is not necessary to understand the document to use a Web Service.

Invoking a Web Service from a Browser

- **Enter the URL for the Web Service with parameters**
- **Syntax:**

  http://webservername/vdir/webservicename.asmx/ MethodName?parameter=value

- **Example:**

```
http://www.nwtraders.msft/Shopping/User.asmx/AddUser?strName=Joe
```

You invoke a Web Service from a browser by entering the URL of the service, specifying the method name to run, and specifying any parameter values.

Syntax

You use the following syntax to invoke a Web Service:

```
http://webservername/vdir/webservicename.asmx/
  MethodName?parameter=value
```

Example

The following example shows how to invoke a Web Service. This code calls the *AddUser* method of the *User.asmx* Web Service in the *Shopping* virtual directory on the *nwtraders.msft* Web server. It also passes in a parameter value of the user name *Joe*.

```
http://www.nwtraders.msft/Shopping/User.asmx/
AddUser?strName=Joe
```

The Web Service will return XML output containing the results of the execution as shown in the following example. The results show a **String** value of *43-124-21* being returned as the new identity of the added user.

```
<?xml version="1.0" ?>
<string xmlns="http://tempuri.org/">43-124-21</string>
```

This approach uses the HTTP-GET protocol and would most commonly be used for testing purposes; real application-to-application communication would use the more powerful SOAP protocol.

Invoking a Web Service from a Client

- **Visual Basic .NET creates a proxy class for early binding**
- **Steps required:**
  1. Add a Web reference
  2. Enter the URL for the .asmx file
  3. Create client code that uses appropriate namespaces

```
Sub btnSubmit_Click(…) Handles btnSubmit.Click
    Dim usr As New Services.User() 'Services is the given namespace
    MessageBox.Show(usr.AddUser(txtName.Text))
End Sub
```

You can invoke a Web Service from a client application in several ways, depending on the client. If the client is written in Visual Basic .NET, you can use the following process for either a Windows Forms or a Web Forms application:

1. Add a Web reference to the Web Service.
2. Enter the URL for the .asmx file.
3. Create your client code for accessing a component. Use the appropriate namespaces.

When you add a Web reference to your client project, Visual Basic .NET creates a proxy class that hides the complexity of calling a Web Service. This proxy allows you to use early binding when connecting to the service, as if the components were accessible within a local assembly.

Example

In the following example, the required Web Service has taken a Web reference, and the Web reference has been renamed as the **Services** namespace. A command button named **btnSubmit** and a **TextBox** named **txtName** have been placed on a Windows Forms form with the following code for the **btnSubmit_Click** event handler:

```
Private Sub btnSubmit_Click(ByVal sender As System.Object, _
  ByVal e As System.EventArgs) Handles btnSubmit.Click
    'Services is the given namespace
    Dim usr As New Services.User( )
    MessageBox.Show(usr.AddUser(txtName.Text))
End Sub
```

When the preceding code is executed, a new user is created. The **txtName** text box specifies the name of the new user, and the **AddUser** method creates a message box that displays the new identity.

Demonstration: Using a Web Service

In this demonstration, you will learn how to access a Web Service from a simple browser client as well as from a rich Visual Basic .NET-based, Windows-based application.

Multimedia: How Web Services Work

In this animation, you will see how you can use Web Services in your Microsoft Visual Basic .NET–based applications, how the Web Services Description Language provides information about the Web Services, and how Visual Basic .NET uses SOAP to create proxies.

Script: How Web Services Work

A bride can plan every detail of her wedding, but if she is planning to change her name, she might not be prepared for how complicated that can be.

At her job, how many phone calls do you think she will need to make to get her name changed? How many internal and external Web sites do you think she will need to update? How many hours of unproductive work do you think she will spend, just to make the name change?

She needs to change her e-mail alias and contact payroll. She needs to change her name with her health insurance company. She also needs to order new business cards. All these different vendors use different platforms.

Imagine how astonished she will be to find out that she only needs to enter her new information one time! How is that possible? It is possible because of Web Services. Web Services are applications that are remotely activated over the Web by a simple XML or SOAP-based message.

Here is how it works: An astute developer at her company built a portal based on Web Services that aggregates all employee services. Web Services allow client applications to access business logic by using Internet protocols, which means that any business can interact with any other business without encountering problems related to company-specific protocol.

When the Visual Basic .NET–based application running on this client needs to use a Web Service, it uses a process called discovery to find out what services are available from a specific company. To provide this flexible approach, certain details must be provided by the Web Service in a discovery document.

A discovery document contains information in XML format about one or more Web sites that provide Web Services. The document contains URL links to descriptive documents or contracts for a specific Web Service. Visual Basic .NET automatically creates a discovery document when you create a Web Service. The client application uses the discovery document to locate individual services and contracts.

With this information, the client can explore the contract documents to find the requirements of the Web Service methods. These contracts are also in XML format, but they follow specific standards that have been established to describe the methods, arguments, and return values of a Web Service.

ASP.NET uses the Web Services Description Language, or WSDL, to describe the services available. WSDL documents describe the details of each method for three different protocols: HTTP-Get, HTTP-Post, and the Simple Object Access Protocol (SOAP).

From these requirements, the Visual Basic .NET client automatically constructs a proxy class to ease communication between the developer's client code and the service. Visual Basic .NET applications use the SOAP method descriptions when creating this proxy. SOAP supports some enhanced features such as by-reference parameters and the ability to pass objects, structs, and ADO.NET DataSets.

The Visual Basic .NET client application can then call the proxy class as if it were talking directly to the real service. In fact, the proxy hides all of the network communications.

The proxy then makes requests to the Web Service, passing any parameters across the Internet as SOAP messages. The Web Service processes the incoming request and performs the required action. If values need to be sent back to the client, the Web Service creates these values and returns them as SOAP messages.

The message is received by the proxy and converted into .NET base types that the Visual Basic .NET client can work with. This layer of abstraction allows developers to work with a Web Service as if it were a component running locally to the client.

So, using Web Services, the Web server receives XML messages by means of ASP.NET. The Web server activates Web Service functions using SOAP, and the name change tasks are performed.The newlywed will be able to enter her name in one location that:

- Uses the discovery process to find out what services are available.
- Uses the ASP.NET WSDL to define methods to call, the address of the SOAP endpoint, schemas for SOAP messages and responses, and the data types returned.
- Creates a proxy client class.

In this animation, you saw how you can use Web services in your Visual Basic .NET applications, how the Web Service Description Language provides information about the Web service, and how Visual Basic .NET uses SOAP to create proxies.

Lab 7.2: Creating and Using the CustomerService Web Service

Objectives

After completing this lab, you will be able to:

- Create Web Services.
- Consume Web Services from a rich client.

Prerequisites

Before working on this lab, you must be familiar with creating Web Services in Visual Basic .NET.

Scenario

In this lab, you will create a Web Service that allows retrieval and storage of customer details. You will also create a Windows Forms application to test the Web Service methods. Web Services are often used by other Web Services or Web Form applications. A Windows Forms application will be used as the test application in this lab to contrast using a class from a form with using a Web Service from a form.

The **Customer** class from Lab 5.1, Creating the Customer Class, of Course 2373B, *Programming with Microsoft Visual Basic .NET*, is provided and will be used as a basis for the Web Services application to replicate data retrieval and storage. The test form from the same lab has been modified and supplied to test these lab exercises.

Starter and Solution Files

There are starter and solution files associated with this lab. The starter files are in the *install folder*\Labs\Lab072\Ex0*x*\Starter folder, and the solution files are in the *install folder*\Labs\Lab072\Ex0*x*\Solution folder (where *x* is the exercise number).

Estimated time to complete this lab: 45 minutes

Exercise 1
Creating the CustomerService Web Service

In this exercise, you will create the CustomerService Web Service and define its methods.

▶ To open the starter project

1. Open Visual Studio .NET.
2. On the **File** menu, point to **Open**, and click **Project**.
3. Set the folder location to *install folder*\Labs\Lab072\Ex01\Starter, click **Ex01.sln**, and then click **Open**.

▶ To create the CustomerService Web Service

1. On the **Project** menu, click **Add Web Service**. Rename the item **CustomerService**.
2. Open the Code Editor for CustomerService.asmx, locate the Public Class CustomerService definition, and then modify the **WebService** attribute to include the following **Description** parameter value:

   ```
   Stores and retrieves Customer information.
   ```

3. Verify that the class definition now looks as follows:

   ```
   <WebService(Namespace:="http://tempuri.org/", _
   Description:="Stores and retrieves Customer information." _
   )> Public Class CustomerService
   ```

▶ To define the Web Service methods

1. On the **File** menu, point to **Open**, and then click **File**.
2. In the **Files of type** box, click **Text Files**.
3. Set the folder location to *install folder*\Labs\Lab072\Ex01\Starter, click **Code.txt**, and then click **Open**.
4. Copy all of the code in **Code.txt** into the Web Service class definition in CustomerService.asmx.
5. Examine each of the three methods to ensure that you understand the purpose of the code.
6. Add the **WebMethod** attribute to each of the three method definitions. This will change them from standard methods into Web Service methods.
7. Add the following descriptions to each **WebMethod** attribute, using the same syntax as that used for the **WebService** attribute shown in step 3 of the previous procedure.

Method	Description
AddCustomer	Adds a customer to the system.
GetDetails	Retrieves customer details based on the Customer ID.
LogOn	Retrieves customer details based on logon details.

► To test the Web Service

1. Build the project.
2. In Solution Explorer, right-click **CustomerService.asmx**, and then click **View in Browser** to display the HTML description page.
3. Click the **Service Description** hyperlink and examine the WSDL document.
4. Click the **Back** button on the **Web** toolbar to move back to the HTML description page.
5. Click the hyperlink for each method of the Web Service to view the method details. Note that you can only test the **AddCustomer** method from this page because it is the only method that does not use by-reference parameters.
6. Test the **AddCustomer** method by entering any information for the input fields and then clicking **Invoke**. View the XML results to confirm that the value **1200** was generated and returned.

Exercise 2
Creating the LogOn Test Code

In this exercise, you will test the **LogOn** method of the Web Service from a simple form.

▶ To open the starter project

1. On the **File** menu, point to **Open**, and then click **Project**.
2. Set the folder location to *install folder*\Labs\Lab072\Ex02\Starter, click **Ex02.sln**, and then click **Open**.

▶ To create the Web reference

1. On the **Project** menu, click **Add Web Reference**.
2. Type **http://localhost/2373/Labs/Lab072/Ex01/Starter/CustomerService.asmx** in the **Address** box, and then click **Go**.
3. When the discovery document information is displayed, click **Add Reference**.
4. In Solution Explorer, rename localhost as **Services** to provide an appropriate namespace.

▶ To add the test code for the Logon method

1. In frmLogon.vb, locate the **btnLogon_Click** event handler.
2. Declare and instantiate a **Services.CustomerService** variable named **cusCustomer**.
3. Call the **LogOn** method of the **cusCustomer** object, using the following parameters.

Parameter	Value
strEmail	txtEmail.Text
strPassword	txtPassword.Text
intID	intId
strFName	strFName
strLName	strLName
strAddress	strAddress
strCompany	strCompany

4. Assign the following values to the text boxes following the call to the **LogOn** method.

Text box	Value
txtID	**CStr(intId)**
txtFName	**strFName**
txtLName	**strLName**
txtAddress	**strAddress**
txtCompany	**strCompany**

5. Destroy the **cusCustomer** reference by using the **Nothing** keyword.
6. Save the project.

► To test the LogOn code

1. On the **Debug** menu, click **Start**.
2. Click the **Test 'Logon'** button to display the test form.
3. Enter the following values in the appropriate text boxes.

Text box	Value
E-mail	**karen@wingtiptoys.msn.com**
Password	**password**

4. Click the **Logon** button and confirm that the customer information is displayed correctly in the text boxes.
5. Close the application.

Exercise 3
Testing the GetDetails Procedure

In this exercise, you will test the **GetDetails** Web Service method from the test form. Continue working with the project from the previous exercise. If you did not complete the previous exercise, you can use the Ex03.sln project located in the *install folder*\Labs\Lab072\Ex03\Starter folder.

► **To add the test code for the GetDetails method**

1. In frmRetrieve.vb, locate the **btnRetrieve_Click** event handler.
2. Declare and instantiate a **Services.CustomerService** variable named **cusCustomer**.
3. Call the **GetDetails** method of the **cusCustomer** object, using the following parameters. Note that all parameters except for **intID** are by reference, so values are returned from the method.

Parameter	Value
intID	**CInt(txtID.Text)**
strEmail	**strEmail**
strPassword	**strPassword**
strFName	**strFName**
strLName	**strLName**
strAddress	**strAddress**
strCompany	**strCompany**

4. Assign the following values to the text boxes following the call to the **GetDetails** method.

Text box	Value
txtEmail	**strEmail**
txtPassword	**strPassword**
txtFName	**strFName**
txtLName	**strLName**
txtAddress	**strAddress**
txtCompany	**strCompany**

5. Destroy the **cusCustomer** reference by using the **Nothing** keyword.
6. Save the project.

▶ To test the Retrieve code

1. On the **Debug** menu, click **Start**.
2. Click the **Test 'Get Details'** button to display the test form.
3. Enter the value **1119** in the **CustomerID** text box, and then click the **Retrieve** button.
4. Confirm that your code retrieves the customer information and displays it correctly in the text boxes.
5. Close the application.

Exercise 4
Testing the AddCustomer Procedure

In this exercise, you will test the **AddCustomer** Web Service method from the test form. Continue working with the project from the previous exercise. If you did not complete the previous exercise, you can use the Ex04.sln project located in the *install folder*\Labs\Lab072\Ex04\Starter folder.

► To add the test code for the AddCustomer method

1. In frmNew.vb, locate the **btnNew_Click** event handler.
2. Declare and instantiate a **Services.CustomerService** variable named **cusCustomer**.
3. Call the **AddCustomer** method of the **cusCustomer** object and display the return value in a message box. Use the following values for the parameters of the **AddCustomer** method.

Parameter	Value
strEmail	**txtEmail.Text**
strPassword	**txtPassword.Text**
strFName	**txtFName.Text**
strLName	**txtLName.Text**
strAddress	**txtAddress.Text**
strCompany	**txtCompany.Text**

4. Destroy the **cusCustomer** reference by using the **Nothing** keyword.
5. Save the project.

► To test the AddCustomer code

1. On the **Debug** menu, click **Start**.
2. Click the **Test 'New Customer'** button to display the test form.
3. Enter values in all the text boxes.
4. Click the **New Customer** button, and confirm that an ID is displayed in the message box. Note that adding customers does not actually add a customer to the system, because this part of the application is hard-coded.
5. Close the application.

If Time Permits
Using a Web Service from a Web Application

In this optional exercise, you will use the Web Service from a Web application.

▶ To open the starter project

1. Open Visual Studio .NET.
2. On the **File** menu, point to **Open**, and then click **Project**.
3. Set the folder location to *install folder*\Labs\Lab072\Ex05\Starter, click **Ex05.sln**, and then click **Open**.
4. In the Solution Explorer, right-click **Logon.aspx** and click **Set As Start Page**.
5. View Logon.aspx in the design window and then Logon.aspx.vb in the Code Editor to understand what functionality the Web Form provides.

▶ To create the Web reference

1. On the **Project** menu, click **Add Web Reference**.
2. Enter **http://localhost/2373/Labs/Lab072/Ex01/Starter/CustomerService.asmx** in the **Address** box, and then click **Go**.
3. When the discovery document information is displayed, click **Add Reference**.
4. In Solution Explorer, rename localhost as **Services** to provide an appropriate namespace.

▶ To add the test code for the LogOn method

1. Locate the **btnSubmit_Click** event handler.
2. In the line before the **Try...Catch...Finally** code block, declare and instantiate a **Services.CustomerService** variable named **cusCustomer**.
3. Inside the **Try** block, call the **LogOn** method of the **cusCustomer** object, using the following parameters.

Parameter	Value
strEmail	**txtEmail.Text**
strPassword	**txtPassword.Text**
intID	**intID**
strFName	**strFName**
strLName	**strLName**
strAddress	**strAddress**
strCompany	**strCompany**

4. Assign the user name to the **Session** object, as follows:

```
Session("User_FullName") = strFName & " " & strLName
```

5. Redirect the user to the Welcome.aspx Web Form, as follows:

```
Response.Redirect("Welcome.aspx")
```

6. Save the project.

► **To test the LogOn code**

1. On the **Debug** menu, click **Start**.
2. Enter the following values in the appropriate text boxes.

Textbox	Value
E-mail	**karen@wingtiptoys.msn.com**
Password	**karen**

3. Click the **Submit** button to confirm that the error message is displayed.
4. Enter the following values in the appropriate text boxes.

Textbox	Value
E-mail	**karen@wingtiptoys.msn.com**
Password	**password**

5. Click the **Submit** button, and confirm that the correct name is displayed on the Welcome page.
6. Close the browser and Visual Studio .NET.

Review

- Introduction to ASP.NET
- Creating Web Form Applications
- Building Web Services
- Using Web Services

1. Describe some of the features of ASP.NET.

2. Explain why updates to an ASP.NET application do not require you to restart IIS.

3. Create a line of code that uses the **Response** object to retrieve a *userCounter* session variable and display it to the user.

4. Convert the following HTML control tag into a server-side control.

```
<input type=text id=mytext value="hello">
```

5. What attribute do you add to class methods when creating a Web Service?

6. Visual Basic .NET allows early binding to a Web Service. True or false?

msdn® training

Module 8: Using ADO.NET

Contents

Overview

- ADO.NET Overview
- .NET Data Providers
- The DataSet Object
- Data Designers and Data Binding
- XML Integration

In this module, you will learn how to use ADO.NET from Microsoft® Visual Basic® .NET version 7.0. You will learn about the Microsoft .NET providers included in the .NET Framework and about how to use the **DataSet** object. You also will learn how to use the Microsoft Visual Studio® .NET data designers and how to bind data to Microsoft Windows® Forms and Web Forms. Finally, you will learn about the integration of Extensible Markup Language (XML) with ADO.NET.

After completing this module, you will be able to:

- List the benefits of ADO.NET.
- Create applications using ADO.NET.
- List the main ADO.NET objects and their functions.
- Use Visual Studio .NET data designers and data binding.
- Explain how XML integrates with ADO.NET.

◆ ADO.NET Overview

- Introduction to ADO.NET
- Benefits of ADO.NET

ActiveX® Data Objects for the .NET Framework (ADO.NET) provide many enhancements for accessing data in a disconnected environment. ADO.NET contains objects that are similar to those of ADO, allowing you to update your skills easily.

In this lesson, you will learn where ADO.NET is within the .NET Framework, and about the benefits ADO.NET provides.

After completing this lesson, you will be able to:

- Describe the role of ADO.NET in the .NET Framework.
- List the major benefits of ADO.NET.

Introduction to ADO.NET

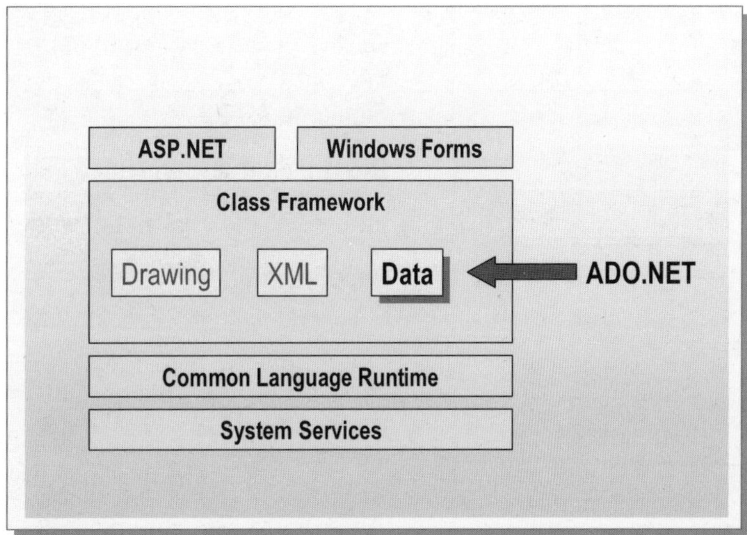

ADO.NET is a set of classes that allow .NET -based applications to read and update information in databases and other data stores. You can access these classes through the **System.Data** namespace provided by the .NET Framework.

ADO.NET provides consistent access to a wide variety of data sources, including Microsoft SQL Server™ databases, OLE DB–compliant databases, non-relational sources such as Microsoft Exchange Server, and XML documents.

Earlier data access methods, such as Data Access Object (DAO), concentrate on tightly coupled, connected data environments. One of the main purposes of ADO.NET is to enhance the disconnected data capabilities. Many of the common ADO objects that you have worked with correlate to ADO.NET objects, although there are also many new classes to enhance the data access model.

ADO.NET uses .NET data providers to link your applications to data sources. .NET data providers are similar to the OLE DB providers used in ADO, although they are primarily concerned with moving data into and out of a database rather than providing interfaces over all of a database's functionality.

ADO.NET includes two .NET data providers:

- SQL Server .NET Data Provider

  For use with SQL Server 7.0 and later.

- OLE DB .NET Data Provider

  For use with data sources exposed by OLE DB.

The ADO.NET data providers contain tools to allow you to read, update, add, and delete data in multitier environments. Most of the objects in the two libraries are similar and are identified by the prefix on their name. For example, **SqlDataReader** and **OleDbDataReader** both provide a stream of records from a data source.

Benefits of ADO.NET

- Similar to ADO
- Designed for disconnected data
- Intrinsic to the .NET Framework
- Supports XML

ADO.NET provides many benefits to experienced Visual Basic developers, including:

- Similar programming model to that of ADO

  This makes it easy for Visual Basic developers who are familiar with ADO to update their skills. You can still use ADO in Visual Basic .NET, so you can keep existing code, but use the features of ADO.NET in new projects.

- Designed for disconnected data

  ADO.NET is designed for working with disconnected data in a multitier environment. It uses XML as the format for transmitting disconnected data, which makes it easier to communicate with client applications that are not based on Windows.

- Intrinsic to the .NET Framework

  Because ADO.NET is intrinsic to the .NET Framework, you have all the advantages of using the .NET Framework, including ease of cross-language development.

- Supports XML

  ADO and XML have previously been incompatible: ADO was based on relational data, and XML is based on hierarchical data. ADO.NET brings together these two data access techniques and allows you to integrate hierarchical and relational data, as well as alternate between XML and relational programming models.

◆ .NET Data Providers

- Using the Connection Object
- Using the Command Object
- Using the Command Object with Stored Procedures
- Using the DataReader Object
- Using the DataAdapter Object

The .NET data providers allow access to specific types of data sources. You can use the **System.Data.SQLClient** namespace to access SQL Server 7.0 and later databases, and the **System.Data.OLEDB** namespace to access any data source exposed through OLE DB.

Each of these providers contains four main objects that you can use to connect to a data source, read the data, and manipulate the data prior to updating the source.

After completing this lesson, you will be able to:

- Use the **Connection** object to connect to a database.
- Use the **Command** object to execute commands and, optionally, to return data from a data source.
- Use the **DataReader** object to create a read-only data stream.
- Use the **DataAdapter** object to exchange data between a data source and a **DataSet**.

Using the Connection Object

- **Connecting from a Web application**
  - Add a line to Web.config file

```
<identity impersonate="true" userName="Karen"
password="Password"/>
```

- **SqlConnection**

```
Dim conSQL As New SqlClient.SqlConnection( )
conSQL.ConnectionString = "Integrated Security=True;" & _
       "Data Source=LocalHost;Initial Catalog=Pubs;"
conSQL.Open( )
```

To connect to a database, you set the connection type, specify the data source, and connect to the data source. When you are finished working with the data, you close the connection.

1. Set the connection type.

   You can use the **Connection** object to connect to a specific data source. You can use either the **SqlConnection** object to connect to SQL Server databases or the **OleDbConnection** object to connect to other types of data sources.

2. Specify the data source.

   After you set the connection type, you use the **ConnectionString** property to specify the source database and other information used to establish the connection. The format of these strings differs slightly between the **SqlClient** namespace and the **OleDb** namespace.

3. Connect to the data source.

   Each **Connection** object supports an **Open** method that opens the connection after the connection properties have been set, and a **Close** method that closes the connection to the database after all transactions have cleared.

Connecting from a Web application

Because the ASP.NET aspnet_wp service runs as a local account named ASPNET, you must use impersonation when connecting to SQL Server 2000 from a Web application. To do this, you must add a line to the Web.config file specifying the username and password you want to use to access the server.

The following example specifies to connect to SQL Server as a user named Karen with a password of Password.

```
<identity impersonate="true" userName="Karen"
password="Password"/>
```

SqlConnection

The **SqlConnection** object is optimized for SQL Server 7.0 and later databases by bypassing the OLE DB layer. It is recommended that you use this object, not **OleDbConnection**, when working with these types of data sources.

The SQL Client .NET Data Provider supports a **ConnectionString** format that is similar to ADO connection strings. This consists of name-value pairs providing the information required when connecting to the data source. The following table lists the most commonly used pairs.

Keyword name	Description	Default value
Connection Timeout (or **Connect Timeout**)	Length of time to wait for a connection to succeed before returning an error.	**15 seconds**
Initial Catalog	Name of the database.	None
User ID	SQL Server logon account (if using SQL Server security).	None
Password (or **Pwd**)	SQL Server password (if using SQL Server security).	None
Data Source (or **Server** or **Address** or **Addr** or **Network Address**)	Name or network address of SQL Server.	None
Integrated Security (or **Trusted_Connection**)	Whether the connection is a secure connection.	**False**

The following example shows how to connect to a SQL Server database by using the SQL Client .NET Data Provider:

```
Dim conSQL As New SqlClient.SqlConnection( )
conSQL.ConnectionString = "Integrated Security=True;" & _
"Data Source=LocalHost;Initial Catalog=Pubs;"
conSQL.Open( )
```

OleDbConnection

The **OleDbConnection** object exposes methods similar to those of the **SqlConnection** object, but certain data sources will not support all the available methods of the **OleDbConnection** class.

The OLE DB .NET Data Provider uses a **ConnectionString** that is identical to that of ADO, except that the **Provider** keyword is now required, and the **URL**, **Remote Provider**, and **Remote Server** keywords are no longer supported.

The following example shows how to connect to an Access database by using the OLE DB .NET Data Provider:

```
Dim conAccess As New OleDb.OleDbConnection( )
conAccess.ConnectionString =
"Provider=Microsoft.Jet.OLEDB.4.0;Data Source=C:\NWind.MDB"
conAccess.Open( )
```

Note The examples in the remainder of this module use the **SQL Client** namespace. For more information about the **OLE DB** namespace, search for "OleDBConnection" in the Visual Basic .NET documentation.

Using the Command Object

- **Two ways to create a Command:**
  - **Command** constructor
  - **CreateCommand** method
- **Four ways to execute a Command:**
  - **ExecuteReader**
  - **ExecuteScalar**
  - **ExecuteNonQuery**
  - **ExecuteXMLReader**

```
Dim commSQL As New SqlClient.SqlCommand( )
commSQL.Connection = conSQL
commSQL.CommandText = "Select Count(*) from Authors"
MessageBox.Show(commSQL.ExecuteScalar( ).ToString)
```

You can use the ADO.NET **Command** object to execute commands and, optionally, to return data from a data source. You can use the **SqlCommand** with SQL Server databases and the **OleDbCommand** with all other types of data sources.

Creating Commands

You can create a command in one of two ways:

- Use the **Command** constructor, passing the **Connection** name as an argument.
- Use the **CreateCommand** method of the **Connection** object.

You can use the **CommandText** property of the **Command** object to set and retrieve the SQL statement being executed. You can use any valid SQL statement with the specified data source, including data manipulation, definition, and control statements.

Executing Commands

You can only execute a **Command** within a valid and open connection. The **Command** object provides four methods that you can use to execute commands:

- **ExecuteReader**

  Use this method when the query will return a stream of data such as a **Select** statement returning a set of records. This method returns the records in a **SqlDataReader** or **OleDbDataReader** object.

- **ExecuteScalar**

  Use this method when the query will return a singleton value; for example, a **Select** statement returning an aggregate value. It executes the query and returns the first column of the first row in the result set, ignoring any other data that is returned. This method requires less code than using the **ExecuteReader** method and accessing a single value from the **SqlDataReader** object.

- **ExecuteNonQuery**

  Use this method when the query will not return a result; for example, an **Insert** statement.

- **ExecuteXMLReader**

  Use this method when the query includes a valid FOR XML clause. This is only valid when using the **SQLCommand** object.

The following example shows how to use the **Command** object to query a database and retrieve data:

```
Dim conSQL As New SqlClient.SqlConnection( )
conSQL.ConnectionString = "Integrated Security=True;" & _
"Data Source=LocalHost;Initial Catalog=Pubs;"
conSQL.Open( )

Dim commSQL As New SqlClient.SqlCommand( )
commSQL.Connection = conSQL
commSQL.CommandText = "Select Count(*) from Authors"
MessageBox.Show(commSQL.ExecuteScalar( ).ToString)
```

This code determines how many rows are present in the Authors table of the Pubs database and displays the result.

Using the Command Object with Stored Procedures

1. **Create a Command object**
2. **Set the CommandType to StoredProcedure**
3. **Set the CommandText property**
4. **Use the Add method to create and set parameters**
5. **Use the ParameterDirection property**
6. **Call ExecuteReader**
7. **Use records, and then close DataReader**
8. **Access output and return parameters**

You can also use the **Command** object to execute stored procedures in a database. You may need to perform some additional steps when preparing the **Command** to allow for the use of parameters in the stored procedure.

Use the following steps to execute a stored procedure with the **Command** object:

1. Create a **Command** object.
2. Set the **CommandType** property to **StoredProcedure**.
3. Set the **CommandText** property.
4. Use the **Add** method to create and set any parameters.
5. Use the **ParameterDirection** property to set parameter type.
6. Call the **ExecuteReader** method.
7. Use the **DataReader** object to view or manipulate the records, and close it when finished.
8. Access any output and return parameters.

The following example shows how to execute a stored procedure using ADO.NET.

```
Imports System.Data.SqlClient

Private Sub Button1_Click(ByVal sender As System.Object, ByVal
e As System.EventArgs) Handles Button1.Click

  Dim conSQL As New SqlClient.SqlConnection( )
  conSQL.ConnectionString = "Integrated Security=True;" & _
  "Data Source=LocalHost;Initial Catalog=Pubs;"
  conSQL.Open( )

  Dim commSQL As New SqlClient.SqlCommand( )
  commSQL.Connection = conSQL
  commSQL.CommandType = CommandType.StoredProcedure
  commSQL.CommandText = "byroyalty"

  Dim paramSQL As New SqlClient.sqlParameter( _
      "@percentage", SqlDbType.Int)
  paramSQL.Direction = ParameterDirection.Input
  paramSQL.Value = "30"
  commSQL.Parameters.Add(paramSQL)

  Dim datRead As SqlClient.SqlDataReader
  datRead = commSQL.ExecuteReader( )
  Do While datRead.Read( )
      MessageBox.Show(datRead(0).ToString)
  Loop
  datRead.Close( )
End Sub
```

Tip If you are running a query that will only return one row, you can improve the performance of your application by returning this data as output parameters from a stored procedure.

Using the DataReader Object

- Reading data

```
Dim commSQL As New SqlClient.SqlCommand( )
commSQL.Connection = conSQL
commSQL.CommandText ="Select au_lname,au_fname from authors"
Dim datRead As SqlClient.SqlDataReader
datRead = commSQL.ExecuteReader( )
Do Until datRead.Read = False
      MessageBox.Show(datRead.GetString(1) & " " _
      & datRead.GetString(0))
Loop
datRead.Close( )
```

- Retrieving data
- Returning multiple result sets

You can use the **DataReader** object to create a read-only, forward-only stream of data. This is an efficient method for accessing data that you only need to read through once. You can improve application performance by using this object because it holds only a single row of data at a time in memory instead of caching the entire set of records.

There are two versions of this object:

- **SqlDataReader** for SQL Server databases
- **OleDbDataReader** for other data sources

The **SqlDataReader** object contains some methods that are not available to the **OleDbDataReader**. These are **GetSQL***type* methods that you can use to retrieve SQL Server–specific data type columns from the data source.

Reading Data

You can instantiate the **DataReader** object by using the **ExecuteReader** method of the **Command** object. After you create the **DataReader**, you can call the **Read** method to obtain data in the rows. You can access the columns by name, ordinal number, or native type in conjunction with ordinal number.

You must ensure that you use the **Close** method of the **DataReader** object before accessing any output or return parameters from a stored procedure.

The following example shows how to retrieve data by using the **DataReader** object:

```
Dim conSQL As New SqlClient.SqlConnection( )
conSQL.ConnectionString = "Integrated Security=True;" & _
"Data Source=LocalHost;Initial Catalog=Pubs;"
conSQL.Open( )

Dim commSQL As New SqlClient.SqlCommand( )
commSQL.Connection = conSQL
commSQL.CommandText = "Select au_lname, au_fname from authors"

Dim datRead As SqlClient.SqlDataReader
datRead = commSQL.ExecuteReader( )
Do Until datRead.Read = False
  MessageBox.Show(datRead(1).ToString & " " & _
  datRead(0).ToString)
Loop
datRead.Close( )
```

Retrieving Data

Because you will often know the data types of your return data, you can use the **Get** methods to retrieve data in columns by specifying their data type. This approach can improve application performance because no type conversion is required, but your data and output types must be identical.

The following example shows how to use the **GetString** method to retrieve data. With **GetString**, you no longer need the **ToString** method shown in the preceding example.

```
Do Until datRead.Read = False
  MessageBox.Show(datRead.GetString(1) & " " & _
  datRead.GetString(0))
Loop
```

Returning Multiple Result Sets

Sometimes you will issue commands that return more than one result set. By default, the **DataReader** will only read the first result set. You can use the **NextResult** method of the **DataReader** to retrieve the next result set into the **DataReader** object. If there are no more result sets, this method returns **False**.

The following example shows how to create a stored procedure that returns two result sets from a SQL Server database:

```
CREATE PROCEDURE MultiResult AS
Select * from authors
Select * from titles
Return 0
GO
```

The following example shows how to execute the stored procedure **MultiResult** and access the information contained in each result set:

```
Dim conSQL As New SqlClient.SqlConnection( )
conSQL.ConnectionString = "Integrated Security=True;" & _
"Data Source=LocalHost;Initial Catalog=Pubs;"
conSQL.Open( )

Dim commSQL As New SqlClient.SqlCommand( )
commSQL.Connection = conSQL
commSQL.CommandType = CommandType.StoredProcedure
commSQL.CommandText = "MultiResult"

Dim datRead As SqlClient.SqlDataReader
datRead = commSQL.ExecuteReader( )
Do
  Do Until datRead.Read = False
      MessageBox.Show(datRead.GetString(1))
  Loop
Loop While datRead.NextResult

datRead.Close( )
```

Using the DataAdapter Object

- **Used as a link between data source and cached tables**

```
Dim adaptSQL As New SqlClient.SqlDataAdapter( _
    "Select * from authors", conSQL)

Dim datPubs As New DataSet( )
adaptSQL.Fill(datPubs, "NewTable")

' Manipulate the data locally

adaptSQL.Update (datPubs, "NewTable")
```

You can use the **DataAdapter** object to exchange data between a data source and a **DataSet**. You can use it to retrieve appropriate data and insert it into **DataTable** objects within a **DataSet**, and to update changes from the **DataSet** back into the data source.

Creating the DataAdapter

There are two ways to create a **DataAdapter** object:

- Use an existing, open **Connection** object.
- Open the **Connection** as needed.

Using an Existing Connection Object

Create a **Command** object within a **Connection** object, and assign the **SelectCommand** property of the previously instantiated **DataAdapter** object to that command. This technique is useful if you need to create a **Connection** object specifically for the **DataAdapter** object to use.

The following example shows how to use **Connection** and **Command** objects to instantiate a **DataAdapter**:

```
Dim conSQL As New SqlClient.SqlConnection( )
conSQL.ConnectionString = "Integrated Security=True;" & _
"Data Source=LocalHost;Initial Catalog=Pubs;"
conSQL.Open( )

Dim comSQL As New SqlClient.SqlCommand( )
comSQL.Connection = conSQL
comSQL.CommandText = "Select * from authors"

Dim adaptSQL As New SqlClient.SqlDataAdapter( )
adaptSQL.SelectCommand = comSQL
```

Using a Closed Connection

Instantiate the **DataAdapter** object, passing a query string and a **Connection** object. The **DataAdapter** will check whether the **Connection** is open, and, if it is not open, it will open it for you and close it when your method call is complete. This method is useful if you have already set the properties of a **Connection** object in your application and only need the connection to be opened to populate the data tables.

The following example shows how to instantiate a **DataAdapter** object:

```
Private conSQL as SqlClient.SqlConnection

Private Sub Form1_Load(ByVal sender As System.Object, ByVal e
As System.EventArgs) Handles MyBase.Load
  conSQL = New SqlClient.SqlConnection( )
  conSQL.ConnectionString = "Integrated " & _
      "Security=True;Data Source" & _
      "=LocalHost;Initial Catalog=Pubs;"
End Sub

Private Sub Button1_Click(ByVal sender As System.Object, ByVal
e As System.EventArgs) Handles Button1.Click
  Dim adaptSQL As New SqlClient.SqlDataAdapter( _
  "Select * from authors", conSQL)
End Sub
```

Filling the DataTable

After the **DataAdapter** object is created, you use the **Fill** method, passing a **DataSet** and, optionally, the required **DataTable** name as parameters. You can then work with the data in your application, and, if required, you can use the **Update** method of the **DataAdapter** to synchronize those changes back to the data source.

You can use a single **DataAdapter** to fill and update multiple **DataSets**. A single **DataAdapter** is linked to a particular **DataSet** only when a method is actually being called. The following example shows how to use a **DataAdapter** to fill a **DataSet**:

```
Dim conSQL As New SqlClient.SqlConnection( )
conSQL.ConnectionString = "Integrated Security=True;" & _
"Data Source=LocalHost;Initial Catalog=Pubs;"
conSQL.Open( )

Dim adaptSQL As New SqlClient.SqlDataAdapter("Select * from
authors", conSQL)

Dim datPubs As New DataSet( )
adaptSQL.Fill(datPubs, "NewTable")

'Manipulate the data locally using the DataSet

adaptSQL.Update(datPubs, "NewTable")
```

Demonstration: Retrieving Data Using ADO.NET

In this demonstration, you will learn how to retrieve data from a SQL Server database by using the **SQLDataReader** object in a Visual Basic .NET–based application.

◆ The DataSet Object

- Disconnected Data Review
- The DataSet Object
- Populating DataSets
- Using Relationships in DataSets
- Using Constraints
- Updating Data in the DataSet
- Updating Data at the Source

DataSets are the primary object that you will work with when accessing disconnected sets of data. They are similar in concept to groups of ADO disconnected recordsets, but in ADO.NET, there are many enhancements, including the ability to relate tables together.

In this lesson, you will learn how to create DataSets and populate tables within them. You will also learn how to edit these tables and propagate those changes to the data source.

After completing this lesson, you will be able to:

- Create DataSets and populate tables within them.
- Edit tables within DataSets.
- Propagate changes to the data source.

Disconnected Data Review

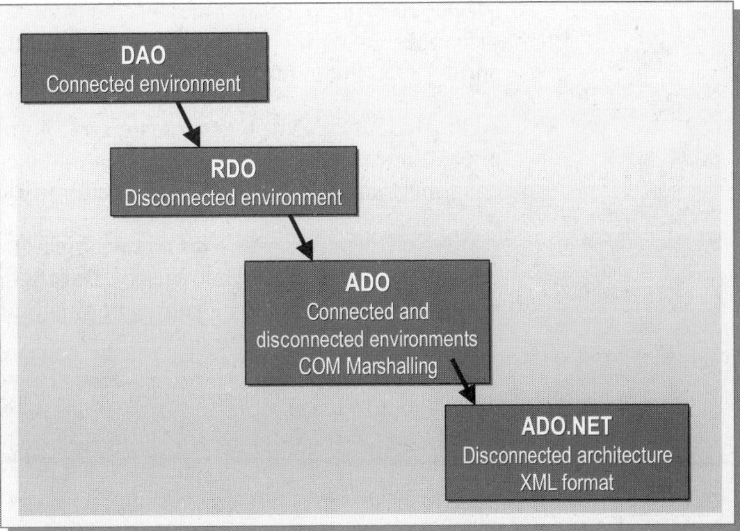

Each new data access technology has improved on the concept of disconnected data, but ADO.NET is the first one to provide a truly enterprise-wide solution.

Problems with Two-Tier Applications

In traditional two-tier applications, a data source connection was often made at the start of the application and held open until the application ended. This can cause many problems, including:

- Poor performance

  Database connections use valuable system resources, such as memory and CPU utilization. The database server performance will be affected if a large number of connections are needlessly held open.

- Limited scalability

  Applications that consume a large number of database connections are not scalable because most data sources can only support a limited number of connections.

Disconnected Data in RDO and ADO

To overcome these problems, Remote Data Objects (RDO) and ADO introduced the concept of disconnected data. This was implemented so that you could retrieve a set of records, disconnect from the data source, and work with the data locally. You could then reconnect and submit your changes to the database. The **Recordsets** were marshaled between the tiers as COM objects, requiring that both the server and client computer could handle COM components.

Disconnected Data in ADO.NET

ADO.NET is designed for use in the Internet world, whereas COM may not be supported by all tiers, and may not be transmitted through firewalls. The disconnected architecture has been updated from the previous two-tier, RDO, and ADO architectures.

ADO.NET uses XML as its transmission format. This is a text-based format, alleviating the problems associated with the transmission of COM objects and ensuring true cross-platform interoperability.

ADO.NET provides you with a new object for the caching of data on the client computer. This object is known as a **DataSet**. This object is automatically disconnected from the data source but maintains the ability to later update the source based on changes made at the client.

The DataSet Object

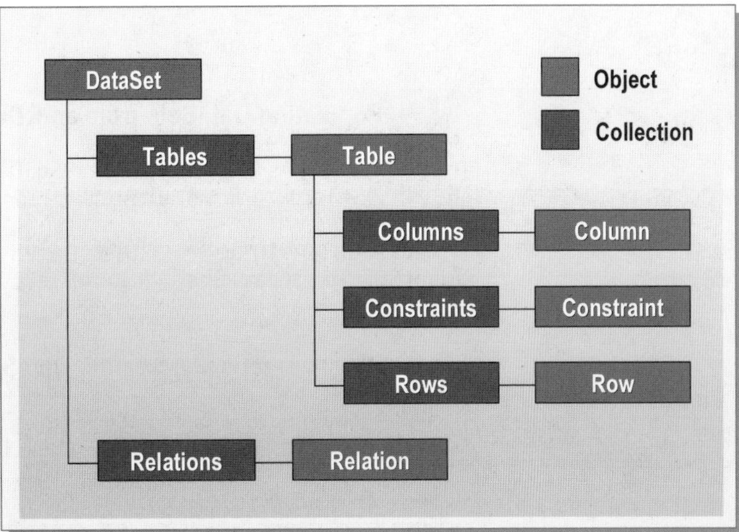

The **DataSet** object is a disconnected, memory resident cache of data. It is structured in a similar manner to a database in that it contains **DataTable**, **DataRelation**, and **Constraint** objects.

DataSets

A typical use of a **DataSet** is through Web Services. A client application will make a request for data to a Web Service that will populate a **DataSet** (using a **DataAdapter**) and return it to the client. The client can then view and modify the **DataSet** by using properties and methods that are consistent with database operations, and then pass it back to the Web Service. The Web Service will then update the database with the clients' changes. The **DataSet** is transmitted between tiers as XML, which means that it can be also be used by non-ADO.NET clients.

DataTables and DataRelations

The **DataSet** contains the **Tables** and **Relations** collections. Using objects within these two collections, you can build up a group of related tables within your **DataSet**. The **DataTable** object consists of the **Columns** collection and the **Rows** collection. You can use the objects in these collections to manipulate the fields and query their properties. The **Relations** collection contains definitions of all the relationships between the **DataTable** objects in the **DataSet**. You can use these to enforce constraints on your data or to navigate across tables.

The System.Data Namespace

The **System.Data** namespace contains the **DataSet** and its objects because they are generic ways of handling data. Unlike the Provider objects, there are not different objects for different data sources.

Populating DataSets

- **Populating DataSets from an RDBMS**

```
Dim adaptSQL As New SqlClient.SqlDataAdapter( _
    "Select * from authors", conSQL)

Dim datPubs As DataSet = New DataSet( )
adaptSQL.Fill(datPubs, "NewTable")
```

- **Programmatically creating DataSets**

```
Dim datPubs As New DataSet( )
Dim tblAuthors As DataTable = New DataTable("authors")
tblAuthors.Columns.Add("AuthorID", System.Type.GetType _
                        ("System.Int32"))
```

Because a **DataSet** is simply a memory resident representation of data, you do not necessarily need to take it from a traditional data source, such as a relational database management system (RDBMS) or a message store. You can create it at run time to manipulate data created within an application, or you can use it to view XML data.

Populating DataSets from an RDBMS

You use a **DataAdapter** to access data stored in a database, and store the data in **DataTable** objects within a **DataSet** in your application.

The following example shows how to populate a **DataTable** called *NewTable* with data from a SQL Server database:

```
Dim conSQL As New SqlClient.SqlConnection( )
conSQL.ConnectionString = "Integrated Security=True;" & _
  "Data Source=LocalHost;Initial Catalog=Pubs;"
conSQL.Open( )

Dim adaptSQL As New SqlClient.SqlDataAdapter("Select * from
authors", conSQL)

Dim datPubs As New DataSet( )
adaptSQL.Fill(datPubs, "NewTable")
```

Programmatically Creating DataSets

You sometimes need to work with non-standard data sources. In this situation, you can programmatically create **DataSets**, **DataTables**, **DataRelations**, and **Constraints**, and then populate the tables with your data. This will give you the ability to use standard ADO.NET functions to access your data.

The following example shows how to create a **DataSet** containing a **DataTable** with three **DataColumns**. This could then be extended to add more columns, and then populate them with data.

```
Dim datPubs As New DataSet( )
Dim tblAuthors As New DataTable("authors")
tblAuthors.Columns.Add("AuthorID", _
  System.Type.GetType("System.Int32"))
tblAuthors.Columns.Add("au_lname", _
  System.Type.GetType("System.String"))
tblAuthors.Columns.Add("au_fname", _
  System.Type.GetType("System.String"))
datPubs.Tables.Add(tblAuthors)
```

Using Relationships in DataSets

- **Creating relationships**

```
Dim relPubsTitle As New DataRelation("PubsTitles", _
        datPubs.Tables("Publishers").Columns("pub_id"), _
        datPubs.Tables("Titles").Columns("pub_id"))
datPubs.Relations.Add(relPubsTitle)
```

- **Accessing related data**

```
Dim PubRow, TitleRow As DataRow, TitleRows( ) As DataRow

PubRow = datPubs.Tables("Publishers").Rows(0)
TitleRows = PubRow.GetChildRows("PubsTitles")
```

The basis of most RDBMSs is the ability to relate tables to each other. ADO.NET provides this ability within **DataSets** through the **DataRelation** class.

Each **DataRelation** object contains an array of **DataColumn** objects that define the parent column or columns, or primary key, and the child column or columns, or foreign key, in the relationship. Referential integrity is maintained by the relationship, and you can specify how to deal with related changes.

Creating Relationships

The following example shows how to create a relationship between two **DataTable** objects in a **DataSet**. The same **DataAdapter** is used to populate the **DataTable** objects, and then a **DataRelation** is created between the two.

```
Dim conSQL As New SqlClient.SqlConnection( )
conSQL.ConnectionString = "Integrated Security=True;" & _
  "Data Source=LocalHost;Initial Catalog=Pubs;"
conSQL.Open( )

Dim adaptSQL As SqlClient.SqlDataAdapter
Dim datPubs As New DataSet( )

adaptSQL = New SqlClient.SqlDataAdapter("Select pub_id," & _
  "pub_name, city, state from publishers", conSQL)
adaptSQL.Fill(datPubs, "Publishers")
adaptSQL = New SqlClient.SqlDataAdapter("Select pub_id," & _
  "title, type, price from titles", conSQL)
adaptSQL.Fill(datPubs, "Titles")

Dim relPubsTitle As New DataRelation("PubsTitles", _
  datPubs.Tables("Publishers").Columns("pub_id"), _
  datPubs.Tables("Titles").Columns("pub_id"))
datPubs.Relations.Add(relPubsTitle)
```

Accessing Related Data

The main use of a **DataRelation** is to allow access to related records in a different table. You can do this by using the **GetChildRows** method of a **DataRow** object that returns an array of **DataRow** objects. The following example shows how to use this method to access the child rows that match the first publisher by using the relationship created in the previous example:

```
Dim PubRow, TitleRow As DataRow
Dim TitleRows( ) As DataRow 'Array of DataRow objects

PubRow = datPubs.Tables("Publishers").Rows(0)
TitleRows = PubRow.GetChildRows("PubsTitles")

For Each TitleRow In TitleRows
  ListBox1.Items.Add(TitleRow("title").ToString)
Next
```

Using Constraints

- Creating new constraints
  - ForeignKeyConstraints
  - UniqueConstraints
- Using existing constraints

```
adaptSQL = New SqlClient.SqlDataAdapter("Select title_id" _
      & ", title, type, price from titles", conSQL)
adaptSQL.FillSchema(datPubs, schematype.Source, "Titles")
adaptSQL.Fill(datPubs, "Titles")
'Edit some data
adaptSQL.Fill(datPubs, "Titles")
```

You can create your own constraints within a **DataSet**, or you can copy the existing constraints from the data source. Each of these options is available to you in ADO.NET.

Creating New Constraints

You can apply two types of constraint classes to **DataColumns**: **ForeignKeyConstraint** and **UniqueConstraint**.

ForeignKeyConstraint

This constraint controls what happens to a child row when a parent row is updated or deleted. You can specify different behaviors for different circumstances. The following table shows the values for the **DeleteRule** and **UpdateRule** properties of the **ForeignKeyConstraint**.

Value	Description
Cascade	Deletes or updates any child records based on the parent record.
SetNull	Sets related values to **DBNull**.
SetDefault	Sets related values to their defaults.
None	Does not affect related rows.

The following example shows how to apply a foreign key constraint with specific actions between two tables in an existing **DataSet**. If a row in the parent table is deleted, the child value will be set to **DBNull**. If a row in the parent table is updated, the child values will be also be updated.

```
Dim colParent As DataColumn
Dim colChild As DataColumn
Dim fkcPubsTitles As ForeignKeyConstraint

colParent = datPubs.Tables("publishers").Columns("pub_id")
colChild = datPubs.Tables("titles").Columns("pub_id")
fkcPubsTitles = New _
  ForeignKeyConstraint("PubsTitlesFKConstraint", colParent, _
  colChild)

fkcPubsTitles.DeleteRule = Rule.SetNull
fkcPubsTitles.UpdateRule = Rule.Cascade

datPubs.Tables("titles").Constraints.Add(fkcPubsTitles)
datPubs.EnforceConstraints = True
```

UniqueConstraint

This constraint can be added to one column or to an array of columns. It ensures that all values in the column or columns are unique. When this constraint is added, ADO.NET verifies that the existing data does not violate the constraint and maintains the setting for all changes to that **DataTable**.

The following example shows how to add a **UniqueConstraint** to a column:

```
Dim ucTitles As New UniqueConstraint("UniqueTitles", _
  datPubs.Tables("titles").Columns("title"))
datPubs.EnforceConstraints = True
```

Using Existing Constraints

If constraints already exist in the RDBMS, you can copy them directly into your **DataSet**. This can save a lot of time that might be spent coding for frequently occurring problems. For example, if you fill a **DataSet**, modify some data, and then use **Fill** again to return to the original data, all the rows will be appended to your existing **DataTable**s, unless you define primary keys. You can avoid this type of problem by copying the table schema.

The following example shows how to use the **FillSchema** method to copy constraint information into a **DataSet**:

```
adaptSQL = New SqlClient.SqlDataAdapter("Select title_id," & _
  "title, type, price from titles", conSQL)
adaptSQL.FillSchema(datPubs, schematype.Source, "Titles")
adaptSQL.Fill(datPubs, "Titles")
'Edit some data
adaptSQL.Fill(datPubs, "Titles")
```

Note Constraints are automatically added to columns when you create a relationship between them. A **UniqueConstraint** is added to the primary key, and a **ForeignKeyConstraint** is added to the foreign key.

Updating Data in the DataSet

- Adding rows

```
Dim drNewRow As DataRow = datPubs.Tables("Titles").NewRow
'Populate columns
datPubs.Tables("Titles").Rows.Add(drNewRow)
```

- Editing rows

```
drChangeRow.BeginEdit( )
drChangeRow("Title") = drChangeRow("Title").ToString & " 1"
drChangeRow.EndEdit( )
```

- Deleting data

```
datPubs.Tables("Titles").Rows.Remove(drDelRow)
```

After you have created a **DataSet** of **DataTables**, you might want to add, update, and delete data. Any changes you make to the data are stored in memory and later used to apply the changes to the data source.

Adding Rows

Use the following steps to add new rows to a table:

1. Instantiate a **DataRow** object by using the **NewRow** method of the **DataTable**.
2. Populate the columns with data.
3. Call the **Add** method of the **DataRows** collection, passing the **DataRow** object.

The following example shows how to add rows to a **DataSet**:

```
Dim drNewRow As DataRow = datPubs.Tables("Titles").NewRow
drNewRow("title") = "New Book"
drNewRow("type") = "business"
datPubs.Tables("Titles").Rows.Add(drNewRow)
```

Editing Rows

Use the following steps to edit existing rows:

1. Call the **BeginEdit** method of the row.
2. Change the data in the columns.
3. Call **EndEdit** or **CancelEdit** to accept or reject the changes.

The following example shows how to edit data in an existing column:

```
Dim drChangeRow As DataRow = datPubs.Tables("Titles").Rows(0)
drChangeRow.BeginEdit( )
drChangeRow("Title") = drChangeRow("Title").ToString & " 1"
drChangeRow.EndEdit( )
```

Deleting Data

Use either of the following methods to delete a row:

- **Remove** method

  Call the **Remove** method of the **DataRows** collection. This permanently removes the row from the **DataSet**.

- **Delete** method

  Call the **Delete** method of the **DataRow** object. This only marks the row for deletion in the **DataSet**, and calling **RejectChanges** will undo the deletion.

The following example shows how to delete an existing row from a **DataSet**:

```
Dim drDelRow As DataRow = datPubs.Tables("Titles").Rows(0)
datPubs.Tables("Titles").Rows.Remove(drDelRow)
```

Confirming the Changes

To update the **DataSet**, you use the appropriate methods to edit the table, and then call **AcceptChanges** or **RejectChanges** for the individual rows or for the entire table.

You can discover whether any changes have been made to a row since **AcceptChanges** was last called by querying its **RowState** property. The following table describes the valid settings for this property.

Value	Description
Unchanged	No changes have been made.
Added	The row has been added to the table.
Modified	Something in the row has been changed.
Deleted	The row has been deleted by the **Delete** method.
Detached	The row has been deleted, or the row has been created, but the **Add** method has not been called.

Updating Data at the Source

- **Explicitly specifying the updates**

```
Dim comm As New SqlClient.SqlCommand("Insert titles" & _
"(title_id, title, type) values(@t_id,@title,@type)")
comm.Parameters.Add("@t_id",SqlDbType.VarChar,6,"title_id")
comm.Parameters.Add("@title",SqlDbType.VarChar,80,"title")
comm.Parameters.Add("@type",SqlDbType.Char,12,"type")
adaptSQL.InsertCommand = comm
adaptSQL.Update(datPubs, "titles")
```

- **Automatically generating the updates**

```
Dim sqlCommBuild As New SqlCommandBuilder(adaptSQL)
MsgBox(sqlCommBuild.GetInsertCommand.CommandText)
adaptSQL.Update(datPubs, "titles")
```

After you have updated the tables in your **DataSet**, you will want to replicate those changes to the underlying data source. To do this, you use the **Update** method of the **DataAdapter** object, which is the link between **DataSet** and data source.

The **Update** method, like the **Fill** method, takes two parameters: the **DataSet** in which the changes have been made and the name of the **DataTable** in which the changes are. It determines the changes to the data and executes the appropriate SQL command (Insert, Update or Delete) against the source data.

Explicitly Specifying the Updates

You use the **InsertCommand**, **UpdateCommand**, and **DeleteCommand** properties of the **DataAdapter** to identify the changes occurring in your DataSet. You specify each of these as an existing command object for an Insert, Update, or Delete SQL statement. For any variable columns in the statements, you use **SqlParameter** objects to identify the column, data type, size, and data to be inserted.

The following example shows how to use the **InsertCommand** property to add a row to the Titles table in the Pubs database:

```
Dim conSQL As New SqlClient.SqlConnection( )
Dim adaptSQL As SqlClient.SqlDataAdapter
Dim datPubs As New DataSet( )

conSQL.ConnectionString = "Integrated Security=True;" & _
  "Data Source=LocalHost;Initial Catalog=Pubs;"
conSQL.Open( )

adaptSQL = New SqlClient.SqlDataAdapter("Select pub_id," & _
  "title_id, title, type, price from titles", conSQL)
adaptSQL.Fill(datPubs, "Titles")

Dim drNewRow As DataRow = datPubs.Tables("Titles").NewRow
drNewRow("title_id") = "hg3454"
drNewRow("title") = "New Book"
drNewRow("type") = "business"
datPubs.Tables("Titles").Rows.Add(drNewRow)

Dim comm As New SqlClient.SqlCommand("Insert titles" & _
"(title_id, title, type) values (@title_id,@title,@type)")

comm.Parameters.Add("@title_id", SqlDbType.VarChar, 6, _
  "title_id")
comm.Parameters.Add("@title", SqlDbType.VarChar, 80, "title")
comm.Parameters.Add("@type", SqlDbType.Char, 12, "type")

adaptSQL.InsertCommand = comm
adaptSQL.Update(datPubs, "titles")
```

Automatically Generating the Updates

If your DataTable is generated from only one table in the data source, you can use the **CommandBuilder** object to automatically create the **InsertCommand**, **UpdateCommand**, and **DeleteCommand** properties.

The following example shows how to use the **CommandBuilder** object to achieve the same results as the previous example:

```
Dim conSQL As New SqlClient.SqlConnection
Dim adaptSQL As SqlClient.SqlDataAdapter
Dim datPubs As New DataSet( )

conSQL.ConnectionString = "Integrated Security=True;" & _
  "Data Source=LocalHost;Initial Catalog=Pubs;"
conSQL.Open( )

adaptSQL = New SqlClient.SqlDataAdapter("Select pub_id," & _
  "title_id, title, type, price from titles", conSQL)
adaptSQL.Fill(datPubs, "Titles")

Dim drNewRow As DataRow = datPubs.Tables("Titles").NewRow
drNewRow("title_id") = "hg8765"
drNewRow("title") = "New Book"
drNewRow("type") = "business"
datPubs.Tables("Titles").Rows.Add(drNewRow)

Dim sqlCommBuild As New SqlCommandBuilder(adaptSQL)
adaptSQL.Update(datPubs, "titles")
```

Note Even though the automatically generated commands can simplify your coding, you will improve performance by using the **InsertCommand**, **UpdateCommand**, and **DeleteCommand** properties.

Practice: Using DataSets

In this practice, you will update existing data in a SQL Server database by using automatically generated commands.

► To review the application

1. Open Microsoft Visual Studio .NET.
2. On the **File** menu, point to **Open**, and then click **Project**. Set the location to *install folder*\Practices\Mod08\DataSets\Starter, click **DataSets.sln**, and then click **Open**.
3. Run the application, and click **Populate DataSet** and **Refresh List from Data Source**. Note that the list on the left displays data from a **DataSet**, and the list on the right uses a **DataReader** object. Quit the application.
4. Review the code in Form1.vb to see how the **DataSet** was created.

► To update the local DataSet

1. In the **btnEditName_Click** procedure, locate the comment "add code to update the dataset here."
2. Add the following lines below the comment to update the local dataset:

```
objDataTable = dsCustomers.Tables("customers")
objDataRow = objDataTable.Rows(iCust)
objDataRow("lastname") = strNewName
```

▶ **To automatically generate a command**

1. In **btnUpdate_Click** procedure, locate the comment "add code to update the data source here."
2. To generate the update command automatically, add the following lines below the comment:

```
Dim sqlCommBuild As New _
SqlClient.SqlCommandBuilder(adaptCustomers)
adaptCustomers.Update(dsCustomers, "customers")
```

▶ **To test your code**

1. Run the application, and click **Populate DataSet** and **Refresh List from Data Source**.
2. Click the first name in the **Local DataSet** box. Click **Edit Name**, type your last name, and then click **OK**. Click **Refresh List from DataSet**, and note that the change has been made to the local dataset. Click **Refresh List from Data Source**, and note that the underlying data source still contains the original data.
3. Click **Update Changes**. Click **Refresh List from Data Source**, and verify that the changes have now been replicated to the underlying data source.
4. Quit the application, and quit Visual Studio .NET.

◆ Data Designers and Data Binding

- Designing DataSets
- Data Form Wizard
- Data Binding in Windows Forms
- Data Binding in Web Forms

Data binding has been an important part of Visual Basic data development for a long time. The tools included in Visual Basic .NET have been enhanced to allow easier creation of data-bound forms and to take advantage of the new features in ADO.NET.

After completing this lesson, you will be able to:

- Describe the data designers available in Visual Basic .NET.
- Create data-bound Windows Forms and Web Forms.

Designing DataSets

- **DataAdapter Configuration Wizard**
  - Generates a **DataAdapter** object in the **InitializeComponent** procedure for use in your code
- **Generate DataSet Tool**
  - Generates a **DataSet** based on data from an existing **DataAdapter**

Visual Basic .NET includes a number of designers to simplify the process of DataSet creation. These include the Connection Wizard, DataAdapter Configuration Wizard, and the Generate DataSet Tool.

DataAdapter Configuration Wizard

This wizard leads you through the steps needed to create a **DataAdapter** object within an existing connection. You can initiate the wizard by adding a **SqlDataAdapter** or **OleDbDataAdapter** from the Toolbox to a form at design time. It requires the following information to generate a **DataAdapter** object for use in your form:

- Connection name
- Query type
  - SQL statement
  - New stored procedure
  - Existing stored procedure
- Details of the chosen query

Once you have created the **DataAdapter**, you can view the code created by the wizard in the **InitializeComponent** procedure.

Generate DataSet Tool

This tool allows you to generate a **DataSet** automatically from a **DataAdapter**.

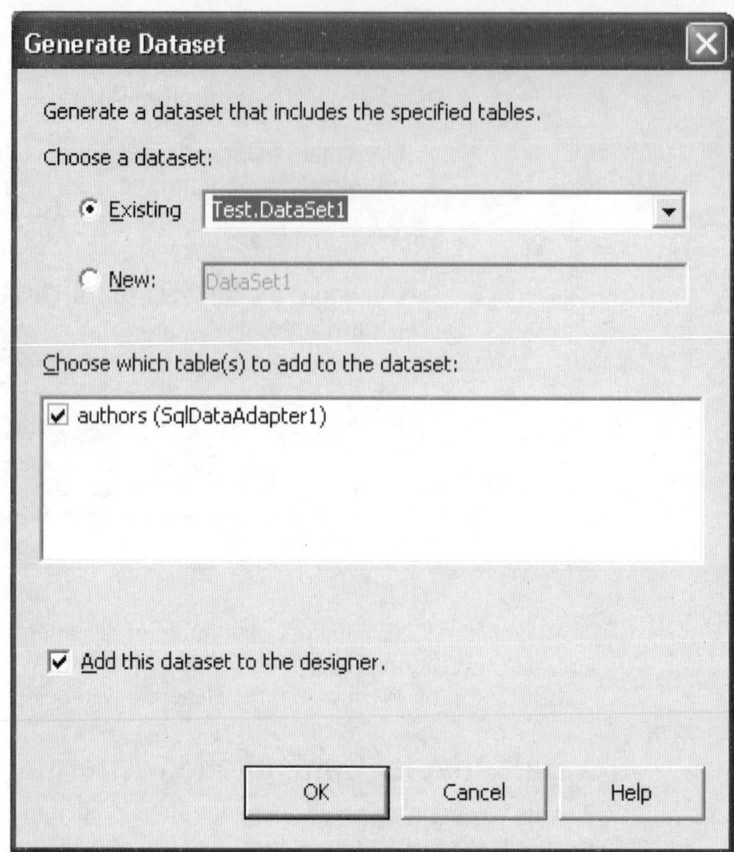

Again, once created, you can use this **DataSet** in the usual way in your code.

Data Form Wizard

- **Information required:**
  - Name of **DataSet**
  - Connection to be used
  - Which tables or views, and which columns within them
  - How to display the data
  - Which buttons to create

You can use the Data Form Wizard to automatically bind data to controls on a form. You can specify to use an existing DataSet in the project, which will then use your pre-written methods for data access, or to create a new DataSet based on information supplied to the wizard.

If you want to create a new DataSet, the Data Form Wizard will require the following information:

- Name of the DataSet to create
- Connection to be used (you can create a new connection at this point)
- Which tables or views to use (if more than one, you can also identify the relationship between them)
- Which columns to include on the form
- How to display the data (data grid or bound controls)
- Whether to include navigation and editing buttons

Demonstration: Using the Data Form Wizard

In this demonstration, you will learn how to use the Data Form Wizard to create a data-bound form from a new **DataSet**.

Data Binding in Windows Forms

- **Simple binding**

```
da = New SqlClient.SqlDataAdapter("Select au_lname, " & _
       "au_fname from authors", sqlconn)
da.Fill(ds, "authors")
TextBox1.DataBindings.Add("Text", _
       ds.Tables("authors"), "au_fname")
```

- **Complex binding**

```
da = New SqlClient.SqlDataAdapter("Select au_lname, " & _
       "au_fname from authors", sqlconn)
da.Fill(ds, "authors")
DataGrid1.DataSource = ds.Tables("authors")
```

If you want more control over the appearance of your forms, you can use data binding to design them yourself.

There are two general types of binding that can be used: simple binding and complex binding. Both can be performed at design time by using the Properties window or at run time by using code.

Simple Binding

You use simple binding to link a control to a single field in a **DataSet**. For example, you would use simple binding for a **TextBox** control. Using the **DataBindings** property of a data-aware control, you can specify which **DataSet** and which field to bind to which property.

The following example shows how to bind data to a **TextBox** control:

```
Dim sqlconn As New SqlClient.SqlConnection( )
Dim da As SqlClient.SqlDataAdapter
Dim ds As New DataSet( )
sqlconn.ConnectionString = "Integrated Security=True;" & _
  "Data Source=LocalHost;Initial Catalog=Pubs;"
sqlconn.Open( )
da = New SqlClient.SqlDataAdapter("Select au_lname, " & _
  "au_fname from authors", sqlconn)
da.Fill(ds, "authors")

TextBox1.DataBindings.Add("Text", _
  ds.Tables("authors"), "au_fname")
TextBox2.DataBindings.Add("Text", _
  ds.Tables("authors"), "au_lname")
```

Complex Binding

You use complex binding to link a control to multiple fields in a **DataSet.** For example, you would use complex binding for a **DataGrid** control. These controls have a **DataSource** property that allows you to specify the table to be used.

The following example shows how to use the **DataSource** property of a **DataGrid** control:

```
Dim sqlconn As New SqlClient.SqlConnection( )
Dim da As SqlClient.SqlDataAdapter
Dim ds As New DataSet( )
sqlconn.ConnectionString = "Integrated Security=True;" & _
  "Data Source=LocalHost;Initial Catalog=Pubs;"
sqlconn.Open( )
da = New SqlClient.SqlDataAdapter("Select au_lname, " & _
  "au_fname from authors", sqlconn)
da.Fill(ds, "authors")
DataGrid1.DataSource = ds.Tables("authors")
```

Updating Data

As with manual coding of data access, changing values in data-bound forms only applies to the local **DataSet**. To write these changes to the underlying data source, you must add your own code by using the **Update** method of the **DataAdapter**.

Data Binding in Web Forms

- **Use impersonation**

```
<identity impersonate="true" userName="Karen"
password="Password"/>
```

- **Binding to read-only data**

```
Dim sqlComm As New SqlClient.SqlCommand("Select * from " & _
        "authors", sqlconn)
Dim sqlReader As SqlClient.SqlDataReader
sqlReader = sqlComm.ExecuteReader
DataGrid1.DataSource( ) = sqlReader
DataGrid1.DataBind( )
```

Most data displayed on Web Forms will be read only, so you do not need to incorporate the overhead of using a **DataSet** in your Web Form applications; you can use the more efficient **DataReader** object instead. If you want your users to be able to edit data on the Web Form, you must code the edit, update, and cancel events yourself.

Use Impersonation

You must configure impersonation when connecting to SQL Server from a Web form. To do this, add an <identity> tag similar to the following example to the Web.config file:

```
<identity impersonate="true" userName="Karen"
password="Password"/>
```

Binding to Read-Only Data

You use the **DataBind** method of the **DataGrid** server control to bind data to a grid on a Web Form. The following example shows how to do this using a **DataReader** object:

```
Dim sqlconn As New SqlClient.SqlConnection( )
sqlconn.ConnectionString = "Integrated Security=True;" & _
  "Data Source=LocalHost;Initial Catalog=Pubs;"
sqlconn.Open( )

Dim sqlComm As New SqlClient.SqlCommand("Select * from " & _
  "authors", sqlconn)
Dim sqlReader As SqlClient.SqlDataReader
sqlReader = sqlComm.ExecuteReader
DataGrid1.DataSource( ) = sqlReader
DataGrid1.DataBind( )
```

The **DataGrid** will not be visible until you call the **DataBind** method.

◆ XML Integration

- Why Use Schemas?
- Describing XML Structure
- Creating Schemas
- Using XML Data and Schemas in ADO.NET
- DataSets and XmlDataDocuments

Traditionally, XML and ADO data have been two distinct entities, but ADO.NET brings them together and allows you to work with both types in the same way.

XML is tightly integrated into the .NET platform. You have already seen how DataSets are transmitted by using XML format, and now you will learn how DataSets are literally represented as XML and how their structure is defined in an XML Schema Definition (XSD).

After completing this lesson, you will be able to:

- Describe what an XML schema is.
- Explain why XML schemas are useful to the Visual Basic .NET developer.
- Create schemas.
- Manipulate XML data within an ADO.NET DataSet by means of an **XMLReader**.

Why Use Schemas?

- **Define format of data**
- **Use for validity checking**
- **Advantages over DTDs**
  - XML syntax
  - Reusable types
  - Grouping

When working with traditional database applications, you often need to write validation code to ensure that the data you are inputting matches the database schema. If you do not do this, then you need to write error-handling code for the potential errors that may occur. Either way, there must be some way of checking. The solution to this problem when you are working with XML data is XML schemas.

XML schemas are similar in concept to database schemas. They define the elements and attributes that may appear in your XML documents, and how these elements and attributes relate to each other. Schemas are very important to ensure that the data you are using conforms to your specification. When loading XML data, you can check it against the schema to validate that none of the data entering your system is in an incorrect format. This is becoming more of an issue as business-to-business and business-to-customer commerce becomes more prevalent in the Internet world.

Visual Studio .NET uses XSD to create schemas. This syntax is currently at working-draft status at the World Wide Web Consortium (W3C), but it has many advantages over document type definitions (DTDs).

- XML syntax

  DTDs are written using a DTD syntax, which is not related to any of the other Internet standards currently in use. XSD uses XML syntax, which enables developers to validate data without needing to learn yet another language.

- Reusable types

  XSD allows you to define complex data types and reuse those within your schema.

- Grouping

  You can specify that a set of elements always exists as a group and stipulate the order in which they must appear.

Describing XML Structure

- **Schemas can describe:**
  - Elements in the document
  - Attributes in the document
  - Element and attribute relationships
  - Data types
  - The order of the elements
  - Which elements are optional

Schemas describe the structure of an XML document, and you can use them to validate data within that document. A schema document can describe all or some of the following:

- Elements and attributes contained within the XML document
- Element and attribute relationships
- Data types
- The order of the elements
- Which elements are optional

For example, consider the following XML document:

```
<?xml version="1.0" ?>
<pubs>
  <Publishers>
      <pub_id>0736</pub_id>
      <pub_name>Lucerne Publishing</pub_name>
      <city>Boston</city>
      <state>MA</state>
      <country>USA</country>
  </Publishers>
  <Publishers>
      <pub_id>0877</pub_id>
      <pub_name>Litware, Inc.</pub_name>
      <city>Washington</city>
      <state>DC</state>
      <country>USA</country>
  </Publishers>
</pubs>
```

This document consists of a <pubs> element containing individual <Publishers> elements. Each of these contains a <pub_id>, <pub_name>, <city>, <state>, and <country> element. This defines the structure of the document.

After the XML document is linked to a schema document describing the structure, the schema can be used to verify data being input into the document.

The following example shows the schema generated for this document:

```
<?xml version="1.0" ?>
<xsd:schema id="pubs"
  targetNamespace="http://tempuri.org/Publishers.xsd"
  xmlns="http://tempuri.org/Publishers.xsd"
  xmlns:xsd="http://www.w3.org/2001/XMLSchema"
  xmlns:msdata="urn:schemas-microsoft-com:xml-msdata"
  attributeFormDefault="qualified"
  elementFormDefault="qualified">
  <xsd:element name="pubs" msdata:IsDataSet="true"
      msdata:EnforceConstraints="False">
      <xsd:complexType>
          <xsd:choice maxOccurs="unbounded">
              <xsd:element name="Publishers">
                  <xsd:complexType>
                      <xsd:sequence>
                          <xsd:element name="pub_id"
                              type="xsd:string" minOccurs="0" />
                          <xsd:element name="pub_name"
                              type="xsd:string" minOccurs="0" />
                          <xsd:element name="city"
                              type="xsd:string" minOccurs="0" />
                          <xsd:element name="state"
                              type="xsd:string" minOccurs="0" />
                          <xsd:element name="country"
                              type="xsd:string" minOccurs="0" />
                      </xsd:sequence>
                  </xsd:complexType>
              </xsd:element>
          </xsd:choice>
      </xsd:complexType>
  </xsd:element>
</xsd:schema>
```

Creating Schemas

- Creating schemas from existing XML documents
- Creating schemas from databases
- Working with schemas
- Validating XML documents against schemas

Schemas are automatically generated for you when you work with DataSets. You may find that there are situations when you want to create your own. One example would be when you are exchanging data with a business partner and want to define the structure of that data.

Creating Schemas from Existing XML Documents

You can add an existing XML document to a project and automatically create a schema based on the contents of the document.

When you are working with XML data, an XML menu becomes available. This menu allows you to generate a schema and validate data against the schema. When you create schemas from existing documents, all data types are declared as strings. You can alter this manually in the XML Designer.

Creating Schemas from Databases

You can also create an XSD schema from the structure of existing data. To do this, you add a new schema item to your project and drag on the chosen tables or views from the hierarchy displayed in the Data Connections of Server Explorer. Again, the data types will need editing.

Working with Schemas

You can view schemas in Visual Studio .NET either as XML or in the Designer Window, which is a user-friendly display of the schema. In this window, you can edit existing schemas (adding, removing, or modifying elements and attributes) and create new schemas.

The following illustration shows the Designer Window:

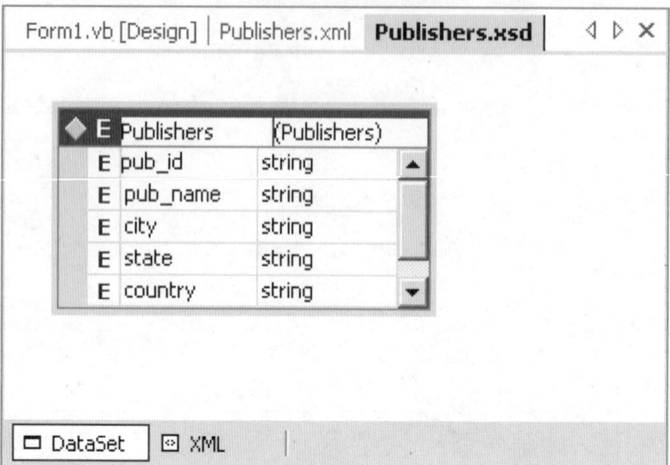

Validating XML Documents Against Schemas

You can use the XML Designer to validate data against XML schemas. If you have an existing document that you are adding data to, you can use this technique to validate that the new data conforms to the structure described in the schema.

Use the following steps to validate an XML document against an XML schema.

1. Load the XML document into the XML Designer.
2. On the XML menu, click Validate XML Data.

Any validation errors will be noted in the Task List.

Using XML Data and Schemas in ADO.NET

- **Loading XML data into a DataSet**

```
Dim datXML As DataSet = New DataSet()
datXML.ReadXml("c:\publishers.xml")
MessageBox.Show(datXML.Tables(0).Rows(0)(0).ToString)
```

- **Using a typed DataSet**
  - Increases performance
  - Simplifies coding

```
MessageBox.Show(pubs.Publishers(0).pub_id)
```

One of the issues experienced by developers in the past has been trying to manipulate XML data within their applications. In earlier data access technologies, there was no ability to do this. In ADO.NET, you can populate a **DataSet** from an XML document. This allows you to access the data in a simple fashion.

Loading XML Data into a DataSet

You can load an existing XML document into a **DataSet** by using the **ReadXML** method of the **DataSet**. This requires one argument of the fully qualified path and file name of the XML document to be loaded.

The following example shows how to load the data and display the first column in the first row:

```
Dim datXML As DataSet = New DataSet( )
datXML.ReadXml("c:\publishers.xml")
Dim drFirstRow As DataRow = datXML.Tables(0).Rows(0)
MessageBox.Show(drFirstRow(0).ToString)
```

Using Typed DataSets

DataSets can be *typed* or *untyped.* A typed **DataSet** is simply a **DataSet** that uses information in a schema to generate a derived **DataSet** class containing objects and properties based on the structure of the data.

You can create a typed **DataSet** by using the **Generate DataSet** command from the Schema view. You can add a DataSet object to a form, and link it to the typed dataset already in the project, and then work with the DataSet in the usual way.

In untyped DataSets, you have been accessing the columns and rows as collections in the hierarchy. In a typed **DataSet**, you can access these directly as objects, as shown in the following example:

```
MessageBox.Show(pubs.Publishers(0).pub_id)
```

Typed **DataSets** also provide compile-time type checking and better performance than untyped **DataSets**.

Note **DataSets** created using the XML Designer tools are automatically typed.

DataSets and XmlDataDocuments

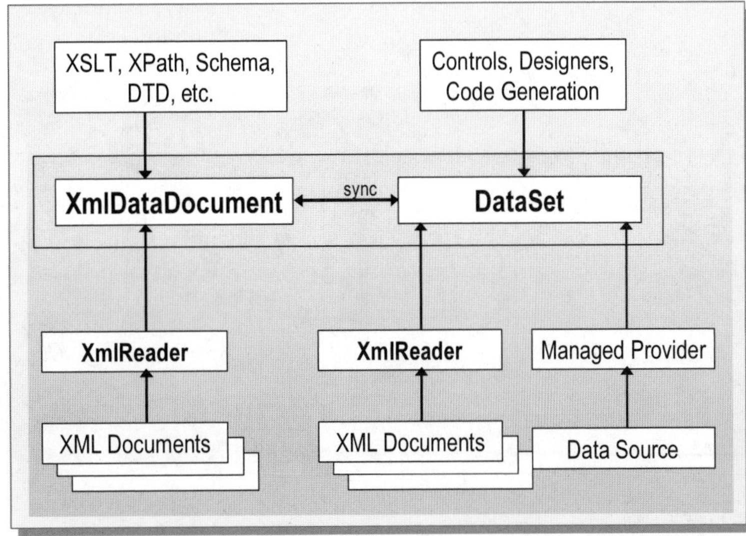

XML developers have traditionally used the Document Object Model (DOM) to manipulate their XML documents. This is a standard COM interface to XML data, and it allows access to the elements and attributes contained within the document.

The **XmlDataDocument** in the .NET Framework extends the **DOMDocument** object in the XML DOM to allow .NET developers to use the same functionality. This object is tightly integrated with the ADO.NET **DataSet**, and loading data into either object synchronizes it with the other.

Any manipulation of data by means of the **DataSet** or the **XmlDataDocument** is synchronized in the other. Therefore, if you add a row to the **DataSet**, an element is added to the **XmlDataDocument**, and vice versa.

Demonstration: Using XML Schemas

In this demonstration, you will learn how to create an XML schema from an existing XML document, and how to then use the schema to validate the document.

Lab 8.1: Creating Applications That Use ADO.NET

Objectives

After completing this lab, you will be able to:

- Retrieve, insert, and update data by using ADO.NET.
- Use data binding on a Web Form.
- Use the XML Designer to create a typed dataset.

Prerequisites

Before working on this lab, you must be familiar with:

- Creating Visual Basic .NET Windows Forms and Web Forms.
- Using ADO.NET data readers.
- Using ADO.NET DataSets.
- Working with XML and XSD.

Scenario

In this lab, you will use ADO.NET to access data for the Cargo application. You will create both Windows Forms and Web Forms that access both customer and invoice information. You will also use the XML Designer to create a typed DataSet.

Starter and Solution Files

There are starter and solution files associated with this lab. The starter files are in the *install folder*\Labs\Lab081\Ex0*x*\Starter folders, and the solution files are in the *install folder*\Labs\Lab081\Ex0*x*\Solution folders (where *x* is the exercise number).

Estimated time to complete this lab: 60 minutes

Exercise 1
Retrieving Data

In this exercise, you will create a Windows Forms application to display a list of customers and their details. You will create a **DataSet** object in a class module and use this data set to obtain the customer details for the selected customer.

▶ To create the project

1. Open Microsoft Visual Studio .NET.
2. On the **File** menu, point to **New**, and then click **Project**.
3. In the **Project Types** box, click **Visual Basic Projects**.
4. In the **Templates** box, click **Windows Application**.
5. Change the name of the project to **CustomerProject**, set the location to *install folder*\Labs\Lab081\Ex01, and then click **OK**.

▶ To create the Windows Form

1. In Solution Explorer, rename the default form to **frmCustomer.vb**.
2. In the Properties window, change the **Text** property of the form to **Customer Details**, and change the **Name** property to **frmCustomer**.
3. Open the project Properties dialog box, change the Startup object to **frmCustomer**, and then click OK.
4. Add controls to the form, as shown in the following illustration.

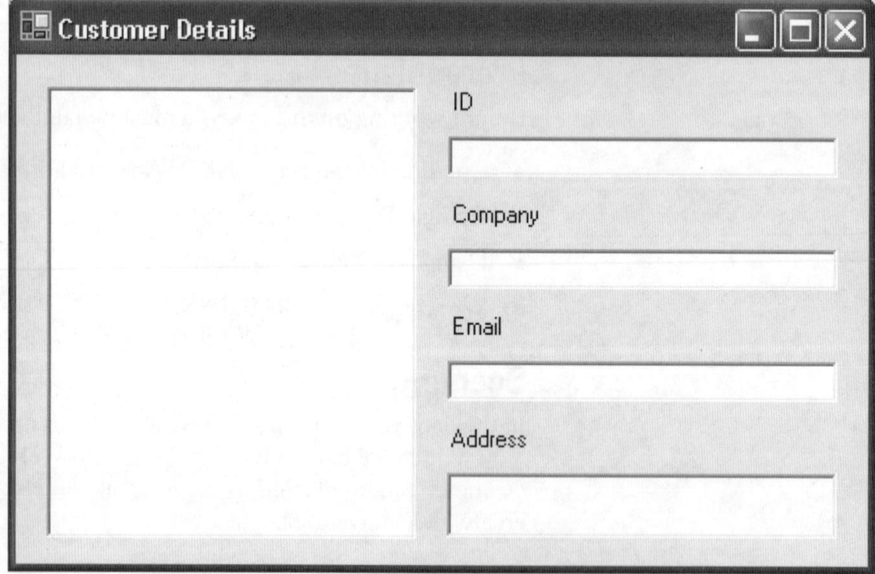

5. Set the properties of the controls as shown in the following table.

Control	Property name	Property value
ListBox1	**Name**	**lstCustomers**
Label1	**Name**	**lblID**
	Text	**ID**
TextBox1	**Name**	**txtID**
	Text	**<empty>**
Label2	**Name**	**lblCompany**
	Text	**Company**
TextBox2	**Name**	**txtCompany**
	Text	**<empty>**
Label3	**Name**	**lblEmail**
	Text	**Email**
TextBox3	**Name**	**txtEmail**
	Text	**<empty>**
Label4	**Name**	**lblAddress**
	Text	**Address**
TextBox4	**Name**	**txtAddress**
	Text	**<empty>**
	Multiline	**True**
	Size.Height	**32**

6. Save the project.

► To create the Cargo class

1. On the **Project** menu, click **Add Class**.
2. Rename the class **Cargo.vb**, and then click **Open**.
3. At the top of the class, add an **Imports** statement to reference the **System.Data.SqlClient** namespace.
4. In the **Cargo** class, create private class-level variables, using the information in the following table.

Variable name	Type
dstCargo	**DataSet**
conCargo	**SqlConnection**

▶ To create the connection

1. Create a constructor for the class.
2. Instantiate the *conCargo* **Connection** object.
3. Using the information in the following table, set the **ConnectionString** property of *conCargo*.

Name	Value
Data Source	**localhost**
Initial Catalog	**Cargo**
Integrated Security	**True**

▶ To create the GetCustomers method

1. Create a method called **GetCustomers** for the class. The method takes no arguments and has no return value.
2. In this method, declare and instantiate a **SqlDataAdapter** object called *adpCust.* Pass the following information to the constructor.

Argument	Value
selectCommandText	**Select CustomerID, FirstName, LastName, CompanyName, Email, Address from Customers**
selectConnection	**conCargo**

3. Instantiate the **DataSet** object.
4. Use the **Fill** method of *adpCust* to pass the following information.

Argument	Value
dataSet	**dstCargo**
srcTable	**CustTable**

▶ To create the CustList property

1. Define a read-only property called **CustList** that returns a **DataTable**.
2. In the **Get** clause, return the **CustTable** table from *dstCargo*.
3. Save and build the project.

▶ To populate the list box

1. Open the frmCustomer Code Editor.
2. Declare and instantiate a private class-level variable called *objCargo* of type **Cargo**.
3. Create the **frmCustomer_Load** event handler.
4. Call the **GetCustomers** method of the *objCargo* object.
5. Add the following code to loop through the customers and populate the list box:

```
Dim CurRows( ) As DataRow, CurRow As DataRow
CurRows = objCargo.CustList.Select( )
For Each CurRow In CurRows
   lstCustomers.Items.Add(CurRow("FirstName").ToString & _
   " " & CurRow("LastName").ToString)
Next
```

6. Call the SetSelected method of lstCustomers to select the first item in the list.

▶ To populate the text boxes

1. Create the **lstCustomers_SelectedIndexChanged** event handler.
2. Declare an **Integer** variable called *RowNum*, and then store the **SelectedIndex** property of the list box in the variable.
3. Declare a **DataRow** variable called *CurRow*, and then store the row identified by *RowNum* in it by using the following line of code:

```
objCargo.CustList.Rows(RowNum)
```

4. Using the information in the following table, populate the text boxes with data from this row.

Text box	Column name
txtID	CustomerID
txtCompany	CompanyName
txtEmail	Email
txtAddress	Address

5. Save the project.

▶ To test the application

1. On the **Build** menu, click **Build CustomerProject**, and resolve any build errors.
2. On the **Debug** menu, click **Start**. You should see that the list box and text boxes are populated with data.
3. Click on a different customer in the list and verify that the text boxes display the relevant data.
4. Quit the application.
5. Quit Visual Studio .NET.

Exercise 2
Updating Data

In this exercise, you will extend the class created in the previous exercise to allow editing of data. The form in the starter file has been modified to make the text boxes read-only by default and to include a button that you will code to test the functionality.

▶ To prepare the form

1. Open Visual Studio .NET.
2. On the **File** menu, point to **Open**, and then click **Project**.
3. Set the location to *install folder*\Labs\Lab081\Ex02\Starter, click **CustomerProject.sln**, and then click **Open**.
4. In the frmCustomer.vb code window, create the **btnEdit_Click** procedure and write code to set the **ReadOnly** property of the following text boxes to **False**.
   - txtCompany
   - txtEmail
   - txtAddress

▶ To update the DataSet

1. Open the code window for Cargo.vb.
2. Create a new public method called **EditDetails** that takes the following parameters by value and has no return value.

Parameter name	Type
RowNum	**Integer**
ID	**Integer**
strCompany	**String**
strEmail	**String**
strAddress	**String**

3. Using the information in the following table, declare and initialize a variable.

Name	Type	Initialization Value
editRow	**DataRow**	`dstCargo.Tables("CustTable").Rows(RowNum)`

4. Call the **BeginEdit** method of the **editRow** object.

5. Update the data in the **DataSet** with the arguments passed to the procedure. Use the information in the following table.

editRow item	Argument
CompanyName	**strCompany**
Email	**strEmail**
Address	**strAddress**

6. Call the **EndEdit** method of the **editRow** object.

► To update the underlying data

1. Using the information in the following table, declare and instantiate a variable.

Name	Type	Construction Value
commUpdate	**SqlCommand**	`"Update customers set CompanyName= @company, email=@email, address=@address where customerid=@id", conCargo`

2. Use the **Add** method of the command's **Parameters** collection to create parameters for this command. Use the information in the following table.

parameterName	sqlDbType	size	sourceColumn
@id	**SqlDbType.Int**	**4**	**CustomerID**
@company	**SqlDbType.VarChar**	**50**	**CompanyName**
@email	**SqlDbType.VarChar**	**255**	**Email**
@address	**SqlDbType.VarChar**	**255**	**Address**

3. In the **GetCustomers** procedure, locate the declaration for *adpCust*.
4. Remove the declaration for *adpCust* (leaving the instantiation code), and then declare *adpCust* as a class-level variable.
5. In the **EditDetails** procedure, set the **UpdateCommand** property of *adpCust* to the **commUpdate** command.
6. Call the **Update** method of *adpCust*, and pass it the existing **DataSet** and the name of the **DataTable** object.

▶ **To call the EditDetails method**

1. Open the frmCustomer.vb code window, and create a handler for the **btnSave_Click** event.
2. Add code to call the **EditDetails** method of the **objCargo** object to pass the appropriate parameters. Use the information in the following table.

Parameter	Value
RowNum	**lstCustomers.SelectedIndex**
ID	**txtID.Text**
strCompany	**txtCompany.Text**
strEmail	**txtEmail.Text**
strAddress	**txtAddress.Text**

3. Set the **ReadOnly** property of the following text boxes to **True**.
   - txtCompany
   - txtEmail
   - txtAddress

▶ **To test your code**

1. Run the application.
2. Click **Edit Details**, replace the company name with **Microsoft**, and then click **Save**.
3. Quit the application.
4. Run the application again, and verify that the changes have been saved.
5. Quit the application.
6. Quit Visual Studio .NET.

Exercise 3
Using Data Binding in Web Forms

In this exercise, you will create a Web Form that displays invoice data in a bound data grid by using a **DataReader** object.

Note If you want to run the solution code for this project, you must ensure that the **userName** attribute of the <identity> element in Web.config matches a user account on your computer.

▶ To create the project

1. Open Visual Studio .NET.
2. On the **File** menu, point to **New**, and then click **Project**.
3. In the **Project Types** box, click **Visual Basic Project**.
4. In the **Templates** box, click **ASP.NET Web Application**.
5. Set the location to http://localhost/2373/Labs/Lab081/Ex03/Invoices, and then click **OK**.

▶ To create the Web Form

1. Open the design window for WebForm1.aspx.
2. In the Properties window, click **DOCUMENT**, and change the **title** property to **Cargo Invoices**. This will alter the text in the Internet Explorer title bar.
3. From the Toolbox, add a **DataGrid** control to the form.
4. Save the project.

▶ To configure impersonation

1. Open the code window for Web.config.
2. Within the **<system.web>** element, create an **<identity>** element by using the information in the following table.

Attribute	Value
impersonate	true
userName	Student*x* (where *x* is your student number)
password	password

▶ To create the connection

1. Open the code window for WebForm1.aspx.
2. Add an **Imports** statement to access the **System.Data.SqlClient** namespace.
3. Locate the **Page_Load** procedure, and declare a procedure-level variable, using the information in the following table.

Name	Type
sqlConn	**SqlConnection**

4. Instantiate the connection object, and then set the **ConnectionString** property, using the information in the following table.

Name	Value
Data Source	**localhost**
Initial Catalog	**Cargo**
Integrated Security	**True**

5. Call the **Open** method of the connection object.

▶ To bind the data

1. In the **Page_Load** procedure, declare and instantiate a **SqlCommand** object called **comInvoices**, and pass the parameters listed in the following table.

Parameter	Value
cmdText	**Select * from Invoices**
Connection	**sqlConn**

2. Declare a **SqlDataReader** object called **drInvoices**.
3. Call the **ExecuteReader** method of the command object, and store the results in **drInvoices**.
4. Set the **DataSource** property of the **DataGrid** to **drInvoices**.
5. Call the **DataBind** method of the **DataGrid**.

▶ To test your code

1. Run the application and verify that the invoices are displayed in a grid on the Web Form.
2. Close Internet Explorer, and then close Visual Studio .NET.

Exercise 4
Creating Typed DataSets

In this exercise, you will create an XSD schema from the Invoices table of the Cargo database and use it to create a typed dataset for use in a Windows Form.

► To create the project

1. Open Visual Studio .NET.
2. On the **File** menu, point to **New**, and then click **Project**.
3. In the **Project Types** box, click **Visual Basic Project**.
4. In the **Templates** box, click **Windows Application**.
5. Change the name of the project to **InvoiceApp**, set the location to *install folder*\Labs\Lab081\Ex04, and then click **OK**.

► To create the connection

1. In Server Explorer, right-click **Data Connections**, and then click **Add Connection**.
2. In the **Data Link Properties** dialog box, enter the following information, and then click **OK**.

Setting	Value
Server name	**localhost**
Security	**Use Windows NT Integrated Security**
Database name	**Cargo**

► To create the schema

1. In the **Solution Explorer**, click **InvoiceApp**. On the **Project** menu, click **Add New Item**.
2. In the **Templates** box, click **XML Schema**, rename the item to **InvSchema.xsd**, and then click **Open**.
3. In Server Explorer, expand **Data Connections**, expand the connection that you just created, expand **Tables**, and then click **Invoices**.
4. Drag **Invoices** onto the **Schema Designer**.
5. Review the schema in both XML view and Schema view.

► To create the DataSet

1. In Schema view, on the **Schema** menu, click **Generate Dataset**.
2. In Solution Explorer, click **Show All Files**, and expand **InvSchema.xsd**. You will see that an InvSchema.vb file has been created containing code to generate a typed DataSet.
3. Review the code in InvSchema.vb.

► **To create the form**

1. Open the design window for Form1.vb.
2. Add three **Label** controls, three **TextBox** controls, and a **Button** control to the form. Use the information in the following table to set their properties.

Control	Property	Value
Label1	Name Text	**lblInvoiceID** **Invoice ID**
Label2	Name Text	**lblCustomerID** **Customer ID**
Label3	Name Text	**lblAmount** **Amount**
TextBox1	Name Text	**txtInvoiceID** **<empty>**
TextBox2	Name Text	**txtCustomerID** **<empty>**
TextBox3	Name Text	**txtAmount** **<empty>**
Button	Name Text	**btnFill** **Fill**

3. From the **Data** tab of the Toolbox, add a DataSet control to the form, using the information in the following table.

Setting	Value
Type of DataSet	**Typed**
Name	**InvoiceApp.Document**

► **To populate the DataSet**

1. Create an event handler for the **btnFill_Click** event.
2. Declare and instantiate a **SqlClient.SqlConnection** object called **sqlConn** using the information in the following table.

Name	Value
Data Source	**localhost**
Initial Catalog	**Cargo**
Integrated Security	**True**

3. Call the **Open** method of **sqlConn**.
4. Declare and instantiate a **SqlClient.SqlDataAdapter** object called **sqlAdapt** using the information in the following table.

Parameter	Value
selectCommandText	**Select * from Invoices**
selectConnection	**sqlConn**

5. Declare and instantiate a variable, using the information in the following table.

Name	Type
invTable	**Document.InvoicesDataTable**

6. Call the **Fill** method of **sqlAdapt**, passing the following parameters.

Parameter	Value
DataSet	**Document1**
srcTable	**invTable.TableName**

▶ To populate the text boxes

1. In **btnFill_Click**, add code to populate the text boxes with the appropriate data. Use the information in the following table.

Control	Text property
txtInvoiceID	**Document1.Invoices(0).InvoiceID**
txtCustomerID	**Document1.Invoices(0).CustomerID**
txtAmount	**Document1.Invoices(0).Amount**

2. Build and save the project.

▶ To test your code

1. Run the application.
2. Click **Fill**, and verify that the text boxes are correctly populated with data.
3. Quit the application, and quit Visual Studio .NET.

Review

- ADO.NET Overview
- .NET Data Providers
- The DataSet Object
- Data Designers and Data Binding
- XML Integration

1. State three benefits that ADO.NET has over earlier data access technologies.

2. You have the following code in your application. What would you do to make the code more efficient? Why?

```
Dim sqlConn As New SqlClient.SqlConnection("Integrated
Security=True;Data Source=LocalHost;Initial Catalog=Pubs;")
sqlConn.Open( )
Dim sqlAdapt As New SqlClient.SqlDataAdapter("Select
au_lname from authors", sqlConn)
Dim sqlDataSet As New DataSet( )
sqlAdapt.Fill(sqlDataSet, "Authors")
Dim i As Integer
For i = 0 To sqlDataSet.Tables("Authors").Rows.Count - 1
MessageBox.Show(sqlDataSet.Tables("Authors").Rows(i).Item(0
).ToString)
Next
```

3. If you change the contents of a DataTable in a DataSet, will those changes be reflected in the underlying data source? Why, or why not?

4. You have the following code in the **Page_Load** event of a Web Form, but the **DataGrid** does not appear. What is wrong, assuming all objects are correctly declared and instantiated?

```
sqlReader = sqlComm.ExecuteReader
DataGrid1.DataSource( ) = sqlReader
```

5. Write the code to load an XML document called Books.xml into a DataSet.

ReadXML

msdn® training

Module 9: Developing Components in Visual Basic .NET

Contents

Microsoft®

Overview

- Components Overview
- Creating Serviced Components
- Creating Component Classes
- Creating Windows Forms Controls
- Creating Web Forms User Controls
- Threading

As a Microsoft® Visual Basic® developer, you probably already know how to develop and use components in your applications. In Visual Basic .NET version 7.0, you can use the new design-time features to easily create components and extend their functionality.

After completing this module, you will be able to:

- Describe the different types of components that you can create in Visual Basic .NET.
- Create components that can be used by managed and unmanaged client applications.
- Create serviced components.
- Create component classes.
- Create Microsoft Windows® Forms controls.
- Create Web user controls.
- Use threading to create multithreaded applications.

◆ Components Overview

- Types of Components
- Using Modules As Components
- Using Classes As Components
- Using Components in Unmanaged Client Applications
- .NET Remoting Overview

In Visual Basic .NET, you can create several types of components that are accessible from both managed client applications (those built on the services of the Microsoft .NET Framework common language runtime) and unmanaged client applications (for example, client applications created in Visual Basic 6.0).

After you complete this lesson, you will be able to:

- Describe the types of components that you can create in Visual Basic .NET.
- Use modules and classes as components.
- Use Visual Basic .NET–based components in unmanaged environments.
- Explain the key concepts of .NET Remoting.

Types of Components

- Structures
- Modules
- Classes
- Component classes
- Serviced components
- User controls
  - Windows Forms user controls
  - Web Forms user controls

In Visual Basic .NET, you can create several different types of components, including:

- Structures
- Modules
- Classes
- Component classes
- Serviced components
- User controls

Structures

You can use structures as components by declaring them as public when you define them. Structures support many features of classes, including properties, methods, and events, but are value types, so memory management is handled more efficiently. Structures do not support inheritance.

Modules

You can use modules as components by declaring them as public when you define them. Declaring modules as public allows you to create code libraries that contain routines that are useful to multiple applications. You can also use modules to create reusable functions that do not apply to a particular component, class, or structure.

If you have used the **GlobalMultiUse** or **GlobalSingleUse** classes in previous versions of Visual Basic, the concept of a code library is not new to you. These classes provide the same functionality in Visual Basic .NET; the client code does not need to qualify these classes by the class name to call the functions.

Classes

You can use classes as components by declaring them as public within an assembly. You can use public classes from any .NET-based client application by adding a reference to the component assembly. You can extend the functionality of classes through mechanisms such as properties, methods, and events. Classes are also extensible through inheritance, which allows applications to reuse existing logic from these components.

Component Classes

A class becomes a component when it conforms to a standard for component interaction. This standard is provided through the **IComponent** interface. Any class that implements the **IComponent** interface is a component. Component classes allow you to open your class in a visual designer, and they allow your class to be sited onto other visual designers.

Serviced Components

Serviced components are derived directly or indirectly from the **System.EnterpriseServices.ServicedComponent** class. Classes configured in this manner are hosted by a Component Services application and can automatically use the services provided by Component Services.

User Controls

User controls are components that are created by a developer to be contained within Windows Forms or Web Forms. Each user control has its own set of properties, methods, and events that make it suitable for a particular purpose. You can manipulate user controls in the Windows Forms and Web Forms designers and write code to add user controls dynamically at run time, just as you can for the controls provided as part of the .NET Framework.

Note In this module, you will learn how to create and use component classes, serviced components, and user controls. For more information about structures, modules, and classes, see Module 5, "Object-Oriented Programming in Visual Basic .NET," in Course 2373B, *Programming with Microsoft Visual Basic .NET.*

Using Modules As Components

- Declare the module as public
- Reference and import the assembly into client code

```
Public Module MyMathFunctions
    Public Function Square(ByVal lng As Integer) As Long
        Return (lng * lng)
    End Function
   ...
End Module

'Client code
Imports MyAssembly
...
Dim x As Long = Square(20)
```

In Visual Basic .NET, you can use modules as components outside of the assembly in which they are defined. To make this possible, declare the module as public when you define it. You then need to create a reference in the client assembly to the component assembly and use the **Imports** statement to allow access to the module methods.

The following example shows how to create a public module named *MyMathFunctions* that defines the function **Square**. This module is defined within the *MyAssembly* assembly. The module can then be used as a component in client code, as shown in the second part of the example.

```
Public Module MyMathFunctions
    Public Function Square(ByVal lng As Long) As Long
        Return (lng * lng)
    End Function
   ...
End Module

'Client code
Imports MyAssembly
...
Dim x As Long = Square(20)
```

Note For more information about assemblies, see Module 10, "Deploying Applications," in Course 2373B, *Programming with Microsoft Visual Basic .NET*. For the purposes of this module, you can think of them as similar to Visual Basic 6.0 Microsoft ActiveX® dynamic-link libraries (DLLs).

Using Classes As Components

- **Declare the class as public**
- **Reference and import the assembly into client code**

```
Public Class Account
    Public Sub Debit(ByVal AccountId As Long, Amount As Double)
        'Perform debit action
    End Sub
    Public Sub Credit(ByVal AccountId As Long, Amount As Double)
        'Perform credit action
    End Sub
End Class

'Client code
Imports MyAssembly
Dim x As New Account( )
x.Debit(1021, 1000)
```

You can use classes as components outside of the assembly in which they are defined by marking the class as public. You then reference the component assembly from the client assembly, and use the **Imports** statement to allow direct access to the class.

The following example shows how to create a public class called **Account** that defines the **Debit** and **Credit** methods. This class is defined in the **MyAssembly** assembly. A separate client assembly then references the assembly, and the class can then be used to created object instances.


```
Public Class Account
  Public Sub Debit(ByVal AccountId As Long, Amount As Double)
      'Perform debit action
  End Sub
  Public Sub Credit(ByVal AccountId As Long, Amount As Double)
      'Perform credit action
  End Sub
End Class

'Client code
Imports MyAssembly
Dim x As New Account( )
x.Debit(1021, 1000)
```

Using Components in Unmanaged Client Applications

- **Setting assembly properties**
  - Generate a strong name
  - Select **Register for COM Interop** in **Build** options
- **Exposing class members to COM and Component Services**
  - Define and implement interfaces
  - Use the **ClassInterface** attribute with **AutoDual** value
  - Use the **COMClass** attribute

You can create Visual Basic .NET components that can be used by unmanaged client applications. This interoperability allows you to use Component Services features such as object pooling and transactions. In order to expose your components to COM and Component Services, you must set specific assembly properties and create your classes appropriately.

Setting Assembly Properties

You must provide your assembly with a strong name if you want the assembly to be accessible to unmanaged code. To create a strong-named assembly, use a private and public key pair when you build the application, so that the assembly is guaranteed to be unique and cannot be inappropriately altered after you build it.

Naming Your Assembly

You can generate a strong name for your assembly by using the strong name tool (sn.exe) that ships with the .NET Framework. The following code shows how to use sn.exe to generate a key file called KeyFile.snk:

```
sn.exe -k KeyFile.snk
```

After you have generated the key file, you can add it to the project and reference it in AssemblyInfo.vb by using the following code:

```
<Assembly: AssemblyKeyFile("KeyFile.snk")>
```

Your assembly will then be strong-named the next time you build it.

Note For more information about creating strong-named assemblies, see Module 10, "Deploying Applications," in Course 2373B, *Programming with Microsoft Visual Basic .NET.*

Registering Your Assembly

You can automatically register an assembly for COM interoperability in the **Configuration Properties** section of the assembly property pages. The **Build** section provides a **Register for COM Interop** check box. If you select this check box, your assembly is registered with COM when it is next built. If you subsequently rebuild your assembly after the initial registration, it will first be unregistered before being re-registered. This process ensures that the registry does not contain outdated information.

Exposing Class Members to COM and Component Services

Creating a class that has public properties and methods does not make the class members accessible to COM and Component Services. Unless you expose the class members, the class itself will be accessible, but the methods will not be accessible except through late binding. You can expose the class members and enable early binding by:

- Defining a public interface.
- Using the **ClassInterface** attribute.
- Using the **COMClass** attribute.

Defining a Public Interface

Defining a public interface and implementing it within your public class allows unmanaged client applications to view and bind to the methods of the interface. This approach provides the most consistent and safe way to expose components to COM because use of interfaces prevents many problems associated with versioning.

The following code shows how to create a public interface and then use the interface in a class that will be accessible to unmanaged client applications through COM:

```
Public Interface IVisible
    Sub PerformAction( )
End Interface

Public Class VisibleClass
    Implements IVisible
    Public Sub PerformAction( ) _
                Implements IVisible.PerformAction
      'Perform your action
    End Sub
End Class
```

Using the ClassInterface Attribute

The **System.Runtime.InteropServices** namespace provides the **ClassInterface** attribute. This attribute allows you to create a class with a dual interface so that all members of the class (and base classes) are automatically accessible to unmanaged client applications through COM. The following code shows how to use the **ClassInterface** attribute:

```
Imports System.Runtime.InteropServices
<ClassInterface(ClassInterfaceType.AutoDual)> _
Public Class VisibleClass
    Public Sub PerformAction( )
      'Perform your action
    End Sub
End Class
```

Using the COMClass Attribute

The **Microsoft.VisualBasic** namespace provides the **COMClass** attribute that you can use within a class to expose all of the public class members to COM. Visual Basic .NET provides a class template item called **COM Class** that you can add to any type of project that uses the **COMClass** attribute. Any assembly that contains this type of class will register itself when it is built and subsequently rebuilt.

Caution All three approaches can cause versioning problems if public method signatures are altered between versions. For this reason, implementing interfaces is the preferred approach because new interfaces with new method signatures can be created without causing versioning difficulties.

.NET Remoting Overview

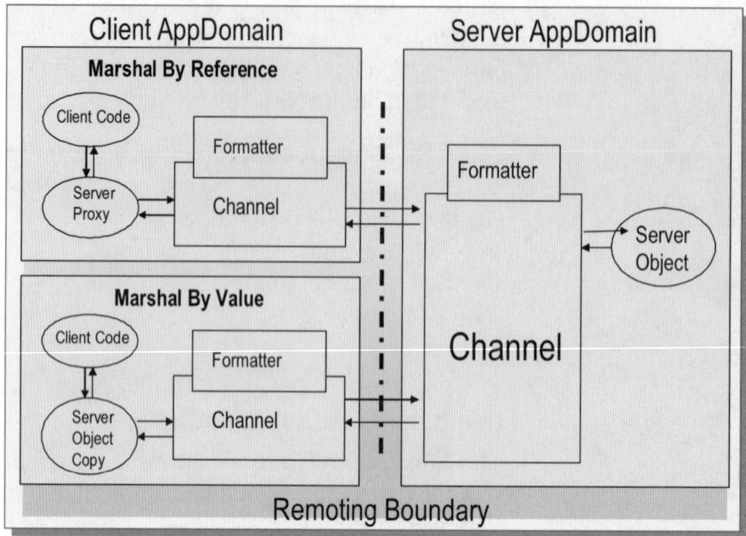

Previous versions of Visual Basic use COM and the distributed version of COM (DCOM) to communicate with components in different processes or on different computers. Visual Basic .NET uses .NET Remoting to allow communication between client and server applications across application domains.

The .NET Framework provides several services that are used in remoting:

- Communication channels are responsible for transporting messages to and from remote applications by using either a binary format over a Transmission Control Protocol (TCP) channel or Extensible Markup Language (XML) over a Hypertext Transfer Protocol (HTTP) channel.
- Formatters that encode and decode messages before they are transported by the channel.
- Proxies that forward remote method calls to the proper object.
- Remote object activation and lifetime support for marshal-by-reference objects that execute on the server.
- Marshal-by-value objects that are copied by the .NET Framework into the process space on the client to reduce cross-process or cross-computer round trips.

Note For more information about .NET Remoting, see ".NET Remoting Technical Overview" in the Microsoft Visual Studio® .NET documentation.

◆ Creating Serviced Components

- Hosting Components in Component Services
- Using Transactions
- Using Object Pooling
- Using Constructor Strings
- Using Security
- Using Other Component Services
- Configuring Assemblies for Component Services

After completing this lesson, you will be able to:

- Describe the requirements for hosting .NET-based components in a Component Services application.
- Enable transaction processing in your components.
- Use object pooling to improve performance for objects that need extra resources.
- Use security attributes to specify how components interact with Component Services security.
- Add constructors to control how a component is initialized.
- Explain how to use other Component Services, such as Just-In-Time activation, from Visual Basic .NET components.
- Set assembly-level attributes to improve the installation of your application.

Hosting Components in Component Services

- **Add a reference to System.EnterpriseServices in your assembly**
- **The System.EnterpriseServices namespace provides:**
  - **ContextUtil** class
  - **ServicedComponent** class
  - Assembly, class, and method attributes

You must add a project reference to the **System.EnterpriseServices** namespace if you want to host a Visual Basic .NET component in a Component Services application. This namespace provides the main classes, interfaces, and attributes for communicating with Component Services.

The **System.EnterpriseServices** namespace provides the following features.

Feature	Usage
ContextUtil class	Use this class to participate in transactions and to interact with security information. The functionality of this class is similar to the functionality of the **ObjectContext** class in Visual Basic 6.0.
ServicedComponent class	All component classes that need to be hosted within a Component Services application must inherit this class. This class defines the base type for all context bound types and implements methods similar to those found in the **IObjectControl** interface used in Visual Basic 6.0–based Component Services applications.
Assembly, class, and method attributes	You can define several assembly attributes for Component Services interrogation in the AssemblyInfo.vb file. These values are used to set the application name and description and other values when the application is installed as a Component Services application. Several class and method attributes are also defined by the **System.EnterpriseServices** namespace, including **TransactionAttribute**, **AutoCompleteAttribute**, **ObjectPoolingAttribute**, and **ConstructionEnabledAttribute**.

Note The "Attribute" part of an attribute name is optional, so, for example, you can use either **AutoComplete** or **AutoCompleteAttribute** in your code.

Using Transactions

- **Transaction attribute specifies how a class participates in transactions**
- **ContextUtil class provides transaction voting**
- **AutoComplete attribute avoids using the SetAbort, SetComplete, and ContextUtil methods**

```
<Transaction(TransactionOption.Required)> Public Class Account
    Inherits ServicedComponent
    Public Sub Debit(...)
        'Perform debit action
        ContextUtil.SetComplete( )
    End Sub
    <AutoComplete( )> Public Sub Credit(...)
        'Perform credit action
        'No SetComplete because AutoComplete is on
    End Sub
End Class
```

Transactions are often required to maintain data integrity and to synchronize updates to data in multiple data sources. You can enable transaction processing in serviced components by including the appropriate attributes and classes in your component code.

Transaction Attribute Options

You use the **Transaction** attribute to specify how a class participates in transactions. You can set transaction support to the one of the following options.

Option	Effect
Disabled	The class instance will not use transactions and will ignore any transactions from parent objects.
NotSupported	The class instance will not be created within the context of a transaction.
Required	The class instance will enlist in an existing transaction that is supplied by the calling object's context. If no transaction exists, one will be created.
RequiresNew	The class instance will always create a new transaction regardless of any transactions already created by calling objects.
Supported	The class instance will enlist in a transaction if provided by the calling object's context but will not create a transaction if one does not already exist.

Using the Transaction Attribute

The following example defines an **Account** class and sets the **Transaction** attribute as **Required**.

```
Imports System.EnterpriseServices

<Transaction(TransactionOption.Required)> Public Class Account
    Inherits ServicedComponent

    Public Sub Debit(ByVal id As Integer, _
                ByVal amount As Double)
        'Debit code
    End Sub
End Class
```

Transaction Voting Options

You can vote for a transaction outcome by using methods of the **ContextUtil** class, which is supplied by the **System.EnterpriseServices** namespace. This static class provides many methods and properties that will be familiar to you if you have created components that use MTS or Component Services. Several of the common methods are outlined below.

ContextUtil method	Use this method to:
SetAbort	Vote for the failure of a transaction. The transaction can only succeed if all objects involved in the transaction vote unanimously for success. This method also allows the object to be deactivated after the method call is complete.
SetComplete	Vote for the success of a transaction. If all objects involved in the transaction vote for success, then the transaction can be completed. This method also allows the object to be deactivated after the method call is complete.
EnableCommit	Vote for a successful completion of the transaction, while not allowing the object to be deactivated after the method call is complete. This is useful if you want to maintain state across multiple method calls, but you do not need further action to successfully complete the transaction if so requested by the top-level serviced component.
DisableCommit	Vote for an unsuccessful completion of the transaction, while not allowing the object to be deactivated after the method call is complete. This is useful if you want to maintain state across multiple method calls and you need other actions to occur before the transaction can be successfully completed.

Using the ContextUtil Class

The following example shows how to use the **ContextUtil** class to complete or abort transactions in the **Debit** method of the **Account** class, based on any exceptions encountered.

```
Public Sub Debit(ByVal id As Integer, ByVal amount As Double)
    Try
        'Perform update to database
        ...
        ContextUtil.SetComplete( )
    Catch ex As Exception
        ContextUtil.SetAbort( )
        Throw ex
    End Try
End Sub
```

Processing Transactions

To avoid using the **SetAbort** and **SetComplete** methods of **ContextUtil**, you can set the **AutoComplete** attribute of specific methods of the component. If no exceptions occur during the method execution, the object behaves as if **SetComplete** has been called. If exceptions do occur, the object behaves as if **SetAbort** has been called.

Using the AutoComplete Attribute

The following example shows how to use the **AutoComplete** attribute:

```
<AutoComplete( )>Public Sub Credit( _
   ByVal fromAccount As Integer, ByVal amount As Double)
    'Perform update to database
    ...
    'No SetComplete or SetAbort is required
End Sub
```

Using Object Pooling

- **Object pooling allows objects to be created in advance**
- **ObjectPooling attribute specifies MinPoolSize and MaxPoolSize**
- **ServicedComponent provides CanBePooled method**

```
<ObjectPooling(Enabled:=True, MinPoolSize:=5, _
               MaxPoolSize:=50)> _
Public Class Account
    Inherits ServicedComponent
    ...
    Protected Overrides Function CanBePooled( ) As Boolean
        Return True
    End Function
End Class
```

In Visual Basic .NET, you use the **ObjectPooling** attribute and the **ServicedComponent** base class to create serviced components that use object pooling.

What Is Object Pooling?

Object pooling allows a preset number of objects to be created in advance, so they are ready for use by client requests when the application first starts up. When a client application requests an object, one is taken from the pool of available objects and is used for that request. When the request is finished, the object is placed back in the pool for use by other client requests.

You can use pooling to improve the performance of objects that require significant periods of time to acquire resources and complete an operation. Objects that do not require such resources will not benefit significantly from object pooling.

Enabling Object Pooling

You specify the **ObjectPooling** attribute so that Component Services can place the component in an object pool. You can also specify optional arguments to the attribute that set the **MinPoolSize** and **MaxPoolSize** values of the pool.

- **MinPoolSize**

  To set the minimum number of objects to be created in advance in the pool, use the **MinPoolSize** argument.

- **MaxPoolSize**

  To set the maximum number of objects that can be created in the pool, use the **MaxPoolSize** argument.

  - If no objects are available in the pool when a request is received, the pool can create another object instance if this preset maximum number of objects has not already been reached.
  - If the maximum number of objects have already been created and are currently unavailable, requests will begin queuing for the next available object.

Returning Objects to the Object Pool

Use the **CanBePooled** method to specify whether your component can be returned to the object pool. Objects can only be returned to the pool when they are deactivated. This happens when the **SetComplete** or **SetAbort** methods are called when the object is transactional, or if a **Dispose** method is explicitly called if the object is not transactional.

- **True**

  If your component supports object pooling and can safely be returned to the pool, the **CanBePooled** method should return **True**.

- **False**

  If your component does not support object pooling, or if the current instance cannot be returned to the pool, the **CanBePooled** method should return **False**.

Note If object pooling is disabled for a component, the **CanBePooled** method will not be executed.

Using the CanBePooled Method

The following example shows how to create an object pool for the **Account** object with a minimum of five objects and a maximum of 50 at any one time. The **CanBePooled** method returns **True** to inform Component Services that the object can be returned to the pool.

```
<ObjectPooling(Enabled:=True,MinPoolSize:=5, _
    MaxPoolSize:=50)>Public Class Account
    Inherits ServicedComponent

    Public Sub Debit(ByVal id As Integer, _
                     ByVal amount As Double)
    ...
    End Sub

    Protected Overrides Function CanBePooled( ) As Boolean
        Return True
    End Function
End Class
```

Using Constructor Strings

- **Specify the ConstructionEnabled attribute to indicate that a construction string is required**
- **Override the Construct method to retrieve information**

```
<ConstructionEnabled(True)>Public Class Account
    Inherits ServicedComponent
    Protected Overrides Sub Construct(ByVal s As String)
       'Called after class constructor
       'Use passed in string
    End Sub
End Class
```

You can use a constructor string to control how serviced components are initialized. This allows you to specify any initial information the object needs, such as a database connection string, by using the Component Services management console. You can use the **ConstructionEnabled** attribute to enable this process in a serviced component. Your Visual Basic .NET component can then receive this constructor information because the inherited **ServicedComponent** class provides the overridable **Construct** method.

Using the ConstructionEnabled Attribute

You specify the **ConstructionEnabled** attribute at the class level so that a constructor string can be passed to the object during object construction. You can modify this value when the component is installed as a Component Services application using the Component Services management console.

Using the Construct Method

You override the **Construct** method of the **ServicedComponent** base class to receive the string value sent to the component during construction.

The following example shows how to enable a constructor, override the **Construct** method, and pass in a constructor string stored in a local variable.

```
<ConstructionEnabled(True)>Public Class Account
    Inherits ServicedComponent

    Private strValue As String

    Protected Overrides Sub Construct(ByVal s As String)
        'Called after class constructor
        strValue = s
    End Sub
End Class
```

Using Security

- **Security configuration attributes enable security and role configuration**
- **SecurityCallContext class provides role checking and caller information**

```
<ComponentAccessControl(True), SecurityRole("Manager")> _
Public Class Account
    Inherits ServicedComponent

    Public Function GetDetails( ) As String
        With SecurityCallContext.CurrentCall
            If .IsCallerInRole("Manager") Then
                Return .OriginalCaller.AccountName
            End If
        End With
    End Function
End Class
```

When working with serviced components, you can use pre-defined attributes and objects to configure and test security options.

Security Attribute Options

You can set security options by using attributes in your classes. Component Services will use these attributes when configuring your components as described in the following table.

Attribute	Usage
ApplicationAccessControl	Use this assembly-level attribute to explicitly enable or disable application-level access checking.
ComponentAccessControl	Use this component-level attribute to explicitly enable or disable component-level access checking.
SecurityRole	Use this attribute at the assembly level to add a role to the application. Use the attribute at the component level to add a role to the application and link it to the particular component.

Setting Security Options

The following example shows how to set the assembly-level **ApplicationAccessControl** attribute, enable security for the **Account** component, and create the *Manager* role, which will be linked to the **Account** component:

```
<Assembly: ApplicationAccessControl(True)>
<ComponentAccessControl(True), SecurityRole("Manager")> _
Public Class Account
    Inherits ServicedComponent
    ...
End Class
```

Retrieving Security Information

You can discover security information about the caller of a serviced component by using the **SecurityCallContext** class. This class provides information regarding the chain of callers leading up to the current method call. The static **CurrentCall** property of the **SecurityCallContext** class provides access to the following methods and properties.

Method or property	Usage
DirectCaller property	Retrieves information about the last user or application in the caller chain that directly called a method. The property returns an instance of the **SecurityIdentity** class that you can use to determine information about the identity, such as the **AccountName**.
OriginalCaller property	Retrieves information about the first user or application in the caller chain that made the original request for the required action. The property also returns an instance of the **SecurityIdentity** class.
IsCallerInRole method	Tests whether a caller belongs to a particular role; returns a **Boolean** value.
IsUserInRole method	Tests whether the user belongs to a particular role; returns a **Boolean** value.

Using the SecurityCallContext Class

The following example shows how use **SecurityCallContext** to determine whether security is enabled, check whether a caller is in the *Manager* role, and return the **AccountName** string from the **OriginalCaller** property, which is a **SecurityIdentity** instance.

```
<ComponentAccessControl(True), SecurityRole("Manager")> _
Public Class Account
    Inherits ServicedComponent

    Public Function GetDetails( ) As String
        If ContextUtil.IsSecurityEnabled Then
            With SecurityCallContext.CurrentCall
                If .IsCallerInRole("Manager") Then
                    Return .OriginalCaller.AccountName
                End If
            End With
        End If
    End Function
End Class
```

Using Other Component Services

- **Other Component Services include:**
  - Just-in-time activation
  - Queued components
  - Shared properties
  - Synchronization

Component Services provides a series of other services that you can use from Visual Basic .NET components.

Just-in-Time Activation

When just-in-time (JIT) activation is enabled, an object is automatically instantiated when a method is called on a serviced component (activation), and then automatically deactivated when the method is complete (deactivation). When this option is enabled, an object does not maintain state across method calls, and this increases the performance and scalability of the application.

You can override the **Activate** and **Deactivate** methods inherited from the **ServicedComponent** class to perform custom functionality during JIT. If object pooling is enabled, the activation occurs when an existing object has been taken from the pool, and the deactivation occurs when the object is placed back in the pool.

JIT is automatically enabled if a component is transactional, and it cannot be disabled. You can manually enable or disable JIT for non-transactional components by using the **JustInTimeActivation** attribute.

Queued Components

Queued components provide asynchronous communication. This allows client applications to send requests to queued components without waiting for a response. The requests are "recorded" and sent to the server, where they are queued until the application is ready to use the requests. These requests are then "played back" to the application as if they were being sent from a regular client.

You can mark an application for queuing by using the assembly-level **ApplicationQueuing** attribute. Mark individual components with the **InterfaceQueuing** attribute.

Shared Properties

You can use the Shared Property Manager (SPM) components to share information among multiple objects within the same application process. Use the SPM components as you use them from components created in Visual Basic 6.0.

Synchronization

Distributed applications can receive simultaneous calls from multiple clients. Managing these simultaneous requests involves complex program logic to ensure that resources are accessed safely and correctly. Component Services provides this service automatically to components that use transactions. You can also use the **Synchronization** attribute to specify this behavior.

Configuring Assemblies for Component Services

- **Setting assembly attributes**
  - **ApplicationName**
  - **Description**
  - **ApplicationActivation**: library or server application
  - **AssemblyKeyFile**
- **Using Regsvcs to register and create Component Services applications**
  - Regsvcs.exe myApplication.dll
- **Using Lazy Registration**
  - Application registered on first use by client

You can specify some assembly level attributes that provide information when your assembly is installed as a Component Services application. The information is stored in the AssemblyInfo.vb file that is part of your Visual Basic .NET project.

Assembly attribute	Usage
ApplicationName	If you use this attribute to specify the name of the application, a Component Services application with the same name when your assembly is deployed and installed.
Description	Use this attribute to set the Component Services application description value when the assembly is deployed and installed.
ApplicationActivation	Use this attribute to specify whether you want to implement your Component Services application as either a library or a server application. The acceptable values for this attribute are **ActivationOption.Server** or **ActivationOption.Library**.
AssemblyKeyFile	Use this attribute to specify the name and location of the file that contains the key pair used to generate a shared name.

Setting Assembly Attributes

The following example shows a section of an AssemblyInfo.vb file that specifies the application name, the description, and information about where the application should be activated (that is, in a server or library process).

```
<Assembly: ApplicationName("BankComponent")>
<Assembly: Description("VB .NET Bank Component")>
<Assembly: ApplicationActivation(ActivationOption.Server)>
<Assembly: AssemblyKeyFile("KeyFile.snk")>
```

Registering Your Assembly

You can register your assembly with Component Services either manually or automatically.

- Manual registration

  You can use the Regsvcs.exe utility to manually register your assembly. This utility uses the information provided by your assembly attributes so that the Component Services application can be created with the correct default information. The basic syntax for using Regsvcs.exe is shown in the following example:

  ```
  Regsvcs.exe myApplication.dll
  ```

- Automatic registration

  If you do not register your application manually, registration will automatically occur when a client application attempts to create an instance of a managed class that inherits from the **ServicedComponent** class. All of the **ServicedComponent** classes within your assembly will then be registered as part of the Component Services application. This is known as Lazy Registration.

Demonstration: Creating a Serviced Component

In this demonstration, you will learn how to create a serviced component that uses object pooling and how to call the component from a managed client.

Lab 9.1: Creating a Serviced Component

Objectives

After completing this lab, you will be able to:

- Create a serviced component.
- Reference a serviced component.

Prerequisites

Before working on this lab, you must be familiar with creating and using components in MTS or Component Services.

Scenario

In this lab, you will create a serviced component based on a preexisting class. The class contains a single method that customers use to logon. You will register this assembly with Component Services and create a test harness application that references and tests your component. The test harness will use a preexisting form that allows you to enter a customer's e-mail address and password to retrieve the customer details by using the component.

Starter and Solution Files

There are starter and solution files associated with this lab. The starter files are in the *install folder*\Labs\Lab091\Ex0*x*\Starter folders, and the solution files are in the *install folder*\Labs\Lab091\Ex0*x*\Solution folders (where *x* is the number of the exercise).

Estimated time to complete this lab: 60 minutes

Exercise 1
Creating the Serviced Customer Component

In this exercise, you will create a serviced component. The component is based on a prewritten interface called **ICustomer** and a class called **Customer** that implements the interface. You will add a reference to the **EnterpriseServices** assembly and mark the class as a serviced component that requires transactions and a construction string. You will add assembly-level attributes that will be used when you place the component under the control of Component Services.

▶ To open the CustomerComponent project

1. Open Microsoft Visual Studio .NET.
2. On the **File** menu, point to **Open**, and click **Project**.
3. Set the location to *install folder*\Labs\Lab091\Ex01\Starter, click **CustomerComponent.sln**, and then click **Open**.
4. Review the Customer.vb code for the **ICustomer** interface and **Customer** class so that you understand the purpose of the **LogOn** function.

▶ To reference the EnterpriseServices assembly

1. On the **Project** menu, click **Add Reference**.
2. On the .**NET** tab, in the **Component Name** list, click **System.EnterpriseServices**, click **Select**, and then click **OK**.
3. Open the Customer.vb Code Editor. At the start of the code, insert an **Imports** statement that references the **System.EnterpriseServices** namespace.

▶ To mark the Customer class as a serviced component

- Between the **Public Class Customer** definition and the **Implements ICustomer** statement, add an **Inherits ServicedComponent** statement.

▶ To add transactional behavior to the Customer component

1. Modify the class definition to include the **Transaction** class attribute, specifying a value of **TransactionOption.Required**. This is necessary because a "Last_Logon" date-time field is updated each time a customer logs on to the system.
2. In the **Try** block of the **LogOn** method, before the statement that executes **Return datCustomer**, add a call to **ContextUtil.SetComplete**.
3. Within the **Catch** block, before the statement that throws the exception to the calling application, add a call to **ContextUtil.SetAbort**.

▶ To add construction string behavior to the Customer component

1. Modify the class definition to include the **ConstructionEnabled** class attribute, specifying a value of **True**.
2. Override the **Construct** method of the inherited **ServicedComponent** class, and assign the passed in value to the local *connString* variable.

► To add the serviced component assembly attributes

1. Open AssemblyInfo.vb.
2. At the beginning of the file, add an **Imports** statement that references the **System.EnterpriseServices** namespace.
3. Add the following assembly attributes.

Assembly attribute	Parameters
ApplicationName	"Customers"
Description	"Customer Component"
ApplicationActivation	ActivationOption.Server

► To generate a key file

1. Click **start**, point to **All Programs**, point to **Microsoft Visual Studio .NET**, point to **Visual Studio .NET Tools**, and then click **Visual Studio .NET Command Prompt.**
2. In the Visual Studio .NET Command Prompt window, navigate to *install folder*\Labs\Lab091\Ex01\Starter.
3. Use the following command to create a Strong Name Key for your component:

```
sn.exe -k CustomerComponent.snk
```

4. Leave the Command Prompt window open. You will use it in the next exercise.

► To link the key file to the component

1. Open AssemblyInfo.vb.
2. Add the following assembly attribute:

```
<Assembly: AssemblyKeyFile("CustomerComponent.snk")>
```

► To compile the assembly

- On the **Build** menu, click **Build Solution**, and then quit Visual Studio .NET.

Exercise 2
Creating the Serviced Component Application

In this exercise, you will place the component under the control of Component Services and set the construction string for the database connection.

► To create the serviced component application

1. Switch to the Command Prompt window and navigate to *install folder*\Labs\Lab091\Ex01\Starter\bin.
2. Execute the following command to register the assembly and create the serviced component application:

```
Regsvcs.exe CustomerComponent.dll
```

3. Close the Command Prompt window.

► To confirm that the assembly is now a serviced component application

1. Open Control Panel, click **Performance and Maintenance**, click **Administrative Tools**, and then double-click **Component Services**.
2. Expand Component Services, expand Computers, expand My Computer, and then expand COM+ applications.
3. Right-click the **Customers** application, and then click **Properties**. Your screen should appear similar to the following screen shot.

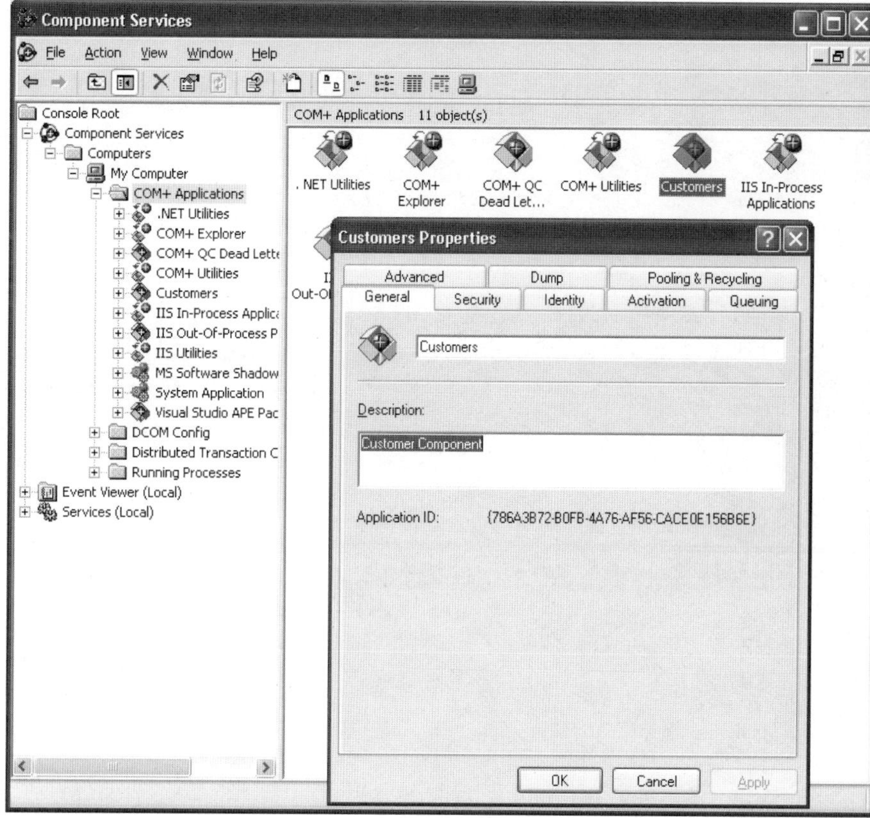

4. Confirm that the assembly-level attributes that you specified in your project have been set in the application.
5. Close the **Customers Properties** dialog box.

► **To set properties for the Customer component**

1. Expand the **Customers** application, and locate **CustomerComponent.Customer** within the list of components.
2. Right-click the **CustomerComponent.Customer** component, and then click **Properties**.
3. Click the **Transactions** tab to view the transactional setting for the class.
4. Click the **Activation** tab, set the Constructor String to the following value, and then click **OK**:

```
Data Source=LocalHost;Initial Catalog=Cargo;Integrated
Security=True;
```

5. Close the Component Services window.

Exercise 3
Testing the Serviced Customer Component

In this exercise, you will modify a prewritten test harness application to reference the serviced **Customer** component. You will then test the application.

► To open the test harness project

1. Open Visual Studio .NET.
2. On the **File** menu, point to **Open**, and then click **Project**.
3. Set the location to *install folder*\Labs\Lab091\Ex03\Starter, click **TestHarness.sln**, and then click **Open**.

► To set a reference to the serviced component assembly

1. On the **Project** menu, click **Add Reference**.
2. In the **Add Reference** dialog box, click **Browse**, and then locate the *install folder*\Labs\Lab091\Ex01\Starter\bin folder.
3. Click **CustomerComponent.dll**, and then click **Open**.
4. From the existing list of .NET components, click **System.EnterpriseServices**, and then click **Select**.
5. Click **OK** to close the **Add Reference** dialog box.

► To call the Customer object

1. In the frmTestCustomer code window, add an **Imports CustomerComponent** statement.
2. Locate the **btnLogon_Click** method. Within the **Try** block, declare an **ICustomer** variable called **cust**, and instantiate it by creating a new **Customer** object. Your code should look as follows:

   ```
   Dim cust As ICustomer = New Customer( )
   ```

3. Call the **LogOn** method of the **cust** object, passing in the following values.

Parameter	Value
Email	txtEmail.Text
Password	txtPassword.Text

4. Use the **ds** Dataset object to store the value returned from the **LogOn** method.

▶ To test the application

1. On the **Debug** menu, click **Start**.
2. Enter the following values.

TextBox	Value
E-mail	**john@tailspintoys.msn.com**
Password	**password**

3. Click **Log on**, and confirm that a record is successfully retrieved from the component.
4. Click **Close** to quit the test harness application.
5. Quit Visual Studio .NET.

◆ Creating Component Classes

- Architecture of a Component Class
- Creating a Component Class

After completing this lesson, you will be able to:

- Describe the architecture of a component class.
- Create a component class.

Architecture of a Component Class

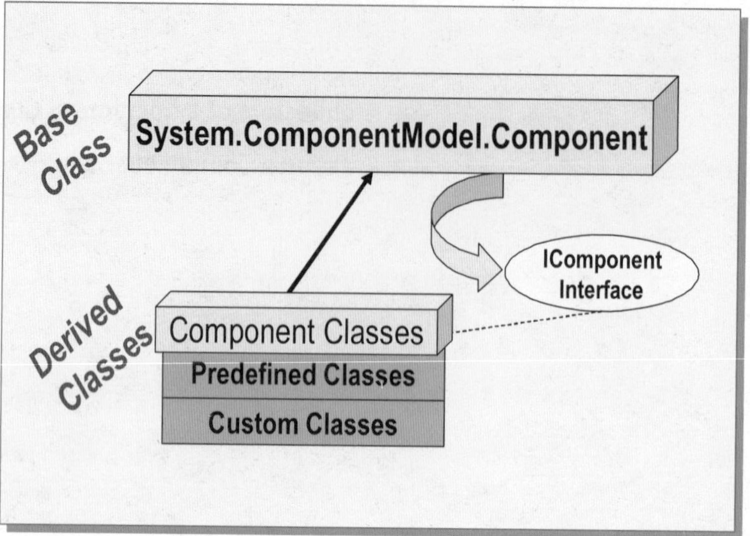

In addition to supporting classes and structures, the **System** namespace provides a library of components designed to make component development easy. When you create a component class based on the **ComponentModel.Component** base class, you automatically inherit the basic architecture for your class.

IComponent Interface

The **IComponent** interface allows you to create custom components or to configure existing components such as the **MessageQueue** or **Timer** components within the visual designer for your component. After you place any existing components on your component (*siting*), you can access them in your component code in the same way as you can when they are placed in the component tray of a Windows Form.

ComponentModel.Component Base Class

The **ComponentModel.Component** base class automatically implements the **IComponent** interface and provides all of the necessary code for handling the siting of components. This is useful because implementing the **IComponent** interface directly would require you to manually create the functionality for handling sited components in addition to the functionality for your component to be sited on another component.

Enhanced Design-Time Features

The **IComponent** interface provides enhanced design-time features. You can add your component class to the Toolbox and the component tray of a Windows Form, a Web Form, or any other item that implements the **IContainer** interface, including another component class. Developers using your component can then use the Properties window to set properties of the component in the same way that they would for .NET Framework components.

To add a compiled component class to the Toolbox, perform the following steps:

1. On the **Tools** menu, click **Customize Toolbox**.
2. In the **Customize Toolbox** dialog box, click the **.NET Framework Components** tab.
3. Browse for the component assembly that you want to add.
4. Select the component from the displayed list of compiled components to add it to the Toolbox.

Creating a Component Class

1. **Inherit the System.ComponentModel.Component**
   - Perform any initialization in constructor
   - Override **Dispose** method
2. **Add any sited components**
   - Use Server Explorer or Toolbox items
3. **Create required functionality**
   - Properties, methods, and events
4. **Build the assembly**

The procedure for creating a component class with Visual Basic .NET is similar to the procedure for creating standard classes, but there are a few extra steps.

1. Inherit the **System.ComponentModel.Component** class.

   The **Component Class** template item contains the required code to inherit the **System.ComponentModel.Component** class, including the constructor code required to add your component class to a container. Add any initialization code for your component class as part of the construction process by placing code in the prewritten **Sub New** method.

   You can override the **Dispose** method of the inherited **Component** class to free any resources before the instance of your component is destroyed.

2. Add any sited components.

   If your component class requires other components in order to fulfill its purpose, you can add them within the Design view by dragging them from the Toolbox or Server Explorer to your component class. These components can then be programmatically accessed from within the code for your component class.

3. Create required functionality.

   Your component class can provide public properties, methods, and events to allow the user of your component to interact with it at both design time and run time.

4. Build the assembly.

   Building the assembly enables other managed clients to make a reference to your component.

The following example shows how to create a component class that is derived from the **System.ComponentModel.Component** class. It extends the functionality of the standard **Timer** class by defining additional properties and events.

```
Imports System.ComponentModel

Public Class Hourglass
  Inherits System.ComponentModel.Component

  Public Event Finished(...)
  Private WithEvents localTimer As System.Timers.Timer

  Public Sub New( )
    MyBase.New( )

    'This call is required by the Component Designer.
    InitializeComponent( )

    'Initialize the timer for 1 minute (60000 milliseconds)
    localTimer = New System.Timers.Timer( )
    localTimer.Enabled = False
    localTimer.Interval = 60000
  End Sub

  Public Property Enabled( ) As Boolean
    Get
      Return localTimer.Enabled
    End Get
    Set(ByVal Value As Boolean)
      localTimer.Enabled = Value
    End Set
  End Property

  Private Sub localTimer_Tick(...) Handles localTimer.Elapsed
    'Raise the finished event after localtimer_Tick is raised
    RaiseEvent Finished( )
  End Sub

  Public Overloads Overrides Sub Dispose( )
    'Disable the localTimer object
    localTimer.Enabled = False
    localTimer.Dispose( )
    MyBase.Dispose( )
  End Sub
End Class
```

When examining the code, note the following:

- The component behaves as an hourglass that raises a **Finished** event one minute after it is enabled.
- The component can be turned on by using the **Enabled** property at design time or run time.
- The **localTimer** is initialized as part of the **Sub New** constructor and set for a timer interval of 60,000 milliseconds, or one minute.
- The **Dispose** method is overridden to ensure that the **localTimer** object is safely disposed of.

Demonstration: Creating a Stopwatch Component

In this demonstration, you will learn how to create a component class that can be used by another assembly.

◆ Creating Windows Forms Controls

- Inheriting from the UserControl Class
- Inheriting from a Windows Forms Control
- Providing Control Attributes

In previous versions of Visual Basic, you can create ActiveX controls that can be reused by different client applications. In Visual Basic .NET, you can also use inheritance to create controls.

After completing this lesson, you will be able to:

- Create a control based on the **System.Windows.Forms.UserControl** class.
- Create a control based on an existing Windows Forms control.
- Add attributes to your controls that enable advanced design-time functionality.

Inheriting from the UserControl Class

- Inherit from System.Windows.Forms.UserControl
- Add required controls to designer
- Add properties and methods that correspond to those of constituent controls
- Add any additional properties and methods
- No InitProperties, ReadProperties, or WriteProperties
  - Property storage is automatic

In previous versions of Visual Basic, you can create a unique new control by placing one or more existing controls onto a UserControl designer. You can then create custom properties, methods, and events to set and retrieve values for the contained controls. This type of control is useful when several forms require the same layout of controls, such as forms for addresses or contact details.

Adding Required Controls

In Visual Basic .NET, you can create the same type of user controls by inheriting your control from the **System.Windows.Forms.UserControl** class, which is automatic if you create a control using the **User Control** template item. You can inherit from this base class to use a designer similar to the one used in previous versions of Visual Basic. By using this method, you can:

- Place as many controls on the designer as you need to in order to create your own user control.
- Access these controls within your user control class, because they are declared as private variables.
- Add your own properties and methods that correspond to the properties and methods of the constituent controls.
- Add public properties, methods, and events in exactly the same way that you do for a regular class.

Adding Properties and Methods

In previous versions of Visual Basic, you persist the properties to a **PropertyBag** object, so the control retains its settings between design time and run time. To do this, you write code in the **ReadProperties** and **WriteProperties** events of the **UserControl** class.

In Visual Basic .NET, this persisting of information is automatic and requires no extra code.

Example

The following example shows how to create a simple user control that contains a label and a text box:

```
Public Class LabelAndTextControl
    Inherits System.Windows.Forms.UserControl

    Public Property TextBoxText( ) As String
        Get
            Return TextBox1.Text
        End Get
        Set(ByVal Value As String)
            TextBox1.Text = Value
        End Set
    End Property

    Public Property LabelText( ) As String
        Get
            Return Label1.Text
        End Get
        Set(ByVal Value As String)
            Label1.Text = Value
        End Set
    End Property
    ... 'Windows Form Designer generated code
End Class
```

The TextBox1 and Label1 controls are privately declared variables within the user control that are only accessible using the public properties **TextBoxText** and **LabelText**.

Inheriting from a Windows Forms Control

- **Allows enhanced version of a single control**
- **Inherit from any System.Windows.Forms control**

```
Public Class MyTextBox
    Inherits System.Windows.Forms.TextBox
    Private strData As String
    Public Property HiddenData( ) As String
        Get
            Return strData
        End Get
        Set(ByVal Value As String)
            strData = Value
        End Set
    End Property
    ...
End Class
```

In previous versions of Visual Basic, you can create enhanced versions of an existing control by placing an instance of the control on the UserControl designer. You can then create public properties, methods, and events that correspond to the equivalent items of the constituent control, adding any custom items to create your enhanced behavior.

In Visual Basic .NET, you can create a control that inherits from any **System.Windows.Forms** class, such as the **TextBox** or **Label** class. Because this approach uses inheritance, there is no need to create public properties, methods, and events that map to the constituent control. This greatly reduces the amount of code required. You only need to create any extra functionality, as described for user controls in the previous topic.

The following example shows how to create a control that inherits from **SystemWindows.Forms.TextBox** and adds a public property:


```
Public Class MyTextBox
    Inherits System.Windows.Forms.TextBox

    Private strData As String

    Public Property HiddenData( ) As String
        Get
            Return strData
        End Get
        Set(ByVal Value As String)
            strData = Value
        End Set
    End Property
    ...
End Class
```

This code creates a new control that inherits all of the **TextBox** class functionality and adds a property called **HiddenData**.

Note For some existing controls, you can create a new graphical front end by overriding the **OnPaint** method of the base class. However, some controls, such as the **TextBox** control, are painted directly by Windows and cannot be overridden.

Providing Control Attributes

- **System.ComponentModel provides control attributes**
- **Class level – DefaultProperty, DefaultEvent, ToolboxBitmap**
- **Property level – Category, Description, DefaultValue**

```
Imports System.ComponentModel
<ToolboxBitmap("C:\txticon.ico"), DefaultEvent("Click")> _
Public Class MyTextBox
    Inherits System.Windows.Forms.UserControl
    <Category("Appearance"), _
     Description("Stores extra data"), _
     DefaultValue("Empty")> _
    Public Property HiddenData( ) As String
        ...
    End Property
    ...
End Class
```

In previous versions of Visual Basic, you can use the **Procedure Attributes** dialog box to set control attributes, such as property descriptions and their categories, which can be viewed in the Object Browser. You can supply similar information in Visual Basic .NET by using the attributes provided by the **System.ComponentModel** namespace.

Setting Class-level Attributes

You can specify several attributes for the control, including **DefaultProperty**, **DefaultEvent**, and **ToolboxBitmap**. The following example shows how to set the **ToolboxBitmap** and **DefaultEvent** attributes for the **MyTextBox** class:

```
<ToolboxBitmap("C:\txticon.ico"), DefaultEvent("Click")> _
Public Class MyTextBox
    Inherits System.Windows.Forms.UserControl
...
End Class
```

Setting Property-level Attributes

You can specify property-level attributes for any public properties, including the **Category**, **Description**, and **DefaultValue** attributes. The following example shows how to set these attributes for the **HiddenData** property:

```
Imports System.ComponentModel

Public Class MyTextBox
    Inherits System.Windows.Forms.UserControl

    <Category("Appearance"), _
     Description("Stores extra data"), _
     DefaultValue("Empty")> _
    Public Property HiddenData( ) As String
        ...
    End Property
    ...
End Class
```

Demonstration: Creating an Enhanced TextBox

In this demonstration, you will learn how to create a Windows Forms user control based on the existing **TextBox**.

◆ Creating Web Forms User Controls

- **Extending Existing Controls**
- **Creating Web User Controls**

In Visual Basic .NET, you can create controls for use within ASP.NET Web Forms.

After completing this lesson, you will be able to:

- Create a Web Forms user control based on other controls in the **System.Web.UI.UserControl** class.
- Use a Web Forms user control within a Web Form.

Extending Existing Controls

1. **Add a Web user control to an ASP.NET Web project**
2. **Use the Toolbox to drag existing controls to the Web user control designer**
3. **Add properties and methods**
4. **Save the .ascx file**
5. **Drag the .ascx file from Solution Explorer to the Web Forms Designer**
6. **Create Web Form code as usual**

Creating your own Web user control allows you to extend the controls provided with ASP.NET. You can extend a single control with added features or create a new control that is a combination of existing controls.

► To create your own Web user control

1. Add a Web user control to your ASP.NET Web project.
2. Use the Toolbox to drag-and-drop existing Web server controls to the Web user control designer.
3. Add properties and methods in the code-behind file.
4. Save the .ascx Web user control file.

► To use your Web user control

1. Open your Web Form.
2. Drag the .ascx file from Solution Explorer to the Web Forms Designer.
3. Create any Web Form code that accesses the Web user control, as you would for existing Web server controls.
4. Test your control by running your application and displaying the Web Form.

Creating Web User Controls

```
<%@ Control Language="vb" AutoEventWireup="false"
  Codebehind="SimpleControl.ascx.vb"
  Inherits="MyApp.SimpleControl"%>
<asp:TextBox id="TextBox1" runat="server"></asp:TextBox>
```

```
Public MustInherit Class SimpleControl
 Inherits System.Web.UI.UserControl
 Protected WithEvents TextBox1 As System.Web.UI.WebControls.TextBox
 Public Property TextValue( ) As String
     Get
         Return TextBox1.Text
     End Get
     Set(ByVal Value As String)
         TextBox1.Text = Value
     End Set
 End Property
End Class
```

To create a Web user control, you need to create:

1. The graphical layout of the controls in the .ascx file.
2. The code that executes in the.ascx.vb code-behind file.

The following example shows how to create a Web user control based on the existing **TextBox** control while inheriting from the **UserControl** class. It also provides a custom property for setting the **TextBox1.Text** value.

The following code is located in the Web user control .ascx file:

```
<%@ Control Language="vb" AutoEventWireup="false"
  Codebehind="SimpleControl.ascx.vb"
  Inherits="MyApp.SimpleControl"
  TargetSchema="http://schemas.microsoft.com/intellisense/ie5"
%>
<asp:TextBox id="TextBox1" runat="server"></asp:TextBox>
```

The example code shows the similarity between Web Forms and Web user control code, the main difference being the **@ Control** directive and the lack of any <html>, <body>, or <form> tags.

The following code is located in the .ascx.vb code-behind file.

```
Public MustInherit Class SimpleControl
  Inherits System.Web.UI.UserControl
  Protected WithEvents TextBox1 _
            As System.Web.UI.WebControls.TextBox

    Public Property TextValue( ) As String
        Get
            Return TextBox1.Text
        End Get
        Set(ByVal Value As String)
            TextBox1.Text = Value
        End Set
    End Property
End Class
```

The **SimpleControl** class is similar to most classes in that it allows public access to private members of the class. However, note that it is through inheriting the **UserControl** class that the Web user control functionality is provided.

Demonstration: Creating a Simple Web Forms User Control

In this demonstration, you will learn how to create a simple Web Forms user control that contains a **Label** and a **TextBox** as its constituent controls.

Lab 9.2: Creating a Web Forms User Control

Objectives

After completing this lab, you will be able to:

- Create a Web Forms user control.
- Use a Web Forms user control on a Web Form.

Prerequisites

Before working on this lab, you must be familiar with creating Web Form applications, and have completed Lab 9.1.

Scenario

In this lab, you will create a Web Forms user control that requests logon information for a customer. The control will retrieve the customer information by means of the serviced component that you created in the previous lab. You will then use this control on a Web Form and test the control.

Starter and Solution Files

There are starter and solution files associated with this lab. The starter files are in the *install folder*\Labs\Lab092\Ex0*x*\Starter folders, and the solution files are in the *install folder*\Labs\Lab092\Ex0*x*\Solution folders (where *x* is the number of the exercise).

Estimated time to complete this lab: 30 minutes

Exercise 1
Creating the LogOn Web Forms User Control

In this exercise, you will open a preexisting Web Forms application that allows you to logon as a customer of the system. You will create a LogOn Web Forms user control that uses text boxes and validation controls. This user control allows users to enter their e-mail address and password and then click a **Submit** button.

▶ To open the existing Web Forms application

1. Open Visual Studio .NET.
2. On the **File** menu, point to **Open**, and then click **Project**.
3. Set the location to *install folder*\Labs\Lab092\Ex01\Starter, click **LogonControl.sln**, and then click **Open**.

▶ To create the Web user control interface

1. On the **Project** menu, click **Add Web User Control**. Rename the item **Logon.ascx**, and then click **Open**.
2. From the **Web Forms** tab of the Toolbox, insert the following controls, and set their property values as shown.

Control	Property name	Property value
Label	**(ID)**	**lblEmail**
	Text	**E-mail:**
TextBox	**(ID)**	**txtEmail**
RegularExpressionValidator	**(ID)**	**revEmail**
	ErrorMessage	**Your e-mail address is invalid**
	ControlToValidate	**txtEmail**
	ValidationExpression	**Click the browse button and select Internet E-mail Address**
	Display	**Dynamic**
RequiredFieldValidator	**(ID)**	**rfvEmail**
	ErrorMessage	**Please enter an e-mail address**
	ControlToValidate	**txtEmail**
	Display	**Dynamic**
Label	**(ID)**	**lblPassword**
	Text	**Password:**
TextBox	**(ID)**	**txtPassword**
	TextMode	**Password**

(*continued*)

Control	Property name	Property value
RequiredFieldValidator	**(ID)**	**rfvPassword**
	ErrorMessage	**Please enter a password**
	ControlToValidate	**txtPassword**
	Display	**Dynamic**
Label	**(ID)**	**lblNotFound**
	Text	**Not found message**
	ForeColor	**Red**
	Visible	**False**
Button	**(ID)**	**btnSubmit**
	Text	**Submit**

3. Arrange your controls as shown in the following screen shot:

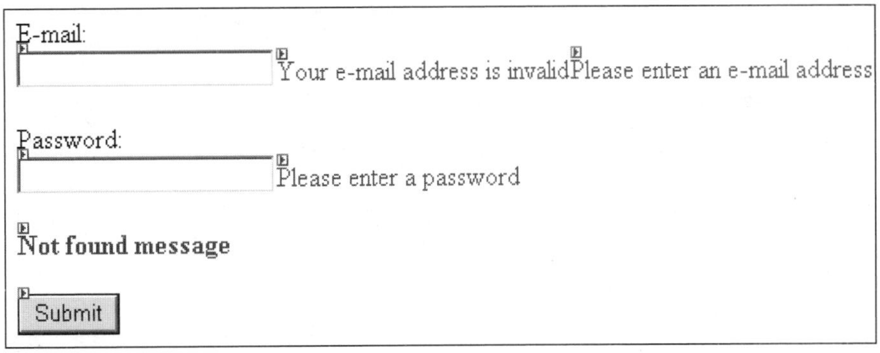

E-mail:
Your e-mail address is invalidPlease enter an e-mail address

Password:
Please enter a password

Not found message

Submit

▶ **To create the Web user control code**

1. View the Code Editor for **Logon.ascx**.
2. Declare an event with the following signature:

```
Public Event SubmitPressed(ByVal Email As String, _
                           ByVal Password As String)
```

3. Create a **Click** event handler for the **btnSubmit** event. In this method, set the **Visible** property of the lblNotFound label to **False**, and raise the **SubmitPressed** event, passing the following parameters:

Parameter	Value
Email	**txtEmail.Text**
Password	**txtPassword.Text**

4. Create a **DisplayMessage** subroutine that accepts a single string argument called **Message**. Within the subroutine, set the following values for the lblNotFound label.

Control property	Value
Text	**Message**
Visible	**True**

5. Save your project.

Exercise 2
Testing the LogOn Web Forms User Control

In this exercise, you will create a simple Web Form that uses the **Logon** user control to get customer logon information from the user. This information will then be passed to the serviced customer component for validation and information retrieval that you created in an earlier exercise. You will then redirect the browser to a preexisting Web Form that displays a welcome message with the customer's first name.

▶ To open the starter project

- If you did not complete the previous exercise, open the **LogonControl.sln** located in the *install folder*\Labs\Lab092\Ex02\Starter folder.

▶ To set a reference to the serviced component assembly

1. On the **Project** menu, click **Add Reference**.
2. In the **Add Reference** dialog box, click **Browse**, and then locate the *install folder*\Labs\Lab091\Ex01\Starter\bin folder.
3. Click **CustomerComponent.dll**, and then click **Open**.
4. From the existing list of .NET components, click **System.EnterpriseServices**, and then click **Select**.
5. Click **OK** to close the **Add Reference** dialog box.

▶ To create the logon page

1. On the **Project** menu, click **Add Web Form**, and rename the file **LogonPage.aspx**.
2. Drag Logon.ascx from Solution Explorer to the LogonPage Web Forms Designer to create an instance of the control on the Web Form.
3. In the LogonPage code window, add an **Imports CustomerComponent** statement.
4. Add the following variable declaration after the **Inherits System.Web.UI.Page** statement:

```
Protected WithEvents Logon1 As Logon
```

5. Create an event handler procedure for the **SubmitPressed** event of Logon1, and add the following code:

```
Dim ds As DataSet, dr As DataRow
Dim cust As ICustomer = New Customer( )
Try
    ds = cust.Logon(Email, Password)
    dr = ds.Tables(0).Rows(0)
    Session("FirstName") = dr("FirstName")
    Response.Redirect("Welcome.aspx")
Catch ex As Exception
    Logon1.DisplayMessage _
    ("No match was found. Please reenter your details.")
End Try
```

6. Save the project.

▶ To test the application

1. In Solution Explorer, right-click **LogonPage.aspx**, and then click **Set As Start Page**.
2. On the **Debug** menu, click **Start**.
3. Click **Submit** without entering any values in the text boxes to test the validation controls.
4. Enter the following deliberately incorrect values in the text boxes, and then click **Submit**.

Control	Value
E-mail	**john@tailspintoys.msn.com**
Password	**john**

5. Confirm that an error message is displayed by the user control.
6. Enter the same e-mail address as in step 4, but use the correct password of **password**, and then click **Submit**. Confirm that the welcome message is displayed and that the customer has been recognized.
7. Quit Microsoft Internet Explorer and Visual Studio .NET.

◆ Threading

- What Is a Thread?
- Advantages of Multithreading
- Creating Threads
- Using Threading
- When to Use Threading

Previous versions of Visual Basic have limited threading support. Visual Basic .NET allows developers to use the full power of threads when necessary. When you use threading correctly, you can enhance the performance of your application and make it more interactive.

After you complete this lesson, you will be able to:

- Explain the basic concepts of threading.
- List the advantages of incorporating multithreading into your applications.
- Create and use threads by using the **System.Threading** namespace.
- Avoid some potential problems in your multithreaded applications.

Warning Be aware that this section is an overview of how to use threading in Visual Basic .NET. This is a very complex subject, and you must be sure that you fully understand the implications before using these methods. For more information, see the .NET Framework SDK.

What Is a Thread?

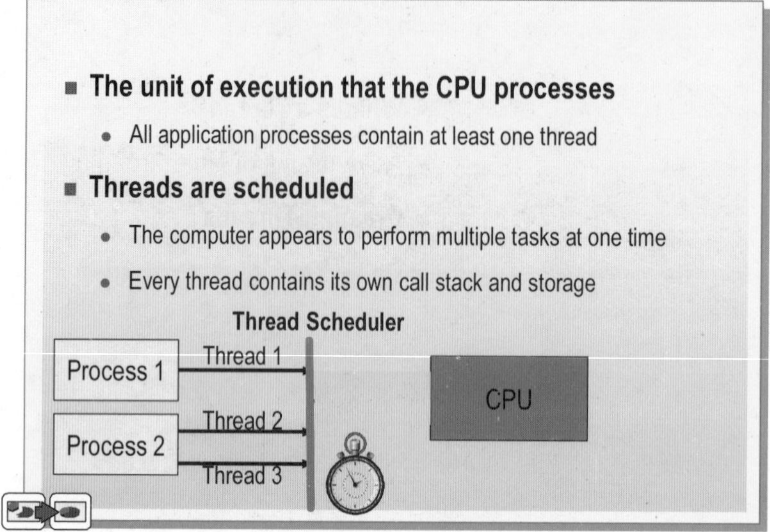

An application running on a computer is known as a process. Each process gets work done by using one or more *threads*. The thread is the unit of execution that is processed by the CPU of the computer.

Threading Process

A CPU can only execute a single thread at any one instant, so a thread scheduler allocates a certain amount of CPU time for each thread to get as much work done as possible before allowing another thread to access the CPU. This scheduling makes a computer appear to perform multiple tasks at once. In reality, the following is what happens:

1. Every thread contains its own call stack and storage for local variables. This information is kept with the thread and passed to the CPU whenever the thread is scheduled for processing.
2. When the time is up, the thread scheduler removes the thread from the CPU and stores the call stack and variable information.

The more threads that are running on the system, the less frequently a thread is scheduled to run in the CPU. This is why a computer can appear to be running slowly when you have multiple applications open and functioning at the same time.

Threading Types

Different programming languages support different types of threading:

- Previous versions of Visual Basic support the apartment threading model.

  This model places some restrictions on the types of applications that these versions are best suited for creating. One of these restrictions is that an object is tied to the thread that it is created on, and cannot be used for object pooling in Component Services. However, this model makes development easy because you do not need to be involved with more complex issues such as synchronization.

- Visual Basic .NET supports the free threading model.

  This model allows you to use multithreading and features such as object pooling or to continue using single threads as you have in applications created with previous versions of Visual Basic.

Advantages of Multithreading

- Improved user interface responsiveness
  - Example: a status bar
- No blocking
- Asynchronous communication
- No thread affinity
  - Objects are not tied to one thread

A multithreaded application has several advantages over a single-threaded application.

Improved User Interface Responsiveness

You can use multiple threads in a single process to improve the responsiveness of the user interface. The following is an example:

- Use threads for lengthy processing operations, such as using the spelling checker or reformatting pages. These extra threads can then raise events to the main user interface thread to update items such as a status bar.
- Assign each thread a priority level so that particular threads can run as a higher priority than other lower priority threads. In an application that relies heavily on user interaction, you should run the user interface thread as a higher priority thread.

No Blocking

Blocking occurs because a call to a single-threaded application must wait until any previous call by another client application has been fully satisfied before executing any other code. In server-based applications, blocking will occur if multiple clients make simultaneous requests of a process and only a single thread is available.

Multithreaded applications are able to perform actions on different threads simultaneously (through thread scheduling) without waiting for other threads to finish their current execution. This allows multiple clients to be handled by different threads without any blocking in a server-based application.

Asynchronous Communication

Asynchronous communication is possible in a multithreaded application because one thread can make a request to another thread. The calling thread can continue with other processing because the request executes on a separate thread. An event can be raised when the second thread finishes executing the requested functionality, informing the first thread that it has completed its work.

No Thread Affinity

Visual Basic .NET uses the free threading model. This model does not restrict you to using an object only on the thread where it was initially created. You can create an object on one thread and then pass it to another thread without difficulty. This improves scalability when used in conjunction with Component Services and object pooling.

Creating Threads

- **Use the System.Threading.Thread class**
  - Constructor specifies delegate method
  - Methods provide control of thread processing
  - Properties provide state and priority information
- **Use a class if parameters are required**
  - Allow public access to class variables
  - Raise an event when finished

The .NET Framework provides a simple way to create and work with multiple threads.

Using the System.Threading.Thread Class

Use the **Thread** class to create multiple threads within a Visual Basic .NET–based application.

Constructing the Thread

When a **Thread** instance is created, the **AddressOf** operator passes the constructor a delegate representing the method to be executed, as shown in the following example:

```
Dim th As New Threading.Thread(AddressOf PerformTask)
...
Sub PerformTask( )
    ...
End Sub
```

Threading Methods

The **Thread** class also provides several methods to control the processing of a thread.

Method	Purpose
Start	Begins execution of the method delegate declared in the thread constructor.
Abort	Explicitly terminates an executing thread.
Sleep	Pauses a thread. Specifies the number of milliseconds as the only parameter. If you pass zero as the parameter, the thread gives up the remainder of its current time slice. This is similar to **DoEvents** in previous versions of Visual Basic.
Suspend	Temporarily halts execution of a thread.
Resume	Reactivates a suspended thread.

Threading Properties

The **Thread** class provides properties to retrieve information about the thread state and to manipulate the thread priority.

Property	Purpose
ThreadState	Use the **ThreadState** property to determine the current state of a thread, such as **Running**, **Suspended**, or **Aborted**.
Priority	Modify the priority of a thread by setting its **Priority** property by using the **ThreadPriority** enumeration. The enumeration provides the following values: **AboveNormal**, **BelowNormal**, **Highest**, **Lowest**, and **Normal**.

Warning If you set thread priorities to a value of **Highest**, this may affect vital system processes by depriving them of CPU cycles. Use this setting with extreme caution.

Creating and Testing Threads

The following example shows how to create a thread, test the state of the thread, and change its priority:

```
Dim th As New Threading.Thread(AddressOf PerformTask)
th.Start( )
If th.ThreadState = ThreadState.Running Then
    th.Priority = Threading.ThreadPriority.AboveNormal
End If
```

Using Classes to Supply Parameters

You cannot specify a method delegate that accepts arguments in the thread constructor. If your procedure requires information to perform its required action, you can:

- Use classes to provide methods that perform operations on local data.
- Use public properties or variables to supply the local data.

To use classes to supply parameters, you must create an instance of the class before calling the thread constructor. Use the **AddressOf** operator to pass a reference to the method of the class as the constructor parameter. You can then use the properties or public variables to supply any data required by the method. When the worker method finishes its execution, you can raise an event to inform the calling thread that the operation is completed.

Using Threading

```
Class Calculate
  Public iValue As Integer
  Public Event Complete(ByVal Result As Integer)
  Public Sub LongCalculation( )
    'Perform a long calculation based on iValue
    ...
    RaiseEvent Complete(iResult)      'Raise event to signal finish
  End Sub
End Class
```

```
Sub Test( )
  Dim calc As New Calculate( )
  Dim th As New Threading.Thread(AddressOf calc.LongCalculation)
  calc.iValue = 10
  AddHandler calc.Complete, AddressOf CalcResult
  th.Start( )
End Sub
Sub CalcResult(ByVal Result As Integer)
  ...
End Sub
```

This topic shows how to prepare a class for threading, create a thread, start the thread, and perform calculations on the new thread.

Preparing a Class for Threading

The following example shows how to create a **Calculate** class and prepare it for threading by using the **Complete** event:

```
Class Calculate
   Public iValue As Integer
   Public Event Complete(ByVal Result As Integer)
   Public Sub LongCalculation( )
    'Perform a long calculation based on iValue
     ...
     RaiseEvent Complete(iResult)'Raise event to signal finish
   End Sub
End Class
```

When examining the previous code, note the following:

- The class provides a **LongCalculation** worker function, which will be executed on a separate thread.
- The worker function uses information stored in the public *iValue* integer variable to calculate its result.
- The **Calculate** class provides a **Complete** event to notify the calling thread that the calculation is finished.

Creating and Using a Thread

The following example shows how to create a thread and use threading to perform calculations:

```
Sub Test( )
   Dim calc As New Calculate( )
   Dim th As New Threading.Thread( _
               AddressOf calc.LongCalculation)
   calc.iValue = 10
   AddHandler calc.Complete, AddressOf CalcResult
   th.Start( )
End Sub

Sub CalcResult(ByVal Result As Integer)
   'Perform appropriate action when calculation is finished
   ...
End Sub
```

When examining this code, note the following:

- The **Test** subroutine instantiates a **Calculate** object and specifies the **LongCalculation** delegate in the **Thread** constructor.
- A value is assigned to the *iValue* variable for use by the worker function.
- An event handler is created to detect completion of the calculation.
- The **Start** method is called on the separate thread to begin the processing of the calculation.

When to Use Threading

- **Use threads carefully**
  - Using more threads requires more system resources
- **Synchronize access to shared resources**
  - Prevent two threads from accessing shared data simultaneously
  - Use **SyncLock** statement to block sections of code

```
Sub Worker( )
    SyncLock(theData)          'Lock this object variable
        theData.id = iValue
        'Perform some lengthy action
        iValue = theData.id
    End SyncLock               'Unlock the object variable
End Sub
```

Using multiple threads is a useful programming concept in enterprise development; however, improper use of threads can cause performance problems, create inconsistent data, and cause other errors.

System Resources

Threads consume memory and other valuable resources, such as CPU processing time. If your application creates multiple threads, it may do so at the expense of other applications or other threads within your own process. The more threads you create, the longer the delay between CPU time slices for each thread. If all applications created an excessive number of threads and used them constantly, the system would spend most of its time swapping threads in and out of the CPU, since the thread scheduler itself requires the CPU to perform the swapping logic.

Shared Resources

If multiple threads need to access the same information at the same time, a concurrency problem may arise. Two threads accessing a shared global resource may get inconsistent results back from the resource if other threads have altered the data.

The following is an example of a situation in which this can occur:

- Thread A updates a value on a shared resource such as an integer, setting the value to 10 before performing some lengthy action.
- Thread B updates the same integer value to 15 during the delay of thread A's lengthy action.
- When this action is completed, thread A may read the integer value back from the resource whose value is now 15.

Synchronizing Shared Resources

You can avoid inconsistent results by locking the resource between the time that the value is initially set and the time that it is read back. You can use the **SyncLock** statement to lock a reference type such as a class, interface, module, array, or delegate.

The following example defines a shared resource called **SharedReference** that exposes an integer variable. The **ThreadObj** class defines the method that will be executed by different threads. This method uses the **SyncLock** statement to lock the shared resource object while it is in use. The module code shows how you can test this behavior by creating two threads and two worker objects, and then starting both threads consecutively.

```
Imports System.Threading

'Shared data
Public Class SharedReference
    Public Id As Integer
End Class

'Class for running on other threads
Public Class ThreadObj
    Private sr As SharedReference
    Private Count As Integer

    'Constructor with reference and Id
    Public Sub New(ByRef sharedRef As SharedReference, _
                ByVal ID As Integer)
        sr = sharedRef
        Count = ID
    End Sub

    'Actual worker method
    Public Sub RunMethod( )
        SyncLock (sr)   'Lock sr object
            sr.Id = Count

            'Execute lengthy code
            'sr.Id could have changed without SyncLock

            Count = sr.Id
        End SyncLock    'Release sr object lock
    End Sub
End Class

Module MainModule
    Sub Main( )
        'Create shared data object
        Dim sr As New SharedReference( )

        'Create two worker objects
        Dim worker1 As New ThreadObj(sr, 1)
        Dim worker2 As New ThreadObj(sr, 2)

        'Create two threads
        Dim t1 As New Thread(AddressOf worker1.RunMethod)
        Dim t2 As New Thread(AddressOf worker2.RunMethod)

        'Start both threads
        t1.Start( )
        t2.Start( )
    End Sub
End Module
```

Demonstration: Using the SyncLock Statement

In this demonstration, you will learn how to use the **SyncLock** statement when using multiple threads in an application created in Visual Basic .NET.

Review

- Components Overview
- Creating Serviced Components
- Creating Component Classes
- Creating Windows Forms Controls
- Creating Web Forms User Controls
- Threading

1. An unmanaged client application uses a class created in Visual Basic .NET but cannot access any methods of the class. What is the likely cause of this problem, and how would you fix it?

2. Modify the following code to use auto completion of transactions rather than the explicit **SetAbort** and **SetComplete** methods.

```
<Transaction(TransactionOption.Required)> _
Public Class TestClass
    Public Sub MySub( )
        Try
            'Perform action
            ContextUtil.SetComplete( )
        Catch ex As Exception
            ContextUtil.SetAbort( )
            Throw ex
        End Try
    End Sub
End Class
```

3. Create assembly attributes so Component Services can automatically create an application named "TestComponents" that runs as server activation.

4. Why would you use the **IComponent** interface?

5. The following code causes a compilation error. Explain what is causing the error and how it could be fixed.

```
Sub Main( )
    Dim t As New Thread(AddressOf MySub)
    t.Start(10)
End Sub

Sub MySub(ByVal x As Integer)
    ...
End Sub
```

Course Evaluation

Your evaluation of this course will help Microsoft understand the quality of your learning experience.

At a convenient time between now and the end of the course, please complete a course evaluation, which is available at http://www.metricsthatmatter.com/survey.

Microsoft will keep your evaluation strictly confidential and will use your responses to improve your future learning experience.

msdn® training

Module 10: Deploying Applications

Contents

Overview

- Describing Assemblies
- Choosing a Deployment Strategy
- Deploying Applications

After you create and test an application, you will want to distribute it for use on other computers. The users may be end users running a Web application or an application based on Microsoft® Windows®, or other developers using a code library.

In this module, you will learn how to deploy assemblies for use by client applications, how to decide what type of distribution strategy to implement, and how to deploy Windows-based and Web-based applications.

After completing this module, you will be able to:

- Describe an assembly.
- List the different types of application deployment.
- Deploy a component assembly.
- Deploy an application based on Windows.
- Deploy a Web-based application.

◆ Describing Assemblies

- Assemblies Overview
- Benefits of Strong-Named Assemblies
- Creating Strong-Named Assemblies
- Versioning Strong-Named Assemblies
- Using the Global Assembly Cache

In this lesson, you will learn about the role of assemblies in Microsoft Visual Basic® .NET version 7.0. You will learn about the benefits of strong-named assemblies and how to create them. Finally, you will learn how to version assemblies.

After completing this lesson, you will be able to:

- Describe the benefits of using strong-named assemblies.
- Create strong-named assemblies.
- Version assemblies.

Assemblies Overview

- Contains code, resources, and metadata
- Provides security, type, and reference scope
- Forms a deployment unit
- Versionable
- Side-by-side execution allows multiple installed versions
- Global assembly cache allows assembly sharing

An assembly is the building block of a Microsoft .NET-compatible application. It is a built, versioned, and deployed unit of functionality that can contain one or more files. An application can be composed of one or more assemblies.

You can think of an assembly as a collection of types and resources that form a logical unit of functionality and are built to work together. Using existing assemblies to add extra functionality to your application is similar to the way that you use Microsoft ActiveX® libraries in previous versions of Visual Basic. You also can create your own assemblies for other applications to use.

What makes assemblies different from .exe or .dll files in earlier versions of Windows is that they contain all the information you would find in a type library, in addition to information about everything else necessary to use the application or component.

Assemblies Contain Code, Resources, and Metadata

An assembly contains:

- Intermediate language (IL) code to be executed
- Any required resources, such as pictures and assembly metadata, which exists in the form of the assembly manifest.
- Type metadata

  Type metadata provides information about available classes, interfaces, methods, and properties, similar to the way that a type library provides information about COM components.

An assembly can be grouped into a single portable executable (PE) file, such as an .exe or .dll file, or it can be made up of multiple PE files and external resource files, such as a bitmap.

The assembly manifest contains assembly metadata. It provides information about the assembly title, description, version information, and so on. It also provides information about linking to the other files in the assembly. This enables the assembly to be self describing, which allows you to distribute it using the XCOPY command. The information in the manifest is used at run time to resolve references and validate loaded assemblies.

The assembly manifest can be stored in a separate file but is usually compiled as part of one of the PE files.

Assemblies Provide Boundaries

Assemblies provide the following boundaries:

- Security boundary

  You set security permissions at an assembly level. You can use these permissions to request specific access to an application, such as file I/O permissions if the application must write to a disk. When the assembly is loaded at run–time, the permissions requested are entered into the security policy to determine if permissions can be granted.

- Type boundary

  An assembly provides a boundary for data types, because each type has the assembly name as part of its identity. As a result, two types can have the same name in different assemblies without any conflict.

- Reference scope boundary

  An assembly provides a reference scope boundary by using the assembly manifest for resolving type and resource requests. This metadata specifies which types and resources are exposed outside the assembly.

Assemblies Form a Deployment Unit

Assemblies are loaded by the client application when they are needed, allowing for a minimal download where appropriate.

Assemblies Are Versionable

An assembly is the smallest versionable unit in a .NET-compliant application. The assembly manifest describes the version information and any version dependencies specified for any dependent assemblies. You can only version assemblies that have a strong name.

Side-by-Side Execution Enables Multiple Installed Versions

Multiple versions of an assembly can run side-by-side simultaneously on the same computer or even in the same process. This ability greatly aids a client's compatibility with previous versions, because clients can specify which version they want to use regardless of how many new versions are deployed on the computer. This avoids the .dll conflicts that happen when a client application is expecting a particular version of an assembly but that version has been overwritten with an inappropriate version by another installation.

The Global Assembly Cache Enables Assembly Sharing

If an assembly is to be shared by several applications on a particular computer, you can install the assembly into the global assembly cache. Deploying assemblies into the cache can enhance performance because the operating system must only load one instance of the assembly. It also increases file security because only users with local Administrator privileges can delete assemblies in the global assembly cache.

Serviced component applications, such as COM+ applications, are often deployed into the global assembly cache so that all clients access only a single copy of the component assembly.

Note The .NET Framework assemblies are installed into the global assembly cache.

Benefits of Strong-Named Assemblies

- **Guaranteed uniqueness**
  - No two strong names can be the same
- **Protected version lineage**
  - Only legitimate assembly versions can be loaded
- **Enforced assembly integrity**
  - Assemblies are tested for unauthorized modification before loading

You can use strong-named assemblies to ensure safe use of the components contained within the assembly. A strong-named assembly is a requirement for serviced components because only a single instance of the assembly is loaded regardless of the number of client applications.

Guaranteed Uniqueness

Strong names guarantee that an assembly name is unique and cannot be used by anyone else. You generate strong names through the use of public and private key pairs when the assembly is compiled.

Protected Version Lineage

By default, applications can only run with the version of the assembly that they were originally compiled with, unless a setting in a configuration file overrides it. If you want to update a component, you can use a publisher policy file to redirect an assembly binding request to the new version. This link ensures that a client application cannot use an incorrect component assembly unless the client application is explicitly recompiled.

Enforced Assembly Integrity

The .NET Framework provides an integrity check that guarantees that strong-named assemblies have not been modified since they were built. This ensures that no unauthorized alterations can be made to the component assembly after the client application is compiled.

Creating Strong-Named Assemblies

- **Requires identity, public key, and digital signature**
- **Generating the public-private key pair**
  - Create a .snk file
  - Modify AssemblyInfo.vb

```
<Assembly: AssemblyKeyFile("KeyFile.snk")>
```

The.NET Framework can create a strong-named assembly by combining the assembly identity (its name, version, and culture information), a public key, and a digital signature.

You must generate the strong name key file (.snk extension) that contains the public-private key pair before you build the assembly. You can do this manually by using the Strong Name tool (sn.exe) utility.

In **AssemblyInfo.vb**, you can use the **AssemblyKeyFile** attribute to link the key file to the component. The public key is inserted into the assembly manifest at compile time, and the private key is used to sign the assembly.

Versioning Strong-Named Assemblies

- **When a client makes a binding request, the runtime checks:**
  - The original binding information inside the assembly
  - Configuration files for version policy instructions
- **Use a publisher policy file to redirect the binding request**

```
<bindingRedirect  oldVersion="1.0.0.0"
                  newVersion="1.0.1.0"/>
```

Often, you will want to update a component without redeploying the client application that is using it. However, by default, an application only functions with the original component that it was compiled with. To overcome this behavior, you must ensure that your components have strong names, which enables you to version them at a later date.

When a client application makes a binding request, the runtime performs the following tasks:

- Checks the original assembly reference for the version to be bound
- Checks the configuration files for version policy instructions

You can use a publisher policy file to redirect a binding request to a newer instance of a component. The following example shows a publisher policy file. Note the **publicKeyToken** attribute, a hexadecimal value, which is used to identify the strong name of the assembly. This value can be obtained by using sn.exe with the **–T** switch, or from the Assembly Cache listing in the .NET Framework Configuration snap-in in the Microsoft Management Console.

```
<configuration>
  <runtime>
      <assemblyBinding>
          <dependentAssembly>
              <assemblyIdentity name="myasm"
                  publicKeyToken="e9b4c4996039ede8"
                  culture="en-us"/>
              <bindingRedirect
                  oldVersion="1.0.0.0"
                  newVersion="1.0.1.0"/>
              <codeBase version="1.0.1.0"
                  href="http://www.Microsoft.com/Test.dll"/>
          </dependentAssembly>
      </assemblyBinding>
  </runtime>
</configuration>
```

You can compile this XML file into a publisher policy assembly, to be shipped with the new component, using the Assembly Generation tool (Al.exe). This signs the assembly with the strong name originally used.

Using the Global Assembly Cache

- **Performance**
  - Quicker binding
  - Only one instance ever loaded
- **Shared location**
  - Can use machine configuration file to redirect bindings
- **File security**
  - Only administrators can delete files
- **Side-by-side versioning**
  - Can install multiple copies using different version information

You can store your shared components inside the global assembly cache. To do this, you must create a strong name for the assembly, and when deploying the component, you must specify that it is stored in the global assembly cache, as opposed to the common files folder for the client application. Using the global assembly cache has the following benefits.

Performance

If the component is stored in the cache, the strong name does not need to be verified each time the component is loaded. This method also guarantees that only one instance of the component is loaded in memory, reducing the overhead on the target computer.

Shared Location

You can use the computer configuration file to redirect all bindings to the global assembly cache, providing simpler administration of assemblies.

File Security

Only users with administrative privileges can delete files from the cache.

Side-by-Side Versioning

You can install multiple copies of the same component, with different version information, into the cache.

◆ Choosing a Deployment Strategy

- Deployment Overview
- Copying Projects
- Deploying Projects
- Types of Deployment Projects

There are a variety of options available when deploying Visual Basic.NET–based applications. Choosing what option to use depends on the type of application that you are deploying and the version of Windows you are deploying it to.

Before you can begin the distribution process, you must understand the differences in the various strategies available to you. Some of these simply involve copying the application to an appropriate place, some involve creating a deployment project to copy the application and register any components, and some involve creating a complete setup application for use by the end user.

After completing this lesson, you will be able to:

- Describe the deployment options available to you.
- Match deployment options with specific scenarios.

Deployment Overview

- No-impact applications
- Private components
- Side-by-side versioning
- XCOPY deployment
- On-the-fly updates
- Global assembly cache

Application developers have traditionally faced many issues when deploying their applications. Use of the deployment features in Microsoft Visual Studio® .NET alleviates some of these issues.

The following table lists some of the advantages of using Visual Studio .NET deployment.

Feature	Description
No-impact applications	All applications are isolated, which results in fewer .dll conflicts.
Private components	By default, components are installed into the application directory. Therefore, you can only use it in that application.
Side-by-side versioning	You can have more than one copy of a component on a computer, which can prevent versioning problems.
XCOPY deployment	Self-describing components can just be copied to the target computer.
On-the-fly updates	.dlls are not locked when in use and can be updated by an administrator without stopping the application.
Global assembly cache	You can share assemblies between applications by installing them into the global assembly cache. This can also increase performance because only one copy of the assembly is loaded.

Copying Projects

- **Copying a project**
  - There is an extra menu command for Web applications
  - You can copy a project directly to a Web server
- **Using the XCOPY command**
  - Use the DOS command
  - You can use it for any type of application

Deploying simple applications with no dependencies can be as easy as copying the application to the target computer. Using this method can be quick, although it does not take advantage of the all the new features available in Visual Studio .NET deployment.

Copying a Project

When you are working with a Web application, you have an extra menu item available, **Copy Project**, which allows you to copy the project directly to a Web server. You can specify the access method, for example with Microsoft FrontPage® Server extensions, and whether to copy just the necessary application files, the entire project, or all files in the project directory.

Consider the following facts when using the **Copy Project** command:

- Assemblies are not registered for unmanaged client access.
- The locations of assemblies are not verified.

Using the XCOPY Command

You can use the Microsoft MS-DOS® XCOPY command to deploy any type of application. Consider the following facts when deploying with the XCOPY command:

- Assemblies are not registered for unmanaged client access.
- The locations of assemblies are not verified.
- Project-to-project references are not copied.
- Internet Information Server (IIS) is not configured for Web applications.
- You cannot take advantage of the Zero Administration initiative for Windows feature in Microsoft Windows Installer.

Deploying Projects

- **Windows Installer**
  - Is used for Windows-based and Web-based deployment
  - Copies all required files and registers components
  - Configures IIS for Web-based applications
- **Merge modules**
  - Are used for reusable components
  - Are included in an .msi file

In general, you will create applications that have dependencies on other assemblies or components. In this situation, you must create a deployment package to ensure that the external references are correctly registered and located.

Windows Installer

You can use the Windows Installer to package all your data and installation instructions in one file, an .msi file, for easy distribution. Using the Windows Installer provides the following advantages:

- Support for the Zero Administration initiative for Windows

  This helps overcome the problems of overwriting shared components.

- Safe uninstall options

  Windows Installer provides an uninstall program that detects shared components and does not remove them.

- Rollback

  If the install fails before it is complete, for example, if the connection to the network share containing the source files is lost, then the Windows Installer will return the computer to its original state.

You can use the Windows Installer to package both Windows-based and Web-based applications.

Merge Modules

You can use merge module projects to package shared components that will be used by more than one application on the target computer. You can then incorporate these modules into .msi packages whenever that component is used in a solution. Using merge modules has the following advantages:

- Eliminates versioning problems
- Captures the dependencies of the component
- Creates reusable setup code

Types of Deployment Projects

- Cab Project – for downloading from Web server
- Merge Module Project – for shared components
- Setup Project – for Windows-based applications
- Setup Wizard – to walk through deployment project creation
- Web Setup Project – for Web-based applications

There are five options available to you when creating a deployment project in Visual Studio .NET. The following table lists the types of projects and their uses.

Project type	Use
Cab Project	Use this to create compressed CAB files for downloading from a Web server.
Merge Module Project	Use this to create a setup for a shared component.
Setup Project	Use this to create a setup for a Windows-based application.
Setup Wizard	Use this to initiate the Setup Wizard that leads you through the steps of creating one of the four main deployment projects.
Web Setup Project	Use this to create a setup for a Web-based application.

To create a new deployment project, click **Setup and Deployment Projects** in the **New Project** dialog box, as shown below:

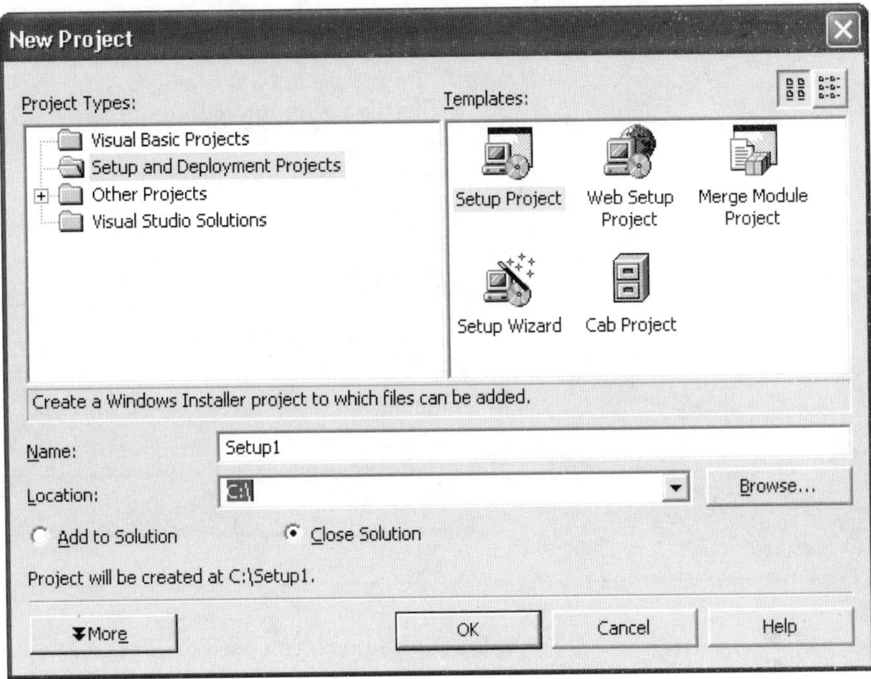

◆ Deploying Applications

- Creating a Merge Module Project
- Creating a Setup Project
- Using the Editors
- Creating Installation Components
- Deploying the Application

To deploy applications, you need to create a setup project with all your installation preferences and build the project for distribution.

After completing this lesson, you will be able to:

- Describe the two types of setup projects used for Windows-based and Web-based applications.
- Configure your installation process by using the Visual Studio .NET editors.

Creating a Merge Module Project

- **Never installed directly – included in client application deployment project**
- **Contains**
  - DLL
  - Any dependencies and resources
  - Information for the Windows Installer
- **Store one component only in one merge module**
- **If component changes, create a new merge module**

After you create the strong-named assembly, you need to package it within a merge module for it to be included in the deployment project for a client application. The merge module provides you with a standard way of distributing components and ensuring that the correct version is installed.

The merge module is never installed directly, but it is distributed within a Windows Installer project. It includes the .dll file, any dependencies, any resources, and any setup logic. This method of deployment ensures that whenever this shared component is used, it is installed on the target computer in the same way. It also contains information that the Windows Installer database uses to determine when you can safely remove a component during application removal.

To package a component assembly, complete the following steps:

1. Create your component and build the .dll.
2. Add a merge module project to your solution.
3. Add the component to the Common Files folder or the global assembly cache.
4. Build the merge module project.
5. Add the merge module project to a Windows-based or Web-based setup project.

Lab 10.1: Packaging a Component Assembly

Objectives

After completing this lab, you will be able to create a merge module project.

Prerequisites

Before working on this lab, you must have:

- Knowledge of the merge module project template.
- Knowledge of the deployment editors.
- Knowledge of the setup project template for Windows-based applications.

Scenario

In this lab, you will create a merge module project to package a component assembly.

Starter and Solution Files

There are starter and solution files associated with this lab. The starter files are in the *install folder*\Labs\Lab101\Starter folder, and the solution files are in the *install folder*\Labs\Lab101\Solution folder.

Estimated time to complete this lab: 15 minutes

Exercise 1
Packaging the Component Assembly

In this exercise, you will create a strong name for a component assembly and then package the component in a merge module project that is ready for deployment with the client application.

▶ To generate a key file

1. Click **start**, point to **All Programs**, point to **Microsoft Visual Studio .NET**, point to **Visual Studio .NET Tools**, and then click **Visual Studio .NET Command Prompt**.
2. In the Visual Studio .NET Command Prompt window, navigate to *install folder*\Labs\Lab101\Starter\Component.
3. Use the following command to create a Strong Name Key for your component:

```
sn.exe -k Component.snk
```

4. Close the Command Prompt window.

▶ To attach the key pair to the assembly

1. Open Microsoft Visual Studio .NET.
2. On the **File** menu, point to **Open**, and then click **Project**.
3. Browse to the *install folder*\Labs\Lab101\Starter\Component folder, click **Component.sln**, and then click **Open**.
4. In Solution Explorer, click **Show All Files**.
5. Right-click **Component.snk**, and then click **Include In Project**.
6. Open AssemblyInfo.vb.
7. Add the following assembly attribute:

```
<Assembly: AssemblyKeyFile("Component.snk")>
```

8. Build the component.

▶ To create the merge module project

1. In Visual Studio .NET, on the **File** menu, point to **Add Project**, and then click **New Project**.
2. In the Project Types pane, click **Setup and Deployment Projects**.
3. In the Templates pane, click **Merge Module Project**. Set the location to *install folder*\Labs\Lab101\Starter, and then click **OK**.
4. In the left pane of the File System Editor, right-click the **Common Files Folder**, point to **Add**, and then click **Project Output**.
5. In the **Add Project Output Group** dialog box, select **Primary output** and **Content Files**, and then click **OK**.
6. On the **Build** menu, click **Build MergeModule1**.
7. Close Visual Studio .NET.

► To verify that the package has been created

- Open Windows Explorer, browse to the *install folder*\Labs\Lab101\Starter\MergeModule1\Debug folder, and verify that MergeModule1.msm has been created.

Creating a Setup Project

- **Creates a blank setup project with relevant folders in File System Editor**
- **Windows-based application**
  - Application Folder
  - User's Desktop
  - User's Programs Menu
- **Web-based application**
  - Web Application Folder

You can use the Setup Project and Web Setup Project templates to create Windows Installer packages for Windows-based and Web-based applications, respectively. You specify which of these project types you want to use when you create a new project in Visual Studio .NET. You can also use the Setup Wizard to lead you through the process of gathering the necessary information resulting in the required project type.

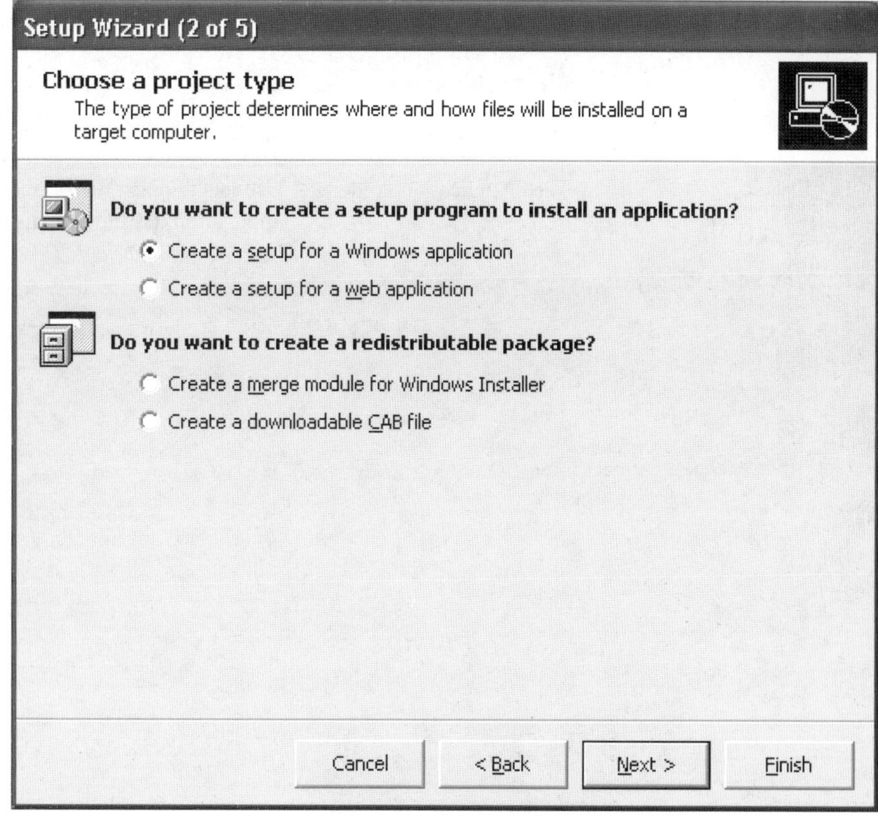

Both project types start in the File System Editor window, which you use to specify where to install the included files on the target computer. You can allocate files, folders, shortcuts, and components to these folders. For example, you can include a ReadMe.htm or a merge module project containing a shared component in these folders. In addition to using the default folders, you can also use a predetermined set of special folders (for example the Windows folder), and you can also create your own subfolders.

Windows-Based Setup Project

When you create a setup project for a Windows-based application, you are given a set of default folders.

Folder name	Description
Application Folder	Where the user specifies that the application is to be installed on the target computer, the application is installed in the Program Files*Manufacturer**ProductName* folder by default. Use this folder for the standard files used to run the application.
User's Desktop	Use this folder to create desktop shortcuts for the application. When the user installs the application, they can choose whether this application is for all users or just themselves, which determines where this folder is located.
User's Programs Menu	Use this folder to create **start** menu shortcuts for the application. When users install this application, they can choose whether this application is for all users or just themselves, which determines where this folder is located.

Web Setup Project

A Web setup project also presents you with a set of folders, but these are different because of the differences in the base project type.

Folder name	Description
Web Application Folder	Use this to place files in the default folder for the Web application. By default this will be http://*ComputerName*/*ProductName*

Using the Editors

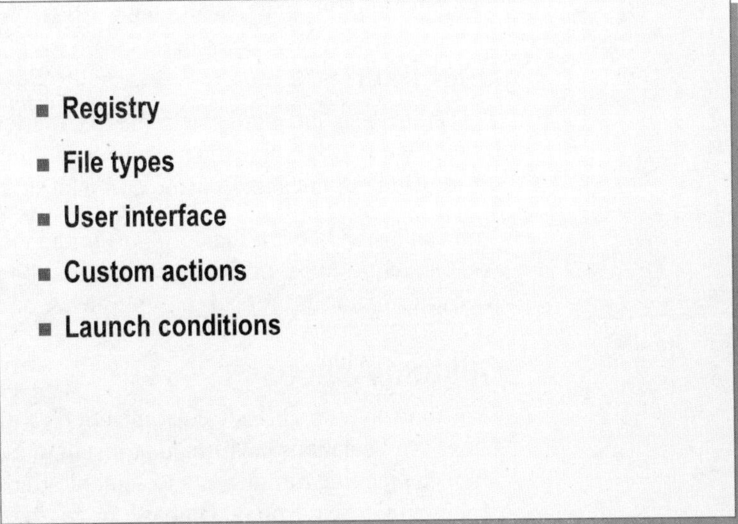

Registry
File types
User interface
Custom actions
Launch conditions

In addition to the File System Editor, you can use a range of other editors to further define your setting for the installation process. You can access these editors by using the toolbar buttons in Solution Explorer, as shown below.

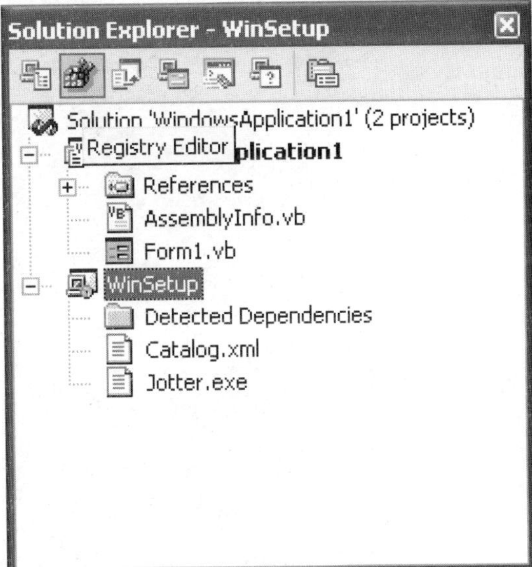

Registry

This gives you access to the commonly used registry hives and keys, such as **HKEY_CURRENT_USER\Software** and **HKEY_LOCAL_MACHINE\Software**. These vary according to whether your application is a Windows-based or Web-based application. In this editor, you can define your own keys and write their default values during the installation process.

File Types

This editor allows you to define new file types to be configured on the target computer and the actions associated with those types.

User Interface

This editor lists the windows in the Installation Wizard that the user sees and allows you to customize the messages and images displayed in them. You can customize both the standard and administrative installation programs.

You can also add extra dialog boxes to the installation process. For example, you can request user preferences with text boxes and option buttons, request user information for registration purposes, or display license agreements.

Custom Actions

This allows you to include custom actions within your main setup program. These can be actions performed at install, commit, rollback or uninstall time. They can include running any executable file, .dll, or script file; adding users to or removing users from a database; or adding a support contact to the address book in Microsoft Outlook®.

Launch Conditions

This editor allows you to define conditions for installing the application or performing custom actions. For example, if a database is not present on the server, you will not want to add users to it and may not want to install the application. You can check for files, registry keys, and Windows Installer installations. You can also customize the message given to the user if the condition is not satisfied.

Creating Installation Components

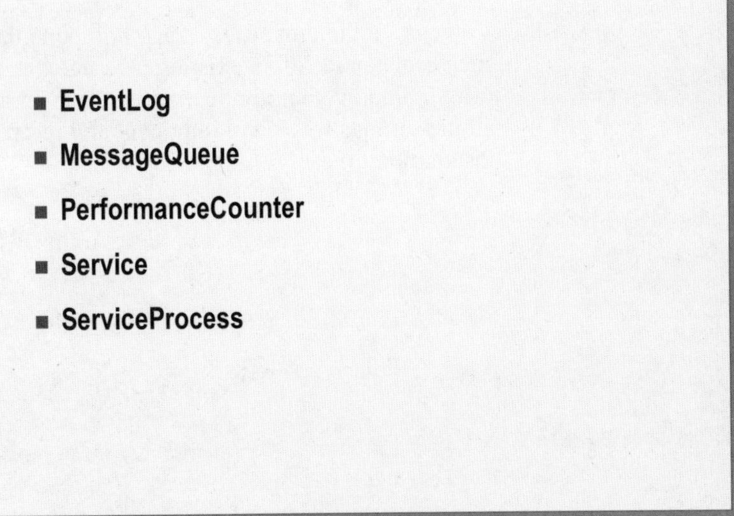

When you are developing an application, you often use Windows resources such as event logs and message queues. These types of objects are available to you on the **Components** tab of the Visual Basic .NET toolbox.

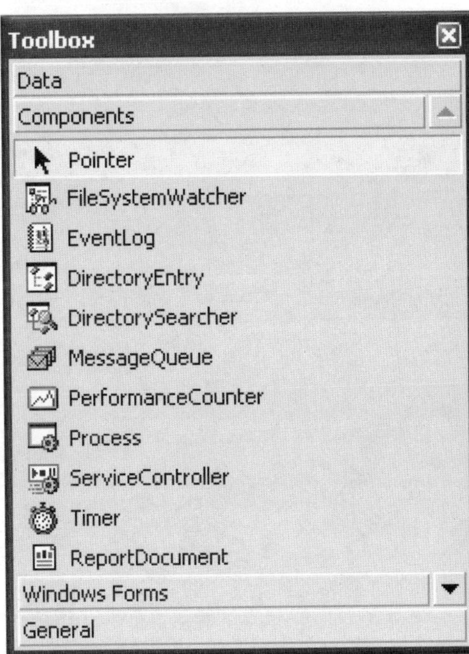

The Visual Studio .NET installation process allows you to create these components on the target computer as part of your application installation process. You accomplish this by using installation components.

You can set the properties of any component. These properties include elements such as the name of an existing message queue or name of the log. When you want to deploy your application, you can create ProjectInstaller files that copy all the settings for your component and re-create it on the target computer at installation time.

Deploying the Application

- **Windows-based setup project**
  - Copies all files
  - Registers components
  - Performs other installation tasks
- **Web setup project**
  - Copies all files
  - Registers components
  - Creates a Web application

After you configure settings using the editors in Visual Studio .NET for your custom setup program, you can build the project ready for deployment. Because this is a standard Visual Studio .NET project, you can build or deploy the project in the usual ways, although building a Visual Basic solution will not build any setup projects included in it.

Building the project creates an .msi file that you distribute to users so that they can run the setup program for your application. To install the application, you can run the .msi file on the target computer or click **Install** on the **Project** menu.

Windows-Based Setup Project

Installing a Windows-based application copies all the specified files to the appropriate locations on the target computer, creates any shortcuts that are specified, adds registry entries, creates file types, and creates any installation components included in the project.

Web Setup Project

When you install a Web project, all the actions performed are the same as those performed during the installation of a Windows-based project. The Web application is also created and configured within IIS.

Demonstration: Deploying a Web-Based Application

In this demonstration, you will learn how to use the Setup Wizard to create a deployment project for a Web-based application. You will also learn how to use the Launch Conditions Editor to verify that a database is present on the target computer before installing the application.

Lab 10.2: Deploying a Windows-Based Application

Objectives

After completing this lab, you will be able to:

- Create a Windows Installer project.
- Deploy a Windows-based application.

Prerequisites

Before working on this lab, you must have:

- Completed Lab 10.1.
- Knowledge of the deployment editors.
- Knowledge of the setup project template for Windows-based applications.

Scenario

In this lab, you will deploy a Windows-based application. You will begin by creating a Windows Installer package that includes the merge module that you created in the previous lab and the client application. Then, you will deploy the application and ensure that it installs all sections successfully.

Starter and Solution Files

There are starter and solution files associated with this lab. The starter files are in the *install folder*\Labs\Lab102\Starter folder, and the solution files are in the *install folder*\Labs\Lab102\Solution folder.

Estimated time to complete this lab: 30 minutes

Exercise 1
Creating a Windows Installer Project

In this exercise, you will create a Windows Installer project for a client application. This will include the merge module that you created in the previous lab. You will create shortcuts for the application on the desktop and **All Programs** menu and include a ReadMe file in the distribution.

▶ **To reference the component**

1. Open Visual Studio .NET.
2. On the **File** menu, point to **Open**, and then click **Project**.
3. Browse to the *install folder*\Labs\Lab102\Starter\Customers folder, click **Customers.sln**, and then click **Open**.
4. In Solution Explorer, right-click **Customers**, and then click **Add Reference**.
5. Click **Browse**, browse to the *install folder*\Labs\Lab102\Starter\Component\bin folder, click **Component.dll**, click **Open**, and then click **OK**.
6. View the properties of this component and verify that it is a strong-named assembly.
7. Run the application to test that it functions correctly.

▶ **To create a Windows Installer project**

1. On the **File** menu, point to **Add Project**, and then click **New Project**.
2. In the Project Types pane, click **Setup and Deployment Projects**.
3. In the Templates pane, click **Setup Project**. Set the location to *install folder*\Labs\Lab102\Starter, and then click **OK**.
4. In Solution Explorer, right-click **Setup1**, point to **Add**, and then click **Merge Module**.
5. Browse to the *install folder*\Labs\Lab102\Starter\MergeModule1\Debug folder, click **MergeModule1.msm**, and then click **Open**.
6. In the left pane of the File System Editor, open the Application Folder. Right-click the folder, point to **Add**, and then click **File**. Browse to the *install folder*\Labs\Lab102\Starter\Customers\bin folder, click **Customers.exe**, and then click **Open**.

► To customize the installation

1. In the File System Editor, open the User's Desktop folder. Right-click in the right pane and click **Create New Shortcut**.
2. In the **Select Item in Project** dialog box, open the Application Folder, click **Customers.exe**, and then click **OK**.
3. In the Properties window, change the name of the shortcut to Customers.
4. Use the same method to create a shortcut to Customers.exe in the User's Programs Menu.
5. Right-click the **Application Folder**, point to **Add**, and then click **File**.
6. Browse to the *install folder*\Labs\Lab102\Starter folder, click **ReadMe.rtf**, and then click **Open**.
7. On the Solution Explorer toolbar, click **User Interface Editor**.
8. Under **Install**, right-click **Start**, and then click **Add Dialog**.
9. In the **Add Dialog** dialog box, click **Read Me**, and then click **OK**.
10. Select the new **Read Me** dialog box in the editor.
11. In the Properties window, in the **ReadmeFile** property drop-down, click **(Browse...)**. In the **Select Item in Project** dialog box, open the **Application Folder**, click **ReadMe.rtf**, and then click **OK**.

► To build the project

1. On the **File** menu, click **Save All**.
2. On the **Build** menu, click **Build Setup1**.
3. When the project is successfully built, quit Visual Studio .NET.

Exercise 2
Running the Installation

In this exercise, you will run the Windows Installer project that you created in the previous exercise and verify that it installs correctly.

▶ To run the installation program

1. Open Windows Explorer.
2. Browse to the *install folder*\Labs\Lab102\Starter\Setup1\Debug folder, and then double-click **Setup1.msi**.
3. Follow the setup program, accepting the default options, wait for the deployment to finish, and then click **Close**.

▶ To verify the installation

1. Minimize all windows, and check that there is a shortcut to your application on the desktop.
2. On the **All Programs** menu, click **Customers**, and verify that the application functions correctly.
3. Quit the application.

▶ To remove the application

1. Open Control Panel, and then click **Add or Remove Programs**.
2. Click **Setup1**, and then click **Remove**. Confirm that you want to remove the application.
3. After the removal is complete, verify that the shortcuts and application folder have been removed.

Review

- Describing Assemblies
- Choosing a Deployment Strategy
- Deploying Applications

1. Name the four ways of distributing a Visual Studio .NET project and describe what each is used for.

2. How do you create a strong-named assembly?

3. Describe the use of the Launch Conditions Editor.

msdn® training

Module 11: Upgrading to Visual Basic .NET

Contents

Microsoft®

Overview

- Deciding Whether to Upgrade
- Options for Upgrading
- Recommendations
- Performing the Upgrade

As you have seen throughout this course, there are some fundamental changes in Microsoft® Visual Basic® .NET version 7.0. These changes are necessary because Visual Basic .NET is a significant upgrade that takes full advantage of the Microsoft .NET Framework.

Because of these changes, you will find that upgrading applications to Visual Basic .NET might take time and effort, but it does allow you to take advantage of the new features in the .NET Framework. The Visual Basic Upgrade Wizard has been provided as a step in the upgrade process to help you upgrade, but there are tasks that you should complete both before and after its use.

In this module, you will learn the factors you must consider when deciding whether to upgrade an existing application, the options you have for upgrading, and how to use the Upgrade Wizard.

After completing this module, you will be able to:

- Make an informed decision about whether to upgrade an application.
- Describe the various upgrade options available to you.
- Use the Upgrade Wizard.

◆ Deciding Whether to Upgrade

- Advantages Gained
- Cost Incurred
- Ease of Upgrade

You must consider various factors when deciding whether to upgrade an application. In some situations, the advantages gained from porting the application to the .NET Framework will greatly outweigh the costs involved. In other situations, you might decide that the advantages are not worth the investment. Upgrading is not a necessity, and you should carefully examine the advantages and disadvantages before starting the process.

After completing this lesson, you will be able to:

- Evaluate the advantages and disadvantages of the upgrade process.
- Identify how to decide when to upgrade your applications to Visual Basic .NET.

Advantages Gained

- Scalability
- Performance
- Deployment
- Access to rich set of base classes
- Better debugging
- Solves DLL conflicts
- Maintenance

The .NET Framework provides many benefits to the application developer that may enhance applications created in Visual Basic version 6.0.

Advantages

Three major advantages upgrading your application to Visual Basic .NET provides are:

- Scalability

  ADO.NET enhances scalability by means of the disconnected data architecture, which reduces the number of concurrent database connections necessary, thereby reducing the overhead needed to run the application.

  The ASP.NET state management system improves upon that of Active Server Pages (ASP). Session state can be shared among many servers in a Web farm, allowing for greater scalability.

- Performance

  ADO.NET is a simplified version of Microsoft ActiveX® Data Objects (ADO). It is designed around Extensible Markup Language (XML) to work seamlessly with disconnected data. The **DataReader** object is designed for speed and greatly increases the performance of data intensive applications.

  ASP.NET has improved performance over ASP and other Web development technologies. ASP.NET is a compiled .NET-based environment, which will run faster than existing applications, and allows you to use early binding throughout your applications.

- Deployment

  Deployment is greatly simplified in the .NET Framework. Depending on the complexity of your application, deployment can entail running an application directly from a server, using XCOPY to copy the application to a workstation or Web server, or installing by using Microsoft Windows® Installer.

Other advantages include:

- Maintenance
- Access to Rich Set of Base Classes
- Better Debugging
- Solves DLL Conflicts

Cost Incurred

- Time to upgrade may trade-off against future maintenance time
- May require redesign, as well as upgrading and recoding
- Financial costs can be spread by upgrading an application section by section

The costs you may incur in upgrading an application can be measured in terms of time, effort, and ultimately finance.

It will take you time to upgrade your applications from Visual Basic 6.0 to Visual Basic .NET; however, that time may actually recoup itself in the reduced maintenance time associated with the upgraded application or be outweighed by the benefits obtained by the upgrade. Visual Basic .NET–based applications can require less maintenance because of the improvements associated with the .NET Framework. XCOPY deployment ends DLL conflicts.

Some applications will gain little benefit from simply upgrading the existing application to Visual Basic .NET. These include applications that may have been upgraded through various versions of Visual Basic and never redesigned to take full advantage of the current systems architecture. The costs of redesigning an application will greatly increase the overall cost, and may be a deciding factor in your choice.

Some application architectures lend themselves to a gradual upgrade process over a period of time. For example, an application using a number of classes that contain data access code can be upgraded in a number of steps. First you can upgrade the user interface, then you can upgrade the middle-tier components, and then you can recode the existing ADO code to ADO.NET in the data tier.

Ease of Upgrade

- Modularity of code
- Project types
- Control types
- Language constructs

There are a variety of factors that will affect how easy it is to upgrade an application. These include the original application architecture, the modularity of the code in the application, the types of projects and controls used in application, and the language constructs used.

Modularity of Code

Because Visual Basic .NET supports object-oriented features not available in Visual Basic 6.0, it is easier to upgrade modular code than non-modular code. If an application has been designed in a modular fashion, changes to one component should not adversely affect another, and this results in a simpler upgrade path.

Project Types

Visual Basic .NET does not support some of the Visual Basic 6.0 project types, such as dynamic HTML (DHTML) applications and ActiveX Documents. These applications cannot be upgraded and should be left in Visual Basic 6.0 or rewritten in Visual Basic .NET by using Web Forms.

Control Types

Some Visual Basic 6.0 controls are not supported in Visual Basic .NET and will upgrade to substitute controls. For example, the **Shape**, **Line**, and **OLE Container** controls are all unsupported and will upgrade to **Label** controls in Visual Basic .NET. If your application makes extensive use of these types of control, it may require more work to upgrade the application to a working solution.

Language Constructs

Some Visual Basic 6.0 keywords are not supported in Visual Basic .NET. For example, **Option Base**, **LSet**, and **GoSub** are not supported. Extensive use of these keywords in your projects will require manual work after the upgrade process.

◆ Options for Upgrading

- Complete Rewrite
- Complete Upgrade
- Partial Upgrade

There are three options available if you decide to upgrade an existing application: You can completely rewrite the application, gaining all the benefits of the .NET Framework. You can use the Upgrade Wizard on all sections of the application, gaining some of the benefits. Finally, you can do a partial upgrade, leaving legacy sections in Visual Basic 6.0.

After completing this lesson, you will be able to:

- Identify the three upgrade options.
- Describe the advantages and disadvantages of each upgrade approach.

Complete Rewrite

- **Use if:**
  - Upgrading is impractical
  - Performance is essential
- **Advantages**
  - Best performance
  - Best scalability
  - Cleanest design
  - Reduced code base
  - Uses all new features
- **Disadvantages**
  - Labor intensive
  - Steep learning curve
  - Wasted investment in existing code
  - Introduction of errors

A complete rewrite of the application is the best way to gain all of the benefits of the .NET Framework, but this can also be the most costly solution. It is most commonly used when the application contains sections that are not upgradeable but that need to take advantage of the .NET Framework.

Advantages

- Performance can be improved through the use of new technologies such as ASP.NET and ADO.NET.
- Scalability is increased when using ASP.NET rather than ASP or other Visual Basic 6.0 Web project types.
- If you rewrite your application from the very beginning, you will have the chance to redesign it to take advantage of the object-oriented features of Visual Basic .NET.
- Your code base will be reduced due to some of the new features in Visual Basic .NET; for example, resizing code can be replaced by using the Anchor properties of a control.

Disadvantages

- Rewriting an application can be labor intensive, as it will potentially involve software analysts as well as developers.
- Learning Visual Basic .NET by rewriting an application can be very difficult for those involved.
- Any existing code that has been written will not be reused, and this results in wasted investment of the existing code.

Complete Upgrade

- Not as elegant as a rewrite
- Use if time or resources are limited

- Advantages
  - Improved performance
  - Improved scalability
  - Preserved investment in existing code
- Disadvantages
  - Some sections may not upgrade
  - Not best performance

You will probably find that this is the easiest option for upgrading, but it will not be a common occurrence. Even if the application is completely upgradeable, it may not result in the most efficient code, so you are likely to need to revisit sections anyway.

Advantages

- You will gain performance and scalability from the upgraded sections of the code.
- You will preserve the earlier investment made in the existing code by reusing the code.

Disadvantages

- Some sections of the application may not be upgradeable (for example, ADO code), so this will not take advantage of .NET.
- Some upgraded sections may use COM interoperability to communicate with the .NET components, resulting in lower performance. Other sections may use the Visual Basic compatibility library, again introducing overhead into the system.

Partial Upgrade

- Most likely option
- COM interoperability is only a problem if large number of client server calls

- Advantages
  - Improved performance
  - Improved scalability
  - Preserves investment in existing code
  - Quick upgrade, and retain non-upgradeable code
- Disadvantages
  - Use of COM interoperability adds overhead
  - Difficult to maintain
  - Difficult to deploy

A partial upgrade is the most likely option for migrating your application to Visual Basic .NET. This allows you to upgrade the sections of your code that will make the most benefit of using the .NET Framework while continuing to use the ones that will be difficult to upgrade. Sometimes you will use this method as a progressive upgrade option, allowing you to focus the upgrade process on small sections of the application at a time.

Advantages

- Performing a partial upgrade can allow you to take advantage of the particular performance and scalability enhancements in the .NET Framework that are appropriate to your application.
- It preserves the investment made in your existing code, and allows reuse of as much or as little as you want.

Disadvantages

- A partial upgrade may result in using COM interoperability to communicate between COM and .NET components. This may degrade performance.
- Applications that mix Visual Basic 6.0 and Visual Basic .NET are harder to deploy and maintain than single-language applications.

Recommendations

- **Web client server**
  - Complete upgrade
  - ASP to ASP .NET and Web Forms, COM components to .NET components, and ADO to ADO .NET
- **Traditional N-tier applications**
  - Partial upgrade
  - Leave client in Visual Basic 6.0
- **Enterprise legacy applications**
  - Complete rewrite
  - Encapsulate legacy system in Web Service
- **Stand-alone Windows-based applications**
  - Little benefit to upgrading

You have seen that the various upgrade options will lend themselves to particular application architectures. The following recommendations can be used as general guidelines to help you decide on the best upgrade process for your particular needs.

Web Client Server

This type of application will typically use ASP as a front end, business logic in COM components in the middle tier, and ADO code for the data access layer. It will gain the greatest benefits from upgrading to Visual Basic .NET because it will be performance driven and need to be extremely scalable. All the technologies used in Visual Basic 6.0 will correspond directly to technologies available in Visual Basic .NET, making the upgrade path relatively simple.

Traditional N-Tier Applications

This type of application will be fairly similar to the thin client server, but it will include some of the logic on the client side. The middle tier and data tier will benefit from upgrading, but unless the front end is extremely simple, it is best left as a Visual Basic 6.0–based application.

If the main goal of the upgrade is to improve performance, then you should rewrite any ADO code to ADO.NET.

Enterprise Legacy Applications

This type of application will typically be client/server with a legacy data source at the back end. They are perfect examples of applications that will benefit from being rewritten in Visual Basic .NET. You can encapsulate the legacy system in a managed component and expose it to many clients by using a Web Service.

Rewriting sections of these applications will provide the greatest improvements in scalability and performance.

Stand-Alone Windows-based Applications

These applications might benefit from the Windows Forms package and they can provide excellent environments to learn the upgrade process.

◆ Performing the Upgrade

- Preparing for the Upgrade
- Using the Upgrade Wizard
- Results of the Upgrade Wizard
- Completing the Upgrade

You can use the Upgrade Wizard to assist you in upgrading your Visual Basic 6.0–based applications to Visual Basic .NET. Opening a Visual Basic 6.0–based application in Visual Basic .NET will create a new application and leave the existing application as it is.

Because of the differences between the two products, the Upgrade Wizard cannot perform the entire process, but it can simplify some of the tasks involved.

After completing this lesson, you will be able to:

- Identify tasks you need to perform before, during, and after using the Upgrade Wizard.

Note The Upgrade Wizard should only be used to upgrade applications created in Visual Basic 6.0. If you want to upgrade projects created in earlier versions of Visual Basic, open and compile them in Visual Basic 6.0 before using the wizard.

Preparing for the Upgrade

- Early binding
- Null propagation
- Date variables
- Constants
- Data access

There are certain tasks that you can perform before using the Upgrade Wizard to maximize the usefulness of its output. These are tasks that make the wizard able to upgrade what would otherwise be ambiguous code.

It is easier to modify your Visual Basic 6.0 code and allow the wizard to upgrade it than to need to address the issues after the upgrading has occurred. You can identify these issues by upgrading your application, reading the comments added by the wizard, and then modifying your Visual Basic 6.0–based project before beginning the upgrade process again.

Early Binding

Late-bound objects can cause problems during the upgrade process when default properties are resolved, and when calls to updated properties, methods, and events are upgraded.

Example

In the following example, a **Label** object is declared as type **Object**, meaning that the Upgrade Wizard is unable to upgrade the **Caption** property to the Visual Basic .NET equivalent of the **Text** property:

```
Dim objLabel as Object
Set objLabel = Form1.Label1
objLabel.Caption = "Enter your password" 'Cannot be upgraded
```

To avoid this, you should declare all of your variables as the explicit type.

```
Dim objLabel as Label
Set objLabel = Form1.Label1
objLabel.Caption = "Enter your password" 'Can be upgraded
```

Null Propagation

Null propagation is the behavior in Visual Basic 6.0 that dictates that if you add **Null** to another data type, the result will always be **Null**.

Example

```
a = Null
b = 5
c = a + b
```

In Visual Basic 6.0, the above code will result in variable *c* evaluating to **Null**. In Visual Basic .NET, this code will return an invalid cast exception. To avoid this error, you should always check the contents of a variable that could potentially be **Null** prior to performing operations on it.

The following code shows how to write your Visual Basic 6.0 code to ensure compatibility with Visual Basic .NET:

```
a = Null
b = 5
If IsNull (a) Then
  ' Take appropriate action
Else
  c = a + b
End If
```

Note The Upgrade Wizard will upgrade the Visual Basic 6.0 **Null** constant to **System.DBNull.Value** and the **IsNull** function used in Visual Basic 6.0 to **IsDbNull**.

Date Variables

In Visual Basic 6.0, dates are stored internally as **Double**, so you can declare them as either **Date** or **Double**, and implicit type conversion will occur. In Visual Basic .NET, dates are not stored internally as **Double**, so they need to be declared as explicit **Date** types.

Because there is no way for the Upgrade Wizard to determine which **Doubles** were intended as **Dates**, it cannot upgrade dates declared as **Doubles**. To avoid this problem when upgrading, declare all dates explicitly in Visual Basic 6.0 as the **Date** data type.

Constants

Some of the underlying values of intrinsic Visual Basic constants have changed. If your Visual Basic 6.0 code uses the constants, the Upgrade Wizard will automatically upgrade them to the new constants storing the new underlying values; however, if you have used explicit values in your code, the Upgrade Wizard will leave these unaltered, and errors may occur.

The following example shows how to correctly use Visual Basic constants in your Visual Basic 6.0 code:

Example

```
'Incorrect use of underlying values
Response = MsgBox("Do you want to continue?", 4)
If Response = 6 Then
  'Do something
End If

'Correct use of predefined constants
Response = MsgBox("Do you want to continue?", vbYesNo)
If Response = vbYes Then
  'Do something
End If
```

Data Access

The only forms of supported data binding in Visual Basic .NET are ADO and ADO.NET. For this reason, it is recommended that you upgrade all Data Access Object (DAO) or Remote Data Objects (RDO) data binding to ADO in your Visual Basic 6.0 applications before upgrading to Visual Basic .NET.

DAO, RDO, ADO, and ADO.NET code are all supported in Visual Basic .NET, so you do not need to change these before upgrading. However, you may decide to take advantage of the disconnected ADO.NET architecture and upgrade your code to ADO.NET after the upgrade process has been completed.

Using the Upgrade Wizard

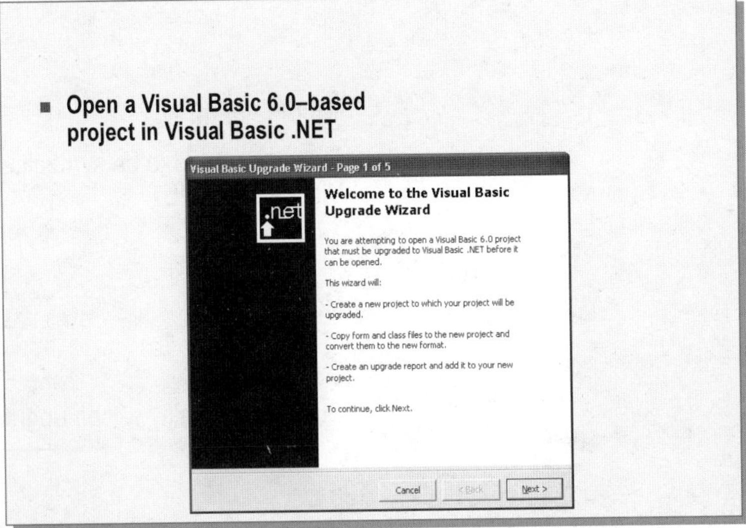

Once you have prepared your application for upgrade, use the Upgrade Wizard to perform the process. It is recommended that you begin by upgrading the user interface tier of your application, and work back through the other tiers.

You can launch the Upgrade Wizard by opening a Visual Basic 6.0–based application in Visual Basic .NET. This will gather the information necessary to upgrade your application.

The Upgrade Wizard will not modify your original application; it will create an upgraded copy at the location you specify.

Results of the Upgrade Wizard

- **Language changes**
  - Code upgraded to be syntactically correct in Visual Basic .NET
- **Form changes**
  - Most controls will upgrade
- **Other changes**
  - Other functionality will be upgraded to similar objects

When you have upgraded your application, the resulting project will still be very similar to the original.

Anything that can be upgraded is upgraded, and anything that cannot be upgraded, or anything that is ambiguous, will be marked with comments and entered in the Upgrade Report. Links are created to relevant topics in the documentation files to help you resolve any outstanding issues.

Some Visual Basic 6.0 functions do not have equivalents in Visual Basic .NET, and these will be retained through use of compatibility functions.

Language Changes

The Upgrade Wizard modifies the code where possible to take into account the syntax changes in Visual Basic .NET. This includes:

- Resolving parameterless default properties.
- Adding the **ByRef** keyword to procedure parameters.
- Changing property procedures to the new syntax.
- Adding parentheses to all function calls.
- Changing all data types to their new equivalents.

Form Changes

Visual Basic forms will be upgraded to Windows Forms, although a few controls cannot be upgraded because they have no counterpart in Visual Basic .NET. These include the following, which all upgrade to Visual Studio® .NET **Label** controls:

- **OLE Container** control
- **Shape** controls
- **Line** controls

Other Changes

Other functionality in applications created in Visual Basic 6.0 may not have a direct counterpart in Visual Basic .NET but will be left as is or upgraded to similar objects. For example:

- Resource files will upgrade to .resx files that can store any .NET data type.
- Web classes will not upgrade.
- ADO data environments will not upgrade.
- ADO code and ADO data binding will remain unchanged.
- Property pages are no longer used in Visual Basic .NET.

Completing the Upgrade

- Upgrade Report
- Upgrade comments
- Task List entries
- Testing
- Other tasks

The Upgrade Wizard also identifies any potential issues in the upgraded project. It creates an Upgrade Report that lists all potential problems, and adds tasks to the Task List for changes you need to make. These changes are also marked with comments in the code.

Upgrade Report

The Upgrade Report lists all upgrade errors and warnings, grouped by the file in which they occur. It contains details of the issue, the location, and the Help topic associated with the issue. This Help topic will explain why there is a problem with the code and what you should do to correct the code.

Upgrade Comments

The Upgrade Wizard adds fours types of comments to your code:

- UPGRADE_ISSUE

  These mark any lines of code that will prevent your code from compiling.

- UPGRADE_TODO

  These mark any code that will compile but that will still cause a run-time error.

- UPGRADE_WARNING

  These mark code that will compile but that may cause run-time errors.

- UPGRADE_NOTE

  These mark code that will compile and run but for which the changes in Visual Basic .NET may cause unwanted side effects.

The comments also include a hyperlink to the Help topic associated with the issue.

Task List Entries

The Task List shows all upgrade comments that you must resolve to ensure the correct running of your application. This includes Issues, ToDos, and Warnings. It will also list any other issues in your code that have not been introduced by the Upgrade Wizard. You can use this list to quickly find all the comments in the code.

Testing

You must ensure that you complete a full test cycle after the upgrade process, to check that the application is still functioning as you would expect.

Other Tasks

There are a number of other modifications that you can make to your code to improve it. The first of these should be done immediately; the rest can be done in the next phase of the upgrade.

- Replace compatibility functions and controls with .NET code.

  These are only provided for convenience during the upgrade process and should not be used in deployed applications.

- Upgrade ADO code to ADO.NET.

  This will take advantage of the benefits of ADO.NET.

- Replace COM components with NET components.

  This will reduce the number of managed to unmanaged calls, which will improve the performance of your application.

- Replace error handling code.

  You should replace any existing Visual Basic 6.0 error handling code with Visual Basic .NET exception handling using Try..Catch blocks to ensure a more structured approach to your error handling.

Demonstration: Using the Upgrade Wizard

In this demonstration, you will see how to upgrade a Visual Basic 6.0 application to Visual Basic .NET. You will see the original Visual Basic 6.0 application, how to use the Upgrade Wizard, and some of the tasks that could be completed afterwards.

This application is a simple invoice viewing system for the Cargo system. It is currently running as a Visual Basic 6.0 form-based application, interacting with class modules providing the data access code.

You will see the projects being upgraded by the Upgrade Wizard and review the issues identified in the comments and Upgrade Report.

Once the critical issues have been solved, there are other considerations for the project. All the data access code is ADO and could be upgraded to ADO.NET to take advantage of the disconnected architecture.

Review

- Deciding Whether to Upgrade
- Options for Upgrading
- Recommendations
- Performing the Upgrade

1. List two benefits of upgrading an application and how those benefits are gained.

2. What is the most commonly followed upgrade path? Why?

3. Which upgrade comments are not listed in the Task List? Why?

Course Evaluation

Your evaluation of this course will help Microsoft understand the quality of your learning experience.

To complete a course evaluation, go to http://www.metricsthatmatter.com/survey.

Microsoft will keep your evaluation strictly confidential and will use your responses to improve your future learning experience.

Notes

Notes

Notes

Notes

CHILDREN'S ILLUSTRATED DICTIONARY

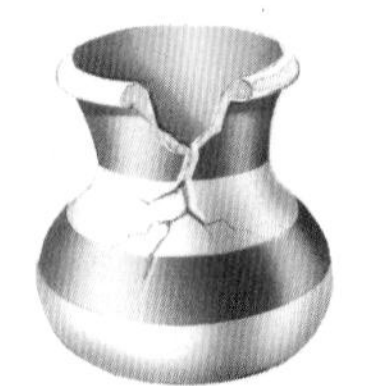

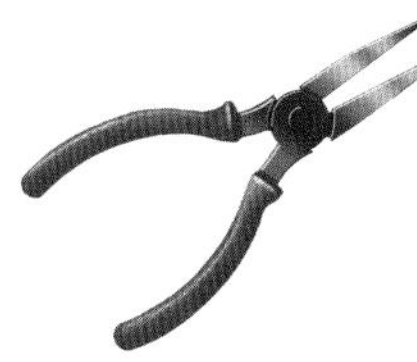
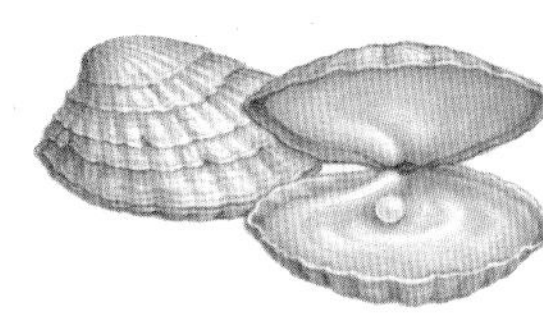

CHILDREN'S ILLUSTRATED DICTIONARY

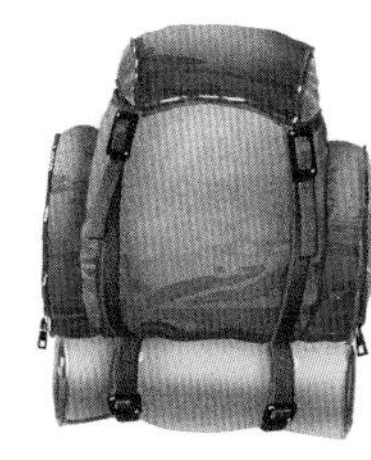

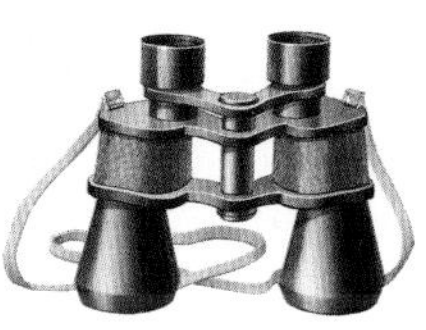

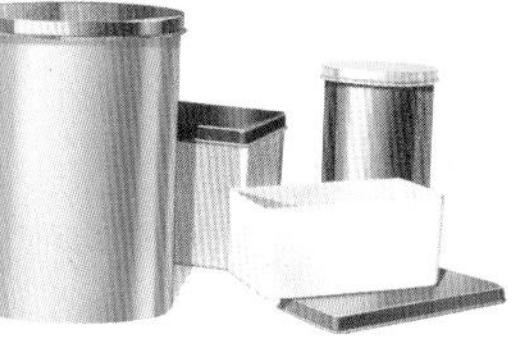

p

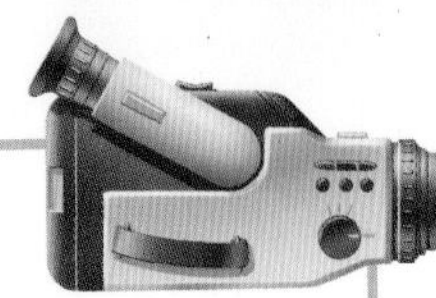

Authors
John Grisewood, Neil Morris, Ting Morris

This is a Parragon Book
This edition published in 2001
Parragon, Queen Street House, 4 Queen Street, Bath, England, BA1 1HE, UK

Produced by Miles Kelly Publishing Ltd
Bardfield Centre, Great Bardfield, Essex, England CM7 4SL

Hardback ISBN 0-75256-450-1
Paperback ISBN 0-75256-448-X

Printed in Dubai

Introduction

Have you ever played the game in which you try to describe something in words only – without using any gestures – and other people have to work out what you are describing? How would you describe a horse or a television?

This dictionary describes a horse as follows: 'a big, four-legged animal with hooves, a long mane and a tail, which can be used for riding or for pulling things like carts and ploughs'. The television is described as 'a box-shaped instrument that receives programmes that have been broadcast, and shows them on a screen as moving pictures with sound'.

That is exactly what a dictionary does. It tells us what words mean. A good dictionary should describe things well by being clear and concise. If a word has two or more meanings, it should tell us. 'Post', for example, has two quite different meanings: firstly, mail (letters, parcels etc.) and secondly, a pole, like a telegraph pole. The noun 'bear' is an animal but the verb means 'to carry or support'.

A good dictionary has certain other features:

It tells you how words are spelled ('accommodation' has two 'c's and two 'm's).

It tells you how awkward words are pronounced ('gnome', 'handkerchief', 'scythe', 'qualm', 'typhoon', for example).

It tells you what the part of speech is. Is it a noun, verb, adjective or adverb? This is useful. For instance, the noun 'object' meaning 'a thing' is pronounced '**ob**-ject' but the verb, meaning 'to protest' is pronounced 'ob-**ject**'.

It provides example sentences or phrases to help you understand how a word should be used. For instance: 'This is just (exactly) the colour I'm looking for' and 'There's just about (almost not) enough to eat.'

To be really useful, a dictionary must be up-to-date. New words enter the language and old words may die or acquire a new meaning. If you looked at a dictionary that is only a few years old, you probably would not find the second definition of 'mouse': 'a small device on your desk that you move on the surface with your hand to control the position of the cursor on a computer screen'. And the word 'cursor' in the definition would probably not be in the dictionary.

This dictionary has some other features that make it rather special:

- It is superbly illustrated with photographs, diagrams and drawings that complement the definitions and add more visual information.
- Special notice-board panels provide fascinating facts on such things as word histories, spelling, grammar and homophones plus much general information associated with a particular word.

We hope you will find this dictionary both useful and interesting. How would you describe it – without using gestures?

John Grisewood, Neil Morris, Ting Morris

How to use this dictionary

All the entries are in alphabetical order. A page letter or thumb-index shows you the pages on which all the entries beginning with the same letter appear. A guide word at the top outside corner of each page also helps you find the word you're looking for. The guide word on the left-hand page gives the first word on that page and the guide word on the right gives the last.

Parts of speech

These show how words behave in a sentence. They are: adjective, adverb, conjunction, noun, preposition, pronoun, verb. Look up the entry in the dictionary to find out more about each of these parts of speech.

Headwords

Headwords or entries are printed in bold, black type. Other forms of the same word (related words) are in less bold type, for example: **baptize** *verb*. **baptism** *noun*. **baptismal** *adjective*.

Derivatives

Derivatives or other irregular forms of the headword are shown in brackets as in the verb give (give, gives, giving, gave), the noun goose (geese) and the adjective big (bigger, biggest). Regular forms are not given, for example, dog (dogs).

Pronunciation

For some of the more difficult words there is a guide to how to say it correctly, for example: **gnash** *verb* (say nash).

Definition

This tells you what a word means. If a word has more than one meaning, each meaning is numbered. For example: temple noun 1 a building... 2 the flat part on either side of your head...

---

chariot

C

Around 1200 BC the Hittites, who lived in modern-day Turkey, used chariots for warfare.

charity *noun* 1 an organization that helps those who need it. *A charity for stray cats.* 2 kindness towards others.

charm *noun* 1 the ability to be attractive and to please. *He used all his charm to win her over.* 2 an act, saying or object that has magical powers. 3 an ornament on a bracelet or chain. **charm** *verb* 1 *He charmed her with his flattery.* 2 to control something by using magical powers.

charming *adjective* delightful, pleasing. *She is a charming person.*

chart *noun* 1 a map of the sea and coast or sky and stars. 2 a map with special information in curves and graphs. *A weather chart.* 3 a list of information in a particular order. *The charts list the most popular records.* **chart** *verb. Explorers charted the coastline.*

chase *verb* to go after somebody or something in order to try and catch them or make them go away. *The cat chased the mouse.* **chase** *noun.*

chasm *noun* 1 a deep crack in the ground. 2 a large difference between two things or groups. *The chasm between us widened.*

chat *noun* a friendly talk. **chat** *verb. We chatted all afternoon.*

chat show *noun* a TV or radio programme in which famous people are interviewed.

chatter *verb* 1 to talk non-stop about unimportant things. 2 to make a rattling sound. *His teeth were chattering with cold.*

chauffeur *noun* (say **shoh**-fer) a person employed to drive somebody's car.

The chauffeur wears a smart uniform and waits by his employer's car.

AMAZING FACT

Cheetahs can reach speeds of up to 60 mph (100kph) over short distances when chasing gazelles.

WORD HISTORY

The original 'chauffeur', in French, was not a driver but a stoker or fireman, who put coal on the furnace of a steam engine. Early motor cars gave off a lot of smoke and steam, so their drivers were jokingly called stokers.

chauvinist *noun* (say **shoh**-vin-ist) a person who shows great prejudice, especially against women. *He's a real male chauvinist.*

cheap *adjective* 1 not costing very much. *Food is cheaper in Portugal than in Spain.* 2 of poor quality, not very good. *Cheap housing is hard to come by.*

cheat *verb* to lie or trick somebody, often in order to do well. *He always cheats in exams.* **cheat** *noun* 1 a person who cheats. 2 a dishonest action.

check *noun* 1 an examination to find out if something is correct. *He made a thorough check.* 2 keeping somebody or something under control. *It's impossible to keep the disease in check.* 3 in chess the position of the king when under attack.

check *noun* a pattern of squares in different colours. **checked** *adjective.*

Tartan is a traditional Scottish fabric pattern, based on colourful overlaid checks.

check *verb* 1 to make sure something is correct or satisfactory. *Have you checked the bill?* 2 to hold back or stop doing something. *The bad weather checked their progress.* **check in** to register at a hotel or report at an airport. *You have to check in an hour before take-off.* **check out** to pay the bill and leave a hotel.

checkout *noun* a place in a supermarket where goods are packed and paid for.

check-up *noun* a medical examination.

cheek *noun* the side of the face below the eye. *Rosy cheeks are a sign of health.*

cheek *noun* rude behaviour. **cheeky** *adjective. Don't be cheeky to your mother!*

cheer *noun* 1 a shout of praise or happiness. *The crowd gave a big cheer.* 2 If you are full of cheer, you are very happy. **cheer** *verb. The fans cheered wildly throughout the match.* **cheer up** to become happy and stop feeling sad.

cheerful *adjective* 1 looking, sounding and feeling happy. 2 something pleasant, that makes you happy. **cheerfully** *adverb.*

cheese *noun* a soft or hard food made from milk. *Let's have bread and cheese for lunch.*

cheetah *noun* a wild animal, like a big spotted cat. Cheetahs are the fastest land animals in the world.

72

Illustrations
The illustrations have been carefully selected to extend and complement the definitions. All have informative captions or labels. 'A good picture,' they say, 'is worth a thousand words.'

Phrasal verbs
Phrasal verbs are included as a distinct part of many definitions. They are simple verbs like make, get, go, together with an adverb or preposition (as in get up, get away, get on etc.). They function like a single word but the meaning cannot be worked out from the literal meaning of the words. The ability to use and understand phrasal verbs is very important in writing and speaking clear English.

chip

C

chef *noun* a cook in a restaurant.

A chef has to deal with many pans at once. His job is both hot and demanding.

chemical *adjective* used in, made by or connected with chemistry. **chemical** *noun*. **chemically** *adverb*.

chemist *noun* 1 a trained person who makes up and sells medicines. 2 a shop selling medicines and toilet articles. 3 a scientist who specializes in chemistry.

chemistry *noun* the study of how substances are made up and how they react with other substances.

cheque *noun* a printed form telling the bank to pay money from your account to the person you have written the cheque to. *Can I pay by cheque?*

cherry (cherries) *noun* 1 a small round fruit with a stone. Ripe cherries are red. 2 the tree on which cherries grow.

chess *noun* a game for two players in which each player moves pieces on a chessboard.

chest *noun* the upper front part of the body enclosing the heart and the lungs.

chest *noun* a big, strong box for keeping things in. *A treasure chest.*

chestnut *noun* 1 a reddish brown nut inside a prickly green case. 2 the tree on which these nuts grow. **chestnut** *adjective* having a reddish-brown colour. *Chestnut hair.*

When the chestnut is ripe, the case falls to the ground and splits open. The shiny nuts roll out.

chest of drawers *noun* a piece of furniture with a set of drawers.

chew *verb* to move food about in your mouth and grind it with your teeth, so it is easy to swallow. **chew over** to think about something very carefully.

chewing gum *noun* a sweet gum that you chew and don't swallow.

chick *noun* a young bird.

Chile is a long thin country that runs along the backbone of South America.

DID YOU KNOW

China has a population of more than 1,200 million, more people than any other country in the world. Yet China has a smaller area than either Russia or Canada.

chicken *noun* 1 a young bird, especially a hen. 2 the bird's meat used as food. *We had chicken for dinner.* 3 (slang) a coward or frightened person. **chicken out** not to do something because you are frightened.

chickenpox *noun* a disease with red itchy spots on the skin.

chief *noun* a leader or highest official. **chief** *adjective* most important. **chiefly** *adverb*.

chilblain *noun* a painful swelling or sore in the fingers or toes caused by extreme cold.

child (children) *noun* 1 a young boy or girl. 2 a son or daughter.

childhood *noun* the time when you are a child. *Now he's old, he often thinks back to his childhood.*

childish *adjective* behaving like a child, often in silly way. *It's very childish to shout and scream like that.*

children plural of child.

Chile *noun* a country in South America.

chill *noun* 1 an unpleasant coldness. *In the morning there is often a chill in the air.* **chilly** *adjective*. 2 an illness caused by cold in which you might have a temperature, a headache and feel shivery. 3 a feeling of fear and doom. **chill** *verb* 1 to make something colder. 2 to become cold with fear. **chilling** *adjective*. *A chilling film.*

chimney *noun* a hollow passage in a roof through which smoke goes up into the air.

chimpanzee *noun* an African ape.

chin *noun* the front of the lower jaw.

china *noun* 1 a kind of fine white clay. 2 cups, saucers, plates and ornaments made of china. *The china cupboard.*

China *noun* a country in East Asia.

Chinese *noun* a person who comes from China. **Chinese** *adjective*. *An excellent Chinese restaurant.*

chip *noun* 1 a fried strip of potato. *We bought fish and chips.* 2 a small piece of wood, brick or paint, broken off something. 3 a crack that has been left in a cup or glass, when a small piece has been broken off. 4 a flat plastic counter used as money in games. 5 a very small electronic circuit in a computer. *A silicon chip.* **have a chip on your shoulder** to be rude or behave badly, because you think you have been treated unfairly in the past. **chip** (chipping, chipped) *verb* to damage something by breaking off a small piece of it. *I'm afraid I've chipped a plate.* **chip in** 1 to interrupt a conversation. 2 to give money to a fund, so that something can be paid for by a number of people.

73

Examples of use
A sentence or phrase may be given to show how to use the word correctly.

Gazetteer
The dictionary is also a useful mini-gazetteer. It includes as 'definition' all the countries of the world and their capitals, from Abu Dhabi, capital of the United Arab Emirates, to Zimbabwe, a country in Africa.

Notice-board
The narrow centre column has been used as a kind of notice-board on which to 'pin' different kinds of notes – tips, words of advice and warnings about problem words and how to use them well. There are notes on grammar and spelling, on confusable words ('lightening' and 'lightning', for example), on how to make new words by building them with prefixes, as well as notes on the history of words and an interesting series of asides called 'Did you know'.

Aa

aardvark *noun* an African mammal with a long snout and a long sticky tongue that it uses for catching insects.

abacus (abacuses) *noun* a frame with beads that slide along wires, used for counting.

abandon *verb* 1 to leave someone or something without returning. *They abandoned the sinking boat.* 2 to stop doing something. *She abandoned her search when it got dark.*

abbey *noun* a church and a group of buildings where monks or nuns live, work and pray.

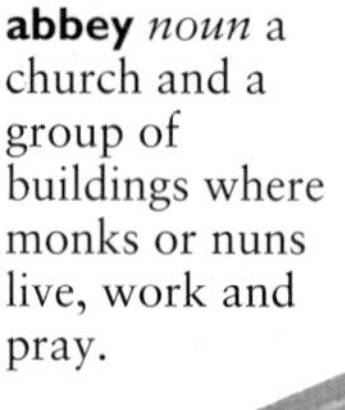

abbot *noun* the head of an abbey of monks.

abbreviation *noun* a short way of writing a word or group of words. *Maths is an abbreviation for mathematics.* **abbreviated** *adjective.*

abdicate *verb* to give up a position, especially that of king or queen. **abdication** *noun.*

abdomen *noun* 1 the part of the body that contains the stomach. 2 the back part of an insect's body.

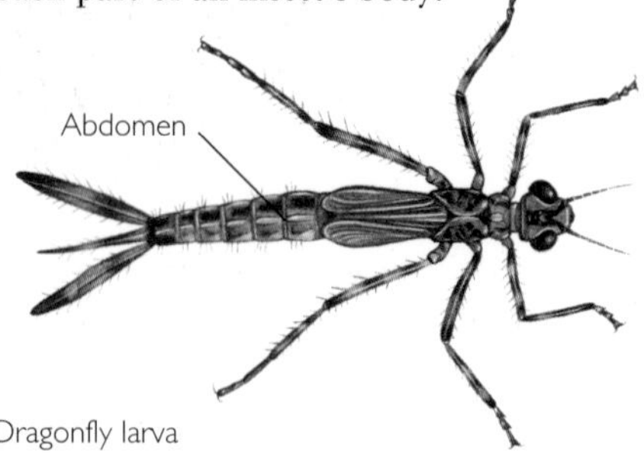

Dragonfly larva

WORD HISTORY

Dutch settlers in South Africa gave the aardvark its name. It means 'earth pig', although an aardvark is really a type of anteater.

Some large abbeys were like walled towns, where the monks or nuns lived in seclusion from the rest of the world.

DID YOU KNOW

Abbreviations such as Mr and Dr that end in the final letter of the word do not need a full stop. Abbreviations of names of countries and organizations, e.g. USA and EU, do not usually have full stops either.

An insect's body is clearly divided into head, thorax and abdomen.

abhor (abhors, abhorring, abhorred) *verb* to look on something with horror and hate. **abhorrence** *noun.*

ability *noun* the power or skill to do something. *Cats have the ability to see in the dark.*

able *adjective* 1 having the power, time, opportunity etc. to do something. *I wasn't able to leave work early.* 2 clever or skilled. *An able cook.* **ably** *adverb.*

abnormal *adjective* strange, peculiar and not normal. *It's abnormal for it to snow in summer.* **abnormality** *noun.*

aboard *adverb, preposition* in or on a ship, bus, train or aeroplane. *The ferry is leaving. All aboard!*

abolish (abolishes, abolishing, abolished) *verb* to get rid of or put an end to. *Capital punishment was abolished years ago.* **abolition** *noun.*

abominable *adjective* bad and very unpleasant. **abominably** *adverb. He was rude and noisy and behaved abominably.*

aborigine (or now preferred) **aboriginal** *noun* (say ab-or-**ij**-in-ee and ab-or-**ij**-in-ul) one of the original people who lived in Australia. **aboriginal** *adjective.*

The art of Australian aboriginals often recalls their ancient myths and legends with bold patterns and pictures of animals.

abortion *noun* ending a woman's pregnancy by removing the foetus from her womb. **abort** *verb.*

abortive *adjective* unsuccessful. *An abortive attempt to seize power.*

about *preposition* 1 concerning, in connection with. *The film is about space travel.* 2 near to. *I'll ring you at about six o'clock.* 3 all round. *Old papers were scattered about the room.* **about** *adverb* all over the place. *The dogs were dashing about.*

above *preposition* 1 higher than. *A bee is buzzing above my head.* 2 more than. *Above normal temperature.* **above** *adverb* overhead. *Look at the sky above.*

abreast *adverb* side by side and facing the same way. *The boys marched four abreast.*

abridge *verb* to make a book etc. shorter. **abridged** *adjective. The abridged novels of Dickens.* **abridgement** *noun.*

abroad *adverb* in another country. *Holidays abroad.*

abrupt *adjective* 1 sudden and unexpected. *The bus came to an abrupt stop.* 2 rude and unfriendly. *An abrupt answer.*

abscess *noun* (say **ab**-sess) a swelling on the body containing a yellow liquid called pus.

abseil *verb* (say **ab**-sail) to lower yourself down a cliff by holding on to ropes.

Henry abseiled slowly down the cliff face.

absent *adjective* not there but away. *Anne was absent from school because she had a cold.* **absence** noun.

absent-minded *adjective* forgetful or not paying attention.

absolute *adjective* 1 complete. *I'm telling the absolute truth.* 2 unlimited. *Dictators have absolute power to do what they want.*

absorb *verb* 1 to soak up a liquid. *Sponges absorb water.* **absorbent** *adjective.* 2 to take up somebody's attention. *She is absorbed in her work.* **absorbing** *adjective.*

Litmus paper absorbs liquid and turns pink if the liquid is acid. It turns blue if the liquid is alkaline. This experiment is called the litmus test.

abstain *verb* 1 to keep yourself from doing something, especially if it is something you enjoy. *She abstained from drinking alcohol.* **abstinence** *noun.* 2 to choose not to vote in an election. **abstention** *noun.*

abstract *adjective* concerned with thoughts and ideas rather than real things.

WORD BUILDER

The suffix '-able' can be added to certain verbs and nouns to form adjectives, e.g. 'adaptable' and 'advisable'. But some adjectives end in '-ible', e.g. 'audible', 'credible' and 'edible'. This has given rise to a lot of confusion and misspellings!

AMAZING FACT

In the 1950s a group of playwrights founded a type of drama called the Theater of the Absurd which examined the meaning of life. They included Beckett, Ionesco and Pinter.

abstract *noun* a noun that is concerned with qualities and ideas. *Love and courage are abstract nouns.* The opposite of 'abstract' is 'concrete'.

absurd *adjective* stupid and ridiculous. **absurdity** *noun.*

Abu Dhabi *noun* the capital of the United Arab Emirates.

Locals hunt for bargains in this shopping bazaar in Abu Dhabi, United Arab Emirates.

Abuja *noun* the capital of Nigeria.

abundant *adjective* available in large amounts, plentiful. *Abundant supplies of fruit.* **abundance** *adjective.*

abuse *verb* (say a-**bewz**) 1 to treat a person or an animal in an unkind or violent way. 2 to misuse or use in a wrong way.

abuse *noun* (say a-**bewss**) 1 rude or cruel words. 2 the wrong and harmful use of something. *Drug abuse.* **abusive** *adjective.*

abysmal *adjective* very bad. *What an abysmal film!*

abyss *noun* a very deep pit.

academic *adjective* concerned with education and learning. *Academic studies.* **academic** *noun.*

Academics wearing traditional gowns talk outside a college at Oxford University.

academy *noun* a school or college, especially one for training in a particular subject. *The Academy of Speech and Drama.*

accelerate *verb* to go faster and faster. **acceleration** *noun.*

accelerator *noun* a pedal that you press with your foot to make a motor vehicle go faster.

A

accent *noun* (say **ak**-sent) 1 a way of pronouncing a language in a particular region or country. *An American accent.* 2 a mark that is put above or below a letter of the alphabet in some languages to show you how to pronounce it. **accent** *verb* (say ak-**sent**) to pronounce a syllable in a word with more force. *You accent the second syllable in 'tomato'.*

accentuate *verb* to emphasize or to make more noticeable.

accept *verb* 1 to take something that is offered. 2 to agree to or say yes to something. *I accept your decision.* 3 to believe something to be true. *You must accept that abseiling is dangerous.* **acceptance** *noun.*

acceptable *adjective* satisfactory. *Your homework is not acceptable.*

access *noun* a way to get into a place. *The access to the castle is over the drawbridge.*

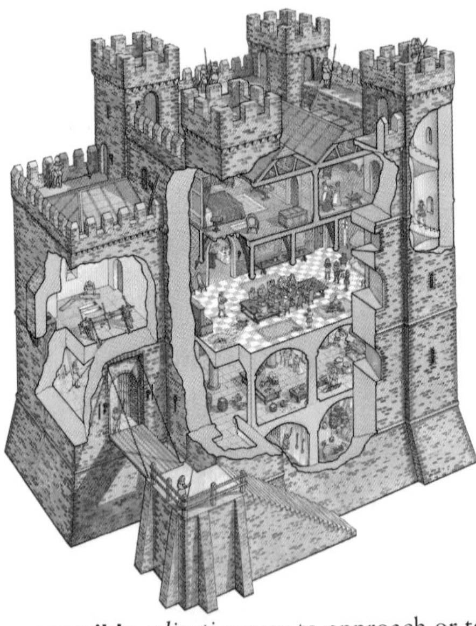

People must cross a drawbridge to gain access to this fortress.

accessible *adjective* easy to approach or to reach.

accessory *noun* 1 an extra part that goes with the main part. 2 somebody who helps to carry out a crime.

accident *noun* an unexpected and usually unpleasant happening, especially one in which people are hurt. *An aeroplane accident.*

accidental *adjective* by chance and not on purpose. **accidentally** *adverb.*

accommodate *verb* to provide a place for somebody to live. **accommodation** *noun.*

accompany (accompanies, accompanying, accompanied) *verb* 1 to go along with somebody or something. 2 to play a musical instrument while somebody else sings or dances. **accompanist** *noun.*

AMAZING FACT

Everyone who speaks has an accent, although it may not seem like it unless the accent is different from ours.

We often make judgements about people based on their accents – without realizing that we are doing it.

We may also form opinions of people's character based on how quickly they speak, how loudly they speak and how much they speak.

SPELLING NOTE

'Accommodation' has two 'c's and two 'm's. There is no plural form.

AMAZING FACT

The accordian was invented in Vienna, Austria in 1829 by Cyrill Damien.

accomplice *noun* a person who helps somebody carry out a crime.

accomplish *verb* to succeed in completing something. **accomplishment** *noun.*

A student who has accomplished a degree is awarded a certificate.

accomplished *adjective* talented or skilful at something. *An accomplished violinist.*

according to *preposition* as said by or in the opinion of somebody. *According to Jack, the visit has been postponed.* 2 in a suitable way. *Your pension is bigger according to how many years you've worked.*

accordingly *adverb* therefore, as a result.

accordion *noun* a portable musical instrument that you play by pressing keys and squeezing bellows to force air through reeds.

The accordion is a popular musical instrument in Madeira, Portugal.

account *noun* 1 a description of something. *There was a full account of the accident in the papers.* 2 the money that a person keeps in a bank. *Which bank is your account with?* 3 a bill or a record of money received or owed. **on account of** because of. *She stayed at home on account of the strike.* **by all accounts** according to what other people say.

account *verb* To account for means to give an explanation or reason for something. *How do you account for this broken window?*

accountant *noun* a person whose job it is to look after money and the accounts of businesses or people.

Accra *noun* the capital of Ghana.

accumulate *verb* to collect things in large quantities or to let things pile up. Dad has accumulated a pile of magazines over the years. **accumulation** *noun.*

accurate *adjective* correct and exact. **accuracy** *noun.*

For accurate measurement of time, athletes use a stopwatch.

accuse *verb* to blame and say that somebody has done something wrong. **accusation** *noun.*

accustomed *adjective* used to something. *It will take a little time to get accustomed to your new computer.*

ace *noun* 1 a playing card with a single symbol on it. *The ace of spades.* 2 a person who is very skilled at something. *He was a diving ace.*

ache *noun* a pain that goes on hurting for a long time. **ache** *verb* to hurt. *I'm aching badly all over.*

achieve *verb* to do or finish something successfully, especially after trying hard. **achievement** *noun.*

acid *noun* a chemical substance that can dissolve metals and turn blue litmus paper pink. **acidic** *adjective.*

acid *adjective* a sharp, sour taste. *Lemons have an acid taste.*

acid rain *noun* rain that contains chemicals from factories and cars and that damages plants and rivers.

Trees damaged by acid rain are unable to produce leaves, and so slowly die.

DID YOU KNOW

Some common acronyms are 'laser' (light amplification by stimulated emission of radiation), 'Nato' (North Atlantic Treaty Organization), 'radar' (radio detection and ranging) and 'sonar' (sound navigation ranging).

acknowledge *verb* to admit or agree that something is true. *She acknowledged that she'd been badly mistaken.* **acknowledgement** *noun.*

acne *noun* a lot of red pimples on the face, especially common in young people.

acorn *noun* the nut or seed of an oak tree.

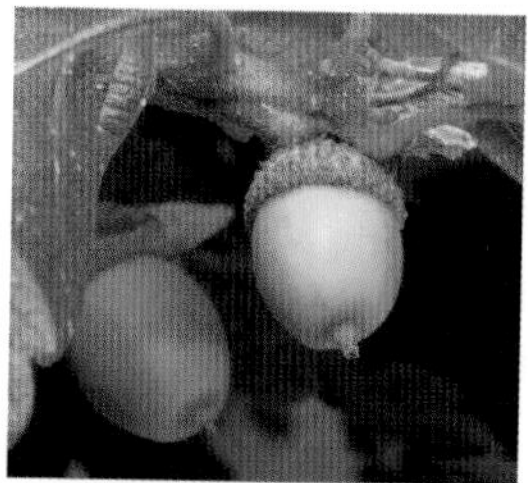

Acorns are a favourite food of squirrels. They bury them to provide a stock of winter food.

acoustics *plural noun* 1 the science of sound. 2 the effect a room has on the quality of sounds you hear in it. **acoustic** *adjective. An acoustic guitar.*

acquaintance *noun* 1 a person you know, but not a close friend. 2 a knowledge of something. *I have some acquaintance with the Japanese language.*

acquire *verb* to get something, especially by your own efforts.

acre *noun* an area of land equal to 4,047 square metres.

acrobat *noun* a person who is skilled in doing difficult and exciting gymnastic actions (acrobatics), especially at a circus. **acrobatic** *adjective.*

Trapeze artists are among the most daring of circus acrobats, swinging high over the ring, often without a safety net.

acronym *noun* a word made from the first letter of other words, such as VAT (Value Added Tax).

acrophobia *noun* a fear of great heights.

across *adverb, preposition* from one side of something to the other. *It measures almost 3 metres across.*

act *verb* 1 to do something. *She acted quickly to rescue the child from the blazing car.* 2 to perform a part in a play or film. **acting** *noun.* 3 to behave. *He's acting in a peculiar way.*

act *noun* 1 something that somebody does. *A kind act.* 2 a part of a play. 3 an Act of Parliament, a law passed by the government.

A

action *noun* 1 something that is done. *His fast action prevented the fire from spreading.* 2 a gesture or physical movement. 3 a law suit. 4 a battle. *He was killed in action.* **take action** to do something. **out of action** not working.

active *adjective* busy and full of energy. The opposite of 'active' is 'inactive'.

activity *noun* 1 lively action and movement. *The market is full of activity.* 2 something that people do, for example a hobby or playing games.

actor *noun* a man who performs in plays, in films or on television.

These actors are performing on stage against a painted backdrop.

actress *noun* a woman who performs in plays, in films or on television.

actually *adverb* really, in fact. *Did you actually talk to the president?*

acute *adjective* 1 severe and great. *An acute shortage of water.* 2 sharp. *Acute toothache.*

acute accent a sloping symbol placed over a vowel in some languages to show how it is pronounced, e.g. é in café.

acute angle an angle of less than 90°.

'Acute' also means sharp, and an acute angle has a narrow point.

AD *abbreviation* Anno Domini, the Latin words meaning 'in the year of our Lord', used for all dates after the birth of Jesus Christ.

adamant *adjective* unwilling to change your mind. *He's adamant that he will go.*

AMAZING FACT

Some species of adder, although they are poisonous, are so small that they can only bite humans in very delicate places, such as the skin between the toes or fingers.

DID YOU KNOW

By tradition the abbreviation 'AD' is placed before the year number, e.g. AD 2006, whereas 'BC' (standing for Before Christ) follows the year number, e.g. 20 BC.

adapt *verb* to change or make something suitable for a new situation or purpose. *We adapted the old shed into an office.* **adaptable** *adjective.*

adaptor *noun* a device that can connect two or more electrical plugs to one socket.

add *verb* to put two or more things together. *If you add four and three you get seven.* **addition** *noun*. The opposite of 'add' is 'subtract'.

adder *noun* a small snake, also sometimes known as a viper.

The adder has a distinctive zigzag pattern along its back.

addict *noun* somebody who likes or needs something (especially harmful drugs) so much that they cannot give it up.

addiction *noun* something that people find it hard to do without, especially harmful drugs. **addictive** *adjective.*

Addis Ababa *noun* the capital of Ethiopia.

additional *adjective* extra, more than usual. *It was so cold she put on an extra jersey.*

address *noun* the name of the house, street and town where somebody lives. **address** *verb* to write an address on an envelope, parcel etc.

If the address on a letter contains a postcode, it can get to its destination more quickly.

adenoids *plural noun* soft lumps of flesh at the back of your nose, which sometimes swell and make it difficult to breathe.

adequate *adjective* just enough, suitable. *Adequate food supplies.*

adhere *verb* to stick. *Please adhere strictly to the rules.*

adhesive *noun* a substance, like glue, that sticks things together. **adhesive** *adjective* sticky. *Adhesive tape.*

adjacent *adjective* very close or next to. *The playing fields are adjacent to the school.*

The settlers built their wooden homes adjacent to each other.

adjective *noun* a word that tells us something about nouns. In the phrase 'big, brown bear' the words 'big' and 'brown' are adjectives that describe the noun 'bear'.

adjust *verb* to arrange or change something slightly so as to improve it. *She adjusted the curtains.* **adjustment** *noun.*

administer *verb* 1 to be in charge of and manage. *She administers the company's finances.* 2 to give out. *The nurse who was on duty always administered the medicine at the correct time.*

administration *noun* 1 the management of a company etc. 2 the government of a country. *The last Liberal administration.* **administrate** *verb* to admininster.

admirable *adjective* very good and worthy of being admired. *An admirable achievement.*

admiral *noun* a very senior officer in the navy.

Admiral Lord Nelson was the hero of the Battle of Trafalgar.

admire *verb* 1 to like and to think somebody or something is very good, to respect. *They admired him for his courage.* 2 to look at something with pleasure. *We admired the view.* **admiration** *noun.*

DID YOU KNOW

'Admission' usually refers to permission to enter a public place, or the price of a ticket for entry. 'Admittance' is a more formal word for the act of entering a private place not usually open to the public.

admission *noun* 1 permission to enter somewhere. *Admission is by invitation only.* 2 the price charged to enter a place. *Admission is free.* 3 a statement that something is true. *She was guilty by her own admission.*

Tickets give admission to National Trust properties.

admit (admits, admitting, admitted) *verb* 1 to agree or own up that something is true. *They admitted they were wrong.* 2 to let somebody enter.

adobe *noun* 1 a clay brick hardened in the Sun. 2 a building made of such brick.

adolescent *noun* a young person who is changing from a child to an adult. **adolescence** *noun.*

adopt *verb* to take somebody's child into your home and make it legally your own son or daughter. **adoption** *noun.*

adore *verb* to love and admire somebody very much. **adoration** *noun.*

adorn *verb* to decorate something to make it look pretty.

adrift *adverb* floating and drifting without being secured. *The yacht was adrift.*

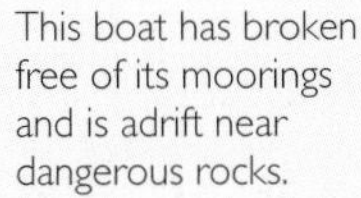

This boat has broken free of its moorings and is adrift near dangerous rocks.

adult *noun* a grown-up person or animal. **adult** *adjective* grown-up. **adulthood** *noun.*

adulterate *verb* to spoil something by adding to it something that is less good or harmful. **adulteration** *noun.*

A

advance *verb* 1 to move forward. *The army advanced towards the enemy.* **advance** *noun.* 2 to suggest an idea. *The detective advanced a new theory.*

advance *noun* 1 progress. *Medicine has made great advances.* 2 a loan of money. **in advance** before a certain date.

advantage *noun* something that helps you to succeed and perhaps do better than others. *It's a great advantage to be able to speak Japanese.* **take advantage of** to make use of a person or situation to help yourself.

advent *noun* 1 the beginning or arrival of something. *The advent of television.* 2 the four weeks before Christmas in the Christian Church.

adventure *noun* a happening that is exciting and perhaps dangerous. **adventurous** *adjective. She led an adventurous life in Africa.*

The South Pole was first reached by a Norwegian, Roald Amundsen, in 1911. The expedition was the greatest adventure of his life.

adverb *noun* a word that tells us more about a verb, an adjective or another adverb. In the sentence 'My grandmother talks very quickly,' the words 'very' and 'quickly' are adverbs.

advertise *verb* to tell people in a newspaper, on television etc. about something that is for sale.

advertisement *noun* a notice in a newspaper, on a hoarding, on television etc. that advertises something.

advice *noun* a helpful suggestion made to somebody about what they should do.

SPELLING NOTE

'Advertise' is one of the words in British English ending in '–ise' that must never be spelled with '–ize'. Other words are 'despise', 'supervise', 'surprise' and 'televise'.

A television mast or aerial placed on high ground ensures good reception for viewers and listeners in the surrounding area.

AMAZING FACT

Roald Amundsen was beaten to the North Pole by Robert Peary, a US polar explorer, the year before he succeeded in being the first person to reach the South Pole in 1911.

SPELLING NOTE

Try not to confuse 'advice' with a 'c' (the noun) and 'advise' with an 's' (the verb).

advisable *adjective* sensible and worth doing. *It's advisable to get an early night before setting off on holiday.*

advise *verb* to recommend and tell somebody what you think they ought to do. *The dentist advised me to brush my teeth twice a day.* **adviser** *noun.*

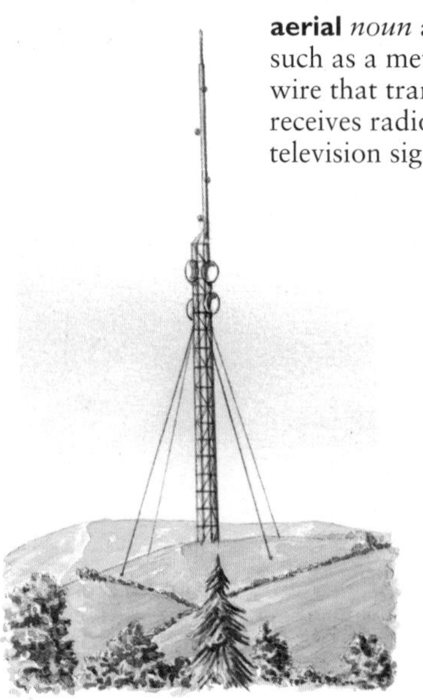

aerial *noun* a device such as a metal rod or wire that transmits or receives radio or television signals.

aerobics *plural noun* energetic physical exercises performed to music.

aerodynamics *plural noun* the science of objects moving through the air. **aerodynamic** *adjective.*

The aerodynamic shape of the Bullet train enables it to reach an average speed of 160 kph.

aeronautics *plural noun* the science of designing and building aircraft.

aeroplane *noun* a machine with wings that flies through the air carrying passengers or freight, driven by one or more engines.

aerosol *noun* a container that holds a liquid such as paint under pressure and lets it out as a fine spray.

affair *noun* 1 an event. *A barbecue is usually an informal affair.* 2 a relationship between two people, usually temporary. *A passionate love affair.*

affairs *plural noun* business and things that have to be done.

affect *verb* to influence or to cause a change in something. *The cold weather affects her health really badly.*

affected *adjective* pretended, not natural or sincere. *An affected smile.*

affection *noun* a feeling of love for somebody. **affectionate** *adjective.*

affluent *adjective* wealthy. **affluence** *noun.*

afford *verb* to have enough money to buy something.

afforestation *noun* the covering of land with forest. The opposite of 'afforestation' is 'deforestation'.

Afghanistan *noun* a country in central Asia.

afloat *adjective, adverb* floating on water or another liquid.

afraid *adjective* 1 frightened. *Are you afraid of the dark?* 2 apologetic. *I'm afraid you'll have to wait outside.*

Africa *noun* one of the Earth's seven continents.

Africa is a vast continent with deserts, high mountains, lush rainforests and grassy plains.

African *noun* a person who comes from Africa. **African** *adjective. An African sportswoman.*

aft *adverb* towards the back or stern of a ship or an aircraft. *The captain went aft.*

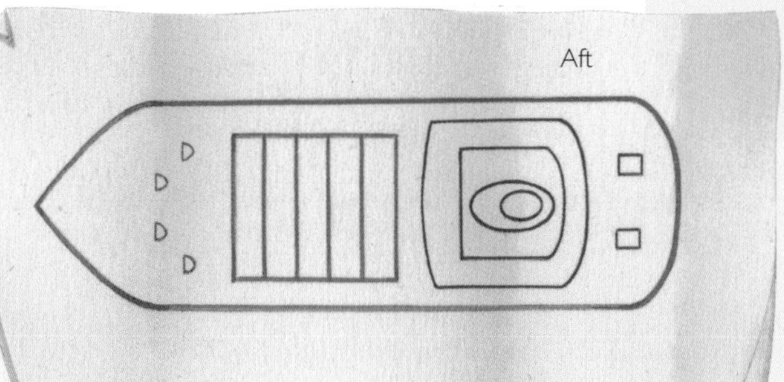

The plan shows the two flagpoles at the aft of the boat.

after *preposition* 1 later. *Come round after school.* 2 following behind. *The lamb ran after her.* **after** *adverb* later. *I met her the day after.*

SPELLING NOTE

'Agenda' is a noun with a Latin plural ending (the singular form is 'agendum'). However, it is used as a singular noun. 'What's on the agenda for today?'

afternoon *noun* the part of the day between midday and the evening.

afterwards *adverb* later. *We swam first and had breakfast afterwards.*

again *adverb* once more. *Please would you sing it again.*

against *preposition* 1 touching or next to something. *She propped the ladder against the wall.* 2 opposed to *They are against all hunting.* 3 in opposition to. *Who are you playing against tomorrow?*

agate *noun* a semi-precious stone striped with different colours.

This flint was used as a tool during the Iron Age.

age *noun* 1 the length of time that somebody has lived or that something has existed. *What age are you?* 2 a length of time in history. *The Iron Age.* **age** *verb* to become old.

aged *adjective* 1 (say **ay**-jid) very old. *An aged witch.* 2 (rhymes with 'paged') having a certain age. *A woman aged 50.*

ageism *noun* unfair treatment of somebody because of their age.

ageless *adjective* showing no signs of getting old.

agenda *noun* a list of things that are to be discussed at a meeting.

agent *noun* 1 a person who organizes things and does business for other people. *A travel agent.* 2 a spy.

The secret agent has a glamorous image thanks to fictional characters like James Bond.

aggression *noun* forcefulness, or an attack without being provoked.

A

aggressive *adjective* violent and likely to attack people. *An aggressive dog.* **aggressor** *noun.*

agile *adjective* nimble. Moving quickly and easily. **agility** *noun.*

The ballet dancer displayed astonishing agility.

agitate *verb* 1 to make somebody nervous or worried. *She was agitated because she was late.* 2 to campaign or argue strongly for something. *They agitated for bigger pensions.* **agitator** *noun.*

agitation *noun* 1 a strong feeling of worry. 2 a campaign or protest.

ago *adverb* in the past. *Napoleon lived years ago.*

agonizing *adjective* very painful.

agony *noun* great pain or suffering.

agoraphobia *noun* (say agra-**foh**-bee-uh) a great fear of open spaces.

agree *verb* 1 to say 'yes' to something. *Angela agreed to babysit.* 2 to share the same ideas or opinions about something. *We all agree that cruelty is wrong.* **agree with** to be good for or to suit. *Curry doesn't agree with him.*

agreeable *adjective* pleasant. *An agreeable evening.*The opposite of 'agreeable' is 'disagreeable'.

agreement *noun* a promise or an understanding between two or more people, countries etc.

agriculture *noun* farming. **agricultural** *adjective.*

DID YOU KNOW

Do not use 'ago' with 'since' – you should use either one or the other. 'It's years since I last went to Greece,' or 'It was years ago that I last went to Greece.'

Agriculture began when humans realized that sowing seeds would yield food crops. They settled to farm because it was more efficient than gathering food. Agriculture has shaped our land – not always for the better.

aground *adverb* If a boat runs aground, it touches the bottom of the sea or lake and cannot move.

ahead *adverb* 1 in front of. *She walked ahead.* 2 in the future. *Plan ahead.*

aid *verb* to help. **aid** *noun* 1 help or support, something that helps you do something. *He walks with the aid of a stick.* 2 money, food etc. for people in need.

Aids *noun* (short for or an acronym for acquired immune deficiency syndrome) a serious illness that destroys the body's natural defences (immunity) against disease and infection.

ailment *noun* an illness that is not very serious.

aim *verb* 1 to point at something, especially with a weapon. *He aimed the gun at the target.* 2 to plan or try to do something. *Alan aims to be the finest athlete in his school.* **aim** *noun* line of sighting. *He took aim.*

An archer takes careful aim. He fires arrows that are stored in a quiver belted to his waist.

aimless *adjective* without any purpose. *An aimless existence.*

air *noun* 1 the invisible mixture of gases that surrounds us and which we breathe. 2 general appearance or impression. *You have an air of calm about you.* 3 a tune. *The Londonderry Air.*

air-conditioning *noun* a system of controlling a building's temperature and keeping it cool in summer. **air-conditioner** *noun.* **air-conditioned** *adjective.*

aircraft any machine that flies, such as an aeroplane, glider or helicopter.

aircraft carrier *noun* a warship with a large deck from which aircraft can take off and land.

airfield *noun* a place where aircraft take off and land.

A plane lifts off the runway at an airfield. In the background are the airport buildings, including the control tower.

airforce *noun* the part of a country's forces that uses aircraft for fighting.

airline *noun* a company that owns aircraft and provides a regular service.

airport *noun* a place you leave from or arrive at when travelling by aeroplane.

airscrew *noun* an aircraft's propeller.

airship *noun* a large balloon with engines and that can be steered. Airships have a compartment beneath for carrying passengers or freight.

airtight *adjective* tightly sealed so that no air can get in or out. *Food can be preserved in airtight containers.*

airy (airier, airiest) *adjective* full of fresh air. *A large, airy room.*

aisle *noun* (rhymes with 'pile') 1 a narrow passage where you can walk between rows of seats in an aeroplane, cinema etc., or rows of shelves in a supermarket.

AMAZING FACT

HMS Hermes, which was completed in 1913, was the first purpose-designed aircraft carrier.

WORD HISTORY

'Alcohol' is one of a number of words that we have taken from Arabic. Others include 'algebra', 'assassin' and 'sofa'.

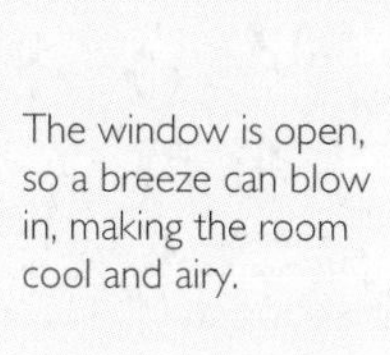

The window is open, so a breeze can blow in, making the room cool and airy.

ajar *adverb, adjective* When a door or window is slightly open, it is ajar.

alarm *verb* to make somebody suddenly afraid or anxious that something bad will happen. *They were alarmed to see smoke pouring out of their house.*

alarm *noun* 1 a sudden fear or danger. 2 a bell, buzzer etc. that warns people of danger. *A fire alarm.*

Albania *noun* a country in southeastern Europe.

The Albanian flag shows a black eagle against a red ground.

Albanian *noun* a person who comes from Albania. **Albanian** *adjective. Albanian wine.*

albatross (albatrosses) *noun* a large white seabird with long wings.

album *noun* 1 a blank book in which to keep photographs, stamps etc. 2 a CD or tape or record with a collection of songs.

Keeping a photograph album is a good way to record your family's history.

alchemy *noun* (say **al**-kem-ee) the medieval science of trying to turn metals into gold. **alchemist** *noun.*

alcohol *noun* 1 a colourless chemical liquid that catches fire quickly. 2 drinks such as beer, whisky and wine that contain alcohol and which can make people drunk.

alcoholic *adjective* containing alcohol. *alcoholic drink.* **alcoholic** *noun* a person who is addicted to alcohol and cannot stop drinking it.

alcove *noun* a recess or a small part of a room with the wall set back.

ale *noun* a kind of beer.

A

alert *verb* to warn people of a possible danger. *The doctor alerted her to the danger of eating too much.*

alert *adjective* quick-thinking and watchful of what is going on. **on the alert** ready for any possible danger.

algae *noun* (say **al**-ghee) water plants such as seaweed that have no root or stem.

algebra *noun* a branch of mathematics that uses symbols and letters to represent numbers. 3X + Y = 10 is an example of an algebraic equation.

Algeria *noun* a country in Africa.

The Algerian flag shows a red star and crescent moon against a green and white ground.

Algiers *noun* the capital of Algeria.

alias *noun* (say **ail**-ee-uss) a false or pretended name. **alias** *adverb* also known as. *Ron Chalky, alias Ronald White.*

alibi *noun* (say **al**-ee-beye) a proof or claim that a person charged with a crime was somewhere else when it was committed.

alien *noun* 1 a foreigner or stranger 2 a creature from space. **alien** *adjective. An alien being.*

It's difficult to imagine what an alien creature from outer space might look like....

alight *adjective* on fire, burning.

alike *adjective* similar. *The brothers are very alike.* **alike** *adverb* equally. *She treats them all alike.*

alive *adjective* living, not dead. **alive** *adverb* full of life.

alkali (alkalis) *noun* a chemical substance that can turn pink litmus paper blue. It reacts with acid to form a salt.

SPELLING NOTE

'Allege' is a word that is often misspelt. People often put '–edge' at the end instead of just '–ege'.

all *adjective* the whole amount or number. *All babies sleep a lot.* **all** *adverb* completely. *He was dressed all in black.* **all along** all the time. **all at once** 1 suddenly. *All at once the house shook.* 2 all at the same time. *Try not to spend it all at once.* **after all** all things considered. *After all he's no longer young.*

Allah *noun* the name given to God in the Islamic religion.

allege *verb* (say al-**edge**) to say that something is true or that somebody has done something, usually without having any proof. **allegation** (say al-eg-**ay**-shun) *noun.*

allergy *noun* an illness caused by substances such as dust, fur or certain foods, which do not normally make people ill. **allergic** *adjective* reacting badly to. *Andy is allergic to eggs.*

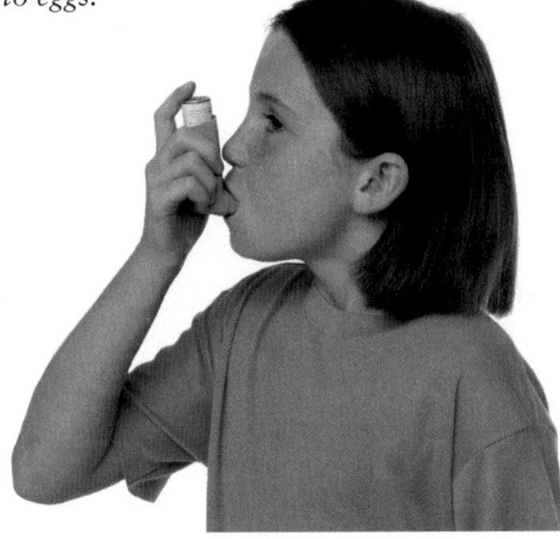

Some people suffer from allergies that cause them difficulty in breathing. They can often get relief by using an inhaler to breathe in a fine spray of medicine.

alley (alleys) *noun* a very narrow street with only one way out. **a blind alley** a situation without a way out.

alliance *noun* a union or friendly agreement between two or more different countries, political parties etc.

alligator *noun* a large reptile with a long body and tail, sharp teeth and strong jaws. Alligators are similar to crocodiles and live in rivers in the southern states of the US.

You can tell an alligator from a crocodile, because when an alligator shuts its mouth, the fourth pair of teeth on the lower jaw disappears into pits in the upper jaw. A crocodile's teeth stick out when its mouth is shut!

alliteration *noun* the repetition of the same sound at the beginning of each word in a phrase or sentence. *The Sun sank slowly.*

allocate *verb* to share out or to set aside something for a particular purpose. *The charity allocated £1,000 for the children's home.* **allocation** *noun.*

allotment *noun* a piece of land that people can rent for growing vegetables etc.

allow *verb* to permit or let somebody do something. *Nobody is allowed to smoke on public transport.*

allowance *noun* a fixed amount of money that is paid to somebody regularly. **make allowances for** to take someone's circumstances into account.

alloy (alloys) *noun* a metal made from mixing other metals. **alloy** *verb* to mix metals together.

Some knives and forks are made of alloy.

all right *adjective* If you are all right, you are not ill, hurt or in difficulties. **all right!** *interjection* a phrase you can say when you agree to something. *'Will you do the washing up?' 'Oh, all right.'*

allude *verb* to talk about something in an indirect way or to mention it in passing. **allusion** *noun.*

alluring *adjective* very attractive, appealing and charming.

alluvium *noun* fertile soil washed down by rivers and floods.

ally *noun* (say al-eye) a country or person that helps and supports another. *America, France and Great Britain were allies in World War II.*

almanac *noun* a kind of calendar or book with information about the movements of the Moon and stars.

Almaty *noun* the capital of Kazakhstan.

almond *noun* the oval nut that grows on the almond tree.

Almonds are a nutritious source of food.

AMAZING FACT

Alliteration is a powerful poetic device but many of familiar phrases and cliches are also examples of alliteration.

For example:
She's 'cool as a cucumber'.
He's 'fit as a fiddle'.

WORD HISTORY

The word 'alphabet' comes from the first two letters of the Greek alphabet, 'alpha' and 'beta'.

Our alphabet has 26 letters.

SPELLING NOTE

Don't confuse 'already' with 'all ready' – 'Are you all ready to go?

almost *adjective* very nearly but not quite. *Arthur is almost as tall as Angela.*

alone *adjective, adverb* with no other people, by yourself.

along *preposition, adverb* 1 from one end to the other. *They drove along the road.* 2 in the company of. *He brought his sister along.*

alongside *preposition, adverb* next to and by the side of. *He put the bench alongside the wall.*

aloud *adverb* in a voice loud enough to be heard. *Archie read the letter aloud.*

The teacher is reading aloud from a storybook to a group of children.

alphabet *noun* all the letters we use to write words, arranged in order. *Our alphabet begins with A and ends with Z.*

Aa Bb Cc Dd Ee
Ff Gg Hh Ii Jj
Kk Ll Mm Nn
Oo Pp Qq Rr Ss
Tt Uu Vv Ww
Xx Yy Zz

alphabetical *adjective* in order according to the alphabet. *The words in this dictionary are arranged in alphabetical order.*

alphabetize *verb* to put words in the order of the alphabet.

already *adverb* before this time. *I've already had my lunch.*

alsatian *noun* a large wolf-like breed of dog, also called a German Shepherd, often used as a guard dog and by the police.

also *adverb* as well, too. *He can play and also sing, but rather badly.*

altar *noun* a table used for religious ceremonies in a church or temple.

A cross and two candlesticks stand on the altar.

alter *verb* to change or to become different. *The village has altered a lot since my grandmother was a child.*

alternate *verb* (say **awl**-ter-nate) to happen by turn or to change first one way and then the other. *Barbara alternates between being happy and sad.* **alternate** *adjective* (say awl-ter-nat) *Alternate weeks of good weather and bad weather.* **alternately** *adverb.*

alternative *noun* 1 a choice between two or more things or possibilities. *The alternative to flying is to travel by train.* 2 different from what is usual. *Alternative medicine can involve taking herbs to cure illness.*

although *conjunction* even if, in spite of the fact. *Although it was snowing, we drove through the mountains.*

altitude *noun* the height above sea level.

altogether *adverb* 1 completely. *Are you altogether pleased with the plan?* 2 counting everybody or everything. *There are eight of us altogether.*

aluminium *noun* a lightweight silver-coloured metal.

Because aluminium is a very lightweight metal, it is much used in building planes.

always *adverb* something that always happens, happens all the time or very often. *Sally Remblance is always smiling.*

SPELLING NOTE

Try not to confuse 'alternate' with 'alternative'.

SPELLING NOTE

Try not to confuse 'altogether' with 'all together'. 'The puppies sat all together in a line. It was altogether an amusing sight.'

a.m. *abbreviation* the initial letters of the Latin words 'ante meridiem', which mean before noon. 7 a.m. is 7 o'clock in the morning.

amalgam *noun* a mixture of metals. *Dentists use an amalgam of mercury and silver to fill teeth.*

amalgamate *verb* to combine to make something bigger. *The two companies have amalgamated.* **amalgamation** *noun.*

amateur *noun* a person who does something such as paint or play games just for pleasure and not for payment. **amateur** *adjective. Amateur dramatics.*

Amateur dramatics can be fun for anyone who likes dressing up.

amateurish *adjective* not professional or skilful. *Debbie turned in a very amateurish design job.*

amaze *verb* to surprise or astonish somebody very much. **amazement** *noun. We watched the bungee jumping with fear and amazement.*

amazing *adjective* surprising. *What amazing tricks!*

ambassador *noun* an important official who represents his or her country abroad.

amber *noun* a hard yellowish-red fossil substance that you can see through, used in making jewellery. 2 the yellowish-red colour of amber.

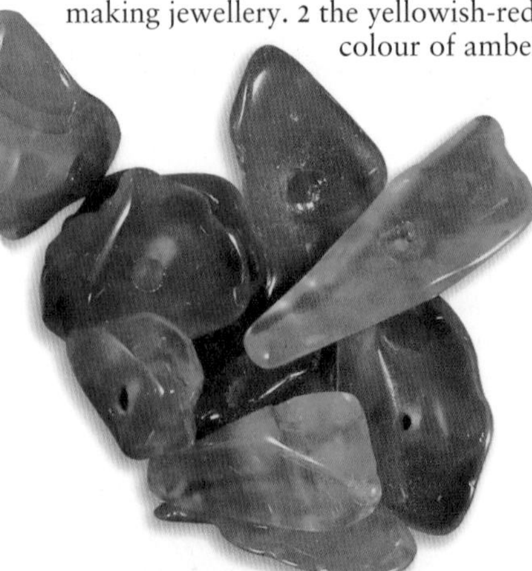

Sometimes you can be lucky enough to find pieces of amber on the beach.

ambi- *prefix* meaning 'both'. **ambidextrous** able to use both hands equally well.

ambiguous *adjective* not clear, having more than one possible meaning. 'They are eating apples' is an ambiguous sentence. It could mean 'the apples are for eating', or 'those people are eating apples.' **ambiguity** *noun* of uncertain meaning.

ambition *noun* a very strong wish to do something well or to have success and fame. *Her burning ambition is to be a vet.* **ambitious** *adjective.*

amble *verb* to walk slowly. **amble** *noun.*

ambulance *noun* a vehicle for carrying people who are ill or injured.

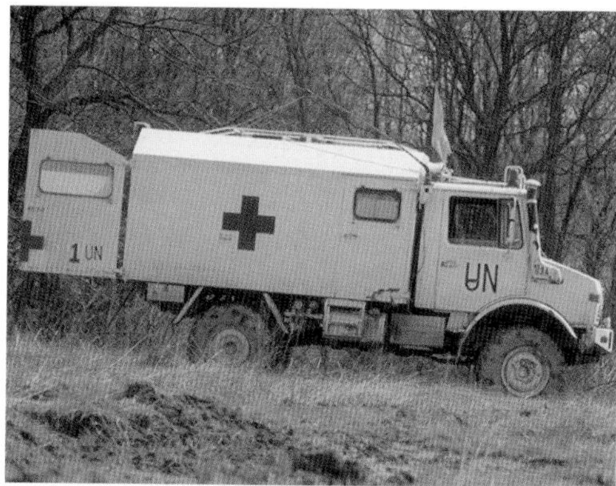

You can often recognize an ambulance by a red cross on a white background.

ambush *verb* to wait in hiding in order to attack somebody by surprise. **ambush** *noun.*

amend *verb* to alter or correct something slightly in order to improve it. *Some laws are out of date and need amending.* **amendment** *noun.*

American *noun* a person who comes from the United States. **American** *adjective* belonging to the United States.

amiable *adjective* pleasant and friendly. **amiably** *adverb.*

Amman *noun* the capital of Jordan.

ammonia *noun* a strong-smelling gas that dissolves in water.

ammonite *noun* a fossilized shell shaped like a flat coil.

Ammonites were molluscs, related to squid. This is a fossilized ammonite.

AMAZING FACT

The amoeba feeds by flowing around and surrounding its food. It reproduces by splitting in half.

DID YOU KNOW

The preposition 'among' or 'amongst' is used when talking about more than two people: 'The teacher handed the books among the pupils.' Use 'between' when talking of two people. 'The twins shared the sweets between them.'

ammunition *noun* things such as bullets and shells that can be fired from a gun or other weapon.

amnesia *noun* loss of memory.

amnesty *noun* a general pardon given by the state to, usually political, prisoners.

amoeba *noun* a microscopic, one-celled animal that moves about by constantly changing its shape.

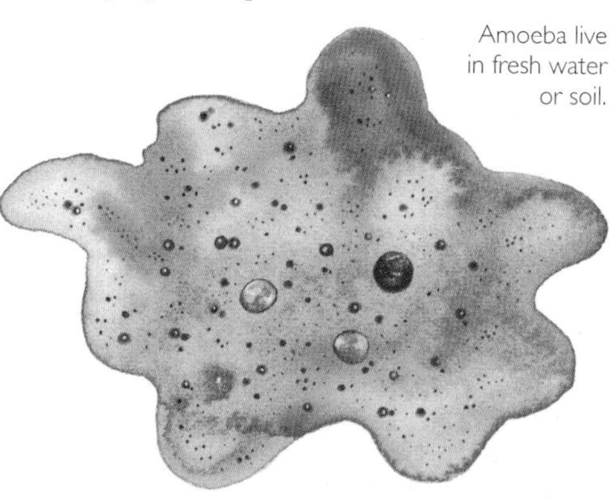

Amoeba live in fresh water or soil.

among *or* **amongst** *preposition* 1 in the middle of, surrounded by. *She lived among the islanders.* 2 one of. *Canada is among the biggest countries in the world.* 3 between. *Share these sweets among your friends.*

amount *noun* the quantity of something, or how much there is. *A large amount of money was spent on renovating the palace.*

amount *verb.* to add up to or be equal to. *The bill amounts to £50.*

ampersand *noun* the sign '&' that means 'and'.

amphibian *noun* an animal that lives mainly on land and breathes air but breeds in water. Frogs and newts are amphibians. **amphibious** *adjective.*

Frogs are amphibians. This is the poison arrow frog that lives in South American rainforests. The bright colours warn predators that they are poisonous and should be left alone.

amphitheatre *noun* a circular building with rows of seats surrounding a central open space. Amphitheatres were used for sporting events and plays in Roman times.

ample *adjective* more than enough, plenty. *The car has ample room for five passengers.*

A

amplifier *noun* an electrical device for making sounds louder.

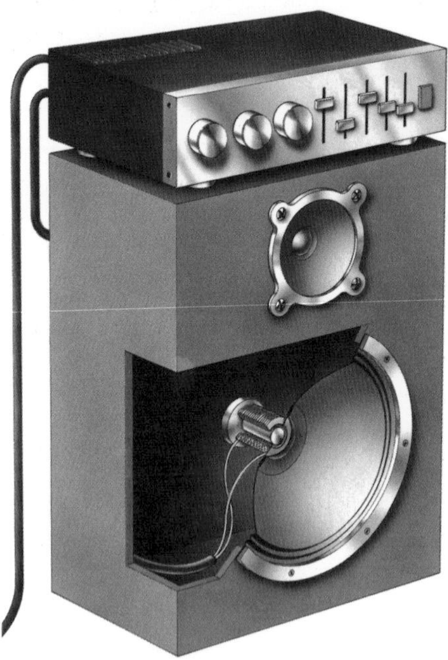

Small electrical signals from the pickup of a record player are strengthened in the amplifierer before being passed to the loudspeaker.

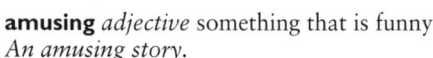

amplify (amplifies, amplifying, amplified) *verb* to make louder. **amplification** *noun.*

amputate *verb* to cut off a limb because it is diseased or badly broken. *He had his leg amputated in the war.* **amputation** *noun.*

amputee *noun* a person who has had a limb amputated.

Amsterdam *noun* the capital of the Netherlands.

Amsterdam is a city of fine old buildings and many canals.

amuse *verb* to make somebody laugh or smile or to keep them happy and busy. *They amused themselves by drawing, reading and listening to records.*

amusement *noun* 1 the feeling of being amused. 2 something that gives enjoyment or entertainment.

The word 'anaemia' comes from Greek words for 'no' ('an') and 'blood'. 'Anaesthetic' comes from the Greek for 'no' and 'feeling', and 'anarchy' from the words 'no' and 'ruler'.

SPELLING NOTE

In British English the '–yse' ending of 'analyse' should never be replaced with a '–yze' ending.

amusing *adjective* something that is funny. *An amusing story.*

anaemia *noun* (say a-**neem**-ya) an illness caused by a shortage of red cells in the blood. **anaemic** *adjective. Anaemic people are always tired and look pale.*

anaesthetic *noun* (say an-iss-**thet**-ik) a substance that is given to patients before an operation to stop them feeling pain. **anaesthetize** *verb.*

anagram *noun* a word made by changing all the letters of another word. 'Horse' is an anagram of 'shore'.

analyse *verb* to examine something in great detail, often to find what it is made of. *She analysed the water and found that it was polluted.* **analysis** *noun.*

analyst *noun* a person who analyses something.

anarchist *noun* a person who believes there should be no government and no laws.

anarchy *noun* disorder and lack of control by the government.

anatomy *noun* 1 the structure of the body of an animal or person. 2 the study of the structure of the body of living things.

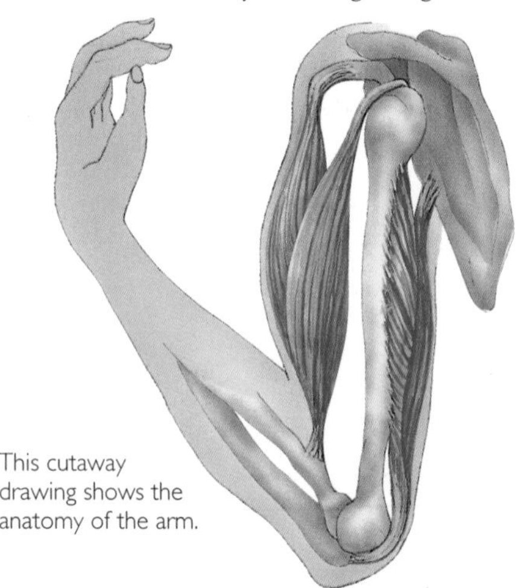

This cutaway drawing shows the anatomy of the arm.

ancestor *noun* Your ancestors are members of your family who lived before you. **ancestral** *adjective.*

ancestry *noun* all your ancestors, the people you are descended from. *Many Canadians have Scottish ancestry.*

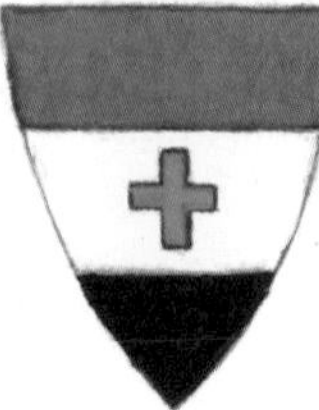

In the Middle Ages a knight's shield displayed his coat of arms and told something of his ancestry.

A

anchor *noun* a heavy metal hook that is lowered on a long chain from a boat to lodge in the seabed and stop the boat from moving. *They threw the anchor overboard.*

ancient *adjective* (say **ane**-shunt) 1 very old. *Ancient ruins.* 2 of a time long ago. *Ancient Rome was the centre of a great empire.*

The arrangement of the seats and the cages for the wild animals in the Coliseum can tell us a lot about life in ancient Rome, where visiting the amphitheatre was a popular entertainment.

Andorra *noun* a country in the Pyrenees Mountains of Europe.

Andorra la Vella *noun* the capital of Andorra.

anecdote *noun* a very short, amusing story.

anemone *noun* a small woodland or garden plant, usually red, blue, white or purple.

angel *noun* 1 a spiritual being and messenger from God. 2 a very kind person. *Be an angel and bring me my glasses.* **angelic** *adjective.*

An angel descended from heaven and appeared to the shepherds.

anger *noun* a strong feeling you have when you are not pleased with somebody or something, bad temper.

angle *noun* a corner, the space between two straight lines that meet.

angler *noun* a person who fishes using a rod.

Angola *noun* a country in Africa.

The civil war in Angola has left a great many children orphaned.

DID YOU KNOW

You are usually 'angry' or 'annoyed' with somebody, but you are 'angry' or 'annoyed' at or about something.

AMAZING FACT

Wedding anniversaries have different materials connected to them. The first anniversary is cotton, the fifth is wood and the twentieth is china.

angry (angrier, angriest) *adjective* annoyed and feeling full of anger. *I'm very angry with her for being so late.* **angrily** *adverb.*

anguish *noun* a very great feeling of sorrow or pain. **anguished** *adjective.*

animal *noun* 1 any living creature that is not a plant. 2 all mammals except human beings. **animal kingdom** one of the three basic groups into which all things in nature are divided. The other two are the mineral kingdom and the plant kingdom.

animate *adjective* (say **anny**-mut) alive. Animals and plants are animate. The opposite is 'inanimate'. Stones and metals are inanimate.

animation *noun* a kind of film, e.g. a cartoon in which photographs of a series of drawings of people and things are shown in quick succession and appear to move.

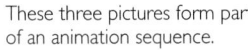

These three pictures form part of an animation sequence.

Ankara *noun* the capital of Turkey.

ankle *noun* the joint that connects your leg to your foot.

annexation *noun* the act of annexing a territory or of taking possession of it. *The annexation of Poland.*

annexe *noun* an additional building joined on to or near the main building. **annexe** *verb* to seize or take possession of.

annihilate *verb* to destroy completely. *The volcano annihilated all the farms for miles around.* **annihilation** *noun.*

anniversary *noun* a day each year when you remember something special that happened on the same day in a previous year. *A wedding anniversary.*

announce *verb* to make known publicly something important. *The king announced his abdication over the radio.* **announcement** *noun.*

announcer *noun* a person who makes an announcement. *A radio announcer.*

A

annoy *verb* to irritate or make somebody angry. **annoyance** *adjective.*

annual *adjective* happening every year or once a year. *Annual medical check-up.* **annual** *noun* 1 a plant that lives for one year only. 2 a book or magazine that appears once a year. **annually** *adverb.*

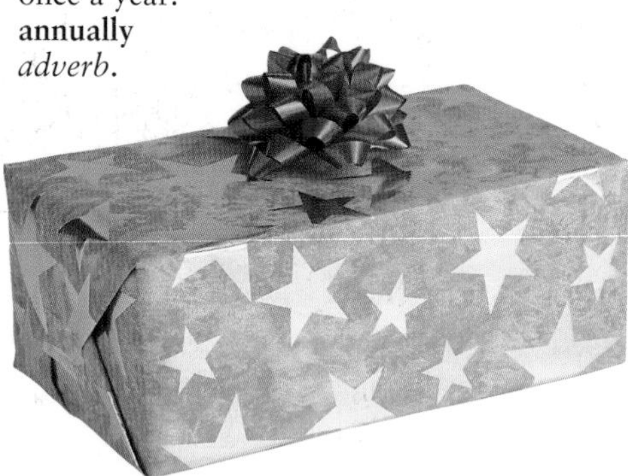

A birthday is an annual event. Most people are given presents on their birthday.

anoint *verb* to smear oil on somebody, usually as part of a religious ceremony.

anonymous *adjective* without the name being known or given. *An anonymous author.* **anonymity** *noun.*

anorak *noun* a zip-up waterproof jacket with a hood.

anorexia *noun* an illness that makes the sufferer afraid of becoming fat and so not want to eat anything. **anorexic** *adjective.*

another *adjective* 1 one more *He ate another sweet.* 2 different. *Can you find me a dress in another colour?*

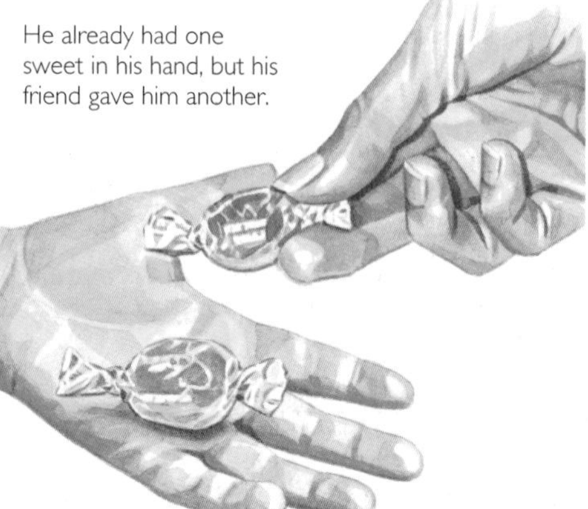

He already had one sweet in his hand, but his friend gave him another.

answer *verb* 1 to speak or write in reply to a question or to something that somebody has said. *'Where are you going?' 'To the stables,' she answered.* 2 to respond to a signal etc. *'Can you answer the phone?'*

answer *noun* 1 reply. *Have you had an answer to your letter?* 2 a solution. *I can't find an answer to this problem.* **answer back** to give a rude or cheeky reply to somebody.

answerable *adjective* responsible for.

WORD HISTORY

'Answer' is made up of two Anglo-Saxon words: 'swear' and 'an' (meaning against). So the whole word meant 'to swear against'. 'Answer' has two synonyms: to reply and to respond.

SPELLING NOTE

Try not to confuse the prefixes 'ante–' meaning before, e.g. 'anteroom', a small room giving access to another, and 'anti–', against or opposite, e.g. 'anti-aircraft'.

answering machine *noun* a machine that records telephone messages from people who ring you when you are out.

ant *noun* a small sociable insect that lives with other ants in an underground colony. **anthill** *noun* a heap of earth made by ants above their nest.

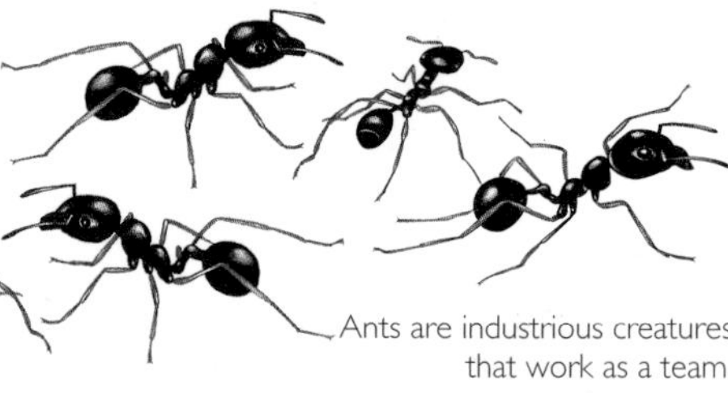

Ants are industrious creatures that work as a team.

antagonist *noun* an enemy or opponent.

antagonize *verb* to make somebody angry, unfriendly or hostile to you. **antagonism** *noun.* **antagonistic** *adjective.*

Antananarivo *noun* the capital of Madagascar.

Antarctic *noun* the area around the South Pole. **Antarctic** *adjective. An Antarctic expedition with sledges and husky dogs.*

Antarctica *noun* one of the Earth's seven continents, situated at the South Pole.

ante- *prefix* before. 'Antenuptial' means before marriage and 'antenatal' means before birth.

anteater *noun* a toothless mammal from South America that uses its long snout and long sticky tongue to catch ants and other insects on which it feeds.

antelope *noun* any one of several kinds of deer-like animals of Africa and Asia. They include gazelles, impala and springboks.

Antelopes are fast running animals that live in South Africa's grassy savanna.

antenna (antennae) *noun* 1 one of the feelers on an insect's head. 2 an aerial.

anthem *noun* a hymn or a song written for special occasions. 'The Star-Spangled Banner' is the national anthem of the United States.

anther *noun* part of a flower's stamen where pollen matures.

anthology *noun* a collection of poems, stories etc.

anthropology *noun* the study of human beings, especially their customs and beliefs.

anti- *prefix* against, opposed to, opposite. *Anti-Communist demonstrations.*

antibiotic *noun* a powerful medicine that kills harmful bacteria that cause diseases.

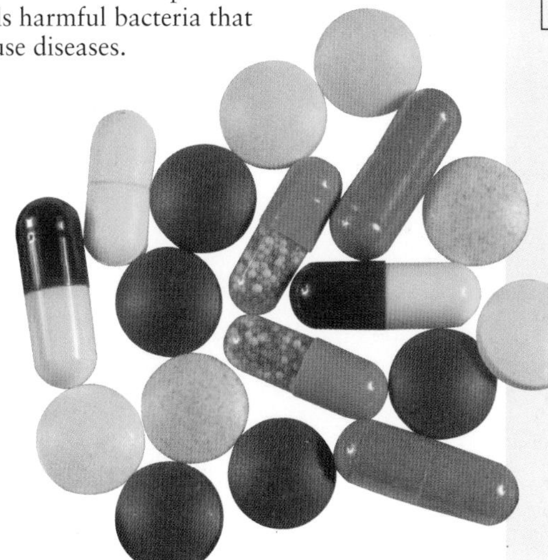

It is important not to take antibiotics too often, or the body will get immune to them.

anticipate *verb* to look forward to or expect something to happen. *We anticipated that these books would sell well, so we stocked up.* **anticipation** *noun.*

anticlockwise *adjective*, *adverb* moving in the opposite direction to the hands of a clock. Not clockwise.

anticyclone *noun* air moving away from an area of high pressure, usually bringing calm weather. The opposite of 'anticyclone' is 'cyclone'.

antidote *noun* a medicine that acts against the harmful effects of poison.

antifreeze *noun* a chemical that you put in a car's radiator to stop the water freezing.

Antigua and Barbuda *noun* a country in the West Indies.

The colourful flag of Antigua and Barbuda shows that the Sun and the sea are part of everyday life.

antiquated *adjective* old and out of date. *Antiquated rules.*

AMAZING FACT

In 1928, Alexander Fleming dicovered that penicillin could kill harmful germs. It was first used extensively in WWII on soldiers with serious wounds and saved many lives.

DID YOU KNOW

The opposite of 'antique' is 'modern'. Another word meaning old is 'antiquated', but whereas 'antique' is old and valuable, 'antiquated' is old and almost laughably useless.

antique *noun* something that is old and also very valuable. **antique** *adjective* valuable, old. *Antique furniture.*

Valuable antiques, like this chest of drawers, are often sold at auctions.

antiquity *noun* ancient times, especially the times of Ancient Greece and Rome.

antiseptic *noun* a substance that kills harmful germs and prevents infection and disease. **antiseptic** *adjective* clean and germ-killing. *Antiseptic soap.*

antler *noun* one of the branching horns on a stag's head.

During the mating season, stags fight by locking antlers until one brings the other to its knees.

antonym *noun* a word that has the opposite meaning to another word. 'Hot' is the antonym of 'cold'.

anus *noun* the opening at the end of the bowels through which solid food waste leaves the body.

anxious *adjective* 1 worried, concerned. **anxiety** *noun.* 2 eager. *Annie is extremely anxious to help.*

any *adjective* 1 one of. *Take any record you like.* 2 some. *Is there any pudding left?* 3 at all. *Are you any happier?* 4 every. *Any athlete could jump that fence.* (**anybody anyhow anyone anything anytime anyway anywhere**).

apart *adverb* 1 separate and at a distance away from each other. *The two villages are about a mile apart.* 2 into parts or pieces. *Andrea took her bike apart.* **apart from** except for. *Apart from a few showers the weather is lovely.*

apartment *noun* a flat (especially US).

A

apathy *noun* a lack of interest or feeling.

ape *noun* an animal like a monkey but with no tail. Gorillas and chimpanzees are apes.

Gorillas are apes that live in the rainforests of West and Central Africa.

ape (apes, aping, aped) *verb* to imitate how somebody behaves, usually in a silly way.

aperture *noun* a small hole or opening.

apex (apexes) *noun* the highest point.

aphid or **aphis** *noun* a tiny insect that damages or kills plants by sucking juices from them.

Apia *noun* the capital of Samoa.

apologize *verb* to say that you are sorry for doing something. *We apologized sincerely for causing so much trouble.* **apology** *noun.* **apologetic** *adjective.*

apostle *noun* one of the original twelve disciples or followers of Christ.

The apostles listened to Christ's teachings and spread the Christian message after his death.

apostrophe *noun* (say a-poss-tra-fee) a punctuation mark (') that shows that letters have been left out of a word (*we've* for *we have*) or to show the ownership of something (*Margaret's pencil*).

appal (appals, appalling, appalled) *verb* to cause horror or shock. *I was appalled by the chairman's rude and unkind remarks.* **appalling** *adjective.*

apparatus *noun* the tools or equipment needed for a particular purpose.

DID YOU KNOW

Apostrophes are often used – for clarity – to form the plural of a number of short words, e.g. do's and dont's, but dos and donts are acceptable too.

apparent *adjective* 1 obvious and easily seen. *It was quite apparent that she was bored.* 2 seeming to be true or real.

apparition *noun* a ghost or something that you think you have seen.

appeal *verb* 1 to ask for something urgently and seriously. *They appealed for help for the orphans.* 2 to be interesting or attractive. *The plan doesn't appeal to me at all.* **appealing** *adjective.* 3 to ask for a legal decision to be changed by going to a higher court. **appeal** *noun.*

appear *verb* 1 to come into view. *He suddenly appeared from behind the wall.* 2 to seem. *Fiona appears to be quite ill.* 3 to take part in. *Actors appear in films and plays.*

appearance *noun* 1 the act of coming into view. *The sudden appearance of the bull frightened everybody.* 2 the way somebody or something looks.

appendicitis *noun* painful inflammation of the appendix.

appendix (appendixes or appendices) *noun* 1 a small tube inside the body at the end of the intestines. 2 additional information after the main text at the end of a book.

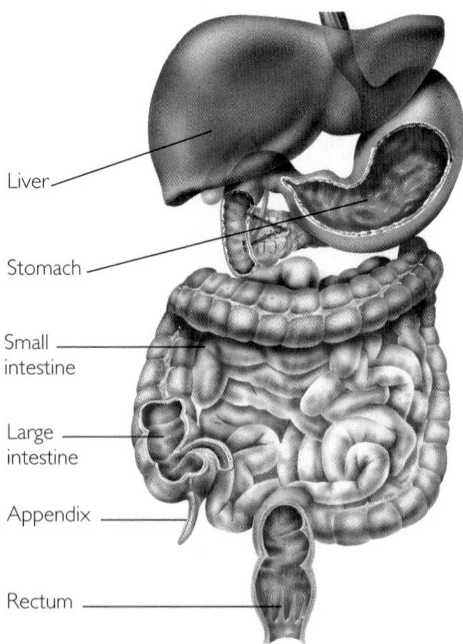

Inflammation of the appendix is common. The usual treatment is to remove the appendix by surgery.

appetite *noun* 1 hunger or a desire for food. 2 a desire or enthusiasm.

appetizing *adjective* smelling and looking so good that you want to eat it.

applaud *verb* to show that you like something by clapping your hands. **applause** *noun.*

apple *noun* the hard, round fruit of the apple tree. **in apple pie order** in perfect order.

The Golden Delicious is the most popular apple in the world.

appliance *noun* a tool or piece of equipment designed to do a specific job, especially in the home, such as a vacuum cleaner.

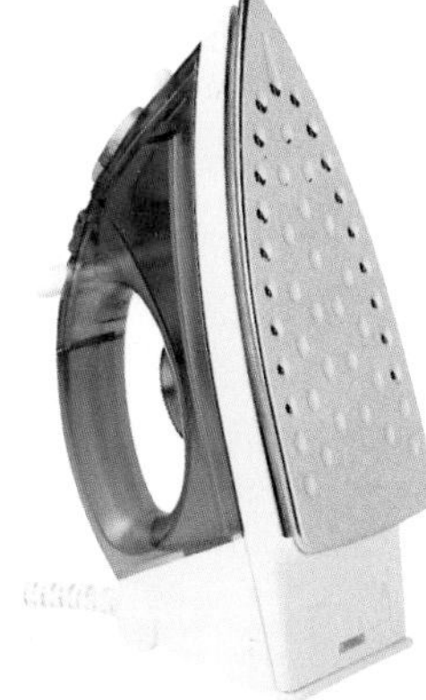

The steam iron is one of the most commonly owned electrical appliances.

applicant *noun* a person who applies or asks for something. *There were lots of applicants for the job.*

apply (applies, applying, applied) *verb* 1 to ask for something formally. *She applied for the job of editor.* 2 to be relevant or suitable to a person or situation. *These rules apply to everyone.* 3 to spread on. *She applied the ointment to the cut.* **application** *noun.*

appoint *verb* to choose somebody to do a job. *Mrs Bartholomew has been appointed chief accountant.*

appointment *noun* 1 a job. 2 a time and place that you have arranged to see somebody.

Write your appointments down to help you remember them.

appreciate *verb* 1 to know about and understand the value or good points of something. *She appreciates good food.* 2 to be grateful for something. *I appreciate all the valuable help you've given me.* 3 to rise in value. *House prices have appreciated.* **appreciation** *noun.*

appreciative *adjective* showing gratitude.

approach *verb* 1 to come nearer. *She approached the stray dog.* 2 to speak to somebody about a request or an offer. *Dean approached his uncle to ask for some money towards a new car.*

approach *noun* 1 a road or path leading somewhere. 2 the course followed by an aeroplane before landing.

AMAZING FACT

Apricots are originally from the Far East. They were cultivated in Armenia for many years and were later introduced to Europe and the US from there.

WORD HISTORY

Like all the months of the year, 'April' comes from a Latin word. It is named after 'Aprilis', meaning to open. April was the second month in the early Roman calendar.

approachable *adjective* easy to talk to and willing to listen. The opposite of 'approachable' is 'unapproachable'.

appropriate *adjective* suitable and correct for a certain place or event. *Trainers are appropriate footwear for running.*

approval *noun* 1 good opinion. *Does this plan meet with your approval?* 2 permission. *You have to get approval from the council to build a summerhouse.*

approve *verb* to agree to, to be in favour of something. *She doesn't approve of my clothes.* The opposite is disapprove.

approximate *adjective* nearly but not exactly correct. *What is the approximate length of the Nile?*

apricot *noun* a yellowish-orange fruit like a small peach.

Apricots grow best in a warm climate. This fruit is rich in vitamin A.

April *noun* the fourth month of the year. April has 30 days. **April fool** somebody who has been fooled by a trick played on them on the morning of 1 April, April Fools' Day.

apron *noun* a piece of clothing you wear around the front of your body to protect the clothes underneath when you are cooking or cleaning etc.

apt *adjective* 1 suitable. *An apt time to leave.* 2 likely to do something. *He's apt to fall asleep when he's bored.*

aptitude *noun* an ability to learn and do something well.

aqualung *noun* equipment that divers wear to breathe underwater.

aquarium *noun* a glass tank for keeping fish and other water animals, or a building (in a zoo) where many such tanks are kept.

It is fun to breed tropical fish in an aquarium at home.

aquatic *adjective* living or growing in water, or to do with water. *Aquatic plants.*

aqueduct *noun* a bridge with a canal or pipes for carrying water across a valley etc.

Arab *noun* a person who comes from Arabia and other parts of the Middle East and North Africa. **Arabian** *adjective*.

Arabic *noun* the language spoken by the Arabs. **Arabic numerals** the numerical figures 1 to 9.

arable *adjective* ploughed and suitable for growing crops. *Arable land.*

arbitrary *adjective* decided by a person's random opinion and not according to reason or rules. *An arbitrary decision.*

arc *noun* 1 a curved line. 2 in geometry, a section of the circumference of a circle.

arcade *noun* 1 a row of arches supported on columns. 2 a covered passageway usually with small shops on either side. 3 a place where there are slot machines for games etc. *An amusement arcade.*

arch *noun* a curved part of a building, bridge or wall. *verb* to form the shape of a curve. *The rainbow arches across the sky.*

This spectacular arch leads to the Murder Corridor in Alnwick Castle, Northumberland.

arch- *prefix* chief or most important. *archbishop.*

archaeology or **archeology** *noun* (say ar-kee-**ol**-oh-jee) the study of the past and how people lived, by the examination of remains of buildings, tools etc. **archaeological** *adjective. An archeological dig.* **archaeologist** *noun.*

DID YOU KNOW

Arabic numerals were originally brought to Europe from India by the Arabs. Before that, people in Europe used Roman numerals: I II III IV V VI VII VIII IX X.

archaic *adjective* (say ar-**kay**-ik) very old or antiquated.

archer *noun* a person who shoots with a bow and arrow.

archery *noun* a sport in which people shoot at a target with a bow and arrow.

This archer is using a longbow. Nowadays, archery is a popular competitive sport, testing steadiness of aim.

archipelago *noun* (say ar-kee-**pel**- agoh) a group of small islands.

architect *noun* a person who designs and plans buildings.

architecture *noun* 1 the skill or activity of designing buildings. 2 a style of architecture. *Greek architecture.*

Arctic *noun* the region around the North Pole. **Arctic** *adjective*.

The Arctic Circle is an imaginary line around the northern part of the globe.

arduous *adjective* difficult and tiring to do. *Arduous work.*

Stonehenge is a site of special archaeological interest. The stones are said to have been brought across the River Severn to the south of England from the Preselli Mountains in Wales.

area *noun* 1 the size of a flat surface. *The barn has an area of 15 square metres.* 2 a part of a place. *The residential area of Bristol.* 3 a part of somewhere used for a special purpose. *Non-smoking areas.*

arena *noun* a large area with seats around it where you can watch sports and various other entertainments.

Argentina *noun* a country in South America.

Argentinian *noun* a person who comes from Argentina. **Argentinian** *adjective.*

argue *verb* 1 to talk angrily with somebody you disagree with, to quarrel. 2 to give your reasons for or against something. *Mrs Earnshaw argued against joining the club.* **argument** *noun.*

argumentative *adjective* often arguing and tending to disagree for the sake of it.

arid *adjective* very dry and having little rainfall. Deserts are arid.

aristocracy *noun* the nobility, the social class that aristocrats belong to.

aristocrat *noun* a person of high social rank and with a title, a nobleman or noblewoman.

arithmetic *noun* the study and use of numbers, especially addition, subtraction, division and multiplication.

ark *noun* a ship in the Bible that Noah built for his family and animals to live in during the Great Flood.

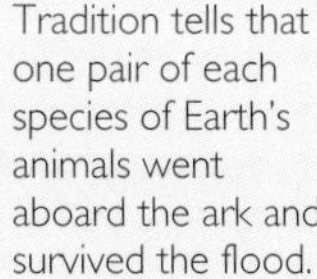

Tradition tells that one pair of each species of Earth's animals went aboard the ark and survived the flood.

arm *noun* 1 the part of your body between your shoulder and your hand. 2 anything shaped like an arm. *The arm of a chair.* **arm in arm** with arms joined in friendship.

arm *verb* to supply with weapons (arms). **armed** *adjective* carrying weapons. *The armed forces.*

armada *noun* a fleet of ships, especially the fleet that was sent from Spain to attack England in 1588.

armadillo (armadillos) *noun* a South American mammal covered with a shell of bony plates.

WORD HISTORY

'Arena' comes from the Latin word for sand. Sand was put on central areas of amphitheatres where Roman gladiators fought.

WORD HISTORY

'Armadillo' is a Spanish word meaning a small armoured man.

armaments *plural noun* guns, ammunition and other war supplies.

armchair *noun* a comfortable chair with supports for the arms.

Armenia *noun* a country in West Asia.

armour *noun* 1 a strong metal or leather covering that protects a soldier's body in battle. *Knights in armour.* 2 a metal protection for tanks, ships etc. **armoured** *adjective.*

This suit of armour is made of shaped metal plates fitted carefully together. It dates from around 1450. The most expensive suits of armour were decorated with engraved patterns or polished gold.

armoury (armouries) *noun* a place in which to store arms.

armpit *noun* the hollow place under your shoulder.

arms *plural noun* 1 weapons. 2 a coat of arms, a symbol or design on a shield etc. used as the badge of a noble family, city etc. **up in arms** very angry and ready to fight.

army *noun* a large number of soldiers who have been trained to fight on land.

aroma *noun* a pleasant, distinctive smell. **aromatic** *adjective. The chef liked to use plenty of aromatic herbs.*

around *adverb* on all sides. *He looked around but there was nobody there.* **around** *preposition* in all directions, in a circle. *She walked around the room.*

arouse *verb* 1 to stir up or excite feelings. *The terrible news aroused great anger in everybody.* 2 to wake somebody up.

arrange *verb* 1 to put in a certain order or position. *He arranged his books in alphabetical order.* 2 to plan or prepare something. *Can you arrange a meeting for next week?* **arrangement** *noun.*

arrest *verb* 1 to hold somebody as a prisoner. *The police arrested her for shop-lifting.* 2 to stop or prevent. *Progress was arrested because Richard did not bring the digger.* **arrest** *noun.* **arresting** *adjective* attractive, holding your attention.

A

arrival *noun* 1 the act of arriving or reaching a place. 2 a person or thing that has arrived. *The new arrivals were welcomed by the committee.*

arrive *verb* to reach somewhere. *They arrived home last night.*

arrogant *adjective* having an unpleasantly high opinion of yourself. **arrogance** *noun.*

arrow *noun* 1 a stick with a point at one end that you shoot from a bow. 2 a sign that tells you which way to go.

The head of an arrow points in the direction you need to go. An arrow is also a useful symbol meaning 'this way up'.

arsenic *noun* a very powerful poison made from a metallic element.

arson *noun* the crime of deliberately setting fire to a house etc. **arsonist** *noun* someone who intends criminal damage by fire. *The arsonist was sent to gaol.*

art *noun* 1 the ability to create beautiful paintings, sculpture, music, poetry etc. 2 an activity requiring a great skill. *The art of good conversation.* **artful** *adjective* 1 skilful. 2 cunning.

artery *noun* one of the thick-walled tubes that carries blood from your heart to all parts of your body.

Artery

The heart's job is to pump blood to the lungs and then all round the body. The right side of the heart takes in blood from the body and pumps it to the lungs. The left side of the heart takes blood filled with oxygen from the lungs and pumps it to the rest of the body.

DID YOU KNOW

'An' is the form of the indefinite article used before words beginning with a vowel, as in 'an apple', and before words beginning with a vowel sound, as in 'an hour'.

arthritis *noun* a disease that makes joints painful and swollen. **arthritic** *adjective.*

arthropod *noun* an animal such as an insect, spider or crab, with a skeleton on the outside of its body.

article *noun* 1 an object of some kind. *A belt is an article of clothing.* 2 a piece of writing published in a newspaper etc. 3 the words 'a' or 'an' (indefinite articles) and 'the' (definite article).

articulate *adjective* able to express thoughts and feelings clearly in words. **articulate** *verb* to pronounce words clearly.

articulated lorry *noun* a lorry made in two parts, a cab and a trailer.

An Australian road train is a very powerful articulated truck that often has several trailers.

artificial *adjective* not found in nature but made by people. *These flowers are artificial because they are made of plastic.*

artillery *noun* large guns used by the army.

artist *noun* a person who can paint, draw or produce other works of art.

This Russian artist has set up his easel outside and is painting from life.

artiste *noun* a professional entertainer in a circus, theatre etc.

artistic *adjective* liking art or showing skill in creating art. *An artistic family.*

artistry *noun* the skill of an artist. *This pianist's artistry is much admired.*

a.s.a.p. *abbreviation* as soon as possible.

ascend *verb* (say az-**send**) to go or move up, to climb. *The plane ascended quickly after take-off.* **ascent** *noun.* The opposite of 'ascend' is 'descend'.

A

ASCII *abbreviation* American Standard Code for Information Interchange (a computer term).

ash (ashes) *noun* the grey powder that is left after something has burned completely. *Wood ash is good for the garden.*

ash *noun* a hardwood tree with a silver-grey bark. *A whole forest of ash trees.*

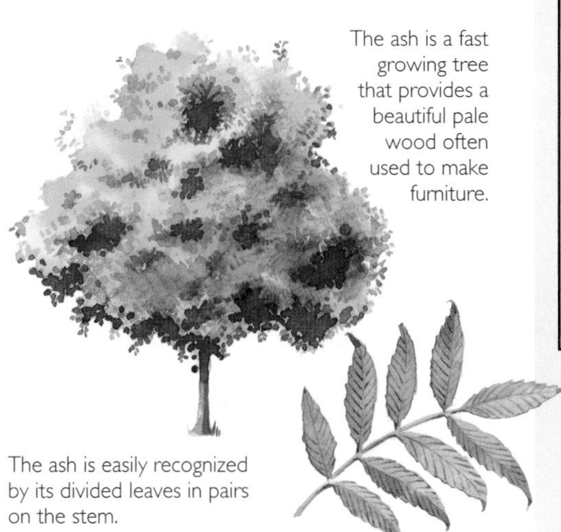

The ash is a fast growing tree that provides a beautiful pale wood often used to make furniture.

The ash is easily recognized by its divided leaves in pairs on the stem.

ashamed *adjective* feeling guilty or embarrassed about something.

Ashkhabat *noun* the capital of Turkmenistan.

ashore *adverb* on shore or land. *The sailors stepped ashore on the island.*

Asia *noun* one of the Earth's seven continents.

Asian *noun* a person from Asia. **Asian** *adjective. Asian countries include India and Sri Lanka.*

ask *verb* 1 to speak in order to get the answer to a question. 2 to make a request or to say that you would like somebody to do something for you. 3 to invite. *Ask him to the meeting on Monday.*

asleep *adjective* sleeping. *He was still asleep when I called, although it was after lunch.* The opposite of 'asleep' is 'awake'.

When you are asleep you are not aware of what is going on around you. The brain blocks incoming signals unless they are so strong they wake you up.

WORD HISTORY

The word 'assassin' – and note its two double 's's – comes from an Arabic word meaning an eater of the drug hasish. Many people under the influence of the drug committed murders.

AMAZING FACT

Although aspirin has been used as a painkiller for many years, it was not known how the drug works until recently.

SPELLING NOTE

Try not to confuse 'assent' (meaning agreement) with 'ascent' (meaning a climb or an act of ascending).

Asmera *noun* the capital of Eritrea.

asp *noun* a small poisonous snake.

Queen Cleopatra of Egypt is said to have committed suicide by putting an asp to her breast.

aspect *noun* a side, feature or look of something. *Let's consider every aspect of the problem before making a decision.*

asphalt *noun* a tar-like substance that is used for making road surfaces etc.

aspiration *noun* an ambition or goal in life.

aspirin *noun* a medicine that helps to ease pain and reduce fever.

ass (asses) *noun* 1 a wild donkey. 2 a stupid person.

Asses are used in many countries as beasts of burden.

assassin *noun* a person who assassinates or murders. *The assassin was arrested.*

assassinate *verb* to murder somebody, especially an important person like a king or president. **assassination** *noun.*

assault *verb* to attack someone violently. **assault** *noun. It was a ferocious assault.*

assemble *verb* 1 to bring or collect together in one place. *A small crowd assembled in the square.* 2 to put or fit the parts of something together.

assembly *noun* 1 a meeting, often regular like a school assembly. 2 putting together different parts of something to make a whole. *A car assembly plant.*

assent *verb* to agree to something. **assent** *noun* agreement. *He gave his assent.*

A

assert *verb* to declare or state something forcefully so people pay attention. **assertion** *noun. He made a false assertion about me.*

assess *verb* to judge the quality or value of something. *He assessed the damages.* **assessment** *noun.*

This wine taster is assessing the quality of a glass of red wine. He must smell the wine as well as taste it.

asset *noun* somebody or something that is useful or valuable. *She is good at maths and this is a great asset to the finance company.*

assist *verb* to help. **assistance** *noun. Can I be of any assistance?*

The girl is giving her mother valuable assistance with the washing-up.

assistant *noun* 1 a person who helps. *My aunt is the head teacher's assistant.* 2 a person who serves in a shop. *A shop assistant must be polite to the customers.*

associate *verb* 1 to spend time with a group, to work together. *He associates mainly with sports people.* 2 to connect two things in your mind. *He associates snow with skiing.*

association *noun* 1 a club or a group of people working together, an organization. 2 a connection made in your mind.

assorted *adjective* of different kinds. Mixed. *We found assorted oddments of clothing strewn all over the lawn.* **assortment** *noun.*

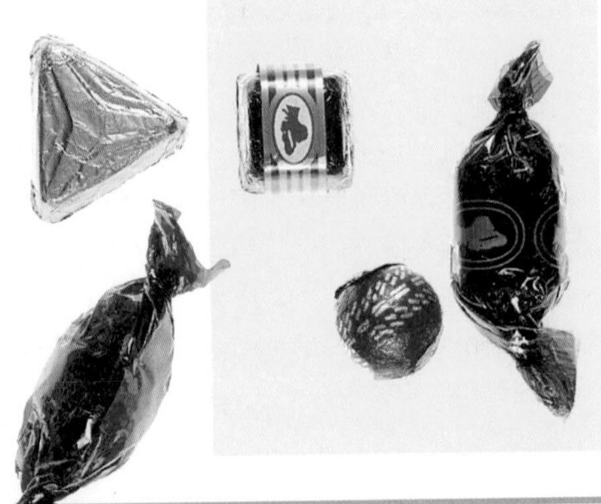

An assortment of sweets usually contains chocolates, toffees and sweets with fruity centres.

SPELLING NOTE

'Asthma' comes from a Greek word meaning panting or breathing hard.

Over 3,200 asteroids have been identified so far. The biggest, Ceres, is 1,000 km across, but most are much smaller.

assume *verb* 1 to accept something as true without question, to suppose. *We assumed she had no money because she dressed so badly.* **assumption** *noun.* 2 to take over. *The vice-president assumed absolute control of the country.*

assurance *noun* 1 a confident statement or promise. *He gave every assurance that the bridge was safe.* 2 confidence. *She is playing the piano now with more assurance.* 3 insurance.

assure *verb* to tell somebody something confidently and definitely. *The nurse assured him that he would soon be better.*

asterisk *noun* a small star (*) used in printing.

astern *adverb* towards the stern or back of a boat.

asteroid *noun* a small planet that orbits the Sun between Mars and Jupiter.

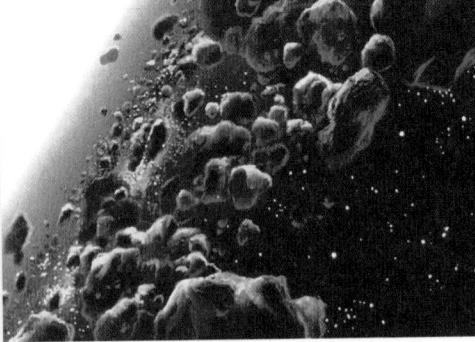

asthma *noun* a chest illness that makes it difficult to breathe. **asthmatic** *adjective.*

astonish *verb* to surprise somebody very much, to amaze. **astonishment** *noun.*

astound *verb* 1 to surprise or shock somebody very much. *She was astounded to hear that he had failed the final examination.*

astride *preposition* with one leg on each side of something. *He sat astride the horse.*

A

astrologer *noun* a person who studies the stars to try to predict the future. *The astrologer predicted a win.* **astrology** *noun.*

astronaut *noun* a man or woman who travels in a spacecraft.

Astronauts on the Moon could jump high in heavy spacesuits because the Moon is much smaller than Earth and its gravity is weaker.

astronomer *noun* a person who scientifically studies the planets, the stars and other heavenly bodies.

astronomical *adjective* 1 concerned with astronomy. 2 very large. *The house prices were astronomical.*

astronomy *noun* the scientific study of the planets and stars.

It is not clear who invented the telescope, but Galileo was the first person to put it to use in the study of astronomy.

astute *adjective* clever and quick of mind, shrewd. *She is an astute businesswoman.*

Asuncion *noun* the capital of Paraguay.

asylum *noun* 1 a refuge or a place to shelter from persecution etc. *The refugees were given political asylum.* 2 in the past, a place for treating people with mental illnesses.

ate *verb* past tense of eat. *He ate too much.*

atheism *noun* the rejection of a belief in God or gods.

WORD HISTORY

Atlas is named after a Greek god who was made to carry the heavens on his shoulders as a punishment for his rebelliousness.

atheist *noun* a person who does not believe in God or gods.

Athens *noun* the capital of Greece.

athlete *noun* a person who is good at athletics. **athletic** *adjective.*

athletics *plural noun* competitive sports such as running, jumping, vaulting and throwing the javelin or discus.

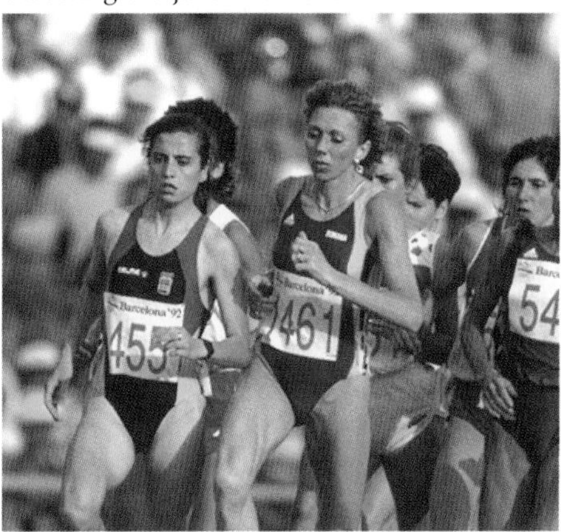

People from many countries compete in athletics championships.

atlas (atlases) *noun* a book of maps.

atmosphere *noun* 1 the air that surrounds and protects the Earth. 2 the air in a particular place. *The atmosphere in this city is badly polluted.* 3 the general feeling of a place. *The hotel has a warm and friendly atmosphere but is excessively expensive.*

atoll *noun* a coral island in the shape of a ring surrounding a lagoon.

atom *noun* the smallest possible part of a chemical element that can take part in a chemical reaction. An atom consists of a nucleus surrounded by electrons. **atomic** *adjective. Atomic energy.*

The atom was first split by the New Zealand-British physicist Ernest Rutherford in 1919.

A

atrocious *adjective* very bad, terrible. *Atrocious spelling mistakes.*

atrocity *noun* a very cruel act, a crime.

attach *verb* to fasten or join two things together. *She attached another link to the chain.* **to be attached to** to be very fond of somebody or something.

attachment *noun* 1 something extra that can be attached. *The vacuum cleaner has a special attachment for cleaning upholstery.* 2 fondness or friendship.

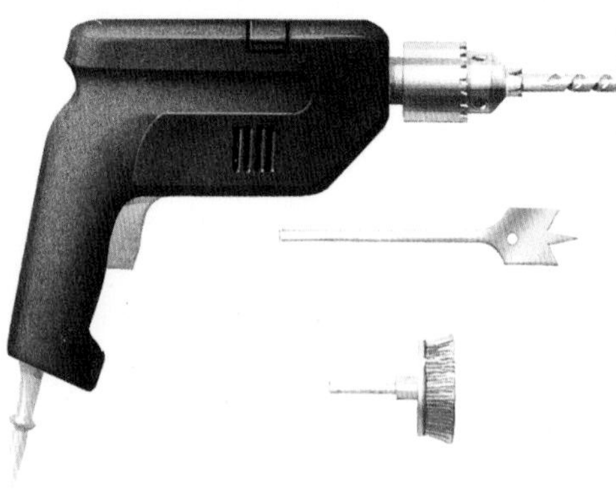

Electric drills usually come with several attachments designed for different jobs.

attack *verb* 1 to use violence against a person or place. *The army attacked the village.* 2 to criticize or speak strongly against. *The architects were attacked for their bad design.*

attack *noun* 1 a violent attempt to hurt someone or something. 2 a fit or sudden illness. *An asthma attack.*

attain *verb* to reach or achieve something, to succeed. *She attained a ripe old age.* **attainment** *noun.* **attainable** *adjective.*

attempt *verb* to try to do something. *Jo attempted to climb the tree.* **attempt** *noun.*

attend *verb* to be present at a place or happening. *We all attended the public meeting.* **attendance** *noun.* **attend to** 1 to concentrate. *Please attend to what I'm saying.* 2 to deal with or look after. *He attended to the accident victims.*

A crowd is gathering in the square to attend a public meeting.

SPELLING NOTE

Whether words like 'attendance', 'acquaintance' and 'intelligence' should end in '–ance' or in '–ence' causes people a lot of trouble. There are no easy rules. You just have to learn the spelling!

attention *noun* giving thought or care or being interested in something. *She gave all her attention to her studies.* **attract attention** to make somebody notice something.

attentive *adjective* 1 taking care to notice or listen. 2 kind and gentle. *He was very attentive to his grandfather's needs.*

attic *noun* a room just under the roof of a house.

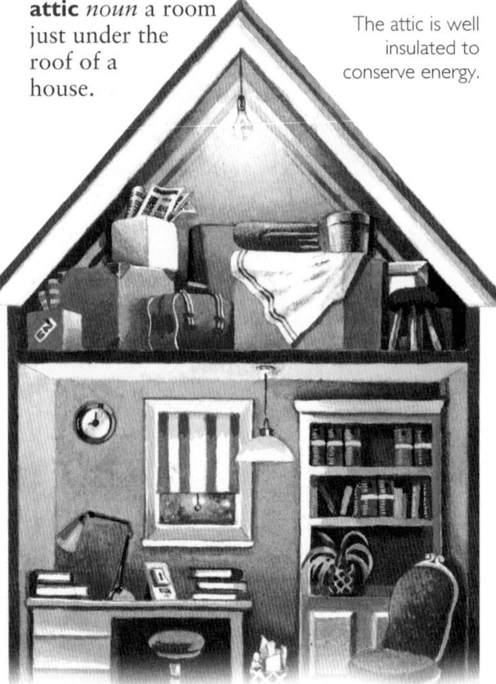

The attic is well insulated to conserve energy.

attitude *noun* an opinion or a way of thinking about somebody or something, a way of behaving. *She has a very mean attitude towards her children.*

attract *verb* 1 to like and find somebody or something interesting. *Katie was attracted to the boy next door.* 2 to catch the attention of. *The elephant caught the child's attention and he stopped crying.* 3 to make something come nearer. *Bright flowers attract butterflies.* **attraction** *noun.*

attractive *adjective* 1 interesting and pleasing. *An attractive idea.* 2 good-looking. *An attractive boy.*

aubergine *noun* (US eggplant) a vegetable with a shiny purple skin.

Aubergines grow in warm climates. They are a favourite vegetable in Mediterranean lands and in the Middle East.

A

auburn *adjective* reddish-brown. *Jill had long auburn hair.*

auction *noun* a public sale in which goods are sold to the person who will bid (offer to pay) the highest price. **auction** *verb*.

An auctioneer is someone in charge of an auction. Items such as paintings are sold to the highest bidder.

audible *adjective* loud enough to be heard. The opposite of 'audible' is 'inaudible'.

audience *noun* a group of people who watch or listen to something. *The play is attracting huge audiences.*

audio-visual *adjective* using recorded sound and pictures for teaching etc. *The school's audio-visual equipment includes CDs and cassettes.*

Audio-visual material such as CDs and cassettes make learning more fun.

audition *noun* a short performance to test whether an actor, singer or musician is suitable for a particular job.

auditorium *noun* the place in a theatre, concert hall etc. where the audience sits.

August *noun* the eighth month of the year. August has 31 days.

aunt *noun* Your aunt is the sister of your father or mother, or the wife of your uncle.

au pair *noun* a young foreign person, usually a young woman, who lives for a short time with a family to learn the language and in return looks after the children and does light housework. *The au pair was looking after three children.*

AMAZING FACT

Australia is the smallest continent and the largest island in the world.

WORD HISTORY

August was named in honour of the Roman Emperor, Augustus Caesar.

SPELLING NOTE

The name 'Australia' comes from the Latin word 'australis', meaning southern.

austere *adjective* simple and without luxury, severe. **austerity** *noun*.

Australasia *noun* one of the Earth's seven continents.

Australia *noun* a country in Australasia.

Australian *noun* a person who comes from Australia. **Australian** *adjective*. *The Australian outback.*

Austria *noun* a country in Central Europe.

The red and white stripes of the Austrian flag also appear on the country's eagle crest.

Austrian *noun* a person from Austria. **Austrian** *adjective*. *The Austrian alps.*

authentic *adjective* real, genuine and not copied. *An authentic painting by Picasso.* **authenticity** *noun*.

The archaeologists found an authentic African mask.

author *noun* a person who writes a book, article, poem, play etc.

authoritative *adjective* 1 showing power and authority. 2 reliable and coming from somebody in authority. *An authoritative atlas contains up-to-date information.*

authority *noun* 1 the power to tell others what to do. *The police have the authority to breathalyze people.* 2 a group or organization that has the power to control what is going on. *The local authority refused our planning application.* 3 an expert. *She's an authority on dolls' houses.*

A

authorize *verb* to give somebody power or permission to do something.

autism *noun* an abnormal condition in children in which they are unable to respond to or communicate with people. **autistic** *adjective*.

auto- *prefix* self, self-caused, or same.

autobiography *noun* a book that somebody writes about her or his own life. **autobiographical** *adjective*.

autograph *noun* a person's name written in their own handwriting, a signature. **autograph** *verb*. *The pop star autographed our programmes.*

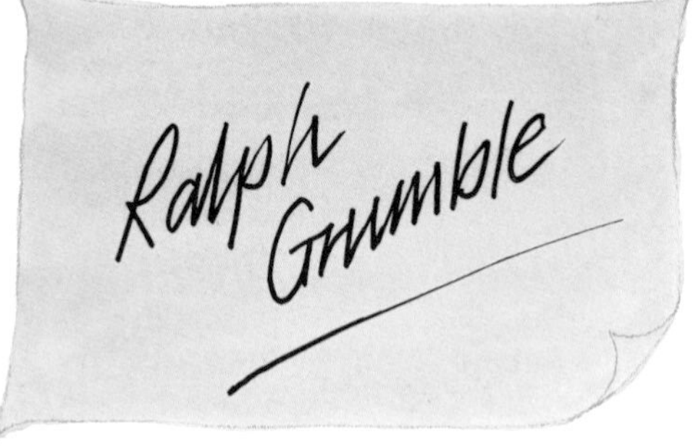

The autograph of a famous person could one day be worth a lot of money.

automatic *adjective* 1 working by itself without the control of a human being. *An automatic central-heating system*. 2 done without thinking about it. *Breathing is automatic.* **automatically** *adverb*.

automation *noun* using machines instead of people to do monotonously repetitive jobs in factories etc.

SPELLING NOTE

Try not to confuse 'adverse' (which means harmful or unfavourable) with 'averse' (which means unwilling or disinclined).

automobile *noun* a motor car (mainly US).

autopsy *noun* the examination of a body after death, a post-mortem.

autumn *noun* the season of the year between summer and winter.

available *adjective* 1 obtainable and ready to be used. *Raspberries are not available all the year round.* 2 free to see people. *She'll be available to interview you next week.* **availability** *noun*.

avalanche *noun* a huge mass of snow and ice suddenly falling down a mountain.

avenge *verb* to harm or punish somebody in return for a wrong they have done to somebody else. *He avenged his father's murder.* **avenger** *noun*.

average *noun* in maths, the sum of several amounts divided by the number of amounts. The average of 4+6+9+13 = 8. (4+6+9+13=32 divided by 4 = 8.) **average** *adjective* 1 normal, ordinary. *It's been a very average week.* 2 not extreme or special. *Her work is about average.*

averse *adjective* opposed to or disliking. *Averse to hard work.*

aversion *noun* a strong dislike. *He has a great aversion to jellyfish.*

aviary *noun* a large cage for keeping birds.

aviation *noun* the science of building and flying aircraft.

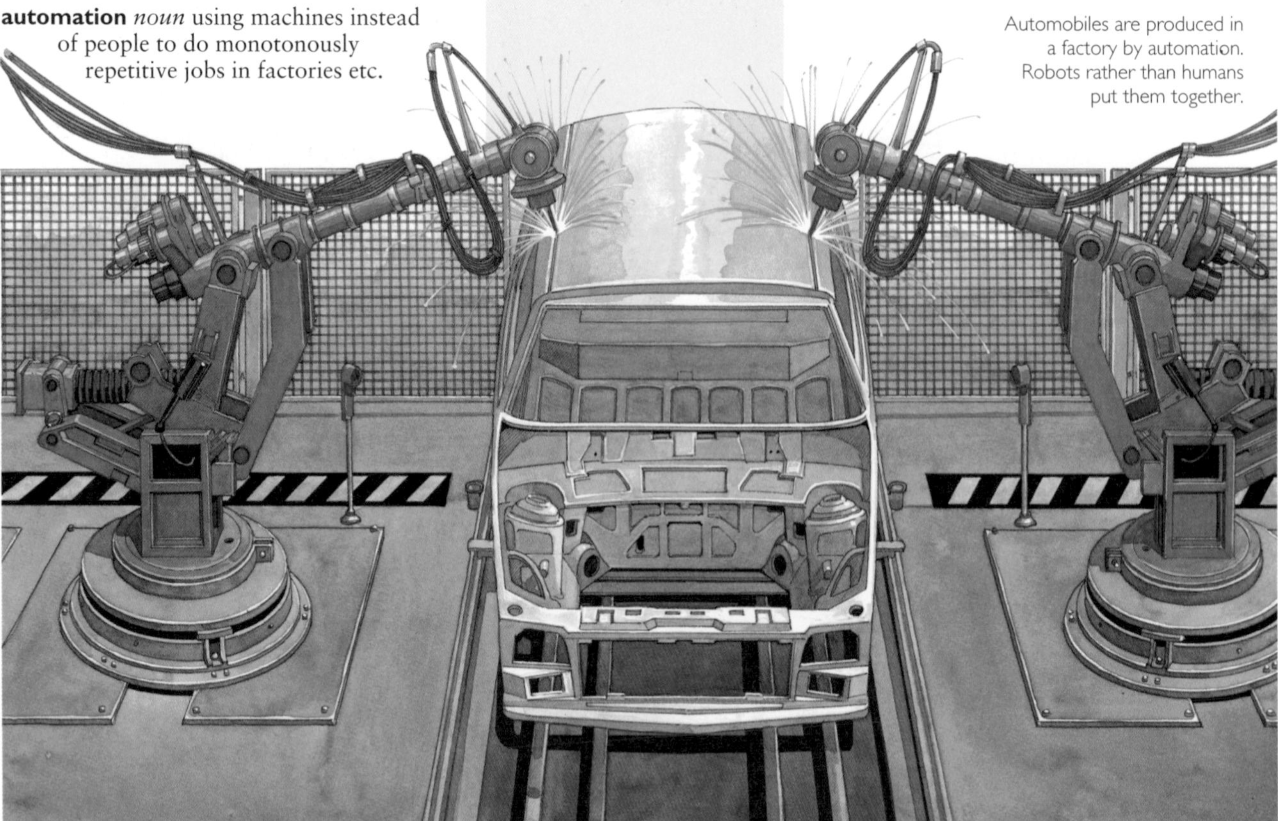

Automobiles are produced in a factory by automation. Robots rather than humans put them together.

aviator *noun* (old-fashioned) an aircraft pilot. *The aviator wore flying goggles and a leather hat with earflaps.*

The Sopwith Camel was flown by British aviators in World War I.

avid *adjective* 1 keen, enthusiastic. *An avid reader.* 2 greedy. *The pupil waved her arm in the air, avid for the teacher's attention.*

await *verb* to wait for, to expect. *We are awaiting the arrival of the president.*

awake *adjective* not sleeping. **awake** (awakes, awaking, awoke, awoken) *verb* to wake up. *I awoke at dawn.*

award *noun* something, such as a prize or money, given to somebody for doing well. **award** *verb* to present. *She was awarded first prize for singing.*

She was awarded a gold medal for coming first in the swimming contest.

aware *adjective* knowing about. *Andy wasn't aware of the dangers of mountaineering.* **awareness** *noun.*

away *adverb* 1 not here, not at home. *He's gone away for a few weeks.* 2 at a distance. *The next town is miles away.* 3 into the distance. *The music faded slowly away.* 4 ceaselessly. *She worked away at her exercises.* **do away with** *verb* to get rid of.

awe *noun* a mixture of wonder, fear and respect. *She is in awe of her teacher.* **awe-inspiring** *adjective* causing a feeling of awe. *An awe-inspiring poem.*

SPELLING NOTE

An award is something that you win or are given for a special reason. 'She was awarded the Nobel peace prize.' A reward is something you get for doing something useful or helpful. 'The police are offering a reward for any information about the accident.'

awful *adjective* 1 very bad or unpleasant. *What an awful smell!* 2 very great. *She's done an awful lot of knitting.*

awfully *adverb* very. *I'm awfully sorry.*

awkward *adjective* 1 clumsy and embarrassed. *The boy feels awkward among adults.* 2 not convenient. *We are eating, so this is an awkward time to call.* **awkwardness** *noun.*

awoke past tense of awake. *He awoke when the alarm went off.*

axe *noun* a tool with a sharp blade on a long handle used for chopping wood.

An axe can be used for felling trees as well as for splitting timber.

axiom *noun* a statement that everyone generally agrees to be true.

axis *noun* 1 a real or imaginary line through the middle of an object around which it spins. *The Earth rotates on its axis, which passes through the North and South Pole.* 2 a line along the side or bottom of a graph.

The Earth tilts on its axis as it spins through space.

axle *noun* the rod that goes through the centre of a wheel and on which it turns.

Azerbaijan *noun* a country in West Asia.

azure *adjective* bright blue like an unclouded sky.

Bb

babble *verb* to chatter and talk in a confused and excited way.

babe *noun* a baby. *A babe in arms.*

baboon *noun* a large monkey from Africa.

A baboon needs nearly 7,000 kJ of energy from food each day, half the amount of an adult man.

baby *noun* a very young child. *The baby's first smile.* **babyish** *adjective.*

babysitter *noun* a person who is paid to look after children when their parents are away. **babysit** (babysits, babysitting, babysat) *verb.*

bachelor *noun* a man who has never been married. *A bachelor pad.*

back *noun* 1 the part of your body along the spine between your shoulders and bottom, also the top part of an animal. *She climbed on to the horse's back.* 2 the opposite side to the front, the part situated behind. **back** *adjective* at the rear. *The back door was wide open and the dog had run away.* **back-breaking** very tiring. *Back-breaking work.*

The staple food in Southeast Asia is rice. Cultivating the paddy fields is back-breaking work.

back *adverb* to an earlier place or time. *He thought back to when he was young.*

AMAZING FACT

The human backbone, or spinal column, is a flexible S-shaped arrangement allowing us to bend forward and backward and to stand up without falling over.

SPELLING NOTE

The commonest error in spelling 'bachelor' is to put a 't' before the 'ch'.

back *verb* 1 to move backwards. *She backed away from the fierce dog.* 2 to support or help. *Will you back me?* 3 to put money (bet) on an animal etc. *Uncle Ben backed the winning horse in the race.* **back down** to give up or change your mind. **put your back into** to work hard. **back out** to decide not to keep an agreement. *You promised to come to the party. You can't back out now.*

backbone *noun* the set of joined bones along the back. The spine.

The backbone is made up of individual bones called vertebrae. They interlock with each other in sliding joints.

backfire *verb* to have the opposite result to the one intended. *The plan backfired and the robbery was discovered.*

background *noun* 1 the part of a scene or picture that is behind the main objects or people. *The picture shows a lake with mountains in the background.* 2 the different facts that surround an event and which help to explain it. 3 a person's past experience or family history and education. *She comes from a farming background.*

backpack *noun* a large bag that climbers, campers etc. carry on their backs. **backpacker** *noun.*

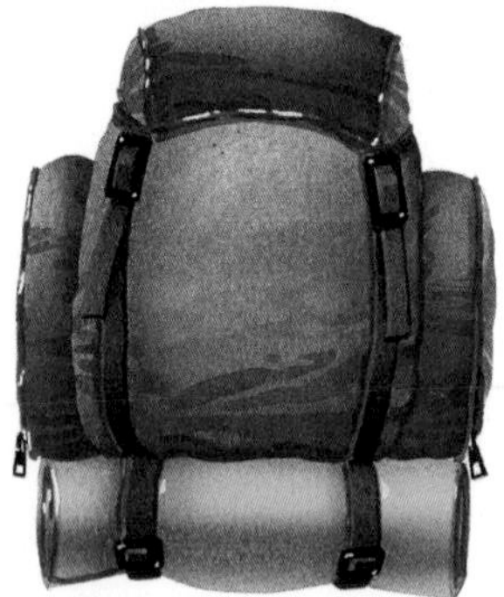

This backpack is ready for the hike. It is stuffed with warm clothes and has a bed-roll strapped beneath it.

backward *adjective* 1 towards the back. *A backward look.* 2 slow to learn or develop. *This baby is backward at walking.*

backwards *adverb* 1 towards the back. *She took a step backwards and fell over the rug, breaking her leg.* 2 in the reverse way from normal. *Counting backwards.*

backyard *noun* a yard with a hard surface at the back of a house. In US a garden with a lawn at the back of a house.

bacon *noun* thin slices of salted or dried meat from a pig.

bacteria *plural noun* microscopic living things. Some bacteria cause diseases.

bad (worse, worst) *adjective* 1 not good. Unpleasant. *I've got some bad news.* 2 naughty, wicked. *You're a bad girl to tell so many lies.* 3 harmful. *Eating too many sweets is bad for you.* 4 hurt or in bad health. *I've got a bad leg.* 5 rotten and not good to eat. *The food has gone bad.* 6 serious. *A bad accident.* **go bad** to decay.

badge *noun* a piece of cloth, metal or plastic that is pinned or sewn on to clothes, with a picture or message on it. *All employees must wear a badge with their name on it.*

badger *noun* a wild animal with grey fur and a black and white striped head. Badgers live in underground holes called sets and are active at night.

Badgers' hands and feet are broad with wide claws for digging.

badger *verb* to annoy somebody by pestering them to do something.

badminton *noun* a game like tennis that is played by hitting a shuttlecock over a high net with rackets.

baffle *verb* to confuse or puzzle. *I was baffled by so many questions and couldn't think of what to say.* **baffling** *adjective.*

bag *noun* a container for carrying things. *Never put a plastic bag on your head.*

baggage *noun* bags and suitcases that travellers use. Luggage.

baggy *adjective* baggy clothes are too big and so hang in loose folds.

Baghdad *noun* the capital of Iraq.

bagpipes *plural noun* a musical instrument. Air is squeezed from a bag into pipes on which the music is played.

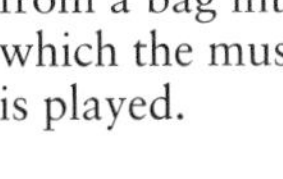

Bagpipe music is traditional in Scotland at Hogmanay, or New Year.

Bahamas *noun* a country in the West Indies.

Bahrain *noun* a country in Southwest Asia.

bail *noun* one of a pair of pieces of wood placed on top of the stumps on a cricket wicket. *The bowler knocked off the bail.*

AMAZING FACT

A badger's sett is an elaborate underground network of tunnels and rooms. There are usually several entrances.

WORD HISTORY

'Badminton' is named after Badminton House in England where the game was first played in the middle of the 19th century.

bail *noun* money that is paid to allow somebody accused of a crime to go free until their trial. *She was released on bail for £100,000.*

bail *verb* to scoop water from a boat to prevent it sinking. **bail out** (also bale out) to jump from an aircraft, using a parachute.

bait *noun* 1 a small amount of food used to attract fish, birds or animals to help you catch them. 2 something that is tempting.

bake *verb* to cook in an oven. *He baked a cake for their birthday tea.*

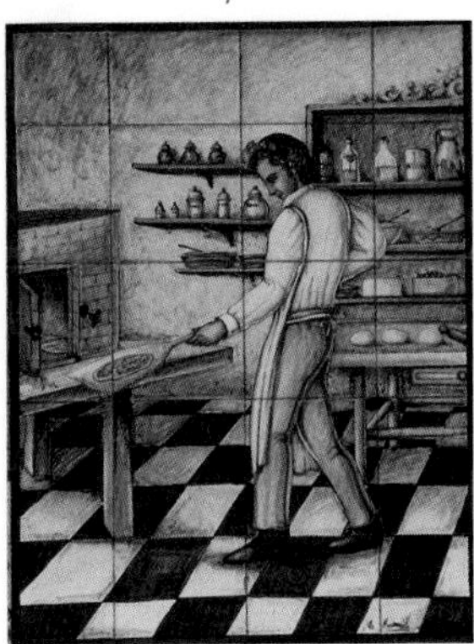

baker *noun* a person who works in a bakery and makes and sells bread, cakes etc.

This decorative tile shows a scene in a bakery in Seville, Spain.

Baku *noun* the capital of Azerbaijan.

balance *verb* to keep something steady and not let it fall over. **balance** *noun. Jack has good balance. He can stand on one leg without falling over.*

balance *noun* 1 an instrument for weighing things. 2 the amount of money somebody has in the bank.

balcony *noun* a platform on the outside wall of a building with a wall or railings around it.

A beautiful girl stands on the balcony waiting for her lover.

bald *adjective* (rhymes with 'crawled') with little or no hair on the head. **baldness** *noun.*

bale *noun* a large bundle of something soft. *A bale of hay.*

ball *noun* 1 a round object used to play games. 2 something that is round in shape. *A cannon ball.* 3 a grand, formal party at which people dance.

ball bearings *plural noun* very small steel balls that help different parts of a machine move smoothly against each other.

ballad *noun* a poem or song that tells a story. *He sang a romantic ballad.*

ballerina *noun* a female ballet dancer.

ballet *noun* (say **bal**-ay) a form of highly artistic dancing, usually telling a story, and performed on a stage. **ballet-dancer** *noun.*

balloon *noun* 1 a small bag made of thin material such as plastic or rubber and filled with gas. *The children blew up red and blue balloons.* 2 a large bag made of strong material and filled with gas or hot air (hot-air balloon), which carries people in a basket underneath. **balloonist** *noun.*

A colourful hot air balloon drifts through a blue sky.

ballot *noun* a way of voting secretly in an election. *The ballot box was full of votes.*

Bamako *noun* the capital of Mali.

bamboo *noun* a giant tropical grass-like plant with a hollow, woody stem used to make furniture etc.

ban (bans, banning, banned) *verb* to forbid or say that something must not be done. *She was banned from driving for six months.* **ban** *noun.*

banana *noun* a long tropical fruit with soft white flesh and a yellow skin when ripe.

band *noun* a group of musicians or a group of people who get together for a purpose. *A band of hooligans.* **band together** *verb. The villagers banded together to stop the motorway being built.*

band *noun* a narrow strip of material that goes around something. *An elastic band.*

bandage *noun* a strip of material used to tie around an injury or to cover a wound. **bandage** *verb. The nurse bandaged his knee.*

Bandar Seri Begawan *noun* the capital of Brunei.

bandit *noun* a robber who works with others in a group or band. *The travellers were attacked by bandits.*

Gangs of bandits often hide in remote wooded hills and ambush unsuspecting travellers.

WORD HISTORY

'Ballot' comes from an Italian word meaning little ball. Little balls were dropped into a container to vote – white for yes, black for no. Hence the expression 'to blackball' or vote against somebody.

bang *noun* 1 a sudden, very loud noise. *She shut the lid with a bang.* 2 a heavy knock. **bang** *verb. He banged on the door.*

banger *noun* 1 (slang) a sausage. 2 (slang) an old car. 3 a firework that makes a loud banging noise.

Bangkok *noun* the capital of Thailand.

Visitors to Bangkok often shop for local produce in Thailand's floating markets.

Bangladesh *noun* a country in South Asia.

Bangui *noun* the capital of the Central African Republic.

banish *verb* to send somebody away, usually from their own country, as a punishment. **banishment** *noun.*

banister or **bannister** *noun* a hand-rail along the side of a staircase.

Banjul *noun* the capital of Gambia.

bank *noun* 1 a place that looks after money for people and which provides financial services. **bank** *verb. She banked all her savings.* 2 a place for storing things or leaving things for collection. *A bottle bank.* **bank holiday** in UK a public holiday when banks close. **bank on** to rely on. *You can bank on me. I'll be there.*

bank *noun* 1 the sides of a river, lake or canal. 2 a piece of raised, sloping land.

bankrupt *adjective* unable to pay debts. **bankruptcy** *noun.*

banner *noun* a large flag with a design or message on it, hung up or carried on a pole or between two poles.

The suffragettes carried banners demanding votes for women.

banquet *noun* a large, formal dinner, usually for a special occasion. *The mayor held a banquet in honour of the king.*

baptize *verb* in the Christian religion, to sprinkle or pour water over a person as a sign that they have become a Christian. To christen. **baptism** *noun.* **baptismal** *adjective.*

bar *noun* 1 a long, straight piece of metal or wood. *A cage with iron bars.* 2 a room or a long table or counter in a pub or hotel at which drinks etc. are served. 3 a solid block of something. *A bar of soap.* 4 the equal sections into which music is divided.

bar (bars, barring, barred) *verb* 1 to keep out. *Children are barred from the premises.* 2 to block. *She barred the door.*

Barbados *noun* a country in the West Indies.

Neptune's trident appears on the flag of the island nation of Barbados.

barbarian *noun* a cruel, rough, uncivilized person. In the ancient world barbarians were people who were not Greek or Roman.

barbaric or **barbarous** *adjective* brutally cruel. **barbarity** *noun.*

barbecue *noun* an outdoor party at which food is cooked on a grill over a charcoal fire. **barbecue** *verb.*

barbed wire *noun* fencing wire with sharp spikes sticking out of it.

barber *noun* a men's hairdresser.

bar code *noun* an arrangement of thick and thin lines and spaces printed on goods in shops, containing information about price, size etc., and which can be 'read' by a computer.

Bar codes save time at a supermarket checkout.

bare *adjective* 1 uncovered, naked. *bare arms.* 2 empty. *The removal van has gone and the house is bare.* **bare** *verb* to expose. *The dog bared its teeth.*

barely *adverb* scarcely, only just. *She could barely lift the heavy box.*

bargain *noun* 1 something that you buy at a price that is cheaper than usual. *This book is a real bargain!* 2 an agreement between two people in return for something.

bargain *verb* to haggle or argue over the price of something.

barge *noun* a long boat with a flat bottom, used on canals mainly to carry heavy goods.

barge *verb* to push your way roughly through people. To bump clumsily into people or things. *Jim barged his way through the crowd and grabbed the money.*

AMAZING FACT

Barometers measure the air pressure and interpret its changes. If the pressure is high, that generally means that the weather is good, low pressure signals changing or bad weather.

WORD HISTORY

'Barbarian' comes from the Greek word 'barbaros', meaning foreign. The Greeks invented the word because it resembled the strange sounds of the languages spoken by non-Greeks.

SPELLING NOTE

Try not to confuse the spellings of 'bare', meaning naked, and 'bear', the verb meaning to support.

bark *noun* the sharp sound made by a dog, fox etc. **bark** *verb. The dog barked at the postman and then bit his leg.*

bark *noun* the rough, hard covering of the trunk and branches of trees.

barley *noun* a grain used for food and in making beer.

bar mitzvah *noun* a religious ceremony that takes place on a Jewish boy's 13th birthday to celebrate his becoming an adult.

barn *noun* a farm building for keeping animals or storing crops.

barnacle *noun* a shellfish that fixes itself firmly to rocks and the sides of boats.

barometer *noun* an instrument that measures the air pressure and shows changes in the weather.

The barometer was invented in 1643 by Italian scientist Torricelli, who discovered air pressure.

baron *noun* a nobleman or peer of the lowest rank.

baroness *noun* the wife of a baron or a noblewoman or peer of the lowest rank.

baroque *noun* a highly ornate style of European architecture of the late 16th to early 18th century.

barracks *plural noun* buildings where soldiers live.

barrage *noun* 1 a dam or barrier built across a river. 2 continuous heavy gunfire. 3 a huge number of something. *A barrage of complaints.*

barrel *noun* 1 a large container with curved sides for storing liquids such as beer. *The beer barrels are in the cellar.* 2 the tube of a gun through which a bullet is fired.

barren *adjective* the soil of barren land is so poor that crops cannot grow.

barricade *noun* a barrier that has been quickly put up to block a road. **barricade** *verb* to block. *The demonstrating students barricaded the streets.*

A barricade hastily put together out of any objects to hand blocks the road.

B

barrier *noun* a fence, railing or some other obstacle designed to stop people or things getting past.

barrow *noun* 1 a cart that you can push or pull. 2 a cart from which fruit, vegetables etc. are sold in the street.

The builders' barrow is full of sand.

barrow *noun* a prehistoric mound of earth and stones over a grave.

barter *noun* to exchange goods for other goods rather than for money. To swap.

base *noun* 1 the lowest part of something, especially the part on which it stands. *The base of the vase.* 2 the headquarters or main place from which things are controlled. *The expedition returned to base.* **base** *verb. The company is based in Edinburgh.*

base *verb* to use something as a basis or starting point. *The new musical is based on a famous novel.*

baseball *noun* an American game played with a bat and ball by two teams of nine players.

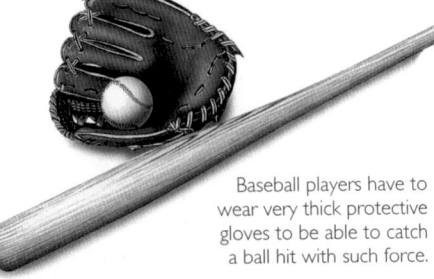

Baseball players have to wear very thick protective gloves to be able to catch a ball hit with such force.

basement *noun* a room or an area below the level of the street.

bashful *adjective* shy and lacking in confidence. **bashfulness** *noun.*

basic *adjective* 1 the most important and necessary. *The basic rules of grammar.* 2 very simple, essential. *Basic needs.*

basically *adverb* 1 concerned with what is basic or fundamental. 2 most important.

basil *noun* a herb used to flavour food.

basin *noun* 1 a large bowl for mixing food. 2 a bowl fixed to a wall in a bathroom where you can wash. 3 A river basin is the area of land it gets its water from.

AMAZING FACT

Bats are the only mammal that is capable of genuine flight.

There is great variety among the 2000 + species of bats. Some have wingspans of only about 10 inches while others have a wingspan of up to four or five feet.

Bats have leathery wings and very poor eyesight. They hunt and navigate using ultrasonics and echo-location.

DID YOU KNOW

'Basically' is far too often used nowadays to mean simply 'importantly' – or even nothing at all. Try to avoid sentences like: 'Basically, I think it's time I went to bed.'

basis (bases) *noun* the main principle or idea behind something.

basket a woven container with a handle.

basketball *noun* a game for two teams in which the players try to score points by throwing a ball through a high net at each end of the court.

bass *adjective* 1 the lowest sounds in music. *Deep bass notes.* 2 A double bass is a very large violin-shaped instrument that plays very low notes.

Basseterre *noun* the capital of St Kitts and Nevis.

bat *noun* a mouse-like animal with wings that flies at night hunting for insects.

bat *noun* a piece of wood or metal that players use to hit a ball in games like baseball, cricket and table tennis. **bat** (bats, batting, batted) *verb. Nick batted the ball to Jim.*

batch *noun* a group of things that were made at one time or have to be dealt with together. *A large batch of letters arrived for my grandmother this morning.*

bath *noun* a long, deep container that you fill with water and sit in to wash your whole body. **bath** *verb.*

bathe *verb* 1 to go swimming in the sea. 2 to wash a part of the body very gently. *The nurse bathed the wound.* 3 (US) to take a bath or to bath.

bathroom *noun* a room with a bath or shower and usually a basin and toilet.

batik *noun* an Eastern way of printing designs on cloth by covering parts of the cloth with wax patterns and dyeing the rest.

Cotton and silk can be dyed with brilliant colours to make batik.

baton *noun* 1 a short, thin stick the conductor uses to beat time for an orchestra or choir. 2 a short stick that is passed from one runner to the next in a relay race.

battalion *noun* an army unit made up of smaller units called companies.

batter *noun* to hit something heavily again and again. *Battered to death.* **batter** *adjective. A battered old car.*

batter *noun* a mixture of flour, milk and eggs for making pancakes etc.

battery *noun* 1 a container that makes and stores electricity. You put batteries in things such as radios and torches to make them work. 2 a number of big guns. 3 a large group of small cages in which hens or other animals are kept for the mass production of eggs or meat. *Battery farming.*

battle *noun* a fight between two armies or opposing groups. **battle** *verb. She battled against poor health.*

battleship *noun* a large, heavily armed warship. *Battleship grey.*

bay (bays) *noun* a part of the seashore that curves inwards. An inlet. **bay window** a window that forms a recess by sticking out from the wall of a house. **at bay** facing an enemy and fighting them off. *A stag at bay.*

bay *adjective* a reddish-brown colour of a horse. **bay** *noun. This horse is a bay.*

bayonet *noun* a knife that can be attached to the end of a rifle.

bazaar *noun* 1 a market in Eastern countries. 2 a sale to raise money for something. *A church bazaar.*

Men selling beaten metalware wait for their customers. When buying goods at a bazaar it is customary to haggle over the prices.

AMAZING FACT

Bears are omnivores, which means that they eat plants and animals. They do not have very good eyesight but have an excellent sense of smell.

WORD HISTORY

The word 'bayonet' is named after the town of Bayonne in France, where the weapons were originally made.

BC *abbreviation* Before Christ, used for dates before the birth of Jesus Christ. *Alexander the Great died in 323 BC.*

beach *noun* the area of sand or pebbles where the land meets the sea.

beacon *noun* a light or fire used as a guide or warning. *A beacon was lit on the hilltop.*

bead *noun* a small piece of glass or other material with a hole through it, which can be threaded on string or wire to make a necklace etc.

beak *noun* the hard pointed outer part of a bird's mouth. *The eagle has a hooked beak.*

beaker *noun* 1 a drinking mug without a handle. 2 a glass vessel used for pouring liquids in chemistry.

beam *noun* a large, heavy bar of wood, metal or concrete used for supporting the roof or floors of a building.

beam *noun* a band or ray of bright light. *The beam from the torch dazzled us.*

bean *noun* a plant that produces seeds (beans) that grow in a pod and are eaten as a vegetable. *Broad beans.* **full of beans** lively and full of energy.

Beans are one of the world's most nutritious foods. Young broad beans can be eaten raw, and even the pods can be made into a soup. Older beans are lightly steamed or boiled.

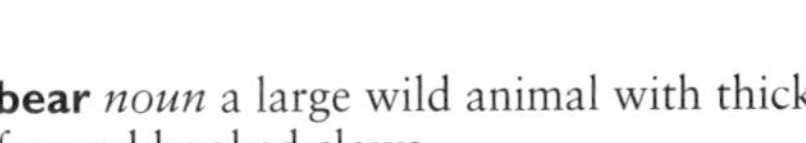

bear *noun* a large wild animal with thick fur and hooked claws.

bear (bears, bearing, bore, borne) *verb* 1 to support the weight of something. *That little chair won't bear your heavy weight.* 2 to carry from one place to another. *Seeds borne by the wind.* 3 to produce. *The plum tree bears fruit in the autumn.* 4 to accept or tolerate something unpleasant. *She cannot bear rudeness.* **bear with** to be patient with. *Bear with me and I'll tell you.*

beard *noun* the hair on a man's face.

beast *noun* 1 a large wild animal. 2 (slang) a cruel, unpleasant person. **beastly** *adjective.*

B

beat (beats, beating, beat, beaten) *verb* 1 to hit somebody or something hard and often. *The hail beat against the window.* 2 to stir something with a whisk or fork. *The chef beat the batter.* 3 to defeat or win against somebody. *He always beats me at chess.* 4 to make a regular sound or movement. *The bird was beating its wings.* **beat** *noun* rhythmic knocking. *The beat of the music.*

beauty *noun* the quality of something that makes it attractive to look at or listen to. Loveliness. *The inspiring beauty of the lakes and mountains.* **beautiful** *adjective.* **beautifully** *adverb.*

beaver *noun* a North American furry wild animal with a broad flat tail and strong front teeth. Beavers cut branches to build dams and homes called lodges in rivers.

A beaver gnaws at a stick in front of its dam. The beaver's staple food is fish.

because *conjunction* for the reason that. *The tennis match stopped because it had started to rain.*

become (becomes, becoming, became, become) *verb* 1 to come to be. To start feeling. *We became very good friends.* 2 to change into. *Caterpillars become moths and tadpoles develop into frogs.*

bed *noun* 1 a piece of furniture to sleep on. 2 the bottom of the sea or a river. 3 an area for growing flowers etc. *Flower bed.*

A bee sucks nectar from a flower. At the same time, it pollinates the flower by carrying pollen on its legs from one bloom to the next.

WORD HISTORY

The word beauty – and take care how you spell it! – comes via the French from the Latin 'bellus'. We usually use the word 'beautiful' to describe women, children and things, but not men. It is more usual to call a man 'handsome' or 'good-looking'.

There are over 300,000 species of beetle worldwide.

bedridden *adjective* permanently in bed because of illness or old age.

bedroom *noun* a room to sleep in. *The twins share a bedroom.*

bedsitter or **bedsit** *noun* a rented room for eating and sleeping in.

bee *noun* a flying insect with a yellow and black body that lives in large groups and makes honey. Some bees can sting.

beech *noun* a hardwood tree with a smooth bark. Beeches are deciduous, so their leaves drop in autumn.

beef *noun* the meat of cattle.

beefy (beefier, beefiest) *adjective* A beefy person is big and has strong muscles.

beehive or **hive** *noun* a small wooden house in which bees are kept.

beeline *noun* a straight line between two places. **make a beeline for** to go directly and swiftly towards something. *The boys made a beeline for the beach.*

beer *noun* an alcoholic drink brewed from malt, barley and hops.

beeswax *noun* the wax produced by bees to build the combs in which they store honey.

beet or **sugarbeet** *noun* a plant with a bulbous root that can be eaten as a vegetable (beetroot) or that can be used to make sugar.

beetle *noun* an insect with hard covers for its wings.

beetroot *noun* a variety of beet with a red root that is cooked as a vegetable.

bedding *noun* 1 blankets, duvets, sheets etc. for a bed (also bedclothes). 2 straw etc. for animals to lie on.

Water beetles, snails and small fishes are some of the creatures that feed on the bed of the river.

before *preposition* 1 earlier than or sooner than now. *The day before yesterday.* 2 in front of. *She stood before the statue.* **before** *adverb* previously. *We've never met before.*

beg (begs, begging, begged) *verb* 1 to ask somebody for money or food, especially in the street. *She begged for enough money to buy a bowl of soup.* **beggar** *noun.* 2 to ask for something very earnestly and eagerly. *He begged to be allowed to go swimming.*

begin (begins, beginning, began, begun) *verb* to start. *The meeting began at 7 o'clock.* The opposite of 'begin' is 'end'.

beginner *noun* a person who is just starting to do or learn something.

When you begin to learn to ride a bike, stabilizers can give you confidence.

beginning *noun* the start of something, the origin. *At the beginning of the week.*

behave *verb* 1 the way we act or do things is how we behave. *She's been behaving in a funny way lately.* 2 to act in a good or proper way. *You can come with me only if you behave.*

behaviour *noun* a way of behaving.

behind *preposition* 1 on the other side of or towards the back. *She hid behind the curtain.* 2 not making good progress. *He's behind with his studies.* 3 supporting or encouraging somebody. *We're behind you in your campaign.* **leave behind** *verb* to leave without something. *Peter was always leaving his keys behind.*

Beijing *noun* the capital of China.

being *noun* a living creature. *The first human beings lived in Africa.*

Beirut *noun* the capital of Lebanon.

Belarus *noun* a country in eastern Europe.

This is the flag of Belarus,. which used to be part of the Soviet Union. The capital of Belarus is Minsk.

WORD HISTORY

The word 'beggar' may have come from an Old French word 'bégard', a begging monk, named after Lambert e Begue, the founder of an order of nuns.

AMAZING FACT

Belize was the last British mainland colony in the Americas. It gained independence in 1981. Both English and Spanish are spoken in Belize.

belch *verb* 1 to let wind from your stomach come noisily out of your mouth, to burp. *It is rude to belch at the table.* 2 to send out gases, fire smoke etc. like a volcano.

Belfast *noun* the capital of Northern Ireland.

belfry (belfries) *noun* a tower attached to a church, where the bells are hung.

Belgian *noun* a person from Belgium. Belgian *adjective. Belgian chocolates.*

Belgium *noun* a country in Northwest Europe.

Belgrade *noun* the capital of Yugoslavia.

belief *noun* 1 the things you believe to be true. The feeling that something is true.

believe *verb* 1 to think or feel strongly that something is true or real. *I believe in ghosts.* 2 to think that somebody is telling the truth. 3 to think or have an opinion. *I believe he's coming tomorrow.*

Belize *noun* a country in Central America.

bell *noun* a hollow metal object shaped like an upside-down cup that makes a ringing sound when struck. Any device that makes a ringing sound. *An electric door bell.*

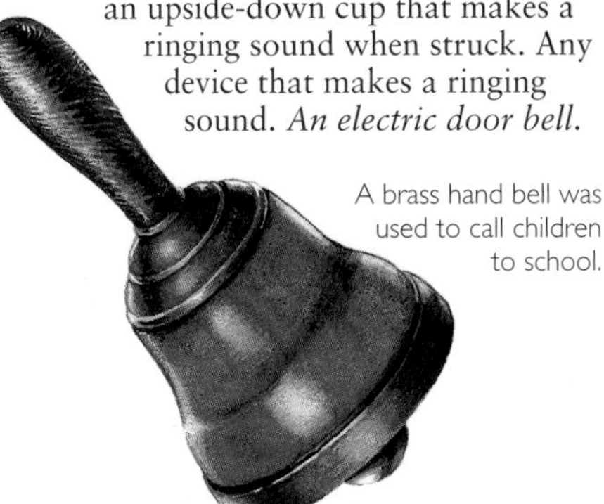

A brass hand bell was used to call children to school.

bellow *noun* a deep roaring sound made by a bull. **bellow** *verb. The bull bellowed with rage and the children ran for cover.*

bellows *plural noun* an instrument used for pumping air into a fire or a church organ.

To get a fire to light, people used to pump air under it with bellows.

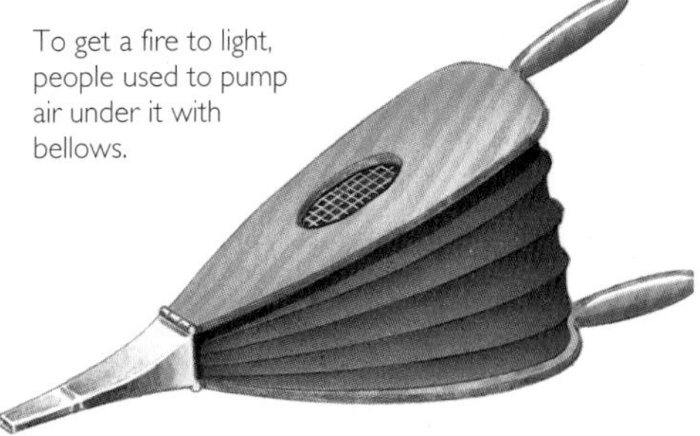

belly (bellies) *noun* the abdomen or the part of a person's or animal's body containing the stomach and intestines. *He ate until his belly was full.* **belly button** the navel.

Belmopan *noun* the capital of Belize.

belong *verb* 1 to be the property of somebody. *This book belongs to you, it is yours.* 2 to be a member of a group. *Brian belongs to the bowling club.* 3 to have its right place. *Put the tools back in the cupboard where they belong.*

belongings *plural noun* all the things that are yours and which you own.

below *preposition* 1 lower than. *Your chin is below your mouth.* 2 less than. *The temperature is below freezing.* **below** *adverb* beneath. *He looked down at the moat below.* The opposite of 'below' is 'above'.

belt *noun* 1 a long strap of leather or other material that you wear around your waist. 2 a narrow area of land. *The corn belt.* **belt** *verb* to hit. *He belted me round the ear.*

bench *noun* 1 a long wooden seat that two or more people can sit on. 2 a table that people put things on when they work. *A work bench.*

A work bench is an essential piece of furniture for the do-it-yourself enthusiast.

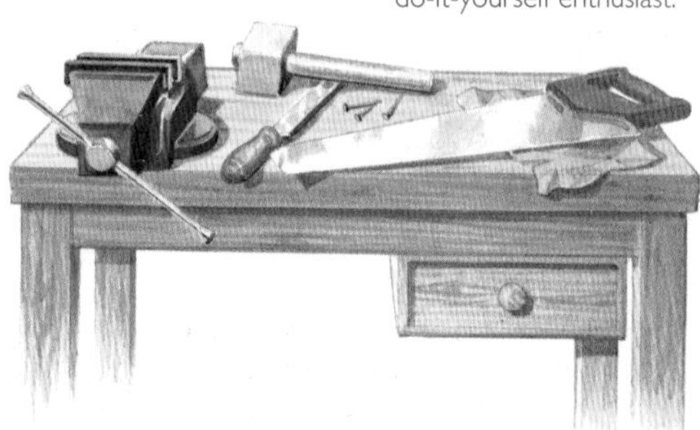

bend *verb* 1 to change the shape of something straight so that it curves or is at an angle. 2 something that bends changes direction. *The trees bend in the wind.* 3 to move the top part of your body downwards. *Ben bent down to examine the beetle.*

beneath *preposition*, *adverb* 1 under, below. *The cat was asleep all day beneath the bed.* 2 not worthy or not good enough. *The business executive thought it was beneath him to do the housework.*

benefit *noun* 1 an advantage or something that helps you. 2 money that the government pays to people who are ill, unemployed, or very poor. **benefit** (benefits, benefiting, benefited) *verb*. *She benefited from her seaside holiday and felt much better.*

Benin *noun* a country in Africa.

beret *noun* (say **bare**-ay) a soft, round, flat cap made of wool.

Berlin *noun* the capital of Germany.

Berne *noun* the capital of Switzerland.

SPELLING NOTE

Try not to confuse the spelling of the words 'berry' and 'bury', which sound exactly the same.

berry *noun* a small, round, juicy fruit with lots of seeds such as a strawberry, blackberry or gooseberry.

Blueberries, raspberries and strawberries make a lovely dessert.

berserk *adjective* **go berserk** *verb* to become violently angry.

berth *noun* 1 a bed in a ship or train. 2 a place in a port where a ship can be moored.

beside *preposition* at the side of, next to. *A house beside the sea.*

besides *adverb* as well as. *What games can you play besides rugby?*

besiege *verb* to lay siege to a place or surround it with soldiers in order to make it surrender. *The soldiers besieged the castle.*

SPELLING NOTE

Remember 'i' comes before 'e' except after 'c'. Take care with the spelling of 'besiege' (not to be confused with 'seize'), which is an exception to the 'i' before 'e' rule.

best *adjective*, *adverb* better than all the others. *The best film I've ever seen.* **best man** a friend of the bridegroom who helps him at his wedding. **best-seller** *noun* a book that sells a very large number of copies.

bet (bets, betting, bet or betted) *verb* 1 to forecast the result of a race etc. and to risk money on the result. *She bet £3 on the bay horse.* **bet** *noun* the money risked. 2 to be certain. *I bet I can swim farther than you.*

betray *verb* 1 to let somebody down and hurt them by being disloyal. *She betrayed me by giving away all my secrets.* 2 to show signs of your real feelings etc. *His face betrayed his sadness.*

better *adjective* 1 something that is better has more good about it but is not the best. 2 recovered from an illness. *When you're better you can go back to school again.*

The patient is sitting up in bed reading, so he must be getting better.

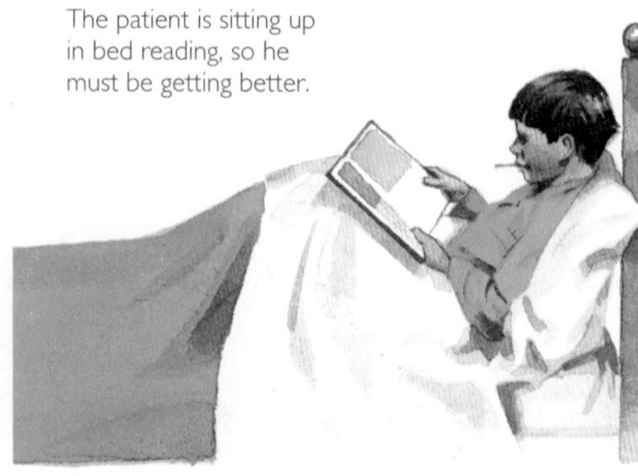

between *preposition* 1 in the space or time after one thing and before another. *Between the school and the hospital is a field where we play football between teatime and bedtime.* 2 in shares or parts. *They shared the money between them.* 3 used in comparing. *What's the difference between jam and marmalade?*

beverage *noun* a drink.

beware *interjection* be careful and look out for something dangerous. *Beware of the bull!*

Bulls can be dangerous, so beware of entering a field with a bull in it.

bewilder *verb* to confuse and worry somebody. *He was bewildered by all the street signs.* **bewildering** *adjective.*

beyond *preposition* 1 on the other side or farther than. *Don't drive beyond the crossroads.* 2 outside the limit of, past. *The camera is beyond repair.* 3 too difficult or confusing. *Algebra is quite beyond me.*

Bhutan *noun* a Himalayan country in South Asia.

bi- *prefix* two or twice. **biannual** happening twice a year. **bilateral** with two sides. **bilingual** speaking two languages.

biased *adjective* unfairly preferring one side to another, prejudiced. *She's biased against all foreigners.* **bias** *noun.*

bib *noun* a cloth or piece of plastic tied under a child's chin to protect its clothes when it is eating.

Bible *noun* A sacred book that has two main parts. First, the Old Testament, the holy book of the Jewish religion. Second, the New Testament, which, with the Old Testament, is the holy book of the Christian religion. **biblical** *adjective.*

A bicycle provides an environmentally friendly way of getting about.

AMAZING FACT

Although we have a saying, 'like a red rag to a bull', it is misleading. Bulls, like most mammals, are colour-blind.

Television is banned in mountainous Bhutan and the people are required by law to wear national costume.

WORD HISTORY

'Billabong' is an Australian aboriginal word that means 'dead river'.

bicker *verb* to quarrel continuously over unimportant things.

bicycle *noun* a two-wheeled vehicle that you ride by pushing pedals and steering with handlebars. The short form of bicycle is bike. *I love riding my new bike.*

bid (bids, bidding, bid) *verb* to offer to pay a certain amount of money for something, especially at an auction. *What am I bid for this vase?* **bid** *noun.*

bid *noun* an attempt to achieve something. *She's going all out in her bid to become ice-dance champion.*

big (bigger, biggest) *adjective* 1 large in size. *Elephants are big.* 2 important. *The big match is on today.* The opposites of 'big' are 'small' and 'unimportant'.

bigot *noun* a bigot is somebody who has strong and usually unreasonable views, which they obstinately refuse to change.

bike *noun* a bicycle or motorbike.

bill *noun* 1 a piece of paper on which is written how much you owe for something. *The gas bill.* 2 a written statement of a proposed new law to be discussed by parliament. 3 in the US, a piece of paper money. *A 10$ bill.*

bill *noun* a bird's beak.

billabong *noun* in Australia, a pool of water that is left when a river has run dry.

billiards *noun* a game played with balls and long sticks (cues) on a cloth-covered table with pockets along the sides and at the corners. *Let's have a game of billiards.*

billion *noun* 1 in North America and now generally in UK, a thousand million. 2 previously in UK, a million million.

billygoat *noun* a male goat.

bin *noun* a container. *A rubbish bin.*

B

binary *adjective* consisting of two parts. **binary system** *noun* a number system used in computers in which only two numbers, 0 and 1, are used.

bind (binds, binding, bound) *verb* 1 to tie or fasten together. *He bound the magazines into a bundle with string.* 2 to wrap. *She bound the bruise with a bandage.* 3 to join the pages of a book together and put a cover or binding on it.

binder *noun* a stiff cover or folder for holding papers.

binoculars *plural noun* an instrument with lenses you look through to make distant things seem closer.

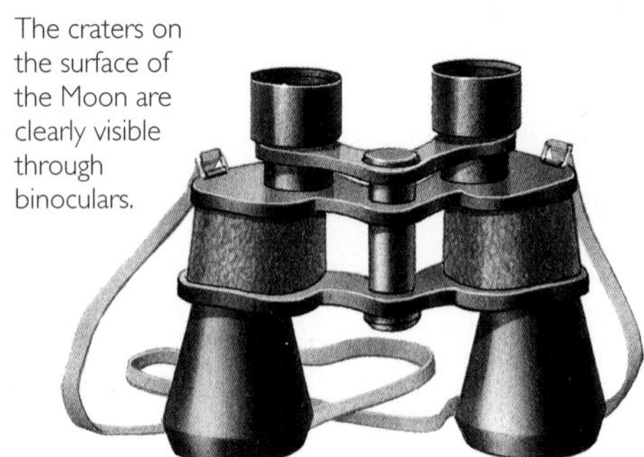

The craters on the surface of the Moon are clearly visible through binoculars.

biodegradable *adjective* Things that are biodegradable decay naturally. *Paper is biodegradable.*

biography *noun* the story of somebody's life written by somebody else. **biographical** *adjective*. **biographer** *noun* someone who writes a biography.

biologist *noun* a person who studies biology. *The biologist examined the newt.*

biology *noun* the scientific study of living things. *Human biology.* **biological** *adjective*. **biological warfare** the use of germs as weapons in warfare.

biped *noun* an animal with two feet. *Birds and humans are bipeds.*

biplane *noun* an aeroplane with two sets of wings. *The biplane looped the loop.*

bird *noun* a creature that is covered with feathers, has two legs, two wings and a beak. All female birds lay eggs and most birds can fly. **bird of prey** any bird that kills other birds and small animals for food. *Eagles are birds of prey.* **bird-watcher** *noun* a person who studies birds.

The toucan is a bird that lives in the rainforests of South America.

WORD HISTORY

The word 'biscuit' – a French word – means 'twice cooked' – from the two Latin words 'bis coctus'. Remember the 'u' in the spelling.

WORD HISTORY

The prefix 'bio–' in words like 'biology', 'biography' and 'biopsy' comes from the Greek word 'bios', meaning 'life'.

birth *noun* being born, the beginning of anything. *The birth of the universe.*

birth control *noun* ways of preventing a woman becoming pregnant.

birthday *noun* the anniversary or day each year when you celebrate the day you were born. *Birthday cake.*

biscuit *noun* a crisp, flat cake.

bisect *verb* to divide into two equal parts.

Bishkek *noun* the capital of Kyrgyzstan.

bishop *noun* 1 a high-ranking priest in some Christian churches, in charge of a diocese or group of churches. 2 a chesspiece in the shape of a bishop's mitre (hat).

bison *noun* (*plural* bison) a wild ox (the buffalo of North America).

The bison has been saved from extinction and lives in protected wildlife parks in America.

Bissau *noun* the capital of Guinea-Bissau.

bit *noun* a very small piece.

bit *noun* the metal bar part of a bridle that fits into a horse's mouth.

bit *noun* the smallest unit of information, expressed in binary numbers, in a computer.

bitch *noun* a female dog.

bite (biting, bit, bitten) *verb* 1 to grasp and cut through something with your teeth. 2 to sting. *The gnats have bitten me.* **bite** *noun*. *The insect bite has left a red mark.*

bitter *adjective* 1 having a sharp, nasty taste. *Bitter medicine.* 2 angry and full of hatred. *Bitter enemies.* 3 very cold. *We expect bitter weather in the winter months.*

bizarre *adjective* strange and unusual.

black *adjective* the darkest of colours. *A black cat is thought to bring good luck.* **Black** *noun* a person with black skin.

blackberry *noun* the fruit of a wild, prickly bush called a bramble.

blackbird *noun* a common European songbird.

blackboard *noun* a large board painted in a dark colour for writing on with chalk.

A cat is drawn in white chalk on this child's blackboard.

blackbox *noun* an electronic machine on an aircraft that automatically records details of the flight.

blacken *verb* to make or become black. *Soot from the fire has blackened the bricks.*

blackmail *noun* the crime of trying to get money from somebody by threatening to reveal a secret. **blackmail** *verb. He was arrested for blackmail.* **blackmailer** *noun.*

blacksmith *noun* a person who makes things out of metal, including horseshoes.

bladder *noun* a bag-like organ in your body where urine collects until it leaves your body.

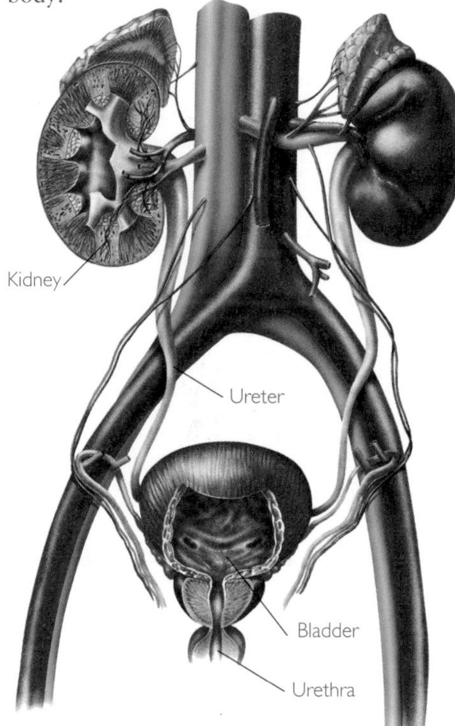

Urine leaves the bladder through the urethra when a circle of muscle relaxes to open the entrance to the tube.

blade *noun* 1 the sharp part of an axe, knife, sword etc. 2 a narrow leaf. *A blade of grass.* 3 the flat, thin parts of oars, propellers etc.

WORD HISTORY

The 'mail' in 'blackmail' is a Scottish word meaning 'payment', 'tax' or 'tribute'. Blackmail was the tribute in money, corn or cattle demanded by rebel chiefs in the 16th century in return for their protection.

blame *verb* to say that somebody has done something wrong and that it is their fault. *She blamed me for spilling the paint all over the sofa.* **blame** *noun. My sister took the blame.* **blameless** *adjective.*

blank *adjective* 1 unmarked, with nothing on it. *A book of blank pages.* 2 empty. *My mind went blank.*

blanket *noun* 1 a thick warm covering for a bed. 2 any sort of covering. *A thick blanket of snow lay over the fields.*

blare *verb* to make a loud, harsh, unpleasant noise. *The taxi horn blared.*

blaspheme *verb* (say blass-**feem**) to speak without respect about God and holy things. To swear. **blasphemy** *noun.* **blasphemous** *adjective.*

blast *noun* 1 a sudden strong gust of air or wind. 2 a sudden loud noise, especially the noise of an explosion. *He gave a deafening blast on the trumpet.*

blast-off *noun* the moment when a rocket or spacecraft takes off. **blast off** *verb.*

It is always a thrilling moment when a rocket blasts off the launchpad.

blaze *noun* a very bright light or fire. *The blaze of the headlights.* **blaze** *verb* to give off bright light. *The fire is blazing.*

blazer *noun* a jacket, often coloured with a badge on it, and part of a school uniform.

bleach *noun* a strong chemical liquid used to kill germs and to make things such as cloth white. **bleach** *verb* to make white. *He bleached his grey shirt.*

bleak *noun* 1 cold, bare and miserable. *The moor is windswept and bleak.* 2 not very hopeful. *Bleak prospects.*

bleat *verb* to make a noise like a sheep or goat. *Stop bleating about how terribly hungry you are.* **bleat** *noun.*

bleed (bleeds, bleeding, bled) *verb* to lose blood. *A bleeding nose.*

blend *verb* 1 to mix things together. *He blended the ingredients into a smooth paste.* 2 When things like colours or sounds come together in a pleasing way, they blend. **blend** *noun. A nice blend of coffee.*

bless (blesses, blessing, blessed *or* blest) *verb* to ask God to protect someone or something from harm.

blew past tense of blow.

B

blind *adjective* not able to see. *Guide dogs for the blind.* **blindness** *noun.*

blind *noun* a screen or covering for a window. *Pull up the blind to let in the sun.*

A venetian blind is made up of slats that tilt to allow more or less light into a room.

blindfold *noun* a piece of cloth tied over someone's eyes. **blindfold** *verb.*

blink *verb* to close and open your eyes again very quickly. *He blinked in the bright light.*

blinkers *plural noun* leather flaps placed at the side of a horse's eyes so that it can only see forwards.

blister *noun* a sore swelling like a bubble on your skin, filled with liquid, caused by a burn or by rubbing. *A blood blister.*

blizzard *noun* a heavy snowstorm with strong winds. *They were lost in the blizzard.*

block *verb* to be in the way of, or put something in the way of so that nothing can pass. *A broken-down tractor blocked the road and stopped us from getting home.*

block *noun* 1 a lump or solid piece of something with flat sides like a block of wood. 2 a large building or group of buildings. *A block of flats.*

blockade *verb* to isolate or cut off a place and stop supplies getting through.

blockage *noun* something in, e.g. a pipe, that stops anything passing through.

blond *adjective* having fair hair (of a boy or man).

blonde *adjective* having fair hair (of a girl or woman).

blood *noun* the red liquid that flows around inside the bodies of humans and animals.

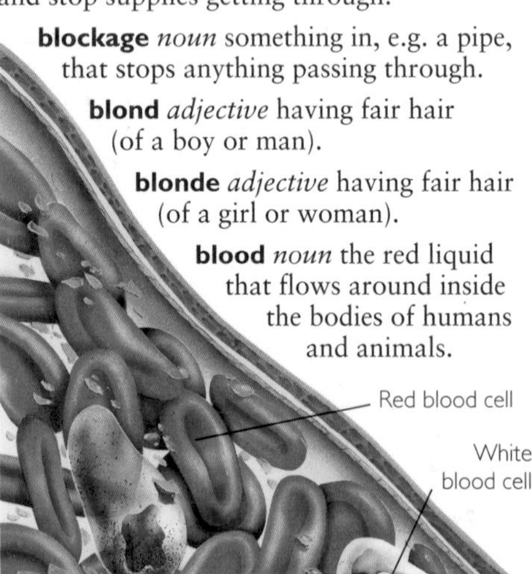

DID YOU KNOW

In Australia and New Zealand a 'block' is also a plot of land or settlement. And 'to do your block' means to get very angry.

AMAZING FACT

Wind blows when some air masses are warmer than others.

Each drop of your blood contains up to 5 million red blood cells that give blood its colour.

blood-curdling *adjective* terrifying.

blood donor *noun* a person who gives some blood to be stored in a blood bank to be given to others in operations etc.

bloodhound *noun* a large dog with a keen sense of smell.

bloodshed *noun* the loss or spilling of blood in war etc.

blood-thirsty *adjective* keen for violence or killing. *A bloodthirsty film.*

blood vessel *noun* one of the tubes in your body that blood flows along.

bloom *noun* a flower. **bloom** *verb. The roses are blooming.*

The bright red blooms of the poppy are very short-lived.

blossom *noun* the flowers that grow on trees in spring. **blossom** *verb* 1 to grow blossom. 2 to grow and improve. *The girl blossomed into a beautiful woman.*

blot *noun* 1 a mark or spot made by a spilled drop of ink or paint. 2 a stain or fault that spoils something. **blot** *verb.*

blouse *noun* a loose shirt, usually worn by girls and women.

blow (blows, blowing, blew, blown) *verb* 1 to push air quickly through your mouth. 2 to move about in or be moved by the wind. *The wind blew the gate shut.* **blow over** to pass or become forgotten. *The fuss will soon blow over.* **blow up** 1 to destroy with an explosion. *Guy Fawkes tried to blow up the Houses of Parliament.* 2 to enlarge. *She blew up the photo.*

It used to be thought that the winds had personalities, both kind and unkind.

B

blow *noun* 1 a hard hit. *A blow to the head.* 2 a cause of unhappiness or disappointment. *Her dad's death was a terrible blow.*

blubber *noun* the fat from whales.

blubber or **blub** *verb* to cry.

blue *noun* the pure colour of a cloudless sky. **blue** *adjective* 1 of the colour blue. 2 sad and miserable. **out of the blue** suddenly. *The money arrived out of the blue.*

The blue hamlet is one of the world's most beautiful fish.

blues *noun* a slow, sad kind of jazz.

blunder *noun* a bad and stupid mistake. **blunder** *verb* to stumble or make a clumsy mistake. *He blundered into the room.*

blunt *adjective* 1 not sharp. *A blunt knife.* 2 plain and to the point. *The language my father used was very blunt.*

blur (blurs, blurring, blurred) *verb* to make something indistinct or less clear. To smear. *The photograph is very blurred.* **blur** *noun* a smear, something that is unclear. *In my memory, the accident is all a blur.*

The sign is blurred. It is not shown in clear focus.

blurb *noun* a publisher's description praising a book.

blurt out *verb* to say something suddenly and without thinking.

blush *verb* to go red in the face, usually because you are shy, embarrassed or ashamed.

boa constrictor *noun* a large South American snake that crushes its prey to death by winding its body around it.

boar *noun* 1 a male pig. 2 a wild pig.

board *noun* 1 a plank or long flat piece of wood or card. 2 a piece of wood or card used for playing games etc. *A chess board.* 3 a group of people who manage an organization. *The company's board of directors met to discuss the merger.*

DID YOU KNOW

The words 'blush' and 'flush' mean 'to go red in the face'. People blush because they are embarrassed or out of shame or guilt. People who flush may be angry or may have had too much alcohol to drink!

board *verb* to get on an aircraft, ship or train. *We got on board ship and set sail.*

boarding school *noun* a school where pupils eat and sleep.

boast *verb* to talk proudly about what you possess and how good and clever you think you are in order to impress people, to brag. **boast** *noun.* **boastful** *adjective.*

boat *noun* a small vessel for carrying people and things on water. **in the same boat** in the same difficult or unpleasant situation.

A fishing boat is called a trawler. Its nets trawl deep waters to catch fish.

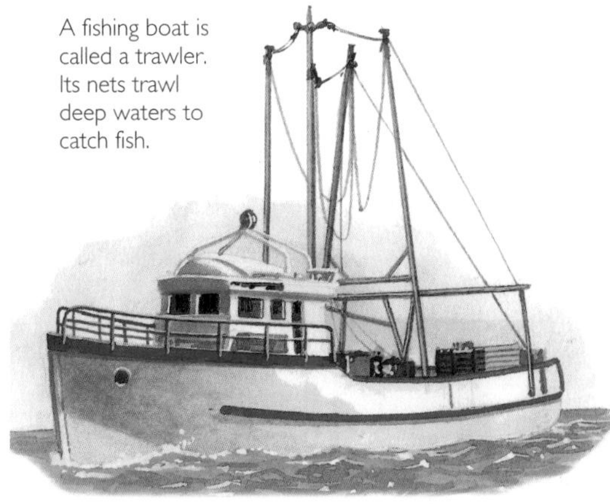

body *noun* 1 all the physical parts of a person or animal, both inside and outside. 2 the main part of a body without the limbs. 3 a dead body, a corpse. 4 the main part of something. 5 a group of people. **bodily** *adjective.*

bodyguard *noun* a person or group of people who protects someone.

bog *noun* soft, wet ground. A marsh.

bogged down *adjective* stuck and unable to make progress. *Bogged down with work.* **bog down** *verb.*

The body moves by means of its muscles. The body has about 650 muscles, and they work in pairs.

Bogota *noun* the capital of Colombia.

bogus *adjective* false, not genuine.

boil *verb* 1 When a liquid boils, it becomes so hot that it bubbles and steams. 2 to cook food in boiling water. *He prefers to eat boiled beef and carrots, like his mother used to make.* **boiling point** the temperature at which a liquid boils.

The pan of boiling water is steaming up the mirror.

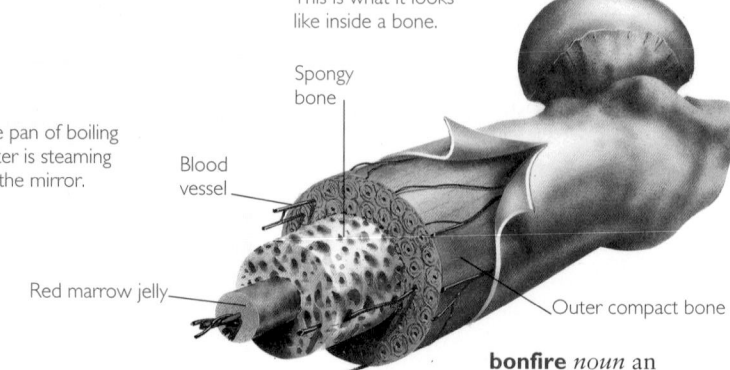

boil *noun* a red, painful lump under your skin. *He had horrible boils all over his face.*

boisterous *adjective* noisy, cheerful and lively. *The children were too boisterous.*

bold *adjective* 1 showing no fear, brave. 2 clear, easy to see and impressive. *Bold lettering.* **boldness** *noun.*

Bolivia *noun* a country in South America.

bollard *noun* a short, thick post in a road to keep traffic away from the area.

bolt *noun* 1 a metal bar that slides across to lock a door, window etc. **bolt** *verb. She bolted the door every night.* 2 a metal pin with a screw that fits into a part called a nut to hold things together.

The bolt screws into the nut to make a secure fastening.

bolt *verb* 1 to run away suddenly. *The horses bolted.* 2 to eat something very quickly. *Don't bolt your food!*

bomb *noun* a weapon containing explosive chemicals that is used to destroy buildings etc. **bomb** *verb. Coventry was badly bombed in the war.* **bombshell** *noun* a surprise. *The news that she had been chosen for the job came as a bombshell.*

bombard *verb* 1 to attack with gunfire. 2 to attack or overwhelm. *They bombarded the chairman with difficult questions, but he was unable to give satisfactory answers.*

WORD HISTORY

In the Middle Ages a 'bonfire' was a 'bone fire'. Burning bones as a source of fuel was quite common until the beginning of the 19th century.

bone *noun* any of the hard, white pieces forming the skeleton of a person or animal. **bone idle** very lazy.

This is what it looks like inside a bone.

Spongy bone

Blood vessel

Red marrow jelly

Outer compact bone

bonfire *noun* an outdoor fire. *We made a massive bonfire yesterday to burn all the rubbish.*

bonnet *noun* 1 the part of a car that covers the engine (US hood). 2 a hat tied under the chin, worn by women or babies.

bonus *noun* a reward or extra payment added to your pay.

bony (bonier, boniest) *adjective* 1 thin and with little flesh. *A bony cow.* 2 having large bones. 3 full of bones. *This fish is very bony.*

book *noun* a set of pages, usually printed, bound together in a cover. *A leather-bound book of poems.*

book *verb* to reserve or arrange a place in a theatre, hotel, airline etc. before you need it. *Let's book up to go to Spain.* **booking** *noun.*

bookcase *noun* a piece of furniture with shelves for books.

bookmaker or **bookie** *noun* a person whose job is to take bets on horses etc.

bookworm *noun* a person who likes reading books a lot.

boom *noun* 1 a deep, loud sound. *The boom of the guns.* 2 a period of sudden increase. *A boom in computer sales.*

boomerang *noun* a curved stick used by Australian aboriginals as a weapon. It is thrown at its target and returns to the thrower if it misses.

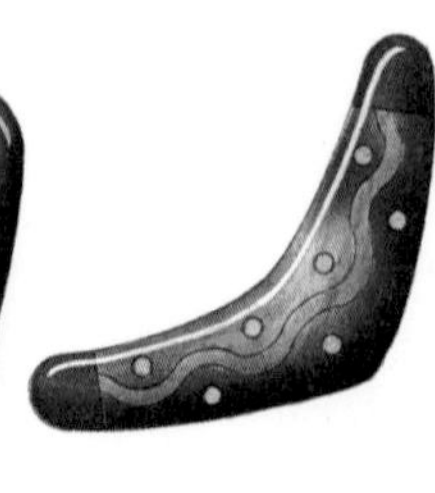

Boomerangs are often decorated by aboriginal hunters with beautiful patterns.

boost *verb* to increase, push up or encourage. *The advertisement has boosted sales considerably.* **boost** *noun.*

B

boot *noun* 1 a shoe with high sides covering the ankle and sometimes lower leg. *Cowboy boots.* 2 a place in a car where you can put luggage etc. (US trunk).

boot up *verb* to turn on a computer.

booty *noun* valuable things stolen after a battle. Plunder.

border *noun* 1 a frontier or the line along which two countries meet. **border** *verb. Canada borders the United States.* 2 a strip along an edge.

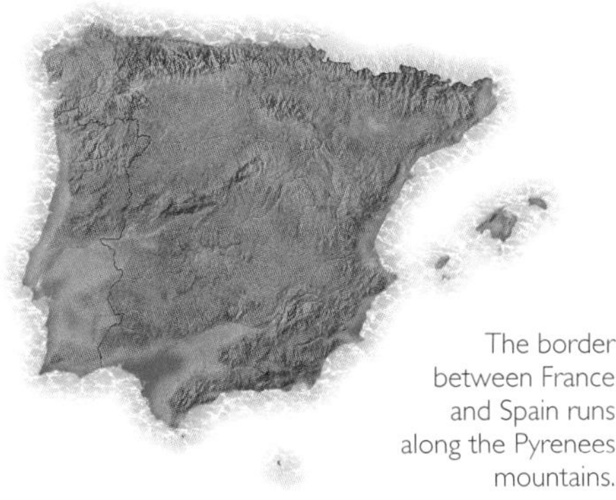

The border between France and Spain runs along the Pyrenees mountains.

bore *verb* 1 to pierce or drill a hole into something. 2 to tire through lack of interest. **boring** *adjective* dull. *What a boring book!*

bore *noun* a dull person who makes you feel weary. *The boss is a real bore.*

bore past tense of bear. *The knight bore a coat of arms on his helmet.*

boredom *noun* tiredness caused by dull or monotonous work etc.

born *verb* When people or animals are born they start a life of their own. *Mum was born in Singapore in 1970.*

borrow *verb* to take something belonging to somebody else and use it for a short time before returning it. **borrower** *noun.* The opposite of 'borrow' is 'lend'.

Bosnia-Herzegovina *noun* a country in Southeast Europe.

The flag of Bosnia-Herzegovina shows a blue shield with yellow fleurs-de-lys on a white ground.

bosom *noun* a woman's chest or breasts. **bosom friend** a very close friend.

boss *noun* a person in charge of workers. **boss** *verb* to tell people what to do.

bossy *adjective* enjoying giving orders and telling people what to do. **bossiness** *noun.*

AMAZING FACT

Many computer terms are new uses for old words like 'boot' (to start up a computer), 'mouse' (the device that is used alongside the keyboard to work on screen), and 'bookmark' (to record an Internet address on your computer).

SPELLING NOTE

Try not to confuse 'borne', past participle of the verb 'bear', with 'born', which means giving birth.

HANDY HINT

Words that sound alike but that are spelled differently – like 'bough' and 'bow' are called homophones. Be careful not to confuse them when you're writing.

botany *noun* the scientific study of plants. **botanist** *noun. She's studying to become a botanist.* **botanical** *adjective.*

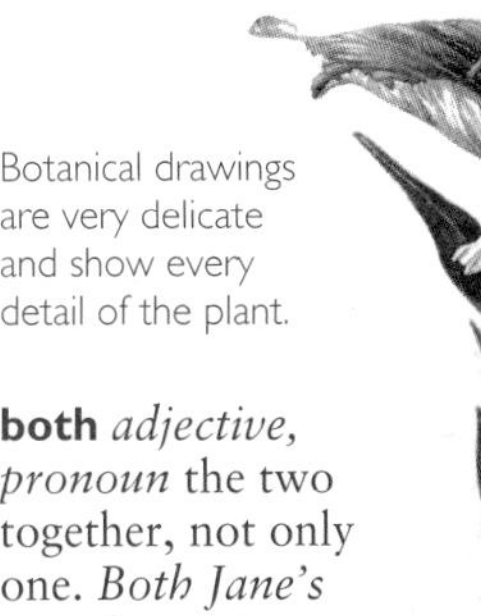

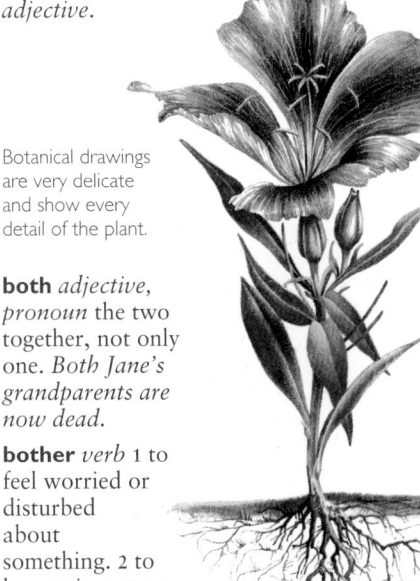

Botanical drawings are very delicate and show every detail of the plant.

both *adjective, pronoun* the two together, not only one. *Both Jane's grandparents are now dead.*

bother *verb* 1 to feel worried or disturbed about something. 2 to be a nuisance or worry somebody. **bother** *noun* nuisance. *I'm sorry to be a bother.* 3 to take care, time and trouble over something. *He can't be bothered to do his homework.*

Botswana *noun* a country in Africa.

bottle *noun* a container made of glass or plastic for holding liquid. **bottle** *verb. He bottled the delicious homemade lemonade.*

This beautiful blue glass bottle has been hand-blown. You can tell this because of irregularities in the glass.

bottleneck *noun* a place where a road becomes narrower and traffic cannot flow freely. Anything that slows down work or progress.

bottle up *verb* to keep your feelings and thoughts to yourself.

bottom *noun* 1 the lowest part or underside of something. *The bottom of the sea.* 2 the part of your body that you sit on. **get to the bottom of** *verb* to solve or explain a mystery etc. *Let's get to the bottom of the problem.*

bough *noun* (rhymes with 'how') a large branch of a tree. *An apple bough.*

bought past tense of buy.

boulder *noun* a large, round rock.

bounce *verb* to spring back after hitting something. *The ball hit the floor and bounced back.* **bounce** *noun.* **bouncy** *adjective. A bouncy castle.*

B

bound *verb* to move along by making large leaps. **bound to** certain to. *You're bound to win the competition.* **out of bounds** a place where you are not allowed to go.

boundary *noun* a line that marks an edge.

bouquet *noun* (say boo-**kay**) a gift of a bunch of flowers.

The bouquet is made up of lovely summer flowers.

bout *noun* a short period of something. *A serious bout of ill health.*

bow *noun* (rhymes with 'so') 1 a piece of wood curved by a string attached at each end, used in shooting arrows. 2 a long thin stick used for playing stringed instruments such as violins. 3 a knot with loops. *He tied his shoelaces in a neat bow.*

bow *noun* (rhymes with 'cow') the front part of a ship.

bow *verb* (rhymes with 'cow') 1 to bend your head or the top part of your body forwards. *At the end of the show the actors bowed.* 2 to give in. *They refused to bow to his unreasonable demands.*

bowels *plural noun* the intestines in the lower part of your body, which carry waste matter from your body.

bowl *noun* a deep, uncovered dish. *A sugar bowl.*

bowl *verb* to throw a ball towards the batsman in cricket. **bowl** *noun* a big hard wooden ball used in the game of bowling.

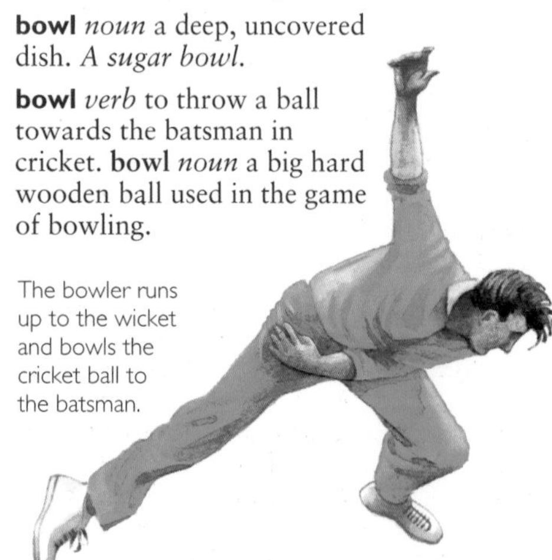

The bowler runs up to the wicket and bowls the cricket ball to the batsman.

box *noun* a wooden or cardboard container with straight sides and usually with a lid.

WORD HISTORY

Boxing Day gets its name from the boxes or gifts traditionally given on this day.

WORD HISTORY

'Boycott' is named after a British estate manager in Ireland whose tenants refused to pay unreasonable rents.

DID YOU KNOW

Braille was invented in the 19th century by a Frenchman called Louis Braille.

box *verb* to punch or fight with your fists wearing heavy leather gloves in a sport called boxing. **boxer** *noun. He is a not a heavyweight but a middleweight boxer.*

boxer *noun* a short-haired breed of dog related to the bulldog.

Boxing Day *noun* the first weekday after Christmas Day.

boy (boys) *noun* a male child. **boyhood** *noun* the childhood of a man. *In my boyhood things were different.*

boycott *verb* to refuse to have any dealings with somebody, as a protest or to bring about a change.

boyfriend *noun* 1 a girl or woman's usual and regular male friend. *She lives with her boyfriend.* 2 a gay man's partner.

bra or **brassiere** *noun* a piece of underwear that supports a woman's breasts.

brace *noun* 1 something that straightens or supports. *She wears a wire brace on her teeth.* 2 a carpenter's tool for drilling holes. 3 two things of the same kind. *A brace of pheasant.* 4 **braces** *plural noun* straps worn over the shoulders to hold up trousers.

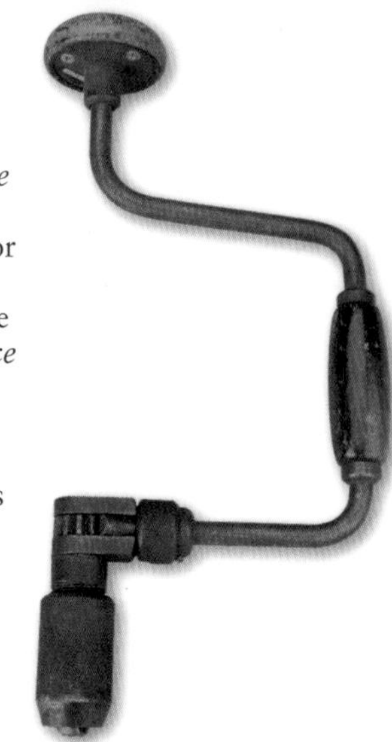

The brace gives the carpenter a good grip for drilling holes.

brace *verb* to prepare yourself for something nasty. *He braced himself to go to the dentist and have six fillings.*

bracelet *noun* an ornamental band worn around the arm or wrist.

bracing *adjective* fresh and strength-giving. *Bracing sea breezes are good for the health.*

bracket *noun* 1 a support fixed to a wall for a shelf etc. 2 **brackets** *plural noun* the signs ( ) used in writing or maths to enclose words or symbols. **bracket** *verb* to group together.

brag (brags, bragging, bragged) *verb* to boast and talk too proudly about yourself. **braggart** *noun* boaster.

braid *noun* 1 a narrow strip of decorative material used for trimming. 2 (mainly North American) a plait of hair. **braid** *verb*.

Braille *noun* a system of printing for blind people using raised dots that can be felt and read with the fingers.

B

brain *noun* the part inside your head that controls how your body works and which enables you to think and feel.

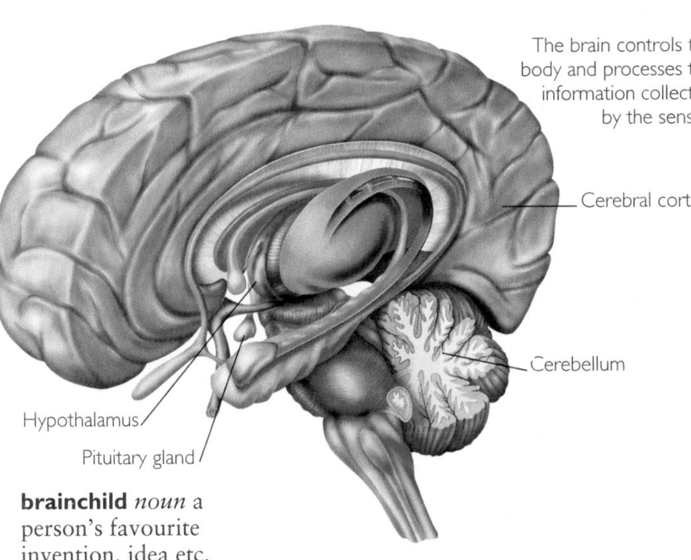

The brain controls the body and processes the information collected by the senses.

brainchild *noun* a person's favourite invention, idea etc.

brainteaser *noun* a difficult problem or puzzle. *This crossword is a real brainteaser.*

brainwave *noun* a good idea.

brainy (brainier, brainiest) *adjective* clever and intelligent. *A very brainy pupil.*

brake *noun* the part of a vehicle that you use to slow it down or to stop it. *The brakes failed and the car crashed.* **brake** *verb.*

bramble *noun* a prickly bush that blackberries grow on.

bran *noun* what is left after flour has been made from the grain of wheat, the husks or outside parts of the seed.

branch *noun* 1 a part of a tree that sticks out from the trunk. 2 a division of a group or subject. *What branch of science are you studying?* 3 a bank, office or shop belonging to a big organization. *The supermarket has branches in most towns.* **branch** *verb* to divide. *The railway line branches here.* **branch out** to strike out in a new direction. *They've branched out on their own.*

In spring, the branch sprouts new leaves.

brand *noun* a particular kind or make of goods. *An expensive brand.* **brand new** *adjective* unused and completely new.

brandy *noun* a strong alcoholic drink.

WORD HISTORY

'Brandy' is the shortened form of a Dutch word, 'brandewijn', meaning 'burnt wine'. In fact the wine was not burned but distilled over a fire.

Brasilia *noun* the capital of Brazil.

brass *noun* a yellow metal made from mixing two other metals, copper and zinc. **brass band** a group of musicians who play instruments made of brass.

Bratislava *noun* the capital of Slovakia.

brave *adjective* willing to do dangerous things and face danger, fearless. **bravery** *noun. He was awarded a medal for bravery.*

brave *noun* a Native American warrior.

brawl *noun* a rowdy quarrel or rough fight. *A drunken brawl.* **brawl** *verb.*

brawn *noun* great physical and muscular strength. **brawny** *adjective.*

bray *noun* the loud sound that a donkey makes. **bray** *verb.*

brazen *adjective* 1 made of brass. 2 without shame. *A brazen lie.*

Brazil *noun* a country in South America.

Brazilian *noun* a person from Brazil. **Brazilian** *adjective. Brazilian coffee.*

Brazzaville *noun* the capital of the Republic of the Congo.

Brazil is the largest country in South America. It has the world's greatest rainforest, the Amazon.

bread *noun* a food made from flour, water and yeast and baked in an oven. **breadwinner** the person who earns money for a family to live on.

Brown bread is healthier than white bread because it contains more roughage.

breadth *noun* how wide something is from one side to the other.

break *verb* 1 to split into pieces, to smash. *The glass fell off the table and broke.* **breakages** *plural noun* things that are broken. *All breakages must be paid for.* 2 to damage something so it does not work. *The radio is broken.* 3 to fail to keep. *He broke his promise.* **break down** 1 If a car breaks down, it stops going because something has gone wrong. 2 If somebody has a breakdown, they cry and are overcome by nervous exhaustion. **break into** to enter a building with force. **break off** to stop doing something. *They broke off for lunch.*

B

break *noun* 1 a rest. *You've worked long enough. Take a break.* 2 a sudden change. *A lucky break was well deserved.*

breaker *noun* a large wave that crashes against the rocks.

breakfast *noun* the first meal of the day. *I like a cooked breakfast.* **breakfast** *verb.*

breakthrough *noun* an important achievement or discovery.

breakwater *noun* a wall or barrier protecting a harbour or shore from the full force of waves.

breast *noun* 1 one of the two soft parts on a woman's chest that produces milk when she has had a baby, the bosom. 2 the chest.

breath *noun* the air that you draw in and let out of your lungs. **out of breath** panting. **under your breath** very quietly. *She said it under her breath so they wouldn't hear.*

breathalyser *noun* a device that the police ask a person to breathe into to find out how much alcohol is in their blood. **breathalyse** *verb. He was breathalysed by the police.*

breathe *verb* to draw air into your lungs through your nose and mouth and send it out again. *Breathe deeply and calm down.*

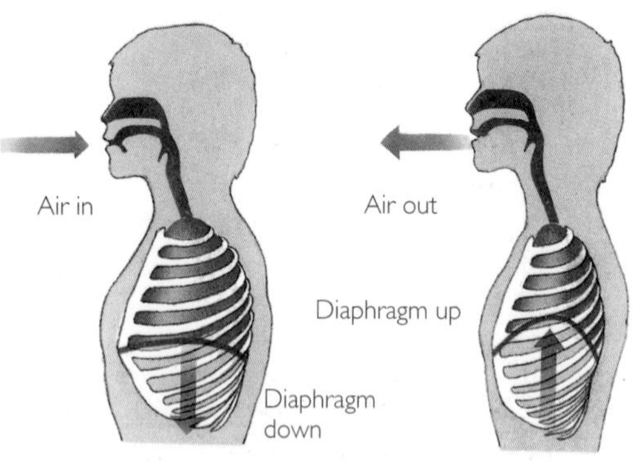

The diaphragm and the muscles between the ribs make you breathe in and out.

breed *verb* 1 to mate and produce young. 2 to raise animals to sell. *Tom and Mary breed pigs.* **breed** *noun* animals that mate and produce others of the same kind. *Bloodhounds and collies are breeds of dog.*

The collie is a very popular breed of dog.

WORD HISTORY

The 'groom' in 'bridegroom' has nothing to do with horses. It is a misspelling of an original word 'gome' that simply meant 'man'.

WORD HISTORY

'Breathalyser' is a 'blend' word made up of two words put together – 'breath' and 'analyser'. ('Motel', 'Eurovision' and 'smog' are other examples.) Note that in British English the word must always be spelt with '–yse', never '–yze'.

breeze *noun* a soft wind. **breezy** *adjective.*

brewery *noun* a place where beer is made (brewed). *Malt is delivered to the brewery.*

bribe *noun* a gift or money given to somebody to persuade them to do something unlawful or dishonest. *He gave them a bribe to keep them quiet.* **bribe** *verb.*

brick *noun* a small block of hardened clay used for building.

bride *noun* a woman who is about to get married. **bridal** *adjective.*

bridegroom *noun* a man who is about to get married. *The bridegroom is nervous.*

bridesmaid *noun* a girl or young woman who helps the bride on her wedding day.

bridge *noun* 1 a structure built over a canal, river, road etc. so that people and vehicles can cross from one side to the other. *A railway bridge.* 2 a high platform from which a ship is steered. *The captain stands on the bridge.* 3 a piece of wood that holds up the strings stretched along a violin, guitar etc. **bridge** *verb. Bridge that gap.*

A bridge carries the road across the river.

bridge *noun* a card game for four players.

Bridgetown *noun* the capital of Barbados.

bridle *noun* the leather straps that fit over a horse's head and to which the reins are attached. *The bridle is part of the tack.*

brief *adjective* lasting or taking only a short time. *A brief encounter.*

brief *verb* to give instructions, information or advice. *She briefed her staff on the best tactics.* **briefing** *noun.*

briefcase *noun* a flat case for papers etc.

briefs *plural noun* short underpants or knickers. *His briefs were too tight.*

bright *adjective* 1 giving out a lot of strong light. 2 a clear, strong colour. *Bright orange.* 3 clever. *A bright student.* **brightness** *noun. The brightness of the Sun.* The opposite of 'bright' is 'dull' or 'dim' or 'dark'.

brighten *verb* to make or become brighter.

brilliant *adjective* 1 shining very brightly. *Brilliant stars.* 2 very clever or able. *A brilliant dancer.* **brilliance** *noun.*

The dancers wear brilliant flowers round their necks, heads and ankles.

brim *noun* 1 the top of a container. *The glass is full to the brim.* 2 the part of a hat that sticks out.

brine *noun* salty water.

bring (brings, bringing, brought) *verb* 1 to carry something or to take somebody with you. *Can you bring your CDs when you come?* 2 to cause or start something happening. *The sad story brought tears to his eyes.* **bring back** to cause to return. *Bring back the old days.* **bring up** 1 to look after and educate a child. 2 to mention a subject. *Don't bring up the War.*

brink *noun* the edge of a steep place such as a cliff.

brisk *adjective* 1 lively and efficient. *Brisk manner.* 2 fast. *A brisk walk by the sea.*

bristle *noun* a short, stiff hair on an animal or on a man's unshaven face. **bristly** *adjective.*

British *adjective* relating to Great Britain and its people.

brittle *adjective* hard and easily broken. *Brittle twigs.*

broad *adjective* (rhymes with 'lord') measuring a lot from one side to the other, wide. **broaden** *verb* to make wider. *They are going to broaden the road.*

broadcast (broadcasts, broadcasting, broadcast) *verb* to send out a programme by radio or television. **broadcast** *noun.*

When a television programme is broadcast, the signal leaves the studios and is sent via a transmitter to a satellite in space. The satellite beams the signal to a receiver on your house and into your television set.

DID YOU KNOW

'Britain' is an abbreviation of 'Great Britain', a country made up of England, Scotland and Wales. The United Kingdom is correctly called the United Kingdom of Great Britain and Northern Ireland. The two kingdoms that united were those of England (and Wales) and Scotland.

broad-minded *adjective* tolerant and accepting opinions and behaviour that you may not agree with.

broccoli *noun* a vegetable like a cauliflower with a green stalk and small green flowerheads. *Broccoli is very good for you.*

brochure *noun* a pamphlet or small book containing information.

broke, broken past and past participle of break.

bronchitis *noun* an illness of the lungs that makes you cough a lot.

bronco *noun* (US) a wild or half-tamed pony. *The bucking bronco threw off the cowboy who was trying to break him in.*

bronze *noun* a reddish-brown metal made by mixing copper and tin. **bronze** *adjective.*

Bronze Age *noun* a time in history when people made tools of bronze.

These urns were made by people who lived in the Bronze Age.

brooch *noun* (rhymes with 'poach') an ornament that you can pin to your clothes.

brood *noun* a family of young birds hatched at the same time. *The mother hen sat on her brood of chicks.* **brood** *verb* 1 to sit on eggs to hatch them. 2 to worry about things for a long time. *Helen was brooding over her poor examination results.*

brook *noun* a small stream. *The brook rushed down the mountainside.*

broom *noun* a large brush with a long handle for sweeping floors. *A new broom sweeps away old problems.*

broth *noun* a thin soup containing vegetables and barley. *The doctor recommended a good thick broth.*

brother *noun* a boy or man who has the same parents as you. A half-brother has only one parent the same as you. **brotherly** *adjective. Brotherly love.*

brother-in-law *noun* the brother of a person's husband or wife.

brought past tense of bring.

B

brow *noun* 1 the part of your face between your eyes and the top of your head, forehead. 2 the arch of hair over each eye, eyebrow. 3 the top of a hill.

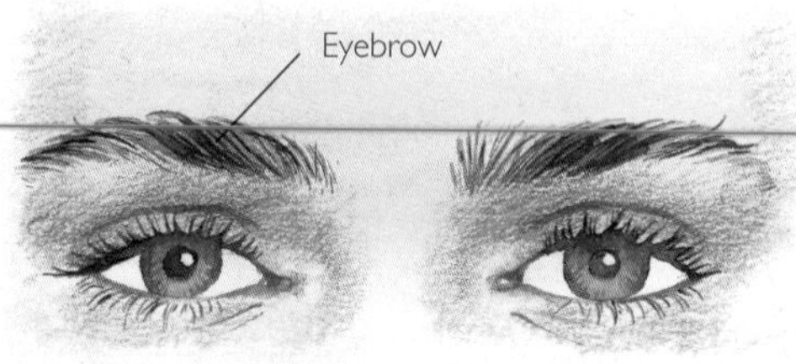

Eyebrows protect the eyes from sweat running into them down the brow.

brown *noun, adjective* the colour of wood or chocolate. *As brown as a nut.*

browned off *adjective* bored.

browse *verb* to glance at things such as books or goods in a shop in a casual way. *He browsed through the catalogues.* **browser** *noun.*

bruise *noun* a bluish-black mark on your skin caused by a knock. **bruise** *verb. She bruised her knee when she fell.*

Brunei *noun* a country on the island of Borneo, in Southeast Asia.

The flag of Brunei has a red crest on a yellow, black and white ground.

brush *noun* a tool with stiff hairs called bristles used for sweeping, painting etc. *A hairbrush.* **brush** *verb* 1 to use a brush. *He brushed the floor.* 2 to touch gently while passing. *The cat brushed against her legs.*

Brussels *noun* the capital of Belgium.

brutal *adjective* cruel, violent and without feeling. **brutality** *noun.*

brute *noun* 1 a cruel person. 2 a wild, savage animal.

bubble *noun* a thin ball of liquid filled with air or gas, especially one that floats. *A soap bubble.* **bubble** *verb. The water is bubbling on the stove.* **bubbly** *adjective. Bubbly lemonade.*

buccaneer *noun* an old word for pirate.

The buccaneers boarded the ship wielding their daggers. Then they took all the valuables on board.

SPELLING NOTE

Be careful with the spelling of 'Buddha' and 'Buddhism' and note the double 'd' and the position of the 'h'. The word 'Buddha' means 'the enlightened one'.

Bucharest *noun* the capital of Romania.

buck *noun* 1 a male deer or rabbit. 2 (slang) a dollar. *That will cost you several bucks.*

buck *verb* When a horse bucks it leaps into the air with its head down.

bucket *noun* a container with a handle for carrying water etc.

buckle *noun* a metal fastener for joining the ends of a belt. **buckle** *verb.*

bud *noun* a small, round swelling on a plant that will grow into a leaf or flower. **bud** *verb. The trees are starting to bud.* **budding** *adjective.* **nip in the bud** *expression* to deal with a problem etc. while it is still small.

Budapest *noun* the capital of Hungary.

Buddhism *noun* the religion founded by the Buddha in the 500s BC. **Buddhist** *adjective, noun. Buddhist monks.*

The young Buddhist monks are praying in the temple. Their heads are shaved and they wear robes dyed with saffron, a valuable crocus flower.

budge *verb* to move a little.

budgerigar *noun* a small, parrot-like bird, often kept as a pet.

budget *noun* a plan of how money should be spent. **budget** *verb.*

Buenos Aires *noun* the capital of Argentina.

buff *noun* 1 a dull yellow colour. 2 (slang) a person who knows a lot about a subject. *A cricket buff.*

buffalo *noun* 1 one of a variety of wild oxen from Asia and Africa with long curved horns. 2 a North American bison.

buffet *noun* (say **buh**-fay) a meal set out on a table from which guests help themselves.

B

bug *noun* 1 an insect, especially an unpleasant one. *Bed bugs.* 2 a germ causing a minor illness. *A tummy bug.* 3 a fault in a computer program. 4 a hidden microphone that records conversations.

bugle *noun* a brass musical instrument like a small trumpet used mainly in the armed forces. **bugler** *noun.*

build (builds, building, built) *verb* to make something by joining different pieces together. *The house that Jack built.*

The truck is at the building site, pouring concrete into the foundations

build *noun* the shape and size of a person. *A woman of slender build.*

builder *noun* a person who earns a living by putting up buildings.

building *noun* a construction such as a house or supermarket with walls and a roof.

built-up *adjective* A built-up area is covered with houses, shops and other buildings.

Bujumbura *noun* the capital of Burundi.

bulb *noun* 1 the roundish part of plants like daffodils and tulips from which the flowers grow. 2 (or **light bulb**) the pear-shaped glass part of an electric lamp that gives the light.

The pressure of the electric current through the bulb's thin wire filament makes it glow.

Wire filament

Bulgaria *noun* a country in eastern Europe.

bulge *verb* to swell or stick out. *His sack was bulging with presents.*

DID YOU KNOW

The expression 'like a bull in a china shop' means to behave in a rough, coarse and clumsy way, likely to cause damage.

AMAZING FACT

Early buildings were made from the materials that were most readily available. In Europe, houses were made of woven branches filled with mud. Other cultures used birchbark laid over poles or sometimes animal hides over bones.

bulk *noun* 1 great in size. 2 most of. *The bulk of the work has been done.* **bulky** *adjective. A bulky package.*

bull *noun* a male cow, elephant, seal or whale. *A bull elephant has huge tusks.*

bulldog *noun* a strong, fearless breed of dog. *The fierce bulldog bit the postman.*

bulldozer *noun* a powerful vehicle with a big metal blade in front for moving earth and clearing land.

A bulldozer clears up after logging in a sustainable plantation.

bullet *noun* the small pointed piece of metal that is fired from a gun.

bullion *noun* large bars of gold or silver.

bull's eye *noun* the small round centre of a target. *Peter hits the bull's eye every time.*

bully *noun* somebody who tries to frighten or hurt a weaker or smaller person. **bully** *verb. The bully was expelled from school.*

bump *verb* to collide or knock into something. *Things that go bump in the night.* **bump** *noun.* **bump into** to meet accidentally. *I bumped into Adam.*

bump *noun.* a round lump caused by something hitting you. **bumpy** *adjective. A very bumpy road.*

bumper *noun* a bar fixed to the front and back of a motor vehicle to protect it from bumps. (US) fender.

bumptious *adjective* A bumptious person is full of self-importance.

bun *noun* 1 a small, round cake. 2 a round coil of hair at the back of a woman's head.

Buns are made of white flour and sugar and may be iced.

B

bunch *noun* 1 a group of things of the same kind tied or joined together. *An enormous bunch of keys.* 2 a group of people. *A nice bunch of kids.* **bunch** *verb.*

bundle *noun* a number of things tied loosely together or wrapped in a cloth. *A bundle of old newspapers.* **bundle** *verb* 1 to tie up loosely. 2 to push or hurry away. *The children were bundled into the bus.*

A bundle of towels was tied together with a blue ribbon.

bungalow *noun* a house with all the rooms on the ground floor.

bungee jumping *noun* a sport in which a person jumps from a great height with elastic ropes tied to their legs to stop them hitting the ground.

bungle *verb* to do something awkwardly and badly. **bungler** *noun.*

bunk *noun* 1 a narrow bed attached to a wall on a ship, train etc. 2 **bunkbeds** a bed that has one or more beds above or below it. *The children slept in bunkbeds.*

bunny *noun* a child's name for a rabbit.

buoy *noun* a floating, anchored marker in the sea that warns ships of danger etc.

buoyant *adjective* 1 able to float. 2 A buoyant person is cheerful.

The life jacket saved his life by keeping him buoyant.

burden *noun* 1 a heavy load. 2 something that is difficult to carry or put up with. *The responsibility is a great burden to him.* **burden** *verb.*

burglar *noun* a person who breaks into a building to steal things. **burglary** *noun.* **burgle** *verb.*

WORD HISTORY

'Bungalow' comes from a Hindi word 'bangla', meaning 'a house in the style of Bengal', a region in Northeast India where thatched, single-storey houses are common.

burial *noun* the act of putting a dead body in a grave. *The burial was a sad affair.*

Burkina Faso *noun* a country in Africa.

The flag of Burkina Faso has a gold star on a red and green ground.

burn (burns, burning, burned or burnt) *verb* 1 to set fire to something. To be destroyed by fire. *He burnt the rubbish.* 2 to hurt or damage with fire. *He burnt his hand very badly while cooking.* **burn** *noun. She has a nasty burn right across her face.*

burp *verb* to let wind from your stomach come noisily out of your mouth, to belch. **burp** *noun. He let out a loud burp.*

burrow *noun* a hole made in the ground by an animal as a shelter. **burrow** *verb* to dig or make a tunnel. *Lots of rabbits have been burrowing in the field.*

burst (burst, bursting, burst) *verb* to explode. To break apart suddenly. *The balloons burst in the heat.* **burst into** *He burst into the room. She burst into tears.*

Burundi *noun* a country in Africa.

bury (buries, burying, buried) *verb* 1 to put a dead body or thing in the ground. *The dog buried its bone in the garden.* 2 to hide. *He wept and buried his head in his hands.*

bus *noun* a large road vehicle for carrying a lot of passengers.

bush *noun* a shrub or large plant like a small tree with many branches. **bushy** *adjective. Bushy eyebrows.* **the bush** wild, uncultivated land, especially in Australia. **bushman** a native of the African bush. **bushranger** an outlaw living wild in the Australian outback or bush.

The burning bush threw out such a lot of light that the shepherd was blinded.

B

business *noun* (say **biz**-ness) 1 buying and selling goods and services. The company or organization that makes, buys or sells things. *Business is very good at the moment.* 2 concerns, events or situations in general. *What she did is none of your business.*

businesslike *adjective* efficient, methodical.

businessman, businesswoman a man or woman who works in a business or who owns a business.

busker *noun* a singer, musician etc. who performs in the street for money. **busk** *verb.*

bust *noun* 1 a statue of a person's head and the top part of the chest. 2 a woman's breasts. *What is your bust size?*

This bust of William Lyon Mackenzie can be seen in Queen's Park, Toronto, Canada.

bust *adjective* (slang) 1 broken. *The television is bust.* 2 bankrupt. *The haulage company has gone bust.*

bustle *verb* to hurry because you are busy. *He bustled about putting things away.* **bustle** *noun. The bustle of the supermarket.*

busy (busier, busiest) *adjective* 1 If you are busy, you have a lot to do. *I'm too busy to see you today.* 2 full of people or activity. *A busy office.* **busily** *adverb.* **busybody** *noun* a person who interferes with other people's business and gives unwanted advice.

butcher *noun* a person who cuts up meat and sells it.

butler *noun* the chief male servant in a house. *The butler's pantry.*

butt *verb* to push or hit with the head or horns like a bull or goat, to ram. **butt in** to interrupt. *Don't butt in when I'm talking.*

butt *noun* 1 a large barrel. 2 the thick end or handle of a gun etc. 3 the end of a finished cigarette. 4 a person that others joke about or criticize. *I am the butt of all his jokes.*

butter *noun* a soft yellow food made from cream and milk. **butter** *verb. Please butter the bread and pass it to your Aunt Maud.*

AMAZING FACT

There are more than 17,000 varieties of butterfly.

Some species migrate. The monarch butterfly spends the summer months in Canada and the northern US, then flies to southern California and Mexico for the winter.

WORD HISTORY

'Butler' comes from the French 'bouteillier', a man who puts wine into bottles. The Normans brought the word to England at the time of the conquest in 1066.

buttercup *noun* a small plant with yellow petals that grows in fields.

butterfly *noun* an insect with large white or colourful wings.

The habitat of many butterflies is under threat because of urban development.

buttocks *plural noun* the fleshy parts of your body on which you sit.

button *noun* 1 a small, round thing sewn on to clothes to hold them together. 2 a small thing or device that you press to make a machine work. *Which button do I press to get this machine to start printing?*

buttress *noun* a support for an outside wall. **buttress** *verb.*

buy (buys, buying, bought) *verb* to get something by paying money for it, to purchase. *He bought a new car.*

buzz *verb* to make a low humming sound like a bee. *The buzz of many flies.*

buzzard *noun* a large bird of prey that hunts other animals for food.

A buzzard glides on a warm air current, waiting to spot its prey.

byelection *noun* a special election that is held when an MP dies or resigns.

bypass *noun* a road that takes traffic around a town etc. and not through it. **bypass** *verb.*

bystander a person who looks on at something but takes no part in it, a spectator. *The bystanders cheered loudly.*

byte *noun* a group of bits or units of information in a computer's memory.

Cc

cab *noun* 1 a taxi. 2 the front part of a lorry, train or crane in which the driver sits.

cabbage *noun* a large round vegetable with thick green leaves. *A red cabbage has purple leaves that go blue when cooked.*

cabin *noun* 1 a small wooden house. *A log cabin.* 2 a room or compartment in a ship or plane.

In Canada, a log cabin in the pine forests makes an ideal holiday home.

cabinet *noun* 1 a cupboard used for storing things in. *We keep our documents in a filing cabinet.* 2 **Cabinet** the group of senior ministers who decide on government policy.

cable *noun* 1 a thick rope of fibres or wire. 2 a bundle of wires inside a plastic casing through which electricity flows. *An electric cable.* 3 a telegram.

cable car *noun* a cabin hanging from a cable which carries people up and down a mountainside.

cable television *noun* a system in which TV programmes are sent to sets along electric cables instead of as radio waves.

cackle *verb* to laugh in a loud and nasty way. *The witch cackled as she cast her spell.*

cactus (cacti) *noun* a fleshy plant covered with spines that grows in hot countries.

cadge *verb* to get something by begging for it. *Can I cadge a lift?*

café *noun* (say **kaf**-ay) a small restaurant that serves refreshments and light meals.

cafeteria *noun* (say kaf-it-**eer**-ee-uh) a self-service restaurant.

cage *noun* a container with wires or bars in which animals or birds are kept.

Cairo *noun* the capital of Egypt.

cajole *verb* to persuade somebody into doing something by flattering them. *He cajoled her into giving him the information.*

AMAZING FACT

The forerunner of today's calculator was the abacus – invented about 5000 years ago!

SPELLING NOTE

'Café' is the French word for 'coffee' or 'coffee house' and is usually spelt with an acute accent on the 'e' (é).

cake *noun* a sweet mixture of flour, eggs and sugar baked in an oven. *I had a piece of her birthday cake.* **a piece of cake** really easy.

This gorgeous cake is layered with jam and topped with pink icing, cherries and cream.

calamity *noun* a disaster, such as losing all your money. **calamitous** *adjective.*

calcium *noun* a chemical substance found in limestone, teeth and bones.

calculate *verb* 1 to work out an amount by using numbers. *We calculated that we'd arrive at about 10 o'clock.* 2 to plan. *The ads are calculated to attract students.* **calculation** *noun.*

calculator *noun* a small electronic machine for doing sums.

calendar *noun* a list that shows the days, weeks and months of the year, so you can look up the date. Calendars also list important events in the year.

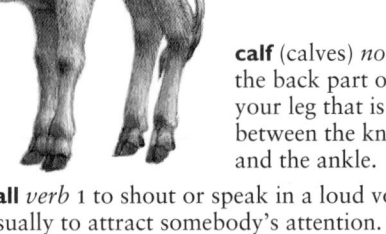

calf (calves) *noun* a young cow, elephant or whale.

A calf learns to walk in the first couple of hours after birth.

calf (calves) *noun* the back part of your leg that is between the knee and the ankle.

call *verb* 1 to shout or speak in a loud voice, usually to attract somebody's attention. 2 to tell somebody to come to you. *Why don't you come when I call you?* 3 to telephone. 4 to give a name to somebody or something. *Her brother is called John.* 5 to describe something or somebody. *I wouldn't call her fat.* 6 to get somebody to come. *We had to call the doctor.* 7 to make a short visit. 8 to wake somebody up. *Call me at seven in the morning.* **call** *noun* 1 a shout or cry. 2 a visit. 3 a telephone call. **call for** to collect somebody. *I'll call for you on my way to school.* 2 to require. *This calls for prompt action.* **call off** to stop something. *The meeting was called off.* **call out** 1 to shout. 2 to summon in an emergency. *The fire brigade was called out twice last night.* 3 to order workers to strike.

calling *noun* an occupation, especially a profession that involves helping others.

callous *adjective* not caring about other people's feelings. *His behaviour was selfish and callous.*

calm *adjective* 1 not windy. 2 When the sea is calm, it is still and without waves. 3 not excited and not showing any worry. *Please stay calm when we land.* **calm** *noun.*

calorie *noun* 1 a unit for measuring the energy that food produces. *One slice of brown bread has 95 calories, which is less than a slice of cake.* 2 a unit of heat.

calves plural of calf.

Cambodia *noun* a country in Southeast Asia.

camcorder *noun* a video camera and recorder all in one.

With a camcorder you can film family events such as weddings.

came past tense of come.

camel *noun* an animal with a long neck and one or two humps on its back. Camels are used in the desert for riding and carrying goods. *A camel train.*

camera *noun* an apparatus for taking photographs or making films and television pictures. *Smile at the camera, please!*

Cameroon *noun* a country in Africa.

camouflage *noun* (say **kam**-off-lahzh) a way of hiding things by making them blend in with their surroundings. *A polar bear's white fur is good camouflage in the snow.* **camouflage** *verb. The enemy camp was well camouflaged behind the bushes.*

camp *noun* a place where people live in tents, huts or caravans, usually for a short time. **camp** *verb* to make a camp. **camping** *noun. Scouts and guides go camping.*

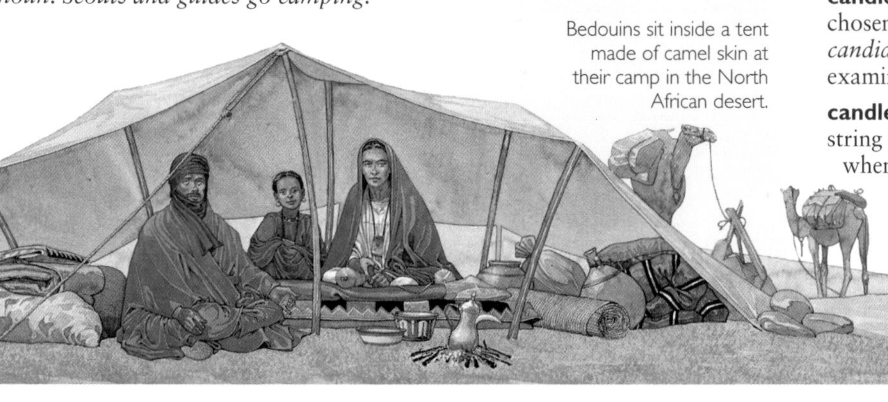

Bedouins sit inside a tent made of camel skin at their camp in the North African desert.

AMAZING FACT

Canada is the second largest country in the world.

Canada's northern lands reach deep into the frozen Arctic, but most Canadians live in the south, close to the border with America.

DID YOU KNOW

A one-humped camel is called an Arabian camel or a dromedary. The two-humped animal is a Bactrian camel.

campaign *noun* a series of planned activities to achieve a particular result. *A successful advertising campaign.* **campaign** *verb. He's campaigning for the president.*

campus *noun* the grounds of a university or college. *Most first-year students live on campus in halls of residence.*

can *noun* a metal container for holding food or drink. *A can of worms.*

can (could) *verb* 1 to be able to. *Can you carry that heavy box?* 2 to know how to do something or have the ability to do it. *She can speak German.* 3 to be allowed to do something. *The teacher says we can go home after the break.* 4 a polite way of asking somebody to do something. *Can you tell me the time?*

Canada *noun* a country in North America.

Canadian *noun* a person who comes from Canada. **Canadian** *adjective. A Canadian film.*

canal *noun* 1 a man-made waterway for boats to travel along or to bring water to an area. 2 a tube in a plant or an animal that carries food.

canary (canaries) *noun* a small yellow bird that sings.

Canberra *noun* the capital of Australia.

cancel (cancelling, cancelled) *verb* 1 to say that a planned activity will not take place. *The concert was cancelled because the singer had flu.* 2 to stop an instruction for something. *I decided not to go and cancelled the booking.* 3 to mark a ticket or stamp to stop it from being used again. When you cancel a cheque, it is no longer valid. **cancellation** *noun.* **cancel out** to balance and be equal to each other.

cancer *noun* 1 a serious disease in which abnormal growths form in the body. *Smoking can cause lung cancer.* 2 **Cancer** a sign of the zodiac (21 June to 22 July).

candid *adjective* honest. If you're candid, you tell the truth even when it is unwelcome. **candour** *noun.*

candidate *noun* 1 a person who wants to be chosen for a special position. *The Labour candidate was elected.* 2 a person taking an examination.

candle *noun* a stick of wax with a piece of string (a wick) through it, which gives light when it burns.

candlestick *noun* a holder for a candle. *Brass candlesticks.*

candy (candies) *noun* a sweet.

cane *noun* a long thin stick. Cane is the hollow stem from a plant such as bamboo. **cane** *verb* to hit with a cane.

C

cannabis *noun* 1 a kind of hemp plant. 2 a drug made from the plant.

cannibal *noun* 1 a person who eats other people. 2 an animal that eats its own kind. **cannibalism** *noun*.

cannon *noun* a big gun that fires cannon balls.

Cannons were the first guns and appeared in the early 14th century.

cannot = can not, see can. *Unfortunately we cannot come to the party.*

canoe *noun* a light, long and narrow boat that is moved by using a paddle. **canoe** *verb* to go in a canoe. **canoeing** *noun*.

can't short for cannot, see can. 'Can't' is mainly spoken rather than written.

canteen *noun* a restaurant in a factory, office, school or college.

canter *noun* the movement of a horse, faster than a trot but slower than a gallop. **canter** *verb*.

canvas *noun* 1 a strong, rough cloth used for tents, sails and bags. *We spent the night under canvas.* 2 a stretched piece of cloth on which oil paintings are done. 3 an oil painting on canvas. 4 the floor of a boxing or wrestling ring.

canvass *verb* to go to people to ask for their vote, support or opinion. *They canvassed the neighbours for support.*

canyon *noun* a deep, steep valley, usually with a river running through it.

America's Grand Canyon is regarded as one of the seven wonders of the natural world.

cap *noun* 1 a hat with a peak. 2 a lid or top on a bottle or tube. 3 a piece of paper covered with a tiny amount of explosive that makes a bang when used in a toy gun. **cap** *verb* to put a cap or top on something.

capable *adjective* having the ability to do something. **capability** *noun*.

SPELLING NOTE

Note that the cloth called canvas has one 's' at the end, while the verb asking for support has two – to canvass. The two words sound exactly the same.

AMAZING FACT

The main difference between a canoe and a kayak is that kayak paddles are double-bladed – one on each side, and canoe paddles are single-bladed.

capacity *noun* 1 the amount that can be held. *The stadium has a capacity of 30,000.* If a place is filled to capacity, it is completely full. 2 the ability to do something. *Algebra is beyond my capacity.* 3 a position. *In my capacity as head teacher.*

cape *noun* a loose cloak without sleeves and fastened at the neck.

cape *noun* a large piece of land going out into the sea. *The Cape of Good Hope is in South Africa.*

Cape Town *noun* the legal capital of South Africa.

Cape Verde *noun* a country in the Atlantic Ocean off West Africa.

The flag of Cape Verde has a circle of yellow stars on a striped red, blue and white ground.

capital *noun* 1 a city where the government of a country is. *Paris is the capital of France.* 2 a letter written or printed in a large form (A, B, C), used at the beginning of a sentence or a name. *Write your name in capitals.* 3 a sum of money used to start up a business, as well as money or property used to make more money. *He put up the capital for the new company.* **capital** *adjective*.

capitalism *noun* (say **kap**-it-ul-izm) a system in which a country's trade and industry are controlled by the owners of capital and are run for profit.

capitalist *noun* 1 a person who lends his money to businesses, to make more money. 2 a person who supports capitalism. **capitalist** *adjective*.

capital punishment *noun* punishment in which the criminal is killed.

capitulate *verb* to admit that you have lost and give in under agreed conditions. **capitulation** *noun*.

capsize *verb* to overturn in water. *The boat capsized in deep water.*

The friends wait to be rescued on top of the capsized boat.

capsule *noun* 1 a pill containing medicine. 2 the seed case of a plant. 3 the part of a spaceship that holds the crew and instruments and can be separated from the craft in space.

captain *noun* 1 the leader of a team or group. *Who's the captain of your football team?* 2 a person in command of a ship or an aircraft. 3 an officer in the army or navy. **captain** *verb* to be captain of a sports team.

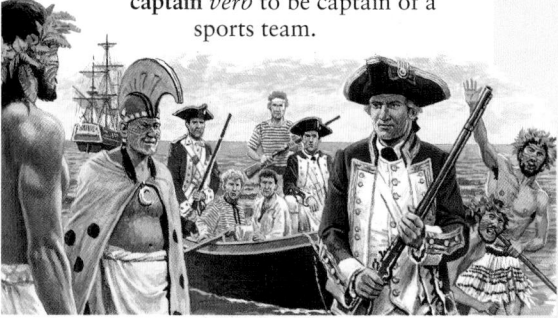

Captain James Cook and the crew of the *Endeavour* step ashore in New Zealand and meet the Maoris for the first time.

caption *noun* 1 words put with a picture to explain what it is about. 2 a heading or short title in a newspaper or magazine.

captive *noun* a person or an animal taken prisoner. If you are taken captive, you are taken as a prisoner. **captive** *adjective* kept as a prisoner. **a captive audience** a group of people who have to listen to somebody. *TV viewers are a captive audience for advertisers.* **captivity** *noun.*

capture *verb* 1 to make a person or an animal a prisoner. 2 to get something by force, skill, attraction or trickery. *Her beauty captured his heart.* 3 to put data into a computer. 4 to describe something in words or pictures. *The film captures the loneliness of old age.* **capture** *noun* 1 the act of capturing. 2 somebody or something that has been taken by force.

car *noun* 1 a car has four wheels and an engine and room for a driver and passengers. Cars drive on roads and motorways. *We usually go by car.* 2 a railway carriage. *This train has a dining car.*

Most cars have the engine at the front.

Caracas *noun* the capital of Venezuela.

carat *noun* 1 a unit for measuring the weight of precious stones such as diamonds, equal to 0.2 grams. 2 a unit for measuring gold. Pure gold is 24 carats.

caravan *noun* 1 a home on wheels in which people live or spend their holidays. Caravans are usually pulled by a car. 2 a group of people travelling across the desert.

DID YOU KNOW

The phrase 'on the cards' comes from fortune-tellers who predict the future by reading and interpreting special cards.

WORD HISTORY

The cardigan is named after the Earl of Cardigan, who led the Charge of the Light Brigade in the Crimean War in 1854.

carbon *noun* 1 a substance that is found in all living things. Diamonds and coal are made of carbon. 2 a thin piece of paper with a coloured coating on one side which is put between two sheets of paper for making copies of what is written or typed, also called carbon paper. 3 a copy made by using carbon paper, a carbon copy.

carbon dioxide *noun* a gas that is present in the air and is also formed when animals and people breathe out.

carbon monoxide *noun* a poisonous gas produced especially by car engines.

carburettor *noun* the part of a car engine in which petrol and air are mixed to provide power. *The carburettor needs replacing.*

carcass (carcasses) *noun* the body of a dead animal.

Bearded vultures gather at a carcass to feed.

card *noun* 1 a folded piece of stiff paper with a picture on the front and a message inside which you send to somebody on special occasions. *A birthday card.* 2 a piece of stiff paper for writing information on. 3 a postcard. 4 a small piece of printed plastic which you use if you have an account at a bank or a shop. *I paid with my credit card.* 5 one of a pack of 52 playing cards, used for games like whist, bridge or poker. *We played cards all afternoon.* **on the cards** likely or possible. **put your cards on the table** to make your plans known.

cardboard *noun* thick stiff paper used for making boxes. *A cardboard box.*

Cardiff *noun* the capital of Wales.

cardigan *noun* a knitted jacket that usually buttons up at the front.

care *verb* to be interested and feel that something is important. *We care about the environment.* If you don't care about something, it doesn't matter to you and you don't worry. **care** *noun* 1 serious attention, in an effort to avoid making any mistakes. *She plans her essays with great care.* 2 If you take care of somebody or something, you look after them. 3 a person or object you are responsible for. *Children in care are looked after by the authorities because their parents can't care for them.* 4 worry and sorrow. 5 **care of** (c/o *abbreviation*) written when sending a letter or parcel to somebody who is living at another address.

C

care for 1 to look after somebody or something. 2 to like a person. *Although he's nasty to her, she still cares for him.* If you care for something, you enjoy it. *I don't care for dancing.*

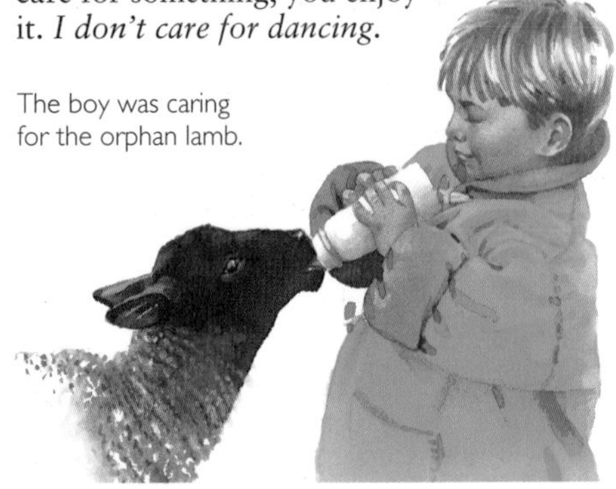

The boy was caring for the orphan lamb.

career *noun* 1 a job or profession that you do for a long time and hope to be successful in. *He's chosen a career in teaching.* 2 the development and progress through a person's working life. **career** *verb* to move very fast and in an uncontrolled way. *The car careered into a wall.*

careful *adjective* 1 paying attention to what you do in order to avoid danger or damage. *Be careful when crossing the road.* 2 done with care and thought. *A careful report.* **carefully** *adverb*. **carefulness** *noun*.

careless *adjective* 1 not paying attention or taking care about something and making mistakes. 2 thoughtless. *Careless driving costs lives.* 3 untroubled and not worried. *She's careless with money.* **carelessly** *adverb*.

caress *verb* to stroke or kiss somebody to show your love for them. **caress** *noun* a loving touch.

cargo (cargoes) *noun* goods carried in a ship or plane.

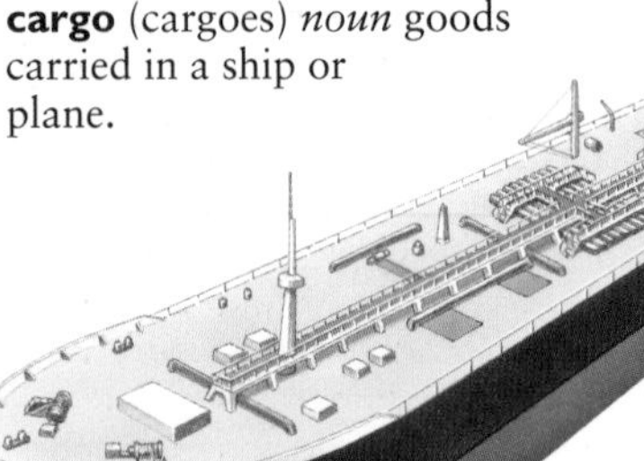

Supertankers designed to carry oil are among the world's biggest cargo ships.

caricature *noun* an amusing picture or description of somebody, so that parts of his character seem odder than they really are. **caricature** *verb* to make a caricature of a person. *He's brilliant at caricaturing all sorts of politicians.*

carnation *noun* a scented garden flower.

carnival *noun* a public festival with music, dance and processions of people in wild make-up and fancy dress.

AMAZING FACT

Carnivores generally have very good hearing and eyesight, a keen sense of smell and are able to move fast enough to hunt and catch their prey.

In the 18th century Russians travelled the snowy roads in sledge carriages drawn by a team of horses.

WORD BUILDING

The suffix '-ful' means full of. It is usually spelt with just one 'l'. 'Careful' means full of care or taking care. The suffix '-less' means without, e.g. careless.

AMAZING FACT

Carnival in Latin American countries is a major celebration that may last a full week or more.

In New Orleans, Louisiana, it is known as 'Mardi Gras' and marks the period of festivity before Lent.

carnivore *noun* an animal that eats meat. Lions and tigers are carnivores. **carnivorous** *adjective*.

carol *noun* a Christmas song.

carpenter *noun* a person who makes or repairs wooden things.

carpet *noun* a thick woven covering for floors and stairs. **sweep something under the carpet** to keep something secret.

carriage *noun* 1 a section of a train for passengers. 2 an old-fashioned passenger vehicle pulled by horses. 3 the cost of carrying goods from one place to another. *Carriage paid.* 4 the movable part of a machine. *The typewriter carriage holds the paper.*

carrier *noun* 1 a construction usually fixed to a car or bicycle for carrying things. 2 a person who has a disease and passes it on to others without suffering from it.

carrion *noun* the flesh of dead animals.

carrot *noun* a plant with an orange root grown as a vegetable.

carry (carries, carrying, carried) *verb* 1 to hold something or somebody and go from one place to another. *The porter carried my suitcase.* 2 to hold something up, e.g. a roof or ceiling. 3 to pass something like a disease from one person to another. *Mosquitoes can carry dangerous diseases.* 4 to make sound move through the air. *Her voice carried right to the back of the hall.* 5 to win the support of others in a debate when voting is involved. *The motion was carried by 20 votes to 10.* 6 to print something. *The newspapers carried pictures of the funeral.* 7 to have as a result. *In some countries murder still carries the death penalty.* 8 to keep goods in stock. 9 If somebody carries weight, people respect that person's opinion. **get carried away** to be very excited. **carry on** 1 to continue. *I tried to speak to him but he just carried on reading.* 2 to manage in a difficult situation. 3 to complain and make a fuss about something. *My mother carried on all day about the noise.* 4 (informal) If a person is carrying on with somebody, they are having an affair.

carry out *verb* to fulfil, to do what you have promised or have been told to do. *We carried out our plan and explored the cave.*

cart *noun* a vehicle for carrying goods, usually drawn by a horse. **cart** *verb* 1 to carry in a cart. 2 to carry something heavy and find it tiring. *I don't want to cart those bags around town.*

carton *noun* a plastic or cardboard container for food or drink.

cartoon *noun* 1 an amusing drawing or set of drawings, often showing something of interest in the news. *There was a funny cartoon about the strike in the newspaper.* 2 an animated film. *Have you seen the latest Disney cartoon?* **cartoonist** *noun.*

cartridge *noun* 1 a container holding film for a camera, a tape, a typewriter ribbon or ink for a pen or printer. 2 a tube holding explosive for a bullet. 3 a small case that holds the stylus of a record-player.

carve *verb* 1 to make something by cutting a special shape out of wood or stone. *This statue is carved from marble.* **carving** *noun. An African wood carving.* 2 to cut up cooked meat into slices.

cascade *noun* a waterfall. **cascade** *verb* to fall in a cascade.

case *noun* 1 a container. *A case of wine.* 2 a suitcase. *I packed my case and left.*

Lightweight suitcases are ideal for air travel.

case *noun* 1 an event or a situation of a particular kind. *In this case I wouldn't pay the fee.* 2 an event the police are investigating or a question which will be decided on in court. *A murder case.* 3 an example of something bad, or of a disease. *A case of Asian flu.* 4 a patient, a solicitor's client, or a person looked after by a social worker. 5 facts and arguments for and against a plan used in a discussion. *The case for giving up smoking.* 6 in grammar, the change in the form of a word showing how it relates to other words in the sentence. Emma's is the possessive case of Emma. **in case** an action taken in advance referring to a particular thing that might happen. *I've brought a map in case we get lost.* **in any case** anyway. *I'll come in any case.*

DID YOU KNOW

The first full-length cartoon made as a feature film was Disney's 'Snow White and the Seven Dwarfs', which came out in 1938.

cash *noun* money in coins and notes. *Please pay in cash.* **cash** *verb* When you cash a cheque, you get money for it.

cash-and-carry *noun* a large supermarket that sells goods cheaper than other shops.

cashier *noun* a person who takes in or pays out money in a bank or shop.

cashpoint *noun* an automatic machine, usually in or outside a bank, from which customers can withdraw cash.

cask *noun* a container like a barrel for holding liquids.

casket *noun* a small box for jewellery or other valuable things.

cassette *noun* a small flat plastic container with tape or film inside it.

cassette recorder *noun* a machine for recording and playing music and other sounds on cassettes.

Most cassette recorders are manufactured in the Far East.

cast *noun* 1 all the actors in a film or play. 2 an object made from liquid metal, plastic or plaster poured into a mould. 3 a hard covering made of plaster that keeps a broken bone in place while it is mending. **cast** *verb* 1 to throw. *The fishermen cast their nets into the sea.* 2 To cast doubt on something means that you're not sure about it. 3 to give your vote in an election. *Have all the votes been cast?* 4 to choose actors for a film or play. 5 to make an object by pouring liquid into a mould and leaving it to harden. *A beautiful figure cast in bronze.* **cast off** 1 to get rid of something. 2 to set off in a boat by untying the rope. 3 In knitting, you cast off when you take the stitches off the needle to finish a piece. **cast on** You cast on when you start knitting something and put the first stitches on to the needle.

castaway *noun* a shipwrecked person.

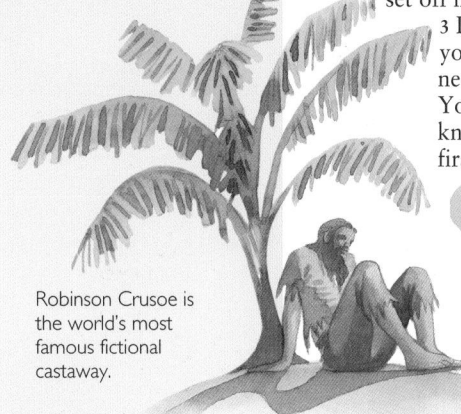

Robinson Crusoe is the world's most famous fictional castaway.

castle *noun* 1 a large, strong building with high walls that was built to protect kings, queens and others from their enemies. 2 a chesspiece, also called a rook. *He took the pawn with the castle.*

Castries *noun* the capital of St Lucia.

casual *adjective* 1 happening by chance, without planning. *A casual chat.* 2 relaxed and not doing things very seriously, sometimes seeming uninterested. *The teacher didn't like his casual attitude.* 3 informal. *I wear casual clothes at home.* 4 not permanent or regular. *Casual work.* **casually** *adverb.*

casualty *noun* a person who is injured or killed in a war or an accident. *There were five casualties in the car crash.*

cat *noun* 1 a small furry pet animal. 2 a large wild animal of the cat family. Lions, tigers and leopards are all big cats. **let the cat out of the bag** to tell a secret.

Today's domestic cat is believed to have originated in Egypt.

catalogue *noun* a list of names, places, goods and other things put in a particular order so that they can be found easily. *I buy all my clothes from a catalogue.* **catalogue** *verb* to list something in a catalogue. *The library books are all catalogued.*

catalyst *noun* (say **kat**-uh-list) something that causes a change or speeds up an event. One person's actions can also act as a catalyst to others.

catapult *noun* 1 a Y-shaped stick with an elastic band, used by children to shoot small stones. 2 an ancient military machine used to hurl stones and rocks at the enemy. **catapult** *verb* to launch, as if from a catapult. *She was catapulted to stardom.*

cataract *noun* a large waterfall.

cataract *noun* a growth over the eyeball that blurs a person's vision. *My grandfather had a cataract removed.*

The cataract is rushing down the mountainside.

catarrh *noun* (say ku-**tar**) an inflammation of the nose and throat similar to a cold.

catastrophe *noun* (say ku-**tass**-trof-ee) a disastrous event that causes suffering and great damage. **catastrophic** *adjective. A catastrophic mistake.* **catastrophically** *adverb. It went catastrophically wrong.*

Anglers often tend to exaggerate the size of the fish they catch.

WORD HISTORY

The expression 'to let the cat out of the bag' probably started in market places hundreds of years ago. Traders would sometimes secretly put a cat in a bag and pretend it was a pig, which was worth much more.

catch (catches, catching, caught) *verb* 1 to get hold of an object that is moving through the air. *He threw the ball and I caught it.* 2 to capture an animal or a person after chasing them. *You can catch fish in a net and mice in a trap.* 3 to be in time for a bus or train. *Leave now if you want to catch the train.* 4 to suddenly discover a person doing something wrong. *The teacher caught them smoking in the loo.* 5 to become stuck. *I caught my shirt on a nail.* 6 to manage to hear. *I didn't catch his name.* 7 to become infected by an illness. *The baby caught a cold.* 8 to overtake. *He's only just left, you can still catch him.* 9 If you catch sight of somebody or something, you see them for just a moment. **catch fire** to start burning. **catch somebody's eye** to attract their attention. **catch the post** to post a letter just before the next collection.

catch *noun* 1 catching something like a ball. *He saved the game with a brilliant catch.* 2 something caught or worth having. *She's a good catch, I should marry her if you can.* 3 a trick, a hidden difficulty. *That car's too cheap, there must be a catch.* 4 a hook or another method of fastening something or locking a door. *The catch on the door is broken.* 5 a game in which children throw a ball to each other. **catch on** 1 to become popular. *The new fashion soon caught on.* 2 to understand. *I didn't catch on at first.* **catch up** 1 to reach somebody who is in front of you. *You go on, I'll soon catch up with you.* 2 to make up work that you are behind on. *I stayed up late to catch up on my homework.* 3 If something catches up with a person, they have to deal with an unpleasant situation they wanted to avoid. *My laziness caught up with me at last.*

catcher *noun* a person or thing that catches. *Grandpa was a mole catcher.*

catching *adjective* spreading quickly from one person to another. *Is the disease that you are suffering from very catching?*

category *noun* a division or class.

cater *verb* 1 to provide food and drink for parties. **caterer** *noun.* 2 to provide whatever is needed. *They don't cater for children.*

caterpillar *noun* a small worm-like creature with many legs. *Caterpillars turn into beautiful butterflies.*

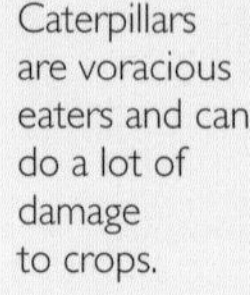

Caterpillars are voracious eaters and can do a lot of damage to crops.

cathedral *noun* a large church. The main church of a district.

Catholic *noun* a member of the Roman Catholic Church. **Catholic** *adjective*. *Their children go* to a Catholic school. **Catholicism** *noun*.

catseye *noun* a spot in the road that reflects cars' lights at night.

These cattle are Friesians. Commercial dairy cows can produce 18 litres of a milk a day.

cattle *noun* farm animals, especially cows. Cattle are kept for beef and milk.

caught past tense of catch.

cauliflower *noun* a vegetable with green leaves and a large head of white flower buds. Only the white part is eaten.

cause *noun* 1 a person or thing that makes something happen. *Nobody knows the cause of the fire.* 2 reason. *You've got no cause for complaint.* 3 a purpose for which people work, such as a charity. *The money is for a good cause.* **cause** *verb* to make something happen. *The accident was caused by negligence.*

causeway *noun* a raised road or footpath across wet ground.

caution *noun* 1 a warning. 2 the act of taking care to avoid danger or making mistakes. **caution** *verb* to give a warning to somebody. **cautious** *adjective*.

cavalry *noun* soldiers on horses.

cave *noun* an underground hollow, sometimes in the side of a cliff or hill. **cave in** *verb* to fall down. *The roof caved in.*

caveman *noun* a person living in a cave. *The caveman killed a mammoth.*

caving *noun* exploring caves.

cavity *noun* a hole.

CD *abbreviation* compact disc.

CD-ROM *abbreviation* compact disc read-only memory, a disc used in a computer for reading information.

cease *verb* 1 to end. 2 to stop doing something. *Cease this idle chat!*

ceiling *noun* 1 the top part of a room forming the upper surface. 2 the highest limit of something.

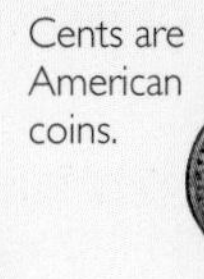

The CD has largely replaced vinyl records and cassettes.

Some people keep wine in their cellars. Others use them for storing junk.

DID YOU KNOW

The Celsius scale was invented by the Swedish astronomer Anders Celsius (1701–1744).

Cents are American coins.

celebrate *verb* to do something special to show that a day or an event is important. *We had a party to celebrate granny's 80th birthday.* **celebration** *noun*.

celebrity *noun* 1 fame. 2 a famous person.

celery *noun* a plant with long stems grown as a vegetable and often eaten raw.

cell *noun* 1 a small room in which a prisoner is kept. 2 a small room in which a monk or a nun lives. 3 the smallest part of humans, plants or animals. 4 one of the compartments of a honeycomb. 5 a unit of an apparatus, such as a battery for producing electric current.

cellar *noun* an underground room of a building, often used for storing things.

cello *noun* (say **chel**-oh) a musical instrument with strings that looks like a very large violin. **cellist** *noun*.

cellular *adjective* 1 made up of cells. 2 Cellular blankets are loosely woven and very warm. 3 A cellular phone is a mobile phone.

Celsius *adjective* (say **sel**-see-us) from the Celsius scale for measuring temperature. Water boils at 100° Celsius.

cement *noun* 1 a grey powder, made from lime and clay, used for building. When cement is mixed with water and left to dry, it becomes hard as stone. 2 a strong glue. **cement** *verb* 1 to cover with cement. *Unfortunately the garden has been cemented over, so we can't plant anything.* 2 to strengthen an agreement or a friendship.

cemetery *noun* (say **sem**-et-ree) a place where dead people are buried.

census *noun* the official count of population.

cent *noun* the 100th part of a dollar and some other currencies. *I've only got a few cents left in my pocket.*

centenary *noun* (say sen-**teen**-u-ree) a 100th anniversary.

centimetre *noun* a measure of length. There are 100 centimetres in a metre.

centipede *noun* a long crawling creature with many legs.

central *adjective* 1 in the middle of something, near the centre. 2 most important. *The government's central aim is to improve education.* **centrally** *adverb*.

C

Central African Republic *noun* a country in Africa.

Central America *noun* a narrow strip of seven countries between Mexico and South America.

central heating *noun* a system of heating buildings from a central boiler through pipes and radiators.

centre *noun* 1 the middle part or point, such as the point around which a circle is drawn. *She likes to be the centre of attention.* 2 an important place of interest and great activity. *Cambridge is a centre of learning.* 3 in sport, a player in a team who plays near the middle of the field. **centre** *verb* 1 to put something near or in the middle. 2 to concentrate your thoughts or ideas on something.

centurion *noun* (say sent-**yoor**-ee-un) a commander of 100 men in the ancient Roman army.

century *noun* 1 a period of 100 years. *The 21st century starts in the year 2000.* 2 in cricket, 100 runs made by a batsman.

cereal *noun* 1 any grain such as wheat, rice or maize used for food. 2 a breakfast food make from grain.

ceremony *noun* 1 a special event or occasion, such as a wedding. 2 the things said and done during such an occasion. *I don't like all the ceremony at big church weddings.* **ceremonious** *adjective*.

certain *adjective* 1 sure, having no doubt. *I'm certain that's right.* If you make certain of something, you find out first. 2 not named. *A certain person was involved in the crime.* 3 some but not much. *He seems to get a certain pleasure out of it.*

certificate *noun* an official document giving facts about a person. *A birth certificate.* **certify** *verb*.

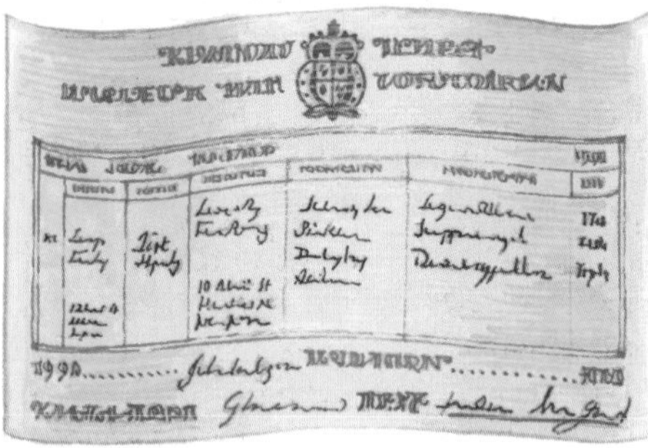

A birth certificate gives proof of identity and entitles its owner to a passport.

CFC *abbreviation* chlorofluorocarbon. A substance used in things such as fridges and aerosols. CFCs have caused the ozone layer to shrink.

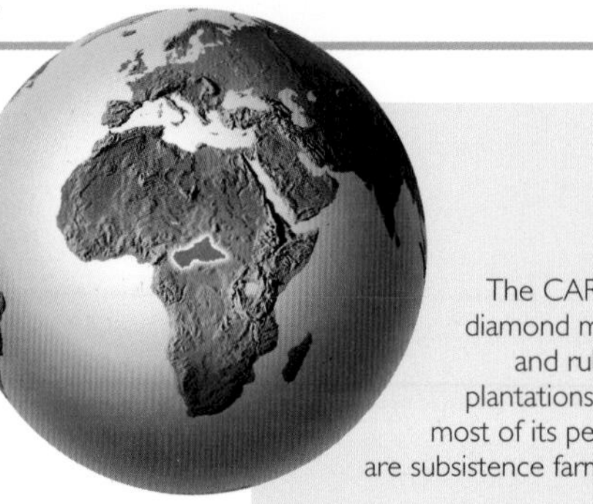

The CAR has diamond mines and rubber plantations, but most of its people are subsistence farmers.

SPELLING NOTE

'Cereal' is pronounced the same as 'serial', but the two words have completely different meanings. The word for grain comes originally from Ceres, who was the Roman goddess of agriculture.

Chad *noun* a country in Africa.

chaffinch *noun* a small songbird.

chain *noun* 1 metal rings fitted into one another. *She wore a silver chain around her neck.* 2 a number of connected events, or shops, mountains and restaurants. **chain reaction** a number of events in which each causes the next. **chain-smoke** to smoke all the time. **in chains** kept as a prisoner.

Strong chains such as this one are often used in heavy industry.

chair *noun* 1 a seat with legs and a back for one person to sit on. 2 a person in control of a discussion. *Who is in the chair?* **chair** *verb* to chair a meeting.

chalk *noun* 1 a soft white stick used for writing and drawing on a blackboard. 2 a soft white rock. Chalk is a common form of limestone.

challenge (challenging, challenged) *verb* 1 to demand to have a fight, play a game or run a race to see who is stronger or better. *I challenged my brother to a game of tennis.* 2 to question the truth or rightness of something. **challenge** *noun* 1 a demand to see who is stronger or better. 2 a difficult project which demands effort and willpower. *Mountaineering is a great challenge.* **challenger** *noun*.

chamber *noun* 1 a large room used for meetings or for a special purpose. *The House of Lords is the upper chamber of Parliament.* 2 A Chamber of Commerce is a group of people in businesses who work together. 3 an enclosed space in a body or a machine. *The human heart has four chambers.* 4 in old use, a room, especially the bedroom.

champion *noun* 1 a person or team who wins a race or game. *A tennis champion.* 2 somebody who speaks or fights for other people and defends ideas. *She is a champion of women's rights.* **champion** *verb*.

The champion was presented with this fine cup by the mayor.

championship *noun* a competition to find the best player or team. *Wimbledon is the oldest tennis championship.*

chance *noun* 1 something unplanned. *I met her by chance.* 2 the possibility that something might happen. *What are our chances of winning?* 3 an opportunity. *This is your last chance.* If you take a chance, you do something although it might fail. **by any chance** a polite way of asking for something. *You wouldn't have a pencil by any chance?* **chance it** to take a risk.

chancellor *noun* a high state official. *The Chancellor of the Exchequer is the country's finance minister.*

change *verb* 1 to become different or make something different. *She's changed a lot since I last saw her.* 2 to take something back and get something else instead. *I changed the jeans because they were too tight.* 3 to put on different clothes or coverings. *I always change when I get home from work.* 4 to get off one bus or train and get on to another. *We changed at Oxford.* 5 to give something up and get something else. *I've changed my job.* **change your mind** to come to have another opinion. **change money** to exchange a sum of money for the same amount in coins or notes. **change** *noun* 1 the act of changing or the result of changing. *A change in the weather.* 2 the money returned to the payer when the cost of the goods is less than the amount given. *It costs 50p and you gave her a pound, so you get 50p change.* 3 the same amount of money in coins or smaller notes. *Have you got change for a pound?* 4 A change of clothes is a clean set. **for a change** something different from what usually happens. *Why don't we go out for a pleasant change of scene?*

channel *noun* 1 a stretch of water that connects two seas. *The English Channel.* 2 a passage along which water flows. 3 a wavelength for television or radio programmes. *I often watch Channel 5.* **channel** (channelling, channelled) *verb* 1 to form a channel in something. 2 to direct. *He channelled his energy into the new project.*

chant *noun* 1 a word or a group of words that is repeated over and over again. 2 a religious song. **chant** *verb.*

chaos *noun* a state of disorder and confusion. *The accident caused chaos on the motorway in both directions.*

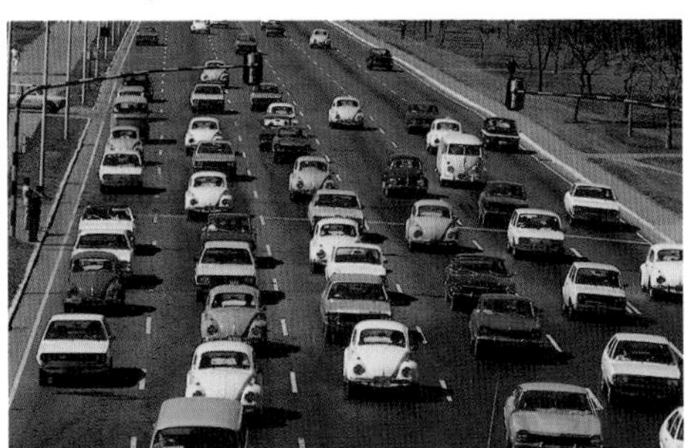

The holiday traffic threatened to cause chaos on the motorway.

WORD HISTORY

'Chancellor' comes from the Latin word 'cancelli', meaning a lattice or grating. This is because a Roman court official used to stand at a grating to separate the public from judges. Today, the head of a British university and the head of the German government are both chancellors.

AMAZING FACT

'Chaos theory' is the theory that changes in the physical world, and their consequences, are unpredictable.

chapel *noun* 1 a small church, sometimes as part of a hospital or school. *A Methodist chapel.* 2 a part of a church with its own altar. 3 the members of a trade union.

chapter *noun* 1 a division of a book, usually with its own number or title. 2 a special period in history. 3 all the members of a religious group. **chapter and verse** the exact place where detailed information can be found.

char (charring, charred) *verb* to become black from burning.

character *noun* 1 the qualities that make a person or a place what they are. *The twins have quite different characters.* 2 a person in a story, film or play. 3 a character is somebody interesting or different from others. *He's a real character.* 4 a letter, number or other symbol. **characteristic** *adjective.* **characterize** *verb.*

The cartoon character gasped with exhaustion as he continued his journey.

charade *noun* (say shu-**rahd**) 1 a scene in a game in which players guess words acted out by others. 2 an act that can easily be seen by others to be false or foolish. *The trial was just a charade.*

charge *noun* 1 a price asked or paid for goods or a service. 2 a written or spoken statement blaming a person for breaking the law. *He was arrested on a murder charge.* 3 the care and responsibility for a person or thing. If you are in charge of somebody or something, you are in control of them and responsible for them. 4 a sudden attack. 5 an amount of explosive to be fired. 6 electricity in a battery or other electrical apparatus. **take charge** to become responsible for something. *I'll take charge of the children if you do the washing up.*

charge *verb* 1 to ask a price for something. *He didn't charge me for the phone call.* 2 to accuse somebody of a crime. 3 to rush forward in an attack. *The bull charged at the crowd and killed three children.* 4 When you charge a battery, it lasts longer. 5 If you are charged with something or charged to do something, you are given a duty or task.

chariot *noun* an ancient horse-drawn vehicle with two wheels, used in battles and races.

Around 1200 BC the Hittites, who lived in modern-day Turkey, used chariots for warfare.

charity *noun* 1 an organization that helps those who need it. *A charity for stray cats.* 2 kindness towards others.

charm *noun* 1 the ability to be attractive and to please. *He used all his charm to win her over.* 2 an act, saying or object that has magical powers. 3 an ornament on a bracelet or chain. **charm** *verb* 1 *He charmed her with his flattery.* 2 to control something by using magical powers.

charming *adjective* delightful, pleasing. *She is a charming person.*

chart *noun* 1 a map of the sea and coast or sky and stars. 2 a map with special information in curves and graphs. *A weather chart.* 3 a list of information in a particular order. *The charts list the most popular records.* **chart** *verb. Explorers charted the coastline.*

chase *verb* to go after somebody or something in order to try and catch them or make them go away. *The cat chased the mouse.* **chase** *noun.*

chasm *noun* 1 a deep crack in the ground. 2 a large difference between two things or groups. *The chasm between us widened.*

chat *noun* a friendly talk. **chat** *verb. We chatted all afternoon.*

chat show *noun* a TV or radio programme in which famous people are interviewed.

chatter *verb* 1 to talk non-stop about unimportant things. 2 to make a rattling sound. *His teeth were chattering with cold.*

chauffeur *noun* (say **shoh**-fer) a person employed to drive somebody's car.

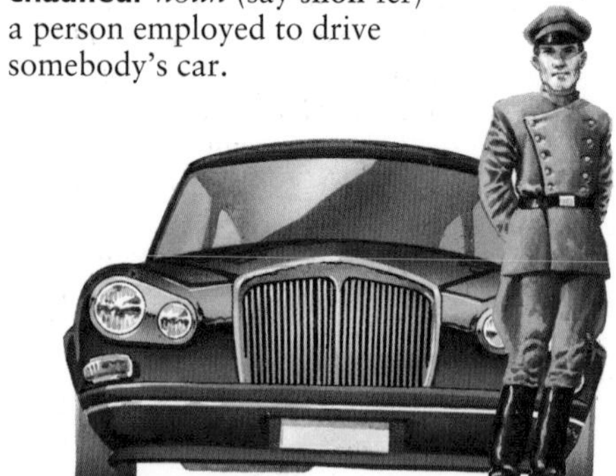

The chauffeur wears a smart uniform and waits by his employer's car.

AMAZING FACT

Cheetahs can reach speeds of up to 60 mph (100kph) over short distances when chasing gazelles.

WORD HISTORY

The original 'chauffeur', in French, was not a driver but a stoker or fireman, who put coal on the furnace of a steam engine. Early motor cars gave off a lot of smoke and steam, so their drivers were jokingly called stokers.

chauvinist *noun* (say **shoh**-vin-ist) a person who shows great prejudice, especially against women. *He's a real male chauvinist.*

cheap *adjective* 1 not costing very much. *Food is cheaper in Portugal than in Spain.* 2 of poor quality, not very good. *Cheap housing is hard to come by.*

cheat *verb* to lie or trick somebody, often in order to do well. *He always cheats in exams.* **cheat** *noun* 1 a person who cheats. 2 a dishonest action.

check *noun* 1 an examination to find out if something is correct. *He made a thorough check.* 2 keeping somebody or something under control. *It's impossible to keep the disease in check.* 3 in chess the position of the king when under attack.

check *noun* a pattern of squares in different colours. **checked** *adjective.*

Tartan is a traditional Scottish fabric pattern, based on colourful overlaid checks.

check *verb* 1 to make sure something is correct or satisfactory. *Have you checked the bill?* 2 to hold back or stop doing something. *The bad weather checked their progress.* **check in** to register at a hotel or report at an airport. *You have to check in an hour before take-off.* **check out** to pay the bill and leave a hotel.

checkout *noun* a place in a supermarket where goods are packed and paid for.

check-up *noun* a medical examination.

cheek *noun* the side of the face below the eye. *Rosy cheeks are a sign of health.*

cheek *noun* rude behaviour. **cheeky** *adjective. Don't be cheeky to your mother!*

cheer *noun* 1 a shout of praise or happiness. *The crowd gave a big cheer.* 2 If you are full of cheer, you are very happy. **cheer** *verb. The fans cheered wildly throughout the match.* **cheer up** to become happy and stop feeling sad.

cheerful *adjective* 1 looking, sounding and feeling happy. 2 something pleasant, that makes you happy. **cheerfully** *adverb.*

cheese *noun* a soft or hard food made from milk. *Let's have bread and cheese for lunch.*

cheetah *noun* a wild animal, like a big spotted cat. Cheetahs are the fastest land animals in the world.

chef *noun* a cook in a restaurant.

A chef has to deal with many pans at once. His job is both hot and demanding.

chemical *adjective* used in, made by or connected with chemistry. **chemical** *noun*. **chemically** *adverb*.

chemist *noun* 1 a trained person who makes up and sells medicines. 2 a shop selling medicines and toilet articles. 3 a scientist who specializes in chemistry.

chemistry *noun* the study of how substances are made up and how they react with other substances.

cheque *noun* a printed form telling the bank to pay money from your account to the person you have written the cheque to. *Can I pay by cheque?*

cherry (cherries) *noun* 1 a small round fruit with a stone. Ripe cherries are red. 2 the tree on which cherries grow.

chess *noun* a game for two players in which each player moves pieces on a chessboard.

chest *noun* the upper front part of the body enclosing the heart and the lungs.

chest *noun* a big, strong box for keeping things in. *A treasure chest.*

chestnut *noun* 1 a reddish brown nut inside a prickly green case. 2 the tree on which these nuts grow. **chestnut** *adjective* having a reddish-brown colour. *Chestnut hair.*

When the chestnut is ripe, the case falls to the ground and splits open. The shiny nuts roll out.

chest of drawers *noun* a piece of furniture with a set of drawers.

chew *verb* to move food about in your mouth and grind it with your teeth, so it is easy to swallow. **chew over** to think about something very carefully.

chewing gum *noun* a sweet gum that you chew and don't swallow.

chick *noun* a young bird.

DID YOU KNOW

China has a population of more than 1,200 million, more people than any other country in the world. Yet China has a smaller area than either Russia or Canada.

chicken *noun* 1 a young bird, especially a hen. 2 the bird's meat used as food. *We had chicken for dinner.* 3 (slang) a coward or frightened person. **chicken out** not to do something because you are frightened.

chickenpox *noun* a disease with red itchy spots on the skin.

chief *noun* a leader or highest official. **chief** *adjective* most important. **chiefly** *adverb*.

chilblain *noun* a painful swelling or sore in the fingers or toes caused by extreme cold.

child (children) *noun* 1 a young boy or girl. 2 a son or daughter.

childhood *noun* the time when you are a child. *Now he's old, he often thinks back to his childhood.*

childish *adjective* behaving like a child, often in silly way. *It's very childish to shout and scream like that.*

children plural of child.

Chile *noun* a country in South America.

Chile is a long thin country that runs along the backbone of South America.

chill *noun* 1 an unpleasant coldness. *In the morning there is often a chill in the air.* **chilly** *adjective*. 2 an illness caused by cold in which you might have a temperature, a headache and feel shivery. 3 a feeling of fear and doom. **chill** *verb* 1 to make something colder. 2 to become cold with fear. **chilling** *adjective*. *A chilling film.*

chimney *noun* a hollow passage in a roof through which smoke goes up into the air.

chimpanzee *noun* an African ape.

chin *noun* the front of the lower jaw.

china *noun* 1 a kind of fine white clay. 2 cups, saucers, plates and ornaments made of china. *The china cupboard.*

China *noun* a country in East Asia.

Chinese *noun* a person who comes from China. **Chinese** *adjective*. *An excellent Chinese restaurant.*

chip *noun* 1 a fried strip of potato. *We bought fish and chips.* 2 a small piece of wood, brick or paint, broken off something. 3 a crack that has been left in a cup or glass, when a small piece has been broken off. 4 a flat plastic counter used as money in games. 5 a very small electronic circuit in a computer. *A silicon chip.* **have a chip on your shoulder** to be rude or behave badly, because you think you have been treated unfairly in the past. **chip** (chipping, chipped) *verb* to damage something by breaking off a small piece of it. *I'm afraid I've chipped a plate.* **chip in** 1 to interrupt a conversation. 2 to give money to a fund, so that something can be paid for by a number of people.

C

chipmunk *noun* a small American animal like a squirrel with a long bushy tail.

Chipmunks are friendly animals. They often come up to visitors in America's national parks, looking for titbits.

chirp *verb* to make a short, sharp sound like a bird or insect.

Chisinau *noun* the capital of Moldova.

chivalry *noun* (say **shiv**-ul-ree) good manners, helpfulness and polite behaviour, in particular by men towards women. **chivalrous** *adjective*.

chocolate *noun* 1 a sweet food made from cocoa beans. *A bar of chocolate.* 2 a sweet covered with a layer of chocolate. *A box of chocolates.* 3 a hot drink made from the powder of crushed cocoa beans.

choice *noun* 1 a number of things you can choose from. *There is a choice of three films.* 2 the thing or things you have decided on. *The French film was my choice.* 3 the right, act or possibility of choosing. *My friend had no choice but to come.* **choice** *adjective* of high quality, best. *We only sell choice wines.*

choir *noun* a group of people who sing together, e.g. in a church or school.

choke *verb* 1 to be unable to breathe properly because something is blocking the air passages. *He choked on a fish bone.* 2 to stop the breathing by pressing on the throat or squeezing the neck. *The victim was choked to death.* 3 If a place is choked with cars or people, it is so full that it is impossible to move.

choke *noun* a device controlling the amount of air going into the engine that makes it easier to start a car.

cholesterol *noun* (say kol-**est**-er-ol) a fatty substance found in animals and food. Too much cholesterol is bad for the heart.

choose (choosing, chose, chosen) *verb* 1 to pick out a person or thing from a greater number. *I chose my favourite music.* 2 to decide to do something. *We chose to stay.*

chop (chopping, chopped) *verb* to cut wood or food into small pieces with a chopper, an axe or a knife. **chop and change** to keep changing your mind about what to do. **chop** *noun* 1 a quick, heavy blow with a chopper or an axe. 2 a slice of meat with a bone in it. *A pork chop.*

chopper *noun* a heavy tool, like an axe, for cutting wood or meat.

chopsticks *noun* a pair of thin sticks held in one hand and used by the Chinese and others to eat food.

Lots of trees are cut down every year and made into chopsticks. But other chopsticks are made of plastic.

chord *noun* (say kord) a number of musical notes sounded at the same time.

chord *noun* (say kord) in geometry, a straight line connecting two points on a curve.

SPELLING NOTE

It's easy to confuse 'chord' and 'cord', which are pronounced the same. Musicians play chords, and mathematicians use them to connect points on a curve. Both words come from the Latin 'chorda', the string of a musical instrument.

chore *noun* (say chor) a small everyday task or duty that is usually boring.

choreography *noun* (say ko-ree-**og**-ru-fee) the art of planning and arranging dances for the stage. **choreographer** *noun*.

chorus *noun* 1 a group of people who sing together. 2 a part of a song that is repeated after each verse by all the singers. 3 a group of singers or dancers who act together in a show. *She dances in the chorus.* **in chorus** at the same time. **chorus** *verb* to sing or say something at the same time.

chose past tense of choose.

chosen past participle of choose.

Christian *noun* a person who believes in Jesus Christ and his teachings. A member of the Christian Church. **Christian** *adjective* believing in the Christian religion. **Christianity** *noun*.

Christmas (Christmases) *noun* the day when people celebrate the birth of Jesus Christ, 25 December. **Christmas Eve** the day before Christmas Day. **Christmas tree** a tree decorated at Christmas time.

Christmas is celebrated throughout the Christian world.

chrome *noun* (say krohm) a hard, silver-coloured metal used for covering objects such as taps.

chronic *adjective* lasting for a long time. *A chronic illness kept him away from work.*

AMAZING FACT

Chocolate originally came from the Aztec people of Mexico who valued it as a drink.

chronological *adjective* arranged in the order in which things happened, according to time. *I've listed the events in strict chronological order.* **chronologically** *adverb.*

chrysalis *noun* 1 a butterfly or moth in the stage between being a caterpillar and the time when it flies, also called a pupa. 2 the hard covering of a chrysalis during that time.

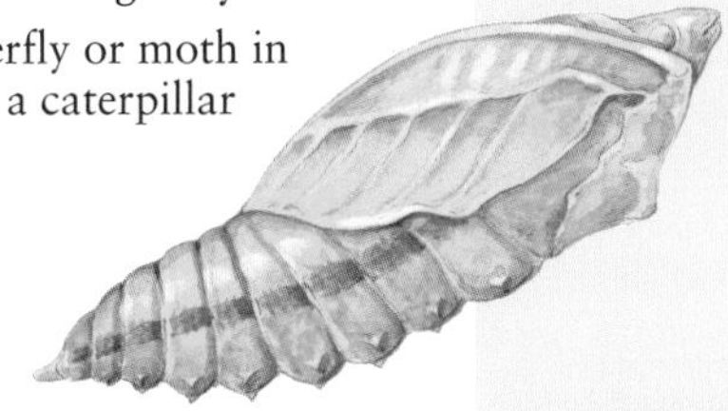

Inside this chrysalis a beautiful butterfly is waiting to emerge.

church *noun* 1 a building in which Christians pray. 2 a religious service in a church. 3 The Church is a group of people within the Christian religion. *The Pope is head of the Catholic Church throughout the world.*

AMAZING FACT

Inside the chrysalis, the caterpillar's body is broken down by hormones and is gradually replaced with the butterfly's body.

cigar *noun* a roll of dried tobacco leaves that people smoke. *Cigars are usually much bigger than cigarettes.*

cigarette *noun* finely cut tobacco wrapped in a roll of thin paper which people smoke.

cinema *noun* a place where you can watch films. *Let's go to the cinema tonight.*

cipher *noun* (say sy-fer) a secret way of writing. *Inscribed with strange ciphers.*

circa *preposition* about, approximately. *He died circa 1850.*

circle *noun* 1 a round flat shape enclosed by a line. Every part of the line is the same distance from the centre. 2 something that makes the shape of a circle. 3 a group of people who like the same thing or have similar interests. *He is well respected in political circles.* 4 seats on the upper floor of a theatre. **circle** *verb* to go round in a circle.

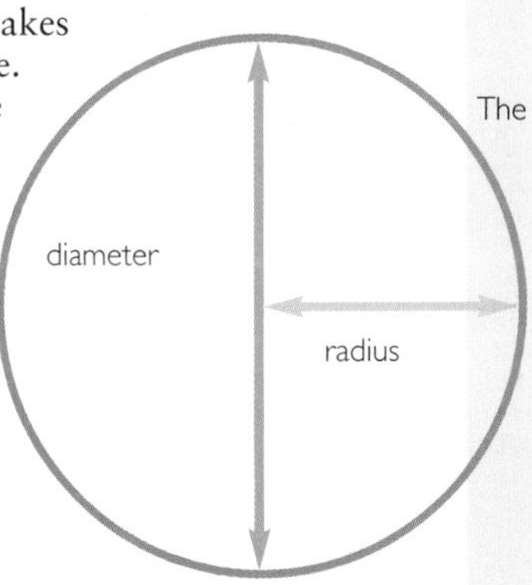

diameter

radius

The diameter of a circle is twice the length of its radius.

circular *adjective* 1 round, shaped like a circle. 2 moving in a circle, starting from a point and ending up in the same place. *A circular route.*

circular *noun* a printed letter, advertisement or notice sent to a large number of people.

circulation *noun* 1 the process of passing something round a number of people. *When will the Euro be put into circulation?* 2 the flow of blood through the body. *She's got poor circulation.* 3 the movement of any substance around a system. *Air circulation.* 4 the number of sold copies of a newspaper or magazine. *This magazine has a high circulation.* **circulate** *verb.*

circumcision *noun* cutting off the foreskin of the penis for medical or religious reasons. **circumcise** *verb.*

circumference *noun* the line that marks out a circle or the distance all the way around a circular object.

circumstance *noun* the conditions connected with an event or person and influencing a particular situation. *Mysterious circumstances surrounded her disappearance.* **in the circumstances** because of the way things are. *I decided it was the best thing to do in the circumstances.* **under no circumstances** never.

circus (circuses) *noun* a show with clowns, animals and acrobats in a big tent. *The circus travels from one town to another.*

The large tent that houses a circus is called a big top.

cistern *noun* a tank for storing water. *Flush the lavatory and the cistern empties.*

citizen *noun* 1 a member of a state. *She's a British citizen.* 2 the inhabitant of a city.

citrus fruit *noun* a fruit, such as a lemon, orange, lime or grapefruit, with a sour-sweet taste.

city *noun* 1 a large town. 2 *The City of London is a centre for financial matters.*

civil *adjective* 1 belonging to the people, not military or religious. *Civil rights include freedom and equality.* 2 The Civil Service includes all government departments, except the armed forces. 3 polite and helpful. *He gave me a civil response.* **civility** *noun.*

Lemons and other citrus fruit grow around the warm Mediterranean Sea.

civilian *noun* a person who is not a member of the armed forces.

civilization *noun* 1 a society that has reached a high level of education and culture. *The Greek civilization.* 2 the state of making or becoming civilized.

C

civilize *verb* to educate and bring culture to people. *The civilized world.*

civil war *noun* a war between people of the same country.

The Battle of Bull Run, which took place in Virginia in 1861, was the first major battle of the American Civil War. Confederate forces (right) defeated the Union army (left).

claim *verb* 1 to say that something belongs to you and ask for it. *Who claimed the lost umbrella?* 2 to say that something is a fact. *He claims to have written to me, but I haven't received the letter.* **claim** *noun* 1 *His claim to have written is a lie.* 2 a demand for something you have a right to. *A pay claim.* 3 a piece of ground or property belonging to somebody. **lay claim to something** to say that something belongs to you.

clan *noun* a group of families who all come from one common family. *The Scottish clans were gathering for Hogmanay.*

clap (clapping, clapped) *verb* 1 to hit your hands together loudly, to show that you are pleased or to attract attention. *Everybody clapped when the music started.* 2 to hit somebody in a friendly way. *He clapped him on the shoulder and said, 'Hello'!* **clap** *noun* 1 the sound of people clapping. 2 a friendly slap. 3 a clap of thunder.

clarinet *noun* a wooden musical instrument, shaped like a tube, which you blow into.

The clarinet is a wind instrument that gives a lovely mellow sound.

clarity *noun* clearness. *He explained it with such clarity that I understood immediately.*

clash *verb* 1 to fight, argue or disagree with somebody. *Gangs of hooligans clashed with the police.* 2 When colours clash, they don't look good together. 3 to take place at the same time and therefore be difficult. *The football clashes with the tennis.* 4 to make a loud sound, like the noise of metal objects being hit together. **clash** *noun.*

GRAMMAR NOTE

There are two types of clauses in grammar. A main clause stands alone and forms a complete sentence, e.g. 'I switched on the light.' A subordinate clause cannot stand on its own and has to go with a main clause to form a sentence, e.g. 'I switched on the light when it got dark.'

A bird's claws help it grip its perch.

clasp *noun* 1 a metal fastener for holding two things or parts of something together. *I can't close my bag because the clasp has broken.* 2 a tight hold with your fingers or arms. **clasp** *verb* to take something in your hand or arms and hold it tightly.

class (classes) *noun* 1 a group of pupils or students who are taught together. **in class** during the lesson. *We aren't allowed to talk in class.* 2 people of the same social group. *People used to divide society into upper, middle and lower classes.* 3 people, animals or things that are similar. 4 an examination result. *A first-class degree in History.* 5 good style. *You can see from the way she dresses that she's got class.* **class** *verb* to say that somebody or something belongs to a group of things, to put them in a class. *You can't class all pop music as rubbish.*

classic *adjective* 1 of very high quality, outstanding. *A classic novel.* 2 well known and serving as a good example for what is expected. *This is a classic case of measles.* **classic** *noun* 1 a book or film of very high quality. 2 classics is the study of ancient Greek and Roman customs, language and literature.

Students of the classics know that Julius Caesar was murdered on the Ides (15) March by Brutus and Cassius.

classical *adjective* 1 thought of as best, because it follows old traditions. Serious and lasting. *I prefer classical ballet to modern dance.* 2 going back to Roman or Greek customs, art and literature. *In classical times, women were often treated as badly as slaves.*

classroom *noun* a room in a school or college in which children or students are taught. *The classroom was full of students.*

clause *noun* 1 a part of a written agreement or legal document. *It was covered by a clause in the contract written in small print.* 2 a group of words with its own verb forming part of a sentence.

claustrophobia *noun* fear of being in a small closed space.

claw *noun* 1 a sharp nail on the toe of an animal or bird. *Cats have sharp claws.* 2 Crabs and lobsters catch and hold things with their claws. 3 an instrument like a hook on machines for lifting things. **claw** *verb* to pull and scratch with a claw or hand. *The cat clawed a hole in my tights.*

clay *noun* a kind of earth that is soft when it is wet and hard when it is dry. Bricks and pots are made from clay.

The first clay pots were made in Japan around 10,500 BC.

clean *adjective* 1 without any dirt or marks. *I put on clean clothes.* 2 not yet used. *Can I have a clean sheet of paper?* 3 fair. *A clean fight.* 4 morally pure, not dirty. *He only tells clean jokes when there are girls about.* **come clean** to decide to be honest about something you've kept as a secret.

clean *verb* to make something clean from dirt or dust. *I cleaned the car for you.* **clean up** 1 to make an area or a person clean and tidy again. *Before my parents came back, we cleaned up the mess.* 2 You clean up when you win a bet and take all the money.

clean *adverb* completely. *I clean forgot about the money.*

clear *adjective* 1 easy to see through. *The water is so clear, you can see the bottom of the lake.* 2 not cloudy. *A clear sky.* 3 easy to understand or hear. *A clear description.* 4 empty, free from blocks, unwanted things or dangers. *A clear road ahead.* 5 free from doubt, guilt or difficulty. *I'm quite clear about my plans.* 6 complete. *Allow three clear days for the cheque to clear.* **make yourself clear** to say something so that it is understood and there is no doubt about your wishes. **clearly** *adverb.*

clear *adverb* 1 easily heard or seen. *He said it loud and clear.* 2 out of the way, not near or touching. *Stand clear of the doors.*

clear *verb* 1 to become free of something like clouds, traffic or unwanted objects. *The mist has cleared.* 2 *The tablets will clear your headache.* 3 to get past something without touching it. *The horse cleared the fence.* 4 to state that somebody is not guilty. *The jury cleared him of all charges.* 5 to get somebody's permission for something. *You'll have to clear your plans with the manager.* **clear away** to take away things that are no longer needed. **clear off** to go away. **clear up** 1 to stop raining or being cloudy. 2 to tidy up. 3 to solve or settle a mystery or misunderstanding.

clench *verb* to close your teeth or fist tightly.

clergy *noun* ministers of the Christian Church. *The clergy wear surplices in church.*

SPELLING NOTE

Though pronounced 'clark', the word 'clerk' is spelt with an 'e'. It originally meant a clergyman, and is rather an old-fashioned word in British English. But in America, 'clerk' rhymes with 'Turk' and means a shop assistant.

WORD HISTORY

'Climax' comes from the Greek for ladder. As you near the top of a series of rungs, you reach the climax.

Ice cubes are sparkling clear lumps of frozen water.

clerk *noun* (rhymes with bark) a person who works in an office, bank or law court and looks after accounts, records and paperwork. *The clerk of the court.*

clever *adjective* 1 intelligent and able to learn and understand things quickly. 2 showing skill. *The pocket calculator was a clever invention.* **cleverness** *noun.*

cliché *noun* (say **klee-shay**) a phrase that has been used so much that it has become meaningless.

click *noun* a short, sharp sound. **click** *verb* 1 *I heard the camera click.* 2 to suddenly understand something. *It suddenly clicked that I had met them before.*

cliff *noun* a steep rock-face, usually at the coast. *The white cliffs of Dover.*

Waves hollow out caves in a rocky cliff. Blow holes form above the caves.

climate *noun* the weather conditions of a place. *Oranges don't grow in cold climates.*

climax *noun* the most important and exciting moment in a story, usually near the end. *The film built up to a climax.*

climb *verb* 1 to go up, down or over something. *We climbed over the wall.* 2 to go higher. *Prices have climbed.* 3 to grow upwards. *A rose climbing up the fence.* **climb** *noun. It was a hard climb to the top.*

climber *noun* a person or plant that climbs.

cling *verb* to hold on to somebody tightly. If you cling to an idea, you keep it firmly in your head and believe in it.

cling film *noun* thin plastic material used for wrapping up food.

clinic *noun* a place where people go to get medical treatment or advice.

clip *noun* a small metal or plastic fastener for holding things together. **clip** *verb.*

clip *noun* a short piece of a film or television programme. **clip** *verb* to cut. *Diane clipped the hedge with her shears.*

cloak *noun* 1 a loose coat without sleeves that fastens at the neck. 2 a disguise to hide the truth. *Under the cloak of darkness.* **cloak** *verb* to hide or cover secrets.

C

clock *noun* an instrument that tells the time. **turn the clock back** to go back to things or ideas how they were a long time ago. **clock in** *verb* to record the time when you start work. **clock out** to record the time you stop work. *The workers clocked out at 4 p.m.*

No one would be able to sleep through the loud ringing of this alarm clock.

clockwise *adjective* moving in the same direction as the hands of the clock. *To switch on, you turn the knob clockwise.*

clockwork *noun* a mechanism with wheels and springs that is wound up. **clockwork** *adjective. Clockwork toys.*

clod *noun* a lump of earth.

clog *noun* a shoe with a wooden sole.

clog (clogging, clogged) *verb* to become blocked with grease or dirt. **clog up** *I need a plunger because the sink is clogged up.*

cloister *noun* a covered path round a square in a monastery or college.

clone *noun* an animal or plant that has been produced in a laboratory from the cells of another animal or plant. A clone looks exactly like the animal it was made from. **clone** *verb.*

close *verb* (say klohz) 1 to shut. *She closed the door.* 2 to end. *The offer closes at the end of the month.* **close down** to stop work. *Most of the coal mines have closed down.* **close in** to come nearer and nearer. *Winter is closing in.* **close** *noun* the end of an activity or a period of time.

close *noun* (say klohss) 1 an enclosed area around a church. 2 a short street closed at one end. *A close of houses.*

close *adjective* (say klohss) 1 near. *My cousins are my close relatives.* 2 trusted and liked. *Sophie is my closest friend.* 3 tight, with little space between, especially in competitions and games. *It was a close contest.* 4 thorough and careful. *A close examination of the document showed that it was a forgery.* 5 warm and stuffy. **closely** *adverb.* **closeness** *noun.*

close *adverb* (say klohss) 1 near. *I live quite close.* 2 almost. *Close to 30 years ago.*

The section of the caterpillar that is under the magnifying glass is seen in close-up.

AMAZING FACT

The four main types of clouds are called 'cirrus', 'nimbus', 'cumulonimbus' and 'stratus'.

DID YOU KNOW

Clubs are one of the four suits in a pack of playing cards. The other suits are diamonds, hearts and spades.

closed *adjective* 1 not open. *We could hardly breathe with all the windows closed.* 2 not open to the public, especially a shop or museum. *Closed on Mondays and Wednesdays.* **behind closed doors** in secret.

closet *noun* a small room for storing things. **closet** (closeting, closeted) *verb* to shut away. *They were closeted in the study.*

close-up *noun* a photograph or film that is taken from very near.

closure *noun* the closing down of a factory, shop or other business. *There have been more pit closures in the south of Wales.*

cloth *noun* 1 woven fabric used for making clothes, coverings and other things. 2 a piece of material for cleaning, e.g. a dish cloth.

clothes *plural noun* things you wear, such as trousers, shirts and dresses.

clothing *noun* the clothes people wear. *You'll need waterproof clothing for mountain biking.*

cloud *noun* 1 a mass of small drops of water that floats in the sky. *Clouds are usually white or grey.* 2 a mass of smoke or dust in the air. **under a cloud** out of favour, in disgrace. *He had a row and left under a cloud.* **cloud** *verb* to become unclear. **cloudy** *adjective.* **cloud over** *The sky clouded over.*

It was a bright summer's day, but now the sky is beginning to cloud over.

clover *noun* a small plant with three leaves on each stalk.

clown *noun* 1 a person in a circus or pantomime who wears funny clothes and make-up, and says and does silly things to make people laugh. 2 a person who acts like a clown. **clown** *verb.*

club *noun* 1 a group of people who meet because they have the same interests. *My brother has joined the football club.* 2 the place where the club members meet.

club *noun* 1 a big, heavy stick with a thick end that can be used for fighting. 2 a specially shaped stick for hitting a golf ball. 3 a playing card with black clover leaves on it. *The king of clubs.* **club** *verb* to hit somebody with a heavy stick. **club together** to give money to share the cost with others. *We all clubbed together to buy a present.*

clue *noun* something that helps you to find the answer to a question or problem. *The footprints provided a clue.* **not to have a clue** not to know much about something.

clump *noun* a group. *A clump of daffodils.* **clump** *verb* to walk with heavy footsteps. *Don't clump about in those big heavy boots.*

Daffodils grow in clumps as the bulbs under the ground multiply.

clumsy *adjective* 1 A clumsy person moves about awkwardly, walks into things, knocks things over and breaks them. 2 tactless and not very skilful. *A clumsy explanation.*

cluster *noun* a small group of people or things close together. *A cluster of bright stars.* **cluster** *verb* to form a tight group.

clutch (clutches) *noun* 1 a tight hold. If you are in somebody's clutches, they have control over you. 2 the pedal you press in a car while changing gear.

clutch *verb* to hold tightly.

coach (coaches) *noun* 1 a bus for long-distance journeys. 2 a train carriage designed for passengers. 3 a four-wheeled horse-drawn carriage that was used to carry passengers and mail.

coach (coaches) *noun* 1 a person who trains sportspeople. *The football team has a new coach.* 2 a teacher who gives private lessons. **coach** *verb. She was coached by her dad.*

coal *noun* 1 a hard black or brown mineral substance from under the earth that gives heat when it is burned. Coal is dug out of mines. 2 a piece of coal.

coarse *adjective* 1 rough, not smooth. 2 rude, vulgar. **coarseness** *noun.*

coast *noun* land right next to the sea. **coastal** *adjective.* **the coast is clear** there is nobody around to see you or catch you out.

coastline *noun* the outline of the coast. *A rocky coastline.*

This coastline has rocky headlands, sandy beaches and two rivers running down to the sea.

DID YOU KNOW

Real cockneys are born within hearing distance of Bow Bells in London. Some cockneys still use a rhyming slang: 'apples and pears' mean stairs, and your 'plates of meat' are your feet.

Inside a coconut there is white flesh and a thin milk that makes a refreshing drink.

coat *noun* 1 a piece of clothing with sleeves that you wear over other clothes when you go out. 2 an animal's fur or hair. 3 a layer of paint or varnish. *A coat of paint.* **coat** *verb.*

coating *noun* a thin covering or layer spread over a surface.

coax *verb* to gently try to talk somebody into doing something.

cobra *noun* (say **koh**-bruh) a poisonous snake. *A cobra was coiled up in the grass.*

cobweb *noun* a spider's web.

cock *noun* a male bird.

cockerel *noun* a young male bird.

A cockerel has a bright red comb and shiny tail feathers. A cock is usually more colourful than a hen.

cockney *noun* 1 a person born in East London. 2 the way people from East London speak.

cockpit *noun* a compartment for the pilot of a plane or the driver of a car.

cocoa *noun* 1 a brown powder made from cocoa seeds. 2 a hot drink made from cocoa powder and water or milk.

coconut *noun* 1 a large round nut with a hard, hairy shell from the coconut palm. 2 the white flesh inside the nut, which is used in cooking and baking.

cocoon *noun* a covering of silky threads produced by a caterpillar before it develops into an adult insect.

cod (cod) *noun* a large sea-fish. *We had cod and chips for dinner.*

code *noun* 1 a set of signals or a system of words, letters or numbers used to write messages. *You can only crack a code if you know the system.* 2 a set of laws or rules. *You must know the Highway Code if you want to pass your driving test.* **code** *verb* You code a message by replacing the letters or numbers in it with other letters or numbers. **coded** *adjective. A coded message.*

coffee *noun* 1 a drink made by pouring hot water on to the roasted and ground seeds, called coffee beans, of a tropical plant. *A cup of strong coffee.* 2 the coffee beans or powder the drink is made from.

coffin *noun* a box in which a dead person is buried. *A vampire rose up out of the coffin.*

C

cog *noun* one of a number of teeth round the edge of a wheel which is used to move another wheel or part in a machine.

cogwheel *noun* a wheel with cogs.

coil *noun* a loop of rope or wire or a series of loops wound into a spiral. **coil** *verb* to wind into a coil. *The snake coiled its body around a tree.* **coil up** to wind round and round.

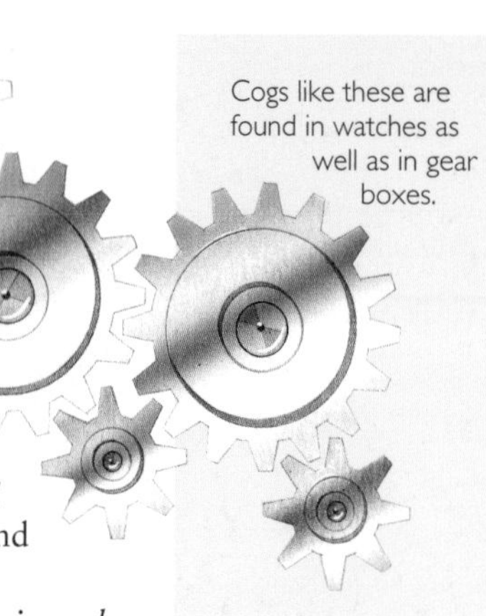

Cogs like these are found in watches as well as in gear boxes.

coin *noun* a piece of metal money. **coin** *verb* 1 to manufacture coins. 2 to invent a new word or phrase.

coincide *verb* to happen at the same time as something else. *Her holiday coincided with his trip to Italy.*

coincidence *noun* a remarkable set of events. *By coincidence they met on the plane to New York.*

cold *adjective* 1 not warm, having a low temperature. 2 unfriendly or unkind. *She seems very cold and unloving.* If something leaves you cold, you can't get excited about it. **coldness** *noun.*

cold *noun* 1 low temperature, cold weather. *Wrap up warm if you're going out in the cold.* 2 an infectious illness that makes you sneeze and cough. *If you don't wrap up warm, you'll catch a cold.*

cold-blooded *adjective* Cold-blooded animals change their body temperature according to the temperature around them. Reptiles are cold-blooded. A cold-blooded person is cruel.

Reptiles like this iguana are cold-blooded. They need to sit on a rock to warm up in the Sun before they get active.

cold sore *noun* a blister on the lips or in the mouth. *Philip had a cold sore on his mouth.*

colic *noun* a stomach-ache.

collaborate *verb* to work together or with someone else on a job. **collaboration** *noun.*

collapse *verb* 1 to fall down suddenly. *The roof collapsed in the storm.* 2 If you collapse, you become weak or ill. 3 If a plan collapses, it doesn't work out. 4 to fold up, e.g. a table or chair. **collapse** *noun. Disagreements on both sides caused the collapse of the talks.* **collapsible** *adjective. Collapsible chairs are easy to store.*

collar *noun* 1 the part of a shirt, dress or coat that stands up or folds down round the neck. 2 a leather band round the neck of a dog, cat or horse. **collar** *verb* to catch somebody. *I collared him just as he was leaving the office.*

colleague *noun* a person you work with.

collect *verb* 1 to gather from various places. *We collected wood for the fire.* 2 If you collect things, you are interested in them. *I collect comics.* 3 to come together. *People collected around the singer.* 4 to ask for money from people. 5 to fetch. *My sister is collecting the children from school.* 6 When you collect your thoughts, you prepare and calm yourself. **collection** *noun.*

collector *noun* a person who collects things. *A stamp collector.*

college *noun* a place where people can carry on studying after they have left school.

Colombia was named by its Spanish conquerors after Christopher Columbus, the first European to discover it.

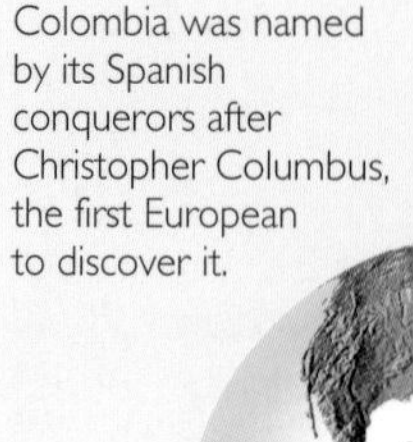

collide *verb* to crash into something. *The two cars collided.* **collision** *noun.*

Colombia *noun* a country in South America.

Colombo *noun* the capital of Sri Lanka.

colon *noun* a mark (:), often put before listing a number of things.

colon *noun* the large part of the intestine.

colonel *noun* (say **ker**-nul) an army officer in charge of a regiment.

colony *noun* 1 a country that is controlled by another more powerful country. 2 a group of people of the same kind living close together. 3 a group of animals living together. *A colony of bees.*

colossal *adjective* very large. *There was colossal interest in the new project.*

colour *noun* 1 Colour is what you see when light is broken up into parts. Red, blue and green are colours. 2 something seen in all its colours, not just in black and white. 3 the quality that makes things interesting or more exciting. *He'll add a bit of colour to the party.* **colour** *verb* 1 to colour in a picture with crayons. 2 to influence somebody's opinion or feelings. 3 to become red in the face. **coloured** *adjective.*

Red, blue and yellow are the primary colours from which all other colours can be made.

colt *noun* a young male horse.

column *noun* 1 a tall stone structure holding up part of a building or standing on its own. A pillar. 2 a long, narrow shape. *A column of smoke.* 3 an article usually written by the same person in a newspaper or magazine. 4 part of a page. *There are three columns on this page.* 5 a group of people or animals that move in a long line.

C

coma *noun* (say **koh**-muh) a state of unconsciousness from which it is difficult to wake up, usually due to illness or an accident.

comb *noun* a piece of plastic or metal with a row of teeth for tidying your hair. **comb** *verb* 1 to comb your hair. 2 to search thoroughly. *We combed the house for clues.*

Viking comb

combination *noun* 1 a mixture of things. *The members are a good combination of young and old.* 2 a code of numbers or letters for opening a lock.

combine *verb* to join together. *It's not always easy to combine work and play.*

combine harvester *noun* a machine that reaps and threshes grain.

combustion *noun* the process of burning.

come (coming, came, come) *verb* 1 to move towards a place or the speaker. 2 to arrive at a particular place or reach something like a decision. *I've come to the conclusion that I don't like meat.* 3 to happen. *How did you come to be invited to the party?* 4 to exist. *The T-shirts come in all colours.* 5 to become. *My laces have come undone.* **come about** to happen. **come across** to meet or find. **come by** to get. **come in** 1 to enter. 2 to become fashionable. 3 to be received. *A report of the accident has just come in.* **come in for** to get a share of something. *She's come in for some criticism.* **come into** to inherit. **come off** 1 to take place or succeed. *Our holiday didn't come off.* 2 to become unfastened. *A button has come off.* 3 to fall from something. *He came off his bike.* **come through** to survive a difficult situation. **come to** 1 *The bill came to £20.* 2 to wake up after having been unconscious. *I was in hospital when I came to.* **come up** 1 to come to attention, be mentioned or discussed. *My question came up at the meeting.* 2 to happen. *An interesting job has come up.* 3 to win. *Your number might come up next time.* **come up against** to meet something, such as a difficult situation. **come up with** to think of. *He came up with a new plan for the school play.*

comedian *noun* an actor who plays a funny part or a person who makes people laugh.

comedy *noun* a funny play, film or situation.

comet *noun* an object travelling across the sky that looks like a star with a bright tail of light.

WORD HISTORY

'Coma' comes from the Greek for 'deep sleep'. Some people have fully recovered after being in a coma for years.

GRAMMAR NOTE

We usually write a comma in places where we would make a slight pause if we were speaking the words. A comma can also show that one part of a sentence is separate: 'When you leave, please shut the door'.

Napoleon was in command of the French navy as well as the French army.

Spectacular comets are just dirty iceballs a few kilometres across.

comfort *noun* 1 a pleasant and relaxed situation or feeling. 2 kindness and sympathy given to a person who is unhappy. 3 a person or thing that gives hope or makes pain easier for an unhappy person. **comfort** *verb* to make somebody less unhappy. *I tried to comfort her after the accident.* **comforting** *adjective.*

comfortable *adjective* 1 relaxing and pleasant to be in or on. *A comfortable chair.* 2 having enough money. *We are comfortable and can afford most things now.* 3 free from pain or worry. *I don't feel comfortable with people I don't know.*

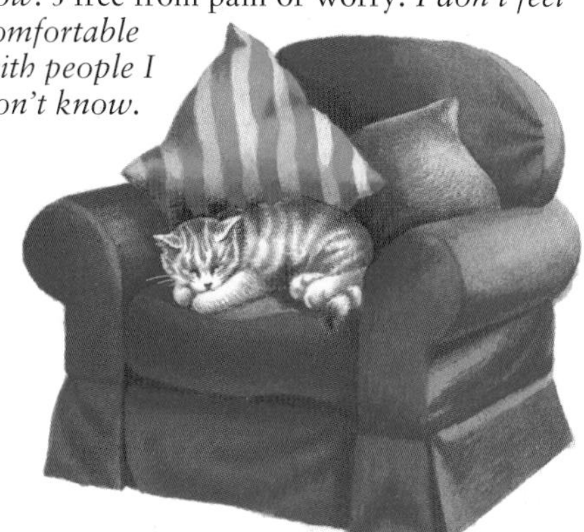

Cats usually like to sit in the most comfortable chair in the house.

comic *noun* 1 a magazine with picture stories. 2 a person who makes people laugh or an actor who plays funny parts. **comic** *adjective. A comic strip.*

comma *noun* a mark (,) used in writing to show a pause or separate items in a list. *Oranges, apples and pears are all fruit.*

command *noun* 1 an order, telling people what to do. *The soldier obeyed the officer's commands.* 2 control. *The troops are under the general's command.* 3 knowledge and ability. *She has a good command of French.* **command** *verb* 1 to order. 2 to be in control and responsible for a person or group. 3 to deserve and get. *Her position commands respect.* **commanding** *adjective.*

commence *verb* to begin.

comment *noun* an opinion or explanation about an event, a book or a person. *I have made a few comments on your essay.* **comment** *verb.*

commentary *noun* 1 opinions and descriptions spoken during an event. *I listened to the exciting commentary on the big match.* 2 a collection of written opinions and explanations on an event, a book or a person. *I read the commentary with interest.*

commerce *noun* the buying and selling of goods on a large scale.

commercial *adjective* 1 used in commerce. 2 profitable, out to make money. *His film is a commercial success.* 3 Commercial television and radio are paid for by advertisements.

commercial *noun* an advertisement on television or radio.

Some people enjoy the commercials on television more than the programmes.

commit (committing, committed) *verb* 1 to do something wrong or bad. To commit a crime. 2 to put somebody into care or prison. 3 If you commit yourself to something, you promise to do it. **commitment** *noun.*

committee *noun* a group of people chosen by others to carry out special duties.

common *adjective* 1 shared by two or more. *It is our common aim to stop the war.* If people have something in common, they share the same interest or are somehow the same. 2 ordinary or happening often. *Smith is a common name.* 3 generally known. *It is common knowledge that smoking is bad for you.* 4 If something is done for the common good, it is done for all people. **common law** unwritten law based on customs. **common sense** good sense and the ability to make the right decision, gained from experience.

common *noun* a grassy area where everybody is allowed to go.

communicate *verb* to make news, information or your feelings known to other people. *She communicates very well.*

communication *noun* 1 sharing and exchanging news or information. 2 a message. 3 Communications are the links between people and places, such as television, radio, telephone, fax, e-mail, roads and railways.

communism *noun* a political system in which production is owned and controlled by the state. **communist** *noun.* **communist** *adjective.*

community (communities) *noun* 1 people living in one particular place or area. 2 a group of people living together and sharing interests, religion or nationality.

GRAMMAR NOTE

The comparatives of short words add '-er' at the end: 'older', 'younger', 'taller'. Longer words use 'more' in front: 'more beautiful', 'more cowardly', 'more thrilling'. Do not ever use 'more' and '–er' together.

commuter *noun* a person who travels regularly between home and work. **commute** *verb. I commute by train.*

Comoros *noun* a country in the Indian Ocean off East Africa.

compact *adjective* closely packed and neatly fitted together. *A compact kitchen.*

compact disc *noun* a disc from which recorded sound is reproduced. CD stands for compact disc.

companion *noun* a person you spend time with. *A travelling companion.*

company *noun* 1 being with other people. When you keep somebody company, you stay or go with them. 2 visitors. 3 a business firm. *He works for a toy company.*

comparative *adjective* judged by looking and thinking about things, by comparing. *Despite the war raging around them, they live in comparative peace.* **comparatively** *adverb.* **comparative** *noun* the form of an adjective or adverb that shows 'more'. The comparative of 'good' is 'better'.

compare *verb* to look at and examine things or people to find out in what ways they are similar or different. *It's cold compared to yesterday.* **comparison** *noun.*

compartment *noun* 1 a separate section in a train carriage. 2 a separate part in a bag or box for keeping things in.

compass (compasses) *noun* (say **kum**-puhss) an instrument used for finding directions. The needle of a compass always points north.

You should always take a compass when walking in the mountains, in case a fog descends and you lose your way.

compasses *noun* a V-shaped instrument used for drawing circles.

compatible *adjective* able to exist together or work well with another. *Good holidays at prices compatible with most people's income.* The opposite of compatible is incompatible.

compel (compelling, compelled) *verb* to make somebody do something they don't want to do.

compensate *verb* to make up for loss, injury or damage, usually by paying money. **compensation** *noun. They asked for compensation for their ruined holiday.*

The Muslim community prays to Allah five times a day, not always at a mosque. The most important worship is at noon on Friday.

compete *verb* to take part in a game, race or examination.

The fastest cars in the world compete against each other at a Grand Prix race.

competent *adjective* able to do something. *She is a competent teacher.*

competition *noun* 1 a game, race or other test that people try to win. 2 the act of trying to win or get something. *I was in competition with two other applicants for the job.* In business, competition means trying to get people to buy one thing rather than another. *Competition helps to keep prices down.*

competitive *adjective* 1 keen to take part in tests and enjoy competition. 2 Competitive prices are low. *Selling at competitive rates.*

competitor *noun* a person, firm or product competing with others.

compile *verb* to collect information and put it together in a list or book. *Lots of people helped to compile this dictionary.*

complain *verb* to say that you are not happy about something. *The neighbours complained about the noise.*

complaint *noun* 1 a statement expressing unhappiness with a particular situation. *He made an official complaint.* 2 an illness.

complete *adjective* 1 whole. 2 finished. *When will work on the new house be complete?* 3 total, full. *The party was a complete surprise.* **complete** *verb* to finish doing something or add what is needed. **completion** *noun.*

complex *adjective* difficult to understand or explain. *A complex problem.*

$$X^2 = 109(a + b), (x + y)$$

Simon could not work out the complex equation his teacher set him.

complex *noun* 1 a group of buildings or things connected with each other. *A new housing complex.* 2 an emotional problem that influences a person's behaviour. *If you keep blaming me, I'll get a guilt complex.*

complexion *noun* the natural colour and quality of the skin of your face. *She has a beautiful complexion.*

WORD HISTORY

The ancient Greeks believed that the body contained four vital fluids, or humours – blood, phlegm, yellow bile and black bile. Your complexion, from the Latin 'weaving together', showed how your humours were combined.

complicated *adjective* difficult. *A complicated problem.* **complication** *noun.*

compliment *noun* an expression of praise and admiration. *He paid her a compliment on her new dress.* **compliment** *verb.*

component *noun* a part of a larger object or machine. *The bike's components are made in southern Italy.*

A spark plug is one of the components of a car's engine.

compose *verb* 1 to make up or form something. *The firm is composed of managers, secretaries and builders.* 2 to write music or poetry. 3 to make yourself calm. *Compose yourself before you speak.*

composer *noun* a person who writes music.

composition *noun* 1 a piece of music. 2 an essay or story written at school. 3 the various parts something is made up of. *A chemical composition.*

comprehend *verb* to understand. *I don't comprehend.* **comprehension** *noun.*

comprehensive *adjective* including everything needed. *The Prime Minister gave a comprehensive explanation of his plans.*

comprehensive school *noun* a secondary school for pupils of all abilities.

compress *verb* (say kum-**press**) to squeeze something together so it takes up less space.

A car crusher can compress a whole car into a small cube for recycling purposes.

compress *noun* (say **kom**-press) a soft pad pressed on a wound to stop it bleeding.

compromise *noun* the settlement of an argument or differences of opinion by each side accepting less than it had asked for. *After a long discussion we reached a compromise.* **compromise** *verb* 1 *We compromised and went by bus.* 2 If you compromise yourself, you act unwisely or make people doubt you.

C

compulsive *adjective* not being able to stop yourself from doing something, even though it is wrong or harmful. *Compulsive liars rarely tell the truth.* **compulsion** *noun.*

compulsory *adjective* having to do something. If something is compulsory, it must be done. *Education is compulsory for all children in Europe.* The opposite of compulsory is optional.

computer *noun* an electronic machine that can make calculations, store information or control other machines. **computerize** *verb* 1 to store information on a computer. 2 to equip a business with computers.

Businesses and schools have all benefited from the invention of the computer.

Conakry *noun* the capital of Guinea.

concave *adjective* curved inwards, like the inside of a hollow ball. The opposite of concave is convex.

conceal *verb* to hide or keep secret. *The scarf concealed the hideous scar.*

conceited *adjective* being too proud of yourself and your abilities. **conceit** *noun.*

concentrate *verb* 1 to give all your attention to something. *You must concentrate more on your homework.* 2 to bring or come together. *Industry is concentrated in the north.* **concentrated** *adjective. Concentrated orange juice has to be diluted with water.*

concentration *noun* 1 If something needs concentration, it requires all your attention. 2 a gathering. *A concentration of troops at the border.*

concept *noun* an idea.

concern *noun* 1 something that is very important to you. *Her diet is no concern of mine.* **concern** *verb.* 2 a business. *A very profitable concern.*

concert *noun* a musical performance. *They played a symphony at the concert.*

The concert is in full swing, with the conductor directing the percussionist to bang the drums.

The type on the right has been squashed up, or condensed.

CONDENSED

WORD HISTORY

'Concave' comes from the Latin 'cavus', a cave. 'Convex' comes from the Latin 'convexus', arched.

concise *adjective* short and to the point, not saying anything unnecessary.

conclude *verb* 1 to end. 2 to come to believe something after having thought it over. To decide. *When they didn't ring back, he concluded that they had gone away.*

conclusion *noun* 1 an ending. 2 an opinion or judgement. *The jury reached the conclusion that he was guilty.*

concrete *noun* building material made by mixing together cement, sand, gravel and water. *A concrete bridge.*

concrete *adjective* definite, real. *Can you give me a concrete example?*

condemn *verb* 1 to say that you find something wrong and unacceptable. *We condemn violence.* 2 to judge a person guilty or sentence a criminal. 3 to force somebody to suffer. *After her husband's death, she was condemned to a life of loneliness.*

condense *verb* 1 to make a speech or piece of writing shorter. *He condensed his report to a few sentences.* 2 to change from gas or vapour into liquid. 3 to become thicker. **condensed** *adjective. Condensed milk.*

condition *noun* 1 the state somebody or something is in. *My bike is in very good condition.* 2 The conditions people live or work in are the surroundings that affect their well-being. *It is impossible to work under these conditions.* 3 something that is dependent on another thing, or necessary for something else. *You can come to stay on condition that you help with the baby.*

condom *noun* a rubber covering for the penis used as a means of birth control or to prevent infection.

conduct *verb* (say kun-**dukt**) 1 to behave. *They conducted themselves well.* 2 to lead or guide a person. 3 to control or manage a group. *To conduct a meeting.* 4 to direct. *To conduct an orchestra.* 5 to act as a path for electricity or heat.

conduct *noun* (say **kon**-dukt) 1 behaviour. *Conduct at school has improved.* 2 the manner in which something is managed.

conductor *noun* 1 a person who conducts musicians in an orchestra. 2 a person who collects fares from passengers on buses and trains. 3 something that conducts heat or electricity. *Copper is a good conductor.*

cone *noun* 1 a shape with a round base ending in a point at the top. 2 the fruit of pine or fir trees. 3 an ice-cream cone.

Cones are the seed pods of conifers or evergreen trees.

confuse *verb* 1 to make a person feel puzzled. To make something difficult to understand. *He confused me with his long explanation.* 2 to get things mixed up. *I'm always confusing her with her sister.*

confusion *noun* 1 mixing a thing, person or situation up. 2 a situation where nobody knows what is going on. **confusing** *adjective. A confusing explanation.*

Congo *noun* one of two countries in Africa; the Republic of the Congo is also called Congo-Brazzaville; the Democratic Republic of the Congo was fomerly called Zaire.

The flag of the Congo has a diagonal yellow stripe on a green and red ground.

congratulate *verb* to tell a person that you are pleased about their success or something that they have done. *My friend congratulated me on passing my driving test.* **congratulation** *noun.*

conifer *noun* (say **kon**-if-er) a type of tree that has needle-like leaves and bears its fruit in cones. *A conifer plantation.*

conjure (say **kun**-juh) *verb* to do magic tricks. *The magician conjured a large white rabbit out of a hat.* **conjuror** *noun.* a person who does magic tricks. **conjure up** to make something appear.

conker *noun* a round brown nut of the horse chestnut tree.

connect *verb* 1 to join together. 2 to link by telephone. *Don't hang up, I'm trying to connect you.* 3 to be related or linked. *The families are connected.* **connection** *noun.*

conquer *verb* 1 to defeat and take over. To conquer a country. 2 to overcome an illness or a difficult situation. **conqueror** *noun.*

conquest *noun* 1 the conquering of something. *The conquest of Mount Everest.* 2 overcoming something.

conscience *noun* the part of your mind that tells you if what you are doing is right or wrong. *You have a guilty conscience when you do something wrong.*

conscious *adjective* 1 noticing what is happening. *He was conscious of everybody looking at him.* 2 awake. *The patient is not conscious.* **consciousness** *noun.*

consent *verb* to agree to do something. **consent** *noun* permission given. *She left school without her parents' consent.*

DID YOU KNOW

Except for the larch, nearly all conifer trees are evergreen. This means they don't lose their leaves in autumn. Trees that drop their leaves are called deciduous.

Many of the constellations, such as the Great Bear, were named after mythical creatures.

consequence *noun* something that happens as a result of something else. *He dreaded the consequences of his actions.*

conserve *verb* to store up, or keep from going bad or being wasted. *We need to conserve energy.* **conservation** *noun.*

consider *verb* 1 to think about something in order to make a decision. *I'm considering changing my job.* 2 to regard as. *I consider him an idiot.* **consideration** *noun.* **take into consideration** to allow for something. *I will take your illness into consideration when marking your paper.*

considerable *adjective* fairly large. *A considerable amount of money.*

consist *verb* to be made up of. *Europe consists of many different countries.*

The Low Countries consist of many islands.

console *verb* to give somebody sympathy to make them less sad. **consolation** *noun.*

consonant *noun* any of the letters of the alphabet except for the vowels a, e, i, o and u. *How many consonants are in your name?*

conspiracy *noun* a secret plan to do something that is against the law. A plot.

conspirator *noun* a person who takes part in a conspiracy.

constant *adjective* 1 unchanging, fixed. *We were driving at a constant speed.* 2 loyal and faithful. **constancy** *noun.*

constellation *noun* a group of stars.

constipated *adjective* If you are constipated, you are unable to empty your bowels. **constipation** *noun. Constipation is unpleasant.*

constituency *noun* a town or area that elects a Member of Parliament to represent them.

constitution *noun* 1 the system of laws that states how a country is governed. *The constitution requires elections to be held every five years.* 2 the general condition of a person's body. 3 the way in which something is made up.

C

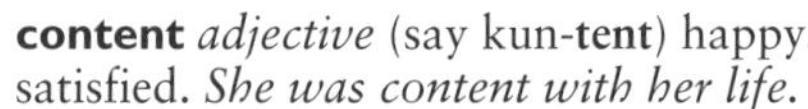

construct *verb* to build or put together.

construction *noun* 1 a building. 2 the process of building. *The bridge is under construction.* 3 words put together to form a phrase or sentence. *The construction of a sentence.* 4 an explanation. *The wrong construction was put on his behaviour.*

constructive *adjective* helpful.

consult *verb* to go to a person or book for information. *Consult a doctor about your illness before it gets any worse.*

consultant *noun* a person who gives advice.

consume *verb* 1 to eat or drink something. 2 to use up. *The car consumes a lot of petrol.* 3 to destroy. *Fire consumed the entire village in a matter of hours.*

consumer *noun* a person who buys and uses goods and services.

contact *noun* 1 the process of touching or coming together. Communication. *I'm not in contact with him.* 2 a person. **contact** *verb. He's got some useful contacts.*

contact lens *noun* a tiny piece of plastic shaped to fit over the eye to make you see better. *Disposable contact lenses.*

contagious *adjective* spreading from person to person. *A contagious disease.*

contain *verb* to hold. *The book contains all the information you need.*

container *noun* 1 a box, barrel or bottle to hold things in. 2 a large metal box used for transporting goods.

Different shaped plastic containers are useful for storing food.

contemporary *adjective* 1 happening now, modern. 2 belonging to the past and happening at the same time as something else. *Contemporary politicians were critical of Disraeli.* **contemporary** *noun. Our fathers were contemporaries at school.*

contempt *noun* lack of respect, thinking that somebody or something is not important. *I hold him in contempt.*

AMAZING FACT

The continents, Africa, Asia, Antartica, Europe, Australia, North America and South America, formed a single continent millions of years ago called Pangaea.

Cranes work from above to finish the construction of this skyscraper.

GRAMMAR NOTE

Words like 'I've', 'won't' and 'shouldn't' are called contractions. These shorter forms (for 'I have', 'I will not' and 'I should not') use an apostrophe to show where letters have been missed out.

content *adjective* (say kun-**tent**) happy, satisfied. *She was content with her life.*

content *noun* (say **kon**-tent) something contained. *The contents had gone off.*

contents *plural noun* things contained. *He emptied the contents of the packet.*

contest *noun* (say **kon**-test) a struggle or fight in which people take part in order to win. *It was an even contest.*

contest *verb* (say kun-**test**) to compete or fight for a place. *To contest an election.*

continent *noun* one of Earth's huge land masses. *Europe, Asia and Africa are continents.*

The continent of Antarctica surrounds the South Pole.

continual *adjective* without stopping.

continue *verb* 1 to go on doing or being something without stopping. 2 to start again after stopping. **continuation** *noun.*

continuous *adjective* without a break. **continuity** *noun.*

contract *noun* (say **kon**-trakt) a written agreement between people. **contract** *verb* (say kun-**trakt**) 1 *We have been contracted to do the music.* 2 to get a disease. *My sister has contracted German measles.*

contract *verb* (say kun-**trakt**) to make or become smaller or shorter. *'Has not' is often contracted to 'hasn't'.* **contraction** *noun.*

contradict *verb* to say that something said or written is wrong. *Don't contradict me.* **contradiction** *noun.*

contrast *noun* (say **kon**-trast) the difference seen between things when they are compared. *There was a big contrast between their results.* **contrast** *verb* (say kun-**trast**).

contribute *verb* 1 to join with others in doing things or giving money to help make something successful. *She contributed towards my success.* 2 to write an article for a newspaper or magazine. **contribution** *noun. He made a contribution of £100.*

control *noun* the power to influence, make decisions or give orders. **control** *verb* to have control of something. *The teacher can't control the class.*

convenience *noun* 1 ease of use. *I always buy frozen food for convenience when I'm busy at work.* 2 a useful appliance, such as a dishwasher. 3 a public lavatory.

convenient *adjective* 1 easy to use or suitable. 2 easy to get to. *The flat is convenient for the shops.*

convent *noun* a place where nuns live.

converge *verb* to come together towards the same point. *The crowds converged on the stadium.*

The roads converged just south of the mountains.

conversation *noun* a talk between people.

converse *verb* to talk. *Let's converse.*

convex *adjective* curved outward, like the outside of a ball. The opposite of convex is concave. *A convex mirror.*

convey *verb* 1 to carry from one place to another. 2 to make known. *Words cannot convey my sympathy.*

convict *verb* (say kun-**vikt**) to find somebody guilty of a crime. *He was convicted of murder.* **convict** *noun* (say **kon**-vikt) a person who has been found guilty.

convoy *noun* a group of ships or vehicles travelling together.

A convoy of vehicles is heading for the ferry.

cook *verb* to make food. **cook** *noun. She's a wonderful cook.*

cooker *noun* an apparatus on which food is cooked. *Your tea is in the cooker.*

cookie *noun* a biscuit.

cool *adjective* 1 between warm and cold. 2 calm. *She manages to keep cool even when she is annoyed.* **cool** *verb* to make or become cool.

cooperate *verb* to work together for a common purpose. **cooperation** *noun.*

cooperative *adjective* 1 helpful. 2 owned by its members. *A cooperative business.*

cope *verb* to deal with something successfully. *She manages to cope with all the family's problems.*

Copenhagen *noun* the capital of Denmark.

WORD BUILDING

The prefix 'co-' gives a sense of together. People who cooperate (sometimes spelled with a hyphen, co-operate), work together.

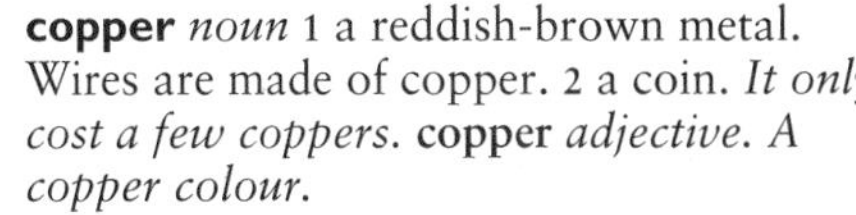

copper *noun* 1 a reddish-brown metal. Wires are made of copper. 2 a coin. *It only cost a few coppers.* **copper** *adjective. A copper colour.*

copy *noun* 1 a thing that looks exactly like another. *Can I have a copy of the picture?* 2 an example of a book, newspaper or magazine of which there are many others. *His copy of the book was torn.* **copy** *verb* 1 to make a copy of something. 2 to do the same as another person. *He's always copying me.*

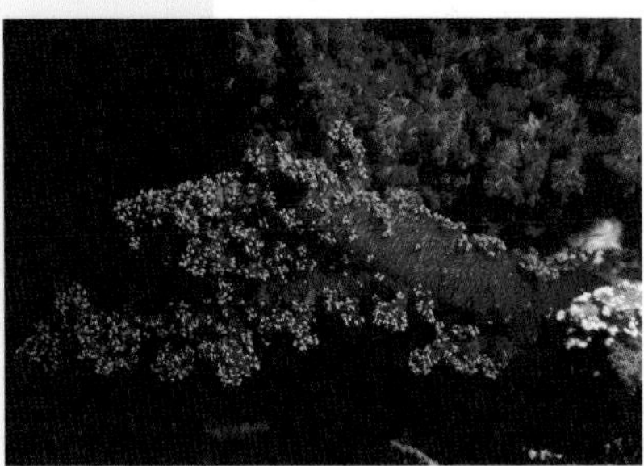

coral *noun* a hard red, pink or white substance formed from the skeletons of tiny sea animals. *A coral necklace.*

A coral reef is a fascinating place for underwater explorers to observe tropical fish.

cord *noun* 1 a thick string. 2 wires inside a plastic casing for electrical equipment. 3 a part of the body. *We use our vocal cords to make sounds.*

corduroy *noun* thick velvety cotton material with thin ridges. *A corduroy jacket.*

core *noun* 1 the hard middle of an apple or pear which contains the pips. 2 the central, most important part of something.

cork *noun* 1 the soft, light bark of the cork oak. Cork tiles are used as a floor covering. 2 a stopper for a bottle made of cork or other material.

corn *noun* 1 the crop of wheat, barley and other types of grain. *The farmer stored his corn in a barn.* 2 maize. *Corn on the cob.*

corn *noun* a painful, hard lump of skin on the foot. *He trod on my corn.*

corner *noun* 1 the place where two edges, lines, walls or streets meet. 2 a kick from the corner of a football field. *They scored from a corner.* 3 a region. *The four corners of the world.* **in a corner** in a difficult situation. **corner** *verb* 1 to drive round a corner. 2 to force somebody into a difficult situation. *He finally cornered me about the mistake.*

cornflakes *noun* toasted flakes made from corn, usually eaten with milk for breakfast.

coronation *noun* the crowning of a king or queen. *We watched the coronation of the new king on television.*

corporal punishment *noun* punishing a person by beating them.

corpse *noun* a dead body.

correct *adjective* 1 without any mistakes. 2 proper, most suitable in a particular situation. **correct** *verb* 1 to put something right and mark the mistakes. 2 to point out a person's faults in order to improve their behaviour. **correction** *noun*.

correspond *verb* 1 to write letters to each other. 2 to be the same or in agreement with something. *Her report of the accident doesn't correspond with his.* 3 to be like or match closely. *Our prime minister corresponds to their president.*

correspondence *noun* 1 writing and exchanging letters. 2 the letters you receive. *A pile of correspondence.* 3 likeness or relationship between particular things.

corridor *noun* a passage in a building.

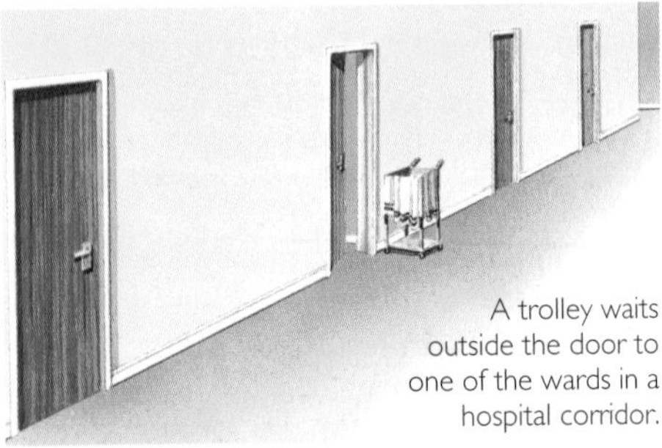

A trolley waits outside the door to one of the wards in a hospital corridor.

corrode *verb* to destroy by chemical action or by rust. *Acid corrodes metal.* **corrosion** *noun*. **corrosive** *adjective*.

corrugated *adjective* shaped into ridges or folds. *Corrugated paper is used for packing.*

corrupt *adjective* immoral or wicked. *The newspaper exposed the corrupt politicians.*

corrupt *verb* to make somebody change from good to bad. *Power corrupts.* **corruption** *noun*.

cosmetics *noun* substances such as lipstick and eyeshadow, used to beautify the face.

cosmic *adjective* related to the universe. *Cosmic rays from outer space.*

The galaxy is surrounded by cosmic dust.

cosmonaut *noun* a Russian astronaut.

cosmos *noun* (say **koz**-moss) the universe.

DID YOU KNOW

Costa Rica, the 'rich coast', actually has two coastlines. One is on the Pacific Ocean and the other on the Caribbean Sea.

GRAMMAR NOTE

'Could' is used with another verb to express possibility or permission: 'You could be right.' 'He said we could smoke.' 'Could' is also used to make a polite request: 'Could you help me carry the bags?' 'Could not' is the negative of 'could'. If you could not do it, you were unable to do it.

SPELLING NOTE

'Council' and 'councillor' have different meanings from 'counsel' and 'counsellor', though they sound exactly the same.

cost *noun* the price of something. **at all costs** no matter what the cost may be. **cost** (costing, cost) *verb* 1 to have a certain price. 2 to cause a loss or disadvantage to somebody. *Drunken driving costs many lives.* 3 to estimate. *The garage costed the repairs at about £100.*

Costa Rica *noun* a country in Central America.

The flag of Costa Rica has a coloured emblem on a striped red, blue and white background.

costly *adjective* expensive.

costume *noun* clothes worn by actors or at a particular time in history. *National costume is worn on historic occasions.*

cot *noun* a bed with high sides for a baby or young child.

cottage *noun* a small house, especially in the country.

cotton *noun* 1 cloth made from the soft white fibres covering the seeds of the cotton plant. 2 a tall tropical plant. 3 cotton thread.

cotton wool *noun* soft, fluffy cotton used for putting cream on your skin or cleaning wounds. *A packet of cotton wool.*

couch *noun* a sofa. *Sit on the couch.*

cough *verb* to push air out of your throat and make a harsh noise. **cough** *noun* 1 the sound of coughing. 2 an illness that makes you cough. *The baby had a nasty cough.*

could past tense of can.

council *noun* a group of people chosen to make laws and decisions and run a town or county. *The parish council.*

councillor *noun* a member of a council.

counsel *noun* 1 advice. 2 a group of lawyers acting for somebody in court. **counsel** (counselling, counselled) *verb*. *She counsels families who have problems.*

counsellor *noun* a person trained to give advice and help.

count *verb* 1 to say numbers in order. *He counted up to 10.* 2 to say or name objects or people to find the total number in a collection. *The teacher counted the children.* 3 to include. *There are four of us, counting me.* 4 to have importance or value. *It's the thought that counts.* 5 to consider. *I count myself lucky.* **count** *noun* 1 counting. 2 a number reached by counting. 3 one of a number of crimes somebody is accused of. *He was found guilty on all counts.* **lose count** not know the exact number.

count *noun* a European nobleman equal to an earl. *The count married the countess.*

counter *noun* 1 a flat surface like a table on which goods are shown and where customers are served in a shop or bank. 2 a small, flat, round piece of plastic or wood used in board games.

counter *verb* 1 to act against something. 2 to meet an attack by hitting back.

counterfeit *noun* a copy of something made in order to deceive, a fake. **counterfeit** *adjective. Counterfeit money.* **counterfeit** *verb. It is illegal to counterfeit money.*

country *noun* 1 a land with its own people, government and language. 2 all the people who live in a particular country. *The Queen spoke to the country.* 3 land away from towns. *We live in the country.*

county (counties) *noun* a region that has its own local government.

couple *noun* 1 two people or things. 2 two people who are married or live together.

couple *verb* to connect or link together.

coupon *noun* a ticket or piece of printed paper allowing the holder to receive goods or information or pay less money for something than usual.

courage *noun* the ability to control fear and face danger or difficulty. **courageous** *adjective.* **pluck up courage** to become brave enough to do something.

The lion is known as the king of the jungle because of its great courage.

courier *noun* 1 a messenger who takes letters and parcels from one place to another. 2 a person who works for a travel company and looks after tourists.

course *noun* 1 lessons or lectures on a particular subject. 2 a series of events or things you can do in a particular situation. 3 the direction or route in which something goes. 4 part of a meal. *What would you like for your main course?* 5 a ground for certain games. *A golf course.* **in the course of** during. **of course** certainly, naturally.

court *noun* 1 a place where law cases are heard and judged. 2 a place where a king or queen, their family and officials live. 3 an area for games. *A tennis court.*

court *verb* to try and win somebody's love. *He courted her for many years.*

courtesy *noun* (say **ker**-tuh-see) polite behaviour. **courteous** *adjective.*

DID YOU KNOW

Your mother's or father's cousin is your cousin once removed. Your grandmother's or grandfather's cousin is your cousin twice removed.

cousin *noun* the child of your uncle or aunt.

cove *noun* a small bay on the coast.

They bathed in the sea in the beautiful cove.

cover *verb* 1 to put something on or round something else to protect or hide it. *I covered my eyes.* 2 to spread over. *Snow covered the fields.* 3 to travel a certain distance. 4 to be enough money for something. *£10 should cover the petrol.* 5 to deal with or discuss a subject or topic. *The book covers the whole of modern history.* 6 to insure against damage or loss. *The policy doesn't cover jewellery.*

cover *noun* 1 a thing put on to cover another thing. 2 the binding of a book or magazine. If you read a book from cover to cover, you read it from beginning to end. 3 something that hides something illegal or shelters you from bad weather. *We had to spend the whole day under cover.* 4 a guarantee from an insurance company against loss or damage. **take cover** to hide or protect yourself.

cow *noun* 1 a fully grown female animal that farmers keep for its milk. 2 a female elephant, whale or seal.

coward *noun* a person who shows fear and avoids dangerous situations. *Cowards lack courage.* **cowardly** *adjective.*

cowardice *noun* cowardly behaviour.

cowboy *noun* a man who looks after cattle on a ranch in America.

A cowboy on horseback rounds up a steer that has strayed from the herd.

cox (coxes) *noun* a person who steers a rowing boat.

coy *adjective* pretending to be shy and modest. *She gave him a coy smile.*

crab *noun* a sea animal with a shell-covered body and five pairs of legs.

C

crack *verb* 1 to split or make something split. *The hot water cracked the glass.* 2 to make a sudden loud noise. *To crack a whip.* 3 to break down. *After days of questioning, he finally cracked.* **crack a problem** to finally solve a problem. **crack a joke** to tell a joke. **get cracking** to get on with a task. **crack up** to break down. **crack** *noun* 1 a thin line on the surface of a glass or plate, for example, where they have cracked but not come completely apart. 2 a narrow gap. 3 a sudden loud noise. **at the crack of dawn** very early in the morning. **have a crack at something** to try to do something difficult.

cracker *noun* 1 a hollow cardboard tube with toys inside that cracks when you pull apart a snap inside it. 2 a firework that explodes with a crack. 3 a thin, dry biscuit.

cradle *noun* a small bed for a baby. **from the cradle to the grave** from birth to death.

cradle *verb* to hold gently.

craft 1 a job that needs skill, especially making things skilfully with your hands. 2 the skill of tricking people. **crafty** *adjective*. *I wouldn't trust him, he's very crafty.*

craft *noun* a ship, boat or plane. *A spacecraft is a craft for travelling in space.*

Sputnik was the first craft ever to be sent into space. It was launched on 4 October 1957.

cram (cramming, crammed) *verb* 1 to push lots of things or people into a small space. 2 to fill. *His head was crammed with facts.*

crane *noun* 1 a machine for lifting and moving heavy objects. 2 a large bird with a long neck and long legs.

crane *verb* to stretch out your neck in order to see something better.

crash *noun* 1 a loud noise made by something falling or breaking. 2 a bad accident. 3 a business failure. **crash** *verb* 1 to make a loud noise when falling, or hitting something violently. 2 to hit something and be damaged. *She crashed the car.* 3 to move noisily or break through something with force. *He crashes through the house like an elephant.* 4 to fail, especially in business or money matters. *The stock market crashed.*

crate *noun* a box made of wood for putting goods in. *A crate of oranges.*

DID YOU KNOW

Craters in extinct volcanoes are often filled with water. Most other craters, on Earth and other planets, were caused when meteorites crashed into them.

WORD HISTORY

'Crafty' used to mean skilful, before it got today's meaning of cunning.

AMAZING FACT

The Whooping Crane was once a common bird in the United States but was hunted nearly to extinction. In 1945 there were only 16 individual birds left. Then a successful breeding program was started and the chicks were reared by humans. But the chicks couldn't be released because they were so used to the humans that fed them. So now the chicks are fed using hand puppets that look like adult cranes.

crater *noun* 1 a round hole in the top of a volcano. 2 a round hole in the ground or on the surface of another planet.

crawl *verb* 1 to move on your hands and knees with the body close to the ground. 2 to move slowly. *The traffic was crawling along.* 3 to be full of or covered with crawling things. *Don't sit on the grass, it's crawling with ants.* 4 If something makes your skin crawl, it gives you a nasty feeling. **crawl** *noun* 1 a slow crawling movement. 2 a fast swimming stroke.

Babies learn to crawl before they can walk.

crayon *noun* a pencil or stick of coloured wax for drawing.

crazy *adjective* 1 foolish, mad. 2 very interested or excited. *Crazy about football.* **crazily** *adverb*. **craziness** *noun*.

creak *verb* to make a sound, usually when something is moved or moves. **creak** *noun* the sound of wood bending or an unoiled door opening.

cream *noun* 1 the fatty part of milk. *We had strawberries and cream.* 2 food that looks and tastes like cream. *Ice-cream.* 3 a soft substance that you put on your skin to make it soft or soothe it. 4 the best part of something. *The cream of society.* **creamy** *adjective*. **cream** *verb* to mix food until it is like cream. **cream** *adjective* a cream colour.

Cream and fruit are two of the ingredients of ice-cream.

crease *noun* 1 a line made on cloth, paper or clothes by folding, crushing or pressing. 2 a line on a cricket pitch. **crease** *verb*. *I can't sit down because my dress will crease.*

create *verb* 1 to make something new. *They have created a garden in the desert.* 2 to produce or cause something to happen. *His film created a lot of controversy.*

creation *noun* 1 making something. *The creation of great works of art.* 2 a thing created. *All my own creation.*

creative *adjective* able to invent and produce new ideas and things.

creator *noun* a person who makes or invents something.

C

creature *noun* a living being.

crèche *noun* (say kresh) a day nursery for babies and young children.

credit *noun* 1 the practice of allowing somebody to buy something and pay for it later. 2 the money a bank or business has agreed somebody can borrow. 3 the time you are allowed to pay a debt. *They gave us a month's credit.* 4 somebody with a good reputation. *He's a credit to the school.* 5 trust. *Don't give any credit to what he says.* 6 Credits are the list of people who helped to make a film or programme. **credit** *verb* 1 to believe. 2 to say that somebody has done something. *She is credited with many achievements.* 3 to increase an account with a sum of money. *We will credit your account with the refund.*

credit card *noun* a plastic card you can use to buy goods on credit.

Credit cards are sometimes also called smart cards.

creditor *noun* a person money is owed to.

creed *noun* a set of beliefs or opinions.

creek *noun* a small inlet on the sea coast.

creep (crept) *verb* 1 to move slowly and quietly. *She creeps around the house.* 2 to move slowly towards or across something. **creep** *noun* an unpleasant person you dislike. *That creep always flatters the boss.* If someone or something gives you the creeps, they make you feel nervous. **creepy** *adjective. A creepy story.*

cremate *verb* to burn a dead body to ashes. **cremation** *noun.*

crematorium *noun* a place where people are cremated.

crescent *noun* 1 a curved shape like a crescent moon. 2 a curved street.

crevice *noun* an opening or crack in a rock.

crew *noun* 1 all the people working on a ship, plane or spacecraft. 2 a group of people working together. *A film crew.*

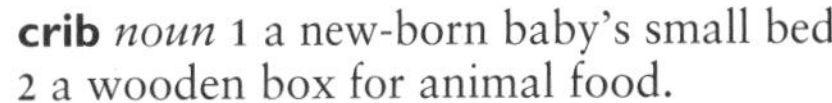

crib *noun* 1 a new-born baby's small bed. 2 a wooden box for animal food.

crib *verb* to copy somebody else's work and pretend that it is your own.

cricket *noun* an outdoor game for teams played with a ball, bats and two wickets.

cricket *noun* an insect like a grasshopper.

On warm summer nights you can hear the crickets chirping.

cried past tense of cry.

crime *noun* 1 an unlawful activity. 2 an action that is wrong, but not a matter for the police. *It would be a crime not to enjoy the sunshine.*

criminal *noun* a person who has committed a crime. **criminal** *adjective. A criminal act.*

crimson *adjective* purplish red.

cringe *verb* to move back with fear.

The poor creature cringed with fear when he heard the man's voice.

crisis *noun* a serious or dangerous situation.

crisp *adjective* 1 dry and easily broken. *Crisp pastry.* 2 fresh or newly made. *A crisp shirt.* 3 fresh and cold. *A crisp morning.* 4 quick and clear. *A crisp hello.* **crisp** *noun* a thin piece of fried potato.

critic *noun* 1 a person who gives his opinion about books, films, music or art. 2 a person who points out mistakes.

The air crew greet the passengers as they board the plane.

critical *adjective* 1 finding faults or mistakes. *He made critical remarks about my work.* 2 very important or dangerous. *A critical illness.* **critically** *adverb.*

criticism *noun* 1 pointing out faults and mistakes. 2 a critic's opinion on books, films, music or art. **criticize** *verb.*

croak *verb* to make a deep low sound. *Frogs croak in spring.* **croak** *noun* a deep hoarse sound.

Croatia *noun* a country in Southeast Europe.

The flag of Croatia has a colourful crest on a striped red, blue and white background.

crockery *noun* cups, plates and other dishes. *He smashed all their crockery.*

crocodile *noun* a large reptile with a long body. Crocodiles live in rivers.

crocus *noun* a small plant with white, yellow or purple flowers that grows in spring. *Crocuses grew on the lawn in spring.*

croissant *noun* (say **krwah**-sahn) a crescent-shaped bread roll.

crook *noun* 1 a shepherd's stick. 2 a dishonest person. 3 the inside of your elbow or knee. *The crook of my arm.*

crooked *adjective* 1 not straight, twisted. 2 dishonest, criminal.

crop *noun* 1 plants such as grain, fruit or vegetables grown for food. 2 the plants collected at harvest time. 3 a group of things appearing at the same time. *A crop of questions.* **crop** *verb* to cut short. *Cropped hair.* **crop up** to appear or happen. *A problem has cropped up.*

cross *noun* 1 a mark that looks like an X. *He marked the place with a cross.* 2 an upright post with another shorter bar across the top or any similar design used for decoration or as jewellery. The cross is an important Christian symbol. 3 a mixture of two animals or plants. *A mule is a cross between a horse and a donkey.*

Christian relics were highly prized in the Byzantine Empire, which began in AD 476. This gold crucifix, or cross, is an example.

AMAZING FACT

Although crocodiles' jaws are powerful enough to crush the bones of their prey, they are also sensitive enough to carry their young hatchlings safely to water.

WORD HISTORY

In crossword puzzles, words have to fit both across and down and so cross each other. The first crossword was published in a New York magazine called 'World' in 1913, so the puzzle is not as old as you might think.

AMAZING FACT

The Crown Jewels are a collection of crowns, swords and other valuable articles that belong to the kings and queens of Britain. In 1671, a man called Colonel Blood tried to steal the jewels. He was captured just outside the Tower of London where the Crown jewels were kept.

cross *verb* 1 to go across something, or move from one side to another. 2 to draw a line or lines across something. 3 When roads or railways cross, they meet and go across each other. 4 to put one arm, leg or finger on top of the other. *I crossed my fingers for luck.* 5 to mix one animal or plant with another. 6 to oppose somebody's plans or go against somebody's wishes. *If you cross me, I'll get angry.* **cross out** to draw a line through something to show that it is wrong or not wanted.

cross *adjective* angry.

crossing *noun* 1 a journey by ship to the other side of a sea. 2 a place where people can cross a road or railway. 3 a place where two roads or railways cross.

crossroads *noun* a place where two roads meet and cross each other.

crossword *noun* a puzzle in which you work out answers to clues and write the answers into numbered squares.

crouch *verb* to lower your body close to the ground by bending your knees and back.

crow *noun* a large black bird with a loud cry. **as the crow flies** in a straight line. **crow** *verb* to make a loud cry like a crow.

crowd *noun* a large group of people in one place. **crowd** *verb* 1 to come together in a large group. 2 to fill completely. *The new museum was crowded with tourists carrying cameras.* 3 to cram in.

crown *noun* 1 a headdress like a ring made of gold and jewels, worn by a king or queen. 2 The Crown is the governing power of a monarchy. 3 the top part of your head. 4 an old British coin that is no longer used, worth 25 pence. **crown** *verb* 1 to put a crown on somebody who has become king or queen. 2 to complete something successfully. *Crowned with glory.*

The crown was made of gold and studded with precious jewels.

crucial *adjective* (say **kroo**-shuhl) extremely important. *A crucial appointment.*

crucify (crucifying, crucified) *verb* to punish by nailing or binding a person to a cross and leaving them to die. **crucifixion** *noun.* The Crucifixion is the death of Jesus Christ on the Cross.

crude *adjective* 1 in a raw or natural state. *Crude oil.* 2 rough, not skilfully made. *A crude drawing.* 3 not showing sensitive feeling, vulgar. *Crude jokes.*

cruel (crueller, cruellest) *adjective* causing pain or suffering to people or animals. **cruelty** *noun.*

cruise *noun* a holiday on a ship visiting a number of places. **cruise** *verb* to move in a car or ship at a comfortable speed.

A cruise in the warm blue waters of the Mediterranean makes a luxurious summer holiday.

crumb *noun* a very small piece of bread, cake or biscuit.

crumble *verb* 1 to break or fall into lots of small pieces. 2 to come to an end or to nothing. *Her hopes soon crumbled.* **crumble** *noun* cooked fruit covered with a mixture of flour, butter and sugar.

crumple *verb* to become full of creases and folds. *She crumpled up the invoice.*

crunch *verb* 1 to crush hard food noisily with your teeth. *The dog was crunching a bone.* 2 to make a crushing or breaking noise. **crunch** *noun* 1 crunching. 2 a crunching noise. *The crunch of footsteps on the gravel drive frightened me.* **come to the crunch** to reach a point when a difficult decision has to be made.

crusade *noun* 1 an expedition to Palestine made by Christian knights in the Middle Ages. 2 a movement against something bad or for something good. *A crusade against smoking in public places.*

crust *noun* 1 the hard surface of something baked, such as bread. 2 a hard surface. *The Earth's crust.*

crustacean *noun* (say krust-**ay**-shuhn) an animal with a shell. Crabs and lobsters are crustaceans.

Crabs and other crustaceans have delicately flavoured meat.

AMAZING FACT

Cuckoos live in all the continents of the world except Antarctica. There are 136 species of cuckoo in all and 45 of these lay their eggs in the nests of other birds. Their eggs are then incubated, and hatched by the 'adopted' parent.

crutch *noun* a stick, with a piece that fits under the arm, which people who have difficulty walking use as a support.

cry (cried) *verb* 1 to shed tears from your eyes, because you are unhappy or in pain. 2 to shout or say something loudly. *She cried for help.* **cry** (cries) *noun* 1 a sound you make when you feel excited or frightened. *A cry of pain.* 2 a shout to attract somebody's attention. 3 weeping.

crypt *noun* an underground room in a church. *A tryst in the crypt.*

crystal *noun* 1 a natural mineral that looks like ice. 2 a shaped piece of this mineral used in jewellery or decoration. 3 high-quality glass, often cut. **crystal** *adjective.*

Crystals are prized for their brilliance and clarity. Some people believe they have the power to heal illness.

cub *noun* a young wild animal. *Tiger cubs.*

Cuba *noun* a country in the West Indies.

cube *noun* 1 an object with six square sides which are all the same size. *A cube of sugar.* 2 the number made by multiplying a number by itself twice. The cube of 2 is 2 x 2 x 2, which makes 8. **cube** *verb* 1 to multiply a number by itself twice. 2 to cut something into cubes. **cubed** *adjective.*

cubicle *noun* a small room, especially for changing clothes.

cuckoo *noun* 1 a bird that lays its eggs in other birds' nests. 2 the sound a cuckoo makes.

cucumber *noun* a long thin vegetable with a green skin, eaten raw in salads.

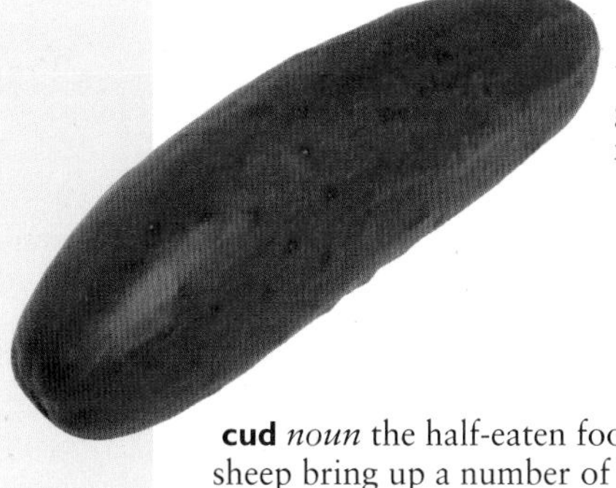

Cucumbers can be served in salads or sandwiches.

cud *noun* the half-eaten food that cows and sheep bring up a number of times, before finally swallowing it.

cuddle (cuddled, cuddling) *verb* to hold somebody or something closely in your arms. **cuddle** *noun.* **cuddly** *adjective.*

cue *noun* a signal for somebody to do or say something.

cue *noun* a long stick for hitting the ball in snooker or pool.

C

culprit *noun* a person who has done something wrong.

cultivate *verb* 1 to use land to grow crops on. 2 to develop something and make it strong. *He has cultivated a love of art.* **cultivation** *noun.*

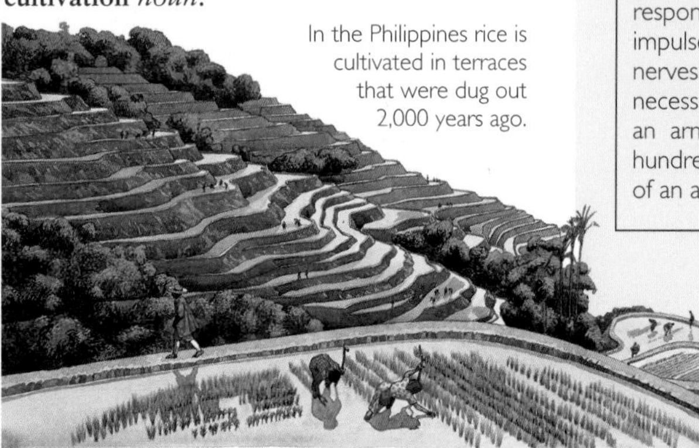

In the Philippines rice is cultivated in terraces that were dug out 2,000 years ago.

culture *noun* 1 an understanding of literature, art, music and other activities of the mind. 2 the shared customs and traditions of a group of people at a particular time. *He studied the Inca culture.* 3 a group of cells grown in a laboratory for medical study. 4 raising animals and growing plants. **cultural** *adjective.*

cultured *adjective* well educated, with good manners and a knowledge of the arts.

cunning *adjective* clever in deceiving others. *He's as cunning as a fox.* **cunning** *noun.*

The fox is an animal renowned for its cunning.

cup *noun* 1 a container with a handle for drinking from, or its contents. 2 a metal trophy given as a prize to a winning team or player. 3 anything shaped like a cup. **cup** *verb* to make your hands into a cup shape.

cupboard *noun* a piece of furniture with shelves and a door for keeping things in.

curb *verb* to keep something under control. *The government has curbed the powers of the police.* curb *noun.*

cure (cured, curing) *verb* 1 to make an illness disappear or a person well again. *There are still many diseases that drugs cannot cure.* 2 to stop something bad. *It is impossible to cure his meanness.* 3 to preserve something to make it last longer. *Fish and meat can be cured by drying, smoking or salting.* **cure** *noun. Doctors are searching for a cure for Aids.*

AMAZING FACT

'Amp' or 'ampere' is the unit of electric current. Our muscles respond to electric impulses from our nerves. The current necessary to raise an arm is about one hundred thousandth of an amp.

Most of the world's currencies are made up of paper notes and metal coins.

SPELLING NOTE

'Currant' and 'current' sound the same but are spelt differently. Currants get their name from Corinth, in Greece, where they grew in ancient times. 'Current' comes from the Latin word for to run or flow.

curious *adjective* 1 interested in things and wanting to find out. *I'm curious to know what he said to my mother the other day.* 2 unusual and interesting. *That's a curious story!* **curiosity** *noun.*

curl *noun* 1 hair shaped into curves and circles. *Goldilocks had golden curls.* 2 a spiral shape. *A curl of smoke.* **curl** *verb* to twist hair into curls or be in curls. **curl up** 1 to form curls or twists. *The leaves have gone brown and curled up.* 2 to lie with your arms and legs drawn close to the body. *She curled up in front of the fire.*

curler *noun* a pin or roller put in the hair to make it curly.

curly *adjective* full of curls.

currant *noun* 1 a small dried grape used in baking and cooking. 2 a soft red, black or white berry.

currency (currencies) *noun* 1 the money used in a country. *The value of foreign currencies is always changing.* 2 the common use of something. If an idea gains currency, more people get used to it and accept it.

current *adjective* happening or being used now. *The current fashion for body piercing.*

current *noun* 1 water or air moving in one direction. *The river has a strong current.* 2 the flow of electricity. *An electric current.*

curry (curries) *noun* food cooked with hot-tasting spices. *An Indian curry.*

curse *noun* a word, phrase or sentence asking supernatural powers to harm somebody or something. *There must be a curse on our family, because everything is going wrong.* **curse** *verb* 1 to swear or say rude words because you are angry. 2 to use a curse against somebody.

cursor *noun* a small movable point on a computer screen used to identify a position.

curtain *noun* 1 a piece of material hung up at a window or door. 2 the heavy sheet of material lowered in front of a theatre stage. 3 something that covers or hides. *A curtain of mist descended on the hills.*

curve *verb* to bend. *The road curves at the top of the hill.* **curve** *noun* a bending line, like the edge of a circle. *A curve in the road.* **curvy** *adjective.*

C

cushion *noun* 1 a case filled with soft material to sit on or lean against. 2 anything soft or springy in the shape of a cushion. *We floated on a cushion of air.* **cushion** *verb* to protect from shock, a knock, hardship or change. *The branches must have cushioned his fall.*

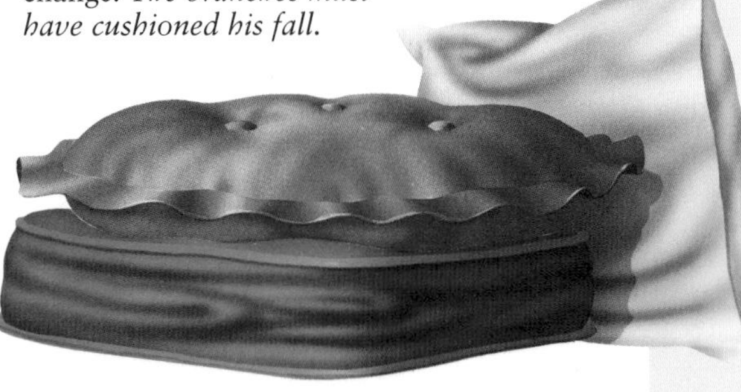

Big soft cushions add to the comfort of any home.

custody *noun* 1 the legal right of caring and looking after a child. *The mother was given custody of the children.* 2 imprisonment. **take into custody** to arrest.

custom *noun* 1 something which is accepted behaviour among people or that people of a particular society always do. *Different countries have different customs.* 2 regular business given to a shop by customers. *The corner shop lost most of its custom to the new supermarket.*

At the spring festival of Holi, it is the custom for Hindu children to throw coloured powder over each other.

customer *noun* a person who buys goods from a shop or uses a bank or other business. *The customer is always right.*

customs *plural noun* a place where government officers check your luggage for goods on which you need to pay duty (tax) when your enter or leave a country. *We were stopped at customs.*

WORD HISTORY

'Cute' comes from 'acute,' which itself comes originally from the Latin word for 'sharp'.

DID YOU KNOW

Cyclones are usually called hurricanes in Europe and America. In the Far East and the Pacific they are usually called typhoons.

cut (cutting, cut) *verb* 1 to make an a opening in your skin with something sharp. *I cut my finger.* 2 to divide, break or make something shorter with a knife, scissors or another sharp instrument. *I've cut some flowers.* 3 to reduce time, size or quantity. *Shops are cutting prices.* 4 to shorten something. *The film was cut by twenty minutes.* 5 to make a recording. *We cut a disc.* **cut and dried** already decided and impossible to change. **cut back** to reduce. *Factories are cutting back on staff.* **cut in** to interrupt. **cut off** 1 to stop a person while speaking. *He cut me off when I was in the middle of asking a question.* 2 to stop a telephone connection. *We were cut off and the line went dead.* 3 to cut off a flower. 4 to stop the supply. *The electricity was cut off because we couldn't pay the bill.* **cut** *noun* 1 the act of cutting. 2 the result of cutting. *There's a cut in the cloth.* 3 an opening or small wound. 4 a reduction. *A price cut.* 5 a part that is cut out. *I noticed quite a few cuts in the film.* 6 a style or shape. *A good hair cut.* 7 a share. *She promised me a cut of her winnings.*

cute *adjective* 1 pretty, attractive. *She's a cute little girl.* 2 clever. *That's a cute idea.*

cutlery *noun* knives, forks and spoons.

cycle (cycling, cycled) *verb* to ride a bicycle or tricycle. *I usually cycle to school, but today I'm walking.* **cyclist** *noun.*

cyclone *noun* (say **seye**-klohn) a tropical storm that moves very fast round a calm central area, a hurricane.

cygnet *noun* (say **sig**-nit) a young swan.

cylinder *noun* an object or container with a long tubular body.

cynic *noun* (say **sin**-ik) a person who sees no good in anything and believes that people always behave in a selfish way. **cynical** *adjective.*

Cypriot *noun* a person who comes from Cyprus. **Cypriot** *adjective. A Cypriot dance.*

Cyprus *noun* an island country in the eastern Mediterranean Sea.

The island of Cyprus appears in yellow on the country's flag.

czar *noun* (say zar) the title of the former emperor of Russia.

Czech *noun* (say chek) 1 the language spoken in the Czech Republic. 2 a person who comes from the Czech Republic. **Czech** *adjective. A Czech tennis player.*

Czech Republic *noun* a country in eastern Europe.

D

Dd

dab (dabs, dabbing, dabbed) *verb* to touch quickly and gently with something soft. *She dabbed the dirty mark with a damp cloth.*

dachshund *noun* a small black or brown dog with a long body and short legs.

dad *or* **daddy** (daddies) *noun* an informal word for father.

daddy-long-legs *noun* also known as a cranefly, a flying insect with very long legs.

daffodil *noun* a tall plant with a yellow, bell-shaped flower that grows from a bulb in spring.

daft *adjective* silly or foolish. *You really look daft in that hat!*

dagger *noun* a weapon for stabbing that looks like a short, pointed knife.

Dáil *noun* the lower house in the parliament of the Republic of Ireland, the equivalent of the British House of Commons.

daily *adjective* happening or done every day. **daily** *adverb*. **daily** (dailies) *noun* a newspaper that is published every day except on Sunday.

dainty (daintier, daintiest) *adjective* small, pretty and delicate. *Dainty feet.* **daintiness** *noun*. **daintily** *adverb*.

dairy (dairies) *noun* a place where milk is put into bottles and where milk products such as butter and cheese are made and sold. **dairy** *adjective*.

daisy *noun* a wild flower with a yellow centre and white petals.

Dakar *noun* the capital of Senegal.

dam *noun* 1 a strong barrier or concrete wall built across a river to hold back the water. 2 the water held back. **dam** (dams, damming, dammed) *verb*.

damage *verb* to harm or spoil something. **damage** *noun*. **damaging** *adjective*.

The Aswan Dam in Egypt provides the country with hydroelectric power.

DID YOU KNOW

'Dáil' is the Irish word for assembly. The Dáil Éireann (Irish Assembly) has 144 members, who are elected every five years.

WORD HISTORY

Flower names often have an interesting history. 'Daisy' comes from Old English 'day's eye', because it opens in the morning. 'Dandelion' comes from the French 'dent de lion', meaning 'lion's tooth', from the shape of its leaves.

Graceful Balinese dancers enact a traditional story. Their elaborate costumes are decorated with gold threadwork.

damages *noun* money that somebody is paid for injury or harm done to them.

Damascus *noun* the capital of Syria.

damp *adjective* moist or slightly wet. **dampness** *noun*. **dampen** *verb*.

dance *verb* to move your feet and body to the rhythm of music. **dancer** *noun*.

dance *noun* 1 a style of dancing with special set steps e.g. a waltz or gavotte. 2 a party at which there is dancing.

dandelion *noun* a wild plant with a yellow flower.

dandruff *noun* small flakes of dead skin found on the scalp of some people.

danger *noun* 1 the chance that something may happen that will cause harm or injury. 2 a situation that is not safe. *The tunnel is in danger of collapsing.* **danger** *interjection*. *Danger! Falling rocks.* **dangerous** *adjective*.

dangle *verb* to swing to and fro or to hang down loosely. *He dangled his legs over the side of the pool.*

Danish *adjective* of Denmark or its people. *A Danish ship.* **Danish** *noun*. The language spoken in Denmark.

dank *adjective* damp and cold.

dappled *adjective* marked with patches or spots of dark and light colours.

dare *verb* 1 to be brave enough or rude enough to do or try to do something. *How dare you contradict me!* 2 to challenge somebody to do something brave. *I dare you to jump.* **dare** *noun*.

daring *adjective* brave and not afraid to take chances. **daring** *noun*.

dark *adjective* 1 with little or no light. **dark** *noun* darkness. 2 not light or fair in colour. *She has dark hair.* **in the dark** not knowing about something. **a dark horse** somebody who may have unexpected, hidden abilities.

darken *verb* to make or become dark.

darn *verb* to mend a hole in a piece of clothing by sewing threads across it.

dart *noun* a small arrow that players throw at a round board marked with numbers in a game called darts.

D

dart *verb* to move suddenly and quickly. *She darted across the road.*

dash *verb* to rush somewhere. **dash** *noun.*

dash *noun* a short line (–) used in writing.

dash *noun* a small amount. *A dash of salt.*

data *noun* facts and information.

All the data about the new business venture was presented in a huge sheaf of papers.

database *noun* a large amount of information stored on a computer.

date *noun* 1 the day, month and/or year of a particular event. 2 an appointment to meet somebody, particularly a boyfriend or girlfriend. **date** *verb* 1 to put a date on a letter etc. 2 to guess or give a date when something was made. *This church dates from 1400.* **out of date** 1 old-fashioned. 2 no longer valid. *An out of date ticket.* **up to date** modern.

date *noun* the brown, sticky fruit of the date palm.

daughter *noun* somebody's female child.

daughter-in-law *noun* the wife of somebody's son.

daunt *verb* to make somebody afraid that they won't be able to do something. *He was daunted by the huge task that lay ahead of him.* **daunting** *adjective.*

dawdle *verb* to waste time by moving or doing something very slowly.

dawn *noun* the beginning of the day when the Sun rises.

At dawn the sky was full of warm apricot coloured light.

day (days) *noun* 1 the 24 hours from one midnight to the next midnight. 2 the part of the day from sunrise to sunset when it is light. **call it a day** to stop doing something in order to return to it later.

daybreak *noun* dawn.

daydream *noun* pleasant, distracting thoughts that some people have when they are awake. **daydream** *verb.*

GRAMMAR NOTE

A dash is usually used to show a pause or an interruption in a sentence. Two dashes – such as these – can act like brackets.

SPELLING NOTE

Don't confuse the spelling of 'dear', as in 'Dear Mrs Earnshaw', with 'deer', the animal.

dazed *adjective* bewildered and unable to think clearly, perhaps because of a shock.

dazzle *verb* 1 to blind briefly or make somebody dazed with a bright light. 2 to amaze or impress somebody. *She was dazzled by his wit.* **dazzling** *adjective.*

de- *prefix* By adding de- to a noun or verb it changes the meaning to its opposite or negative. **defrost** to remove ice from something. *Please defrost the fridge.*

dead *adjective* no longer alive.

deadline *noun* a time or date by which some work or a job must be finished.

deadlock *noun* a situation in which people cannot settle a disagreement. *The talks ended in deadlock.*

deadly (deadlier, deadliest) *adjective* fatal or likely to kill. *Deadly poison.*

deaf *adjective* unable to hear well or to hear at all. **deafness** *noun.*

deafen *verb* to make unable to hear because the noise is so loud. **deafening** *adjective.*

deal (deals, dealing, dealt) *verb* 1 to do business by buying and selling. *They deal in silver.* 2 to give out cards to people in a card game. **dealer** *noun.* **deal with** 1 to take action to sort out a problem. 2 to be about or concerned with. *This book deals with religion in Africa.*

The cards were dealt into four piles.

deal *noun* 1 a business agreement. 2 a bargain. *I got a good deal on this car.*

dear *adjective* 1 loved very much. *A dear friend.* 2 the way of beginning a letter before putting the name of the person you are writing to. *Dear Mrs Smith.* 3 costing a lot of money. The opposite of dear is cheap.

dear *noun* 1 a person you love or who is loveable. 2 an interjection, used when surprised or angry. *Oh dear, I'm late!*

death *noun* the end of life. **put to death** to kill, execute. **frightened/sick to death** very scared/fed up.

death penalty *noun* the punishment of death for a person who has committed a crime such as murder.

death trap *noun* a building, vehicle or something else that is very dangerous.

deathly *adjective*, *adverb* like death. *Deathly cold hands.*

debate *noun* a discussion, especially at a public meeting. **debate** *verb.*

debris *noun* (say **deb**-ree) scattered pieces of things that have been destroyed, or rubbish. *The debris left after the bomb attack.*

The beach was littered with all kinds of debris.

debt *noun* (say det) 1 money you owe somebody. *Pay off your debts before you buy a new car.* If you are in debt, you owe money. 2 a feeling that you owe somebody for something they have done for you. *A debt of gratitude.*

debtor *noun* a person who owes money. The opposite of debtor is creditor.

debug (debugging, debugged) *verb* 1 to remove faults or problems from a computer. 2 to remove a listening device.

decade *noun* a period of ten years. *The first decade of the 21st century.*

decaffeinated *adjective* with the caffeine removed. *My grandmother has a heart problem, so she drinks decaffeinated coffee.*

decapitate *verb* to cut off someone's head.

decathlon *noun* a competition in which athletes take part in ten different events, involving running, jumping, hurdling, shot put, discus, pole vault and javelin.

decay *verb* 1 to go bad. *Sugar can decay your teeth.* 2 to lose health or power, to become weak. **decay** *noun. The building is falling into decay.* **decayed** *adjective.*

Decaying fruit attracts wasps and other insects.

deceased *noun* a person who has recently died. *The deceased was a very rich man.*

deceit *noun* being dishonest by making people believe something that is not true. **deceitful** *adjective.*

deceive *verb* to make somebody believe something that is not true. *He deceived everybody with his terrible lies.*

December *noun* the twelfth month of the year. December has 31 days.

decent *adjective* 1 socially acceptable, honest and respectable. 2 acceptable, good. *A decent wage.* **decency** *noun. He had the decency to apologize.*

deception *noun* deceiving somebody or being deceived. **deceptive** *adjective. Her charm is very deceptive.*

WORD HISTORY

A decibel is actually a tenth of a bel, which is rarely used. The unit was named after Alexander Graham Bell (1847–1922), the inventor of the telephone.

WORD BUILDING

The prefix 'deci–', as in 'decibel' and 'decimal', comes from the Latin 'decimus', which means tenth.

decibel *noun* (say **dess**-ib-el) a unit for measuring the loudness of sound.

decide *verb* 1 to do something after thinking about it; to make up your mind. *I've decided to go away.* 2 to settle something or bring it to an end. *Lack of money decided the issue.*

decided *adjective* clear and definite, easily seen. *You have a decided advantage.*

deciduous *adjective* (say dis-**id**-yoo-us) deciduous trees shed their leaves every autumn. (Trees that never shed their leaves are called evergreen.)

decimal *adjective* counting units in tens. *Decimal currency.* The dot in a decimal fraction (such as 1·5) is called a decimal point. **decimal** *noun.*

decipher *verb* (say dis-**eye**-fer) to work something out that is difficult to read or understand. *I can't decipher his writing.*

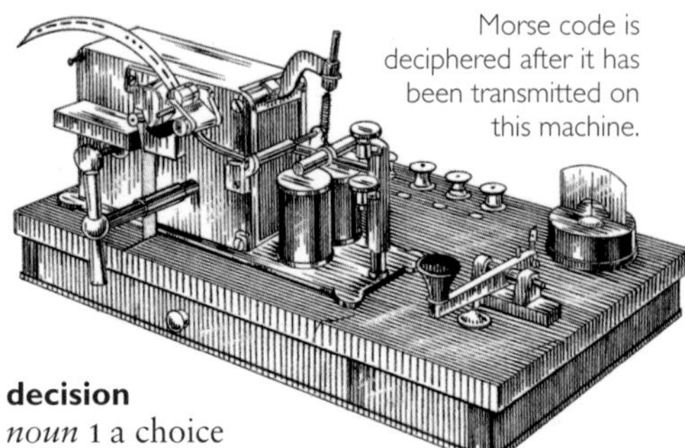

Morse code is deciphered after it has been transmitted on this machine.

decision *noun* 1 a choice made about what should be done. Deciding. *She made the right decision.* 2 the ability to decide and act quickly.

decisive *adjective* 1 full of decision and acting quickly. 2 having a definite result or making certain that there will be a particular result. *A decisive victory.* **decisively** *adverb.*

deck *noun* 1 a floor on a ship or bus. 2 a piece of equipment for playing records on or tapes in. *A tape deck.* 3 a pack. *A deck of playing cards.*

declaration *noun* something declared. *A declaration of war.*

declare *verb* 1 to make known or say something clearly. *I have declared my support.* 2 to tell Customs that you have bought goods abroad or tell the tax office about your income.

decline *verb* 1 to refuse politely. *We declined the invitation.* 2 to become smaller, weaker or worse. *Her health is declining rapidly.* **decline** *noun* a gradual loss of strength or importance.

decode *verb* to work out the meaning of a code. *He tried to decode the message.*

decompose *verb* to rot or decay after having died. **decomposition** *noun.*

decorate *verb* 1 to make something look more attractive by adding things to it. *The cake was decorated with sweets.* 2 When you decorate a room, you paint or wallpaper it. 3 to give somebody a medal. *The soldier was decorated for bravery.* **decoration** *noun.*

The decorator is wearing rubber gloves to protect her hands against the paint.

decorator *noun* a person who paints houses or paints and wallpapers rooms.

decrease *verb* to become smaller or weaker. *The number of voluntary workers is sadly decreasing.* **decrease** *noun.* **decreasing** *adjective.*

decree *noun* an official order or decision, especially by a ruler or a government. **decree** *verb. The king decreed an end to the war.*

decrepit *adjective* very old and in bad condition. *A decrepit old man.*

dedicate *verb* 1 to give a lot of time and effort to something. *She dedicates her life to prayer.* 2 to declare a book or performance to be in honour of somebody. *I dedicated this book to my mother.* **dedication** *noun.*

dedicated *adjective* devoted to something or somebody. *Dedicated to her job.*

deduce *verb* to work something out by looking at the facts and reaching a conclusion. *They have been silent all year, and from this I deduce that they must have moved away.* **deduction** *noun.*

deed *noun* 1 something done, especially a good deed. 2 The deeds of a house are the official documents given to its owner.

deep *adjective* 1 going a long way down from the surface. *A deep hole.* 2 measured from back to front. *The drawers are 20 centimetres deep.* 3 serious, strong or to a great extent. *Deep feelings* 4 low. *A deep voice.* **deeply** *adverb.* **deep in thought** thinking very hard about something.

deep-freeze *noun* a refrigerator for keeping frozen food in, a freezer.

deer (*plural* deer) *noun* a large fast animal. Male deer usually have antlers.

A male red deer has magnificent antlers. It uses them to attract a mate and to fight off other stags.

DID YOU KNOW

Male deer (note that the plural word stays the same, like sheep) are called stags, bucks or harts. Female deer are called hinds or does. Deer range in size from the small Pudu of South America to the huge elk of northern Europe, Asia and North America.

deface *verb* to spoil something, especially a wall or a notice, by scribbling all over it. *The white wall was defaced with graffiti.*

default *verb* to fail to do something you have agreed to do. **default** *noun.* If you win a game by default, you have won because the other player has not turned up.

defeat *verb* 1 to beat. *Chelsea were defeated in the final.* 2 to cause to fail. *My hopes were defeated.* 3 to be too difficult to solve. *The problem defeated me.* **defeat** *noun.*

defect *noun* (say **dee**-fekt) a fault or imperfection. *His radio had a defect.*

Two of these pots are perfect, but the middle one is cracked and broken. This may be due to a defect in manufacturing techniques.

defect *verb* (say di-**fekt**) to leave your own country, party or army and join the other side. **defector** *noun.*

defective *adjective* having faults, not working properly.

defence *noun* 1 something used for defending or protecting. *The trees act as a defence against the wind.* 2 the act or action of defending. 3 the arguments put forward by a defendant in court. 4 the lawyers representing an accused person in a trial. 5 a group of players in a team who try to stop the opposition from scoring.

defend *verb* 1 to protect, guard or speak in support, especially when attacked. She is always defending her little brother. 2 to try to prove in court that an accused person is not guilty. 3 to play in a position that stops an opponent from scoring points or goals. If a champion defends her title, she wants to win to keep it. **defender** *noun.*

defendant *noun* a person who has been accused of a crime.

defensive *adjective* 1 used for defending. *Defensive weapons.* 2 behaving in an unsure or threatened way. *She is very defensive about her friends.* **on the defensive** behaving as if expecting an attack.

defer (defers, deferring, deferred) *verb* 1 to arrange that something will take place at a later date. *She deferred her studies for a year.* 2 to agree with a person or an opinion out of respect.

defiance *noun* openly refusing to obey. If you act in defiance of something, you do something although it is forbidden. **defiant** *adjective. Defiant teenagers stay out late.*

deficient *adjective* lacking in a particular thing, short of something. **deficiency** *noun. A deficiency in vitamin C.*

D

define *verb* to say exactly what something is or explain what a word means. *Let's define the problem.* **definition** *noun.*

definite *adjective* firm and unlikely to change. *I need a definite answer.* **definite article** the word 'the' is the definite article. ('A' and 'an' are indefinite articles.) **definitely** *adverb.*

deforestation *noun* the cutting down of forests.

Deforestation is a huge problem in the Amazon, where more trees are felled every day to make way for building and farming land.

deformed *adjective* abnormally shaped. **deformity** *noun.*

defrost *verb* 1 to get rid of ice or frost, especially in a refrigerator or on a windscreen. 2 When you defrost food, it becomes unfrozen.

defuse *verb* 1 to remove the fuse from an unexploded bomb so it cannot explode. 2 to make a situation less dangerous. *He defused the situation by apologizing.*

defy (defies, defying, defied) *verb* 1 to refuse to obey. *Criminals defy the law.* 2 to challenge somebody to do something that seems impossible. *I defy you to swim across the river.* 3 to be impossible to understand or solve. *The problem defies solution.*

degree *noun* 1 a unit for measuring temperature, usually written with a degree sign (°). 2 a unit of measurement of angles. *A right angle is a 90° angle.* 3 the extent or amount of feeling. *I admire him to a degree.* 4 an academic grade given by a university or a college to a person who has finished a course or passed an examination. *A degree in German.* **by degrees** gradually.

deity (deities) *noun* (say **day**-it-ee) a god or goddess. *They worshipped several deities.*

delay *verb* 1 to put something off until later. *We have decided to delay the meeting until the middle of this afternoon.* 2 to make somebody or something late.

delete *verb* to cross out something written or printed.

deliberate *adjective* (say dil-**ib**-er-ut) 1 planned, done on purpose and not by accident. *A deliberate lie.* 2 slow and careful, especially when moving or speaking. **deliberately** *adverb.*

WORD HISTORY

The delta of a river got its name from its triangular shape. It was named after the shape of the Greek letter D.

deliberate *verb* (say dil-ib-er-**ayt**) to think carefully. **deliberation** *noun* careful consideration of a subject.

delicacy (delicacies) *noun* 1 something soft, fine and graceful. 2 something that needs careful and tactful handling. *He didn't appreciate the delicacy of the situation.* 3 delicious and often expensive food.

delicate *adjective* 1 soft, fine and graceful. *Delicate silk.* 2 fragile, easily broken or becoming ill easily. *A delicate child.* 3 not strong, especially when talking about colour, taste or smell. *A delicate flavour.* 4 needing careful treatment or tactful handling. *Don't mention her old boyfriend, it's a delicate subject.* **delicately** *adverb.*

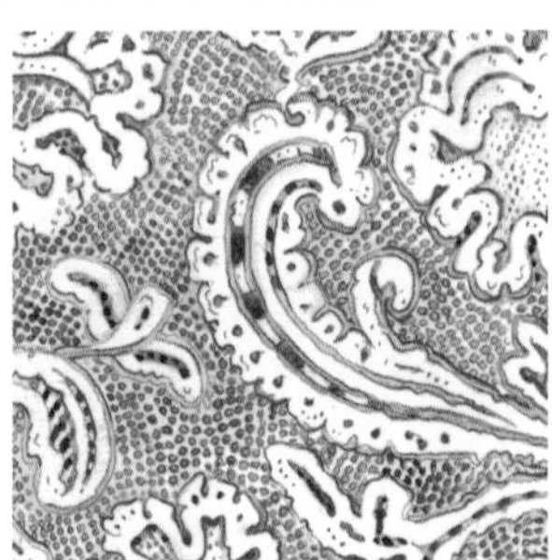

Lace is a strong yet very delicate fabric.

delicatessen *noun* a shop or section of a supermarket selling cooked meats, cheeses and other prepared foods.

delicious *adjective* giving great pleasure, having a pleasant taste or smell. *The food was delicious.*

delight *noun* great pleasure. *To our delight the exam was cancelled.* **delight** *verb* to give or feel a lot of pleasure. **be delighted** *I'd be delighted to come to Marianne's party.* **delightful** *adjective.*

deliver *verb* 1 to take something, especially goods or messages, to somebody's house or office. *The postman delivered the letters.* 2 to give a speech. 3 to help with the birth of a baby. *The baby was delivered this morning.* **delivery** *noun.*

delta *noun* 1 the Greek letter D (written Δ). 2 the fan-shaped area at the mouth of a river, where it splits up into many channels. *The Nile delta.*

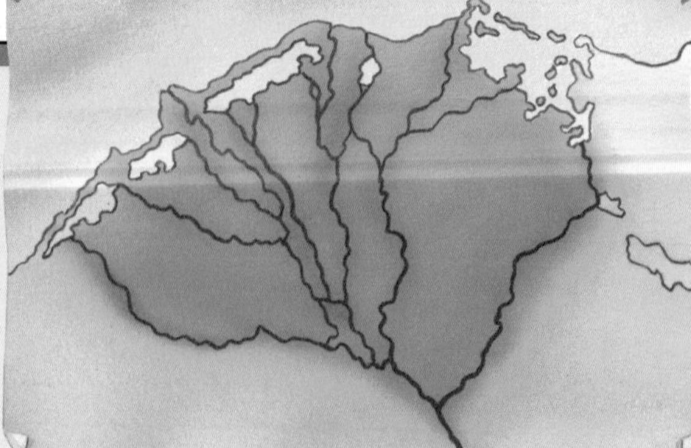

At the delta of a river a lot of silt flows into the sea.

deluge *noun* 1 a heavy fall of rain, a great flood. 2 things arriving in large numbers. *We had a deluge of applications for the job we advertised.* **deluge** *verb.*

demand *verb* 1 to ask for something firmly, as if ordering it. *I demand an explanation.* 2 to need. *Teaching demands a lot of patience.* **demand** *noun* 1 a firm request. 2 a desire to buy or get something. **in demand** wanted. *Mobile phones are in great demand even though expensive to run.*

demanding *adjective* needing attention, time or energy. *Looking after small children is a very demanding job.*

demo (demos) *noun* a demonstration.

democracy *noun* 1 a system of government in which people elect the leaders of their country. 2 a country governed by democracy. **democrat** *noun.* **democratic** *adjective. A democratic decision.*

demolish *verb* to pull down old buildings or destroy something. **demolition** *noun. Demolition work began early.*

The crane operator began the demolition work and soon the old house began to crumble.

demon *noun* a devil or evil spirit.

demonstrate *verb* 1 to show how something works or prove a point by giving examples. 2 to take part in a march or meeting, to show support for a cause. *The students are demonstrating against grant cuts.* **demonstration** *noun.*

demonstrative *adjective* showing your feelings. *He rarely kisses his children, he is not a very demonstrative father.* 'This', 'that', 'these', 'those' are **demonstrative adjectives.** They are used to point out a person or thing.

den *noun* 1 the home of a fox or wolf. 2 a person's private room. *He invited me to a game of billiards in his den.*

denial *noun* 1 denying or refusing something. *A denial of justice.* 2 saying that something somebody is accused of is not true. *He printed a denial in the newspaper.*

Denmark *noun* a Scandinavian country in Europe.

The flag of Denmark has a white cross against a red background.

AMAZING FACT

George Washington, the first President of the United States, wore dentures, or false teeth. Several sets are on show at the Smithsonian Institution in Washington, DC. Early dentures were made of various materials including ivory and wood.

DID YOU KNOW

Denmark is a small country, made up of a peninsula and about 100 inhabited islands. The island of Greenland, thousands of kilometres away, belongs to Denmark and is over 50 times bigger than the mother country.

denounce *verb* to speak or write against somebody. *He was denounced as a traitor.* **denunciation** *noun.*

dense *adjective* 1 thick, crowded together or difficult to see through. *A dense forest.* 2 stupid. **density** *noun.*

dent *noun* a hollow in a hard surface made by a collision or by pressure. *There was a big dent in the side of the car.* **dent** *verb* to make a dent.

dental *adjective* of or for the teeth. *Free dental treatment for children.* A dental surgeon is a dentist.

dentist *noun* a person trained to treat people's teeth.

dentures *plural noun* false teeth.

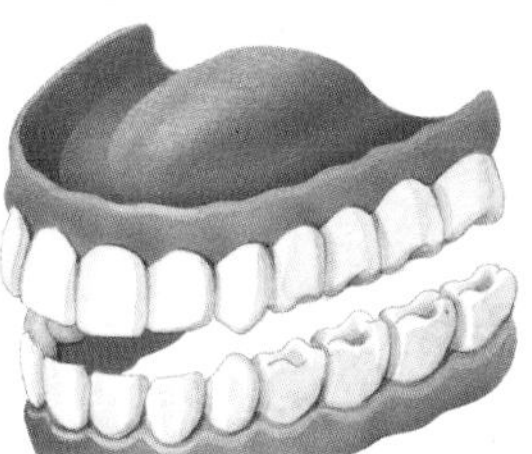

Some people take out their dentures and put them in a glass beside the bed overnight.

depart *verb* to go away, leave. *The train to Oxford is about to depart from platform three.* **departure** *noun.*

department *noun* a part of a large business, government, college or shop.

department store *noun* a large shop in which all sorts of goods are sold in different departments.

depend *verb* 1 If you depend on somebody or something, you need them. *Our group depends on your help.* 2 to trust somebody or rely on something. *You can always depend on me.* 3 to vary according to circumstances. *The success of the trip will depend on the weather.* **it depends** said when you are not sure about what will happen. *'Are you going to the cinema?' 'I don't know. It depends.'*

deport *verb* to send an unwanted person out of a country. **deportation** *noun.*

deposit *noun* 1 a sum of money paid into a bank account. *I'd like to make a deposit, please.* 2 money paid as part payment for something. *If you want to order the goods, you will have to pay a deposit.* 3 a layer of a substance left somewhere. *There were deposits of sugar at the bottom of the bottle.* 4 a natural layer of sand, coal or rock. **deposit** *verb* 1 to put something down. *Sand was deposited by the wind.* 2 to pay money as a deposit.

depot *noun* (say **dep**-oh) 1 a place for storing goods. 2 a place where buses or trains are parked and repaired.

depressed *adjective* very sad. **depression** *noun. She felt depressed and anxious.*

D

deprive *verb* to take or keep something away from somebody. *The children have been deprived of love.*

depth *noun* the distance between the top and bottom surfaces or the distance from the front to the back of something. How deep something is. **in depth** thoroughly, looking at all aspects. **out of your depth** 1 to be in water that is too deep to stand in. 2 to try and do something that is too difficult.

Divers wear special breathing apparatus so they can explore the ocean depths.

derive *verb* 1 to get from. *She derives great satisfaction from her work.* 2 to come from. *The word democracy derives from the Greek for 'people'.*

descend *verb* to go down. **be descended from** to be related to and come from a certain family. **descent** *noun.*

descendant *noun* a person or an animal related to another who lived a long time ago. *She is a descendant of Mary Stuart.*

describe *verb* 1 to say what something or somebody is like. 2 to mark out. *To describe a circle.* **description** *noun.* **descriptive** *adjective.*

desert (say **dez**-ut) *noun* a large sand-covered area of land where very little rain ever falls.

The cactus can survive in the harsh conditions of the desert. It stores water in its thick stems and its spines protect it against getting eaten by animals.

SPELLING NOTE

They sound the same but they are spelt differently: 'desert' is an empty area, 'dessert' (with two 's's) is a pudding.

desert (say diz-**ert**) *verb* 1 to go away with no intention of returning, to abandon. *He deserted his wife and children.* 2 to run away from military service. **desertion** *noun. The soldier was accused of desertion.* **deserter** *noun.* **deserted** *adjective* empty, abandoned.

deserts *plural noun* what somebody deserves. *He got his just deserts.*

deserve *verb* to be worthy of something. *He deserves to win after all the hard training he has done.*

desiccate *verb* to dry. *Desiccated coconut.*

design *noun* 1 a drawing that shows how something is to be made or built. *He showed the designs for his new fashion collection.* 2 the way something is made or built. *I don't like the design of the car.* 3 a pattern of shapes to decorate something. *Curtains with a floral design.* 4 a thought-out plan. **design** *verb* 1 to invent the look of something. *He designs for a jeweller.* 2 to plan. *This dictionary is designed for children.* **designer** *noun.*

desire *noun* a strong wish for something. *I have no desire to meet him.* **desire** *verb.*

desk *noun* a table at which you sit to read, write and work.

despair *noun* a complete loss of hope. **despair** *verb. He quite despaired of ever seeing her again.*

despatch see dispatch.

despise *verb* If you despise somebody, you think that they are worthless.

dessert *noun* (say diz-**ert**) sweet food eaten at the end of a meal.

destination *noun* the place to which a person or thing is going.

destiny *noun* 1 Your destiny is what will happen to you in your life. *It was her destiny to marry the king.* 2 the force that controls your life. Fate. **destine** *verb. They were destined to meet again.*

destroy *verb* to ruin something, or break it to pieces. *The criminals destroyed all the vital evidence before their capture.* **destruction** *noun.* **destructive** *adjective.*

detail *noun* a small point or fact. *The police officer noted down the essential details.* **detailed** *adjective.*

detective *noun* a person, especially a police officer, whose job it is to find out what has happened in a crime.

deteriorate *verb* to become worse. *Her health has deteriorated within the last year.* **deterioration** *noun.*

determined *adjective* having firmly decided to do something in order to be successful. *She is determined to win the tennis tournament.* **determination** *noun.*

devastate *verb* 1 to destroy or damage. *The floods have devastated the whole area.* 2 to shock. *I was devastated when he gave me the terrible news.* **devastation** *noun.*

develop *verb* 1 to grow or become bigger. *Her small company soon developed into a major business.* 2 to come into existence, to become more serious. *She has developed a huge appetite.* 3 to make prints from a photographic film. 4 to use an area of land for building houses, shops and factories. **development** *noun.*

device *noun* something made or built for a particular purpose. *She has invented an unusual listening device.*

A corkscrew is a device for opening bottles.

devise *verb* to invent or think up. *He devised a cunning plan.*

devote *verb* to spend time or energy on something or somebody. *He devotes all his spare time to football.* **devotion** *noun.*

devour *verb* to eat greedily.

dew *noun* tiny drops of water that form during the night on the ground or cool surfaces. *Dew lay on the grass.*

Dhaka *noun* the capital of Bangladesh.

diabetes *noun* (say die-uh-**bee**-teez) an illness in which there is too much sugar in a person's blood. **diabetic** *adjective* (say die-uh-**bet**-ik). *Diabetic marmalade.*

diagnose *verb* to find out what is wrong with a person and what illness they might have. *The doctor diagnosed a case of measles.* **diagnosis** *noun.*

diagonal *adjective* (say die-**ag**-un-ul) A diagonal line goes in a slanting direction, joining opposite corners. **diagonal** *noun* a straight line going diagonally across.

diagram *noun* a simple drawing that shows the parts of something, often used to explain how things work.

dial *noun* an indicator, like a clock face or a meter, with numbers or letters around it. **dial** (dials, dialling, dialled) *verb* to ring a telephone number by turning a dial or pressing buttons.

DID YOU KNOW

Diamond is made of carbon and is the hardest mineral in the world. Because of this, diamonds are used in cutting and grinding tools.

AMAZING FACT

Dr Samuel Johnson (1700–84) wrote one of the first major dictionaries of the English language.

dialect *noun* a form of language spoken in a particular region, which has different words and pronunciation from other forms of the same language.

dialysis *noun* (say die-**al**-iss-iss) a process of removing harmful products from the blood, especially when the kidneys are not functioning properly.

diameter *noun* (say die-**am**-it-er) the length of a straight line going from side to side through the centre of a circle or sphere.

diamond *noun* 1 a very hard precious stone that looks like cut glass. 2 a shape with four straight sides of equal length that stands on one of its points. 3 a playing card with red diamond shapes on it. *The ace of diamonds.* **diamond** *adjective.*

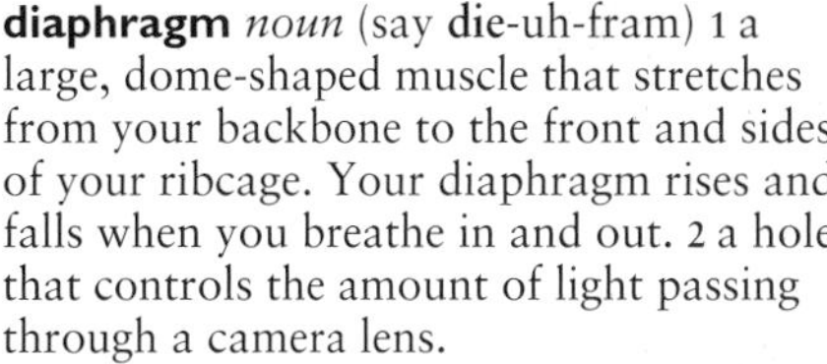

A diamond is a beautiful clear and sparkling stone.

diaphragm *noun* (say **die**-uh-fram) 1 a large, dome-shaped muscle that stretches from your backbone to the front and sides of your ribcage. Your diaphragm rises and falls when you breathe in and out. 2 a hole that controls the amount of light passing through a camera lens.

diary (diaries) *noun* 1 a book with spaces for each day of the year used for writing down appointments. 2 a book for keeping a record of daily events.

dice *noun* ('Dice' is the plural of 'die', but is used as both singular and plural.) a small six-sided cube marked with dots from one to six on each of its sides, used in board games and gambling.

Dice are used in many games of chance.

dice *verb* to cut something, especially food, into cubes.

dictate *verb* 1 to say aloud what somebody should write down. *She dictated a letter to her secretary.* **dictation** *noun.* 2 to give orders. *I won't be dictated to by my parents.*

dictator *noun* a ruler who has total power over a country. Most dictators take power by force. *A ruthless dictator ran the country.*

dictionary *noun* a book in which words are listed in alphabetical order, from A to Z. You look up a word in the dictionary to find out what it means and how to spell it.

D

did past tense of do.

die singular of dice.

die *noun* a block of hard metal for pressing coins and other metal or plastic objects into shape. *This component was cast in a die.*

die (dies, dying, died) *verb* 1 to stop living. *She died of cancer.* 2 to come to an end or disappear. *My love will never die.* **die down** to become less strong. *The noise eventually died down.* **die for** to want something very much. *I'm dying for a drink.*

diesel *noun* 1 a vehicle that has a diesel engine. 2 fuel for a diesel engine.

A diesel engine is more economical and less polluting than a petrol engine.

diet *noun* 1 the sort of food usually eaten by a person or an animal. *A healthy diet.* 2 special kinds of food eaten in order to be healthy or to lose weight. *I'm on a very strict diet.* **diet** *verb.*

difference *noun* 1 being different. A way of being unlike each other. *The difference between boys and girls.* 2 the amount left between two numbers when one is subtracted from the other. *The difference between 10 and 4 is 6.* 3 When people have their differences, they have a disagreement. 4 When something makes a difference, it is important. *It makes no difference to me.*

different *adjective* 1 not the same. *Every time I see her, she has a different boyfriend.* 2 various. *The dress comes in different colours.*

These two houses are the same, but they have different coloured doors and different windows.

difficult *adjective* 1 not easy, hard to do or understand. 2 a difficult person is somebody who is not easily pleased and hard to get on with. **difficulty** (difficulties) *noun.*

dig (digs, digging, dug) *verb* 1 to make a hole in the ground, usually by moving soil. *To dig the garden.* 2 to poke or push in. *Don't dig your knife into the cake.* **dig up** 1 to remove something from the soil. *I dug up the bush.* 2 to discover something. *The newspapers have dug up another scandal.*

AMAZING FACT

The human digestive tract is approximately eight to ten metres long.

WORD HISTORY

A diesel (car or locomotive) has a diesel engine that burns diesel oil. They were all named after Rudolf Diesel (1858–1913), a German engineer.

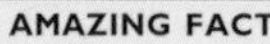

AMAZING FACT

Dinosaurs died out about 65 million years ago but, although there are several theories, no one knows why.

dig *noun* 1 a small push or poke. *She gave him a dig in the ribs.* 2 an archaeological site. 3 a remark against a person, intended to upset. *That teacher loves having a dig at me.*

digest (say die-**jest**) *verb* 1 to make food change so the body can use it. *Fruit is easy to digest.* 2 to take in information and think it over. **digestion** *noun.*

digest (say **die**-jest) *noun* a summary of information or news.

digit *noun* 1 any of the numbers from 0 to 9. 2 a finger or toe.

digital *adjective* 1 giving a reading by displaying numbers rather than by moving hands. *A digital clock.* 2 working with signals or information represented by numbers. *A digital recording.*

The watch is digital. It has no hands.

dilemma *noun* a difficult situation in which you have to choose between two or more possible actions.

dilute *verb* to make a liquid weaker or thinner by mixing it with water or other liquid. *I like to dilute my orange juice.*

dim (dimmer, dimmest) *adjective* 1 not bright or clear, difficult to see. *The light was very dim.* 2 stupid.

dim (dims, dimming, dimmed) *verb* to make something dim. *Dim the lights.*

dime *noun* an American 10 cent coin.

dimension *noun* 1 a measurement, especially of length, height or width. *The exact dimensions of the room.* 2 The dimensions of a problem are the extent and importance of it.

diminish *verb* to become smaller.

din *noun* a loud, annoying noise.

dine *verb* to have dinner. **dine out** to eat in a restaurant or at friends.

dinghy (dinghies) *noun* (say **ding**-ee) a small boat, especially an inflatable rubber boat.

dingy (dingier, dingiest) *adjective* (say **din**-jee) dark, depressing and dirty-looking. *He's got a dingy little room.*

dining room *noun* a room where people have their meals.

dinner *noun* the main meal of the day.

dinner party *noun* a party at which guests eat dinner together.

dinosaur *noun* a large extinct reptile that lived in prehistoric times.

dip (dips, dipping, dipped) *verb* 1 to put into a liquid. *He dipped his biscuit in the tea.* 2 to move downward or drop slightly. *The Sun dipped below the horizon.*

dip *noun* 1 a downward slope or slight drop. 2 a quick swim or bathe. *A dip in the sea.* 3 a creamy mixture that is eaten with raw vegetables or biscuits.

diplomacy *noun* 1 the building of relations between countries and different people. 2 the skill of doing and saying the right thing at the right time. *She handled the delicate situation with tact and diplomacy.*

diplomat *noun* 1 a government official who represents their country in another country. Diplomats usually work in an embassy. 2 a tactful person. **diplomatic** *adjective.* **diplomatically** *adverb.*

direct *adjective* 1 straight towards a place. *A direct flight.* 2 honest and frank. *Please give me a direct answer.* 3 exact. *The direct opposite.* **directly** *adverb.*

direct *verb* 1 to tell somebody the way. *Can you direct me to the station?* 2 to order somebody to do something. 3 to organize and manage something. *Who is directing the new Batman film?* **director** *noun.*

direction *noun* 1 the course in which a person or thing is moving or the line they are pointing in. *What direction is the reform taking?* 2 control or management. *The film was made under his direction.*

directions *plural noun* instructions on how to do, use or find something. *Can you give me directions?*

The arms of the signpost point in the directions of some of the world's most famous cities.

dirt *noun* earth, soil, or anything that is not clean.

dirty (dirtier, dirtiest) *adjective* 1 not clean. *My hands are dirty.* 2 vulgar. *Dirty jokes.* 3 mean, unfair. *That was a dirty trick.*

dis- *prefix* forming the opposite of a word. Dishonest is the opposite of honest.

SPELLING NOTE

A disc is thin, flat and circular. It is sometimes spelt 'disk', and this is the usual spelling for computer storage devices, such as hard and floppy disks.

disabled *adjective* physically or mentally unable to do something. *There are special parking spaces reserved for disabled people.* **disability** *noun.*

disadvantage *noun* a condition that causes problems and makes success difficult. The opposite of advantage. *You are at a disadvantage if you can't use a computer.*

disagree *verb* to have different opinions and so not agree. If food disagrees with you, it makes you feel ill. **disagreement** *noun.*

disappear *verb* to stop being seen, to go out of sight. **disappearance** *noun.*

disappoint *verb* to fail to come up to somebody's hopes or expectations. *My parents were disappointed in me.* **disappointment** *noun.*

disaster *noun* 1 an unexpected event that causes great damage and suffering. *Floods and earthquakes are natural disasters.* 2 a failure, something unsuccessful. *Our holiday was a disaster.* **disastrous** *adjective.*

disc *noun* 1 a gramophone record. 2 a round flat object. 3 a layer of cartilage between the bones in your back. *She's suffering from a slipped disc.*

disc jockey or usually **DJ** *noun* a person who plays records and tapes on radio, TV, or in discos and clubs.

disciple *noun* a person who believes in and follows the teachings of a leader. *Jesus and all his disciples sat in a circle.*

discontinue (discontinues, discontinuing, discontinued) *verb* to stop something.

discover *verb* 1 to find or find out. 2 to be the first person to find something. *Christopher Columbus was the first European to discover America.* **discovery** *noun.*

Marco Polo is believed to have discovered spaghetti. He ate it in the form of noodles while exploring China.

discreet *adjective* 1 tactful in what you say or do. 2 not attracting a lot of attention. *Discreet pastel colours.* **discretion** *noun.*

discriminate *verb* 1 to notice a difference between two or more things. *We must discriminate between right and wrong.* 2 to treat things or people differently. If you discriminate against somebody, you treat them unfairly. **discrimination** *noun. Racial discrimination is a crime.*

discuss *verb* to talk about something. *I often discuss politics while drinking coffee with my friends.* **discussion** *noun.*

D

disguise *verb* to make somebody or something look or sound different so they are not recognized by other people. *The prince disguised himself as a servant.* **disguise** *noun. She wore a red wig as a disguise.* **in disguise** disguised.

If you wear this cunning disguise to school, none of your friends will know who you are.

disgust *noun* a feeling of strong dislike caused by an unpleasant smell, sight or sound. *He left the meeting room in utter disgust.* **disgust** *verb.*

disgusting *adjective* very unpleasant. *Wendy noticed a truly disgusting smell.*

dish (dishes) *noun* 1 a shallow bowl for food. 2 part of a meal. **do the dishes** to wash up. **dish up** to serve food.

dishevelled *adjective* (say di-**shev**-uld) untidy, especially somebody's hair or clothes. *The bed was dishevelled.*

dishonest *adjective* not honest. *It is dishonest to cheat.* **dishonestly** *adverb.*

dishwasher *noun* a machine that automatically washes dishes.

disinfectant *noun* a substance used to destroy germs.

disk *noun* a flat round object for storing information, used in computing.

dislike *verb* to not like. *I dislike long car journeys intensely.* **dislike** *noun.*

disloyal *adjective* not loyal. *He was disloyal to his regiment.* **disloyally** *adverb.*

dismay *noun* a feeling of worry and disappointment. **dismay** *verb.* **dismayed** *adjective. I was dismayed at her truly pathetic attitude.*

dismiss *verb* 1 to send somebody away or tell a person that they will no longer have a job. *He was dismissed for constantly being late for work.* 2 to stop thinking about something or somebody or considering an idea. *We dismissed the idea.* **dismissal** *noun.*

disobedience *noun* not doing what you are told to. Not obeying. **disobedient** *adjective.*

dispatch *verb* to send somebody or something off to a destination. *The message was dispatched early this morning.*

dispatch *noun* an official report.

dispense *verb* to give out. *The chemist dispenses medicines.* **dispenser** *noun. A cash dispenser outside the bank.*

WORD HISTORY

'Disgust' and 'disgusting' come from the Latin 'gustus', meaning taste. The prefix 'dis–' shows the opposite, so disgusting food is food that doesn't taste very good.

display *verb* 1 to put something in a place so it can easily be seen. *The shop displayed the new range in the window.* 2 to show. *He displayed his ignorance.* **display** *noun.*

dispute *noun* a quarrel between people. *The dispute over university grants.* **in dispute** being argued about.

dispute *verb* 1 to argue or quarrel. 2 to say that something is not true, to raise objections. *I don't dispute that the homeless need our support.*

disqualify (disqualifies, disqualifying, disqualified) *verb* to stop somebody from doing something because they have broken the rules. **disqualification** *noun. He took his disqualification badly.*

disrupt *verb* to bring into disorder and prevent something from continuing normally. **disruption** *noun.*

dissatisfied *adjective* not satisfied.

dissect (say dis-**sekt**) *verb* to cut something up in order to examine it, especially a dead animal or plant. **dissection** *noun.*

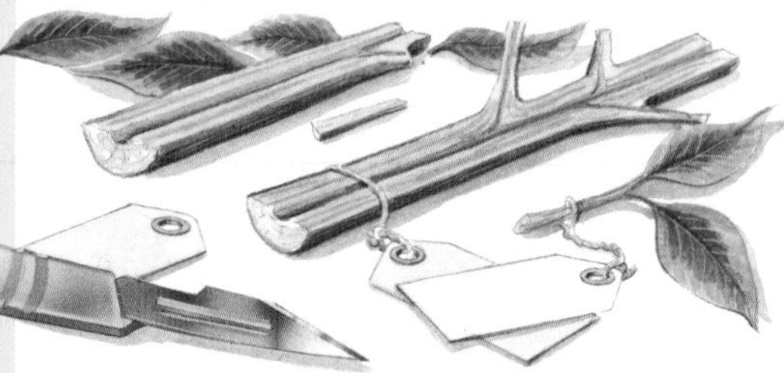

Part of the botanist's job was to dissect the plants for research purposes.

distance *noun* the amount of space between two places. *My new flat is within easy walking distance of the office.* **in the distance** far away. **from a distance** a long way away from something in space or time. **distant** *adjective.*

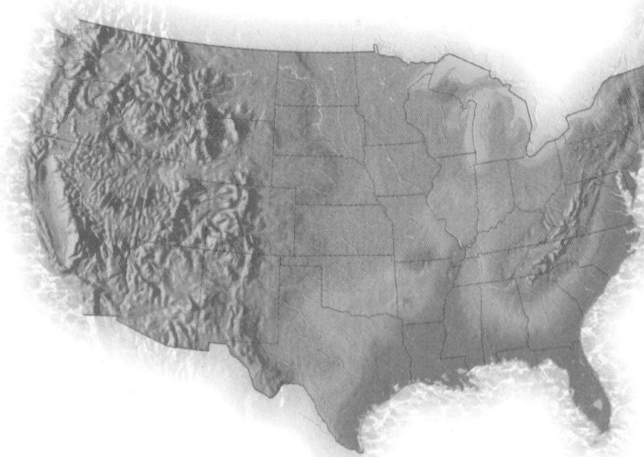

From one side of North America to the other is a huge distance to travel.

distinct *adjective* 1 easily heard or seen. *I noticed a distinct bruise on his leg.* 2 clearly different. **distinctly** *adverb.*

distinction *noun* 1 a clear difference. 2 excellence, or an award for excellence. *She got a distinction in her exam.*

distinguish *verb* 1 to make or notice differences between things. *I can't distinguish one from the other.* 2 to show excellence. *He distinguished himself by his bravery in the face of the enemy.*

district *noun* a part of a town or country.

disturb *verb* 1 to spoil somebody's rest or interrupt what they are doing. *That noise disturbs my concentration.* 2 to cause somebody to be upset or worried. 3 to move things from their position. *Nothing in the room had been disturbed.* **disturbance** *noun.*

ditch (ditches) *noun* a channel dug in the ground for water to flow along.

ditch *verb* to get rid of or leave behind. *The robbers ditched their get-away car.*

dive *verb* 1 to plunge head first into the water. *She dived off the top board.* 2 to swim under water. *They went diving for pearls.* 3 to go down steeply. *The eagle dived from a great height.* 4 to move quickly and suddenly. *He dived for cover.* **diver** *noun.*

Diving is a skill that requires courage and stamina. It can sometimes be dangerous.

divert *verb* 1 to turn something in another direction. *The traffic has been diverted because of road works.* 2 to turn somebody's attention away from something else. 3 to amuse or entertain. **diversion** *noun.*

divide *verb* 1 to split up or be separated into smaller parts. *We divided the sweets between us.* 2 in maths, to find out how many times one number is contained in another. *Divide 12 by 3.*

division *noun* 1 the process or result of dividing or being divided. *We have a fair division of work in our family.* 2 in maths, the process of dividing one number by another. 3 a vote in parliament which separates members into two sections. 4 a group having a special purpose within an organization. *The soccer team were relegated to the second division.*

divorce *noun* the legal ending of a marriage. **divorce** *verb* 1 to end a marriage. 2 to separate things. *He has become divorced from reality.*

WORD HISTORY

'Diwali' comes from the ancient Sanskrit for 'row of lights'. During the festival, which is celebrated in October or November, lamps are lit in honour of the Hindu god Rama.

Diwali (say di-**wah**-lee) *noun* a Hindu religious festival.

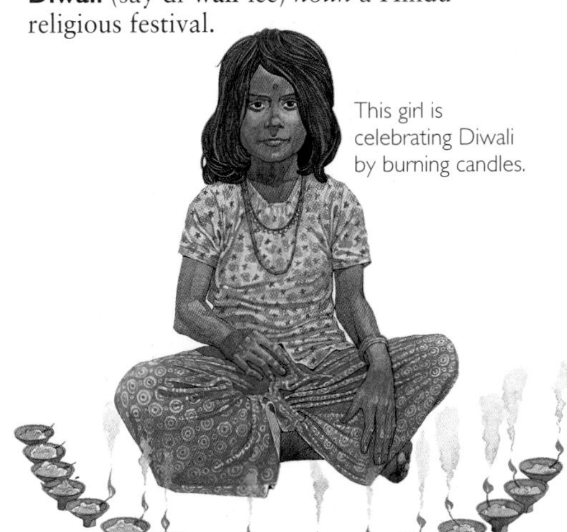

This girl is celebrating Diwali by burning candles.

DIY *abbreviation* do-it-yourself.

dizzy (dizzier, dizziest) *adjective* feeling that everything is going round and round. *I felt dizzy after the roller-coaster ride.*

Djibouti *noun* a country in Africa, and its capital city.

The flag of Djibouti is blue, green and white with a red star.

do (does, doing, did, done) *verb* 1 to carry out or deal with something, perform an action or activity. *I'm doing the cooking.* 2 to be enough. *That will do.* 3 in questions with another verb. *Do you know him?* 4 in statements with 'not' forming the negative. *I do not know him.* 5 to stress something. *He hasn't received the invitation, but I did send him one.* 6 instead of repeating a verb that has already been used. *We earn as much money as they do.* 7 at the end of a statement to form a question. *He won the match, didn't he?* **do away with** to get rid of. **do up** 1 to fasten. *Do up your laces.* 2 to repair or improve. *They are doing up the house.*

dock *noun* a place where ships are loaded and unloaded or repaired. **docker** *noun* a worker at the docks.

dock *verb* 1 to come or go into dock. *The ship docked at Dover.* 2 to join with another spacecraft in space. 3 to take money away, especially wages. *Our pay was docked.*

dock *noun* the place in a court where the accused person stands.

dock *noun* a plant with broad leaves that grows as a weed.

doctor *noun* 1 a person who treats people who are ill. 2 an academic title, a high university degree. *A Doctor of Law.*

document (say **dock**-you-munt) *noun* an official piece of paper giving proof or information about something. **document** (say **dock**-you-ment) *verb. To document the past we have used records from the library.*

dodge *verb* to move away quickly in order to avoid being hit or seen.

Dodoma *noun* the capital of Tanzania.

doe *noun* a female deer, rabbit or hare.

dog *noun* an animal that is kept as a pet. Dogs bark.

Doha *noun* the capital of Qatar.

dole *noun* a weekly payment made to unemployed people. *He's on the dole.*

doll *noun* a child's toy that looks like a baby girl or boy. *A Barbie doll.*

dollar *noun* money used in the USA, Canada and some other countries.

dolphin *noun* a sea animal like a small whale with a long nose. Dolphins are mammals and breathe through a blowhole.

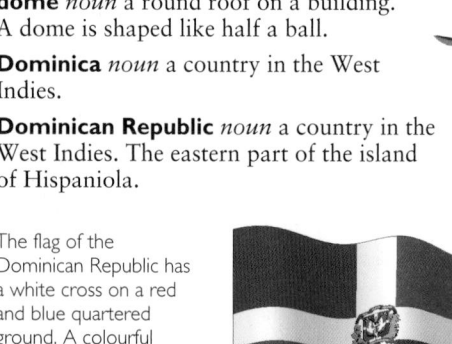

dome *noun* a round roof on a building. A dome is shaped like half a ball.

Dominica *noun* a country in the West Indies.

Dominican Republic *noun* a country in the West Indies. The eastern part of the island of Hispaniola.

The flag of the Dominican Republic has a white cross on a red and blue quartered ground. A colourful crest lies at its centre.

domino *noun* a small rectangular piece of wood or plastic marked with two sets of spots used for playing an old game called dominoes. *She beat me at dominoes.*

donate *verb* to give something, especially money, to a good cause. *I donated some money to charity.* **donation** *noun.*

WORD HISTORY

'Dormant', 'dormitory' and 'dormouse' all come from the Latin word 'dormire', to sleep. The dormouse is probably called a 'sleeping mouse' because it has a long winter sleep, or hibernation.

Dolphins are among the most friendly and intelligent of animals.

done past tense of do.

done *adjective* **not done** socially not acceptable.

donkey (donkeys) *noun* an animal like a small horse with long ears.

door *noun* a movable flat surface that opens or closes the entrance to a building, room or cupboard. **answer the door** to open the door to a visitor.

door-to-door *adjective* visiting homes to sell something. *A door-to-door salesman.*

dormant *adjective* not active. *A dormant volcano is no longer dangerous.*

dormitory (dormitories) *noun* a room with a number of beds for people to sleep in, especially in a school or hostel.

dormouse (dormice) *noun* a woodland animal like a large mouse with a long furry tail. *As sleepy as a dormouse.*

The dormouse was a delicacy roasted with honey in Roman times.

DOS *abbreviation* disk operating system (in a computer).

dose *noun* the amount of medicine to be taken at one time. **dose** *verb. I dosed myself with aspirin against the flu.*

dot *noun* a small spot. **dot** *verb* to mark or cover with dots. **dotted** *adjective.*

double *adjective* 1 twice as much or twice as many. *A double portion of spaghetti.* 2 for two people or things. *A double bed.* 3 having two parts. *Double glazing.* 4 having two different uses. *A word with a double meaning.* **doubly** *adverb.*

double *noun* 1 a double thing, an amount or size that is twice as large. *I paid £5 for it and sold it for double.* 2 a person or thing that looks exactly like another. *He's his father's double.* **double** *verb* 1 to become twice as large, strong or fast. *Sales have doubled in the last year.* 2 to have a second use. *My bedroom doubles as a study.*

doubt *noun* a feeling of not being sure about something. *There's no doubt that he'll pass the exam.* **doubt** *verb* to feel doubt. **doubtful** *adjective.*

doughnut *noun* a round cake or ring fried in hot fat and covered with sugar.

dove *noun* a bird like a pigeon.

dowdy (dowdier, dowdiest) *adjective* not fashionable, dull. *Dowdy clothes.*

down *adverb, preposition* 1 towards, at or into a lower position. *Could you get the book down from the shelf?* 2 in a lower place or from one place to another. *We walked down to the shops.* 3 to a smaller size, grade or standard. *Prices are down.* 4 to put something in writing. *To take down notes.* 5 on to a surface. *Sit down.*

down *noun* 1 a bird's soft feathers. 2 fine soft hair. *The down on the baby's head.*

downcast *adjective* 1 sad, depressed. 2 looking downwards, especially when feeling sad. *With downcast eyes.*

downfall *noun* 1 a fall from power, ruin. *Drink was his downfall.* 2 a fall of rain, a downpour.

downstairs *adverb, adjective* to, at or in a lower floor. *I'll wait downstairs.*

Downstairs there is a sitting room that leads off the kitchen.

doze *verb* to sleep lightly or be half asleep.

dozen *noun* 1 twelve. *A dozen eggs.* 2 lots of. *I've asked him dozens of times.*

Dr *abbreviation* doctor.

drab (drabber, drabbest) *adjective* not colourful, dull.

drag (drags, dragging, dragged) *verb* 1 to pull a heavy load along or pull somebody roughly. *He dragged the case across the street.* 2 to go on slowly, to seem to last a long time. *The meeting dragged on.* 3 to move along while touching the ground or search for something by pulling a heavy net along the bottom of a river or lake. *Her dress dragged in the mud.*

dragon *noun* an imaginary animal or monster in children's stories that has scales and wings and breathes fire.

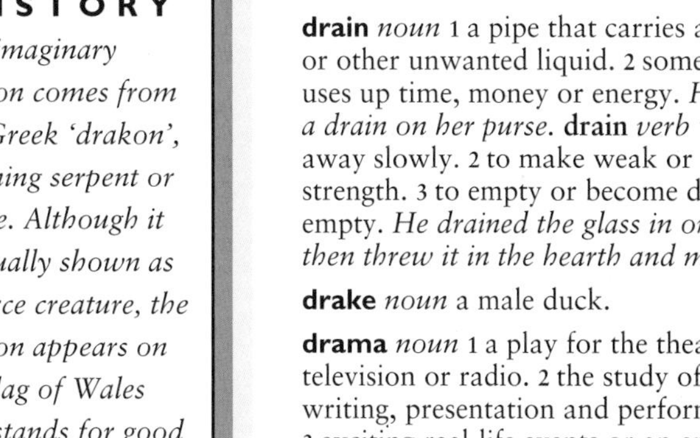

WORD HISTORY

The imaginary dragon comes from the Greek 'drakon', meaning serpent or snake. Although it is usually shown as a fierce creature, the dragon appears on the flag of Wales and stands for good luck in China.

dragonfly (dragonflies) *noun* an insect with a long body and two pairs of large thin wings. *The dragonflies darted and hovered over the pond in the warm summer sun.*

The wings of a dragonfly shimmer in the sunlight with rainbow colours.

drain *noun* 1 a pipe that carries away water or other unwanted liquid. 2 something that uses up time, money or energy. *Her sons are a drain on her purse.* **drain** *verb* 1 to flow away slowly. 2 to make weak or take away strength. 3 to empty or become dry or empty. *He drained the glass in one gulp, then threw it in the hearth and made a wish.*

drake *noun* a male duck.

drama *noun* 1 a play for the theatre, television or radio. 2 the study of plays, their writing, presentation and performance. 3 exciting real-life events or an emotional situation. *Our visit turned into a big drama when the house caught fire.*

dramatic *adjective* 1 impressive, exciting. *The new government has made some dramatic changes.* 2 showing feeling in a lively way. *His speech was very dramatic, but not many people appreciated it.*

drank past tense of drink.

drastic *adjective* having a strong and often violent effect. *A drastic decision had to be taken to save the day.*

The dragon is a mythical beast that can fly and breathe fire.

D

draw (draws, drawing, drew, drawn) *verb* 1 to make pictures, patterns or diagrams with a pencil or pen. 2 to pull something heavy along. *Two horses drew the carriage.* 3 to pull something out of a place, to take out. *To draw money out of the bank.* 4 to attract. *The concert drew a large crowd.* 5 to come or move in the direction mentioned. *Our holiday is drawing to an end.* 6 to end a game or contest with the same points on both sides. *Arsenal and Spurs drew two all.* 7 to form an idea. *To draw a conclusion.* **draw ahead** to move in front of somebody. **draw the curtains** to open or close the curtains. **draw up** 1 to come near and stop. *A car drew up outside my door.* 2 to prepare, especially a report or document.

draw *noun* 1 equal marks in a game or contest. 2 the drawing of lottery tickets. *The luck of the draw.*

drawback *noun* a disadvantage, something that can cause trouble or difficulty. *The high price is a drawback.*

drawbridge *noun* a bridge over a moat or river that can be pulled up by chains to protect a castle or let ships pass.

drawer *noun* 1 a box-like container which is part of a cupboard or a table that slides in and out. 2 a person who writes out and signs a cheque.

drawing *noun* 1 making pictures with a pen or pencil. 2 a picture made by drawing.

drawing pin *noun* a short pin with a flat top used for fastening papers to a flat surface. *Please pass me four drawing pins.*

drawn past tense of draw.

dread *noun* great fear. **dread** *verb* to fear something greatly. *I dread the exam.* **dreadful** *adjective. A dreadful headache.*

dreadlocks *plural noun* hair worn in tight plaits. *Bob Marley's dreadlocks.*

DID YOU KNOW

When you are dreaming, your eyes move about rapidly behind your closed eyelids. Experts believe that most people dream every night, but they do not always remember their dreams.

This Bulgarian woman is wearing national dress.

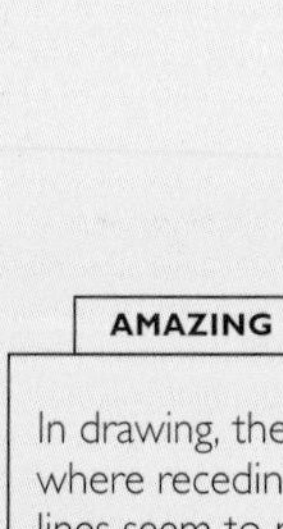

I pinned the drawing of our house on the wall.

AMAZING FACT

In drawing, the point where receding parallel lines seem to meet when you look at them in perspective is called the Vanishing Point.

dream *noun* 1 thoughts, feelings and pictures you see or live through while you are asleep. A bad dream is called a nightmare. 2 something ideal you think about and that you would like to come true. *It's my dream to sail around the world.* 3 something beautiful. *She dances like a dream.* **dream** (dreams, dreaming, dreamt or dreamed) *verb* 1 to have a dream or dreams while sleeping. 2 to imagine that something you want might happen. *I dream of winning the lottery.* **dreamer** *noun.*

dredge *verb* to dredge a river means to clear it by removing mud. **dredger** *noun* a boat or barge used for dredging.

drench *verb* to make or be very wet. *We were caught in a storm and got drenched.*

dress (dresses) *noun* 1 a piece of clothing with a top and a skirt for a woman or a girl. 2 clothing in general. *The children wore national dress.*

dress *verb* 1 to put on clothes. 2 to wear clothes. *She was dressed in black.* 3 to add sauce to food. *I haven't dressed the salad.* 4 to cover with a bandage. *To dress a wound.* 5 to arrange goods for display. *To dress a shop window.* **dress up** 1 to put on smart clothes. 2 to wear something else for fun, to put on clothes in a game. *The children dressed up as pirates.* **get dressed** to put on clothes.

dresser *noun* 1 a kitchen sideboard with shelves above for displaying dishes. 2 a person who is employed to help actors and actresses to dress for the stage.

The jugs, plates and dishes were displayed on the kitchen dresser.

dressing *noun* 1 a bandage for covering a wound. 2 a sauce for food. *Salad dressing.*

dressing gown *noun* a robe worn over pyjamas or a nightie.

drew past tense of draw.

dribble *verb* 1 to let drops of spit (saliva) trickle out of your mouth. *Babies dribble.* 2 to move the ball forward with short kicks. *He dribbled into the penalty area.*

dried past tense of dry.

drier *noun* a device for drying hair or clothes. *The hair drier blows hot or cold.*

drift *verb* 1 to float or be carried along gently by the wind or waves. 2 to move about without a plan. *She just drifts from one job to another.*

drift *noun* 1 sand or snow that the wind has blown into a pile. 2 a general movement or the direction in which something is moving. *There is a drift away from higher education.* 3 the meaning of something, especially a speech. *I didn't catch the drift of their discussion.*

drill *noun* 1 a tool for making holes. *A dentist's drill.* 2 practising an emergency routine. *We had a fire drill this morning.* 3 training by repeating an exercise. *They have a lot of drill in the army.* **drill** *verb* 1 to drill a hole. 2 to do something repeatedly. *We were drilled to say 'thank you'.*

The driver pulled the lever and the powerful drill began to bite into the road.

drink (drinks, drinking, drank, drunk) *verb* 1 to swallow liquid. *You should drink plenty of water.* 2 to drink too much alcohol. *He drinks too much.* **drink** *noun* 1 something you drink. *A drink of water.* 2 alcohol, an alcoholic drink. *He's very fond of drink.*

drip (drips, dripping, dripped) *verb* to fall slowly or let something fall in small drops. *The tap is dripping.* **drip** *noun* 1 a drop of liquid falling, the sound of falling drops. 2 an apparatus for dripping liquid into a blood vessel.

drive (drives, driving, drove, driven) *verb* 1 to travel in a vehicle or make it go. *My brother drives a tractor.* 2 to take somebody in a car. *I'll drive the children home.* 3 to force to go. *She drives all the customers away.* 4 to make somebody do something. *His illness has driven him to drink.* 5 to direct force into or on to something. *To drive a nail into the wall. The engine is driven by steam.* **driver** *noun.*

GRAMMAR NOTE

Be careful to use 'drank' and 'drunk' correctly. 'Drank' is the past tense of 'drink'. 'He drank the whole can in one go.' 'Drunk' is the past participle and goes with have. 'I've drunk my tea.' A person who is drunk has had too much alcohol.

drive *noun* 1 a journey in a car or bus. 2 a private road to a house or garage. 3 energy and enthusiasm. *People with a lot of drive are often very successful.* 4 the act of hitting a ball or the force with which it is hit, especially in golf or cricket. 5 a planned effort by a group for a particular purpose. *We are having a sales drive.*

The drive to our house sweeps through the gates and up to the front door.

drizzle *noun* light rain. **drizzle** *verb.*

drone *noun* 1 a male bee. 2 a low humming sound. **drone** *verb* 1 to make a low humming sound. 2 to talk in a low, boring voice. *He droned on and on.*

drool *verb* 1 If you drool over something, you are very exited and show foolish pleasure in looking at it. 2 to dribble.

droop *verb* to bend or hang down. *The flowers were drooping after the heavy rain.*

drop *noun* 1 a small spot of liquid, a small amount. *Drops of rain.* 2 a fall. *A drop in temperature. A drop of 100 metres.*

drop (drops, dropping, dropped) *verb* 1 to fall. *Water dropped into the bucket.* 2 to let fall. *I dropped my spoon on the floor.* 3 to become less. *Prices have dropped.* 4 to let somebody get out of the car. *Could you drop me at the station?* 5 to stop doing something or meeting somebody. *He's dropped his girlfriend for someone else.* 6 to not select somebody for a team. *The goalkeeper let the ball into the net too many times and was dropped for the next match.* **drop in** to visit somebody without warning. **drop out** to stop taking part in something or doing something. *She dropped out of the race.*

The girl dropped the ball to see how high it would bounce.

D

drove past tense of drive.

drown *verb* 1 to die under water by not being able to breathe. *Hundreds drowned in the* Titanic *disaster.* 2 to cover something with water or make something very wet. *The peaches were drowned in brandy.* 3 to make a sound impossible to hear by making more noise. *Her voice was drowned by the children's shouting.*

drowsy *adjective* sleepy. **drowsiness** *noun.*

drug *noun* 1 a medicine. 2 a substance that affects your mind and feelings and is addictive. *Most drugs are illegal, except for nicotine and alcohol.* **drug** (drugs, drugging, drugged) *verb.* When you drug somebody, you give them a drug to make them unconscious.

drug addict *noun* somebody addicted to drugs, who cannot stop taking them.

drugstore *noun* a shop where you can buy medicines and other goods. You can also have drinks and snacks in a drugstore.

drum *noun* 1 a musical instrument made of a hollow round frame with a skin stretched tightly over it. *To beat the drum.* 2 a round container for liquids. *A large drum full of oil.* **drum** (drums, drumming, drummed) *verb* 1 to play a drum. 2 to tap. *He drummed his fingers on the table.* **drummer** *noun.*

Bongo drums are fun to play.

drumstick *noun* a stick for beating a drum.

drunk *adjective* having had too much alcohol. *He drank too much beer and got extremely drunk.* **drunk** *noun* a person who often gets drunk.

dry (drier, driest) *adjective* 1 not wet. Without water. *The washing is dry.* 2 not rainy. *It was a dry day.* 3 uninteresting, boring. *He's a dry old stick.* 4 without butter. *Dry toast.* 5 witty. *She has a dry sense of humour.*

dry (dries, drying, dried) *verb* to make or become dry.

dry-clean *verb* to clean clothes with chemicals, without using water.

dry-cleaner's *noun* a shop where clothes are taken to be dry-cleaned.

DID YOU KNOW

There are two main types of duck: dabbers and divers. Dabbers feed on the surface of the water, and divers swim under the water to get food. The Aylesbury duck was bred originally in the town in Buckinghamshire, but a Bombay duck isn't a duck at all – it's a kind of dried fish!

dual *adjective* having two parts or two functions. *The driving instructor's car had dual controls.*

Dublin *noun* the capital of Ireland.

duck *noun* a water-bird with a wide beak.

duck *verb* 1 to bend down quickly, to avoid being seen or hit. *When he saw the policeman, he ducked behind a wall.* 2 to dip under water. *My horrible brother ducked me in the swimming pool.* **duck out of** to avoid doing something.

duel *noun* a fight with guns or swords between two people in order to settle a quarrel. **duel** *verb* to fight a duel. **duellist** *noun.*

The fencing champion challenged his friend to a duel.

duet *noun* 1 a performance by two singers or musicians. 2 a piece of music for two singers or players. *A piano duet.*

dug past tense of dig.

dull *adjective* 1 not bright, clear or shining. *A dull colour. The weather was dull.* 2 slow in understanding, stupid. *Some of his pupils are rather dull.* 3 uninteresting, boring. *A dull lesson.* 4 not sharp. *He felt a dull pain. It made a dull sound.* **dullness** *noun.*

dumb (say dum) *adjective* 1 unable to speak. 2 unwilling to speak, silent. *He remained dumb throughout the trial.* 3 stupid. *You aren't really that dumb.*

dump *noun* 1 a place where rubbish is left. 2 an unpleasant, dull and dirty place. *I couldn't live in such a dump.*

There is all sorts of rubbish at the dump, including old furniture and carpets.

dump *verb* 1 to get rid of something unwanted. *People shouldn't dump dangerous chemicals at sea.* 2 to leave or put something down carelessly. *She dumped her things in the hall.*

dune *noun* a sand hill on a seashore or in the desert piled up by the wind.

dung *noun* solid waste matter from the bowels of large animals, especially cattle.

dungeon *noun* (say **dun**-jun) a dark underground prison cell in a castle.

The prisoner was thrown into the filthy dungeon without food or water.

duplicate *adjective* exactly the same. *Duplicate keys.* **duplicate** *noun* something that is exactly the same as something else; an exact copy. *Luckily I had a duplicate of the missing photograph.* **duplicate** *verb* to make or be a duplicate.

during *preposition* 1 throughout, something that happens continuously within a period. *We never go to the cinema during the week.* 2 at some point within a period. *He rang twice during the morning.*

Dushanbe *noun* the capital of Tajikistan.

dusk *noun* the time when it is not completely dark, just before nightfall.

dust *noun* tiny specks of earth, sand or dirt that look like dry powder. *There is a lot of dust on the books.* **dust** *verb* 1 to wipe away dust. *She dusts her room every day.* 2 to cover with dust or fine powder. *To dust a cake with icing sugar.*

duster *noun* a cloth for dusting.

dusty (dustier, dustiest) *adjective* 1 covered with dust. 2 like dust. *A dusty brown.*

Dutch *noun* the language spoken in Holland. **Dutch** *adjective*. *Dutch people.* **go Dutch** to share expenses. *We always go Dutch when I go out with my boyfriend.* **Dutch courage** so-called courage that comes from being drunk.

WORD HISTORY

'Duvet' comes from an Old French word for down, a bird's soft feathers that are used inside the quilt. A duvet is also called a continental quilt.

duty (duties) *noun* 1 something a person must do because they think it right. *It's my duty to look after my sick uncle.* 2 a task, something you have to do as part of your job. *He told me what my duties would be.* 3 a tax on certain goods. *A duty on cigarettes.* **on duty** at work. *The doctor is on duty tonight.* **off duty** not at work.

duvet *noun* (say **doo**-vay) a thick soft quilt used as a bed covering.

dwarf (dwarfs or dwarves) *noun* a very small person, animal or plant. **dwarf** *verb* to make something seem very small by comparison. *The new office block dwarfs the other buildings.*

dwell (dwells, dwelling, dwelt) *verb* to live. *Strange creatures dwell in the forest.* **dwell on** to think or talk about something for a long time. *It's no good dwelling on the past.*

dwelling *noun* a place to live in.

High in the mountains of South America, people make their dwellings from reeds.

dwindle (dwindles, dwindling, dwindled) *verb* to get gradually smaller or fewer. *Numbers are dwindling.*

dye (dyes, dyeing, dyed) *verb* to colour something, especially hair or cloth, by soaking it in a coloured liquid. *I want to dye my hair red.* **dye** *noun* the substance used for dyeing things.

dynamo *noun* a machine that turns mechanical power into electricity.

dynasty (dynasties) *noun* (say **din**-a-stee) a line of rulers of a country who all belong to the same family. *The Tudor dynasty.*

dyslexia *noun* (say dis-**leks**-ee-a) great difficulty with reading and spelling. **dyslexic** *adjective*.

Windmills are a major feature of the Dutch landscape. The wind blows fiercely across the flat land and its power used to be harnessed to grind the corn into flour.

Ee

each *adjective, pronoun* 1 every person or thing in a group. *Each student.* 2 for one. *The tickets are £10 each.* **each other** one another. *They loved each other.*

eager *adjective* wanting to do something very much, keen. **eagerly** *adverb.*

eagle *noun* a large meat-eating bird, or bird of prey, with very good eyesight.

ear *noun* the organ of hearing. You have two ears, one on either side of your head. **all ears** listening with great interest. *Tell us what she did, we're all ears.* **play it by ear** to act from moment to moment, without making plans in advance.

Sound waves travel down the ear canal to the eardrum. The ear is also the body's organ of balance.

Cochlea

Eardrum

ear *noun* the part at the top of a cereal plant that contains the seeds. *Ears of corn stood in a vase on the altar.*

early (earlier, earliest) *adjective, adverb* 1 before the expected time. *The train was 10 minutes early.* 2 happening near the beginning. *Early last week.*

earn *verb* 1 to get money in return for working. 2 to get something, especially praise, because you deserve it. *That will earn him our respect.* **earnings** *plural noun.*

earnest *adjective* very serious. **in earnest** very seriously.

earring *noun* a piece of jewellery worn on the ear.

earth *noun* 1 the planet we live on. *The spacecraft has returned to Earth.* 2 the soil in which plants thrive and grow. 3 the ground. 4 a wire that passes from electrical equipment to the ground and makes the equipment safe. 5 the hole that a fox lives in.

SPELLING NOTE

The planet we live on can be spelt with or without a capital 'e' ('Earth' or 'earth'). When you use it together with the names of other planets, such as Mars and Venus, write 'Earth'.

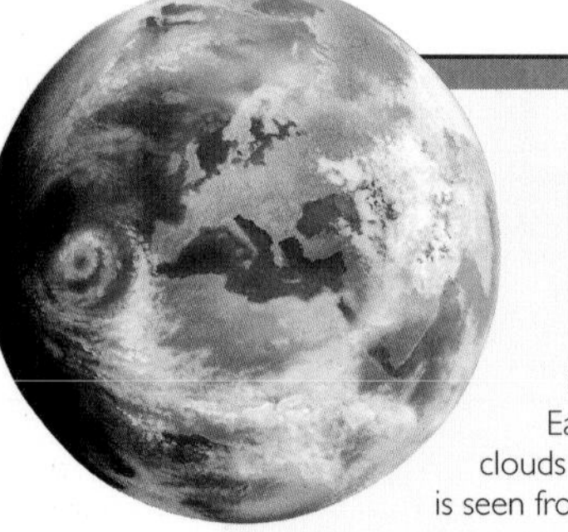

Here the Earth, with clouds above it, is seen from space.

earth *verb* to connect a piece of electrical equipment to the ground.

earthquake *noun* a sudden violent shaking of the Earth's surface.

earthworm *noun* a long thin worm that lives under the ground.

earwig *noun* a crawling insect.

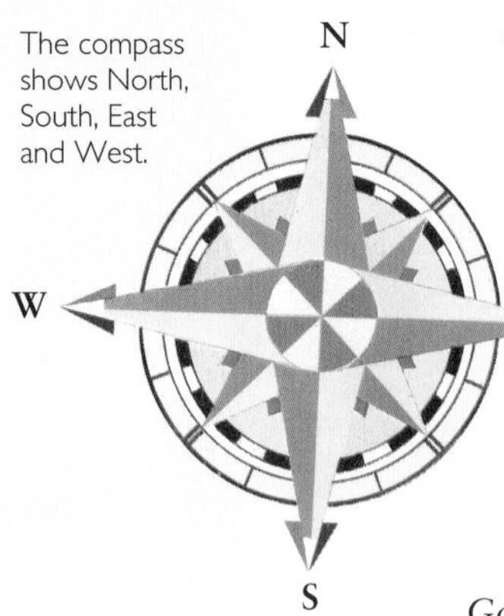

The compass shows North, South, East and West.

easily *adverb* 1 without difficulty or very likely. *I'll easily finish my essay by tonight.* 2 without doubt. *I'm easily the fastest runner in the class.*

east or **East** *adjective, adverb* to or in the direction in which the Sun rises (the opposite of west). *An east wind.* **east** *noun* 1 *The Sun rises in the east.* 2 the eastern part of a country or continent. *Good news from the east.*

Easter *noun* a religious festival when Christians remember the death and resurrection of Christ.

easterly *adjective* towards or in the east. *We walked in an easterly direction.*

eastern *adjective* in or from the east. *A small village in eastern Russia.*

easy (easier, easiest) *adjective, adverb* 1 not difficult, not needing much effort. *It was easy to persuade him to come.* 2 without any problems. *She has an easy life.* **take it/things easy** to relax and not do or work too much. **go easy on something** to avoid using too much of it.

easy-going *adjective* not easily worried or upset. *My parents are very easy-going, they don't mind what I do.*

eat (eats, eating, ate, eaten) *verb* 1 to put food in your mouth and swallow it. 2 to have a meal. 3 to damage or destroy, especially by chemical action. *The acid has eaten a hole in the metal.* **eat in** to have a meal at home. **eat out** to have a meal in a restaurant. **eat up** to finish a meal.

eavesdrop (eavesdrops, eavesdropping, eavesdropped) *verb* to listen secretly to somebody else's conversation.

ebb *verb* 1 to flow back from the land to the sea. 2 to become weaker or grow less. *Her strength is ebbing.* **ebb** *noun* 1 *The ebb and flow of the tides.* 2 a low mood. *He felt at a very low ebb.*

ebony *noun* a hard black wood. **ebony** *adjective. Ebony skin.*

eccentric (say ek-**sen**-trik) *adjective* behaving strangely, having odd habits. **eccentric** *noun* an eccentric person. **eccentricity** *noun.*

echo (echoes) *noun* a sound that is heard again as it is sent back from a wall or inside a cave. **echo** (echoes, echoing, echoed) *verb* 1 to make an echo. *Our footsteps echoed in the tunnel.* 2 to repeat somebody else's words or actions. *His views echoed those of his elder sister.*

eclipse *noun* the disappearance of the Sun's or Moon's light when the Moon or the Earth is in the way. *A total eclipse of the Sun.* **eclipse** *verb* to do or be much better than somebody or something. *His paintings eclipsed all the other exhibits.*

This solar eclipse was photographed on 16 February 1980, over Africa.

ecology *noun* the pattern of relationships between plants, animals and people to each other and their surroundings. **ecologist** *noun.* **ecological** *adjective.*

economic *adjective* 1 relating to economics. 2 making a profit. *It's not economic to run buses to the village.*

economical *adjective* using money, time or goods carefully, not wasteful. *He's very economical with the stationery, if nothing else.* **economically** *adverb.*

economics *noun* the science of the production and distribution of wealth.

economy (economies) *noun* 1 the system by which a country spends its money and organizes its industry and trade. 2 the careful spending of money or use of goods in order to save money.

ecosystem *noun* a system relating all the plants, animals and people in an area to their surroundings.

ecstasy (say **ek**-stuh-see) *noun* a feeling of extreme joy and happiness. **ecstatic** *adjective.* **ecstatically** *adverb.*

Ecuador *noun* a country in South America.

edge *noun* 1 the thin cutting part of a knife or another cutting tool. 2 the place or line where something stops and something else begins. The side of something. *The edge of the cliff.* **on edge** nervous.

The Galapagos Islands in the Pacific Ocean belong to Ecuador, a country on the west coast of South America.

SPELLING NOTE

The noun 'effect' goes with the verb 'affect'. 'It had no effect on me; it didn't affect me.' The verb 'effect' has a different meaning, to make happen.

edge *verb* 1 to form the edge of something or put an edge on something. *The lawn was edged with flowers.* 2 to move slowly and carefully. *He edged towards me.*

edible *adjective* fit to be eaten, eatable.

edifice (say **ed**-if-iss) *noun* a large building.

Edinburgh *noun* the capital of Scotland.

edit *verb* 1 to plan and work on a newspaper, magazine or book. *This manuscript needed a lot of editing.* 2 to choose, arrange and put parts of a film or recording together.

edition *noun* 1 the form in which a book or magazine is printed. *A paperback edition.* 2 the number of copies of a book or magazine printed. *The first edition has already sold out.*

editor *noun* 1 a person who edits a book, magazine or newspaper. 2 the person who is in charge of a newspaper.

educate *verb* to teach or train somebody. **education** *noun.*

eel *noun* a long thin fish that looks like a snake.

The young of the eel is called an elver.

effect *noun* 1 a condition caused by something, a result. *He could feel the effects of the drink.* 2 an impression produced on the mind. *Sound effects are very important in a film.* **effect** *verb* to produce or make something happen. *The changes in the law will be effected soon.* **in effect** really. *In effect the reply told her nothing.* **take effect** to start happening.

effective *adjective* 1 impressive. 2 producing the result you set out to achieve. *Petrol can be an effective stain remover.* 3 actual or real. *She took effective control.* **to become effective** to come into force. *The new opening hours become effective on Tuesday.* **effectiveness** *noun.* **effectively** *adverb.*

efficient *adjective* working well without wasting time or effort. *He's very efficient at his job.* **efficiency** *noun.*

effort *noun* trying hard to do something, or the result of it. *I make an effort to be polite.*

egg *noun* 1 an oval object laid by female birds, fishes and reptiles which contains new life. 2 a hen's egg used as food. 3 a female reproductive cell in humans, animals and plants. The scientific term for a human egg is an ovum.

e.g. *abbreviation* for example. *In certain countries, e.g. Italy, France and Holland.*

Egypt *noun* a country in Africa.

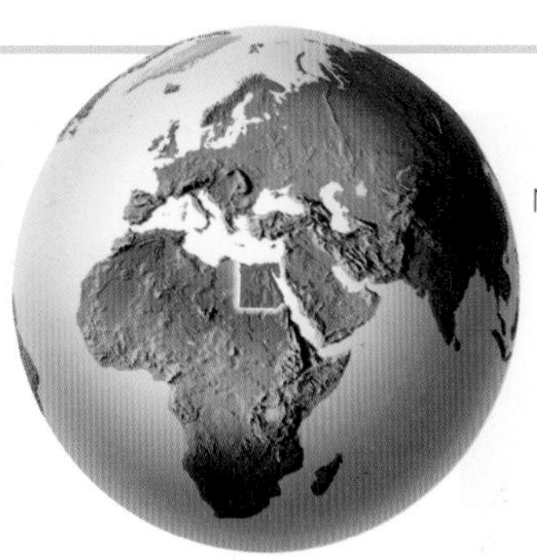

Egypt lies on the Mediterranean Sea in North Africa.

Eid (say eed) *noun* a Muslim festival celebrating the end of the fast of Ramadan (Eid ul-Fitr), or the end of a journey to Mecca (Eid ul-Adha).

either *adjective, pronoun* 1 one or the other of two. *Both computers work, you can use either.* 2 one and also the other, both. *'Which do you prefer?' 'I don't like either.'* **either** *adverb* also (used in negative statements). *I don't like cats and I don't like dogs either.* **either** *conjunction* the first of two or more possibilities. *I'll either write or ring you when I feel better.*

eject *verb* 1 to throw somebody out of a place. *They were forcibly ejected from the stadium.* 2 to push out with force. *The machine ejected the coins.*

El Salvador *noun* a country in Central America.

elaborate (say i-**lab**-uh-rut) *adjective* full of detail with a number of complicated parts. *The curtains had an elaborate pattern of flowers.* **elaborate** (say i-**lab**-uh-rate) *verb* When you elaborate on something, you describe or explain it in detail.

elapse *verb* (of time) to pass by. *Three months have elapsed since the wedding.*

elastic *adjective* able to stretch and go back to its original shape. *An elastic band.* **elasticity** *noun.*

elastic *noun* material that stretches.

elbow *noun* the joint where the arm bends.

Joints, such as the elbow joint, are cushioned by soft, squashy cartilage, which is more flexible than bone.

elder *noun* a tree with white flowers and red or black berries.

elder *adjective* older. *My elder sister.* **elder** *noun* 1 the older of two people. 2 an older person. *We should respect our elders.*

elect *verb* 1 to choose by voting. *A new government was elected.* 2 to decide to do something. *They elected to stay.*

election *noun* voting to choose a person or party to hold an official position. *She stood for parliament in the general election.*

DID YOU KNOW

An element is one of more than 100 substances that consist of atoms of the same type. Everything in the Universe, whether living or non-living, is made up of combinations of chemical elements. For example, water combines the elements hydrogen and oxygen.

electric *adjective* 1 producing or produced by electricity. *An electric toaster.* 2 very exciting. *The atmosphere at the concert was simply electric.*

electrical *adjective* relating to electricity. *An electrical fault.*

electrician *noun* a person whose job is to fit and repair electrical equipment.

electricity *noun* a form of energy that is used for heating and lighting or for driving machines. Electricity is produced by generators or batteries.

electrode *noun* the point where an electric current enters or leaves a battery.

electron *noun* a tiny particle of matter with a negative electric charge.

electronic *adjective* produced or worked by electrons, usually using microchips. *Electronic music.* **electronics** *noun.*

elegant *adjective* showing good taste in design and style. Graceful and pleasing. *An elegant new dress.* **elegance** *noun.*

element *noun* 1 a single part that combines with others to make a whole. *Listening is an important element of her job.* 2 an amount of something. *There is an element of truth in what she said.* 3 the heating part of an electrical appliance. 4 the most important parts or the basics of a subject. *The elements of mathematics.* 5 in science, an element is a substance that consists of only one type of atom. Gold and oxygen are elements. 6 a suitable surrounding. *He was in his element talking about films.* **the elements** the weather, especially wind and rain.

elementary *adjective* easy, simple. *I took an elementary course.*

elephant *noun* the largest living land animal, with a trunk and tusks.

The elephant uses its trunk for taking food from high in the trees. It can also smell, drink and shower with its trunk.

elevator *noun* a lift.

eligible *adjective* 1 entitled to be chosen. *You are eligible for a grant.* 2 desirable or suitable. *An eligible bachelor.*

elite (say ay-**leet**) *noun* the most important or powerful group of people in a community. *He was hoping to join the elite.*

elm *noun* a tree with broad leaves.

E

eloquent *adjective* able to make good speeches that persuade and influence others. **eloquence** *noun*.

else *adverb* 1 besides, in addition, other. *What else can I do?* 2 otherwise. *You must pay the fine, or else you'll lose your membership card.*

elusive *adjective* difficult to catch or find. *Success proved elusive.*

e-mail *noun* electronic mail. *I'll send it to you by e-mail.*

emancipate *verb* to free somebody from things that are holding them back. **emancipated** *adjective*. *Today's women are much more emancipated than their grandmothers.* **emancipation** *noun*.

embankment *noun* a wall of stones or earth to hold back a river or carry a road or railway.

embark *verb* to go on board a ship or plane. **embark on** to start. *She embarked on a new life.*

embarrass *verb* to make somebody feel awkward or self-conscious. *The questions embarrassed me so much that I blushed.* **embarrassment** *noun*.

embroider *verb* to sew a design on cloth. *She embroidered the tablecloth with pink flowers.* **embroidery** *noun*.

embryo (say **em**-bree-oh) *noun* an unborn baby or animal as it starts to grow in its mother's womb. **embryonic** *adjective* undeveloped.

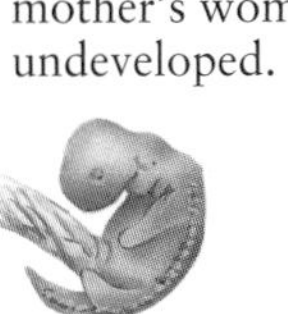

This sequence of pictures shows the development of the embryo in the womb.

emerald *noun* 1 a green precious stone. 2 a clear green colour.

emergency (emergencies) *noun* an unexpected dangerous event that needs immediate action. *Ring 999 in an emergency.*

emigrate *verb* to leave your own country to live in another country. **emigration** *noun*. **emigrant** *noun*.

eminent *adjective* an eminent person is somebody famous and admired.

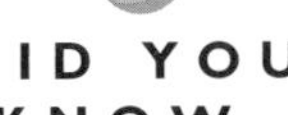

DID YOU KNOW

An e-mail address is made of a group of letters, numbers and dots, with no spaces in between any of them, such as info@bbc.co.uk for the information department of the BBC. E-mail users sometimes call the ordinary postal system 'snail mail', because they think it is so slow.

Emmeline Pankhurst led the campaign to emancipate women. She was arrested and imprisoned several times.

SPELLING NOTE

When they start their journey from their original country, people are called emigrants. At the end of the journey, when they arrive in their new country, they are called immigrants.

emotion *noun* a strong feeling. Love and jealousy are emotions. *She was overcome with emotion.* **emotional** *adjective*.

emotive *adjective* causing emotion. *It was a very emotive issue.*

emperor *noun* the ruler of an empire. If the ruler is a woman, she is called an empress.

emphasize *verb* to give special importance to something. *He emphasized that he wanted to be on his own.* **emphasis** *noun*.

empire *noun* 1 a country or group of countries controlled by one person. *The former British Empire.* 2 a large group of firms or shops controlled by one person. *She has built up a huge empire.*

employ *verb* 1 to pay somebody to do work for you. *The firm employs 20 people.* 2 to make use of something or somebody. *He employed all his charm to win her over.*

employee *noun* a person who is paid to work for somebody else.

employer *noun* a person who employs people. *The workers were in dispute with their employer.*

employment *noun* 1 having a paid job. Employing or being employed. *I have never been out of employment.* 2 a person's regular job.

empty (emptier, emptiest) *adjective* 1 with nothing or nobody in it. 2 with no meaning. *They were empty promises.* **empty** *noun*. *The milkman collects the empties.* **empty** (empties, emptying, emptied) *verb* to make empty. **emptiness** *noun*. **emptily** *adverb*.

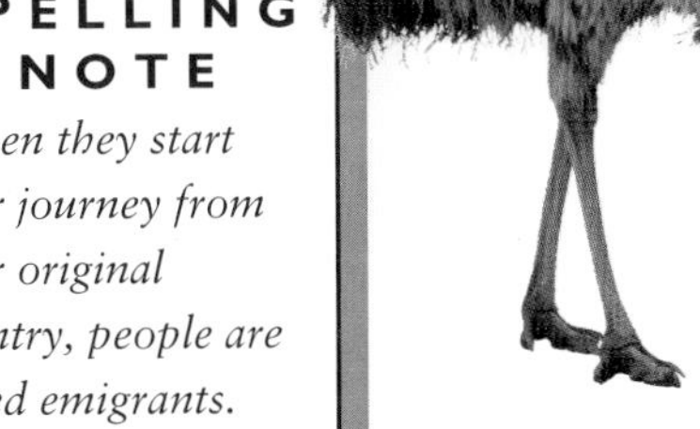

The emu can run very fast but it cannot fly.

emu *noun* a large Australian bird, like an ostrich.

enable *verb* to make somebody able to do something or give somebody the means to do something.

enamel *noun* 1 a shiny substance that is put on to metal, glass or pottery to decorate and protect it. 2 the outer covering of a tooth. **enamel** *adjective*. *Enamel paint.*

enchant *verb* 1 When you enchant somebody, you charm and delight them. 2 to put somebody or something under a magic spell. **enchanted** *adjective* magic. *An enchanted forest.*

enclose *verb* 1 to put a wall or fence around something to shut it in. 2 to put something with a letter or a parcel. *I'm enclosing a photograph.* **enclosure** *noun*.

E

encounter *verb* 1 to meet unexpectedly. 2 to be faced with something bad, especially danger or prejudice. *We encountered many difficulties.* **encounter** *noun.*

encourage *verb* 1 to give courage or hope to somebody. *I encouraged her to take up painting.* 2 to support or help develop. *Don't encourage his laziness.* **encouragement** *noun.* **encouraging** *adjective. Encouraging news from the hospital.*

end *noun* 1 the point or place where something stops, the last part of something. *At the end of the street.* 2 finish. *It was the end of our friendship.* 3 a small piece left. *There were lots of cigarette ends in the ashtray.* 4 death. *His was a cruel end.* 5 purpose. *He is doing this for his own selfish ends.* **in the end** finally. **make ends meet** to have just enough money to live on. **end** *verb* to finish. *How did the play end?*

endanger *verb* to cause danger to. *Smoking seriously endangers your health.*

endeavour (say in-**dev**-uh) *verb* to try. **endeavour** *noun.*

endurance *noun* the ability to endure or bear something. *Henry very much admired the soldiers' endurance.*

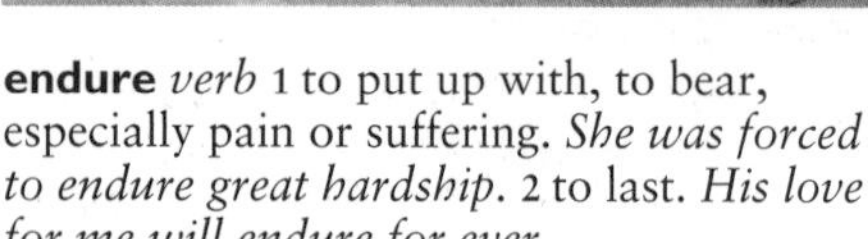

The 20,000 men who survived the 9,700 km Long March in China in 1934–35 performed an astonishing feat of endurance. 80,000 men died on the journey.

endure *verb* 1 to put up with, to bear, especially pain or suffering. *She was forced to endure great hardship.* 2 to last. *His love for me will endure for ever.*

enemy (enemies) *noun* 1 somebody who hates or wants to hurt another person. When two people hate each other, they are enemies. 2 a country or army that is at war with another. *The enemy attacked at night.*

energetic *adjective* full of energy.

energy *noun* 1 the strength and ability to do a lot. 2 the effort put into work. *She concentrated all her energy on her job.* 3 the power that works and drives machines.

engage *verb* 1 to employ. If you are engaged in something, you are doing it or working on it. 2 to attract somebody's attention. 3 to fit into or lock together parts of a machine. *To engage the clutch.*

DID YOU KNOW

English is an official language in 57 countries of the world. But more people speak Mandarin Chinese in China and Hindi in India as their first language. After Mandarin, Hindi and English, the next most common language is Spanish.

engaged *adjective* 1 having agreed to marry. 2 occupied or in use. *This number seems to be constantly engaged.*

engagement *noun* 1 an agreement to marry. *She called off their engagement.* 2 the period of time during which two people are engaged. 3 an arrangement to meet somebody or do something. *A dinner engagement is something I look forward to.*

engaging *adjective* attractive, interesting.

engine *noun* 1 a machine that produces power which makes a vehicle move. 2 a machine that pulls a railway train, also called a locomotive.

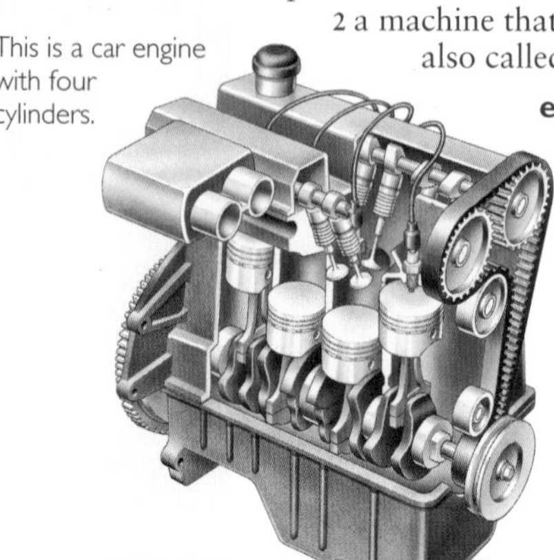

This is a car engine with four cylinders.

engineer *noun* 1 a person who designs machines, roads and bridges. 2 a person who repairs machines or electrical devices. 3 a person in control of an engine or engines, especially on a ship.

engineer *verb* to plan or cause something to happen. *He engineered an interview with the top boss.*

England *noun* a country that is part of the United Kingdom.

England is part of the British Isles. It is separated from the mainland of Europe by the English Channel.

English *noun* 1 the people of England. 2 the language spoken in Great Britain, America, Canada, Australia and elsewhere. **English** *adjective. English customs and traditions.*

enjoy *verb* to get pleasure from something. **enjoyment** *noun.*

enlarge *verb* to make or get bigger. *The house was enlarged by the previous owners.* **enlargement** *noun. I'd like an enlargement of this photograph.*

enormous *adjective* very big.

enough *adverb* having the right amount or to the right degree. *He's not old enough to understand.* **enough** *adjective* as much or as many as necessary. *Have we got enough time for a cup of coffee?* **enough** *pronoun. Not enough is known about the universe.*

enquire, enquirer, enquiry. See inquire, inquirer, inquiry.

enrol (enrols, enrolling, enrolled) *verb* to become a member, especially on a course. *I have enrolled at the local college.*

ensure *verb* to make certain (of). *This medicine will ensure a good night's sleep.*

enter *verb* 1 to come in or go into. *He entered the room.* 2 to become a member, especially of a university or profession. 3 to write down in a book or type into a computer. *He entered the amount in the cash book.* 4 to take part in a competition.

entertain *verb* 1 to give food and drink to guests at your home. 2 to amuse and interest. *He entertained us with stories about his trip around the world.* 3 to think about. *I didn't even entertain the idea.*

entertainer *noun* a person whose job it is to entertain, especially a comedian or singer. *Frank Sinatra was a great entertainer.*

entertainment *noun* 1 the act of being entertained or being entertaining. *He told stories for the children's entertainment.* 2 a performance at the theatre or cinema.

enthusiasm *noun* a strong feeling of interest, liking and excitement. *She was full of enthusiasm.* **enthusiast** *noun. He's a fitness enthusiast.* **enthusiastic** *adjective.*

entire *adjective* whole. *They spent the entire evening arguing.* **entirely** *adverb.*

entrance *noun* 1 a way into a place, for example a door or gate. 2 the arrival in a room. *She made a dramatic entrance.* 3 the right to go into a place. *He was refused entrance.*

entry (entries) *noun* 1 coming or going in. 2 the right to enter. *No entry.* 3 something entered in a list or book. *A dictionary entry.*

envelop (say in-vel-up) *verb* to cover or surround completely. *The hills were enveloped in mist.*

envelope (say en-vuh-lope) *noun* a paper cover for a letter.

envious *adjective* feeling envy. *He was envious of his successful brother.*

environment *noun* the surroundings and conditions in which people, animals and plants live. **environmental** *adjective. Environmental pollution.* **environmentalist** *noun. Environmentalists are protesting about the new bypass.*

The main entrance to Mycenae in ancient Greece was through the Lion Gate.

SPELLING NOTE

Don't confuse 'ensure' and 'insure'. To ensure is to make certain, which is quite a different meaning from to insure.

WORD HISTORY

Early in its ancient Greek history, 'enthusiastic' meant 'possessed by a god'. In old English 'enthusiasm' was used to mean great religious emotion.

DID YOU KNOW

In huge amounts of geological time, epochs make up a period, and periods make up an era.

envy (envies, envying, envied) *verb* wishing you had something that somebody else has. *I envied her her beauty.* **envy** *noun* a feeling of resentment towards somebody who has something that you would like. *His car was the envy of all his friends.*

epic *noun* 1 a long poem about heroes and heroic deeds. 2 a historic, grand book or film. **epic** *adjective. An epic adventure.*

epidemic *noun* a large number of cases of an infectious disease in one area at the same time. *A flu epidemic has been forecast.*

episode *noun* 1 one separate and important event. *That holiday was one of the funniest episodes in my life.* 2 one of several parts of a radio or TV series.

epoch (say ee-pok) *noun* a period of time in history or life. *A new epoch in the history of space travel.*

epoch-making *adjective* very important, remarkable. *An epoch-making discovery.*

equal *adjective* the same amount, size or degree. *Women demand equal rights and opportunities.* **equal to something** having enough strength and courage for something. *Will he be equal to running the business on his own?* **equally** *adverb.*

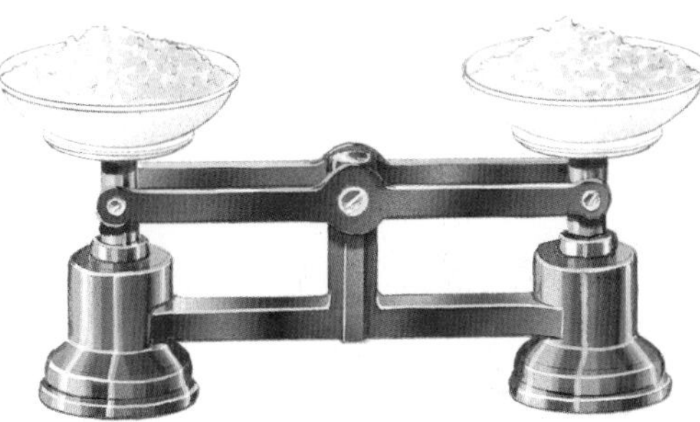

The scales are equally balanced.

equal *noun* a person or thing with the same qualities as another. *The two brothers are always treated as equals.*

equal *verb* 1 to be the same as another one in amount, size or value. *His salary doesn't equal mine.* 2 to be as good or do as well as somebody else. *With this win, they have equalled the record.*

equality *noun* being equal, having the same rights and opportunities.

equate *verb* to consider two things or people to be equal. *It is impossible to equate his novels with his films.*

equator *noun* an imaginary circle around the middle of the Earth.

The Earth is at its hottest at the equator.

E

Equatorial Guinea *noun* a country in Africa.

The flag of Equatorial Guinea has vertical red, yellow and green stripes.

equestrian *adjective* to do with horses and horse-riding. *An equestrian event.*

equinox *noun* the time of the year when day and night are equally long, about 20 March and 22 September.

equip *verb* to supply with what is needed. *The gym is fully equipped with weights and exercise machines.*

equipment *noun* things needed for certain activities. *Office equipment, climbing equipment, cleaning equipment.*

equivalent *adjective* same, equal in value or meaning. *That sum of money is almost equivalent to a day's work.* **equivalent** *noun.*

era *noun* a period of time that starts from a particular point. *The Christian era.*

eradicate *verb* to get rid of something or destroy it completely. *We are determined to eradicate crime.*

erase *verb* 1 to rub out. 2 to wipe out a recording. *I erased the tape by mistake.*

eraser *noun* a rubber used to erase marks or writing, usually on paper.

erect *adjective* upright. *He stood erect.*

erect *verb* to build or set up. *They erected a statue in the town.* **erection** *noun.*

Eritrea *noun* a country in Africa.

err (say er) *verb* to make a mistake or do something wrong. *It is better to err on the side of mercy.*

errand *noun* a short journey that you make to get something, especially buy things, or to deliver a message. *Could you do a few errands for me in town?*

error *noun* a mistake.

erupt *verb* 1 to explode and spurt out lava. *The volcano erupted.* 2 to break out or happen suddenly. *Violence erupted after the football match.* **eruption** *noun.*

escalate *verb* to increase by stages. *The violence soon escalated.*

escalator *noun* a moving staircase that goes up or down.

escape *verb* 1 to get away from a person or place, to get out. *Three prisoners escaped last night.* 2 to avoid, especially something unpleasant. *They escaped the accident unhurt. To escape punishment.* **escape** *noun. They had planned the escape for weeks.*

GRAMMAR NOTE

You can use the word 'to' with the adjective 'equivalent'. 'That's equivalent to £10.' With 'equivalent' as a noun, use the word 'of'. 'That's the equivalent of £10.'

especially *adverb* specially, in particular. *I love chocolate, especially milk chocolate.*

espionage *noun* spying.

essential *adjective* 1 absolutely necessary. *A knowledge of languages is essential for foreign correspondents.* 2 most important. *I only read the essential books on the reading list.* **essential** *noun. Just tell me the bare essentials.*

establish *verb* 1 to set up, especially a new government or business. 2 to place or settle yourself or somebody else. *Once he has established himself in the firm, he'll make progress very quickly.* 3 to find out or make certain. *We must establish the truth first.*

estate *noun* 1 a large piece of land in the country owned by one person. 2 an area of land with houses or factories on it. *A housing estate.* 3 everything, including money and property, that a person leaves when they die.

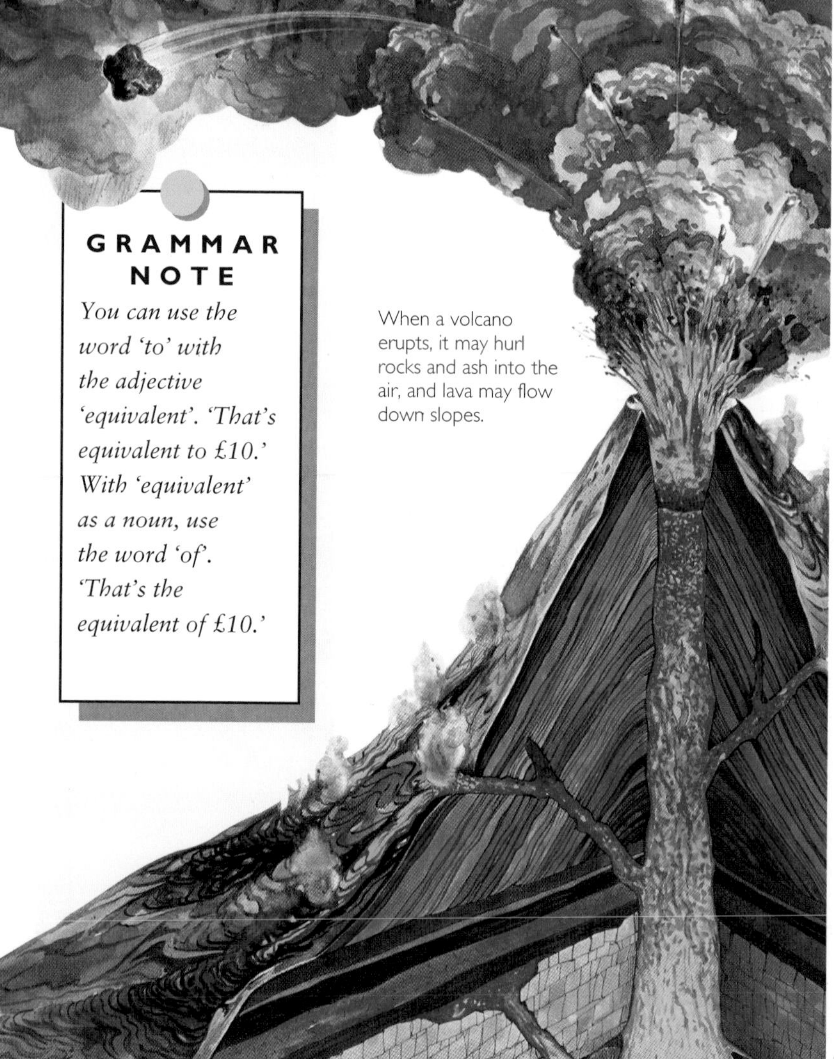

When a volcano erupts, it may hurl rocks and ash into the air, and lava may flow down slopes.

E

estate agent *noun* a person or a business that sells and lets property for others.

Estonia *noun* a Baltic country in Europe.

estuary (estuaries) (say **ess**-tew-uh-ree) *noun* the wide mouth of a river where it flows into the sea.

etc. *abbreviation* et cetera (Latin for 'and other things'), and so on.

eternal *adjective* lasting for ever.

Ethiopia *noun* a country in Africa.

ethnic *adjective* relating to people's race or culture. *Ethnic minorities must have the same rights as everybody else.*

etymology (etymologies) *noun* (say et-im-**ol**-uh-jee) 1 the history and source of a word. 2 the study of the origins and meanings of words. **etymological** *adjective.*

EU *abbreviation* European Union.

The flag of the European Union has a circle of 12 gold stars on a blue background.

DID YOU KNOW

The European Union (EU) began in 1957 as the European Economic Community, when it was made up of six countries: Belgium, France, Italy, Luxembourg, the Netherlands and West Germany. Now the EU has nine more countries as members. They include the United Kingdom, Spain and Sweden.

Europe *noun* one of the Earth's seven continents.

European *adjective* coming from or relating to Europe. *A common European currency.*

evacuate *verb* to leave a place or move people out of a place, especially because of a crisis. *You must evacuate the building immediately. Thousands were evacuated after the earthquake.* **evacuation** *noun.*

During World War II, many children were evacuated from cities to the country, where they would be safe from bombing.

evade *verb* to avoid a person or thing. *He cleverly evaded the question of money.* **evasion** *noun. He was fined for tax evasion.*

evaporate *verb* 1 to change from a liquid into a gas called water vapour. *Water evaporates in the heat of the Sun.* 2 to disappear. *My hopes evaporated.* **evaporation** *noun.*

even *adjective* 1 flat, smooth. *The floor is not very even.* 2 regular, unchanging. *Indoor plants do best in an even temperature.* 3 equal, especially when talking about things that can be measured. *An even distribution of wealth. We both won a game, now we're even.* 4 Even numbers are numbers that can be divided by two. *Four and 26 are even numbers.* **evenly** *adverb.* **evenness** *noun.*

even *adverb* 1 used to stress a word or statement. *Even the teacher was surprised how difficult the exam was.* 2 used before a comparison, meaning still. *He is even taller than his father.* **even so** nevertheless. *She says she doesn't get on with her parents, but even so, she doesn't want to leave home.* **even though** despite the fact that. *Even though she's upset, she won't say anything.* **even out** to make or become even. *Things even themselves out in the end.*

evening *noun* the end of the day, before nightfall. *We usually go to the cinema on Saturday evening.*

event *noun* 1 something that happens, especially something unusual or important. 2 one of the races or other sporting activities in a competition. **in any event** whatever happens.

Russian astronaut Yuri Gagarin was the first man in space. It was a great event in the history of space exploration.

eventual *adjective* happening at last. *He deserved his eventual success.*

ever *adverb* 1 at any time. *Getting a computer was the best thing I ever did.* 2 all the time. *They lived happily ever after.* 3 (used for stress) very. *I had ever such a nice letter from him.* **ever since** since the time. *Ever since I've known him, he has never been late.*

evergreen *adjective* having green leaves all the year round. *Evergreen trees.*

every *adjective* 1 each one. *Every word she says is true.* 2 happening at regular intervals. *Every time I ask her she refuses.* 3 all possible. *He has every reason to be unhappy.* **every now and then** sometimes. *I see my parents every now and then.*

everybody *pronoun* each person or all people. *Everybody wants to come to Marianne's birthday party.*

everyone *pronoun* everybody.

everything *pronoun* each thing or all things. *Money isn't everything.*

everywhere *adverb* in, at or to every place. *I've looked everywhere for it.*

evidence *noun* proof, something that makes a matter or statement clear. *The thieves destroyed the evidence by burning their clothes.* **give evidence** to tell what is known about somebody or something in a court of law.

evil *adjective* very bad, wicked, usually causing harm. *He's an evil man.* **evil** *noun. The difference between good and evil.*

evolution *noun* the change and development that takes place over a long period of time, during which animals and plants evolve. **evolutionary** *adjective.*

WORD BUILDING

In words such as 'excavate' the prefix 'ex–' means 'out'. In Latin, 'excavare' means to hollow out, from 'cavus', meaning a hollow or a cave.

As early people evolved, they gradually became less like apes and more like humans.

evolve *verb* to develop gradually.

ewe (rhymes with 'boo') *noun* a female sheep. *Ewe's milk.*

ex- *prefix* former, no longer the thing the noun refers to. *An ex-minister is no longer a minister. My ex-wife has married again.*

exaggerate *verb* to say that something is bigger, better or worse than it really is. *You can't believe his stories, he always exaggerates.* **exaggeration** *noun.*

examine *verb* 1 to test somebody's knowledge. 2 to look at a person or thing carefully. *The doctor examined the patient.* **examination** *noun.*

example *noun* 1 something that shows how a rule works or what others of the same kind are like. *The penguin is an example of a flightless bird.* 2 a person or thing worth copying. *Her courage is an example to us all.* **for example** *Some birds can't fly – penguins, for example.*

exasperate *verb* to annoy or make angry. *Her stupidity is extremely exasperating.* **exasperation** *noun.*

excavate *verb* to dig out. *Archaeologists are excavating an ancient Roman site.* **excavation** *noun.*

exceed *verb* to be greater than something. *The whole cost of the journey must not exceed £100.*

excel (excels, excelling, excelled) *verb* to be extremely good. *He excels at maths.*

excellent *adjective* extremely good. *He's an excellent tennis player.*

except *preposition* not including. *The film's all right, except that it's too long.* **except** *verb* to leave out. *No one can be excepted.*

exception *noun* somebody or something that does not follow the general rule. *The exception proves the rule.*

exceptional *adjective* 1 very unusual. *Only in exceptional circumstances.* 2 unusually or extremely good. *Her results were quite exceptional.*

excess (excesses) *noun* more than is needed, too much of something. *She cleans the house to excess.* **excess** *adjective. You will have to pay an excess fare.*

exchange *verb* to get something else for something. *I exchanged my pounds for pesetas. We exchanged addresses.* **exchangeable** *adjective.*

The penpals exchanged addresses and started a regular correspondence.

exchange *noun* 1 getting something else for something. *They gave us a bottle of wine in exchange for some bread.* 2 changing places with somebody. *We went on an exchange to France.*

The emperor penguin is an example of a bird that cannot fly. The penguin has waterproof feathers and a thick layer of fat to keep out the cold of Antarctica.

excite *verb* to arouse strong feelings. *We were very excited when we got tickets for the concert.* **exciting** *adjective. An exciting adventure.* **excitable** *adjective. He is very nervous and excitable.* **excitement** *noun.*

exclaim *verb* to shout out with strong feeling. *'No!' he exclaimed. 'You are never to go there again.'* **exclamation** *noun.*

exclamation mark *noun* the punctuation mark (!) which shows an exclamation.

exclude *verb* to keep or leave somebody or something out. *If you are not a member, you will be excluded from the meeting.* **exclusion** *noun.*

exclusive *adjective* 1 excluding many people and so catering for just a few. *An exclusive club.* 2 not appearing anywhere else. *The newspaper has an exclusive interview with the American film star.*

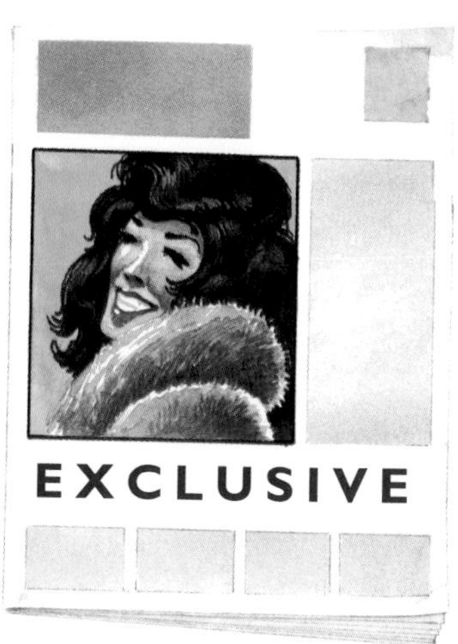

The exclusive interview was the scoop of the year. It was printed on the front page.

excursion *noun* a short journey. *We went on an excursion to the country.*

excuse (say iks-**kewz**) *verb* 1 to forgive. You excuse a person for doing something wrong or inconvenient. *Please excuse me for being late.* 2 to free somebody from a duty. *He asked to be excused from rugby training because of injury.* **excuse me** used as an apology or when asking for something or interrupting somebody.

excuse *noun* (say iks-**kewss**) the reason given or an explanation for something that has been done. *That's no excuse.*

execute *verb* 1 to kill somebody as a punishment for a crime. *The murderer was executed.* 2 to perform or carry out something, especially a plan or an order. *This task is not easy to execute.* **execution** *noun.* **executioner** *noun.*

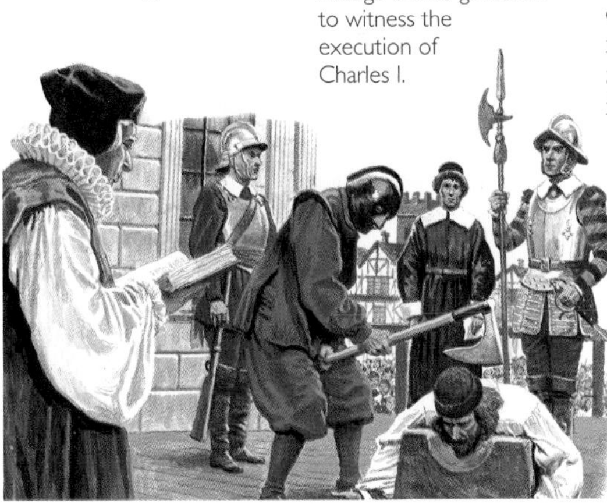

A large crowd gathered to witness the execution of Charles I.

GRAMMAR NOTE

An exclamation mark (!) is used at the end of sentences that express a strong command ('Shut up! Put it down!') or surprise (What an extraordinary idea!). It is also used for warnings (Look out!) and after interjections (Ouch!).

executive *noun* a senior person with authority in a business.

executor *noun* somebody appointed to carry out a person's instructions in their will. *Her son was the executor of her will.*

exercise *noun* 1 movements done to keep healthy or train for a particular sport. *Cycling and swimming are good forms of exercise. Gymnastic exercises.* 2 a short piece of work, especially a set of questions for practice at school. *A grammar exercise.*

exercise *verb* 1 to do exercises to become fit and healthy. *I try to exercise every day.* 2 If a problem exercises your mind, you think a lot about it.

Some people exercise every day to keep fit.

exert *verb* to use power or influence in order to achieve something. If you exert yourself, you make an effort. **exertion** *noun.*

exhaust *verb* 1 to tire out. *I'm exhausted.* 2 to use up completely. *Our food supplies were soon exhausted.* **exhausting** *adjective.*

exhaust *noun* 1 the waste gas produced by an engine. 2 the pipe through which waste gas escapes, also called an exhaust pipe.

exhaustion *noun* the state of being tired out. *Physical and mental exhaustion set in after we had worked all day at a boring job.*

exhaustive *adjective* thorough, comprehensive. *An exhaustive search.*

exhibit *verb* 1 to show in public in a museum or a gallery. *The gallery exhibited the artist's latest paintings.* 2 to show your feelings to other people. *His manner exhibited signs of distress.*

exhibit *noun* something exhibited in a museum or gallery. *Please do not touch the exhibits.*

exhibition *noun* a collection of things shown in a public place.

exile *noun* 1 a person who has been forced to leave his country, usually for political reasons. 2 having to live away from your own country. *He died alone and in exile.* **exile** *verb.*

exist *verb* 1 to be real. *Do you think ghosts really exist?* 2 to stay alive. *She exists on love alone.* **existence** *noun.*

exit *noun* 1 a way out. *Where's the exit?* 2 leaving a room or the stage. *She made a quick exit.* **exit** *verb* to leave.

exorcize *verb* to get rid of an evil spirit. *They had special rituals to exorcize ghosts.* **exorcism** *noun.* **exorcist** *noun.*

exotic *adjective* unusual and interesting. *There are many exotic flowers in the botanical gardens.*

The orchid is a very exotic flower. Orchids grow wild in tropical countries.

expand *verb* to become larger. *Scientists say the universe is expanding.* **expansion** *noun.*

expand *verb* When you expand on something, you tell a story in more detail.

expect *verb* 1 to think that something will happen. *I never expected to win the race. She expects them to make their own beds.* 2 to believe that somebody will come. *We are expecting them at five o'clock.* **expectation** *noun. The holiday didn't come up to our expectations.*

expel (expels, expelling, expelled) *verb* 1 to send somebody away, usually for doing wrong. *He was expelled from school for severe misbehaviour.* 2 to force out. *When you breathe out, air is expelled from your lungs.*

expend *verb* to spend or use up. *She expended a lot of energy.*

expenditure *noun* the spending of money or effort.

expense *noun* spending money. If you spare no expense, you don't worry about the cost of something. *I've had a lot of expenses during this past month.*

expensive *adjective* costing a lot of money. *He drives an expensive car.* **expensively** *adverb. Expensively dressed.*

experience *noun* 1 knowledge or skill gained from doing or seeing things. *Most shops only employ people with sales experience.* 2 an event that has happened to you. *Riding a camel is a strange and wonderful experience.* **experience** *verb* to have something happen to you. *She has experienced great sadness in her life.*

experiment *noun* a test made in order to learn or prove something. *A scientific experiment.* **experiment** *verb* to try things out and make experiments. *We know that it's dangerous to experiment with drugs.* **experimental** *adjective.*

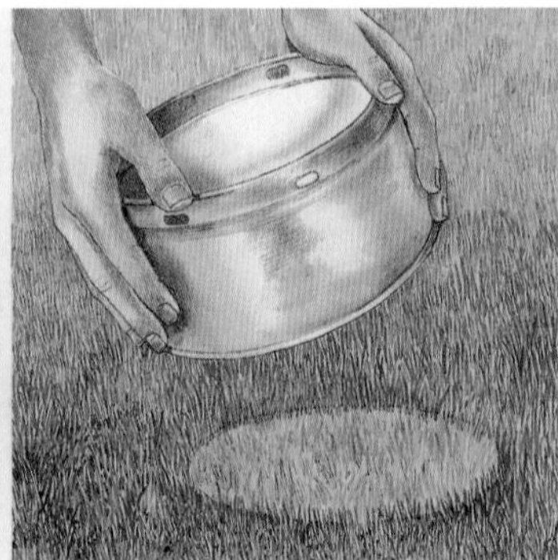

In this experiment, a tin is left on the grass for a few days. Starved of light, the grass under the tin turns yellow.

explain *verb* 1 to make something clear so it can be understood. *He explained how to use the computer.* 2 to give a reason for something. *That explains his strange behaviour.* **explanation** *noun.*

explode *verb* 1 to blow up, especially of a bomb. 2 to burst out suddenly or show violent feelings. *She exploded with anger.* **explosion** *noun.* **explosive** *adjective. Explosive materials.*

exploit (say **eks**-ploit) *noun* a brave or adventurous deed.

exploit (say iks-**ploit**) *verb* 1 to use or develop, especially a country's natural resources. *Exploiting the country's diamond wealth.* 2 to use unfairly and selfishly for your own profit. *The poor have always been exploited.* **exploitation** *noun.*

explore *verb* 1 to travel to places in order to find out what they are like. 2 to examine something and learn about it. *Have you definitely explored all the possibilities?* **exploration** *noun.*

explorer *noun* somebody who explores. *An Arctic explorer.*

export *verb* to send goods to another country for sale. **export** *noun* 1 exporting goods. *The export of ivory has been banned.* 2 exported goods. Exports are products sold in another country. *Exports are up this year.*

DID YOU KNOW

Exports are sent to and sold in another country, while imports are bought in and sent from another country.

Sir Walter Raleigh first brought tobacco and potatoes from South America to Britain. Now tobacco is one of South America's main exports.

E

expulsion *noun* expelling or being expelled. *The football hooligans faced expulsion.*

extend *verb* 1 to stretch out or make bigger. *They extended the garden.* 2 to offer. *They extended a warm welcome to the delegation of foreign visitors.*

extension *noun* 1 an extra period of time. *I should have handed my essay in today, but the teacher gave me an extension.* 2 something added on, especially a room or building. *The new extension to the school will house the library.* 3 an additional telephone connected to the same line. *I'll take the call on the extension in my office.*

extensive *adjective* covering a large area or amount. *There was extensive damage to the building from the bomb blast.*

exterior *noun* the outside of something. **exterior** *adjective. The exterior walls are gradually crumbling away.*

exterminate *verb* to destroy or kill. *Many tribes have been exterminated.* **extermination** *noun.* **exterminator** *noun.*

extinct *adjective* 1 not existing any more. *Dinosaurs have been extinct for millions of years.* 2 no longer active. *An extinct volcano.*

Extinct animals such as dinosaurs can be studied from their fossilized remains.

extra *adjective, adverb* more than usual, additional. *She says the vitamin tablets give her extra strength.*

extract (say iks-**trakt**) *verb* 1 to pull or take something out. *The dentist had to extract two teeth.* 2 to obtain, against a person's will. *They used force to extract information.*

extract (say **eks**-trakt) *noun* 1 a small part taken from a book or film. *They printed extracts from the new book in the newspaper.* 2 something that has been extracted. *Meat extract.*

extraordinary *adjective* 1 very strange or unusual. *It was an extraordinary sight.* 2 unusually great. *She has an extraordinary musical talent.*

extravagance *noun* 1 spending more money than is reasonable or you can afford. 2 something that is very expensive. *A sports car is a real extravagance.* **extravagant** *adjective. She has extravagant tastes.*

exuberant *adjective* full of energy and cheerfulness. *They greeted us noisily with lots of exuberant shouting and waving.* **exuberance** *noun.*

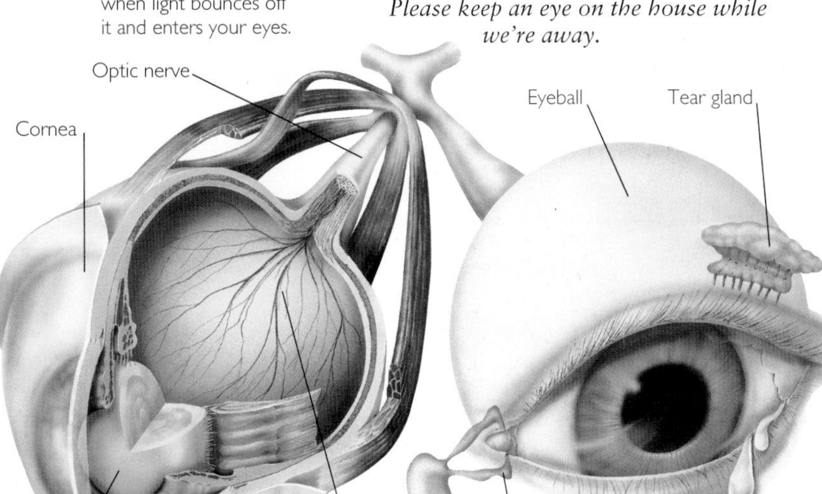

You see something when light bounces off it and enters your eyes.

eye *noun* 1 one of two organs in the face to see with. *We close our eyes when we go to sleep.* 2 the power of seeing. *To have sharp eyes.* 3 the hole in a needle through which the thread passes. 4 a dark spot on a vegetable, such as a potato, from which a new plant grows. **eye** *verb* to watch or look at closely. *He eyed her jealously.* **keep an eye on** to watch somebody or something. *Please keep an eye on the house while we're away.*

eyeball *noun* the whole of the eye, formed like a ball, including the part concealed behind the eyelids.

eyebrow *noun* the line of hairs growing above the eyes.

eyelash *noun* one of the hairs that grow on the edge of your upper and lower eyelids.

eyelid *noun* either of the two pieces of covering skin that move down when you close your eyes or blink.

eyesight *noun* the power to see. *He wears glasses because he has poor eyesight.*

eyewitness *noun* a person who has seen an accident or a crime happen and can describe it. *Will eyewitnesses to the accident please contact the police.*

eyrie (rhymes with 'weary') *noun* an eagle's nest. *The eagle builds its eyrie of large twigs.*

WORD BUILDING

The prefix 'extra–' comes from the Latin for outside or beyond. So something that is extraordinary is 'outside the usual order'.

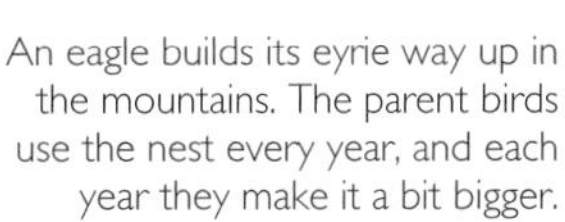

An eagle builds its eyrie way up in the mountains. The parent birds use the nest every year, and each year they make it a bit bigger.

F

Ff

fable *noun* a short story, usually one with animals, that teaches a lesson about behaviour or truth.

fabric *noun* 1 cloth. 2 the structure of a building or the system of a society.

face *noun* 1 the front part of the head. 2 a look or expression on the face. *A sad face.* 3 the front, upper side or surface of something. *The north face of the mountain.* **face to face** looking straight at each other.

face *verb* 1 to have or turn the front towards a certain direction. *Our house faces the park.* 2 to be brave enough to deal with something unpleasant or dangerous. *I can't face the truth.* 3 to cover a surface, such as a wall, with a layer of different material.

facsimile (say fak-**sim**-il-ee) *noun* an exact copy or reproduction.

fact *noun* something that is true or has actually happened. **in fact** really.

factor *noun* 1 one of the things that influences an event and brings about a result. *Money was a very important factor in the decision.* 2 a number by which a larger number can be divided. *2 and 4 are factors of 8.*

factory (factories) *noun* a large building where goods are made, usually by machines.

Smoke from factories pollutes the atmosphere.

factual *adjective* based on facts. *She gave a factual account of events.*

faculty *noun* 1 any of the powers of the mind or body, such as speech or understanding. *After the accident her faculties were impaired.* 2 a large department in a university.

fade *verb* 1 to become less strong or clear. *The colours have faded in the sunshine.* 2 to disappear gradually.

Fahrenheit *adjective* measuring temperature on a scale where water freezes at 32° and boils at 212°.

DID YOU KNOW

The most famous collection of fables was supposedly written by a Greek slave over 2,500 years ago. The writer's name was Aesop.

WORD HISTORY

The word 'fairy' comes from the French 'faie' and the Latin 'fata', which means 'the Fates'. These were three goddesses who controlled people's lives.

WORD HISTORY

The Fahrenheit scale was named after its inventor, the German scientist Daniel Gabriel Fahrenheit (1686–1736).

fail *verb* 1 to try to do something and not succeed. *All my plans failed.* 2 not to do or remember something. *You failed to warn me that she doesn't like dogs.* 3 not to produce the expected result or work as expected. *The brakes failed.* 4 If a teacher fails you, she grades you as not having passed a test. **failed** *adjective* unsuccessful.

failing *noun* a weakness or fault.

failure *noun* 1 lack of success, failing to do something. *After many failures, he has succeeded at last.* 2 an unsuccessful person.

faint *adjective* weak, not clear. *The writing was very faint.*

faint *verb* to lose consciousness suddenly. *He faints at the sight of blood.*

fair *noun* 1 a festival with roundabouts, shows and other amusements. 2 a market or exhibition where goods are displayed and sold. *A trade fair.*

fair *adjective* 1 honest and just. 2 pale or light in colour. 3 fine, especially when talking about the weather. 4 fairly good. *After living in France for a year, he has a fair knowledge of French.* **fairness** *noun.*

fairground *noun* the place where a fair is held. *Fairground rides.*

We had fun at the fairground.

fairly *adverb* 1 quite, to some extent. *This restaurant is fairly cheap.* 2 in a fair way. *The election was conducted fairly.*

fairy (fairies) *noun* a small imaginary person with magical powers.

fairy tale *noun* a story about fairies and other creatures with magical powers.

faith *noun* 1 a strong belief or trust. 2 a particular religion. *The Christian faith.*

faithful *adjective* trustworthy and loyal. **faithfully** *adverb.*

fake *noun* a person or thing that is not what it is supposed to be or looks like. *The painting is a fake.* **fake** *verb* 1 to make something look better or more valuable in order to deceive people. 2 to pretend. *He faked a stomach ache to get off school.*

falcon *noun* a bird of prey that can be trained to hunt other birds and animals. **falconry** *noun.*

fall (falls, falling, fell, fallen) *verb* 1 to come or go down, to drop to a lower place. *A brick fell on his head.* 2 to become lower. *The temperature fell.* 3 to happen. *Silence fell.* 4 to become or pass into another state. *I have fallen in love.* 5 to die in battle. **fall apart** to break into pieces. **fall behind** to not produce something on time, especially money. *He's fallen behind with the rent.* **fall for** 1 If you fall for somebody, you are attracted to them. 2 to be deceived by. *I don't fall for his tricks.* **fall out** to quarrel. **fall through** to fail. *The plan fell through.*

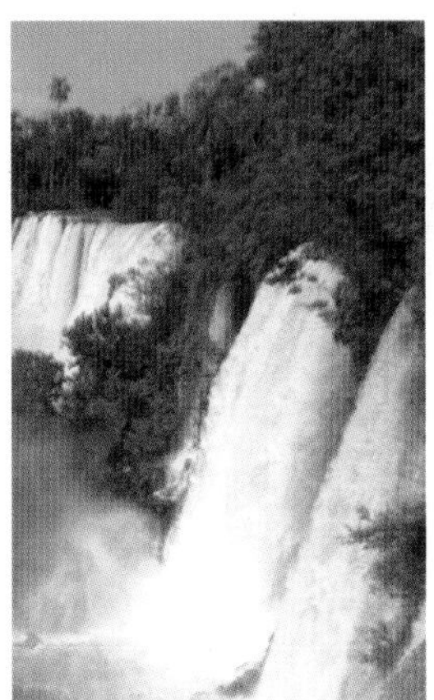

fall *noun* 1 a drop from a higher to a lower place. 2 getting lower or less. 3 a waterfall. *Niagara Falls.* 4 (US) autumn, the season between summer and winter.

The spectacular Iguaçu Falls are a string of 275 waterfalls on the border between Argentina and Brazil.

false *adjective* 1 not true, wrong. *She gave a false address to the police.* 2 not natural, artificial. *False teeth.*

falsehood *noun* 1 something not true, a lie. 2 telling lies.

fame *noun* being famous. *Her fame soon spread throughout the country.*

familiar *adjective* 1 well known. 2 knowing something well. *Are you familiar with this play?* 3 very friendly.

family *noun* 1 parents and their children, grandparents and other relations. 2 a group of related things, especially animals or plants. *Lions belong to the cat family.*

famine *noun* a severe lack of food in a region. *There is a terrible famine in Africa.*

famous *adjective* well known by many people. *A famous actor.*

fan *noun* something that moves the air to make you or a room cooler.

fan (fans, fanning, fanned) *verb* to make the air move.

fan *noun* an admirer or supporter. *Dean is a football fan.*

fancy (fancies, fancying, fancied) *verb* 1 to want to do or have something. *Do you fancy a game of tennis?* 2 to imagine. *He fancies himself as a dancer.* **fancy** (fancies) *noun* 1 an imagined or unlikely idea. 2 a liking. *I have taken a fancy to that restaurant.* **fanciful** *adjective.*

In summer, a fan is essential in a hot office.

GRAMMAR NOTE

When talking about distance you can use 'farther' or 'further', and 'farthest' or 'furthest'. But when talking about time, you can only use 'further/furthest'. 'Remain here until further notice.'

fancy *adjective* brightly coloured and decorated. *Fancy dress.*

fang *noun* a long sharp tooth.

fantasy (fantasies) *noun* something imagined, a situation that you think about. *His mind is crammed full of fantasies.* **fantastic** *adjective.*

far (farther/further, farthest/furthest) *adverb* 1 at or to a great distance. *I live not far from here.* 2 much. *That's far too expensive.* **far** *adjective* distant, a long way off.

far-fetched *adjective* unlikely or impossible, especially an idea or example. *His story was too far-fetched for us to believe.*

far-reaching *adjective* having wide influence or effect over a long period of time. *Far-reaching reforms.*

farce *noun* 1 a play in which lots of silly things happen. 2 an event that is treated too lightly and becomes ridiculous. *The election was a farce as the winner had already been decided on.* **farcical** *adjective.*

fare *noun* 1 the money paid by passengers for a journey. 2 food and drink.

The farmer is at work in the tractor, baling the hay.

fare *verb* to get along. If you fare badly, you are unsuccessful or treated badly.

farm *noun* 1 a place where crops are grown and animals are kept. 2 a farmhouse. **farm** *verb* to grow crops or raise animals.

farmer *noun* a person who owns or works on a farm. *My ambition is to be a farmer.*

farther *adjective*, *adverb* at or to a more distant point. *I'm too tired, I can't walk any farther up the mountain.*

farthest *adjective*, *adverb* at or to a most distant point.

fascinate *verb* to attract and be very interesting. *He has always been fascinated by space travel.* **fascination** *noun.* **fascinating** *adjective.*

fashion *noun* 1 the style of clothes or the way of doing something at a particular time. *Short skirts are back in fashion this autumn.* 2 a way of doing something. *She walks in a strange fashion.* **fashionable** *adjective.* **fashionably** *adverb.*

fast *adjective* 1 quick. *A fast car.* 2 firmly fixed. *Wash the shirt separately, the colours aren't fast.* 3 showing a time that is later than the real time. *My watch is fast.* **fast food** hot food that is cooked and served quickly after ordering.

F

fast *adverb* 1 quickly. *He was driving too fast.* 2 fully. *She was fast asleep.*

fast *verb* to eat no food. *Lent is a time of fasting.* **fast** *noun.*

fasten *verb* 1 to fix one thing to another. 2 to close or lock. *Fasten your seatbelts.* **fastener** *noun.* **fastening** *noun.*

fat *noun* 1 the greasy part of human flesh or animal meat. *Fat under the skin keeps us warm.* 2 oil or grease used for cooking.

fat (fatter, fattest) *adjective* 1 Fat people have a lot of flesh on their body. *He is fat because he eats too much.* 2 thick or large. *A fat book.* **fatness** *noun.*

fatal *adjective* bringing or ending in death. *A fatal accident.* **fatally** *adverb.*

fate *noun* 1 the power that is believed to control events. *Fate was against us.* 2 what will happen or has happened to somebody. *It was her fate.*

father *noun* a male parent. *Your father and mother are your parents.*

father-in-law *noun* the father of your wife or husband.

fatigue *noun* 1 a feeling of great tiredness. 2 weakness in metals caused by stress.

fault *noun* 1 something wrong, a mistake or imperfection. *An electrical fault.* 2 a bad point about a person or thing. *He's always finding fault with me.* 3 a crack in the surface of the earth. *Earthquakes usually occur along faults.* **fault** *verb* to find fault with something or somebody. *His attitude can't be faulted.* **faulty** *adjective.*

Earthquakes occur along faults.

fauna *noun* all the wild animals living in a region. *She was studying the flora and fauna of the Alps.*

favour *noun* 1 a liking of somebody or something. *He is trying to win her favour.* 2 If you are in favour of something, you like the idea of it. If somebody is in favour, he is liked. If he is out of favour, he is not liked. 3 a kind act. *Could you do me a favour and take me to the station?* **favour** *verb* 1 to like or support, especially a plan or an idea. *The government favours free school meals.* 2 to be kinder to one person than another. *The teacher tends to favour the girls.*

AMAZING FACT

'Phobia' means 'fear of'. There is a state called 'phobophobia' which means 'fear of fear'.

Some people have an irrational fear of spiders.

WORD HISTORY

The phrase 'a feather in your cap' comes from a Native American custom. Indian braves were given a feather for their headdress for every warrior they killed in battle.

WORD HISTORY

Fauna was the name of a Roman goddess of the countryside. She was the sister of Faunus, who was associated with the Greek god Pan.

favourable *adjective* good, approving. *The teacher gave her a favourable report.*

favourite *adjective* liked more than all others. *What is your favourite TV programme?* **favourite** *noun* 1 a person or thing preferred over others. *This book is my favourite.* 2 in sport, the competitor expected to win.

favouritism *noun* being unfairly kinder to one person than another. *It's not fair if teachers show favouritism.*

fear *noun* 1 an unpleasant feeling that something dangerous or painful might happen. *She has a fear of flying.* 2 danger. *There is no fear of failure.* **fear** *verb* to be afraid or worry about something or somebody. *They feared for their lives.* **for fear of** because of worry about something. *I didn't ring the bell last night for fear of disturbing you.* **never fear** there is no danger of that.

fearful *adjective* 1 causing fear or being afraid. *A fearful storm.* 2 bad, terrible, great. *Your room is always in a fearful mess.*

fearless *adjective* without fear, not afraid. *She was fearless in the face of danger.* **fearlessly** *adverb.*

fearsome *adjective* terrible or frightening. *The monster was a fearsome sight.*

feasible *adjective* possible, that can be done. *Is it feasible to rebuild the bridge?*

feast *noun* 1 a large and very good meal. *A wedding feast.* 2 a religious festival. **feast** *verb* to eat and drink very well.

feat *noun* a courageous or skilful action that is difficult to do.

feather *noun* one of the many soft, light things that cover a bird's body. **as light as a feather** very light. **a feather in your cap** an achievement that you can be proud of.

feature *noun* 1 an important part. *Sand is a feature of the desert.* 2 an important part of your face. *Your eyes, mouth and nose make up your features.* 3 an article in a newspaper or a special programme on radio or television.

feature *verb* to be an important part of something. *The film features an unknown but very beautiful actress.*

February *noun* the second month of the year. February has 28 days, but in leap years it has 29.

fed past tense of feed.

federation *noun* a united group of states with one government.

fee *noun* a sum of money paid for services. *The agency charges a fee for arranging holidays abroad.*

feeble *adjective* weak, having very little power. *He made rather a feeble attempt.* **feebly** *adverb.*

feed (feeds, feeding, fed) *verb* 1 to give food to. *Don't forget to feed the cat.* 2 to eat. *Horses feed on hay.* 3 to put something in. *All the data has been fed into the computer.* **feed** *noun* food for animals.

feedback *noun* comments about something that you have done, so that possible changes can be made. *Most shops welcome feedback from their customers.*

feel (feels, feeling, felt) *verb* 1 to touch something with your fingers or hold it. *Just feel the quality of the fabric.* 2 to be a certain sensation – wet, dry, soft or sticky, for example. *My clothes feel damp.* 3 to be aware of a mood or to know that something is happening to your body. *I'm not feeling well.* 4 to think something or have an opinion. *I feel strongly that the action is wrong.* 5 to search, usually with your hands, feet or a stick. *He felt in his pockets for money.* **feel** *noun. I like the feel of silk.* **feel like** to want. *I feel like a swim.*

feeler *noun* the long, thin part on the front of an insect's head with which it touches things. **put out feelers** to suggest something in order to find out what others think or want to do.

Feelers

An insect uses its feelers to help it find its way about.

feeling *noun* 1 the power to feel things. *I'm so cold, I've lost all feeling in my hands.* 2 an emotion or physical sensation. *An itchy feeling.* If you have a feeling for somebody or something, you like them. 3 what you think, an idea. *I have a feeling that he'll do very well in the exams.* 4 sympathy and understanding. *He read the poem with great feeling.*

feet plural of foot. **fall on one's feet** to have good luck. *He's fallen right on his feet with that new job.*

feint (say faynt) *noun* a pretend attack, especially in fencing or boxing. **feint** *verb.*

feline (say fee-line) *adjective* like a cat.

fell past tense of fall.

felt past tense of feel.

female *adjective* 1 referring to a woman or girl. *Male and female workers.* 2 A female animal or plant can have babies, lay eggs or produce fruit. *A bitch is a female dog.* **female** *noun* a female person or animal.

WORD HISTORY

'Fence' is a shortened form of the word 'defence', which makes sense both for the wooden barrier and the sport of sword-fighting.

AMAZING FACT

Fencing was once a form of sword practice and a preparation for fighting in duels. Now it is an Olympic sport.

feminine *adjective* 1 with the qualities of a woman. *She designs very feminine clothes.* 2 in grammar, referring to words that are classed as female. *French nouns are either masculine or feminine.* **femininity** *noun.*

feminist *noun* a person who believes that women should have the same rights and opportunities as men. **feminism** *noun.*

fence *noun* a barrier made of wood or wire round an area or used to divide two areas of land. **fence** *verb* 1 to build a fence round an area or along something. *We fenced in the garden to keep the cows out.* 2 to fight with a long thin sword as a sport. **fencing** *noun.*

ferment (say fer-**ment**) *verb* to change chemically; to turn liquid into an alcoholic drink by the action of yeast, for example. **fermentation** *noun.*

fern *noun* a plant with green, feathery leaves and no flowers.

ferocious *adjective* fierce, savage. *A ferocious dog guards the entrance to the house.* **ferocity** *noun.*

ferret *noun* a small animal with a pointed nose. Ferrets are used for catching rats and rabbits. **ferret out** *verb* to search for something or find out information.

ferry (ferries) *noun* a boat that goes across a river or other narrow channel of water carrying people and cars. **ferry** (ferries, ferrying, ferried) *verb* to transport people or goods. *She ferried the children to and from school every day.*

fertile *adjective* 1 land or soil is fertile when plants grow well in it. *Silt from the river makes the land very fertile.* 2 able to produce babies or seeds. 3 full of ideas. *My brother has a very fertile imagination.* **fertility** *noun.*

fertilize *verb* 1 to put pollen into a plant or sperm into an egg to make them grow. 2 When you fertilize the soil you add things to it to make it more fertile. **fertilization** *noun.*

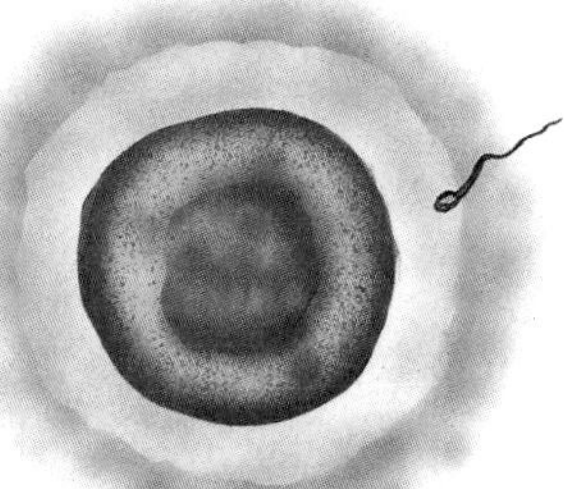

A sperm swims towards an egg. In a moment, fertilization will occur.

fertilizer *noun* a natural substance or chemical added to soil to make it more fertile. *Organic fertilizers are best.*

fester *verb* 1 to become infected, especially of a wound or cut. 2 to poison the mind, causing bitterness over a period of time. *Hatred still festers between the brothers.*

F

festival *noun* 1 a day or time for public celebration which is usually a holiday. *Christmas is a Christian festival.* 2 a number of events like a concert, ballet or other entertainment at a stated time in a place.

festive *adjective* joyful and suitable for a festival. *It was Christmas and we were all in a very festive mood.* **festivity** *noun*.

At New Year the Chinese celebrate by dressing up as a dragon and parading through the streets.

fetch *verb* 1 to get and bring back. *We must fetch a doctor.* 2 to be sold for a certain price. *These old books might well fetch a lot of money.*

fetching *adjective* attractive.

fetlock *noun* the back part of a horse's leg near the foot.

feud *noun* (say fewd) a long-lasting quarrel, especially between families.

feudal *adjective* (say **few**-dal) relating to a method practised in the Middle Ages in which people were given land in exchange for fighting and working for the owner.

fever *noun* 1 a body temperature that is higher than usual, because of illness. 2 an illness that causes a high body temperature. 3 great excitement. *There was a fever of anticipation in the hall.* **feverish** *adjective*.

few *adjective*, *pronoun* not many, a small number. *A few went home early.* **fewer than** not as many as. *Fewer than ten students passed the exam.*

fiancé *noun* (say fee-**ahn**-say) a man engaged to be married. *She introduced her friends to her fiancé.* **fiancée** *noun* (say fee-**ahn**-say) a woman engaged to be married.

fiasco *noun* (say fee-**ass**-koh) an absurd failure. *Everything went wrong and the holiday was a complete fiasco.*

fibre *noun* 1 a very thin thread, especially one used to make cloth or rope. 2 parts of plants or seeds which the body cannot digest. Brown bread and beans are high in fibre. 3 a thin piece of flesh, like thread, in the body. *Muscles are made of fibres.* **fibrous** *adjective*.

These are artificial fibres seen under the microscope.

GRAMMAR NOTE

'Fewer' is the comparative form of 'few' and is the right word to use with plural nouns to mean 'not as many'. 'There were fewer people in the shop today.' Use 'less' with singular nouns. 'We had less time today.'

The Earth's magnetic field is called the magnetosphere.

fickle *adjective*. Fickle people always change their mind. They are not loyal in love or friendship. **fickleness** *noun*.

fiction *noun* writing or stories about something that is not true. *Is the report I read in the paper fact or fiction?* **fictional** *adjective*.

fictitious *adjective* imaginary, invented. *He gave the police a fictitious name.*

fiddle *noun* 1 a violin. *He gave us a tune on the fiddle.* 2 a dishonest action, a swindle. **as fit as a fiddle** in very good health.

fiddle *verb* 1 to play the violin. 2 to get or change something, especially a bill or an account, dishonestly. *He fiddled the figures.* 3 to touch or move things around with your fingers. *Stop fiddling with the matches.* **play second fiddle** to be less important. *He gets fed up playing second fiddle to his brother.* **fiddler** *noun*.

fidget *verb* to move around restlessly and never sit still. *Some children fidget a lot.* **fidget** *noun*.

field *noun* 1 a piece of land with grass or crops growing on it. 2 an area of grass marked out for a game. *A football field.* 3 a battlefield. 4 a piece of land where oil, coal, gold or other things might be found. 5 a subject, an area of study or activity. *She is an expert in the field of medical research.* 6 an area of space where something is strong. *A magnetic field.* Your field of vision is the whole area you can see.

field *verb* 1 to catch the ball in cricket, baseball or other games. 2 to be on the side whose turn it is to bowl rather than bat in cricket or other games. 3 to play players or a team. *Our school fields three rugby teams.*

fierce *adjective* 1 angry and violent. 2 very strong. *In the fierce heat.*

fiery *adjective* flaming, like fire. *He has a fiery temper.*

fig *noun* a soft fruit full of seeds that grows on trees in hot countries. **I don't give a fig** I don't care at all.

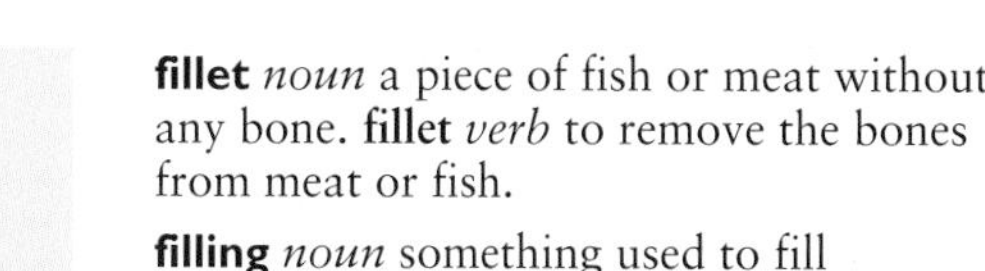

Figs ripened in the Sun are one of the most delicious of all fruits.

fight (fights, fighting, fought) *verb* 1 to use your hands, weapons or words against another in order to try and win. When people fight, they try to hurt each other. 2 to try to overcome or stop something. *We must fight crime.* When you fight for something, you try to get or keep it. 3 to quarrel. **fight** *noun* 1 the act of fighting somebody, using hands or weapons. 2 a struggle to overcome something. *The fight against poverty.*

fighter *noun* 1 a person who fights. 2 a fast military aircraft.

figure *noun* 1 a sign that stands for a number. 1, 3 and 9 are figures. 2 an amount, how much money something costs. *A huge figure.* 3 a diagram or drawing, usually in a book. 4 the shape of the body. *She's got a very good figure.* 5 the shape of a person or an animal in a picture or carved in wood or stone. *A wooden figure of an African tribesman.* 6 a person. *He was a great figure in the world of pop music.* **figure of speech** a word or an expression used to produce an impression, making your meaning stronger. 'As pretty as a picture' is a figure of speech.

figure *verb* 1 to take part in something. *He doesn't figure much in the article.* 2 to believe, imagine or work out. *I figure they'll make him captain.*

Fiji *noun* a country of many islands in the Pacific Ocean.

The flag of Fiji has the Union Jack and a crest against a turquoise blue background.

file *noun* a tool with a rough surface for smoothing, cutting or shaping things. *A nail file.* **file** *verb* to smooth, shape or cut with a file. *The woman sat filing her nails.*

file *noun* 1 a holder for keeping papers and documents in order. 2 a set of papers kept in a file. 3 information stored in a computer. 4 a line of people or things one behind the other. **file** *verb* 1 to put papers or documents in a file. 2 When you file an application, you apply for something officially. 3 to walk one after another. *The class filed into the room.*

fill *verb* 1 to make or become full. 2 to block up. *She pulled the nails out of the wall and filled the holes.*

DID YOU KNOW

There are 176 different kinds of bird in the finch family. They are found in most regions of the world except Australia, and range in size from 10 to 27 cm long. The finch family includes chaffinches, canaries and crossbills.

fillet *noun* a piece of fish or meat without any bone. **fillet** *verb* to remove the bones from meat or fish.

filling *noun* something used to fill something. *I went to the dentist and had two new fillings.*

film *noun* 1 moving pictures taken with a film camera which can be seen in the cinema or on television. 2 a roll of thin plastic that is put in a camera for taking photographs or shooting a film. 3 a thin layer. *A film of dust.* **film** *verb* 1 to make a film. 2 to take moving pictures with a film camera.

John took his film to the chemist's to be developed.

filter *noun* 1 a device through which liquids are passed to make them clean. 2 a piece of glass or plastic used on a camera lens to hold back light.

filter *verb* 1 to pass through a filter. *It's a good idea to filter drinking water.* 2 to pass or move slowly, especially of people, traffic or ideas. *Light filtered through the curtains.*

filth *noun* a disgusting amount of dirt. **filthy** *adjective. Your bedroom looks filthy.*

fin *noun* 1 a wing-like part that a fish uses in swimming. 2 something shaped like a fish's fin, such as a swimmer's flipper or the surface of a car or plane.

final *adjective* last, at the end. *The final word on the page.* **final** *noun* the last match in a competition or the last examination. *They are in the Cup Final.* **finalist** *noun.*

finally *adverb* 1 lastly or at last. *Finally, I'd like to thank the headmaster.* 2 after a long time. *I finally found out where he lives.*

finance *noun* the control and management of money. **finances** *plural noun* money, especially of a business. *How are the firm's finances?* **finance** *verb* to provide money for something. *Who is financing the trip?*

finch *noun* a small songbird.

find (finds, finding, found) *verb* 1 to get or see somebody or something by searching or by chance. 2 to learn by working, experimenting or by experience. *Doctors are hoping to find a cure for Aids.* **find** *noun* something found.

fine *adjective* 1 excellent. *We had a fine time on Sunday.* 2 dry, bright and sunny. *In fine weather.* 3 very thin. *Fine hair.* **fine** *adverb* very well. *That suits me fine.* **cut it fine** to just make it on time.

fine *noun* a sum of money to be paid as punishment. *I had to pay a parking fine.* **fine** *verb* to make somebody pay a fine.

F

finger *noun* 1 one of the parts of the hand. You have five fingers on your hand. 2 a thin piece of something. *Fish fingers.* **finger** *verb* to touch with your fingers.

fingernail *noun* the hard flat piece at the end of your finger.

fingerprint *noun* the mark made by the lines on the skin of the finger. *The thieves left no fingerprints.*

finish *verb* to reach the end or bring to the end.

finish (finishes) *noun* 1 the end or last part of something. *The finish of a race.* 2 the coating, especially of painted or polished articles.

Everyone has different fingerprints, even identical twins.

Finland *noun* a Scandinavian country in Europe.

Finnish *noun* the language spoken by the Finns.

The capital of Finland is Helsinki.

Finnish *adjective. A Finnish lake.*

fir *noun* an evergreen tree with leaves that look like needles. The seeds are formed in cones. *A plantation of firs.*

fire *noun* 1 burning with flames. *The house is on fire.* If you set fire to something, you light it in order to burn it. 2 burning coal or wood or an apparatus using gas or electricity for heating or cooking. 3 the shooting of guns. *The enemy opened fire.* **catch fire** to begin to burn.

fire *verb* 1 to shoot a gun or propel bullets, missiles or arrows. 2 to let off other things. *He fired lots of questions at us.* 3 to bake pottery. *Clay pots are fired in a kiln.* 4 to dismiss somebody from a job. *He was fired for misconduct.* 5 to excite. *His speech fired our enthusiasm.*

firearm *noun* a gun.

fire engine *noun* a large vehicle that carries firefighters and equipment for putting out fires. *The fire engine raced towards the fire.*

firefighter *noun* a person who puts out fires. *The firefighter was awarded a medal.*

fireplace *noun* a place in a room for a fire.

fireproof *adjective* fireproof things cannot be damaged by fire or heat.

firework *noun* an object filled with chemical powder that makes sparks and noises when lit.

DID YOU KNOW

Finnish is one of two official languages in Finland. The other is Swedish. An English word borrowed from Finnish is 'sauna'. Finland joined the European Union in 1995.

AMAZING FACT

A fish's fins are used primarily for steering and balance. Most fish propel themselves by beating their tail from side to side.

firm *adjective* 1 hard, not changing shape when pressed. *Firm muscles.* 2 steady, not shaking or moving. *Keep a firm grip on it.* 3 strong and sure, not likely to change. *We need a firm decision.*

firm *noun* a business or organization. *He works for a computer firm.*

first *adjective, adverb* before all others or everything else. *He came first in the race.* **at first** in the beginning. *They didn't like each other at first.* **first** *noun* the first thing, person or event. *I was the first to know.*

first aid *noun* emergency treatment given to an injured person, usually before a doctor arrives. *She went on a first aid course.*

first name *noun* your given or Christian name. *My first name is Jane.*

first-rate *adjective* excellent. *A first-rate performance.*

fish (fish or fishes) *noun* an animal that lives and breathes in water. Fish use their fins and tail to swim.

fish *verb* 1 to try and catch fish. *We went fishing on holiday.* 2 to try to get something, especially information or compliments. *She is fishing for praise.* 3 to pull something out.

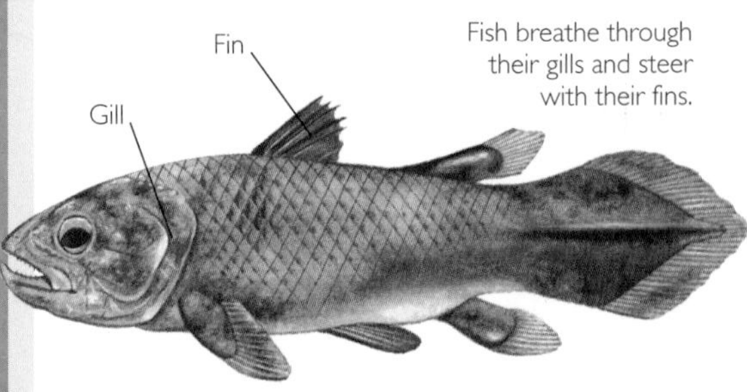

Fish breathe through their gills and steer with their fins.

fisherman *noun* a man who catches fish, usually for a living.

fist *noun* a hand with the fingers tightly closed. *In boxing you fight with your fists.*

fit (fitter, fittest) *adjective* 1 right or good enough. *The meal was fit for a king.* 2 healthy. *She goes jogging every day to keep fit.* **fitness** *noun.*

fit (fits, fitting, fitted) *verb* 1 to be the right size or shape. *The shoes don't fit, they're too small.* 2 to make clothes the right size and shape for somebody. *He had a suit fitted.* 3 to put into place. *We had a new lock fitted on the door.* 4 to be or make suitable. *The description fits her well.* **fit in** 1 to feel comfortable among a group of people. 2 to find time to do something. *We'll fit in an extra lesson before the exam.*

fit *noun* 1 the way something fits. 2 a sudden attack of an illness or loss of consciousness. *A coughing fit.* 3 an outburst. *He hit him in a fit of anger.* **have someone in fits** to make someone laugh uncontrollably.

fix *verb* 1 to make something firm, to attach it. 2 to decide or arrange. *We have fixed the date for our holiday.* 3 to repair. *He managed to fix the bike.* 4 to treat colours or a photographic film with chemicals to protect them from light. 5 to prepare or cook, especially food or a drink. *I'll fix myself dinner.* **fix up** to arrange.

fix *noun* 1 something arranged, especially by deception. *The election was a fix.* 2 an injection of illegal drugs. **in a fix** in a difficult situation.

fixture *noun* 1 built-in furniture or equipment that is fixed to a house or flat and left behind when you move. *The bath and lights are fixtures.* 2 a match or other competition that has been arranged to take place on a particular date. *All the football matches are in the fixture list.*

fizzy *adjective* bubbling. *A fizzy drink.*

fjord *noun* (say **fee**-ord) a long narrow inlet of sea between steep cliffs, especially in Norway. *Norwegian fjords.*

The fjords of Norway were created by glaciers during the Ice Age.

flabby *adjective* too soft, fat. *He's a bit flabby around the waist.*

flag *noun* a piece of cloth with a design on it, which is used as a signal or sign of something, especially a country.

Flamingoes, with their soft pink feathers, are among the world's most beautiful birds.

WORD HISTORY

'A flash in the pan' referred originally to a flash in the lock-pan of an old gun called a musket. Sometimes it only flashed instead of lighting the charge and firing when the trigger was pulled.

flamingo (flamingos or flamingoes) *noun* a tropical water bird with long legs and pink feathers. *Flamingo pink.*

flammable *adjective* likely to catch fire or burn easily. Flammable is the same as inflammable. The opposite of flammable is non-flammable.

flank *noun* the side of something, especially an animal. **flank** *verb* to be placed on one or both sides. *The actress was flanked by two tall men in dinner suits.*

flap (flaps, flapping, flapped) *verb* 1 to move up and down or from side to side. *The bird flapped its wings and took off.* 2 to panic or become anxious.

flap *noun* 1 a piece of material or flat part of something that covers an opening. *A cap with ear flaps.* 2 the sound of flapping. 3 a state of anxiety or panic. *I got into a terrible flap when I couldn't find my purse.*

flare *noun* 1 a sudden bright flame or light. 2 a device producing a bright light that is used as a signal. **flare** *verb* to burn with a bright flame for a short time. **flare up** to show sudden anger.

flared *adjective* shaped so as to get wider towards the bottom. *Flared trousers.*

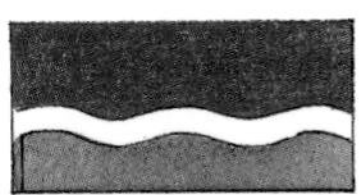

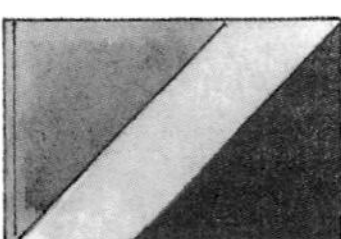
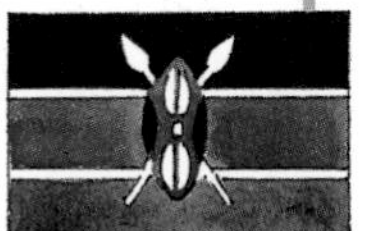

Each country is represented by its own flag.

flag (flags. flagging, flagged) *verb* 1 to become weak. *My interest is flagging.* 2 to signal with a flag. **flag down** to wave, especially at a car, to make it stop.

flagstone *noun* a stone slab used for paving.

flair *noun* instinctive talent. *She has a real flair for fashion.*

flake *noun* 1 a small, thin piece of something. *Flakes of paint.* 2 a piece of falling snow. **flake** *verb* to come off in flakes. *The paint is starting to flake.*

flame *noun* a portion of fire or burning gas. *The car burst into flames.* **in flames** burning.

AMAZING FACT

Signal flags for sending messages at sea include a flag for each letter of the alphabet and the numbers 1–10.

flash (flashes) *noun* 1 a sudden bright light. *Flashes of lightning.* 2 a sudden idea or display of wit. *She had a flash of inspiration.* 3 a device producing a sudden bright light for taking photographs in the dark. 4 a short news report. **flash in the pan** a sudden short-lived success. **in a flash** quickly. *The ambulance was there in a flash.*

flash *verb* 1 to shine brightly once or several times. *Lights flashed across the sky.* 2 to suddenly think of something. *It flashed through my mind that he was lying.* 3 to move very fast or appear suddenly. *Cars flashed past me.* 4 When you flash a look at somebody, you look at them very quickly.

F

flashback *noun* a scene in a film or story that shows events that happened in the past.

flat (flatter, flattest) *adjective* 1 not curved, smooth with no bumps. 2 spread out. *Lie down flat on the ground.* 3 dull or boring. *Everything seems very flat since our holiday.* 4 not deep or high. *She is wearing flat shoes.* 5 complete or absolute. *A flat refusal.* 6 A flat tyre has no air in it. A flat drink is not fizzy. A flat battery no longer produces electricity. **flat** *adverb* 1 exactly. *He arrived in five minutes flat.* 2 If something falls flat, it is unsuccessful. **flat out** 1 at top speed. 2 using all your energy. *I'm working flat out.*

The farmlands of Arizona, USA are flat and featureless.

flat *noun* a set of rooms on one floor of a building. *A rented flat.*

flatten *verb* to make or become flat.

flatter *verb* 1 to say that a person or thing is better, more important or beautiful than they really are. 2 to show somebody or something as better then they really are. *The picture flatters her.* **flattery** *noun.*

flavour *noun* the taste of something. **flavour** *verb* to give a taste to something. *Flavour it with vanilla.* **flavouring** *noun.*

flaw *noun* something that makes a person or thing imperfect, something wrong. **flawed** *adjective.*

flea *noun* a small jumping insect that bites and sucks blood from people and animals.

fledgling *noun* a young bird.

flee (flees, fleeing, fled) *verb* to run away from something or somewhere. *We had to flee the country.*

fleece *noun* the woolly covering of sheep.

fleece *verb* to trick a person out of their money. *We were fleeced in the market.*

fleet *noun* a group of ships, planes or other vehicles belonging to one country or company. *A fleet of taxis.*

flesh *noun* 1 the soft substance that includes fat and muscle between the bones and the skin of people and animals. 2 the soft part of fruit and vegetables. **fleshy** *adjective.* **in the flesh** in real life. *He doesn't look so tall in the flesh.* **flesh out** to give more details.

AMAZING FACT

Flint was used by Stone Age people to make tools and weapons.

DID YOU KNOW

There are about 1,600 different kinds of fleas around the world. Some are tiny, and the largest is 8 mm long. One of the best jumpers is the cat flea, which is known to have reached a height of 34 cm in a single jump.

flew past tense of fly.

flex *verb* to bend or stretch, especially a muscle, leg or arm. *He flexed his muscles.*

flex (flexes) *noun* a long flexible covered wire for electricity.

flexible *adjective* 1 easily bent. 2 easily changed to suit new conditions, or adaptable. *I prefer flexible working hours.* **flexibility** *noun.*

flicker *verb* 1 to burn or shine unsteadily. 2 to move lightly or jerkily. *His eyelids flickered.* **flicker** *noun.*

flight *noun* 1 flying. 2 a plane journey. 3 a set of stairs. 4 the act of running away and escaping. 5 a group of birds flying together. *A flight of geese.*

flimsy (flimsier, flimsiest) *adjective* thin or light and easily damaged. **flimsily** *adverb. The wardrobe is very flimsily built.* **flimsiness** *noun.*

fling (flings, flinging, flung) *verb* 1 to throw quickly or carelessly. *She flung a few clothes in a case and left.* 2 to move quickly and violently. *She flung her head back angrily.*

fling *noun* 1 throwing something quickly. 2 a short, wild time of fun and enjoyment. 3 a dance.

flint *noun* 1 a hard grey stone. 2 a small piece of flint or hard metal that can be struck to produce sparks and light things.

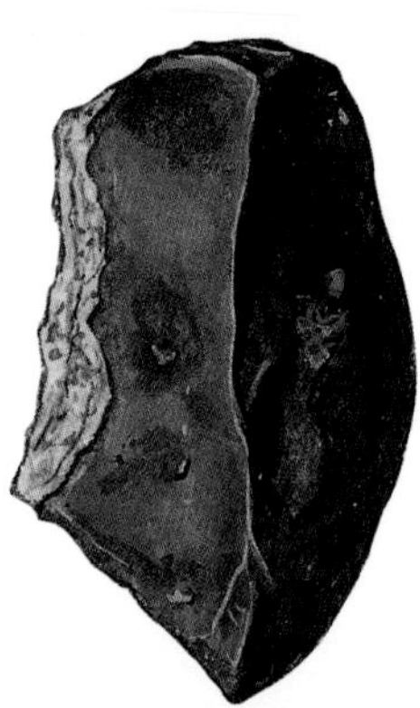

Flints were shaped by Stone Age people and used as tools.

flip (flips, flipping, flipped) *verb* 1 to turn something over quickly. 2 to move something into a different position or send it spinning in the air with a quick push or light hit. *She flipped open her diary and searched for the appointment.* **flip** *noun.*

flippant *adjective* not serious, especially when trying to be amusing. *She made some very flippant remarks.* **flippancy** *noun.*

flipper *noun* 1 the flat limb of some sea animals used for swimming. 2 Flippers are attachments you can wear on your feet to help you swim more quickly.

flirt *verb* to behave in a playful way as if you were attracted to somebody. *She flirts with all the boys.* **flirt** *noun* somebody who flirts a lot. **flirtatious** *adjective.*

float *verb* 1 to stay or move in a liquid or in the air. *We floated down the river.* 2 to move aimlessly about. *She floats from one job to another without ever settling down.*

float *noun* 1 a light object, such as a cork, that is used to help somebody or something float. 2 a lorry on which special shows of people and things travel through the streets in a festival procession. 3 a sum of money kept, especially by shopkeepers, for giving change or paying small bills.

floating voter *noun* somebody who does not always vote for the same party.

flock *noun* a group of sheep, goats or birds. **flock** *verb* to gather or move in large crowds. *People flocked to the fair.*

floe *noun* (rhymes with glow) a sheet of floating ice. *Ice floes.*

flog (flogs, flogging, flogged) *verb* 1 to beat a person or an animal, especially with a whip or rod. 2 (slang) to sell. *He flogged us his old car and bought a new one.* **flogging** *noun.*

flood *noun* 1 a large amount of water in a place that is usually dry. *The village was almost destroyed by the flood.* 2 a large amount. *A flood of complaints.* **flood** *verb* 1 to cover with a flood. 2 to arrive in large amounts. *Calls flooded in.*

The flood washed away the houses and made the people homeless.

floor *noun* 1 the surface, especially of a room, that you walk on. 2 all the rooms that are on the same level in a building. *Our flat is on the second floor.* 3 The ground at the bottom of the sea, a cave or a valley.

floor *verb* 1 to knock down. *The punch floored him.* 2 to confuse. *His question completely floored me.*

flop (flops, flopping, flopped) *verb* 1 to sit or lie down suddenly and heavily. 2 to fail or be unsuccessful. *The play flopped.* **flop** *noun* 1 a flopping movement or sound. 2 a total failure.

floppy *adjective* not firm, hanging loosely. *They wore floppy hats.*

floppy disk *noun* a disk that can be put into a computer to transfer information, also called a diskette.

WORD HISTORY

An ice floe comes from the Norwegian word 'flo', which originally meant a layer. Other Norwegian words are 'fjord' and 'ski'.

DID YOU KNOW

To the British, the first floor of a building is the one above the ground floor. To Americans this is the second floor, because they call the ground floor the first floor.

flora *noun* all the plants growing in a region. *Flora and fauna.*

Mountain flora, such as edelweiss and mountain avens, grow well in the poor rocky soil above the tree-line.

florist *noun* a person or shop that sells flowers. *The florist's art is arranging flowers.*

flour *noun* a powder made from ground grain, especially wheat, used to make bread and cakes. **floury** *adjective.*

flourish (flourishes, flourishing, flourished) *verb* 1 to grow healthily. 2 to be well and successful. *The shop is flourishing, we are going to expand.* 3 to wave something about for people to notice it. *He rushed into the room flourishing a cheque.* **flourish** *noun.*

flow *verb* 1 to move along smoothly. *The conversation soon began to flow really well.* 2 to hang down loosely, especially of clothing or hair. **flow** *noun.*

flower *noun* 1 the coloured or white part of a plant which produces seeds and fruit. 2 the flower and its stem. **flower** *verb* to produce flowers. *Daffodils flower in spring.*

flown past tense of fly.

flu *noun* short for influenza, an illness in which you may have a cold, a temperature and aching muscles.

fluent *adjective* able to speak and write a language easily. *She speaks fluent French.* **fluently** *adverb.* **fluency** *noun.*

fluff *noun* 1 soft bits from woolly material. 2 soft newly grown hair on young animals.

fluff *verb* 1 to shake or push something to make it seem larger and lighter. *The bird fluffed out its feathers.* 2 to do something badly or unsuccessfully. *She fluffed her test.*

fluffy *adjective* like or covered with fluff.

fluid *noun* a substance that can flow, such as a liquid or a gas.

F

fluid *adjective* 1 able to flow, not solid. 2 not fixed, likely to change. *Her ideas were totally fluid.* 3 smooth and graceful. *The dancer's fluid movements.*

fluke *noun* an unexpected piece of accidental good luck. *He won the match, but only by a fluke.* **fluke** *verb.*

flung past tense of fling.

flush *verb* 1 to become red, to blush. 2 to clean something with a sudden flow of water. *Don't forget to flush the lavatory every time you use it.* **flush** *noun.*

fluster *verb* to make somebody nervous and confused. *I got flustered when they all started asking me questions.*

flute *noun* a musical instrument shaped like a long tube with holes.

The flute is a woodwind instrument.

flutter *verb* 1 to move quickly and irregularly, up and down or from side to side. *The flags fluttered prettily in the wind.* 2 to move through the air with small quick movements. *Ticker tape fluttered down.*

flutter *noun* 1 a fluttering movement. 2 a feeling of panic or excitement. *He was in a flutter because of moving house.*

fly (flies, flying, flew, flown) *verb* 1 to move through the air like a bird or plane. 2 to control a plane or transport passengers in a plane. *A helicopter flew the injured to the nearest hospital.* 3 to make something fly. *To fly a kite.* 4 to move at speed or pass quickly. *Time flies when you enjoy your work.* 5 to move or wave about. *Flags were flying.* **send somebody flying** to hit a person so they fall over. **fly at somebody** to attack a person suddenly and violently.

fly (flies) *noun* 1 a small flying insect. 2 (usually in the plural, flies) the front opening on trousers.

Flies often carry germs and can spread disease.

foal *noun* a young horse.

foam *noun* 1 a mass of small white air bubbles, especially on top of a liquid. 2 rubber with plastic air bubbles inside, used for making mattresses and cushion stuffing, also called foam rubber.

WORD HISTORY

'Focus' comes from the Latin for hearth, or fireplace. This was the central point of a Roman home, and all members of every Roman household worshipped the goddess Vesta at the hearth. The round temple of Vesta, in Rome, was thought to represent the original hearth of the king of the city.

focus (focuses) *noun* 1 a point or distance from an eye or lens at which an object is sharpest. *The picture is out of focus.* 2 the point at which beams of light or heat or sound waves meet. 3 the centre of interest or attention. **focus** (focused, focusing or focussed, focussing) *verb* 1 to adjust a lens so that things can be seen clearly. *He focused the telescope on the Moon.* 2 to concentrate. *All Jean's attention is focused on her work.*

fodder *noun* food for farm animals.

foe *noun* an enemy.

foetus (foetuses) *noun* (say **fee**-tus) a developing embryo, especially a baby inside its mother.

fog *noun* very thick mist.

foggy *adjective* thick with fog. **I haven't got the foggiest.** I have no idea at all.

foil *noun* 1 metal sheet as thin as paper, especially for wrapping up food. 2 somebody or something that makes another person or thing look better. *Richard acted as a foil for his friend.*

foil *noun* a long thin sword with a covered point used in the sport of fencing.

foil *verb* to stop somebody from carrying out a plan. *The police managed to foil the robbers after hearing of their plan.*

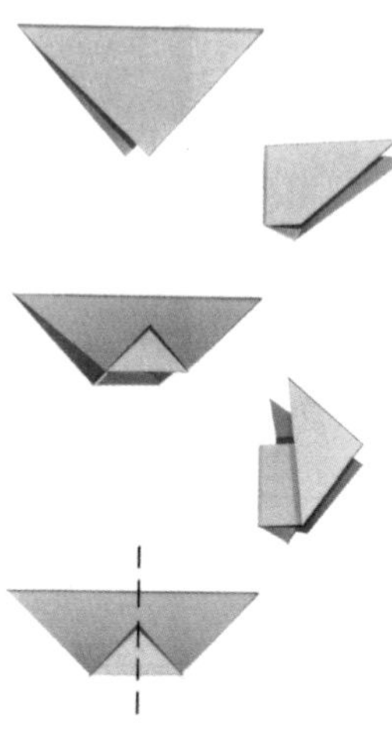

Origami is the Japanese art of folding paper to make models.

fold *verb* 1 to turn back a part of something, especially paper or cloth, and cover it with another part. When you fold something, you make it into a smaller shape. 2 to bring together or cross, especially your arms or hands. *The old woman folded her hands and prayed.* 3 to bend back or close up furniture or equipment. **fold** *noun* a line where something is folded, a crease. **fold up** 1 to make something into a smaller shape. 2 to fail. *The business has folded up.*

fold *noun* a fenced-in area for sheep.

-fold *suffix* meaning 'by the number of times stated', showing that something has a particular number of parts or kinds. 'Fivefold' means five times. *My problem is twofold. I don't have any money or time.*

folder *noun* a folded piece of cardboard for keeping papers in.

foliage *noun* leaves of plants and trees.

folk (folk or folks) *noun* people.

follow *verb* 1 to come or go after, to move behind in the same direction. 2 to go in the same direction. *I followed the route on the map.* 3 to come next on a list. *Tuesday follows Monday.* 4 to do what somebody says or suggests. *I followed his advice.* 5 to take an interest in something. *He follows his local football team.* 6 to understand. *I couldn't follow his line of thought.* 7 to be true or logical. *It doesn't follow that because you don't like school, you don't have to go.* **follower** *noun.* **following** *adjective.* **following** *noun. She has a large following of fans.*

fond *adjective* 1 To be fond of somebody or something means liking them. *She is very fond of children.* 2 loving and kind. *His fond parents.* 3 foolishly hopeful. *Fond hopes.* **fondly** *adverb.*

fondle *verb* to stroke gently.

font *noun* a typeface, such as you choose on a computer.

font *noun* a stone water basin in a church that is used for baptisms.

food *noun* something that is eaten by people or animals, or taken in by plants to help them to grow and live.

food chain *noun* a series of animals in a community, in which each member feeds on another in the chain. Humans are at the top of the food chain.

fool *noun* 1 a silly person who acts stupidly. If you make a fool of somebody, you make them look stupid. 2 a clown. 3 a pudding made of cream and crushed fruit. *Gooseberry fool.* **fool** *verb* 1 to trick somebody. *She fooled me into thinking it was her car.* 2 to behave in a silly way. *Please stop fooling about.* **foolish** *adjective* unwise or stupid.

Autumn foliage is a beautiful sight, with the leaves turning red and gold.

WORD HISTORY

The word 'fool' has a very interesting history. It comes originally from the Latin 'follis', which means bellows – a bag that blows air. It could be that people thought fools were full of hot air and spoke nonsense, or that their heads were full of air, in other words empty.

All sorts of food was spread on the ground for a wonderful picnic.

foolproof *adjective* Something that is easy to use and cannot go wrong is foolproof. *My plan is absolutely foolproof.*

foot (feet) *noun* 1 the part at the end of the leg below the ankle that people and animals stand on. 2 the lowest part or the bottom end. *At the foot of the hill.* 3 a measurement of length (*abbreviation* ft, equal to 12 inches or 30·5 centimetres). **on foot** walking. *What's the quickest way on foot?* **fall on your feet** to be lucky. **have cold feet** to be nervous. **stand on your own two feet** to be financially independent. **have one foot in the grave** to be very old. **put your foot in it** to say the wrong thing or make a mistake.

football *noun* 1 a game played by two teams of eleven players who kick a ball and try to score goals. 2 the ball used in this game. **footballer** *noun.*

footnote *noun* a note at the bottom of a page. *This book has too many footnotes.*

footprint *noun* a mark made by a foot.

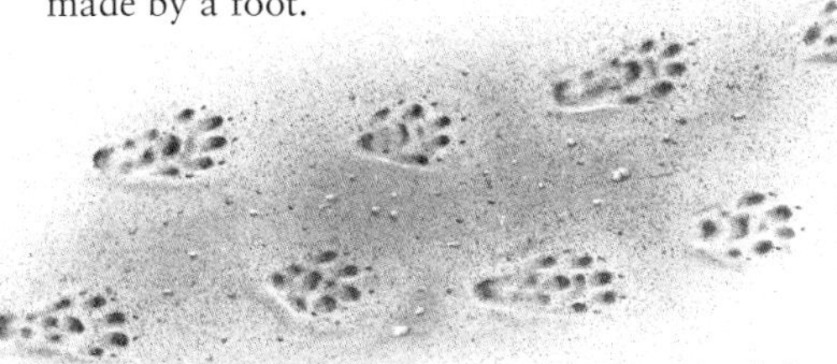

The footprints led us to the animal's lair.

for *preposition* 1 to show that something is intended to be given to or aimed towards somebody. *This huge present is for you.* 2 towards, in order to reach. *This train is for London.* 3 for the purpose of. *The computer is for my office.* 4 in order to have, get or do something. *I'm doing it for your own good.* 5 to show distance, time or price. *For the first time.* 6 in favour of. *How many people are for a strike and how many are against it?* 7 because of something. *I was told off for being late.* 8 as being or meaning. *She looked so old I took her for your grandmother.* 9 with reference to something surprising. *She looks amazingly young for her age.* 10 being suitable. *The right person for the job.* **for ever** always.

forbid (forbids, forbidding, forbade, forbidden) *verb* to order somebody not to do something. *I forbid you to go out.*

force *noun* 1 power or strength. *He had to use force to open the door.* 2 a power that produces changes of movement in a body. *The force of gravity.* 3 a person, thing, belief, influence or idea that causes changes. *The forces of good and evil.* 4 an organized group of police or soldiers. *The police force.* **in force** in large numbers. **join forces** to combine efforts.

force *verb* 1 to make somebody do something, although they are unwilling. *He forced the children to tidy their room.* 2 to use force to do or get something. *I had to force the lock to get in.* **forced** *adjective. A forced smile.*

ford *noun* a shallow place where you can cross a river. *The ford was liable to flood.*

After heavy rains, the road was impassable at the ford.

forecast *noun* a statement that tells you what is likely to happen. *The weather forecast was good.* **forecast** (forecasts, forecasting, forecast) *verb.*

forehand *noun* a stroke played in tennis with the palm turned forward. The opposite of forehand is backhand.

forehead *noun* (say **for**-hed) the part of the face above the eyebrows and below where your hair grows.

foreign *adjective* 1 belonging to a country that is not your own. *Foreign languages.* 2 not natural or belonging. *She is such an honest person, lying is foreign to her.*

foreigner *noun* a person from another country. *Foreigners are always welcome.*

foresee (forsees, forseeing, foresaw) *verb* to know what is going to happen in the future. *I forsee trouble.* **foresight** *noun.*

forest *noun* a large area of land covered with trees. *A pine forest.*

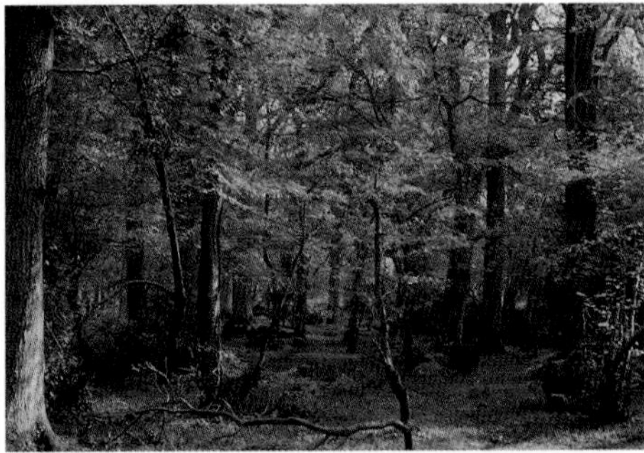

The forest is a mysterious place where many small animals live.

forever *adverb* continually. *He was forever complaining about his mother-in-law.*

foreword *noun* an introduction to a book.

forfeit *verb* (say **for**-fit) to lose something because you have done something wrong or broken a rule. *If you don't pay the bill within two weeks, you forfeit your discount.* **forfeit** *noun* 1 something lost, a price to be paid. 2 something you have to do when you lose in games. *She lost the round and was made to pay a forfeit.*

SPELLING NOTE

The foreword that sometimes acts as the introduction to a book is spelt differently from 'forward' (meaning to or towards the front). A foreword is often written by a person other than the book's author.

AMAZING FACT

Forests in the United States cover over 700 million acres. The US Government owns and manages about a third of this land.

forge *verb* 1 to copy things, especially banknotes, paintings or documents, in order to deceive people. 2 to shape something by heating and hammering it. *The blacksmith forged an iron staircase and a fire grate.* 3 to form or create something, especially links or a friendship. **forger** *noun.*

forge *noun* a place where metal is heated and shaped. *Horseshoes are made in a forge.*

forgery *noun* 1 a crime of forging things like banknotes. 2 something forged. *The painting was discovered to be a forgery.*

forget (forgets, forgetting, forgot, forgotten) *verb* 1 to not remember. 2 to stop thinking about. *Let's forget about the money you owe me.* **forget yourself** to behave thoughtlessly, to lose your temper. *When she kept on complaining, he forgot himself and shouted at her.*

forgive (forgives, forgiving, forgave, forgiven) *verb* to say or feel that you are no longer angry with somebody about something. *He still hasn't forgiven his sister for forgetting his birthday.* **forgivable** *adjective. A forgivable error.* **forgiveness** *noun. He begged for forgiveness.*

fork *noun* 1 an instrument with prongs at the end of a handle for eating food. 2 a large tool with prongs for digging the garden. 3 a point, especially in the road, which divides into two parts in the shape of a Y. **fork** *verb* 1 to lift, dig or move with a fork. 2 to divide in a Y-shape. *Turn right where the road forks.* **fork out** to pay out money, usually unwillingly.

fork-lift truck *noun* a truck with a platform at the front for lifting, lowering and moving heavy goods.

A fork-lift truck works by hydraulics.

form *noun* 1 the shape or appearance of something or somebody. *A pencil sharpener in the form of a crocodile.* 2 a particular kind or a particular way of behaving. *Ice and snow are forms of water. It's bad form to whisper.* 3 a piece of paper with questions to be answered and filled in. 4 a class in school. 5 a way in which a word may be spoken, written or spelt. *The irregular forms of verbs are listed in this dictionary.* **on form** fit, performing well. **off form** not fit.

form *verb* 1 to take shape, develop or come into existence. 2 to shape or create something. *He can hardly form a sentence.*

formal *adjective* correct, according to accepted rules or customs. *I'm expecting a formal apology from my boss.* **formally** *adverb. We dressed formally for the dance.* **formality** (formalities) *noun.*

format *noun* the shape and size of something, or the way it is presented. *I like the format of this book.*

former *adjective* 1 of an earlier period. *Her former husband has married again, to a very wealthy woman.* 2 the first of two people or things just mentioned. *Extra trains and buses are needed. The former will be more expensive.* (The second of two things just mentioned is called the latter.)

formerly *adverb* in earlier times.

formidable *adjective* very difficult to overcome. *They faced some formidable problems in their first year of marriage.*

formula (formulae) *noun* 1 a group of letters, signs or numbers that make up a rule. *The chemical formula for water is H_2O.* 2 a list of substances or directions for making or achieving something. *My formula for success is plenty of sleep.* 3 a set of words or behaviour used regularly for a particular occasion. *They changed the formula of the meetings.* 4 a plan, or suggestions worked out to deal with a problem.

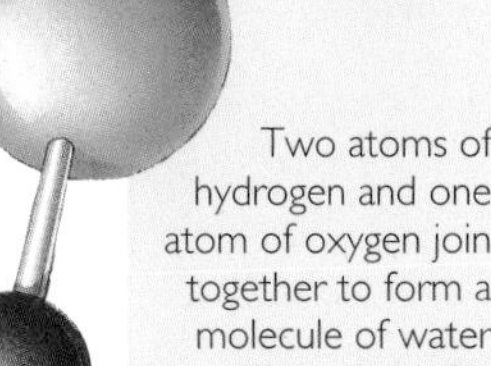

Two atoms of hydrogen and one atom of oxygen join together to form a molecule of water (formula H_2O).

forsake (forsakes, forsaking, forsook, forsaken) *verb* to leave. *He has forsaken his wife and children.*

fort *noun* a strong building used as a military base. **hold the fort** to look after things while somebody is away.

fortify (fortifies, fortifying, fortified) *verb* 1 to strengthen a place against attack. 2 to eat or drink something to make you stronger. **fortification** *noun.*

fortnight *noun* a period of two weeks. *A fortnight's holiday.* **fortnightly** *adverb.*

fortress (fortresses) *noun* a castle or other strong building that is difficult to attack.

The fortress came under heavy cannon fire and was eventually engulfed in flames.

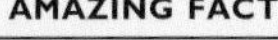

AMAZING FACT

Most fossils are found in places that were once under or near seas.

WORD HISTORY

'Fortnight' is a shortened form of the Old English words 'feowertiene niht', which meant 'fourteen nights' or two weeks.

fortuitous *adjective* by chance, especially by lucky chance, accidental.

fortunate *adjective* lucky. **fortunately** *adverb. Fortunately he didn't notice that I was very late.*

fortune *noun* 1 (good) luck. 2 fate, what will happen in the future. *The old woman told him his fortune.* 3 a large amount of money. *She earns a fortune in advertising.*

forward *adjective, adverb* 1 to or towards the front, towards the future. *A step forward.* 2 advanced or early in development. *The boy is very forward for his age.* 3 to be sure or eager in an unpleasant way. *She is too forward for my liking.* **forward** *noun* an attacking player in the front line of a team, especially in football, hockey and rugby.

forward *verb* to send on a letter, parcel or information. *Please forward letters to my new address in Spain.*

forwards *adverb* to or towards the front or future. *Let's move forwards.*

fossil *noun* the remains of an animal or a plant that lived long ago and has hardened into rock. *A fossil of a dinosaur tooth.* **fossilize** *verb.*

This fossil was once an ammonite, a creature like a squid.

foster *verb* 1 to bring up a child as if you were her/his father or mother. 2 to help something grow or develop. *France is fostering good relations with Germany.*

fought past tense of fight.

foul *adjective* 1 dirty, having a disgusting taste or smell. 2 very bad, unpleasant or angry. *She's got a foul temper.* **foul play** unfair play, actions against the rules. **foul** *noun* an action against the rules in sport. **foul** *verb* 1 to dirty. 2 to commit a foul against another player.

found past tense of find.

found *verb* 1 to establish or give money to start something. *The school was founded by monks.* 2 to base on. *Her success was founded on hard work.*

foundation *noun* 1 concrete and stonework that support the walls of a building or other structure, often in the plural, foundations. 2 the things that beliefs and ideas are based on. **be without foundation** to be untrue.

F

founder *verb* 1 to fill with water and sink. *The ship foundered on the rocks.* 2 to fail or collapse. *The company foundered and eventually went bankrupt.*

fountain *noun* an apparatus, often hidden in a stone figure or bowl, that pumps a stream of water up into the air.

The sound of the water splashing in the fountain was like music to his ears.

fox *noun* a wild animal that looks like a dog with a long bushy tail.

foxglove *noun* a tall straight plant that has flowers shaped like the fingers of a glove.

foyer *noun* (say **foy**-ay) the entrance hall in a theatre, cinema or hotel.

fraction *noun* 1 a small part or bit. *For a fraction of a second.* 2 a number that is not a whole number, a part of a whole number. $^{1}/_{2}$ and $^{1}/_{3}$ are fractions.

fracture *noun* a crack or break, especially in a bone. **fracture** *verb.*

fragile *adjective* easy to break or easily damaged. **fragility** *noun.*

fragment *noun* 1 a small piece that has broken off. *She dropped the vase and it broke into a million fragments.* 2 a small piece or part of something, especially an unfinished work of art.

fragrance *noun* a sweet or pleasant smell. **fragrant** *adjective.*

frame *noun* 1 the border into which something like a picture or window is fitted. 2 the main structure that forms the support for something. *A bicycle frame.* 3 the part that holds the lenses of a pair of glasses in place. 4 the shape or body of a person or animal. *Years of hardship had weakened his powerful frame.* 5 one of a number of small photographs that make up a film. **frame of mind** the mood somebody is in at a particular time. **frame** *verb* 1 to put a frame on or around. 2 to give shape to or express in a particular language, especially words or a plan. 3 to make an innocent person seem guilty and look as if they had committed a crime. *He was framed and sent to prison, but he didn't commit the crime.*

The mirror had an elegant gold frame.

DID YOU KNOW

The word 'fraction' comes from the Latin for break, referring to a whole number broken up into little parts. $^{1}/_{2}$ is called a vulgar fraction ('vulgar' meaning common), and 0·5 is called a decimal fraction.

framework *noun* 1 a supporting frame for something. 2 a basic plan or set of rules.

France *noun* a country in western Europe.

France is famous for the excellent food and wine enjoyed in homes across the land.

frank *adjective* honest and direct. The open way in which you say what you think. *I will be frank with you, I don't think he'll pass the exam.* **frankly** *adverb.* **frankness** *noun.*

frank *verb* to stamp a letter or parcel to show that postage has been paid.

frantic *adjective* wild and desperate; extremely anxious. *He was frantic with worry.* **frantically** *adverb.*

fraud *noun* 1 a swindle, a crime of getting money by trickery. 2 a person who pretends to be something he is not, a swindler. **fraudulent** *adjective.*

freak *noun* 1 an unusual or very strange person, animal, thing or happening. *That was a pure freak, it will never happen again.* 2 a person who takes a fanatical interest in something. *A football freak.* **freak** *adjective. A freak storm.* **freakish** *adjective.*

freckle *noun* a small brown spot on the skin, caused by the Sun. **freckly** *adjective.*

The freckles on her face always appear in early summer.

free (freer, freest) *adjective, adverb* 1 able to do what you want, go where you want, not shut up, be held in prison or controlled by anybody. *He set the prisoners free.* 2 without payment, costing nothing. *Entrance to the museum is free.* 3 not fixed on to anything. *The free end of the sail has been torn in the storm.* 4 not busy. *Are you free on Wednesday?* 5 not being used. *Is this seat free?* 6 without obstruction or anything being in the way. *A free flow of water.* **have a free hand** to be able to do things, without having to ask others for permission. **free with** If you are free with something, you are generous and ready to help. **freely** *adverb.* **free** (frees, freeing, freed) *verb* to set free. **freedom** *noun.*

Freetown *noun* the capital of Sierra Leone.

freeze (freezes, freezing, froze, frozen) *verb* 1 to harden into ice or become covered with ice. 2 to preserve food by making it very cold and storing it below freezing point. 3 to be extremely cold. *I'm absolutely freezing.* 4 to stop moving and stand completely still. *The boy froze at the sight of the snake.* 5 to fix prices or wages for a certain time so they cannot be increased. **freeze** *noun.*

The trees look beautiful when they freeze. They are covered with frost and snow.

freezer *noun* a refrigerator in which food can be frozen, because the temperature inside it is below freezing-point.

freezing-point *noun* the temperature at which water freezes into ice. Freezing-point is 0° Celsius.

freight *noun* (say frayt) 1 the transport or transportation of goods by lorries, ships, trains or planes. 2 goods. **freight** *verb.*

French *noun* 1 the people of France. 2 the language of France. **French** *adjective. The French flag is red, white and blue.*

French fries *plural noun* thin pieces of potato fried in oil, chips.

frequent *adjective* (say **freek**-wunt) happening often. *My brother is a frequent visitor, he comes every day.* **frequently** *adverb.* **frequency** *noun.*

frequent (say frik-**went**) *verb* to be or go somewhere often.

fresh *adjective* 1 newly made, picked, grown or arrived. Not old or stale, tinned or cooked. *I prefer fresh fruit to tinned.* 2 cool, refreshing and unused. *She put fresh sheets on the bed.* 3 new. *Let's make a fresh start.* 4 Fresh water is not salty. **freshly** *adverb. Freshly caught fish.* **freshness** *noun.*

friction *noun* 1 the rubbing of one thing against another. *Oil is used in machines to stop friction.* 2 disagreement and quarrels. *There is always friction between them.*

Friday *noun* the sixth day of the week, following Thursday.

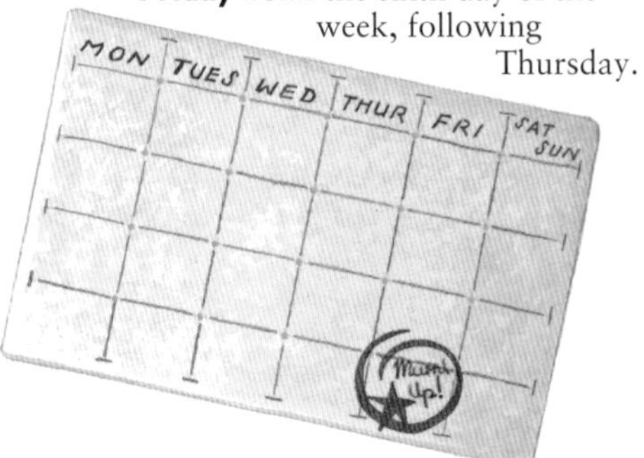

Sarah made an appointment to see the dentist on Friday.

fridge *noun* a refrigerator.

fried past tense of fry.

DID YOU KNOW

Frogs, toads and newts belong to a group of animals called amphibians. They spend part of their lives on land, but always go back to water when it is time to lay their eggs. Most frogs lay between 1,000 and 20,000 eggs.

friend *noun* 1 a person you know and like. 2 a helpful person or an object that you know well and like using. **make friends** to become somebody's friend. **be friends** If you are friends with somebody, you like spending time together.

friendly *adjective* acting as a friend. *A friendly gesture.* **friendship** *noun.*

frighten *verb* to fill with fear. *The big dog frightened the little girl.* **fright** *noun.*

frill *noun* 1 a pleated strip of paper or cloth attached to something as a decoration. *A frill on a dress.* 2 an unnecessary extra. **frilly** *adjective. A frilly lampshade.*

fringe *noun* 1 hair cut to hang in a straight line over the forehead. 2 a decorative border of many threads hanging down loosely, especially on shawls and rugs. 3 the part furthest from the centre, the edge of something. *They live on the fringes of London.* **fringed** *adjective.*

frisk *verb* 1 to run and jump about playfully, especially children or animals. 2 to search somebody with your hands for hidden weapons or goods. *The police frisked the man and found a gun on him.* **frisky** *adjective. A frisky little dog.*

frivolous *adjective* 1 not serious, light-heartedly looking for pleasure. *Clubbing is a frivolous way of spending your time.* 2 amusing, not important.

frock *noun* a dress.

frog *noun* a jumping animal, usually brownish-green, that lives in water and on land. Frogs croak.

Frogs develop from tadpoles.

from *preposition* 1 showing a starting point in time, place or number. *We took the train from London to Cardiff.* 2 showing who gave or sent something. *He got the money from the bank.* 3 showing what something is made of, what it is based on or where you might find it. *It was cut from cardboard.* 4 out of the possession of, showing separation. *He took the doll from his little sister.* 5 judging by. *From the noise they are making, it must be a party.* 6 showing difference or change. *I can't tell one from the other.* 7 because of, showing the reason for something. *In Africa people are suffering terribly from the famine.*

F

front *noun* 1 the side that is normally seen and faces forward. *The front of the house.* 2 the part that is ahead of others. *He went to the front of the queue.* 3 a road along the seashore. *We walked along the front.* 4 the place where two armies are fighting in war. 5 a line of separation where masses of cold air meet masses of warm air. *A cold front.* **in front** ahead of others. **in front of** facing somebody or something. *He spends too much time in front of the television.*

frontier *noun* the border where one country meets another country.

The frontiers were clearly marked on the map.

frost *noun* 1 weather at a temperature below freezing-point. *Unfortunately, the frost has killed our new plants.* 2 a thin layer of powdery ice crystals that form on the ground when there is a frost. **frost** *verb* 1 to become covered with frost. 2 to cover with sugar, especially a cake.

froth *noun* small white bubbles on liquid that look like foam. **frothy** *adjective.*

frown *verb* to move your eyebrows towards each other and wrinkle your forehead because you are annoyed or worried. **frown** *noun. He frowned with disapproval.*

froze past tense of freeze.

frugal *adjective* 1 careful with money or food, not wasteful. 2 small and costing little. *A frugal meal.* **frugally** *adverb.*

fruit (fruits or fruit) *noun* 1 Fruit grows on trees and bushes, contains seeds and is used for food. *Apples, oranges and strawberries are all kinds of fruit.* 2 good or bad results of something. *Now you can enjoy the fruits of your hard work.* **fruity** *adjective.*

Fresh fruit forms an important part of a healthy diet.

fruitful *adjective* producing good results. *We had a fruitful meeting.*

AMAZING FACT

Fruits are actually the seed-cases that a plant uses to protect and distribute its seeds.

Many fruits are distributed by the animals that eat them but some fruits scatter their seeds when they are ripe.

GRAMMAR NOTE

When 'full' is used as a suffix at the end of a word, it is usually spelt '–ful': 'beautiful', 'useful', 'fruitful', etc. This also applies if the suffix is used to mean 'the amount needed to fill': e.g.'bucketful', 'handful' etc.

frustrate *verb* 1 to stop you from doing what you would like to do or to stop plans from being carried out. *Our plans for a picnic were frustrated by bad weather.* 2 to make you feel disappointed and angry. *It's frustrating not to be able to see you when I want to.* **frustration** *noun.*

fry (fries, frying, fried) *verb* to cook something in hot fat, usually in a frying pan.

fudge *noun* a soft brown sweet made with butter, sugar and milk.

fudge *verb* to avoid taking firm action or making a clear decision. *The government have fudged the issue.*

fuel *noun* something that is burnt to produce heat, especially coal and oil. **fuel** (fuels, fuelling, fuelled) *verb* 1 to supply something with fuel or take in fuel. 2 to make a situation worse or cause an argument. *His anger was fuelled by a tremendous jealousy of his brother.*

fugitive *noun* (say few-jit-iv) somebody who is running away from something. *A fugitive from justice.*

fulcrum *noun* the point on which a bar (called a lever) is fixed or is supported in lifting something.

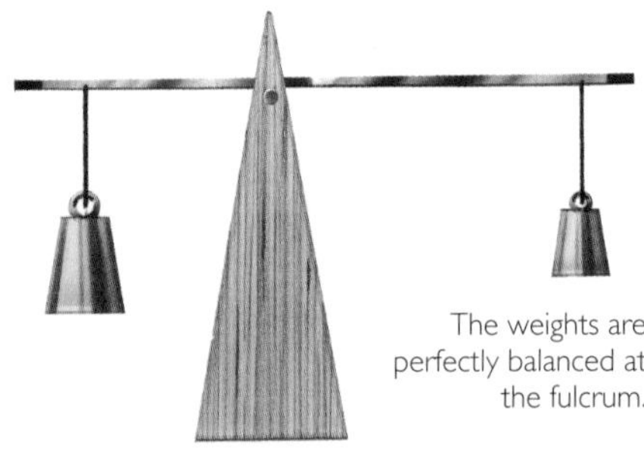

The weights are perfectly balanced at the fulcrum.

fulfil (fulfils, fulfilling, fulfilled) *verb* 1 to do what was promised, to carry out what is required. *He didn't fulfil his promises.* 2 to make true or come true. **fulfilment** *noun.*

full *adjective* 1 completely filled, holding as much or as many as possible. 2 containing a large number of people or things. *He is always full of ideas.* 3 complete, with nothing missing. *She wrote down her full name and address.* 4 as much or great as possible. *He drove at full speed.* 5 rounded. *She has a full figure.* 6 wide and loosely fitting. *A full skirt.* **full of something** to be talking about something with great enthusiasm. **in full** not leaving out anything. *She told me the story in full.* **full up** with no space left. **fully** *adverb.* **fullness** *noun.*

full stop *noun* a dot (.) which is put at the end of a sentence as a punctuation mark.

fumble *verb* to handle or search for something clumsily. *He fumbled in his pocket for his keys.*

fun *noun* amusement, something enjoyable. **make fun of** to tease or laugh at somebody in an unkind way.

Funafuti *noun* the capital of Tuvalu.

function *noun* 1 a special duty or purpose. What somebody or something is there to do. *One of the chairman's functions is to conduct meetings.* 2 an important party or event. *We were invited to a function at the embassy.* 3 an activity a computer can carry out. **function** *verb* to be in action or work.

fundamental *adjective* very important or basic. **fundamentally** *adverb*.

funeral *noun* the ceremony of burying or cremating a dead person.

fungus (fungi, say **fung**-guy) *noun* a plant-like organism without flowers, leaves or green colouring. Mushrooms, toadstools and mould are all fungi.

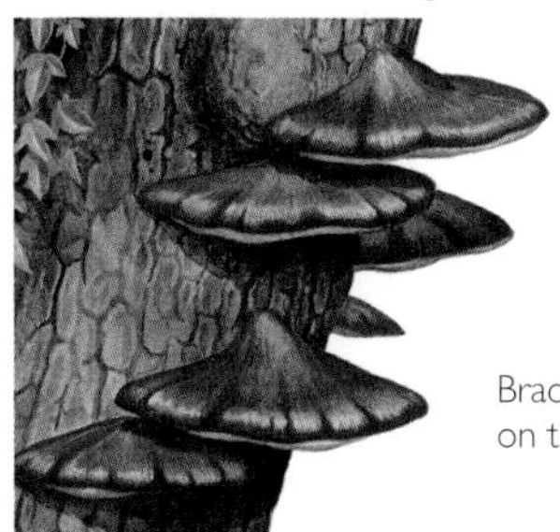

Bracket fungus grow on the trunk of a tree.

funnel *noun* 1 a chimney on a steamship or steam engine for letting out smoke. 2 an object with a wide round top and a tube at the bottom used for pouring liquids and powders into a container with a narrow opening. **funnel** *verb* to move as if through a funnel. *Crowds funnelled through the gateway and into the square.*

funny (funnier, funniest) *adjective* 1 amusing, making you laugh. 2 strange or unusual. *The car is making a funny noise.*

fur *noun* 1 the thick hair that covers the bodies of many animals. 2 the fur-covered skin used for making clothes, especially fur coats. *The fur traders sold mink and beaver furs.* 3 a coat made from real fur or fabric that looks like fur.

furnace *noun* a container with a very hot fire, used for burning things, melting metal, making glass or producing steam in a factory. *A burning fiery furnace.*

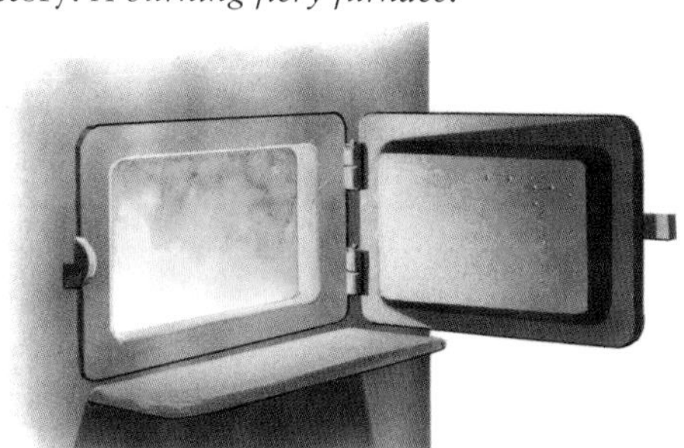

The heat was white hot inside the furnace.

DID YOU KNOW

There are about 50,000 different kinds of fungi. They are different from green plants because they cannot make their own food. They get their food mainly from decaying plants, and sometimes from living plants or animals.

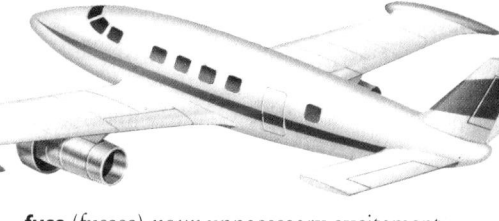

The fuselage of an aircraft can be used for transporting passengers or freight.

furnish *verb* 1 to put furniture in a place. *The flat is not furnished.* 2 to supply what is necessary. *Luckily we were furnished with a dictionary for the translation.*

furniture *noun* movable things like tables, chairs and beds that are put in a room or needed in a place.

furry *adjective* like or covered with fur. *The little boy likes furry toys.*

further *adjective, adverb* 1 at or to a more distant point or greater degree. *We can't walk any further.* 2 more or additional. *He works in further education.* **further** *verb* to help to be successful. *We will do everything to further peace.*

furtive *adjective* done secretly, hoping not to be seen. *The thief gave a furtive glance at my handbag.* **furtively** *adverb*.

fury *noun* great anger, rage. **furious** *adjective*. *I am furious that you are late.*

fuse *noun* 1 a short thin piece of wire, e.g. in an electric plug, that acts as a safety device by melting if too much electricity is passed through it. *The lights went out when a fuse blew.* 2 a tube or cord on a bomb or firework used for setting it off. **fuse** *verb* 1 to stop working because a fuse has melted. *Suddenly all the lights in the house fused.* 2 to melt in great heat or become joined by melting. *The wires have fused together.*

fuselage (say **few**-zuh-lahzh) *noun* the main body of an aircraft.

fuss (fusses) *noun* unnecessary excitement or anger, especially about unimportant things. *Don't make such a fuss.* **make a fuss of somebody** to pay a lot of attention to a person. **fuss** *verb* to behave in an unnecessarily excited or anxious way. **fussy** (fussier, fussiest) *adjective*.

futile (say **few**-tile) *adjective* of no use, not successful. *It's futile to argue with me because I know I'm right.* **futility** *noun*.

future *noun* the time or events that come after the present, the things that will happen. *We all wish you a very happy future.* **in future** from now on. **future** *adjective*. *What are your future plans?*

fuzz *noun* 1 something fluffy and soft, especially from wool. 2 short curly hair. 3 *slang* the police. **fuzzy** (fuzzier, fuzziest) *adjective* 1 not clear in shape, blurred. *Some of the photographs were very fuzzy.* 2 soft and curly. *Fuzzy hair.*

Gg

gabble *verb* to speak so quickly that people cannot understand you.

gable *noun* the triangular outside end of a house between two sloping roofs. **gabled** *adjective. Gabled houses.*

Gabon *noun* a country in Africa.

Gaborone *noun* the capital of Botswana.

gadget *noun* a small, useful instrument or tool for a particular job. *This gadget is called a garlic press.*

gag (gags, gagging, gagged) *verb* 1 to put something over or into somebody's mouth to stop them speaking. **gag** *noun.* 2 to retch or feel like being sick.

gag *noun* a joke.

gain *verb* 1 to win, earn or obtain something. 2 to increase. *He's gained half a stone.* **gain** *noun* 1 a profit. 2 an increase.

gala *noun* a special public event or entertainment.

galaxy *noun* a huge group of stars and planets. The Milky Way is a galaxy.

gale *noun* a very strong, violent wind. *A force-10 gale.*

gallant *adjective* 1 brave. *A gallant knight.* 2 honourable and polite.

galleon *noun* a large Spanish sailing ship of the 16th century. *A galleon in full sail.*

gallery *noun* 1 a building or long room for displaying paintings and other works of art. 2 the highest floor of seats in a theatre.

galley (galleys) *noun* 1 the kitchen on a ship or aircraft. 2 a single-decked ship of ancient times that was driven by both sails and oars.

gallop *noun* the fastest pace of a horse.

gallon *noun* a measure for liquids. There are eight pints or 4.5 litres in a gallon. (US 3.8 litres.)

gallop *verb. We galloped across the moor.*

gallows *singular and plural noun* a wooden structure on which criminals used to be hanged. *The gallows on the hill.*

galore *adverb* in large numbers or amount, in plenty. *The library has got books galore.*

WORD HISTORY

Like the letter C, the shape of the letter G comes from an ancient Egyptian symbol for a boomerang or throwing stick. The Romans used it for two sounds – C and G. They later added a stroke to the C (G) and used the new letter for the G sound and the old letter for the K sound.

Galaxies are classified according to their shapes. This one is a spiral galaxy.

AMAZING FACT

Our galaxy, the Milky Way, is one of many. The other galaxies are moving away from us. The farther away a galaxy is, the faster it is moving. The most distant galaxies are receding at almost the speed of light.

galvanized *verb* 1 to cover a metal with zinc to protect it from rusting. 2 to shock into doing something. *The threat of flooding galvanized the men into action.* **galvanized** *adjective. A galvanized dustbin.*

Gambia *noun* a country in Africa.

The flag of Gambia has red, blue and green stripes, divided by narrow white stripes.

gamble *verb* to risk something, particularly money, for possible gain, especially on the result of a game or race. *He's gambled away all his family fortune on cards.* **gamble** *noun.* **gambler** *noun.*

game *noun* 1 an activity or contest with rules. Football, baseball, chess and bridge are all different kinds of game. **games** athletic competitions. *The Olympic Games take place every four years.* 2 wild animals and birds that are hunted for food and as a sport.

Farmers breed game birds because they bring in a lot of money in the shooting season.

game *adjective* brave and willing to try something.

gamekeeper *noun* a person who looks after game animals and birds.

gander *noun* a male goose.

gang *noun* a group of people who regularly go about and do things together.

gangster *noun* one of a gang of criminals.

gangway *noun* 1 a gangplank or movable bridge for passengers between a ship and the shore. 2 a space between rows of seats in an aeroplane, train or cinema, etc.

gaol *noun* (also spelt jail) a prison.

gap *noun* an opening or empty space.

gape *verb* 1 to stare with your mouth wide open, usually in surprise. 2 to be wide open. *A gaping hole in the ground.*

garage *noun* 1 a place where cars and other motor vehicles are kept. 2 a place that sells petrol or where cars can be repaired.

garbage *noun* (especially North American) kitchen rubbish.

garden *noun* land, usually near a house, where flowers and vegetables are grown. **gardener** *noun.* **gardening** *noun.*

gargle *verb* to wash your throat with a medicated liquid without swallowing it and then to spit it out.

gargoyle *noun* a grotesque carving on a building of a human or animal head forming part of a gutter.

This gargoyle comes from an Oxford college.

garish *adjective* (say **gair**-ish) over-coloured and too bright, gaudy.

garlic *noun* a strong-tasting bulb like an onion that is used in cooking to add flavour to food.

garment *noun* a piece of clothing such as a jacket or skirt.

garnish *verb* to decorate food. *He garnished the vegetables with sprigs of parsley.*

garret *noun* a small room in the attic of a house. *The poet lived in a garret.*

garter *noun* a band of cloth or elastic at the top of a sock or stocking to hold it up.

gas (gases) *noun* 1 any of many substances like air that are neither liquid nor solid. Oxygen and nitrogen are gases. 2 the kind of gas we use as a fuel in our homes for heating and cooking. 3 (in US, short for gasoline) petrol.

gash *noun* a deep, long cut, a slash. **gash** *verb. She gashed her knee on the rock.*

gasoline see gas.

gasp *verb* to breathe quickly and noisily through your mouth because you have been running etc. or because you are ill. **gasp** *noun. A gasp of surprise.*

gastric *adjective* relating to or belonging to the stomach. *A gastric ulcer.*

gate *noun* 1 a kind of outside door or barrier across an opening in a fence, hedge or wall. 2 the number of people who pay to see a sporting event.

gatecrash *verb* to go to a party when you have not been invited. **gatecrasher** *noun.*

gateway (gateways) *noun* 1 an opening with a gate. 2 an opportunity or an opening to something. *The gateway to stardom.*

gather *verb* 1 to come together as a group, to bring together. *A crowd gathered in the square.* 2 to pick. *He gathered nuts and blackberries.* 3 to understand or find out something. *We gather you're going away.*

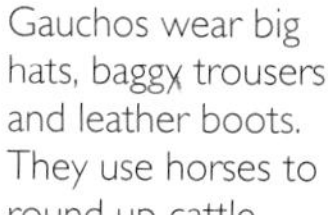

gathering *noun* a meeting or coming together of people for some purpose.

gaucho *noun* a cowboy of South America.

Gauchos wear big hats, baggy trousers and leather boots. They use horses to round up cattle.

AMAZING FACT

Birthstones are gemstones that symbolize the month of a person's birth.

Do you know what yours is?

January – garnet
February – amethyst
March – aquamarine
April – diamond
May – emerald
June – pearl
July – ruby
August – peridot
September – sapphire
October – opal
November – topaz
December – turquoise

gaudy (gaudier, gaudiest) *adjective* (say gaw-dee) Something that is gaudy is too brightly coloured and showy.

gauge *noun* (rhymes with cage) an instrument for measuring. *A fuel gauge.* **gauge** *verb. She tried to gauge (measure or estimate) the depth of the pond.*

gaunt *adjective* very thin, bony and haggard. *His gaunt face.*

gauntlet *noun* a long, thick glove with special protection for the wrist, worn by motorcyclists etc. **take up the gauntlet** take up a challenge.

gauze *noun* a thin net-like cloth often used with bandages.

gave past tense of give.

gay *adjective* 1 homosexual. **gay** *noun. A club for gays.* 2 bright and cheerful. *Gay colours.* **gaiety** *noun.* **gaily** *adverb.*

gaze *verb* to look steadily at something or somebody for a long time. **gaze** *noun.*

gazelle *noun* a small, graceful antelope of Africa and Asia.

gazetteer *noun* a geographical dictionary that lists and describes places.

gear *noun* a wheel with teeth around the edge which can work with other gears in a machine. Gears in a car or on a bicycle send power to the wheels.

gear *noun* clothes or equipment needed for a special purpose. *Climbing gear.*

geese plural of goose.

gelding *noun* a castrated (neutered) horse.

gem *noun* a precious stone that has been cut. Diamonds, emeralds and rubies are kinds of gems.

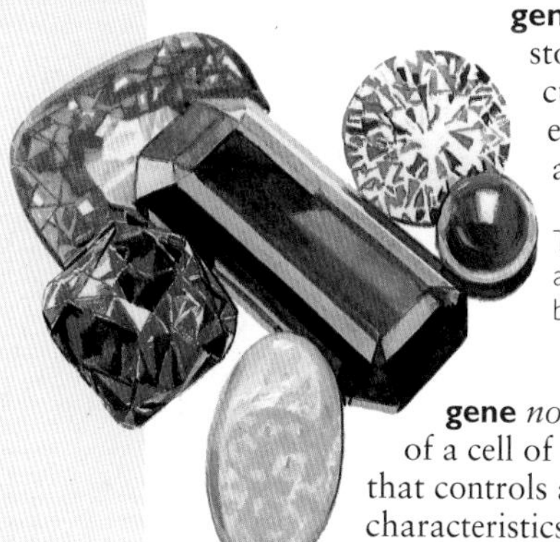

The empress built up a huge collection of beautiful gems.

gene *noun* one of the parts of a cell of all living things that controls and passes on characteristics from parents to offspring.

general *noun* a very senior officer in the army. *General Custer.*

general *adjective* 1 concerning several or most people or things. *General knowledge.* 2 not in detail but in broad outline. *A general description.* **in general** mainly, usually. *In general, I prefer cats to people.*

generate *verb* 1 to produce electricity. *Electricity is generated in power stations.* 2 to bring into being, to cause. *The Viking exhibition generated a great deal of interest.*

G

generation *noun* all the people now living who were born at about the same time. The period of time between generations (about 25 years). *The beat generation.*

generator *noun* a machine that generates (produces) electricity.

generous *adjective* A generous person is kind and helpful and gives freely of their time and money. **generosity** *noun.*

genetic *adjective* concerning the genes or inherited through the genes. *He was suffering from a genetic disorder.*

genitals *plural noun* the sexual organs.

genius *noun* (say **jee**-nee-us) an exceptionally clever and creative person.

gentile *noun* a person who is not Jewish. **gentile** *adjective.*

gentle *adjective* 1 a gentle person is quiet, kind and thinks of others. 2 not rough or violent. 3 not extreme. **gentleness** *noun.* **gently** *adverb.*

genuflect *verb* to bend a knee, especially in church as a sign of reverence. **genuflexion** *noun. Genuflexion shows humility.*

genuine *adjective* real and not fake or untrue. *A genuine need for help.*

genus (genera) *noun* a group of similar plants or animals but containing different species or kinds. Foxes and hyenas are two species of the dog genus.

geography *noun* the study of the Earth, its natural features, its people, resources, weather etc. *World geography.* **geographer** *noun.* **geographic** *adjective.*

geology *noun* the study of the Earth's rocks and layers of soil. **geological** *adjective.* **geologist** *noun.*

Rocks were Carl's passion. He had wanted to study geology since childhood.

geometry *noun* a branch of mathematics concerned with the study of angles, lines, shapes and solids. **geometric** *adjective.*

Georgetown *noun* the capital of Guyana.

Georgia *noun* a country in Southwest Asia.

geranium *noun* a plant with clusters of pink, red or white flowers.

gerbil *noun* a small desert rodent with long back legs, often kept as a pet.

WORD HISTORY

Some words borrowed from German are 'angst' ('anxiety'), 'kaput' ('broken'), 'kindergarten', 'kitsch' ('in bad taste'), 'spanner', 'waltz' and 'zinc'.

AMAZING FACT

Old Faithful, in Yellowstone National Park in the northwestern United States, is a famous geyser. It is called Old Faithful because it erupts at the same time every day. Yellowstone became the world's first national park in 1872.

The steam from the geyser seemed to rise for miles into the sky.

geriatric *adjective* relating to or concerning old people. *A geriatric ward in the hospital.*

germ *noun* a microscopic living thing that can cause diseases.

German *noun* 1 a person who comes from Germany. 2 the language spoken in Germany, Austria and parts of Switzerland. **German** *adjective. German music.*

German Shepherd dog another name for an alsatian.

Germany *noun* a country in central Europe.

germinate *verb* when seeds germinate, they begin to sprout.

Once the seeds had germinated they began to grow very quickly.

gesture *noun* 1 a movement of the hand or head intended to mean something. *She wrung her hands in a gesture of despair.* 2 an action that expresses feelings. *He invited them to supper as a friendly gesture.*

get (gets, getting, got) *verb* 1 to obtain. *I must get a new book from the library.* 2 to receive. *I got a lot of presents at Christmas.* 3 to bring. *Can you get me a glass of lemonade?* 4 to become. *You'll get wet if you stand in the rain.* 5 to prepare. *Dad got the supper.* 6 to catch an illness. *I hope you don't get my cold.* 7 to cause to happen. *You must get your watch repaired.* 8 to own something. *Have you got a dog?* 9 to understand. *I don't get the joke.* 10 to ask somebody to do something. *We got the builders to move the bricks.* 11 to arrive. *We got home at midnight.* **get about** 1 *How do these stories get about?* 2 *He's over 90 but still manages to get about.* **get ahead** *She got ahead through hard work.* **get along with** *He's friendly and gets along with everybody.* **get at** 1 *The truth is difficult to get at.* 2 *Why are you always getting at me?* **get by** *He gets by on his small pension.* **get down to** *She's getting down to some serious work.* **get off** 1 *Don't get off the train until it has stopped.* 2 *She got off with a small fine.* **get on** 1 *How are you getting on with you homework?* 2 *She's over 80, so she's getting on a bit.* **get on to** *Get on to (contact) the press immediately.* **get over** *He's got over his illness.* **get up to** *He's always getting up to mischief.*

geyser *noun* a natural spring from which hot water and steam erupt, often at regular intervals.

Ghana *noun* a country in Africa.

ghastly *adjective* very unpleasant, horrible. *A ghastly accident.* **ghastliness** *noun.*

ghost *noun* the spirit or shape of a dead person that some people believe walks about at night. **ghostly** adjective.

giant *noun* in fairy stories, a huge and often frightening and cruel man. **giant** *adjective. A giant marrow.*

gibberish *noun* speech that makes no sense at all. *Don't talk gibberish.*

gibbon *noun* an ape with very long arms.

giddy (giddier, giddiest) *adjective* feeling dizzy, light-headed and about to fall over. **giddiness** *noun.*

gift *noun* 1 something that you give somebody, a present. 2 a talent. *He has a gift for languages.* **gifted** *adjective.*

gig *noun* a public performance of pop music or jazz. *A gig in the park.*

gigantic *adjective* (say jie-**gan**-tik) of giant size, enormous.

giggle *noun* a silly, nervous laugh. **giggle** *verb. Granny giggled into her soup.*

gill *noun* an organ on each side of a fish through which it breathes.

gimmick *noun* something clever or unusual that is done to attract attention, especially to advertise something. **gimmicky** *adjective.*

gin *noun* a colourless alcoholic drink.

ginger *noun* 1 a hot spice made from the root of a tropical plant used to flavour food or drinks such as ginger ale and gingerbeer. 2 an orange-brown colour. **ginger** *adjective. Ginger hair.*

gingerbread *noun* a sweet biscuit or cake flavoured with ginger.

gingerly *adjective, adverb* carefully and timidly. *Gingerly, he peeled off the label.*

giraffe *noun* an African animal with long legs and a very long neck. It has yellow fur with brown patches as camouflage.

girder *noun* a long metal beam used as a support in buildings, bridges etc.

girl *noun* a female child. **girlish** *adjective.*

girlfriend *noun* 1 a boy or man's usual and regular female friend. 2 the female friend of a woman. 3 the partner of a lesbian woman.

gist *noun* the rough outline or main points of something. *He gave us the gist of the story while we were on the way there.*

AMAZING FACT

Nearly two million years ago, North America was almost completely covered by huge ice sheets. The ice melted, forming rivers and river valleys. The Great Lakes were also formed from ice that melted. Glaciers have given us some of our most dramatic and beautiful scenery.

Snow falls on the mountains. At the highest levels, the snow piles up year on year.
Snow in mountain basins, called cirques, becomes glacier ice.
At the end of the glacier the ice melts, creating streams that sweep away the glacier's rocky load.
The ice melts, creating streams that sweep away the glacier's rocky load.

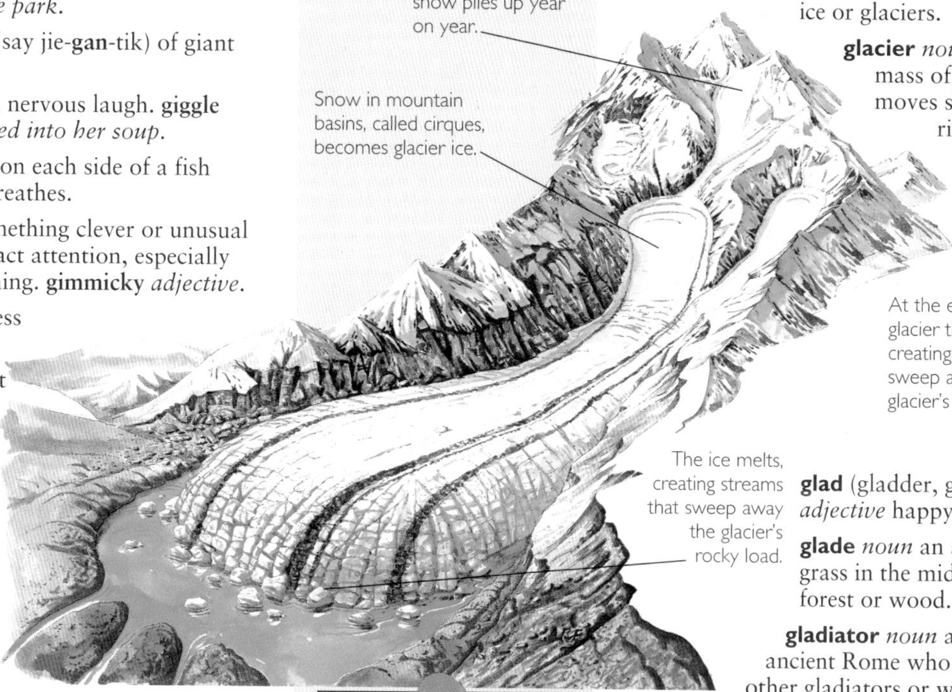

WORD HISTORY

Until the 17th century giraffes were called 'cameleopards' because of their camel-like necks and leopard-like spots.

give (gives, giving, gave, given) *verb* 1 to hand something over to somebody. 2 to bend or collapse. *The fence gave under her great weight.* 3 to organize or present something. *They are giving a concert tonight.* 4 to do something suddenly. *Pat gave a sigh of relief.* **give away** *I'm giving away all my money.* **give back** *Jack gave back the tapes he'd borrowed.* **give in** 1 *They gave in their guns to the police.* 2 *He won't give in (succumb) to your threats.* 3 *You don't know the answer, so why don't you give in (admit defeat)?* **give off** 1 *The bonfire is giving off a lot of smoke.* **give out** 1 *She gave out (distributed) the prizes.* 2 *The engine has finally given out (broken).* **give up** 1 *We gave up (renounced) the idea of moving away.* 2 *Mum has given up (stopped) smoking.*

glacial *adjective* 1 concerning ice or glaciers.

glacier *noun* a huge mass of ice that moves slowly like a river down a mountain valley.

glad (gladder, gladdest) *adjective* happy, pleased.

glade *noun* an area of open grass in the middle of a forest or wood.

gladiator *noun* a warrior in ancient Rome who fought other gladiators or wild animals for the entertainment of spectators.

glamorous *adjective* exciting and charming. *She has got a glamorous job in the fashion business.* **glamour** *noun.*

glance *verb* 1 to look at something for a moment. *She glanced at her watch.* **glance** *noun.* 2 to hit and then bounce off something at an angle. *The ball glanced off the bat and smashed the window.*

gland *noun* an organ in the body that produces substances for the body to use or that removes unwanted substances. *Sweat glands.* **glandular** *adjective. Glandular fever.*

glare *verb* 1 to look at somebody fiercely and angrily. 2 to shine with strong, dazzling light. **glare** *noun.*

G

glaring *adjective* 1 very bright. *Glaring headlights.* 2 obvious. *Glaring gaps in your general knowledge.*

glass *noun* 1 a hard, brittle and usually transparent material used in making window panes, bottles, mirrors, etc. 2 a container made of this material, for drinking. 3 a mirror. **glassy** *adjective.*

glasses *plural noun* a pair of lenses in a metal or plastic frame that people with poor eyesight wear over their eyes to help them see better, also called spectacles.

He needed glasses for reading and watching television.

glaze *verb* 1 to fit glass into something. *He glazed the windows.* **glazier** *noun.* 2 to cover something with a coating of shiny material called glaze.

gleam *verb* to shine softly. *The furniture is gleaming.* **gleam** *noun.*

glen *noun* a Scottish word for a long narrow valley. *The lochs and glens.*

glide *verb* 1 to move smoothly and silently. 2 to fly smoothly.

glider *noun* a small aircraft without an engine that floats on air currents.

glimmer *verb* to flicker or to shine very faintly. **glimmer** *noun. A glimmer of hope.*

glisten *verb* to shine or gleam, especially of a wet or polished surface.

glitter *verb* to sparkle. *The glittering lights of the city.* **glitter** *noun.*

global *adjective* relating to the whole world. *Global issues.*

globe *noun* a ball-shaped object with a map of the Earth on it.

Sheila kept a globe on her desk to remind her of her travels around the world.

AMAZING FACT

Glass has been used to correct weak eyesight since the 1300s, although eyeglasses did not became common until the 1500s.

In 1760, Benjamin Franklin invented the bifocal lens.

DID YOU KNOW

The 'g' in most words beginning with 'gn' was once pronounced. We have dropped the 'g' sound in words like 'gnarled', 'gnash' and 'gnat' but kept the spelling.

The gnomes invited the fairies and elves to a tea party under their toadstool.

gloom *noun* 1 near-darkness, dimness. 2 sadness and a feeling of depression. **gloomy** *adjective. A gloomy cave.*

glorious *adjective* 1 magnificent, causing great happiness. *A glorious holiday.* 2 worthy of glory or praise. *A glorious victory was won by the Persians.*

glory *noun* 1 great fame, praise. 2 splendour. *The glory of the mountains.* **glory** *verb. They gloried in their achievements.*

glossy *adjective* shiny and smooth. *A glossy magazine.* **gloss** *noun.*

glove *noun* a covering for your hand with parts for each finger and thumb.

glow *verb* to give out a warm, steady light without flames. **glow** *noun.*

glow-worm *noun* an insect that gives out a greenish glow from its tail.

Katharine saw the glow-worms in the Botanical Gardens at Munich.

glucose *noun* a natural sugar found in plants. *Glucose is good for athletes.*

glue *noun* a thick, sticky substance used for sticking things together. **glue** *verb. Sue glued the handle on to the cup.*

glum (glummer, glummest) *adjective* gloomy and sad, depressed.

glut *noun* a much greater supply of something than is needed. *A glut of fruit.*

glutton *noun* a person who always eats too much. **gluttony** *adjective.*

GMT *abbreviation* for Greenwich Mean Time.

gnarled *adjective* (say narld) twisted and full of lumpy knots. *A gnarled old oak.*

gnash *verb* (say nash) to grind or strike your teeth together with anger or pain.

gnat *noun* (say nat) any of many small, mosquito-like insects that bite. *A swarm of gnats.*

gnaw *verb* (say naw) to chew on something hard for a long time. *A dog gnaws a bone if it's hungry.*

gnome *noun* (say nowm) a little old man in fairy stories who lives under the ground.

gnu *noun* (say new) an African ox-like antelope, also known as a wildebeest.

go (goes, going, went, gone) *verb* 1 to move away from or to somewhere, to travel. 2 to visit. 3 to leave. 4 to disappear. *My tools have gone.* 5 to do something. *I'm going to mow the lawn.* 6 to become. *This fruit is going bad.* 7 to work correctly. *The car won't go.* 8 to fit or have a place somewhere. *The knives go in that drawer.* 9 to lead somewhere. *The road goes to the sea.* 10 to make a certain sound. *Cats go 'miaow'.* **go about** *There's a bug going about.* **go ahead** *Despite the weather, we decided to go ahead with the game.* **go back** *We're going back home to Ireland.* **go in for** *George is going in for the competition.* **go off** 1 *The bomb went off with a bang.* 2 *The milk tastes sour, it must have gone off.* 3 *I don't eat hamburgers any more, I've gone right off them.* **go on** *She keeps going on about how clever she is.* **go with** *Does this tie go with (look good with) this shirt?*

goal *noun* 1 the space or net between two posts that players have to kick or hit a ball into in games like hockey and football. 2 A goal is something you hope to achieve, an ambition.

goat *noun* a farm animal with short hair and horns.

The milk of goats is recommended to anyone suffering from allergies.

gobble *verb* to eat quickly, noisily and greedily. *Peter gobbled up his Big Mac.*

gobsmacked *adjective* (slang) stunned and shocked. *I was gobsmacked by the result.*

god *noun* any one of many supernatural beings that were thought to control the world. *The gods lived on Mt Olympus.*

God *noun* the creator of the universe in Christianity, Islam and Judaism.

godparent *noun* a godfather or godmother who at a child's baptism promises to help their godchild be brought up as a Christian.

goggles *plural noun* special glasses that fit tightly around the eyes to protect them from dirt, water, etc.

go-kart *noun* a small racing car.

gold *noun* a very valuable yellow metal that is found in rocks and streams, used for making jewellery. **gold** *adjective.*

golden *adjective* made of gold or of the colour of gold. **golden wedding** *noun* the 50th anniversary of a wedding.

AMAZING FACT

Some golf courses in desert areas are all sand, the 'greens' are not green at all!

SPELLING NOTE

Try not to confuse 'goal' with 'gaol', which means 'prison'.

The gondola made its way down the narrow canal.

SPELLING NOTE

Take care not to confuse 'gorilla' ('ape)' with 'guerrilla' ('a soldier who fights by surprise attacks'). And notice one 'r' and two 'l's in 'gorilla' and two 'r's and two 'l's in 'guerrilla'.

Rich seams of gold run underground in South Africa.

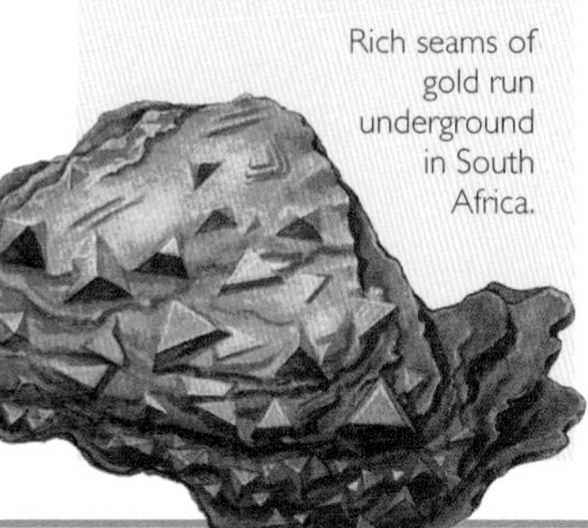

goldfish *noun* a small orange fish related to carp. *Lots of goldfish in our pond.*

golf *noun* an outdoor game in which players use long-handled sticks called golf clubs to hit a small ball from one hole to another around a large grassy area called a golf course. **golfer** *noun.*

gondola *noun* a long narrow boat with high pointed ends used on the canals of Venice. **gondolier** *noun* a person who operates a gondola. *The gondolier earned lots of tips.*

gone past participle of go.

good (better, best) *adjective* 1 of a high quality or standard. 2 kind and helpful. 3 able to do something well. 4 obedient and behaving well. 5 health-giving. 6 enjoyable. **goodness** *noun.* **good-looking** *adjective.*

goodbye *interjection* what we say when we leave somebody.

Good Friday *noun* the Friday before Easter when Jesus was crucified.

goods *plural noun* things that can be bought and sold or that are carried on trains and lorries.

gooey *adjective* (slang) sticky. *A gooey pudding.* **gooeyness** *noun.*

goose (geese) *noun* a water bird with webbed feet, similar to a large duck. It makes a loud, honking sound. **wild goose chase** a useless journey. **cook someone's goose** to ruin somebody's chances.

gooseberry *noun* the small, round green fruit of the gooseberry bush.

goosepimple *noun* (also goosebump and gooseflesh) tiny bumps on the skin caused by cold or fear.

gorilla *noun* the largest and strongest of the apes. It lives in Africa.

gorge *noun* a deep valley with steep sides.

gorge *verb* to eat your fill greedily.

gorgeous *adjective* 1 very pleasant. 2 beautiful.

gosling *noun* a young goose.

gospel *noun* one of the first four books of the New Testament which describe the life and teachings of Jesus.

gossip *noun* talking about other people's personal affairs and saying things that are sometimes untrue. **gossip** *verb*.

got past tense of get.

govern *verb* to manage or be in charge of a country or organization and make laws and rules for it.

government *noun* a group of people who govern or rule a country.

governor *noun* 1 a person elected to manage or govern a state in the US. 2 a person who controls an organization. *A school governor*.

gown *noun* 1 a long, formal dress worn by a woman. 2 a long, flowing robe worn by such people as lawyers, judges and lecturers.

GP *abbreviation* General Practitioner, a family doctor who is not a specialist and who works in the community rather than in a hospital.

grab (grabs, grabbing, grabbed) *verb* to take or seize something suddenly and roughly, to snatch. **grab** *noun*. *The mugger made a grab for the old woman's handbag*. **how does it grab you?** What do you think about it?

grace *noun* 1 a beautiful and easy way of moving. **graceful** *adjective*. 2 the love and favour of God. 3 a short prayer of thanks said before and after meals.

gracious *adjective* pleasant and polite. *A gracious smile*.

grade *noun* 1 a scale that sorts people or things according to quality, rank, size, etc. *Vegetables of the highest grade*. 2 marks given in an exam. 3 (US) a class of a particular level or year. *He's in the fourth grade*. **grade** *verb*. *The eggs were graded according to size*.

gradient *noun* the measure of how steep a slope is. *That hill has a gradient of one in seven. It rises one metre for every seven*.

gradual *adjective* changing or happening slowly. *A gradual improvement*.

graduate *noun* a person who has finished a course of studies and taken a university degree. **graduate** *verb*.

graffiti *plural noun* (say gra-**fee**-tee) drawings and writing scribbled on buildings, trains, etc.

Grain can be ground into flour for making into pasta or bread.

According to a very old tradition, a judge still wears a wig and gown.

DID YOU KNOW

Words that include 'ph' (pronounced 'f') as part of the spelling come from the Greek, as in 'graphic' and 'photograph'.

grain *noun* 1 the seed of cereal plants like maize, rice and wheat. 2 tiny bits of something. *Grains of salt, sand and sugar*. 3 the pattern of lines made by the fibres in wood.

gram *noun* a metric unit of weight. There are 1000 grams in a kilogram.

grammar *noun* the rules of a language and how the words are put together properly.

grand *adjective* 1 large, important and magnificent. *Blenheim Palace is very grand*. 2 very pleasant. *We had a grand time at the theme park*.

grandchild, granddaughter, grandson the child of a person's son or daughter.

grandparent, grandfather, grandmother the parent of one of a person's parents.

grandstand *noun* a covered area at a sports ground with rows of raised seats.

granite *noun* (say **gran**-it) a very hard rock used in building.

granny *noun* grandmother.

grant *verb* to agree to, to give something. *The government granted the island independence*. **take something for granted** to feel sure something will happen without checking or without appreciating it.

grant *noun* a sum of money given for a particular purpose. *A university grant*.

grape *noun* a small, round green or purple fruit that grows in bunches on a bush called a grapevine. Wine is made from grapes.

grapefruit (grapefruit or grapefruits) *noun* a round fruit like a big orange but with a yellow skin.

graph *noun* (rhymes with half) a diagram or chart that shows how numbers, amounts etc. compare or are related.

The graph showed how sales figures had risen dramatically.

graphic *adjective* 1 clear and vivid. *A graphic account of the murder*. 2 relating to painting and drawing. *The graphic arts*.

graphics *plural noun* pictures and patterns.

grasp *verb* 1 to hold something tightly, to seize. 2 to understand. **grasp** *noun. Get a good grasp on the rope.*

grass *noun* a plant with long, thin, green leaves that grows in fields. **grassy** *adjective.*

grasshopper *noun* a small jumping insect with long back legs. It makes a chirping sound by rubbing its wings together.

grate *noun* a metal frame in a fireplace, for holding the burning fuel.

grate *verb* 1 to rub or shred into little pieces against a tool with a rough surface called a grater. 2 to make an unpleasant, scraping sound by rubbing something.

grateful *adjective* pleased and wanting to thank somebody, thankful.

gratitude *noun* a feeling of being grateful, thankfulness. *Helen was full of gratitude.*

grave *adjective* very serious or important. *A grave illness.*

grave *noun* a hole in the ground in which to bury a corpse. **gravestone** a carved stone slab placed over a person's grave. **graveyard** a place where people are buried.

gravel *noun* small stones used to cover paths and roads.

gravity *noun* 1 seriousness. 2 the natural force that draws things to the Earth so that they stay there and do not float away.

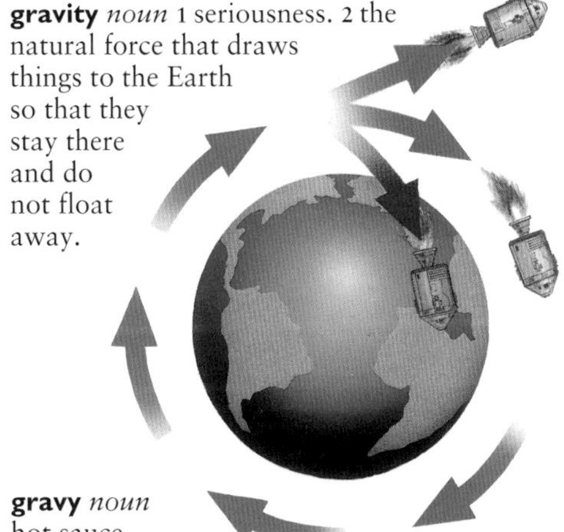

The Earth's pull of gravity holds satellites and rockets in orbit around the planet.

gravy *noun* hot sauce made from the juices of cooked meat.

graze *verb* 1 when animals graze, they eat grass as it grows. 2 to scrape your skin by rubbing it against something rough.

grease *noun* a thick, oily substance. **greasy** *adjective.*

great *adjective* 1 big or heavy. 2 important, famous or clever. *A great composer.* 3 Very good. *It's great to be here.* **greatness** *noun.*

Great Britain *noun* the main island and small islands of England, Scotland and Wales.

great-grandparents, great-grandfather great-grandmother the grandparents of somebody's father or mother.

AMAZING FACT

Grasshoppers can jump up to 20 times the length of their own bodies. Because they eat leaves and the shoots of young plants, they can become a pest to farmers. Locusts can travel great distances when they swarm and may do serious damage to large areas.

AMAZING FACT

Not all greenhouse gases are produced by burning fossil fuels such as gasoline and coal. Large amounts of methane are produced by termites and cattle digesting cellulose.

Greece *noun* a country in Southeast Europe.

The flag of Greece is blue and white with a cross in the corner.

greed (greedier, greediest) *adjective* a selfish wish to have more of something than you need. **greedy** *adjective.*

Greek *noun* 1 a person who comes from Greece. 2 the language spoken in Greece. **Greek** *adjective. Greek civilization.*

green *noun* 1 the colour of grass. 2 an open piece of grassy ground for use by everybody. **green** *adjective* 1 *A green light means 'go'.* 2 *They are interested in such green issues as protecting the environment.* 3 young and without much experience.

greenhouse *noun* a building made of glass used for growing plants. **greenhouse effect** the effect of the atmosphere around the Earth warming up because gases such as methane and carbon dioxide are trapped in the atmosphere and become heated by the Sun.

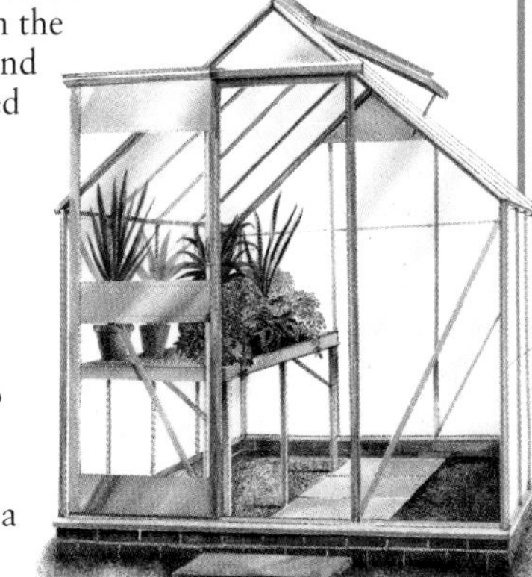

A greenhouse is the ideal place for growing pot plants as well as vegetables.

greet *verb* to meet and welcome somebody in a friendly way. **greeting** *noun.*

Grenada *noun* a country in the West Indies.

grew past tense of grow.

grey *noun* a colour that is a mixture of black and white. *Rain clouds are grey.*

greyhound *noun* a slim breed of dog that can run very fast and is used in racing.

grid *noun* 1 a pattern of squares formed by straight lines crossing each other at right angles. 2 a network of cables carrying electricity.

grief *noun* (rhymes with leaf) great sorrow or sadness, especially after a death or misfortune. **grieve** *verb. He is grieving for his dead wife.*

grievance *noun* a reason to complain or be angry about something.

grievous *adjective* very serious or harmful. *A grievous injury.*

grill *noun* a part of a cooker where food is cooked under or above direct heat. **grill** *verb. They grilled sausages for breakfast.*

G

grim (grimmer, grimmest) *adjective* 1 stern and unsmiling. *A grim look of disapproval.* 2 unpleasant. *Grim news.*

grime *noun* dirt rubbed deeply into a surface. **grimy** *adjective.*

grin *noun* a broad, cheerful smile. **grin** (grins, grinning, grinned) *verb.* **grin and bear it** to put up with something unpleasant without complaint.

grind (grinds, grinding, ground) *verb* to crush something into very small pieces. *The coffee beans have just been ground.* **grind to a halt** slowly to come to a complete stop.

grip (grips, gripping, gripped) *verb* 1 to hold something very firmly, to grasp. **grip** *noun.* 2 to hold somebody's complete attention. *She was gripped by the news of his death.*

grit *noun* tiny pieces of stone. **grit** *verb. The council grit the roads in icy weather for safety.* **gritty** *adjective.*

groan *noun* a long, deep sound showing pain or unhappiness. **groan** *verb.*

groceries *plural noun* things such as flour, tea, jam and sugar that you buy from a grocer's shop or from a supermarket.

groin *noun* the place where the top of your legs meet.

groom *verb* to clean and brush an animal, particularly a horse. **groom** *noun* 1 a person who looks after horses. 2 a man who is about to get married, a bridegroom.

groove *noun* a long, narrow cut into the surface of something.

grope *verb* to feel your way or search with your hands for something you cannot see.

grotesque *adjective* (say grow-**tesk**) weird and unnatural.

ground *noun* 1 the solid surface of the Earth. The floor. 2 a sports field. **gain ground** to make progress. **break new ground** to do something new or for the first time.

ground past tense of grind.

grounded *adjective* If an aircraft is grounded it is unable to fly.

grounds *plural noun* 1 the land around a large building. *The school grounds.* 2 reasons. *What grounds have you for believing her?* 3 the little bits that fall to the bottom of a drink like coffee.

group *noun* a number of people, animals or things that are in one place or that belong together in some way. A family group. *Lions, tigers and leopards belong to the same group of animals.* **group** *verb.*

A tadpole will soon grow into a frog.

AMAZING FACT

The largest North American frog, the bullfrog is very slow to mature. Although the eggs hatch in only about five or six days, it may take from two to five years for the tadpoles to grow into adult bullfrogs.

Dorian cut a groove in the wood with his chisel.

SPELLING NOTE

Note the 'u' in words like 'guarantee' and 'guard'. Before 'i' and 'e' the 'g' is usually soft, as in 'gem' and 'ginger'. Inserting 'u' makes the 'g' hard' as in 'guest' and 'guide'.

grovel (grovels, grovelling, grovelled) *verb* to behave in an over-humble and respectful way to somebody because you think they are important.

grow (grows, growing, grew, grown) *verb* 1 to become larger and taller, to develop. 2 to plant in the ground. *We are growing vegetables this year.* 2 to become. *He's growing stronger every day.* **grow up** to become an adult. **grow out of** *She'll grow out of biting her nails.*

growl *verb* to make a deep, low and angry sound. *The dog growled when I tried to take her bone.*

growth *noun* 1 growing, developing. *The population growth.* 2 a lump growing in a part of person's body.

grown-up *noun* an adult. **grown-up** *adjective. He has a grown-up son.*

grub *noun* 1 the larva or worm-like creature that will grow into an insect. 2 (slang) food.

One day the grub would turn into a beautiful moth.

grubby (grubbier, grubbiest) *adjective* dirty. *Wash your grubby hands.*

grudge *noun* a long-lasting feeling of dislike or resentment towards somebody because they harmed you in the past.

gruelling *adjective* very tiring, severe. *A long, gruelling journey.*

gruesome *adjective* revolting and shocking. *A gruesome murder.*

gruff *adjective* unfriendly and rough. *A gruff voice.*

grumble *verb* to mutter and complain in a bad-tempered way. *He's always grumbling about the noise.*

grumpy (grumpier, grumpiest) *adjective* irritable and bad-tempered. **grumpiness** *noun. Gary's grumpiness got them down.*

grunt *verb* to make a short, gruff sound like a pig. **grunt** *noun.*

guarantee *noun* 1 a promise by a manufacturer etc that something is of a certain quality and that it will be repaired or replaced if it goes wrong within a certain time. *The computer has a year's guarantee.* 2 a promise that something will definitely happen. *There's no guarantee that we'll win the match.* **guarantee** *verb.*

guard *verb* to watch over and protect somebody or something. *Police officers guarded the palace.*

guard *noun* 1 a person or group etc. that guards. *A guard dog.* 2 some device or thing that guards or protects. *A fire guard.* 3 a person in charge of a train (US brakeman). **on guard** prepared to defend and protect. **off guard** unprepared.

guarded *adjective* 1 protected. 2 cautious and careful not to say too much. *A guarded reply.*

Guatemala *noun* a country in Central America.

Guatemala City *noun* the capital of Guatemala.

guess *verb* 1 to say what you think is the answer without having enough information to know whether it is really correct. *Joe guessed the weight of the cake.* 2 to think. *I guess I'd better be going.* **guess** *noun. My guess is that she is older than she looks.* **guesswork** making guesses or the result of guesses. *He cooked the cake by guesswork.*

guest *noun* 1 a person who has been invited to stay for a short time in somebody's house, a visitor. *Be my guest!* 2 a person staying in an hotel.

guide *noun* somebody who leads or shows the way; a person who helps or advises. *A guide showed us around the magnificent cathedral.* **guide** *verb.*

guidebook *noun* a book containing information for visitors to a place.

guide dog *noun* a dog that has been trained to help a blind person.

guideline *noun* advice or rules on how something should be done.

guillotine *noun* (say **gill**-uh-teen) a machine used in France to cut off people's heads (behead). It consists of a blade that slides down between two posts.

guilt *noun* 1 the miserable feeling you have when you know you have done something wrong. 2 the fact that you have done something wrong.

guilty *adjective* 1 having done something wrong or committed a crime. *She was guilty of shop-lifting.* 2 the feeling of guilt or shame.

Guinea *noun* a country in Africa.

Guinea-Bissau *noun* a country in Africa.

Guinea pigs make ideal pets.

AMAZING FACT

Guinea pigs are rodents, not pigs, and they are originally from Peru, not Guinea.

The tame Guinea pigs that we keep as pets are actually descendants of the cavy, an animal that lives in the Andes mountains.

Some Guinea pigs have very long coats. They may be white, black, gray or brown.

SPELLING NOTE

The guillotine was first used during the French Revolution (1789–95) and is named after its inventor, Dr Joseph Guillotin.

Marie Antoinette, Queen of France, lost her head on the guillotine.

guinea pig *noun* 1 a furry, tail-less South American rodent, often kept as a pet. 2 somebody used in a scientific experiment.

guitar *noun* a musical instrument with six strings that you pluck with your fingers or with a plectrum. **guitarist** *noun.*

Gujurati *noun* the language spoken in the state of Gujurat in western India.

gulf *noun* a bay or large area of the sea almost surrounded by land.

gull *noun* a large sea bird (seagull) with grey and white feathers and webbed feet.

gum *noun* 1 the firm pink flesh in your mouth that holds your teeth. 2 glue or sticky liquid for sticking things together. **gum** *verb.* 3 chewing-gum.

gun *noun* a weapon that shoots bullets through a metal tube. **gunfire** the repeated firing of guns.

gunpowder *noun* a powder that explodes easily. Gunpowder is used in fireworks.

gush *verb* When a liquid such as water gushes, it flows out suddenly and in large quantities. **gush** *noun.*

gust *noun* a strong and sudden rush of wind. **gusty** *adjective.*

guts *plural noun* 1 the intestines. 2 bravery.

gutter *noun* a channel for rainwater to flow along, fixed to the edge of a roof or built along a street.

Guyana *noun* a country in South America.

gym short for gymnasium and gymnastics.

gymnasium *noun* a room or building with special equipment for doing physical exercises. *Sarah goes to the gymnasium at least once a week.*

gymnast *noun* a person who is trained in gymnastics.

gymnastics *noun* highly skilled physical exercises using equipment such as bars, ropes and jumping horses.

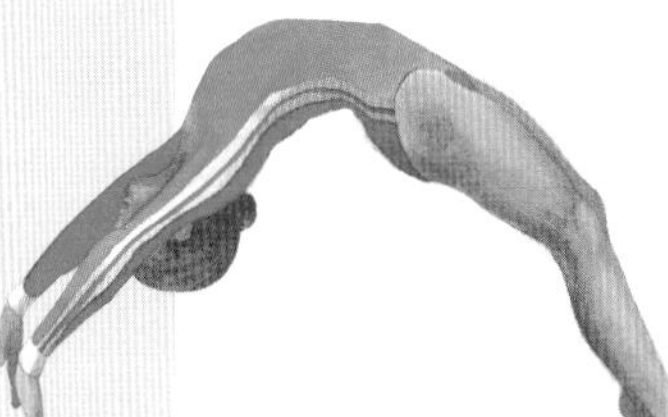

Gymnastics is one of the most respected events at the Olympic Games.

gypsy *noun* a member of a dark-haired race of people who travel from place to place, usually in caravans. *The gypsies danced and played music by the camp fire.*

Hh

habit *noun* 1 something that you do regularly, usually without thinking about it. A custom. *She has an annoying habit of twisting her hair.* **habitual** *adjective*. 2 the loose clothes worn by a monk or nun.

habitat *noun* the place where an animal or plant naturally lives or grows.

hack *verb* 1 to cut something, roughly, with repeated blows. *He hacked his way through the undergrowth.* 2 to ride a horse in open countryside. 3 to get information from a computer system illegally. **hacker** *noun*.

haddock *noun* an edible sea fish, related to cod. *Smoked haddock with poached egg.*

hag *noun* an offensive word meaning ugly old woman.

haggard *adjective* looking thin, ill and tired. *Worry has made her look terribly haggard.*

haggle *verb* to argue over the price of something, to bargain.

hail *noun* frozen rain. **hail** *verb*. **hailstone** *noun* a frozen raindrop.

hail *verb* to call out or wave to get attention. *She hailed a taxi.*

hair *noun* 1 a fine thread that grows on the skin of people and animals. 2 the soft mass of these threads covering a person's head. *Harry has fair hair.* **let your hair down** to behave in a very relaxed way. **keep your hair on** to stay calm and not get excited. **split hairs** to argue about unimportant details.

haircut *noun* the act of cutting somebody's hair. The style in which the hair has been cut.

hairdresser *noun* a person who cuts and arranges (styles) hair.

hair-raising *adjective* terrifying.

hairy (hairier, hairiest) *adjective* 1 covered in hair. 2 (slang) exciting and risky. *A hairy ride on the roller-coaster.*

Haiti (say **hay**-tee) *noun* a country in the West Indies, the western part of the island of Hispaniola.

halal *noun* meat from animals that have been killed according to Islam's religious laws. *A halal butcher.*

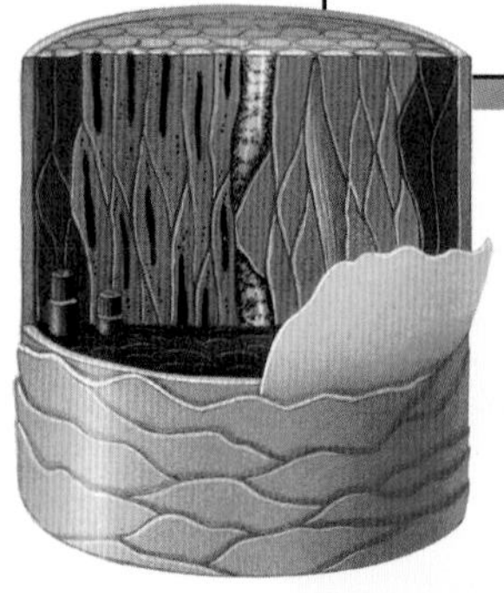

This section through a hair shaft shows how layers of keratin (a protein) make up the outer coating or cuticle. Inside, more keratin makes up the cortex and the inner layer, or medulla.

WORD HISTORY

The shape of the letter H comes from the ancient Egyptian symbol for a twist of rope. In the Greek alphabet it has an 'ee' sound. The Romans gave it its present 'h' sound.

SPELLING NOTE

Hallowe'en comes from All Hallows Eve, the eve of All Saints' Day, 31 October. 'Hallow' is an Old English word for saint.

half (halves) *noun* one of two equal parts. *Half an apple.* **half** *adverb* partly, not completely. *The meat is still half-frozen.* **half** *adjective A half bottle of wine.* **half-hearted** *adjective* not very keen or enthusiastic. *A half-hearted effort.*

Jackie likes prawn cocktail made with half an avocado.

half-time *noun* a short break between two halves of a game such as football or hockey.

halfmast *noun* the position half-way down a pole at which a flag is flown as a sign that somebody important has died.

hall *noun* 1 a room or passageway at the entrance to a house. 2 a large room or building for public meetings, concerts etc.

Halloween *noun* the evening of 31 October, the day before All Saints' Day when some people believe that ghosts and witches roam about.

hallucinate *verb* to hear or see things that are not really there. **hallucination** *noun*.

halt *verb* to come or bring to a stop. *The train halted at the station.* **halt** *noun*.

halve *verb* 1 to divide or cut something into two equal parts. 2 to reduce by half.

ham *noun* 1 salted meat from a pig's back leg. 2 (slang) an actor who is not very good and who overacts.

hamburger *noun* a bread roll containing a round cake of chopped beef.

hamlet *noun* a small village (in Britain), usually without a church.

hammer *noun* a tool with a long handle and a heavy head used mainly for hitting (hammering) nails into things. **hammer** *verb*.

hammock *noun* a swinging bed made of strong cloth or rope that is hung up at the ends between two supports.

Andy lazed all day in the hammock.

hamper *noun* a large basket with a lid, for carrying things. *A picnic hamper.*

hamper *verb* to prevent or make something difficult to do, to hinder. *Her tight jacket hampered her movements.*

hamster *noun* a small, furry, tail-less rodent that can store food in its cheeks. Hamsters are often kept as pets.

Lola's hamster won first prize in the show.

hand *noun* 1 the part of your body at the end of your arm and below your wrist with four fingers and a thumb. 2 a pointer on a clock. *My watch has an hour hand, a minute hand and a second hand.* 3 help. *Can you give me a hand, please?* 4 a worker. *A farm hand.* 5 the cards a player holds in his or her hand in a card game. *I had a winning hand.* 6 The measure of the height of horses and ponies (equal to 10 centimetres). **hand** *verb* to give. *She handed me the letter.* **at first hand** directly and not through other people. **in hand** being dealt with, under control. **hand out** to give out, share. **on hand** ready and available. **out of hand** out of control.

handbag *noun* a small bag usually carried by women for money and personal belongings (US purse).

handbook *noun* a book with instructions or useful facts about something.

handcuffs *plural noun* a pair of metal rings joined by a chain and locked around a prisoner's wrists to stop them escaping. **handcuff** *verb*.

handicap *noun* 1 a disadvantage or something that makes it difficult to do what you want to do. *His lack of experience was a handicap.* 2 a disability of the body or mind. *Being deaf can be a terrible handicap.*

handicraft *noun* work such as pottery or weaving that needs skilful use of the hands.

handkerchief *noun* (say **hang**-ker-cheef) a small piece of cloth or tissue used for blowing and wiping your nose.

handle *noun* the part of an object that you can hold it by or make it work by. *Turn the handle to open the door.* **handle** *verb* 1 to hold, touch or move something with your hands. 2 to deal with or control. *Grooms handle horses.*

handlebars *plural noun* the bar with a handle at each end at the front of a bicycle or motorbike that the rider holds and steers with. *Hold on to the handlebars.*

WORD HISTORY

'Handsome' once meant 'easy to handle'. The meaning then changed to 'pleasant' and then to the present meaning of 'pleasant to look at, noble, gracious and generous.'

SPELLING NOTE

Try not to confuse 'hangar' with an 'a' and 'hanger' with an 'e'.

AMAZING FACT

'Hangman' is a game that you can play to improve your spelling. Play with a friend. Take turns. Think of a word. Put a blank – for each letter of the word on a piece of paper. The other person guesses a letter. If the word contains that letter, write it in the correct blank. If not, draw one part of the 'hangman'. There are 10 parts.

handsome *adjective* attractive, good-looking. *A handsome man.*

handy (handier, handiest) *adjective* 1 nearby and easy to reach. *There's a handy shop round the corner.* 2 useful and easy to use. *Penknives are handy tools.* 3 skilful in the use of tools. *He's handy around the house.*

hang (hangs, hanging, hung) *verb* 1 to attach something by its top part so that the lower part is free. *She hung her coat on a hook.* 2 to swing loosely. *The dog's tongue is hanging out of its mouth.* 3 **hang** (hangs, hanging, hanged) to kill somebody by putting a rope around their neck and letting them drop from a support. **hang about** to wait about a place with nothing to do. **hang back** to be unwilling to do something. **hang on** 1 to hold tightly. 2 to wait. *Hang on a minute, wait for me!*

hangar *noun* a large building where aircraft are kept. *Aircraft hangar.*

hanger *noun* something on which to hang clothes to be stored in a cupboard.

I bought some plastic hangers so you can keep your bedroom tidy.

hang-glider *noun* a kite-like glider to which you are strapped and can then fly from the top of cliffs etc. in the sport of hang-gliding.

hanker *verb* to want something very badly, to long for. *She is hankering after a ride in the helicopter.*

Hanoi *noun* the capital of Vietnam.

Hanukkah *noun* the Jewish festival of lights, which is held in December.

haphazard *adjective* unplanned, happening by accident. *A haphazard arrangement.*

happen *verb* 1 to take place. *What happened next in the story?* 2 to occur by chance. *I just happened to see him.*

happening *noun* an event. *Great happenings in history.*

The space walk was the greatest happening of his life.

happy (happier, happiest) *adjective* 1 the feeling of being pleased and cheerful. 2 willing. *I'd be happy to go instead of you.* **happiness** *noun.* **happily** *adverb.*

Harare *noun* the capital of Zimbabwe.

harass *verb* to annoy or bother somebody repeatedly. **harassment** *noun.* **harassed** *adjective. Sarah feels very harrassed today.*

harbour *noun* a place where ships stop to load or unload cargoes and where they can shelter. A port.

hard *adjective* 1 solid and difficult to shape or break, not soft. *Concrete becomes hard when it sets.* 2 difficult. *A hard jigsaw.* 3 severe and tough. *Hard discipline.* **hard** *adverb* with great energy or effort. *Work hard, play hard.* **hardness** *noun.*

hardback *noun* a book with a long-lasting, stiff cover.

harden *verb* to make or to become hard and stiff. *The concrete hardened.*

hard-copy *noun* a printed copy of information created on a computer, also called a printout.

hard-disk *noun* a device inside a computer that holds a large amount of data.

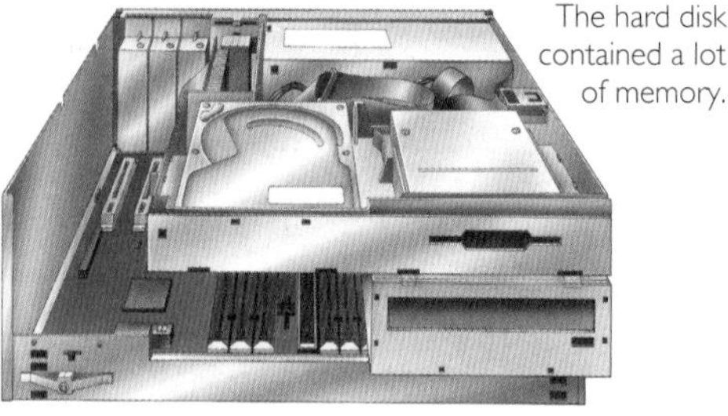

The hard disk contained a lot of memory.

hardly *adverb* almost but not completely, scarcely. *He was so tired he could hardly keep his eyes open.*

hardship *noun* causing suffering or difficulty. *He suffered great hardship.*

hardware *noun* 1 all the pieces of machinery that make up a computer, e.g. the printer and VDU. 2 tools and equipment used in the home, ironmongery.

hardy *adjective* strong, robust and able to endure severe conditions. *Hardy plants.*

hare *noun* an animal like a large rabbit.

harm *verb* to hurt or damage somebody or something. **harm** *noun.*

harmful *adjective* bad for you. *Too much sugar is harmful to your teeth.*

harmless *adjective* safe and not dangerous or harmful. *A harmless insect.*

harmony *noun* 1 musical notes played at the same time and which sound pleasant. 2 agreement and cooperation. **harmonious** *adjective.* **harmonize** *verb.*

The harp is a favourite instrument in Wales.

SPELLING NOTE

Note the one 'r' and two 's's in 'harass'. But remember that 'embarrass' has two 'r's'.

harness *noun* the leather straps fastened to a horse to control it. The bridle, reins and saddle are parts of the harness. **harness** *verb.*

harp *noun* a musical instrument that you play by plucking its strings. **harpist** *noun.*

harpoon *noun* a spear with a rope attached that is used to hunt whales. **harpoon** *verb.*

harpsichord *noun* a keyboard instrument similar to a piano with strings that are plucked.

harsh *adjective* 1 stern, unkind and severe. *Harsh treatment.* 2 rough and unpleasant. *A harsh sound.*

harvest *noun* the time when grain and other crops are cut and gathered. *Harvest is the busiest time of the year for the farming community.* **harvest** *verb.*

hassle *noun* a bother or a cause of trouble. *It's too much hassle to go by bus.* **hassle** *verb* (slang) to pester or bother somebody. *Stop hassling me!*

haste *noun* a hurry. *She was late and left in great haste.* **hasten** *verb. He hastened home.*

hasty (hastier, hastiest) *adjective* done quickly, and sometimes too quickly and without care. *A hasty decision.*

hat *noun* a covering for the head, usually with a brim. *A hat keeps your head warm.* **talk though your hat** to talk nonsense.

AMAZING FACT

Some animals have special words for the young, for males, for females, a group of the animal and for the place the animals live.

For example, a young hare is called a leveret, a male hare is a buck, a female is a doe. A group of hares is called a drove and the home of a hare is a form. These specialized words probably developed during the Middle Ages, when hunting was a main source of food.

Hats can be decorated with feathers, bows and coloured bands.

hatch *noun* a movable covering for a hole in a floor, wall or ceiling etc. *An escape hatch on an aeroplane.* **hatchback car** a car with a door at the back that opens upwards.

hatch *verb* 1 An egg hatches when it breaks open and a chick or reptile comes out. 2 to plan. *What scheme are you hatching?*

hate *verb* to dislike somebody or something very much, to loathe. **hate, hatred** *noun.*

hateful *adjective* causing hatred, unpleasant. *What a hateful person he is.*

haul *verb* to pull or drag something heavy with a lot of effort.

haunt *verb* If a ghost haunts a place, it visits it regularly. **haunted** *adjective.*

Havana *noun* the capital of Cuba.

have (has, having, had) *verb* 1 to own. *She has 20 pairs of shoes.* 2 to experience or enjoy something. *Let's have a party.* 3 to be forced to do something. *I have to go home today.* 4 to receive. *I had a lot of cards on my birthday.*

havoc *noun* great damage, chaos.

hawk *noun* a bird of prey with good eye-sight and sharp talons.

hay *noun* grass that has been cut and dried for feeding to animals. **make hay while the sun shines** to do things while you have the opportunity to.

hayfever *noun* an illness like a bad cold caused by an allergy or bad reaction to breathing in the pollen of grasses or flowers.

hazard *noun* a risk or something that can cause harm. *That loose step is a hazard.*

hazel *noun* 1 a small tree on which hazelnuts grow. 2 a yellowish-brown colour. *Hazel eyes glow with a special warmth.*

hazy (hazier, haziest) *adjective* 1 misty. *A hazy day.* **haze** *noun.* 2 not clear, confused. *I have only a hazy idea of how to get there.*

head *noun* 1 the top part of your body above your neck, containing your face, hair and skull. 2 the leader or person in charge of something. *The head of department.* 3 the front or upper part of something. *The head of a letter.* **heads** the side of a coin showing somebody's head. **head** *verb* 1 to move in a direction. *They headed for the beach.* 2 to be in charge of. *She heads the news team.*

headache *noun* 1 a pain in your head. 2 a problem.

headland *noun* a piece of land jutting out into the sea.

headlight *noun* one of the strong lights at the front of a motor vehicle.

headline *noun* 1 heading or words printed in large, bold print at the head of a story in a newspaper. 2 **headlines** the main items of news. *The news headlines in brief.*

headquarters *noun* the main place from which a business or organization is controlled. *The headquarters of the bank.*

headway *noun* progress. *He's making some headway in Japanese.*

heal *verb* to make or become better or healthy again. *Physician, heal thyself.*

AMAZING FACT

A group of hawks is called a cast of hawks.

The hawk is a fearsome predator.

GRAMMAR NOTE

'To hear' means to receive sounds through your ears, and 'to listen' means to pay attention to what you hear.

AMAZING FACT

Headlines are short and contain only the most important information in a news story. They are supposed to get your attention and be easy to read. Space is often limited, too, so headlines are rarely complete sentences. Next time you read a newspaper, look at the language of headlines – not only is the grammar different, certain words are more common in headlines than in any other form of writing.

health *noun* the condition of your body and how well or ill it is.

healthy (healthier, healthiest) *adjective* 1 well and not suffering from any illness or injury, fit. 2 something that is good for you. *Healthy exercise.* **healthily** *adverb.*

heap *noun* 1 an untidy pile or mass of things. *A heap of dirty dishes.* 2 **heaps** a large amount. *There's heaps of time before the train goes.* **heap** *verb. She heaped the rubbish in the corner.*

Dad left a heap of dirty dishes in the sink.

hear *verb* 1 to receive or pick up sound with our ears, to listen to. 2 to receive information. *We hear you are going away.*

hearing *noun* One of the body's five senses is the ability to hear.

hearing-aid *noun* a small device that makes sounds louder and which people with poor hearing wear in or behind their ears to help them hear better.

hearse *noun* a vehicle for carrying a coffin to a cemetery etc.

heart *noun* 1 the organ inside your chest that pumps blood around your body. 2 the main or most important part. *The heart of the matter.* 3 courage and enthusiasm. *She put her heart into the job.* 4 **hearts** one of the four suits in a pack of playing cards.

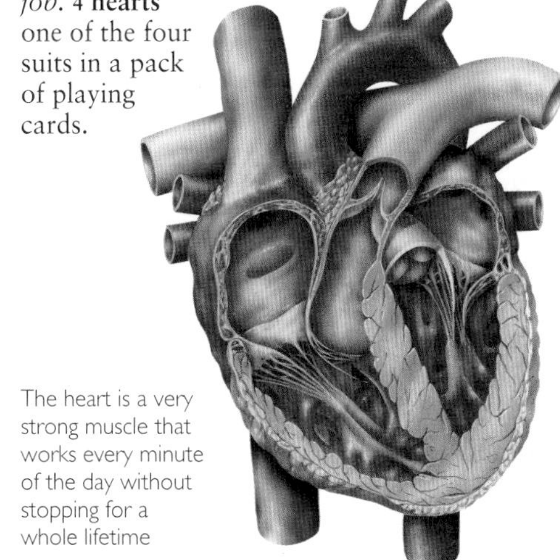

The heart is a very strong muscle that works every minute of the day without stopping for a whole lifetime

heart-attack *noun* a serious condition when the heart suddenly does not work properly and may even stop, causing death.

heart-breaking *adjective* causing great sadness. *I am so sorry to hear your heart-breaking news.*

heartbroken *adjective. She was heartbroken when her budgie died.*

H

heart-felt *adjective* very sincere. *My heart-felt thanks to all concerned.*

heartless *adjective* cruel and pitiless. **heartlessness** *noun.*

hearth *noun* the floor of a fireplace.

hearty (heartier, heartiest) *adjective* 1 enthusiastic and friendly. *They gave us a hearty welcome.* 2 strong, big and healthy. *A hearty meal was enjoyed by all.*

heat *adjective* 1 the hotness or warmth of something. *The heat of the fire.* 2 one of a number of races in a competition, the winners of which go forward into the next trial. **heat** *verb* to make something hot. *The fire heated the room.* **heated** *adjective.*

heath *noun* a wild and open area of land covered with grass and shrubs.

heather *noun* an evergreen shrub with pink, purple or white flowers that grows on moors and heaths.

Heather is the national flower of Scotland.

heave *verb* to lift, move or throw something using a lot of effort.

heaven *noun* a place of great happiness and the home of God, where good people are said to go when they die.

heavy (heavier, heaviest) *adjective* 1 having great weight and hard to lift. *A heavy suitcase.* 2 great amount or force. *Heavy rain fell in sheets.* 3 (slang) serious, boring and complicated. *She gets heavy when she talks about her work.* **heaviness** *noun.* **heavily** *adverb.*

Hebrew *noun* the original language of Judaism.

hectare *noun* a measure of an area of land, equal to 10,000 square metres.

hectic *adjective* very busy and full of exciting activity. *A hectic day.*

hedge *noun* a fence around a field or garden made of closely planted shrubs or small trees. **hedge** *verb* 1 to surround land with a hedge. 2 to avoid giving a straight answer. *She hedged around the subject.*

hedgehog *noun* a small animal covered in needle-like prickles. Hedgehogs come out at night. They roll up into a ball if frightened.

SPELLING NOTE

A word with the same sound as 'heel' is 'heal'.

DID YOU KNOW?

'Heir' is one of a small number of words beginning with 'h' in which the 'h' is not pronounced. Others are 'hour', 'honour' and 'honest'.

Hedgehogs can get quite tame if you feed them on bread and milk.

hedgerow *noun* a row or line of bushes forming a hedge around a field or along a country road.

heel *noun* 1 the back part of your foot. 2 the part of sock, shoe etc. that covers or supports the heel. *She's wearing shoes with very high heels.*

heifer *noun* (say **heff**-er) a young cow that has not yet had a calf.

height *noun* 1 how high something is from top to bottom. *The height of the room is nearly three metres.* 2 the highest, best or most important point or part of something. *The height of fashion.*

heighten *verb* to make something higher or become greater. *Their excitement heightened as they approached the park.*

heir *noun* (say air) an heir is a person who will have (inherit) the money, title etc. of somebody when they die.

heiress *noun* (say **air**-ess) a female heir.

heirloom *noun* a special or valuable object that is passed down in a family from one generation to the next.

held past and past participle of hold.

helicopter *noun* an aircraft with a large, fast-turning blade (rotor) on top, which acts as both a propeller and wings.

helium *noun* a colourless gas that is lighter than air and does not burn. It is used to fill balloons and airships.

hell *noun* a place where some people believe the devil lives and where wicked people go to be punished after they die.

hello *interjection* a word we use to attract somebody's attention or to greet somebody. *'Hello! Can you help me?'*

helm *noun* a ship's steering wheel, a tiller.

helmet *noun* a strong, hard covering to protect the head.

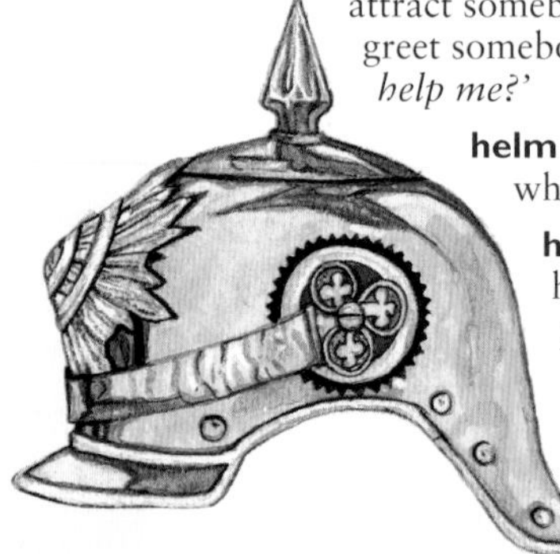

He wore the splendid golden helmet when he went on parade.

help *verb* 1 to do something that is needed or useful for somebody else, to assist. *'Can you help me move this sofa, please?'* 2 **can't help** unable to prevent or control. *She can't help sneezing.* **help** *noun.* **helper** *noun.*

helpful *adjective* useful and willing to help. *That was helpful advice.*

helping *noun* a share or amount of food put on your plate. *A big helping of pudding.*

helpless *adjective* not able to take care of yourself. *Babies are quite helpless.*

Helsinki *noun* the capital of Finland.

hem *noun* the edge of a piece of cloth that is folded over and sewn. **hem** (hems, hemming, hemmed) *verb. She hemmed her skirt.* **hem in** to surround closely and prevent from escaping.

hemisphere *noun* 1 the shape of half a sphere. 2 one half of the Earth. *Europe is in the northern hemisphere.*

hen *noun* a female chicken, especially one kept for its eggs. 2 any female bird. *A hen pheasant.*

The brown hen lays an egg for my breakfast every day.

hence *adverb* 1 therefore, for this reason. *There's been no rain, hence it's very dry.* 2 from now on. *From this day hence.*

herald *verb* 1 to say that something is going to happen. 2 to be a sign that something is going to happen. *Dark clouds herald storms.*

heraldry *noun* the study of coats-of-arms and family histories.

herb *noun* a plant used to add flavour in cooking or for making medicines. **herbal** *adjective. Herbal remedies.*

herbivore *noun* an animal that eats only plants. Horses and cattle are herbivores. **herbivorous** *adjective.*

herd *noun* a group of animals of one kind that graze and live together. *A herd of cows.* **herd** *verb* to crowd together.

here *adverb* at or to this place. *Come here immediately!*

hereafter *adverb* in the future, after this time. *Hereafter, things will be different.*

heretic *noun* (say **hair**-it-ik) a person who supports an opinion (usually religious or political) that is against the official view or what most people generally accept. **heretical** *adjective.* **heresy** *noun.*

heritage *noun* traditions, buildings etc. that are passed from one generation to the next.

hermit *noun* somebody who chooses to live alone and away from people, usually for religious reasons.

AMAZING FACT

Herons use their long beaks to grasp their prey rather than to spear it.

Florence Nightingale was a heroine to all the men she nursed.

AMAZING FACT

Animals hibernate during the cold, winter months when food is scarce. They eat as much as they can before finding a safe place to curl up for the winter. Hibernation isn't the same as sleeping, though. Sleeping takes more energy than hibernation. To conserve energy, the breathing and heartbeat of a hibernating animal slows down so much that they may appear to be almost dead.

hero (heroes) *noun* 1 a man or boy admired for having done something brave or especially good. **heroism** *noun.* **heroic** *adjective. Heroic deeds are related in many myths and fairytales.* 2 the most important male character in a book, film or play.

heroin *noun* a very strong drug that some people become addicted to.

heroine *noun* a woman or girl admired for having done something brave or especially good. **heroism** *noun.* **heroic** *adjective.* 2 the most important female character in a book, film or play.

heron *noun* a bird with long legs and a long thin beak that lives near ponds or rivers.

hesitate *verb* to pause or to stop doing something for a short time because you are uncertain, undecided or worried. **hesitation** *noun. He agreed to help without any hesitation.* **hesitant** *adjective.*

heterosexual *adjective* sexually attracted to people of the opposite sex. Most people are heterosexual. **heterosexuality** *noun.*

hew (hews, hewing, hewed, hewn or hewed) *verb* to cut with an axe.

hexagon *noun* a shape with six equal sides. **hexagonal** *adjective.*

A hexagon is a shape with six equal sides.

hibernate *verb* when animals hibernate, they spend the winter in a deep sleep. Bears, hedgehogs and tortoises all hibernate. **hibernation** *noun.*

hiccough *noun* (say **hik**-up) a sudden, repeated sound in your throat which people sometimes make after eating or drinking.

hide (hiding, hid, hidden) *verb* 1 to go to a place where you cannot be seen. *She hid in the attic.* 2 to put something in a place where people will not see it. *She hid the presents in a cupboard.*

hide *noun* the skin of an animal used for making leather.

hideous *adjective* very ugly, unpleasant. *A hideous smell wafted up out of the drain.*

hieroglyphics *plural noun* (say **hy**-er-uh-glif-iks) the ancient Egyptian system of writing that uses pictures to represent words and sounds.

high *adjective* 1 a long way above the ground. 2 the distance from the top to the bottom of something. *The door is two metres high.* 3 greater than normal. *The police car drove at a high speed.* 4 not deep or low. *Children have high voices.* 5 important or above others in rank.

highlands *plural noun* a hilly region, especially the Highlands of northern Scotland.

In the Highlands of Scotland you can see lochs, mountains and castles.

highlight *noun* the most interesting part of something. *Seeing the game park was the highlight of the visit.* **highlight** *verb* 1 to draw attention to something. *He highlighted the importance of good spelling when he spoke to the class.* 2 to use a coloured pen to mark important parts of a document.

high-pitched *adjective* shrill and high in sound. *A high-pitched wail.*

high-rise *adjective* High-rise buildings are very tall.

High-rise buildings lined the waterfront.

highly-strung *adjective* sensitive and nervous. *The horse is very highly-strung.*

high tech *noun* high technology. The use of advanced computers, electronics etc.

high tide *noun* the time when the sea reaches its highest level.

highway *noun* a main road.

WORD HISTORY

'Hieroglyphics' comes from two Greek words, 'hieros', 'sacred or priestly' and 'glyphe', 'carving' or 'writing'. The Greeks believed that only the Egyptian priests understood and used this system of writing.

SPELLING NOTE

The word 'hippopotamus' comes from two Greek words and means 'river horse'. Hippos are in fact more closely related to pigs than horses.

highwayman (highwaymen) *noun* in the past, a robber on horseback who stopped travellers at gunpoint.

hijack *verb* to take control of an aircraft, car etc. by force and make it go somewhere. **hijack** *noun. The hijack ended in disaster.*

hijacker *noun* a person who hijacks.

hike *verb* to go on a long walk. *I hiked all over Wales.* **hike** *noun.* **hiker** *noun.*

hilarious *adjective* very funny in a noisy way. **hilarity** *noun.*

hill *noun* an area of ground that is higher than the ground around it. **hilly** *adjective. Hilly countryside.*

hilt *noun* the handle of a sword or dagger. **up to the hilt** completely. *I support my team right up to the hilt.*

hinder *verb* to get in the way and so make things difficult for somebody, to prevent and delay. **hindrance** *noun.*

Hindu *noun* (say hin-**doo**) a follower of Hinduism, an Indian religion which has many gods and teaches that people will return to Earth in a different form after death. **Hindu** *adjective.*

Hindustani *noun* a dialect of the language Hindi, and one of the main languages of India. *Fluent Hindustani.*

hinge *noun* a moving metal joint on which such things as doors, gates, windows and lids to boxes can swing when opened.

hint *verb* to mention something without actually saying it. *Jack hinted that it was time to go by looking at his watch.* **hint** *noun* 1 a suggestion or clue. 2 helpful advice. *Gardening hints.*

hip *noun* one of the two joints on either side of your body between the top of your legs and your waist.

hippopotamus (hippopotamuses) *noun* a very large African animal with short legs and thick skin that lives in or near lakes and rivers. It is often called a hippo for short.

A hippopotamus was bathing in the water hole, enjoying wallowing in the mud.

hire *verb* to pay money to employ somebody or use something for a short time. *She hired two men to mend the roof.*

hiss *verb* to make a long S sound to show anger or disapproval. **hiss** *verb. The audience hissed at the actors.*

historian *noun* a person who studies and writes about history.

historic *adjective* famous or important in the past. *Historic houses.*

The Parthenon is a historic building in Athens.

historical *adjective* concerned with events and people in history. *Was Hamlet a historical person?*

history *noun* 1 the study of the people and events of the past. 2 a description of the past. *A history of Wales.*

hit (hits, hitting, hit) *verb* to strike with a blow, to touch something violently. *She hit the ball with a bat.* **hit** *noun* 1 a blow. *A hit on the nose.* 2 a great success.

hitch-hike *verb* to travel by getting free rides from passing vehicles by holding up your thumb.

HIV short for human immunodeficiency virus, a virus that weakens a person's resistance to diseases and may lead to Aids.

hive *noun* bee-hive, a box-like structure for keeping bees in.

The bees buzzed round the hive, busy making honey.

hoard *noun* a secret store of money, treasure, food etc. **hoard** *verb. Squirrels hoard nuts for the winter.* **hoarder** *noun.*

hoarding *noun* a large board or temporary wooden fence covered in advertisements.

hoarse *adjective* a rough, low voice caused by a sore throat or by shouting too much.

hoax *noun* a practical joke, a trick or deception. *We had to evacuate the building, but the bomb scare was a hoax.* **hoax** *verb.*

hobble *verb* to limp or walk with difficulty. *He twisted his ankle and hobbled about in pain for more than a month.*

hobby *noun* an activity such as model-making that you enjoy doing in your spare time. *His hobby is collecting stamps.*

SPELLING NOTE

Try to distinguish between 'historic', meaning 'famous' or 'important in history'; and 'historical', meaning 'having actually happened in history' or 'concerned with history'. 'Hitler is a historical person.'

SPELLING NOTE

Another word that sounds like 'hoarse' is 'horse'.

hockey *noun* an outdoor game played with curved sticks and a ball by two teams of 11 players who try to score goals.

hoe *noun* a garden tool with a long handle and a short blade, used for weeding.

hog *noun* a male pig that has been neutered.

hog (hogs, hogging, hogged) *verb* to be very selfish and, for example, take much more of something than you can use.

Hogmanay *noun* New Year's Eve in Scotland. *A glorious Hogmanay.*

hoist *verb* to raise or lift up something, usually with ropes or a special machine. *The soldiers hoisted the flag.*

hold (holds, holding, held) *verb* 1 to carry something in your hand or mouth, to grasp. 2 to contain a certain amount. *The bottle holds a pint of milk.* 3 to arrange or carry on. *They held a dance in the hall.* 4 to have in control or in your possession. *Who holds the land speed record?* 5 to support or to keep something steady. *The pillars hold up the roof.* **hold off** to stay away. *I hope the rain holds off for the match.* **hold on** 1 to continue holding something. 2 to wait. *Hold on a minute.* **hold up** 1 to delay or hinder. *The roadworks held us up for an hour.* 2 to stop and rob somebody with threats. *She was held up at gunpoint.*

hold *noun* a place in a ship or aircraft where cargo is kept.

hole *noun* an opening or gap in something, a hollow space. *There's a hole in my sock. She hit the golf ball into the hole.*

holiday *noun* a day or a longer period of time away from school or work when you can enjoy doing what you want. *We're going to Mexico for our summer holidays.*

hollow *adjective* not solid, having an empty space inside. *Bottles and pipes are hollow.* **hollow** *noun* 1 a hole. 2 a small valley.

holly *noun* an evergreen tree with shiny, spiky leaves and sometimes red berries in winter.

Holly has beautiful red berries that the birds eat in winter.

hologram *noun* a photograph created by laser beams that appears to be three-dimensional (seeming to have width, depth and height).

holy *noun* relating to or belonging to God or a religion. Churches and temples are holy places. **holiness** *noun.*

H

home *noun* the place where you usually live or where you were brought up. **feel at home** to feel relaxed with somebody or something.

homeless *adjective, noun* without a place to live in. *How can we help the homeless?* **homelessness** *noun.*

homely *adjective* 1 pleasantly plain and simple. 2 (US) ugly.

homesick *adjective* unhappy and lonely because you are away from your family and home. *I was homesick for America.*

homework *noun* work that teachers give their pupils to do at home.

homicide *noun* (say **hom**-uh-side) the killing of a human being.

homosexual *adjective, noun* sexually attracted to somebody of the same sex, gay. **homosexuality** *noun.*

Honduras *noun* a country in Central America.

The flag of Honduras is blue and white striped. Five blue stars decorate the central white stripe.

honest *adjective* (say **on**-est) an honest person is somebody who always tells the truth and whom you can trust. **honesty** *noun. Honesty is always the best policy.*

honey *noun* (rhymes with bunny) the sweet, sticky food made by bees from the nectar of flowers. *Toast and honey for tea.*

honeycomb *noun* rows of six-sided wax containers made by bees to store their honey and eggs.

honeymoon *noun* a holiday spent together by two people who have just married.

honeysuckle *noun* a climbing shrub with sweet-smelling flowers.

Honiara *noun* the capital of the Solomon Islands.

honour *noun* (say **on**-ur) 1 to give great respect to somebody. *He was honoured by everybody for his great achievements.* 2 to praise and reward somebody publicly. 3 to keep an agreement. **honour** *noun* good reputation. **honourable** *adjective. She behaved in an honourable way and told the absolute truth.*

He fetched the honeycomb out of the hive and it was dripping with honey.

AMAZING FACT

Animals that have hooves are divided into two major groups: animals with an even number of claws or 'toes' such as sheep, goats and camels; and those with an odd number such as horses and zebras.

WORD HISTORY

'Hooligan' comes from the name of an unruly Irish family that lived in southeast London in the 19th century.

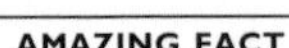

AMAZING FACT

Be careful when writing 'horde' (a crowd) and 'hoarde' (a secret store of something). They sound the same but are spelled differently.

hood *noun* 1 a part of a coat that you can pull up to cover your head and neck. 2 a soft roof for a car or pram that you can fold back. 3 (US) the bonnet of a car.

hoodwink *verb* to trick somebody. *He was hoodwinked into paying a lot of money for a worthless clock.*

hoof (hooves or hoofs) *noun* the hard covering on the feet of some animals such as horses, cows and sheep.

hook *noun* 1 a bent piece of metal or plastic for hanging things on. *Hang your raincoat on the hook to dry.* 2 a bent piece of metal for catching fish. **by hook or by crook** by any means possible. **get off the hook** to get out of a difficult situation.

For fly-fishing, anglers use hooks decorated with colourful feathers.

hooked *adjective* 1 shaped like a hook. *A hooked nose.* 2 (slang) fascinated by or addicted to. *He's hooked on bird watching.*

hooligan *noun* a violent, noisy person who gets into trouble and breaks things. **hooliganism** *noun.*

hoop *noun* a large ring made of metal or wood. At the circus we saw an acrobat jump through a hoop of fire.

hoot *verb* to make a sound like the horn of a car or the long 'oo' cry of an owl. *We hooted with laughter.* **hoot** *noun. We heard the hoot of the owl.*

hop (hops, hopping, hopped) *verb* 1 to jump on one foot. 2 (of animals) to make short jumps. *The rabbit hopped across the lawn and disappeared under the fence.*

hop *noun* a climbing plant used to flavour beer. *Hops grow well in the county of Kent.*

hope *verb* to want something to happen and be expecting it to happen. *I hope you will win first prize.* **hope** *noun* a feeling that something you want will happen. *She has no hope of passing her exams.*

hopeful *adjective* feeling confident and full of hope. **hopefulness** *noun.*

hopefully *adverb* if all goes well. *Hopefully I'll be home tomorrow.*

hopeless *adjective* 1 without hope. 2 very bad, useless. *He's hopeless at drawing, but very good at maths.*

horde *noun* a large crowd. *Hordes of tourists swarmed into the piazza.*

horizon *noun* the line in the distance where the sky and land or sea seem to meet.

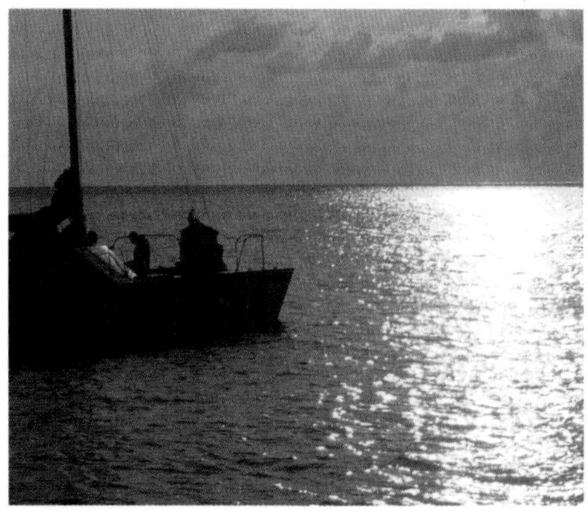

The Sun dropped behind the horizon, leaving a golden path across the sea.

horizontal *adjective* lying flat to the ground in line with the horizon, going from side to side and not up and down.

hormone *noun* a chemical substance produced in your body and that controls particular functions of the body. Some hormones, for example, control growth and others control digestion.

horn *noun* 1 one of the hard, bony growths on the heads of certain animals such as cows and goats. 2 a brass musical instrument that you play by blowing into it. 3 a device on a vehicle that makes a loud, warning sound. *The driver sounded her horn, but it was too late.*

horoscope *noun* a forecast of somebody's future, based on the position of the stars at the time of that person's birth.

AMAZING FACT

A horse's height is measured in hands, not feet. A hand is equal to ten centimetres.

horse-chestnut *noun* a large tree that has clusters of white flowers in the spring and shiny brown nuts called conkers in autumn.

horse-play *noun* rough and noisy play by children. *Too much horse-play!*

horseshoe *noun* a curved piece of iron nailed to a horse's hoof to protect it.

horticulture *noun* the science of gardening and the growing of fruit, flowers and vegetables. **horticultural** *adjective*.

hose *noun* a long rubber or plastic tube that water can go through. Firefighters use hoses for putting out fires.

hospice *noun* a hospital where people who are suffering from incurable diseases are looked after by doctors and nurses.

hospitable *adjective* friendly and generous to guests and strangers. *A most hospitable welcome.* **hospitality** *noun*.

hospital *noun* a place where people who are ill or injured are treated and looked after.

host *noun* 1 a person who invites guests and looks after them. 2 a person who introduces guest performers on a TV or radio show. 3 a very large number. *We now have a whole host of problems.*

hostage *noun* a person who is held prisoner by people who will not release her or him until their demands have been carried out.

hostel *noun* a place where people such as students or hitch-hikers can stay cheaply.

hostile *adjective* behaving in an unfriendly way. *The president was met by a hostile group of pensioners.*

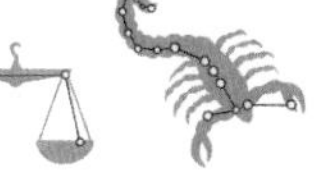

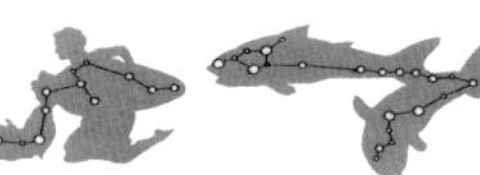

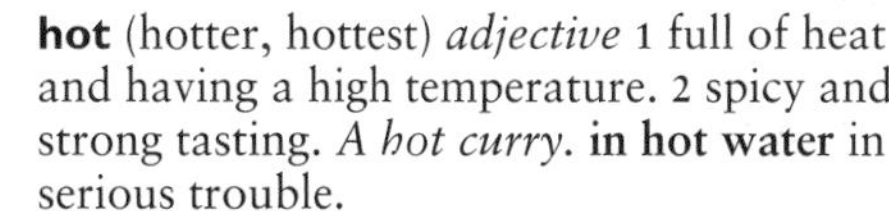

When you want to read your horoscope, you have to look up your sign of the zodiac in the newspaper.

horrible *adjective* terrible, very unpleasant. *What a horrible noise!*

horrid *adjective* horrible, unkind or hateful. *What a horrid person she is.*

horrify (horrifies, horrifying, horrified) *verb* to shock or fill with great horror and disgust. *I was horrified to hear about the earthquake in Armenia.*

horror *noun* a feeling of shock or fear. *He watched the snake slide towards him with horror.*

horse *noun* 1 a big four-legged animal with hooves, a long mane and a tail that can be used for riding or for pulling things like carts or ploughs. 2 a piece of equipment in a gym used for jumping over and doing exercises.

The horse's coat glowed from so much grooming.

hot (hotter, hottest) *adjective* 1 full of heat and having a high temperature. 2 spicy and strong tasting. *A hot curry.* **in hot water** in serious trouble.

hot dog *noun* a thin, hot sausage in a bread roll, a frankfurter. *Hot dogs with mustard and tomato ketchup.*

We ate delicious hot dogs at the fair.

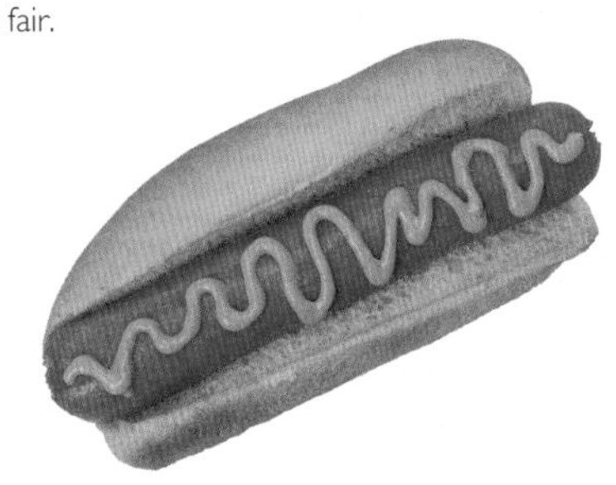

H

hotel *noun* a building with many bedrooms where people pay to stay and have meals.

hound *noun* a breed of dog that is used for hunting and racing. Foxhounds, deerhounds and bloodhounds are all different kinds of hound. **hound** *verb* to follow or harass somebody. *The princess was hounded by photographers wherever she went.*

hour *noun* a period of time consisting of 60 minutes. There are 24 hours in a day. **hourly** *adjective, adverb. The hourly rate for the job is not very impressive.*

house *noun* 1 a building where people live. 2 a building used for a particular purpose. *The White House.* **house** *verb* to provide a place for somebody to live.

A cross-section through this house shows all the rooms from cellar to attic.

household *noun* all the people who live together in one house.

householder *noun* the person who owns a house.

househusband *noun* a man who normally looks after the house for the family.

housekeeper *noun* a person who is paid to look after a house.

housewife *noun* a woman who normally looks after the house for the family.

housework *noun* cleaning, washing and cooking and other work that has to be done in a house.

hovel *noun* a small, filthy and broken house or hut. *The hermit lived in a hovel.*

hover *verb* 1 to remain in the air over one spot without moving. 2 to linger or to stay near one place.

hovercraft *noun* a boat that can fly over sea or land, lifted up on a cushion of air.

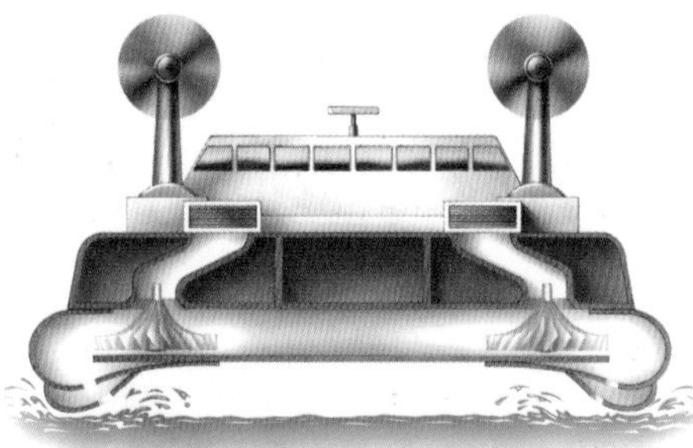

The hovercraft runs between Calais and Dover.

howl *verb* to make a long cry like an animal makes when it is in pain. **howl** *noun.*

howler *noun* a ridiculously funny mistake of fact. *A real howler in your essay.*

HQ *abbreviation* Headquarters.

hub *noun* the centre part of a wheel.

AMAZING FACT

'Hug' probably comes from an old Norse word that meant 'to console'.

SPELLING NOTE

Some howlers!
1 The practice of having only one wife is called monotony. 2 She's at her wick's end. 3 Calm down - don't get so historical. 4 Russia uses the acrylic alphabet.

huddle *verb* to crowd closely together. *They huddled under the tree to shelter from the rain.* **huddle** *noun.*

hue *noun* a colour or shade of colour.

hug (hugs, hugging, hugged) *verb* to put your arms around somebody and hold them tightly. **hug** *noun. He gave his cousin a big hug to welcome him home.*

huge *adjective* very big, enormous.

hull *noun* the body or frame of a ship.

hum (hums, humming, hummed) *verb* 1 to sing a tune with your mouth shut. 2 to make the low, continuous sound of an insect. **hum** *noun. The hum of the traffic.*

human *noun* human being. A man, woman or child. **human** *adjective* having natural and understandable feelings. *It's only human to cry when you are upset.*

humane *adjective* kind and gentle, not cruel. *Humane treatment of animals.*

humanity *noun* 1 all people. 2 being kind and humane.

humble *adjective* modest and not vain or self-important. *He's very clever, but in spite of his achievements, he's modest too.*

humid *adjective* damp and sometimes warm. *Humid weather.* **humidity** *noun.*

humiliate *verb* to make somebody feel ashamed or appear stupid to other people. **humiliation** *noun.*

hummingbird *noun* a very small, brightly coloured bird with a long slender beak. It hovers over flowers, beating its wings so fast that they make a humming sound.

The hummingbird sucked nectar from the flower.

humorous *adjective* funny. *A very humorous book.*

humour *noun* 1 what makes people laugh or smile. 2 a mood. *Is she in a good humour today?* **sense of humour** the ability to see what is funny and to laugh at it.

hump *noun* a small, round lump. A camel has a hump on its back.

hunch *verb* to lean forward with your shoulders raised and your head bent down.

hunch *noun* a feeling about something but not based on facts. *I had a hunch you would be on this train.*

hung past tense of hang.

H

Hungarian *noun* 1 a person who comes from Hungary. 2 the language spoken in Hungary. **Hungarian** *adjective. Hungarian dances.*

Hungary *noun* a country in eastern Europe.

The Hungarian flag has red, white and green stripes.

hunger *noun* a strong wish or need to eat. **hunger** *verb. She hungered for fame and fortune.*

hungry (hungrier, hungriest) *adjective* feeling hunger or the need for food. *The hungry dog hurried to eat all its supper.* **hungrily** *adverb.*

hunk *noun* a large piece or slice of something. *A hunk of bread.*

hunt *verb* 1 to look for and chase wild animals and then kill them for food or sport. 2 to search carefully for something. *I hunted everywhere for her phone number.* **hunt** *noun.*

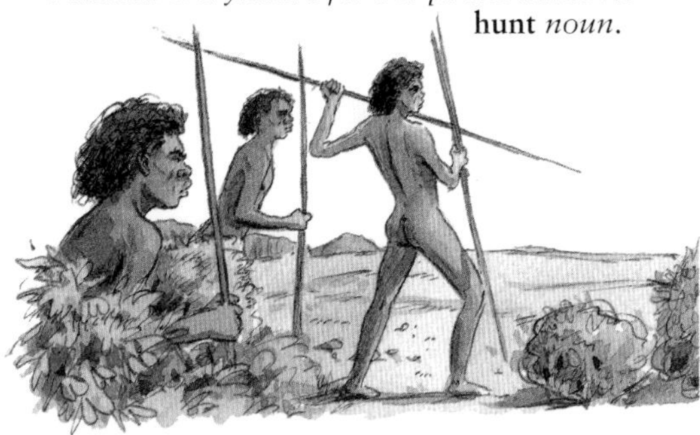

Australian aborigines hunt with spears and boomerangs.

hurdle *noun* 1 a small fence a runner jumps over in a race called hurdling. 2 a difficulty or problem to be overcome.

hurl *verb* to throw something with force as far as you can.

hurricane *noun* a violent storm with strong winds. *The hurricane tore off the roof.*

hurry (hurries, hurrying, hurried) *verb* to move quickly or do something as fast as you can. **hurry** *noun. Why are you in such a hurry, when we have all day to spare?*

hurt *verb* 1 to cause pain or harm to a person or an animal. *I didn't mean to hurt you.* 2 to feel pain. My bruised knee hurts.

husband *noun* a husband is the man that a woman has married.

hush *interjection* Be quiet! **hush** *noun* a sudden silence. *A hush fell over the concert hall and the music began.*

hush-hush *adjective* secret and in confidence. *A hush-hush story.*

husk *noun* the outer covering of some fruits and cereals. *Don't eat the husk.*

husky *adjective* (of a voice) low and rough.

husky *noun* a strong dog used to pull sledges in Arctic regions.

AMAZING FACT

Hyenas have very powerful jaws that they use to crush the bones of their prey. The spotted hyena has the most powerful jaws of any mammal.

WORD HISTORY

'Husband' comes from an Old Norse word meaning 'master of a household'. It was generally applied to all men who were masters of a household whether married or single.

hut *noun* a small house or temporary shelter, usually made of wood.

hutch *noun* a wooden cage for pet rabbits or other small animals.

hybrid *noun* a plant or animal produced from two different kinds (species) of plant or animal. A mule is a hybrid of a horse and a donkey. **hybrid** *adjective. A hybrid rose.*

hydrant *noun* an outdoor water tap to which a hose can be attached to supply water for fires or other emergencies.

hydroelectricity *noun* electricity produced by using water power, at a dam or a waterfall, for example.

hydrofoil *noun* a fast, light boat that skims over the surface of water on fin-like foils attached to its hull.

hydrogen *noun* hydrogen is the lightest of all gases and the simplest of all chemical elements. It combines with oxygen to make water.

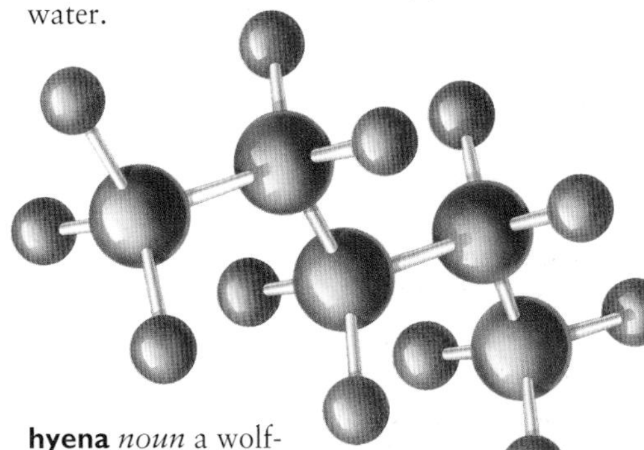

Hydrogen is the most abundant element in the whole universe.

hyena *noun* a wolf-like wild animal from India and Africa that hunts in packs and lives off the flesh of dead animals. The howl of a hyena is like hysterical laughter.

hygiene *noun* (say **hy**-jeen) the science and practice of cleanliness and good health. **hygienic** *adjective.*

hymn *noun* (say him) a religious song of praise. *We sang hymns in church.*

hype *noun* exaggerated and excessive publicity about something in order to sell it.

hyphen *noun* a mark (-) used in writing to join two parts of a divided word at the end of a line or to join two words to make a new word. *Stage-coach, self-defence, record-player.*

hypocrite *noun* a person who pretends to have feelings, good qualities or beliefs which he or she does not really have.

hypodermic needle *noun* a thin, hollow needle that is used to inject drugs into a vein. *Never re-use a hypodermic needle.*

hysteria *noun* uncontrollable excitement or distress. *She had a fit of hysteria.*

hysterical *adjective* extremely emotional and uncontrollably excited.

hysterics *plural noun* a fit of hysteria.

I

Ii

ice *noun* water that has frozen hard.

ice *verb* to spread icing sugar on a cake.

ice-age *noun* a time long ago when large areas of the Earth were covered with ice.

iceberg *noun* a huge lump of ice floating in the sea. Most of an iceberg is hidden under the surface of the sea. **the tip of the iceberg** only a small part of a problem.

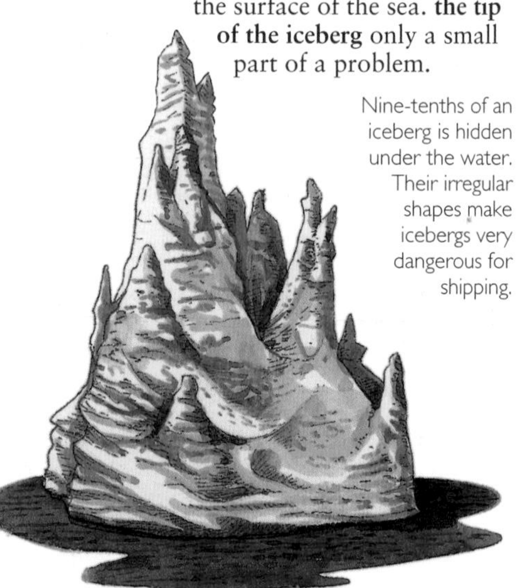

Nine-tenths of an iceberg is hidden under the water. Their irregular shapes make icebergs very dangerous for shipping.

ice-cream *noun* a smooth, sweet frozen food usually made with milk or cream.

ice cube *noun* a small block of ice used to cool drinks.

ice hockey a game played on ice by two teams in which the skaters try to score goals by hitting a rubber puck (ball) with a long stick. *Canada won the ice hockey match.*

Iceland *noun* a Scandinavian country in Europe.

The flag of Iceland shows a red on white cross, on a blue ground.

ice skate *noun* a boot with a metal blade on the bottom for sliding smoothly over the ice. **ice skate** *verb* to move on ice wearing ice skates.

icicle *noun* a long, pointed stick of ice formed by water freezing as it drops.

WORD HISTORY

The shape of the letter I comes from an ancient Egyptian symbol of a hand. The Romans gave the letter its present shape.

SPELLING NOTE

Try not to confuse 'idle', a lazy person, with 'idol', a god.

icing *noun* a mixture of sugar and water that is spread on cakes to decorate them.

icon *noun* 1 a picture of Jesus Christ or a saint painted on wood seen in many Greek or Russian Christian (orthodox) churches. 2 a small picture on a computer screen representing a program and which can be selected by clicking the mouse.

icy (icier, iciest) *adjective* 1 very cold. *Icy weather.* 2 covered in ice. *Icy roads.*

idea *noun* 1 a thought or picture in your mind. 2 a plan. *She had the idea of becoming a vet.* 3 purpose. *The idea of the game is to score as many goals as possible.*

ideal *adjective* perfect or very suitable. *He's an ideal father.* **ideal** *noun* the best possible person, thing, situation or example.

identical *adjective* exactly the same in every way. *Identical twins.*

identify (identifies, identifying, identified) *verb* to recognize somebody or something and be able to name them. *The police identified the body.* **identification** *noun.*

identity *noun* a person's distinguishing characteristics that make them individual.

idiom *noun* an expression or special way of saying something in which the words have a meaning different from what they appear to have. 'To drop off' means to fall asleep; and 'heads will roll' means that some people will get into trouble.

idiot *noun* a very stupid person. **idiotic** *adjective. What an idiotic idea.*

idle *adjective* 1 lazy and work-shy. **idleness** *noun.* 2 not working. *During the strike the machines were left idle.* 3 worthless or not really meant. *Idle threats.*

idol *noun* 1 something, such as a statue, that is worshipped as a god. 2 a famous person who is greatly admired. *A pop idol.*

This statue of Zeus, the Greek king of the gods, was probably worshipped as an idol.

igloo *noun* a house made out of blocks of snow and ice in the shape of a dome by the Inuits of the Arctic region.

ignite *verb* to set fire to or to catch fire.

ignition *noun* a device in a motor vehicle that starts the engine working by igniting the fuel. *Turn the key to start the ignition.*

ignorant *adjective* knowing very little about something, badly educated. *He's ignorant about computers.* **ignorance** *noun.*

ignore *verb* to take no notice of somebody or something, to disregard. *She totally ignored me when I asked her a question.*

il- *prefix* used before many words beginning with l to indicate against or negation. *illiterate* (not literate or able to read), *illegal* (against the law).

ill (worse, worst) *adjective* 1 not in good health, unwell. **illness** *noun.* 2 bad or harmful. *The ill effects of smoking.* **ill at ease** feeling unhappy and uncomfortable with other people. **ill disposed** unfriendly. **ill-founded** without good reasons. *Ill-founded suspicions.* **ill-timed** happening at a bad time. **ill-treat** to treat cruelly.

illegal *adjective* not allowed by the law. *It is illegal to drive at over 70 mph.*

illegible *adjective* handwriting that is so poor that it is difficult or impossible to read.

illiterate *adjective* unable to read or write. **illiteracy** *noun.*

illogical *adjective* not obeying logic and therefore not making sense.

illness *noun* a disease such as flu or measles that makes people unwell.

illuminate *verb* 1 to light up or shine a light on something. *The castle is illuminated at night.* **illuminations** *plural noun. The streets are decorated with Christmas illuminations.* **illuminating** *adjective. An illuminating idea.* 2 to decorate a book such as a Bible with gold and coloured letters and pictures. **illumination** *noun.*

In the Middle Ages, monks spent a lot of time copying texts and illuminating the manuscripts with coloured painting.

DID YOU KNOW

The word 'illustrate' had the same meaning as 'illuminate' – to throw light upon. The word had nothing to do with pictures until the 17th century.

illusion *noun* a false idea or image of something that is really not there. *An optical illusion.*

Sometimes when people have been travelling for a long time in the desert, they see a mirage. This is an illusion, perhaps brought about by exhaustion, and also the sand in the air seen though a heat haze. This mirage is of a camel at an oasis, something that desert travellers would dearly love to see.

im- *prefix* like in- , used before certain words beginning with b, m and p and meaning against, negation or without. *immeasurable* (too great to be measured). *immature* (not mature).

image *noun* 1 a picture or statue. 2 any picture in a book, film, or on television. 3 your reflection in a mirror. 4 a picture of something in your mind. 5 a very close likeness. *He is the image of his twin brother.* 6 a person's image is the general opinion that others have of them.

imagery *noun* the descriptive words used by writers to create pictures in the minds of readers. *Beautiful imagery.*

imaginary *noun* not real but existing only in the mind. Goblins and elves are imaginary creatures.

This imaginary creature is a goblin. He lives underneath the toadstool.

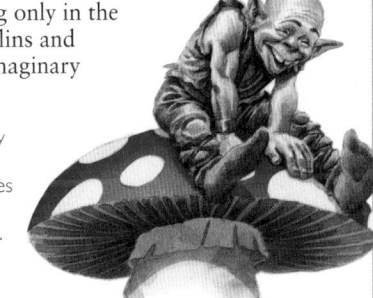

imagination *noun* 1 the ability to create pictures in the mind. *Use your imagination and write a story about space travel.* 2 the ability to create new ideas.

imaginative *adjective* having a lot of imagination. *Imaginative ideas.*

imagine *verb* 1 to have a picture of something in your mind. *Can you imagine life without cars?* 2 to think you see or hear things that are not really there. *You're just imagining there's a ghost under your bed.*

imitate *verb* to copy or behave like somebody or something. *She can imitate her mother's voice perfectly.* **imitation** *noun. He does a good imitation of a dog barking.*

immature *adjective* 1 not fully grown or developed, unripe. 2 behaving childishly and not like an adult. **immaturity** *noun.*

I

immediately *adverb* at once and without delay. **immediately** *conjunction* as soon as. *I knew I'd get on with her immediately I met her.* **immediate** *adjective.*

immense *adjective* very big. *The Sahara is an immense desert in North Africa.* **immensity** *noun.*

immerse *verb* to put something into a liquid until it is completely covered. **immerse yourself in** to give all your attention to something.

Pat immersed the dirty plate in the soapy water and began to wash up.

immigrant *noun* somebody who immigrates to and comes to settle in a country. **immigration** *noun.*

immigrate *verb* to come to live and settle in a country. *They immigrated quite recently.*

imminent *adjective* Something that is imminent is expected to happen very soon. *The forecast says that snow is imminent.*

immobile *adjective* not moving or able to move. **immobility** *noun.* **immobilize** *verb* to make immobile and unable to move. *All traffic has been immobilized by the snow.*

immoral *adjective* behaving in a way that is considered wrong. **immorality** *noun.*

immortal *adjective* never dying but living and lasting for ever.

immune *adjective* protected against a disease and so unable to catch it. **immunity** *noun.* **immunize** *verb* to give somebody an injection so that they cannot catch a disease.

imp *noun* a mischievous little creature in fairy stories.

The mischievous imp was exhausted after all the damage he had done in the shoe shop.

impact *noun* 1 the force of one object colliding with another. 2 the strong effect or impresssion that something has. *Computers have had a great impact on the way we learn, both at home and at school.*

AMAZING FACT

The impala is an extremely fast animal, speed is its main defence. It can also leap as far as ten metres, which it does to escape predators, but also, it seems, because it just enjoys leaping!

SPELLING NOTE

Try not to confuse 'immigrate' (to come from another country) with 'emigrate' (to go to another country).

impala *noun* a small African antelope that lives in great herds.

The impala is a graceful creature that lives in herds in the South African veld.

impartial *adjective* fair and not favouring one person or side more than another. **impartiality** *noun.*

impassable *noun* not able to be passed through or across. *Heavy snowstorms made the mountain roads impassable.*

impatient *adjective* unwilling to wait and easily annoyed. **impatience** *noun.*

impede *verb* to get in the way of somebody or something and so slow down progress.

impenetrable *adjective* 1 impossible to get through. *An impenetrable forest.* 2 impossible to understand. *He posed us an impenetrable problem.*

imperfect *adjective* 1 not perfect and having some fault. **imperfection** *noun.* 2 a verb tense indicating a repeated or incomplete action in the past. *She was sitting in a chair.*

imperial *adjective* 1 of or having to do with an empire or an emperor or empress. 2 The imperial system is a traditional non-metric British system of weights and measures using inches, feet, yards and miles, ounces pounds and hundredweight, and pints and gallons.

impersonal *adjective* unfriendly and showing no personal feelings or warmth. *Her manner was cold and impersonal.*

impersonate *verb* to pretend to be somebody else by copying their behaviour. **impersonation** *noun.*

impertinent *adjective* rude and impudent, especially to somebody in authority.

impetuous *adjective* an impetuous person acts suddenly and without thinking first.

implement *noun* a tool or instrument. *Garden implements.*

The gardening tools were useful implements.

imply (implies, implying, implied) *verb* to suggest or hint at something without actually saying it directly. *By questioning everything he said, she implied that he was lying.* **implication** *noun*.

impolite *adjective* rude and bad-mannered.

import *verb* (say im-**port**) to buy goods from another country to sell in your own country. **import** *noun* (say **im**-port). *One of our main imports is cloth.* The opposite of import is export.

Coffee beans are imported to Europe from South America and Africa.

important *adjective* 1 of great interest and which matters a lot. *Your birthday is an important day for you.* 2 having influence and power. *An important writer.*

imposing *adjective* large and making a great impression. *An imposing palace.*

impossible *adjective* not possible, something that cannot be done or happen.

impostor *noun* someone who pretends to be somebody else in order to deceive and get things they want.

impracticable *adjective* not possible to use or put into practice. *An impracticable idea.*

impractical *adjective* not useful and lacking common sense. *He's quite impractical and couldn't boil an egg.*

impress *verb* to cause somebody's admiration or respect. *I was impressed by his knowledge.* **impressive** *adjective*.

impression *noun* 1 the way something appears to you and the effect it has on you. *His kindness made a great impression on us.* 2 a vague idea or belief. *I have the impression I've been here before.* 3 a mark made by something pressing on to a surface. *Our cats, Onion and Plumage, left the impressions of their paws in the wet concrete.* 4. an impersonation or attempt at copying how somebody talks and behaves, usually in order to entertain people.

The cat left the impression of her feet in the wet concrete.

impressionable *adjective* very easily influenced or impressed by others. *Some young people are very impressionable.*

WORD BUILDER

You can make many words negative by adding the prefix 'in–' to certain words, as in 'incurable', 'informal'. It is often only necessary to look up the definition of a word to discover its negative meaning.

AMAZING FACT

The system of weights and measures used in the United States is called the English system and is based on the system that was used in Britain until it was officially replaced by the metric system. In 1975, Congress passed the Metric Conversion Act, which called for a voluntary changeover to metric.

imprison *verb* to put somebody in prison. **imprisonment** *noun*. *His punishment was imprisonment.*

improve *verb* to become better or to make something better. *Her health is improving.* **improvement** *noun*.

improvise *verb* 1 to do something as you go along without planning or rehearsing beforehand. *She had lost her notes and had to improvise the speech.* 2 to make something quickly with whatever materials are available. *We improvised a table from cardboard boxes.* **improvisation** *noun*.

impudent *noun* rude and showing no respect, insolent. **impudence** *noun*.

in- *prefix* meaning 'not' when added to the beginning of certain words. *inadequate* (not adequate), *inactive* (not active), *inconsistent* (not consistent).

inarticulate *adjective* unable to express yourself well when speaking.

inaudible *adjective* not loud enough to be heard clearly **inaudibility** *noun*.

inborn *adjective* natural and present in a person or animal from birth. *Birds have an inborn ability to build nests.*

Birds have an inborn capacity to build nests.

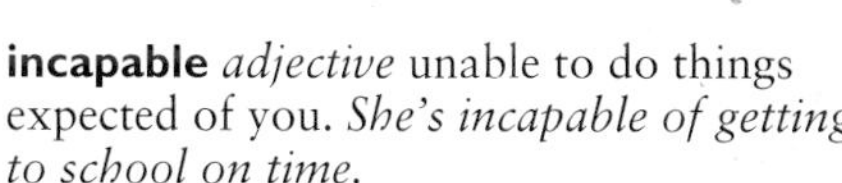

incapable *adjective* unable to do things expected of you. *She's incapable of getting to school on time.*

incentive *noun* something that encourages you to do something. *He was promised a bike as an incentive to work hard.*

incessant *noun* going on and on and never stopping. *The incessant noise of the traffic.*

inch *noun* a measurement of length, equal to 2.55 centimetres. There are 12 inches in a foot. **inch by inch** very slowly.

incident *noun* a single event or happening.

incidentally *adverb* by the way. *Incidentally, I haven't eaten all day, so I'm ravenously hungry.*

incinerator *noun* a container for burning rubbish. *Please put all these papers straight in the incinerator.*

incision *noun* a cut into a patient's body made by a surgeon during an operation.

incite *verb* to stir up and encourage people to do something, usually bad and violent. *The leader incited the crowd to riot, and the troops retalliated with tear gas and batons.*

inclination *noun* a tendency or slight preference to do something. *My inclination is to take the right-hand turning.*

incline *verb* 1 to lean or slope towards something, to bend. 2 to have a tendency or preference for doing something. *He's inclined to be a bit slow in the morning.* **incline** *noun* a slope.

include *verb* to consider or count something as a part of a whole or a group of other things. **inclusion** *noun.*

including *preposition* forming part of a larger group. *Everybody went on holiday, including our dog and cat.*

inclusive *adjective* including everything. *The price is inclusive of tax.*

incoherent *adjective* speaking in a rambling way that is not easy to follow or understand. **incoherence** *noun.*

income *noun* the money a person regularly earns. *She has an income of £30,000 a year.* **income tax** a tax that is charged on a person's income.

incompetent *adjective* lacking the ability to do a job well. **incompetence** *noun.*

incomplete *adjective* unfinished, not complete. *An incomplete set of encyclopedias was delivered to the school.*

When Jane left the room, the puzzle was still incomplete.

incongruous *adjective* strange and out of place. *A skyscraper would look incongruous in a small village.*

inconsiderate *noun* thoughtless and not considering the feelings of others.

inconspicuous *adjective* small and not easily noticeable.

incorporate *verb* to include something and make a part of the whole. *The sports wing incorporates a gym and a swimming pool.*

incorrect *adjective* wrong. *The man always seemed to give the incorrect answer.*

increase *verb* (say in-**krees**) to make bigger or to become bigger. **increase** *noun* (**in**-krees) *A sharp increase in prices.*

A microscope gives an increased ability to examine the structure of a leaf.

AMAZING FACT

The prefixes 'il-', 'im-', 'in-' and 'ir-' are all used to form the negative of various words (illogical, improbable, indigestible, irresponsible), but they are not interchangeable. Check the spelling in your dictionary if you're not sure which prefix to use.

DID YOU KNOW

'Bungalow', 'khaki', 'polo', 'jungle' and 'shampoo' are all words that come from India.

incredible *adjective* 1 difficult or impossible to believe. *An incredible adventure story.* 2 amazing, very good. *An incredible film.*

incriminate *verb* to show that somebody is guilty of a crime.

incubator *noun* 1 a container in which premature and weak babies are kept alive and safe until they are strong. 2 a heated container for keeping eggs warm until the chicks hatch. **incubate** *verb* to keep eggs warm until they hatch.

Stephanie put the eggs in the incubator to hatch.

incurable *adjective* not able to be cured or made better. *An incurable disease.*

indecent *adjective* shockingly rude and offensive. **indecency** *noun.*

indefinite *adjective* vague, not fixed or limited. *He's gone away to Outer Mongolia for an indefinite time.* **indefinite article** the adjectives 'a' and 'an'.

independent *adjective* free, not controlled by or needing help from others. *Most colonies have become independent.* **independence** *noun.*

index *noun* a section at the end of some books giving an alphabetical list and page number of all the subjects mentioned in the book. *The index in this book is very useful.*

India *noun* a country in South Asia.

India is the seventh largest country in the world and has the second largest number of people.

Indian *noun* 1 a person who comes from India. 2 a Native American. **Indian** *adjective. An Indian temple.*

indicate *verb* 1 to show or point out something. *He indicated on the map where the village is.* 2 to be a sign of. *Dark clouds indicate rain.* 3 to show which way you are turning, to signal. *Indicate left.* **indication** *noun. He gave no indication of his plight.*

indicator *noun* a flashing light on a motor vehicle that shows other drivers which way you are going to turn.

indifferent *adjective* 1 having no feelings and not caring. *She is indifferent to what people think of her.* 2 not very good. *An indifferent meal.* **indifference** *noun.*

indigestion *noun* pain you get in your stomach when you have eaten too much and have difficulty in digesting your food. **indigestible** *adjective.*

indirect *adjective* not direct or straightforward. *An indirect route.*

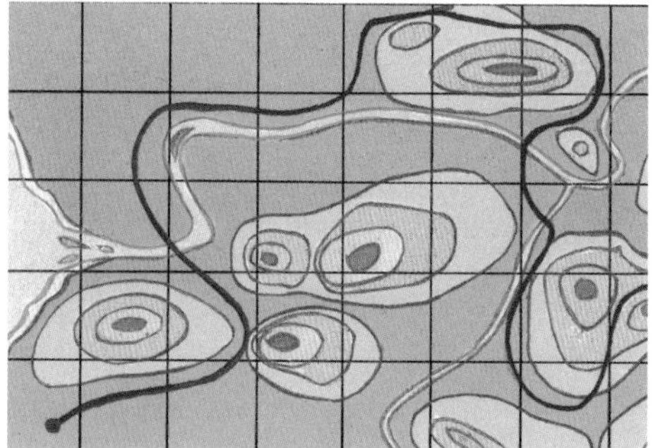

Because of the mountainous landscape, the road had to take an indirect route across country.

individual *adjective* 1 relating to one person or thing and not to a group. *She has individual tennis coaching from the champion.* 2 having an unusual quality or way of behaving. *He has an individual way of walking.* **individual** *noun* a single person. **individually** *adjective* separately.

individuality *noun* a quality that makes a person or thing different and stand out from others. *Striking for its individuality.*

Indonesia *noun* a country in Southeast Asia, made up of Sumatra, Java and many other islands.

indulge *verb* 1 If you indulge in something you take great pleasure in it, even if it is bad for you. 2 To indulge somebody is to let them have or do what they want, to spoil them. **indulgence** *noun.* **indulgent** *adjective. Indulgent grandparents.*

industrial *adjective* concerning industry and factories. *The industrial regions of Italy.* **Industrial Revolution** the name given to the widespread use of machines in factories during the 18th and 19th centuries, particularly in Britain.

industrialist *noun* a person who owns an industry.

industrious *adjective* hardworking.

industry *noun* 1 work and the making of things in factories. 2 a particular business or branch of industry. *The car industry.* 3 hard work.

inefficient *adjective* not working well and wasting time or energy.

AMAZING FACT

'Infantry' refers to soldiers who fight on foot, 'cavalry' used to refer to soldiers who fought on horseback but now it is more likely to mean soldiers who fight from vehicles.

GRAMMAR NOTE

Indirect speech is reported speech and not the exact words of the speaker. 'He said he was happy to be home,' is indirect speech. 'I am happy to be home,' is direct speech.

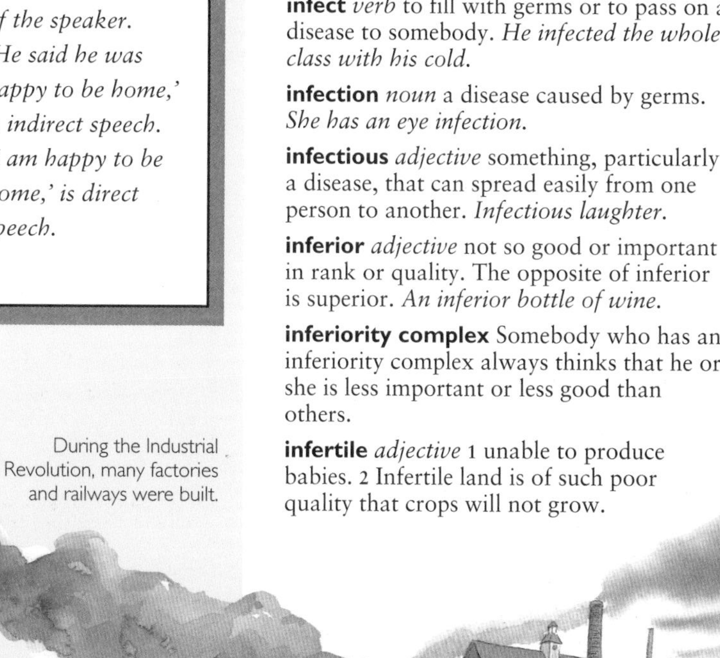

During the Industrial Revolution, many factories and railways were built.

inert *adjective* without power and unable to move. **inertia** *noun* lack of energy.

inevitable *adjective* sure to happen or impossible to stop. **inevitability** *noun.*

infamous *adjective* well known or famous for being bad. *An infamous thief.*

infant *noun* a very young child. **infancy** *noun* the time of being an infant.

infantry *noun* soldiers who fight on foot.

Soldiers in the infantry have to be very fit, because they march long distances carrying heavy equipment.

infatuated *adjective* to have such a strong love for somebody that you cannot think sensibly about them. **infatuation** *noun.*

infect *verb* to fill with germs or to pass on a disease to somebody. *He infected the whole class with his cold.*

infection *noun* a disease caused by germs. *She has an eye infection.*

infectious *adjective* something, particularly a disease, that can spread easily from one person to another. *Infectious laughter.*

inferior *adjective* not so good or important in rank or quality. The opposite of inferior is superior. *An inferior bottle of wine.*

inferiority complex Somebody who has an inferiority complex always thinks that he or she is less important or less good than others.

infertile *adjective* 1 unable to produce babies. 2 Infertile land is of such poor quality that crops will not grow.

infested *adjective* full of pests such as insects or rats. *The house was infested with a plague of fleas.*

infinite *adjective* endless and without limits, so great that it cannot be measured or imagined. *I loved him for his infinite kindness towards animals.* **infinity** *noun.*

infinitive *adjective* the basic form of a verb, having 'to' in front of it. *To go, to dream, to plan, to talk, to visit.*

inflammable *adjective* catching fire easily.

inflate *verb* to make something expand by filling it with air or gas. *They inflated the balloons with a pump.*

Jim inflated the raft on which he hoped to shoot the rapids.

inflation *noun* a rise in prices.

inflexible *adjective* unable to bend or change in any way. *Inflexible rules.*

inflict *verb* to make somebody suffer pain or something unpleasant.

influence *noun* 1 the power you have to make somebody do something or cause something to happen. 2 a person who has such power. *His uncle was a great influence on his decision to become an actor.* **influence** *verb.* **influential** *adjective.*

influenza or flu *noun* an infectious disease that gives you headache, fever and aching muscles. *I was in bed for a week with flu.*

inform *verb* to tell somebody about something. *Please keep me informed.*

informal *adjective* 1 friendly and relaxed, not following rules. *Informal clothes.* 2 used in ordinary conversation or writing. 'Bangers and mash' is an informal way of saying 'sausages and mashed potatoes'. **informality** *noun.*

information *noun* all the facts or knowledge about something. *Can you give me any information about the crash?*

information technology the use of computers to store, arrange and send out information.

informative *adjective* giving useful or helpful facts. *An informative programme about endangered animals.*

ingenious *adjective* clever and imaginative. *An ingenious invention.* **ingenuity** *noun.*

SPELLING NOTE

The opposite word for 'inflate' is 'deflate', and the opposite word for 'inhale' is 'exhale'.

AMAZING FACT

Influenza is a very common disease and is not normally serious. But in 1918–19, a flu epidemic killed about 20 million people around the world.

ingot *noun* a lump of metal, usually in the shape of a brick. *The Queen was presented with a gold ingot.*

Ingots are pieces of cast metal moulded into a form useful for transport and storage.

ingredient *noun* any one of a number of things that go into a mixture from which something is made, particularly in cooking. *Flour, eggs and milk are ingredients of the batter used for making pancakes.*

inhabit *verb* to live in a place. *The island is not inhabited.*

inhabitant *noun* the people or animals that live in a place or country. *The inhabitants of the mental asylum were treated kindly.*

inhale *verb* to breathe in. *She inhaled deeply the fresh sea air.*

inhaler *noun* a container that people who suffer from diseases such as asthma use to breathe in medicine. *The doctor gave him an inhaler to ease his breathing.*

inherit *verb* 1 to receive something such as money or property from somebody who has died. *She inherited the house from her aunt.* 2 to have the same qualities or characteristics as your parents or ancestors. *He has inherited his father's bad temper!* **inheritance** *noun.*

inhuman *adjective* cruel, showing no kindness or pity. **inhumanity** *noun.*

initial *noun* (say in-**ish**-ul) the first letter of a word or name. *Robin Ashe's initials are R.A.* **initial** *adjective* first or at the beginning. *My initial reaction is good.*

initiative *noun* the ability to do things on your own and to lead the way. *Marcus showed a lot of initiative and got the job done in extra quick time.*

inject *verb* to use a hollow needle to put liquid medicine into somebody's body. **injection** *noun. Billy didn't like having injections at the dentist's.*

The doctor used a syringe to inject the patient.

injure *verb* to hurt or damage a part of a person's or an animal's body. *She injured her arm when she fell.* **injury** *noun.*

ink *noun* a coloured liquid used for writing with a pen or for printing.

Margaret prefers to write with a fountain pen and blue or black ink.

inkling *noun* a slight idea, a hint. *She had no inkling I'd be coming.*

inland *adjective* away from the sea and towards the middle of a country.

inn *noun* a small hotel or pub, usually in the country.

inner *adjective* on the inside and near the middle. *The inner tube of a bicycle tyre.*

innocent *adjective* 1 without blame or guilt. *The prisoner was innocent.* 2 harmless. *Innocent fun.* **innocence** *noun.*

innovation *noun* something that is completely new. A new invention or way of doing things. *Computers were a major innovation in schools and businesses.*

innumerable *adjective* too many to be counted. *Innumerable stars in the sky.*

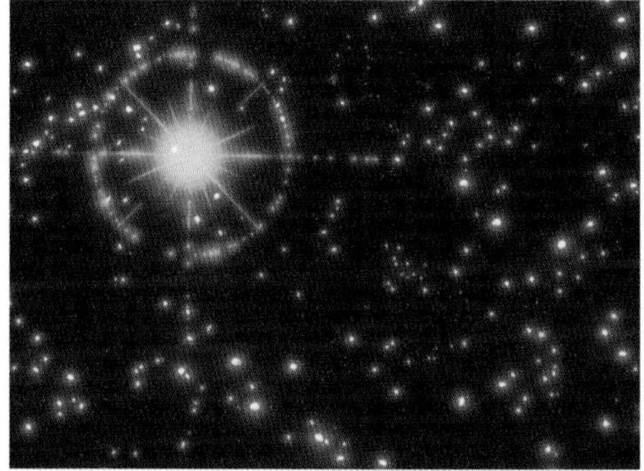

On a clear night, you can see innumerable stars in the sky.

inoculate *verb* to protect somebody from a disease by injecting them with a weak form of the disease. **inoculation** *noun.*

input *noun* information that you put into a computer. **input** *verb.*

inquest *noun* an official inquiry to find out why somebody suddenly died.

inquire *verb* to ask questions to find out about something. *Madge inquired about the times of trains.*

inquiry *noun* 1 a question. 2 a detailed and official investigation. *There was an inquiry into the cause of the fire.*

inquisitive *noun* eager to find out about things, always asking questions.

SPELLING NOTE

Note that 'inoculate' has only one 'n' and one 'l'. Also note that 'inquire' and 'inquiry' can be spelled 'enquire', 'enquiry'.

AMAZING FACT

Edward Jenner first inoculated a person in 1796. He injected a boy with cowpox as a vaccine against smallpox.

insanitary *adjective* unclean and likely to harm people's health by causing disease.

inscribe *verb* to write or carve words on to the hard surface of something.

inscription *noun* words written or carved on something.

insect *noun* a small animal with six legs, no backbone, and usually with wings. An insect has three parts to its body. Beetles, butterflies and flies are insects.

Butterflies are some of the world's most beautiful insects.

insecticide *noun* a poison that is used to kill insects that are pests.

insert *verb* to put something inside something else.

inside *noun* the interior and centre part of something, near the middle. *The inside of my mouth is sore.* **inside** *preposition. The owl lives with its young family inside the hollow tree.* **inside** *adverb. Come inside a minute.* **inside out** the inside of a piece of clothing turned to the outside. The opposite of inside is outside.

insight *noun* having a clear understanding of something. *An insight into his behaviour.*

insincere *adjective* not honest and pretending to have feelings about something. *He said he liked me but I knew he was insincere.*

insipid *adjective* without taste, dull. *An insipid cup of tea.*

insist *verb* to demand and be very firm in asking or doing something. *He insisted on buying me an ice cream.* **insistent** *adjective.*

insolent *adjective* rude and insulting. *Insolent behaviour.* **insolence** *noun.*

insoluble *adjective* 1 If something is insoluble, it will not dissolve. 2 A problem that is insoluble cannot be solved.

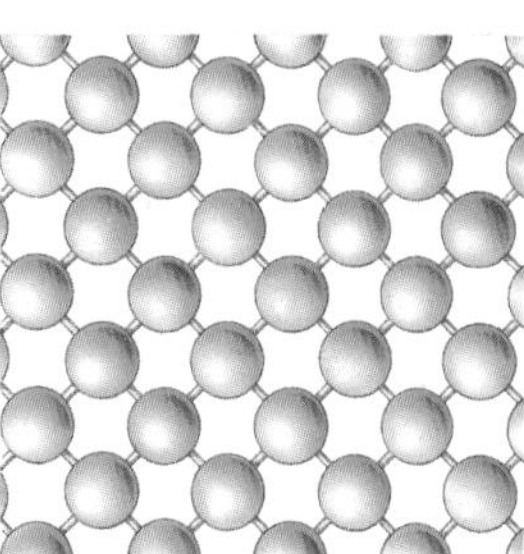

The molecules of an insoluble solid are joined together in a regular pattern.

insomnia *noun* sleeplessness or difficulty in going to sleep.

inspect *verb* to look at every part of something very carefully, to check. **inspection** *noun.*

inspire *verb* to influence somebody and encourage them to feel confident and enthusiastic about what they are doing. *The teacher inspired me to practise harder.* **inspiration** *noun.* **inspiring** *adjective.*

install *verb* 1 to put something in a place ready to be used. *He installed a new cooker.* 2 to give somebody an important position. *She was ceremonially installed as mayor.*

instalment *noun* 1 one of the parts into which something is divided. An episode. *An instalment of the story was read every evening on the radio.* 2 one of a series of regular payments for something.

instant *noun* a very short time. *He paused for an instant.* **instant** *adjective* 1 happening straight away. *An instant success.* 2 able to be prepared very quickly. *Instant soup.*

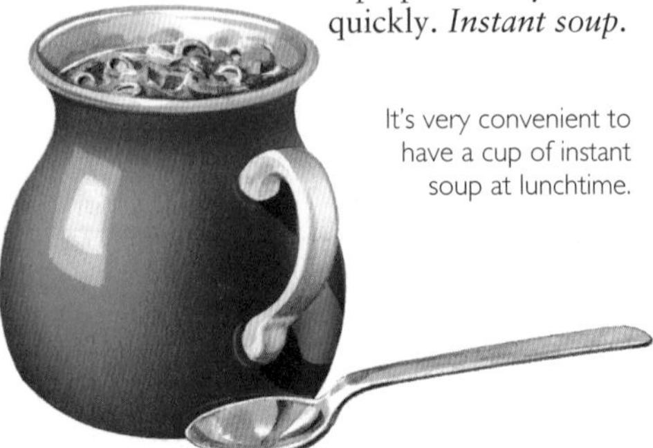

It's very convenient to have a cup of instant soup at lunchtime.

instead *adverb* in place of something or somebody. *Can I have milk instead of cream in my coffee?*

instinct *noun* behaviour that is natural and does not have to be thought about or learnt. *Birds build their nests by instinct.* **instinctive** *adjective. Instinctive behaviour.*

institute *noun* an organization that is established for a particular purpose. *A medical research institute.* **institute** *verb* to start something. *To institute reforms.*

institution *noun* 1 a large or important organization. *Hospitals, prisons, universities and other institutions.* 2 an established custom, habit or tradition. *Putting up decorations at Christmas is an institution.*

instruct *verb* 1 to teach or tell somebody how to do something. 2 to tell somebody what to do. *The teacher instructed the boys to wait until the bell rang.* **instruction** *noun.*

instructions *plural noun* directions or words that tell you how to do something. *Read the instructions carefully before connecting the computer.*

instructive *adjective* giving helpful information. *An instructive talk.*

AMAZING FACT

'Inspire' comes from a word that originally meant 'breathe in'.

SPELLING NOTE

Try not to confuse 'intense', meaning 'extreme' or 'very strong', as in 'intense heat' with 'intensive', meaning 'thorough' or 'concentrated', as in 'intensive language course'.

instructor *noun* a person who instructs you to do something. *A driving instructor.*

instrument *noun* 1 a device or tool you use to help you with your work. *Scientific instruments.* 2 A musical instrument is an object such as a piano or a guitar that you play to make music.

insulate *verb* to cover something with a material that will not let heat or electricity escape from it. *Electric wires are insulated with rubber or plastic.* **insulation** *noun.*

Safety demands that electric wires should be fully insulated.

insult *verb* (say in-**sult**) to upset somebody by saying something rude to them or behaving in a bad way. **insult** *noun* (say **in**-sult). *It was an insult to my intelligence.*

insurance *noun* small sums of money (premiums) you pay regularly to an organization (an insurance company) that agrees to protect you and give you a large amount of money to replace something of yours that has been stolen or damaged, or to pay medical bills if you injure yourself or become ill etc.

intact *adjective* not damaged, complete and not changed. *My feelings for her remain intact, despite the way she has behaved.*

intake *noun* 1 the number of people taken in. *A high intake of students.* 2 the process of taking something in. *The news was greeted by a sharp intake of breath.*

integrate *verb* 1 to combine people, often of different races, into one community. 2 to fit different parts together. **integration** *noun.*

integrity *noun* complete honesty and trustworthiness. *A woman of integrity.*

intelligent *adjective* clever and able to learn and understand things quickly and easily. **intelligence** *noun.*

Chimpanzees are intelligent creatures that can be taught many human skills.

intend *verb* to plan or have in mind to do something. *She intends to visit her sister.*

intense *adjective* 1 very strong or great. *Intense cold.* 2 very serious and with strong feelings. *He gets very intense about his work.* **intensity** *noun.*

intensive *adjective* 1 very thorough. *Intensive investigations.* 2 concentrated. *The patient is in intensive care.*

intention *noun* what you intend or plan to do. *Please state your intentions clearly.*

intentional *adjective* intended or done on purpose. *Intentional damage.*

inter- *prefix* among or between. *Interplanetary travel.*

interact *verb* to have an effect on one another. *All the chemicals in this experiment interact with one another.*

interaction *noun* the action or influence of people or things on one another.

interactive *adjective* (in computers) the exchange of information between a computer and the user.

intercept *verb* to stop somebody or something that is moving from one place to another. *He intercepted the ball with a fine catch.*

The player cleverly intercepted the ball and passed it back to her own team.

interest *verb* to want to learn or find out more about something. **interest** *noun* 1 *He has a great interest in geology.* 2 extra money you pay to a bank etc. for money you have borrowed.

interested *adjective* wanting to find out or learn more about something.

interesting *adjective* If something is interesting you want to find out more about it. *Archaeology is a very interesting subject.*

interface *noun* in computing, a connection that allows two pieces of equipment to be operated together.

interfere *verb* to meddle or take part in something that has nothing to do with you. **interference** *noun.*

interior *noun* the inside part of something. **interior** *adjective. Interior design.*

interjection *noun* a word or phrase used to express surprise, pain etc. *'Ouch! It hurts.'*

The plan of the new house showed internal features, such as the staircase.

AMAZING FACT

Be careful not to confuse the two prefixes 'inter-' meaning 'between' and 'intra-' meaning 'within'. Think of the Internet, a system of connected computers around the world, and 'intranet' which is a system of connected computers, usually within a company.

DID YOU KNOW

'Interfere' was once used about horses and referred to when a horse struck its fetlock with the hoof of the opposite foot. It then came to mean 'to collide' and later 'to intervene'.

internal *adjective* relating to the inside of something or somebody. *The internal organs of the body.*

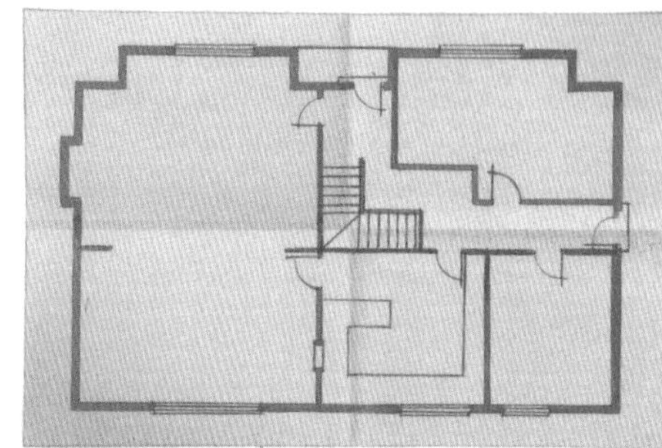

international *adjective* concerning several nations or countries. *An international peace-keeping force flew into the country.*

interpret *verb* 1 to translate or put the words of one language into another. 2 to decide or explain what something means. *He interpreted her nod as meaning 'yes'.* **interpretation** *noun.*

interpreter *noun* a person who translates from one language into another.

interrupt *verb* 1 to stop somebody while they are talking or doing something. *I'm reading, so don't interrupt me.* 2 to disturb or stop something happening for a short time. *Thunder interrupted the lesson.* **interruption** *noun.*

interval *noun* 1 a period of time between two dates or events. 2 a short break in a play or concert. **at intervals** happening sometimes but not regularly.

intervene *verb* to become involved in or join in something such as a quarrel in order to stop it happening. **intervention** *noun.*

intervening *adjective* the time between two events. *The intervening years.*

interview *noun* a meeting at which a person is asked questions to see if he or she is suitable for a job. A meeting at which things are discussed. **interview** *verb. He was interviewed for the job.*

intestines *plural noun* the long tube that food passes through after it has left our stomach.

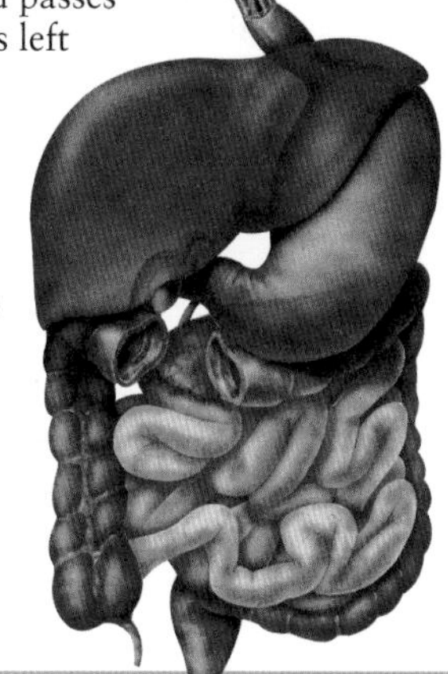

The intestines are coiled inside the abdomen.

intimate *adjective* (say **in**-tim-at) 1 very friendly and close. *Intimate relations.* 2 personal and private. *Intimate details.*

intimidate *verb* to frighten somebody violently to make them do something you want, to threaten. **intimidation** *noun.*

intolerant *adjective* unable to put up with people with ideas or beliefs that are different from yours. **intolerance** *noun.*

intoxicated *adjective* having drunk too much alcohol. *Peter was intoxicated.*

intrepid *adjective* brave and bold, without fear. *Intrepid astronauts.*

intricate *adjective* complicated and hard to follow, detailed. *An intricate pattern.*

The silk scarf was designed with an intricate pattern in gorgeous colours.

intrigue *noun* (say **in**-treeg) a scheme or plot. *Intrigue was rife in the office.*

intrigue *verb* (say in-**treeg**) to interest or fascinate somebody. *Animal behaviour has always intrigued him.*

introduce *verb* 1 to bring people together for the first time and make them known to one another. 2 to bring in something or use it for the first time. *The company introduced a new computer.*

introduction *noun* 1 the act of introducing somebody or something. 2 a piece of writing at the beginning of a book telling you what it is about. 3 a first experience of something. *An introduction to swimming.*

The introduction to the book told how fruits are formed.

intrude *verb* to enter somewhere or join in something when you are not wanted or have not been invited. To disturb. **intrusion** *noun.* **intrusive** *adjective.*

intruder *noun* somebody who intrudes or breaks in, such as a burglar.

intuition *noun* a feeling or understanding about something that you do not have to think about but cannot explain in a logical way. *His intuition told him that something was very badly wrong.*

WORD HISTORY

'Intoxicate' comes from the Latin word 'toxicum', meaning 'poison'.

DID YOU KNOW

'Invent' originally had the sense of 'to discover something that already exists'. Only much later did it acquire the meaning of 'to think up or create something entirely new'.

inundate *verb* 1 to flood. 2 to receive so much of something that you cannot cope with it, to overwhelm. *She was inundated with job offers.* **inundation** *noun.*

invade to send troops into another country or place to fight the people living there and to take control of it. **invasion** *noun.*

invalid *noun* (say **in**-val-id) a person who is ill or disabled.

invalid *adjective* (say in-**val**-id) something that is not legal and so cannot be used. *Your ticket is out of date and therefore invalid.*

invaluable *adjective* very valuable or priceless, very useful. *Learning to ride a bike is an invaluable experience.*

invent *verb* 1 to make something or think of something for the first time. *Who invented the computer?* 2 to make something up that is not true. *She invented an excuse so as not to go to the dentist.*

invention *noun* something that has been invented. *A terrific new invention.*

inventive *adjective* able to think up new ideas, original. *Peter is very inventive.*

inventor *noun* a person who invents things.

invertebrate *noun* any animal without a backbone such as an insect, slug or worm.

The common garden worm is an invertebrate.

inverted commas *plural noun* the marks (') and (') used in writing to show what somebody has said. *'Hello,' he whispered.*

investigate *verb* to try to find out all the facts about something, to examine carefully. *The police are investigating the boy's disappearance.* **investigation** *noun.*

invisible *adjective* something that cannot be seen. *Air is invisible.*

invitation *noun* written or spoken words asking you to come to something such as a party. *I've lost your kind invitation.*

invite *verb* to ask somebody to come to something or to go somewhere. *He asked me to stay for the Easter holidays.*

inviting *adjective* tempting or attractive. *An inviting warm fire.*

invoice *noun* a document asking for payment for goods that have been sent or for work that has been done.

involve *verb* 1 to be necessary as a part of a job. *The job involves a lot of letter writing.* 2 to be interested in and concerned with. *I don't want to be involved with your problems.* **involvement** *noun.*

IQ *abbreviation* intelligence quotient, a way of measuring a person's intelligence by asking special questions.

Iran *noun* a country in Southwest Asia.

Iranian *noun* a person who comes from Iran. **Iranian** *adjective*. *Iranian oil wells.*

Iraq *noun* a country in Southwest Asia.

Iraq is an Arab state at the top of the Persian Gulf. Its economy is built on reserves of oil.

irate *adjective* (say eye-rate) angry and complaining. *She wrote an irate letter to the council.*

Ireland *noun* a country in Northwest Europe.

iris *noun* 1 a tall garden flower. 2 the coloured part of your eye.

Irish *adjective* connected to or relating to Ireland and its people (the Irish). *Irish eyes are smiling.*

iron *noun* 1 a heavy grey metal that is one of the chemical elements. 2 a heavy electrical tool that heats up and which you use to smooth creases from clothes. **ironing** *noun*. *Have you got any ironing to do?*

irony *noun* the use of words to say the very opposite of what they mean. *'That was clever of you to smash my best plate!'* **ironic** *adjective*. *An ironic chain of events.*

irregular *adjective* 1 not regular or usual. *He works irregular hours, so I never know when he'll be home.* 2 not even or smooth.

irrigate *verb* to supply water for crops on dry land by means of ditches, pipes, canals etc. **irrigation** *noun*.

An irrigation channel brought water to the parched fields.

irritable *adjective* easily annoyed, in a bad mood. *Father was in an irritable mood.*

irritate *verb* 1 to make somebody annoyed, cross and impatient. 2 to make your skin feel sore or itchy. **irritation** *noun*.

Islam *noun* a religion that Muslims follow. It is based on the teachings of the prophet Muhammad. **Islamic** *adjective*.

AMAZING FACT

Be careful when you are writing 'it's' (a contraction of either 'it is' or 'it has') and 'its' (which means 'a characteristic of or something that belongs to it').

In 'it's' the apostrophe takes the place of the letters that are left out. for example, 'It's a nice day for a picnic.'

'Its' doesn't have an apostrophe: 'A robin built its nest in a tree in our back yard.'

Islamabad *noun* the capital of Pakistan.

island *noun* a piece of land surrounded by water. *She is buried on an island in the lake.*

isle *noun* an island, usually used as part of its name. *Isle of Skye.*

isobar *noun* a line on a weather map that connects places with the same or equal atmospheric pressure.

isolate *verb* to place something apart from others and by itself, to separate. *She had to be isolated because she had an infectious disease.* **isolation** *noun*.

Israel *noun* a country in Southwest Asia.

The flag of Israel features the star of David on a white ground bordered with blue stripes.

issue *noun* 1 an edition of a newspaper or magazine brought out at a particular time. *Today's issue has the latest news.* 2 something that is given out, a supply. 3 a problem or an important topic for discussion. *The issue of bullying.* **issue** *verb* to supply with. *The hikers were issued with special boots.* **take issue with** to disagree.

isthmus *noun* a narrow strip of land that joins two larger pieces of land.

IT *abbreviation* information technology, the use of computers to store and retrieve information.

Italian *noun* 1 a person who comes from Italy. 2 the language spoken in Italy. **Italian** *adjective*. *Italian opera.*

Italy *noun* a country in southern Europe.

itch *noun* an uncomfortable, tingling feeling on your skin that makes you want to scratch yourself. **itch** (itches, itching, itched) *verb*. *The mosquito bite itches.*

item *noun* a single thing on a list or in a group of other things. *An item of news.*

ivory *noun* the hard, smooth white material that the tusks of elephants and some other animals are made of.

Ivory Coast *noun* a country in Africa.

ivy *noun* a climbing evergreen plant with shiny, pointed leaves.

Holly and ivy are traditional Christmas decoration plants. Bringing green leaves indoors in midwinter looks forward to springtime.

J

Jj

jab (jabs, jabbing, jabbed) *verb* to hit or stab with something pointed. **jab** *noun* an injection. *A flu jab.*

jack *noun* 1 a tool for lifting something heavy such as a car off the ground. 2 a picture playing card with a value between the ten and the queen. A jack is sometimes called a knave.

jackal *noun* a wild animal of the dog family that feeds off the dead bodies of other animals. Jackals come from Asia and Africa.

jackass *noun* a male donkey.

jacket *noun* 1 a short coat that covers the top half of your body. 2 a covering for something. *A book jacket.*

jackknife *verb* when the trailer of an articulated lorry suddenly bends round towards the cab. *The lorry jackknifed on the black ice.*

jackpot *noun* the biggest prize to be won in a game or a lottery.

jacuzzi *noun* a bath with underwater jets that make the water swirl.

jade *noun* a precious green stone used in making jewellery.

jaded *adjective* bored and tired and lacking in enthusiasm.

jagged *adjective* with many sharp, rough and uneven points. *Jagged rocks.*

jaguar *noun* a South American wild cat with yellow and black spots like a leopard.

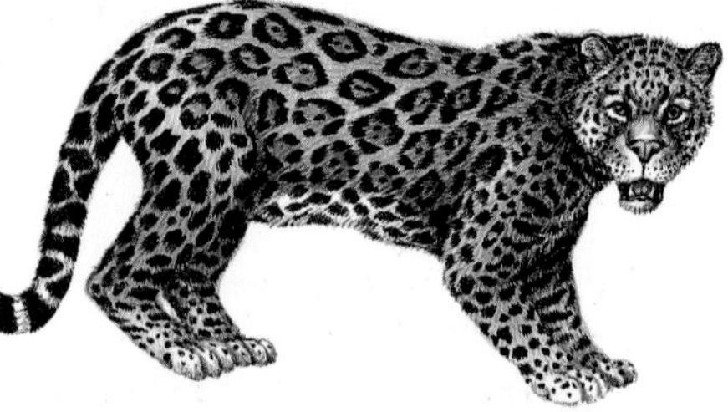

The jaguar turned and growled as it heard us approach.

jail *noun* another spelling for gaol, a prison where people are kept as a punishment for committing a crime.

Jakarta *noun* the capital of Indonesia.

jam *noun* 1 a sweet, sticky food made by boiling fruit and sugar together 2 a lot of vehicles or people crowded so closely together that they cannot move easily. *A traffic jam.* **in a jam** in a difficult situation.

SPELLING NOTE

The letter J developed from the letter I during the Middle Ages and was used to show an I at the beginning of a word. Later it became a symbol for the consonant J as in 'jewel' and 'jolly'.

jam (jams, jamming, jammed) *verb* 1 to get stuck or to make something get stuck so that it cannot move. *The door has jammed and I can't open it.* 2 to fill and press things tightly in a place. *Kevin jammed the bag into the boot of the car.* **jam-packed** packed very tightly.

The Jamaican flag has a diagonal yellow cross bisecting a green and black ground.

Jamaica *noun* a country in the West Indies.

Jamaican *noun* a person who comes from Jamaica. **Jamaican** *adjective. Jamaican sugar.*

jangle *verb* to make a ringing noise like pieces of metal banging together. *The bracelets jangled as she threw up her arms.*

January *noun* the first month of the year. January has 31 days.

Japan *noun* a country in East Asia.

Japanese *noun* 1 somebody who comes from Japan. 2 the language spoken in Japan. **Japanese** *adjective. Japanese gardens.*

Sumo wrestling is a very popular sport among the Japanese.

jar *noun* a glass container with a lid for storing food such as jam.

jar (jars, jarring, jarred) *verb* 1 to make an irritating noise that has an unpleasant effect on people. *The loud music jarred her nerves.* 2 to jolt or give a sudden shock.

jargon *noun* the special technical language used by a particular group of people. *Computer jargon.*

jaunt *noun* a trip or short journey made for pleasure. *A jaunt to the seaside.*

The javelin is one of the events in the Olympic Games.

jaunty *adjective* cheerful and carefree. *A jaunty walk.* **jauntiness** *noun.*

javelin *noun* a short, light spear thrown by hand, usually in athletic sports.

jaw *noun* one of two large bones in your mouth that hold your teeth. Your jaws move up and down when your speak and eat.

jazz *noun* a type of music with a very strong rhythm. Jazz was first played by the Black people of America.

jealous *adjective* unhappy because you want what somebody else has. **jealousy** *noun. Jealousy poisons the mind.*

jeans *noun* trousers made from a strong cotton material called denim.

jeer *verb* to make fun of somebody in a rude, loud and unkind way, to mock.

jelly *noun* a clear, soft, sweet food flavoured with fruit juice. Jellies wobble. They are made from a substance called gelatine.

jellyfish *noun* a sea animal without a backbone (invertebrate) that looks like an umbrella made of jelly. Jellyfish have tentacles that can sting.

Because of their transparent bodies, it is sometimes hard to spot jellyfish floating in the sea.

jeopardy *noun* (say jep-ur-dee) If somebody or something is in jeopardy they are in danger or somehow threatened.

jerk *verb* to move or pull something suddenly and quickly. **jerk** *noun.*

jersey (jerseys) *noun* a kind of knitted shirt or pullover with sleeves, a sweater.

Jerusalem *noun* the capital of Israel.

jest *noun* a joke or something said or done for fun. **in jest** as a joke.

jester an entertainer at a royal court during the Middle Ages.

The jesters danced and sang for the entertainment of the court.

jet *noun* 1 a strong stream of liquid or gas forced under pressure. *The fountain threw up jets of water.* 2 an aircraft that is driven forward by a strong jet of air forced out of the back of the engine (a jet engine).

jet-lag *noun* great tiredness and a feeling of confusion that some people suffer after a long plane journey.

jetty *noun* a pier or landing stage where boats can moor and unload.

SPELLING NOTE

'Jewellery' is one of several words that are spelled differently in American English. The American spelling is 'jewelry'.

WORD HISTORY

The name 'jeans' comes from the name of the material they are made from: 'jenes' or 'geanes', the French names for the city of Genova where the cloth was first made.

Jew *noun* 1 a person of the Hebrew race described in the Old Testament of the Bible. 2 a person who follows the religion of Judaism. **Jewish** *adjective.*

jewel *noun* a beautiful and precious stone such as a ruby or emerald.

jewellery *noun* rings, bracelets, necklaces and other ornaments that people wear.

This gold necklace is part of a collection of jewellery that dates from the Bronze Age.

jiffy *noun* a very short time. *I'll be back in a jiffy to make the tea.*

jig *noun* a lively folk dance. **jig** *verb.*

jigsaw *noun* a puzzle made up of pieces of cardboard or wood cut in different shapes that you fit together to form a picture.

jingle *noun* 1 the ringing sound made by small bells or keys knocking together. **jingle** *verb. She jingled the coins in her purse.* 2 a simple but catchy tune or song used in radio and TV adverts.

jinx *noun* something that is thought to bring bad luck. *There is a jinx on this job.*

job *noun* 1 the work that somebody does regularly to earn money. 2 a task or a particular piece of work that has to be done. **just the job** exactly what is required. **job centre** a place where people can go to find out about jobs that are available. **job lot** an assortment of things that you buy together.

jockey (jockeys) *noun* a person whose job it is to ride horses in races.

The jockey urged the horse on to win the race.

jodhpurs *plural noun* (say **jod**-purz) close-fitting trousers that you wear for riding a horse. *Jodhpurs and riding boots.*

jog (jogs, jogging, jogged) *verb* 1 to run at a slow steady pace for exercise. 2 to push or shake something gently. *She jogged my arm and I upset the jug.* **jog somebody's memory** to make somebody remember something.

join *verb* 1 to fasten, tie or somehow connect things together. **join** *noun.* 2 to become a member of a club or organization. 3 to unite or come together. **join in** take part in. *They all joined in the fun.* **join up** to become a member of the armed forces.

J

joint *noun* 1 a place where two things join and are fixed. 2 a place where two bones in your body are joined together, such as your elbow or knee. **joint** *adjective* shared by two or more people. *I can't take all the credit, it was a joint effort.*

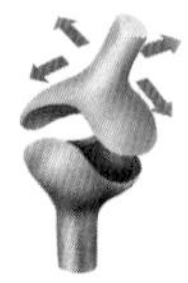

The joints found in the human body are, from left to right, ball and socket, pivot, saddle and hinge.

joke *noun* something that you say or do that makes people laugh. **joke** *verb*. **beyond a joke** not at all funny but very serious.

joker *noun* 1 somebody who tells jokes. 2 an extra card in a pack of playing cards which in certain games may have any value.

jolly (jollier, jolliest) *adjective* happy, cheerful and full of fun.

jolt *verb* to move suddenly and roughly, to jerk. *The train jolted to a halt.*

Jordan *noun* a country in the Middle East.

The flag of Jordan has a red triangle with a white star on a black, white and green background.

Jordanian *noun* a person who comes from Jordan. **Jordanian** *adjective*. *Jordanian oil.*

jostle *verb* to shove or push and bump into people roughly.

jot (jots, jotting, jotted) *verb* to write down something quickly and briefly. *He jotted down a list of things he wanted.*

journal *noun* (say **jer**-nul) 1 a diary or daily record of things you have done etc. 2 a magazine, especially one that deals with a particular subject. *The Nursing Journal.*

journalese *noun* (say jer-nul-**eez**) a style of careless and far-fetched writing used in some newspapers and magazines.

journalism *noun* (say **jer**-nul-izum) the job of gathering news and writing articles for newspapers and magazines.

journalist *noun* (say **jer**-nul-ist) a person who writes or edits articles for a newspaper or magazine.

journey (journeys) *noun* (say **jer**-nee) the act of travelling from one place to another, a trip. **journey** *verb*.

joust *noun* (say **jow**-st) a sporting fight in the Middle Ages between two knights on horses, using long spears. **joust** *verb*.

WORD HISTORY

'Jubilee' comes from a Hebrew word 'yobel', meaning a ram's horn. The ram's horn was blown to proclaim a year of celebration, especially a celebration held every 50 years.

joy *noun* 1 a feeling of great happiness. 2 success or luck. The opposite of joy is sorrow.

joyride *noun* a ride in a stolen car, to experience danger. **joyrider** *noun*.

jubilee *noun* a celebration to commemorate an important event. **silver jubilee** a celebration of a 25th anniversary. **golden jubilee** a celebration of a 50th anniversary. **diamond jubilee** a celebration of a 60th anniversary.

Judaism *noun* the religion of the Jewish people. *He converted to Judaism.*

judge *noun* 1 a person who hears cases in a court of law and decides how a guilty person should be punished. 2 a person who decides who is the winner of a competition. 3 a person who forms an opinion about something. *She's a good judge of character.* **judgement** *noun*.

judo *noun* a Japanese sport of self-defence in which two people wrestle, using special movements, and try to throw each other to the ground.

jug *noun* a container with a handle and a lip part for pouring liquids.

juggle *verb* to keep throwing and catching a number of objects, such as balls, in the air without dropping them. *We learned to juggle at camp last summer. I'm pretty good at it now.* **juggler** *noun*.

juice *noun* (rhymes with loose) the liquid you can squeeze from fruit and vegetables. **juicy** *adjective*. *Mavis bit into a juicy orange.* **juiciness** *noun*.

juke-box *noun* a machine that plays music you select when you put coins into it.

Jousting only takes place in pageants and fairs these days.

July *noun* the seventh month of the year. July has 31 days.

jumble *verb* to mix things up so that they are an untidy mess. *She jumbled up the pieces of the jigsaw puzzle.* **jumble** *noun* a messy and mixed collection of things. *The floor of my closet is a jumble of clothes and shoes.*

jumbo *adjective* very large. **jumbo jet** a large passenger plane, a 747.

The jumbo jet took off with the 350 passengers aboard.

jump *verb* 1 to leap or throw your body up into the air. 2 to go over something by leaping. **jump** *noun* something you jump over. *The horse is coming to the last jump.* **jump at** to accept enthusiastically. *He jumped at the chance to go riding.*

jumper *noun* a dress without sleeves that you usually wear a blouse under.

jumpy (jumpier, jumpiest) *adjective* nervous. *My mistake made me feel jumpy.*

junction *noun* a place where railroad lines or roads join or cross over.

June *noun* the sixth month of the year. June has 30 days.

jungle *noun* a dense forest in a tropical country. *I spent a year exploring the jungle.*

The toucan, the monkey and the chameleon are all creatures of the jungle.

WORD HISTORY

The name 'July' comes from the Latin word for this month. The month was named by the Romans in honour of the general and statesman Julius Caesar.

junior *adjective* 1 of lower rank or importance. *A junior executive.* 2 of or for younger people. *A junior dictionary.*

junk *noun* 1 things that are old and useless or worthless. 2 a Chinese sailing boat with a flat bottom.

Traditional junks can still be seen in modern Hong Kong harbor.

junk food *noun* food that is not good for you but may be quick and easy to prepare.

junkie *noun* a drug addict.

junk mail *noun* leaflets and advertisements that are sent to you in the mail and which you do not want.

junk shop *noun* a place that sells second-hand clothes etc.

jury *noun* a group of people who are chosen to hear a case in a court of law and decide whether an accused person is guilty or not.

just *adjective* fair and right, honest. *A just decision was eventually reached.*

just *adverb* 1 not long ago. *She just went home.* 2 only. *Just a minute!* 3 exactly. *This is just the right color.* 4 almost not. *There is just enough to eat.*

justice *noun* 1 treatment that is just, fair and right. 2 a country's system of laws and how they are operated by the law courts. 3 a judge. *A justice of the peace.*

justify (justifies, justifying, justified) *verb* to defend or to prove that something is just and fair. *How can you justify hitting the child?* **justification** *noun.*

jut (juts, jutting, jutted) *verb* to stick out farther than other things around it, to project *The balcony juts out from the side of the house.*

jute *noun* a fiber used to make rope and coarse cloth for sacks etc.

juvenile *adjective* 1 concerning young people. 2 childish and silly. *Juvenile behavior is inappropriate here.*

Kk

Kabul *noun* the capital of Afghanistan.

kaleidoscope *noun* a tube that you turn as you look through it to see changing patterns of colour made by mirrors and pieces of glass fitted at one end of it.

Kampala *noun* the capital of Uganda.

kangaroo *noun* a large Australian animal with strong back legs for jumping. The female has a pouch on her stomach in which she carries her baby, called a joey. Kangaroos belong to a group of pouched animals called marsupials.

A kangaroo with her baby in her pouch is a familiar sight to travellers in Australia.

karaoke *noun* (say ka-ree-**ok**-kee) a kind of entertainment from Japan in which people sing pop songs to recorded music and follow the words of the song on a screen.

karate *noun* a self-defence sport originating from Japan in which two people fight one another using special kicks and blows.

Kathmandu *noun* the capital of Nepal.

kayak *noun* (say **kye**-ak) a canoe covered in canvas, originally used by the Inuit people.

Kazakhstan *noun* a country in West Asia.

Kazakhstan exports oil, metals, chemicals, grain and wool.

kebab *noun* small pieces of meat or vegetable cooked on a skewer. *A chicken kebab.*

WORD HISTORY

The shape of the letter K comes from the ancient Egyptian symbol for an open hand. Its sound comes from 'kaph', a Semitic word for an open palm of a hand.

AMAZING FACT

Kangaroos, wallabies oppossums and other marsupials begin carrying their babies in their pouches before they are fully developed. The baby may stay inside its mother for only 11 days, it continues to develop in the pouch.

keel *noun* the long piece of steel that lies along the bottom of a ship's frame.

keen *adjective* 1 eager and interested. 2 sensitive and sharp. *A keen sense of smell.* 3 clever and quick. *A keen wit.*

keep (keeps, keeping, kept) *verb* 1 to have something and not to give it to anybody. 2 to look after something for somebody. *Can you keep my place for me please?* 3 to remain. *Please keep still!* 4 to remain fresh or in a good condition. *Will this meat keep till Sunday?* 5 to look after and feed. *Mary keeps goats.* **keep** *noun* the food and money etc. a person needs to live. *He earns his keep by gardening.* **keep away** stay away. **keep down** *The food disagrees with her and she can't keep it down.* **keep on** to continue. **keep to** *Keep to the footpath all the way.* **keep up** *Keep up with your studies.*

keep *noun* the main tower in a castle.

keeper *noun* a person whose job it is to look after animals in a zoo or who is responsible for the objects in a museum.

keg *noun* a small barrel.

kelp *noun* a kind of seaweed used as a fertilizer. *Sea otters eat kelp.*

kennel *noun* 1 a small shelter or hut for keeping a dog in. 2 **kennels** a place where dogs are bred or where dogs can be looked after when their owners are away.

Kenya *noun* a country in Africa.

kept past tense of keep.

kerb *noun* the line of stones along the edge of a pavement. *Don't trip up the kerb.*

kernel *noun* the edible middle part of a nut, inside the shell.

kestrel *noun* a small falcon. Kestrels kill and eat small animals.

Kestrels are becoming more common in urban areas of Britain.

ketchup *noun* a thick sauce, usually made from tomatoes.

kettle *noun* a container for boiling water in. Kettles have a lid, a handle and a narrow spout for pouring.

K

key *noun* 1 a shaped metal object that you turn to open a lock or to start an engine. 2 the buttons on typewriters and computers or the black and white bars on a piano or organ that you press with your fingers. 3 the answers to a problem or mystery. *The key to the crime.* 4 a set of musical notes in a scale based on one note. **key** *adjective* important. *A key witness.*

keyboard *noun* 1 the set of keys on a computer, piano etc. that you press when you use them. 2 an electronic musical instrument. *A keyboard player.*

This diagram shows what is inside the keyboard of your computer.

keyhole *noun* a hole in a lock where you put the key.

keystone *noun* the stone in the centre of an arch. It holds the other stones in the arch in place. *A marble keystone.*

kg *abbreviation* kilogram.

khaki *noun* (say **kah**-key) a yellowish-brown colour. *Soldiers wear khaki.*

Khartoum *noun* the capital of Sudan.

kick *verb* 1 to hit somebody or something with your foot. 2 to move your legs about with force. **kick** *noun* 1 *The pony gave Peter a nasty kick.* 2 a thrill. *She gets a kick out of pop music.* **kick-off** the kick of a ball that starts a match. **kick out** to get rid of.

kid *noun* 1 a young goat. 2 a child.

kid *verb* to tease somebody by pretending that something is true. *It's not broken. I was just kidding.*

kidnap (kidnaps, kidnapping, kidnapped) *verb* to capture somebody and keep them prisoner until you get what you demand, e.g. money. **kidnapper** *noun.*

kidney (kidneys) *noun* Your kidneys are organs in your body that keep your blood clean by removing waste products and passing them out in the form of urine.

Kiev *noun* the capital of Ukraine.

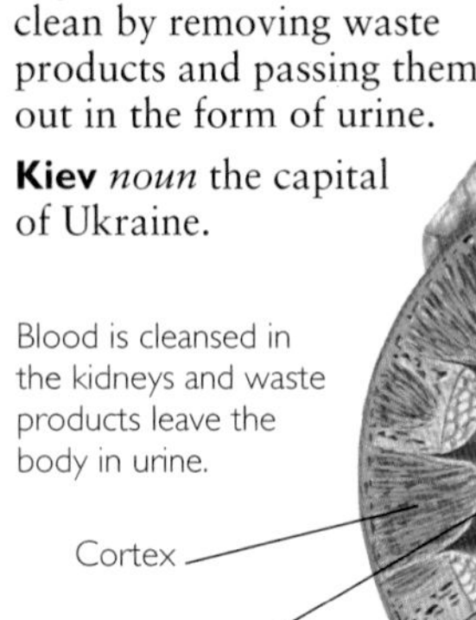

Blood is cleansed in the kidneys and waste products leave the body in urine.

WORD BUILDER

'Kilo' is a Greek word meaning a thousand. So a kilogram is a thousand grams, a kilowatt is a thousand watts and kilobyte is a thousand bytes.

AMAZING FACT

'Kindergarden' comes from the German words 'kind' (child) and 'garten' (garden) – so its orignal meaning was 'children's garden'.

Kigali *noun* the capital of Rwanda.

kill *verb* to end the life of a person or animal, to destroy something. **kill** *noun* 1 the act of killing. 2 the animal killed. *The tiger stood over its kill.*

killer *noun* a person or animal that kills.

kiln *noun* a very hot oven for baking pottery and bricks to make them hard.

Pottery is baked in a kiln.

kilogram or **kilogramme** *noun* a measure of weight equal to 1,000 grams. Also called a kilo. *A kilo of sugar.*

kilometre *noun* a measure of length equal to 1,000 metres.

kilt *noun* a knee-length pleated skirt made from tartan cloth, traditionally worn by Scottish men.

kimono *noun* a long loose robe with wide sleeves, traditionally worn by Japanese women.

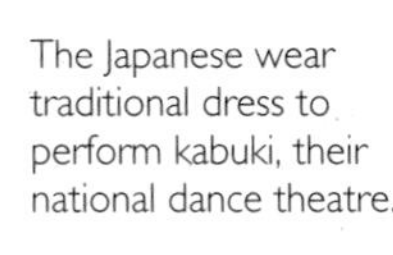

The Japanese wear traditional dress to perform kabuki, their national dance theatre.

kin *noun* (old-fashioned) your family and relations. **next of kin** your closest relation.

kind *adjective* helpful and friendly to people, gentle. *It was kind of you to visit me in hospital.* **kindness** *noun.*

kind *noun* a group of things that are similar. A type or sort of something. *What kind of dog is this?* **kind of** something like. *An igloo is a kind of a house built of ice.*

kindle *verb* to set light to and start something burning.

kindergarten *noun* a small school for very young children.

K

king *noun* 1 a male ruler of a country. Kings are not elected but inherit their position by succeeding the previous ruler. 2 a playing card with a picture of a king on it. 3 a chesspiece. When the king is taken the game is lost.

King Henry VIII of England had six wives. He divorced two wives and had two others executed. One wife died a natural death and his last wife survived him.

kingdom *noun* 1 a country that is ruled by a king or queen. 2 a division of the natural world. *The animal kingdom.*

kingfisher *noun* a bird with bright blue and brown feathers and a dagger-like beak that it uses to catch fish from lakes and rivers.

Kingston *noun* the capital of Jamaica.

Kingstown *noun* the capital of St Vincent and the Grenadines.

Kinshasa *noun* the capital of the Democratic Republic of the Congo (formerly Zaire).

kiosk *noun* (say **kee**-osk) a small hut-like shop on the street where you can buy things like newspapers and sweets.

Kiribati *noun* a country of many islands in the Pacific Ocean.

kiss *verb* to touch somebody with your lips as a sign of love or friendship. **kiss** *noun. He gave me a kiss.*

kiss of life a way of helping somebody to breathe again after an accident by blowing air into their lungs.

kit *noun* 1 the clothes and equipment you need to do something. *Cricket kit.* 2 all the things you need to make something. *A model ship kit.*

David got his tennis kit ready for the match.

SPELLING NOTE

'K' is not pronounced when it comes before 'n' at the beginning of a word, as in 'knave', 'knee', 'knot' and 'knuckle'.

AMAZING FACT

'Knickers' were originally called 'knickerbockers' after the pretended author of Washington Irving's 'History of New York', 1809.

kitchen *noun* a room in a house that is used for preparing and cooking food.

kite *noun* 1 a toy that you fly in the wind. It consists of a light frame covered in paper or cloth on the end of a long piece of string. 2 a bird of prey belonging to the hawk family.

kitten *noun* a very young cat. **kittenish** *adjective* behaving like a kitten, playful.

kitty *noun* a sum of money put in by several people for everybody in the group to use.

kiwi *noun* (say **kee**-wee) a New Zealand bird that cannot fly.

The kiwi is the national bird of New Zealand.

km *abbreviation* kilometre.

knack *noun* the ability to do something difficult with ease and skill.

knave *noun* 1 a picture playing card with a value between the ten and the queen. A knave is often called a jack. *The knave of hearts.* 2 a dishonest person.

knead *verb* to squeeze and stretch dough with your hands before baking.

knee *noun* the joint in the middle of your leg where it bends.

kneecap *noun* the movable bone in front of your knee.

The kneecap is also called the patella.

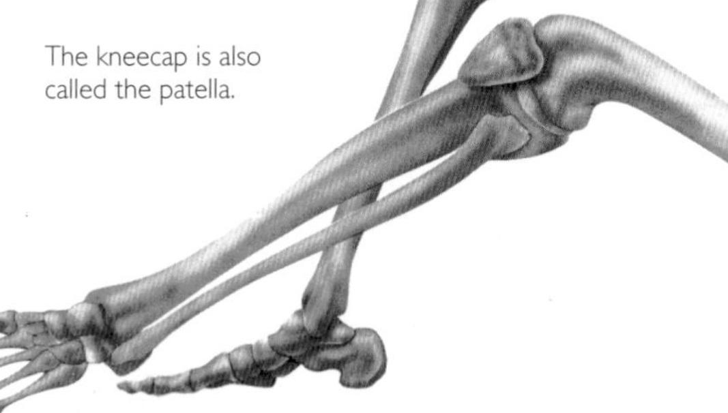

kneel *verb* to bend your knees and go down on them. *They knelt to pray for forgiveness.*

knew the past tense of know.

knickers *plural noun* underpants worn by women and girls.

knife (knives) *noun* a metal tool with a handle and a sharp blade that you use for cutting. **knife** *verb* to stab with a knife.

knight *noun* 1 in the Middle Ages a soldier who fought on horseback for his king or lord. 2 a man who has been given the title 'Sir' by the monarch. *Sir Andrew Marvell.* 3 a chesspiece with a horse's head.

The noble knight was training a falcon to hunt for him.

knit (knits, knitting, knitted) *verb* 1 to make clothes by looping wool together with two long needles. 2 to join closely. *The broken bones will soon knit together.*

knob *noun* a round handle on a door or drawer. *Knobs and knockers.*

knock *verb* 1 to hit or strike something hard. *Is there somebody knocking at the door?* 2 to hit something so that it falls. *Sue knocked her mug off her desk.* **knock** *noun.* **knock out** to hit somebody so hard they become unconscious.

knocker *noun* a hinged metal ring, knob or hammer on a door that you use for knocking. *He banged the door knocker.*

knot *noun* 1 a join or fastening made by tying pieces of string, rope or cloth together. 2 a hard, dark part in wood where a branch joined the tree. 3 a measure of speed for ships. 1 knot is about 1.85 kph.

knot (knots, knotting, knotted) *verb* to fasten something by tying its ends into a knot. *Fishermen's knots.*

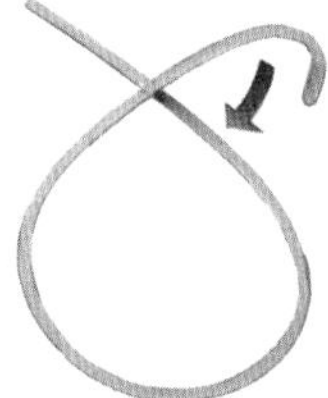

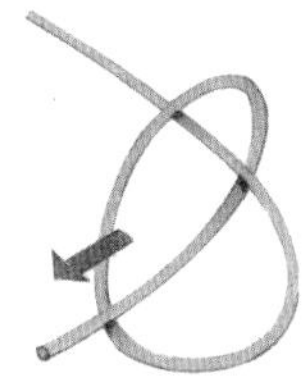

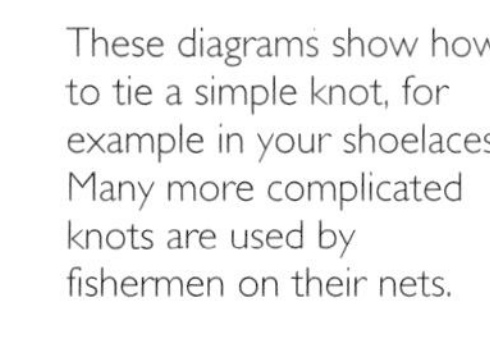

These diagrams show how to tie a simple knot, for example in your shoelaces. Many more complicated knots are used by fishermen on their nets.

know (knows, knowing, knew, known) *verb* to have learnt something or to have information about something and to have it in your mind. *Do you know French?* 2 to remember or to recognize somebody or something. *I know Sharon very well.*

WORD HISTORY

The word 'knight' comes from an Old English word 'cniht', meaning a boy servant or warrior.

DID YOU KNOW

The lord of a manor provided horses and armour for his knights. In time it became a great honour to be a knight, and knights formed an important part of the feudal system of the Middle Ages.

knowing *adjective* showing that you know something secret. *He knew she was lying and gave her a knowing look.*

knowledge *noun* the things that you know and understand, things that you learn by study. *A good knowledge of French.*

knowledgeable *adjective* clever and well-informed about a subject.

know-all *noun* somebody who thinks they know a great deal about everything.

know-how *noun* practical knowledge and ability. *I admire your know-how.*

knuckle *noun* the bones at the joint of a finger. *Knuckles swollen with arthritis.*

koala *noun* an Australian animal that looks like a small bear. Koalas live in eucalyptus trees and feed on their leaves.

Koala bears sleep for 22 out of every 24 hours.

kookaburra *noun* an Australian bird of the kingfisher family that makes a loud laughing noise. *The kookaburra has a strange laugh.*

Koran or **Qu'ran** *noun* the holy book of Islam, the religion of the Muslims.

kosher *adjective* (say **koh**-shur) food that has been prepared in accordance with the laws of the Jewish religion.

kph *abbreviation* kilometres per hour.

Kuala Lumpur *noun* the capital of Malaysia.

Kuwait City *noun* the capital of Kuwait.

Kuwait *noun* a country in Southwest Asia.

Kuwait is a country that has grown rich because of its vast reserves of oil.

Kyrgyzstan *noun* a country in central Asia.

Ll

lab *noun* a laboratory.

label *noun* a piece of paper, cloth or plastic that is attached to something and that gives information about it. **label** (labels, labelling, labelled) *verb* to put a label on something.

laboratory *noun* a room or building where scientists work.

laborious *adjective* difficult and needing a lot of hard work or effort. *Digging is a laborious job.*

labour *noun* 1 hard, physical work. 2 workers considered as a group. 3 the pain a woman feels when giving birth. 4 **Labour Party** one of the three main political parties in Great Britain. **labour** *verb* to work hard. **labourer** *noun* an unskilled worker.

labyrinth *noun* a maze.

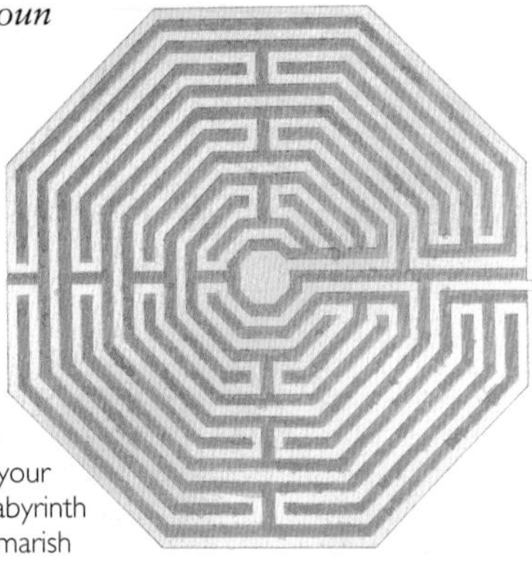

Trying to find your way out of a labyrinth can be a nightmarish experience.

lace *noun* 1 a delicate material made of fine threads woven into a pretty pattern with holes in it. 2 a long, thin cord that is threaded through holes and used, for example, to tie up a shoe or a boot. **lace** *verb. Lace up your trainers tightly.*

lack *verb* to be without something that is needed or wanted. *She lacks the intelligence to be a good teacher.* **lack** *noun.*

lacquer *noun* (say **lack**-ur) a varnish or glossy paint.

lad *noun* a boy or young man.

ladder *noun* 1 two long wooden or metal poles with cross-pieces called rungs used for climbing up or down. A set of steps. 2 a tear in a pair of tights or stockings.

ladle *noun* a large, deep spoon with a long handle used for lifting out liquids such as soup. *A generous ladle of soup.*

WORD HISTORY

The shape of the letter L comes from the ancient Egyptian symbol for a shepherd's crook. Its sound comes from 'lamed', a Semitic word for a shepherd's crook. The Greeks called the letter 'lambda'.

SPELLING NOTE

A word that sounds like 'lain' is 'lane'. Try not to confuse the two.

AMAZING FACT

Labyrinths are created by carefully planting hedges in an intricate pattern. When the plants are fully grown, they are taller than a person and so you cannot see which path to take. If you succeed in finding your way to the middle of the puzzle, there is usually a reward – a beautiful fountain or a peaceful place to sit.

lady *noun* 1 a woman, especially one with very good manners. 2 the title of a noblewoman. *Sir John and Lady Brown.* **ladylike** *adjective. Ladylike behaviour.*

ladybird *noun* (US ladybug) a small round flying beetle, usually with black spots on red wings. Ladybirds eat aphids and other harmful plant pests.

Ladybirds are the gardener's friend because they eat aphids (greenfly).

lag (lags, lagging, lagged) *verb* to move or develop more slowly than others and so be unable to keep up. *Catch up! You're lagging behind everybody else.* **time lag** the time that passes between one event and another.

lager *noun* a kind of beer that is light in colour. **lager lout** a young man who behaves rudely and violently when he has drunk too much alcohol.

lagoon *noun* a seawater lake separated from the sea by sandbanks or rocks.

laid past tense of lay.

laid-back *adjective* (slang) relaxed and unworried. *A laid-back kind of guy.*

lain past participle of lie.

lair *noun* a den or hidden place where a wild animal sleeps.

lake *noun* a large area of fresh water with land all around it.

lamb *noun* 1 a young sheep. 2 the meat of a young sheep. *Roast lamb and mint sauce.* **lamb** *verb* to give birth (to lambs).

lame *adjective* 1 unable to walk properly because of an injured leg. *The pony is lame and walks with a limp.* **lameness** *noun.* 2 weak and not good enough. *A lame excuse.* **lame duck** a person or company that cannot manage without help.

lamp *noun* a device that gives light by burning electricity, gas, oil or a candle. **lamp-post** *noun* a tall post holding a street lamp. **lampshade** *noun* a cover placed over a lamp to soften its light.

lance *noun* a long spear once used by knights on horseback.

The knights charged at each other, their lances poised to strike.

land *noun* 1 all the dry surface of the Earth that is above the sea. 2 the ground used for farming, gardening, building etc. 3 a country or nation. **land** *verb* 1 to arrive on land from a ship. 2 to bring an aircraft down to the ground. *The plane landed at noon.* 3 to get into trouble. *He landed up in prison.*

landing *noun* 1 a level area at the top of a flight of stairs. 2 bringing into ground or shore. *An emergency landing.*

landlady, landlord *noun* 1 a person who rents a house or flat to somebody. 2 a person who runs a public house.

landmark *noun* some building or object that you can see clearly from a distance. *The church spire is a clear landmark.*

The American presidents carved in the rock at Mount Rushmore in South Dakota are an instantly recognizable landmark.

landscape *noun* a wide view or all that you can see from one place.

lane *noun* 1 a narrow country road. 2 one of the strips on a motorway that is wide enough for a single line of traffic. 3 a strip of track or water for a runner or swimmer.

language *noun* 1 all the words that we use to talk or write to one another. Human speech. 2 the system of words used in one or more countries. *Spanish is the language spoken in Spain and in most of South America.* 3 any other system of communicating. *Sign language.*

lanky *adjective* tall and thin.

lantern *noun* a container, often with glass sides, for holding a candle or oil lamp.

Laos *noun* a country in Southeast Asia.

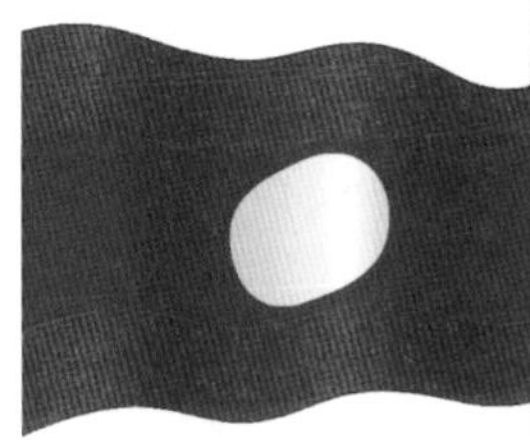

The flag of Laos shows red and blue stripes and a white circle.

lap *noun* 1 the top, flat part of your legs when you are sitting down. 2 one journey around a race track.

lap (laps, lapping, lapped) *verb* An animal laps up water by flicking it into its mouth with its tongue.

DID YOU KNOW

'Laser' is an acronym for 'light amplification by stimulated emission of radiation'.

WORD HISTORY

'Larva' is a Latin word meaning 'mask' or 'ghost'. Because the larva of an insect looks so different from the actual insect it was thought to mask or be the ghost of the fully developed insect.

La Paz *noun* the seat of government of Bolivia.

lapel *noun* the part below the collar of a jacket that folds back on the chest.

lapse *noun* 1 a small careless mistake. 2 a period of time that has passed.

laptop *noun* a small portable computer that you can use on your lap.

lard *noun* fat from pigs, used in cooking.

large *adjective* big in size, amount etc., not small. **largeness** *noun.* **at large** free after escaping. *The zoo's lion is still at large.*

largely *adverb* mostly.

lark *noun* a small brown bird that flies high in the sky and sings beautifully.

larva (larvae) *noun* an insect at its first stage of development after coming out of the egg and before becoming a pupa. A grub. A larva looks like a worm.

laser *noun* a device that produces a very narrow and powerful beam of light, used for cutting in surgery.

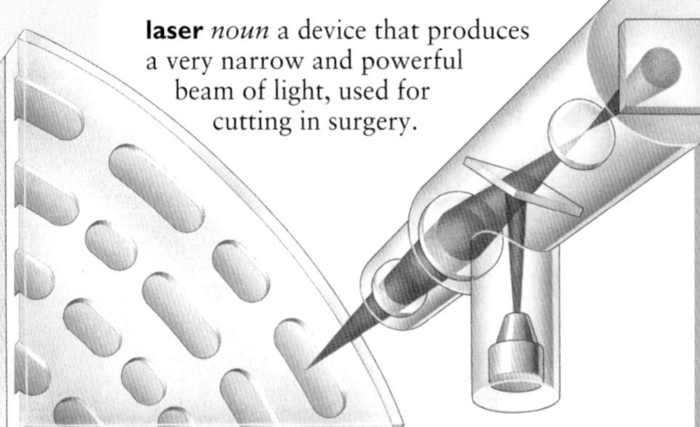

Precision cutting can be carried out with a laser.

lash *verb* 1 to hit violently, as with a whip. *The waves lashed against the rocks.* 2 to make rapid movements like a whip. *The cat lashed its tail in anger.* **lash** *noun* 1 a whip. 2 one of the small hairs growing around the eye (eyelash).

lass *noun* a girl or young woman.

lasso *noun* (say lass-**oo**) a long rope with a loop or noose at one end, used to catch cattle and horses. **lasso** *verb.*

last *adjective* 1 coming after all the others. *The last horse in the race.* 2 the only one remaining. *The last slice of cake.* 3 most recent, just past. *Last night.* 4 previous or one before this one. *Her last job.*

last *verb* 1 to continue. *The concert lasted four hours.* 2 to remain in good condition for some time. *These shoes are already worn out – they haven't lasted long.*

late *adjective, adverb* 1 not early but after the usual or expected time. *She was an hour late for her appointment, but she always arrives late.* 2 near the end of a period of time. *They arrived home late in the evening.* 3 previous, recently dead. *The late queen.* **lateness** *noun.* **lately** *adverb* recently.

later *adverb* after some time.

lateral *adjective* concerned with the side, sideways. *Lateral movement.*

lathe *noun* a machine that holds and turns wood or metal while it is being shaped with a cutting tool.

lather *noun* the bubbles or foam you get when you mix soap or detergent in warm water. *This soap makes a good lather.*

Latin *noun* the language spoken by the ancient Romans.

latitude *noun* a position or distance measured in degrees on a map north or south of the equator.

The lines of latitude run horizontally round the globe.

latter *adjective* the second of two things, compared with the former, which is the first of two things.

Latvia *noun* a Baltic country in Europe.

laugh *verb* to make sounds that show that you are very happy or think something is funny. *We laughed at the joke.* **laugh** *noun. He has a laugh like a drain.* **laughter** *noun. The sound of laughter shook the room.*

laughable *adjective* ridiculous and absurd.

launch *verb* 1 to send a boat or ship into the water. 2 to send a rocket into space. 3 to start something new or important. *They launched the company with a champagne party.* **launch** *noun.*

launchpad *noun* a place from which rockets are sent into space.

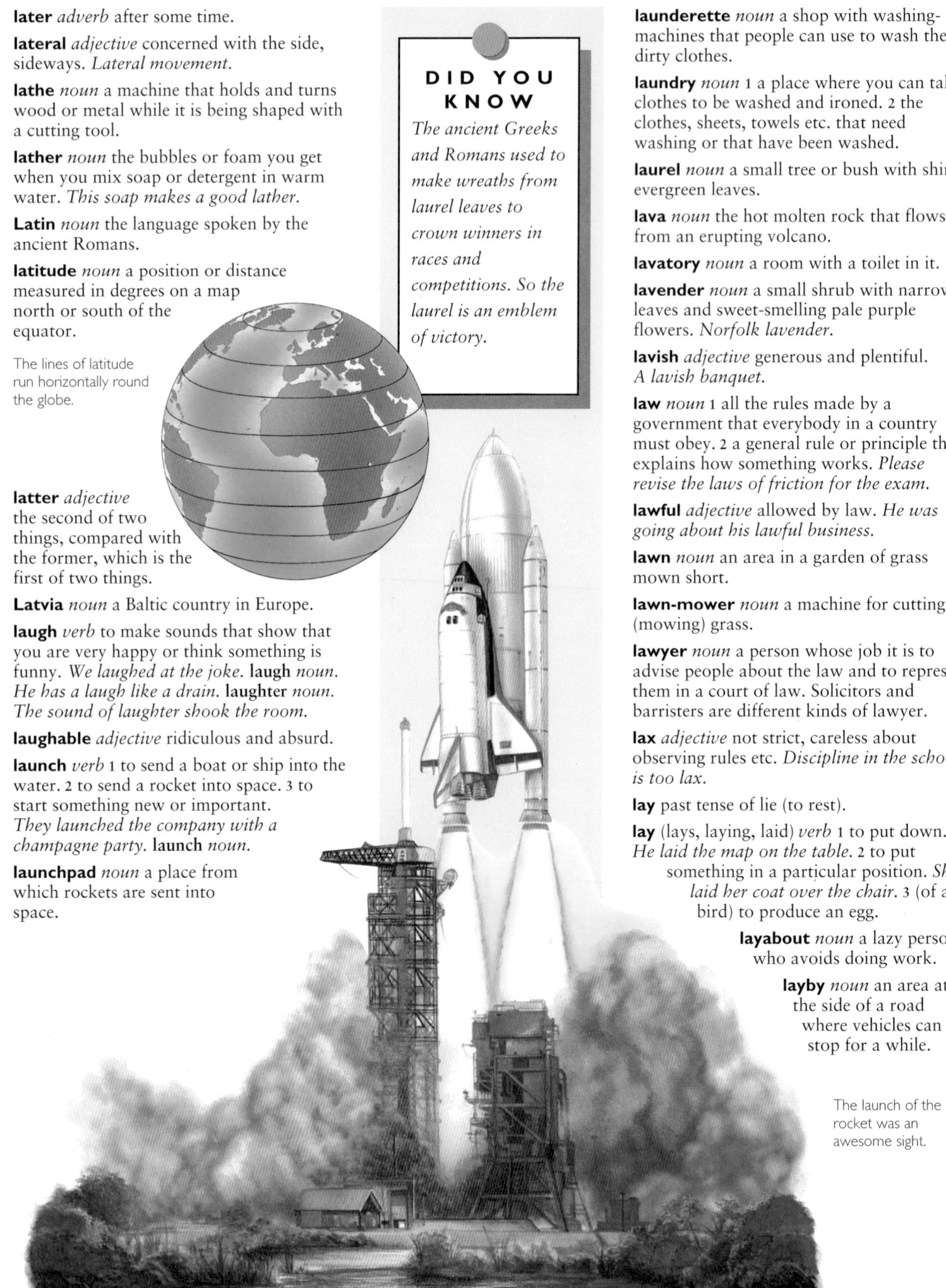

The launch of the rocket was an awesome sight.

DID YOU KNOW

The ancient Greeks and Romans used to make wreaths from laurel leaves to crown winners in races and competitions. So the laurel is an emblem of victory.

launderette *noun* a shop with washing-machines that people can use to wash their dirty clothes.

laundry *noun* 1 a place where you can take clothes to be washed and ironed. 2 the clothes, sheets, towels etc. that need washing or that have been washed.

laurel *noun* a small tree or bush with shiny evergreen leaves.

lava *noun* the hot molten rock that flows from an erupting volcano.

lavatory *noun* a room with a toilet in it.

lavender *noun* a small shrub with narrow leaves and sweet-smelling pale purple flowers. *Norfolk lavender.*

lavish *adjective* generous and plentiful. *A lavish banquet.*

law *noun* 1 all the rules made by a government that everybody in a country must obey. 2 a general rule or principle that explains how something works. *Please revise the laws of friction for the exam.*

lawful *adjective* allowed by law. *He was going about his lawful business.*

lawn *noun* an area in a garden of grass mown short.

lawn-mower *noun* a machine for cutting (mowing) grass.

lawyer *noun* a person whose job it is to advise people about the law and to represent them in a court of law. Solicitors and barristers are different kinds of lawyer.

lax *adjective* not strict, careless about observing rules etc. *Discipline in the school is too lax.*

lay past tense of lie (to rest).

lay (lays, laying, laid) *verb* 1 to put down. *He laid the map on the table.* 2 to put something in a particular position. *She laid her coat over the chair.* 3 (of a bird) to produce an egg.

layabout *noun* a lazy person who avoids doing work.

layby *noun* an area at the side of a road where vehicles can stop for a while.

layout *noun* 1 the way text and pictures are arranged on a page. 2 the way things are arranged on a plan. *The layout of the new supermarket.*

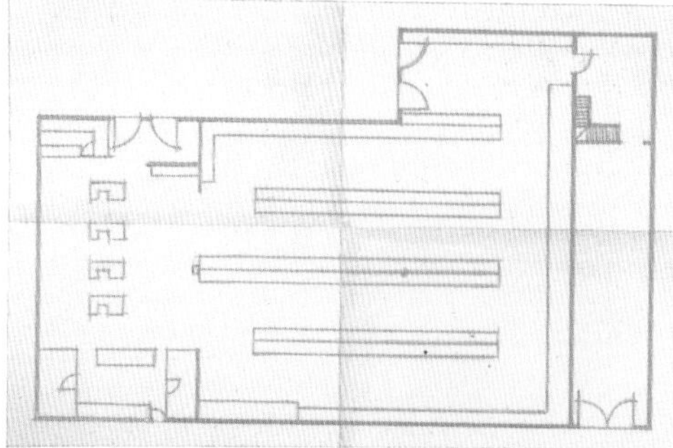

The managers studied the architect's plan for the layout of the new supermarket.

layer *noun* a thickness of something that lies between two other pieces of it or on top. *The cake was covered with a layer of icing.*

lazy (lazier, laziest) *adjective* not liking work, effort or exercise. *Cats are lazy and sleep a lot.* **laziness** *noun.* **lazily** *adverb.*

lead *noun* (rhymes with bed) 1 a soft, grey metal. 2 the substance in the middle of a pencil that makes a mark.

lead (leads, leading, led) *verb* (rhymes with need) 1 to go in front and show the way, to take in a certain direction. *He led me out of the maze.* 2 to be in the first place. *The grey horse was leading for most of the race.* 3 to be in charge of other people. *The captain led her team bravely.* 4 to live a certain way of life. *Our dog leads a happy life.* **lead** *noun* 1 the front position. *The grey horse is in the lead.* 2 a strap you attach to a dog's collar to lead or control it. 3 a cable that carries electricity. 4 a piece of information or a clue that helps you to solve a crime etc.

leader *noun* somebody who leads or who goes first, a person in charge of a group.

leaf (leaves) *noun* 1 one of the flat, usually green, parts of a plant that grows from a stem or twig. 2 a page of a book.

The green leaves of summer provided a dappled shade for the picnickers.

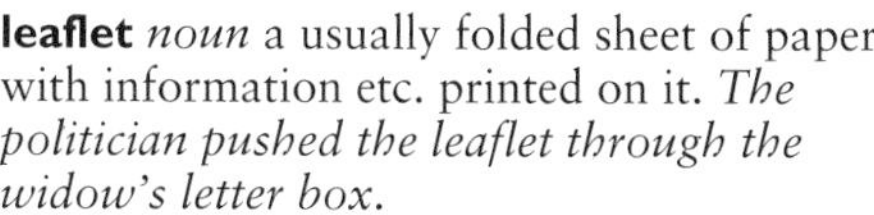

leaflet *noun* a usually folded sheet of paper with information etc. printed on it. *The politician pushed the leaflet through the widow's letter box.*

AMAZING FACT

In green plants, leaves make food to nourish the plant. This process is called photosynthesis. The chlorophyll in the leaf uses a combination of carbon dioxide, water and light to make sugar. It then passes the sugar to the rest of the plant through tubes.

SPELLING NOTE

Do not confuse the past tense of 'lie' to rest ('I lay in bed thinking') with the verb 'lay' meaning 'put down'. ('When you've finished reading, lay the book on the table.')

leak *noun* a hole in a container or pipe through which liquid or gas can escape. **leak** *verb* 1 (of a gas or liquid) to escape through a hole or crack. *This pipe is leaking.* 2 to give away secret information.

lean *adjective* having little or no fat. *Lean meat.* **leanness** *noun.*

lean (leans, leaning, leaned or leant) *verb* 1 to bend towards something. *Tom leant out of the window and waved to his friends.* 2 to rest against something for support. *Lean the ladder against the wall.*

leap (leaps, leaping, leapt or leaped) *verb* to jump up high or to jump over something. **leap** *noun.* **leap year** every fourth year in which February has 29 days instead of 28. Leap years have 366 days instead of 365.

learn (learns, learning, learnt or learned) *verb* to find out about something or how to do something. *Joe's learning French.*

learned *adjective* A learned person knows a lot. *A learned monk.*

learning *noun* having a great deal of knowledge. *His learning is phenomenal.*

lease *noun* an agreement between the owner of a property and a person renting it for a stated period of time. *They signed a 20-year lease on the house.*

leash *noun* a lead attached to a dog's collar so that you can take it for walks.

least *adjective* smallest or less than all the others. *This is the least expensive bike.* **at least** the minimum, but likely to be more. *It will cost at least £50.*

leather *noun* the skin of animals used to make such things as shoes, handbags and belts. **leathery** *adjective* tough like leather.

Tom was given a leather executive briefcase for his birthday.

leave *verb* 1 to go away from somewhere. The opposite of leave is arrive. 2 to let something remain where it is. *She left her clothes all over the floor.* 3 to forget about something by not taking it with you. *I left my coat indoors.* 4 what remains after the main part has been used or taken away. *Seven from eight leaves one.* 5 to pass on something to somebody after you die. *My uncle left me his gold watch.* **leave out** not to include or forget to put in.

leave *noun* 1 a holiday or time away from a job. 2 permission to do something.

L

leaves plural of leaf. *In autumn the leaves turn red and gold before they fall.*

Lebanon *noun* a country in Southwest Asia.

The flag of Lebanon has red and white stripes and a central symbol in green and gold.

lecture *noun* 1 a formal talk about a particular subject given to a class or audience. 2 a scolding or telling off. *The teacher gave him a lecture on how to behave.* **lecture** *verb.*

led past tense of lead. *The dog led the children out of danger.*

ledge *noun* a shelf-like space on a cliff, rock or wall. *The bird nested on the ledge.*

leek *noun* a long white vegetable with green leaves at one end. It tastes like an onion.

leer *verb* to look and smile at somebody in an evil way. *The old man gave her a leer.*

leeward *adjective* on the sheltered side, turned away from the wind.

left past tense of leave.

left *noun* You are reading these words from left to right. **left** *adjective. Close your left eye.*

left-overs *plural noun* food that has not been eaten after a meal. *I like eating left-overs.*

left-wing *adjective* in politics supporting socialism and big social changes. The opposite of left-wing is right-wing.

leg *noun* 1 one of the parts of the body that animals and humans use for walking, running and standing on. 2 one of the parts that support a chair or other piece of furniture. **pull somebody's leg** to tease or make a fool of somebody by trying to make them believe something that is not true.

legal *adjective* 1 allowed by the law. *Cock-fighting is no longer legal.* 2 concerned with the law. *The legal system.* The opposite of legal is illegal.

legend *noun* an old, well-known story that may or may not be true. *The legend of King Arthur.* **legendary** *adjective.*

legible *adjective* clear enough to be read easily. *The writing is very faded but it is just legible.* **legibility** *noun.*

Lemons grow in sunny countries around the Mediterranean Sea.

DID YOU KNOW

Native American legends are stories that explain things like how the sun and moon were created and where fire comes from.

Janet put her left leg forward and marched off, swinging her left arm high in the air.

legion *noun* a large division of the ancient Roman army (from three to six thousand soldiers).

legitimate *adjective* allowed by the law, lawful. **legitimacy** *noun.*

leisure *noun* free time when you can do what you like and you do not have to work. **leisurely** *adjective. A leisurely life is the life for me.*

lemon *noun* a bright yellow, oval citrus fruit with a sour-tasting juice.

lemonade *noun* a sweet, and sometimes fizzy, drink with a lemon flavour.

lend (lends, lending, lent) *verb* to let somebody have something for a short time, before they give it back to you. *It was raining so I lent him my umbrella.* The opposite of lend is borrow.

length *noun* 1 how far it is from one end of something to the other horizontally. *A length of cloth.* 2 how long something lasts. *We were surprised at the length of her prison sentence.*

lengthen *verb* to make or become longer.

lengthy (lengthier, lengthiest) *adjective* long, lasting a long time.

lenient *adjective* not severe or strict. *A really lenient teacher.* **lenience** *noun.*

lens *noun* 1 a piece of curved glass or plastic used in a camera, a pair of glasses etc. that bends light and makes it go where it is needed. 2 a part of the eye that focuses light on to the retina.

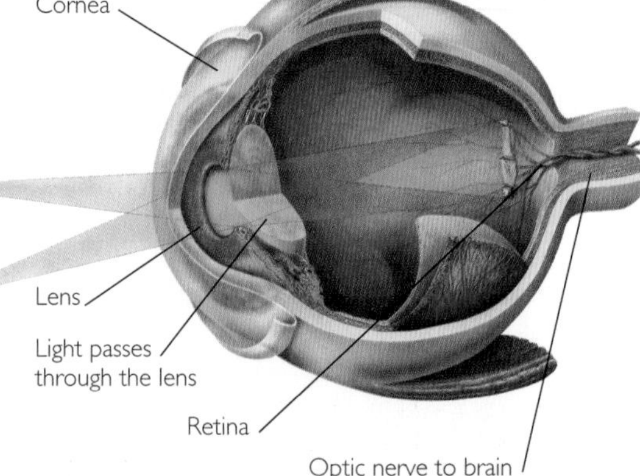

This diagram shows how the lens of the eye reverses an image on to the retina. The brain then interprets it, so that we see things the right way up.

Lent *noun* in the Christian Church a period of 40 days fasting and penance before Easter. *Sarah gave up chocolate for Lent.*

lent the past tense of lend.

leopard (say **lep**-urd) *noun* a large wild, spotted cat of Africa and Asia.

There is a saying: 'A leopard never changes its spots.' It means that you can't expect people to change their habits.

leper *noun* a person who has leprosy.

leprosy *noun* a disease of the skin and nerves which can lead to fingers and toes dropping off.

lesbian *noun* a woman who is attracted to other women, a gay woman.

Lesotho *noun* a country in Africa.

-less *suffix* without. *Colourless, smokeless.*

less (lesser, least) *adjective* not so much. *Please make less noise.* **less** *adverb. You should eat less and sleep more.* **less** *preposition* minus. *Six less four equals two.*

lessen *verb* to make or become smaller in size, importance etc.

lesson *noun* 1 a period of time when you are taught something by a teacher. 2 an experience that is a warning or example. *His accident was a lesson to him to be more careful in the future.*

let *verb* 1 to allow. *He let me borrow his bike.* 2 to allow somebody to rent a house and use it if they pay money. **let's** to suggest something. *Let's go swimming.* **let off** 1 to set light to a firework or to fire a gun. 2 to allow somebody to go without punishing them. **letdown** disappointment. *The film was a big letdown.* **let go** to set free.

lethal *adjective* able to cause death, deadly. *A lethal weapon.*

letter *noun* 1 one of the signs we use to write words. 2 a written message we send to somebody by post.

Jamie wrote a letter to his cousins thanking them for the birthday present.

lettuce *noun* a plant with large green leaves that we eat in salads.

leukemia *noun* (say loo-**kee**-mee-uh) a serious cancer-like disease in which the blood produces too many white cells.

level *adjective* smooth and horizontal, not sloping. *A level surface.* **level** *adverb* equal or at the same height or distance.

lever *noun* 1 a strong bar that you use to lift something heavy by placing one end under the object and pushing down on the other end. 2 a long handle that you use to work a machine.

GRAMMAR NOTE

'Fewer' is the comparative of 'few', and means 'a smaller number of'. 'Less' is the comparative of 'little', and means 'a smaller quantity or amount'. 'Fewer' is followed by a plural noun, as in: 'There were fewer than 100 women in the hall.' 'Less' is followed by a singular noun or a noun describing an amount, as in: 'Put less milk in my tea, please.'

AMAZING FACT

Lichens are very simple plants. They don't have any true leaves, roots or flowers. They grow very slowly and are an ancient form of life. A small, hand-sized patch of lichen on a rock could be hundreds of years old.

liable *adjective* 1 legally responsible for something. *You are liable for damaging the machine.* 2 likely to. *In winter the lake is liable to freeze.*

liar *noun* a person who tells lies.

liberal *adjective* generous and tolerant. *A liberal attitude.*

Liberal Democrat *noun* one of three main political parties in Great Britain.

liberate *verb* to set somebody or an animal free. **liberation** *noun.*

Liberia *noun* a country in Africa.

liberty *noun* freedom from control, slavery etc. **take liberties** to behave rudely and without respect.

The Statue of Liberty in New York Harbour was a present to the US from the people of France.

librarian *noun* a person who is in charge of or who works in a library.

library (libraries) *noun* a room or building where a lot of books, records etc. are kept, usually for people to borrow.

Libreville *noun* the capital of Gabon.

Libya *noun* a country in Africa.

Libyan *noun* a person who comes from Libya. **Libyan** *adjective. The Libyan coast.*

lichen *noun* (say **litch**-in or **lie**-kin) a flat, green or yellowish plant that grows in patches on rocks and tree trunks.

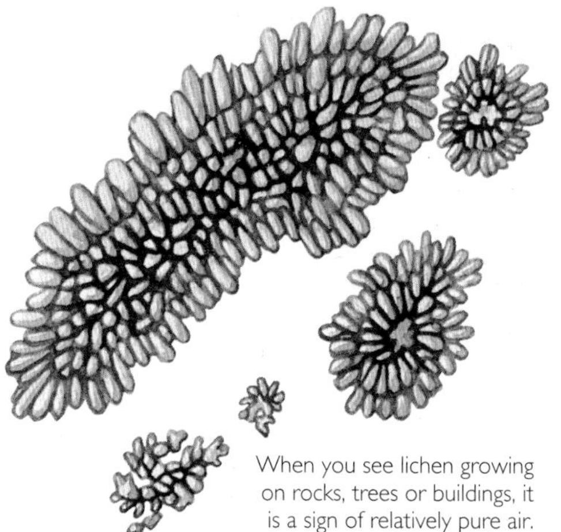

When you see lichen growing on rocks, trees or buildings, it is a sign of relatively pure air.

lick *verb* 1 to touch something with your tongue. *The dog licked my hand.* 2 (informal) to defeat or overcome. *He is determined to lick the problem.* **lick** *noun.*

L

lid *noun* 1 a cover for a box, jar, pot etc. that you can remove or lift up. 2 the eyelid, the piece of skin that covers the eye.

The eyelid shields the eye from light and protects it against dust flying in the air.

lie (lies, lying, lied) *verb* to say something that you know is untrue. *She lied to the police about the theft.* **lie** *noun. It is dishonest to tell lies.*

lie (lies, lying, lay, lain) *verb* 1 to rest your body in a flat position. *She felt ill so she lay on the sofa.* 2 to remain. *The snow lay on the ground for weeks.* 3 to be located in a certain place. *The village lies 10 kilometres north of Newtown.*

Liechtenstein *noun* a country in central Europe.

life *noun* 1 the time between a person's or an animal's birth and death when they are alive. 2 the ability of plants and animals to grow and develop, unlike such things as rocks, metals etc. 3 a way of living. *She leads a very exciting life.* 4 liveliness. *He is full of life.* **take somebody's life** to kill somebody

lifebelt *noun* a ring or belt that floats and which a person holds on to or wears to prevent them sinking or drowning.

lifeboat *noun* a boat that rescues people who are shipwrecked or in danger at sea.

The lifeboat set out to rescue the holidaymakers who had capsized their dinghy.

lifeguard *noun* a person who has been trained to help rescue swimmers in danger.

lifejacket *noun* an inflatable jacket that keeps you afloat in the water.

lifeless *adjective* 1 dead. *Her lifeless body.* 2 uninteresting. *Lifeless acting.*

lifelike *adjective* looking like a real person or animal. *A lifelike painting.*

lifestyle *noun* the way people live their lives, where they live and what their interests are.

SPELLING NOTE

Try not to confuse 'lightning' in 'thunder and lightning' (no 'e') with the present participle of 'lighten' (with an 'e') meaning 'to become brighter'.

All lighthouses used to be manned, with the lighthouse-keeper living there full-time. Nowadays, lighthouses are operated automatically and no one lives in them.

lift *verb* 1 to pick something up and raise it to a higher place. *He lifted the child on to his knee.* 2 to rise. *The plane lifted into the air.* **lift** *noun* 1 a container for carrying people or goods up or down between floors inside a building (US elevator). 2 a short ride in somebody's car, lorry etc.

lift-off *noun* the launching of a rocket.

light (lights, lighting, lit or lighted) *verb* 1 to make something start burning. *Let's light the candles.* 2 to give light to a place. **light** *noun* 1 what makes us able to see things, not dark. *The Sun gives us light.* 2 something that gives out light. **light** *adjective* 1 (of colour) pale and not strong. *Light blue.* 2 full of bright light. *A light room.*

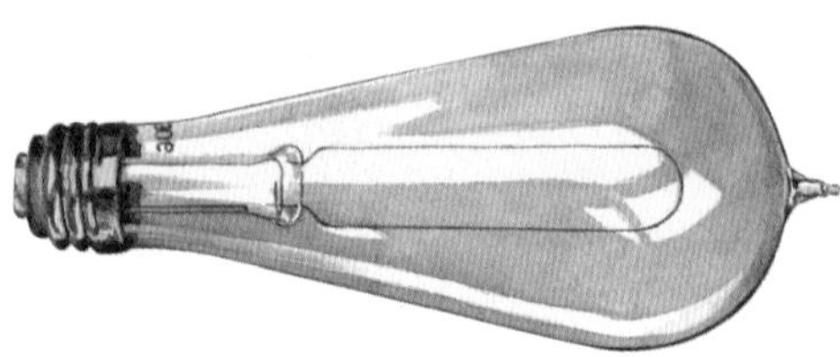

The electric current flows through a thin coil of wire called a filament to light up the bulb.

light *adjective* 1 weighing little, not heavy. *As light as a feather.* 2 gentle or small in amount. *We ate a light meal.* 3 not too serious. *Light music on the radio.*

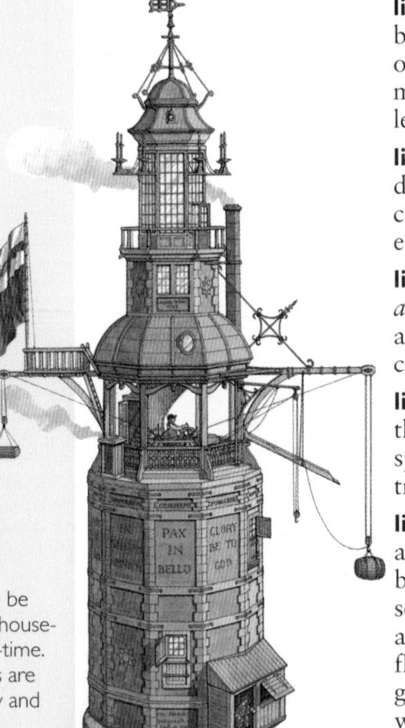

lighten *verb* 1 to become brighter or less dark. 2 to make something less heavy.

lighter *noun* a device for lighting cigarettes or a fire etc.

light-hearted *adjective* cheerful and without a care.

light year *noun* the distance in space that light travels in a year.

lighthouse *noun* a tower-like building by the sea that sends out a very bright flashing light to guide ships or warn them off dangerous rocks.

lighting *noun* artificial lights such as candles and electric light.

lightning *noun* a bright flash of electricity that lights up the sky during a thunderstorm. *Thunder and lightning.*

like *verb* 1 to be fond of and to find somebody pleasant. 2 to enjoy something.

like *preposition* 1 nearly the same as or similar to, resembling. *He looks like his dad.* 2 in the same way as. *He roared like a lion.* 3 typical of or in the character of. *It's not like Laura to be early.* 4 for example, such as. *Indoor games like chess and snooker are my favourites.*

likely (likelier, likeliest) *adverb* probable and expected to happen. *I think it's likely to rain, if not today, then tomorrow.*

likeness *noun* a resemblance. *There's a great likeness between the brothers.*

lilac *noun* a small tree or shrub with sweet-smelling purple or white flowers.

Lilongwe *noun* the capital of Malawi.

lily (lilies) *noun* a plant that grows from a bulb with white, yellow or red flowers.

Lima *noun* the capital of Peru.

limb *noun* an arm or a leg or the wing of a bird.

lime *noun* 1 an oval, green citrus fruit similar to a lemon. 2 a substance obtained from limestone and used in making cement.

limerick *noun* a humorous poem in five lines. *An Irish limerick.*

limestone *noun* a kind of rock from which lime is obtained for making cement.

Stalactites and stalagmites form in limestone caves. Stalactites hang from the ceiling and stalagmites grow from the floor.

limit *noun* 1 a boundary or some point beyond which you should not go. *A 70 mph speed limit.* **limit** *verb* to prevent going beyond a certain limit or point, to restrict. *She limits herself to one small bar of chocolate a day.*

limp *adjective* drooping, soft and floppy. *A limp handshake.*

limp *verb* to walk with difficulty and unevenly because you have an injury to your leg or foot. **limp** *noun*.

AMAZING FACT

A group of lions is called a pride. This term probably dates from the Middle Ages and arose because lions look majestic and proud.

A female lion is called a lioness. In fact, the lioness does most of the hunting and feeds the cubs and the rest of the pride.

Waterlilies thrive in ponds. Their large waxy flowers and leaves float on the surface of the water.

DID YOU KNOW

This is a limerick:
'There was a young lady of Wilts,
Who walked up to Scotland on stilts;
When they said it is shocking
To show so much stocking,
She answered, "Then what about kilts?'"

line *noun* 1 a long, thin mark on a surface. *She tried to draw straight lines on the paper.* 2 a group of people, things or words in a row. *Count the lines on this page.* 3 a rope, string etc. with a special purpose. *A washing line.* 4 a system of buses, trains or aircraft that travel regularly. 5 **lines** the words that actors have to say. **line** *verb*. *Great crowds lined the streets.*

line *verb* to sew material inside something. *I am going to line the jacket with blue silk.*

linen *noun* a strong cloth made from the fibres of the flax plant and used for sheets, tablecloths etc.

liner *noun* a large passenger ship or aircraft.

linger *verb* to dawdle, wait around, seeming unwilling to leave.

lining *noun* a layer of material to line the inside of something. *Most jackets have a lining, and in some, it's quilted, for warmth.*

linguist *noun* a person who studies foreign languages and is good at learning and speaking them.

link *noun* 1 a ring or loop in a chain. 2 a connection between two things. *The Eurotunnel is a link between England and France.* **link** *verb* to join up. *They linked arms.*

The links in a chain are extremely strong.

lion *noun* a large wild cat with light brown fur that lives in Africa and Asia. The male has a thick mane. Lions live in family groups called prides.

lioness *noun* a female lion.

The lioness was proudly guarding her cubs.

lip *noun* Your lips are the soft edges of your mouth. *Luscious lips.*

lip-read *verb* (of a deaf person) to understand what somebody is saying by looking carefully at their lips while they are speaking. *Sally learned to lip-read.*

liquefy (liquefies, liquefying, liquefied) *verb* to make or become liquid.

L

liquid *noun* any substance that flows, such as water. Any substance that is not a gas or a solid. **liquid** *adjective*. **liquidize** *verb* to crush food like fruit and vegetables into a liquid in a liquidizer. **liquidizer** (*noun*).

Lisbon *noun* the capital of Portugal.

lisp *verb*, *noun* a speech problem in which the 's' sounds like a 'th'.

list *noun* a series of names or things written down one under the other. *A list of the club's members.* **list** *verb* to write things down on a list.

list *verb* (of a ship) to lean over to one side.

listen *verb* to pay attention to what you hear. **listener** *noun*.

lit past tense of light.

literally *adverb* exactly as the words state. *He literally knocked me flying.*

literate *adjective* able to read and write.

literature *noun* 1 novels, plays and poetry that are especially good. 2 printed material on a particular subject. *Is there any literature about this washing machine?*

Lithuania *noun* a Baltic country in Europe.

The flag of Lithuania has three stripes, yellow, green and red.

litre *noun* a measure of liquids equal to 1,000 millilitres.

litter *noun* rubbish such as paper and bottles left lying around.

litter *noun* all the animals born to the same mother at the same time.

little *adjective* 1 small in size or quantity. 2 not much. *There's very little time left.*

live *verb* (rhymes with give) 1 to be alive, to have life. Plants and animals live. 2 to continue to stay alive. *The tortoise lived for 50 years.* 3 to have your home in some place. *My gran lives in Jersey.*

live *adjective* (rhymes with dive) 1 not dead, but living. *There was a live rabbit under the bed.* 2 full of electricity. *This wire is live.* 3 a performance on radio or television that is happening as you listen or watch.

SPELLING NOTE

Try not to confuse 'liquefy' or 'liquify', meaning 'to make something liquid' with 'liquidize', meaning 'to crush fruit etc. in a blender'.

Mum left the shopping list behind when she went to the supermarket.

AMAZING FACT

In order to survive, lizards have evolved in some very bizarre ways. Some lizards have adapted to their surroundings by becoming snake-like; their legs have become tiny, but movable flaps. The komodo dragon, which may grow to ten feet long, has well-developed limbs and is a good climber and swimmer.

livelihood *noun* the way a person earns money to live. *He earns a good livelihood from doing up old houses and selling them.*

lively *adjective* full of energy. *He has a very lively mind and is interesting company.*

liver *noun* 1 a large and important organ in your body that helps to clean your blood and helps to process food. 2 this organ from an animal used as food.

lives plural of life. *Do cats really have nine lives, as it is thought?*

livestock *noun* animals kept on a farm. *John keeps cattle and other livestock.*

living *adjective* alive not dead. **living** *noun* how a person earns money to live. *What do you do for a living?*

lizard *noun* a small reptile with a long scaly body, four legs and a tail. Most lizards live in warm countries.

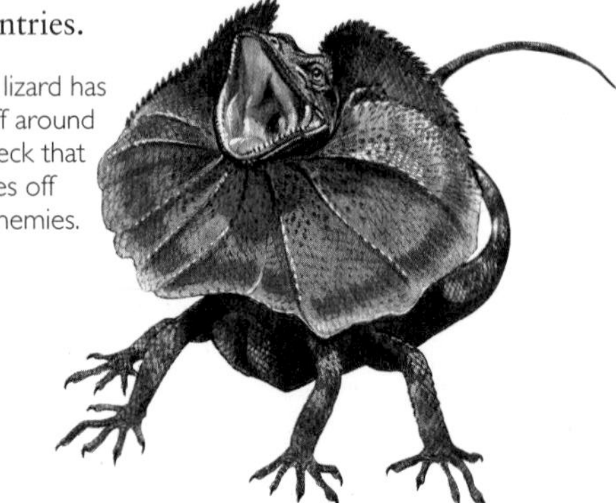

This lizard has a ruff around its neck that scares off its enemies.

Ljubljana *noun* the capital of Slovenia.

llama *noun* a South American animal similar to a camel, but without a hump. *Llamas make good sheep guards, and one llama can guard over 100 animals.*

load *noun* something heavy that is carried. An amount of something to be carried. *A load of wood.* **load** *verb* 1 to put a load on to something that will carry it. *He loaded the wood on to the lorry.* 2 to put bullets in a gun, a film into a camera or data into a computer. **loads of** a lot of something.

loaf (loaves) *noun* a large piece of bread baked in a shape. *A farmhouse loaf.*

loan *noun* something that somebody lends you, usually money.

loathe *verb* (rhymes with clothe) to hate or to dislike something very much.

lob (lobs, lobbing, lobbed) *verb* 1 to hit or throw something slowly or high in the air. 2 (in cricket) to bowl underhand. **lob** *noun*.

lobby *noun* an entrance hall in a theatre, hotel etc. *I met him for drinks in the lobby of the hotel.*

lobe *noun* the soft part of the ear that hangs down. *Her ear lobes were pierced several times, and she wore many earrings.*

lobster *noun* a shellfish or sea animal with a long body covered in a hard shell. It has eight legs and two large claws in front. Lobsters can be eaten.

Lobsters turn pink when boiled.

local *adjective* belonging to or affecting a particular area or place. *The local newspaper carried daily reports of our campaign.* **locally** *adverb.*

locality *noun* an area. *This is a very well-to-do locality.*

locate *verb* 1 to find the exact position of. *Joe located the source of the river on the map.* 2 to be situated in a particular place. *The supermarket is located out of town, for the convenience of shoppers.*

loch *noun* a Scottish word for lake. *Loch Lomond is so beautiful in spring.*

lock *noun* 1 a device that fastens a door or lid and that you open and shut with a key. **lock** *verb* to fasten with a lock and key. 2 a section of a canal or river between gates that can be opened and shut to raise or lower ships by altering the level of the water. *The barge went through the lock.*

locust *noun* a large kind of grasshopper that travels in huge swarms and destroys crops. *A plague of locusts.*

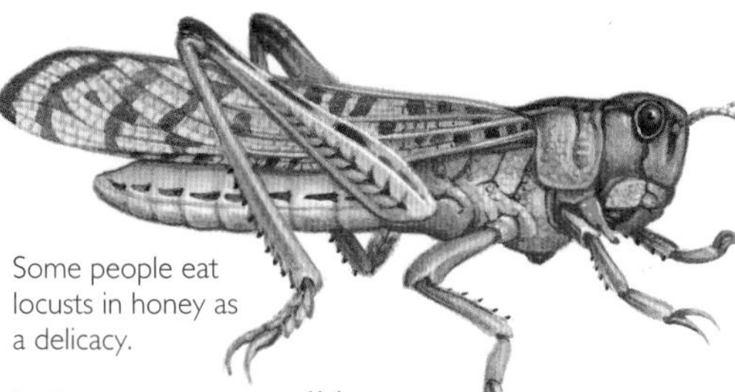

Some people eat locusts in honey as a delicacy.

lodge *noun* 1 a small house, usually at the gates leading to a large house. 2 a beaver's home. **lodge** *verb* 1 to live in rented rooms (lodgings). 2 to become firmly fixed in.

lodger *noun* somebody who pays to live in a room in another person's house.

loft *noun* a room or space under the roof of a building. *I put the junk in the loft, rather than throw it away.*

log *noun* 1 a length of wood that has been cut from a branch of a felled tree. 2 a written record of the journey of a ship or aircraft. *The log book.*

AMAZING FACT

When a lobster is in danger, it curls its tail under its body, pushing the animal backwards and helping it to escape.

SPELLING NOTE

Some -logies
anthropology (the study of mankind)
astrology (the stars)
chronology (dates)
cosmology (universe)
dendrology (trees)
etymology (word origins)
meteorology (weather)
ornithology (birds)
pathology (diseases)
vexillology (flags)

logic *noun* the science of careful and correct reasoning. *I rely on logic, not imagination.*

logical *adjective* 1 following the rules of logic. 2 sensible and reasonable.

logo *noun* a symbol or lettering that represents a company or organization, an emblem or trademark. *The diaries were printed with the company's logo.*

-logy *suffix* the study of some subject. *Geology, anthropology, biology.*

loiter *verb* to stand around somewhere with nothing to do. *The woman loitering near that car looks suspicious.*

Lomé *noun* the capital of Togo.

London *noun* the capital of England and the United Kingdom.

lonely (lonelier, loneliest) *adjective* 1 unhappy at being alone. 2 far away and not often visited. *A lonely island off the north coast of Scotland.*

long *adjective* 1 measuring far from one end to the other. The opposite of long is short. *The longest bridge in the world is in Japan.* 2 taking a lot of time. *It's a long journey from London to Beijing.* 3 a certain amount of distance or time. *An hour-long flight.* **no longer** not any more.

long *verb* to want something very much. *She longed to go home.* **longing** *noun.* **longingly** *adverb. He looked longingly at the shiny bike.*

longitude *noun* the position of a place measured as a distance in degrees east or west of a line on a map that runs through Greenwich near London from the North and South Poles.

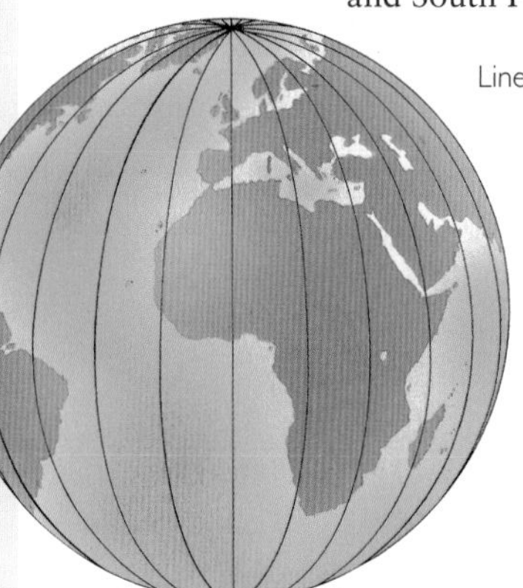

Lines of longitude run vertically around the globe.

loo *noun* a lavatory.

look *verb* 1 to move your eyes to see something. 2 to seem or appear to be so. *Dick looks happy today.* **look after** to take care of somebody or something. **look for** to search. *Betty is looking for her trainers.* **look forward to** to wait for something eagerly. **look into** to investigate. **look out** Be careful! **look up to** to admire.

L

loom *noun* a machine for weaving thread into cloth.

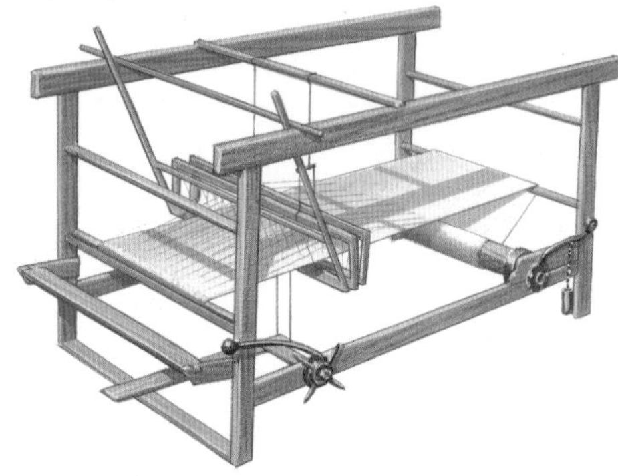

Many different kinds of fabrics can be woven on a loom.

loop *noun* a circular shape made in a rope or piece of string. **loop** *verb. He looped the rope around the post.*

loose *adjective* 1 not held firmly in place. *My loose tooth fell out.* 2 not attached or fastened. *The ponies were loose in the paddock all day.* 3 (of clothes) not fitting tightly, too big.

loosen *verb* to make or become loose. *His tie was too tight so he loosened it.*

loot *noun* goods and money that have been stolen. **loot** *verb. During the riots people looted shops and houses.*

lord *noun* 1 the title of a nobleman, bishop or male judge. 2 **Lord** the name given to God and Jesus. 3 **Lords** short for House of Lords, the unelected upper house in the British parliament. **lordly** *adjective. Lordly behaviour doesn't suit you.*

lorry (lorries) *noun* a big motor vehicle that carries heavy goods by road, a truck.

In Australia, lorries hauling several trucks are called road trains.

SPELLING NOTE

Try not to confuse 'loose', meaning 'set free', 'undo', and 'loosen', meaning 'to make less tight'.

lot *noun* 1 large amount or number. *What a lot of presents!* 2 **lots** *Put lots of jam on the bread.* 3 an article in an auction. **the lot** everything. *You can take the lot.*

lotion *noun* a liquid or cream that you put on your skin to clean, soften or protect it. *Suntan lotion.*

lottery *noun* a way of making money by selling a lot of tickets to try to win prizes.

loud *adjective* 1 making a large amount of sound, not quiet. 2 unpleasantly bright and colourful. *He was wearing a loud purple shirt.* **loudness** *noun.*

loudspeaker *noun* a piece of equipment in a radio, televison or stereo system etc. that turns electrical waves into sound. A device for making sounds louder.

When a sound signal from the amplifier of a loudspeaker passes through the metal coil, it makes the cone vibrate, producing sound.

lounge *noun* a sitting room with comfortable chairs where you can relax. **lounge** *verb* to sit around in a lazy way doing nothing.

love *verb* to like somebody very much and want to be with them all the time. **lovable** *adjective* easy to love. **lover** *noun.*

lovely (lovelier, loveliest) *adjective* 1 beautiful to look at, listen to or touch. 2 very pleasant.

lose (loses, losing, lost) *verb* 1 If you lose something, you do not have it any more and cannot find it. 2 to fail to win. *They lost the match.* 3 to go astray. *We lost our way.*

loser *noun* somebody who seems never to be successful. *I always back the loser.*

loss *noun* something that has been lost and that you no longer have. *She was very upset by the loss of her precious bracelet.*

lost past tense of lose.

loving *adjective* showing love. *She gave him a loving smile.*

low *adjective* 1 not high but near the ground. 2 not loud. *He talked in a low voice so nobody could hear.* **the Low Countries** the Netherlands and Belgium.

low *verb* to moo or make a noise like a cow.

lower *verb* to move or let something down. *The soldiers lowered the flag.* The opposite of lower is raise.

loyal *adjective* always faithful and true to your friends. **loyalty** *noun.*

Luanda *noun* the capital of Angola.

lubricate *verb* to put oil or grease on parts of a machine so that they move easily and smoothly. **lubrication** *noun.*

lucid *noun* 1 easy to understand. *A lucid explanation.* 2 clear, not confused. *Despite the accident his mind was lucid.*

luck *noun* 1 something that happens to you by chance and that you have not planned or cannot control. *Winning a lottery is pure luck.* 2 something good but unexpected that happens to you. *Wish me luck!*

lucky (luckier, luckiest) *adjective* 1 something lucky happens by chance. *She was lucky to win the lottery.* 2 bringing good luck. *A lucky charm.*

ludicrous *adjective* (say loo-dee-kruss) very silly, absurd. *You look ludicrous in those clothes.*

luggage *noun* the suitcases and bags that travellers take with them.

lukewarm *adjective* 1 A liquid that is lukewarm is only just warm. 2 not enthusiastic. *The film received only lukewarm praise.*

We had so much luggage that we had to pay excess charges.

lull *noun* a short period of quiet when little is happening. *There was a lull in the traffic noise.*

lull *verb* to soothe and make somebody relaxed and calm. *The gentle music lulled her to sleep.*

lullaby *noun* a gentle song that helps a child go to sleep. *Mum sang the baby a lullaby.*

lumber *noun* rough timber.

Jake looked in the lumber pile for a piece of wood he could make into a chair leg.

lumber *verb* to walk slowly in a heavy, clumsy way. **lumber with** to give somebody something they do not want. *Lizzie was lumbered with mowing the lawn.*

lumberjack *noun* in North America, a person who cuts down and saws up trees.

lump *noun* 1 a bump or swelling. *Luke has a lump on his knee.* 2 a small solid piece of something without shape. *A lump of clay.*

DID YOU KNOW

The formal word for the midday meal, 'luncheon', is really a long form of the original but less formal word 'lunch'.

AMAZING FACT

The lynx has a much shorter tail than most of the other 'big cats'. It is a nocturnal animal that lives on rodents and young deer.

lunar *adjective* concerned with the Moon. *A lunar journey.* **lunar month** the time it takes for the Moon to orbit the Earth – 29 days.

lunatic *noun* somebody who is foolish or insane. **lunatic** *adjective. A lunatic idea.*

lunch *noun* a meal eaten in the middle of the day. **lunch** *verb.*

lung *noun* one of two organs inside your chest that you use for breathing. The lungs take in oxygen from the air and give out carbon dioxide.

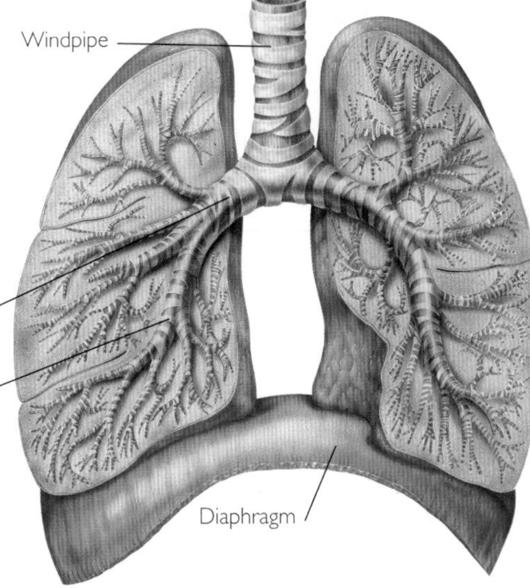

The lungs are the organs of breathing.

lunge *verb* to make a sudden thrust forward. *She lunged at the dog with a stick.* **lunge** *noun.*

lure *verb* to attract and tempt, to lead astray. *They were lured by the bright lights of the fair.* **lure** *noun.*

lurk *verb* to wait around out of sight with a dishonest purpose, to prowl. *There is somebody lurking under the trees.*

Lusaka *noun* the capital of Zambia.

lush *adjective* growing thickly and healthily, fertile. *Lush vegetation.*

lust *noun* a very strong desire. *A lust for fame got him nowhere.*

lute *noun* an old-fashioned stringed musical instrument in the shape of half a pear.

Luxembourg *noun* a country in Northwestern Europe, and its capital city.

luxury *noun* 1 something expensive that is very nice to have but that you do not really need. 2 great comfort and having a lot of expensive luxuries. *She grew up in luxury.* **luxurious** *adjective. A luxurious house.*

lynx *noun* a wild cat with a short tail and tufts of hair in its ears.

lyre *noun* a musical instrument like a small harp. *A gentle tune on the lyre.*

lyrics *plural noun* the words of a popular song. *I really like these lyrics.*

Mm

macabre *adjective* strangely frightening and gruesome. *A macabre film.*

macaroni *noun* tube-shaped pasta.

Macedonia *noun* a country in Southeast Europe. *Macedonian wine.*

machine *noun* a piece of equipment with moving parts that uses electricity or an engine to do a job or make work easier.

machinery *noun* 1 the parts of a machine. 2 machines. 3 an organized system of doing something. *The machinery of local government runs very slowly.*

macho *adjective* (say **match**-oh) (of a man) aggressively and exaggeratedly masculine. Strong and virile.

mackintosh *noun* a raincoat that keeps the water out.

mad (madder, maddest) *adjective* 1 mentally ill, insane. 2 wildly foolish, not sensible. *What a mad idea to run across a busy road.* 3 very angry. **madness** *noun.*

Madagascar *noun* a country in the Indian Ocean off East Africa.

madam *noun* a formal and polite way of addressing a woman without using her name. *Can I help you, madam?*

madden *verb* to make somebody angry. *It maddens me when you bite your nails.*

made past tense of make.

Madrid *noun* the capital of Spain.

magazine *noun* a publication with a paper cover that comes out usually every week or month and which contains articles, photographs, stories etc.

maggot *noun* the larva or grub of the house-fly. Maggots look like small worms.

Maggots are used to catch fish.

magic *noun* 1 in stories, a strange power that makes wonderful or impossible things happen. 2 clever tricks that look as though they happen by magic. *She pulled a pigeon out of the hat by magic.*

magical *adjective* 1 produced by magic. 2 strange and exciting. *A magical evening was had by all.*

magician *noun* (say maj-**ish**-un) a person who can do tricks or magic.

When the paperclips come within the magnet's magnetic field, they become magnetized too, and so attract other paperclips.

WORD HISTORY

The shape of the letter M comes from an Ancient Egyptian symbol for water. Its sound comes from 'mem', a Semitic word meaning 'water'.

AMAZING FACT

The forerunner of the mainframe computer, and all the personal computers that we use today, was actually a tabulating and adding machine designed in 1837 by Charles Babbage. His machine was only partially built and was never completed. In fact, the records of his work were lost for 100 years.

magistrate *noun* a person who acts as a judge in a court of law that deals with less serious offences.

magnet *noun* a piece of metal that has the power to attract or make iron or steel move towards it. **magnetic** *adjective. A magnetic compass.* **magnetism** *noun.* **magnetize** *verb.*

magnificent *adjective* beautiful and very impressive. *A magnificent castle stood on the hill.* **magnificence** *noun.*

magnify (magnifies, magnifying, magnified) *verb* to make something seem larger than it really is by looking at it through a magnifying glass or microscope. *Astronomers use telescopes to magnify the stars.*

magnifying glass *noun* a special lens with a handle that makes objects look bigger than they really are.

mahogany *noun* a very hard, reddish-brown wood used in making furniture. *A mahogany table.*

maid *noun* a female servant.

maiden *noun* (old-fashioned) an unmarried young woman. **maiden name** a woman's surname before she marries. **maiden voyage** a ship's first voyage.

The maiden waited shyly for her knight to arrive.

mail *noun* 1 letters and parcels sent by post. **mail** *verb* (mainly US) to send by post. 2 a kind of armour made from small metal rings.

maim *verb* to injure somebody so badly that they are disabled for life.

main *adjective* the most important. *The main shopping area is near our house.*

mainframe *noun* a big, powerful computer that can be used by several people at once.

mainland *noun* the principal and largest mass of land without its islands.

M

mains *plural noun* the chief cable or pipes that carry electricity, gas, or water to a street. *They repaired the burst mains.*

maintain *verb* 1 to keep in good condition. *The council maintains the grass verges.* 2 to support and look after. 3 to state as true or as a belief. *She maintains that she is always right.* 4 to continue. *The pupils have maintained high standards.*

maize *noun* a tall plant that produces cobs of sweetcorn, a cereal with large seeds.

Maize is used as cattle fodder.

majesty *noun* 1 impressive greatness, splendour. *The majesty of the mountains.* 2 **Your Majesty** the title people use when speaking to a king or queen. **majestic** *adjective.*

major *adjective* important, main. *The new government made major changes.* **major** *noun* an officer in the army above a captain.

majority *noun* 1 more than half of a total. *The majority of people watch television every day.* 2 the number of votes by which somebody wins an election.

Majuro *noun* the capital of the Marshall Islands.

make (makes, making, made) *verb* 1 to put things together to produce something new, to create or build. 2 to prepare. 3 to cause or force something to happen. *The aeroplane made a forced landing.* 4 to add up or produce. *Three and six make nine.* 5 to earn or gain. *How much money does a waiter make?* **make** *noun* the maker's name or brand. *What make of car is this?* **make somebody's day** to make somebody feel happy all day long.

make do *verb* to use something to replace what you really want. *You'll have to make do with this old saucepan.*

make-up *noun* special coloured creams and powders (cosmetics) that women and actors put on their faces.

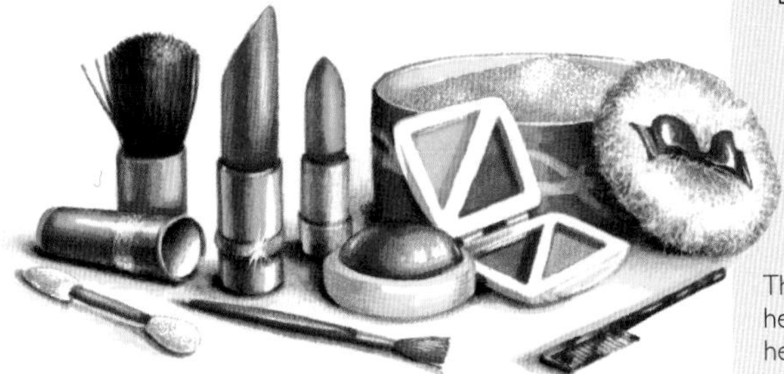

The actress kept her make-up on her dressing table.

make up *verb* 1 to invent. *Make up a story about a monster.* 2 to become friends again after quarrelling. 3 to put on make-up.

WORD HISTORY

'Malaria' comes from two Italian words, 'mal aria', meaning 'bad air'. People once thought the disease was caused by breathing the 'bad air' of marshy places.

AMAZING FACT

Mammals were the last major animal group to appear on Earth. During the period that dinosaurs lived, the only existing mammals were small rodents that looked like shrews.

make-believe *verb* to pretend and imagine things. *Let's make-believe we are cowboys.*

makeshift *adjective* temporary and only meant to last until something better can be used. *Makeshift accommodation.*

mal- *prefix* bad or ill. *Malformed, malfunction, malnutrition.*

Malabo *noun* the capital of Equatorial Guinea.

malaria *noun* a tropical disease that is carried from person to person by the bite of a female mosquito.

Malawi *noun* a country in Africa.

Malaysia *noun* a country in Southeast Asia.

The Malaysian flag is red and white striped with a yellow Moon and Sun on a square blue ground.

Malaysian *noun* a person who comes from Malaysia. **Malaysian** *adjective. Malaysian rubber plantations.*

Maldives *plural noun* a country of many islands in the Indian Ocean.

Malé *noun* the capital of the Maldives.

male *noun, adjective* a human or animal belonging to the sex that does not produce babies or eggs. Boys and men are males. *A male horse is called a stallion.* The opposite of male is female.

Mali *noun* a country in Africa.

malicious *adjective* (say mal-**ish**-uss) unkind and wishing to see others hurt or unhappy, spiteful. *She has a very malicious tongue.* **malice** *noun.*

mall *noun* (mainly US) a shopping centre.

mallard *noun* a kind of wild duck.

mallet *noun* a large wooden hammer.

malnutrition *noun* illness caused by eating too little food or the wrong kind of food.

malt *noun* dried barley that is used to make beer and whisky.

Malta *noun* a country in southern Europe.

Maltese *noun* 1 a person who comes from Malta. 2 the language of Malta. **Maltese** *adjective. The Maltese Cross.*

maltreat *verb* to treat a person or animal roughly or unkindly. *We should never maltreat our pets.*

mammal *noun* any animal of which the female feeds her young with milk from her own body. Humans, elephants and whales are mammals.

mammoth *noun* a kind of large hairy elephant that lived thousands of years ago during the Ice Age. Mammoths are now extinct.

man *noun* 1 a fully grown male human. 2 humans in general. *When did man first appear on Earth?* **mankind** *noun. A giant step for mankind.*

manage *verb* 1 to control or be in charge of something. *Lucy manages the production department.* 2 to be able to do something, especially something difficult or awkward, to succeed. *She managed to solve the crossword.* **manager** *noun.* **management** *noun. Bad management.*

Managua *noun* the capital of Nicaragua.

Manama *noun* the capital of Bahrain.

mane *noun* the long thick hair on the neck of a horse or male lion.

manger *noun* a long narrow container in a barn or stable from which cattle and horses feed.

The baby Jesus was wrapped in swaddling clothes and laid in a manger.

mangle *verb* to damage something by crushing and twisting it out of shape.

manhood *noun* the state or condition of being a man.

mania *noun* a strong desire or enthusiasm for something. *He has a mania for motorbikes.*

maniac *noun* 1 a person suffering from a mental illness that makes them behave violently. 2 (informal) an over-enthusiastic person. *She drives like a maniac.*

Manila *noun* the capital of the Philippines.

mankind *noun* all people in general.

manner *noun* 1 the way in which something is done. *Let's do this in a professional manner.* 2 the way a person behaves or talks. *She has a very friendly manner.* 3 **manners** polite behaviour.

Animals such as mammoths adapted to the Ice Age by growing thick woolly coats.

AMAZING FACT

The word 'marathon' comes from a long distance run made by a messenger from Marathon, Greece, to Athens in 490 BC to report a Greek victory in the battle at Marathon.

DID YOU KNOW

Some people object that the use of 'man', as in 'the origins of man' for people in general is sexist. You can get round the problem by using words such as 'person', 'people', or 'human'.

manoeuvre *noun* (say man-**oo**-ver) a skilful or difficult movement or clever trick.

manor *noun* a large, important house in the country with land around it.

mansion *noun* a large, impressive house.

manslaughter *noun* killing somebody through carelessness but not with the intention of doing so.

mantelpiece *noun* a shelf above a fireplace.

manual *noun* a book with instructions on how to use or work something. **manual** *adjective* worked with the hands. *Manual controls, manual labour.*

manufacture *verb* to make things in large quantities by machine in a factory.

manure *noun* dung or animal waste used as a fertilizer to help produce better crops.

manuscript *noun* a handwritten or typed copy of a book etc. before it is printed.

Manx *adjective* relating to the Isle of Man. *Manx cats do not have tails.*

many *adjective, pronoun* a large number of people or things.

Maori (Maori or Maoris) *noun* (say **mow**-ree) the original people who lived in New Zealand.

map *noun* a drawing of an area, country etc. showing things like mountains, rivers, roads and towns. *A map of Treasure Island.*

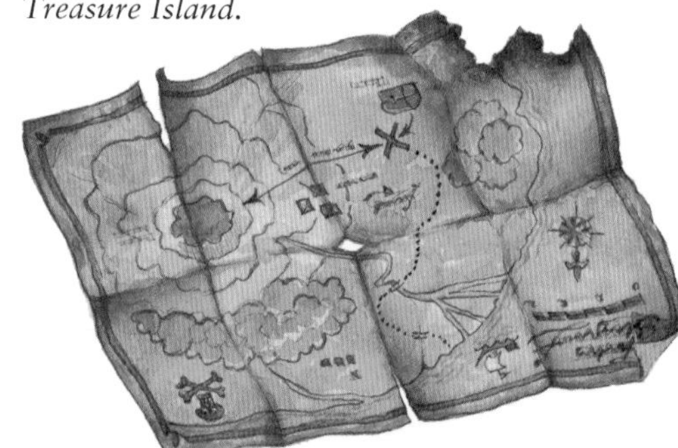

The map showed exactly where the treasure had been buried.

maple *noun* a tree with large leaves with five points. The maple leaf is the national emblem of Canada.

Maputo *noun* the capital of Mozambique.

marathon *noun* a race in which people run 26 miles (42 km).

marble *noun* 1 a very hard stone that can be polished to show its pattern or colour. 2 a small coloured glass ball used in children's games. *A game of marbles.*

march *verb* to walk with regular steps and arm movements in time with one another, like soldiers. **march** *noun* 1 a piece of music with a regular beat suitable for marching to. 2 a boundary. *The Welsh marches.*

March *noun* the third month of the year. March has 31 days.

mare *noun* a fully grown female horse. The opposite of a mare is a stallion.

margarine *noun* a soft yellow butter-like fat made mainly from vegetable oils.

margin *noun* the blank space or gap down the sides of a page.

marigold *noun* a plant of the daisy family with large orange or yellow flowers.

marine *adjective* to do with the sea. *Whales are marine mammals.* **marine** *noun* a soldier who serves at sea on board ship.

A school party visited the museum of marine life, where they saw many different sea creatures swimming in huge tanks.

mark *noun* 1 a stain or scratch on something. *There's a dirty mark on my shirt.* 2 a special sign on something. 3 a number or sign on a piece of schoolwork to show how good it is. *She got full marks, ten out of ten.* **mark** *verb*.

market *noun* a place where things are sold, usually from stalls in the open.

marmalade *noun* a jam made from oranges or some other citrus fruit and usually eaten at breakfast. *Orange marmalade.*

maroon *noun*, *adjective* dark reddish-brown. *Maroon socks.*

maroon *verb* to abandon or leave somebody alone in an isolated place such as a desert island.

marquee *noun* a very large tent used for summer parties, circuses etc.

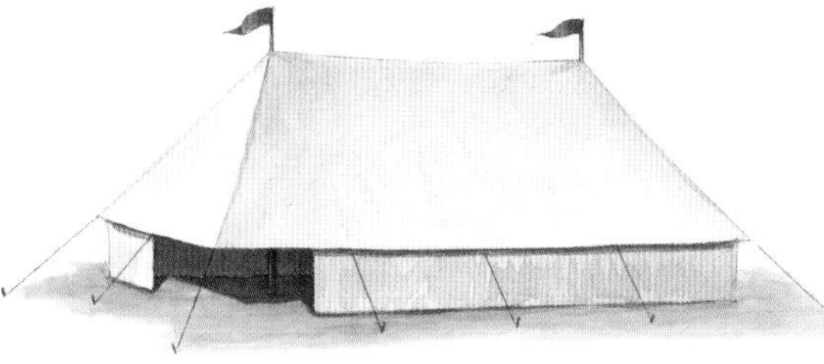

She hired a marquee and gave a big party when her daughter got married.

marriage *noun* 1 a wedding ceremony. 2 the state of being married. *My sister got married last year.*

marrow *noun* 1 a long, large green vegetable like a huge cucumber. 2 a soft substance containing blood vessels in the hollow parts of bones.

marry (marries, marrying, married) *verb* 1 to take somebody as your husband or wife. *My uncle married an American.* 2 to carry out the ceremony of marriage.

WORD HISTORY

'Marmalade' is from a Portuguese word 'marmelada', named after the quince ('marmelo' in Portuguese), from which fruit the preserve was originally made.

AMAZING FACT

Newly-born marsupials are very small and have not finished developing when they crawl into their mother's pouch. The babies drink their mothers' milk inside the pouch and grow strong.

marsh *noun* an area of low-lying land that is always wet, a bog. *The house was always damp because it was so near the marsh.*

Marshall Islands *plural noun* a country of many islands in the Pacific Ocean.

marshmallow *noun* a soft jelly-like sweet. *Toasted marshmallows for tea.*

marsupial *noun* an animal the female of which carries her young in a pouch on her stomach. Kangaroos are marsupials.

martial *adjective* to do with wars, battles, fighting, soldiers etc. *The band played marches and other kinds of martial music.* **martial arts** systems of self-defence such as karate, kendo and judo that come from China and Japan.

Martian *noun* an imaginary person from the planet Mars.

martin *noun* a bird with a forked tail similar to a swallow.

martyr *noun* somebody who chooses to suffer or be killed rather than give up their beliefs. **martyrdom** *noun*.

marvel (marvels, marvelling, marvelled) *verb* to be astonished or surprised. *I always marvel at how clever sheepdogs are.* **marvel** *noun*. *A computer is an electronic marvel.*

marvellous *adjective* excellent, very good.

mascara *noun* a colouring substance used on eyelashes to make them look longer or thicker. *Black mascara.*

mascot *noun* an animal or thing that people think brings good luck. *The team's mascot is a rabbit.*

masculine *adjective* concerned with men or typical of men, manly. **masculinity** *noun*. The opposite of masculine is feminine.

Maseru *noun* the capital of Lesotho.

mask *noun* a covering worn over the face to hide, disguise or protect it. **mask** *verb* to cover or disguise something.

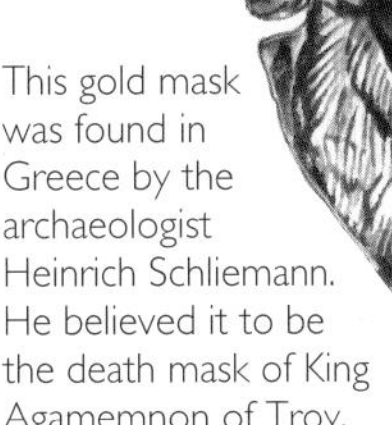

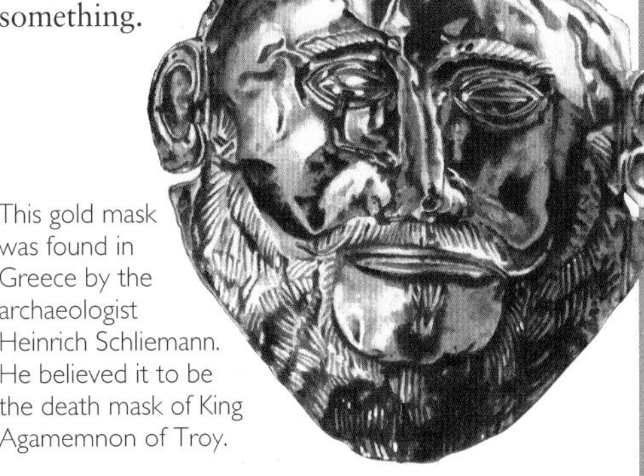

This gold mask was found in Greece by the archaeologist Heinrich Schliemann. He believed it to be the death mask of King Agamemnon of Troy.

mason *noun* a person who makes or builds things from stone.

masonry *noun* stonework.

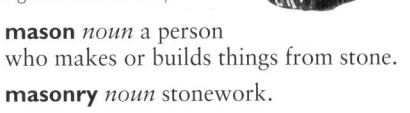

M

mass *noun* 1 a large number or quantity. *The plant was covered in a mass of flowers.* 2 a large shapeless lump of something. 3 **the masses** the ordinary people. **mass** *verb* to gather into a group or mass. *The crowd massed on to the pitch.* **mass-media** ways of communicating through such things as newspapers, radio and television, from which most people get their news and information. **mass-produced** made by machines in great quantities.

mass *noun* the celebration of the Holy Communion service in Roman Catholic and some other Christian churches.

massacre *noun* (say **mass**-uh-ker) the brutal killing of a large number of people. **massacre** *verb. The troops stormed the castle and massacred all the prisoners.*

massage *verb* to rub and knead parts of a person's body to get rid of pain or stiffness and to help them relax. **massage** *noun.*

massive *adjective* huge in size and heavy. *A massive rock blocked the road.*

mast *noun* a pole that holds a flag or supports a ship's sails.

Tom the cabin boy climbed to the top of the mast and searched the horizon for sight of land.

master *noun* 1 a male teacher. 2 the male owner of an animal. *The dog obeys its master.* 3 a man who controls other people. *He is master in his own house.* 4 a person who is very skilled at something. **master** *verb* 1 to learn something and become skilled in it. *She mastered Japanese in six months.* 2 to control. *He mastered his fear of flying and took off for the States.*

masterly *adjective* showing skill. *A truly masterly performance.*

masterpiece *noun* an outstandingly skilful work of art.

mastery *noun* 1 having complete control of something. *Mastery over his phobia.* 2 skill. *Mastery of the piano.*

mat *noun* 1 a small piece of material for covering a part of a floor. *Please wipe your feet on the mat.* 2 a small piece of material placed on a table to protect it from hot or wet plates, cups etc.

match *verb* to be like or equal to something, to go well together. *These two socks don't match.* **match** *noun* 1 an equal to. *At exams, she's no match for her sister.* 2 a game between two teams. *A tennis match between two champion players.*

AMAZING FACT

Matter is anything – gas, solid or liquid – that takes up space. And nearly all matter can exist in all three of these forms. You may or may not be able to see and touch matter in all three forms, however.

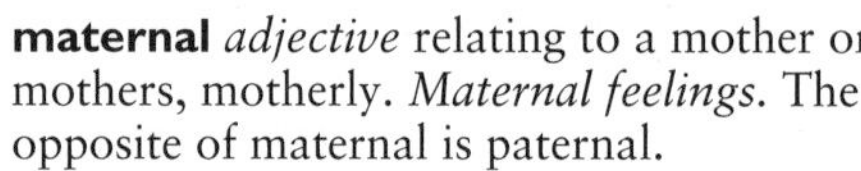

The building materials stood waiting for Colin to arrive, but he was busy on another job.

GRAMMAR NOTE

Try not to confuse 'masterful', meaning 'showing authority' or 'overbearing' with 'masterly', which means 'showing skill'.

match *noun* a thin piece of wood with one end tipped with a material that ignites when you rub it against something rough.

mate *verb* (of animals) to come together to breed in order to produce offspring. **mate** *noun* 1 one of the two animals brought together to breed. 2 a friend. *My best mate.*

material *noun* 1 a substance from which you can make other things. *Wood, glass, bricks and cement are some of the materials used in building houses.* 2 cloth for making clothes from.

maternal *adjective* relating to a mother or mothers, motherly. *Maternal feelings.* The opposite of maternal is paternal.

maternity *adjective* relating to a mother-to-be or birth. *A maternity ward.*

mathematics *plural noun* the study of the science of numbers, measurements, quantities and shapes. **mathematical** *adjective. I was given an extremely tricky mathematical problem.* **mathematician** *noun* an expert in mathematics.

maths *abbreviation* for mathematics.

matrimony *noun* marriage or the state of being married. **matrimonial** *adjective.*

matron *noun* 1 (old-fashioned) a senior nurse in charge of a hospital. 2 a person in a school responsible for the health of the children. *Matron bandaged his knee.*

matter *verb* to be important. *You can go or stay – it doesn't matter.*

matter *noun* 1 the substance or material from which all things are made. Matter can be a solid, a gas or a liquid. 2 a subject of interest. *Financial matters.* 3 a problem. *What's the matter with you today?*

mattress *noun* the thick oblong padding you put on a bed to lie on.

My father bought a new mattress designed to help his bad back.

mature *adjective* 1 fully developed and adult, grown up. 2 ripe. **mature** *verb. Puppies mature into dogs.*

maul *verb* to injure somebody badly by attacking or handling them savagely.

Mauritania *noun* a country in Africa.

Mauritius *noun* a country in the Indian Ocean off East Africa.

mauve *noun, adjective* pale purple colour.

maxim *noun* a general rule or wise piece of advice. *'Look before you leap' is an old maxim, and a wise one.*

maximum *noun* the greatest number or amount possible. *The box holds 50 matches at the maximum.* **maximum** *adjective. 70 mph is the maximum speed on motorways.* The opposite of maximum is minimum.

May *noun* the fifth month of the year. May has 31 days.

maybe *adverb* perhaps, possibly. *Maybe we'll see you later.*

mayhem *noun* general chaos.

mayor *noun* a person in charge of the council or government of a town or city.

maze *noun* a system of complicated paths or lines to follow and which is difficult to find your way through.

The children got lost in the maze.

Mbabane *noun* the capital of Swaziland.

meadow *noun* a grassy field where animals can graze. *A meadow full of buttercups.*

meal *noun* the food that people eat at a particular time. Breakfast, lunch, tea and dinner are all meals.

mean *adjective* unwilling to give, not generous or kind. **meanness** *noun.*

mean (means, meaning, meant) *verb* 1 to intend or plan to do something. *I meant to telephone, but I forgot.* 2 to intend to show or express. *Red means danger.* **mean well** to intend to be helpful. *She is very slow, but she means well.* **by all means** certainly.

meaning *noun* 1 what something means. *Dictionaries tell us the meaning of words.* 2 the importance, purpose or intention of something. *What is the meaning of poetry?*

GRAMMAR NOTE

'May' or 'might'? 'Might' is the past of 'may'. Both express possibility. 'It may snow tonight.' 'I thought you might have come yesterday.'

AMAZING FACT

The ancient Egyptians had a system of measurements that was based on the human body. The smallest unit, based on the hand, was a digit. Four digits made a palm. The distance between the little finger and thumb of an outstretched hand was called a span. A cubit was equal to 2 spans, 7 palms or the distance from fingertips to elbow.

meaningful *adjective* full of significance, important. *A meaningful debate.*

meaningless *adjective* without any purpose. *His life seems meaningless.*

means *plural noun* 1 a method or way of doing something. *The prisoner found some means of escape.* 2 wealth. *A woman of substantial means.*

meantime *noun* the time between two things happening. *I'm going to the shop, and in the meantime you can lay the table.*

meanwhile *adverb* at the same time as. *The rain fell. Meanwhile, Megan slept.*

measles *noun* a mainly children's infectious disease causing a fever and a rash of small red spots on the skin.

measure *verb* to find out or to show how long, tall, wide or heavy something is. *Ian measured the length of his desk.* **measure** *noun* 1 a unit of measure. A metre is a measure of length. 2 an action or law. *The government took measures to reduce crime.*

Jane took a ruler to measure the space exactly.

measurement *noun* how much something measures. *What are the measurements of the room?*

meat *noun* the flesh of animals or birds that we eat.

mechanic *noun* a person who understands machines and is skilled at making and mending them.

mechanical *adjective* 1 relating to machinery. 2 worked by machines. *A funny mechanical mouse.* 3 automatic and done without thought.

mechanism *noun* the system of the working parts of a machine.

medal *noun* a flat round piece of metal or plastic similar to a large coin with words or a symbol on it, which is given as a reward.

Henry was awarded a medal for his achievements in athletics.

meddle *verb* to interfere in things when you have not been asked. **meddlesome** *adjective. He's turned into a meddlesome old man.*

media see mass-media.

medical *adjective* concerning doctors and their work in preventing and treating disease. **medical** *noun* a complete examination of your body by a doctor.

medicine *noun* 1 the tablets and liquid substances you swallow to try to treat and cure an illness. *The medicine tasted horrible.* 2 the science of treating illnesses.

medieval *adjective* relating to the Middle Ages, a period in European history that lasted between about AD 1100 and 1450.

meditate *verb* to think about something quietly and deeply. **meditation** *noun.*

meek *adjective* timid and patient and sometimes too obedient.

meet (meets, meeting, met) *verb* 1 to come face to face with somebody or something. 2 to come together by plan. *Shall we meet in the club this evening?* 3 to join or come together from different places. *The place where two rivers meet is called a confluence.*

meeting *noun* a time and place planned for people to come together to discuss or contest something.

mega- *prefix* very big. *Megawatt.*

megabyte *noun* a unit of memory in a computer (about a million bytes).

megalith *noun* a very large stone put up in prehistoric times.

The megalith marked an ancient burial ground.

melancholy *noun, adjective* very sad or gloomy. *A melancholy tale.*

mellow *adjective* 1 (of fruit) sweet and juicy. 2 (of light) soft and golden. 3 (of people) older but pleasanter. **mellow** *verb. She has mellowed with age.*

melodious *adjective* nice to listen to. *A beautifully melodious voice.*

melody (melodies) *noun* a sweet, pleasing tune. *I played a lovely melody on the flute.*

melon *noun* a large round juicy fruit with a green or yellow skin and lots of seeds inside.

melt *verb* to change from a solid to a liquid by heating. *The ice-cream melted in the Sun.*

member *noun* somebody or something that belongs to a group, team, club, family etc. **membership** *noun.*

memorable *adjective* worth remembering, famous, easy to remember. *A memorable day at the fair.*

memorize *verb* to learn something so well that you can remember it word for word. *Actors have to memorize their lines.*

memory *noun* 1 the ability to remember things. *He has a good memory for telephone numbers.* 2 things that you can remember about the distant past. *Childhood memories.* 3 the part of a computer that stores and retrieves information.

Janice mended the rip in her skirt by sewing it up with a needle and thread.

SPELLING NOTE

In British English we 'meet people'. The British may also 'meet with' opposition, disapproval or an accident. Americans 'meet with' people as well as with accidents etc.

AMAZING FACT

Because Mercury is so close to the Sun, it has a very short year. A year on Mercury is only 88 Earth days.

Mercury is also the name of a planet, the planet nearest to the Sun.

men *noun* the plural of man.

menace *noun* somebody or something that is a threat or danger and may cause damage. *Black ice is a menace to drivers.*

mend *verb* to repair or to make something that is broken useful again. *When is somebody coming round to mend the washing machine?*

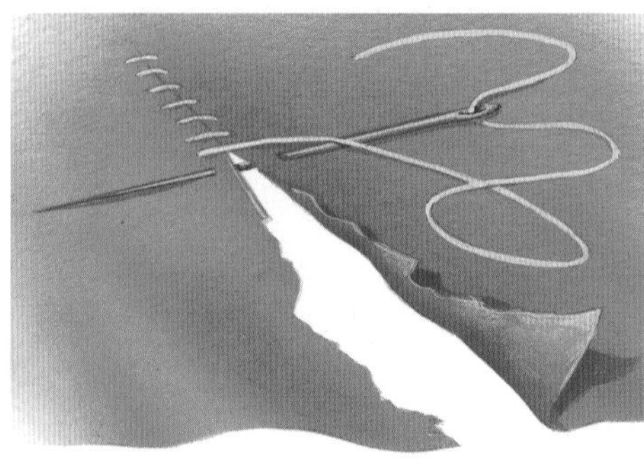

menstruation *noun* blood that comes from a woman's womb about once a month. A period. **menstruate** *verb.*

mental *adjective* relating to the mind, done in the head. *Mental arithmetic.*

mention *verb* to make a casual or brief remark about something. *I think she did mention you would be away.* **mention** *noun.*

menu (menus) *noun* 1 a list of the dishes you can choose from in a restaurant. 2 a list of choices displayed on a computer screen.

MEP *abbreviation* Member of the European Parliament.

merchandise *noun* goods for sale.

merchant *noun* a person who buys and sells large quantities of goods of a particular kind. *A coffee merchant.* **merchant navy** a nation's ships that carry goods.

merciful *adjective* willing to forgive somebody and not punish them.

merciless *adjective* cruel and showing no pity, ruthless.

mercury *noun* a silvery metal that is usually liquid. Mercury is used in thermometers.

mercy *noun* ready to show kindness and forgiveness to somebody who has done something wrong.

merely *adverb* simply, only. *She merely laughed when I fell down.* **mere** *adjective. Lucy is a mere child.*

merge *verb* to combine or blend together. *The two firms decided to merge.* **merger** *noun.*

merry (merrier, merriest) *adjective* 1 cheerful and happy. *Have a merry Christmas.* 2 (informal) very slightly drunk.

mesmerize *verb* to be so fascinated by something that you can think of nothing else. To be hypnotized.

mess *noun* untidy with things lying everywhere, a confused muddle. *What a mess your desk is!* **messy** *adjective.*

message *noun* information sent from one person or group to another. *Are there any telephone messages for me?*

met past tense of meet.

metal *noun* a hard material that goes soft and can be bent when heated. Metals are usually shiny and conduct heat well. Copper, gold, iron and silver are all metals.

metamorphosis *noun* the complete change in form that some animals go through as they develop. *The metamorphosis of a tadpole into a frog.*

metaphor *noun* an expression in which something or somebody is described as though they were something else. *She has green fingers and he has a heart of gold.*

meteor *noun* a large piece of metal or rock that travels through space and normally burns up if it enters Earth's atmosphere.

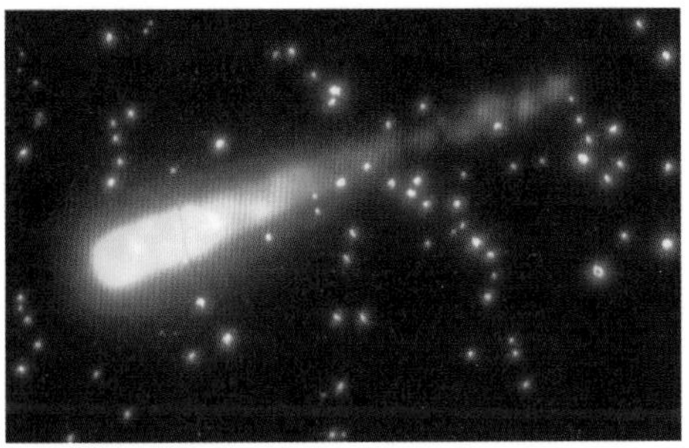

The meteor shower was spectacular, with up to six shooting stars lighting up the sky at once.

meteorite *noun* a meteor that has fallen to Earth from space.

meteorology *noun* the scientific study of the atmosphere and weather. **meteorologist** *noun* a person who forecasts the weather.

meter *noun* an instrument that measures how much electricity, gas, water etc. has been used. *He came to read the meter.*

method *noun* a certain way of doing something, a system. *There are several methods for making coffee.*

methodical *adjective* in an orderly, well-organized way, according to plan.

metre *noun* a measure of length equal to 1,000 millimetres. **metric** *adjective* to do with the metre or metric system. **metric system** a system of weighing and measuring based on 10 and multiples of 10. Kilograms, litres and metres are all metric measures.

metropolis *noun* a very large city.

Mexican *noun* a person who comes from Mexico. **Mexican** *adjective. A Mexican hat.*

Mexico City *noun* the capital of Mexico.

DID YOU KNOW

You can mix metaphors in a really confusing way. Can you unravel these? 'She took the bull by the tail.' 'You can't teach an old dog to suck eggs.'

SPELLING NOTE

Try not to confuse 'meter', a measuring instrument, and 'metre', a measure of length. In American English both words are spelled 'meter'.

There are 12 hours between midnight and midday, so the hands of the clock move once around its face in that time.

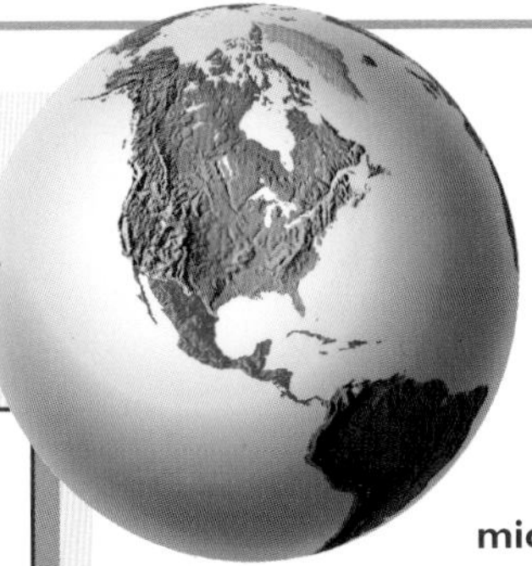

Mexico *noun* a country in North America.

In Mexico 90 per cent of the population belongs to the Roman Catholic Church.

mice plural of mouse.

micro- *prefix* very small. *Microchip, microfilm, microsecond.*

microbe *noun* a living thing that is so tiny that it can be seen only through a microscope. *Swarming with microbes.*

microchip or **silicon chip** *noun* a tiny piece of silicon with electronic circuits printed on it, used in computers and other electronic equipment. *The microchip industry.*

Micronesia *noun* a country of many islands in the Pacific Ocean.

microphone *noun* an electrical instrument that is used to help record sound, or to make sounds louder than they really are.

microscope *noun* an instrument with lenses that makes tiny objects look much larger. *We looked at the ant under the microscope.*

microscopic *adjective* so tiny that it cannot be seen except through a microscope.

microwave *noun* an oven that cooks food very quickly by using energy in very short waves (electronic microwaves).

midday *noun* the middle of the day, 12 noon.

middle *noun, adjective* the part of something that is half-way or the same distance from its ends or its sides. *A cherry has a stone in the middle.* **middle age** the time of a person's life between about the ages of 40 and 60. **Middle Ages** a period in European history between about 1100 and 1450. **Middle East** an area at the eastern end of the Mediterranean Sea and including Egypt and Iran.

midge *noun* a tiny gnat-like insect that bites.

midget *noun* an exceptionally short person.

midnight *noun* 12 o'clock in the middle of the night. **midnight** *adjective. A midnight feast.*

midwife *noun* a person whose job it is to help women at the birth of their babies.

migraine *noun* (say mee-grane) a very severe, throbbing headache that makes you feel sick.

M

migration *noun* the movement from one place to another to live. **migrate** *verb*. *Swallows migrate every autumn.* **migratory** *adjective*. **migrant** *noun* 1 a person who is moving or migrating from one country to another. 2 a bird that migrates each year.

mild *adjective* 1 gentle. *She has a mild nature.* 2 not too bad or severe. *A mild fever.* 3 (of weather) rather warm. *A mild winter.* 4 (of food or drink) not strong or too spicy. *A mild curry.*

mildew *noun* a greyish fungus that grows on plants or decaying matter.

mile *noun* a measure of distance equal to 1,760 yards or 1.6 km. **to be miles away** to daydream. *I was miles away when you rang.*

militant *adjective* aggressive and ready to fight, very active in support of a cause.

military *adjective* relating to armed forces and warfare. *In some countries, all young men have to do military service.*

WORD HISTORY

'Mile' comes from a Latin word for a thousand (as do 'millennium', 'milligram', 'millipede', etc). A mile was a Roman unit of length – 'mille passuum', or a thousand paces.

Military life was hard during the war.

milk *noun* 1 the white liquid that female mammals make in their bodies to feed their young. 2 the milk of cows and goats used as food for humans and to make such things as cheese and butter. **milk** *verb* to take milk from a cow. **milky** *adjective*. **milk-tooth** one of the first, temporary teeth in young mammals. Milk teeth fall out and are replaced by teeth that should last you the rest of your life.

mill *noun* 1 a building with machinery for grinding grain into flour. 2 a factory. *A steel mill.* 3 a small grinding tool. *A pepper mill.*

millennium (millennia) *noun* a period of a thousand years.

milligram *noun* a very small measure of weight. There are 1,000 milligrams in a kilogram.

millilitre *noun* a very small liquid measure. There are 1,000 millilitres in a litre.

millipede *noun* a small worm-like creature with many pairs of legs.

mime *noun* a kind of acting without words in which the actors use gestures and facial expressions. **mime** *verb*.

mimic (mimics, mimicking, mimicked) *verb* to imitate somebody's actions or speech, usually to amuse people. **mimic** *noun*. *He's a good mimic.*

minaret *noun* a tall tower near a mosque from the top of which the muezzin calls people to prayer.

A muezzin, a holy man, calls Muslims to prayer from the minaret on a mosque.

mince *verb* to chop food into tiny pieces. **mince** *noun* meat that has been minced or ground into small pieces.

mincemeat *noun* finely chopped dried fruit and spices, used in making mincepies.

mind *noun* the part of you that thinks, feels, learns, understands and remembers. *He has a very fine mind.* Your intelligence. **make up your mind** to decide.

mind *verb* 1 to care about or feel unhappy about something. *Do you mind if I turn on the TV?* 2 to look after something. *She is minding the baby for me.* 3 Be careful. *Mind your head on that door!*

mindless *adjective* stupid and unthinking.

mine *noun* 1 an underground place where people dig to obtain such things as gold or diamonds. 2 a bomb buried under the ground or in the sea. *The car was blown up by a mine.* **mine** *verb*. **minefield** *noun* an area covered with buried explosive mines.

miner *noun* a person who works down a mine. *The miners went on strike.*

mineral *noun* a natural substance such as coal, gold and salt, which is mined from the earth. **mineral** *adjective* of or containing minerals. *Mineral water.*

This beautiful blue-green mineral is Mexican selenite.

mingle *verb* to mix with or blend. *The police mingled with the crowd.*

mini- *prefix* smaller or shorter than normal.

miniature *adjective* very small. *A miniature railway.* **miniature** *noun* a small version of something much larger, such as a painting.

M

minim *noun* a musical note equal to the time value of two crotchets.

minimize *verb* 1 to make something seem unimportant. *She tried to minimize the problem.* 2 to make as small as possible.

minimum *noun* the smallest amount or number of something you can have. *You need a minimum of ten people for the trip.* **minimum** *adjective. The minimum cost will be £10.* The opposite of minimum is maximum.

mining *noun* the process or industry of extracting minerals from the earth. *The coal-mining industry.*

minister *noun* 1 a member of the clergy who holds services in a Protestant church. 2 the head of a government department. *The Minister of Health.*

ministry *noun* 1 the work of a clergyman. 2 a government department. *The Ministry of Agriculture.*

minnow *noun* a tiny fish found in lakes and rivers. *He caught only minnows.*

A shoal of minnows flashed past as the children watched from the bridge.

minor *adjective* small, unimportant, not serious. *A minor accident.* The opposite of minor is major. **minor** *noun* a young person who is under the age of 18.

minority *noun* 1 the smaller of two groups of people or things. *Only a minority voted against.* 2 a small number of people of one race, culture or religion living among a much larger group of people of a different race, culture or religion. The opposite of minority is majority.

Minsk *noun* the capital of Belarus.

mint *noun* 1 a plant whose leaves are used as a flavouring. 2 a place where coins are made.

minus *noun* a mathematical term or symbol (–) meaning subtraction or taking away. *Seven minus five equals two, or 7–5 = 2.*

minute *noun* (**min**-it) a period of time consisting of 60 seconds. There are 60 minutes in an hour.

minute (**my**-newt) *adjective* 1 very small, tiny. *A minute speck of soot.* 2 very detailed. *A minute examination.*

miracle *noun* an amazing and unexpected happening for which there is no explanation. *His escape from the blazing car was a miracle.* **miraculous** *adjective.*

WORD BUILDING

The prefix 'mini-' (a shortening of 'miniature') has become a very useful word builder, producing such new words as: 'minibreak' (short holiday), 'minibus', 'minicab' and 'minicomputer'.

AMAZING FACT

Dividing the day into 24 hours, the hour into 60 minutes, and the minute into 60 seconds is an ancient system of time measurement but it did not come into general use until about AD 1600.

Today, not all cultures measure the day in the same way, though. In Kenya, for example, seconds, minutes and hours are the same but the day is split into two halves – from dawn until sunset, then sunset to sunrise. The two halves are more or less equal because the country is on the Equator.

mirage *noun* something that you imagine you see but that is not really there, an optical illusion. *The travellers saw a mirage of an oasis in the desert.*

mirror *noun* a piece of special glass, metal or plastic that reflects light and whatever is in front of it.

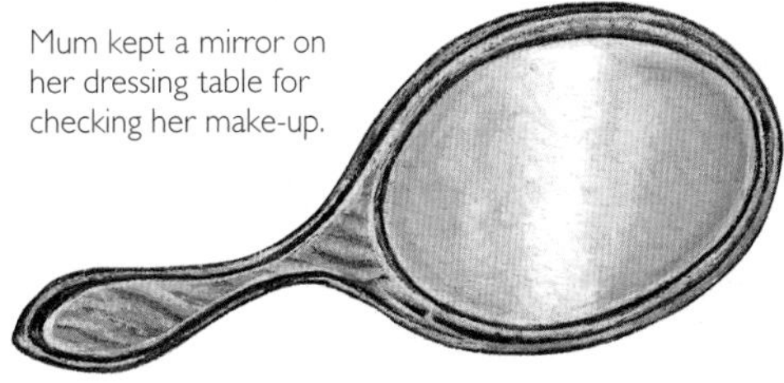

Mum kept a mirror on her dressing table for checking her make-up.

mis- *prefix* wrongly. *Misbehave, misjudge.*

misbehave *verb* to behave badly. **misbehaviour** *noun.*

miscellaneous *adjective* a mixture or assortment of various things.

mischief *noun* annoying but harmless behaviour. **mischievous** *adjective. A mischievous child.*

miser *noun* a very mean person who likes to hoard money but who will not spend it. **miserly** *adjective.*

The miser spent a lot of time alone, enjoying counting his money.

misery *noun* 1 a feeling of great unhappiness, wretchedness. 2 (informal) a person who is always complaining. *She's a real misery.* **miserable** *adjective. Jane is miserable because she can't go to the concert with her friends.*

misfit *noun* somebody who does not belong to a group because they are in some way strange or different.

misfortune *noun* bad luck.

mishap *noun* an unfortunate accident.

mislay (mislays, mislaying, mislaid) *verb* to lose something for a short time because you have forgotten where you put it. *I seem to have mislaid my glasses.*

mislead *verb* to give somebody a false idea by making them believe something that is untrue. To deceive or give wrong information. **misleading** *adjective. This newspaper article is very misleading.*

M

miss *verb* 1 to fail to do something such as hitting or catching. *Peter threw me a ball but I missed it.* 2 to fail to be somewhere at the right time. *Matt missed the train by a minute.* 3 to be sad because somebody is no longer with you. *She missed her friend when he was sent abroad.*

Miss *noun* a polite title often put before the name of a girl or unmarried woman.

missile *noun* a weapon that is sent through the air and which explodes when it hits its target. *The missile hit the ammunition store.*

missing *adjective* 1 lost. *A missing dog.* 2 absent. *Two men are missing from the team.*

mission *noun* 2 an important job that somebody is sent somewhere to do. *The astronauts were sent on a mission to Mars.* 2 important work that somebody thinks they should do. *Her mission in life was to help the poor.*

Their mission to the Moon was a milestone in the history of humankind.

missionary *noun* somebody who is sent to another country to tell the people about a religion. *The missionaries were eaten by tigers, or so the local people said.*

mist *noun* a low cloud of damp air that is difficult to see through.

mistake *noun* something that is wrong or incorrect, an error. *Can you see a spelling misstake?*

mistake (mistakes, mistaking, mistook) *verb* 1 to misunderstand or to make an error about something. *She mistook my instructions and went the wrong way.* 2 to confuse one person or thing for another. *I mistook you for your brother.*

mistaken *adjective* wrong and not correctly understood. *He has the mistaken belief that the Sun spins around the Earth.*

misty *adjective. Misty autumn mornings.*

mistreat *verb* to treat in a bad, cruel or unfair way. **mistreatment** *noun.*

misunderstand (misunderstands, misunderstanding, misunderstood) *verb* not to understand the meaning of something correctly, to get the wrong idea.

misunderstanding *noun* 1 a wrong or false idea about the meaning of something. *There must be some misunderstanding.* 2 a quarrel or disagreement.

AMAZING FACT

Since the 1970s, many women, whether married or unmarried, prefer to use the title 'Ms' instead of 'Miss' or 'Mrs'.

WORD HISTORY

Mob comes from the Latin words 'mobile vulgus'. 'Vulgus' means 'masses' or 'crowd' and 'mobile' means 'moveable', 'fickle' or 'easily swayed'.

SPELLING NOTE

'Moccasin' is often misspelled. Note that it has two 'c's and only a single 's'.

mitten *noun* a kind of glove that either leaves the tips of the fingers bare or that has one part for the thumb and one part for four fingers.

mix *verb* to combine or put different things together. **mixture** *noun. A cake mixture.* **mix-up** *noun* a confusion or muddle. *There's some mix-up in the dates.*

mixer *noun* a machine that you use to mix things together. *A cement mixer.*

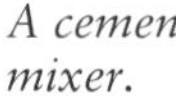

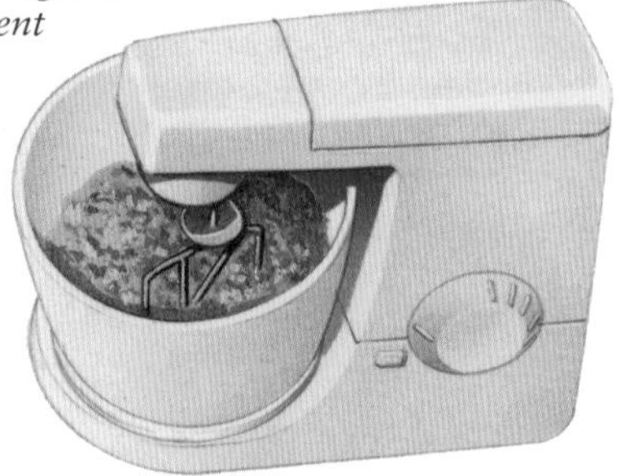

Stephen put the ingredients for the crumble topping in the food mixer.

mnemonic *noun* (say nem-**on**-ik) an aid, such as a rhyme, to help us remember facts.

moan *verb* 1 to make a low, unhappy sound because you are in pain or sad. 2 to grumble and complain. *He's always moaning about the weather.* **moan** *noun. A moan of grief.*

moat *noun* a deep, wide ditch, usually filled with water, around a castle. Moats helped to protect castles from attack.

mob *noun* a noisy, and often violent, crowd of angry people. **mob** *verb* to crowd around. *The fans mobbed the pop star.*

mobile *adjective* able to be moved about easily and quickly. *A mobile home.*

Mobile phones have become extremely popular in a very short time.

mobile phone *noun* a portable telephone that fits easily into a pocket or handbag. Often shortened to mobile.

moccasin *noun* a soft leather shoe without a heel. Moccasins were first worn by Native Americans.

mock *verb* to make fun of somebody, often by copying them in a cruel and unpleasant way. *She mocked the way he stuttered.* **mock** *adjective* not real, imitation. *Mock diamonds.* **mockery** *noun.*

model *noun* 1 a small, to-scale copy of something. *A model of a castle.* 2 a good example. *He is a model of good behaviour.* 3 a person whose job is to wear new clothes to show them off to people before they buy them. 4 a person who poses for an artist or photographer. 5 a style or particular version of a product. *This computer is the latest model.* **model** *verb.*

M

modem *noun* an electronic device that sends information between one computer and another by telephone.

moderate *adjective* 1 not extreme, neither too big nor too small. *He eats a moderate amount of food.* 2 average or fairly good. *She had quite moderate marks for her exam.*

modern *adjective* happening now, new and not old-fashioned. *Modern technology.*

modest *adjective* 1 quiet and not boastful. 2 not extreme or very large, moderate. *Her needs are very modest.*

Mogadishu *noun* the capital of Somalia.

moist *adjective* a little wet, damp. **moisten** *verb* to make or become slightly wet or damp. *He moistened his lips.*

moisture *noun* dampness. Tiny drops of water such as steam.

Moldova *noun* a country in eastern Europe.

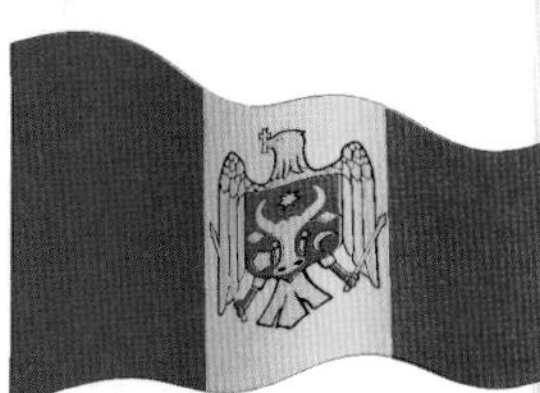

The flag of Moldova has blue, yellow and red stripes with an eagle and crest in the centre.

mole *noun* a small brown spot that is slightly raised on the skin.

mole *noun* a small, dark grey, furry animal that digs tunnels under the ground with its strong front paws. Moles leave behind piles of earth called molehills.

molecule *noun* the smallest amount of a substance that can exist on its own. A molecule of water is made up of two atoms of hydrogen and one atom of oxygen.

mollusc *noun* any animal with a soft body and no backbone such as a snail, slug or octopus.

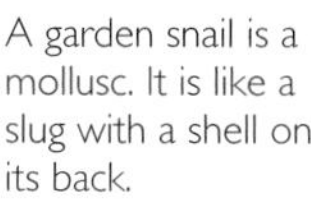

A garden snail is a mollusc. It is like a slug with a shell on its back.

molten *adjective* turned to liquid and melted. *Molten silver.*

moment *noun* a very short period of time. *Wait a moment.* **momentary** *adjective*. *A momentary pause.* **at the moment** now.

momentum *noun* the force gained by an object as it moves. *The sledge gained momentum as it travelled downhill.*

Monaco *noun* a country in southern Europe.

monarch *noun* (say **mon**-ark) a king or queen. **monarchy** *noun*.

AMAZING FACT

There are about 70,000 different types of molluscs. They range in size from a few millimetres to the giant squid, which may grow to be twelve metres.

Monkeys are extremely intelligent animals. Some types are becoming endangered due to hunting or destruction of habitat.

WORD BUILDER

The prefix 'mono' is a useful word builder, as in: 'monoplane' (an aeroplane with one set of wings), 'monorail' (a railway with carriages hanging from one rail), and 'monosyllable' (a word with one syllable).

monastery *noun* a group of buildings in which a community of monks lives and works, an abbey. **monastic** *adjective*.

money *noun* the coins and banknotes we use to buy things.

Mongolia *noun* a country in central Asia.

mongoose (mongooses) *noun* a small African or Asian animal with a long body that kills poisonous snakes.

mongrel *noun* a dog that is a mixture of different breeds. *Many mongrels make very good pets.*

monitor *noun* 1 a pupil at school who has been given special duties or responsibilities. 2 a computer screen. 3 an instrument, usually with a screen, that keeps a check on something and records any changes.

monk *noun* a member of a religious community of men who live, pray and work together in a building called a monastery.

monkey *noun* an animal with long arms and a long tail that climbs trees. Monkeys are primates and belong to the same group as apes and people. **monkey business** some mischievous or illegal activity. **monkey with** play the fool with.

mono- *prefix* one or alone. *Monorail.*

monopoly *noun* having sole control of the manufacture or supply of a product or service. **monopolize** *verb* to control something completely.

monotonous *adjective* dull, boring and lacking any variety. *She has a monotonous voice.* **monotony** *noun*.

Monrovia *noun* the capital of Liberia.

monsoon *noun* a strong prevailing wind around the Indian Ocean that changes directions in winter and summer. The summer monsoon brings heavy rainfall.

monster *noun* 1 a huge, terrifying but imaginary creature. 2 a cruel, wicked person. **monster** *adjective* very big or strange. **monstrous** *adjective* horrible and shocking. *A monstrous crime.*

This monster is the sort of creature that inhabits nightmares.

M

Monte Carlo *noun* the capital of Monaco.

Montevideo *noun* the capital of Uruguay.

month *noun* a period of time and one of the twelve divisions of the year. **monthly** *adjective* happening once a month or every month. *A monthly magazine.* **calendar month** one of the twelve divisions of the year. From 1 March to 31 March is a calendar month. **lunar month** a period of about 29 days, the time it takes the Moon to orbit the Earth.

monument *noun* 1 an old and important building, statue etc. *Ancient monuments.* 2 a building or statue erected so that people will remember an important person or event. **monumental** *adjective.*

mood *noun* the way you feel or your state of mind at a particular time. *Winning the match put him in a good mood.* **moody** *adjective* bad-tempered or liable to change mood quickly for no apparent reason. **moodiness** *noun.*

moon *noun* 1 a natural satellite or small planet that orbits a larger planet. 2 **the Moon** the natural satellite that orbits the Earth once every four weeks (lunar month). The Moon is our closest neighbour in space.

As the Moon waxes and wanes, it passes through various phases.

moonlight *noun* the light from the Sun reflected by the Moon.

moor *noun* a large area of open land usually covered with heather.

moor *verb* to tie up a boat so that it cannot drift away. **moorings** *noun.*

moose (plural moose) *noun* a large brown deer found in the forests of North America. The male has huge, flattened antlers.

The moose uses its antlers to fight off rivals for a mate.

mop *noun* an implement with soft material such as a sponge attached to a long handle, used for cleaning floors and dishes. **mop** (mops, mopping, mopped) *verb* to wipe with a mop or cloth. *He mopped his brow in the midday heat.*

WORD HISTORY

'Mosquito' comes from a Portuguese word that means 'little fly', originally from the Latin 'musca', 'fly'.

AMAZING FACT

'Moose' is a Native American word. Moose and elk are completely different animals – in the US and Canada, that is.

In Europe, the moose is actually called an 'elk', which is an old German name.

mope *verb* to feel sad and sorry for yourself.

moral *adjective* relating to good behaviour and what is right and wrong. *Euthanasia is a moral question.* **moral** *noun* a lesson or point made in a story about what is right and wrong. **morals** *plural noun* standards of behaviour and beliefs in right and wrong.

morale *noun* (say mor-**al**) the spirit of hope, confidence and enthusiasm among members of a group or team. *After its win, the team's morale is very high.*

more *adjective, pronoun* bigger in number, size or amount. *She has more marbles than me.* **more** *adverb. Can you say it once more?*

morgue *noun* a mortuary or place where corpses are kept until they are buried or cremated.

Moroccan *noun* a person who comes from Morocco. **Moroccan** *adjective. A Moroccan mosque.*

Morocco *noun* a country in Africa.

Morocco, in northern Africa, is a Muslim country with many mosques.

Moroni *noun* the capital of Comoros.

morning *noun* the part of the day before midday, from sunrise to noon.

morsel *noun* a very small piece of food.

mortal *adjective* 1 incapable of living for ever. All living things are mortal. 2 causing death. *A mortal illness.* **mortal** *noun* a human being.

mortgage *noun* (say **more**-gage) a loan of money from a building society or bank that you use to buy a house. **mortgage** *verb* to transfer the ownership of your house or property to a bank or building society in return for money they lend you.

mortuary *noun* a place where dead bodies are kept before they are buried or cremated.

mosaic *noun* (say moh-**zay**-ik) a picture or design made from small pieces of coloured glass or stone set in concrete.

Tiles from Turkey are often patterned with intensely coloured mosaic designs.

Moscow *noun* the capital of Russia.

Moslem another spelling for Muslim.

mosque *noun* a building in which Muslims worship. *They prayed in the mosque.*

mosquito *noun* (say moss-**kee**-toe) a small flying insect that bites animals and people and sucks their blood. Some mosquitoes transmit the disease malaria.

moss (mosses) *noun* a small green plant that forms a soft covering on stones in damp places. **mossy** *adjective*.

most *noun*, *adjective* the largest in size, number or amount. *Most apples are green or red.* **most** *adverb*. *The most intelligent boy in the class.*

mostly *adverb* generally, mainly. *What you are saying is mostly nonsense.*

motel *noun* a hotel that caters specially for motorists and their vehicles.

moth *noun* an insect like a butterfly that is usually seen flying at night.

The peppered moth camouflages itself against the bark of trees.

mother *noun* a female parent, the woman who gave birth to you. **mother** *verb* to look after like a mother. **motherly** *adjective*. **motherhood** *noun*. *Motherhood was her greatest joy.*

mother-in-law *noun* the mother of a person's husband or wife.

motion *noun* movement, the action of moving. *The motion of the coach sent him to sleep.* **motion** *verb* to signal or make a movement, usually with the hand. *She motioned him to sit down.*

motion picture *noun* a cinema film.

motionless *adjective* not moving.

motive *noun* a reason that causes somebody to do something. *What was the motive for the crime?*

motor *noun* an engine in a machine that uses fuel to make it work or move. **motor** *adjective* having to do with engines and vehicles. *A motor show.*

motorcycle *noun* a heavy two-wheeled vehicle with an engine.

motorist *noun* a person who drives a motor car. *A tax on motorists.*

motorway *noun* a long wide road with several lanes for traffic to travel quickly over long distances.

mottled *adjective* marked with patches of different colour.

Moss formed on the shady side of the tree.

DID YOU KNOW

'Motel' is a good example of a hybrid or blend word. It is a blend of 'motor car' and 'hotel'. Other examples are 'brunch' ('breakfast' and 'lunch') and 'smog' ('smoke' and 'fog').

The mouse on a computer moves the cursor on the screen.

AMAZING FACT

'The Jazz Singer', starring Al Jolson, was the first 'talkie' – a motion picture that had sound.

motto *noun* a phrase that sums up what is important to a group or a guiding principle to good behaviour. *'Think before you speak' is a good motto.*

mould *verb* to model or to make something into a shape with your hands. *She moulded the clay into a vase.* **mould** *noun* a container into which a liquid is poured, which takes the shape of the container when it sets. *A jelly mould in the shape of a rabbit.*

mould *noun* a fungus found on stale food or damp things.

moult *verb* (of a bird) to lose feathers or (of an animal) to shed hair. *Our dog moults every spring.*

mound *noun* a small hill, a pile or heap. *A burial mound.*

mount *verb* 1 to climb on the back of a horse, pony etc. 2 to increase. *The cost of building is mounting.* 3 to fix something somewhere, for example in a frame so as to display it.

mount *noun* a mountain, usually as part of the name of a mountain. *Mount Everest.*

mountain *noun* a very high and usually steep hill. *Climb every mountain.*

mourn *verb* to feel great sadness because somebody has died, to grieve. **mourning** *noun*. *They mourned their lost loved ones.*

mouse (mice) *noun* 1 a small grey furry animal with a long tail and sharp teeth. Mice are rodents. 2 a small device on your desk that you move on the surface with your hand to control the position of the cursor on a computer screen.

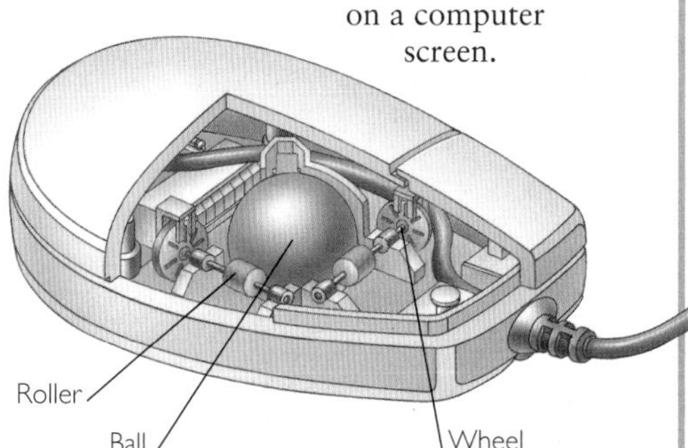

moustache *noun* hair growing above a man's top lip.

mouth *noun* 1 the part of your face that opens when you speak and into which you put food. 2 the place where a river flows out to sea. 3 the entrance to a cave etc.

mouthful (mouthfuls) *noun* the amount you put in your mouth at one time.

mouth-organ *noun* a small musical instrument that you play by moving it along your lips while blowing and sucking.

M

mouthpiece *noun* the part of a musical instrument, pipe etc. that you put in your mouth.

movable *adjective* able to be moved. *The hands of a clock are movable.*

move *verb* 1 to go from one position or place to another. *Don't move, I want to take your photograph.* 2 to change your home. *We moved into a new house.* 3 to make you feel something deeply. *He was moved to pity by the sad film.*

movement *noun* 1 the act of moving. *She made a sudden movement.* 2 a group of people working together for a common cause. *The animal rights movement.* 3 a section into which some pieces of classical music are divided. *Most symphonies have a slow movement.*

movie *noun* a film in the cinema, a motion picture. *Let's go to the movies.*

moving *adjective* touching or moving the feelings. *It was a moving film about orphans.*

mow (mows, mowing, mowed, mown) *verb* (rhymes with go) to cut grass or hay with a machine called a **mower** or **lawnmower** *noun. Sid mowed the front lawn.*

Mozambique *noun* a country in Africa.

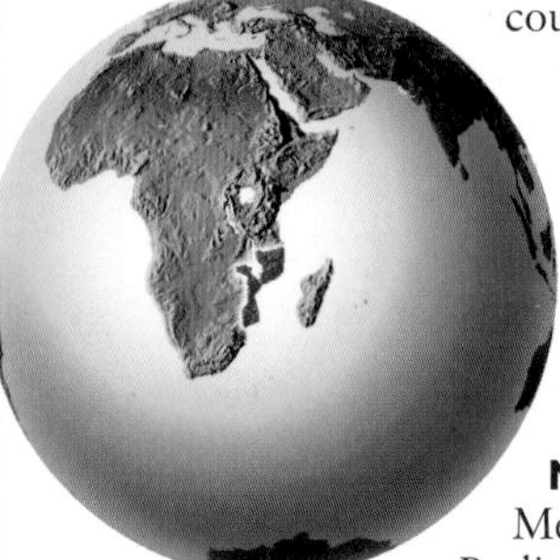

Mozambique lies on the east coast of Africa opposite the island of Madagascar.

MP *abbreviation* Member of Parliament.

mph *abbreviation* miles per hour.

Mr *abbreviation* mister (say **mist**-er) a polite title put before a man's name.

Mrs *abbreviation* mistress (say **miss**-iz) a polite title put before the name of a married woman. *Mrs Jones.*

Ms (say miz) a title that some people put before the name of woman, which does not show whether she is married or single.

much *adjective, adverb, pronoun* a large amount, a lot. *Did you drink much?*

muck *noun* dirt, filth. **muck about** *verb* (slang) to behave in a silly way and waste time. *Pay attention and stop mucking about.* **muck in** *verb* (slang) to join in with other people. **muck out** *verb* to clean stables. **muck up** *verb* (slang) to spoil. *He mucked up our plans.*

mud *noun* soft, wet earth. **muddy** *adjective. Take off your muddy boots.*

AMAZING FACT

In Ancient Egypt, it was not only humans who were mummified. Cats were also preserved.

WORD HISTORY

'Mummy' was originally an Arabic word 'mumiya' meaning 'an embalmed body'. 'Mum' was the Arabic word for the wax used in the process of preserving the corpse.

muddle *noun* a thoroughly confused mess, a jumble. **muddle** *verb* 1 to mix things up in a confused way. 2 to confuse somebody or be confused. *You muddle me with all these complicated questions.*

mudguard *noun* a shield above a wheel on a vehicle that stops water and mud being splashed about.

muesli *noun* a food of mixed crushed cereals, nuts and dried fruit that people usually eat for breakfast.

muezzin *noun* a person who calls Muslims to prayer, usually from a minaret.

mug *noun* a tall cup with straight sides that you use without a saucer. *A mug of cocoa.*

mug (mugs, mugging, mugged) *verb* to attack and rob somebody in the street. *Jane was mugged outside her flat.* **mugger** *noun.*

mule *noun* an animal that is the offspring of a male donkey and a female horse or pony. *The mule carried us up the mountain.*

multi- *prefix* many. *Multi-coloured.*

multi-media *adjective* involving the use of a mixture of different media such as TV, radio, video etc.

multiple *adjective* involving more than one, many. *She suffered multiple injuries in the accident.* **multiple** *noun* any number that can be divided exactly by another number. 20, 30 and 40 are multiples of 2, 5 and 10.

multiply (multiplies, multiplying, multiplied) *verb* to increase a number by adding the number to itself a given number of times. Three plus three plus three make nine or 3 x 3 = 9. **multiplication** *noun.* The opposite of multiply is divide.

multitude *noun* a crowd, a large number of things. *I've a multitude of things to do.*

mumble *verb* to speak in a low, indistinct voice that is not easy to understand.

mummy *noun* a word for mother.

mummy (mummies) *noun* a dead body that has been preserved from decay by being rubbed with special oils and wrapped in cloths, especially in ancient Egypt.

mumps *noun* a painful infectious disease that makes your neck and the sides of your face swell.

munch *verb* to chew something in a noisy way. *The horse munched a crisp apple.*

Mummies were stored in beautifully painted and decorated caskets.

mural *noun* a picture painted on a wall.

murder *verb* to kill somebody on purpose. **murder** *noun. The police are investigating three murders.* **murderous** *adjective.*

murderer *noun* a person who commits a murder. *The murderer was jailed for life.*

Muscat *noun* the capital of Oman.

muscle *noun* a part inside your body that stretches and relaxes to make different parts of your body move. *Tennis players need to have strong arm muscles.*

Thin tissue

Bundles of fibres

Each fibre is made of hundreds of strands called fibrils.

Muscles work in pairs. As one contracts or tightens, the other relaxes.

Muscle fibres are so small that 1 sq cm would contain a million of them.

muse *verb* to think deeply about something.

museum *noun* (say meeyou-zee-um) a place where interesting or rare objects are kept on display for people to look at.

mushroom *noun* a fungus that looks like an umbrella. Some you can eat, but others are poisonous.

music *noun* 1 the pleasing mixture and pattern of sounds made by somebody singing or by musical instruments. 2 the written or printed signs and notes that represent musical sounds.

musical *adjective* 1 relating to music. *Musical instruments.* 2 good at making or understanding music. *She is very musical.* **musical** *noun* a play or film in which singing and dancing form an important part.

musician *noun* a composer of music, a person who plays a musical instrument well.

musket *noun* an oldfashioned kind of gun with a long barrel.

Muslim or **Moslem** *noun* a person who believes in Islam, the religion founded by the prophet Mohammed. **Muslim** *adjective.*

mussel *noun* a small shellfish with two black shells.

must verb that strengthens other verbs 1 to need to, to have to. *I must go to bed now.* 2 to be obliged to. *You must obey the rules.* 3 to be definitely or likely. *You must be happy to have won.*

mustard *noun* a hot-tasting yellow paste made from the seeds of the mustard plant and used to flavour food.

This is what mustard seeds look like under the microscope.

AMAZING FACT

The oldest musical instrument is something called a 'bull-roarer' that was made from a piece of bone with a cord attached to it.

SPELLING NOTE

Scholars and most Muslims prefer the spelling 'Muslim' to 'Moslem', although 'Moslem' is more widespread.

mute *adjective* 1 unable to speak. 2 silent, speechless. *They stared at one another in mute amazement.*

mutilate *verb* to damage somebody or something, usually by cutting off a part of it. *A mutilated body.*

mutiny *noun* a rebellion by sailors or soldiers against officers in charge. **mutiny** *verb.* **mutinous** *adjective. Mutinous troops.* **mutineer** *noun. The mutineers took over the ship and threw the captain overboard.*

mutter *verb* to speak in a very low angry voice that cannot be heard properly, to grumble. *Please don't mutter into your beard because I can't hear you.*

mutual *adjective* 1 shared by two or more people. In common. *We have mutual friends.* 2 done equally one to another. *Mutual respect.*

muzzle *noun* 1 the nose and mouth of an animal such as a dog or wolf. 2 straps put over an animal's muzzle to prevent it biting. *The dog wore a muzzle after it had bitten the postman.* 3 the open end of a gun.

Myanmar *noun* a country in Southeast Asia, formerly called Burma.

mystery *noun* 1 something strange that has happened and which you cannot explain or understand, puzzling. *It's a complete mystery how he disappeared.* 2 a secret. **mysterious** *adjective. A mysterious castle.*

myth *noun* 1 an imaginary story from the distant past, usually about gods and heroes and how the world began. 2 a belief that is imagined and untrue. *It's a myth that spinach builds your muscles.* **mythical** *adjective. A mythical dragon got married to the princess in the fairytale.*

mythology *noun* a collection of myths. *Norse mythology.*

Greek mythology tells of the legend of the minotaur, a monster half-human and half-bull. The minotaur lived inside a maze and was eventually killed by the hero Theseus.

Nn

nag (nags, nagging, nagged) *verb* to annoy somebody by constantly complaining or trying to persuade them to do something. *Mum's always nagging me to tidy my room.* **nag** *noun*.

nail *noun* 1 the hard covering that protects the ends of your fingers and toes (fingernails, toenails). 2 a thin piece of metal with one end pointed and the other end flat that can be used for fastening pieces of wood etc. together. *She hammered a nail into the wall.* **nail** *verb*. *He nailed a notice on the door.*

A nail grows from the cuticle under the skin.

Nairobi *noun* the capital of Kenya.

naked *adjective* with no clothes on, uncovered. **nakedness** *noun*.

name *noun* 1 a word by which a person, animal or place is known or called. *My cat's name is Archie.* 2 a reputation. *The bank has a very good name.* **name** *verb*. *They named their baby Billy.* **name after** to give somebody or something the same name as somebody else. *The city of Adelaide in Australia is named after Queen Adelaide.*

namesake *noun* somebody with the same name as you.

Namibia *noun* a country in Africa.

nanny *noun* a person who is trained to look after young children in their own home.

nanny goat *noun* a female goat.

nap *noun* a short sleep.

nape *noun* the back of your neck.

napkin *noun* a square piece of cloth or paper that you put on your lap to protect your clothes or to wipe your hands or lips during a meal.

These are two deserts in Namibia, the Namib and the Kalahari.

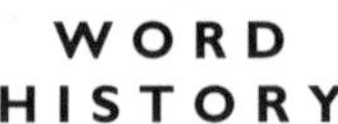

WORD HISTORY

The shape of the letter N comes from an ancient Egyptian symbol for a snake. The sound comes from 'nun', a Semitic word for 'fish'. The Greeks called the letter 'nu'.

AMAZING FACT

The world's first national park, Yellowstone National Park in the western US, was established in 1872. There are 50 national parks in the US, the largest being Wranell-S. Elias in Alaska. There are 32 national parks in Canada.

nappy *noun* a piece of thick, soft paper or cloth that is put around a baby's bottom (US diaper).

narrate *verb* to tell a story or relate an account of something.

narrative *noun* a story or account of things that have happened.

narrator *noun* a person who tells a story or explains what is happening.

narrow *adjective* thin and not measuring very much from one side to the other. *The door is too narrow for the piano to go through.* **narrow** *verb*. *The road narrowed as we climbed the hill.* The opposite of narrow is wide.

narrow-minded *adjective* unwilling to understand or even consider ideas that are new or different.

nasal *adjective* relating to the nose. *The nasal passages.*

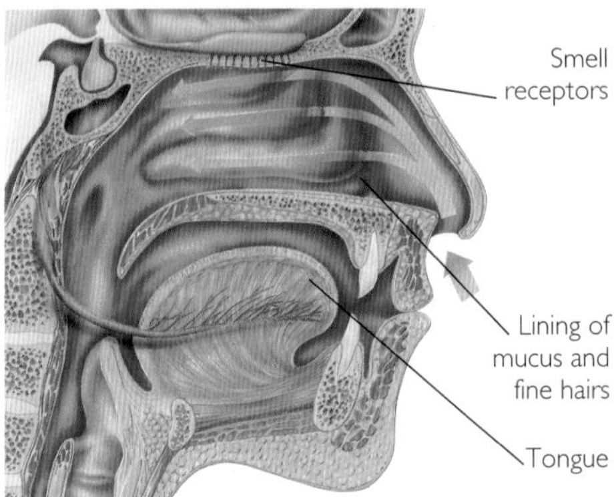

Air is inhaled through the nasal passages, where it is warmed before it is taken into the chest.

Nassau *noun* the capital of the Bahamas.

nasty (nastier, nastiest) *adjective* 1 unpleasant. *A nasty smell.* 2 unkind. 3 serious. *A nasty accident.*

nation *noun* a country with all the people who live there under one government and often sharing the same language, customs etc. *The nations of the world.*

national *adjective* belonging to a nation. *National dress.* **national anthem** a country's official hymn or song. **national park** an area of countryside under the care and ownership of the nation.

nationalism *noun* great pride in the culture, history and success of your own country.

nationalist *noun* 1 person who is very proud of their country. 2 a person who wants their country to be independent. *Scottish nationalist.*

nationality *noun* belonging to a particular nation. *He is of Russian nationality.*

nationalize *verb* to put a privately owned company under state control. **nationalization** *noun*. The opposite of nationalize is privatize.

N

native *noun* 1 one of the first inhabitants of a country. *Native American.* 2 a person who was born in a particular place. *She's a native of Glasgow.* **native** *adjective. What is your native language?*

Native American *noun* a member of the original race of people who lived in North America (often incorrectly called American Indians).

nativity *noun* the birth of Jesus Christ.

natter *verb* to talk busily about this and that, to chatter. **natter** *noun. They had a good natter about old times.*

natural *adjective* 1 relating to or concerned with nature. *Earthquakes are natural disasters.* 2 made by nature and not by humans. *The natural beauty of the mountains.* 3 ordinary and not surprising. *It's natural to laugh if you are amused.*

naturalist *noun* somebody who studies wildlife. *A naturalist in the field.*

nature *noun* (say **nay**-chur) 1 everything in the world around us not made by people, such as plants, animals, oceans, mountains etc. 2 characteristics that make up what a person or animal is really like. Personality. *He has a forgiving nature.*

naughty (naughtier, naughtiest) *adjective* badly behaved, mischievous. **naughtiness** *noun.* **naughtily** *adverb.*

nautical *adjective* relating to ships, sailing and the sea. *A nautical map.*

naval *adjective* relating to the navy or ships of war. *The battle of Trafalgar was fought at sea – it was a naval battle.*

navel *noun* the small round hollow in your stomach where your umbilical cord was attached when you were born.

navigate *verb* to steer a ship or to pilot an aircraft in the right direction with the help of maps and special instruments. **navigation** *noun.*

navigator *noun* somebody who navigates or directs the movement of a ship or aircraft.

navy *noun* the warships and sailors that help defend a country at sea.

navy blue *noun, adjective* very dark blue.

Native Americans lived in conical tents called tepees.

AMAZING FACT

Native Americans came to the Americas from Asia via Siberia and Alaska about 30,000 years ago. Tribes settled in various places and developed distinct languages and cultures. Many states retain their Native American names: Wisconsin means 'grassy place', Ohio is 'fine river' and Michigan means 'great water'.

The compass, sextant and map are three tools of navigation.

N'Djamena *noun* the capital of Chad.

n.b. *abbreviation* Latin words 'nota bene', meaning 'note well'.

near *preposition, adjective, adverb* 1 not far away, close to. *We live near the station.* 2 closely related. **near** *verb. As the boat neared the rocks it slowed down.*

nearby *adjective* not far away. *We stayed in a nearby village.*

nearly *adverb* almost but not quite. *He's nearly as tall as his father.*

neat *adjective* 1 very clean and tidy. *A neat pile of clothes.* 2 well done. *She has extremely neat handwriting.*

necessary *adjective* what must be done or is needed, essential and very important. *The climb is dangerous so please take all necessary precautions.*

neck *noun* the narrow part of a person or animal that joins the head to the body.

necklace *noun* a piece of jewellery that you wear around your neck.

nectar *noun* sweet juice that bees collect from flowers to make honey.

nectarine *noun* a fruit similar to a peach but with a smooth skin.

need *verb* 1 to want something that is a necessity. *We all need air to live.* 2 to have to do something. *I need to go to the vet.* **need** *noun. There's no need for you to hurry.*

needle *noun* 1 a thin piece of steel with a sharp point at one end and a hole (or eye) for thread at the other end that is used for sewing. 2 a long thin pointed stick made of plastic or steel that is used for knitting. 3 an instrument with a long thin part used for giving injections. 4 a moving pointer on a meter. 5 the narrow pointed leaf of a coniferous tree.

needless *adjective* unnecessary. *Needless worry is quite destructive.*

needlework *noun* sewing and embroidery.

negative *adjective* 1 meaning 'no'. 'I will not come' and 'I'll never go' are negative answers. 2 a number less than zero. The opposite of negative is positive. **negative** *noun* 1 a photographic film showing dark areas as light and light areas as dark, used to make prints. 2 (in electricity) the opposite charge to positive.

neglect *verb* to fail to look after or give enough attention to. *The garden is overgrown because he neglected to weed it.* **neglect** *noun. The house fell into neglect.*

negotiate *verb* to discuss something in order to come to an understanding or agreement, to bargain. **negotiation** *noun. The dispute was settled by negotiation.*

N

neigh *noun* the sound that a horse makes. **neigh** *verb. The horse neighed happily.*

neighbour *noun* (say **nay**-bor) somebody who lives near or next door to you.

neighbourhood *noun* the area surrounding where you live.

neighbouring *adjective* next to one another. *Italy and France are neighbouring countries.*

neighbourly *adjective* friendly and helpful like a good neighbour.

neither *adjective, pronoun* not either, not one and not the other. *Neither answer is right.* **neither** *conjunction. I neither like him nor dislike him.*

GRAMMAR NOTE

'Neither' is always followed by a singular verb, as in 'neither Jim nor Jane is clever' (not 'are clever'). And remember that you should always use 'neither... nor', as in 'neither you nor I' and never 'neither you or I'.

neon *noun* a chemical gas. Neon is sometimes used in glass tubes to make them glow orange-red when electricity is passed through (neon light).

Nepal *noun* a Himalayan country in South Asia.

nephew *noun* the son of your brother or sister. *My nephew Tim.*

nerve *noun* 1 a long thin fibre in your body that carries messages and feelings between your brain and body so that your body can feel and move. 2 calm bravery. *You need a lot of nerve to be a paraglider.*

Nerves carry information and instructions to and from the brain and from one part of the brain to another.

nervous *adjective* 1 relating to the nerves. *The nervous system.* 2 timid and easily frightened. *A nervous horse.* **nervousness** *noun.*

nest *noun* a home built by birds, some insects and some animals in which to lay eggs, give birth and raise their young. **nest** *verb. Swallows are nesting in the stable.*

nestle *verb* to curl up close together as if in a nest. *They nestled together in the hay.*

net *noun* 1 a material made of knotted string or rope with a regular pattern of holes between the threads. 2 net material used as a fishing net, tennis net, hairnet etc.

netball *noun* a game in which two teams of seven players try to score goals by throwing a ball through a high net at each end of a court. *May was captain of the netball team.*

Netherlands *noun* a country in northwestern Europe, sometimes called Holland.

The flag of the Netherlands has horizontal red, white and blue stripes.

AMAZING FACT

Most species of newts lay 200–400 eggs at a time but some, such as the rough-skinned newt of North America, lay just one egg at a time.

nettle *noun* (or stinging nettle) a wild plant with leaves covered with hairs that sting you if you touch them.

network *noun* 1 a widespread organization. *The telecommunications network.* 2 an arrangement looking like a pattern of criss-crossing lines. *A network of underground tunnels.* 3 a system of linked computers that share a storage system.

neuter *adjective* (say **new**-ter) neither male nor female, with no sexual organs or with the sexual organs removed.

neutral *noun* 1 not taking sides or having strong feelings for or against in, for example, a disagreement or war. *A neutral country.* 2 (of colours) not too strong. *Grey is a neutral colour.*

neutron *noun* one of the particles that make up the nucleus of an atom but carry no electrical charge.

never *adverb* not ever, at no time in the past or in the future. *I will never let you go.*

new *adjective* 1 just made, built, bought, not used, fresh. *I had a new bike for my birthday.* 2 not known, seen or done before. *A new way of doing things.* 3 different, changed. *We have a new science teacher.* The opposite of new is old.

New Delhi *noun* the capital of India.

news *noun* information about events that have recently happened.

newsagent *noun* a shop that sells newspapers, magazines etc.

newspaper *noun* printed sheets of folded paper containing news reports, articles, photographs, advertisements etc. and published daily or weekly.

newt *noun* an animal with short legs and a long tail that lives on land but lays its eggs in water. Newts are amphibians.

Newts are commonly found in ponds and damp places.

New Year *noun* the beginning of a year, starting on 1 January.

New Zealand *noun* a country in Australasia.

New Zealander *noun* a person who comes from New Zealand. **New Zealand** *adjective. New Zealand lamb.*

next *adjective* 1 the nearest. *She lives in the next house but one.* 2 the one immediately after. *I'll catch the next train.* **next** *adverb. What happens next?*

Niamey *noun* the capital of Niger.

nib *noun* the point at the end of a pen that touches the paper as you write.

nibble *verb* to eat something by biting very small bits of it.

Nicaragua *noun* a country in Central America.

nice *adjective* pleasant and kind. *What a nice girl she is.*

nickel *noun* 1 a silver-coloured metal that is mixed with other metals to make coins. 2 (US) a 5 cent coin.

nickname *noun* a special name that people call you instead of your real name.

Nicosia *noun* the capital of Cyprus.

niece *noun* the daughter of your brother or sister. *I love my niece very dearly.*

Niger *noun* a country in Africa.

Nigeria *noun* a country in Africa.

Nigerian *noun* a person who comes from Nigeria. **Nigerian** *adjective*. *Nigerian gold mines are very productive.*

night *noun* the time when it is dark, between sunset and sunrise. The opposite of night is day.

At night time you can see the Moon shining and the stars twinkling in the sky.

nightfall *noun* the end of the day and the beginning of the night,

nightingale *noun* a small brown bird whose beautiful singing is often heard at night.

nightly *adjective*, *adverb* taking place at night or every night. *The news is broadcast nightly at 9 o'clock.*

nightmare *noun* 1 a terrifying dream. 2 a frightening experience or situation. *Trying to shelter from the gunfire was a nightmare.*

nil *noun* nothing. 0. *The team won the match by three goals to nil.*

nimble *adjective* able to move quickly and easily, active.

nip (nip, nipping, nipped) *verb* 1 to give a small sharp bite, to pinch. *The dog nipped the postwoman on the ankle.* 2 to move quickly and for a short time. *I'll just nip out and buy a paper.*

nipple *noun* the small part that sticks out on each of a person's breasts and from which a baby sucks milk from its mother.

nitrogen *noun* a colourless, tasteless gas that makes up over three-quarters of the Earth's atmosphere and the air we breathe.

WORD BUILDER

The sense of a word with the prefix 'non-' is usually easy to work out, if the meaning of the main or root word is clear. Here are examples: 'non-alcoholic', 'non-believer', 'non-existent', 'non-fiction' and 'non-stop'.

The first inhabitants of America were nomads who walked there from Siberia.

AMAZING FACT

There are still many nomadic peoples in Africa and Asia such as the Bedouin tribes of North Africa and the Middle East and the Maasai of Kenya.

noble *adjective* 1 aristocratic, important and of high social rank. *The Bourbons are a noble French family.* 2 honest and of a good and generous nature. **nobility** *noun*. **nobleman, noblewoman** *noun*.

nobody *pronoun* not one person. *There's nobody at home.* **nobody** *noun* an unimportant person. *She's a nobody.*

nocturnal *adjective* concerned with or active during the night. *Nocturnal animals.*

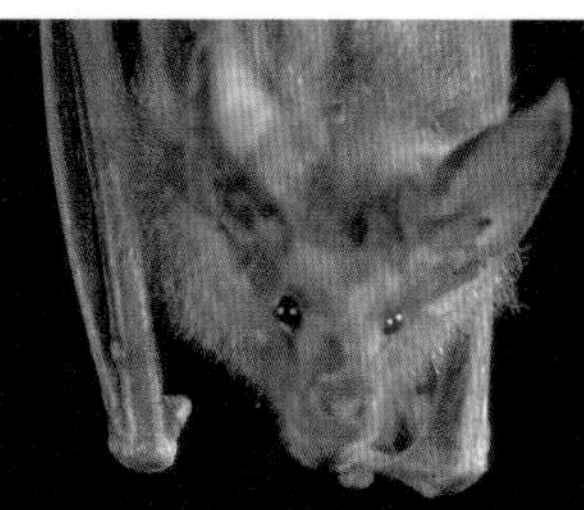

Bats are nocturnal creatures.

nod (nods, nodding, nodded) *verb* to bend your head up and down, perhaps as a sign of agreement or to say yes. **nod off** to half fall asleep by letting your head droop.

noise *noun* sound, usually one that is harsh, loud and unwanted. *Cats make a terrible yowling noise.* **noisily** *adverb*. The opposite of noise is silence.

noisy (noisier, nosiest) *adjective* making a lot of unpleasant noise, full of noise. *Noisy streets.*

nomad *noun* a member of a group of people without a permanent home who wander from place to place with their herds looking for pasture. **nomadic** *adjective*. *A nomadic way of life.*

nominate *verb* to propose that somebody would be the right person to do a job and should be a candidate in an election. To put forward somebody's name. *I nominate Tom Jones, the famous singer, as president of the club.* **nomination** *noun*.

non- *prefix* not, without. *Non-alcoholic drink is recommended for drivers.*

none *pronoun* not one, not any. *You've eaten all the biscuits and there are none left!*

nonfiction *noun* books about real events rather than novels, poetry, plays etc.

nonsense *noun* 1 foolish words that are meaningless. *You're talking utter nonsense.* 2 silly behaviour. *I'll stand no nonsense.*

N

nonstop *adjective* going on without stopping. *A nonstop flight to San Francisco.*

noodles *plural noun* long thin pieces of pasta used in soups etc.

noon *noun* midday, 12 o'clock in the middle of the day.

noose *noun* a loop in a rope that tightens as one end of the rope is pulled.

nor *conjunction* and not (used with neither). *I like neither spinach nor cabbage.*

normal *adjective* ordinary, as expected, usual. *She's a perfectly normal child.* **normality** *noun.*

north *noun* If you face the direction of the Sun as it rises in the morning, north is on your left. The opposite of north is south.

North America *noun* one of the Earth's seven continents.

North Korea *noun* a country in East Asia, officially called the Democratic People's Republic of Korea.

northern *adjective* in the north or of the north. *The lakes of northern Italy are beautiful in spring.*

Northern Ireland *noun* a country that is part of the United Kingdom.

North Pole *noun* the most northerly point on Earth. The north end of the Earth's axis.

northward *adjective*, *adverb* towards the north. *The troops marched northward.*

Norway *noun* a Scandinavian country in Europe.

Norwegian *noun* 1 a person who comes from Norway. 2 the language spoken in Norway. **Norwegian** *adjective. Norwegian fjords were created by glaciers.*

nose *noun* the part sticking out in the middle of your face that you use for breathing and smelling. **pay through the nose** pay too much.

nostalgia *noun* a feeling of sadness for the past and the happy times you had.

nostril *noun* one of the two holes at the end of your nose.

notable *adjective* famous or important. *Notable French cheeses.*

notch *noun* a small cut in the shape of a V.

note *verb* 1 to write something down as a reminder. *He noted down my telephone number.* 2 to call attention to something, to notice. *Note how long the leaves are.*

The magnetic needle of a compass always points to the north.

GRAMMAR NOTE

Where you put 'not' can change the meaning of a sentence. 'He is trying not to win,' is different from 'He is not trying to win.'

SPELLING NOTE

'Nought' or 'naught'? 'Naught' means 'nothing', as in the phrase: 'It came to naught.' 'Nought' is used for the figure 0 or zero.

note *noun* 1 a short letter. *A thank-you note.* 2 a few words you write down as a reminder of something. *He made a note of my address.* 3 a banknote or piece of paper money. *A £20 note.* 4 a single musical sound or a symbol representing the sound.

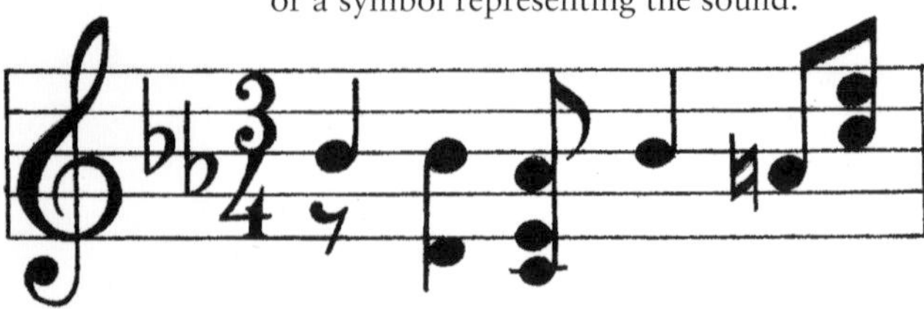

These notes, composed long ago, are the beginning of a popular piece of music.

notebook *noun* a small book in which to write notes. *He scribbled in his notebook.*

noted *adjective* well-known.

nothing *pronoun* no thing, not any thing. *She says she has nothing to wear!*

notice *noun* 1 a written message or announcement that is put in a public place so everybody can read it. *The notice on the wall says: Private.* 2 attention. *Pay no notice to what he says.* 3 warning. *The water may be cut off without notice.* **hand in your notice** to tell your employer that you intend to leave your job.

notice *verb* to become aware of, to see or hear. *She noticed a big crack in the wall.*

noticeable *adjective* easily seen or noticed. *There's been a noticeable improvement in your handwriting.*

noticeboard *noun* a piece wood or cork etc. to which notices can be attached, usually with drawing pins.

We always pin our holiday postcards to the noticeboard.

notify (notifies, notifying, notified) *verb* to tell somebody formally about something. *You should notify the post office when you move.* **notification** *noun. We had official notification to move.*

notion *noun* a general idea or vague belief. *I have a notion that he's gone to India.*

notorious *adjective* well known for being bad or unpleasant, infamous.

Nouakchott *noun* the capital of Mauritania.

nought *noun* (say nawt) the figure 0.

novel *noun* a long written story about imaginary people and events.

novel *adjective* new but different and original. *A novel design.*

novelty *noun* something new, unusual and different. *Gifts and novelties.*

November *noun* the eleventh month of the year. November has 30 days.

AMAZING FACT

November comes from a Latin word meaning 'ninth' because it was the ninth month of the Roman calendar.

novice *noun* 1 a beginner without any experience. 2 a person who is training to be a monk or nun.

now *adverb* 1 the present time. *I am busy now.* 2 immediately and with no delay. *Do it right now, please!*

nowadays *adverb* at this present time. *Few people wear hats nowadays.*

nozzle *noun* the narrow part at the end of a pipe, tube or hose through which a gas, liquid or powder is forced out.

nuclear *adjective* to do with the nucleus, especially that of an atom, and the power created by splitting its nucleus. *Nuclear energy, nuclear missile, nuclear reactor.*

nucleus (nuclei) *noun* the central part or core of something such as an atom or a living cell.

The nucleus is found at the centre of an atom. Negatively charged electrons whirl around it.

nude *adjective* naked, not wearing clothes. **nude** *noun* a person not wearing clothes. **nudity** *noun.*

nudge *verb* to gently poke or push somebody with your elbow.

nugget *noun* a rough lump of precious metal. *A gold nugget.*

nuisance *noun* somebody or something that is annoying. *It's a nuisance I forgot to bring the tapes.*

numb *adjective* unable to feel anything. *My fingers are numb with cold.*

Nuku'alofa *noun* the capital of Tonga.

number *noun* 1 a word or numeral we use for counting. One, two, three. 1, 2,3. 2 a quantity or amount. *She has a large number of CDs.* **number** *verb* 1 count. *The flock numbered 500 sheep.* 2 to put a number on. *The pages are numbered.*

numeral *noun* a symbol or group of symbols you use to write a number. 5, 10, 12 are Arabic numerals and V, X, X11 and C are Roman numerals.

AMAZING FACT

The system of writing numbers that we now use, Arabic numerals, actually originated in India. Most Arabian countries use completely different symbols to represent numbers.

numerate *adjective* able to understand numbers and do calculations. **numeracy** *noun. Literacy and numeracy.*

numerical *adjective* concerning numbers. *Numerical order.*

numerous *adjective* many. *He made numerous visits to the hospital.* The opposite of numerous is few.

numismatics *plural noun* the study of coins and medals.

nun *noun* a member of a religious community of women who live, pray and work together in a building called a convent or an abbey.

nurse *noun* a person who has been trained to look after ill, injured or old people, especially in hospital. **nurse** *verb. Ned nursed his dad when he was ill.*

nursery *noun* 1 a place where young children can go to play during the day while their parents are away. 2 a child's bedroom and playroom in a home. 3 a place where plants are grown to be sold.

nursery rhyme *noun* a short, simple poem that children like to recite.

nut *noun* 1 a fruit with a hard shell and a soft, seed (nut) inside that you can eat. *Brazil nut, hazelnut, walnut.* 2 a piece of metal with a hole through it for screwing on to a bolt. Nuts and bolts are used for holding pieces of metal etc. together. **do your nut** (slang) suddenly to become very angry. *She absolutely did her nut when I broke the mirror.*

nutcracker *noun* an instrument for cracking the shells of nuts.

nutritious *noun* nourishing and good for you as food. *We try to serve three nutritious meals every day.*

Nutritious foods include fruit, vegetables, wholemeal bread, fish, cheese and eggs.

nutty *adjective* 1 tasting of nuts or filled with nuts. *A nutty fruitcake.* 2 (slang) foolish. *I think she's as nutty as a fruitcake.*

nylon *noun* a strong artificial fibre made of chemicals used in making clothes, ropes, brushes etc. *Nylon stockings.*

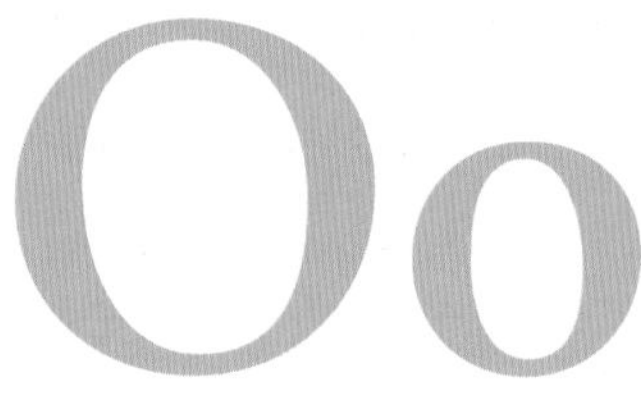

oak *noun* a large deciduous tree with hard wood. The nut of an oak tree is called an acorn. *Mighty oaks from small acorns.*

OAP short for old age pensioner, an old person who receives a pension.

oar *noun* a long pole with a flat part at the end (the blade), used for rowing a boat.

oasis (oases) *noun* an area in a desert where there is water and where plants grow. *At last we arrived at the oasis, where we ate dates and drank mint tea.*

oath *noun* a serious promise to tell the truth, be faithful etc. *I swore an oath on the Bible to tell the truth.*

oatmeal *noun* oats that have been ground to make porridge etc.

oats *plural noun* a type of cereal grain, used as food. *Porridge oats.*

Porridge is a favourite breakfast food in Scotland, where oats grow well.

obedient *adjective* obeying, willing to do what you are told to do. *The children were brought up to be very obedient.*

obese *adjective* (say oh-**beez**) very fat. **obesity** *noun.*

obey *verb* to do what somebody asks or tells you to do. *A sheepdog always obeys commands.* **obedience** *noun.*

obituary *noun* an announcement of somebody's death, usually in a newspaper and with a short account of the person's life and achievements.

object *noun* (say **ob**-ject) 1 a non-living thing that you can see and touch. 2 the purpose or thing you are trying to achieve, aim. *The object of the meeting is to choose a new team.* 3 in grammar, the person or thing towards which the action of a verb is directed. 'Flower' is the object in the sentence 'John picked a flower.'

WORD HISTORY

The shape of the letter O comes from an ancient Egyptian symbol for the eye. Its sound comes from 'ayin', a Semitic word for the eye. The Greeks called it 'omicron'.

object *verb* (say ob-**ject**) to say that you dislike or disapprove of something. *He objected to the woman's rude behaviour.*

objectionable *adjective* disagreeable. *What an objectionable man!*

objective *noun* the aim or goal you are trying to achieve. **objective** *adjective* based on facts and not influenced by feelings, opinions or prejudice. *She wrote a completely objective report on the causes of the famine in the Sudan.*

obligation *noun* something that you have to do, a duty. **obligatory** *adjective. Answering these questions is obligatory.*

oblige *verb* 1 to make somebody do something, to force or compel. *She was obliged to leave the room.* 2 to help or do a favour for somebody. *Please oblige me by closing the door.*

obliging *adjective* willing to help others. *A very obliging young man gave me his seat.*

oblique *adjective* 1 sloping. 2 indirect. *The question seemed rather oblique to me.*

obliterate *verb* to destroy something completely. *Bombs obliterated the town.*

Firemen worked among the rubble of the town that had been all but obliterated by the bombing.

oblong *noun* a shape with four sides with two parallel long sides and two parallel short sides.

obnoxious *adjective* very unpleasant. *An obnoxious smell wafted out of the school dustbins.*

oboe *noun* a woodwind instrument.

Ann clapped loudly when the oboe solo ended.

obscene *adjective* (say ob-**seen**) indecent and sexually offensive. *I will not tolerate obscene behaviour.* **obscenity** *noun.*

obscure *adjective* 1 not well known. *An obscure book by Dickens.* 2 not clear or easy to see or understand. *An obscure problem.* **obscurity** *noun.* **obscure** *verb. The pillar obscured my view of the stage.*

AMAZING FACT

'Obscure' comes from a Latin word meaning 'dark'.

O

observatory *noun* a building with large telescopes for observing the stars, planets and the skies.

From my observatory I can watch the night sky and record my sightings of the planets.

observe *verb* 1 to watch somebody or something carefully. 2 to see and notice something. 3 to obey something such as a law or custom. *Jews observe the festival of Hanukka in December.* 4 to remark. *Tim observed that the post was late.* **observant** *adjective* quick at observing things. **observation** *noun.*

obsolete *adjective* out of date and no longer used. *This computer is obsolete.*

obstacle *noun* something that blocks the way and makes it difficult for you to do something. A hindrance.

obstinate *adjective* refusing to obey or do what somebody wants, stubborn. *An obstinate child.* **obstinacy** *noun.*

obtain *verb* to get something by buying, taking, being given etc. **obtainable** *adjective. Tickets are obtainable in the foyer.*

obtuse angle *noun* an angle between 90 and 180 degrees. An obtuse angle is greater than a right angle.

An obtuse angle is bigger than a right angle.

obverse *noun* the side of a coin showing the head or principal design. The opposite of obverse (heads) is reverse (tails).

obvious *adjective* easy to see and understand, clear. *It's obvious to me that she's broken her finger.*

occasion *noun* a particular time when something happens. *Weddings and birthdays are important occasions.*

SPELLING NOTE

'Occurred', 'occurrence' and 'occurring' are frequently misspelled. Note the 'cc', the 'rr' and the '–ence' (not '–ance').

Some of the world's earliest sea journeys took place across the Pacific Ocean.

The octopus is one of the Greeks' favourite foods. It can be fried gently in olive oil until tender, and served with tomatoes and garlic.

AMAZING FACT

The main defence of the octopus is its ability to squirt a cloud of ink around itself so that it can escape unseen.

occasional *adjective* happening sometimes but not regularly.

occupation *noun* 1 the work a person does for a living, a job. 2 a hobby or something you like doing in your spare time. 3 the invasion and taking control of a town or country by an army. *The German occupation of France during World War II.*

occupy (occupies, occupying, occupied) *verb* 1 to live in. *Who occupies the house next door?* 2 to keep busy. 3 to invade and capture an enemy town, country etc. **occupant, occupier** *noun.*

occur (occurs, occurring, occurred) *verb* to happen. *Thunder storms occur mainly in summer.* **occur to** to suddenly think about something. **occurrence** *noun.*

ocean *noun* any of the great masses of salt water that surround the continents.

o'clock *adverb* 'of the clock', an expression we use when telling the time.

octagon *noun* a flat shape with eight sides. **octagonal** *adjective.*

octave *noun* in music, the eight notes of any scale.

October *noun* the tenth month of the year. October has 31 days.

octopus (octopuses) *noun* a sea creature with a round body and eight tentacles.

odd *adjective* 1 strange, not ordinary. 2 of numbers, not even and not divisible by two. Three, five and 37 are odd numbers. 3 one of a pair and not matching. *An odd sock.* 4 different. *Odd jobs.* 5 **odds** chances or probability of something happening (especially in gambling). **odd one out** the one that is different.

ode *noun* a poem, often addressed to somebody or to something.

odious *adjective* very unpleasant.

O

odour *noun* a strong smell, often an unpleasant one.

odourless *adjective* without smell.

offend *verb* 1 to upset a person's feelings. 2 to do wrong or commit a crime. **offence** *noun*. *Drink-driving is a serious offence.* **offensive** *adjective*. *Offensive behaviour.*

offhand *adjective* 1 unthinking and casual, rude. *An offhand manner.* 2 impromptu and without preparation. *I can't tell you the answer offhand.*

offer *verb* 1 to say that you are willing to do something. 2 to ask somebody if they would like something. To hold out. *She offered him a glass of juice.* 3 to say how much you are willing to give for something. *Harry offered her £100 for the clock.* **offer** *noun*.

office *noun* 1 a place where people work and where a business is carried on. Offices usually contain desks, telephones, computers etc. 2 an important position. *The office of mayor.*

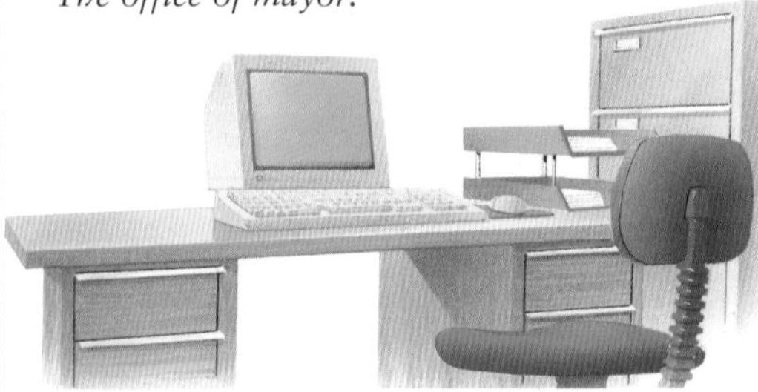

The new office was ready for the company secretary to move into.

officer *noun* a senior person in the armed forces or police who is in charge of other people. *Promoted to the rank of officer.*

official *adjective* coming from or done by people in authority. *An official inquiry.* **official** *noun* a person with a position of authority. *Government officials.*

offspring *noun* the children or young of humans and animals.

often *adverb* frequently, again and again. *We often go swimming in the evening.*

ogre *noun* a frightening and cruel giant in fairy stories.

oil *noun* different kinds of smooth, thick liquids that do not mix with water and which burn easily. You can use oil as a fuel for heating and cooking and for making machines run smoothly. **oil** *verb*.

ointment *noun* a cream that you put on your skin to heal cuts and scratches.

OK or **okay** *adjective*, *adverb* all right.

old *adjective* 1 having lived, existed, or lasted for a long time. 2 having lived for a certain amount of time. *Owen is 11 years old.* 3 belonging to an earlier time. *My old geography teacher.* 4 worn out and no longer new. *Old clothes.* The opposite of old is new.

AMAZING FACT

The first Olympic Games were held at Olympia in Greece in 776BC. The modern Olympic Games began in 1896.

SPELLING NOTE

Try not to confuse 'official', meaning 'authorized' with 'officious', meaning 'meddling' or 'bossy'. So we can talk about 'the official opening of a library' and 'an officious librarian'.

old-fashioned *adjective* out of date, belonging to the past.

olive *noun* a small black or green oval fruit that can be crushed to produce olive oil used in cooking. Olive trees grow in Mediterranean countries.

Olympic Games *plural noun* international competitions in sports held in a different country every four years.

Oman *noun* a country in Southwest Asia.

Oman lies on the Arabian Sea and exports fish as well as petroleum.

omelette *noun* a food made by beating eggs together and frying them, often with a savoury filling.

omen *noun* a sign or warning of good or evil in the future. *Some people believe that putting shoes on a table is a bad omen.*

ominous *adjective* suggesting that something bad is about to happen, threatening. *Those dark clouds look very ominous to me.*

omit (omits, omitting, omitted) *verb* 1 to leave something out. *Your name has been omitted from the list.* 2 to fail to do something. *She omitted some important details.* **omission** *noun*.

omnivore *noun* an animal that eats both plants and flesh. **omnivorous** *adjective*.

once *adverb* 1 at one time in the past. 2 happening one time only. *She comes here once a day.* **once** *conjunction* when. *Once you understand it, you'll never forget it.*

onion *noun* a strong-tasting, rounded bulb eaten as a vegetable.

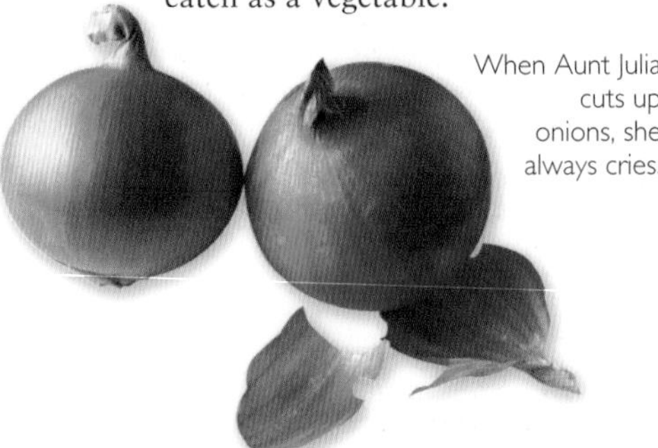

When Aunt Julia cuts up onions, she always cries.

on-line *adjective* a service etc. with a direct connection to and interaction with a computer. *On-line shopping will soon be a reality for many homes.*

onlooker *noun* somebody watching something happen without taking part, a spectator. *The onlookers cheered.*

O

only *adverb* 1 no more than. *It'll only take me a minute to get ready.* 2 just. *She only wants to play for an hour.* **only** *adjective* no others of the same kind. *This is the only watch I have.* **only** *conjunction* but. *I'd love to come, only I can't.* **only child** a child with no brothers or sisters.

ooze *verb* to flow slowly through a narrow opening. *Mud oozed under the door.*

opaque *adjective* If something is opaque, you cannot see through it and it does not let light through.

open *adjective* 1 not shut so people or things can go through, not covered. 2 ready for business. *The shop is open.* 3 honest. *She was very open about her doubts.* **open** *verb* 1 to make open or no longer shut, to become open and no longer shut. *Omar opened the door and let in the cat.* 2 to begin. *The story opens during the Civil War.*

opening *noun* 1 a space. *An opening in the fence.* 2 the beginning of something. *The official opening of the library is next week.* 3 an opportunity. *An opening into the music business would be a dream come true.*

opera *noun* a play with music in which the words are sung. **operatic** *adjective.*

GRAMMAR NOTE

Be sure to place 'only' in the right place in a sentence to express exactly what you mean. 'He drinks beer only on Saturday' is not the same as 'He only drinks beer on Saturday' or 'Only he drinks beer on Saturday.'

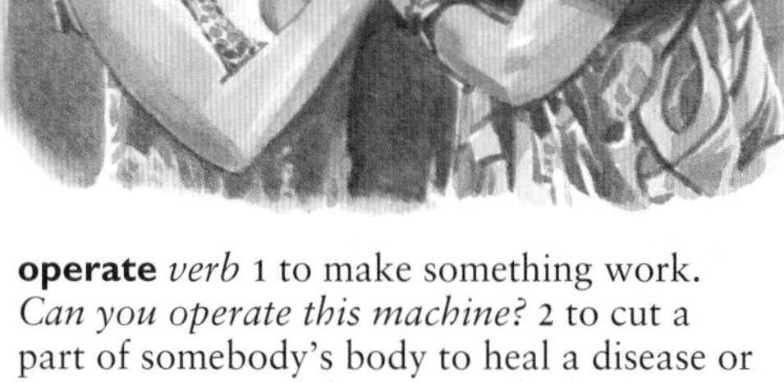

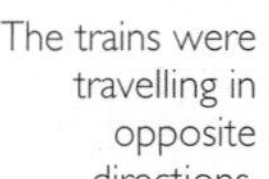

Joan was an overnight success at the opera.

operate *verb* 1 to make something work. *Can you operate this machine?* 2 to cut a part of somebody's body to heal a disease or repair an injury. *The surgeon had to operate on Dick's broken leg.* **operation** *noun.*

opinion *noun* what you think or believe about something. *What is your opinion of the Scottish team?*

opinionated *adjective* stubbornly believing that your opinions are right.

opossum *noun* a small tree-dwelling American marsupial.

The opossum has strong feet and claws for climbing trees.

AMAZING FACT

The opposum is North America's only marsupial. It climbs trees and uses its tail to hold on.

When opposums are in danger, they pretend to be dead. When someone acts as though they have been hurt but haven't, we say they are 'playing possum'.

opponent *noun* somebody who is against you in a contest or fight etc. *Sam outwitted his opponents in the debate.*

Audrey was the chess champion, but she found Steven a formidable opponent.

opportunity *noun* a good time to do something. *Now is your opportunity to learn German.*

oppose *verb* to be against and try to prevent something. *The village opposed the building of a motorway.* **opposition** *noun.*

opposite *noun* something that is completely different in every way from another thing. Happy is the opposite of sad. **opposite** *adjective* 1 different. *They drove in opposite directions.* 2 facing, on the other side. *They stood on opposite sides of the street.*

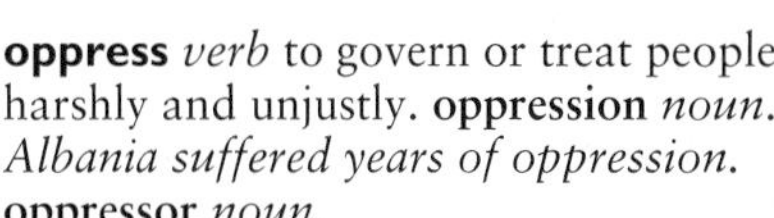

The trains were travelling in opposite directions.

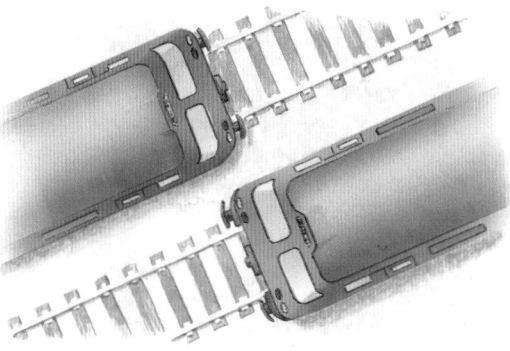

oppress *verb* to govern or treat people harshly and unjustly. **oppression** *noun. Albania suffered years of oppression.* **oppressor** *noun.*

opt *verb* to choose. *We opted to go skiing.* **option** *noun. I have two options, to go or to stay.* **opt out** to decide not to take part.

optical *adjective* relating to the eyes and eyesight. *An optical illusion.*

optician *noun* a person who sells glasses and who is trained to test people's eyesight.

optimism *noun* the belief that only the best will happen and all will end successfully. **optimist** *noun. She is always the cheerful optimist.* **optimistic** *adjective.* The opposite of optimistic is pessimistic.

optional *adjective* not compulsory, that you can choose or not choose.

oral *adjective* relating to the mouth. *Oral hygiene.* 2 spoken not written. *An oral test.*

O

orang-utan *noun* a large Indonesian ape with shaggy reddish fur and long arms.

orange *noun* 1 a round juicy fruit with a reddish-yellow skin (peel). 2 the colour of this fruit. **orange** *adjective*.

orator *noun* a skilled public speaker.

orbit *noun* an imaginary path followed by an object such as a spacecraft or planet as it moves around a planet or star. **orbit** *verb*. *The Moon orbits Earth once a month.*

orchard *noun* a piece of land on which a lot of fruit trees are grown.

AMAZING FACT

The word 'orang-utan' comes from a Malaysian word meaning 'wild man' or 'man of the forest'.

organ *noun* a part inside the body that does a particular job. The heart, kidneys, liver and lungs are organs.

organ *noun* a musical instrument with a keyboard and pipes of different length through which air is pumped to produce sounds. *Rousing chords from the organ.*

organic *adjective* grown without using chemicals or pesticides. *Organic farming.*

organism *noun* any living animal or plant.

We used to love helping with the apple-picking in Grandma's orchard.

orchestra *noun* (say **or**-kess-trah) a large group of people who perform music together, playing different instruments. **orchestral** *adjective*.

orchid *noun* (say **or**-kid) one of many varieties of plant that usually has brightly coloured, strangely shaped flowers.

ordeal *noun* a difficult, unpleasant or dangerous experience.

order *noun* 1 a command given by somebody in control telling people what to do. *The officer gave his orders.* 2 a sequence or a way things are arranged. *Alphabetical order.* 3 neatly arranged, tidy. *He put his papers in order.* **order** *verb* 1 to tell somebody firmly to do something. 2 (in a restaurant) to ask for something to be brought to you, to ask for something to be obtained. *We ordered pie and chips.* **out of order** not working, broken.

ordinary *adjective* not special or interesting. Usual. *A very ordinary sort of guy.*

ore *noun* rock or earth containing metal that can be extracted.

Copper, a reddish-gold metal, is extracted from copper ore.

WORD HISTORY

The orchestra in ancient Greek theatres was a 'dancing place', where dancers and musicians performed in an area between the stage and the audience. Much later the musicians who played there themselves became known as the orchestra.

organization *noun* 1 a group of people working together, a club, business etc. 2 the act of organizing something so it runs smoothly. *The organization of the timetable.*

organize *verb* 1 to plan and prepare something in an orderly way. *Wendy organized a party for her brother's birthday.* 2 to put things in order. **organizer** *noun*.

oriental *adjective* relating to countries of the Far East such as China, India and Japan.

origami *noun* the Japanese art of folding paper into beautiful shapes.

Kylie made a beautiful origami swan.

origin *noun* 1 the start or source of something and why it began. *What is the origin of Halloween?* 2 ancestry or where somebody or something came from. *She's of Jamaican origin.*

original *adjective* 1 the first of its kind to exist or to be made. *The original palace was burned down.* 2 not an imitation. *Original paintings.* 3 different and imaginative. *An original design.*

originate *verb* to start to exist, to have origins. *Cricket originated in England.*

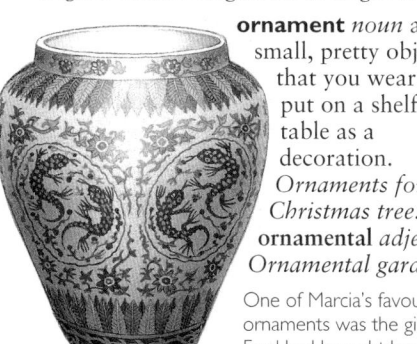

ornament *noun* a small, pretty object that you wear or put on a shelf or table as a decoration. *Ornaments for a Christmas tree.* **ornamental** *adjective. Ornamental gardens.*

One of Marcia's favourite ornaments was the ginger jar Fred had brought back from his travels in China.

ornithology *noun* the scientific study of birds. **ornithologist** *noun.*

orphan *noun* a child whose parents are both dead. *Orphans of the war.*

orphanage *noun* a place where orphans are looked after. *Romanian orphanages.*

orthodontist *noun* a dentist who specializes in straightening and adjusting irregular or crooked teeth.

orthodox *adjective* what is accepted and generally thought to be right by most people. Believing in traditional ideas. *She has very orthodox views.* **orthodoxy** *noun.*

oscillate *noun* to swing backwards and forwards like a pendulum. **oscillation** *noun.*

Oslo *noun* the capital of Norway.

ostrich *noun* a very large bird with long legs and a long neck. Ostriches can run very fast but cannot fly. They come from Africa.

other *adjective* 1 different, not the same as. *The other way is shorter.* 2 opposite. *On the other side of the road.* **other** (others) *pronoun* the rest, more. *Jim's here, but where are the others?*

otherwise *conjunction* or else. *Eat your food, otherwise it will get cold.* 2 except for that. *It was cold, otherwise we had a good time.* **otherwise** *adverb* differently. *He's naughty and cannot behave otherwise.*

ought *verb* must, should.

Ottawa *noun* the capital of Canada.

WORD HISTORY

'Ounce' comes from the Latin word 'uncia', which means a twelfth part of a pound weight. (The Roman pound consisted of 12 ounces).

We travelled into the outback and lived rough for several weeks.

Ostriches are now being farmed in Britain for their meat, which tastes a little like venison.

AMAZING FACT

The ostrich is the world's largest living bird. It cannot fly but is the fastest creature on two legs and is capable of running 45 mph. Ostrich eggs are the largest laid by any bird – one is equivalent to about 40 hen's eggs.

otter *noun* a small animal with brown fur that lives near rivers and eats fish. Otters have webbed feet to help them swim.

Ouagadougou *noun* the capital of Burkina Faso.

ounce *noun* a measure of weight equal to 28.3 grammes. There are 16 ounces to a pound. *An ounce of tobacco.*

out- *prefix* 1 surpassing, more. *Outclassed.* 2 external, outside. *Outhouse.* 3 longer, beyond. *Outlive.*

outback *noun* the huge unpopulated inland areas of Australia.

outbreak *noun* a sudden appearance or start of something. *An outbreak of flu.*

outcome *noun* the result. *What's the outcome of the competition?*

outdoor *adjective* in the open air. *Outdoor activities.* **outdoors** *adverb, noun. In summer we eat outdoors.* The opposite of outdoors is indoors.

outer space *noun* everything beyond the Earth's atmosphere. The universe.

This is a spiral galaxy way beyond planet Earth in outer space.

outfit *noun* a set of clothes, especially for a particular occasion. *Masie wanted a new outfit for the wedding.*

outgrow (outgrows, outgrowing, outgrew, outgrown) *verb* to grow too large or too old for something. *He has outgrown his shoes.*

outing *noun* a day-trip or short journey somewhere for pleasure. *They went on a works outing to the seaside once a year.*

outlaw *noun* a criminal who has not been caught and is hiding. **outlaw** *verb* to make something illegal.

O

outline *noun* 1 a line around the edge of something that shows its shape. *Mike drew the outline of the building.* 2 the main points rather than a detailed description of something. *An outline of the play's plot.* **outline** *verb. She outlined her plans.*

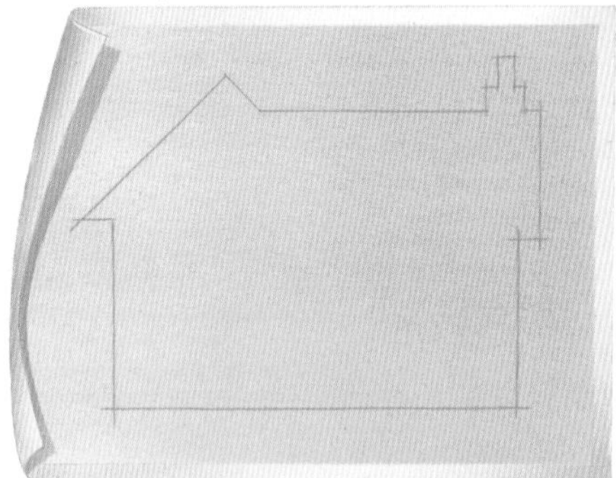

Carl drew the outline of his house on a piece of paper to show the architect.

outlook *noun* 1 a view. *A room with a fine outlook.* 2 a person's general attitude or way of looking at things. *Jennie has a cheerful outlook on life.* 3 what is likely to happen. *The weather outlook is fine.*

output *noun* 1 the amount of something produced in a factory, by a person etc. 2 data produced by a computer.

outrage *noun* a feeling of anger about a shocking or violent act. **outrageous** *adjective* shocking. *Outrageous behaviour.*

outright *adjective* complete, absolute. *She's the outright winner.* **outright** *adverb* instantly. *I told him the bad news outright.*

outset *noun* the beginning. *I knew from the outset she'd win.*

outside *noun* the exterior or outer part of something, the surface of something farthest from the middle. **outside** *adjective, adverb, preposition. The outside lane of the motorway.* The opposite of outside is inside.

We were warm and snug sitting by the fire, but outside it was raining.

outskirts *plural noun* the parts around the outer edges of a town.

outspoken *adjective* saying clearly and strongly what you think even if you offend people. *An outspoken critic of the system.*

outstanding *adjective* 1 excellent. *An outstanding performance.* 2 not paid. *An outstanding bill.*

AMAZING FACT

The saying 'Out of the frying pan and into the fire', meaning to go from a bad situation to a worse one, was originally 'To go from the smoke to the fire' in Greek.

WORD BUILDER

Dozens of new words have been made (and can be made) with the prefix 'over–'. Here are a few: 'over-anxious', 'over-boil', 'over-charge', 'overcook', 'overeat', 'overload' and 'over-optimistic'.

outwit (outwits, outwitting, outwitted) *verb* to be too clever for somebody.

oval *noun* egg-shaped. **oval** *adjective. Rugby balls are oval.*

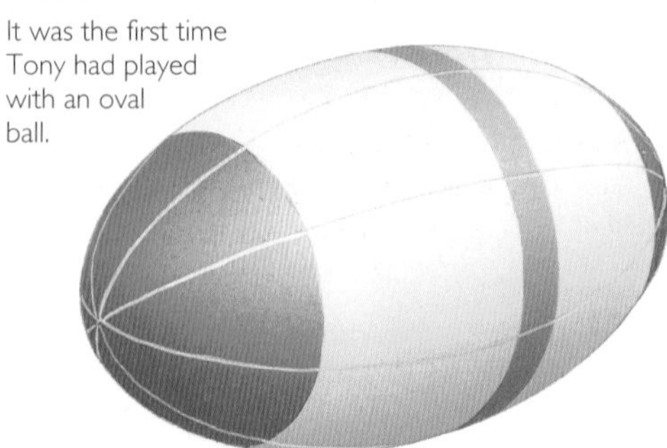

It was the first time Tony had played with an oval ball.

oven *noun* the box-like part of a cooker in which you roast or bake food.

over *preposition* 1 above, higher. *She hung the picture over her bed.* 2 across. *The dog jumped over the stream.* 3 more than. *She's got over a dozen pairs of shoes.* 4 on top of. *He laid blankets over the bed.*

over *adverb* 1 ended. *The ordeal is over.* 2 down from being upright. *I fell over.* 3 upside down. *Flip the pancake over.* 4 not used, remaining. *Any tea left over?* **over and over again** many, many times.

over- *prefix* 1 excessive. *Overconfident.* 2 above, in a higher position. *Overlord.* 3 movement or position above. *Overhang.* 4 extra. *Overcoat.*

overalls *plural noun* a one-piece garment that you wear over your ordinary clothes to keep them clean when doing a messy job.

overboard *adverb* over a ship's side and into the water. *He jumped overboard to rescue the child.* **go overboard** to become too enthusiastic about something.

overcast *adjective* (of the sky) cloudy and dark. *The sky was overcast and it looked very much like rain.*

overcome (overcomes, overcoming, overcame, overcome) *verb* 1 to conquer or defeat, to get the better of. *She has overcome her fear of flying.* 2 to be affected by very strong emotions. *He was overcome with sadness when he heard the news.*

overdue *adjective* behind time, late. *The plane is overdue.*

overflow *verb* to spill or run over the edges of a container. *The river overflowed its banks and flooded the meadow.*

overhaul *verb* to examine something carefully to see if it needs repairing. **overhaul** *noun. She gave her bike a thorough overhaul.*

overhead *adjective, adverb* above you. *An overhead railway.*

overheads *plural noun* all the regular costs involved in running a business such as lighting, heating, insurance and advertising.

overhear (overhears, overhearing, overheard) *verb* to hear accidentally what people are saying when they do not know you are listening.

overlap (overlaps, overlapping, overlapped) *verb* to partly cover or lie across something else. *Roof tiles overlap.*

David fixed on the roof tiles so they overlapped and no rain could get inside.

overlook *verb* 1 to fail to see or do something, to not notice. *You have overlooked how much it will cost!* 2 to forgive and not punish somebody. *I'll overlook your mistake.* 3 to have a view above something. *Your rooms are at the front of the hotel and overlook the sea.*

overrated *adjective* not so good as most people say. *An overrated film.*

overrun (overruns, overrunning, overran) *verb* 1 to spread over; to swarm. *The kitchen was overrun with cockroaches.* 2 to go beyond the time allowed. *The TV programme overran by ten minutes.*

overseas *adjective, adverb* abroad, across the sea. *Overseas visitors.*

overtake (overtakes, overtaking, overtook, overtaken) *verb* to pass another moving person or vehicle. *He overtook the tractor.*

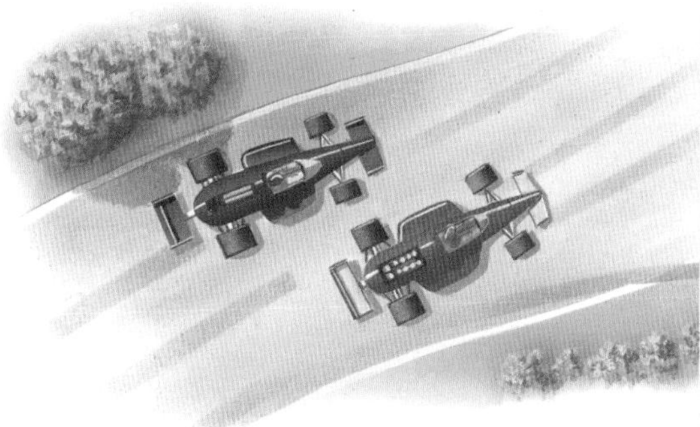

The rivals were running neck and neck, but then Ayrton overtook as they began the last lap.

overthrow (overthrows, overthrowing, overthrew, overthrown) *verb* to defeat or cause something to fall. *The French revolution overthrew the monarchy.* overthrow *noun.*

overtime *noun* extra time spent working outside normal working hours.

overture *noun* a short piece of music at the start of a ballet etc. that sets the mood.

AMAZING FACT

There are over 500 different species of owl. Most owls live in trees but some species actually live in burrows in the ground.

WORD HISTORY

'Ozone' comes from the Greek word for 'to smell', 'ozein'. The name was first given to the gas by the German chemist C.F. Schönbein in 1840 because of its extraordinary smell.

overturn *verb* to fall over or cause something to fall over so that it is upside down. *The lorry crashed and overturned.*

overwhelm *verb* 1 to defeat completely, to crush. 2 to cover completely. *The waves overwhelmed the boat and the twins bailed out frantically.* 3 to put too great a load on. *Paul was overwhelmed with work.*

owe *verb* to have to pay or give something to somebody, especially money that you have borrowed. *I owe you £6 for the tickets.*

owl *noun* a bird of prey with a flat face and large eyes that hunts for small animals such as mice at night. *A wise old owl.*

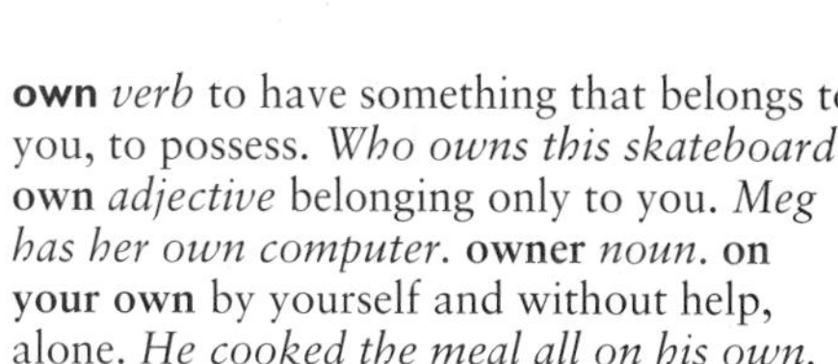

Owls often nest in hollow trees. They fly slowly and almost silently, very close to the ground, so they can spot their prey in the dark without being heard.

own *verb* to have something that belongs to you, to possess. *Who owns this skateboard?* **own** *adjective* belonging only to you. *Meg has her own computer.* **owner** *noun.* **on your own** by yourself and without help, alone. *He cooked the meal all on his own.*

ox (oxen) *noun* a bull that is used in some countries for pulling carts, ploughs etc.

oxygen *noun* a colourless, tasteless gas that makes up about a fifth of the Earth's atmosphere. All life on Earth needs oxygen to live. *Astronauts need to take a supply of oxygen with them into outer space.*

oyster *noun* an edible sea creature that lives inside two shells (a bivalve). Some oysters produce a pearl inside their shell. *David loves oysters and all other shellfish.*

ozone *noun* a gas that is a form of oxygen with three atoms instead of two.

ozone-friendly *adjective* not harmful to the layer of ozone around the Earth. *An ozone-friendly aerosol.*

ozone layer *noun* a layer or belt of ozone high in the atmosphere that protects the Earth by absorbing harmful rays from the Sun. *The ozone layer is becoming depleted, and as a result, many more people who don't wear protective cream in the sun are contracting skin cancer.*

Pp

pace *noun* 1 walking or running speed, or the speed at which something happens. *Work at your own pace.* 2 a single step when walking or running. *She took three paces forwards.* **keep pace with** to go forward at the same rate. *He kept pace with the latest developments.* **pace** *verb* 1 to walk with regular steps. 2 to set the speed, especially for a runner in a race.

pacemaker *noun* 1 a person who sets the speed that others in a race try to keep up with. 2 a machine that is used to keep a weak heart beating.

pacifist *noun* a person who believes that all wars are wrong and who refuses to fight.

pacify (pacifies, pacifying, pacified) *verb* to make calm or quiet.

pack *verb* 1 to put things into a box, bag or case for carrying, storing or moving them. 2 to crowd together, to fit into a space. *The cinema was packed with children.* 3 When you pack something in something, you wrap it up to protect it. *The bowl was packed in newspaper.* **pack in** 1 to stop doing something. *She's packed her job in.* 2 to do a lot of things in a short time. *We packed in a lot of sightseeing.* **pack off** to send somebody away. **send somebody packing** to make somebody leave, especially a person you don't want to be with. **pack up** 1 to pack your belongings. 2 to finish work. *What time do you pack up?* 3 to stop working. *The computer has packed up.*

Jane wrapped the china in newspaper and packed it carefully in the box.

pack *noun* 1 a number of things wrapped or tied together for carrying. *He carried food in a pack on his back.* 2 a group of wild animals, especially wolves or dogs. 3 a group of unpleasant people or a number of bad things. *A pack of lies.* 4 a group of Cub Scouts or Brownies. 5 a complete set of cards. 6 a packet of things. *Alan bought a pack of cigarettes.*

WORD HISTORY

The shape of the letter P comes from the ancient Egyptian symbol for mouse. The sound comes from 'P', a Semitic word for mouse.

DID YOU KNOW

An artificial pacemaker that helps to keep a person's heart beating is operated by a tiny battery. It replaces a small section of the natural heart muscle, which we also call the pacemaker, that regulates our heartbeat.

package *noun* 1 a number of things packed together, a parcel. 2 an offer that includes a number of things. **package** *verb. Juice is packaged in cartons.*

package holiday *noun* a complete holiday at a fixed price, including travel, accommodation and food. *We went on a package holiday to Spain.*

packet *noun* a small parcel.

pact *noun* an agreement. *The two countries signed a trading pact.*

pad *noun* 1 anything filled with soft material used to protect, clean or stuff something. *Skaters wear knee pads.* 2 a number of sheets of paper fixed together at the top or the side that can be torn out. *A writing pad.* 3 the place where a helicopter or rocket takes off. 4 the soft part of an animal's paw. 5 a room, especially in a flat. *We went back to his pad to watch TV.* **pad** (pads, padding, padded) *verb* to put a pad in or on something. *The jacket has padded shoulders.*

John wore protective pads on his knees and elbows while rollerblading.

padding *noun* soft material on or inside something to make it soft.

paddle *noun* a short pole with a flat blade on one or both ends for moving a small boat in water. **paddle** *verb* 1 to move a boat through water. *They paddled really hard in their canoes.* 2 to walk about barefoot in shallow water.

paddock *noun* a field near a house or stables where horses are kept.

paddy field *noun* a field where rice is grown. *The paddy fields of China.*

padlock *noun* a lock that can be put on and taken off, for use on a door, box or locker. **padlock** *verb. He padlocked the shed.*

paediatrician (say pee-dee-uh-**tri**-shun) *noun* a doctor who specializes in children's illnesses. **paediatric** *adjective.*

pagan (say **pay**-gun) *adjective, noun* not believing in the main religions of the world.

page *noun* a piece of paper in a book, newspaper or magazine.

page *noun* 1 a servant, usually a boy, dressed in a uniform who works in a hotel. 2 a boy who attends a bride at a wedding.

page *verb* to call the name of a person, especially in a hotel or hospital. *Can you page Mr Smith?*

pageant *noun* 1 a show, usually outdoors, about the history of a place and its people. 2 a ceremony with a procession of people in costume. **pageantry** *noun.*

pager *noun* a radio device with a bleeper to alert somebody or pass a message.

pagoda *noun* a temple, especially Buddhist or Hindu, shaped like a tower.

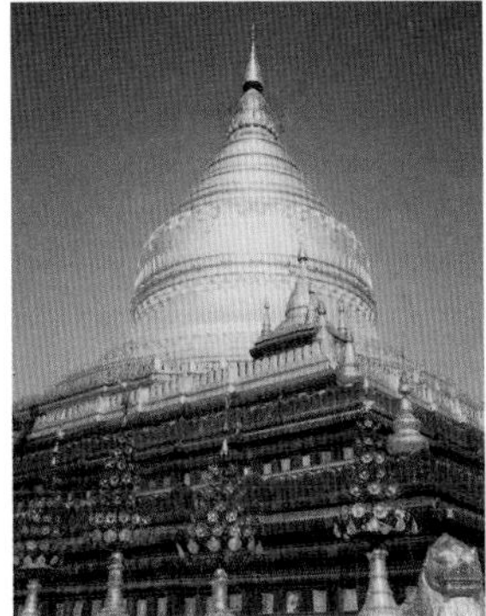

Many of the pagodas of southeast Asia have beautiful gilded roofs.

paid *verb* past tense of pay.

pail *noun* a bucket. *A pail of milk.*

pain *noun* 1 an unpleasant feeling of hurt when you are injured or ill. 2 a feeling of unhappiness when something upsetting happens. **pain** *verb. It pains me to see you unhappy.* **take pains** to make an effort. *She takes great pains with her homework.* **a pain in the neck** an annoying person. **painful** *adjective.* **painless** *adjective* not causing pain. *A painless operation.*

painkiller *noun* medicine that lessens or stops pain.

painstaking *noun* careful and thorough. *A painstaking investigation.*

paint *noun* 1 a coloured liquid or other substance that can be put on a surface. 2 **paints** a set of tubes or cakes of paint, usually in a box, for painting pictures. **paint** *verb* 1 to put paint on something. *He painted the chair black.* 2 to make a picture with paint.

Hannah knocked over the tin of paint, and it spilled all over the floor.

painter *noun* 1 a person whose job is painting and decorating houses or rooms. 2 a person who paints artistic pictures. *A portrait painter.*

painting *noun* a painted picture.

pair *noun* 1 two things, usually used together. *A pair of shoes.* 2 two people. 3 an object made up of two parts. *A pair of scissors.* **pair** *verb* to form a pair.

WORD HISTORY

The first palace was on the Palatium, the Palatine hill in Rome, where the house of the Roman emperor was situated. The Palatine was one of the seven hills on which ancient Rome was built.

AMAZING FACT

Pandas' natural habitat are the forests of Eastern Asia. There are two types of panda. The red panda is about the size of a house cat and has a bushy tail. The giant panda looks like a black and white bear. They aren't bears, though, their closest relatives are raccoons!

Pakistan *noun* a country in South Asia.

palace *noun* a large house which is the home of a king or queen or other important person. **palatial** *adjective* like a palace.

palate *noun* 1 the top of the mouth. 2 a person's sense of taste.

pale *adjective* 1 having little colour. You look pale when your face is almost white or lighter than usual. *She went pale when she heard the bad news.* 2 light, not bright in colour. *In the pale light of dawn.*

palette *noun* a board, with a hole for the thumb, on which an artist mixes colours.

Palikir *noun* the capital of Micronesia.

palindrome *noun* a word or phrase that reads the same backwards or forwards. 'Deed' is a palindrome.

palisade *noun* a fence made of pointed iron or wooden poles.

pallid *adjective* unhealthily pale.

palm *noun* the inner part of the hand between the fingers and the wrist. **palm** *verb* to steal something by picking it up and hiding it in your palm. **palm off** to trick someone into buying or taking something.

palm *noun* a tree that grows in hot countries with large leaves at the top and no branches. *Swaying coconut palms.*

pampas *noun* treeless grassy plains in South America. *Herding cattle on the pampas.*

pamper *verb* to treat too kindly or do too much for somebody.

pamphlet *noun* a small booklet that gives information about something.

pan *noun* 1 a metal container with a handle for cooking. 2 the bowl of a lavatory.

Panama *noun* a country in central America.

Panama City *noun* the capital of Panama.

The flag of Panama has red, blue and white squares and blue and red stars.

pancake *noun* a thin flat cake made of flour, eggs and milk (called batter) and fried on both sides.

Pancake Day *noun* Shrove Tuesday, when people traditionally eat pancakes.

pancreas *noun* a gland near the stomach that produces chemicals to help digestion.

panda *noun* a large bear-like animal with black and white fur that lives in Chinese bamboo forests. Also called a giant panda.

pane *noun* a piece of glass in a window.

panel *noun* 1 a flat piece of wood or other material that is part of a door or larger object. 2 a group of people chosen to discuss or decide something. *An advisory panel.* 3 a piece of material different in colour or fabric that is put in a dress. **panelled** *adjective. A panelled room.* **panelling** *noun.*

pang *noun* a sudden strong feeling. *A pang of sadness.*

panic *noun* a sudden uncontrollable fear. *She got into a panic when she lost her bag.* **panic** (panics, panicking, panicked) *verb* to suddenly become afraid and do things without thinking carefully.

panic-stricken *adjective* afraid, filled with terror. *The panic-stricken burglar fled.*

panorama *noun* a complete view of a wide area. *A panorama of fields spread below.*

pansy (pansies) *noun* a small garden flower.

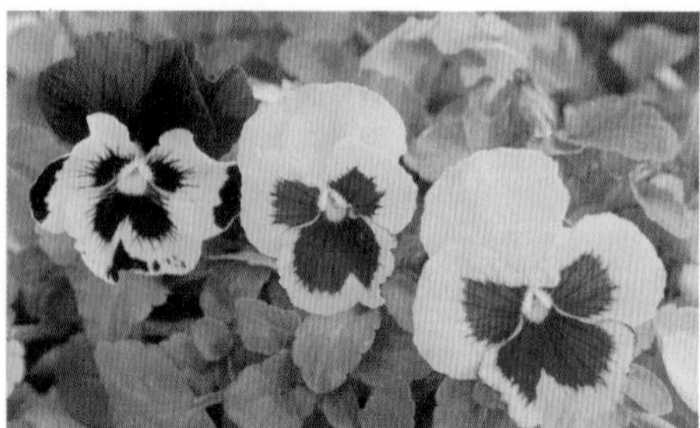

The name 'pansy' came originally from the French word for thought, 'pensée'.

pant *verb* to breathe quickly with your mouth open, usually after running or when you're hot. *The dog panted.*

panther *noun* a wild animal of the cat family, usually black.

panties *noun* underpants worn by girls.

pantomime *noun* a funny musical play for children that is based on a fairy-tale and usually shown at Christmas.

pantry (pantries) *noun* a small room in a house, where food is kept.

pants *plural noun* 1 underpants. 2 (especially US) trousers.

papacy (say **pay**-puh-see) *noun* the power of the Pope or the position of Pope.

papal (say **pay**-pul) *adjective* to do with the Pope. *A papal decree.*

paparazzi *plural noun* photographers who follow famous people to take pictures.

paper *noun* 1 material made in thin sheets from wood or cloth for writing, printing or drawing on or for wrapping and covering things. 2 a newspaper. 3 part of a written examination with questions that have to be answered. 4 **papers** documents showing who a person or thing is. **paper** *verb* to put wallpaper on a wall. *We want to paper the sitting room.* **paper over something** to hide faults by pretending things are going well.

SPELLING NOTE

Note that the words to do with the Pope, 'papacy' and 'papal', are spelt with an 'a' (not 'popacy' or 'popal'!). The origin of all the words is the Latin 'papa', meaning bishop, from the Greek 'papas', meaning father.

paperback *noun* a book with a soft cover.

papoose *noun* a bag on a frame for carrying a baby on a person's back.

Papua New Guinea has a population of four million people.

Papua New Guinea *noun* a country in Australasia, forming part of the island of New Guinea.

par *noun* 1 an average or normal amount, degree or condition. When something is on a par with something else, both are equally good or equally bad. 2 in golf, the number of strokes an average player should take on one hole.

parable *noun* a simple story with a moral point. *Parables from the bible.*

parachute *noun* a device attached to a person or thing to make them fall slowly when dropped from a plane. **parachutist** *noun.*

There was a wonderful parachute display at the airfield.

parade *noun* 1 a procession or gathering of people or things for the purpose of being looked at or to celebrate a special event. *A fashion parade.* 2 soldiers marching together for inspection or for a ceremony. 3 a public square, or a row of shops. **parade** *verb* 1 to march in procession in order to be looked at by other people. *The winners paraded triumphantly around the stadium.* 2 to show something off in order to impress.

paradise *noun* 1 heaven, a place of perfect happiness. 2 in the Bible, the Garden of Eden, home of Adam and Eve.

paradox (paradoxes) *noun* 1 a statement that seems wrong or impossible, but has some truth in it. 2 two facts or ideas that are opposite to what is generally believed to be true. **paradoxical** *adjective.*

paraffin *noun* a kind of oil used for heating or lighting. *A paraffin lamp.*

paragliding *noun* a sport involving cross-country gliding using a parachute shaped like wings.

paragraph *noun* a section of a piece of writing consisting of a number of sentences on a subject. A paragraph starts on a new line. *Please write two paragraphs.*

Paraguay *noun* a country in South America.

parakeet *noun* a small parrot.

parallel *adjective* lines that are at the same distance from each other are parallel. *The road runs parallel to the railway.*

parallel *noun* 1 a line parallel to another. 2 something similar to something else, or a comparison that shows likeness. *She is without parallel.*

parallelogram *noun* a four-sided figure with opposite sides parallel.

paralyse *verb* 1 to make some or all of the body's muscles unfeeling and unable to move. *A stroke paralysed his left arm.* 2 to make somebody or something unable to act, move or work properly. *Paralysed with fear.* **paralysis** *noun.*

Paramaribo *noun* the capital of Suriname.

parapet *noun* a low wall at the edge of a bridge or roof.

paraplegic *noun* (say par-uh-**plee**-jick) a person whose lower body, including both legs, is paralysed. **paraplegic** *adjective.* **paraplegia** *noun.*

parasite *noun* a plant or animal that lives on or in another and gets food from it. **parasitic** *adjective.*

Ticks are parastites that live on sheep. They can also infest humans, dogs and cats.

parasol *noun* an umbrella used as a sunshade. *A dainty parasol.*

parcel *noun* something wrapped up so it can be sent by post or carried. **parcel** (parcels, parcelling, parcelled) *verb.* **parcel up** to make into a parcel.

parchment *noun* a kind of thick yellowish paper. In ancient times parchment was made from the skin of sheep or goats and used for writing on.

pardon *noun* forgiveness. *I beg your pardon.* **pardon** *verb* to forgive or excuse a person. **pardonable** *adjective.*

parent *noun* Your parents are your father and mother. **parental** (say puh-**rent**-ul) *adjective. Parental care.*

parenthesis (parentheses) *noun* (say puh-**ren**-thi-sis) 1 a sentence or a phrase inserted in a sentence, usually in brackets. 2 a bracket.

Paris *noun* the capital of France.

DID YOU KNOW

The term 'parrot-fashion' came about because people sometimes teach parrots to 'talk', or repeat the sounds they make. Today, many people feel it is wrong to keep birds in cages. In the wild, parrots have a harsh, screaming voice. They use their short, hooked bill to open nuts and feed on fruits and seeds.

AMAZING FACT

There are both animal and plant parasites.

Animal parasites such as fleas and ticks, live on birds and mammals and suck blood.

Plant parasites, such as fungus, take nourishment from plants by twining around or growing into the host.

Mistletoe, traditionally used as a decoration at Christmas time, is a parasite that lives off trees.

parish (parishes) *noun* a village or town that has its own church. *The vicar of this parish.* **parishioner** *noun.*

park *noun* 1 a public garden or place, usually in a town, for people to walk in. 2 the large private garden of a country house. *The duke went riding in the park.*

park *verb* to leave a car or other vehicle somewhere for a time. *I parked the car in the car park.*

parliament *noun* an institution made up of a group of people who are elected and make a country's laws. **parliamentary** *adjective.*

parlour *noun* (old-fashioned) a sitting room. *The piano is in the parlour.*

parody (parodies) *noun* a piece of writing or music that makes fun of somebody else's style by copying it.

parrot *noun* a tropical bird with bright feathers and a hooked beak.

Conservationists are working to stop the illegal export of parrots from their native homes. Many parrots die in transit.

parrot-fashion *adjective* mechanical, without understanding. *She repeated everything parrot-fashion.*

parsley *noun* a plant with green leaves, used to add taste to food.

Parsley has a very high vitamin C content.

parsnip *noun* a white or yellowish root vegetable.

parson *noun* a member of the clergy, a vicar. *She took tea with the parson every Tuesday afternoon.*

part *noun* 1 any piece or portion of a whole, anything that belongs to something bigger. *The afternoon is the best part of the day.* 2 an important piece of a machine or other apparatus. *You can order spare parts for the bike.* 3 a share or duty in doing something. *He never takes part in games.* 4 a person's role in a play or film. *She played the part of the witch.* 5 any of several equal amounts in something. *This mixture is two parts milk and one part cream.* **take something in good part** to show that you are not offended by something. **play a part in** to have an important effect on what happens.

P

part *verb* to separate or divide, to leave each other. *Let's part as friends.* **part with** to give away. *I won't part with my dog.*

partial *adjective* 1 not complete. *A partial success.* 2 supporting one person or side, more than the other, especially in a way that is unfair. 3 liking something very much. *I'm very partial to chocolate.* **partiality** *noun.*

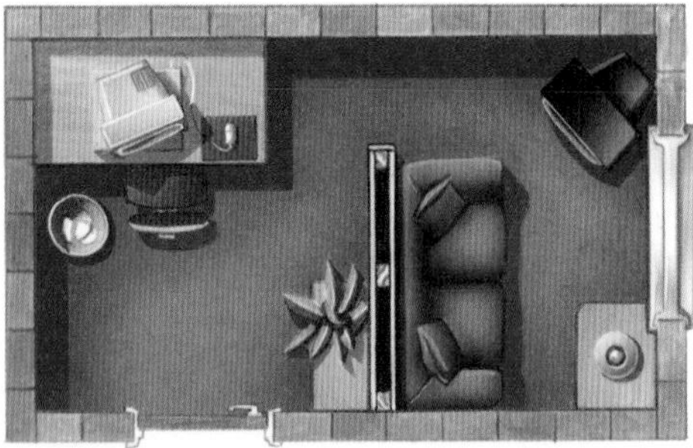

Ann was so partial to television, that she had a tv set and a sofa in her office.

participate *verb* to take part in something or have a share in an event. **participation** *noun. Your participation is appreciated.*

particle *noun* a very small piece or amount. *Food particles.*

particular *adjective* 1 relating to one and not any other. *This particular car is faster than the others.* 2 special. *She takes particular care to please her parents.* 3 difficult to please. *She is very particular about her food.* **particularly** *adverb.*

particular *noun* 1 a detail. *He is right in every particular.* 2 **particulars** facts or details, especially about events. *Fill in your particulars.* **in particular** especially.

parting *noun* the line on the head where the hair is parted.

partition *noun* 1 a thin wall that divides a room. 2 division into two or more parts. **partition** *verb* to divide into two or more parts. *A partition divides these rooms.*

partner *noun* one of two people who do things together or share the same activity. *My tennis partner.* **partner** *verb.* **partnership** *noun.*

Her tennis partner was very good at volleying.

part of speech *noun* one of the classes of words in grammar. Nouns, verbs and adjectives are parts of speech.

partridge *noun* a bird with brown feathers. Partridges are shot for sport and food.

GRAMMAR NOTE

Try to avoid using the passive form of verbs. The active form is more direct and easier to understand. For example: 'Pencils are to be found in the drawer' is not as good as: 'You will find pencils in the drawer.'

DID YOU KNOW

The common or grey partridge ranges across Europe and western Asia. It was also introduced to North America. Partridges eat mainly plant food such as seeds and young shoots.

part-time *adjective, adverb* during a part of a day or week. *She works part-time.* The opposite of part-time is full-time.

party (parties) *noun* 1 a gathering of people who come together to enjoy themselves. *We gave a birthday party for my sister.* 2 a political organization. *The Labour Party.* 3 a group of people who work or travel together. *A party of tourists.* 4 a person who is taking part in a lawsuit. *The guilty party has to pay the costs.* **be party to** to be responsible for something. *I was party to the decision.* **party** *verb* to go to parties.

pass (passes, passing, passed) *verb* 1 to move past something or somebody. 2 to get or go through or between. *No one is allowed to pass this line.* 3 to go by, or spend time. *Three months passed before she heard from him.* 4 to give something to another person. *Can you pass me the jam?* 5 to do well and be successful, especially in an exam. *She passed her driving test.* 6 to accept or agree, especially a law. *The law was passed by Parliament.* 7 in sport to kick, throw or hit, especially a ball, to somebody in your team. **pass on** to tell something to another person. **pass out** to faint.

pass (passes) *noun* 1 a way between two mountains. 2 a successful result in an exam or test. 3 kicking, throwing or hitting a ball to somebody in your team. 4 a document or ticket that allows you to do something, especially go into a place. **make a pass** to try to make somebody of the opposite sex interested in you, usually in an unwelcome approach. *The boss made a pass at me.*

passenger *noun* a person who is driven in a car or is travelling by public transport.

The passenger enjoyed a comfortable ride.

passer-by (passers-by) *noun* a person who happens to pass a place. *A few passers-by saw the accident.*

passion *noun* a very strong attraction or strong feeling about somebody or something. *She has developed a passion for painting.* **passionate** *adjective.*

passive *adjective* 1 not active, showing no feeling or interest in what is said or done to you. 2 in grammar, a form of a verb when it describes what happens or will happen to somebody or something. 'The car was driven by me' is passive. 'I drove the car' is active. **passive** *noun.*

Passover *noun* a Jewish festival in memory of the freeing of the Jews from Egypt.

passport *noun* an official document that has to be shown when entering or leaving a country.

Michael renewed his passport so that he could go abroad on holiday.

password *noun* a secret word or phrase that you have to know to show that you are a friend or to gain access to something.

past *adjective* 1 referring to the time before now. *During the past hours.* The verbs 'went', 'called' and 'wrote' are in the past tense. **past** *adverb, preposition* 1 up to and beyond a point. *The bus drove past.* 2 after. *It's ten past four.* **be past it** to be no longer able to do things, because you are too old. **past** *noun* the time before the present.

pasta *noun* an Italian food made of a mixture of flour, eggs and water. Spaghetti, macaroni and noodles are all forms of pasta. *Pasta with parmesan cheese.*

Pasta may be coloured with spinach, tomato or beetroot.

paste *noun* 1 a soft mixture used for sticking things together. 2 food, especially fish or meat, made into a soft mixture that can be spread on bread. 3 hard shiny glass used for making imitation jewellery. **paste** *verb* to stick something using paste. *I spent all day pasting cuttings into my scrap-book.*

pastel *noun* 1 a coloured crayon. 2 a picture drawn with coloured crayons. *He loves working in pastels.* 3 a light colour.

pasteurize *verb* to remove bacteria from milk by heating and then cooling it.

pastry (pastries) *noun* 1 a mixture of flour, fat and water rolled out and baked in the oven. 2 something made of pastry.

pasture *noun* land covered with grass, suitable for grazing animals such as cattle or sheep. *Lush pasture.*

SPELLING NOTE

Take care not to confuse 'past' with 'passed'. 'Past' is an adjective, adverb or preposition, as in: 'We walked past the school.' 'Passed' is the past tense of the verb to pass, as in: 'A week passed before we received the letter.' 'Past' can also be a noun: 'That's all in the past.'

AMAZING FACT

Italian words for pasta, such as spaghetti, macaroni, linguini and tagliatelli, are all plural forms. The plurals end in 'i'.

This is also true of other Italian plural nouns such as graffiti and paparazzi.

pasty (say pay-stee) (pastier, pastiest) *adjective* looking pale and unhealthy.

pasty (say pas-tee) (pasties) *noun* a small pie made of folded pastry filled with meat, fish, fruit or vegetables.

pat (pats, patting, patted) *verb* to tap lightly with your fingers on something flat. *He patted the dog.* **pat** *noun* 1 a friendly pat. 2 a light sound. 3 a small piece of butter or something else soft. **pat on the back** praise for doing well. **know something off pat** to be prepared for something and have a ready answer. *He had the answer off pat.*

patch (patches) *noun* 1 a small piece of material to put over a hole or damaged place. *She put a patch on her jeans.* 2 a pad worn to protect an eye that has been hurt. 3 a small piece of ground. *A vegetable patch.* 4 a small area of something or a part that is different from the space around it. *Patches of fog.* **A bad patch** is a period of bad luck. **patchy** *adjective.* **not a patch on** not nearly as good. **patch** *verb* to put a patch on something. **patch up** 1 to repair something roughly. 2 to end a quarrel. *They tried to patch things up, but it hasn't worked out.*

Aunt Mary kindly sewed a patch on my trousers.

patent *noun* the official right given to an inventor to make or sell their invention and stop others from copying it. **patent** *verb* to get a patent for an invention. **patent** *adjective* 1 protected by a patent. 2 obvious. *It was a patent lie.* **patent leather** leather that has a shiny surface.

paternal *adjective* like or relating to a father. *Paternal feelings.*

path *noun* 1 a strip of ground for people to walk on or made by people walking over it. *We followed the path through the woods.* 2 a line along which somebody or something moves. *The path to success.*

pathetic *adjective* sad, weak or helpless. *What a pathetic joke!* **pathetically** *adverb.*

patient *adjective* able to wait calmly without getting annoyed. *Please be patient, I'll be as quick as I can.* **patience** *noun.*

patient *noun* a person who has medical treatment from a doctor or hospital.

patio *noun* a paved area next to a house.

patriot *noun* a person who loves and supports his or her country. **patriotic** *adjective.* **patriotism** *noun.*

P

patrol (patrols, patrolling, patrolled) *verb* to go at regular times over an area or a building to make sure that there is no trouble. *Soldiers patrolled the border.* **patrol** *noun* 1 the time of patrolling. *A soldier on patrol.* 2 a person, group of soldiers or vehicles patrolling an area.

patron (say **pay**-trun) 1 somebody important who gives money to or takes an interest in a person, especially an artist. 2 a person who uses a shop regularly.

patronize *verb* 1 to act towards others in a superior way, as if more important. *She has no right to patronize me.* 2 to support and give money to artists.

patron saint *noun* the protecting saint of a person or place. Saint Christopher is the patron saint of travellers.

patter *verb* to make light tapping sounds. **patter** *noun* 1 a number of quick, light tapping sounds. *The patter of children's little feet.* 2 the fast talk of a salesperson or an entertainer.

pattern *noun* 1 an arrangement of lines, shapes or colours, especially a design that is repeated. 2 a particular way in which something is done or happens. *A behaviour pattern.* 3 The shape of something to be copied. *A dress pattern.*

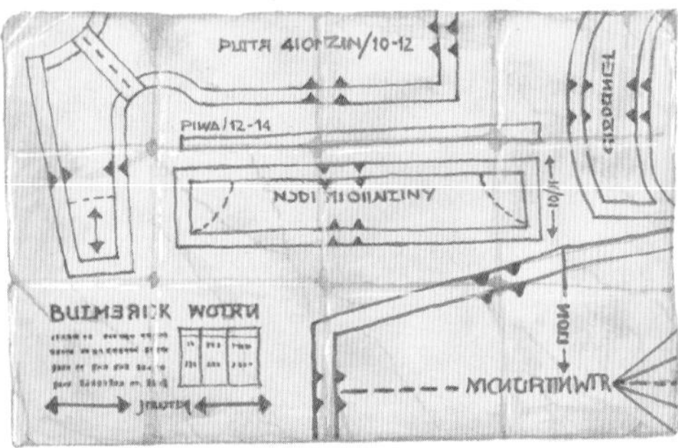

Carrie spread out the dress pattern to see how much material she would need.

pauper *noun* a very poor person.

pause *noun* 1 a moment of silence. 2 a break from doing something. **pause** *verb* to stop for a short while.

pave *verb* to put flat stones or bricks on a path or an area. **pave the way** to make something more likely to happen. *Their meeting paved the way to an agreement.*

pavement *noun* a path at the side of the street for people to walk on.

pavilion *noun* 1 a building next to a sports field for the use of players and spectators. 2 an ornamental building used for dances, concerts or exhibitions.

paw *noun* an animal's foot. **paw** *verb* to feel or touch with a hand or foot.

pawn *noun* 1 the smallest and least valuable playing piece in chess. 2 an unimportant person used by others to their own advantage. *He was a pawn in their game.*

DID YOU KNOW

Most groups of people and occupations have their own patron saint, and some have more than one. Here are some: athletes, St Sebastian; comedians, St Vitus; grocers, St Michael; librarians, St Jerome; scientists, St Albert the Great; students, St Thomas Aquinas and St Catherine of Alexandria.

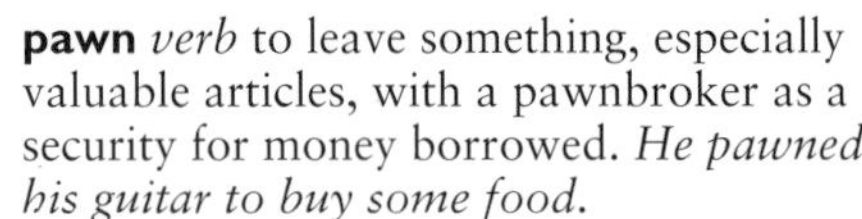

pawn *verb* to leave something, especially valuable articles, with a pawnbroker as a security for money borrowed. *He pawned his guitar to buy some food.*

pawnbroker *noun* a person who lends money to people in exchange for articles which they leave as security.

pay (pays, paying, paid) *verb* 1 to give money for goods bought or work done. *I paid five pounds for his old bike.* 2 to settle a bill or debt. *I'll pay!* 3 to give somebody an advantage, to be worth the trouble or cost. *It doesn't pay to cheat.* 4 to give or say something to a person, especially in certain phrases. *He paid her a compliment.* **pay back** to give back the money that you owe. **pay somebody back** to make somebody suffer for what they did to you. **pay up** to pay fully, to give all the money you owe. **pay** *noun* money received for work.

payee *noun* a person to whom money is paid or should be paid.

payment *noun* 1 paying money or being paid. *When can we expect payment?* 2 an amount of money paid to somebody.

PC *abbreviation* 1 personal computer. 2 police constable. 3 politically correct.

PE *abbreviation* physical education, especially sports at school.

pea *noun* the small round green seed growing inside a pod, eaten as a vegetable.

peace *noun* 1 a time when there is no war between countries, no trouble, quarrelling or fighting among people. 2 calm and quietness. *Leave us in peace.* **make peace** to end a quarrel. **peaceful** *adjective.*

peach *noun* a round juicy fruit with soft yellowish-red skin and a large stone.

peacock *noun* a large male bird with long colourful tail feathers that it can spread out like a fan.

peahen *noun* a large brownish bird, the female of the peacock.

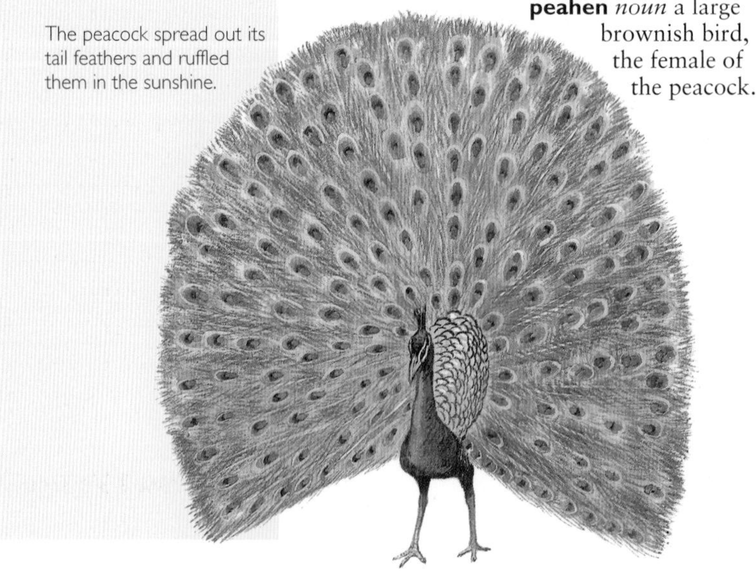

The peacock spread out its tail feathers and ruffled them in the sunshine.

peak *noun* 1 the pointed top of a mountain. 2 the front part of a cap, that sticks out to shade your eyes. 3 the highest level or most successful part of something. *She has reached the peak of her career.* **peak** *verb* to reach its highest point or level of success.

peanut *noun* a small round nut that grows under the ground.

peanut butter *noun* roasted peanuts crushed into a paste and eaten as a spread on bread.

pear *noun* the hard, juicy fruit of the pear tree. *Pear and apple crumble.*

pearl *noun* 1 a hard, round, shiny white object that grows inside the shell of an oyster and is a valuable jewel. *A pearl necklace.* 2 something that looks like a pearl or is a copy of a pearl. **pearly** *adjective.*

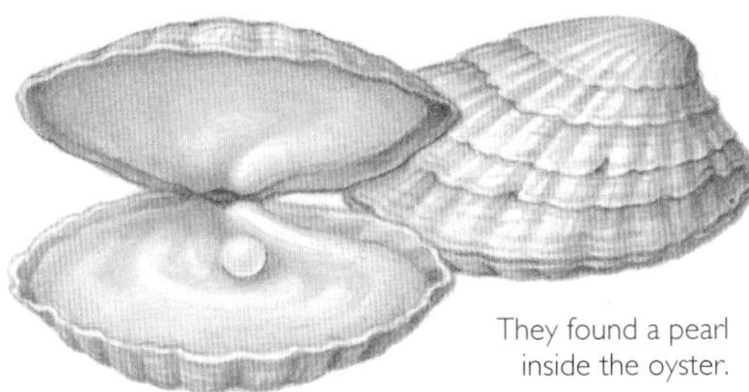

They found a pearl inside the oyster.

peasant *noun* a person who works on a farm or owns a small piece of land.

peat *noun* rotted plant material found under the ground. Peat is used for burning instead of coal or to improve soil and make plants grow better.

pebble *noun* a smooth round stone.

pebbledash *noun* cement with lots of small pebbles in it which is used for covering the outside walls of a house.

peck *verb* 1 to hit, tap or bite with the beak. *The bird pecked a hole in the apple.* 2 to kiss quickly and lightly. **peck** *noun* 1 a quick hit or tap with the beak. 2 a quick kiss. *She gave him a peck on the cheek.*

peculiar *adjective* 1 strange, unusual, often in an unpleasant way. *He gave me a peculiar look.* 2 belonging or relating to a particular thing or person only. *The accent is peculiar to the people in this valley.* **peculiarity** *noun.*

pedal *noun* a bar which is pushed or pressed with the foot to make a bicycle move or work a car or machine. **pedal** (pedals, pedalling, pedalled) *verb* to work something by using pedals. *He had to pedal hard to get up the hill.*

pedant *noun* a person who is very strict about unimportant rules and pays too much attention to detail. **pedantic** *adjective.*

pedestal *noun* the base on which a statue or pillar stands.

DID YOU KNOW

Peanuts are also called groundnuts or earthnuts. They come originally from tropical South America, but now most of the world's peanuts are grown in Africa and Asia. There are usually two peanuts in a pod.

WORD HISTORY

A pedant was originally simply a teacher. The word comes from the Italian 'pedante', meaning teacher, perhaps from the Latin paedagogus, who was originally a slave who looked after his master's son, including taking him to school.

pedestrian *noun* a person walking, especially in a town. **pedestrian** *adjective* 1 for people walking. *A pedestrian crossing.* 2 dull, uninspired. *A very pedestrian speech.*

pedigree *noun* a list showing the families from which a person or animal has come, especially to show the quality of an animal. *A dog with a fine pedigree.* **pedigree** *adjective. A pedigree cat.*

The pedigree dalmatian was in perfect condition and won first prize at the show.

peek *noun* a quick look. **peek** *verb. He peeked round the corner.*

peel *noun* the skin of oranges, apples, potatoes and other fruit and vegetables. **peel** *verb* 1 to take the skin off fruit and vegetables. 2 to come off in layers, strips or flakes. *The paint is peeling.*

peep *verb* 1 to look quickly, often secretly. 2 to look through an opening. 3 to begin to show. *The ticket peeped out of his pocket. noun* 1 a quick look. 2 a high, weak sound.

peer *verb* to look very hard or closely, usually because something is difficult to see.

peer *noun* 1 a member of the nobility. A duke or a baron is a peer. 2 a person who is the same age or has the same rank.

peer group *noun* a group of people of the same age.

peevish *adjective* bad-tempered.

peg *noun* 1 a piece of wood, metal or plastic used to fasten things or to attach washing to a line. *A tent peg.* 2 a hook or knob for hanging things on. **peg** (pegs, pegging, pegged) *verb* 1 to fix with pegs. 2 to keep prices or wages unchanged.

pelican *noun* a large water bird with a long beak and a pouch for storing fish.

Pelicans can be seen on Lake Galilee in Israel.

pellet *noun* a small ball of metal, paper or other material.

pelmet *noun* a piece of wood or material that hides a curtain rod.

pelvis *noun* the round bony frame with the hip bones at the lower end of the spine.

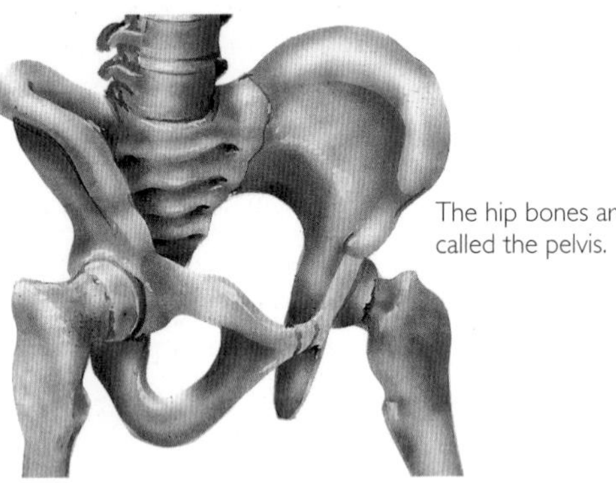

The hip bones are called the pelvis.

pen *noun* an instrument for writing with ink. *A fountain pen.*

pen *noun* a small place, an enclosure, for farm animals or pets. **pen** (pens, penning, penned) *verb* to shut into a small place. *The chickens were penned in for the night.*

penal (say **peen**-ul) *adjective* connected with the punishment of criminals. *Penal laws.*

penalize *verb* to punish.

penalty *noun* 1 punishment. 2 a point or a chance to score a goal, especially in football, rugby or hockey, because an opponent has committed a foul.

pence *plural* of penny.

pencil *noun* a wooden instrument for writing or drawing, with a thin stick of lead or coloured material inside it. **pencil** (pencils, pencilling, pencilled) *verb* to write or draw with a pencil.

pendulum *noun* a weight hanging from a rod so it can swing from side to side. Some old clocks have a pendulum.

The pendulum on a grandfather clock is what makes the comforting 'tick-tock' sound.

penetrate *verb* to force or manage to find a way into something. *A strange smell penetrated the room.* **penetration** *noun*. **penetrating** *adjective*. *Penetrating questions.*

penfriend *noun* a friend, especially somebody from a foreign country, who you write letters to and receive letters from.

penguin *noun* a black and white bird that lives in the Antarctic and cannot fly.

penicillin *noun* an antibiotic used in medicine to destroy bacteria.

peninsula *noun* a piece of land that is almost surrounded by water. *Italy is a peninsula.* **peninsular** *adjective*.

GRAMMAR NOTE

The plural 'pence' is used for a sum of money, and 'pennies' for separate coins. The expressions 'to spend a penny' and 'the penny has dropped' both refer to the old, large penny coin that was in use before 1971. Public lavatories used to have a coin slot for a penny to open the door, so you had to spend a penny to go to the loo.

AMAZING FACT

Penguins are flightless birds, but they are extremely good swimmers and divers.

penis (penises) *noun* the part of the body a man or male animal uses for urinating and for reproducing.

penknife *noun* a small knife with a blade that folds into the handle.

pen-name *noun* the name a writer uses in books instead of his or her own name. A pseudonym. *She writes under a pen-name.*

penniless *adjective* having no money, very poor. *Penniless orphans.*

penny (pennies or pence) *noun* a British coin worth one hundredth of a pound. **spend a penny** to go to the toilet. **the penny has dropped** something has finally been understood.

pension *noun* a sum of money paid regularly by the government or a firm to a retired or disabled person.

pensioner *noun* somebody who gets a pension, a retired person.

pentathlon *noun* an athletic competition made up of five different events.

penthouse *noun* a flat or apartment on the roof or top floor of a tall building

people *plural noun* 1 two or more persons. *Only three people came.* 2 all the men, women and children of a particular place, class or group. *Young people.*

pepper *noun* 1 a hot-tasting powder made from peppercorns and used for making food spicy. 2 a hollow green, red or yellow vegetable.

Peppercorns are spread out in the sun to dry before they are used to flavour food.

peppermint *noun* 1 a mint grown for its strong flavouring. 2 a sweet that tastes of peppermint.

per *preposition* for each. *Ten kilometres per hour.* **per annum** for each year. *She earns £20,000 per annum.* **per cent** in each hundred. *Ten per cent (10%).*

perceive *verb* to notice or see something.

percentage *noun* an amount stated as part of a whole or as a share of one hundred parts. *A large percentage of students pass their exams every year.*

perception *noun* the ability to notice, an understanding.

perceptive *adjective* quick to notice and understand. *A very perceptive guess.*

perch *noun* 1 a branch or other place a bird rests on. 2 a high position taken up by a person. **perch** *verb* to be on something high. *The house perched on top of the cliff.*

percussion *noun* 1 the striking together of two hard things. 2 musical instruments that are hit together, especially drums and cymbals.

It is Jamie's ambition to play the cymbals. They are his favourite percussion instrument.

perennial *adjective* lasting for a long time or for many years. **perennial** *noun* a plant that lives for many years.

perfect *adjective* 1 excellent, without fault. 2 complete. *A perfect stranger.* **perfectly** *adverb. I feel perfectly at home here.*

perform *verb* 1 to do something, especially something difficult. 2 to act in a play or do something in front of an audience. **performer** *noun.*

performance *noun* 1 doing something in front of an audience. *Samantha went to the first performance of the new play.* 2 an action performed.

perfume *noun* 1 a fragrant liquid people put on to smell nice. 2 a nice smell.

perhaps *adverb* it may be, possibly. *Perhaps we'll win the game.*

perimeter *noun* the border or outer edge around something. *We walked all round the perimeter of the grounds.*

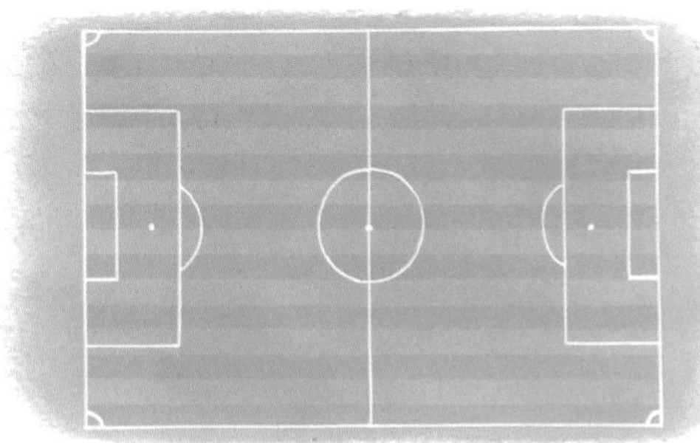

The perimeter of the pitch was marked with a white line.

period *noun* 1 a length or portion of time. *For a short period. Sunny periods.* 2 a woman's monthly flow of blood. **period** *adjective* made at an earlier time in history. *The hotel was full of period furniture, including original four-poster beds.*

periodic *adjective* happening at regular intervals. *Periodic amazement.*

DID YOU KNOW

Periscopes are sometimes used at sporting events or other occasions where there are crowds, so that people can see over the heads of others. They work by reflecting the light across mirrors.

DID YOU KNOW

In American English, a period is a full stop, such as appears at the end of a sentence. Sometimes the word is used at the end of a spoken sentence, meaning 'and that's all there is to it.'

periodical *noun* a magazine that comes out at regular intervals, for example monthly. **periodical** *adjective.*

periscope *noun* a tube with mirrors and lenses through which somebody in a submarine can see things above the water.

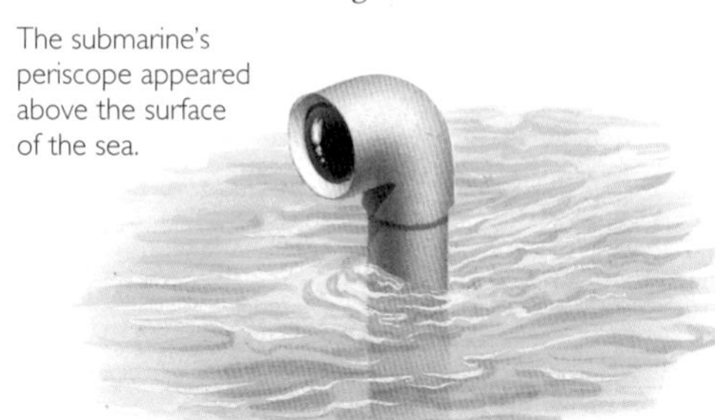

The submarine's periscope appeared above the surface of the sea.

perish *verb* 1 to die or become destroyed. 2 to rot or fall to pieces. *Soft fruit perishes quickly.* **perishable** *adjective.*

perk *noun* an advantage.

perk up *verb* to become or make somebody more cheerful. *She perked up after tea.*

permanent *adjective* lasting for ever, not expected to change. *My permanent address.* **permanently** *adverb.*

permissible *adjective* allowed by the rules.

permission *noun* the right to do something, the act of allowing something. *The teacher gave us permission to leave early.*

permissive *adjective* allowing too much personal freedom.

permit (say per-**mit**) (permits, permitting, permitted) *verb* to allow or make something possible. **permit** (say **per**-mit) *noun* an official document stating that somebody is allowed to do something or go somewhere.

perpendicular *adjective* pointing straight up. *Perpendicular lines.*

perpetrate *verb* to be guilty of something, to do something wrong. **perpetrator** *noun. We caught the perpetrator of the crime.*

perpetual *adjective* never ending or changing. *The perpetual noise of the traffic.* **perpetually** *adverb.*

perpetuate *verb* to preserve from being forgotten. *Let us perpetuate his memory.*

persecute *verb* to continually treat a person or group of people cruelly, especially because of their beliefs. **persecution** *noun.*

persevere *verb* to go on doing something and not give up. **perseverance** *noun. His perseverance won him the match.*

persist *verb* 1 to continue in spite of warning. *If he persists in breaking the rules, he will be expelled.* 2 to continue to exist. *If your headaches persist, take these tablets.* **persistent** *adjective.* **persistently** *adverb.* **persistence** *noun.*

P

person *noun* 1 a human being. *It's too much work for one person.* 2 in grammar, any of the three forms of pronouns or verbs that show who is speaking. **in person** bodily. *I can't come in person, but I'll send my brother to collect the prize.*

personal *adjective* 1 belonging, concerning or done by a particular person. *I want your personal opinion.* 2 concerning a person's private life. *There's no need to be personal.* **personally** *adverb. Don't take it personally.*

personal computer *noun* a computer used by a single person, especially at home.

personality (personalities) *noun* 1 the character or nature of a person. *He has a weak personality.* 2 a famous person. *A well-known television personality.*

personal stereo *noun* a small cassette player or radio with headphones.

personnel *noun* the people employed in a business. *The personnel are very friendly.*

perspective *noun* 1 the art of drawing so that things in the background look further away than things in the foreground. *The house is in perspective.* 2 a particular way of thinking about something. *What happened put everything in perspective.*

The line of the trees in this photograph show perspective.

perspire *verb* to sweat. **perspiration** *noun.*

persuade *verb* to make somebody do or believe something. *We persuaded him to buy a new bike.* **persuasion** *noun.* **persuasive** *adjective. A persuasive salesman.*

perturb *verb* to worry. *The news about the accident perturbed him greatly.*

Peru *noun* a country in South America.

Peruvian *adjective* of Peru. *Peruvian people speak Spanish.* **Peruvian** *noun.*

perverse *adjective* continuing to do something wrong or in a different way from what is wanted. *How perverse of you to like exams.* **perversely** *adverb.* **perversity** *noun.*

pervert (say **per**-vert) *noun* a person whose behaviour, especially sexual behaviour, is not normal or is disgusting. **pervert** (say puh-**vert**) *verb* to turn away from what is right or what it used to be. *He perverted the course of justice.* **perversion** *noun.*

pessimism *noun* thinking that whatever happens will be bad. **pessimist** *noun.* **pessimistic** *adjective.*

AMAZING FACT

Ancient Egyptians believed that all pharaohs were the same god incarnated in the shape of different men. Pharaohs were supposed to be the absolute rulers of the country, but the priests and noblemen actually ran things.

GRAMMAR NOTE

'Phenomena' is sometimes used mistakenly as a singular. Remember that 'phenomena' is the plural of 'phenomenon'. 'The growth in popularity of mobile phones is a remarkable phenomenon.'

pester *verb* to annoy somebody continually, especially by asking questions or wanting something.

pet *noun* 1 an animal kept in the home as a companion. *Cats are my favourite pets.* 2 a person who is a favourite. *The teacher's pet.* **pet** (pets, petting, petted) *verb* to treat or touch with special love.

This lily has pink petals.

petal *noun* one of the bright coloured parts that form a flower.

petrify (petrifies, petrifying, petrified) *verb* 1 to make somebody extremely frightened. *The strange noises petrified him.* 2 to turn into stone. *A petrified forest.*

petrol *noun* a liquid made from oil and used as a fuel for engines.

petty (pettier, pettiest) *adjective* unimportant. *Petty squabbles.*

pew *noun* a long wooden bench in a church. *He sat on the pew and prayed.*

phantom *noun* a ghost.

pharaoh (say **fair**-oh) *noun* a king of ancient Egypt.

Tutankhamun was one of the most famous pharaohs of ancient Egypt.

pharmacy (pharmacies) *noun* 1 a shop where medicines are sold. 2 the making or giving out of medicine. **pharmacist** *noun.*

phase *noun* a stage of development. **phase** *verb* to happen or make something happen in stages. *We can phase payment over three years, if it would make it easier for you.*

pheasant *noun* a long-tailed bird that is hunted for food. *A pheasant shoot.*

phenomenal *adjective* unusual, amazing. *He's got phenomenal strength for his age.*

phenomenon (phenomena) *noun* an unusual fact, event or thing. *Summer snow is an almost unknown phenomenon.*

philately (say fil-**at**-il-ee) *noun* stamp-collecting. **philatelist** *noun.*

-phile *suffix* indicating a person or thing that has a liking for something. *Francophiles like France and everything French.*

Philippines *noun* a country of many islands in Southeast Asia.

The flag of the Philippines is blue, red and white with a design of the Sun and stars.

philistine (say **fil**-ist-ine) *noun* a person who does not like or want to understand art and beautiful things.

philology *noun* the study of the development of language. **philologist** *noun.*

philosopher *noun* a person who studies or teaches philosophy.

philosophy *noun* 1 the study of the meaning of life and how people should live. 2 the ideas and beliefs that a philosopher has, or your own rules for living your life. *The philosophy of the ancient Greeks.* **philosophical** *adjective.*

Phnom Penh *noun* the capital of Cambodia.

phobia (say foh-bee-uh) *noun* a great fear of something. *He's got a phobia about spiders.*

phone *noun* a telephone. **on the phone** speaking to somebody by phone. **phone** *verb* to telephone. *Please phone home.*

Old-fashioned phones had a dial instead of push-buttons.

phone-in *noun* a programme on radio or television in which people ring up and take part. *I took part in a phone-in about pets.*

photo *noun* a photograph.

photocopier *noun* a machine that can quickly copy documents and other papers by photographing them.

photocopy (photocopies) *noun* a photographic copy of a document or page made by a photocopier. **photocopy** (photocopies, photocopying, photocopied) *verb. Can you photocopy this page?*

photogenic *adjective* looking nice in photographs. *She is very photogenic, and will probably be a model when she is old enough to work.*

WORD HISTORY

The original Philistines were driven from Egypt about 1200 BC and settled in Canaan. The region took the name Palestine from the new settlers.

AMAZING FACT

There are many different types of phobia. Most of them are named after the Greek word for the thing that is feared. 'zoophobia' is fear of animals; 'acrophobia' is fear of heights; 'entomophobia' is fear of insects; 'nyctophobia' is fear of night; and 'ophidiophobia' is fear of snakes.

photograph *noun* a picture made with a camera and a film sensitive to light. **photograph** *verb* to use a camera to take a photograph. **photography** *noun.* **photographic** *adjective.*

photographer *noun* somebody who takes photographs. *A wedding photographer.*

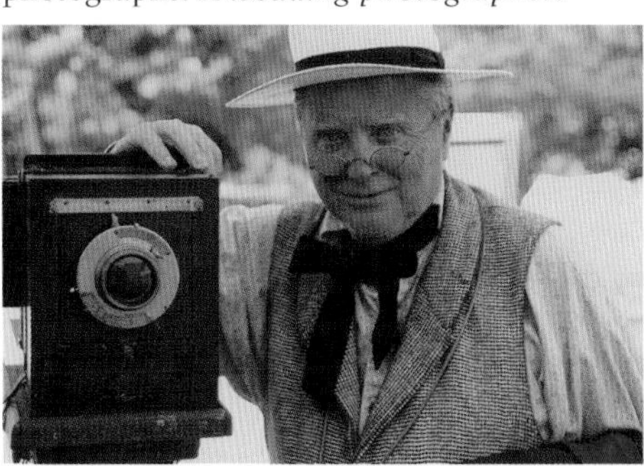
The photographer told the guests to smile for the camera.

photosynthesis *noun* the process by which green plants make food in their leaves, using the Sun's energy, carbon dioxide and water.

phrase *noun* a group of words used together, that form part of a sentence. 'In the park' is a phrase in 'We went for a walk in the park.' **phrase** *verb* to express something in words. *A well-phrased letter.*

physical *adjective* 1 connected with a person's body, not their mind. *Physical exercise.* 2 of things that can be touched and seen. *The physical world.* 3 connected with physics. **physically** *adverb.*

physician *noun* a doctor.

physics (say **fiz**-iks) *noun* the study of forces such as heat, light, sound, electricity and gravity. *She's good at physics and maths.*

physiotherapy (say fiz-ee-o-the-ruh-pee) *noun* treatment by means of exercise, massage, light and heat. **physiotherapist** *noun. The injured player was treated by the physiotherapist.*

physique (say fiz-**eek**) *noun* the shape and size of a person's body, especially a man's.

piano *noun* a large musical instrument that is played by the pianist's fingers pressing down on black and white keys. **pianist** *noun.*

Christine has a grand piano in her living room, but rarely gets time to play it.

piccolo *noun* a small flute that plays high notes. *A piccolo solo.*

pick *verb* 1 to pull or break off part of a plant, especially a flower or fruit. *We picked some strawberries.* 2 to choose carefully. *He always picks the best.* 3 to remove unwanted things or pull bits off something. *Don't pick your nose.* 4 to take up. *Birds picking at the grain.* **pick a lock** to open a lock without a key. **pick a quarrel** to want to have a quarrel with somebody. **pick somebody's pocket** to steal from somebody. **pick holes in** to find weak points in something. **pick up** 1 to lift or take up. 2 to collect. *I can pick the children up from school.* 3 to take somebody as a passenger. *They picked up a hitch-hiker.* 4 to get better. *His health is picking up.* 5 to get to know somebody. *He picked up a girl at the party.* 6 to learn or hear something. *I picked up some Italian on holiday in Tuscany.*

pick *noun* 1 choice. *Take your pick.* 2 the best of many. *The pick of the bunch.*

pick *noun* 1 a pickaxe. 2 a plectrum.

pickaxe *noun* a pointed tool with a long handle used for breaking up rocks or hard ground.

A geologist needs a pickaxe to get samples of rocks for analysis.

pickle *noun* vegetables or fruit preserved in water, salt and vinegar. **pickle** *verb* to preserve food in water, salt and vinegar. **be in a pickle** to be in a difficult situation.

pickpocket *noun* a thief who steals things from people's pockets.

picnic *noun* a meal eaten out of doors, at the beach or in a field. **picnic** (picnics, picnicking, picnicked) *verb* to have a picnic. **picnicker** *noun.*

The picnic hamper was packed full of good things to eat and drink.

pictorial *adjective* with pictures.

DID YOU KNOW

Wild pigs, or boars, were probably first kept by people in Asia about 5,000 years ago. They were used for clearing vegetation and for their meat, which we now call pork and bacon.

picture *noun* 1 a painting, drawing or photograph of somebody or something. 2 a film at the cinema or on television. 3 an idea or impression. *She had quite a different picture of the house in her mind.* 4 a perfect example or a description of an event. *The baby is a picture of health.* **go to the pictures** to go to the cinema to see a film. **get the picture** to understand a situation somebody is telling you about. **put somebody in the picture** to tell somebody about a situation they need to know about. **picture** *verb* to imagine something.

picturesque *adjective* attractive and interesting. *A picturesque mountain village.*

pie *noun* a pastry case filled with meat, fish, vegetables or fruit, usually baked in a dish.

piece *noun* 1 a part or bit of something. *A piece of cake.* 2 one single thing, object or example. *A piece of paper.* 3 something written or composed, especially an article or a play. *A piece of music.* 4 a counter or any object used when playing a board game. *A chess piece.* 5 a coin. *A 50-pence piece.* **piece together** to make something by putting pieces together. *We tried to piece together the facts.*

pier *noun* 1 a bridge-like structure built out into the sea, used as a landing-stage or for people to walk along. 2 a pillar for supporting a bridge or roof.

pierce *verb* to make a hole with something sharp or pointed. *She had her ears pierced.* **piercing** *adjective* sharp in an unpleasant way. *A piercing scream.*

pig *noun* 1 a pink or black fat animal with a snout, usually kept on farms for its meat. 2 a dirty or greedy person.

Pigs are extremely intelligent creatures. More farmers are now rearing pigs outside, instead of confining them in sties and sheds.

pigeon *noun* a grey bird with a fat body.

pigeon-hole *noun* a small open box or one of many compartments on a wall for papers and messages. *He left the letter in my pigeon-hole, so I could collect it later.*

piglet *noun* a young pig.

pigment *noun* a substance that gives a particular colour to things. *The red pigment of blood.* **pigmentation** *noun.*

pigsty (pigsties) *noun* 1 a hut for pigs. 2 a dirty room or home.

pile *noun* 1 a number of things lying on top of each other. 2 a large quantity of things or amount of money. **pile** *verb* to put things in or on a pile. **pile in** to come or get into a place in a large group. **pile out** to leave a place in a large group.

Graham was taking a pile of newspapers to the recycling bank.

pile *noun* a heavy wooden, metal or stone post that is hammered into the ground as a support for a bridge or building. *A pile-driving machine.*

pilfer *verb* to steal small things. *She used to pilfer from my purse.* **pilferage** *noun.*

pilgrim *noun* somebody who travels to a holy place for religious reasons.

pilgrimage *noun* a journey made by pilgrims to visit a holy place.

They set off on a pilgrimage across the desert.

pill *noun* 1 a tablet of medicine. 2 a tablet taken by women, so they do not become pregnant. *She is on the pill.*

pillar *noun* 1 a tall upright stone or wooden post that supports a building. 2 something that looks like a pillar. *A pillar of smoke.* 3 an important member of a group of people. *He's a pillar of society.*

pillow *noun* a cushion for resting your head on, especially in bed.

pillowcase *noun* a cover for a pillow.

pilot *noun* 1 a person trained to fly an aircraft. 2 a person who steers a ship in and out of port. **pilot** *verb* 1 to act as a pilot of an aircraft or a ship. 2 to guide carefully. *He piloted me through the crowd.*

pilot *noun* a test to find out if something will work. *The TV producers are making a pilot of the series.*

pimple *noun* a small spot on the skin. **pimply** *adjective. A pimply complexion.*

WORD HISTORY

The pineapple probably got its name because the fruit looks like a large pine cone. It is thought that pineapples originated in Brazil. Christopher Columbus and his crew were probably the first Europeans to taste the fruit.

DID YOU KNOW

An imperial, or British, pint is equal to 0.565 litres. A US pint is slightly less, being equivalent to 0.551 litres.

pin *noun* 1 a metal needle with a sharp point and a round head for fastening pieces of cloth or paper together. 2 a short pointed piece of metal or wood for fixing or marking something. **pins and needles** a prickly feeling in your hands or legs. **pin** (pins, pinning, pinned) *verb* 1 to fasten with a pin or pins. *She pinned a flower to her dress.* 2 to hold or keep in a particular position, to make unable to move. *She was pinned under the wrecked car.* 3 to fix. *I'm pinning all my hopes on getting the job.*

pincers *plural noun* 1 an instrument used for gripping things or pulling things out. 2 the claws of a crab or lobster.

pinch *verb* 1 to squeeze somebody's skin using your thumb and first finger. *It hurt when he pinched my arm.* 2 to be too tight. *My shoes are too small, they pinch.* 3 to steal. *Don't pinch my sweets.* **pinch** (pinches) *noun* 1 an amount that can be held between thumb and first finger. *A pinch of salt.* 2 a squeeze, usually a painful one. 3 suffering or stress, especially caused by not having enough money to buy things. *We are feeling the pinch, now I have lost my job.* **at a pinch** if absolutely necessary.

pine *noun* an evergreen tree with leaves that look like needles.

pine *verb* to become weak and sad because of wanting something very much. *The dog is pining for his master.*

The seeds of the pine tree are inside the pine cone.

pineapple *noun* a large tropical fruit with spiny leaves, a thick skin and sweet, yellow juicy flesh.

pink *adjective* pale red. You can mix pink by adding a lot of white to red.

pinpoint *verb* to find or discover exactly what or where something is. *Can you pinpoint the problem?*

pint *noun* a measure for liquids. *A pint of beer and a plate of fish and chips, please.*

pioneer *noun* the first person to go to a place or do or study something new. **pioneer** *verb* to help to develop something. *He pioneered the solar car.*

pious *adjective* very religious.

pip *noun* 1 a small fruit seed. *The pips of an apple.* 2 a short, high sound, especially as a time signal on the telephone or radio. **pip** (pips, pipping, pipped) *verb* to just beat somebody in a competition.

pipe *noun* 1 a long hollow metal or plastic tube through which water or gas can flow. 2 an object used for smoking tobacco. 3 a tube-like musical instrument, played by blowing. **pipe** *verb* 1 to carry liquid or gas through a pipe. 2 to send music or other sound through a loudspeaker. 3 to play music on a pipe. 4 to add a strip of decoration (called piping). 5 to pipe icing on a cake. **pipe down** to be quiet.

pipeline *noun* pipes, often underground, for carrying oil, water or gas a long way. **in the pipeline** being planned or on the way. *Plans for a shorter school day are in the pipeline.*

piranha *noun* a small, fierce, meat-eating fish from South America.

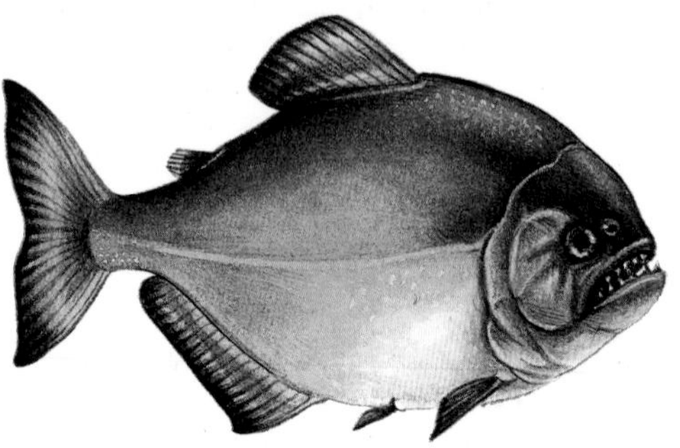

Piranhas have sharp teeth.

AMAZING FACT

Piranhas are not large fish, measuring not more than about 12 inches in length, but they travel in very large schools. Despite their bloodthirsty reputation, carnivorous piranhas feed mainly on fish, seeds and fruit.

pirate *noun* 1 a sailor who attacks and robs other ships. 2 somebody who copies or broadcasts somebody else's work, like books, video tapes or cassettes, without permission. *Pirate radio stations do not pay for the music they play.* **pirate** *verb* to copy or broadcast somebody else's work without permission. **piracy** *noun.*

DID YOU KNOW

There were many pirates, or buccaneers, around the Caribbean Sea in the second half of the 17th century. The word pirate comes from the Greek 'peirates', meaning 'an attacker'.

pit *noun* 1 a deep hole. 2 a coal mine. 3 (usually plural, pits) a place at the side of the racing track where racing cars are repaired and refuelled. *The Ferrari came into the pits.* **pit** (pits, pitting, pitted) *verb* to make a hole in something. *The road was pitted with holes.* **pit against somebody** to set or match a person against another in a competition. *We were pitted against the darts champions.*

pitch (pitches) *noun* 1 a ground marked out and used for playing certain games. *A cricket pitch.* 2 the highness or lowness of a sound. *Her voice dropped to a lower pitch.* 3 the degree or strength of something. *A pitch of excitement.* **pitch** *verb* 1 to set up, especially a tent or camp. 2 to throw or fling something. 3 to fall suddenly or heavily. *I tripped and pitched forward.* 4 to give a particular feeling to something, to set a level. *Her stories are pitched so that even the youngest children can easily understand them.* **pitch in** to join in an activity, to get working or eating.

pitch-dark *adjective* very dark.

pitfall *noun* an unexpected difficulty.

pith *noun* 1 the white substance under the peel of oranges, lemons and other citrus fruit. 2 the soft white substance in the stems of certain plants and trees.

A little of the white pith can be seen on the inside of this strip of lemon peel.

pitiful *adjective* sad and weak, making you feel pity. *A pitiful story.*

pitiless *adjective* showing no feeling or pity. *The boss is pitiless, he makes us pay for every error.*

pity *noun* 1 feeling sorry for somebody who is suffering or unhappy. *Don't help me out of pity.* 2 a state of disappointment. *It's a pity you can't come to the party tonight.* **take pity on** to feel sorry for somebody and help them. **pity** (pities, pitying, pitied) *verb* to feel sorry for somebody.

pivot *noun* 1 a point or pin on which something turns. 2 the most important thing, which everything depends on. **pivot** *verb* to turn round as if on a pivot. **pivotal** *adjective. His mother has a pivotal influence on him.*

Pizzas are often topped with tomatoes, anchovies and olives.

pizza *noun* a round piece of bread dough baked with a mixture of tomatoes, cheese and other food on top.

placard *noun* a large poster or notice. *The demonstrators carried placards with slogans on them.*

place *noun* 1 a particular position where something belongs or should be. *I put the books back in their place.* 2 any point like a building, an area, a country, a town or a village. *This is the place where we used to live.* 3 a seat. *He saved me a place.* 4 a house or home. *Come round to my place after school.* 5 a particular point in a story or book or part of it. *I lost my place because my bookmark fell out.* 6 a position in a group, race or competition. *First place.* 7 somebody's role in relation to other people or things. *It's not my place to tell him off.* 8 a job, a position in a team, a school or at a university. *He got a place in the team.* 9 a point in a series of things, especially in an explanation. *In the first place I don't want to come, and in the second place I haven't been invited.* **all over the place** everywhere. **in place** in the proper position, suitable. **out of place** not in the proper position, unsuitable. **in place of** instead of. **take place** to happen. *When did the party take place?*

place *verb* 1 to put something in a particular place. 2 to say that somebody has achieved a particular position or put somebody in a particular position. *This places him in a difficult position.* 3 When you place an order, you order goods from a firm.

placid *adjective* calm, not easily made angry or upset. *She has a placid nature.*

plague *noun* 1 a dangerous illness that spreads quickly and kills many people. 2 a large number of unpleasant things. *A plague of rats.* **plague** (plagues, plaguing, plagued) *verb* to annoy or trouble all the time. *The child plagued me with questions.*

The procession of people prayed to be spared from the plague.

plaice (plaice) *noun* (say place) a flat sea-fish used for food.

plaid *noun* (say plad) a cloth with a tartan pattern. *A plaid shirt.*

plain *adjective* 1 simple, not decorated, patterned or flavoured. Not complicated. *I prefer plain food.* 2 easy to see, hear or understand. *It was plain he didn't like her.* 3 honest and open, especially about feelings or opinions. 4 not beautiful or handsome. **plainly** *adverb*. **plainness** *noun*.

plain *noun* a large flat area of land.

plait (say plat) *verb* to twist three or more strands, especially hair or rope, under and over one another into one thick length. **plait** *noun* a length of hair or rope that has been plaited. *She wears her hair in plaits.*

plan *noun* 1 an outline or drawing showing all the parts of something. *We were looking at the plans for the new house.* 2 an arrangement for carrying out something that is to be done or used in the future. *We have made plans for our holiday.* 3 a map of a town or district. **plan** (plans, planning, planned) *verb* to make a plan for something.

plane *noun* 1 an aeroplane. 2 a flat surface. 3 a tool with a sharp blade for making wood smooth by shaving small pieces off its surface. **plane** *verb* to smooth wood with a plane. *Peter planed down all the doors.*

plane *noun* a tall tree with big leaves.

DID YOU KNOW?

Nine planets orbit the Sun. From nearest the Sun: Mercury, Venus, Earth, Mars, Jupiter, Saturn, Uranus, Neptune and Pluto.

AMAZING FACT

The nursery rhyme, 'Ring-a-ring-a-roses' originates from the time of the plague in the 1300s when herbs and fragrant flowers were thought be protection against the disease.

WORD HISTORY

Plaster of Paris was first made from gypsum in the Montmartre district of Paris in the 15th century. It is called the same in French: 'plâtre de Paris'.

planet *noun* any of the large bodies in space that travel around the Sun, such as Earth, Venus and Mars. **planetary** *adjective*.

The planet Uranus spins at a tilt.

plank *noun* a long, usually heavy, flat piece of wood. *Two men carried the plank.*

plankton *noun* tiny plants and animals that live in water and are food for many fish.

plant *noun* 1 a living thing that grows in the earth and has leaves and roots. Plants need water and light. 2 large machinery used in industry. 3 a factory. 4 a thing, especially stolen goods, hidden on somebody to make that person look guilty. *The drugs were a plant by the police.* **plant** *verb* 1 to put something in the ground to grow. 2 to fix firmly or place in a position. *She planted herself in the chair next to mine.* 3 to hide something or somebody secretly in order to wrongly accuse an innocent person. *He planted the stolen bike in his friend's garage.*

plantation *noun* 1 a large piece of land, especially in hot countries, on which crops like tea, sugar or cotton are grown. 2 a large group of trees planted especially for wood.

Workers on a plantation, harvesting sugar cane.

plaque (say plak) *noun* 1 a flat metal or stone plate fixed to a wall in memory of a famous person or event. 2 a substance that forms on teeth and gums and in which bacteria can live.

plaster *noun* 1 a mixture of lime, water and sand which hardens when dry and is used for covering walls and ceilings. 2 a piece of sticky material used to cover a wound. 3 a white paste (called plaster of Paris) that dries quickly and is used for making moulds or for casts around broken bones. *His arm was in plaster for five weeks.* **plaster** *verb* 1 to cover with plaster. 2 to cover something thickly, usually too thickly. *They plastered stickers all over the window.*

plastic *noun* a manmade material that can easily be formed into various shapes. Plastic is light and does not break easily. **plastic** *adjective* made of plastic.

P

plastic surgery *noun* an operation to repair and replace damaged skin or injured and deformed parts of the body.

plate *noun* 1 a flat dish from which food is eaten or served. *A dinner plate.* 2 a flat sheet of metal, glass or other hard material. 3 a small piece of metal with a person's name on, usually beside the front door of an office or a house. 4 metal articles, dishes, bowls and cutlery with a thin covering of gold or silver. 5 a picture or photograph usually printed on special paper in a book. 6 a piece of plastic with false teeth on, shaped to fit inside a person's mouth. **plate** *verb* to cover metal objects with a thin layer of gold, silver or tin. *The spoons are silver plated.*

plateau (plateaux) *noun* (say **platt**-oh, **platt**-ohz) a flat area of land high above sea-level.

The high plateau was lit up with brilliant reds and purples in the setting sun.

platform *noun* 1 a flat raised structure, often made of wood, which people stand on when they make speeches or give a performance. 2 the area next to the railway line in a train station where people wait for or get off a train. *The train to Dover leaves from platform 5.* 3 a statement of what a political party will do if they are elected.

platinum *noun* a very valuable metal used for making jewellery.

platypus (platypuses) *noun* an Australian animal with a beak like a duck.

The platypus has a beak for feeding underwater and strong webbed feet for digging.

play *verb* 1 to take part in a sport, a game or other pleasant amusement. 2 to make music with a musical instrument, perform a musical work or operate a tape-recorder or cassette player. *She plays CDs all the time.* 3 to act in a play or film. *He played a king in the school play.* 4 to behave in a certain way. *She played it very cool when offered the job.* **play along** to pretend to agree with somebody. **play up** 1 to not work properly. *The car is playing up again, it keeps stalling.* 2 to be naughty or annoying. *The children always play up when I look after them.*

DID YOU KNOW

The modern pack of playing cards is based on the French pack of 52 cards, which itself came from tarot cards, which were once used for games but are now used for fortune-telling.

AMAZING FACT

The platypus is considered a primitive mammal because it lays eggs and retains some reptilian characteristics.

Because of its extremely odd appearance, when the first specimen arrived at London's Natural History Museum 200 years ago, it was thought to be a hoax.

play *noun* 1 a story performed in a theatre, on TV or on the radio. A piece of writing to be performed. *He has written a new play.* 2 playing. *Children learn through play.* **in/out of play** when the ball is/is not in a position where it is allowed to be played by the rules of the game. **come into play** to begin to be used. *The new rules are coming into play from Wednesday.*

player *noun* a person who plays a game.

playground *noun* a place where children can play. *Skipping in the playground.*

playing card *noun* one of a set of cards used to play games. *We always take a pack of playing cards on holiday.*

plc, PLC *abbreviation* public limited company. The shares of a plc can be bought by the public.

plea *noun* 1 a strong request. *A plea for help.* 2 an excuse. *A plea of insanity.* 3 a statement made by the accused in court stating whether they are guilty or not guilty.

plead *verb* 1 to make a strong request. *He pleaded with the teacher to give him another chance.* 2 to state in court whether one is guilty or not guilty. 3 to offer an excuse.

pleasant *adjective* nice, enjoyable. *We spent a pleasant day together.* A pleasant person is friendly and polite. **pleasantness** *noun.*

please *verb* 1 used when politely asking somebody to do something or asking for something. *Please don't touch.* 2 to give satisfaction, make a somebody happy. *He always tries to please his parents.* **please yourself** to do what you want. **as you please** as you think best. *I'll do as I please.*

pleasure *noun* 1 a feeling of satisfaction, happiness and enjoyment. 2 something that is enjoyable and pleases you.

pleat *noun* a flattened fold in cloth. **pleat** *verb* to make folds. **pleated** *adjective. A pleated skirt.*

The skirt had a kick pleat in the back of it.

plectrum *noun* a small piece of plastic or wood, held in the hand and used for playing the guitar.

pledge *noun* 1 a serious promise or agreement. *He made a pledge of loyalty to the queen and to his country.* 2 something given as a sign of friendship or love. 3 an object given in return for money until that money is repaid. **pledge** *verb* 1 to make a serious promise. *She pledged never to leave home again.* 2 to make a serious promise to give something. *The firm pledged £1,000 to cancer research.*

plenty *pronoun, noun* enough, as much or more than is needed. *We've got plenty of time before the next train.* **plenty** *adverb* quite. *It's plenty big enough for three.*

pliers *plural noun* a gripping tool for holding or pulling out things. *He used a pair of pliers to pull out the nail.*

plight *noun* a difficult situation.

plod (plods, plodding, plodded) *verb* 1 to walk slowly with a heavy step. 2 to work slowly and without much interest.

plot *noun* 1 a small piece of ground. *A vegetable plot.* 2 a secret plan. *The police uncovered a plot to shoot the president.* 3 the story in a film or novel. *The director changed the plot.* **plot** (plots, plotting, plotted) *verb* 1 to make a secret plan. 2 to mark the position or course, especially of a ship or plane, on a map.

plough *noun* (say plow) a farming tool with sharp blades for turning the soil over before seeds are planted. **plough** *verb* to turn over the soil with a plough. To plough a field. **plough through** to make your way through, usually with difficulty. *He ploughed through all the books on the reading list.* **plough back** to put money back into a business. *The firm ploughed back last year's profits.*

Martin used a pair of pliers to pull out all the nails.

GRAMMAR NOTE

The plural of most English nouns is formed by adding an s at the end. But there are exceptions. Nouns ending in '–y' usually change to '–ies': 'sty', 'sties'. Some nouns that end in '–o' change to '–oes': 'hero', 'heroes'; but 'photo', 'photos'. Some nouns ending in '–f' change to '–ves': 'half', 'halves'; but 'roof', 'roofs'. Some nouns have irregular plurals, and these are given in their entries.

plum *noun* 1 a soft juicy fruit with a stone in the middle. 2 a dark reddish-blue colour. 3 something very good. *He's got a plum job in the new company.*

plumber *noun* a person whose job is to fit and repair water pipes. **plumbing** *noun.*

plump *adjective* slightly fat, round. **plumpness** *noun.*

plunder *verb* to rob, especially in a war. *The soldiers plundered the town.* **plunder** *noun.* **plunderer** *noun.*

plunge *verb* 1 to suddenly fall or jump downwards or forwards. *He plunged into the water.* 2 to push quickly and forcefully. *The murderer plunged the knife into his victim's back.* 3 to fall steeply. *Prices have plunged to rock bottom.* **plunge** *noun* a dive. **take the plunge** to decide to do something risky or difficult.

plural *noun* a word that expresses more than one. *Cats is the plural of cat.* **plural** *adjective. Pliers is a plural noun.*

plus *preposition* 1 showing that one number is added to another, often written as a plus sign (+). Three plus three, or 3 + 3. 2 with the addition of. *She lost her job plus the company car.* **plus** *noun* 1 a plus sign (+). 2 an advantage. *Knowing lots of languages is a definite plus.*

plutocrat *noun* a person who is powerful because he or she is very rich.

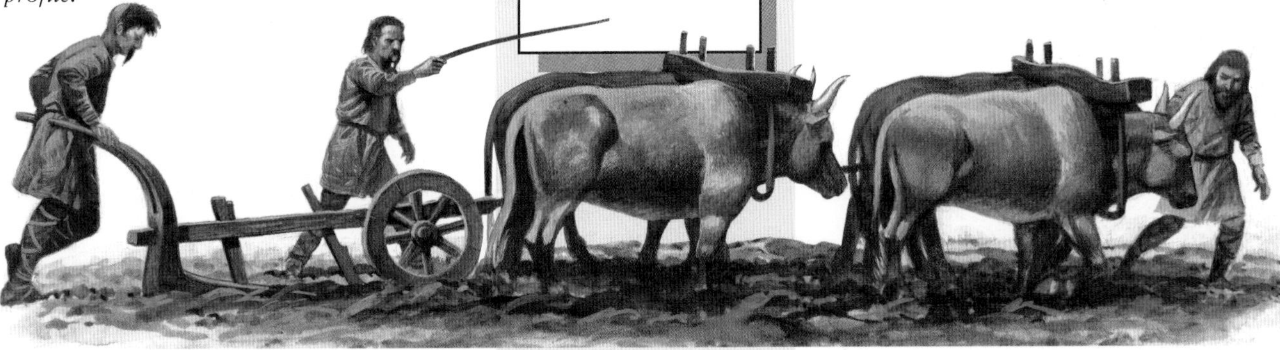

The man in front drives the team of oxen that pull the plough, while the man behind steadies it and keeps the furrow straight.

pluck *verb* 1 to pull feathers off. *The cook plucked a chicken.* 2 to pull out, especially something unwanted. *She plucks her eyebrows.* 3 to pick a flower or fruit. 4 to pull and let go the strings of a stringed instrument. **pluck up courage** to overcome fear to do something. **pluck** *noun* courage.

plug *noun* 1 a plastic object with metal pins that fit into a socket to connect wires to the electricity supply. 2 a piece of rubber, wood or other material to block up a hole. *She pulled the plug out of the bath to let the water out.* 3 a piece of publicity praising a product. *His new song got a plug on TV.* **plug** (plugs, plugging, plugged) *verb* 1 to block up a hole. 2 to advertise something by frequently mentioning it.

AMAZING FACT

'p.m.' is an abbreviation of a Latin phrase – 'p' stands for 'post' meaning after and 'm' stands for 'meridiem' meaning noon or midday.

ply *noun* 1 a thickness of wood or cloth. Three-ply wood has three layers. 2 a thickness of wool, thread or rope measured in strands.

ply (plies, plying, plied) *verb* 1 to go regularly from one place to another. *The ferry plies between Dover and Calais.* 2 to use a tool or weapon. 3 to keep a person supplied, especially with food or questions. 4 to do a particular kind of work regularly. *They plied their trade by night.*

p.m. *abbreviation* written after a number and used to show the time after midday. *Shops close at 5.00 p.m.*

pneumatic *adjective* worked or filled with compressed air. *A pneumatic drill.*

pneumonia *noun* an illness with inflammation of one or both lungs.

poach *verb* to cook an egg, fish or fruit in boiling water or other liquid, sometimes in a special pan. *Poached plums.*

poach *verb* 1 to catch or shoot animals, fish or birds without permission from somebody else's land. *He was caught poaching rabbits.* 2 to take or use unfairly somebody else's ideas or belongings. *The football club has poached our best players.* **poacher** *noun.*

pocket *noun* 1 a small bag-shaped part of an article of clothing. *He put his hands in his pockets.* 2 a small area. *A pocket of cloud.* **to be out of pocket** to have no money or less money than you should have. **pocket** *verb* 1 to put something into a pocket. 2 to steal something. **pocket** *adjective* small enough to fit into a pocket. *A pocket calculator.*

Andrew took his pocket calculator everywhere.

poem *noun* a piece of writing with short lines that often rhyme.

poet *noun* a person who writes poems. **poetic** *adjective.* **poetry** *noun* poems. *A book of poetry.*

pogrom *noun* a planned killing often for racial or religious reasons.

point *noun* 1 a sharp end. *The point of a pencil.* 2 a small dot. *A decimal point.* 3 something that shows an important idea, particular fact or a position from which something is seen. *The point is, he can't act.* 4 a particular place or time. *At that point in the journey I just wanted to go to sleep.* 5 a mark on a scale. *The boiling-point of water.* 6 a score in some games or competitions. *They beat us by three points.* 7 a detail or quality of something or somebody. *He has his good points.* 8 a purpose, use. *There is no point in tidying up before the party.* 9 an electrical socket. *A power point.* 10 (usually plural, points) a junction of railway tracks for changing a train from one line to another. **up to a point** to a certain degree. *I like him up to a point.* **beside the point** of little importance. **come to the point** to give the necessary facts. **point of view** a way of looking at something.

He pointed out the castle on the horizon, our distant destination.

WORD HISTORY

Long ago market traders would try to trick customers by putting a cat in a bag and claiming that it was a pig. Those who failed to check properly would buy 'a pig in a poke' – actually a cat! The 'poke' came from Old French for 'pouch', or 'bag'.

point *verb* 1 to direct or aim. *He pointed the water pistol at his friend.* 2 to show a direction or where something is, especially by holding out a finger. *The sign pointed in the other direction.* 3 to show that something is likely to happen. *Everything points to a war.* 4 to fill in the spaces between the bricks with cement. **point out** to draw attention to something. *She pointed out a mistake.*

point-blank *adjective, adverb* 1 aimed or said very directly or rudely. *She told him point-blank that she didn't like him.* 2 from a very close distance. *At point-blank range.*

pointed *adjective* 1 with a point at one end. 2 said or done in an unfriendly, critical way. *The teacher made a few pointed comments about homework being handed in late.*

pointless *adjective* with no purpose. *A pointless question.*

poison *noun* a substance that harms or kills animals or plants. **poison** *verb* 1 to put poison in or on something. To kill with poison. *The air is being poisoned by car fumes.* 2 to spoil something or influence somebody in a harmful way. *He poisoned her mind against her friend.* **poisonous** *adjective. A poisonous snake.*

poke *verb* 1 to push or jab, usually with something sharp. *She poked him in the ribs.* 2 to stick out or push through. *She poked her head through the door.* **poke** *noun.* **poke about** to search. *He was poking about in the house.* **poke fun at** to make jokes against, have a laugh at. **buy a pig in a poke** to buy something without seeing it and find afterwards that it is useless.

poky (pokier, pokiest) *adjective* too small. *A poky room.*

Poland *noun* a country in central Europe.

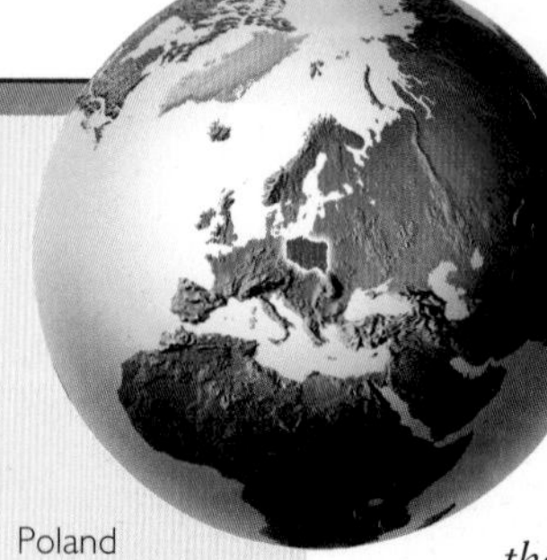

Poland is famous for its shipyards and its sausages.

polar *adjective* near the North or South Pole.

polar bear *noun* a white bear that lives near the North Pole.

pole *noun* a long, round, usually thin stick or post. *One of the tent poles is missing.*

pole *noun* 1 either of the two ends of the earth's axis. The point as far north as the North Pole or as far south as the South Pole. 2 either of the ends of a magnet. 3 either of the two points of an electric battery. *The positive pole, the negative pole.* **be poles apart** to have completely different opinions on a subject.

police *noun* the men and women whose job and duty is to catch criminals and protect people and property. **police** *verb* to keep order by using the police. *Football matches are heavily policed.*

police force *noun* an organized group of police. *The West Midlands police force.*

policeman *noun* a male member of a police force. *The policemen flagged him down.*

police officer *noun* a male or female member of a police force.

policewoman *noun* a female member of a police force.

policy (policies) *noun* a plan of action or statement of aims. *One of our policies is to reduce classroom sizes.*

policy *noun* a document that shows the agreement made with an insurance company. *A life insurance policy.* **policyholder** *noun.*

polish *verb* to make things smooth and shiny by rubbing. **polish off** to finish quickly, especially food or work. **polish up** to make something better, improve it. *I must polish up my French.* **polish** *noun* 1 a substance, like wax, for polishing. 2 a shining surface. 3 elegance and good behaviour. *Samantha has real polish.*

Polish *noun* the language spoken in Poland. **Polish** *adjective. Polish sausages.*

polite *adjective* having good manners. **politely** *adverb. The children thanked their grandmother politely.* **politeness** *noun.*

political *adjective* concerning the government of a country. *A political party.*

politics *noun* the ways in which a country is governed, political affairs. **politician** *noun.*

polka *noun* a dance for couples or the music to which it is danced.

poll *noun* (say pole) 1 voting in an election. 2 a questioning of people chosen by chance to find out the general opinion about something, an opinion poll. **poll** *verb* 1 to receive a stated number of votes at an election. 2 to vote at an election.

pollen *noun* a fine yellow powder on the male part of the flower that fertilizes other flowers to produce seeds. Bees carry pollen from one flower to another.

The hummingbird gets pollen on its beak as it sucks nectar from the flower.

WORD HISTORY

The polka is a 19th-century Bohemian dance with three steps and a hop. The name comes from the Czech 'pulka', meaning 'half-step'.

DID YOU KNOW

Poodles were once used as hunting and retrieving dogs. The breed originated in Germany during the 1500s. The name comes from the German Pudel(hund), from 'pudeln', meaning 'to splash'; the dogs were clearly once used as retrievers in water.

pollinate *verb* to fertilize with pollen. **pollination** *noun.*

pollute *verb* to make dirty and dangerous to live in or use. *Many of our rivers have been polluted.*

pollution *noun* 1 polluting the water, air or atmosphere. 2 substances that pollute. *There's too much pollution on our beaches.*

poly- *prefix* many. Polyatomic means having many atoms.

polygon *noun* a shape with many sides.

This is an irregular polygon.

polymath *noun* somebody who has knowledge in many fields of learning.

polythene *noun* a very light plastic material for making plastic bags and packaging.

polyunsaturated *adjective* containing fats that are healthier and more easily digested. Polyunsaturated margarine is made from vegetable fats.

pompous *adjective* full of self-importance. **pomposity** *noun.*

pond *noun* a very small lake.

ponder *verb* to think deeply and carefully.

ponderous *adjective* 1 slow and clumsy. *His movements were very ponderous.* 2 dull and serious. *He speaks in a ponderous way.* **ponderously** *adverb.*

pony (ponies) *noun* a small horse.

Sophie had always wanted a white pony of her own.

poodle *noun* a dog with curly hair.

pool *noun* 1 a small amount of water or other liquid. *A pool of blood spread across the floor.* 2 a swimming pool.

pool *noun* 1 an amount of money used by gamblers. 2 a common supply of workers or goods that can be shared by a number of people. *Our firm has a pool car that we all use.* 3 an American billiard game. **pool** *verb* to share. *We pooled our money and rented a villa in Spain for the summer.*

P

poor *adjective* 1 having very little money. 2 not good, of low quality or small in quantity. *She's in poor health.* 3 needing help or sympathy. *The poor little boy was crying.* **poorly** *adverb* badly. *Most foreign workers are poorly paid.* **poorly** *adjective* unwell. *She's been poorly for weeks.*

pop *adjective* popular. *A pop singer.* **pop** *noun* popular music.

pop *noun* 1 a short explosive sound. *The cork came out with a pop.* 2 a fizzy drink. **pop** *verb* 1 to make a bursting sound. *The balloon went pop.* 2 If you pop something somewhere, you put it there quickly. *She popped a sweet in the child's mouth.* 3 to go quickly. *Could you pop into the shop?* **pop out** 1 to quickly go out. *I'm just popping out for a coffee.* 2 If something pops out of something, it suddenly comes out. *Her eyes almost popped out when she saw that she had the winning numbers.* **pop over** to make a short visit. **pop up** to spring up or to appear unexpectedly.

popcorn *noun* grains of maize heated until they burst open and look like little balls.

Popcorn is a favourite cinema snack in Britain and America.

pope *noun* the head of the Roman Catholic Church.

poppy (poppies) *noun* a plant with big flowers.

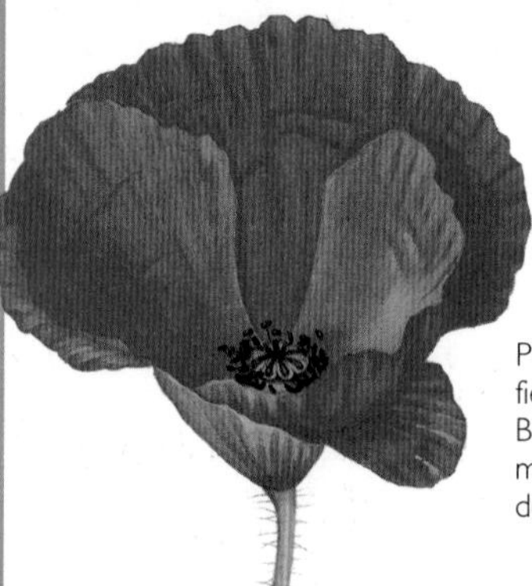

Poppies grow on the fields of Flanders, in Belgium, where so many soldiers fell during World War I.

popular *adjective* 1 liked, enjoyed or admired by many people. *Katie is a very popular name.* 2 of or for the general public. *The popular press pays too much attention to gossip.* **popularity** *noun.*

WORD HISTORY

'Porcupine' comes from the Latin words 'porcus' ('pig') and 'spina' (thorn); it is a thorny or spiny pig. The porpoise is a 'porcus/piscis' ('pig fish'); you could say it has a piglike snout!

If attacked, the porcupine runs backwards at its enemy, driving in its sharp spines.

AMAZING FACT

Porcupines usually give birth to a single offspring after a gestation period of seven months. The baby is well-developed at birth, with fur, open eyes and soft quills that harden in about an hour. It is able to climb trees and eat solid food just a few hours after it is born.

populate *verb* to live in, inhabit. *We live in a heavily populated area.*

population *noun* the people living in a place, especially a country or town. *The population of India is expanding rapidly.*

porcelain *noun* a hard shiny material, used for making cups, plates and other articles, which is produced by baking clay. China.

porch *noun* a roofed entrance to a building.

porcupine *noun* a small animal with long prickles over its back and sides.

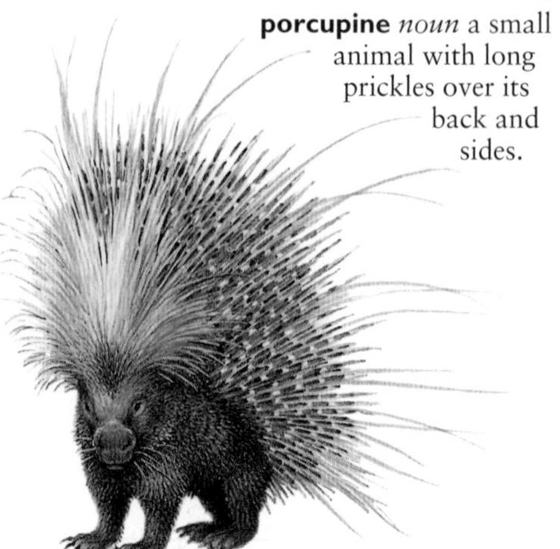

pork *noun* meat from pigs.

porpoise *noun* a large sea animal similar to a dolphin.

porridge *noun* soft food made from oats cooked in water and milk.

port 1 a harbour where goods are loaded and unloaded. 2 a town with a harbour. 3 the left side of a ship when you are facing towards the front of it.

port *noun* a strong sweet red Portuguese wine. *Fine ruby port.*

portable *adjective* able to be carried. *A portable television.*

Port-au-Prince *noun* the capital of Haiti.

portcullis *noun* a framework of pointed bars above the entrance in old castles that could be lowered as a protection against attack. *Let down the portcullis!*

porter *noun* 1 a person who is employed in a building like a hotel or hospital to stand at the entrance and open doors. 2 a person employed to carry people's luggage at a railway station, an airport or in a hotel.

Port Louis *noun* the capital of Mauritius.

Port Moresby *noun* the capital of Papua New Guinea.

Port of Spain *noun* the capital of Trinidad and Tobago.

Porto Novo *noun* the capital of Benin.

portrait *noun* a painted picture, drawing or photograph of somebody.

P

portray *verb* 1 to make a picture of somebody or something. 2 to describe in words. 3 to play the part of a character in a film or play.

Portugal *noun* a country in Southwest Europe.

Portuguese *noun* the language spoken in Portugal and Brazil. Portuguese *adjective. The Portuguese flag.*

Port Vila *noun* the capital of Vanuatu.

The Japanese woman adopted a traditional pose for her photograph.

pose 1 a particular position in or for a photograph or painting. *He sat in an unnatural pose.* 2 a way of behaving in order to impress or deceive people. **pose** *verb* 1 to sit or stand in a pose for a photograph or painting. 2 to behave in a way to impress other people or be admired by them. *I hate the way she is always posing at parties.* 3 to pretend. *The spy was posing as a car mechanic.* 4 to bring into being, to cause. *Lack of money is posing too many problems.* **poser** *noun.*

position *noun* 1 the place where something is or stands. *The house is in a sunny position.* 2 the way of sitting or standing. *He slept in an uncomfortable position.* 3 a situation or condition. *You've put me in an awkward position.* 4 a job. 5 a particular place in a group. 6 an opinion. **position** *verb* to put somebody or something into position. *I positioned the table by the door.*

positive *adjective* 1 sure, certain, having no doubt about something. *I am positive that I have seen you before.* 2 practical, helpful. *Let me give you some positive advice.* 3 agreeing, saying yes. *I got a positive reply to my request.* 4 real, noticeable. *It was a positive delight to see the children playing so happily together.* 5 greater than zero. *A positive number.* The positive sign is +. 6 If a medical test is positive, it shows that something, usually a disease, is present. **positively** *adverb* 1 definitely, really being the case. 2 without doubt. *The food was positively horrible.*

possess *verb* 1 to have or own. *I wish he possessed some of his brother's charm.* 2 to influence somebody's behaviour or thinking. *What possessed you to drive so fast?*

GRAMMAR NOTE

You make the possessive form of a singular noun by adding apostrophe 's' at the end: 'my father's book'. Plural nouns have 's' apostrophe at the end: 'my parents' house'.

WORD BUILDING

The usual opposite of 'post–' is 'pre–', or sometimes 'ante–': 'post-war' and 'pre-war'; ' post-natal' and 'ante-natal'.

AMAZING FACT

In the 1880s a New England post office received a letter with the following address:

John
Hill
Mass.

He realised that it was to John Underhill, Andover, Massachusetts.

possession *noun* 1 ownership, possessing. *How did the paper come into your possession?* 2 the things you possess or own. *He left all his possessions to his best friend.*

possessive *adjective* 1 wanting to keep things for yourself. *My brother is very possessive about his bike.* 2 in grammar, a possessive word shows ownership. 'My' and 'their' are possessive adjectives. **possessiveness** *noun.*

possible *adjective* able to happen, be done or that may be true. *Please come as soon as possible.* **possibility** *noun.* **possibly** *adverb.*

post *noun* 1 an upright bar of wood, metal or concrete fixed into the ground, especially as a support. *A lamp post.* 2 the starting or finishing point in a race. 3 a job. 4 a special place on duty, especially on guard. *The soldiers had to stay at their posts.*

post *noun* 1 the service of collecting, sorting and delivering of letters and parcels. *The cheque is in the post.* 2 the letters and parcels that are delivered. **post** *verb* 1 to put a letter or parcel into a postbox or take it to the post office for collection. 2 to send somebody to a particular place to work or to place soldiers on duty or guard. *Guards were posted around the building.* **postal** *adjective. Postal charges have gone up for the third time this year.* **keep somebody posted** to keep somebody informed.

post- *prefix* later than. *A post-war building.*

postcard *noun* a card for sending a message without an envelope.

Our friends sent a postcard from the seaside.

postcode *noun* a group of letters and figures added to an address to help the post office sort mail.

poster *noun* a large picture or notice that is stuck to a wall or noticeboard.

posthumous *adjective* printed or happening after a person's death. **posthumously** *adverb. Posthumously awarded a medal.*

post-mortem *noun* an examination of a dead body to find the cause of death.

post office *noun* the place that deals with the post and postal business.

postpone *verb* to fix a later date or move to a later time. *The match was postponed because of rain.* **postponement** *noun.*

P

pot *noun* a round container for cooking or keeping things in. **go to pot** to be ruined, especially from lack of care. **take pot luck** to take whatever is offered or available. **pot** (pots, potting, potted) *verb* 1 to put into a pot, especially food for preserving or plants. 2 to hit a ball into one of the pockets in snooker or pool.

potato *noun* a round vegetable with brown or red skin that grows underground.

potential *adjective* capable of happening or being used. Not yet developed, but able to come into existence. *This film is a potential success.* **potential** *noun. The boy shows lots of potential.* **potentially** *adverb.*

potholing *noun* the sport of exploring underground caves. **pothole** *noun.* **potholer** *noun. The potholer called for help.*

pottery *noun* 1 pots, plates and other objects that are made from clay and then baked in an oven. 2 a place where pottery is made. **potter** *noun.*

Classical Greek pottery is often decorated with designs of red and black showing scenes of life in ancient Greece.

potty *noun* a pot used by little children as a toilet. *The baby is being potty-trained.*

pouch (pouches) *noun* a small bag or anything shaped like a bag.

poultry *noun* farm birds like chickens and ducks that are kept for eggs and meat.

pounce *verb* to leap or swoop down quickly, especially in order to get something. *The cat pounced on the mouse as it crept out from behind the cupboard.*

pound *noun* 1 a unit of weight equal to 454 grams or 16 ounces. 2 a unit of money, used in Britain. One pound is divided into a hundred pence. *I earned fifteen pounds (£15) today.*

pound *noun* a place where stray animals and illegally parked cars are taken and kept until collected by the owner.

pound *verb* 1 to hit something loudly and repeatedly. *I can feel my heart pounding.* 2 to crush into a powder or paste.

WORD HISTORY

There are various explanations of where the expression 'to go to pot' comes from. It might have referred originally to putting old used items into a pot, or waste bin; or it might have meant putting food into a pot for stewing; it could even have referred to putting a cremated person's ashes into an urn.

Nuclear power stations generate energy.

DID YOU KNOW

Potatoes first grew in the Andes Mountains of South America. Spanish and Portuguese conquerors took them back to their countries in the 16th century, and Sir Walter Raleigh introduced them to England around 1585.

pour *verb* 1 to flow or make liquid or another substance flow. *He poured me a drink.* 2 to rain. *It's been pouring all day.* 3 to come or go quickly and in large amounts. *Fan mail has been pouring in.* **pour out** to tell freely and with feeling, especially a story or your troubles. *She poured out all her worries.*

poverty *noun* the state of being very poor. *They live in poverty.*

powder *noun* any substance that has been crushed or rubbed to dust. *Washing powder.* **powder** *verb* to put powder on. *She powdered her nose.* **powdered** *adjective* in the form of powder. *Powdered milk.* **powdery** *adjective* like powder.

power *noun* 1 the ability to do something or have a certain effect. *He did everything in his power to help.* 2 force, physical strength. *The power of the waves threw the boat on to the beach.* 3 energy, the force that makes things work. *Electric power.* 4 authority, the right to do something. *The power of the press.* 5 a person or organization that has great influence. *America is a world power.* **in power** having the right to govern. **powerful** *adjective.* **powerless** *adjective* without energy or influence.

practicable *adjective* that can be done.

practical *adjective* 1 good at doing or making things. Clever at dealing with difficulties, sensible. 2 useful, convenient, good for a particular purpose. *A plastic tablecloth is very practical, you can just wipe it clean.* 3 concerned with action and practice, rather than just ideas. A practical lesson is a lesson in which you make things or do experiments. *She didn't get the job because she had no practical experience.* **practicality** *noun.*

practical joke *noun* a funny trick played on a person.

practically *adverb* 1 in a practical way. 2 almost. *He practically walked into her.*

practice *noun* 1 something done regularly or as an exercise. *We have football practice twice a week.* 2 doing something, knowledge of a skill. *In practice this arrangement will never work.* 3 the business of a doctor or lawyer. **out of practice** no longer very good, because of lack of practice.

practise *verb* 1 to do something often in order to be good or get better at it. *I'm practising this piece on my guitar for the concert.* 2 to take part in an activity, do something actively. *People are allowed to practise any religion in this country.* 3 to work as a doctor or lawyer.

The team practised every day before the big match.

pragmatic *adjective* dealing with things in a practical way, a way which is best under the actual conditions. **pragmatist** *noun.*

Prague *noun* the capital of the Czech Republic.

Praia *noun* the capital of Cape Verde.

prairie *noun* flat grassland in North America. *Wheat prairies.*

The pioneers travelled across the prairies of the US.

praise *verb* to say that somebody or something is very good. *He praised her courage.* **praise** *noun* words that praise somebody or something.

prattle *noun* meaningless childish talk. **prattle** *verb. She prattled on about the clothes she wants to buy.*

prawn *noun* a small shellfish like a shrimp.

pray *verb* to speak to God. *She prayed that God would give her strength.*

prayer *noun* 1 the activity of praying. 2 the words used in praying. A set form of words used during service. 3 a strong hope. *My prayers were answered when he asked me out for a meal.*

praying mantis *noun* an insect.

pre- *prefix* before a particular time. *A pre-war building.*

preach (preaches, preaching, preached) *verb* to give a talk, especially a moral or religious talk. **preacher** *noun.*

precaution *noun* something done in order to avoid a possible known danger or trouble. **precautionary** *adjective. We took precautionary measures and put up a fence.*

AMAZING FACT

If you add a word or part of a word (called a prefix) to the beginning of a root word, you can form a new word. The word 'prefix' itself comes from 'pre–' ('before') and 'fix' ('fasten').

GRAMMAR NOTE

If you add a word or part of a word (called a prefix) to the beginning of a root word, you can form a new word. The word 'prefix' itself comes from 'pre–' '('before') and 'fix'('fasten').

precede *verb* to come or go in front.

precinct (say **pree**-sinkt) *noun* 1 a specially built shopping area, in which cars are not allowed. 2 the area around a cathedral or university, often enclosed by walls.

precious *adjective* 1 very valuable. 2 much loved by somebody. *My dolls are very precious to me.* **precious little** very little.

precipice *noun* a very steep side of a rock, mountain or cliff. **precipitous** *adjective. A precipitous mountain path.*

Karen got ready to abseil down the precipice.

precipitation *noun* 1 being too hurried, unwise haste. 2 the amount of rain or snow that falls. **precipitate** *verb.*

precise *adjective* exact, clear. *He gave a precise description of the accident.* **precision** *noun.* **precisely** *adverb. At precisely that moment he appeared at the door.*

precocious (say prik-**oh**-shus) *adjective* seeming older, having developed earlier than is normal in mind or body. *He is a precocious little boy, he talks like an adult.*

predecessor (say **pree**-dis-ess-er) *noun* somebody who has had a job before another person, or something that was used before something else. *The new headmaster is much better than his predecessor.*

predict *verb* to say what will or might happen, to forecast. **prediction** *noun. My prediction is that the idea will be very successful.* **predictable** *adjective. A predictable mistake.*

prefabricated *adjective* made in parts in a factory. *Prefabricated buildings are fitted together on site.* **prefabricate** *verb.*

preface *noun* an introduction to a book or speech. *The preface is by a famous writer.*

prefer (prefers, preferring, preferred) *verb* to like one person or thing better than another. *I prefer coffee to tea.* **preference** *noun. What is your preference?*

prefix (prefixes) *noun* a word or group of letters in front of a word to make a new word. The prefix 'un-' before 'load' makes the word 'unload'.

P

pregnant *adjective* When a woman or female animal is pregnant, a baby develops inside her body. **pregnancy** *noun.*

prehistoric *adjective* of the time before history was written down. *Dinosaurs were prehistoric animals.*

Scientists think that prehistoric animals such as the dinosaur were wiped out when the Earth suffered a dramatic climate change, killing the vegetation on which they fed.

prejudice *noun* an unfair opinion or dislike of somebody or something, not based on knowledge or experience. *They were accused of racial prejudice and brought to trial.* **prejudiced** *adjective.*

premature *adjective* done or happening earlier than usual or expected. *A premature baby may need to be put in an incubator.*

premiere *noun* the first showing or performance of a film or play.

premises *plural noun* a building and its grounds. *Residential premises.*

preoccupied *adjective* thinking a lot about something and therefore not giving attention to other matters. *She is so preoccupied with plans for her wedding that she can't work.* **preoccupation** *noun.*

prepare *verb* to get or make ready. **prepared** *adjective* 1 got ready in advance. 2 willing. *I'm not prepared to help you.*

preposition *noun* in grammar, a word or group of words used with a noun or pronoun to show its connection with another word such as place, position or time. In 'the woman on the stage', 'on' is a preposition.

prescribe *verb* 1 to advise what medicine or treatment a patient should have. *The doctor prescribed a cough mixture.* 2 to state what must be done. **prescription** *noun. I get the drugs on prescription.*

DID YOU KNOW

The youngest ever President of the United States was the 26th president, Theodore Roosevelt (1858–1919), who was 42 when he entered office; he was president from 1901 to 1909.

present *noun* (say **pre**-zunt) something given, a gift. *Christmas presents.* **present** *verb* (say pree-**zent**) 1 to give something formally, especially something like a prize. *They presented her with a bouquet of flowers.* 2 to introduce somebody to an important person or introduce a television or radio programme. *Professor Bird presented the documentary.* 3 to put on a play or show. 4 to offer, show or be the cause of. *He loves sailing because it presents such a challenge.* **presentation** *noun.*

She was thrilled when she saw her present.

present *noun* (say **pre**-zunt) the time that is taking place now or the things that are happening at the moment. *Try to live in the present, not the past.* **at present** now.

present *adjective* (say **pre**-zunt) 1 there, in this or that place. *Is a doctor present?* 2 existing now. *The present government.* 3 being talked or written about now. *We'll make an exception in the present case.* **presence** *noun. I don't talk about it in her presence.* **presently** *adverb.*

president *noun* 1 the leader of a country. *The president of the United States.* 2 a person who has a high position in an organization such as a club, a college or a company. *The president of our golf club.* **presidency** *noun.* **presidential** *adjective.*

Nelson Mandela cast a vote for the ANC in South Africa's first free election. He became the first black president of his nation.

press *verb* 1 to push hard against something or push one thing against another. *You have to press harder to make it work.* 2 to squeeze or flatten. To press flowers in a book. 3 to iron. *Can you press my trousers?* 4 to persuade somebody to do something or make demands. *She's always pressing us to stay longer.* **press on** to go on doing something. **pressed for** If you are pressed for time, you are in a hurry. If you are pressed for money, you do not have enough money at the moment. *I am pressed for time and money.*

P

press (presses) *noun* 1 the action of pushing against something. *At the press of a button.* 2 a device or machine for pressing. *A flower press.* 3 newspapers, magazines and journalists. *He was interviewed by the press.* 4 a business for printing and making books and magazines. 5 a machine for printing books and magazines. *A printing press.*

The newspapers rolled off the printing presses.

press conference *noun* an interview with journalists. *He held a press conference.*

pressure *noun* 1 the action of pressing. 2 the force with which something presses. *The water pressure is very low.* 3 a feeling of being forced to do something, a strain. *She was under pressure to do well at school.* **put pressure on somebody** to force somebody to do something. *They put pressure on her to leave the country.* **pressure** *verb* to forcefully make somebody do something. *They pressured me into going to university.* **pressurize** *verb.*

presume *verb* to think that something is the case or true. *An accused person is presumed innocent until proved guilty.* **presumption** *noun.*

pretend *verb* to act in a way as if something is true or real, although in fact it is not, either as a game or to deceive people. *He's snoring, pretending to be asleep.* **pretence** *noun. He doesn't really like the job, it's all a pretence.*

Pretoria *noun* the seat of government of South Africa.

pretty (prettier, prettiest) *adjective* nice, attractive. *A pretty girl.* **prettily** *adverb.* **prettiness** *noun.*

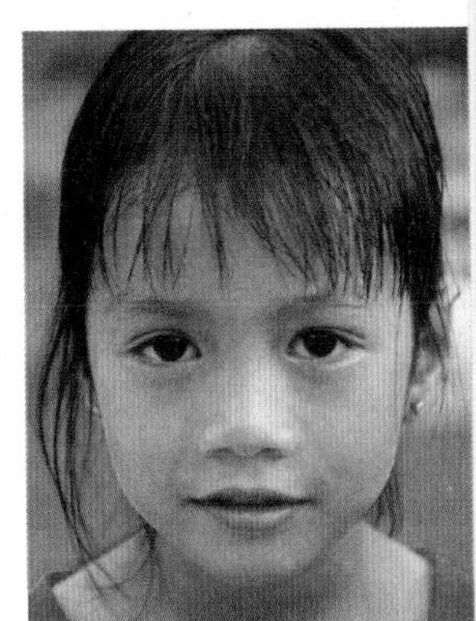

A very pretty girl offered a shell necklace for sale.

pretty *adverb* quite or rather. *It was pretty hot.* **pretty much** very nearly, almost.

We went up into the mountains to observe the birds of prey.

GRAMMAR NOTE

You can pressure or pressurize someone into doing something: 'My father pressured (or pressurized) me into taking the exam again.'

DID YOU KNOW

The South African city of Pretoria was founded in 1855 and named after the Afrikaner leader Andries Pretorius (1799–1853). Today it is the administrative capital of South Africa.

prevailing *adjective* most common or general, especially of a custom or belief. *The prevailing wind is a westerly.*

prevent *verb* 1 to stop somebody from doing something. 2 to make sure something does not happen. *How can we prevent war?* **prevention** *noun. Crime prevention.* **preventive** *adjective. Preventive medicine.*

previous *adjective* happening or being earlier in time or before the one you are talking about. *In my previous job.* **previously** *adverb. They previously lived in Germany.*

prey (say pray) *noun* 1 an animal that is hunted and eaten by other animals. *The lion pounced on its prey.* 2 a helpless person, a victim. **bird of prey** a bird that hunts and eats animals or other birds. **prey on** *verb* 1 to hunt for food. 2 to attack and steal from people. 3 to trouble you greatly, to make you worry about something. *The journey is preying on my mind.*

price *noun* 1 an amount of money for which something is bought or sold. *We have to fix a price.* 2 what you must do in order to get what you want. *He paid the price of becoming rich and famous.* **price** *verb* 1 to fix the price of something. 2 to mark goods in a shop with a price. *I've priced the jam at £2.00 a pot.*

priceless *adjective* worth a lot of money, very valuable. *A priceless painting.*

prick *verb* 1 to make a small hole in something. *I pricked my finger with a needle.* 2 to hurt somebody with a pin or something sharp, or feel a sharp pain on the skin. *The thorns pricked me.* **prick** *noun* 1 a small hole. 2 a sharp pain.

prickle *noun* 1 a small sharp point that sticks out from a plant or an animal. *The prickles of a cactus.* 2 a feeling that something is pricking you. **prickle** *verb* to have or give a pricking feeling. *Wool makes my skin prickle.* **prickly** *adjective. Prickly holly leaves.*

pride *noun* 1 a feeling of delight and pleasure in what you or people you know have done. *She showed him her certificate with pride.* 2 something that makes you feel proud. *The children are her pride and joy.* 3 too high an opinion of yourself, especially because of wealth or position. 4 self-respect. *He swallowed his pride and said sorry.* **pride yourself on** to be proud of. *She prides herself on never having missed a lesson.*

priest *noun* 1 a member of the Christian clergy, a clergyman. 2 a specially trained person who performs religious ceremonies. **priestess** *noun*.

prim (primmer, primmest) *adjective* very correct and easily shocked by anything rude.

primary *adjective* extremely important, main. *A peace agreement is our primary aim.* **primarily** *adverb*.

primary colour *noun* The primary colours are red, yellow and blue. All other colours can made up by mixing them in different ways.

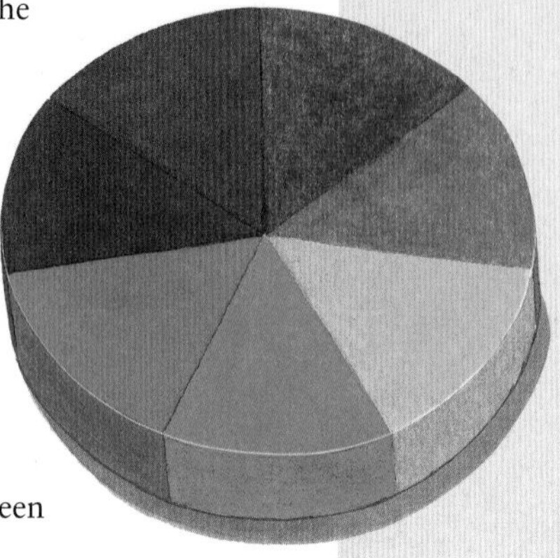

Primary colours can be mixed to form all the other colours of the spectrum.

primary school *noun* a school for children between 5 and 11 years old.

prime *adjective* 1 most important. *Computers are of prime importance in all businesses, hospitals and schools.* 2 of the very best quality, best. *Early evening is the prime time for advertising on television.* **prime minister** the head of a government. **prime number** a number that can be divided only by itself and the number 1. 3, 7 and 11 are prime numbers.

prime *noun* the best or most successful stage of something. *He is past his prime.*

prime *verb* 1 to give somebody information beforehand so that they are prepared, especially for difficulties. *She had primed him before the interview, so he could answer all the questions.* 2 to cover a surface, especially wood, with a coat of paint or oil to prepare it for painting. 3 to get a machine ready for use.

primitive *adjective* 1 belonging to a society of people who lived at an earlier time. *Primitive man made tools from sharp stone and animal bones.* 2 simple or old-fashioned. *This cottage is too primitive for me, it has no central heating.*

primrose *noun* a wild plant that has pale yellow flowers.

prince *noun* a man or boy in a royal family, especially the son of a king or queen.

princess *noun* 1 a woman or girl in a royal family, especially the daughter of a king or queen. 2 the wife of a prince.

principal *adjective* most important.

principal *noun* 1 the head of a school or college. 2 money lent or put into a business on which interest is paid.

AMAZING FACT

An easy way to remember how to spell 'principal' is to think of the principal as your pal or friend!

SPELLING NOTE

As an adjective, 'principal' is spelt '–pal'. As a noun, 'principal' is the spelling for the head of a school or an amount of money. A 'principle' (with '–ple') is a rule.

Light passing through a prism is split into all the colours of the rainbow.

principle *noun* 1 a general rule about how something should be done or how it works. *The principles of grammar.* 2 a rule for behaviour. *It was against his principles.* **in principle** in general. *In principle I agree with you.* **on principle** because of your personal beliefs. *I'm against war on principle.*

print *verb* 1 to produce words or pictures on paper with a machine or shapes covered with ink. To make books, magazines and pictures in this way. *How many copies of this dictionary were printed?* 2 to write words without joining the letters, usually in capitals. *Please print your name and then sign here.* 3 to press a mark on to a surface or make a pattern on cloth. *The pattern has been printed on to the scarf by hand.* 4 to make a photograph from a negative film. **print** *noun* 1 the printed letters and numbers on a page. *The print is too small to read without glasses.* 2 a mark made on a surface showing the shape of the thing pressed on it. *The tyres left prints in the sand.* 3 a printed picture, photograph or pattern. **in print** 1 printed in a book, magazine or newspaper. *Don't believe everything you see in print.* 2 If a book is in print, it is still available and can be bought. **printing** *noun*.

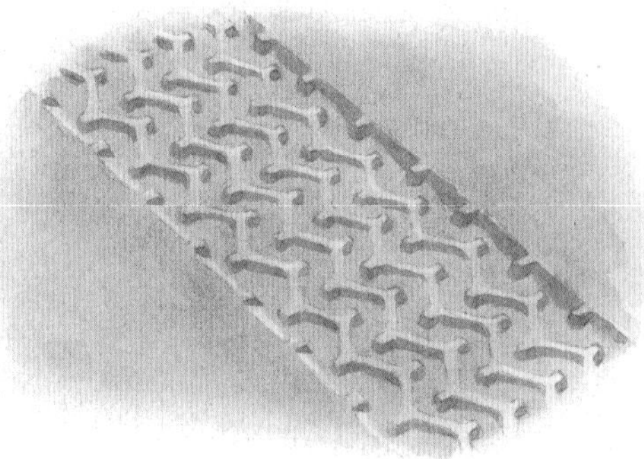

We followed the tyre prints and discovered the stolen car.

printer *noun* 1 a person or firm that prints books, newspapers and other printed material. 2 a machine connected to a computer that prints out what you have written or any other information.

print-out *noun* information from a computer printed on a piece of paper.

prior *preposition, adjective* earlier or more important than something else. *They had already decided prior to the event.*

prior *noun* a monk who is the head of a religious house, called a priory.

priority *noun* something considered more important than other things. *We must do that as a priority.*

prism (say **priz**-um) *noun* 1 a solid shape with a flat base and parallel upright edges. 2 a three-sided block, usually made of glass, that breaks up light into the colours of the rainbow.

prison *noun* a building where criminals are kept locked up as a punishment. *The thief was sent to prison for three years.*

The prison had tall gates with a window to check a visitor's identity.

prisoner *noun* a person kept in prison as a punishment. 2 a person or animal who has been captured and is kept locked up.

privacy *noun* being private, away from others and able to do things without other people seeing you.

private *adjective* 1 for one person or a small group of people, not public, not shared with others, personal. *A house with a private swimming pool.* 2 secret or kept secret. *He has some private information about the president.* 3 personal, rather than to do with work or business. *He never talks about his private life at work.* 4 quiet, sheltered. Somebody who is a private person is shy and does not like to share their feelings with other people. 5 independent, not owned by the state. *Private hospitals and private schools are not paid for by the government.* **in private** without other people listening or hearing, away from others. *Could we have a talk in private?*

privileged *adjective* having an advantage that most other people do not have. *She came from a privileged background.* **privilege** *noun. It was a privilege to be able to work with such a famous director.*

prize *noun* something of value given to the winner of a game, competition or particular good work. **prize** *verb* to value highly. *Italian tomatoes are prized for their taste.*

The first prize for excellence at school went to Jennifer Jones.

pro *noun* a professional. *He turned pro when he was just eighteen.*

pro- *prefix* for somebody or something, in favour of. *He is very pro-Italian.* **pro and con** for and against.

AMAZING FACT

It is best not to begin a sentence with 'probably'. For example, 'Probably I will spend Easter at home.' is not correct. It should read 'I will probably spend Easter at home.'

WORD HISTORY

Originally a privilege was a 'law affecting an individual', from the Latin 'privilegium'. This word itself came from two other Latin words: 'privus', meaning 'private', and 'legis', meaning 'law'.

probably *adverb* very likely. *I'll probably see you tomorrow.* **probable** *adjective. He is the probable winner.*

probation *noun* 1 a period of time during which somebody's abilities at work are tested before they are finally given the job. 2 a system of letting a criminal go free if he behaves well. Somebody on probation is supervised by an official, a probation officer, for a period of time.

probe *noun* 1 a long thin metal instrument used by doctors to search inside the body. 2 an object used for exploring space. **probe** *verb* to search or explore.

problem *noun* something difficult, a question for which an answer is needed. **problematic, problematical** *adjective.*

proboscis (say pro-**boss**-iss) *noun* 1 the long part of an insect's mouth. 2 an elephant's trunk.

The elephant's trunk is technically called a proboscis.

procedure *noun* a way of doing something, especially in a correct way.

proceed *verb* 1 to continue with an action, often after stopping. 2 to go forward in a particular direction.

proceedings *plural noun* 1 a series of happenings. 2 a lawsuit.

process (processes) *noun* (say **proh**-sess) 1 a series of actions for doing or achieving something. *Packing the car was a slow process.* 2 a series of things that happen naturally. *Chemical processes.* 3 an action in law. **process** *verb* 1 to treat food and other materials using a particular process. *To process (develop) a film.* 2 to produce information by putting it through a process. *It will take a week for us to process the applications.*

procession *noun* a group of people or vehicles moving forward, following each other. *A funeral procession.*

proclaim *verb* to make officially known. **proclamation** *noun.*

prod (prods, prodding, prodded) *verb* 1 to push with your finger or something pointed. 2 to get or remind somebody to act. *You have to prod him into action.* **prod** *noun.*

P

prodigal *adjective* wasteful, especially of money. *The prodigal son.*

produce *verb* 1 to make, grow or create. *The Sun produces heat.* 2 to show, bring out to be seen. *He produced a ticket to prove he had paid.* 3 to cause to happen. *Good soil will produce good vegetables.* 4 to organize a film, play, record or programme. *The film was directed and produced by the same person.* **produce** *noun* things produced, especially things grown. **producer** *noun.*

product *noun* 1 something produced, especially something manufactured. *Cleaning products.* 2 the result of thought or conditions. 3 in maths, the number obtained by multiplying two or more numbers.

production *noun* 1 the process of producing, making or growing things in large quantities. 2 something produced, a play, opera or show.

productive *adjective* producing a lot of things, especially in large amounts. *We had a very productive meeting.*

profession *noun* a job that needs special training. *Teaching always has been a poorly paid profession.*

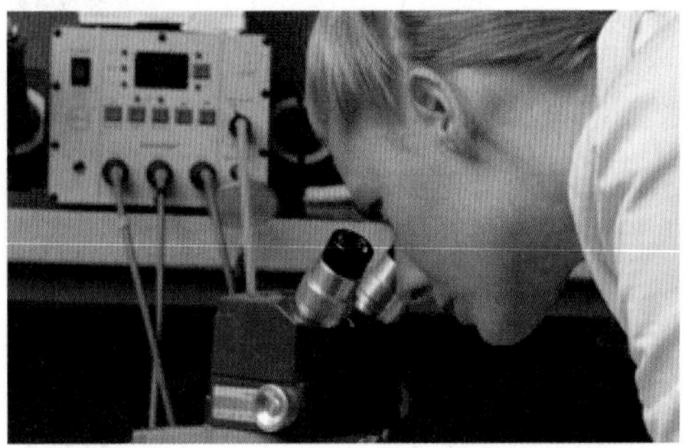

Science is a serious profession.

professional *adjective* 1 of a particular profession. 2 doing work as a proper job for payment. *You can earn a lot of money as a professional footballer.* 3 showing the skill of a professional, competent. **professional** *noun. He is a true professional.* **professionally** *adverb.*

program *noun* a set of instructions for a computer to carry out. **program** (programs, programming, programmed) *verb. Can you program a computer to answers questions?* **programmer** *noun.*

programme *noun* 1 a fixed plan of events, activities or a list of duties. *What is on the programme today?* 2 a booklet or list that gives information about what you have come to see or take part in. *A theatre programme.* 3 a performance, talk or show on radio or television. *A new music programme.* **programme** *verb. The central heating is programmed to come on at six.*

The theatre programme explained the history of the production.

DID YOU KNOW

A prodigal son is a wasteful person who changes his ways, and the expression is sometimes also used just to mean a returned wanderer. This comes from a parable in the Bible.

AMAZING FACT

Computer programs use a system of numbers called the 'binary system'. Instead of using the numbers 0–9, as we do, the binary system uses only 0 and 1.

progress (say **pro**-gress) *noun* 1 forward movement, the process of gradually getting nearer to something. *We made slow progress up the hill.* 2 development or improvement. *You are making good progress in your work.* **in progress** happening now. *When we arrived, the game was already in progress.* **progress** *verb* (say pro-**gress**) to make progress.

progressive *adjective* 1 moving forward or happening gradually over a period of time. *The progressive closure of the coal industry.* 2 having modern ideas how things should be done. *Most progressive schools are against wearing uniform.*

prohibit *verb* to say that something must not be done, to ban. **prohibition** *noun.*

project *noun* (say **pro**-jekt) 1 a plan. 2 a study of a subject by a student. *Our class is doing a project on pop music.* **project** *verb* (say pruh-**jekt**) 1 to stick out above a surface or edge. 2 to make a light or picture from a film appear on a surface. *The pictures were projected on to a screen.* 3 to throw or send through the air with force. *Missiles were projected into space.* 4 to plan. *The minister's projected visit to Spain has been cancelled.* **projection** *noun.*

projector *noun* a machine for showing films or slides on a screen or wall.

We bought a projector so we could see our holiday slides.

prolong *verb* to make longer or make something last longer. *Let's not prolong this ludicrous argument.*

prominent *adjective* 1 important, well known. *The Ritz is full of prominent people.* 2 standing out, noticeable. *Her bottom is unfortunately the most prominent part of her body.* **prominently** *adverb.* **prominence** *noun.*

promise *noun* 1 a statement that you make to somebody to say that you will do or give them something. *She always keeps her promises.* 2 expectation or hope of success. *The singer shows great promise.* **promise** *verb. He promised to buy her a new bike.*

promising *adjective* likely to be successful.

promote *verb* 1 to give somebody a more important job or higher rank. 2 to bring to notice, especially to increase sales or somebody's popularity. *The firm is promoting a new shampoo on television.* **promotion** *noun.* **promoter** *noun.*

prompt *adjective* without delay, punctual. A prompt reply. **promptly** *adverb. He arrived promptly at 9 o'clock.*

prompt *verb* 1 to make you decide to do something. *Poor results prompted the manager to change the team.* 2 to remind an actor or speaker of the next words when they have been forgotten.

prone *adjective* lying face downwards. **be prone to** be likely to do or have something. *He is prone to bad moods.*

prong *noun* a spike of a fork.

The fork has three prongs.

pronoun *noun* in grammar, a word that is used in place of a noun that has already been or will be mentioned. He, she, it, hers, them are pronouns.

pronounce *verb* 1 to make the sound of a letter or word. In the word 'gnaw' the 'g' is not pronounced. 2 to declare formally. He was pronounced dead. **pronunciation** *noun. His French pronunciation is very good.*

proof *noun* 1 a thing or fact that shows that something is true. *He has no proof that the car belongs to him.* 2 a trial copy of something printed, made for checking before other copies are printed.

proof *suffix* showing that something cannot be damaged or gives protection against something harmful. *A waterproof jacket. A foolproof tin-opener.*

prop *noun* 1 a support used to keep something up. 2 (usually plural, props) the furniture and other objects used in a play or film. **prop** (props, propping, propped) *verb* to support or keep in position by putting something under or against. *She propped the door open with a shoe.* **prop somebody up** to help and give support to somebody.

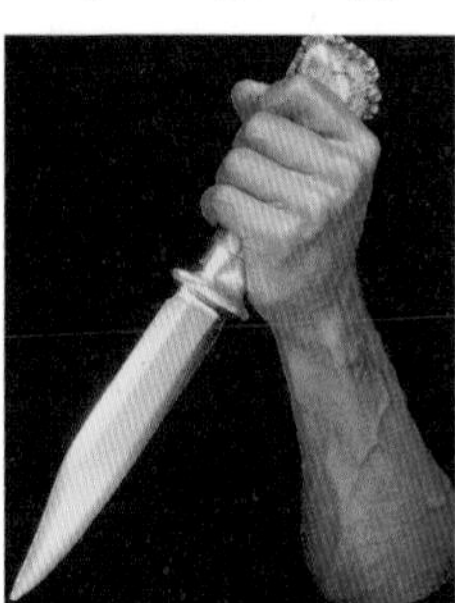

The plastic knife was often used as a prop during theatre productions.

propaganda *noun* information, often false information, given to influence people. *The extremists put out a lot of propaganda.*

DID YOU KNOW

Propellers work by thrusting a vehicle forwards. A ship's propeller is connected to a shaft, which is turned by the engine. As it turns, the propeller pushes water backwards, and this thrusts the ship forwards.

A prophet is often a person who has spent a great deal of time alone among nature, asking difficult questions about religion and existence.

SPELLING NOTE

Note that the noun from 'pronounce' is spelt 'pronunciation': the middle part is spelt – and pronounced! 'Nun' rather than 'noun'.

propel (propels, propelling, propelled) *verb* to push or drive forward.

propeller *noun* blades fixed to a bar which spin round and make an aircraft or ship go.

proper *adjective* 1 suitable, correct, right for the situation. *Everything was in its proper place.* 2 respectable. *Proper behaviour.* 3 great, real. *I felt a proper fool.* **properly** *adverb. She doesn't eat properly, all she has for lunch is bag of crisps.*

prophecy (prophecies) *noun* telling something that will happen in the future.

prophet *noun* 1 a person who is believed to be chosen by God to teach a religion to the people. *Muslims are followers of the Prophet Muhammad.* 2 somebody who makes prophecies.

proposal *noun* 1 a plan or suggestion. 2 an offer of marriage.

propose *verb* 1 to suggest an idea or plan. 2 to ask somebody to marry you. *Tom proposed to Emma.*

prosecute *verb* to accuse somebody of a crime and try and prove it in a court of law. *He was prosecuted for burglary.* **prosecution** *noun* 1 the action of prosecuting somebody. 2 the lawyers who try to prove that the accused person is guilty.

prospect (say **pross**-pekt) *noun* 1 a possibility or hope. *What are the prospects of getting a job?* 2 a wide view.

prospect (say pruh-**spekt**) *verb* to search in the ground, especially for gold, silver or oil. **prospector** *noun.*

prosper *verb* to be successful or rich.

prosperity *noun* success and riches. **prosperous** *adjective.*

prostitute *noun* a person who offers sex for payment. **prostitution** *noun.*

prostrate *adjective* lying face downwards flat on the ground.

protect *verb* to keep safe from harm, danger or enemies. *Vitamin C helps protect against flu.* **protection** *noun. As a protection against the cold.* **protector** *noun.*

P

protective *adjective* 1 giving protection. 2 wishing to protect. *She is very protective towards her children.*

protein *noun* a body-building substance found in all living things. Protein is in foods such as meat, eggs, beans and milk.

protest (say **pro**-test) *noun* an act of saying or showing that you do not agree with something. *There were many protests against experiments on animals.* **protest** (say pruh-**test**) *verb* 1 *The workers protested against poor conditions.* 2 to state firmly. *He protested his innocence.* **protester** *noun.*

protestant *noun* a member of the Christian church which separated from the Catholic church in the sixteenth century.

proton *noun* a very small piece of matter, an atomic particle, that has a positive electric charge.

prototype *noun* the first model of something, from which others have been developed or are copied.

Mark sketched the prototype of the new car.

proud *adjective* 1 feeling pleased about something good that you or somebody else has done. *The Queen's visit was a proud day for the hospital.* 2 having self-respect or having too high an opinion of yourself. *She is too proud to say sorry.* **proudly** *adverb. She proudly showed us her son's medal.*

prove *verb* 1 to show that something is true. *Can you prove that all the doors were locked?* 2 to turn out or to be found to be as expected. *He proved to be a bad loser.*

proverb *noun* a short well-known saying, usually giving a general truth. 'Too many cooks spoil the broth' is a proverb. **proverbial** *adjective. The proverbial ill wind blows no one any good.*

provide *verb* 1 to give things that are needed or useful. *The hostel provides bed and breakfast.* 2 to state arrangements or make special arrangements that must be fulfilled. **provider** *noun.*

provided, providing *conjunction* on the condition that. *I'll lend you some money provided you promise to pay me back.*

AMAZING FACT

Canada is divided into ten provinces and two national territories: The Yukon Territory and the Northwest Territories

Ottawa is the capital of Canada. It is in the province of Ontario.

DID YOU KNOW

There are many proverbs to do with words. 'Actions speak louder than words.' 'Least said, soonest mended.' 'Easier said than done.' 'The pen is mightier than the sword.'

province 1 a part of a country, a state. *Newfoundland is a province of Canada.* 2 (usually plural, the provinces) all the country outside the capital. 3 special knowledge or learning somebody has or is responsible for. *I'm in computing, but games consoles are outside my province.* **provincial** *adjective.*

provoke *verb* 1 to make somebody angry, usually on purpose. *That dog bites if provoked.* 2 to cause or force an action. *The boy's rudeness provoked a fight.* **provoking** *adjective* annoying. **provocation** *noun.* **provocative** *adjective.*

prow *noun* the front part of a boat.

prowess *noun* great ability or skill.

prowl *verb* to move about quietly, trying not to be seen or heard. **prowl** *noun.* An animal on the prowl is looking for food. **prowler** *noun.*

prune *noun* a dried plum.

Prunes are delicious with cream or custard.

prune *verb* to cut off or shorten branches of a tree or bush.

psalm *noun* (say sahm) a religious song from the Bible. The Book of Psalms is part of the Old Testament.

pseudonym *noun* a false name used by a writer. *He writes rather bad novels under the pseudonym John Smith.*

psychiatry *noun* (say sigh-**kie**-uh-tree) the study and treatment of mental illness. **psychiatric** (say sigh-key-**ah**-trik) *adjective.* **psychiatrist** *noun.*

psychology *noun* the study of the human mind and how it works. **psychological** *adjective. Psychological problems.* **psychologist** *noun.*

pub *noun* a public house, a building where people drink alcohol.

puberty *noun* (say **pew**-buh-tee) the time in a young person's life when they physically develop into an adult.

P

pubic *adjective* (say **pew**-bic) relating to the area around the sexual organs.

public *adjective* belonging to, for, connected with or known by everyone. Not private. *Public transport.* **public** *noun* all the people. *The castle is open to the public.* **in public** with other people there. *People sometimes say different things in public from what they say in private.*

public school *noun* a private school that charges fees.

publish *verb* 1 to have books, magazines, newspapers and other material printed and sold. *Her first book was published last spring.* 2 to make known to the public. *They published news of her death the day she died.* **publisher** *noun.*

pudding *noun* 1 a sweet food made with flour, fat, eggs and other ingredients. *I love vanilla pudding.* 2 the sweet dish in a meal, usually eaten at the end of a meal.

puddle *noun* a small pool of liquid, especially rainwater on the ground.

puerile (say **pew**-er-I'll) *adjective* childish.

puffin *noun* a sea-bird with a brightly coloured beak.

Puffins feed on fish from the sea.

pull *verb* 1 to use force to make something come towards or after you. *He pulled the chair up to the table.* 2 to drive, move a vehicle. *The car pulled out of the entrance.* 3 to attract interest or support. *Their concerts always pull big crowds.* 4 to injure. *He pulled a muscle in the race.* **pull a face** to make a strange or funny face. **pull apart** to separate by using force. **pull down** 1 to make something lower. *Pull the blind down if the sun bothers you.* 2 to destroy a building, usually to build a new one. **pull in** 1 to drive a car somewhere and stop. *We pulled in at the petrol station.* 2 to arrive at a station. *The train from London has just pulled in.* **pull off** 1 to take clothes off quickly. *He pulled off his boots.* 2 to succeed in a difficult situation. *He managed to pull the trick off.* **pull out** 1 to take something out. *The dentist pulled out a tooth.* 2 to move or drive out of a place. *The train pulled out of the station.* 3 When you pull out of an agreement, you get out of it. **pull through** to recover from a serious illness or accident. *She was very ill, but fortunately she pulled through.* **pull yourself together** to control your feelings and behave in a sensible way.

A pulley is an essential mechanism on any crane.

AMAZING FACT

In humans, pulse rates between 50 and 85 beats per minute are considered normal. Generally, the normal rate for men is about 72 beats per minute, for women the normal range is 76–80 beats. Children's pulse rates are faster.

You can take your own pulse by gently gripping your wrist with the fingertips of your other hand. Use a watch to count the number of beats per minute. Try taking your pulse after various activites.

WORD HISTORY

You might think that the name of the drink 'punch' came from its power or zing. In fact, it has nothing to do with this. The origin is the Sanskrit word 'panca', meaning five. The number refers to the five ingredients that traditionally went into punch: wine, water, sugar, spice and fruit juice.

pulley *noun* a wheel over which a rope or chain is moved, used for lifting heavy things.

pulp *noun* 1 the soft inner part of a fruit or vegetable. 2 a soft mass of other material. *Wood pulp.* 3 cheap books and magazines. **pulp** *verb* to crush.

pulpit *noun* a small platform for the preacher in a church.

pulse *noun* 1 the regular beating of blood as it is pumped through the body by the heart. You can feel your pulse when you touch your wrists. 2 the regular beat or throbbing of music. **pulse** *verb* to beat or shake with strong, regular movements.

pulverize *verb* 1 to crush into or become fine powder. 2 to destroy. *The town was pulverized by shelling.*

puma (say **pew**-muh) *noun* a large brown wild cat of western America, also called a cougar or mountain lion.

The puma pricked up her ears to hear a rustling in the grass.

pump *noun* a machine with a tube for forcing liquid, air or gas into or out of something. *A petrol pump.* **pump** *verb* 1 to force liquid or air into or from something with a pump. *Her heart was pumping fast. I must pump up my tyres.* 2 to get information, usually by asking questions. *He pumped me about my new job.* 3 to force something into somebody or something. *They have pumped a lot of money into the business.*

pumpkin *noun* a large round fruit with a hard orange skin. People hollow out pumpkins to make lanterns at Halloween.

pun *noun* an amusing use of words that have the same sound but different meanings.

punch *verb* 1 to hit hard with a fist. *He punched him in the stomach.* 2 to make a hole in something. **punch** (punches) *noun* 1 a hit with a fist. *The boxer had to take a lot of punches.* 2 a tool for making holes, especially in paper or leather. 3 a drink made of wine and fruit juice.

P

punchline *noun* the last few words in a joke that make it funny.

punctual *adjective* doing things at the right or fixed time. *He is always punctual, never even a minute late.* **punctually** *adverb.*

punctuate *verb* 1 to put full stops, commas and other punctuation marks in text. 2 to interrupt from time to time, especially a speech. **punctuation** *noun.*

puncture *noun* a small hole made by a sharp object, especially in a tyre. **puncture** *verb* to make or get a puncture. *A nail in the road must have punctured my tyre.*

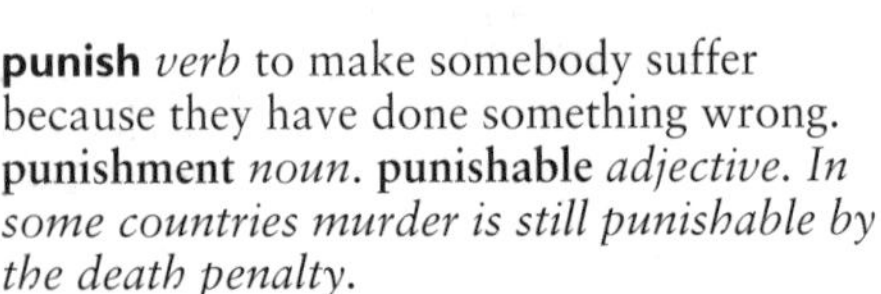

Peter drove into the bonfire and punctured his tyre on a nail.

punish *verb* to make somebody suffer because they have done something wrong. **punishment** *noun.* **punishable** *adjective. In some countries murder is still punishable by the death penalty.*

Punjabi *noun* the language of the Punjab, an area in north-western India and Pakistan. **Punjabi** *adjective. The Punjabi people.*

punt *noun* a flat-bottomed boat pushed along by a pole. **punt** *verb* to travel in a punt. *Let's go punting on the river.*

punt *verb* to kick a ball by dropping it from the hands on to the foot. **punt** *noun.*

punter *noun* 1 a person who bets money, especially on horse races. 2 (slang) a customer. *It's what the punters want.*

pupa (pupae) *noun* (say **pew**-puh) an insect in a covering between the time when it creeps and the time when it flies.

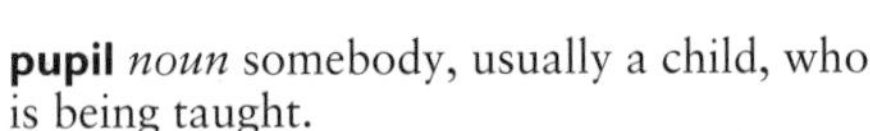

The pupa was waiting to hatch out into a fully-fledged insect.

pupil *noun* somebody, usually a child, who is being taught.

pupil *noun* the small, round black opening in the middle of the coloured part of the eye. *Her pupils dilated.*

puppet *noun* 1 a doll you can move by pulling strings that are fixed to it, or by putting your hand inside its body (called a glove puppet). 2 somebody whose actions are controlled by others. *He is the politicians' puppet.*

AMAZING FACT

Puppies are blind when they are born. Their vision improves as they mature but even when they are fully grown, they are near-sighted and don't see things in colour, just shades of gray.

WORD HISTORY

What's the connection between somebody being taught and the middle of the eye? They are both called 'pupils', but why? They actually come from the same Latin words, 'pupillus' or 'pupilla', meaning little boy or girl. A pupil in school is a boy or girl. The word came to refer to the eye because of the tiny reflection you get of yourself when you look closely into someone else's eye – you see a tiny boy or girl!

puppy (puppies) *noun* a young dog.

The puppies looked identical.

purchase *verb* to buy. **purchase** *noun* 1 something bought. *Most of her purchases were clothes.* 2 buying. *Do you remember the date of purchase?* 3 a firm hold for pulling or stopping something from slipping. *His hands lost their purchase and he fell into the precipice.*

pure *adjective* 1 not mixed with anything else, clean and clear. 2 complete, total. *The hotel is pure luxury.* **purity** *noun.*

purge *verb* to get rid of unwanted people or feelings. *I'll purge this town of crime.*

purple *adjective, noun* reddish-blue.

purpose *noun* 1 a plan, a reason for doing something. *What is the purpose of this machine?* 2 a feeling of having an aim, willpower. *Teaching has given her a sense of purpose.* **on purpose** intentionally, not by accident. *She bumped into him on purpose.*

purr *verb* to make a low sound like a cat when it is pleased. **purr** *noun.*

purse *noun* a small bag for money.

purse *verb* to draw your lips together into a rounded shape. *She pursed her lips in distaste at the horrible smell.*

pus *noun* (say puhss) a thick yellowish liquid that comes out of an infected wound or other part of the body.

push *verb* 1 to press using force in order to make something or somebody move away or to a different position. *He pushed the window up.* 2 to make your way through something by using force. *Don't push in front of me.* 3 to force somebody to do something or force something on people. *The advertisers are pushing a new drink.* 4 to try to sell something illegal. *To push drugs.* **push ahead** to carry out. *We are pushing ahead with the new building.* **push for** to try to get. **push in** to come into a queue in front of other people. **push off** to go away. **push on** to continue to travel or work. **push** (pushes) *noun* 1 the action of pushing. 2 drive or energy. **to get the push** to be dismissed from your job. **to give somebody the push** to end a relationship. *Her boyfriend gave her the push last week.* **at a push** if really necessary, if forced. *I can finish the essay by next week at a push.*

pushy *adjective* unpleasantly keen to get things done so as to make yourself noticed.

pussyfoot *verb* to act very cautiously.

put (puts, putting, put) *verb* 1 to move, place, lay or fix something or somebody in a certain place or position. *Put your bike in the garage.* 2 to cause something or somebody to be in a particular state. *The news put her in a good mood.* 3 to express something in words or write something down. *She put it rather cleverly.* 4 to give money for something, or time or energy to something. *They only put £100 into the business.* **put across** to describe or explain something to somebody. **put away** to put something into a place where it is usually kept. If somebody is put away, they are sent to prison. **put something off** not to do something until later. **put somebody off** 1 to not see somebody until later than planned. 2 to make somebody dislike something or lose interest. *The smell puts me off fish.* **put on** 1 to make a light or piece of equipment work. *To put a CD on.* 2 *He put on his clothes.* 3 to pretend to be something or behave in an unnatural way. *She only puts on that shy voice.* 4 to add more to something. *She has put on weight.* **put out** 1 to stop a candle or fire from burning, to stop a light shining. 2 to make something known. *They put out a warning.* 3 to place things that are needed somewhere ready to be used. *I put out a clean shirt for you.* 4 to annoy or upset. *I was put out when everybody laughed at me.* **put up** 1 to build. *We put up a new fence.* 2 to give somebody a place to sleep. *We can put up your friends.* 3 to raise or unfold. *She put up her hand.* 4 to fix. *To put up a poster.* 5 to provide. *Who is putting up the money for the event?* 6 to increase. *Petrol prices have been put up.* **put up to** If you put somebody up to something, you tell them to do something foolish. **put up with** to accept something or somebody unpleasant, to suffer without complaining. *She puts up with a lot of trouble to keep her job.*

AMAZING FACT

Making your own crossword puzzles is a good way to practice spelling and helps you remember the meaning of words. Make a grid on a sheet of paper. Start with a longish word either across or down the page. Then add words to it, using a letter from the original word. Write short definitions as clues.

WORD HISTORY

The word 'pyjamas' originally referred to just the trousers. The word comes from the Persian 'pay' and 'jama', meaning leg clothing.

putrid (say pew-trid) *adjective* rotting and smelling bad. *Putrid vegetation.*

putty *noun* a soft paste used to fix glass into window frames or fill holes.

puzzle *noun* 1 a game or toy. *A jigsaw puzzle.* 2 a difficult question, problem or something that is hard to understand. *Why she wants to go there is a puzzle to me.* **puzzle** (puzzles, puzzling, puzzled) *verb* to make somebody feel confused because they do not understand. **puzzle out** to think hard to try and find an answer. **puzzle over** to think hard about something confusing. **puzzlement** *noun.*

Muriel is addicted to crossword puzzles.

pyjamas *plural noun* a loose top and trousers worn for sleeping in.

pylon *noun* a tall metal structure used for holding wires that carry electricity over long distances. *Electricity pylons.*

Pyongyang *noun* the capital of North Korea.

pyramid *noun* 1 a shape with a flat base and three or four sloping sides that come to a point at the top. 2 an ancient Egyptian stone building over the tombs of the kings and queens of Egypt in a pyramid shape.

The ancient Egyptians buried their dead on the west bank of the Nile, where the Sun sets, and built their homes on the east bank, where it rises.

pyrotechnics *noun* 1 the art of making fireworks. 2 a fireworks display.

python *noun* a large snake that kills by winding its body round animals and squeezing them.

Qq

Qatar *noun* a country in Southwest Asia.

quack *verb* to make the harsh sound that a duck makes. **quack** *noun.*

quadrangle *noun* 1 a four-sided shape. 2 a four-sided area or courtyard with buildings all around it.

quadrant *noun* 1 a quarter of a circle. 2 an instrument for measuring vertical angles.

quadri- *prefix* four.

quadrilateral *noun* a flat shape with four straight sides.

quadruped *noun* any animal with four legs.

quadruple *verb* to multiply by four. *My wages have quadrupled in the last ten years.* **quadruple** *noun.*

quadruplet *noun* one of four babies born at the same time to the same mother (quad for short). *The quadruplets were doing fine.*

quagmire *noun* a very soft, marshy area of land. *I got bogged down in a quagmire.*

quail *verb* to show fear by trembling.

quail *noun* a small, plump bird related to the partridge, often shot as game.

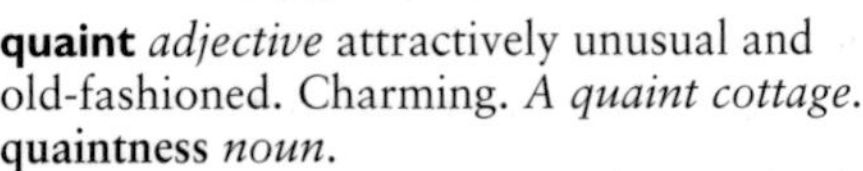

Quail eggs are very popular as starters.

quaint *adjective* attractively unusual and old-fashioned. Charming. *A quaint cottage.* **quaintness** *noun.*

quake *verb* to shake, to tremble. *Quentin quaked with fear at the sight of the ghost.*

qualification *noun* your skills or the training you have had that make you suitable to do a certain job.

qualify (qualifies, qualifying, qualified) *verb* 1 to be suitable for a job, especially by passing a test or exam to reach a certain standard. *Karen has qualified as a vet.* 2 to obtain enough points to go on to the next part of a competition etc. 3 to limit. To make a remark less strong. *He qualified his remark that all his pupils are lazy and said only some are lazy.*

WORD HISTORY

The shape of the letter Q comes from an ancient Egyptian symbol for monkey. The sound probably came from 'qoph', a Semitic word for monkey. The Greeks called it 'koppa'.

AMAZING FACT

Qatar is an 'emirate' or nation that is ruled by a monarch called an 'emir'. Oil was discovered in Qatar in the 1940s.

AMAZING FACT

The biggest quarry in the world is in Utah. It is the Bingham Copper Mine. It is approximately 770 metres deep.

quality *noun* 1 how good or bad something is. *The sound quality is very poor.* 2 what somebody or something is like. Good characteristics. *His best quality is his cheerfulness.*

qualm *noun* (sounds like harm) a feeling of unease or doubt.

quandary *noun* uncertainty. *I'm in a quandary – should I go or should I stay?*

quantity *noun* an amount or number of things. *A large quantity of fodder.* **in quantity** in large amounts.

quantum leap *noun* a dramatic advance. *A quantum leap in space research.*

quarantine *noun* a period when a person or an animal that may be carrying a disease is kept away from others to prevent the disease from spreading.

quarrel (quarrels, quarrelling, quarrelled) *verb* to have an angry argument or disagreement with somebody. To stop being friendly. **quarrel** *noun.* **quarrelsome** *adjective. Quarrelsome children.*

quarry *noun* 1 a place where sand or stone is dug out of the ground for building etc. **quarry** *verb.* 2 an animal that is being hunted. Prey.

quart *noun* a measure of liquid equal to 2 pints or .95 litres.

quarter *noun* 1 one of four equal parts into which something can be divided. A fourth. 2 three months. 3 (in Canada and USA) a 25-cent coin. 4 a district of a city. *The Chinese quarter.* 5 **quarters** a place to stay. *Officers' living quarters.* **quarterly** *adjective* happening every three months. *A quarterly magazine.*

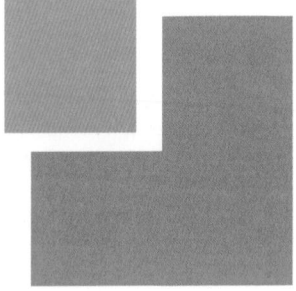

The green square is a quarter of the size of the mauve square.

quartet *noun* 1 a group of four singers or players. 2 a piece of music written for four musicians.

quartz *noun* a crystal-like mineral used in electronic equipment.

quasi- *prefix* almost or seeming to be. *Quasi-official, quasi-scientific.*

quaver *verb* to speak in a trembling voice because of fear or nervousness. **quaver** *noun. There was a quaver in her voice.*

quaver *noun* a note in music equal in length to a quarter of a minim or half a crotchet.

Q

quay *noun* (say key) a place in a harbour for boats to load and unload.

The fishing boats bobbed on the water by the quay.

queasy (queasier, queasiest) *adjective* a feeling that you are going to be sick. **queasiness** *noun*.

queen *noun* 1 a female ruler of a country or the wife of a king. A monarch. Queens are not elected but either inherit their position by succeeding the previous ruler or marry a king. 2 a playing card with the picture of a queen on it. 3 a chesspiece that can move in any direction. **queen mother** the widowed mother of a reigning king or queen.

queer *adjective* strange, unusual.

quell *verb* to prevent by squashing. *The police quelled the riots.*

quench *verb* 1 to drink enough to satisfy your thirst. 2 to put out a fire.

query *noun* a question, a doubt. **query** (queries, querying, queries) *verb*.

quest *noun* a thorough search.

question *noun* 1 what you ask when you want to find out about something. 2 a problem. *The question of finance.* **question** *verb*. *The police questioned her for hours.*

question mark *noun* a punctuation mark (?) that is put at the end of a question.

questionnaire *noun* a list of questions to be answered by a number of people as part of a report etc.

queue *noun* (sounds like cue) a waiting line of people or vehicles. **queue** *verb*. *People are queuing to get into the stadium.*

quibble *noun* a small, unimportant point not really worth arguing about. *Don't quibble!*

quiche *noun* (say **key**-sh) a pastry tart with a filling of beaten egg, cheese, ham etc.

quick *adjective* 1 moving rapidly, fast. 2 done in a short time. *A quick and tasty snack.* 3 fast to understand, lively. *A quick brain.* **quickness** *noun*.

quicksand *noun* dangerously wet sand into which you can sink if you walk on it.

quicksilver *noun* the liquid metal mercury.

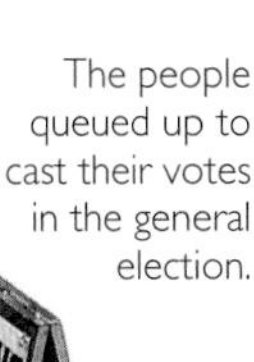

The people queued up to cast their votes in the general election.

GRAMMAR NOTE

Take care how you use 'quite', because this little word can mean 'very' or 'rather'. 'This cake is quite good' could mean fairly good but not very good. But there is no doubt about 'This cake is quite excellent'. So it might be quite a good idea to avoid using 'quite', if it's going to cause offence.

quid *noun* (slang) a pound in British money (£1). *Can you lend me a quid?*

quiet *adjective* 1 without much noise. Silent. 2 calm or without movement. *A quiet life in the country.* **quietness** *noun*.

quill *noun* 1 one of the sharp spines on a hedgehog or porcupine. 2 a long, strong feather used as a pen.

quilt *noun* a light bed covering filled with warm soft material.

quintet *noun* 1 a group of five singers or players. 2 a piece of music written for five musicians. *A string quintet.*

The quintet played some lively music at the dance.

quintuplet *noun* one of five babies born at the same time to the same mother (quin for short). *The quintuplets were a surprise.*

quip *noun* a witty and often cutting remark.

quit (quits, quitting, quitted or quit) *verb* 1 to give up or stop doing something. *She quit smoking.* 2 to go away.

quite *adverb* 1 totally. *I'm quite sure you are right.* 2 to some extent, rather. *It was quite a good meal.*

Quito *noun* the capital of Ecuador.

quiver *verb* to shake slightly but quickly. *Her lip quivered and she started to cry.*

quiver *noun* a long container for arrows.

quiz *noun* a game in which people are asked questions to test their knowledge. *Sue got all the answers right and won the quiz.*

quota *noun* a share of something.

quotation *noun* a person's words repeated exactly by somebody else, a passage from a play or book for example.

quotation marks *plural noun* the punctuation marks (') or ("") used before and after words somebody has said or to highlight words. *'What did you say?' she asked. 'Nothing,' I replied.*

quote *verb* 1 to repeat words that were first said or spoken by somebody else. *He quoted some lines from Shakespeare.* 2 to give a price. *The shop quoted me a price for mending my bike.*

Qu'ran another spelling for Koran.

Rr

Rabat *noun* the capital of Morocco.

rabbi *noun* a Jewish religious leader and teacher. *The rabbi prayed in the synagogue.*

rabbit *noun* a small furry animal with long ears that lives in a hole (called a burrow) in the ground.

rabble *noun* a crowd of noisy people.

rabies *noun* a disease passed on by a bite that makes people and animals go mad and die. *He was bitten by a fox and got rabies.*

raccoon *noun* a small furry animal from North America with a long tail.

race *noun* a competition to see who is the fastest. **race** *verb* 1 to take part in a race. *I'll race you to the end of the road and back again.* 2 to go very quickly.

As they came round the bend into the last lap of the race, Nigel moved into the lead.

race *noun* a group of people with the same ancestors and history, or a division of people with a type of body or colour of skin. The human race. Race relations are the relationships between people of different races who live in the same country.

racial *adjective* relating to people's race. **racially** *adverb. Racially different.*

racist *noun* a person who does not like people from other races because he thinks his own race is the best. **racist** *adjective. Racist remarks.* **racism** *noun.*

rack *noun* 1 a framework with bars, pegs or shelves for holding things or hanging things on. *A plate rack.* 2 a shelf for luggage in a train or bus. 3 an instrument used in the Middle Ages for torturing people by stretching them. **rack** *verb* to hurt a lot. *He left his family for another woman and was racked with guilt.* **rack your brain** to try hard to think of something.

racket *noun* a bat with strings across it for playing tennis, squash or badminton.

SPELLING NOTE

Be careful about the difference between the adjectives 'racial', which refers to race, and 'racist', which refers to racism and so is offensive.

SPELLING NOTE

The word 'radar' is an acronym, which means that is made up of the initial letters of other words. It comes from 'radio detection' and 'ranging'. The system was developed during the 1930s.

racket *noun* 1 a loud noise. 2 a dishonest way of making money, a swindle.

racoon *noun* see raccoon.

radar *noun* a way of finding the position or speed of objects that cannot be seen by using radio signals that show on a screen. *The plane was last seen on radar.*

radiant *adjective* 1 sending out light or heat. *The radiant Sun.* 2 looking very happy. *She looked radiant on her wedding day.*

radiate *verb* to send out light, heat or happiness. **radiation** *noun. Exposure to radiation can cause serious illness and even death.* **radiate from** to spread out from a central point in many directions.

radiator *noun* 1 an apparatus, usually connected to a central heating system, used for heating buildings. 2 a device that keeps a car's engine cool.

radio (radios) *noun* 1 a method of sending or receiving sound through the air by means of electrical waves. 2 a piece of equipment, a radio set, for listening to radio programmes. 3 broadcasting of programmes. *She works in radio.* **radio** *verb. The ship radioed for help.*

radioactive *adjective* Something is radioactive if it has atoms that break up and send out radiation in the form of rays that can be harmful to living things. *After the reactor accident there was radioactive dust in the air.* **radioactivity** *noun.*

radish *noun* a small red vegetable that is eaten raw.

radius *noun* 1 the distance, a straight line, from the centre of a circle to its outside edge. A circle's radius is half its diameter. 2 the distance from a particular central point where something happens or exists. *All citizens living within a three-mile radius of the town centre are allowed free bus travel.*

The radius of the circle is shown by the green line from the centre to the circumference.

raft *noun* 1 logs tied together and used as a boat. 2 an inflatable rubber boat. *The raft saved Jane's life.*

rag *noun* 1 a small, usually torn piece of cloth. 2 a badly written newspaper. 3 a student carnival held to raise money for charity. **rag** (rags, ragging, ragged) *verb* to make fun of, tease.

rage *noun* 1 a strong uncontrollable anger. 2 the latest fashion. *Snowboarding is all the rage.* **rage** *verb* 1 to be very angry. 2 to be very violent. *The storm raged all night.*

R

raid *noun* 1 a sudden attack on an enemy. 2 an unexpected visit by the police. **raid** *verb* to make a raid. *The police raided the minister's office.* **raider** *noun.*

rail *noun* 1 a fixed bar to hang things on or hold on to, or forming part of a fence. *Put the towel on the rail.* 2 one of a pair of metal bars that a train runs on. **by rail** in a train.

railing *noun* (usually plural, railings) a fence made from metal bars. *The child got his head stuck in the railings.*

railway *noun* 1 the track or route between two places on which trains run. 2 a system of rail transport and the organization operating that system.

rain *noun* drops of water that fall from clouds. **rain** *verb* 1 to fall as rain. *It's raining.* 2 to fall like rain. *Tears rained down her cheeks.*

rainbow *noun* an arch of colours that you can sometimes see in the sky when the Sun shines through rain.

Some people say that a crock of gold is buried at the rainbow's end.

raincoat *noun* a waterproof coat that is worn in the rain. *Put on your raincoat, because it's pouring down outside.*

rainfall *noun* the amount of rain that falls in a place in a certain time. *The Atacama Desert in Chile has the lowest rainfall of any place on Earth.*

rainforest *noun* a tropical forest with tall trees in which it rains a lot.

DID YOU KNOW

Because the Islamic calendar is based on the Moon, Ramadan falls at different times of the year. Muslims celebrate Ramadan as the month during which the prophet Muhammad received the first of the revelations that make up the Koran, the holy book of Islam. Fasting during Ramadan is one of the chief duties of a Muslim. It is also a time for other religious activities, and nights are often devoted to special prayers and readings from the Koran.

The world's rainforests are home to many species of plants and animals that may hold the key to health cures of the future.

raise *verb* 1 to move to a higher position. *Raise the flag.* 2 to increase in amount or level. *To raise prices.* 3 to manage to get something together. *The school raised £100 for charity.* 4 to bring up a child, breed animals. 5 to bring up for discussion or attention. *I'm sorry to have to raise the question of money.* 6 to make appear. *It raised doubts in my mind.* **raise** *noun* an increase in salary. *They offered me a raise if I would stay in my job, but I didn't accept.*

rake *noun* a gardening tool with a row of metal teeth attached to a long handle. **rake** *verb* to collect or make smooth with a rake. *He raked the leaves into a pile.* **rake up** 1 to collect. 2 to talk about something unpleasant that should be forgotten. *She kept raking up the past until it drove him out of his mind with guilt.*

rally (rallies) *noun* 1 a large public meeting in support of something. *A peace rally.* 2 a car or cycling competition. 3 a series of shots players exchange in tennis or badminton. **rally** (rallies, rallying, rallied) *verb* 1 to come together in support of something. *My friends rallied round and helped me when I was ill.* 2 to become stronger again, recover.

ram *noun* a male sheep. *The ram with the curly horns can be quite aggressive.*

ram *noun* a device for pushing something. **ram** (rams, ramming, rammed) *verb* to push with great force. *He rammed the post hard into the ground.*

RAM *abbreviation* random-access memory. The amount of memory in a computer that is available and stored directly.

Ramadan *noun* the ninth month of the Muslim year, when no food or drink may be taken between sunrise and sunset. *They sat in the market place waiting for the Sun to go down, so they could eat a bowl of soup.*

ramble *noun* a long walk, often in the country. **ramble** *verb* 1 to go for a ramble. 2 to talk or write in a confused way. *My grandmother often rambles and says strange things.* **rambler** *noun.* **ramble on** to talk for a long time without sticking to the subject.

R

ramp *noun* a slope used instead of a step or stairs. *She pushed his wheelchair up the ramp so fast that he nearly fell out of it.*

rampart *noun* a wide bank of earth built to protect a fort or city.

ramshackle *adjective* badly made and needing repair. *A ramshackle old shed.*

ran *verb* past tense of run.

ranch (ranches) *noun* a cattle-farm in North or South America. **rancher** *noun.*

Jeff herded the cattle on his uncle's ranch.

rancid *adjective* tasting or smelling unpleasant, especially fatty food. *The smell of rancid butter makes me feel sick.*

random *adjective* made or done without any plan. *A random selection of CDs.* **at random** without any plan or pattern. *He asked us questions at random.*

rang *verb* past tense of ring.

range *noun* 1 a connected series of hills or mountains. 2 the distance at which you can see or hear or that a gun can shoot. *Within range, out of range.* 3 a number of different things of the same kind. *We sell a wide range of gardening tools.* 4 the limits that can be measured between two points, the distance between which things vary. *The age range is from 20 to 30.* 5 grassy land in North America for grazing or hunting. 6 an area for shooting practice. 7 a large stove for cooking. **range** *verb* 1 to reach from one limit to another, to vary within limits. *Sizes range from small to extra large.* 2 to place or arrange. 3 to wander.

The distant mountain range was covered in snow.

ranger *noun* somebody who looks after a park or forest. *A forest ranger.*

Rangoon *noun* the capital of Myanmar.

rank *noun* 1 a position or grade in an organization. *He holds the rank of general.* 2 a line of people or things. *A taxi rank.* **rank** *verb* to put or be in a position on a scale. *I rank him as one of the best of the new breed of American writers.*

DID YOU KNOW

The city of Rangoon is also sometimes called Yangon. And the country of which it is capital has the official name Myanmar, but is often called by its old name of Burma. Rangoon became the capital in 1886, and was badly damaged in World War II when it was occupied by the Japanese. A famous golden temple in Rangoon, called the Shwe Dagon Pagoda, is Myanmar's holiest Buddhist shrine.

ransack *verb* 1 to search a place thoroughly, usually leaving it in a mess. *The police ransacked the building in their search for clues.* 2 to search and rob a place.

ransom *noun* a sum of money that has to be paid to free a kidnapped person. **hold to ransom** to keep somebody as a prisoner until money is paid for them to be set free. **ransom** *verb* to set somebody free in exchange for a ransom.

rap *noun* 1 the sound of a quick hit or knock against something. 2 blame or punishment. *I'm always taking the rap.* 3 rhymes with a backing of rock music. **rap** *verb* 1 to hit something quickly and lightly. *He rapped him on the knuckles.* 2 to speak in rhymes with a rock music backing.

rape *verb* to perfoem intercourse against someone's will. **rape** *noun.* **rapist** *noun.*

rapid *adjective* quick. **rapidly** *adverb. The town is growing rapidly.*

rapier *noun* a thin, light sword.

rare *adjective* 1 uncommon, not often found or happening. *A rare plant.* 2 lightly cooked. *I like my steak rare.* **rarely** *adverb* not often. *We rarely go to the cinema.* **rarity** *noun.*

Pandas are now quite rare, because the clearance of bamboo forests has deprived them of their major food source.

rash *adjective* acting foolishly without thinking first. *Don't make rash promises.* **rashly** *adverb.* **rashness** *noun.*

rash (rashes) *noun* an outbreak of small red spots on the skin, caused by an illness or allergy. *An itchy heat rash.*

rasher *noun* a slice of bacon.

raspberry (raspberries) *noun* a small soft red fruit that grows on bushes.

rat *noun* 1 an animal with a long tail that looks like a large mouse. 2 a nasty, untrustworthy person.

Rats are rodents that can carry disease in the wild, though some people love them as pets.

rate *noun* 1 speed. *We were travelling at a steady rate.* 2 an amount, value, cost or speed measured by comparing it to some other amount. *The unemployment rate.* 3 a charge. *Postage rates are rising.* **at any rate** in any case. **at this rate** if things go on in the same way as now. *He'll never find a job at this rate.* **rate** *verb* to consider, to put a value on something. *How do you rate my chances of passing the test?*

rather *adverb* 1 to a slight extent or to a large extent. *It's rather cold today.* 2 more willingly, in preference. *I would rather not say.* 3 more exactly. *I went to bed late last night – or rather, early this morning.* 4 to a greater degree. *I'm looking for something practical rather than fashionable.*

ratio (say **ray**-shee-oh) *noun* the relationship between two numbers or amounts which shows how much greater one is than the other. If there are ten applicants for every five jobs, the ratio of applicants to jobs is two to one.

ration *noun* a fixed amount allowed to one person. *I've eaten my ration of chocolate for this week.* **ration** *verb* 1 to limit somebody to a ration. 2 to limit something. *During the hot weather water was rationed.*

rational *adjective* 1 sensible. *There must be a rational explanation.* 2 able to think, make decisions and judgements. *She's usually a very rational person.* **rationally** *adverb.* **rationality** *noun.*

rat-race *noun* a competitive struggle for success or power.

rattle *noun* 1 short, sharp sounds. 2 a baby's toy that makes a rattling sound. **rattle** *verb* 1 to make short, sharp sounds. *The windows rattled in the wind.* 2 to make somebody nervous. *She gets rattled if you ask her too many questions.* **rattle off** to say something quickly without thinking. *She rattled off the answers automatically.* **rattle on** to continue to talk quickly and without thinking.

rattlesnake *noun* a poisonous American snake that makes a rattling noise with its tail. *He was bitten by a rattlesnake.*

A number of hard rings at the end of the rattlesnake's tail make a rattling noise when shaken together.

raucous (say **raw**-kus) *adjective* loud and unpleasant, especially of voices. *There was a lot of raucous shouting.*

rave *verb* 1 to talk wildly and in an uncontrolled way. *He had a high temperature and was raving all night.* 2 to talk or write enthusiastically about something. **rave** *noun.*

rave-up *noun* a wild party.

WORD HISTORY

The adjective 'ravenous' has nothing to do with the bird called a raven. 'Ravenous' comes from Latin and old French words meaning 'on the prowl for prey', presumably because the prowling person or animal is very hungry.

SPELLING NOTE

The prefix 're–' is usually spelt with a hyphen before a word that begins with an 'e', such as 're-enact', or if it could be confused with another word (to re-form means to form again, to reform is to make or become better).

raven *noun* a large black bird. **raven** *adjective* glossy black. *Raven hair.*

ravenous *adjective* very hungry.

ravine *noun* a very deep, narrow valley.

raw *adjective* 1 not cooked. 2 in the natural state, not treated. *Raw materials.* 3 untrained, new to the job. 4 without skin. *Her fingers were rubbed raw.* 5 cold and wet, especially of weather. **rawness** *noun.*

raw deal *noun* unfair treatment.

ray *noun* 1 a beam of heat, light or energy. *The rays of the Sun.* 2 a small amount. *A ray of hope.* 3 one of a number of lines radiating out from the centre of something.

razor *noun* an instrument used for shaving hair from the skin.

re- *prefix* again. *He remarried last year.*

reach *verb* 1 to arrive at, to get to. *When did the news reach you?* 2 to stretch out a hand to get or touch something. *Can you reach the tin on the top shelf?* **reach** (reaches) *noun* 1 the distance that you can reach. *Put the bottle out of her reach.* 2 the length of an arm. *Sebastian has a very long reach.* 3 a straight stretch of a river between two bends.

She reached up to the top of the cupboard where she hid the children's presents.

react *verb* to behave in a particular way because of something, to behave differently as a result. *How did your boss react when he heard about the strike?* **reaction** *noun.* 1 an effect produced by an earlier action. 2 a change in one chemical substance caused by another. *A chemical reaction.*

reactionary *adjective* against changes in society. **reactionary** *noun.*

reactor *noun* a machine used to produce nuclear energy.

read (reads, reading, read) *verb* (say red) 1 to look at and understand or say out loud something written or printed. *He plays lots of instruments, but he can't read music.* 2 to judge how somebody feels. *I can read her mind.* 3 to say. *The sign reads 'Exit'.* 4 to show, register. *The thermometer reads 35 degrees.* 5 to study. *He is reading English at Oxford.* **read up** to find out about something by reading about it. **readable** *adjective* interesting and easy to read. **reader** *noun.* **reading** *noun. Children learn reading and writing at school.*

R

ready (readier, readiest) *adjective* 1 prepared, able to be used or do something. *Lunch is ready.* 2 willing to do something. *She's always ready to help.* 3 about to do something. *She was ready to cry.* 4 quick and prepared. *My sister always has a ready answer.* 5 easily reached. *Have your tickets ready.* **readiness** *noun.*

real *adjective* actually existing, not imaginary or artificial. *Real pearls.*

realistic *adjective* 1 practical, based on actual facts. *Their prices are realistic.* 2 like people or things in real life. *A realistic painting.* **realism** *noun.*

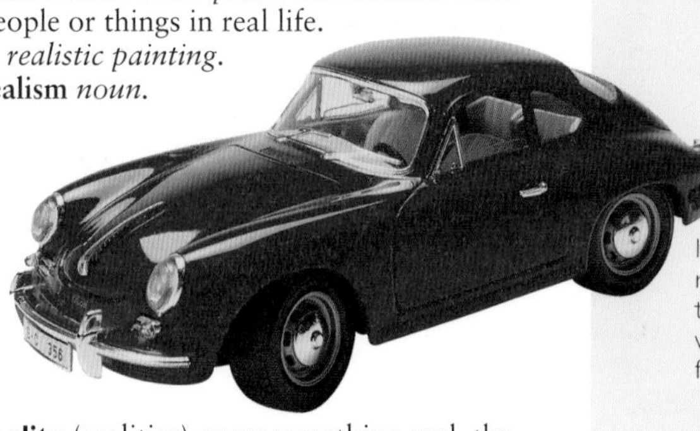

It was not very realistic of Malcolm to want a sportscar when he had a family of five.

reality (realities) *noun* something real, the truth. *He tries to escape reality by going to the cinema.* **in reality** in actual fact.

realize *verb* 1 to understand, to become aware of something. *I never realized that she was your mother.* 2 to make a hope or plan happen. *He realized his dreams of becoming an actor.* 3 to get money by selling something. **realization** *noun.*

really *adverb* 1 truly, without doubt. *It's really hot today.* 2 used for showing interest, doubt or surprise. *'I saw a film all about Batman yesterday.' 'Really?'*

realm *noun* (say relm) 1 a kingdom. 2 an area of thought or knowledge. *Fairies exist only in the realm of fantasy.*

reap *verb* 1 to cut down and gather. *We reaped the harvest.* 2 to gain as a result of something done. *One day she'll reap the benefit of all that hard work.*

The summer was very hot that year and everyone reaped a good harvest.

rear *noun* the back part. *We were at the rear of the queue when it happened.* **rear** *adjective. The rear wheel.*

rear *verb* 1 to bring up a child or animal. 2 to lift up, or rise upright on its back legs. *The snake suddenly reared its head.*

AMAZING FACT

The saying, 'You reap what you sow' means that you get what you deserve in life. If you 'sow' or plant goodness by doing kind things, you will 'reap' benefits.

SPELLING NOTE

Note the spelling of 'receipt', 'receive' and 'receiver': it's 'ei', not 'ie'. An easy way to remember this is the saying 'I before E except after C,' but there are exceptions to the rule, such as 'weird'.

reason *noun* 1 a cause of an event, an explanation for an action. *What's the reason for the strike?* 2 the ability to think and make judgements, common sense. *He won't listen to reason.* **with reason** rightly. **reason** *verb* 1 to think carefully and decide. 2 to argue in order to persuade somebody to do something. *It was impossible to reason with the kidnappers.*

reasonable *adjective* 1 sensible. 2 fair, not too much. *An extremely reasonable price.* **reasonably** *adverb.*

rebel (rebels, rebelling, rebelled) *verb* (say rib-**el**) to fight or protest against anybody in power. *They rebelled against the government.* **rebel** *noun* (say **reb**-ul) somebody who rebels. *The rebels stormed the castle and killed the king.* **rebellious** *adjective.* **rebellion** *noun* fighting or opposition to anybody in power.

rebuke *verb* to give somebody a short telling off. *His boss rebuked him for not wearing a tie.* **rebuke** *noun.*

recall *verb* 1 to remember. 2 to ask somebody to come back. **recall** *noun.*

recede *verb* 1 to move back or further away. *His hair is receding and he will soon go completely bald.* 2 to become less clear.

As we took off in the helicopter, our home receded into the distance.

receipt *noun* (say ris-**eet**) 1 a piece of paper that states that money or goods have been received. *I will need a receipt for the payment.* 2 the act of receiving. *He rang the school on receipt of the letter.*

receive *verb* 1 to get or take something given or sent to you. *The news was received with horror.* 2 to suffer. *She received nasty injuries to the spine.* 3 to welcome a visitor. *We were very well received.*

receiver *noun* 1 the part of a telephone you speak into. *Pick up the receiver and dial this number.* 2 a person who receives something, especially stolen goods. 3 the part of a radio or television set that receives broadcasts. 4 a person officially appointed to take charge of a bankrupt business.

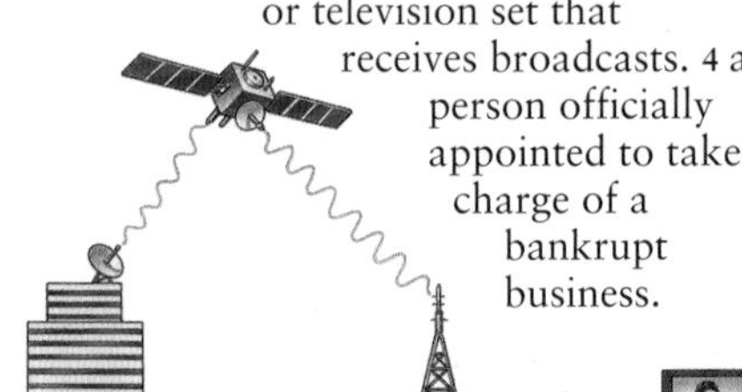

The satellite beamed the television programme to a receiver near Michael's home.

recent *adjective* having happened only a short time ago. *A recent discovery.* **recently** *adverb. I was at college until recently.*

reception *noun* 1 the way somebody or something is received, a welcome. *His new book got a very good reception.* 2 an office or place in a hotel or large organization where appointments, reservations and enquiries can be made. *She left her keys at reception when she went upstairs.* 3 a formal party. 4 the quality of receiving sounds or pictures from radio or television.

recess (recesses) *noun* 1 a period of time when work or business is stopped. *The judge announced a recess.* 2 a space in the wall of a room. *Let's put shelves in the recess.* 3 a hidden part that is difficult to reach. *The recesses of the mind.*

recession *noun* 1 a decline in wealth and economic success. *The government is doing its best to avoid recession.* 2 receding.

recipe *noun* instructions on how to make a particular dish, or something else. *It was a recipe for disaster to use Paul as designer.*

The recipe for winter vegetable soup called for lots of carrots and onions.

recital *noun* 1 a musical performance. *A piano recital.* 2 a detailed account.

recite *verb* to say something learned out loud. *She recited the poem in class.*

reckless *adjective* not caring about danger.

reckon *verb* 1 to consider. *It's reckoned to be one of his best books.* 2 to guess, feel confident. *I reckon he's a liar.* 3 to add up. *The rent is reckoned from the first of July.*

reclaim *verb* 1 to get something back that was taken away from you. 2 to make land ready for use again. *To reclaim land from the sea for agricultural use.*

recline *verb* to lean or lie back.

recognizable *adjective* easy to identify or recognize. *An easily recognizable style.*

recognize *verb* 1 to know what something is or who somebody is. 2 to be willing to agree, to see clearly. *The importance of his work has now been recognized.* 3 to accept as real, welcome or lawful. *The new government was not recognized by the people.* **recognition** *noun.*

WORD BUILDING

The nouns 'reception' and 'receipt' both come from the verb to 'receive'. The reception in a hotel is a place where people are received, and guests are also received at the formal party called a reception (such as a wedding reception).

WORD HISTORY

'Reckless' seems an odd word, because there is no 'reck' or 'reckful'. There used to be a verb 'reck', however, which meant to pay attention or take account. This has now gone out of use.

DID YOU KNOW

A square is a rectangle with four equal sides. A rectangle that is not a square can also be called an oblong.

recollect *verb* to remember.

recommend *verb* to say that somebody or something would be good or useful for a particular job. *I can recommend a good carpenter.* **recommendation** *noun.*

record *noun* (say **rek**-ord) 1 information, especially facts, either written down or stored on a computer. *She keeps a record of how much she spends.* 2 a disc on which sound, especially music, is stored. 3 the best yet done, especially in sport, or the most amazing achievement. *He broke the world record for 400 metres.* 4 facts known about the past or somebody's past life. *This aircraft has a good safety record.* **for the record** to be reported. **off the record** not to be written down or made known. **record** *verb* (say rik-**ord**) 1 to put something down in writing or on a computer. 2 to store sound or television pictures on disc or tape. *We recorded the programme, so we can watch it tomorrow.* **recording** *noun.*

The recording came out on CD as well as on tape.

recover *verb* 1 to become well again. *She is recovering from a very serious illness.* 2 to get something back after it is lost or taken away. **recovery** *noun.*

recruit *noun* a new member of an army, group or society. **recruit** *verb* to get new members. *Lots of people were recruited to put up tents in the field.*

rectangle *noun* a shape with four straight sides and four right angles. **rectangular** *adjective. A rectangular dish.*

recuperate *verb* to get better and become strong again after an illness.

recur (recurs, recurring, recurred) *verb* to happen again, either once or many times. **recurrence** *noun. A recurrence of illness.*

recycle *verb* to treat things that have already been used so that they can be used again. *To recycle newspapers and bottles.* **recyclable** *adjective. Some aluminium drinks cans are recyclable.*

R

red *noun* the colour of blood. **red** *adjective. Red wine.* **see red** to become very angry. **in the red** to have spent more money than is in your bank account. **red herring** something that takes people's attention away from what is important.

redundant *adjective* no longer needed because there is no work or something is no longer used. *The workers were all made redundant when the firm closed down.* **redundancy** *noun.*

refectory (refectories) *noun* the dining hall in a monastery or university.

The monks ate every day in the refectory.

refer (refers, referring, referred) *verb* 1 to speak about or mention. 2 to go to for information. *We were not allowed to refer to a dictionary in the exam.* 3 to send somebody or something, especially a problem, to somebody else for action. *He was referred to a specialist.*

reference *noun* 1 mentioning something. *There were a number of references to the trial in the paper.* 2 referring to somebody or something for information. A note that tells you where information can be found. *I use my computer for quick reference.* 3 a statement, usually a letter, about a person's character. *His old headmaster gave him a good reference.* **with reference to** regarding.

reference book *noun* a book for looking things up in. *Dictionaries, encyclopedias and other reference books.*

referendum *noun* a vote in which all the people in a country or area can decide on a particular political question.

refine *verb* 1 to make substances pure by taking out unwanted substances. *Refined sugar.* 2 to make more cultured. *Refined behaviour can sometimes be unfriendly.*

refinery (refineries) *noun* a factory where substances such as oil or sugar are refined.

reflection *noun* 1 the sending back of light, heat or sound from a surface. 2 an image of something in a mirror or shiny surface. *She looked at her reflection in the lake.* 3 a deep thought. *Reflections on old age.* 4 Something that makes a bad impression. *Hooliganism is a sad reflection on football.* 5 being the result of something. *His meanness is a reflection of his upbringing.* **on reflection** after thinking about something. **reflect** *verb.*

WORD HISTORY

A red herring was originally a specially prepared fish with a very strong smell. The dried smoked herring was used to train hunting dogs. It was pulled along the ground in front of the hounds to draw them away from the foxes' trail.

WORD BUILDING

A refugee is really a person who is seeking refuge. Both words come originally from the Latin for 'to flee'.

WORD HISTORY

'Regatta' is an Italian word that comes originally from the Venetian dialect. A famous regatta is still held on the canals of Venice every September.

reform *verb* to make or become better. *He reformed completely after giving up drink.* **reform** *noun Prison reforms.*

refrain *verb* to hold yourself back from doing something. *I refrained from having another drink in case I was sick.*

refrain *noun* part of a song that is repeated at the end of each verse.

refreshing *adjective* 1 pleasing and interesting, different from what you are used to. *It was refreshing to meet such helpful people.* 2 giving strength. *A most refreshing sleep.* **refresh** *verb.*

refreshments *plural noun* light food or drink. *Refreshments are served.*

refrigerator *noun* a large box or cupboard in which food and drinks are kept cool.

refuge *noun* a place that gives shelter and protection from trouble or danger. *The explorers found a refuge from the cold.*

refugee *noun* a person who has been forced to leave home, usually his or her country, because of war or disaster. *Refugees poured across the border after the earthquake.*

The refugees had walked many miles looking for shelter, taking it in turns to carry their baby.

refuse *verb* (say ri-**fewz**) to say 'no' to something, to not do or accept something. *She refused my offer of help.* **refusal** *noun.*

refuse *noun* (say **ref**-yooss) waste material, rubbish. *There is a weekly refuse collection.*

regal *adjective* (say **ree**-gul) suitable for a king or queen, splendid.

regatta *noun* a meeting for boat races.

region *noun* a large area, especially of land. *Forest regions.* **in the region of** about.

register *noun* 1 a list of things or names. *A register of births, deaths and marriages is kept in the register office.* 2 the range of a voice or musical instrument. **register** *verb* 1 to list something in a register. 2 to show on a scale, record. *The thermometer registered 35 degrees.* 3 to make something clear, usually a feeling or an opinion. *Her face registered fear.* 4 to send a letter or parcel by registered post. *To register a letter you have to pay extra, but it's worth it.*

regret (regrets, regretting, regretted) *verb* to feel sorry about something you have done or not done. *She regretted her mistakes all her life.* **regret** *noun.* **regrettable** *adjective.* **regretful** *adjective.*

regular *adjective* 1 happening, coming or doing something again and again at certain times. *Regular meals.* 2 evenly arranged or shaped, not varying. *Regular, white, shining teeth.* 3 normal, standard or proper. *That's not the regular procedure.* 4 A regular verb is a verb that follows the common pattern. The verb 'write' is not a regular verb. **regularly** *adverb.* **regularity** *noun.*

rehearse *verb* to practise something, especially a play, speech or music, before a performance. **rehearsal** *noun.*

reign *verb* (say rain) 1 to rule a country as a king or queen. 2 to exist. *Silence reigned.* **reign** *noun. During the reign of Queen Elizabeth.*

The coin was issued to commemorate the long reign of the king and queen.

rein *noun* a strap for guiding a horse. *Don't let go of the reins!*

reindeer (reindeer) *noun* a deer with large antlers that lives in the coldest parts of the world. *The people of Lapland herd reindeer.*

reinforce *verb* to make stronger. *Reinforced concrete is strengthened with metal bars.* **reinforcement** *noun.*

reject *verb* 1 to not accept a person or thing. *The machine rejects bent coins.* 2 to throw away or send back as not good enough. *The oranges were rotten and had to be rejected.* **rejection** *noun.*

rejoice *verb* to feel or show great happiness. *Rejoice and be merry!*

relapse *verb* to fall back into a worse state, to return to a previous condition, usually after having been better. **relapse** *noun.*

relate *verb* 1 to see or show a connection, to compare one thing with another. *It is difficult to relate these two results.* 2 to tell a story. 3 to get on with. *He cannot relate to children, not even his own.*

relation *noun* 1 a member of your family. 2 a connection. *There is no relation between her health and her results at school.* **relations** the dealings between people or groups. *Business relations with Germany.*

All the relations gathered together for the naming ceremony of the youngest family member.

AMAZING FACT

The English language has relatively few words for relatives compared to other languages. Many languages have different words for male and female cousins. Others have different terms for paternal or maternal aunts, uncles, or grandparents.

AMAZING FACT

The reindeer is the only deer in which both sexes have antlers.

relationship *noun* 1 how people and things are connected. *The relationship between light and heat.* 2 a family connection. *What is your brother's relationship to her?* 3 a friendship or the way people or groups behave towards each other. *She has never had a lasting relationship.*

relative *noun* a person who is related to another, a relation. *My aunt is my only living relative.*

relative *adjective* 1 compared to each other or to something else. 2 connected with. **relatively** *adverb. Relatively well off.*

relax *verb* 1 to become less stiff, tight or strict. *He relaxed his grip.* 2 to be more calm and rest. *After work I like to relax.*

relay *noun* 1 a relay race. 2 a fresh group taking over from a tired one. *We worked all through the night in relays.* 3 a piece of equipment that receives messages by telephone, television or radio and passes them on to another place. **relay** *verb* to pass on a message or broadcast.

relay race *noun* a team race in which each member runs part of the whole distance.

Clive handed the baton to Mark, who ran the next leg of the relay race.

release *verb* 1 to set free. *He was released from prison.* 2 to let your grip go. 3 to allow to be shown or published. *His new single will be released on Monday and shoot to the top of the charts.* **release** *noun* 1 being released or something released. 2 a new film, record or piece of news that has come out. 3 a handle, button or other device that can be pressed to unfasten something.

relent *verb* to become less stern. *She relented after hearing the explanation.*

relentless *adjective* without pity.

relic *noun* 1 something that was used or made a long time ago. 2 something that belonged to a saint and is usually kept in a church. *This bone is a relic of Saint James.*

relief *noun* 1 a lessening or ending of pain, worry or boredom. *The medicine gave relief.* 2 help for people in trouble, especially food, money and clothes. *Famine relief.* 3 a person or group taking over a duty for another. *We went on relief buses during the train strike.*

R

relieve *verb* 1 to lessen pain, trouble or boredom. 2 to take over a duty from somebody else. *To relieve the guard.* **relieve of** to rob somebody of something.

religion *noun* a belief in god or many gods. **religious** *adjective. A religious text.*

reluctant *adjective* unwilling. **reluctantly** *adverb. He reluctantly agreed to help.*

rely (relies, relying, relied) *verb* to depend on something happening or trust somebody or something. *She has always relied on her parents for help.* **reliance** *noun.*

remain *verb* 1 to be left behind after other parts have gone. *Two of the guests remained.* 2 to continue to be the same, to stay unchanged. *He remained silent.* **it remains to be seen** we will know later on.

remainder *noun* the rest, the part that is left over. *She paid £10 and promised to give me the remainder next week.*

remains *plural noun* 1 parts that are left after everything else has gone. *They found some remains of Greek pottery.* 2 a dead body. *The prince's remains were buried in the family vault.*

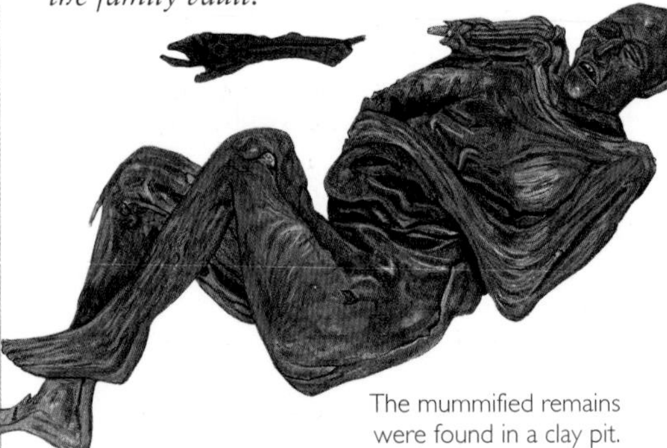

The mummified remains were found in a clay pit.

remark *noun* something said. *He made some embarrassing remarks about her new hairstyle.* **remark** *verb.*

remarkable *adjective* worth speaking about, impressive. **remarkably** *adverb. She did remarkably well in the exam.*

remember *verb* 1 to keep in the mind. *I'll always remember the first time we met.* 2 to call back into mind, especially after having forgotten it for a while. **remembrance** *noun.*

remind *verb* to tell or make somebody remember something. *She reminds me of my mother.* **reminder** *noun.*

remnant *noun* 1 a small part of something left over. *We ate up the remnants of the meal.* 2 a small piece of material.

remorse *noun* a feeling of guilt about something you have done wrong. **remorseful** *adjective. Gary felt very remorseful.*

remove *verb* to take something away, off or out. *How can I remove this stain?* **removal** *noun. The removal of the furniture.*

SPELLING NOTE

Note the spelling of relieve. It has 'i' before 'e' and not 'e' before 'i'.

WORD HISTORY

Rent comes from the Latin word 'reddere', 'to give', so it means something given or paid.

AMAZING FACT

The saying 'Opposites attract' refers to people who have different personalities, rather than magnets, which is where the saying comes from.

renew *verb* 1 to replace something old with something new of the same kind. *Passports have to be renewed every ten years.* 2 to begin or make again. *After meeting up again we renewed our friendship.* 3 to put new strength into something, to make as good as new again. **renewal** *noun.*

renown *noun* fame, being well known for something good. *A writer of extremely high renown.* **renowned** *adjective.*

rent *noun* the amount of money paid for the use of something, especially a flat or house that belongs to somebody else. **rent** *verb. I rent my flat and my television set.* **rent out** to allow something to be used in return for rent.

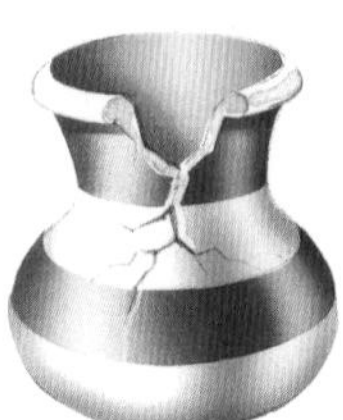

repair *verb* to mend or put something right that has broken or gone wrong. **repair** *noun. I left the car in the garage for repairs.*

The vase was impossible to repair, because a big chunk had been knocked out of it and lost.

repay (repays, repaying, repaid) *verb* to give back, especially money. *He repaid her kindness with insults.* **repayment** *noun.*

repeat *verb* to say or do the same thing again. **repeat** *noun. They show too many repeats on television.*

repel (repels, repelling, repelled) *verb* 1 to drive back. *The army repelled the attack.* 2 to find something horrible or disgusting. *The sight of blood repels him.* **repellent** *adjective, noun. An insect repellent.*

We used powerful magnets in the scientific experiment.

replace *verb* to put something back in its place or take the place of somebody or something else. *She broke one of my best cups but replaced it next day with a new one.*

replica *noun* a copy, especially of a painting. *This is only a cheap replica of the original statue in the British Museum.*

reply (replies) *noun* something said or written as an answer to somebody. *I rang Jane's doorbell, but there was no reply.* **in reply** as an answer. **reply** (replies, replying, replied) *verb* to give an answer.

report *verb* 1 to tell or give information about something. *They reported the accident to the police.* 2 to make a complaint against somebody. *The teacher reported the boy to the headmaster.* 3 to let somebody know that you are there. *We have to report to the manager every morning.* **report** *noun* 1 a written or spoken account of an event. 2 a written account of how well or badly a pupil has done during the school term. 3 the sound of an explosion.

reporter *noun* somebody who writes or broadcasts news reports.

represent *verb* 1 to be a picture, sign or example of something. To show or mean. *Love is often represented by a heart.* 2 to act for another person, especially as a lawyer or leader of a group. *We chose Gregory to represent the class at the school meeting.* **representation** *noun.*

representative *noun* somebody chosen to represent others. *Travel representatives welcome and help holidaymakers.* **representative** *adjective* being an example of what others are like. *This painting is representative of the artist's work.*

repress *verb* to hold back or control. *Steve could hardly repress a grin.* **repression** *noun.*

reprieve *noun* an order to delay or cancel the punishment of a prisoner, especially one who was to die. *She won a last-minute reprieve.* **reprieve** *verb. The prisoner was reprieved and set free at last.*

reprimand *verb* to tell somebody officially that they should not have done a particular thing. **reprimand** *noun. The superintendent gave him a severe reprimand.*

reproduce *verb* 1 to make a copy of something. To cause something to be seen or heard again. *This painting has been reproduced in many books.* 2 to produce young. *Dinosaurs reproduced by laying eggs.* **reproduction** *noun.*

reptile *noun* an animal with scaly skin whose blood changes temperature according to the temperature around it. Snakes, lizards and crocodiles are all reptiles.

republic *noun* a country with an elected president at the head, rather than a king or queen. **republican** *noun.*

DID YOU KNOW

Reptiles are cold-blooded, which means that they need lots of sunshine to warm them up. Reptiles live in all warm parts of the world, and they usually lay eggs which are soft and leathery. Dinosaurs were reptiles, though some scientists think that they may have been warm-blooded creatures. The word reptile comes from the Latin repere, 'to crawl': reptiles are 'crawling animals'.

AMAZING FACT

The first republics in history were Ancient Greece and Ancient Rome. They were considered republics even though many of the people were slaves.

repugnant *adjective* horrible and disgusting. *A repugnant smell.*

repulsive *adjective* horrible. *Some people find eating snails repulsive.* **repulsion** *noun.*

reputation *noun* people's opinion of how good somebody or something is. If you live up to your reputation, you behave in the way people expect you to.

request *noun* asking for something or the thing asked for. *My next request is an early song by Mozart with words by Schiller.* **request** *verb* to ask politely.

require *verb* 1 to need. 2 to demand, make somebody do something. *Students are required to bring their own dictionaries.* **requirement** *noun.*

rescue *verb* to save from danger, to set free. *The fireman rescued the child from the burning house.* **rescue** *noun.* **rescuer** *noun.*

research (researches) *noun* a study of a subject to find out facts and information. **research** *verb. He is researching the feeding habits of monkeys.* **researcher** *noun.*

resemble *verb* to be like or similar. *She resembles her younger sister – they have the same nose.* **resemblance** *noun.*

reservation *noun* 1 an arrangement to keep something for somebody for later use. *Holiday reservations.* 2 doubt in your mind. *I've got reservations about this plan.* 3 a piece of land kept for a special purpose.

reserve *verb* to keep or order something for somebody. *We reserved two rooms in the hotel.* **reserve** *noun* 1 something kept for later use. *Reserves of food.* 2 an extra player who may replace another player before or during a game. 3 a piece of land for a special purpose. *A nature reserve.* 4 not showing your feelings. **reserved** *adjective. She is very reserved, which is why I don't like her.*

reservoir (say **rez-uh-vwar**) *noun* a place where water is stored.

In summer they used to go sailing on the reservoir.

resident *noun* a person who lives in a particular place. *Parking is for residents only.* **resident** *adjective. The resident doctor.*

R

resign *verb* to give up your job or post. *He disagreed with the committee and resigned.* **resign yourself** to accept and put up with something without complaint. *She resigned herself to a very boring evening at the office dinner.* **resignation** *noun.*

resist *verb* to fight back against something or not allow yourself to do something. *I can't resist another piece of cake.* **resistance** *noun.* **resistant** *adjective.*

resolution *noun* 1 being firm. 2 something you make up your mind to do. *My New Year's resolution is to give up smoking.* 3 a decision taken at a meeting by a vote. 4 solving problems.

resolve *verb* 1 to decide. *She resolved to work harder.* 2 to solve a problem or clear up a difficulty.

resort *noun* a holiday place. *Davos is a famous skiing resort.*

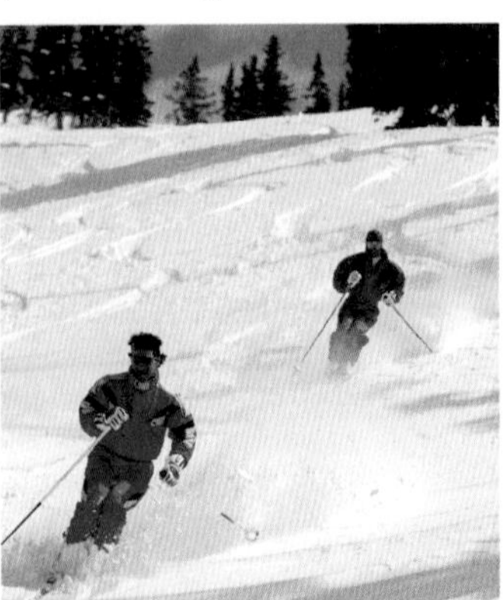

The twins visited a resort in the mountains that was famous for its good skiing facilities.

resort *verb* to turn to, especially something bad. *When he lost his money he resorted to crime and broke into the office safe.*

resourceful *adjective* clever at finding ways of doing things.

resources *plural noun* possessions such as wealth or goods. *Oil is one of the country's main resources.*

respect *noun* 1 a high opinion or admiration of somebody. *She has great respect for his work.* 2 If you show respect to somebody, you are polite. 3 a detail or particular point. *She's like her mother in every respect.* **with respect to** relating to. *With respect to your order, please find the invoice enclosed.* **respect** *verb.*

respond *verb* to reply or react to something. **response** *noun. He made no response to the question.*

responsibility (responsibilities) *noun* 1 the duty of having to deal with something and making decisions. Being responsible. *If you borrow my bike, it's your responsibility to lock it up properly.* 2 a duty, something for which you are responsible. *Parents have a lot of responsibilities.*

WORD HISTORY

'Restaurant' is a French word, meaning the same as in English. It comes from the French 'restaurer', which means to rebuild, restore, or bring back to health.

DID YOU KNOW

Someone who runs a restaurant is properly called a 'restaurateur' (without the 'n'); this is sometimes misspelt with the 'n', like restaurant.

The result was a resounding win for the team from Athens.

responsible *adjective* 1 having the duty of looking after somebody or something, having to take the blame if things go wrong. *She is responsible for keeping her room tidy.* 2 trustworthy. **be responsible for** to be the cause of. *Who is responsible for the damage?* **responsibly** *adverb.*

rest *noun* 1 not doing anything active. Quiet or sleep. 2 a support. **rest** *verb* 1 to take or have a rest. *She never rests for a second.* 2 to support or be supported. *Now rest your head on your knees.* **rest assured** to be certain. **restful** *adjective.* **restless** *adjective.*

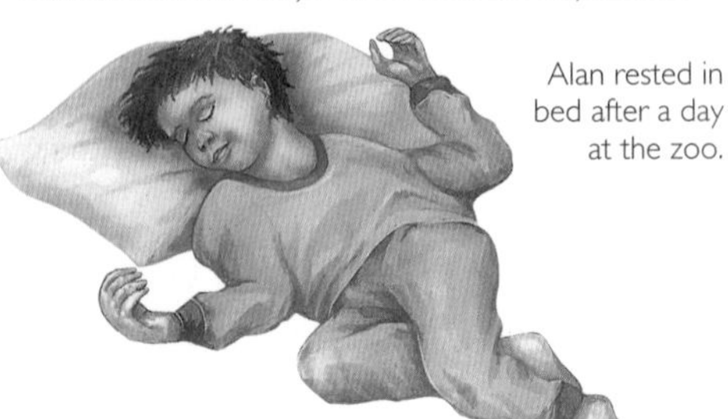

Alan rested in bed after a day at the zoo.

rest *noun* the part that is left, the others. *Take what you want and throw the rest away or give it to charity.*

restaurant *noun* a place where you can buy and eat meals.

restore *verb* 1 to give back, especially something stolen or lost. 2 to put or bring back as before. *The old church has been restored.* **restoration** *noun.*

restrain *verb* to hold back from doing something, to control. *I had to restrain myself from hitting him.* **restraint** *noun.*

restrict *verb* to keep within a limit. *She restricts herself to two cups of coffee a day.* **restriction** *noun.*

result *noun* 1 something that happens because of an event or activity. An effect. *You get good results with this washing powder.* 2 the final score of a game, competition or race. *The football results.* 3 the answer to a sum. *Each time I add up the figures I get a different result.* **result** *verb* to happen as an effect.

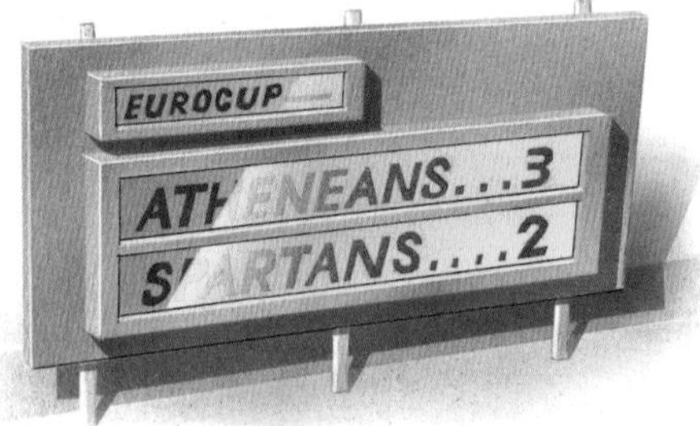

resume *verb* to begin again. *Talks resumed yesterday.* **resumption** *noun.*

résumé *noun* a summary.

R

resurrect *verb* to bring back into use. *I resurrected the old piano.* **resurrection** *noun. The resurrection of some old ideas.*

resuscitate *verb* to revive a person so they become conscious again. **resuscitation** *noun.*

retail *verb* to sell goods. *The camera retails at £50.* **retail** *noun* selling goods to the public. **retailer** *noun.*

retain *verb* to keep or continue to have. *If you don't play football it's very difficult to retain an interest in the World Cup.*

retina *noun* the area at the back of the eye that is sensitive to light. *A damaged retina.*

retire *verb* 1 to give up work, especially when you are old. *My father retired at 60.* 2 to leave a place or room. 3 to go to bed. **retirement** *noun.*

Grandfather was very much enjoying his retirement.

retreat *verb* to go away or move back, especially when forced to do so. *After a three-day battle the enemy retreated.* **retreat** *noun* 1 the act of retreating. 2 a quiet, restful place. *A weekend retreat in the country.*

return *verb* 1 to come or go back. *He returned from holiday yesterday.* 2 to give, put or send back. *She returned the book I lent her.* **return** *noun* 1 the act of returning or returning something. 2 a return ticket. 3 profit on an investment of money. **in return** in exchange. *I gave him my stamp collection in return for a computer game.*

reunion *noun* a meeting of old friends or family members who have not seen each other for some time. *At the school reunion, Clarrie met up with a lot of her old friends.*

reveal *verb* 1 to uncover something so it can be seen. *Her dress revealed a tattoo on her shoulder.* 2 to make known. *To reveal a secret.* **revelation** *noun.*

revenge *noun* hurting in return for having been hurt. *In revenge for her betrayal he refused to return her posessions.* **revenge** *verb.*

revenue *noun* the money that an organization receives from people, especially money paid as tax to the government.

reverse *adjective* opposite in position or order. *The reverse side of the material has lines through it.*

AMAZING FACT

Palindromes are words, phrases, sentences or even longer pieces of text that read the same when you reverse them. 'Dad' 'mom' 'noon' and 'peep' are short ones. 'Was it a car or a cat I saw?' is longer but still works in reverse.

Marie reversed the green car neatly into the parking space.

WORD HISTORY

'Retina' comes from the Latin 'rete', meaning 'net'. Perhaps early doctors saw it as a sort of net at the back of the eye that caught light. If so, they were right in a way. The retina actually contains light-sensitive cells that send signals along the optic nerve to the brain. There are two kinds of cells: rods are sensitive to light and dark, and cones are more sensitive to colour.

The people won a massive victory in the French Revolution.

reverse *noun* 1 the exact opposite. *She always does the reverse from what you expect.* 2 the back. 3 a gear in which you drive a car backwards. **in reverse** in the opposite way from what usually happens. **reverse** *verb* 1 to go backwards. *She reversed the car into the parking space.* 2 to change to the opposite or change round. *Roles are often reversed, with men looking after children and women going out to work.* **reverse the charges** to make a phone call for which the receiver pays. **reversal** *noun.*

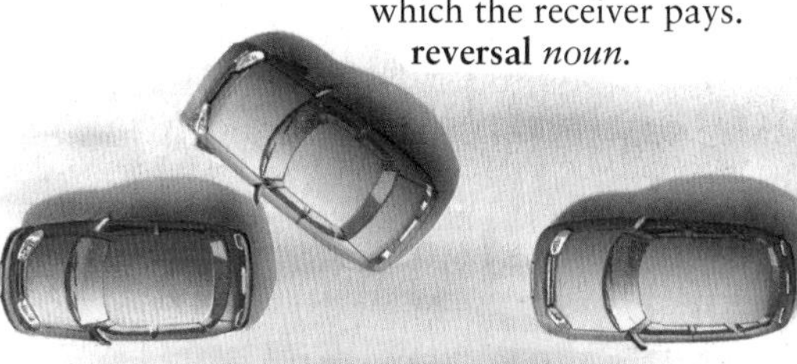

review *noun* 1 a critical opinion in a newspaper, magazine or on radio or television about a book, film, concert or play. *He writes film reviews.* 2 an inspection or examination. *Hospital practices have been under review.* **review** *verb.*

revise *verb* 1 to study facts already learnt, especially for an exam. 2 to change or correct something. *He's been so helpful I'll have to revise my opinion of him.* **revision** *noun. I still have a lot of revision to do.*

revive *verb* to come back to life or strength again. To bring back. *A warm drink will soon revive me.* **revival** *noun.*

revolt *verb* 1 to fight against something. *The army revolted against the dictator.* 2 to be disgusted. **revolting** *adjective. A revolting banana skin was in the wastepaper bin.*

revolt *noun* a fight to change a system.

revolution *noun* 1 a rebellion, especially one overthrowing a political system. 2 complete change in ways of doing things or methods. *The green revolution.* 3 one complete turn of a wheel. **revolutionary** *adjective.* **revolutionize** *verb. Computers have revolutionized office work.*

revolve *verb* to turn or keep turning round.

revolver *noun* a small gun that does not have to be reloaded after each shot.

R

reward *noun* 1 something given in return for something good or useful you have done. 2 an amount of money given to somebody who helps the police. **reward** *verb. The boy was rewarded for his bravery with a medal.*

rewarding *adjective* giving you satisfaction. *Teaching can be a rewarding job.*

Reykjavik *noun* the capital of Iceland.

rheumatism (say **roo**-muh-tizum) *noun* an illness that makes joints or muscles stiff and painful. **rheumatic** *adjective.*

rhino (rhinos) *noun* a rhinoceros.

rhinoceros (rhinoceroses) *noun* a large animal from Africa or Asia with one or two horns on its nose.

The rhinoceros is endangered because poachers value its horn.

rhyme *noun* 1 a similar sound at the ends of words or lines in poetry, as in 'say' and 'day' and 'school' and 'fool'. 2 a word that rhymes with another. 3 a short piece of writing with rhymes. **rhyme** *verb.*

ribbon *noun* 1 a long strip of material for tying things together or used as a decoration. *She tied her hair with a red ribbon.* 2 a narrow strip of inked material that is put into a typewriter. *A typewriter ribbon.*

rice *noun* white or brown grains that are cooked and eaten.

The rice terraces at Luzon in the Philippines were carved out of the rock thousands of years ago.

rich *adjective* 1 having a lot of money or possessions. *A country rich in oil.* 2 containing a lot of goodness or quality of sound or colour. *Rich soil is good for growing things.* 3 containing a lot of cream, oil, sugar or eggs. *Rich food.* 4 expensive, luxurious. **riches** *plural noun.* **richly** *adverb.* **richness** *noun.*

rickety *adjective* not made strongly, likely to break. *The old chairs were very rickety.*

riddle *noun* a difficult question to which you must guess the answer.

DID YOU KNOW

Rhymes can be either masculine or feminine. A masculine rhyme is one in which the two words have the same sounds in their final stressed syllables, such as 'betray' and 'delay'. In a feminine rhyme, the words' same sounds are in stressed syllables before other unstressed syllables, such 'joviality' and 'morality', or 'stocking' and 'shocking'.

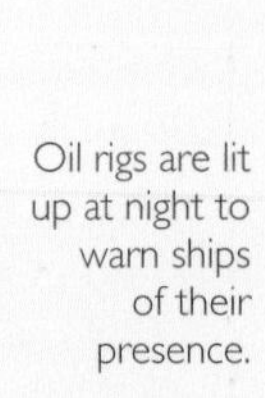

Oil rigs are lit up at night to warn ships of their presence.

AMAZING FACT

The word 'rhinoceros' comes from the Greek word for nose – rhino. When people have plastic surgery on their nose, it is called 'rhinoplasty'.

riddle *verb* to make holes in somebody or something, to make full of holes. *He riddled the target with bullets.* **riddled with** full of. *Your essay is riddled with mistakes.*

ride (rides, riding, rode, ridden) *verb* 1 to sit on a horse, bicycle or motorbike and go along on it. 2 to travel in a car, bus or train. 3 to float on something. *The boat rode the waves.* **rider** *noun.* **ride up** to move up the body. *I hate it when my vest rides up under my dress.* **ride** *noun* a journey on an animal, a bike or in a vehicle. **take for a ride** to cheat somebody.

ridiculous *adjective* silly. *She wore a ridiculous hat to the wedding.*

rifle *noun* a gun with a long barrel, fired from the shoulder.

rifle *verb* to search through and possibly steal things. *Thieves rifled through every drawer and cupboard.*

rig *noun* 1 a large structure that is used for drilling for oil or gas. *An oil rig.* 2 the way a ship's sails and masts are arranged. **rig** (rigs, rigging, rigged) *verb* 1 to fit out a ship with ropes and sails. 2 to arrange an event dishonestly in order to get the results that are wanted. *The race was obviously rigged.* **rig up** to put something together quickly out of materials that are handy. *The scouts rigged up a shelter for the night.*

Riga *noun* the capital of Latvia.

rigging *noun* the ropes and sails of a ship.

right *adjective* 1 of or belonging to the right-hand side. *In Italy cars drive on the right.* 2 correct, true. *Is that the right time?* 3 morally good, just. *Giving her the money back was the right thing to do.* 4 most suitable or healthy. *She is the right person for the job.* **right** *adverb* 1 towards the right-hand side. 2 directly, straight. *He stood right in front of me.* 3 properly, correctly. 4 immediately. *Right now.* 5 expressing agreement. *Right, I'll see you tomorrow afternoon.* **right angle** an angle of 90 degrees. **right-wing** not wanting political change, conservative.

right *noun* 1 the right-hand side, part or direction. *Keep to the right.* 2 a political party or group of people with conservative views. 3 morally good actions. *The difference between right and wrong.* 4 something you are allowed to do or have, a claim. *I know my rights.* **right of way** a right to go before other vehicles. **right** *verb* 1 to make something return to its usual position. *The boat righted itself.* 2 to make something right. *To right a wrong.*

rigid *adjective* 1 stiff, not bending. 2 strict. *The army has rigid discipline.*

rim *noun* the edge of a cup, plate, wheel or other round object.

rind *noun* the tough outer skin of fruit, cheese or bacon. *Orange rind.*

Orange rind is finely chopped and added to marmalade.

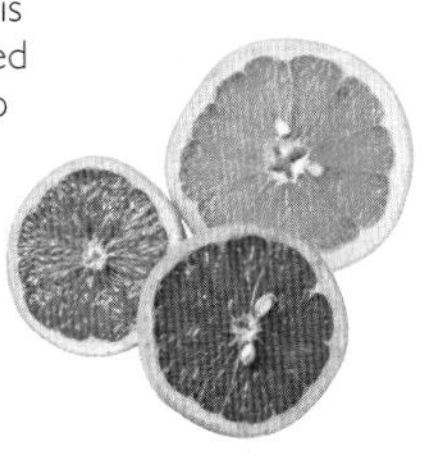

ring *noun* 1 a circle or something the shape of a circle. *Smoke rings.* 2 a small circle of metal worn on the finger. *A wedding ring.* 3 a space with seats around it where a circus performs or a boxing or wrestling match takes place. 4 a group of people who are doing something illegal. **ring** *verb* to put a ring around something. *The teacher ringed all the mistakes in red pen.*

ring (rings, rang, ringing, rung) *verb* 1 to make or cause the sound of a bell. *The telephone is ringing.* 2 to telephone. *She rang her mother.* 3 to be filled with sound. *It was so loud, my ears were ringing.* **ring true/false** to sound true or untrue. **ring** *noun* 1 the action or sound of ringing. 2 a telephone call. *I'll give you a ring either tomorrow or the day after.*

rink *noun* a place for skating.

For her birthday, Jemma took her friends ice-skating at the local rink.

rinse *verb* to wash something with clean water and without soap. She rinsed the plates. **rinse** *noun* 1 rinsing with clean water. 2 a special liquid for colouring the hair.

SPELLING NOTE

Riddles were originally clever puzzles that people had to solve. They occur in many myths and legends, with gods and rulers 'talking in riddles'. In recent times they have tended to be more like jokes, such as those you find in Christmas crackers.

WORD HISTORY

A rival was originally a person using the same stream as another, from the Latin 'rivus', meaning stream. Perhaps in places where there was a water shortage, the two rivals competed with each other for use of the stream. Strangely, the word river is thought to come from the Latin 'ripa', meaning bank.

riot *noun* violent or noisy behaviour by a number of people, usually in a public place. **riot** *verb* to take part in a riot.

rip (rips, ripping, ripped) *verb* 1 to tear quickly. *She ripped her skirt on the barbed wire.* 2 to remove quickly. *He ripped the letter out of her hand.* **rip** *noun.* **rip off** to cheat by asking for too much money.

rip-off *noun* a fraud or swindle.

ripe *adjective* 1 ready to be picked and eaten. 2 ready, fit for something. *The country is ripe for change.* **ripen** *verb. The bananas will soon ripen.*

ripple *noun* a small wave or small waves. *Ripples on the pond.* **ripple** *verb* to make ripples or move in ripples.

I threw a stone in the pond and watched the ripples grow.

rise (rises, rising, rose, risen) *verb* 1 to go up, get higher. *The water is rising.* 2 to come up. *The Sun rises in the east.* 3 to get up from a lying, sitting or kneeling position, to get out of bed. *He rises early.* 4 to get stronger. *The child's voice rose to a scream.* 5 to come up to the surface. 6 to show above the surroundings as a tall shape. *The tower rose above the rooftops.* **rise from the dead** to come back to life. **rise up** to fight against somebody in power. *The people rose up against the dictator.* **rise** *noun* 1 a small hill or upward slope. 2 an increase, such as an increase in wages. A rise in prices or the temperature. 3 the act of growing more powerful. *The rise and fall of the Roman Empire.* **give rise to** to lead to, especially something bad.

risk *noun* a danger of something bad happening. A chance of a loss. *There's a risk of showers.* **risk** *verb* to take a chance. *I don't want to risk losing my place in the queue.* **risky** *adjective. Gambling is a risky business, but Peter enjoys it.*

ritual *noun* a series of actions that people regularly carry out in certain situations. *Religious rituals.*

rival *noun* somebody who competes with you. **rival** *verb* to be as good as somebody or something else. *Nobody else's cooking can rival his mother's.* **rivalry** *noun. A great rivalry between two brothers caused big problems for the family.*

river *noun* a large stream of fresh water. *The River Thames winds its way through London and out towards the east.*

rivet *noun* a short nail with a flat head used for holding pieces of metal together. **rivet** *verb* 1 to fasten with rivets. 2 to attract or hold somebody's attention. *She watched the film, riveted to the screen.* **riveting** *adjective. He gave a riveting performance.*

Riyadh *noun* the capital of Saudi Arabia.

road *noun* 1 a specially made way between places for traffic to travel on. 2 a method or way. *The road to success is often very bumpy.* **on the road** travelling.

roam *verb* to wander about.

roar *noun* a loud, deep noise like the sound a lion makes. *The roar of traffic.* **roar** *verb* 1 to make a loud, deep sound like a lion or thunder. 2 to say or shout something loudly. *She roared with laughter.* **a roaring success** something very successful. **to do a roaring trade** to sell a lot of something.

roast *verb* 1 to cook meat or vegetables in the oven or over a hot fire. 2 to get very hot. *I've been roasting in the Sun all day.* **roast** *noun.* **roast** *adjective* roasted. *Roast meat.*

rob (robs, robbing, robbed) *verb* 1 to take what belongs to somebody else, usually by force. *The thieves robbed the safe.* 2 to take away. *She was robbed of a real opportunity.* **robber** *noun.* **robbery** *noun.*

robe *noun* a long loose piece of clothing.

robin *noun* a small bird with a red breast.

robot *noun* a machine programmed to do things automatically. Some robots look and act like a person. *Cars are put together by robots in factories.* **robotic** *adjective.*

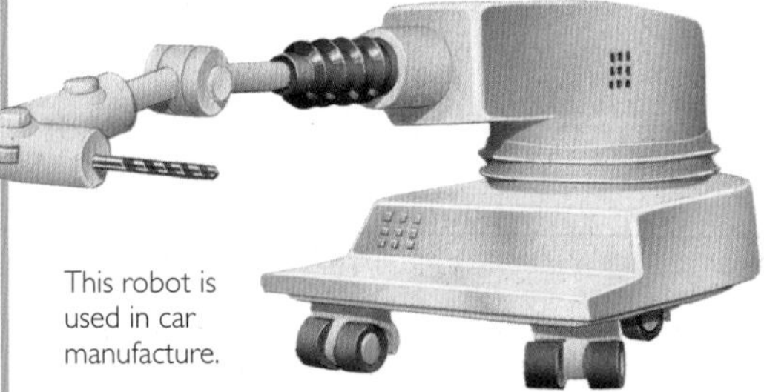

This robot is used in car manufacture.

robust *adjective* strong. *A robust wine.*

rock *noun* 1 the hard stony part that is part of the earth's crust. 2 a large stone that sticks up above the ground or out of the sea. *We climbed up a rock and then jumped off it.* 3 a hard stick of sweet stuff, usually sold at the seaside. **rocky** *adjective.*

rock *verb* 1 to move backwards and forwards or from side to side. *She rocked the baby in her arms.* 2 to shock or shake. *The news of his death rocked the world.* **rock** *noun* 1 a rocking movement. 2 music with a strong beat, rock music.

rock-bottom *adjective* at the lowest point. *Everything was sold at rock-bottom prices.*

AMAZING FACT

Rodeos are still held in the US and Canada. The Stampede in Calgary, Alberta is the most important in Canada. One of the most important events in the US is in Oklahoma City – The National Finals.

SPELLING NOTE

Be careful about the spellings of 'roll' and 'role'. A roll is something that is rolled up, including the round shape of bread. The actor's part or somebody's position is spelt 'role', as in 'role-play' or 'role model'. This word comes from French, and is sometimes still spelt in the French way with a circumflex accent, 'rôle'.

AMAZING FACT

Roller skates were first invented in Belgium in about 1760 by Joseph Merlin who is said to have skated into a ballroom playing the violin.

rocket *noun* 1 a machine in the shape of a long tube that flies by burning gases and is used to send up missiles or spacecraft. 2 a kind of firework. **give somebody a rocket** to tell somebody off. **rocket** *verb* to move up quickly. *The song rocketed to Number One in the charts.*

rocking-chair *noun* a chair in which you can rock backwards and forwards.

The rocking chair stood by the fire in Grandma's house.

rod *noun* 1 a long thin stick. 2 a stick with a line for fishing.

rode *verb* past tense of ride.

rodent *noun* an animal that has sharp front teeth for gnawing. Rats, mice and squirrels are all rodents.

rodeo (rodeos) *noun* (say **roh**-dee-oh) a show at which cowboys ride wild horses and catch cattle with ropes.

rogue *noun* a dishonest person.

role *noun* 1 an actor's part in a play, film or musical. 2 somebody's position in a particular situation. *She didn't like the role of leader, but accepted it gracefully.*

role-play *noun* an exercise in which people play the part of a character.

roll *verb* 1 to move along turning over and over. 2 to make something into the shape of a ball or tube. *Can you roll cigarettes?* 3 to move along on wheels or as if on wheels. *The years rolled by.* 4 to make flat by pressing. *To roll pastry.* 5 to make a deep sound. *Thunder rolled.* 6 to move from side to side. *Drunks rolled down the street.* **roll over** to face the other way by turning over. **roll up** 1 to roll something into a tube or ball. 2 to arrive. *His friends rolled up at midnight.* **roll** *noun* 1 something rolled into a tube. 2 bread in a round shape for one person. 3 a rolling movement. 4 a rolling sound. 5 an official list of people's names. *The electoral roll.*

rollerblades *plural noun* boots fitted with small wheels in a line for roller-skating. **rollerblading** *noun.*

roller-skate *verb* to move over a surface wearing roller-skates. **roller-skate** *noun* a shoe fitted with four small wheels. **roller-skating** *noun.*

ROM *abbreviation* read-only memory. ROM is the memory a computer uses which cannot be changed.

R

Roman Catholic *noun* a member of the Roman Catholic Church, which has the Pope at its head. Roman Catholics believe in the Christian religion. **Roman Catholic** *adjective*.

Romania *noun* a country in eastern Europe.

Romanian *noun* 1 the language of Romania. 2 a person who comes from Romania. **Romanian** *adjective*. *The Romanian flag.*

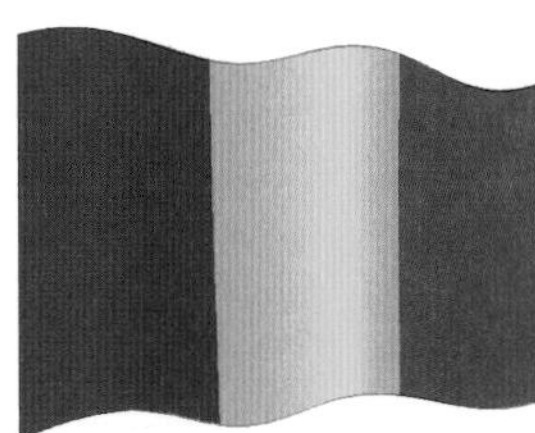

The Romanian flag has blue, yellow and red vertical stripes.

romantic *adjective* having feelings about love and beauty, seeing things in an unreal way. Romantic novels and films are about love and usually have a happy ending. **romantic** *noun*. **romantically** *adverb*. **romance** *noun*.

Rome *noun* the capital of Italy.

roof *noun* 1 the covering on top of a building, tent, car or bus. 2 the upper part of the inside of the mouth.

rook *noun* 1 a black crow. 2 a chess piece, also called a castle.

rook *verb* to get money from somebody by cheating. *I was rooked!*

room *noun* 1 a part in a house or other building that has its own walls, floor, ceiling and door. 2 space. **roomy** *adjective* spacious.

rooster *noun* a cockerel.

root *noun* 1 the part of a plant that grows under the ground. 2 the part of a tooth or hair beneath the skin. 3 the cause or basis of something. *The root of the problem.* 4 in mathematics, a number in relation to the number it makes when multiplied by itself. *The square root of 9 is 3.*

root *verb* 1 to grow roots. *Ivy roots very quickly.* 2 to search through things. *Pigs root around for food.* **rooted to the spot** unable to move.

The tree's roots spread far down into the earth and draw moisture up the trunk and into the branches and leaves.

SPELLING NOTE

You might think that the plant rosemary was named after two women, Rose and Mary. In fact in old English it used to be called 'rosmarine', and it came from the Latin 'ros marinus', which meant 'sea dew'. As the word changed, people probably thought that it had to do with the plant 'rose' and the Virgin Mary.

AMAZING FACT

Helicopters are the slowest aircraft. Because of their rotor, they are able to hover in the air. Planes, on the other hand, have to fly at a certain speed of they or they will crash.

Leonardo da Vinci (1452-1519) first had the idea of a helicopter – he sketched one and may even have built a model.

rope *noun* a strong thick string. **know the ropes** to know how something should be done. **rope** *verb* tie together with a rope. **rope in** to persuade somebody to help you with an activity. **rope off** to separate an area with ropes, usually to keep people away from it. *The accident area was roped off.*

rose *noun* 1 a sweet-smelling flower with a thorny stem that grows on a bush. 2 a pink colour. 3 a nozzle with little holes in it that is fitted at the end of a pipe or watering can for watering the garden.

rose *verb* past tense of rise.

Roseau *noun* the capital of Dominica.

rosemary *noun* a bush with evergreen leaves that are used in cooking.

Rosh Hashanah *noun* a festival marking the Jewish New Year.

rot (rots, rotting, rotted) *verb* to go bad, to decay. *The apples were rotting in the box.* rot *noun* 1 rotting. 2 nonsense. *He talks a load of rot.* **rotten** *adjective*. 1 *Rotten apples.* 2 bad, unpleasant.

rota *noun* (say **roh**-tuh) a list of people who take turns doing a particular job.

rotate *verb* 1 to move round a fixed point. *A wheel rotates.* 2 to take turns or come round in regular order. *We rotate the babysitting.* **rotation** *noun*. *The Earth's rotation is a mystery to me.*

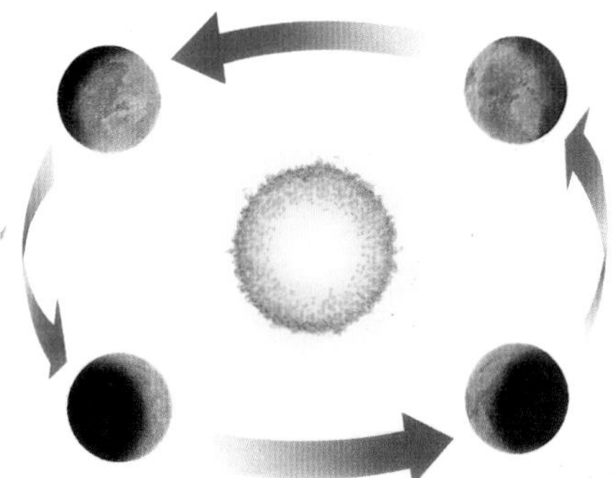

The Earth rotates on its axis as it moves around the Sun.

rotor *noun* a part of a machine that rotates, especially the rotating blades of a helicopter.

rouble *noun* Russian money.

rough *adjective* 1 uneven, not smooth or polished. *Rough skin.* 2 not calm, gentle or polite, using force. *Rough manners.* 3 not exact, without detail. *A rough description.* **roughly** *adverb*. **roughness** *noun*.

rough *verb* to make something untidy. If you rough somebody up, you hit them. **rough it** to live in an uncomfortable way. *Students usually don't mind roughing it for a while on their first trips abroad.* **rough out** to make a quick drawing or plan of something. **rough** *noun* 1 the long grass on a golf course. 2 a rough person. 3 a piece of writing or a drawing without much detail, not finished.

R

round *adjective* 1 shaped like a circle or ball. 2 complete. *A round dozen.* 3 going and returning. *A round trip.* **roundness** *noun.* **in round figures** not exactly, but to the nearest 10, 100, 1000, etc.

round *adverb* 1 in a circle. 2 from one to another, all over the place. *Hand the books round.* 3 to your home. *They invited us round.* 4 facing the other way. *Round the corner.* **round about** 1 about. 2 very near a place.

round *preposition* 1 in a circle. 2 on all the sides of. 3 in every direction or everywhere. 4 in the neighbourhood. **round the clock** all the time. *Paul made us work round the clock.*

round *noun* 1 something round. 2 a regular journey to a number of houses. *A paper round.* 3 a slice of bread or a sandwich made with two slices of bread. 4 a share given out to everyone. *This round of drinks is on me!* 5 one stage in a game or a competition. *Our team is through to the next round.* 6 a bullet or bullets from a gun. 7 in golf, playing all the holes once.

roundabout *noun* 1 a place where a number of roads meet and cars drive in a circle. 2 a merry-go-round.

roundabout *adjective* not in the shortest or most direct way. *He told us in a roundabout way that he was leaving.*

rout *verb* to defeat heavily. **rout** *noun.*

route *noun* (say root) the way you take to get to a place.

routine *noun* (say roo-**teen**) the usual way of doing things. *Getting up late upsets my routine.* **routine** *adjective. A routine job.*

rove *verb* to roam.

row *noun* (rhymes with go) a line of people or things. *A row of houses.*

row *verb* (rhymes with go) to move a boat through the water with oars. **rower** *noun.* **rowing** *noun.*

row *noun* (rhymes with now) 1 a noisy quarrel. 2 a loud noise.

rowdy (rowdier, rowdiest) *adjective* rough and noisy. *The twins are too rowdy.*

The meeting was held at a round table, where all the participants were equal.

Rubies are gemstones valued for their beautiful red colour.

SPELLING NOTE

In British English, people often use 'round' when there's the idea of going in a curve: 'It's just round the corner.' For a more general area, they more often use 'around': 'Do you live around here?' To mean approximately, you should only use around: 'I'll see you around eight.'

rowing boat *noun* a small boat with oars.

royal *adjective* belonging to or connected with a king or queen. **royally** *adjective.* **royalty** (royalties) *noun* 1 people of the royal family. 2 part of the price of a book that is paid to the writer for each copy sold.

rub (rubs, rubbing, rubbed) *verb* to move something backwards and forwards or round and round against something else. *Rub some cream on it to make it better.* **rub out** to remove something, especially pencil marks, with a rubber.

rubber *noun* 1 an elastic substance that keeps out water, made from the juice of some tropical trees. *Rubber gloves.* 2 a small piece of rubber used for rubbing out pencil marks, an eraser. **rubbery** *adjective.*

rubbish *noun* 1 unwanted things to be thrown away. 2 nonsense, foolish talk. *Switch that rubbish off!*

rubble *noun* broken stones or bricks. *Fill the hole with rubble.*

ruby (rubies) *noun* a red precious stone. **ruby** *adjective. Ruby port.*

rudder *noun* a piece of metal or wood at the back of a boat or plane, used for steering.

rude *adjective* 1 impolite. *It's rude to laugh.* 2 vulgar. *Rude jokes.* 3 unexpected and unpleasant. *A rude awakening.* 4 very simple and roughly made. *A rude shelter.* **rudeness** *noun. Her rudeness is appalling.*

rug *noun* 1 a mat, smaller than a carpet. 2 a thick blanket.

rugby *noun* a game similar to football but played with an oval ball that can be handled. *Tim loves playing rugby.*

rugged *adjective* 1 craggy and rocky. *A rugged landscape.* 2 rough and strong. *A rugged face.*

ruin *noun* 1 destruction. *Drink will be the ruin of her.* 2 the state of no longer having any money. *My business is facing ruin.* 3 part or parts of a building still standing after the rest has been destroyed. *The ruins of a castle.* **ruin** *verb* 1 to destroy or harm. 2 to lose all your money.

The castle ruins provided a fascinating introduction to the archaeology lesson.

rule *noun* 1 an order or a law that says what is allowed or not allowed. Instructions on how things are to be done. *The rules of grammar.* 2 power to govern or control. *Under British rule.* **as a rule** usually. **rule** *verb* 1 to govern or control. 2 to decide. *The judge ruled that he must pay a fine.* 3 to make a straight line with a ruler. *Ruled paper.* **rule out** to decide that something is impossible.

ruler *noun* 1 a person who rules. 2 a long, flat piece of wood, metal or plastic with straight edges that are marked with centimetres, used for measuring things or drawing straight lines.

rum *noun* an alcoholic drink made from sugar cane. *Rum and blackcurrant.*

rumble *verb* to make a low rolling sound. *My stomach is rumbling.* **rumble** *noun.*

rumour *noun* talk, especially false information, spread from one person to another. **rumour** *verb* to say as a rumour.

rump *noun* the back part (buttocks) of an animal. *Rump steak.*

run (runs, running, ran, run) *verb* 1 to move quickly on your legs. 2 to take part in a race. *He runs for the school.* 3 to go, travel or drive somebody somewhere. *The bus runs every hour.* 4 to flow. *Shall I run you a bath?* 5 to move quickly. *A strange thought ran through her mind.* 6 to work, operate. *He left the car running.* 7 to organize, control or own. *He runs a shop.* 8 to stretch or continue. *The road runs through the forest.* 9 to continue to go on for a period of time. *The play ran for a week.* **run away** to leave suddenly. **run behind** to be late ending or starting. **run into** 1 to hit a person or thing while driving. 2 to happen to meet or come across. *She ran into an old friend.* **run out** to have used up everything and have nothing left. *We ran out of money.* **run over** to knock somebody or something down when driving. *He ran over his neighbour.*

rung *noun* a bar in a ladder. *My foot was on the bottom rung when I fell off the ladder and broke my arm.*

rung *verb* past tense of ring.

runner *noun* 1 a person who runs, especially in a race. 2 a thin wooden or metal strip on which something slides or moves. *The runners of a sledge.* 3 a messenger. 4 a long strip of carpet.

Anna was a good runner who trained every day.

DID YOU KNOW

From 1922 to 1991 Russia was part of the USSR (Union of Soviet Socialist Republics) or Soviet Union, which was the biggest country in the world. When the Soviet Union broke up into separate republics, the Russian Federation, or Russia, remained the world's largest country. Its area covers more than 17 million square kilometres, much larger than the continent of Europe.

DID YOU KNOW

Rugby, or rugby football, was first played at Rugby School in Warwickshire, which is where the name comes from.

runner bean *noun* a climbing bean, the pods of which are used as food.

runner-up *noun* somebody who finishes second in a race or competition.

runway *noun* the long strip of hard surface on which planes take off and land.

rural *adjective* of or like the countryside, far away from the city.

rush *verb* 1 to hurry, act quickly. *Don't rush me, I have to think about it.* 2 to move quickly. *He was rushed to hospital.* 3 to get through, over or into something by pressing forward. **rush** (rushes) *noun* 1 hurry or hurried activity. 2 a sudden interest or demand for something. *A rush for tickets.*

rush hour *noun* the busy part of the day when most people are travelling to or from work.

Russia *noun* a country in eastern Europe and Asia.

Russia is a vast country that spans eight time zones.

Russian *noun* 1 the language of Russia. 2 a person who comes from Russia. **Russian** *adjective. A Russian church.*

rust *noun* a reddish-brown substance formed on iron when it becomes damp. **rust** *verb. The bike will rust if you leave it out in the rain.* **rusty** *adjective.*

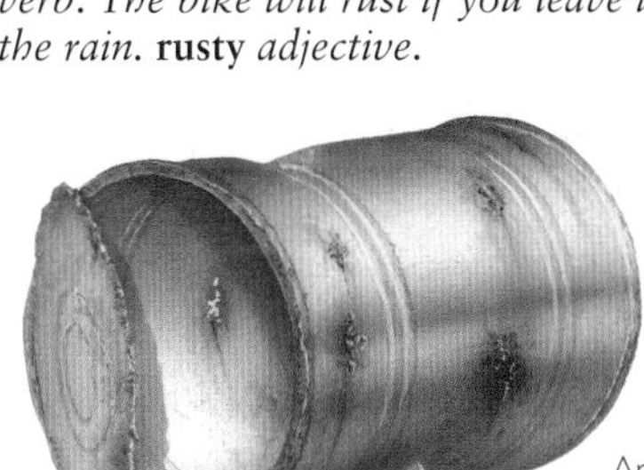

An old rusty can was all that Tom caught when he went fishing.

rustic *adjective* connected with the country, rough and simple. *Rustic furniture.*

rut *noun* 1 a deep, narrow track made in the ground by wheels. 2 a fixed way of thinking or doing things which is difficult to get out of. *The only way to get out of this rut is to leave home and start a new life.*

ruthless *adjective* showing no pity, cruel. *You have to be ruthless in business.* **ruthlessness** *noun.*

Rwanda *noun* a country in Africa.

rye *noun* a grass grown in cold countries, and the grain of that plant which is used for making flour. *Rye bread.*

S

Ss

sabbath *noun* a weekly day of rest, Saturday for Jews, Sunday for Christians.

sabotage *noun* secretly carried-out damage, usually to machines or buildings as a protest, to weaken an enemy or ruin a plan. **sabotage** *verb. The railway lines had been sabotaged by enemy troops.*

sachet *noun* (say **sash**-ay) a small closed plastic or paper bag for holding something. *A sachet of shampoo.*

sack *noun* a large bag made of strong material. *A sack of potatoes.*

sack *noun* taking away somebody's job. *He got the sack for being late.* **sack** *verb.*

sacred (say **say**-krid) *adjective* connected with religion, holy.

sacrifice *noun* 1 giving something to a god as an offering. 2 giving up something you like or value for the good of something else. **sacrifice** *verb* to offer or give up something as a sacrifice. *He sacrificed his job to look after his sick parents.* **sacrificial** *adjective. A sacrificial lamb.*

sad (sadder, saddest) *adjective* unhappy, showing or causing sorrow. **sadly** *adverb.* **sadness** *noun. Tears of great sadness.*

saddle *noun* a seat on a horse or bicycle for a rider to sit on. **saddle** *verb* to put a saddle on a horse or other animal.

safe *adjective* out of danger or free from risk or harm. *Have a safe journey.* **safely** *adverb. They arrived home safely.*

safe *noun* a strong box or cupboard with special locks for keeping money or valuable things in. *Put your jewels in the safe.*

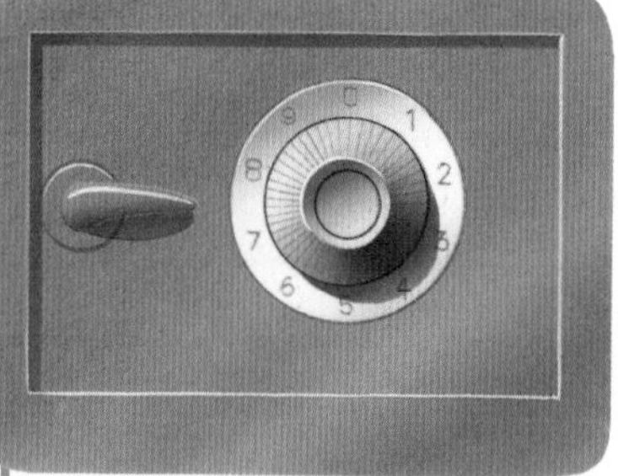

Marcia kept her jewels locked in the hotel's safe.

safeguard *noun* a protection against something unwanted. *She eats a lot of fruit as a safeguard against catching colds and flu.* **safeguard** *verb* to protect.

DID YOU KNOW

S, the 19th letter in the English alphabet, was the 21st letter in the ancient Hebrew and Phoenician alphabets, in which it was called shin.

DID YOU KNOW

The original sagas were long stories of heroic achievement in the Old Norse language. The best sagas were written down in Iceland in the 12th and 13th centuries.

WORD HISTORY

Both 'salad' and 'salary' come originally from the Latin word for salt, 'sal'. 'Salad' simply meant 'salted', since that way your vegetables tasted better. A Roman soldier's pay was his salarium, or salt money, which enabled him to buy salt to improve the flavour of his food.

safety *noun* being safe, freedom from danger or harm.

safety belt *noun* 1 a strap attached to the seat in a car or plane worn by travellers. 2 a belt for fastening to something solid worn by somebody working high up or in a dangerous position.

safety pin *noun* a metal pin for fastening things together.

sag (sags, sagging, sagged) *verb* to hang down loosely or in the middle, usually because of weight. **sag** *noun.*

saga *noun* (say **sah**-guh) a long story. *A family saga is my favourite entertainment.*

sage *noun* a plant used as a herb.

sage *adjective* wise. **sage** *noun* a wise person. *Three sages came on camels.*

said *verb* past tense of say.

sail *noun* 1 a large piece of cloth attached to the mast of a ship to catch the wind and make the ship move. **set sail** to leave a port. 2 the blade of a windmill. **sail** *verb* 1 to travel across the water, to be able to control a sailing boat. 2 to move quickly and easily. *She sailed through the exam.* 3 to begin a voyage. *Our ship sails tomorrow.*

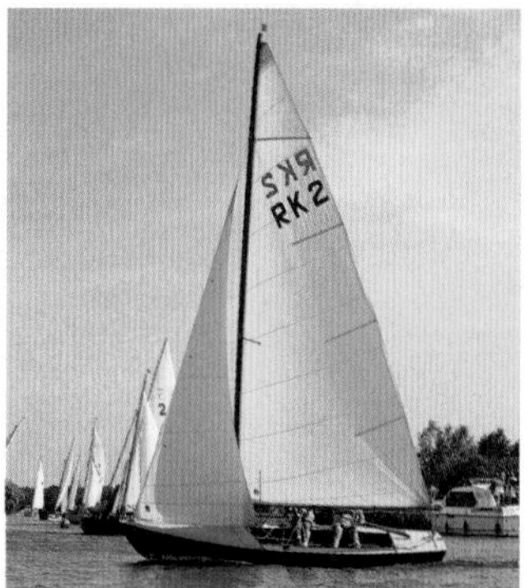

Jonanthan took a course in navigation so he could sail long distances across the sea.

sailboard *noun* the board used for windsurfing. *He bought a new sailboard.*

sailing boat *noun* a boat driven by sails.

sailor *noun* 1 somebody who can sail a boat. 2 a member of a navy, somebody who works on a ship.

saint *noun* a holy person or a very kind and patient person. **saintly** *adjective.*

sake *noun* for the sake of somebody or something, for the good of somebody or for the purpose of something. *For heaven's sake, stop arguing with each other.*

salad *noun* 1 a mixture of uncooked vegetables, such as lettuce, cucumber and tomatoes, eaten cold.

salad dressing *noun* a sauce for putting on salads. *Salad dressing with garlic and herbs.*

salary (salaries) *noun* fixed pay, usually monthly, earned by somebody for work.

S

sale *noun* 1 the selling of goods for money. 2 a special time when goods are sold in shops at lower prices. **on sale** if something is on sale, it can be bought in the shops. **for sale** offered to be sold. *The house is for sale.*

saliva *noun* the watery liquid that naturally forms in the mouth.

salmon (salmon) *noun* (say sam-un) a large fish with pink flesh eaten as food.

Salmon swim upstream in spring to spawn.

salt *noun* a white substance found in seawater, used for making food taste better or for preserving it. Salt crystals. **rub salt into somebody's wounds** to make somebody's pain even worse. **salt** *verb* to put salt in or on food. **salty** *adjective.*

salute *verb* 1 to greet somebody. Soldiers salute by raising their right hand to their forehead. 2 to show respect or admiration. *We salute the enormous efforts you have made.* **salute** *noun. A salute to freedom.*

salvage *verb* to save from something that has been destroyed, so it can be used again. **salvage** *noun.*

salvation *noun* 1 being saved from sin, the saving of the soul, especially in the Christian religion. 2 something that stops loss or damage.

same *adjective* 1 not different, exactly alike. *She wore the same dress as me.* 2 not changed. *She still does the same job for him.* 3 a particular one or one already mentioned. *I saw a flash and at the same moment the car crashed into a tree.* **same** *adverb* in the same way. *I don't feel the same about him now.* **sameness** *noun.*

sample *noun* a small quantity that shows what something or what the rest is like. *A free sample of washing powder.* **sample** *verb* to test a part of something.

Diane took samples of curtain material home to try them against her walls.

WORD HISTORY

The sandwich is named after the 4th Earl of Sandwich, John Montagu (1718–92), who was so addicted to gambling that he never wanted to leave the gaming table. So when the Earl needed something to eat, a servant would bring him some cold beef, which he liked to have between two slices of bread. This snack soon came to be known as a sandwich.

SPELLING NOTE

Santa Claus is the legendary Saint Nicholas, the patron saint of children. Nicholas was a bishop who lived in Asia Minor, present-day Turkey, over 1600 years ago. Stories about Nicholas giving gold to poor children led to the legend of Father Christmas bringing gifts to all children.

San'a *noun* the capital of Yemen.

sanction *noun* 1 permission given to do something. 2 actions taken by countries against a country that is breaking international laws. A punishment ordered when a law or rule is broken. *The sanctions included a total trade ban.* **sanction** *verb* to allow something to be done. *The minister sanctioned the sale of the pictures.*

sanctuary (sanctuaries) *noun* 1 a holy place, especially in a church or temple. 2 a place of safety. 3 a place where animals or birds are protected. *A bird sanctuary.*

sand *noun* a mass of finely crushed stones as on beaches and in deserts. **sandy** *adjective* 1 full of sand. *A sandy beach.* 2 yellowish-red. *Sandy hair.*

sand *verb* to smooth or clean a surface by rubbing sandpaper over it.

sandal *noun* a shoe with straps over the foot, worn in summer.

sandpaper *noun* paper with sand stuck to it, used for smoothing surfaces. **sandpaper** *verb. Please sandpaper the woodwork.*

sandwich *noun* two slices of bread with a filling between. **sandwich** *verb* to put something between two others. *The bag was sandwiched between two big suitcases.*

Trudy packed the sandwiches for the picnic.

sane *adjective* 1 able to think normally, not mentally ill or mad. 2 sensible. **sanity** *noun.*

sang *verb* past tense of sing.

sanitary *adjective* 1 concerning the treatment of waste for the protection of public health. *In the Middle Age, sanitary conditions were very poor.* 2 clean, free from dirt or infection.

San José *noun* the capital of Costa Rica.

sank *verb* past tense of sink.

San Marino *noun* a country in southern Europe. Its capital is also called San Marino.

San Salvador *noun* the capital of El Salvador.

Santa Claus *noun* another name for Father Christmas. Small children are told that Santa Claus comes in a sleigh to bring presents to them at Christmas.

Santiago *noun* the capital of Chile.

S

Santo Domingo *noun* the capital of the Dominican Republic.

São Tomé *noun* the capital of São Tomé and Príncipe.

São Tomé and Príncipe *noun* a country in the Gulf of Guinea off West Africa.

sap *noun* the watery liquid in plants and trees. *The sap rises in the spring.*

sap (saps, sapping, sapped) *verb* to weaken somebody's strength or confidence, especially over a period of time.

sapling *noun* a young tree.

sapphire *noun* a bright blue precious stone.

Sarajevo *noun* the capital of Bosnia-Herzegovina.

sarcasm *noun* amusing, often hurtful things said to mock or upset somebody's feelings, usually by saying the opposite of what is really thought. **sarcastic** *adjective. Your sarcastic tone of voice.* **sarcastically** *adverb.*

sardine *noun* a small seafish. *A tin of sardines is a delicacy.*

sari (saris) *noun* a long piece of material wrapped around the body, usually worn by Indian women.

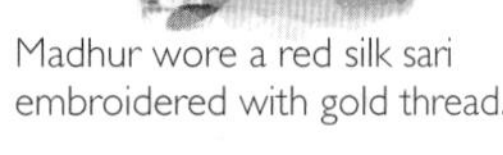

Madhur wore a red silk sari embroidered with gold thread.

sat *verb* past tense of sit.

Satan *noun* the devil, an evil power. **satanic** *adjective. Satanic powers.*

satellite *noun* 1 a heavenly body like a small planet, or a man-made object like a spacecraft, moving around a larger planet. The Moon is a satellite of the Earth. *A weather satellite was sent into space.* 2 a person or country taking orders from another more powerful one.

satellite dish *noun* a dish-shaped aerial for receiving signals from a space satellite.

satin *noun* a shiny cloth, usually made from silk. *Kate dressed up in satin pantaloons.*

satire *noun* amusing writing used to show how foolish or bad people or their ideas are.

satisfy (satisfies, satisfying, satisfied) *verb* 1 to give enough of what is wanted to make somebody pleased. *Nothing satisfies her, she is always complaining.* 2 to be enough or good enough for what is needed. *One bowl of soup is not enough to satisfy my hunger.* 3 to make somebody free from doubt, to convince. *When I had satisfied myself that everybody had gone, I locked the door.* **satisfaction** *noun.* **satisfactory** *adjective* good enough. **satisfying** *adjective* pleasing.

AMAZING FACT

'Saturday' comes from Old English and originally meant 'the day of Saturn', referring to the planet Saturn.

Saudi Arabia is one of the world's richest countries, due to its vast reserves of oil.

WORD HISTORY

Both 'sardine' and 'satin' come from place names. The small fish were originally caught off the coast of the Italian island of Sardinia, and they have been called sardines since the 15th century. The silky fabric called satin comes originally from China. The Arabs called the fabric 'zaytuni', which was their name for the Chinese port of Qingjiang.

saturate *verb* 1 to make very wet. 2 to fill completely so that no more can be held. *The handkerchief was saturated with perfume.* **saturation** *noun.*

Saturday *noun* the seventh and last day of the week. Saturday comes after Friday and before Sunday.

saucepan *noun* a metal cooking pot with a lid and a handle.

saucer *noun* a small dish on which a cup stands. *A cup and saucer.*

Saudi *noun* a person from Saudi Arabia. Saudi *adjective. A Saudi prince.*

Saudi Arabia *noun* a country in Southwest Asia.

sauna *noun* 1 a hot steam bath. 2 a room or place where you have a sauna.

saunter *verb* to walk in a slow, casual way.

sausage *noun* chopped-up meat in a thin casing that looks like a tube. *He had sausage, egg and chips for breakfast.*

savage *adjective* wild, uncontrollable or cruel. *The boy was bitten by a savage dog and had to go to hospital to have stitches.* **savagely** *adverb.* **savage** *noun* a cruel, wild or primitive person.

savannah *noun* a grassy plain with few trees. *The African savannah.*

save *verb* 1 to make somebody or something free from danger. *He saved my life.* 2 to keep something, especially money, for later use. *He has saved enough to buy a new bike.* 3 to make something unnecessary for somebody, so they don't have to do it. *Using a computer saves time.* 4 to stop a player from scoring. **save** *noun.*

savings *plural noun* money saved, especially in a bank. *My savings are under the bed.*

saw *verb* past tense of see.

saw *noun* a tool with a blade with sharp teeth along one edge for cutting wood or metal. *He gave me the saw to cut the wood into lengths.*

Arnold took the saw from the shed and prepared to cut the dead branch from the tree.

say (says, saying, said) *verb* 1 to speak words, using your voice to express something. 2 to give an opinion or thought in words or writing. *He said how nice everybody was to him on his trip to India.* **say** *noun* the power of acting or deciding. *She had no say in the matter.* **have your say** to have a chance to say what you think.

saying *noun* a sentence people often say that makes a wise statement.

scab *noun* 1 a dry crust, mainly of dried blood, which forms over a cut or wound. 2 somebody who does not join a trade union or a strike.

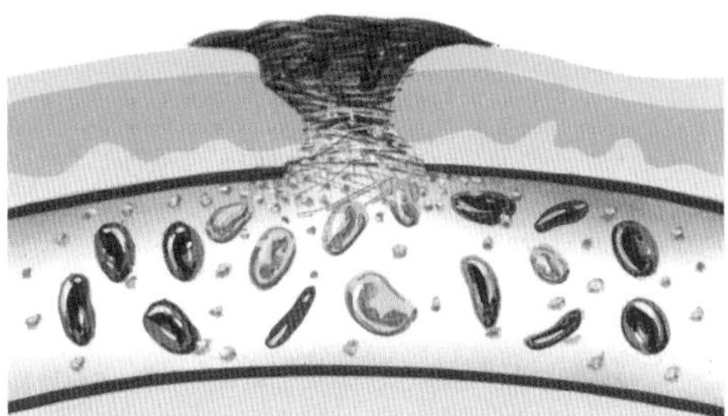

The blood clot dries in the air to form a hard crust called a scab.

scaffolding *noun* a framework of metal poles and boards put up round a building for workers to stand on while building or repairing a house.

scald *verb* 1 to burn yourself with hot liquid or steam. 2 to clean pans or instruments with boiling water or steam. **scald** *noun* a skin burn from hot liquid or steam. **scalding** *adjective. Scalding hot water.*

scale *noun* 1 a small, flat piece of hard skin that covers the skin of fish and reptiles. 2 a hard layer that forms at the bottom of a kettle, in pipes or on teeth. **scale** *verb* 1 to remove the scales, especially from fish. 2 to remove from a surface in thin pieces.

scale *noun* 1 a set of numbers, marks or degrees for measuring. *A ruler with a metric scale.* 2 a set of numbers comparing measurements on a map or model with the measurements in the real world. *The model is to scale.* 3 a size or importance in relation to other things. *The party is going to be on a grand scale.* 4 a set of musical notes arranged in order going upward or downward. *She practises the scales on the piano every day.* **scale** *verb* 1 to climb up. *The thief scaled the wall.* 2 to make a copy of something according to a certain scale. **scale down** to make something smaller in size or amount than it used to be.

scales *plural noun* a weighing machine. *Bathroom scales.*

scalp *noun* 1 the skin under the hair on the head. 2 a piece of skin and hair that was taken as a mark of victory when somebody was scalped. **scalp** *verb* to cut the scalp off a dead enemy.

DID YOU KNOW

Sayings are often clichés or proverbs, and people sometimes use the expression 'as the saying goes' to go with them: 'The left hand didn't know what the right hand was doing, as the saying goes.'

DID YOU KNOW

Some Native Americans scalped their enemies, and the scalp was considered to be a war trophy. This trophy was a symbol of triumph, and in modern American English the verb 'scalp' is used to mean to defeat.

scamper *verb* to run quickly with small, short steps. *Ned scampered up the tree.*

scan (scans, scanning, scanned) *verb* 1 to look closely and carefully, to examine. *Mother scanned our faces to see if anything was wrong.* 2 to look at something quickly without reading it properly or to search through information, especially on a computer. 3 to use special equipment to examine a person or pass an electronic beam over an area in search of something. 4 to count the pattern of beats in each line of poetry. **scan** *noun.*

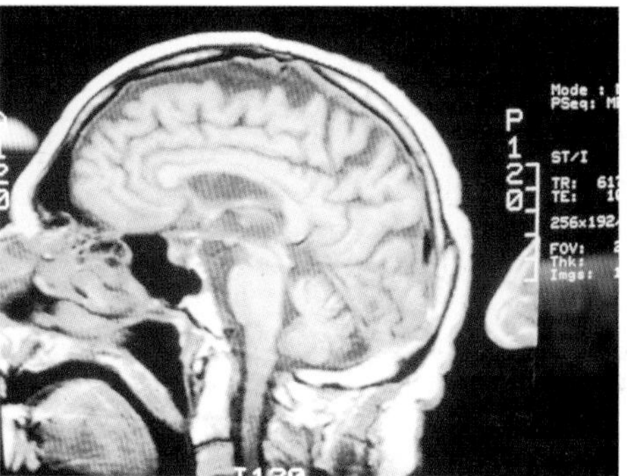

A scan can detect tumours growing inside the brain.

scandal *noun* 1 careless talk, gossip that shocks. *The tabloid newspapers love a bit of scandal.* 2 action that shocks or makes people angry. **scandalous** *adjective.*

Scandinavia *noun* a region covering the countries of northern Europe – Denmark, Finland, Iceland, Norway and Sweden.

The Little Mermaid sits on a rock on the harbour at Copenhagen, Denmark. She is Scandinavia's best-loved sculpture.

Scandinavian *noun* a person from Scandinavia. **Scandinavian** *adjective. Scandinavian languages.*

scanner *noun* 1 a device for putting pictures into a computer. 2 a machine used in hospitals for examining a person by moving a beam of light or X-rays over them.

scanty (scantier, scantiest) *adjective* very small, hardly big enough. **scantily** *adverb. Helen and Sarah were scantily dressed.*

scar *noun* a mark on the skin which is left after a wound or burn has healed. **scar** (scars, scarring, scarred) *verb* to mark with a scar or scars.

scarce *adjective* not enough compared with what is wanted, difficult to find. *Fruit is scarce in winter.* **scarcity** *noun. There is a scarcity of good humour in the office.*

scarcely *adverb* hardly, only just.

S

scare *noun* a sudden fear, alarm. **scare** *verb* to frighten or make you frightened, to become afraid. *I'm scared of the dark.* **scare away** to frighten somebody so that they go away. **scary** *adjective.*

scarecrow *noun* a figure dressed in old clothes that is put up in a field to frighten birds away.

The scarecrow was dressed in the farmer's old clothes.

scarf (scarves) *noun* a piece of cloth worn around the neck or head.

scarlet *adjective*, *noun* bright red.

scarper *verb* to run away.

scatter *verb* to throw or go in different directions. *He scattered his toys about and made a terrible mess.*

scatty (scattier, scattiest) *adjective* being a little mad or forgetful.

scavenge *verb* to look among rubbish for food or other things. *The old man scavenges in dustbins for food.* **scavenger** *noun* 1 somebody who scavenges. 2 a bird or animal that feeds on waste and decaying flesh.

scene *noun* 1 one of the parts of a play, film or book. 2 the background for a play. *There were only three scene changes.* 3 the place where an event or action happens or an area of activity. *The scene of the crime.* 4 a showing of anger. *He made a scene in the restaurant when I arrived late.* 5 a view. *She paints mountain scenes.* **behind the scenes** secretly. **set the scene** to prepare in order to understand what is going to happen next.

scenery (sceneries) *noun* 1 the landscape and everything natural around you. *When we reached the mountains, the scenery suddenly changed for the better.* 2 things used on a theatre stage, like the furniture and painted backgrounds.

Nick and Daphne like walking in the mountains because the air is clear and the scenery is breathtaking.

WORD HISTORY

The word 'sceptic' comes from the Greek 'skepsis', meaning speculation. The original Sceptics were ancient Greek philosophers who thought it was impossible to know things definitely. This philosophy began with Pyrrhon of Elis (c. 365–c.270 BC*), who was influenced by some of the thinkers he met on his travels to India.*

scent *noun* 1 a pleasant smell. *The scent of violets.* 2 a liquid perfume you put on your skin to smell nice. 3 a smell left by an animal that other animals can follow. **scent** *verb* 1 to smell. *The dog scented a fox.* 2 to feel that something is going to happen, to detect. *I scent trouble.* 3 to put scent on something or fill with scent. *The air was scented with flowers and full of the buzz of insects.*

sceptic (say **skep**-tik) *noun* somebody who does not believe things. **sceptical** *adjective I'm sceptical about our chances of winning.*

schedule (say **shed**-yool) *noun* a plan that gives a list of events and times for doing things. **on schedule** on time. **behind schedule** not on time. **schedule** *verb* to put into a plan or timetable. *A scheduled flight to Paris.*

scheme *noun* a plan of action or an arrangement. *I like your colour scheme better than your furniture.* **scheme** *verb* to make clever, secret plans. **schemer** *noun.*

scholar *noun* 1 a person who studies an academic subject and knows a lot about it. 2 a pupil or student who receives money (a bursary or scholarship) to study at a school or university.

school *noun* 1 a place for teaching children. 2 the time when teaching is done and you are at school. 3 all the teachers and pupils in a school. 4 a place for the study of a particular subject, especially a college or university department. 5 a group of people who think the same or have the same methods of work. 6 a group of dolphins or fish. **school** *verb* to train. **schooling** *noun.*

science *noun* the study of nature, natural things and the testing of natural laws. If you study science you might do chemistry, physics or biology. Psychology is a social science. **scientific** *adjective. Microscopes and thermometers are scientific instruments.*

scientist *noun* somebody who studies science or works in one of the sciences.

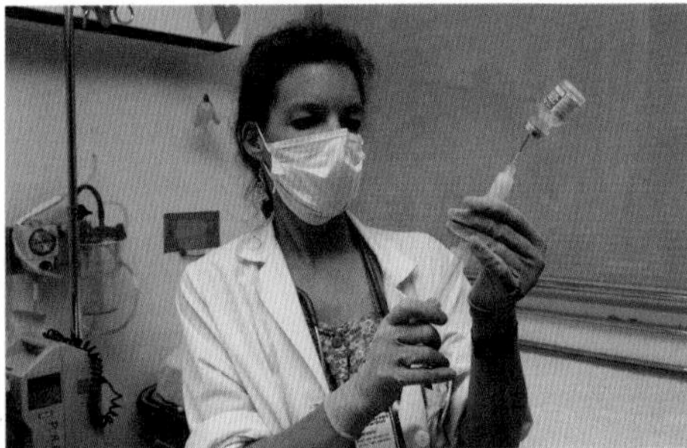

Jane trained as a scientist, then got a job as a lab technician.

scissors *plural noun* a tool with two sharp blades for cutting.

scoff *verb* 1 to speak in a mocking way about somebody or something. 2 to eat food quickly and greedily. *Who scoffed the cake?*

scold *verb* to tell somebody off, to speak angrily. *She scolded the children.*

scone *noun* (say skon rhyming with on, or skohn rhyming with bone) a small flat cake usually eaten with butter.

scoop *noun* 1 a deep round spoon for dishing out soft food such as ice-cream. 2 a shovel-shaped spoon for picking up grain, flour or sugar. *A measuring scoop.* 3 the amount a scoop holds. 4 an exciting news story reported by a newspaper before any other newspapers. 5 a successful piece of business, usually a large profit made from acting faster than others. **scoop** *verb* 1 to lift something or make a hole as if with a scoop. *She scooped out a hole in the sand.* 2 to pick something up with a scoop or spoon. *I scooped out some ice-cream.*

scooter *noun* 1 a kind of small motorbike. 2 a child's vehicle with a long handle and two small wheels attached to a board.

Scooters were very popular in the 1970s with Mods, while Rockers preferred motorbikes.

scope *noun* 1 an opportunity, a chance for action. *I wish there was more scope for doing your own mixing in music lessons.* 2 a range, a whole area of action.

scorch *verb* to burn something so it goes slightly brown. *The grass was scorched by the hot Sun.* **scorching** *adjective* very hot.

score *noun* 1 the number of points, goals or runs made in a game. 2 a written copy of a piece of music for the performers, showing what each one has to play. 3 a piece of music for a film or play. 4 twenty. *Two score and ten is 50.* When you get scores of something, you get a large number. *Scores of complaints.* 5 a reason or point. *He won't let us down, you can trust him on that score.* **score** *verb* 1 to win points in a game or competition, to get a goal, try or run in sport. 2 to keep a record of scores. 3 to gain or win success or an advantage. *She is only interested in scoring over her sister at parties.* 4 to mark or cut lines with a sharp instrument. *Score the card to make it easier to fold.* 5 to write out a musical score. **scorer** *noun. The scorer of most goals gets a medal and a certificate.*

scorn *noun* the feeling that somebody or something is worthless, contempt. **scorn** *verb* to show scorn. *She admires the rich and scorns the poor.* **scornful** *adjective. She is scornful about boys.* **scornfully** *adverb.*

AMAZING FACT

Scorpions belong to the same family as spiders because they have eight legs. They are very ancient creatures.

DID YOU KNOW

The first language of Scotland was Gaelic, which was introduced by Celts from Ireland about 1400 years ago. This became the native tongue of the Highlands and Islands of northern and western Scotland. English was introduced into these areas when it started being used in schools in the mid-18th century, but Gaelic is still spoken in the region today.

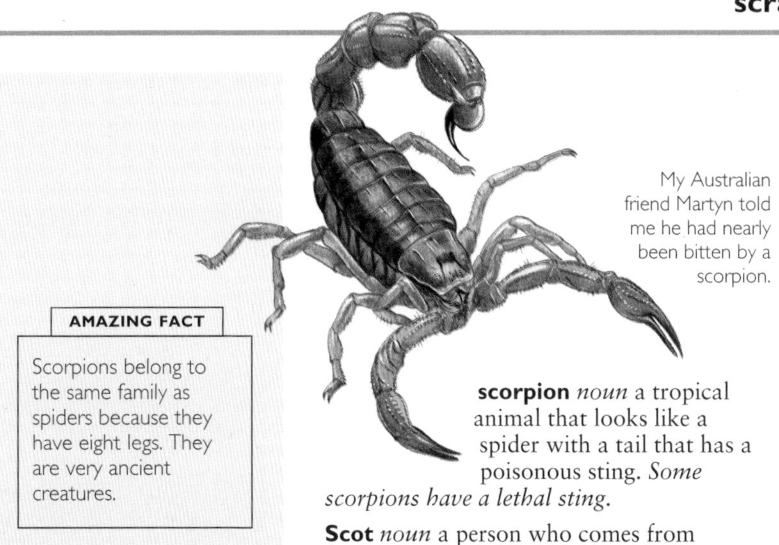

My Australian friend Martyn told me he had nearly been bitten by a scorpion.

scorpion *noun* a tropical animal that looks like a spider with a tail that has a poisonous sting. *Some scorpions have a lethal sting.*

Scot *noun* a person who comes from Scotland. *Most Scots like whisky.*

Scotland *noun* a country that is part of the United Kingdom.

Scots *noun* a dialect of the English language spoken in Scotland. **Scots** *adjective. A Scots writer from Glasgow.*

Scottish *adjective* from or belonging to Scotland. *The Scottish team.*

scour *verb* to clean something by rubbing it with rough material. *She scoured the pans.*

scour *verb* to search everywhere. *She scoured the papers for information.*

scout *noun* 1 somebody sent out to get information or look for talented sportsmen. 2 a member of the Scout Association. **scout** *verb* to go about looking for somebody or something. *We scouted around for a good hotel, but without any luck.*

scowl *noun* an angry expression on the face. **scowl** *verb* to frown to show anger. *He didn't say anything, he just scowled at me.*

scrap *noun* 1 a small piece, especially something unwanted or a small amount. *A scrap of paper.* Scraps are pieces of food that are usually thrown away. 2 waste material, especially metal. *Scrap metal.* **scrap** (scraps, scrapping, scrapped) *verb* to throw something unwanted away or cancel a plan or an idea.

After the accident, Gerry's car was a write-off and he had to send it for scrap.

scrap heap *noun* a pile of waste, unwanted things and ideas. *That plan might as well go on the scrap heap, it'll never work.*

scrape *verb* 1 to remove something by pulling or pushing a knife or other object over it. *He scraped the mud from his boots.* 2 to make something clean or smooth by pulling a knife or something rough over it. *She scraped the carrots before boiling them.* 3 to rub roughly or damage by rubbing. *He scraped his knee.* 4 to get or pass something with difficulty. *She scraped through the exam.* **scrape a living** to get just enough food or money to stay alive. **scrape** *noun* 1 a scraping movement or sound. 2 damage or hurt caused by scraping. 3 a difficult position, usually caused by yourself. *She got into a scrape for not doing her homework.*

scraper *noun* a tool for scraping.

scratch *verb* 1 to rub, cut or mark with something sharp or rough. *The cat scratched me.* 2 to rub the skin to stop itching. 3 to withdraw from a race or competition before it starts. **scratch** *noun* 1 a mark, cut or injury made by scratching. 2 the action or sound of scratching. *The dog likes a good scratch.* **scratchy** *adjective.* **start from scratch** to start from the beginning. **be up to scratch** to be good enough.

scrawl *verb* to write untidily. *He scrawled a message on the pad.* **scrawl** *noun.*

scrawny (scrawnier, scrawniest) *adjective* thin and bony. *A scrawny pigeon.*

scream *noun* 1 a loud cry or noise, usually because of pain or fear. *I could hear screams of laughter.* 2 somebody or something very funny. *You'd like her, she's a scream.* **scream** *verb* to make a scream.

screen *noun* 1 a flat surface on which television pictures, films or photographs are shown. *A computer screen.* 2 an upright frame, usually made to fold, used to divide a room or other area. 3 something that gives protection or hides. **screen** *verb* 1 to shelter, hide, protect or divide something or somebody. *The trees screened her from view.* 2 to show a film on television or in the cinema. 3 to examine or look carefully at somebody's ability or health. *She was screened for cancer.* **screen off** to make part of a room into a separate area.

If you stare at the screen on your computer all day, you may risk eyestrain or headaches.

I bought Basil a set of screwdrivers to thank him for plumbing in my washing machine.

A scroll is like a book on one long sheet of paper. The reader unrolls and rolls it as he or she reads.

WORD HISTORY

'Scuba' comes from the first letters of the words 'self-contained underwater breathing apparatus'.

AMAZING FACT

Word meaning changes as our lifestyles change. For example, the meaning of 'scroll' has changed since computers have become such an important part of our lives. It still has the original meaning of a roll of paper but it also means to move up or down a screen to view more information.

screw *noun* 1 a metal pin with spiral grooves round it used for fastening or holding things together. 2 a turning movement or something that twists like a screw. *He gave it another screw to make sure it was tight.* 3 a propeller on a ship or plane. 4 slang for a prison warder.

screwdriver *noun* a tool for turning screws.

scribble *verb* 1 to write quickly and untidily. 2 to make meaningless marks or rough drawings. **scribble** *noun. I can't read her scribble.*

script *noun* 1 a written form of a play, film or talk. *He writes scripts for television programmes.* 2 handwriting. 3 a particular system of writing. *Arabic script.*

scripture *noun* sacred writing.

scroll *noun* 1 a long roll of paper or other material with writing on it. 2 a spiral design.

scrotum (say **skroh**-tum) *noun* the bag of skin that holds the testicles.

scrounge *verb* to get something, usually money or food, by asking for it without paying or working for it. **scrounger** *noun.*

scrub (scrubs, scrubbing, scrubbed) *verb* 1 to clean by rubbing hard, usually with a brush. *She scrubbed the floor.* 2 to cancel. *The match was scrubbed.* **scrub** *noun.*

scrub *noun* low-growing bushes and trees or land covered with them.

scruffy (scruffier, scruffiest) *adjective* dirty and untidy. **scruffiness** *noun.*

scrum, scrummage *noun* 1 a group of rugby players from both teams pushing against each other to get the ball. 2 a crowd pushing against each other.

scuba *noun* a container of air under pressure which a diver carries on his back and uses for breathing while swimming under water.

scuba-diving *noun* swimming underwater using a scuba.

sculpt *verb* to carve or model shapes in clay, wood or metal. **sculpture** *noun* the art of making shapes in wood, clay or metal or the shape made in this way. **sculptor** *noun* an artist who makes sculptures.

scum *noun* 1 a covering of dirt on top of water or other liquid. 2 worthless people.

scurf *noun* bits of dry, dead skin in the hair.

scurvy *noun* a disease caused by not eating enough fruit and vegetables with vitamin C.

scythe *noun* a tool with a long curving blade on a long handle for cutting grass.

sea *noun* 1 salty water that covers most of the Earth's surface. 2 a particular area of the sea surrounded by land. *The North Sea.* 3 a large number. *A sea of daffodils.* **by the sea** at the seaside. **at sea** 1 on the sea. 2 confused. *She was completely at sea.*

seagull *noun* a seabird.

Seagulls eat worms on land and fish at sea.

sea horse *noun* a very small upright fish with a head that looks like a horse.

seal *noun* a large sea-animal without legs but big flippers that eats fish and lives both on land and in the sea.

seal *noun* 1 something fixed to a letter or container that must be broken before opening. *The seal on the packet was damaged.* 2 a piece of wax or lead stamped with a design or fixed to documents to show that they are official. 3 the metal tool with the design or a small decorative sticker for sealing a letter or document. 4 something made to close an opening to stop gas, air or liquid getting out. **seal** *verb* 1 to close something tightly. *To seal an envelope.* 2 to put a seal on something. 3 to stop something up or close an opening. *He sealed the cracks with mud.* 4 to make something certain. *We sealed the agreement by shaking hands.* **seal off** to close tightly to stop somebody or something from getting in or out. *The police sealed off the street around the accident.*

sea level *noun* the height of the sea halfway between high and low tide, used for measuring height on land and depth at sea. *1,000 metres above sea level.*

sea lion *noun* a kind of large seal.

seam *noun* 1 a line of stitches that joins two pieces of cloth together or a line where two edges meet. 2 a long layer of coal or another mineral in the ground.

SPELLING NOTE

When it is used with names, 'sea' is written with a capital 's': 'the North Sea'. The biggest sea in the world is the South China Sea, which is part of the Pacific Ocean. The next three biggest are the Caribbean Sea, the Mediterranean Sea and the Bering Sea.

AMAZING FACT

Seahorses swim by moving a fin located in the middle of their backs. They are strange, delicate-looking creatures – and their behaviour is unusual, too. The males, not the females, take care of the eggs until they hatch by keeping them in a pouch on their belly.

search *verb* 1 to look carefully through a place to try to find something. *She searched for her purse.* 2 to examine somebody's clothing for something hidden. *They were searched by the police.* **search** *noun.*

seasick *adjective* feeling sick when travelling in a ship. **seasickness** *noun.*

seaside *noun* a place at the edge of the sea, especially one where people go for their holiday. *Let's take a trip to the seaside.*

The children loved their holidays by the seaside.

season *noun* 1 one of four periods of time each year. The four seasons are spring, summer, autumn and winter. 2 the time of year when something usually happens. *The football season.* **in season** available and ready for eating. *Peaches are in season.* **out of season** 1 not available. 2 not busy. *We usually go to Venice out of season, when it is easy to find a cheap hotel.*

As the seasons change, so the leaves bud, open, flourish, dry and eventually drop.

season *verb* 1 to add salt, pepper or other spices to food to give it a special taste. 2 to leave wood to dry so it can be used. **seasoning** *noun* salt, pepper and spices used to season food.

season ticket *noun* a ticket that can be used whenever you like during a fixed period of time.

seat *noun* 1 a place for sitting on or the part you sit on. *I prefer to sit in the back seat.* 2 a place an official member holds. *A seat on the committee.* 3 a place where something is. *London is the seat of government.* **take a back seat** to leave decisions to others. **seat** *verb* 1 to have enough seats for. *The stadium seats 50,000 people.* 2 to sit down.

seat belt *noun* a belt fixed to the seat of a car or plane which you fasten around you for safety. *Fasten your seat belts ready for take-off, please.*

seaweed *noun* a plant that grows in the sea.

S

seaworthy *adjective* in good condition and fit for a sea voyage. **seaworthiness** *noun.*

second *adjective* 1 next in order after the first. *February is the second month of the year.* 2 another or extra. *Many families have a second car.* **second** *adverb.*

second *noun* 1 a length of time. There are 60 seconds in a minute. 2 a very short time, a moment. *Wait a second.* 3 a person or thing that is second. *I was the second to arrive.* 4 a thing that is not the best. Seconds are goods that are sold cheaply, usually because they are of less good quality. **second** *verb* to help or speak in support of somebody. *I seconded her proposal.*

second-hand *adjective* owned by somebody else before. *We bought a second-hand car.*

second-rate *adjective* of poor quality.

secret *adjective* 1 not told or shown to anybody else, not known by everybody. *We made a secret plan to leave before midnight.* **secret** *noun* something secret. **secrecy** *noun* the habit of keeping secrets. **secretive** *adjective. Secretive whisperings.*

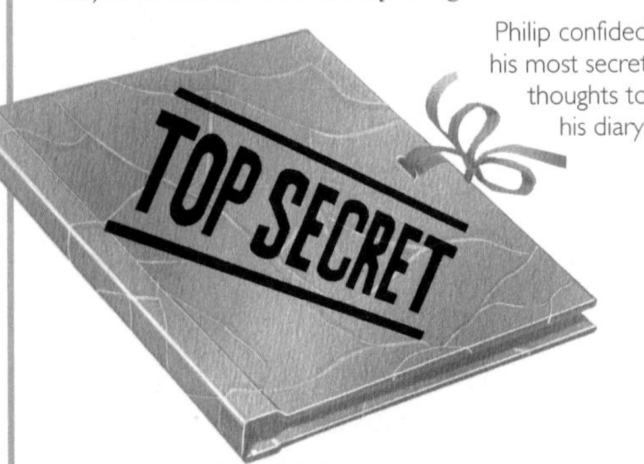

Philip confided his most secret thoughts to his diary.

secretary (secretaries) *noun* 1 somebody whose job it is to deal with letters, telephone calls and arranging meetings and other business affairs. 2 a government minister. *The Secretary of State for Wales.*

sect *noun* a small group of people who have the same religious or political beliefs.

section *noun* 1 a part of something larger. *Picture books go in the children's section.* 2 one of a number of equal parts that can be put together. 3 a cross-section. *This a section through an apple.* **sectional** *adjective.*

secular *adjective* not religious.

secure *adjective* 1 safe, well protected against danger. *Secure locks and windows.* 2 firmly fixed or certain not to be lost. *She has a secure job.* 3 not worried, happy. *Small children need to feel secure with their parents.* **secure** *verb* 1 to make something safe from harm or attack. 2 to get, usually after having made an effort. *We managed to secure two tickets for the concert.* 3 to fix firmly in position. *The shelf was secured to the wall.* **securely** *adverb.* **security** *noun.*

AMAZING FACT

The difference between 'to see' and 'to look' is attention, like the difference between 'hear' and 'listen'. In other words, you can see something, then decide to pay attention and look at it.

WORD HISTORY

The word 'secret' comes from the Latin 'secretus', meaning 'separate' or 'hidden'. 'Secretary' comes from the same source, because it originally referred to a person who was entrusted with a secret.

AMAZING FACT

Plants use a variety of methods to scatter or spread their seeds. Some seeds, such as those from the maple tree, have wings that carry them on the wind. Others, like the acorns produced by oak trees, are stored or eaten by animals. Some seeds have tiny hooks that stick to the fur of animals, allowing them to 'hitch a ride'.

sedative *noun* a drug that calms you or helps you go to sleep.

sediment *noun* solid material that sinks to the bottom of a liquid.

David dredged the sediment from the bottom of the pond and tipped it into a heap.

seduce *verb* to tempt or persuade somebody to do something they might not normally do. *The sales seduced me into buying myself new clothes.* **seductive** *adjective.* **seduction** *noun.*

see (sees, seeing, saw, seen) *verb* 1 to use your eyes, to look at something. 2 to visit or meet. *He has to see the doctor.* 3 to understand. *I can see what you mean.* 4 to watch a film or play. 5 to make sure something is done. *I'll see that dinner is ready.* 6 to imagine or tell what might happen. *I can't see him giving the money back.* 7 to go with somebody, to accompany. *Can you see her home?* 8 to learn something, usually by reading about it. *I see that your team has been promoted.* **see you!** goodbye! **see about** to make arrangements for something to be done. *My brother will see about the tent.* **we'll see about that** perhaps. **see off** to go to the airport or station with somebody who is going on a trip to say goodbye. **see through** 1 to see the truth about somebody or something, not to be fooled. *He made all sorts of promises, but I saw through him.* 2 to support or help until the end. *He earned enough money in one week to see him through the whole summer.* **see to** to take care of, to deal with something.

seed *noun* 1 the small hard part of a plant from which a new plant grows. 2 one of the players named as the best before the start of a competition. *The top seeds don't play against each other in the early rounds.* **seed** *verb* 1 to plant or grow seeds. 2 to place players, especially tennis players, in order of likelihood of winning.

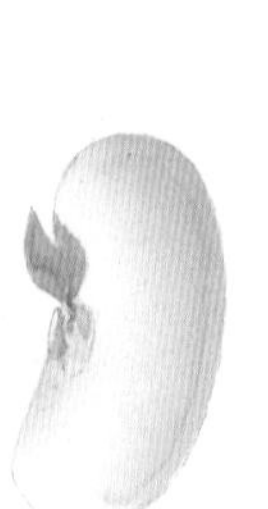
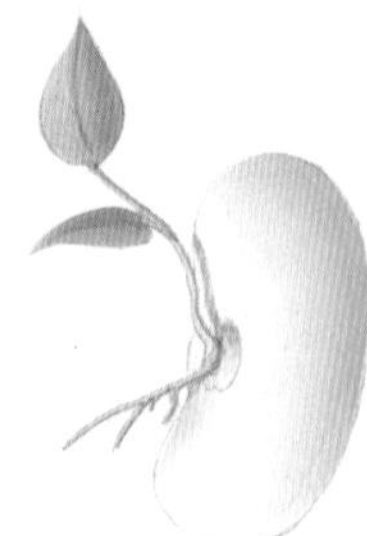

When a seed germinates, it sends up a shoot and sends down a root. It needs water, warmth and light to do this.

seedling *noun* a young plant raised from seed. *The seedlings are in the greenhouse.*

seedy (seedier, seediest) *adjective* looking poor, run-down or uncared for. *He lives in a seedy part of town.*

seek (seeks, seeking, sought) *verb* to search for, to try to get or find.

seem *verb* to appear to be, to give the impression of being something. *It seemed a good idea at the time.* **seemingly** *adverb.*

seen *verb* past tense of see.

seep *verb* to flow slowly through a small opening. *The water seeped slowly away.*

see-saw *noun* a plank balanced in the middle for children to sit on at each end, so that when one end goes down the other goes up. **see-saw** *verb* to move backwards and forwards or up and down. *Prices see-sawed up and down all year.*

seethe *verb* 1 to be very angry, excited, or upset about something. *She was seething with rage.* 2 to bubble as if boiling.

segment *noun* a part marked or cut off from other parts. *An orange segment.*

Annette divided the orange into segments and offered one to each of the triplets.

segregate *verb* to put somebody or something apart from the rest. *It is wrong to segregate people by the colour of their skin.* **segregation** *noun. Religious segregation causes wars.*

seismic *adjective* of earthquakes or sudden shakings of the ground. *There is a lot of seismic activity in the area.*

seismology *noun* the study of earthquakes. **seismologist** *noun.*

seize *verb* 1 to take hold of suddenly and forcefully or to take control of. *Panic seized us.* 2 to take by force, to arrest or capture somebody. *The goods were seized by the police.* 3 to take and use something, especially a chance or an idea. **seize up** to become unable to move. *My back seized up after the tennis match.*

seldom *adverb* not often.

select *verb* to choose somebody or something. **selection** *noun.*

self (selves) *noun* somebody's personality or nature. *She is her old self again.*

self- *prefix* done by or to yourself.

AMAZING FACT

Seismographs show how strong the tremors of an earthquake are. A weight is suspended from a spring, the weight holds a tracer which moves up and down, 'drawing' the strength of the tremor on a drum.

DID YOU KNOW

One of the most famous seismologists was Charles Francis Richter (1900–85). In 1935 he devised the Richter scale, which is still used to measure the strength of earthquakes. Richter's system measured the strength of seismic waves.

self-centred *adjective* interested only in yourself. *A very self-centred child.*

self-confidence *noun* a feeling of power or confidence to do things successfully. **self-confident** *adjective.*

self-conscious *adjective* embarrassed and nervous because you know or think people are looking at you. *I'm too self-conscious to be a good actor.*

self-contained *adjective* complete in itself. *A beautiful self-contained flat.*

self-control *noun* control over your feelings. **self-controlled** *adjective. He is very self-controlled and never loses his temper.*

self-defence *noun* the use or skill of defending yourself.

James always excelled himself in his self-defence class.

self-employed *adjective* working for yourself and not for an employer. **self-employment** *noun.*

self-explanatory *adjective* clear and needing no explanation.

self-important *adjective* having a high opinion of yourself. **self-importance** *noun.*

self-respect *noun* a feeling of pride in your own ability and respect for yourself.

self-sacrifice *noun* giving up what you want, so others can have it.

self-satisfied *adjective* very pleased with yourself. **self-satisfaction** *noun.*

self-service *adjective* a system in shops, restaurants or petrol stations where you serve yourself and pay a cashier.

Luke and Hannah enjoyed choosing their own food at the self-service restaurant.

self-sufficient *adjective* able to make or produce everything that is needed without outside help. A self-sufficient country does not have to buy goods from other countries. **self-sufficiency** *noun. Rod and Hazel decided to try self-sufficiency and bought a farm in Wales.*

S

selfish *adjective* thinking mainly of yourself and what you want. **selfishness** *noun*. **selfishly** *adverb*.

sell (sells, selling, sold) *verb* to give something in exchange for money. **sell out** 1 to sell everything so there is nothing left. *They have sold out of sunglasses.* 2 to agree secretly to work for the other side, to betray. **sell up** to sell everything you have. *I'll sell up and leave.* **seller** *noun*.

Dave and Janice sold meat at the market every Thursday.

semen *noun* (say **seem**-un) the fluid produced by the male sex organs that carries sperm for fertilizing.

semi- *prefix* half or partly. *A semi-detached house is my mother's dream.*

semicircle *noun* one half of a circle. **semicircular** *adjective*.

semicolon *noun* a punctuation mark (;) used in writing that separates different parts of a sentence.

senate *noun* 1 the upper house or council in the government of some countries, for example in the USA, France and Australia. 2 the highest council of state in ancient Rome.

senator *noun* a member of a senate.

send (sends, sending, sent) *verb* 1 to make somebody or something go or be taken somewhere. 2 to make something move quickly in a direction. *The explosion sent glass flying everywhere.* 3 to cause somebody to feel in a particular way. *The noise is sending me crazy.* **send for** to ask somebody to come or order something. *They sent for an ambulance.* **send up** 1 to make something go up. *The coffee shortage has sent the prices up.* 2 to make fun of by imitating something or somebody.

Senegal *noun* a country in Africa.

The flag of Senegal has green, yellow and red strips, with a star in the centre.

senile *adjective* mentally confused because of old age. **senility** *noun*.

senior *adjective* 1 older in age. 2 higher in rank. 3 A senior citizen is an old-age pensioner. **seniority** *noun*.

GRAMMAR NOTE

A semicolon can be used along with commas to separate items in a list in a logical way: 'You will need knives, forks and spoons; cups and saucers; and plates, bowls and glasses.'

SPELLING NOTE

Both ancient and modern senates are usually spelt with a capital 's'. In the USA, the Senate and the House of Representatives together make up Congress.

WORD HISTORY

A sentence was originally a 'way of thinking', and came from the Latin 'sententia', meaning 'opinion'.

sensation *noun* 1 a feeling, especially of heat or pain. 2 a state of excitement. *The new film created a sensation.* 3 a general feeling in the mind that cannot be described. *It gave me a strange sensation to see the house I lived in as a child.*

sensational *adjective* exciting or shocking.

sense *noun* 1 any of the five senses, the ability to see, hear, smell, touch and taste. 2 the ability to make good judgements, be sensible. *He should have shown a little more sense.* 3 a meaning or explanation. *This word has many senses.* 4 an awareness of something. *She has a great sense of humour!* **make sense** to have a clear meaning. **make sense of** to understand. *Can you make sense of his letter?* **sense** *verb* to become aware of something. *He sensed danger.*

During the mating season a warthog's sense of smell becomes highly developed.

sensibility *noun* sensitiveness.

sensible *adjective* able to make good decisions, wise. *It was not very sensible to set off without a map.*

sensitive *adjective* 1 easily hurt in your feelings or offended. 2 quick to feel the effect of something, easily affected by something. *My eyes are very sensitive to bright light.* 3 being aware of other people's feelings or problems. 4 measuring exactly or showing very small changes. *A very sensitive pair of scales.* **sensitivity** *noun*.

sensual *adjective* enjoyable or giving pleasure to your body. *Eating and drinking were sensual pleasures in ancient Rome.* **sensuality** *noun*.

sent *verb* past tense of send.

sentence *noun* 1 a group of words that form a statement, question or command. When you write a sentence, you start with a capital letter and end with a full stop. 2 a punishment for a criminal who is found guilty in court. *He received the death sentence.* **sentence** *verb* to give a punishment to somebody in court.

sentiment *noun* 1 an opinion or judgement based on your feelings or thoughts. *We did not agree with the headmaster's sentiments.* 2 a tender feeling like love, happiness or sadness or memories of the past.

S

sentimental *adjective* having or showing romantic feelings, usually not reasonable or practical ones. Sentimental songs are about love, sadness or childhood memories. *She keeps her old teddy for sentimental reasons.* **sentimentality** *noun.*

sentry (sentries) *noun* a soldier keeping watch. *The sentry fell asleep on duty.*

A sentry in traditional costume stands on duty outside the Vatican in Rome.

Seoul *noun* the capital of South Korea.

sepal *noun* any of the leaves forming the calyx of a bud.

separate (say sep-rut) *adjective* 1 divided, not joined to anything, not shared with another. *She cut it into two separate parts.* 2 different. *He gave her three separate reasons for not going.*

separate (say sep-uh-rate) *verb* 1 to keep apart, to be or become divided. *A wall separates our gardens.* 2 to stop living together. *My parents separated when I was eight.* **separation** *noun* 1 separating or being separated. 2 a time of being or living apart.

September *noun* the ninth month of the year. September has 30 days.

septic *adjective* infected with poison. *The wound has turned septic.*

sepulchre *noun* a tomb. *The king was buried in a sepulchre.*

sequel *noun* 1 a book or film that continues the story of an earlier one. 2 an event or situation that follows something else that happened before.

sequence *noun* 1 a number of things that come one after another. 2 the order in which things are arranged. *Don't mix up the tickets, they have to be kept in sequence.* 3 a part of a film when something particular happens. *In the opening sequence the hero changes into a monster.*

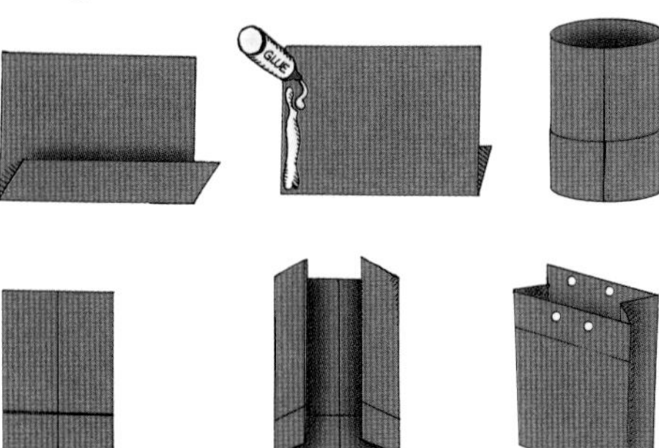

This sequence of diagrams shows step-by-step instructions for making a bag.

DID YOU KNOW

Seoul has been an important settlement since the 11th century. During the Korean War (1950–53) the city was badly damaged and changed hands four times. The city now has a population of more than 10 million.

serene *adjective* calm and peaceful.

sergeant (say sar-junt) *noun* 1 an officer in the army or air force who ranks above corporal. 2 an officer in the police force who ranks below inspector.

serial *noun* a story with a number of separate parts. **serialize** *verb. The book has been serialized on television.*

series (series) *noun* a number of things coming one after another or in order. *A series of books on outer space.*

serious *adjective* 1 thoughtful, not cheerful, joking or funny. If something is serious, it is important and has to be thought about carefully. 2 not slight, causing worry. *A serious illness.* **seriously** *adverb.* **seriousness** *noun.*

sermon *noun* 1 a speech given in church. 2 a lecture or telling-off.

serpent *noun* a snake.

A serpent is a symbol of temptation.

servant *noun* somebody who works for another person, usually in their house.

serve *verb* 1 to work for somebody, an organization or your country. 2 to provide with something necessary or be suitable for something. *That old raincoat has served me well.* 3 to help customers in a shop or restaurant. *A very nice waitress served us.* 4 to give or offer food to people. *Strawberries are usually served with cream.* 5 to spend a time in prison. *He has already served three years of his sentence.* 6 to begin a game of tennis by hitting the ball. **it serves you right** it is your own fault. **serve** *noun* serving, as in tennis. *He has a good serve.* **server** *noun.*

service *noun* 1 something that helps people or provides what the public need. *The train service is poor.* 2 a job done for somebody. *You might need the services of a lawyer.* 3 the serving of customers in a shop or restaurant. *The food is good, but the service is slow.* 4 the repairing of cars and other machines. *I took the car in for a service.* 5 a set of plates and dishes. *A tea service.* 6 a religious ceremony. *Morning service.* 7 serving in tennis. **service** *verb* to check or repair a car or other machine. *Peter made a lovely job of servicing my car.*

session *noun* 1 a formal meeting of an organization. *The court is in session.* 2 a meeting or a time used for an activity. *A recording session.*

set (sets, setting, set) *verb* 1 to put or place in a position. *The story is set in the mountains.* 2 to fix something. *He set a price for the house.* 3 to cause somebody or something to be in a condition. *They set the house on fire.* 4 to prepare something for use or to start doing something. *To set the table.* 5 to go hard. *Wait for the glue to set.* 6 to give yourself or somebody work or a task. *The teacher set the questions for the exam.* 7 to go down. *The Sun was setting.* **set about** to start doing something. *He doesn't know how to set about getting a job.* **set back** 1 to place something at a distance behind something. *The house is set back from the road.* 2 to delay or make late. *The rain has set back the final.* 3 to cost somebody a lot of money. *How much did the car set you back?* **set off** 1 to begin a journey. 2 to make something begin or happen. *Don't set her off crying.* 3 to cause an explosion. *He set off the rocket.* **set out** 1 to present or make something known. *He set out the rules.* 2 to start a journey. **set to** to begin to do something. **set up** 1 to place in position. *We still have to set up the telescope.* 2 to arrange. *He set up a meeting.* 3 to start, establish. *They set up a new school in the village.*

set *noun* 1 a group of people or things that go together. *A set of screwdrivers.* 2 a radio or TV receiver. 3 the place where a play or film is acted. 4 a group of six or more games that make up part of a tennis match.

setback *noun* something that makes your position less good than it was before.

settee *noun* a sofa. *The children hid behind the settee when something frightening came on the television.*

setting *noun* 1 the surrounding or place in which something is or happens. *A dark forest is the perfect setting for a fairy tale.* 2 the positions in which the controls of a machine are set. *The dishwasher has three settings – hot, cold and economy.*

settle *verb* 1 to decide or fix something. *They have finally settled their quarrel.* 2 to become quiet or make calm, to rest. *The medicine will settle your stomach.* 3 to stay in a place or job, to stop being restless. *He travelled the world and finally settled in Canada.* 4 to sink in liquid or come down and cover something. *The snow is settling.* 5 to pay a bill or money owed. **settle down** 1 to become quiet or calm. 2 to start living a quiet life. *He got married and settled down.* 3 to sit down and concentrate on something.

GRAMMAR NOTE

Watch out for sexism in your writing. Many people now object to the use of 'he' and 'his' when what is really meant is 'he or she' and 'his or hers'. One way round this is to use 'they' or 'their': 'If a student is unsure how to register, they should ask their tutor.' You can also easily avoid male-sounding words, for example by using 'the human race' or 'humans' for 'mankind', etc.

The chess set was carved out of black and white wood.

AMAZING FACT

After Daniel Boone blazed the Wilderness Road in 1775, thousands of settlers headed west, beyond the Appalachian Mountains. They, in turn, pushed the Native Americans farther west. Most settlers were not prepared for life in the wilderness and many did not survive.

settlement *noun* 1 a place people have gone to and built homes in, setting up a community. *There was a settlement near the river.* 2 an agreement or decision between two sides. 3 payment of a debt.

The settlement was made up of conical houses with roofs of straw.

settler *noun* a person who goes to live in a new country.

sever *verb* to break or cut. *He severed all links with his family.*

several *adjective, pronoun* some things or people, usually a fairly small number, not many more than two.

sew (sews, sewing, sewed, sewn) *verb* (say soe) to join pieces of material together or make or mend clothing with a needle and thread or a sewing-machine.

sewage (say **soo**-ij) *noun* waste material from houses people live and work in which flows through sewers.

sewer (say **soo**-uh) *noun* a large pipe under the ground that carries sewage away.

sewing machine *noun* a machine for sewing things.

Anita made all her children's clothes on the sewing machine.

sex (sexes) *noun* 1 the condition of being either male or female, gender. *It is difficult to tell what sex the bird is.* 2 the two groups, male and female, into which people and animals are divided. *The opposite sex.* 3 sexual activity by which people and animals produce young and all the activities connected with this act. **sexy** *adjective.*

sexism *noun* the belief that one sex is not as good as the other, especially that women are less able than men.

sexist *adjective* showing sexism. *It's simply sexist to say that women are bad drivers.* **sexist** *noun.*

sexual *adjective* 1 being male or female. *The sexual differences between boys and girls.* 2 connected with sex as male and female activity and the wish for it. 3 connected with the process by which people and animals produce young. *Sexual intercourse.* **sexually** *adverb.* **sexuality** *noun.*

Seychelles *noun* a country in the Indian Ocean off West Africa.

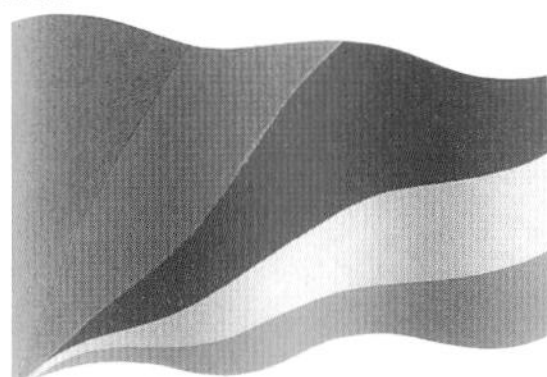
The Seychelles has a flag of unfurling colours, blue, orange, red, white and green.

shade *noun* 1 darkness under or next to an object, made when something blocks out the Sun. *We sat in the shade of a tree.* 2 Something that keeps out light. *The lamp needs a new shade.* 3 the different forms of a colour. How light or dark a colour is. *Many shades of blue.* 4 a little bit. *There was a shade of fear in his voice.* 5. a slight difference. *A word with many shades of meaning.* **shade** *verb* 1 to protect something from bright light. *He shaded his eyes with his hand.* 2 to make part of a drawing darker. *She shaded in the background with a pencil.*

shadow *noun* 1 a dark shape on a surface made when something stands between a light and the surface. *I saw his shadow on the wall.* 2 a dark area. *She has shadows under her eyes.* 3 a darkness in a place due to no light reaching it. *The valley is in shadow.* 4 a form not as real as it used to be. *She is just a shadow of her former self.* 5 a little bit. *A shadow of doubt.* **shadow** *verb* 1 to follow somebody secretly. *The detective shadowed the man on his journey through the town.* 2 to make a shadow on something.

shady (shadier, shadiest) *adjective* 1 giving shade. 2 dishonest. *Shady dealings.*

shaft *noun* 1 a long thin pole or handle. *The shaft of an arrow.* 2 a beam of light coming through an opening. 3 a deep, narrow hole.

shaggy (shaggier, shaggiest) *adjective* untidy and rough hair or fur. *A shaggy beard.*

shake (shakes, shaking, shook, shaken) *verb* 1 to move quickly backwards and forwards or up and down. *He shook the pears from the tree.* 2 to shock or upset. *She was shaken by the bad news.* 3 to tremble. *They were shaking with laughter.* **shake hands** to hold somebody's right hand when meeting or saying goodbye to them. **shake your head** to move your head from side to side to say 'no'. **shake** *noun* 1 the action of shaking. 2 a drink. *Milk shake.* **shaky** (shakier, shakiest) *adjective* weak, not very good or unsafe. **shakiness** *noun.*

The shallow part of the river provided an easy crossing for the buffalo.

WORD HISTORY

The word 'shambles', which is plural but usually treated as if it were singular, comes from the Old English 'sceamul', which meant a stall or stool. Stalls were used by butchers to set out their meat for sale, and the word 'shamble' came to mean a slaughterhouse. Presumably the stalls must often have been scattered about a room or street, leading to the modern meaning of a shambles.

shallot *noun* a small onion.

shallow *adjective* 1 not deep. *A shallow river.* 2 not showing much thought, not very serious. *She lives a shallow life.*

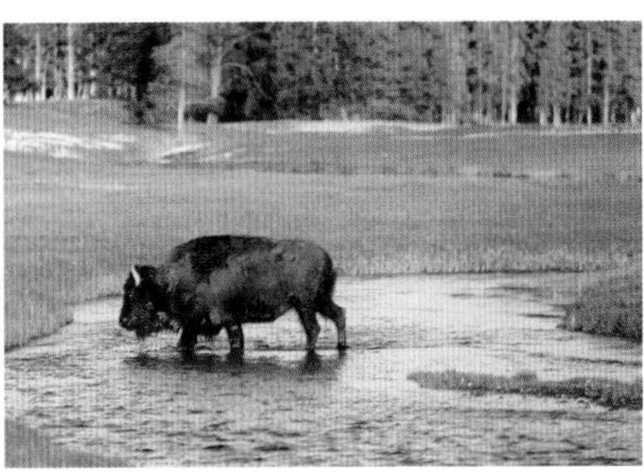

sham *noun* something false pretending to be real. *Her friendliness is just a sham.* **sham** (shams, shamming, shammed) *verb. She shammed interest.* **sham** *adjective.*

shamble *verb* to walk dragging your feet.

shambles *plural noun* a place or scene of disorder, a mess. *After the party the whole house was a shambles.*

shame *noun* 1 a feeling of guilt or embarrassment. *He had a deep sense of shame after the incident.* 2 feeling sorry about something. *It's a shame you can't come.* **shame** *verb* to feel shame or make somebody feel ashamed. **shameful** *adjective.*

shampoo *noun* 1 a special liquid for washing hair. 2 a liquid for cleaning a car or carpet. **shampoo** *verb* to wash or clean with shampoo. *Please shampoo your hair.*

shape *noun* 1 the outer form of something, an outline. *A square and a circle are shapes.* 2 condition. *She looks in good shape.* **take shape** to develop. **shape** *verb* 1 to make something into a particular shape. *The cake was shaped like a heart.* 2 to develop in a particular way. *Being bullied at school shaped her whole life.*

These building blocks are made of many different shapes.

share *noun* 1 a part belonging, given or done by a person. *He does his share of the washing-up.* 2 one of the equal parts into which the ownership of a company is divided. *He owns shares in British Telecom.* **share** *verb* 1 to have or use something with others. *She shares a flat.* 2 to give a portion of something to others, to divide. *They shared the money between them.*

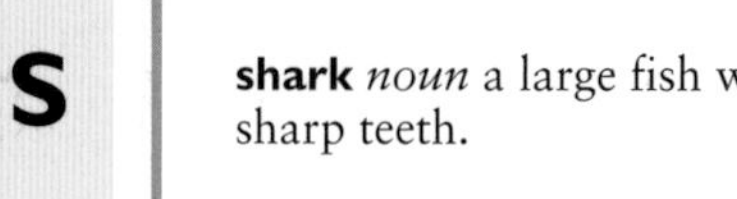

shark *noun* a large fish with sharp teeth.

Contrary to popular belief, most sharks will not attack humans.

sharp *adjective* 1 with a fine cutting edge or point. *A sharp knife.* 2 clear to see. *A sharp outline.* 3 quick in thinking, seeing or hearing, quickly aware of things. 4 having a quick change in direction or steep and sudden. *A sharp bend.* 5 severe and sudden, firm. *A sharp frost.* 6 sudden and loud. *A sharp cry of pain.* 7 sour, fresh in taste. *Gooseberries are too sharp for me, even with sugar sprinkled over them.* 8 a sharp note in music is higher than the normal pitch. **sharply** *adverb*. **sharpness** *noun*.

sharp *adverb* 1 immediately. *Turn sharp left at the church.* 2 exactly, punctually. *We arrived at 3 o'clock sharp.*

shatter *verb* 1 to suddenly break into small pieces. *A stone shattered the windscreen.* 2 to destroy or upset. *My hopes were shattered.* If you are shattered after a hard day, you are very tired.

shave *verb* 1 to cut hair off the skin with a razor. 2 to cut or scrape thin pieces off something. *You'll have to shave some wood off the bottom to make the door shut.* **shave** *noun*. He needs a good shave. **a close shave** a near accident or disaster. **shaver** *noun*.

shawl *noun* a piece of material worn around the head or shoulders or wrapped around a baby. *Wrap the baby warmly in the shawl.*

shear (shears, shearing, sheared, shorn) *verb* to cut off hair or wool from sheep.

David could shear sheep faster than anyone else in the county.

DID YOU KNOW

The Arabic word 'sheikh' is a term of respect and courtesy, dating from pre-Islamic times, that means 'old man'.

WORD BUILDING

The word 'shepherd' is a contraction, or shortening, of the words 'sheep herd', meaning a person who herds sheep.

shears *plural noun* a tool that looks like a large pair of scissors for cutting hedges and long grass. *Shears for shearing sheep.*

shed *noun* a small building for storing things. *A bike shed.*

shed (sheds, shedding, shed) *verb* 1 to flow out or let something fall. *She shed many tears.* 2 to get rid of or give off. *Snakes shed their skin as they grow.*

sheep (sheep) *noun* a farm animal with thick woolly fur. *A flock of sheep.*

sheepish *adjective* embarrassed, usually because you have done something silly. *He gave her a sheepish look.*

sheet *noun* 1 a large piece of cloth, usually cotton, put on a bed. 2 a piece of paper. 3 a large, flat, thin piece of glass, metal or wood. 4 a wide stretch of something thin. *A sheet of ice.*

sheikh (say shake) *noun* an Arab chief or prince. *The sheikh gave the queen a ruby.*

shelf (shelves) *noun* 1 a flat board fixed against a wall or in a cupboard for putting things on. 2 a piece of rock on a mountain that sticks out like a shelf.

shell *noun* 1 the hard outer covering of an animal, egg, fruit, nut or seed. 2 the walls of a building or ship. 3 a metal case filled with explosive for firing from a large gun. **shell** *verb* 1 to take something out of a shell. *She was shelling peas.* 2 to fire explosive shells. *The town was shelled during the attack.*

Karen made a beautiful collection of shells from the beach.

shelter *noun* 1 something that gives protection, usually a small building or covered place. *A bus shelter.* 2 protection or being kept safe. *We took shelter under a tree.* **shelter** *verb* 1 to protect somebody or something from harm. *They sheltered an escaped prisoner.* 2 to take shelter.

shepherd *noun* a person who looks after sheep. *The shepherds watched their flocks.*

shield *noun* 1 a large piece of metal, wood or leather which soldiers used to carry to protect their body. 2 a badge shaped like a shield. 3 a protection, or protective cover. *Sun lotion acts as a shield against the Sun.* **shield** *verb* to protect.

shift *verb* to move from one place to another, to change direction. *She shifted in her seat.* **shift** *noun* 1 a change of position or direction. *A shift in the wind.* 2 the time for which a worker or a group of workers works. *A late shift.* 3 a straight dress.

shifty (shiftier, shiftiest) *adjective* dishonest, not to be trusted.

shilling *noun* 1 a British coin used until 1971 which was worth 12 old pence. 2 an amount of money in some other countries.

shimmer *verb* to shine with a soft light.

shin *noun* the front of the leg between the knee and the ankle.

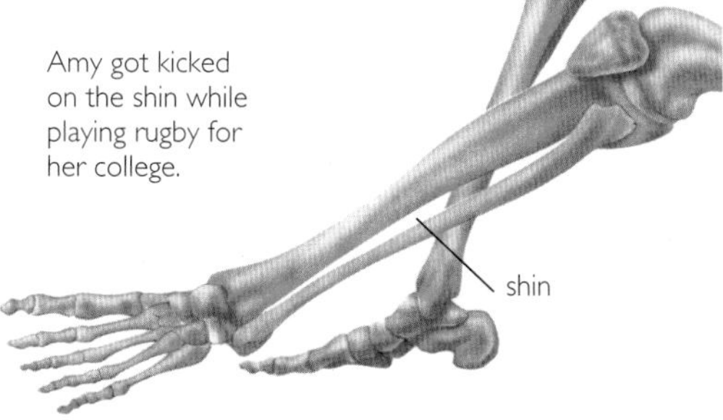

Amy got kicked on the shin while playing rugby for her college.

shine *verb* to polish, make bright by rubbing. **shine** *noun* polishing.

shine (shines, shining, shone) *verb* 1 to give off light, to be bright. *The Sun is shining.* 2 to direct light at something. *Can you shine the torch on the wall?* 3 to be excellent. *He is good at most sports, but he really shines at tennis.* **shine** *noun* a brightness or polish.

shiny (shinier, shiniest) *adjective* looking bright or polished.

ship *noun* a large boat for carrying people or goods.

ship (ships, shipping, shipped) *verb* to take or send goods by ship.

shipshape *adjective* neat and tidy.

shipwreck *noun* 1 the loss of a ship at sea. 2 a ship that has been wrecked. **shipwreck** *verb* to lose a ship at sea. *They were shipwrecked on a desert island.*

DID YOU KNOW

There were 20 old shillings in a pound, and 21 shillings made up a sum called a guinea. An old shilling was worth 5 of today's pence.

WORD HISTORY

The verb 'to shirk' probably comes originally from the German noun 'Schurke', meaning rogue or scoundrel. 'Only a scoundrel shirks the washing-up!'

Terrifying high seas resulted in a shipwreck in which all crew and passengers were drowned.

shipyard *noun* a place where ships are built.

shire *noun* a county.

shirk *verb* to try to get out of doing a job. *He is always shirking the washing-up.*

shirt *noun* a piece of clothing for the top half of the body, worn with trousers or a skirt. *He was wearing a satin shirt.*

shiver *verb* to tremble, especially with cold or fear. **shiver** *noun.* **shivery** *adjective. She has a temperature and feels shivery.*

shoal *noun* a group of fish swimming together. *A shoal of fish among the reef.*

shock *noun* 1 a strong unpleasant feeling of surprise or fear. *It was a shock to hear that he had died.* 2 a movement from something being hit, an explosion or a crash. *We could feel the shock of the bridge crashing.* 3 the effects of electricity passing through the body, an electric shock. *I got a shock when I touched the wire.* **shock** *verb* to surprise or upset somebody, to make somebody feel shocked. *I was shocked by his rudeness.*

shocking *adjective* very bad or wrong. *A shocking waste of money.*

shoddy (shoddier, shoddiest) *adjective* badly made or done. *Katie produced truly shoddy work.* **shoddiness** *noun.*

shoe *noun* 1 a covering you wear on your feet, usually made of leather with a hard sole. 2 a horseshoe. **shoe** *verb* to fix a horseshoe on to a horse's hooves.

shoelace *noun* a strip of material like a piece of string for tying up shoes.

shone *verb* past tense of shine.

shoo *verb* to make somebody, usually an animal, go away by saying 'shoo' and waving your arms.

shook *verb* past tense of shake.

shoot (shoots, shooting, shot) *verb* 1 to fire a gun or an arrow. 2 to kill or injure somebody by shooting. 3 to kick or throw a ball at a goal. 4 to move or send quickly in a direction, to move over or through something. *The pain shot up his arm.* 5 to put out new growth or shoots from a stem. 6 to photograph a scene in a film. *The film was shot in London.* **shoot** *noun* 1 a young growth of a plant. 2 shooting of a film or still photographs for an advertisement or book. 3 a group of people hunting animals or birds for sport.

shop *noun* a building or room in a building where goods are sold. **shop** (shops, shopping, shopped) *verb* to buy things in a shop. **shopper** *noun*. **shopping** *noun*. *Did you do the shopping?*

shoplifter *noun* somebody who steals things from shops. **shoplifting** *noun*.

shore *noun* the land along the edge of a sea or lake. *Let's go down to the sea shore.*

short *adjective* 1 not long, little in distance or length. Having or taking only a little time. If somebody is short, he is not tall. 2 not enough of something. *We are a bit short of money.* 3 rude, usually because you are angry or impatient with somebody. If somebody has a short temper, they get angry easily. 4 Short pastry is made with a lot of fat and is very crumbly. **for short/ short for** abbreviated. *My name is William, Will' for short.* **shortness** *noun*. **short** *adverb* suddenly. *He stopped short at the edge of the cliff.* **short** *noun* 1 a strong alcoholic drink. 2 a short film.

shortage *noun* lack of something, not having enough. *There is a terrible food shortage in Sudan.*

shortcoming *noun* a fault or defect.

shorten *verb* to make or become short.

shorthand *noun* a way of writing that uses special signs or shorter forms for words and phrases, so something can be written down as fast as somebody is saying it.

shortly *adverb* 1 soon, in a little time. 2 in a few words. 3 in a cross way, not politely.

shorts *plural noun* short trousers.

short-sighted *adjective* not able to see things far away properly. *My brother has to wear glasses because he is short-sighted.*

shot *verb* past tense of shoot.

shoulder *noun* the two parts of the body between the neck and the top of the arms. *He put the rucksack over his shoulder.* **shoulder** *verb* 1 to take on something, especially a problem or responsibility. 2 to push with the shoulder. *He shouldered his way through the crowd.*

shout *noun* a loud call or cry. **shout** *verb* to cry or call loudly.

shove *verb* to push roughly. **shove** *noun*.

shovel *noun* a tool like a spade for lifting and moving coal, sand, earth, snow and other things. **shovel** (shovels, shovelling, shovelled) *verb* 1 to move, lift and work with a shovel. *He shovelled a path through the snow.* 2 to push a lot of something quickly into a place. *Don't shovel the food into your mouth like that.*

Dean used the shovel to move the huge mound of stones outside the window.

AMAZING FACT

A West German man, Hans-Gunter Winkler, has won a record number of show-jumping events. He has the Men's World Championship twice, the European Championship and has won five Olympic gold medals.

AMAZING FACT

The phrase, 'a parting shot', which means to say or do something as you leave, was originally 'a Parthian shot'.

The Parthians were an ancient kingdom in Western Asia. As the Parthian troops retreated, they customarily fired a final shot at the enemy.

show (shows, showing, showed, shown) *verb* 1 to allow or offer to be seen. 2 to be seen easily, to be noticeable. *Any marks show on white.* 3 to demonstrate, or make somebody understand something. *He showed me how to use the computer.* 4 to point to a mark or number. 5 to guide. *The waitress showed us to our seats.* 6 to prove or make something clear. *Her marks show that it was worth revising for the exam.* 7 to act towards somebody in a certain way. *He shows no pity for the homeless.* **show off** to show something to impress people. **show up** 1 to arrive at a place. *Only a few people showed up at the party.* 2 to be seen clearly, be noticeable. **show** *noun* 1 a public showing, a collection of things to be looked at. *The Chelsea Flower Show.* 2 a performance in a theatre, on television or in a club. 3 a way of behaving. If something is for show, it is only done to make a good impression. **on show** to be seen by the public. *His paintings are on show at the gallery.* **showy** *adjective* too noticeable, gaudy. *The bride's aunt wore a showy hat.*

There was a wonderful show of tulips in the park that spring.

show business *noun* the business of entertainment. If you are in show business, you work in television, films or the theatre.

shower *noun* 1 a short rainfall. 2 a fall of many small things arriving at the same time. *She was covered in a shower of blossom.* 3 a device, usually in the bathroom, for washing yourself that sprays water on your body. 4 a wash under a shower. *I have a shower every day.* **showery** *adjective*. *It's been showery all day.* **shower** *verb* 1 to fall in a shower. 2 to have a shower.

Peter had a relaxing shower after work.

showjumping *noun* the sport of riding a horse over fences and barriers.

shown *verb* past tense of show.

shred *noun* 1 a small piece torn or cut off something. 2 a very small amount. *There is not a shred of truth in what he says.* **shred** (shreds, shredding, shredded) *verb* to cut or tear into shreds.

shrewd *adjective* having common sense, clever. *She is a very shrewd businesswoman.*

shriek *noun* a sudden loud, wild cry. *A shriek of laughter.* **shriek** *verb.*

shrill *adjective* high-sounding and painful to the ear. *A shrill voice.*

shrimp *noun* a small shellfish with a long legs and a tail like a fan.

shrine *noun* a holy place where people pray. *They left offerings at the shrine.*

The Temple of Angkor Wat become a Buddhist shrine in the 1500s.

shrink (shrinks, shrinking, shrank, shrunk) *verb* 1 to become smaller in size. *The sweater has shrunk in the wash.* 2 to move back, usually in fear. 3 to avoid doing something because it is not pleasant. **shrinkage** *noun.*

shrivel (shrivels, shrivelling, shrivelled) *verb* to become dry and wrinkled.

shrub *noun* a small bush.

shrug (shrugs, shrugging, shrugged) *verb* to raise your shoulders to show that you don't know or don't care. **shrug** *noun.*

shudder *verb* to tremble with fear, cold or horror. **shudder** *noun.*

shuffle *verb* 1 to walk by dragging your feet. 2 to mix up the order of a pack of playing cards before beginning a game. **shuffle** *noun.*

The magician shuffled the pack of cards, and ended with the whole suit in the right order.

WORD HISTORY

The word 'shrewd' used to have a much more negative meaning than it does today. At first it meant 'wicked' or 'cruel'. Then it came to mean 'strict' or 'harsh', before taking on a sly slant.

WORD HISTORY

The original Siamese twins, Chang and Eng (1811–74), were joined at the hip. They were called Siamese because they were born in Siam, which is now called Thailand. Since that time many pairs of Siamese twins have been successfully separated.

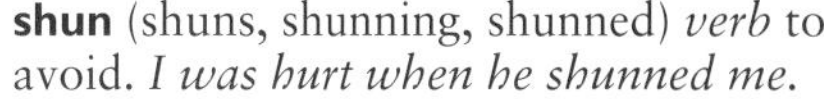

shun (shuns, shunning, shunned) *verb* to avoid. *I was hurt when he shunned me.*

shut (shuts, shutting, shut) *verb* 1 to move into a covered, blocked or folded-together position, to close. 2 to close for a period of time or stop business. **shut down** to stop business or work. *The factory has shut down.* **shut in** to leave or lock in a room. *He shut himself in his room to work.* **shut up** 1 to make a place safe before leaving. 2 to stop talking or stop somebody from talking.

shutter *noun* 1 a cover fitted on the outside of a window that can be opened or shut to keep out the light. *Please close the shutters.* 2 the part in a camera that opens to let in light when a photograph is taken.

The light is regulated by the shutter. It travels through the lens and on to the film inside the camera.

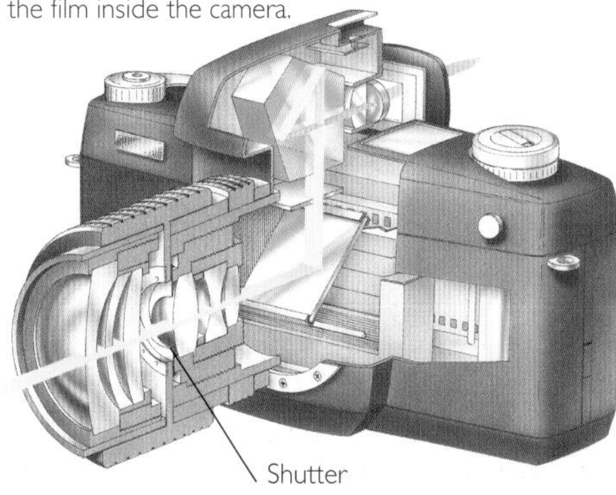

shuttle *noun* 1 a train, bus or aircraft that makes regular journeys between two places. *There is a shuttle service between the sports ground and the college in the centre of town.* 2 a pointed instrument used in weaving by which a thread is carried between other threads. 3 a spacecraft used to make a number of journeys into outer space, a space shuttle. **shuttle** *verb* to move or send backwards and forwards.

shy *adjective* nervous and uncomfortable when with others. *He is too shy to speak up.* **shyly** *adverb.* **shyness** *noun.*

shy (shies, shying, shied) *verb* to move away suddenly. *The horse shied at the sound of the police siren.*

Siamese twins *plural noun* twins who are born with their bodies joined together. *The Siamese twins were successfully separated and grew up happily.*

sibling *noun* a brother or sister.

sick *adjective* 1 ill, not well. 2 likely to vomit or throw up food. *Going on a boat always makes me feel sick.* 3 angry or fed up. *I'm sick of washing-up.* 4 making fun of misfortune or illness. *He told some sick jokes.* **sickly** *adjective.*

sickness *noun* 1 illness or bad health. 2 a disease. 3 feeling sick, vomiting.

S

side *noun* 1 a surface of something that is not the top or the bottom. 2 one of the two surfaces of something flat. *Please write on both sides of the paper.* 3 the two halves of an area which could be divided by a line in the middle, the right or the left part of your body, or a place next to somebody or something. *I've got a pain in my left side.* 4 an edge or border. *Our friends live on the other side of town.* 5 an upright surface of a building or mountain. 6 a particular position in a discussion, or a group which holds a particular position. *Which side is he on?* 7 a team. **on the side** as a sideline. *She sells flowers on the side.* **side by side** next to one another. **to be on the safe side** to be careful and prepared in case something happens. **side** *verb* to take somebody's side. *My mother always sides with my brother.*

side effect *noun* an effect in addition to the intended one. *This drug can have extremely unpleasant side effects.*

siege *noun* an operation, usually by an army, surrounding a place to force it to give in by stopping food reaching the people in it. *The town was under siege for months.*

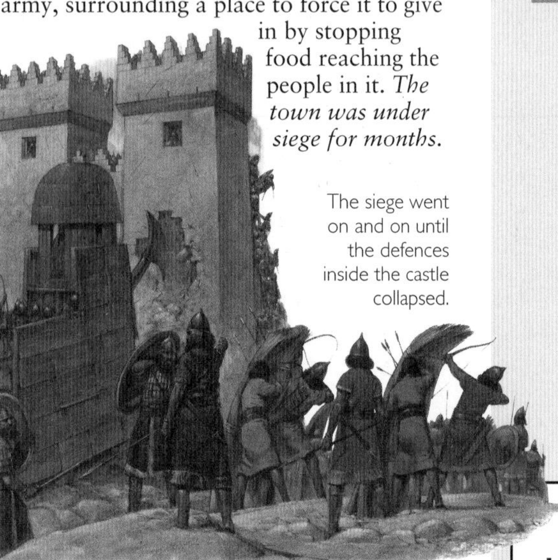

The siege went on and on until the defences inside the castle collapsed.

Sierra Leone *noun* a country in Africa.

siesta (say see-est-uh) *noun* a rest or sleep in the afternoon.

sieve (say siv) *noun* a tool, mainly used in the kitchen, made of wire or plastic net on a metal ring for liquid or soft parts to pass through and large lumps to be left in the net. **sieve** *verb* to put something through a sieve. *Sieve the flour before baking a cake.*

sift *verb* 1 to put something through a sieve. 2 to examine something carefully. *He sifted through his papers to find the letter.*

sigh *verb* to let out a deep breath with a sound as a sign of tiredness, sadness or gladness. **sigh** *noun* the act or sound of sighing. *She breathed a sigh of relief when the job finally came to an end.*

DID YOU KNOW

The longest known siege was that of the Russian city of Leningrad (now called St Petersburg) by the German army during World War II. The siege lasted for 880 days, from August 1941 to January 1944.

The sign of a cross and skull signals danger.

WORD HISTORY

The Spanish word 'siesta' comes from the Latin 'sexta', meaning 'sixth hour'. This must refer to the time at which people originally had their siesta.

sight *noun* 1 the ability to see. 2 the act of seeing something or something seen or worth seeing. *We went to see the sights of Florence.* 3 something that looks very bad or laughable to look at. *Her hair looks a real sight.* 4 the distance within which things can be seen. *She doesn't let the children out of her sight.* 5 a part of a telescope or gun you look through to help you aim. **in sight** likely to happen very soon. *A cure is in sight.* **catch sight of** to see for a moment. **know somebody by sight** to recognize somebody without ever having spoken to them or knowing their name. **sight** *verb* to see something for the first time by coming near. *After a month at sea they sighted land.*

sightseer *noun* a tourist visiting interesting places. **sightsee** *verb.* **sightseeing** *noun.*

sign *noun* 1 a mark or shape that has a particular meaning. *A dove is a sign of peace.* 2 a movement of the body showing a particular meaning. *Putting your finger to your lips is a sign to be quiet.* 3 a board or notice that gives a warning or piece of information. *A road sign.* 4 something that shows that something exists or is happening. *A temperature is the first sign of flu.* **sign** *verb* 1 to make a movement as a sign to somebody. 2 to write your name on a document or form as a sign of agreement. *We signed the contract.*

sign language *noun* a way of talking, usually to deaf people, by using hand movements.

signal *noun* 1 a sound or action that warns, gives a message or causes something else to happen. *Smoke signals.* 2 a piece of equipment, usually with coloured lights, beside a railway which tells drivers if they should stop. 3 a sound or picture sent by radio or TV. **signal** (signals, signalling, signalled) *verb* 1 to make a signal to somebody. 2 to make something known by using a signal. *He signalled right, but went left.* 3 to be a sign of something.

The signal told them to stop because the red light was flashing.

signature *noun* a person's name written by himself or herself, usually at the end of a letter or document.

significant *adjective* meaningful or important. *Significant others.*

Sikh (say seek) *noun* a member of an Indian religious group.

silence *noun* 1 the absence of sound, extreme quietness. 2 not speaking, making a noise, answering questions or mentioning a particular thing. **silence** *verb* to stop somebody or something from speaking or making a noise.

silent *adjective* not speaking, totally quiet.

silhouette (say sil-oo-**ett**) *noun* 1 an outline of a dark shape against a light background. 2 an outline drawing filled in with black or cut out of black paper. **silhouette** *verb. The church was sharply silhouetted against the sky.*

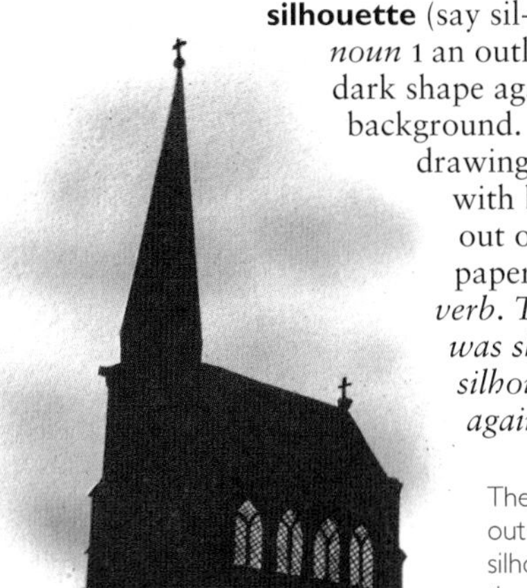

The church stood out in dramatic silhouette against the night sky.

silk *noun* a soft, fine cloth made from the fine thread produced by silkworms. *A luxurious silk scarf.*

silkworm *noun* a type of caterpillar that produces a silk covering for its body (cocoon) which is used to make silk.

sill *noun* a flat shelf at the bottom of a window. *A plant pot on the window sill.*

silly (sillier, silliest) *adjective* foolish. *It was such a silly question.*

silt *noun* fine sand or mud that is carried along by a river. **silt up** to fill or become blocked with silt.

silver *noun* 1 a valuable soft metal used for making ornaments, jewellery and coins. 2 the colour of silver. 3 coins and things made from silver, especially cutlery and dishes. *She always polishes her silver so it sparkles.* 4 a silver medal, given as the second prize. **silver** *adjective* 1 made of silver. 2 like the colour of silver. *Silver paint.*

silver wedding *noun* the 25th anniversary of a wedding.

simile (say **sim**-il-ee) *noun* a comparison of one thing with another, being similar to somebody or something else.

simmer *verb* to cook very gently, just below boiling point. *Simmer the rice for ten minutes, then stir in the beans.*

simper *verb* to smile in a silly way. **simper** *noun. I can't stand the way she simpers when the boss asks her to do something.*

WORD HISTORY

The word 'silhouette' was named after Etienne de Silhouette (1709–67), a finance minister of France, but we are not sure why. Silhouette proposed taxing rich people very heavily, and it could be that this is why his name was applied to a thin, minimal drawing. Or perhaps it was simply that Silhouette himself drew such outlines as a hobby.

GRAMMAR NOTE

In a simile two things are compared in order to point out a feature they share. A simile contains the words 'as' or 'like'. For example: 'as blind as a bat'.

simple *adjective* 1 easy to understand or do, not difficult. *Give me a simple explanation of how it works.* 2 uncomplicated, without much decoration. Ordinary or plain. *Simple food tastes best.* 3 with nothing added. *The simple truth is, she is hopeless at playing the guitar.* 4 without much intelligence or easily fooled. *He's a bit simple.* **simplicity** *noun.*

simplify (simplifies, simplifying, simplified) *verb* to make something easy to understand. **simplification** *noun.*

sin *noun* 1 the breaking of a religious law or something that should not be done. *Stealing is a sin.* **sin** (sins, sinning, sinned) *verb* to break a religious law or do something that is believed to be very bad. **sinner** *noun.*

since *conjunction, preposition, adverb* 1 from that time until now. *I haven't seen her since she left school.* 2 during or at a time after a particular time or event in the past. *He used to play tennis regularly, but has since given up.* 3 because, used to state a reason for doing or not doing something. *Since you say you are too tired, we won't go for a walk along the beach.*

sincere *adjective* honest, not false. **sincerely** *adverb. I sincerely hope that they will believe what he tells them.* 'Yours sincerely' is written at the end of a letter before your signature. **sincerity** *noun.*

sing (sings, singing, sang, sung) *verb* to make musical sounds with the voice, usually by saying words that fit a tune. *Can you hear the birds singing?* 2 to make a buzzing or ringing sound. **singer** *noun.*

Singapore *noun* a city and country in Southeast Asia.

The flag of Singapore has a red stripe with a white Moon and stars, and a white stripe beneath.

singe (say sinj) *verb* to burn slightly.

single *adjective* 1 only one, not more. 2 not married. 3 for or by one person. *She booked a single room at the hotel.* 4 considered by itself, separate. *He repeated every single word I said.* **single ticket** a ticket for a journey from one place to another but not back again. **singly** *adverb.* **single** *noun* 1 a small record with one song on each side. 2 a single person or thing. 3 a single ticket.

single-handed *adjective* without help.

singular *noun* a word that expresses one person or thing. **singular** *adjective.*

sinister *adjective* evil or harmful. *The empty house was a sinister place.*

sink *noun* a basin with taps in the kitchen, especially for washing dishes.

S

sink (sinks, sinking, sank, sunk) *verb* 1 to go down below the surface of water. *The ship sank to the bottom of the sea.* 2 to go or fall down. *She sank to the ground.* 3 to get smaller or less. *Prices are sinking.* 4 to become weaker. *His voice sank to a whisper.* 5 to become depressed. *Her heart sank.* 6 to put money or work into something. *My brother has sunk all his savings into a new car.* 7 to make something hard or sharp go deeply into something. *She sank her teeth into the apple.* **sink in** to be or become understood. *I hope my warning has really sunk in.*

sinus *noun* a space in the bones of the face just behind the nose. If you have a cold, your sinuses often get blocked.

sip *verb* to drink taking in small mouthfuls at a time. **sip** *noun. She took a sip of tea.*

sir *noun* 1 You say 'sir' when you speak politely to a man. It is mainly used by children to a teacher, or by staff in shops or restaurants. 2 a title given to a knight or baronet. 3 used at the beginning of a formal letter to a man. *Dear Sir.*

siren *noun* 1 a device that makes a long, loud warning sound. Police cars and fire engines have sirens. 2 a dangerously beautiful woman.

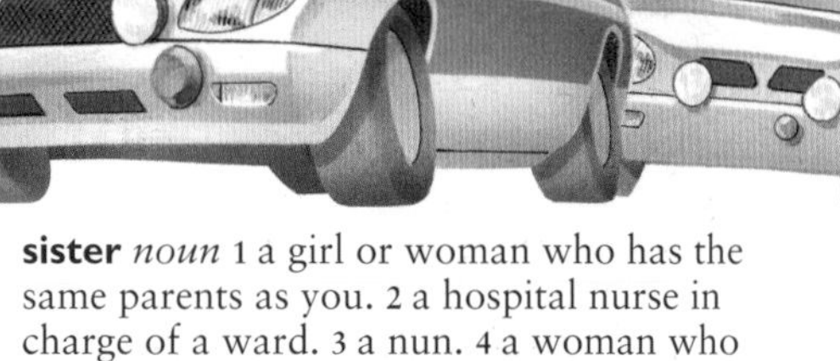

The police cars went into the chase, sirens blaring.

sister *noun* 1 a girl or woman who has the same parents as you. 2 a hospital nurse in charge of a ward. 3 a nun. 4 a woman who stands up for women's rights and feels very close to other women. **sisterly** *adjective.*

sister-in-law (sisters-in-law) *noun* the sister of a person's husband or wife.

sit (sits, sitting, sat) *verb* 1 to be in a position with the upper body upright and the bottom resting on something. 2 to rest on a surface, especially when talking about a bird or animal. *The bird was sitting on a branch.* 3 to take an exam. *We are sitting the exam at the end of term.* 4 to be a member of a committee or of a law court or parliament. To meet and work together. *He sits on the school board.* 5 to be in a place. **sit about** to do nothing for a long time. **sit back** to relax and not do anything while things are happening. **sit tight** to stay in the same place or situation without taking any action. *Sit tight and wait until it's over.*

WORD HISTORY

In Greek mythology, the beautiful Sirens sang such wonderful melodies that sailors passing their rocky island were lured to shipwreck and death. Odysseus ordered his men to plug their ears with beeswax so that they could not hear the Sirens' songs and to tie him to the ship's mast so that he could not swim ashore to them.

site *noun* a place where something was or is happening. *A building site.*

situation *noun* 1 what is happening in a particular place at a particular time or the things that are happening to you. *The situation in Africa looks very bad.* 2 a job. 3 the surroundings of a place. *Our house is in a beautiful situation.*

size *noun* 1 how big or small something is. *The dog had eyes the size of saucers.* 2 a set of measurements, especially for clothes and shoes. *What size does he take?* **size** *verb* to arrange people or things according to their size. **size up** to form an opinion of a person or thing, to decide how to act after thinking about a situation. *It took me a little while to size up the situation.*

sizzle *verb* to make a crackling or hissing sound like the sound made when you fry food. *The bacon sizzled in the pan.*

skate *noun* a boot with a steel blade (ice-skate) or wheels (roller-skate) attached to the sole for skating. **skate** *verb* to move about on ice wearing ice-skates (or on a hard surface wearing roller-skates). *We skated across the frozen lake.*

skate *noun* a large, flat seafish.

skateboard *noun* a board with small wheels at each end for people to ride on for fun. **skateboarding** *noun.*

skeleton *noun* 1 the framework of bones in a human or animal body. 2 something forming a framework or an outline. *The metal skeleton of the building was erected.* **a skeleton in the cupboard** something of which you are afraid or ashamed.

skeleton key *noun* a master key that opens a number of different locks.

sketch (sketches) *noun* 1 a quickly made drawing. *He made a sketch of the castle.* 2 a short description of something. 3 a short, funny piece of writing or acting. **sketch** *verb* 1 to draw something quickly. 2 to give a short description of something with few details. **sketchy** *adjective. A sketchy plan.*

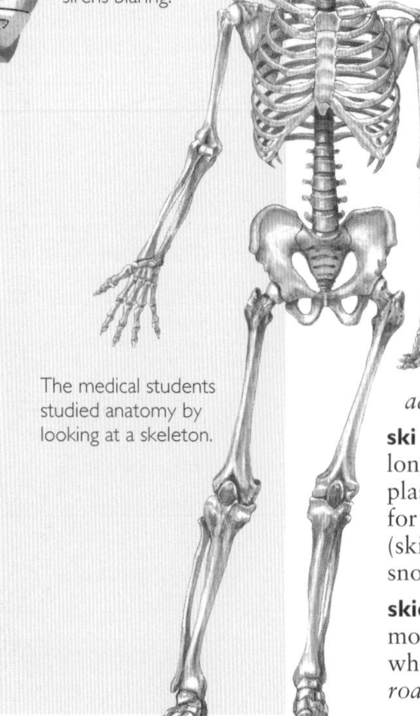

The medical students studied anatomy by looking at a skeleton.

ski *noun* one of a pair of long flat pieces of wood, metal or plastic that are fastened to a ski boot for skiing on the snow. **ski** (skis, skiing, skied) *verb* to move on snow wearing skis. **skier** *noun.*

skid (skids, skidding, skidded) *verb* to move sideways out of control on wheels. *The car skidded on the icy road.* **skid** *noun.*

S

skill *noun* the knowledge or ability to do something well. **skilful** *adjective. She is a very skilful painter.* **skilfully** *adverb.* **skilled** *adjective. A skilled job.*

skim (skims, skimming, skimmed) *verb* 1 to remove cream or other unwanted things from the surface of a liquid. *Skimmed milk.* 2 to read something quickly. *He skimmed the newspaper.* 3 to move quickly along or just above something. *The plane skimmed the treetops, then crashed.*

skin *noun* 1 the outer covering of the body. *Fur coats are made from animal skins.* 2 the outer covering of some fruit and vegetables. *He slipped on a banana skin and broke his ankle.* 3 a thin layer that forms on liquid, especially when it gets cool. *I hate skin on milk.* **skin** (skins, skinning, skinned) *verb* to take the skin off something.

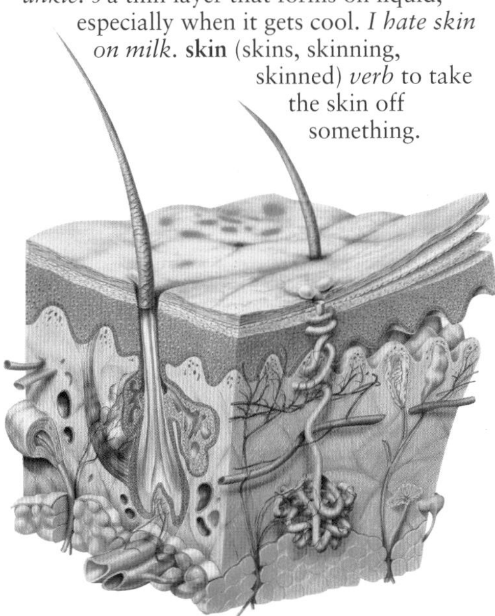

This cross-section through the skin shows how hairs grow and sweat pores reach the surface.

skinny (skinnier, skinniest) *adjective* very thin. *A skinny little boy.*

skint *adjective* having no money. *I'm skint, can you lend me a fiver?*

skip (skips, skipping, skipped) *verb* 1 to jump or hop along lightly. *The children skipped around the garden.* 2 to jump up and down over a rope (skipping rope). 3 to leave something out in order to go on to another subject. *I read the book but skipped the boring bits.* 4 to miss out something you usually do. *I skipped lunch.* **skip** *noun.*

skip *noun* a builder's large metal container for taking away old bricks and rubbish.

skipper *noun* a captain.

skirt *noun* a piece of clothing for women or girls that hangs down from the waist. **skirt** *verb* 1 to go around the edge of something. *The old road skirts the village.* 2 to avoid dealing with something. *She tried to skirt the issue because she was embarrassed.*

Skopje *noun* the capital of Macedonia.

AMAZING FACT

The World's first skyscraper was built in Chicago in 1884 by William Le Baron Jenney.

GRAMMAR NOTE

Many slang words and expressions that work well in spoken English are not effective when written down. Try to use more formal expressions in a serious piece of writing.

skull *noun* the bones of the head that enclose the brain.

skunk *noun* a small North American black and white animal that gives out a nasty smell if it is frightened.

sky (skies) *noun* the space above the Earth that you see when you are outside and look up. *You can see the Moon in the sky.*

skyscraper *noun* a very tall building.

Skyscrapers were originally built so that many people could live in a small area.

slab *noun* a thick flat piece. *A slab of cake.*

slack *adjective* 1 not pulled tight, especially a rope or wire. 2 not firm, weak. *The rules are very slack.* 3 not busy or working hard. *Business is slack.* **slackness** *noun.* **slack** *verb* to not work enough, to be lazy. **slacker** *noun. My brother is a lazy slacker.*

slam (slams, slamming, slammed) *verb* 1 to shut loudly. *Don't slam the door!* 2 to push or put down quickly and with force. *He slammed on the brakes.*

slander *noun* an untrue spoken statement about somebody which damages a person's reputation. **slander** *verb* to harm somebody by making a false statement.

slang *noun* words and expressions used in informal conversation. Dosh, dough and bread are all slang for money.

slap (slaps, slapping, slapped) *verb* 1 to hit somebody or something with the palm of your hand. *She slapped his face.* 2 to put roughly or carelessly. *He slapped paint on the walls.* 3 to put down with force. *He slapped the book on the table.* **slap** *noun.*

slapdash *adjective* careless.

slate *noun* 1 a dark grey rock that splits easily into thin layers. 2 a piece of slate used for covering roofs. 3 a small board made of slate which was used for writing on with chalk. **slate** *verb* 1 to cover a roof with slates. 2 to criticize severely or attack. *The papers slated his new film.*

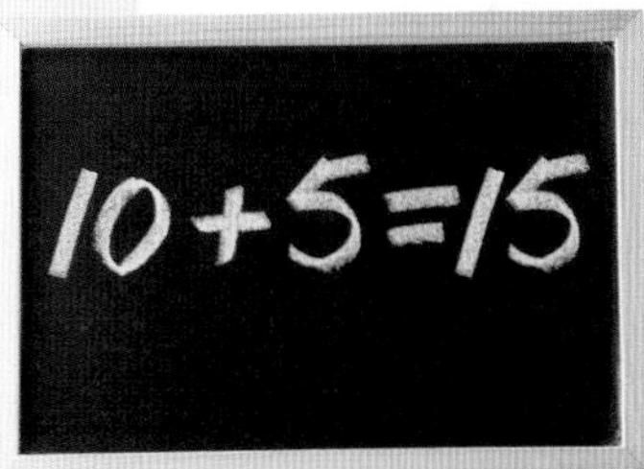

The teacher wrote a sum on the slate.

slaughter *verb* 1 to kill animals for food. 2 to kill cruelly, especially many people. **slaughter** *noun.*

slave *noun* somebody who is owned by another and has to work for that person without getting paid. **slave** *verb* to work very hard, like a slave. *I slaved away cleaning the house all Sunday.* **slavery** *noun.*

slay (slays, slaying, slew, slain) *verb* to kill.

sleazy (sleazier, sleaziest) *adjective* dirty and poor-looking. **sleaze** *noun.* **sleaziness** *noun.*

sled, sledge *noun* a vehicle for sliding across snow and ice on metal blades. **sledge** *verb* to go on a sledge.

sleek *adjective* smooth and shiny, especially hair or fur. *A sleek fat cat.*

sleep *noun* a rest state of the body when the eyes are closed and the mind is not conscious, a period of sleep. *Most people need about eight hours sleep.* **sleep** (sleeps, sleeping, slept) *verb* to be asleep, to have a sleep. **sleepy** *adjective.* **sleepiness** *noun.*

sleeper *noun* 1 a person who sleeps. *I'm a very light sleeper, so any noise will wake me.* 2 one of a row of heavy beams supporting a railway track. 3 a bed on a train. *I booked the sleeper to Rome.*

sleeping bag *noun* a warm bag made of thick material in which you can sleep, usually when camping.

Arthur wanted to sleep under the stars, but he didn't realize that his sleeping bag would get damp in the dew.

sleet *noun* a mixture of rain and snow, frozen rain. **sleet** *verb. It's sleeting.*

sleeve *noun* 1 the part of a piece of clothing that covers the arm. 2 a stiff envelope for a record or a stiff case for a book.

slender *adjective* thin, slim.

sleuth (say slooth) *noun* a detective.

slice *noun* 1 a thin piece cut from something. 2 a part or share of something. **slice** *verb* 1 to cut into slices. 2 to cut off a slice. 3 to cut through something.

slick *adjective* 1 well-made and good-looking, but not meaningful. *The show was too slick.* 2 clever, but not honest. *A slick salesman.* 3 quick and smooth.

slick *noun* a thin sheet of oil floating on water. *The oil slick spoiled Sarah's swim.*

DID YOU KNOW?

Slaves have existed in most countries throughout history. The American Civil War (1861–65) was fought between the northern and southern states partly over the issue of slavery. Abraham Lincoln declared slaves free in 1863, and two years later slavery was officially abolished throughout the United States.

AMAZING FACT

Newborn babies sleep most of the time – about 18–20 hours every day.

slide (slides, sliding, slid) *verb* 1 to move smoothly over or on something. *She slid the door open.* 2 to move quietly and quickly, usually in order to go unnoticed. **slide** *noun* 1 the action of sliding. 2 a structure with a slope for sliding down, usually for children in a playground. 3 a small piece of film in a frame that you can look at on a screen or through a viewer to see it bigger. *Our holiday slides.* 4 a glass plate on which something is put to be looked at under a microscope. 5 a small fastener to keep hair in place, a hair slide.

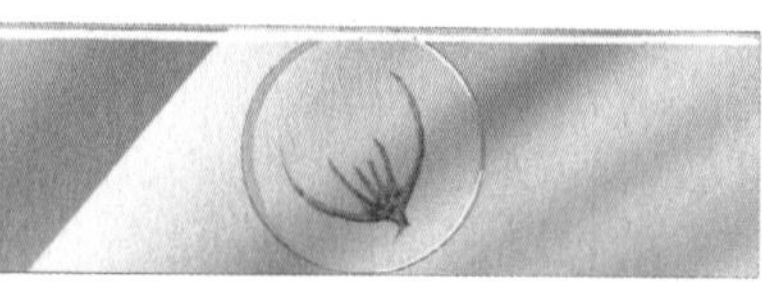

She examined the object under the slide.

slight *adjective* 1 small and thin. 2 small and not important. *A slight headache.* **slightly** *adverb.* **slightness** *noun.*

slight *verb* to treat somebody without respect. **slight** *noun.*

slim (slimmer, slimmest) *adjective* 1 thin, not fat. 2 small. *There is still a slim chance of getting tickets for the concert.*

slime *noun* thick, sticky liquid, usually unpleasant. *The snail left a trail of slime.* **slimy** *adjective.* **sliminess** *noun.*

sling *noun* 1 a piece of material tied round the neck to support a broken arm. 2 a loop or an object made of ropes and straps for carrying or lifting things. *She carries her baby in a sling.* 3 a strap for throwing stones, like a catapult. **sling** (slings, slinging, slung) *verb* 1 to throw carelessly. *He slung his bag in the ditch.* 2 to throw with force. *They were slinging stones.* 3 to attach or hold in a sling.

A broken arm supported in a sling helps the healing process

slip (slips, slipping, slipped) *verb* 1 to slide and almost fall because you have lost your balance. 2 to move, go or put something quickly and smoothly, especially without being noticed. *The girl slipped out of the room.* 3 to put on or take off, especially clothes. 4 to get away, escape or be forgotten. *His birthday slipped my mind.* 5 to get worse or fall in quality. **slip up** to make a mistake. **slip** *noun* 1 the act of slipping. 2 a slight mistake. 3 a small piece of paper. 4 a piece of clothing without sleeves that women wear under a dress. 5 a pillowcase. **give somebody the slip** to escape from somebody.

slipper *noun* a soft shoe worn indoors.

slippery *adjective* difficult to hold or stand on because of being wet or very smooth.

slipshod *adjective* careless.

slip-up *noun* a slight mistake.

slit *noun* a narrow cut or opening. **slit** (slits, slitting, slit) *verb* to cut or make a slit in.

slog (slogs, slogging, slogged) *verb* 1 to do hard dull work without stopping, or to make a long, tiring journey. 2 to hit hard, especially a ball. **slog** *noun*. **slogger** *noun*.

slogan *noun* a short phrase that is easy to remember, mainly used to advertise something. *A catchy slogan.*

slope *noun* 1 a piece of ground that goes up or down. 2 a slanting line or direction. **slope** *verb* to have a slope or to lean to the right or the left. **slope off** to go off quietly, usually in order to avoid work.

As Craig skiied down the slope, he heard the rumblings of an avalanche behind him.

slot *noun* a slit, groove or channel. **slot** *verb* to put into a slot.

slot machine *noun* a machine from which you can buy things by putting coins in a slot. Some slot machines are for gambling.

slouch *verb* to move with shoulders and head drooping down. **slouch** *noun*.

Slovakia *noun* a country in eastern Europe.

The flag of Slovakia has white, blue and red stripes, and a crest.

Slovenia *noun* a country in Southeast Europe.

slovenly *adjective* careless and untidy. *Your room is a slovenly mess.*

slow *adjective* 1 taking a long time or too long, not quick. 2 showing a time that is earlier than the correct time. *My watch is five minutes slow.* 3 not able to understand things quickly, not very active. **slow** *verb* to make or become slower. **slowly** *adverb*. **slowness** *noun*.

slow motion *noun* movement that is much slower than in real life, especially as shown in a film or on television. *They showed the goal again in slow motion.*

AMAZING FACT

The slug belongs to the same family as the snail, gastropods. The main difference between the two animals is that snails have shells while slugs usually do not.

DID YOU KNOW

Slovakia was part of Hungary until 1918, when it became part of Czechoslovakia. It has been an independent republic since 1993.

GRAMMAR NOTE

People often use 'slow' as an adverb in spoken English: 'Drive/eat slower.' In formal writing, it is better to use 'slowly' as the correct adverb: 'Drive/eat more slowly.'

slug *noun* a small slow-moving animal like a snail without a shell.

sluggish *adjective* slow-moving.

slum *noun* an area of a town that is poor, with dirty streets and bad living conditions.

slumber *noun* sleep. **slumber** *verb*.

slur (slurs, slurring, slurred) *verb* 1 to say words unclearly so they are difficult to understand. 2 to say unfair or bad things. **slur** *noun* 1 a slurring way of speaking. 2 unfair or bad remarks that could damage a person's reputation. *His words were a slur on my character.*

sly (slyer, slyest, or slier, sliest are also used) *adjective* cunning and not honest, keeping things secret. *A sly fox tricked the red hen.* **on the sly** secretly.

smack *verb* 1 to hit with the hand. 2 to open and close your lips noisily. 3 to put, throw or hit something so it makes a loud noise. **smack** *noun*. **smack** *adverb*. *He drove smack into the wall and killed his passenger.*

smack *noun* a particular taste. *A smack of lemon.* **smack** *verb* to have a trace of. *She smacks of money.*

smack *noun* a sailing boat used for fishing.

small *adjective* not big, little in size, weight or importance. **smallness** *noun*.

small change *noun* coins.

small-minded *adjective* thinking in a small way, unwilling to change your mind or listen to others. The opposite of small-minded is open-minded.

small talk *noun* conversation about unimportant things. *I loathe small talk.*

smart *adjective* 1 neat and elegant looking. 2 clever. 3 stylish and fashionable. 4 sharp and quick. *We walked at a smart pace.* **smartly** *adverb*. **smartness** *noun*.

smart *verb* 1 to feel a stinging pain. *My eyes are smarting.* 2 to feel upset, especially about something unkind said or done to you.

smash (smashes) *noun* 1 the action or sound of something breaking to pieces. 2 a car crash. 3 a very successful show or film, a smash hit. 4 a disaster in business. 5 a hard stroke, especially in tennis. **smash** *verb* 1 to break noisily into many pieces. 2 to go, drive, hit or throw with great force. *The car smashed into a tree.* 3 to destroy or ruin.

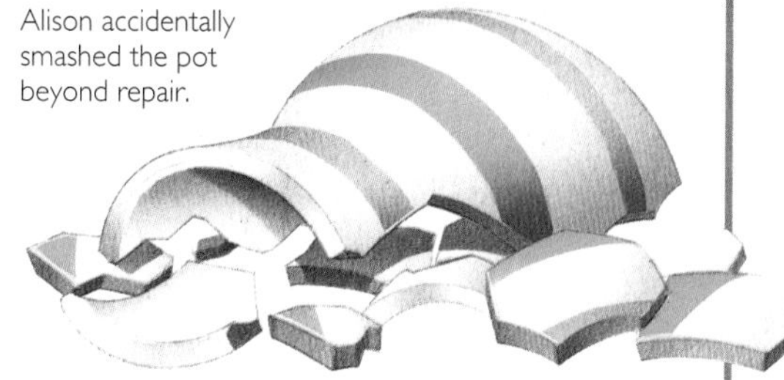

Alison accidentally smashed the pot beyond repair.

smashing *adjective* great, excellent.

smell *noun* 1 the ability the nose has to smell things. *Dogs have a strong sense of smell.* 2 something in things that has an effect on the nose, something you can smell. *A smell of gas.* 3 smelling something. *Have a smell of this cheese!* **smell** (smells, smelling, smelt) *verb* 1 to use your nose to discover a smell. 2 to have or give out a smell. If you say something smells, it has a bad smell. 3 to have a feeling or notice. *She smelt trouble.* **smelly** *adjective.*

smile *noun* an expression on the face with the corners of the mouth turned up that shows happiness or friendliness. **smile** *verb* to give a smile.

Phyllis smiled for the photographer.

smirk *noun* an unpleasant smile. **smirk** *verb* to give a smirk.

smoke *noun* 1 gas and small bits of solid material that are seen in the air when something burns. *Smoke from the chimney.* 2 smoking a cigarette or pipe. *He likes a smoke.* **smoke** *verb* 1 to give out smoke. *The volcano is smoking.* 2 to have a cigarette, cigar or pipe in your mouth and suck in the smoke and blow it out again. 3 the habit of smoking. *Do you smoke?* 4 to preserve meat or fish by hanging it in smoke. **smoky** *adjective.* **smoker** *noun.*

smooth *adjective* 1 having an even surface without lumps or holes, not rough. 2 calm and comfortable without sudden bumps. *A smooth ride.* 3 free from lumps, evenly mixed. 4 very polite, almost too pleasant. *I don't trust Gary, he's really too smooth.* 5 pleasant tasting, not sour or bitter. 6 not harsh. *A smooth voice.* **smooth** *verb* to make smooth. **smooth something over** to make a difficulty seem less serious.

smother *verb* 1 to die from not having enough air, or to kill by covering somebody's mouth so they cannot breathe. 2 to put a fire out by covering it with something. *He smothered the flames with a blanket.* 3 to cover thickly. *The cake was smothered in cream.* 4 to control or hold something back. *She tried to smother a yawn, but he saw she was bored.*

smoulder *verb* 1 to burn slowly without a flame. 2 to have strong feelings without showing them. *She smouldered with hatred.*

smudge *noun* a dirty mark, usually made by rubbing something. **smudge** *verb* to make a smudge on something or become messy.

The smugglers lured a boat on to the rocks with flashing lights by night. The next day, after the ship was wrecked, they brought the treasure ashore.

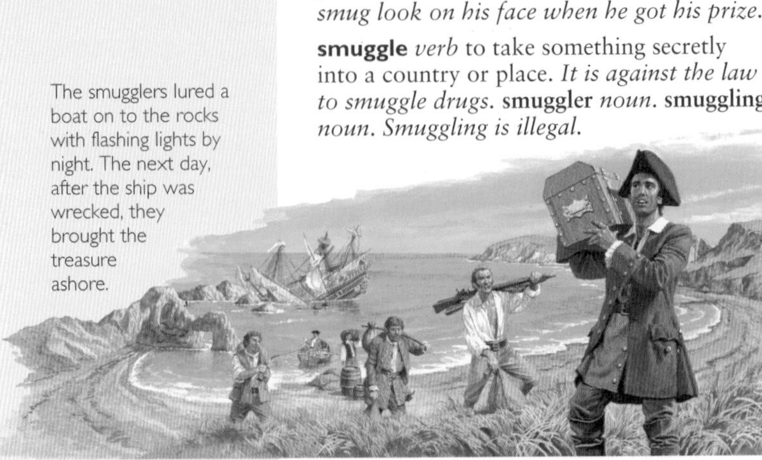

DID YOU KNOW

There are more than 80,000 different species of snails, widely distributed on land, in the sea and in fresh water. Most land snails have two pairs of tentacles, usually with eyes at the tips of the longer ones. Most water-snails have one pair of tentacles, with eyes at the base.

The snake coiled round and hissed dangerously.

AMAZING FACT

Most snakes hatch from eggs, although there are some species that give birth to live young.

Some snakes are very tiny while others, such as the python and anaconda, grow to lengths of up to ten metres.

smug *adjective* being too pleased with yourself and what you can do. *He had a smug look on his face when he got his prize.*

smuggle *verb* to take something secretly into a country or place. *It is against the law to smuggle drugs.* **smuggler** *noun.* **smuggling** *noun. Smuggling is illegal.*

snack *noun* a small, quick meal, especially one eaten between main meals. **snack** *verb.*

snag *noun* 1 a problem or difficulty. 2 a sharp part that sticks out and may catch you in passing. **snag** *verb* to get caught on and tear. *I snagged my tights.*

snail *noun* a small animal with a slimy body and a shell on its back. **at a snail's pace** very slowly. *Mum walks at a snail's pace.*

snake *noun* a long thin reptile with no legs and a fork-shaped tongue. Some snakes are poisonous. *A snake slithered out of the tree.*

snap *noun* 1 the action or sound of snapping. *The trap closed with a snap.* 2 a photograph taken quickly, a snapshot. 3 a small biscuit. *Ginger snaps.* 4 a card game in which players shout 'snap' when they see two of the same cards laid down together. **snap** (snaps, snapping, snapped) *verb* 1 to break with a sharp cracking noise. *His patience finally snapped.* 2 to make a sharp sound like something breaking. 3 to bite or catch something with the teeth. *The dog snapped at her ankle.* 4 to say something quickly and in an angry way. 5 to move or shut quickly into a position with a sharp sound. 6 to take a photograph. *She snapped us at the beach.* **snap at** to take or get something quickly. *We snapped at the chance of spending a week in the sun.* **snap up** to buy something quickly because it is a bargain. *Kate snapped it up in the sales.*

S

snap *adjective* done immediately. *A snap decision may sometimes be regretted.*

snare *noun* a trap for catching birds or small animals. **snare** *verb. He snared a rabbit and ate it for his dinner.*

snarl *verb* to growl angrily or speak in an angry voice. **snarl** *noun.*

snarl *noun* a tangle in wool or a tangled-up situation. *Traffic snarls.*

sneak *verb* 1 to move quietly and secretly, trying not to be seen or heard. 2 to take something somewhere secretly. *He sneaked his pet mouse into school.* 3 to tell tales. *He sneaked on his best friend to the teacher.*

sneak *noun* a person who tells others secretly that somebody else had done something bad, a tell-tale. **sneaky** *adjective.* **sneakily** *adverb.*

sneaker *noun* a sports shoe with a rubber sole, a trainer.

sneeze *noun* a sudden outburst of air through the nose and mouth. **sneeze** *verb. I felt a tickle in my nose and had to sneeze.*

snide *adjective* intending to hurt your feelings by being nasty, especially in a pretended funny way, about something that is important to you. *She made some snide remarks about my friends.*

sniff *verb* 1 to make a sound by breathing in air through your nose. 2 to smell something. *The dog sniffed the ground.* **sniff** *noun.* **sniffer** *noun. A glue sniffer.*

snigger *verb* to laugh quietly and in a disrespectful way, especially at something rude. **snigger** *noun.*

snip (snips, snipping, snipped) *verb* to cut with scissors or shears in short quick cuts. *She snipped at my hair.*

snip *noun.* 1 an act of snipping. 2 a bargain. *I had to buy it, it was a real snip.*

snivel (snivels, snivelling, snivelled) *verb* to speak or cry in a sniffing and whining way.

snob *noun* somebody who admires people with money, power and of a higher social class. **snobbish** *adjective.* **snobbery** *noun.*

snooker *noun* a game played on a special table in which you hit a white ball with a long stick (cue) and get points each time you knock a coloured ball into a pocket at the side of the table.

snooze *noun* a short sleep. **snooze** *verb.*

snore *verb* to breathe noisily while asleep. *Peter claims not to snore, but he makes a funny sawing noise while asleep.* **snore** *noun. Richard gave out a loud snore.*

snorkel *noun* a tube through which you can breathe when you swim under water. **snorkelling** *noun. Gudrun went snorkelling at the Great Barrier Reef.*

DID YOU KNOW

British army officers invented the game of snooker in India in 1875. They developed it as an alternative to billiards.

WORD HISTORY

'Snorkel' comes from the German 'Schnorchel', which was originally a dialect word meaning 'nose' or 'mouth'.

snort *verb* to make a rough noise by breathing out through the nose. **snort** *noun.*

snout *noun* an animal's long nose. *A pig's snout is ideal for rootling in the ground.*

Each snowflake has an individual pattern never to be repeated.

snow *noun* frozen white bits of water (flakes) that fall from the sky in cold weather and cover the ground. **snow** *verb.*

snowball *noun* snow pressed into a hard ball, for throwing at friends.

snowflake *noun* a tiny and unique piece of snow.

snowman *noun* a shape of a person made of snow. *The children built a snowman.*

snug *adjective* 1 cosy, warm and comfortable. *I love being snug in bed, especially when there's a storm.* 2 fitting very closely or tightly. **snugly** *adverb.*

snuggle *verb* to move into a comfortable position, especially close to another person. *The little boy snuggled up to his mother.*

so *adverb* 1 very, to such an extent. *He is so clever.* 2 in this or that way. *He was wrong and she told him so.* 3 also. *My brother has blue eyes and so has my sister.* 4 when agreeing with something that has been said. *'I didn't manage to tidy up my room.' 'So I see.'* **so** *conjunction* that is why, for that reason. *I missed the bus, so I was late.* **so far** up to now. **or so** about that number. *We've been here for a week or so.* **and so on/forth** and other things like this. *They brought their pens, paints, and so on.* **so long!** goodbye! **so as to** in order to. *She asked us to come, so as to get to know us.* **so what?** I don't care, it's not important.

soak *verb* to make or become completely wet. *We were completely soaked.* **soak up** to take in liquid. **soak** *noun.*

The car splashed through a puddle and completely soaked Elizabeth, who was just jumping out of the way.

so-and-so *noun* 1 a certain somebody or something that doesn't need to be specified. *She told me to do so-and-so.* 2 a rude or annoying person. *The headmaster is a real old so-and-so.*

S

soap *noun* 1 a product used with water for washing and cleaning. *A bar of soap.* 2 a soap opera. **soap** *verb.*

soap opera *noun* a light television or radio serial, usually about the daily life of a group of people. *An Australian soap opera.*

soar *verb* 1 to fly or go up in the air. 2 to rise, increase quickly. *Prices are soaring.*

The eagle soared through the mountain air, watching out for prey.

sob (sobs, sobbing, sobbed) *verb* to cry in gasps. *Linda sobbed all night.* **sob** *noun.*

sober *adjective* 1 not drunk. 2 serious and thoughtful, not silly. 3 dull, not bright. *Sober colours.* **soberly** *adverb.* **sober up** to stop being drunk.

soccer *noun* association football.

social *adjective* 1 liking to be with other people, friendly. *We met for a fabulous social evening.* 2 of somebody's position in society or of relations between people. *Social workers are supposed to help people.* 3 living together by nature. *Social animals live in groups.* **socially** *adverb.*

socialism *noun* a political system in which business and industry are controlled by the government with every person getting an equal share of the state's money. **socialist** *noun, adjective.*

society (societies) *noun* 1 a large group of people in a country who have a particular way of life. *In ancient Greek society women did not have an important role.* 2 a group of people with the same interests. *The film society.*

sock *noun* a piece of clothing that covers your foot. *A pair of socks.*

sock *verb* (slang) to punch.

socket *noun* 1 a device usually in a wall into which you put a plug to make an electrical connection. 2 a hollow opening into which something fits.

sofa *noun* a soft seat with a back for two or three people to sit on. *I bought a really comfortable sofa.*

Sofia *noun* the capital of Bulgaria.

WORD HISTORY

The term soap opera came about when they were first broadcast on radio during the 1930s. Their main sponsors were soap manufacturers.

DID YOU KNOW

The solar system contains the Sun, 9 planets, about 50 moons or satellites, more than 1,000 comets, and thousands of smaller bodies known as asteroids and meteoroids.

soft *adjective* 1 not hard, firm. *A soft bed.* 2 smooth to the touch, not rough. *Babies have soft skin.* 3 gentle, not loud or bright. Calm. *Her soft voice.* 4 kind and caring. *A soft heart.* **softly** *adverb.* **softness** *noun.*

soft drink *noun* a drink that is not alcoholic. *Lemonade is a soft drink.*

soften *verb* 1 to make or become soft. 2 to become kinder. 3 to make something less terrible or strong. *He tried to soften the shock by telling some amusing stories.*

software *noun* programs for computers.

soggy (soggier, soggiest) *adjective* unpleasantly wet and heavy. *The ground was very soggy.*

soil *noun* the earth on which plants and trees grow. *The soil here is very sandy.*

soil *verb* to make or become dirty.

solar *adjective* of or from the Sun. If you heat a building with solar power, you make use of the power of the Sun.

solar system *noun* the Sun and all the planets going around it.

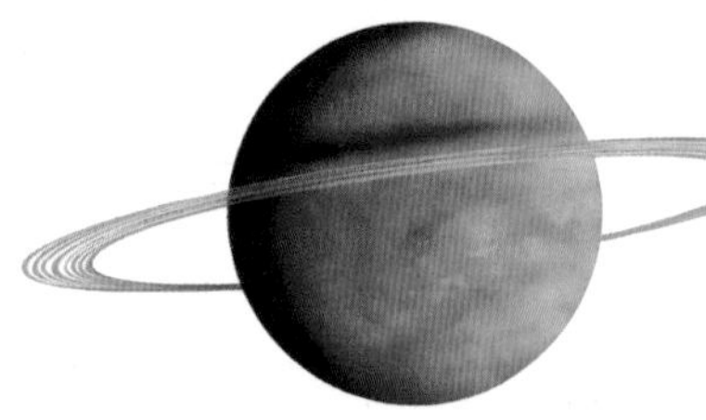

sold *verb* past tense of sell.

soldier *noun* a member of an army.

sole *noun* 1 the bottom of the foot, especially the part you walk or stand on. 2 the flat bottom part of a shoe. 3 a flat fish. **sole** *verb* to put a sole on a shoe.

sole *adjective* being or belonging to only one. *He is the sole survivor.* **solely** *adverb* only. *She acted solely for herself.*

solemn *adjective* 1 serious, not cheerful. 2 formal, in a sincere way. *He made a solemn promise.* **solemnly** *adverb.*

solicitor *noun* a lawyer who gives legal advice to his clients and prepares legal documents. *A solicitor in criminal law.*

solid *adjective* 1 filled up inside, not hollow, with no spaces or gaps. *Solid gold.* 2 not liquid or gas, having a shape. *When milk freezes it turns solid.* 3 of good quality, strong and not flimsy, reliable. *A solid house.* 4 showing complete agreement. 5 continuous, without a break. *I slept for six solid hours.* **solidly** *adverb.* **solidity** *noun.*

solid *noun* 1 something that is solid. *The baby is on solids now.* 2 a solid figure in geometry with length, width and height.

solitary *adjective* 1 alone, without a companion. *A solitary walk.* 2 spending a lot of time alone, lonely. *Bears are solitary animals.* 3 single. *I can't think of a solitary reason for moving.*

solo *noun* a piece or passage performed by one person alone. **solo** *adjective.* **solo** *adverb. He flew solo for the first time.*

soloist *noun* a person who plays a piece of music or sings a song alone. **solo** *noun.*

Solomon Islands *noun* a country of many islands in the Pacific Ocean.

solution *noun* 1 an answer to a question or problem. 2 a liquid in which something has been dissolved. *Bathe the cut knee in a solution of salt and water.*

solve *verb* to find the answer to a problem or puzzle. *Try and solve this riddle.*

Somalia *noun* a country in Africa.

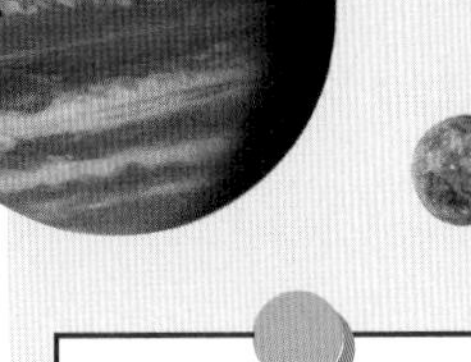

sombre *adjective* dark and gloomy, or serious and sad. *Sombre music filled the chapel at Tracy's funeral.*

some *adjective* 1 a small number or amount, a few. 2 somebody or something that is not named. *Some guy asked me the way to town.* 3 a fairly large number or amount. *She had been dead for some years before we knew about it.* 4 about. *The river is some 10 m deep.* **some** *pronoun* a certain amount, number or part of something. *Some wore red, others pink.*

somebody, someone *pronoun* some person, but not a particular person. *Somebody/someone told me that you were moving house, and now I know it's true.*

somersault *noun* a jump or move in which you bring your legs over your head. **somersault** *verb. He somersaulted on the grass for glee.*

something *pronoun* a thing that is unknown, some thing. *May I have something to drink?* **something like** rather like or about. *She got something like £50 for her old bike.* **something to do with** connected with. *The party is something to do with her birthday.*

sometime *adverb* at one point in time. *I'll see her sometime next week.*

sometimes *adverb* from time to time, not always. *She sometimes walks to school.*

somewhere *adverb* in or to a place, but not a known one. *She lives somewhere in Kent.*

DID YOU KNOW

The first European to visit the Solomon Islands was a Spaniard, Alvaro de Mendana de Neyra, in 1568. Mendana believed that the islands might be the source of King Solomon's gold for the Temple in Jerusalem, which is how they got their name.

son *noun* the male child of a man or woman. *Their son is called Peter.*

son-in-law (sons-in-law) *noun* a daughter's husband. *Their son-in-law is a solicitor.*

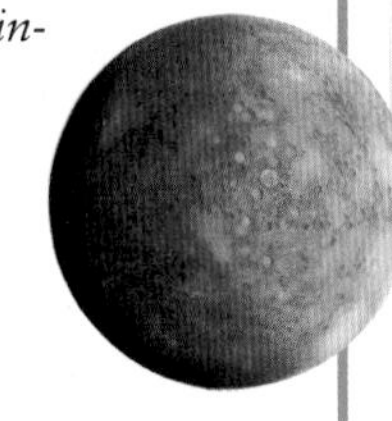

song *noun* 1 a piece of music with words for singing. 2 singing. 3 the sound of a bird. **song and dance** a great fuss about nothing. **for a song** very cheaply.

sonic *adjective* of the speed of sound or sound waves. *A sonic boom.*

sonnet *noun* a poem with 14 lines.

soon *adverb* 1 in a very short time from now. 2 early. *The sooner the better.* **as soon as** 1 quickly. *As soon as possible.* 2 at the moment when. *As soon as I get paid.* **as soon** readily or willingly. *I'd just as soon go home.* **sooner or later** at some time, certainly. *Sooner or later she'll discover the terrible truth about Paula.*

soot *noun* black powder left from burning or carried in the air in smoke. *The chimney is blocked with soot.* **sooty** *adjective.*

soothe *verb* to make less angry or less painful. **soothing** *adjective. A soothing medicine will do your throat good.*

sophisticated *adjective* 1 used to fashionable and elegant ways, not simple. 2 complicated, with many parts. *A highly sophisticated machine.* **sophistication** *noun.*

soppy *adjective* foolishly sentimental.

sorcerer *noun* a man who does magic with the help of evil spirits. *The sorcerer's apprentice.* **sorceress** *noun.* **sorcery** *noun.*

The sorcerer consulted a magic book to find the right spell.

sore *adjective* 1 painful or aching. *A sore throat.* 2 upset or angry. *She is still feeling sore about not being invited.* 3 serious, causing worry. *In sore need.* A sore point is something you do not want to talk about because it upsets you. **soreness** *noun.*

S

sore *noun* 1 a painful place on the body where the skin is infected. 2 a painful memory or subject.

sorry (sorrier, sorriest) *adjective* 1 feeling sadness or pity for somebody, expressing regret. *I'm sorry your dog died.* 2 feeling disappointed with yourself for doing or not having done something, usually said as an apology. *I'm sorry I laughed.* 3 used as a polite way to say that you did not hear or that you do not agree with something. *Sorry, what was the name?* 4 in a bad way, not good. *The house is in a sorry state.*

sort *noun* 1 a particular group of people or things that are the same in certain ways, a kind or type. *I don't like this sort of music.* 2 a person. *He is not the complaining sort.* **out of sorts** slightly ill or annoyed. **sort of** a little, in some way. *Her hair is sort of blond.*

sort *verb* to put things in order or arrange in groups according to their kind. *I spent all day sorting my books.* **sort out** to tidy, deal with or put in order. *She tried to sort out their quarrel, but they remained enemies.*

soul *noun* 1 the part of a person that is believed to live on after the body has died. 2 a person's thoughts and feelings. *That man has no soul, he is hard and unfeeling.* 3 anybody. *She didn't know a soul at the party.* 4 a style of pop music.

soulless *adjective* 1 without feeling or care for others. 2 dull.

sound *noun* 1 something you hear or that can be heard. When you turn the sound down on a television, you make it less loud. 2 an idea or impression from something read or heard. *I don't like the sound of your plans.* **sound** *verb* 1 to make a sound or cause something to make a sound. *The siren sounded a warning.* 2 to say what noise something makes or is. *The rustling of the leaves sounded ghostly.* 3 to seem. *She sounds happy.* **sound out** to find out what somebody thinks or will do.

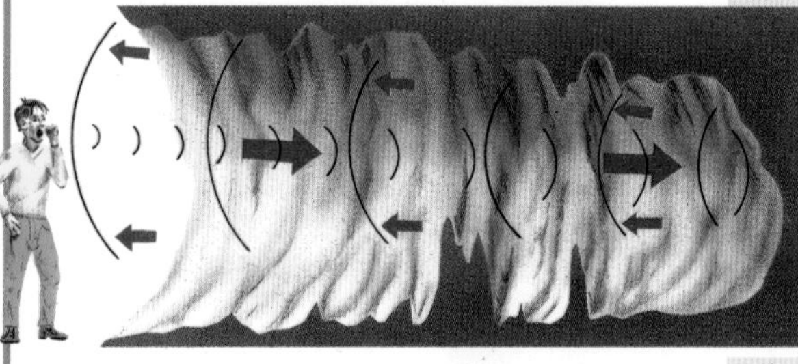

This is how an echo forms in a cave. Sound waves travel to the end wall, then bounce back. The bounce is the echo.

sound *adjective* 1 healthy, in good condition. 2 reliable and sensible. *Sound advice.* 3 deep or strong. **soundly** *adverb*. *Our team was soundly beaten in the first five minutes.* **sound asleep** deeply asleep.

soundproof *adjective* able to stop all sound from getting in or out. *A soundproof room.*

AMAZING FACT

We can taste whether food is sour, salty, sweet or bitter because we have tastebuds that are sensitive to those tastes. All tastebuds are located on the tongue. The tastebuds for sour foods are located at the back of the tongue.

South on the compass is opposite to north (opposite to the magnetic North Pole).

SPELLING NOTE

Note the different spellings of 'sow' and 'sew', which are both pronounced in the same way (rhyming with 'go').

soundtrack *noun* speech and music that go with a film. *I have the soundtrack on CD.*

soup *noun* a liquid food you drink or eat with a spoon. *A nourishing soup.*

sour *adjective* 1 tasting sharp. *Lemons are sour.* 2 not fresh, gone bad. *The milk is sour.* 3 bad-tempered, unfriendly. *She gave me a sour look.* **sour** *verb* to become unpleasant or less friendly.

source *noun* a place where something starts. *The source of the river is in the hills.*

south *noun* the direction of one of the four main points of the compass. South is to the right of a person facing the rising Sun. **south** *adjective*, *adverb* towards, from or in the south. *The south wind is warm.*

South Africa *noun* a country in Africa.

S

South America *noun* one of the Earth's seven continents.

South Korea *noun* a country in East Asia, officially called the Republic of Korea.

southerly (say **suth**-uh-lee) *adjective* in or towards the south. *We drove in a southerly direction until we came to the coast.*

souvenir (say soo-vun-**eer**) *noun* something you buy or keep to remind you of a holiday or another event. *A souvenir of Blackpool.*

sovereign (say **sov**-rin) *noun* 1 a king or queen who rules a country. 2 an old British gold coin. **sovereign** *adjective* 1 independent, not under the control of another country. 2 having the highest power in a country.

sow (sows, sowing, sowed, sown) *verb* (rhymes with go) to plant seeds into the ground that will grow into plants.

sow *noun* (rhymes with cow) a female pig.

soya *noun* a plant that can be made into flour, oil, butter or other food.

soya bean *noun* the seed of soya.

spa *noun* a place with a spring of mineral water where people come to cure illnesses.

space *noun* 1 an empty area in a place. *The desk takes up too much space.* 2 the whole area outside the Earth where the stars and other planets move. 3 an empty area or gap in something. *A parking space.* 4 a period of time. *Within the space of a month.* **space** *verb* to arrange things with gaps between them.

spacecraft *noun* a vehicle for travelling in space. *The spacecraft was in orbit.*

S

space shuttle *noun* a reusable spacecraft that can travel into space and back a number of times. *The space shuttle travelled to Mir.*

spacesuit *noun* a suit for wearing in space with its own air supply.

spade *noun* a tool with a blade and a handle for digging.

spade *noun* a playing card with a picture of a black heart-shaped leaf with a short stem. *The ace of spades.*

spaghetti *noun* long, thin sticks of pasta that you boil before eating.

Spain *noun* a country in Southwest Europe.

span *noun* 1 a period in time from beginning to end, or the length of time over which something exists. *During a ten-year span at the factory he was never late.* 2 the length of something from one end to the other. *The wing span of a glider.* 3 the distance from the tip of the thumb to the tip of the little finger when the hand is spread. 4 the part between two supports of an arch or a bridge. **span** (spans, spanning, spanned) *verb* 1 to last for a length of time or reach across. 2 to form an arch or bridge over.

Spanish *noun* 1 the language spoken in Spain, Mexico and other South American countries. 2 the people of Spain. **Spanish** *adjective. Spanish flamenco dancing.*

spank *verb* to smack on the bottom.

spanner *noun* a tool for holding and turning nuts and bolts.

spare *adjective* 1 kept for use when needed. *She left a spare key with her neighbour.* 2 free or not being used. *Have you got any spare cash?* 3 thin. *A spare figure.* **go spare** to become very angry. **spare** *noun* a spare part for a machine or engine.

spare *verb* 1 not to harm or kill somebody or something, to keep from harming. *Take all I have but spare the children.* 2 to find enough money or time to give to somebody or for a purpose. *Can you spare me a minute?* 3 to keep from using or spending. *No expense was spared.* **enough to spare** more than enough.

sparing *adjective* using or giving very little.

spark *noun* 1 a small bit of burning material that flies up from a fire. 2 a flash of light produced by electricity. 3 a small bit. *A spark of interest.* **spark** *verb* to give out sparks. **spark off** to lead to or be the cause of something. *The discussion sparked off a bitter quarrel between the two families.*

DID YOU KNOW

The first American space shuttle was called Columbia, and its first blast-off was from Kennedy Space Center in Florida in 1981.

Spain is a favourite holiday destination for many Europeans. Tourism is one of its major industries.

WORD HISTORY

Different pasta shapes have different Italian names. Spaghetti are 'little strings', which are thicker than vermicelli ('little worms') and thinner than macaroni (originally from the Greek for 'food made from barley').

AMAZING FACT

The Space Age officially began in 1957, with the launch of the Sputnik, a Soviet satellite that carried a radio transmitter. The first manned space flight was in 1961.

sparkle *verb* 1 to shine with a lot of small flashes of light. 2 to bubble. *Sparkling wine.* 3 to be lively, bright and witty.

sparrow *noun* a small brown bird.

sparse *adjective* small in number or amount, not crowded. *His sparse white hair.* **sparsely** *adverb. Sparsely populated.*

spawn *noun* the eggs of fish, frogs and some other water animals. **spawn** *verb* 1 to lay spawn. 2 to produce something, especially in large numbers. *The latest fashion show has spawned new ideas.*

Our pond was full of frogspawn. We waited eagerly for the tadpoles to hatch.

speak (speaks, speaking, spoke, spoken) *verb* 1 to say things using your voice, to talk. 2 to know and be able to talk a language. *She speaks French.* 3 to give a speech. *He spoke for an hour.* **speak out** to speak freely about something, especially in favour or against it. **speak up** to speak more loudly.

speaker *noun* 1 somebody making a speech. 2 somebody who speaks a language. *English speakers.* 3 a piece of equipment on a radio or cassette player through which the sound comes, a loudspeaker.

spear *noun* a weapon with a long pole and sharp point for throwing or stabbing. **spear** *verb* to make a hole in or catch with a spear or something pointed. *She speared the meat with a fork and stuffed it in her mouth.*

Spears are used for hunting animals for meat.

special *adjective* 1 not usual, better or more important than others. *I'm doing it as a special favour.* 2 for a particular person or thing. *Astronauts wear special suits in space.* **specially** *adverb* 1 more than usual, in a special way. *He was specially nice to me.* 2 for a special purpose. *A school specially for deaf students.*

specialist *noun* a person who has special skills or knowledge in a particular subject, an expert. *A heart specialist is a doctor who treats heart diseases.*

speciality (specialities) *noun* 1 a particular work or study. *Her speciality is French.* 2 fine or best product. *The chef's soup is the speciality of the house.*

specialize *verb* to study one subject or know about one thing so you are an expert in it. *His father specializes in racing bikes.*

species (species) *noun* (say **spee**-sheez) a group of animals or plants that are of the same kind and are the same in all important ways. *This species has become very rare.*

specify (specifies, specifying, specified) *verb* to describe or name something exactly. **specification** *noun. Please give me the exact specifications for the project.*

specimen *noun* 1 a typical thing or example. 2 one piece or a small amount of something that shows what the whole is like. *The doctor took a specimen of blood.*

speck *noun* a small spot.

spectacle *noun* 1 a big show or public performance. 2 a strange or silly sight. *Don't make a spectacle of yourself.*

spectacles *plural noun* a pair of glasses.

spectacular *adjective* grand, impressive. *A spectacular view of the mountains.*

spectator *noun* a person who watches something, especially sport.

spectrum (spectra) *noun* 1 the band of colours as seen in the rainbow. 2 a range of different kinds of things, ideas or opinions.

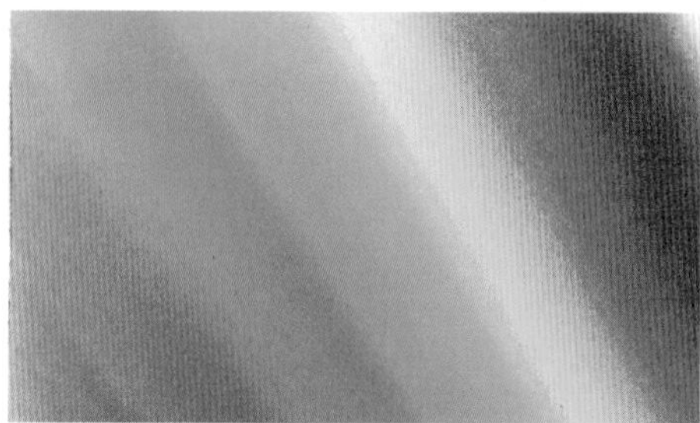

The spectrum contains all the colours of the rainbow.

speech (speeches) *noun* 1 the act or power of speaking. 2 words spoken to a group of people, a talk. *The minister made a speech.*

speed *noun* 1 how quickly something moves, travels or happens. *I was amazed at the speed of his serve.* 2 fastness or swiftness. **at speed** fast. **speed** (speeds, speeding, sped) *verb* 1 to go quickly. *He sped past us.* 2 to go too fast. *He was stopped by the police for speeding.* **speed up** (speeded up) to make something go or happen faster.

speed limit *noun* the fastest speed you are allowed to drive by law.

spell *noun* 1 a period of time. *It rained for a short spell.* 2 a quick period of activity or illness. *A spell in prison.*

spell *noun* words or an attraction that are supposed to have magical powers. *The witch cast a spell on him.*

spell (spells, spelling, spelt) *verb* 1 to put letters of the alphabet in the right order to make a word or words. *Her name is spelt R-o-s-y.* 2 to mean. *Her silence usually spells trouble.* **speller** *noun.*

DID YOU KNOW

In Greek legend the Sphinx was a winged monster with the body of a lion and the head of a woman. She asked travellers a riddle. Those who could not answer were killed. Oedipus got the right answer and the Sphinx then killed herself.

WORD HISTORY

The word 'spider' comes from the Old English 'spinnan' ('to spin'), referring to the spider's web. Spiders look like insects, but actually belong to a group called arachnids, which take their name from the mythological character Arachne, a peasant girl who had great weaving skills.

spelling *noun* the way a word or words are spelt. *American spelling.*

spend (spends, spending, spent) *verb* 1 to give money to pay for something. 2 to pass or use up time. *I spent all day reading.* **spender** *noun. A big spender.*

sperm (sperm or sperms) *noun* the male cell that fertilizes a female egg to produce new life. *Sperm look like tadpoles swimming.*

sphere *noun* 1 a round shape like a ball. 2 a particular area of interest or activity. *The sphere of politics.* **spherical** *adjective.*

sphinx (sphinxes) *noun* an ancient Egyptian stone statue with the body of a lion and a man's head. *The sphinx asked me a riddle.*

The Sphinx stands at Giza, near the Nile in Egypt.

spice *noun* powder or seeds from a plant used to give a taste to food. **spicy** *adjective.*

spider *noun* a small creature with eight legs that spins webs in which it catches other insects. **spidery** *adjective* long and thin. *Spidery handwriting.*

A tarantula is a spider that has hairs on its body and legs which contain an irritant.

spike *noun* 1 a long pointed piece of metal. *The spikes on the fence.* 2 a piece of metal with a sharp point fixed to the bottom of some shoes, especially running shoes. **spike** *verb* 1 to put spikes in or on something. 2 to catch or pierce with a spike.

spill (spills, spilling, spilt or spilled) *verb* 1 to pour out, especially over the edge of a container. *I spilt some milk.* 2 to come out in large numbers. *People spilled out of the stadium.* **spill** *noun.*

spin (spins, spinning, spun) *verb* 1 to make thread by twisting together fibres. 2 When spiders spin, they make a web out of thread from their bodies. 3 to turn around fast or make something go round and round. *My head is spinning.* **spin a yarn** to tell a story. **spin out** to make something last longer. **spin** *noun* 1 the movement of going round and round. 2 a short ride in a car or other vehicle. *A spin in the country would be very pleasant on a sunny afternoon.*

spinach *noun* a vegetable with large green leaves. *Spinach is good for you.*

spindly (spindlier, spindliest) *adjective* long, thin and weak-looking. *Spindly legs.*

spine *noun* 1 the row of bones down the middle of your back, the backbone. 2 a sharp point like a thorn on an animal's body or on a plant. 3 the stiff back part of a book to which the pages and covers are fastened. The title of the book is usually printed on the spine.

When you are making a photocopy, please don't break the spine of my book.

spire *noun* the pointed part on top of a church or tower. *Dreaming spires.*

spirit *noun* 1 a person's mind, the part that is connected with thoughts and feelings. *She was in good spirits.* 2 a supernatural being, a ghost. 3 liveliness and energy, effort shown. *He keeps the team spirit going.* 4 what something really means, not what it actually says. *Making her pay for her food would be against the spirit of our agreement.* 5 a strong alcoholic drink. Whisky and brandy are spirits. **spirit** *verb* If you spirit somebody or something away, you take them quickly and secretly to another place.

spit (spits, spitting, spat) *verb* 1 to force liquid out of your mouth. *She coughed and spat blood.* 2 to rain lightly. **spit out** 1 *She ate a grape and spat out the pips.* 2 to say something quickly and angrily. *She spat out his name.* **spit** *noun* the watery liquid that is produced in the mouth, saliva. **spitting image** an exact likeness. *She is the spitting image of her mother.*

spit *noun* 1 a thin, pointed metal rod for cooking meat over a fire. 2 a point of land sticking out into the sea.

Barry roasted the meat for the barbecue on a spit.

spite *noun* a wish to hurt or annoy somebody. *She said it out of spite.* **spite** *verb*. **in spite of** despite.

AMAZING FACT

Spiders need air to breathe but there is one spider, the Water Spider, that actually lives underwater. It builds a living space underwater, then carries air down to fill it.

WORD HISTORY

The term 'spitting image 'was originally 'spit and image', from the phrase 'the very spit of', which meant the exact likeness. Perhaps this was because everyone's spit looks exactly the same?

spiteful *adjective* being nasty about people you do not like. *A spiteful remark.*

splash *verb* 1 to hit water or throw liquid about so it flies up in drops and makes a noise. If you splash somebody, you make them wet. *We splashed through the waves.* 2 to fall or hit in small noisy drops. *Rain splashed on the window.* 3 to throw liquid on something. *He splashed his face with water.* **splash** (splashes) *noun* 1 the sound made when something hits water. 2 a small amount of liquid that has been spilt. *There is a splash of paint on your skirt.* 3 a bright colour or effect. *A yellow dress with a splash of red.*

splendid *adjective* 1 beautiful and impressive to look at. 2 great.

splendour *noun* impressive beauty. *The utter splendour of the throne room.*

splinter *noun* a small, sharp piece of wood or other hard material that has broken off a bigger piece. *I'm trying to get this glass splinter out of my finger.* **splinter** *verb* to break into splinters.

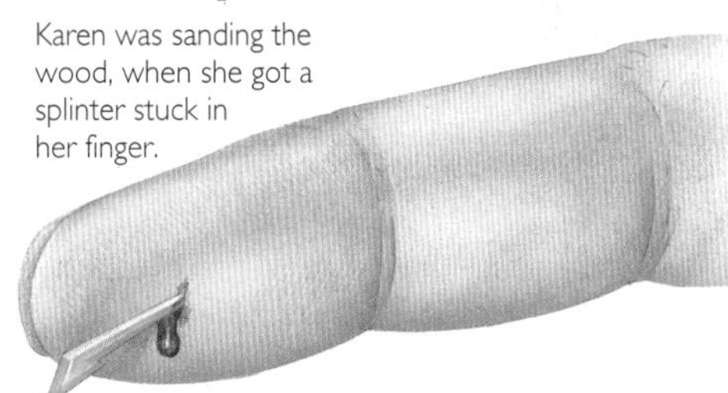

Karen was sanding the wood, when she got a splinter stuck in her finger.

split (splits, splitting, split) *verb* 1 to break, tear or crack. *This wood splits easily.* 2 to divide into parts or share. *The children were split into groups.* **split the difference** to agree on a price which is halfway between the two amounts. **split up** to separate. *We split up and went separate ways.* **split** *noun* 1 a cut or break made by splitting. 2 the splitting or dividing of something. 3 a division between different things. 4 a dish made from cut-up fruit and ice-cream. *A banana split.*

spoil (spoils, spoiling, spoiled or spoilt) *verb* 1 to ruin or damage something so it is no longer any good. *The rain spoilt our holiday.* 2 to harm somebody so they become very selfish by giving them everything they want. *Some parents spoil their children.* 3 to treat very well or too well. *I spoilt myself with an ice-cream.* **spoils** *plural noun* stolen goods, especially those taken in war.

spoilsport *noun* somebody who stops others from having fun and wants to spoil their enjoyment of things.

spoke *verb* past tense of speak.

spoke *noun* each of the bars or wire rods that go from the rim of a wheel to the centre. *Bicycle spokes.*

S

sponge *noun* 1 a small sea animal with a body full of holes. 2 a piece of the body of the sea animal or soft rubber or plastic with holes in for washing or padding things. 3 a soft cake. **spongy** *adjective*. **sponge** *verb* 1 to wash or wipe with a sponge. 2 to live by getting money or things free from people without giving anything in return. *He sponges off his friends.* **sponger** *noun*.

sponsor *noun* a person or business who gives money or help to a person, team or event, usually in return for advertising a product. **sponsor** *verb* to be a sponsor for somebody or something. *We are sponsoring the school football team.*

spook *noun* a ghost. **spooky** *adjective*. *A spooky old house.*

spool *noun* a round holder or roll for winding something on. *A spool of thread.*

spoon *noun* an object with a long handle and a shallow bowl used for eating or stirring food. **spoon** *verb* to lift or take with a spoon. *She spooned soup into bowls.*

spoonerism *noun* an exchange of the first letters of a pair of words, usually with a funny result. 'You have hissed the mystery lesson,' is a spoonerism.

spoonful *noun* the amount a spoon can hold. *Two spoonfuls of sugar.*

sport *noun* 1 an activity, competition or game, usually done outdoors. 2 somebody who is kind, cheerful and does not mind losing or being teased. *He is a very good sport.* **sport** *verb* to have or wear something. *He was sporting a bright blue tie.*

spot *noun* 1 a small round mark or a dirty mark. *A blue dress with red spots.* 2 a lump or pimple on the skin. *Don't squeeze your spots.* 3 a particular place. *This is the spot where the accident happened.* 4 a small amount. *A spot of trouble.* 5 a drop. *Spots of rain.* **on the spot** 1 at once. *He was dismissed on the spot.* 2 If you put somebody on the spot, you make them give an answer or make a decision. **in a tight spot** in a little difficulty. **spot on** exactly right. *Your guess turned out to be spot on.* **spot** (spots, spotting, spotted) *verb* 1 to notice, pick out. *Can you spot the mistake?* 2 to rain lightly. 3 to mark with spots. **spotted** *adjective*. *A spotted scarf.* **spotty** *adjective*. *A spotty face.*

DID YOU KNOW

There are about 10,000 known species of sponges, and they are found in seas all over the world. But there are only about 20 species of freshwater sponges.

The spooky old house on the hill was always lit up at night, though no one had lived there for years.

WORD HISTORY

William Archibald Spooner (1844–1930), an eccentric clergyman and Oxford don, became famous for his silly slips of the tongue. These became known as 'spoonerisms'. He would say, for example, 'a well-boiled icicle', when he meant 'a well-oiled bicycle'.

spotless *adjective* very clean.

spout *noun* 1 the tube or pipe-like opening for pouring liquid from a kettle, jug or pot. 2 a stream of liquid going upwards with great force. **spout** *verb* 1 to stream out with great force. 2 to say a lot in a boring way. *He spouted boring facts all evening.*

Grandma hated teapots with a chipped spout.

sprain *verb* to damage a joint by twisting or bending it. *He sprained his ankle jumping off the cliff.* **sprain** *noun*.

sprawl *verb* 1 to sit or lie with your arms and legs spread out. *He sprawled on the sofa.* 2 to spread over a large area. *The town sprawls across the valley.*

spray *verb* to scatter small drops of liquid on or over something. *She sprayed the room with air freshener.* **spray** *noun* 1 small drops of liquid sent through the air, either blown by the wind or from a special container. *Sea spray.* 2 a special container with liquid in it for spraying. *Hair spray.*

spray *noun* a number of flowers or leaves on a stem or branch.

We ordered a spray of spring flowers to be sent to Sally's bedside.

spread (spreads, spreading, spread) *verb* 1 to open something out so that all of it can be seen, to stretch out. *The bird spread its wings and flew away.* 2 to cover a large area or time. *The rainforest spreads for thousands of kilometres.* 3 to cover something with something. 4 to make or become more widely known or have a wide effect. *The fire spread to the next village and engulfed the huts in flames.* 5 to share or divide evenly. *We spread the work over a period of three years.* **spread** *noun* 1 the act or action of spreading. *The spread of Aids is increasing, especially in Africa.* 2 the distance or time of spreading. 3 a big meal with lots of food and drink. *Claire put on a magnificent spread for the wedding.* 4 a soft food, paste that can be spread with a knife. *Cheese spread.* 5 a number of things, ideas or interests.

spring *noun* 1 the season of the year between winter and summer. 2 a coil of wire that goes back to its normal shape after it is pressed. *One of the springs in the mattress has gone.* 3 a place where water comes up from the ground. *A mountain spring.* 4 being able to stretch and go back to a normal shape. *There is no spring in the sofa.* **spring** (springs, springing, sprang, sprung) *verb* 1 to move quickly and suddenly. 2 to come into being, appear or be the result of. *Her unhappiness springs from her wish to be famous.* 3 to make something happen or known suddenly and unexpectedly. *We sprang a surprise birthday party on him.*

sprinkle *verb* to scatter small drops or tiny pieces on something. *They sprinkled sand on the icy path.*

sprint *verb* to run at full speed for a short distance. sprint *noun* 1 running very fast. *He made a sprint for the bus.* 2 a short race. **sprinter** *noun.*

sprout *noun* 1 a new growth on a plant. 2 a vegetable like a small cabbage. *Brussels sprouts.* **sprout** *verb* to grow or come out.

spruce *adjective* very neat, clean and smart looking. **spruce** *verb* to make yourself look neat. *He spruced himself up to meet his girlfriend's parents.*

spruce *noun* a kind of evergreen tree.

The Norwegians sent a spruce tree to London, where it was put up in Trafalgar Square at Christmas.

spud *noun* (slang) potato.

spun *verb* past tense of spin.

spurn *verb* to refuse with anger or pride. *He spurned her offer of help.*

spurt *verb* 1 to flow out suddenly, to gush out. *Blood spurted from the wound.* 2 to run faster, increase speed suddenly. *She spurted towards the finishing line.* spurt *noun* 1 a sudden spurting. 2 a sudden increase of effort or speed.

spy (spies) *noun* somebody who finds out secret information about other people or countries. **spy** (spies, spying, spied) *verb* 1 to work as a spy to get information. 2 to watch secretly. *He spies on his neighbours.* 3 to notice. *I spied a sweet in your bag.*

squabble *verb* to quarrel about something unimportant. **squabble** *noun. I hope you have made it up after your squabble.*

A square has four equal sides.

DID YOU KNOW

There are about 50 different species of spruce, widely distributed in the forests of the cooler northern regions of the world, especially in China. They also grow as far south as the mountains of Mexico, southern Europe and the Himalayas.

AMAZING FACT

Early settlers are responsible for the word 'squash'. When they began to arrive in the 17th centrury, they had trouble pronouncing Native American words. One of them was 'asquatasquash' which they shortented to 'squash'.

The farmer grew his best crops of squash in years.

squalid *adjective* dirty and untidy. **squalor** *noun. She lives in squalor.*

squander *verb* to spend money or time foolishly and wastefully. *She squandered her youth and now she regrets it.*

square *adjective* 1 having the shape of a square with four equal sides and four right angles. 2 forming a right angle. 3 fair, honest. *He wasn't square with me.* 4 even in points, equal or settled. *I've paid up and now we are square.* 5 having an area equal to that of a square with sides of the length stated or being the length from a corner in both directions. *The room has an area of 3 square metres.* **a square meal** a good meal that fills you. **a square number** any number that is the square of another number. 4 is a square number (4 = 2 x 2). **square root** a number that equals another number when it is multiplied by itself. 2 is the square root of 4 (2 x 2 = 4).

square *noun* 1 a shape with four sides that are all the same length and four corners at right angles. 2 a place surrounded by buildings that is the shape of a square. *Nelson's Column is in Trafalgar Square.* 3 a number equal to another number when it is multiplied by itself. 16 is the square of 4. (16 = 4 x 4). **square** *verb* 1 to make something square, give a square shape to something, or mark squares on something. 2 to multiply a number by itself. 6 squared is 36. 3 to pay or settle something. *He has to square his account first.* 4 to match or fit a particular explanation or situation. *His story does not square with the facts.*

squash (squashes) *noun* 1 a game played with rackets and a small rubber ball that is hit against the walls of an indoor court. 2 a fruit drink. *Orange squash.* 3 a crowd of people in a small place. 4 a vegetable similar to a pumpkin. **squash** *verb* 1 to press something so it goes into a flat shape, to crush. *The grapes got squashed at the bottom of the bag.* 2 to press into a small place. *We all squashed on to the bus.*

squat (squats, squatting, squatted) *verb* 1 to sit on your heels, to crouch. 2 to live in an empty building without being allowed to or paying rent. **squat** *noun. We lived in a squat for a year.* **squatter** *noun.*

S

squat *adjective* short and fat.

squeak *verb* to make a short, very high, loud sound. *Mice squeak.* **squeak** *noun.* **squeaky** *adjective. Squeaky floorboards.*

squeal *verb* 1 to make a long, very high sound or cry. 2 to report a criminal to the police. **squeal** *noun. A squeal of brakes.*

squeamish *adjective* easily upset or made sick, especially if something looks unpleasant. *She is very squeamish and can't stand the sight of blood.*

squeeze *verb* 1 to press from two sides. *He squeezed his finger in the door.* 2 to press to get liquid out of something. *To squeeze an orange.* 3 to manage to get through or into something. *She squeezed herself into her jeans.* **squeeze** *noun.*

squid *noun* a sea creature with a long soft body, eight arms and two long tentacles.

The Greeks love to eat squid cut into rings and deep-fried in batter.

squint *verb* 1 to look with your eyes almost closed. *She squinted in the bright sunlight.* 2 to have eyes that look in different directions. **squint** *noun* a condition in which the eyes look in two different directions.

squirrel *noun* a small furry animal with a long bushy tail that climbs trees and eats nuts. *Squirrels love acorns.*

squirt *verb* to force or come out in a thin stream of liquid. *She squirted the water pistol at me.* **squirt** *noun.*

Sri Lanka *noun* a country in South Asia, formerly called Ceylon.

St *abbreviation* 1 street. 2 saint.

St George's *noun* the capital of Grenada.

St John's *noun* the capital of Antigua and Barbuda.

St Kitts and Nevis *noun* a country in the West Indies.

St Lucia *noun* a country in the West Indies.

St Vincent and the Grenadines *noun* a country in the West Indies.

stab (stabs, stabbing, stabbed) *verb* to strike or pierce with something pointed. *The thief stabbed the policeman with a knife.* **stab** *noun* 1 the act of stabbing. 2 a wound made by something pointed. 3 a sudden painful feeling. *A stab of guilt.* 4 If you have a stab at something, you try something and hope to be successful. *I had a stab at the exam questions, but I didn't do very well.*

SPELLING NOTE

Most people use 'stadiums' as the plural of the sports ground, but 'stadia' can also be used. Most of the original Latin words ending in '–um' have '–a' as their plural.

DID YOU KNOW

Sri Lanka is an island in the Indian Ocean off the southern tip of India. It had a highly developed civilization as early as the 5th century BC.

stable *noun* a building in which horses are kept. *There are two horses in the stable.*

stable *adjective* firmly fixed in a position, not likely to fall or change. *A stable relationship.* **stability** *noun.*

stadium (stadiums or stadia) *noun* a sports ground. *A football stadium.*

Every seat in the stadium was booked for the big match.

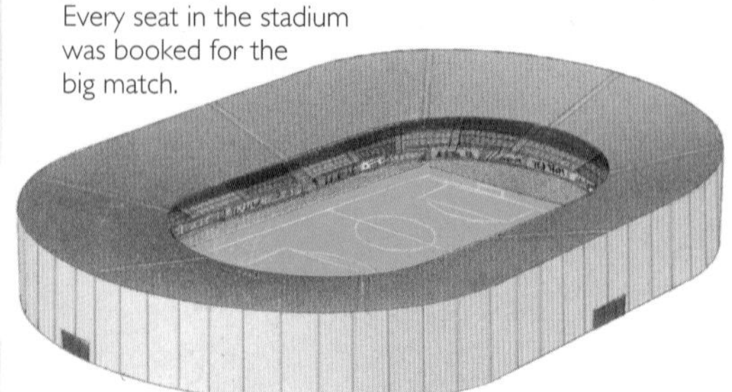

staff *noun* 1 the people who work for an organization, for example an office or a shop. 2 a strong stick. **staff** *verb* to provide workers, supply with staff. *The restaurant is staffed with excellent cooks.*

stag *noun* a male deer.

stage *noun* 1 a period, point or part in a development or journey. *We divided the journey into three easy stages.* 2 the platform on which plays and musicals are performed. 3 acting in theatres. *A stage production.* If you are on stage, you are acting. **stage** *verb* 1 to put on a play or perform a show. 2 to organize. *The students staged a protest.*

stagger *verb* 1 to walk or move unsteadily. *The drunk staggered across the street.* 2 to surprise. *I was staggered that he had left the country.* 3 to arrange things so that they do not happen at the same time. *We staggered our holidays, so that someone was always there to mind the shop.*

stain *noun* 1 a mark that is difficult to remove. 2 a liquid used for darkening or staining wood. 3 a mark of shame or guilt. **stain** *verb* 1 to make a stain on something. *The peach juice has stained my fingers.* 2 to colour with a special liquid. *We stained the chairs red.*

stained glass *noun* glass made up of pieces of different colours fitted together and used for windows and other objects.

The village fair raised hundreds of pounds towards a new stained glass window for the church.

stainless steel *noun* metal made from steel that does not rust or stain.

stair *noun* one of a number of steps. The stairs are a set of steps which go from one floor to another.

staircase *noun* a set of stairs inside a house.

stalactite *noun* a downward-pointing spike of limestone hanging like an icicle from a cave roof.

stalagmite *noun* an upward-pointing spike of limestone standing like a pillar on the floor of a cave.

stale *adjective* not fresh. **staleness** *noun*.

stalemate *noun* a situation in which neither side can win. *We had reached stalemate in our discussions.*

stalk *noun* a stem of a plant or fruit.

stalk *verb* 1 to walk in a stiff, angry or proud way. 2 to follow an animal or person quietly in order to hunt or catch them. **stalker** *noun*.

stall *noun* 1 a table or small shop in a market where things are sold. 2 a place for an animal in a barn or stable. *Cattle in their stalls.* 3 the stalls are the seats on the ground floor in front of the stage in a theatre. **stall** *verb* to stop suddenly or make an engine stop. *The car stalled.*

stall *verb* to not give a clear answer or not do something in order to get more time, to delay. *I'll try and stall them for a while.*

stallion *noun* a male horse, especially kept for breeding. *A beautiful white stallion.*

stamen *noun* the male part of a flower that produces pollen.

stamina *noun* the strength of body or mental energy needed to do tiring things for a long time.

stammer *verb* to repeat sounds of the same word when speaking, to speak with pauses. **stammer** *noun*.

stamp *noun* 1 a small piece of gummed paper with a design on it that is stuck on an envelope before posting to show that postage has been paid. 2 a small pad with a design or letters on one side which is pressed on to a surface. 3 the mark made by using a stamp. *An official stamp on a document.* 4 a mark or sign typical for something. *His songs bear the stamp of youth.* **stamp** *verb* 1 to lift your foot and put it down hard on the ground. *The little boy stamped his foot and cried.* 2 to walk noisily and with heavy footsteps. 3 to put a postage stamp on a letter or parcel. 4 to press a design or letters on something.

Paul collected lots of different stamps and stuck them in an album.

SPELLING NOTE

'Stalactite' comes from an ancient Greek word for 'dripping', and 'stalagmite' from the Greek 'stalagma', 'drop'. Both types of rock formation are formed by dripping, trickling water containing dissolved limestone.

AMAZING FACT

Stamp collecting is also called 'philately' and the person who collects stamps is known as a 'philatelist'.

stand (stands, standing, stood) *verb* 1 to be on your feet in an upright position. 2 to put or be in an upright position. 3 to remain or stay the same. *My invitation still stands.* 4 to put up with or endure. *I can't stand him.* 5 to be a candidate in an election. *He is standing for parliament.* 6 to pay for. *Let me stand you a drink.* **stand between** to be an obstacle. *Only one more election stands between me and a place in parliament.* **it stands to reason** it makes sense or is likely to happen. *It stands to reason she'll fail the exam if she never does any work.* **stand by** to be ready to help or take action. *Ambulances were standing by at the match.* **stand for** 1 to represent or mean. *BT stands for British Telecom.* 2 to put up with, to allow. *She doesn't stand for any nonsense.* **stand out** 1 to be easily seen and clear. *Red stands out well.* 2 to be outstanding. *He stands out as a real artist.* **stand up** 1 to get up. 2 to be accepted as true. *His story won't stand up in court.* 3 to defend. *You must learn to stand up for yourself.* 4 If you stand somebody up, you don't meet them as arranged. **stand up to** 1 to resist attack. 2 to stay in good condition. *The carpet stood up to constant use.*

stand *noun* 1 a piece of furniture for putting things on or in. *An umbrella stand.* 2 a stall or small shop for selling things. *A flower stand.* 3 a position against or in favour. *She took a stand against animal experiments.* 4 a position for sitting or standing in a stadium, from where people can watch a game or other event. *We had seats in the stand.*

standard *adjective* 1 of the usual or accepted kind. *The standard rules of good behaviour.* 2 most widely used or best of its kind. *The standard book on grammar.*

standard *noun* 1 how good something is. *The standard of spelling is very high.* 2 something used for measuring or judging the quality of something. *Different countries use different standards.* 3 a stand or upright base for holding something. *A standard lamp.* 4 a flag of an important person or family. *The royal standard.*

stanza *noun* a verse of poetry.

staple *adjective* regular or main. *Rice is the staple food of India.*

Potatoes are the staple food in Ireland.

staple *noun* 1 a small piece of wire used for holding pieces of paper together. Staples are pushed through the paper with a stapler. 2 a U-shaped nail. **staple** *verb* to fasten papers together with a stapler. **stapler** *noun.*

star *noun* 1 a large ball of burning gas in space, a heavenly body. 2 a shape, an object or a mark with points sticking out round it. If a hotel has five stars, it means that it is extremely good. 3 a famous actor, sports player or performer. *A pop star.* **star** (stars, starring, starred) *verb* 1 to have an important part in a play or film. 2 to mark with a star shape. **starry** *adjective.*

starch (starches) *noun* 1 a white substance in food. There is starch in bread, rice and pasta. 2 a white substance for stiffening clothes, especially clothes made of cotton. **starch** *verb* to stiffen with starch.

stare *verb* to look at somebody or something hard or for a long time. *Don't stare at me, it makes me blush.*

starfish (starfish or starfishes) *noun* a sea animal with five arms that has a star shape.

starling *noun* a small, dark speckled bird.

start *verb* 1 to come into being or to begin, especially something you were not doing before. *She started laughing.* 2 to take place, to begin. *His music started a new craze.* 3 to set out on a journey. *She started as a secretary.* 4 to jerk or move suddenly, usually because you are surprised or frightened. *A sudden noise makes me start.* **start** *noun* 1 the place of starting, the beginning of an activity. *Let's make an early start.* 2 a sudden uncontrolled movement. *She woke up with a start.* 3 an advantage or an amount of time somebody has over somebody else. *We had an hour's start.* **make a fresh start** to start again from the beginning.

startle *verb* to make somebody jump or be surprised. *The noise startled him.*

starve *verb* 1 to suffer or die from not having any food to eat. To make somebody die from hunger. *Thousands starved to death during the drought.* 2 to be very hungry. *When's lunch, I'm starving.* 3 When you are starved of something, you lack that particular thing and need it very much. *The children were starved of love.* **starvation** *noun.* **starving** *adjective.*

state *noun* 1 a condition which somebody or something is in. *His state of health.* 2 the government of a country or a country. *Italy is a European state.* 3 part of a large country. *The state of Texas.*

DID YOU KNOW

An ancient Greek scientist called Thales discovered static electricity over 2,500 years ago, when he rubbed a piece of amber with a cloth.

Starfish cling to the rocks with suckers under their arms.

SPELLING NOTE

Be careful not to mix up the spelling of the adjective 'stationary' (not moving) and the noun 'stationery' (writing materials). Both come from the Latin for 'standing', which came to refer to a shopkeeper as opposed to a 'moving' pedlar.

state *verb* to express something in words, especially in a formal way. *The police stated that no charges had been laid.*

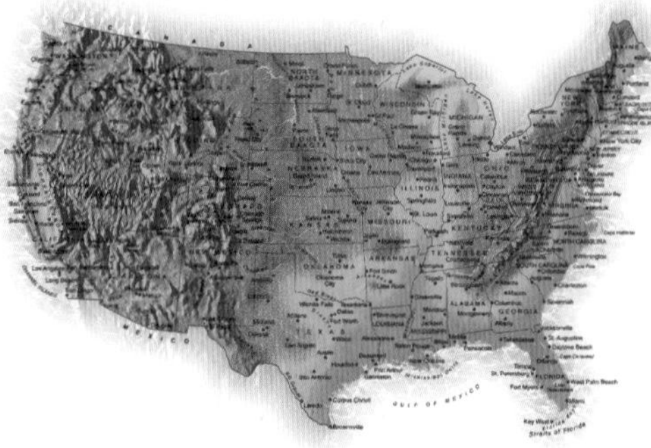

There are 52 states in the USA.

statement *noun* 1 something you state, facts and information given in a written or spoken declaration. *I don't believe the minister's statement.* 2 a printed document showing amounts of money paid in, taken out or owed, usually sent out by your bank. *I get a monthly bank statement.*

static *adjective* not moving or changing.

static electricity *noun* electricity that builds up or is present in certain things like your hair or nylon.

station *noun* 1 a place where trains or buses stop for people to get on and off. *Where is the railway station?* 2 a building for a particular service. *A police station.* 3 a company that sends out radio or television programmes. *The new radio station plays club dance music all day.* **station** *verb* to put people or things in a certain place for a particular purpose.

stationary *adjective* not moving. *The bus was stationary when the accident happened.*

stationery *noun* materials for writing, such as paper, envelopes, pens and pencils.

Jennifer was in charge of the office stationery cupboard.

statistics *plural noun* information shown in numbers that can be compared. *The statistics seem to show that examination results have been getting better every year.* **statistical** *adjective.*

statue *noun* a model of a person or animal in stone, wood or metal. *The statue of the Venus de Milo has no arms.*

stay *verb* 1 to remain in the same place or condition. *The weather stayed fine.* 2 to live at a place as a visitor. *She is staying with her brother in London.* 3 to last out. *The horse stayed the course.* **stay put** to remain in one place. **stay on** to remain in a place or for an extra spell of time. *He stayed on as headmaster.* **stay up** to go to bed after your normal bed time.

stay *noun* 1 a short time spent somewhere. 2 a delay or postponement. *The judge ordered a stay of execution.*

steady (steadier, steadiest) *adjective* 1 not moving, firm. *He is not very steady on his legs.* 2 not changing, regular. *She has now found a steady job.*

steak *noun* a thick slice of meat (especially beef) or fish.

steal (steals, stealing, stole, stolen) *verb* 1 to take something that belongs to somebody else without any right. *He stole some money.* 2 to move quietly and secretly. *She stole out of the room.*

steam *noun* 1 the hot mist that is produced when water is boiled. *The steam from a boiling kettle.* 2 the power from steam used to drive machines. *A steam engine.* 3 energy. If you run out of steam, you have no more energy. **steam** *verb* 1 to give out steam. 2 to cook in steam, not water. *Do you want to steam the fish?* 3 to travel by steam power. *The ship steamed out of the harbour.*

The glorious days of the steam train are long gone, and rail travel is now less exciting but much cleaner.

steel *noun* a very strong hard metal used for making knives and tools.

steep *adjective* 1 rising or falling sharply. *A steep slope.* 2 expensive. *£100 for his old bike is a bit steep.*

steeple *noun* a tall pointed church tower.

steeplechase *noun* a race across country with hedges, fences and ditches.

steer *verb* 1 to control a car, boat or ship so it goes in the direction you want it to go. 2 to guide. *He steered me towards the door.*

steering wheel *noun* the wheel in a car or lorry that the driver holds and turns to steer with. *He gripped the steering wheel.*

AMAZING FACT

Steam fills 1700 times as much space as the water that it has been boiled from. If you compress steam into a small container, it pushes against the sides. If there is a place or thing that the steam can move, such as a piston, the steam will force the piston outward. When the steam cools, it turns back into water, takes less space, and the piston returns to its original position. Early steam engines used this principle to power pumps to pump water out of mines.

WORD HISTORY

The steeplechase gets its name from early races when a local church with a tall steeple was used as a landmark, probably the finish. Steeplechase races using horses can be traced back to 18th-century fox hunting.

stem *noun* 1 the long central part of a plant above the ground. 2 the thin part of a plant that has leaves or flowers on it. 3 the thin part of a wine glass or bowl that looks like a stem. **stem** (stems, stemming, stemmed) *verb* to stop something flowing or spreading. *The nurse tried to stem the flow of blood.* **stem from** to have as its origin, to come from. *Her fear of dogs stems from being bitten as a child.*

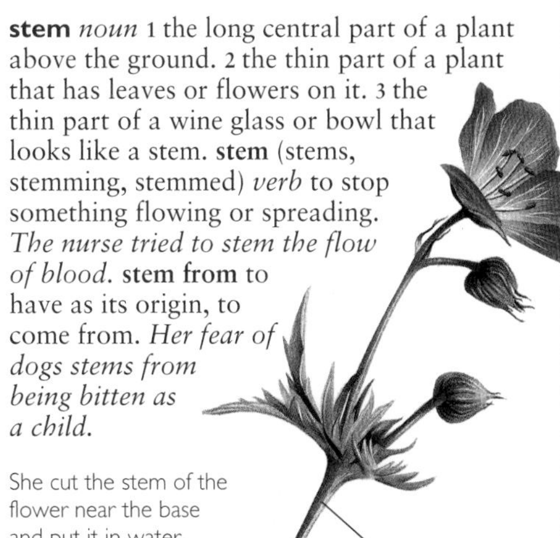

She cut the stem of the flower near the base and put it in water.

stench (stenches) *noun* a very nasty smell.

stencil *noun* a piece of paper, metal or plastic with a design or letters cut out of it, used for making designs or letters on something. **stencil** (stencils, stencilling, stencilled) *verb*.

step *noun* 1 the movement made when lifting a foot and putting it down in a different place. *He takes very big steps.* 2 the sound made when walking. *She could hear steps coming towards her.* 3 a short distance. *The beach is just a few steps from the house.* 4 a flat surface on which you put your foot when you walk up or down, a stair. *Mind the step!* 5 one of a series of actions that are done to get a certain result, or one of a series of stages. *What is the next step?* 6 a movement of the feet in dancing. If you are in step, you are moving your feet forward at the same time as your partner or others walking. If you are out of step, you are not in agreement with the others. **step by step** doing one thing at the time, slowly. **take steps to do something** to get a result. **watch your step!** be careful! **step** (steps, stepping, stepped) *verb* to walk. *She stepped into the house.* **step in** to become involved in order to help. *Her mother stepped in and sorted out her problems.* **step up** to increase in size or speed. *We must step up production.*

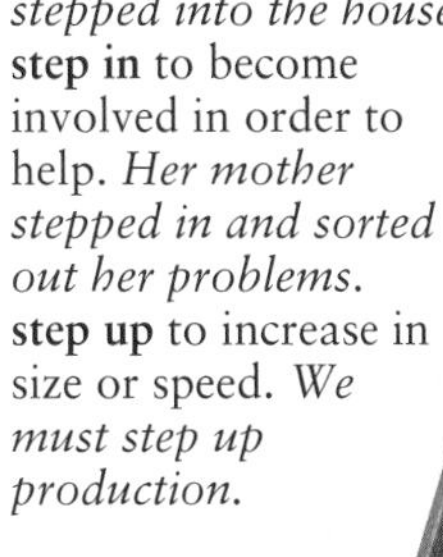

Father climbed up the step ladder to paint the ceiling.

S

stepchild (stepchildren) *noun* a child of a husband's or wife's earlier marriage. **stepbrother** *noun*. **stepsister** *noun*.

stepfather *noun* your stepfather is the man who has married your mother after your real father has died or your parents have divorced. **stepmother** *noun*.

steppe *noun* a large area of grassland without trees, especially in Russia.

stereo *adjective* stereophonic, giving out sound or sound coming from two different places. *Stereo equipment.* **stereo** *noun* 1 a stereo sound or recording. 2 a stereo record/CD player.

stereotype *noun* a fixed idea or typical example of somebody or something. *He is small and thin and does not fit the stereotype of a boxer.* **stereotype** *verb*.

stern *adjective* strict. **sternly** *adverb*. *He looked at her sternly.*

stern *noun* the back end of a ship.

stethoscope *noun* a medical instrument that a doctor uses to listen to somebody's heartbeat. *The stethoscope felt cold.*

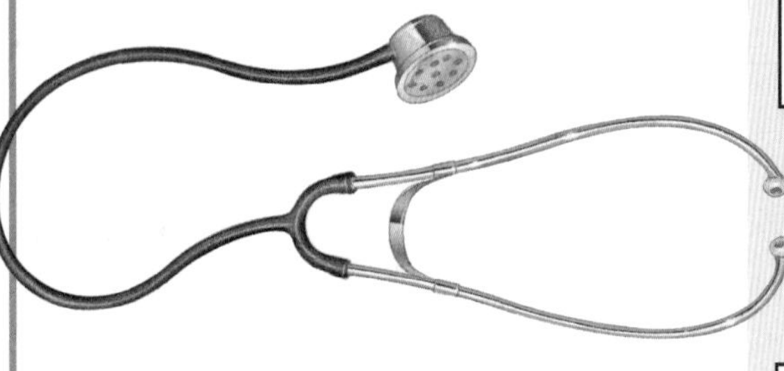

Dr Smith listened to Peggy's heart through his stethoscope.

stew *verb* to cook slowly in liquid. **stew** *noun* a meal with meat and vegetables cooked in liquid.

stick *noun* 1 a long thin piece of wood, a branch broken from a tree. 2 a piece of wood specially made for leaning on when walking. *A walking stick.* 3 any long thin piece of something. *A stick of celery.* **get the wrong end of the stick** to misunderstand something. **stick** (sticks, sticking, stuck) *verb* 1 to push something pointed into something. *She stuck a pin into the noticeboard.* 2 to fix one thing to another thing with glue or another sticky substance. *Don't forget to stick a stamp on the envelope.* 3 to become fixed, unable to move. *My zip sticks.* 4 to not give up, to keep on doing something. *How can you stick having to get up so early every morning?* 5 to stay. *We must stick together.* 6 to put. *Stick your bags in the corner.* **stick at** to continue to work hard at something. *If she sticks at the job, she'll do well.* **stick to** 1 If you stick to somebody, you are loyal to that person and support him. 2 If you stick to something, you refuse to change. *We are sticking to our plan.* **sticky** *adjective*. *A sticky bun.* **stickiness** *noun*.

WORD HISTORY

The prefix 'step–', as in 'stepbrother', 'stepchild', etc. comes from the Old English word 'steop', meaning an orphan or a child whose parent has died.

DID YOU KNOW

The Russian steppes are bordered by forests to the north and by desert to the south. The climate is too cold in winter and too hot and dry in summer for trees to survive. But the steppe grasses have long roots that can tap water from deep under the ground.

stiff *adjective* 1 not bending or moving easily. *Stiff cardboard.* 2 firm, not runny. *Beat the cream until it is stiff.* 3 not friendly, formal. *The new teacher is very stiff with the children.* 4 difficult. *A stiff test.* 5 strong. *A stiff drink.* **stiffness** *noun*.

stile *noun* a step used to climb over a fence or gate. *Let me help you over the stile.*

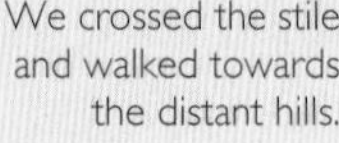

We crossed the stile and walked towards the distant hills.

still *adjective* 1 not moving. 2 silent. 3 not fizzy. *Still water.* **still** *adverb* 1 up to now or up to that moment. *Is he still waiting?* 2 even. *More amazing still, she never spoke again.* 3 nevertheless, in spite of what has been said. *The children were very naughty – still, she shouldn't have hit them.* 4 even so. *He is not the most brilliant footballer, but he still deserves a place in the team.*

still *noun* 1 quietness with no activity. *In the still of the night.* 2 a still photograph taken from a cinema film. 3 an apparatus for making alcoholic spirits.

stimulate *verb* to make more active or interested in something. *Sunlight stimulates growth.* **stimulation** *noun*.

sting *noun* 1 the sharp pointed part of some insects such as bees, or on some plants such as nettles, that can prick and hurt. 2 a sharp pain or wound caused by a sting. **sting** (stings, stinging, stung) *verb* 1 to prick with a sting. 2 to feel a strong pain or to feel hurt. *His eyes were stinging from the smoke.* 3 to take too much money from somebody. *They stung us for ten pounds.*

stink *noun* 1 a nasty smell. 2 a big fuss, usually made by complaining. **stink** (stinks, stinking, stank or stunk) *verb* 1 to smell very badly. *The changing rooms stink of old socks.* 2 to be very unpleasant or bad. *The plan stinks.*

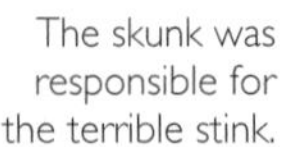

The skunk was responsible for the terrible stink.

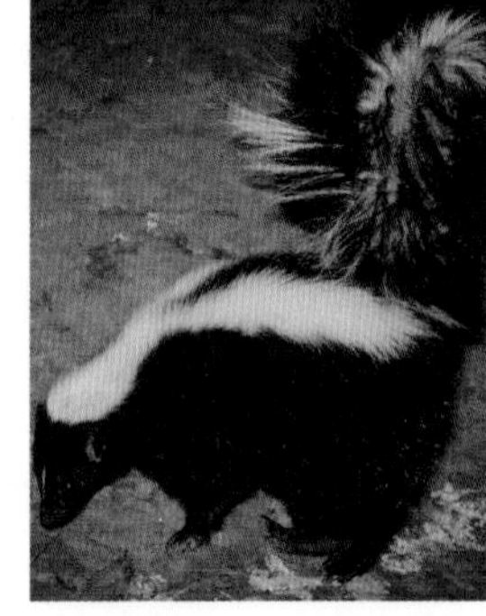

stir (stirs, stirring, stirred) *verb* 1 to mix something by moving it around with a spoon. 2 to move. *She is fast asleep and hasn't stirred.* 3 to excite or be touched by something. *The news stirred him into action.* 4 to cause trouble between others, especially by telling stories. *She loves stirring.* **stir** *noun* 1 the action of stirring. 2 excitement, shock. *The discovery caused quite a stir.*

stir-fry (stir-fries, stir-frying, stir-fried) *verb* to cook small pieces of meat and vegetables quickly by stirring them in a wok or frying pan. **stir-fry** *noun.*

stirrup *noun* a metal loop on a horse's saddle for the rider's foot.

stock *noun* 1 the supply of goods or other things to be sold or used. *A large stock of food.* 2 a group of farm animals used for breeding or kept for their meat. 3 your ancestors or original family, or a type of animal or plant. *Many Americans are of European stock.* 4 a liquid made from vegetables or meat used in cooking. *Vegetable stock cubes.* 5 shares in the ownership of a business company. 6 a garden flower with a sweet smell. **take stock** to think about something before deciding what to do next. **stock** *verb* 1 to keep goods in stock. 2 to fill or supply a place with food or other thing.

stock exchange *noun* a place where shares are bought and sold.

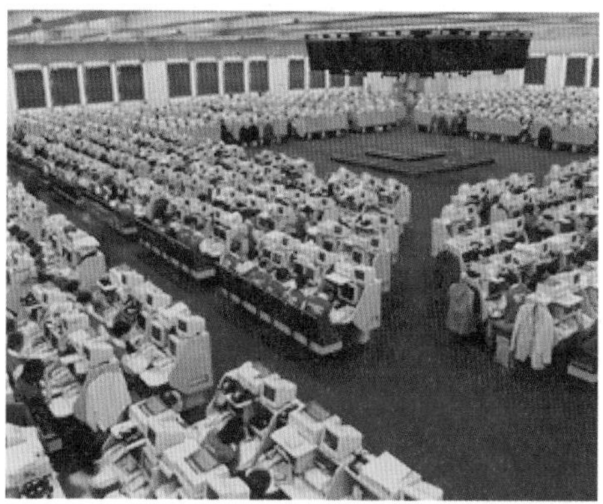

Many people called 'dealers' work at the stock exchange. Their job is to buy and sell shares.

Stockholm *noun* the capital of Sweden.

stodgy (stodgier, stodgiest) *adjective* 1 heavy, sticky and filling, especially food. *Stodgy rice.* 2 dull and uninteresting.

stole *verb* past tense of steal.

stole *noun* a long piece of material worn around the shoulders.

stomach *noun* 1 an organ in the body where food is digested. 2 the front part of the body below the waist. *He is doing exercises to get rid of his big stomach.* **stomach** *verb* to put up with, usually something unpleasant. *How can you stomach his nonsense?*

DID YOU KNOW

The famous London stock exchange, in the City of London, was founded in 1773. It replaced coffee-houses, where financial dealings had previously been made. The New York stock exchange is situated on Wall Street, in the financial district of New York.

AMAZING FACT

The human stomach is a large, muscular bag that has openings at both ends.

The stomach of a human baby is about the size of a chicken egg, while an adult's stomach can hold about one litre or one quart.

stone *noun* 1 very hard material found in the ground, rock. 2 a small piece of rock. *He threw a stone at the window.* 3 a jewel. *A precious stone.* 4 the hard seed in the middle of some fruit such as cherries or peaches. 5 a measure of weight (1 stone = 14 pounds or 6.35 kilograms). **stone** *verb* 1 to throw stones at somebody. *They stoned the traitor to death.* 2 to take the stones out of fruit. **stony** *adjective.*

stone *prefix* completely. *He is stone-deaf.*

stoned *adjective* under the influence of drugs. *Angela gets stoned every night.*

stood *verb* past tense of stand.

Bill sat on the stool to play the guitar.

stool *noun* a seat with legs but without arms or a back. *A milking stool.*

stoop *verb* 1 to stand or walk with your shoulders bent forward. 2 to lower or allow yourself to do something. *I wouldn't stoop to thanking that woman.* **stoop** *noun.*

stop (stops, stopping, stopped) *verb* 1 to come to an end or put an end to an activity or movement. To finish moving, to not continue working. *My watch has stopped.* 2 to prevent somebody from doing something or something from happening. *How can I stop him smoking?* 3 to stay, especially for a short visit. *She stopped for a chat.* 4 to fill a hole, to close. 5 to block. 6 to prevent money from being paid. *She stopped the cheque.* **stop** *noun* 1 the moment something stops, a pause, an end. 2 a place where buses stop. 3 a dot or mark of punctuation, especially a full stop. 4 a knob or lever that changes the level of the notes (pitch) and controls the pipes on an organ.

stopwatch *noun* a watch that can be started and stopped and is used for timing things such as races.

storage *noun* the keeping of things in a special place. *We put our furniture in storage when we went abroad.*

store *noun* 1 a supply of something that is kept for later use. 2 a shop, especially a larger one. **in store** 1 kept ready for later use. 2 about to happen. *There are lots of adventures in store for you.* **store** *verb* to keep things until they are needed. *The wood is stored in the shed.*

storey *noun* a floor of a building. *A block of flats with six storeys.*

stork *noun* a tall bird with a long beak and long legs. *A stork nesting on a chimney pot.*

storm *noun* 1 a very strong wind, usually with rain, thunder or snow. 2 an excited or angry show of feeling. *A storm of protest.* **storm** *verb* 1 to attack or force your way into a place. *The soldiers stormed the stronghold.* 2 to show anger by moving about or shouting loudly and angrily. *He stormed out of the room.* **stormy** *adjective.*

story (stories) *noun* 1 a description of real or made-up events. 2 a lie. *He is always telling stories.*

stout *adjective* 1 thick and strong. *Stout climbing boots.* 2 rather fat. *He is short and stout.* 3 firm. *A stout supporter of the club.*

stout *noun* strong, dark beer.

stove *noun* a device for heating a room or cooking on. *A hot stove.*

The stove roared indoors, keeping us warm while the wind rattled at the windows.

straddle *verb* to sit or stand across something, with one leg on each side. *To straddle a horse.*

straggle *verb* 1 to grow in an untidy way. *Ivy straggled over the wall.* 2 to move forward slowly behind others. **straggler** *noun.* **straggly** *adjective. Straggly hair.*

straight *adjective* 1 going in the same direction, not bent or curved. *Straight hair.* 2 upright. *The picture is not straight.* 3 tidy. 4 honest. *A straight answer.* If you keep a straight face, you look serious and try not to laugh. **straight** *adverb* 1 in a straight line. 2 directly, without stopping. *Go straight home.* **straight away** immediately. **go straight** to leave a life of crime and live an honest life.

straightaway *adverb* immediately.

straighten *verb* to make something straight or become straight.

straightforward *adjective* 1 easy to understand or do. *The instructions are quite straightforward.* 2 honest. *He is a very straightforward person.*

strain *verb* 1 to stretch tightly, usually by pulling. 2 to make a great effort. *She strained her ears to hear.* 3 to damage a part of your body. *I've strained a muscle.* 4 to pour something through a strainer to remove liquid. *He strained the peas.* **strain** *noun* 1 the condition or force of being stretched. *The cable broke under the strain.* 2 a state of worry or tension. Something that tests you or uses up strength. *Looking after children is a great strain.* 3 an injury to a muscle. 4 a tune. *The strains of a song wafted up to where she sat on the deck.*

DID YOU KNOW

The layer of atmosphere just above the Earth's surface, where we live, is called the troposphere; then comes the stratosphere; then the mesosphere, thermosphere, and finally the exosphere.

strain *noun* 1 a type of plant or animal. *A new strain of beans.* 2 a quality that develops, or a characteristic. *There has always been a strain of madness in my family, unfortunately.*

strainer *noun* an instrument for straining solids from liquids.

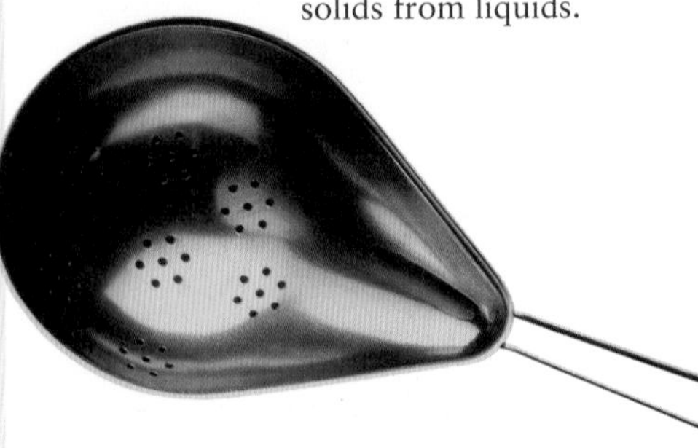

We use a tea strainer because we don't like leaves floating in our tea.

strange *adjective* unusual or surprising, not known or seen before. **strangely** *adverb. Strangely, it seems that she did not leave at her usual time.*

stranger *noun* 1 somebody you don't know. 2 somebody who is in a place he doesn't know. *I'm a stranger in this town.*

strangle *verb* to kill by pressing on the throat. **strangulation** *noun..*

strap *noun* a strip of leather or other material used for fastening. **strap** (straps, strapping, strapped) *verb* to fasten with a strap or straps. *He strapped the child into the car seat.* **be strapped for** to be short of. *I'm a bit strapped for cash at the moment.*

strategy (strategies) *noun* 1 a particular plan to achieve something. *He worked out a clever strategy to get more money.* 2 the planning of the movements of armies in war. *A military strategy.*

stratosphere *noun* the outer part of the air which surrounds the earth, between about 10 and 50 km above the earth's surface.

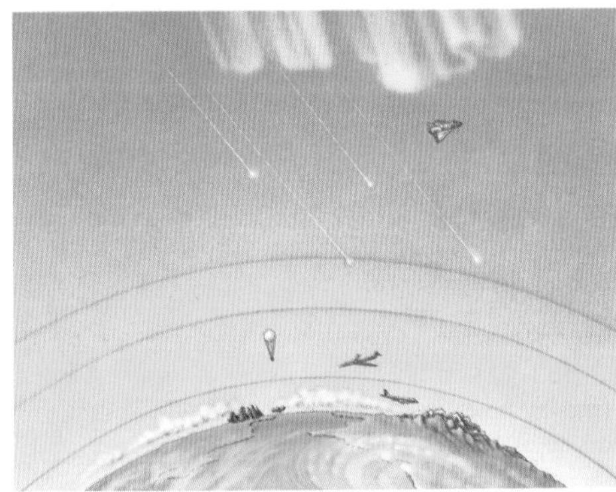

The plane took off and climbed steeply until it reached the stratosphere.

straw *noun* 1 dried stalks of grain. 2 a thin tube of paper or plastic used for drinking through. *Drinking straws.* **the last straw** the last or latest in a row of unpleasant events. *After a terrible day at the office, losing my purse was the last straw.*

S

strawberry (strawberries) *noun* a soft and juicy red fruit.

stray *verb* 1 to wander away from somewhere you are supposed to be. 2 to move away from a subject, to not concentrate. *During the lesson his thoughts strayed to football.* **stray** *adjective* without a home or not in its usual place. *Stray animals need loving homes.*

streak *noun* 1 a long stripe or mark that is different from what is around it. *He has a few grey streaks in his hair.* 2 a quality of character, a trace. *That boy has a streak of cruelty.* **streak** *verb* 1 to move very quickly. 2 to mark with streaks. 3 to run in a public place with no clothes on. **streaker** *noun. At half time a streaker ran on to the pitch.*

stream *noun* 1 a flow of water smaller than a river. 2 a flow of people or things. *A long stream of cars.* **stream** *verb* 1 to flow. *Tears streamed down her face.* 2 to move like a stream or float in the air. *The sun streamed in through the window.*

streamer *noun* a long ribbon or strip of coloured paper.

Streamers hung from the ceiling at David's party.

streamlined *adjective* smooth and regular in shape, able to move easily through air or water. Racing cars and powerboats are streamlined. **streamline** *verb.*

street *noun* a road with buildings along the side in a town or village. *The street where I live.* **streets apart** very different.

streetwise *adjective* used to the ways of modern city life. *If you're not streetwise in New York, you'll get mugged or ripped off.*

strength *noun* 1 the quality of being strong. *Superman has enough strength to lift a lorry.* 2 something that gives power. *Translation is her biggest strength.*

strengthen *verb* to make or become stronger. *Please strengthen your resolve.*

strenuous *adjective* using or needing great effort. *I had a very strenuous day at work.*

stress (stresses) *noun* 1 worries caused by difficulties in life. *She has been under a lot of stress because of her father's illness.* 2 saying a word or part of a word more strongly than another. In the word 'bookshop', the stress is put on 'book'. 3 the force of weight or pressure on something. *The heavy traffic puts stress on the bridge.* **stress** *verb* to give importance to something. *He stressed the need for peace.* **stressful** *adjective.*

DID YOU KNOW

Strawberries belong to the rose family of plants. Wild strawberry plants, bearing tiny fruits, have been picked for food since ancient times. They started to be grown as garden plants in 13th-century France.

WORD BUILDING

Words that are spelt the same can have a different stress to make different meanings. In this dictionary, stress in punctuation is marked by bold letters.

stretch *verb* 1 to become wider or longer. If you pull a rubber band it stretches. 2 to spread out or extend over a distance or period of time. *The forest stretches from the mountains to the sea.* 3 to straighten your body to full length. To push out your arms to reach something. 4 to reach, be long enough. 5 If a job stretches you, you have to work very hard at it. **stretch** (stretches) *noun* 1 stretching or being stretched. *The cat got up and had a good stretch.* 2 an area of land or water, or a period of time. *He was given a long stretch in prison.* **stretchy** *adjective. Stretchy material.*

stretcher *noun* a long piece of cloth between two poles, or something similar, on which a sick or injured person can be carried lying down. *The injured player was carried off on a stretcher.*

The patient was put on a stretcher and taken by ambulance to the hospital.

strict *adjective* 1 firm, making people do what you want. *Our teacher is very strict about punctuality.* 2 exact, complete. *The strict truth.* **strictness** *noun.*

stride (strides, striding, strode, stridden) *verb* to walk with long steps. *She strode across the lawn to meet him.* **stride** *noun* 1 a long step in walking. 2 If you make great strides, you do much better.

strife *noun* trouble between people.

strike (strikes, striking, struck) *verb* 1 to hit somebody or something. *He was struck by lightning.* 2 to stop working for a time, usually to get more money or because you are angry about something. 3 to suddenly happen or come to mind. *It struck me that we should have visited him.* 4 to sound. *The clock struck eight.* 5 to find something in a place. *They struck oil in the desert.* 6 to seem. *She strikes me as very intelligent.* 7 If you are struck by something, you are very impressed by it. *He was struck by her beauty.* 8 to light or produce a flame. *He struck a match.* **strike lucky** to have good luck. **strike off** to cross somebody's name off an official list. *The doctor has been struck off for negligence.* **strike up** 1 to begin a friendship. 2 to begin to play music. **strike** *noun* 1 a time when no work is done. *The train drivers are on strike.* 2 a hit. 3 an air attack. 4 finding oil or gold. **striker** *noun.*

S

string *noun* 1 a thin piece of cord for tying things. 2 nylon or wire in a guitar or other stringed instrument for making sounds. The strings are the stringed instruments in an orchestra. 3 a line or number of things. *A string of accidents.* **string** (strings, stringing, strung) *verb* 1 to put a string or strings on something. *To string a tennis racket.* 2 to thread on a string or hang something on a string. *Flags were strung across the street.* **highly strung** somebody who is easily excited or hurt in feelings.

strip (strips, stripping, stripped) *verb* 1 to take a covering off something. *We stripped the paint off the wood.* 2 to undress. *He stripped off his shirt.* 3 to take somebody's belongings away from them. *He was stripped of his rights.* **strip** *noun* 1 a long narrow piece of material or land. 2 a comic strip. **stripper** *noun.*

stripe *noun* 1 a long line of colour among other colours. 2 a band of cloth sewn on to a soldier's or policeman's uniform to show his rank. **stripy** *adjective.* **striped** *adjective.*

The stripes on her uniform indicated a high rank.

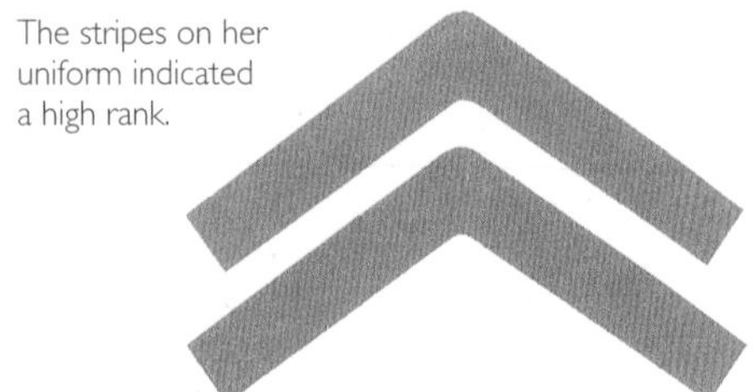

strobe lighting *noun* a light that goes on and off very quickly.

stroke *noun* 1 a hit or blow. *He cut off the giant's head with a single stroke of his sword.* 2 a movement or action with your arms, especially in sports like golf or tennis. *She swims with strong strokes.* 3 a line made by the movement of a pen or brush. *Brush strokes.* 4 the sound made by a clock striking. *He arrived on the stroke of three.* 5 a sudden illness that often makes people unable to move parts of their body. **a stroke of luck** being very lucky.

stroke *verb* to move your hand slowly and gently over something. *She stroked the dear old cat.* **stroke** *noun.*

stroll *verb* to walk slowly and in a relaxed way. **stroll** *noun. A stroll in the park.*

strong *adjective* 1 having great power, especially of the body. *He is very strong and can lift heavy weights.* 2 feeling confident and sure, not easily frightened or upset. *She has a very strong imagination.* 3 not easily broken. 4 having a great effect or taste, not weak. *A strong smell of gas.* 5 having a certain number of people. *Our club is a hundred strong.* **strongly** *adverb.* **strong** *adverb. She is old but still going strong.*

AMAZING FACT

Not all guitars have the same number of strings. The Spanish guitar and most types of electric guitar have six strings. The bass guitar has four strings. Some musicians play a twelve-string guitar which is tuned in six pairs.

The Taj Mahal is one of the world's most beautiful structures.

DID YOU KNOW

Strobe lighting is often used in clubs and discos, to flash in time with the beat of the music. The word 'strobe' comes from the Greek 'strobos', meaning 'whirling'. The stroboscope was perfected in 1931 by the American scientist Harold Edgerton.

The studs around Mike's watch make it look very sporty.

stronghold *noun* 1 a fortified place. 2 a place where many people do or believe the same. *This southern town is a stronghold of Conservatism.*

struck *verb* past tense of strike.

structure *noun* 1 an arrangement of parts, something built. *The bridge is an interesting structure.* 2 the way in which parts are put together or in which something is made. *The structure of a sentence.* **structure** *verb* to arrange or organize. **structural** *adjective.*

struggle *noun* a hard fight. **struggle** *verb* 1 to twist, kick and fight to get free. *She struggled against her attacker.* 2 to make a great effort, fight hard to do something difficult. *He struggles with his homework.*

strum (strums, strumming, strummed) *verb* to play the guitar by moving your fingers up and down the strings.

strut (struts, strutting, strutted) *verb* to walk in a proud way, usually with your head held high and chest out.

stub (stubs, stubbing, stubbed) *verb* to hurt your toe by hitting it against something.

stub *noun* 1 a short end left when something has been used. *The stub of a pencil.* 2 the part of a cheque or ticket that you keep.

stubble *noun* short stiff pieces of something growing, especially a short beard after shaving or corn stalks after harvest.

stubborn *adjective* having a strong will. If you are stubborn, you do what you want.

stuck *verb* past tense of stick.

stud *noun* 1 a small piece of metal like a nail with a large head used as a decoration. *A belt with silver studs.* 2 a kind of fastener, used instead of a button, usually two parts that are pressed together. **stud** (studs, studding, studded) *verb* to decorate with studs. *A watch studded with diamonds.*

S

stud *noun* 1 horses kept for breeding. 2 the place where horses are kept for breeding.

student *noun* somebody who is studying or training, especially at a college or university.

studio *noun* 1 a room where a painter or photographer works. 2 a room where film, radio or television programmes are made.

study (studies, studying, studied) *verb* 1 to spend time learning about a particular subject. 2 to look at something carefully. *He studied her face for a long time.* **study** (studies) *noun* 1 the activity of studying a subject. 2 a subject you study or a piece of writing on a subject. *He made a study of Greek philosophy.* 3 a drawing or painting planned as part of a larger picture. *A study of a rose.* 4 a room used for reading, writing and studying.

stuff *noun* 1 things or personal things. *Take your stuff up into your room.* 2 material of which something is made. *Try this, it's good stuff for a cold.* **stuff** *verb* 1 to fill something. *She stuffed the cushion with feathers.* 2 to push something quickly and carelessly somewhere. *He stuffed the card in his pocket.* 3 to eat a lot. *I stuffed myself with biscuits.*

stuffing *noun* 1 material used to fill something. 2 cut-up food put into meat or vegetables. *Turkey with chestnut stuffing.*

stumble *verb* 1 to trip and almost fall over. 2 to stop or make a mistake while reading or speaking. *He stumbled over a difficult word because he was dyslexic.*

stun (stuns, stunned, stunning) *verb* 1 to make somebody unconscious by hitting them on the head. 2 to shock. *He was stunned by the news of her death.*

stung *verb* past tense of sting.

stunning *adjective* brilliant, beautiful.

stunt *noun* a dangerous and risky act that somebody does in a film or in order to draw attention. *Most actors don't do their own stunts, they hire a stuntman.*

stuntman *noun* somebody who does stunts in a film so the actor does not have to take any risks.

We went into the sty to see Beryl's new litter of pigs.

WORD HISTORY

The word 'style' comes from the Latin 'stilus', meaning a pen. It came to have the wider meaning of 'the manner of writing with a pen', which gave rise to the present senses of style.

The stuffing was poking out of the teddy bear's foot.

The stuntman drove up the ramp and flew over the roofs of several cars.

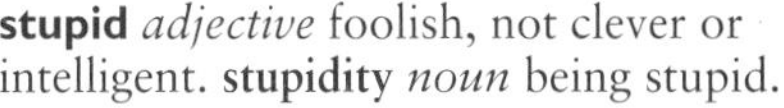

stupid *adjective* foolish, not clever or intelligent. **stupidity** *noun* being stupid.

sturdy (sturdier, sturdiest) *adjective* strong, not easily broken. *A sturdy chair.* **sturdily** *adverb. Sturdily built.* **sturdiness** *noun.*

stutter *verb* to find it difficult to say the first sound of a word, to stammer. **stutter** *noun. He stuttered because he was nervous.*

sty (sties) *noun* a place where pigs are kept.

sty or **stye** (sties or styes) *noun* a red swelling on the edge of the eyelid.

style *noun* 1 a kind or sort. *This is a new style of house.* 2 the way something is written, spoken or performed. *The essay was written in an interesting style.* 3 a superior quality or elegance. *They live in grand style.* 4 a kind of fashion or design. *The latest styles in shoes.* 5 part of a flower involved in pollination. **style** *verb* to design or make in a particular style. **stylish** *adjective* showing superior quality, elegant, fashionable. *Stylish clothes.*

sub- *prefix* 1 below, under. *Submarine.* 2 subordinate, secondary. *Subsection.*

subconscious *adjective* of thoughts and feelings which you are not completely conscious or aware of. **subconsciously** *adverb.* **subconscious** *noun.*

subdue (subdues, subduing, subdued) *verb* 1 to overcome or bring under control. *He managed to subdue his emotions.* 2 to soften. *The restaurant had subdued lighting.*

subject (say **sub**-djikt) *noun* 1 somebody or something being talked or written about. 2 something studied. 3 in grammar, the word or phrase that does the action of a verb. In the sentence 'The flower is red,' 'flower' is the subject. 4 a member of a nation. *The Queen wished a Happy Christmas to all her subjects.* **change the subject** to talk about something different.

S

subject (say **sub**-djikt) *adjective* 1 having to follow or obey something. *We are all subject to the laws of the land.* 2 liable or prone to. *She is subject to colds.* 3 dependent on. *The plan is subject to approval.*

subject (say sub-**djekt**) *verb* 1 to make somebody experience something. *They subjected him to torture.* 2 to bring under control. **subjection** *noun.*

subjective *adjective* depending on your own taste and opinions.

sublime *adjective* grand or extreme. *I think Mozart was a sublime genius.*

submarine *noun* a ship that can travel under water. **submarine** *adjective. A submarine cable.*

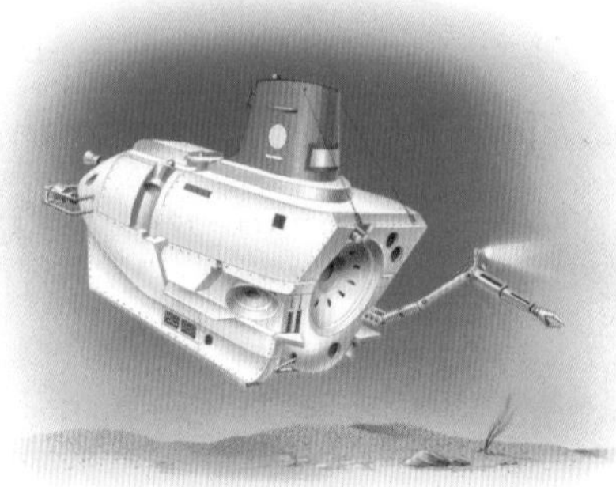

The submarine travelled into the ocean's depths.

submit (submits, submitting, submitted) *verb* 1 to give way. *They had to submit to defeat.* 2 to put forward for consideration. *She submitted her plans to the committee.* **submission** *noun.*

subscribe *verb* 1 to pay regularly for something. *He subscribes to several magazines.* 2 to agree. *I don't subscribe to that theory.* **subscriber** *noun.* **subscription** *noun. Please pay your subscription.*

subside *verb* 1 to sink lower. *The floods finally subsided.* 2 to become less strong. *Her fear subsided.* **subsidence** *noun.*

substance *noun* 1 matter. *Chemical substances.* 2 the main part. *The panel agreed with the substance of the report, but queried some details.*

substitute *noun* a person or thing that takes the place of another. *They put on a substitute in the second half and he scored a goal.* **substitute** *verb* to use in place of another. **substitution** *noun.*

subtle (say **sut**-ul) *adjective* 1 small and hard to grasp. *A subtle difference between the two.* 2 delicate. *A very subtle taste.* 3 clever. *A subtle argument.* **subtlety** *noun.*

subtract *verb* to take away, deduct. *Subtract 5 from 8.* **subtraction** *noun.*

suburb *noun* a housing district at the edge of a town. **suburban** *adjective.* **suburbia** *noun* the suburbs. *They live in suburbia.*

subway *noun* an underground passage.

AMAZING FACT

The first submarine was probably one made of wood and leather in England in 1620. But the first successful submarine was built in 1770. Both of these early attempts were operated by hand.

SPELLING NOTE

'Suède' is French for Sweden. Gloves made from soft Swedish leather were very popular in France. When the English took them up in the 19th century, they abbreviated 'gants de Suède' ('Swedish gloves') into 'suede'.

succeed *verb* 1 to do well. *The plan was good and succeeded.* 2 to come next. *Who will succeed the present chancellor?*

success *noun* 1 doing well, achieving an aim. 2 somebody or something that does well. *The play is a real success in the West End.* **successful** *adjective.*

succession *noun* 1 a series of people or things. *They met with a succession of defeats.* 2 following in order. 3 coming next, especially to the throne. **in succession** one after another.

succulent *adjective* 1 juicy. *A succulent steak.* 2 fleshy. *Succulent plants.*

such *adjective* 1 of this kind. *Such people are to be avoided.* 2 so great. *I had such a fright!* **such-and-such** particular but not specified. *He promises to come at such-and-such a time but is always late.* **such as** of the same kind as. *Big cats such as tigers and lions.* **suchlike** of such a kind. *Ghosts and ghouls and suchlike.*

suck *verb* 1 to take liquid into the mouth by using your lip and tongue muscles. *She sucked the juice from an orange.* 2 to squeeze something in your mouth. *He still sucks his thumb.* 3 to pull. *The boat was sucked into the whirlpool.* **suck up to** to flatter somebody to gain their favour. *He's always sucking up to the teachers.*

sucker *noun* 1 something that sticks to a surface by suction. 2 a person who is easily deceived. *He thinks I am a sucker.*

Sucre *noun* the legal capital of Bolivia.

Sudan *noun* a country in Africa.

Sudan has the biggest sugar factory in Africa, and the third largest in the world.

Sudanese *noun* the people of Sudan. **Sudanese** *adjective. His second wife is Sudanese.*

sudden *adjective* happening unexpectedly or without warning. *A sudden storm broke and lightning flashed.* **all of a sudden** suddenly. **suddenly** *adverb.*

suds *plural noun* froth on soapy water.

sue (sues, suing, sued) *verb* (say soo) to take legal action against somebody. *He sued his employer for damages.*

suede *noun* (say swade) soft leather with a velvety surface. *Blue suede shoes.*

suffer *verb* 1 to feel or experience something bad. *Before the operation he was suffering badly.* 2 to put up with. *He does not suffer fools gladly.* **sufferer** *noun.* **suffering** *noun.*

sufficient *adjective* enough. **sufficiently** *adverb.* **sufficiency** *noun.*

suffix *noun* letters added to the end of a word to make another word. In the word 'forgetful', 'ful' is a suffix.

suffocate *verb* 1 to make it difficult or impossible for somebody to breathe. *The fumes almost suffocated her.* 2 to suffer or die because you can't breathe. **suffocation** *noun. Auntie died of suffocation.*

sugar *noun* a sweet food obtained from the juices of various plants, especially sugar cane and sugar beet. **sugar** *verb* to sweeten, especially with sugar. **sugary** *adjective.*

Sugar can come from either sugarcane or sugarbeet. This is a field of sugarbeet.

suggest *verb* 1 to put forward as a possibility. *She suggested a different plan.* 2 to bring into the mind. *The colour white suggests peace.*

suggestion *noun* 1 a plan or idea. 2 an act of suggesting. 3 a small amount. *A slight suggestion of an accent.* 4 putting beliefs into somebody's mind.

suicide *noun* 1 killing yourself deliberately. *He committed suicide.* 2 somebody who commits suicide. **suicidal** *adjective.*

suit *noun* 1 matching jacket and trousers for men, or jacket and skirt for women. 2 special clothes, such as a spacesuit or swimsuit. 3 one of the four sets of cards in a pack (hearts, clubs, diamonds or spades). 4 a lawsuit.

suit *verb* 1 to go well with, or look good on. *That jacket suits you.* 2 to be suitable or convenient. *Friday doesn't suit me at all.* 3 to adapt. *He suited his style to the audience.* **suit yourself** to do as you want to.

suitable *adjective* right for the purpose, appropriate. *Make sure you wear suitable clothes.* **suitability** *noun.*

suitcase *noun* a case used to hold clothes and other things when travelling. *I packed my suitcase and drove to the airport.*

sulk *verb* to be in a bad mood and show this by being silent. *She hated the party and sulked all evening.* **sulk** *noun.* **sulky** *adjective. A sulky pout.*

sullen *adjective* 1 silent and bad-tempered. *She gave me sullen looks.* 2 dark and gloomy. *A sullen sky.* **sullenness** *noun.*

GRAMMAR NOTE

If you add a word or part of a word (called a suffix) to the end of a root word, you can form a new word.

DID YOU KNOW

The expression 'to suffer fools gladly' comes from the Bible: 'For ye suffer fools gladly, seeing ye yourselves are wise.' (2 Corinthians 11:19).

AMAZING FACT

Although the Sun appears to be small when we look at it from the Earth, it is actually a million times bigger than the Earth.

sultan *noun* a Muslim ruler.

sultana *noun* 1 a seedless raisin. 2 the mother, wife or daughter of a sultan.

sum *noun* 1 a total. The sum of 4 and 3 is 7. 2 a problem in arithmetic. 3 an amount of money. **sum** *verb* to find a total. **sum up** 1 to summarize, especially at the end of a talk. *The judge summed up at the end of the hearing.* 2 to form a judgement. *He summed her up very quickly.*

summarize *verb* to make a summary of. *He summarized the agreement in a few words.* **summarizer** *noun.*

summary *noun* a short account giving the main points. *A quick summary of events.*

summary *adjective* 1 brief. 2 without delay or mercy. *Summary justice.*

summer *noun* the warm season between spring and autumn. **summery** *adjective.*

summit *noun* 1 the top of a mountain. 2 the highest point. *He was at the summit of his career.* 3 a meeting between heads of government. *The prime minister attended a summit meeting.*

summon *verb* 1 to call to appear. *He was summoned to court as a witness.* 2 to call upon. *She summoned him to help her.* **summon up** to build up, gather. *He summoned up all his energy.* **summons** *noun* an official order to appear in a law court.

Sun *noun* 1 the star which the Earth travels around and from which it receives light and warmth. *It's dangerous to look directly at the Sun.* 2 light and warmth from the Sun. She loves sitting in the sun. **sun** (suns, sunning, sunned) *verb* to be in the Sun. *The cat was sunning itself on the terrace.*

The surface of the Sun is a phenomenal 6,000 degrees Centigrade and would melt absolutely anything.

sunburn *noun* reddening of the skin caused by too much sun. **sunburn** *verb* to suffer from sunburn. *She was badly sunburnt.*

Sunday *noun* the first day of the week, after Saturday and before Monday.

sundial *noun* an instrument that shows the time by a shadow on a dial.

sunflower *noun* a very tall plant with a large round flower.

sung *verb* past tense of sing.

sunglasses *plural noun* dark glasses that protect the eyes from strong sunlight.

sunk *verb* past tense of sink.

sunlight *noun* light from the Sun.

sunny (sunnier, sunniest) *adjective* 1 bright with sunlight. *A sunny room.* 2 cheerful. *She gave me a sunny smile.*

sunrise *noun* the rising of the Sun at dawn.

We danced all night and breakfasted at sunrise.

sunset *noun* the setting of the sun.

sunshine *noun* light from the Sun. *We sat in the sunshine and did our knitting.*

suntan *noun* browning of the skin from exposure to the sun. **suntan** *verb.*

super *adjective* exceptional, brilliant.

super- *prefix* 1 above or beyond. *Superstructure.* 2 extra large or good. *Supertankers are the biggest ships.*

superb *adjective* excellent. *A superb wine.*

superficial *adjective* not very deep. *A superficial wound.* **superficiality** *noun.*

superfluous *adjective* more than enough.

superintend *verb* to supervise and inspect. **superintendent** *noun.*

superior *adjective* 1 in a higher position. *A superior officer.* 2 better than average. *Superior quality.* **superior** *noun. She is my superior.* **superiority** *noun.*

superlative *adjective* 1 of the highest quality. 2 in grammar, the highest degree of an adjective. Bravest is the superlative form of brave. **superlative** *noun.*

supermarket *noun* a large self-service store that sells food and other goods. *We buy all our groceries from the supermarket.*

Penny looked at the sundial and saw that it was already half past two.

GRAMMAR NOTE

The superlatives of short words add '–est' on to the end: 'oldest', 'youngest', 'tallest'. Longer words use 'most' in front: 'most beautiful', 'most cowardly'. Don't use '–est' and 'most' with the same word.

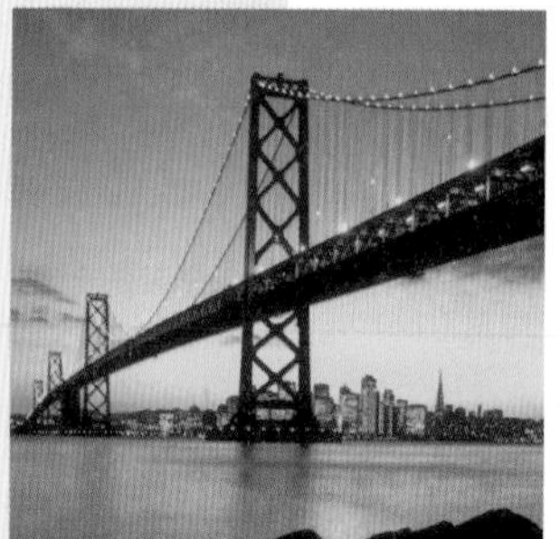

The bridge was supported by a metal framework on concrete pillars.

AMAZING FACT

Superstitions vary from culture to culture. In the US, black cats are considered bad luck, but in the UK, good luck cards often have a black cat on them! Black cats crossing your path are supposed to be bad luck in both places.

supernatural *adjective* magical or mystical. *He thought there were supernatural forces at work.* **supernatural** *noun.*

supersede (say soup-uh-**seed**) *verb* to take the place of somebody or something.

supersonic *adjective* faster than the speed of sound. *Concorde is a supersonic aircraft.*

superstition *noun* a personal belief in the special effects of something. Most superstitions are not based on scientific fact. **superstitious** *adjective. He is very superstitious and won't walk under ladders.*

supervise *verb* to oversee actions or work. *The foreman's job is to supervise the workers.* **supervision** *noun.* **supervisor** *noun.* **supervisory** *adjective.*

supper *noun* an evening meal, especially a light one. *A supper of crackers and cheese.*

supple *adjective* easily bent, flexible. *Athletes have to be supple.* **suppleness** *noun.*

supplement *noun* 1 an added part. *She takes vitamin supplements to add to her diet.* 2 a separate section, especially a colour magazine. *The Sunday supplement.* 3 an extra charge. **supplementary** *adjective.*

supply *verb* to provide something that is needed. **supply** (supplies) *noun* 1 providing what is needed. 2 a stock. *A large supply of tyres.* 3 (plural supplies) provisions and equipment. *The explorers took enough supplies for three months.* **in short supply** scarce. **supplier** *noun.*

supply teacher *noun* a teacher who acts as a substitute for another teacher for a time.

support *verb* 1 to carry the weight of something. *This wall supports the whole house.* 2 to provide with things needed. *He has a family to support.* 3 show the truth of something. *The evidence supports her statement.* 4 to speak in favour. *Most speakers supported the resolution.* 5 to be a fan of. *She supports Manchester United.* **support** *noun.* **supporter** *noun.*

suppose *verb* to assume or think. *I suppose they'll come back.* **be supposed to** to be expected or required to do something. *You were supposed to be there by nine.*

suppress *verb* 1 to prevent from being seen or known. *She tried to suppress a yawn.* 2 to put out of your mind. *She tried to suppress her fear.* **suppression** *noun.*

supreme *adjective* highest in rank, most important. *The case went to the supreme court.* **supremacy** *noun.*

surcharge *noun* an extra charge. **surcharge** *verb. The travel company added a surcharge to my holiday bill.*

sure *adjective* 1 convinced. *I'm sure he's telling the truth.* 2 certain. *She is sure to go.* 3 reliable, definite. *A sure way to find out.* **sure** *adverb* certainly. **for sure** without doubt. **sure enough** certainly. **be sure** not fail to do something. *Be sure to lock up before you leave.*

surely *adverb* 1 certainly. *Slowly but surely.* 2 according to reason. *Surely that can't be right?* 3 safely. *The goat picked its way surely up the cliff.*

surf *noun* foam made by the sea breaking near the shore. **surf** *verb* to ride the surf on a board. **surfing** *noun*. **surfer** *noun*.

Hal thought Bondi Beach in Australia the very best place to surf.

surface *noun* 1 the outside of a solid body. *We have to dust every surface.* 2 the top of a liquid or of the ground. *The diver swam to the surface.* 3 outward appearance. *On the surface everything was quiet.* **surface** *verb* 1 to make a surface. *They surfaced the road.* 2 to rise to the surface. *The submarine surfaced slowly.* 3 to come to light. *The missing papers have suddenly surfaced.*

surgeon *noun* a doctor who performs medical operations.

surgery *noun* 1 medical treatment involving an operation. 2 the place where a doctor or dentist treats patients. 3 the time when a doctor or dentist treat patients. 4 the place where a politician or lawyer gives advice. *My MP holds a surgery every Thursday.*

surgical *adjective* relating to medical surgery. *Surgical instruments.*

Suriname *noun* a country in South America.

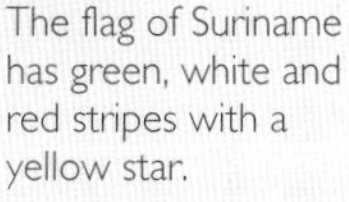

The flag of Suriname has green, white and red stripes with a yellow star.

surly *adjective* bad-tempered and unfriendly. *He had a surly look about him.*

surname *noun* a family name. *Jones is a surname.*

surplus *noun* an extra amount left over when requirements have been met. **surplus** *adjective*. *These items are surplus to government requirements.*

surprise *noun* an unexpected event. *Promotion came as a surprise to her.* **surprise** *verb* 1 to catch by surprise. 2 to shock. *I'm surprised at you!* 3 to take by surprise. *He surprised her taking a chocolate bar.* **surprising** *adjective*. **surprisingly** *adverb*.

WORD HISTORY

The word 'surly' has changed its meaning over the years. It originally meant 'sir-like', in the sense of lordly or masterful, and was spelt 'sirly'. This changed to meaning haughty (misusing a lordly position perhaps), then fell to the present meaning of bad-tempered and unfriendly.

surrender *verb* 1 to give up. *The army surrendered after the heavy defeat.* 2 to hand over. *They surrendered control of affairs.* **surrender** *noun*.

surround *verb* to be all around or enclose. *Trees surround the house.* **surround** *noun* an area or border surrounding something.

surroundings *plural noun* things around somebody or something. *She quickly got used to her new surroundings.*

survey *verb* (say ser-**vay**) 1 to take a general look. *He surveyed the situation.* 2 to examine the condition of something. *They had the house surveyed.* **survey** *noun* (say **ser**-vay) 1 a general view. *The book gave a historical survey.* 2 an examination of property. 3 a report or plan of an examination of property. **surveyor** *noun*.

survive *verb* 1 to continue to live or exist. *They were lucky to survive the earthquake.* 2 to live longer than someone. *He was survived by his wife and two children.* **survival** *noun*. **survivor** *noun*.

suspect *verb* (say suh-**spekt**) 1 to be inclined to believe. *The police suspect murder.* 2 to doubt somebody's innocence. *They suspect him of drug-dealing.* **suspect** *noun* (say **suh**-spekt) a suspected person. **suspect** *adjective* (say **suh**-spekt) not to be trusted.

suspend *verb* 1 to hang up. 2 to put off. *The match was suspended due to bad weather.* 3 to keep away from school. *They were suspended for bad behaviour.*

suspense *noun* anxious or exciting uncertainty. *The film was full of suspense.* **keep in suspense** to make somebody wait for important information. *Don't keep me in suspense – have I passed?*

The suspense was incredible as Tracey leaped from one trapeze to the other.

suspension *noun* 1 the act of suspending or being suspended. 2 springs and other devices that support a vehicle on its axles and give a comfortable ride.

suspension bridge *noun* a bridge with a roadway suspended from cables.

suspicion *noun* 1 feeling inclined to believe or doubt something. *His suspicions were confirmed when she was arrested.* 2 a slight trace. *A suspicion of anger in his voice.* **above suspicion** too good to be suspected. **under suspicion** suspected. **suspicious** *adjective*. *Suspicious circumstances.*

S

Suva *noun* the capital of Fiji.

swagger *verb* to walk or behave in an arrogant way. *The dictator swaggered into the room.* **swagger** *noun.*

swallow *verb* 1 to cause to pass down the throat. *Chew your food well before you swallow it.* 2 to accept something too easily. *I made up an excuse and he swallowed it.* 3 to overcome. *He swallowed his pride and apologized.* **swallow** *noun.*

swallow *noun* an insect-eating bird with a forked tail. *Swallows on the telegraph wires.*

The swallow flew swiftly through the air.

swam *verb* past tense of swim.

swamp *noun* waterlogged land, a bog or marsh. **swamp** *verb* to overwhelm, flood. *The radio station was swamped with letters of complaint.* **swampy** *adjective.*

swan *noun* a large, white waterbird with a long neck. *Black swans are unusual.*

swan *verb* to move aimlessly. *They swanned about the town all day.*

swap *verb* to exchange one thing for another. *He swapped his football for a cricket bat.* **swap** *noun.*

swat (swats, swatting, swatted) *verb* to hit with a sharp blow. *He swatted the fly with a newspaper, but missed.*

sway *verb* 1 to lean in one direction and then another. *The drunk swayed up the road.* 2 to be uncertain. 3 to control or rule over. *He swayed the crowd with his speech.* **sway** *noun* 1 a swaying motion. 2 influence or rule. *Common sense held sway.*

Swaziland *noun* a country in Africa.

swear (swears, swore, sworn) *verb* 1 to promise something faithfully. *He swore that he would never return.* 2 to make somebody promise something. *He swore them to secrecy.* 3 to use vulgar language. *He was sent off for swearing at the referee.* 4 to have great belief in something. *She swears by acupuncture.* **swear to** to be certain. *I couldn't swear to it.* **swearer** *noun.*

sweat *noun* 1 moisture that is given off by the body through the skin. 2 hard effort. *Moving all that furniture was a real sweat.* **sweat** *verb* to give off sweat, to perspire. **sweat it out** put up with a difficulty to the end. **sweaty** (sweatier, sweatiest) *adjective.*

AMAZING FACT

European swallows migrate all the way from their nesting grounds in England, across Europe to the Mediterranean and then to Southern Africa.

AMAZING FACT

Swans are one of the heaviest flying birds in the world. An adult swan might weigh as much as 35 pounds. To take off, a swan runs as fast as it can across the surface of a lake and beats its wings.

The flag of Swaziland has spears and shields against a striped blue, yellow and red background.

sweater *noun* a jersey or pullover.

swede *noun* a yellow kind of turnip.

Sweden *noun* a Scandinavian country in Europe.

Swedish *noun* 1 the language spoken in Sweden. 2 the people of Sweden. **Swedish** *adjective. The Swedish national anthem.*

sweep (sweeps, sweeping, swept) *verb* 1 to clean dust or dirt with a brush. *He swept the floor.* 2 to remove quickly. *The floods swept away the bridge.* 3 to go quickly. *She swept out of the room.* 4 to cover quickly. *The trend swept the country.* **sweep** *noun* 1 an act of sweeping. 2 a chimney sweep. 3 a sweepstake, a kind of lottery. **sweeper** *noun.*

sweeping *adjective* wide-ranging. *They made sweeping changes to the rules.*

sweet *adjective* 1 tasting sugary, not bitter. 2 very pleasant. *Sweet memories.* 3 charming. *A sweet little girl.* **sweet** *noun* 1 a small piece of sweet food, made with sugar or chocolate. 2 a pudding, dessert. **sweetness** *noun.* **sweeten** *verb.*

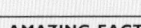

Tom has a sweet tooth and enjoys cakes, milkshakes and fruit.

sweet pea *noun* a climbing plant with sweet-smelling flowers.

swell (swells, swelled, swollen) *verb* to grow larger, to expand. *He swelled with pride.* **swell** *noun* 1 the process of swelling. 2 the rise and fall of the sea's surface.

swelling *noun* a part of the body that has swollen. *There was a swelling on his neck.*

sweltering *adjective* uncomfortably hot.

swept *verb* past tense of sweep.

swerve *verb* to change direction suddenly. **swerve** *noun. She swerved to avoid the car.*

swift *adjective* quick. *A swift response.* **swiftly** *adverb.* **swiftness** *noun.*

swift *noun* a small bird with long wings, similar to a swallow.

swill *verb* to pour water over. *She swilled out the dirty basin.* **swill** *noun* 1 swilling. *Give it a good swill.* 2 sloppy food for pigs.

swim (swims, swimming, swam, swum) *verb* 1 to move through the water. 2 to cover by swimming. *We swam two lengths of the pool.* 3 to float on the surface. 4 to feel dizzy. *My head was swimming.* **swim** *noun. We went for a quick swim.* **swimmer** *noun.* **swimming pool** *noun* an indoor or outdoor pool for swimming.

swindle *verb* to cheat a person. *He swindled her out of her savings.* **swindle** *noun.* **swindler** *noun. A notorious swindler.*

swing (swings, swinging, swung) *verb* 1 to move to and fro or in a curve. *The door swung open.* 2 to change from one opinion or mood to another. *Popular opinion is swinging away from the government.* **swing** *noun* 1 a swinging movement. 2 a seat hanging from ropes or chains, for swinging on. 3 the amount by which opinions change from one side to another. *A big swing against the Tories.* 4 a kind of jazz music. **in full swing** fully active. *A party in full swing.*

swirl (say swurl) *verb* to move round quickly in circles. **swirl** *noun.* **swirly** *adjective. Swirly patterns on her dress.*

Swiss *noun* the people of Switzerland. **Swiss** *adjective. A Swiss watch.*

switch *noun* 1 a device for turning something on and off. 2 a change. **switch** *verb* 1 to turn on or off. *Don't forget to switch off the lights.* 2 to change. *They switched seats.*

Switzerland *noun* a country in southern Europe.

swivel (swivels, swivelling, swivelled) *verb* to turn round. *I swivelled in amazement.*

swoop *verb* to come down with a rush. *The eagle swooped on its prey.* **swoop** *noun.*

sword *noun* (say sord) a weapon with a long metal blade and a handle.

swordfish *noun* a large seafish with a long upper jaw that looks like a sword.

A swordfish has a razor-sharp upper jaw that looks like a sword.

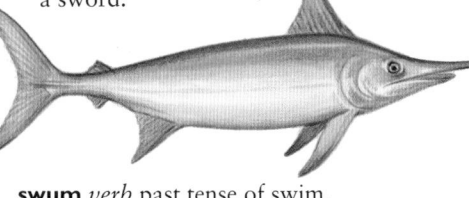

swum *verb* past tense of swim.

swung *verb* past tense of swing.

syllable *noun* a part of a word with one sound. 'Dog' has one syllable, 'tiger' and 'giraffe' have two syllables, and 'gorilla' has three syllables.

syllabus *noun* the programme or outline of a course of study. *The chemistry syllabus.*

symbol *noun* a mark or sign used to represent something. *The dove is a universal symbol of peace.* **symbolic** *adjective.* **symbolically** *adverb.*

symbolize *verb* to be a symbol.

symmetrical *adjective* able to be divided into two halves that are exactly the same. A butterfly shape is symmetrical. **symmetry** *noun. Beautiful symmetry.*

sympathy *noun* 1 the understanding and sharing of another person's feelings or opinions. *My sympathies are with the miners.* 2 feeling pity and sadness for somebody. **sympathetic** *adjective.*

DID YOU KNOW

There is no language called Swiss. In fact, Switzerland has four official languages, German, French, Italian and Romansch.

WORD HISTORY

The word 'syntax' comes from the Greek 'suntaxis', meaning 'arranging together'. The way we arrange words together grammatically is called syntax.

symphony *noun* a long piece of music for an orchestra, usually in three or four parts (called movements). **symphonic** *adjective.*

symptom *noun* 1 a sign that an illness exists. *He has all the symptoms of pneumonia.* 2 a sign of something. *These are symptoms of social unrest.* **symptomatic** *adjective. Headaches may be symptomatic of many different illnesses.*

synagogue (say sin-uh-gog) *noun* the building where Jewish people worship.

Every Friday night they went to the synagogue to pray.

synonym (say sin-uh-nim) *noun* a word that means the same or nearly the same as another. 'Small' and 'little' are synonyms. **synonymous** (say sin-**on**-im-us) *adjective.* 'Shut' is synonymous with 'close'.

syntax (say **sin**-tax) *noun* in grammar, the way words are arranged to form sentences.

synthesizer *noun* an electronic musical instrument with a keyboard that can make a wide range of different sounds.

synthetic *adjective* artificially made, not natural. *Nylon is a synthetic material.*

Syria *noun* a country in Southwest Asia.

Syrian *noun* the people of Syria. **Syrian** *adjective. Her husband is Syrian.*

syringe *noun* a device for injecting liquids into the body, also called a hypodermic needle. **syringe** *verb. I had my ears syringed.*

The syringe was filled with plasma.

syrup *noun* a thick sweet liquid. *Valerie loved syrup sandwiches when she was a child.* **syrupy** *adjective. A syrupy drink contains lots of sugar.*

system *noun* 1 a group of connected parts that work together as a whole. *A new computer system was set up in the office.* 2 an organized set of methods. *A good system of government.* **get something out of your system** get rid of something. **systematic** *adjective. He took a systematic approach to the problem.*

Tt

tab *noun* a small piece of paper or metal attached to something that you can hold or pull. *Pull the tab to open the carton.*

table *noun* 1 a piece of furniture with a flat top supported by one or more legs. 2 a list of facts or figures, especially arranged in columns. **multiplication tables** a list of numbers multiplied. **tablecloth** a cloth for covering a table. **tablespoon** a large spoon used for serving food. **tablespoonful** the amount that a tablespoon can hold.

tablet *noun* 1 a small, usually round, solid piece of medicine that you swallow, a pill. 2 a small flat piece of soap.

table tennis *noun* a game for two or four people who use small bats to hit a small ball over a net on a large table.

tabloid *noun* a small-sized newspaper with lots of photographs and short news stories.

taboo *noun* something that is forbidden or generally disapproved of by custom or tradition. *Cannibalism is a taboo among most people.* **taboo** *adjective*.

tack *noun* 1 a short, sharp nail with a large flat head. 2 the saddle, reins, bridle etc. needed to ride a horse, saddlery.

tack *verb* 1 to use tacks or small nails to fasten something. 2 to sew something roughly with long stitches before sewing it neatly. 3 to sail into the wind on a sideways or zigzag course.

Sophie kept the tack clean and tidy in the tack room at the stables.

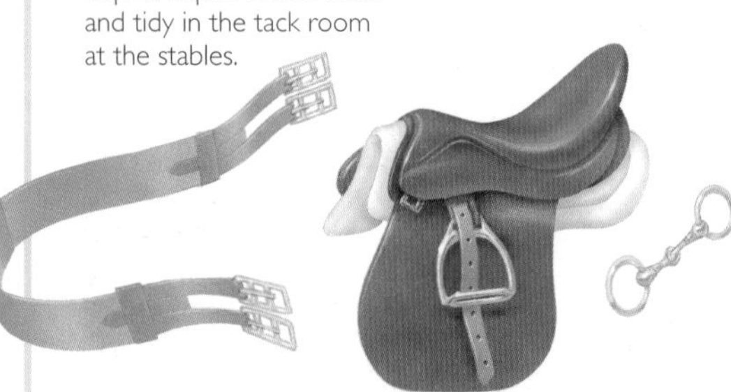

tackle *verb* 1 to try to deal with a problem or difficulty. 2 to try to get a ball from another player or bring a player to the ground in games such as football and rugby. **tackle** *noun*. *He made a brilliant tackle.*

tackle *noun* all the things you need for doing something. *Fishing tackle.*

tacky *adjective* 1 sticky. *The paint is still tacky.* 2 (slang) vulgar, in bad taste.

DID YOU KNOW

The shape of the letter 'T' comes from an ancient Egyptian symbol for ticking things off on a list. It looked like an 'X'. Its sound comes from 'taw', a Semitic word for a mark. The Greeks moved the crossbar to the top and called the letter 'tau'.

Tajikistan used to be part of the Soviet Union, but gained independence in 1991.

WORD HISTORY

'Tabloid' was originally the trademark of a medicine produced in tablet form. The word was then applied to anything produced in a concentrated form, and soon to newspapers that report in a condensed and lively style.

tact *noun* skill in not upsetting people, especially when a situation is difficult. **tactful** *adjective*. **tactless** *adjective*.

tactics *plural noun* the way of organizing or planning things to the best advantage so as to win a game, battle etc. or to achieve what you want. **tactical** *adjective*.

tadpole *noun* a tiny black creature with a long tail that lives in water and that will grow into a frog, toad or newt.

tag *noun* 1 a small paper, cloth or plastic label. *I sewed a name tag on to his pyjamas.* 2 a children's chasing game.

tail *noun* 1 the long part that sticks out of the back of an animal, bird or fish. 2 a part that sticks out at the back of something. *The tail of an aircraft.* 3 **tails** the side of the coin that does not have a head (heads and tails). **tail** *verb* to follow closely.

tailback *noun* a long queue of traffic.

tailor *noun* a person whose business is to make clothes, especially men's suits.

Taipei *noun* the capital of Taiwan.

Taiwan *noun* a country in East Asia.

Tajikistan *noun* a country in central Asia.

take (takes, taking, took, taken) *verb* 1 to reach out for something and to hold or grasp it. 2 to move or lead to another place. *He took the dishes to the sink.* 3 to remove. *Who has taken my ruler?* 4 to perform an action, to do. *I'm going to take a bath.* 5 to photograph. *She took my picture.* 6 to swallow. *Take three tablets a day.* 7 to accept. *Take my advice.* 8 to need or require. *It takes half an hour to get to the airport.* 9 to travel by. *Take the bus.* 10 seize or capture. *The troops took the town.* 11 to choose. *Take which one you like.* **take after** to look or behave like. *He takes after his father.* **take away** 1 to subtract. 2 to remove. **take down** 1 to remove something that is hanging. *They took down the decorations.* 2 to write down. *He took down some notes.* **take in** 1 to deceive. *She took me in with her sad story.* 2 to understand. *I didn't take in all you said.* **take off** 1 to remove clothes. 2 (of an aircraft) to leave the ground. 3 to imitate somebody in an unkind way. **take on** 1 to start to employ somebody. 2 to challenge somebody. **take out** 1 to remove from a place. 2 to invite somebody somewhere. **take over** to take control of. **take place** to happen. *Our wedding took place under the stars.* **takeaway** *noun* a restaurant where you buy cooked food to eat somewhere else.

T

talc (talcum powder) *noun* a soft, scented powder that you sprinkle on your body after a bath.

tale *noun* 1 a story. *A fairy tale.* 2 an untrue or gossipy story, a lie.

talent *noun* great skill or natural ability to do something really well.

talk *verb* to speak, to use words to express feelings ideas etc., to discuss. **talk** *noun* 1 a conversation. 2 a short, informal lecture. **talk down** to to speak to somebody condescendingly as if to a child. **talking to** a telling-off or reprimand.

talkative *adjective* fond of talking a lot. *Are girls more talkative than boys?*

tall *adjective* high or of more than average height. *He's a tall man.* 2 having a certain height. Henry is 2 metres tall. **tall story** a story that is hard to believe.

Tallinn *noun* the capital of Estonia.

talon *noun* a hooked claw of a bird of prey.

tambourine *noun* a small drum with metal discs around the edge that you shake or tap with your fingers.

The gypsies danced around the camp fire banging and shaking their tambourines.

tame *adjective.* A tame animal or bird is not wild and is not afraid of human beings. **tame** *verb.*

tamper *verb* to interfere or meddle with something without permission. *She tampered with the lock and now it's broken.*

tampon *noun* a plug of soft material such as cotton wool. *A sanitary tampon.*

tan *noun* 1 light brown. 2 (suntan) light brown skin caused by its being exposed to the Sun. **tan** *verb.*

tandem *noun* a bicycle with two seats, one behind the other.

tandoori *noun* an Indian way of cooking food in a clay oven.

tangerine *noun* a fruit like a small orange with a loose skin.

tangle *verb* to make things such as wires or string into a twisted and confused muddle. **tangle** *noun. A tangle of wool.*

tank *noun* 1 a large container for storing a liquid or gas. 2 a heavy armoured military vehicle armed with guns.

WORD HISTORY

The word 'tank' was coined during World War I as a secret code name for the newly invented armoured military vehicle. The name was kept when the vehicles eventually went into battle.

WORD HISTORY

Tangerines are named after the Moroccan port of Tangier, from where the fruit was originally imported to Europe.

tanker *noun* a large ship or lorry used for carrying liquids such as oil.

tantrum *noun* a sudden attack of bad temper. *Brian threw a tantrum at school.*

Tanzania *noun* a country in Africa.

Tanzanian *noun* a person who comes from Tanzania. **Tanzanian** *adjective. Tanzanian lakes and mountains.*

Taoiseach *noun* (Say tee-shak) the prime minister of the Republic of Ireland.

tap *noun* a device that you turn on or off to control the flow of a liquid or gas (US faucet). *Turn off the taps – the bath is overflowing!*

Jemima was very thirsty, but the tap had a notice on it saying that the water was not fit for drinking.

tap (taps, tapping, tapped) *verb* 1 to knock gently but repeatedly. *A twig tapped against the window.* 2 to fit a device so that you can take water, information etc. *Her phone was tapped because she was a spy.*

tape *noun* 1 a strip of cloth, paper, plastic etc. used to tie up parcels. *Sticky tape.* 2 a long strip of magnetic material on which sound and pictures can be recorded, usually in a plastic box or cassette.

tape *verb* to record sound on an audio tape or images on a video tape.

tape measure *noun* a metal or cloth strip marked in centimetres or inches for measuring. *Lend me your tape measure?*

tape recorder *noun* an instrument for recording sound on tape and for playing back sound. **tape-record** *verb.*

taper *verb* to become narrower towards the end. *Church spires taper.*

tapestry *noun* a heavy cloth with pictures or designs woven into it and which is hung on a wall. *She wove a beautiful tapestry.*

The tanks went into action and blocked the bridge.

tapir *noun* an animal with a long snout that looks a bit like a pig.

tar *noun* a thick, black sticky substance that is made from wood and coal. **tar** (tars, tarring, tarred) *verb. He tarred the roof to make it waterproof.*

tarantula *noun* a large, hairy poisonous spider. *There was a tarantula in the bath.*

Tarawa *noun* the capital of Kiribati.

target *noun* 1 a mark that you aim at and try to hit. *He shot an arrow at the target.* 2 aim or purpose that you are trying to achieve. *Production targets.*

tariff *noun* 1 a list of prices, especially for hotel rooms and meals. 2 a tax to be paid on exports and imports.

tarmac *noun* a mixture of tar and crushed stones, used to make road surfaces.

tarragon *noun* a plant whose leaves are used to flavour food.

tart *noun* a pastry case with no crust on top, usually with a sweet filling. *A jam tart.* **tart** *adjective* sharp or sour to taste.

tartan *noun* a Scottish woollen cloth with a pattern of different coloured squares.

Tashkent *noun* the capital of Uzbekistan.

task *noun* a job or piece of work that must be done, a duty. *An onerous task.*

taste *noun* 1 the sense by which you can tell the flavour of food and drink. 2 the particular flavour of food. Food can be sweet, sour, salty or bitter. 3 the ability to know what is beautiful or good. **tasteful** *adjective.* **taste** *verb.*

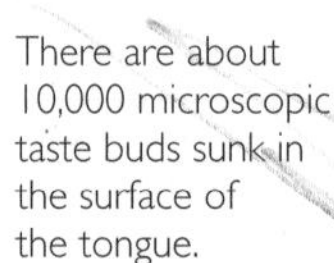

There are about 10,000 microscopic taste buds sunk in the surface of the tongue.

tasteless *adjective* 1 without flavour. 2 unattractive and showing poor taste. *Tasteless furniture.*

tasty *adjective* having a pleasant taste.

tattoo *noun* 1 a permanent coloured pattern on somebody's skin. 2 a military display of music, marching etc. usually held at night.

taught past tense of teach.

taunt *verb* to tease somebody and say hurtful things in order to make them angry. **taunt** *noun. She taunted him about the size of his nose, which really was enormous.*

taut *adjective* stretched or pulled tight so that it is firm. **tauten** *verb.*

AMAZING FACT

Tapirs live mainly in forests and eat vegetation such as leaves, buds and fruit. They are nocturnal creatures and most species are very shy.

WORD HISTORY

Our word 'tea' comes from 'tíe', the word used in Amoy Chinese. The Dutch borrowed the word and renamed it 'thee'. It was then absorbed into other European languages e.g. 'tea' (English) and 'te' (Italian).

tautology *noun* the use of a word that repeats the meaning of a word that has already been used. 'A four-sided square, 'free gifts' and 'a new innovation' are all examples of tautology.

tavern *noun* an old-fashioned word for an inn or public house.

tawny *noun* a light, brownish-yellow colour. **tawny** *adjective.*

tax (taxes) *noun* an amount of money that people and businesses have to pay to the government to help pay for public services. **tax** *verb. The government taxes our income far too much.* **taxation** *noun.*

taxi (taxis) *noun* a car with a driver that you can hire to take you on short journeys. *We took a taxi to the station.*

taxi (taxies, taxiing, taxied) *verb* of an aircraft, to travel along the runway before takeoff or after landing.

Tbilisi *noun* the capital of Georgia.

tea *noun* 1 a drink made by pouring hot water on the dried leaves of a tea plant. 2 a light meal eaten in the afternoon or a main meal eaten in the evening.

Tea bushes grow in China, India and Sri Lanka. The leaves are picked and dried before being exported.

teach (teaches, teaching, taught) *verb* 1 to tell somebody about a subject and to help them learn about it, to educate. 2 to show somebody how to do something. *Jane taught me how to skate.*

teacher *noun* a person who teaches, especially at a school.

The teacher pointed with her stick to a sum on the blackboard and asked if anyone knew the answer.

team *noun* a group of people who work together or who play on the same side in a game. *Our team won the match.*

tear *noun* (rhymes with near) one of the drops of salty liquid that comes from your eyes when you cry. **tearful** *adjective.*

tear (tears, tearing, tore, torn) *verb* (rhymes with fair) 1 to pull something apart, to rip. 2 to make a hole in something. *Tina tore her skirt on a nail.* 3 to pull something violently. *Vic tore the paper off the wall.* **tear** *noun.* 4 to move quickly. *The dog tore across the field and leaped over the fence.*

tease *verb* to annoy somebody by making fun of them for your own amusement.

teaspoon *noun* a small spoon. **teaspoonful** the amount that a teaspoon can hold.

teat *noun* 1 the nipple or soft pointed part on a female mammal through which her babies suck milk. 2 a piece of rubber or plastic on a feeding bottle through which a baby can suck milk etc.

technical *adjective* 1 concerned with science and machines and how they work. *Technical experts.* 2 concerned with a particular specialized subject. *Technical jargon is very boring.*

technique *noun* (say tek-**neek**) a special way of doing something skilfully.

technology *noun* the study of technical ideas and the practical use of science in industry. **technological** *adjective.*

teddy-bear (**teddy**) *noun* a soft toy bear.

tedious *adjective* boring because it is dull and long.

teenager *noun* a person between the ages of 13 and 19. **teenage** *adjective.*

teeth *plural* of tooth.

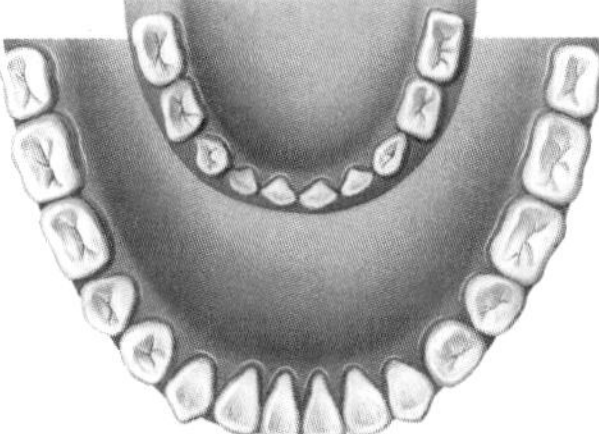

Each person has two natural sets of teeth during their life. The first 20 are called milk teeth, the second 32 are adult teeth.

teetotaler *noun* somebody who never drinks alcohol. **teetotal** *adjective. Many Muslims are teetotal.*

Tegucigalpa *noun* the capital of Honduras.

Tehran *noun* the capital of Iran.

telecommunications *plural noun* the technology of sending information over long distances by radio, telephone, television, etc.

telephone *noun* an instrument that uses electrical current travelling along wires, or radio waves, to allow you to speak to somebody over long distances. **telephone** or **phone** *verb. Please phone me tonight.*

AMAZING FACT

The first television set, made by John Baird, was made of old cans, bike parts, lenses and string.

DID YOU KNOW

Teddy bear is named after 'Teddy' the pet name of Theodore Roosevelt, the US president (1858–1919), who was well known as a bear hunter.

AMAZING FACT

In 1876, Alexander Graham Bell spoke his first words over a telephone when he called out to his assistant to come and help him – he had spilled acid on his leg!

telescope *noun* a tube-shape instrument with lenses that you look through with one eye to make distant objects appear bigger and nearer.

television *noun* a box-shaped instrument that receives programmes that have been broadcast and shows them on a screen as moving pictures with sound.

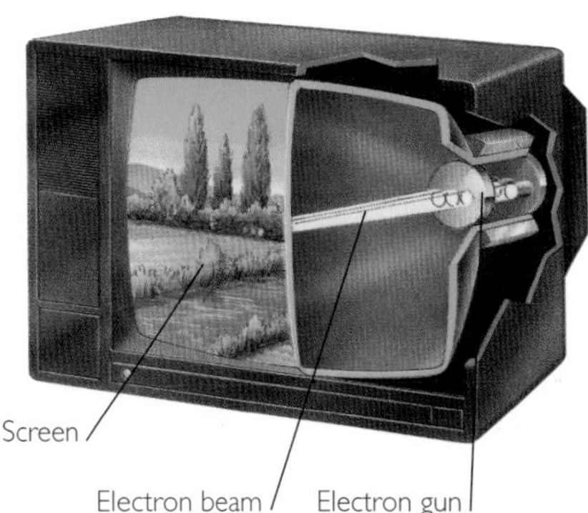

Television signals are picked up by the receiver's TV aerial, demodulated and amplified to work the picture tube and loudspeaker of the TV set.

telex *noun* a system of sending written messages by means of teleprinters.

tell (tells, telling, told) *verb* 1 to pass on information etc. by speaking. 2 to know or recognize. *Can you tell what this is?* 3 to order. *Terry told us to be there on time.* **tell off** to scold. **telling-off** *noun.*

telling *adjective* meaningful and striking. *A telling argument.*

temper *noun* the mood you are in, how you feel. *Is she in a good temper?* **lose your temper** to become angry.

temperament *noun* your personality or the way you usually feel and behave. *She has a very calm temperament.*

temperamental *adjective* liable to sudden changes of mood, excitable.

temperature *noun* 1 a measure of how hot something is. *The temperature has dropped to below freezing.* 2 a fever. *Take your temperature with this thermometer.*

This is Pashupatinath temple near Kathmandu in Nepal. Hindu's are taken here to be cremated on the funeral pyres next to the Bagmati River.

tempest *noun* a violent storm with strong winds. **tempestuous** *adjective. A tempestuous sea.*

temple *noun* 1 a building in which people of some religions worship. 2 the flat part on either side of your head between your ear and forehead.

tempo (tempi) *noun* the speed at which music is played.

tempt *verb* to try to persuade somebody to want to do something they would not normally do, to entice. *He tried to tempt me to cheat in the exam.* **temptation** *noun.*

tempting *adjective* attractive. *It's very tempting to skip classes and go swimming.*

tenant *noun* a person who rents from somebody the place he or she lives in.

tend *verb* to happen often or usually, to be inclined to. *It tends to be cold at night.* tendency *noun. A tendency to eat too much.*

tend *verb* to look after a person or animal.

tender *adjective* 1 sore to touch, painful. *The bruise feels very tender.* 2 easy to chew, not tough. *Tender meat.* 3 loving and gentle, kind. *A tender kiss.* 4 delicate. *Tender seedlings.* **tenderness** *noun.*

tendon *noun* a strong cord-like tissue joining muscles to bones.

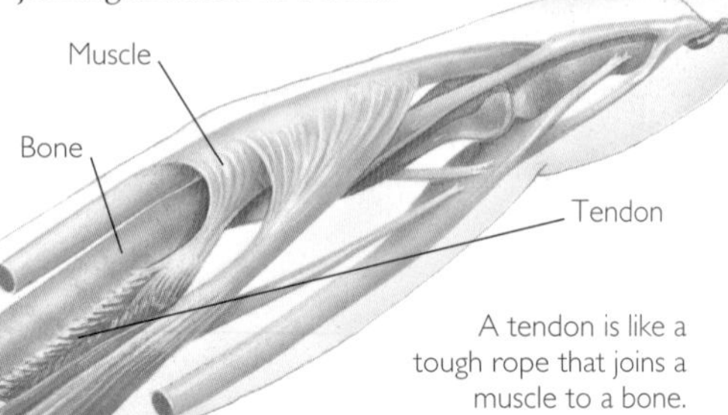

A tendon is like a tough rope that joins a muscle to a bone.

tennis *noun* a game played on a specially marked tennis court by two or four people using rackets to hit a ball to each other over a net.

tenor *adjective*, *noun* the highest normal singing voice for a man.

tense *adjective* 1 showing excitement, stress or nervousness. 2 stiff and tightly stretched, taut. **tension** *noun.* **tense** *verb. She tensed her muscles for the fight.*

tense *noun* a form of a verb that shows when something happens (present tense), happened (past tense) or will happen (future tense).

tent *noun* a shelter made from a waterproof material such as canvas or nylon stretched and supported over poles and held down by ropes.

tentacle *noun* one of the long, snake-like limbs of animals such as octopuses and squid.

A squid has eight tentacles.

SPELLING NOTE

The plural of some English words of Latin origin can be variable. For example, the plural of 'terminus' is usually 'termini' (but it can be 'terminuses').

WORD HISTORY

'Tennis' comes from a French word 'tenez' meaning 'hold' or 'take', which a player called out to his opponent to attract their attention.

tepee *noun* a cone-shaped tent made of animal skins or tree bark, first used by Native Americans.

tepid *adjective* only slightly warm.

term *noun* 1 a length of time. *The school term.* 2 a word or name for something. *ROM is a computer term.* **terms** plural *noun* agreed conditions. *Terms of employment.* **term** *verb* to name. **to be on good terms with somebody** to get on with or to like somebody.

terminal *noun* 1 a building where people begin or end a journey. *Planes for Australia depart from terminal four.* 2 a computer monitor linked to a network. **terminal** *adjective* (of an illness) incurable and liable to cause death.

terminate *verb* to stop, to come to an end.

terminus *noun* a station at the end of a railway line or bus route.

terrace *noun* 1 a row of houses joined together as a single block. 2 a level area cut out of sloping ground. 3 a paved area next to a building where people can sit.

terrapin *noun* a small turtle from North America. Terrapins live in fresh water.

A terrapin can sometimes be kept in an aquarium as a pet.

terrestrial *adjective* 1 relating to the Earth rather than to space. *Terrestrial television.* 2 living on land and not in the air or in water. *Terrestrial animals.*

terrible *adjective* 1 dreadful, causing fear or hardship. 2 bad. *A terrible film.*

terrier *noun* one of several breeds of small dogs. *A fox terrier yaps a lot.*

terrific *adjective.* 1 very good, wonderful. 2 very great, causing terror. *A terrific bang.*

terrify (terrifies, terrifying, terrified) *verb* to make somebody very frightened. *My dog is terrified of thunder.*

territory *noun* 1 an area of land, especially land controlled by the government of a country. 2 an area of land where an animal lives and which it will fight to defend.

terror *noun* great fear.

terrorism *noun* the use of violence and threats to obtain demands. **terrorist** *noun. Terrorists planted bombs along the route.*

test *verb* to try out something, to check to see if something works. *An eye test.* **test** *noun* 1 a set of questions or actions that a person has to answer or perform to find out how much they know or can do. **test tube** *noun* a thin glass container that is closed at one end, used in laboratories to do tests.

tether *verb* to tie an animal by a rope to a post so that it cannot move far or escape. **tether** *noun*. **at the end of your tether** to run out of patience.

testicle *noun* one of two small ball-like glands in a man's scrotum .

text *noun* the printed words in a book or newspaper. *The text was rather dull.*

textbook *noun* a book containing basic information about a particular subject.

textile *noun* woven cloth. **textile** *adjective*. *The textile industry.*

Tartan is a textile that is woven in Scotland.

texture *noun* the way something feels when you touch it, e.g. rough or smooth.

Thai *noun* a person who comes from Thailand. **Thai** *adjective*. *Thai silk.*

Thailand *noun* a country in Southeast Asia.

thank *verb* to tell somebody how pleased you are for something they have given you or done for you. **thanks** *noun* a word we use to say how pleased we are for what somebody has done for us.

thankful *adjective* feeling glad or grateful.

Thanksgiving *noun* a holiday celebrated in the United States on the fourth Thursday in November. Many people eat turkey on this day and give thanks for what they have.

thatch (thatches) *noun* layers of reeds or straw used in roofs.

Thatched houses need to be insured for lots of money because of the risk of fire.

AMAZING FACT

The earliest theatres were in Greece. The theatre at Delphi was so skillfully built that people at the back of the theatre could hear every spoken word.

WORD HISTORY

'Thesaurus' was originally a Greek word meaning 'treasury' and has been used since the 19th century to describe a treasury of information and knowledge or a treasury of words.

thaw *verb* to change from being frozen solid to a liquid through warming, to melt. *The ice on the pond is thawing.*

theatre *noun* 1 a building where you go to see plays performed. 2 a room in a hospital where surgeons perform operations. **theatrical** *adjective* connected with plays or acting. *A theatrical family.*

theft *noun* stealing.

theme *noun* 1 the principal subject. *The theme of the book is poverty.* 2 (in music) the main melody.

theme park *noun* a park with different activities and attractions all based on one particular subject or idea.

theme song *noun* a tune that is often repeated in a film or musical.

theology *noun* the study of God and religion. **theologian** *noun* a person who studies theology. **theological** *adjective*.

theory *noun* 1 an unproved idea put forward to explain something. 2 the rules and principles of a subject rather than the actual practice. *In theory it should work – in practice it doesn't seem to!*

therapeutic *adjective* being good for the health and the treatment of illnesses.

therapy *noun* a treatment for an illness without the use of surgery or drugs. **therapist** *noun*. *I need a therapist.*

therm *noun* a measurement of heat.

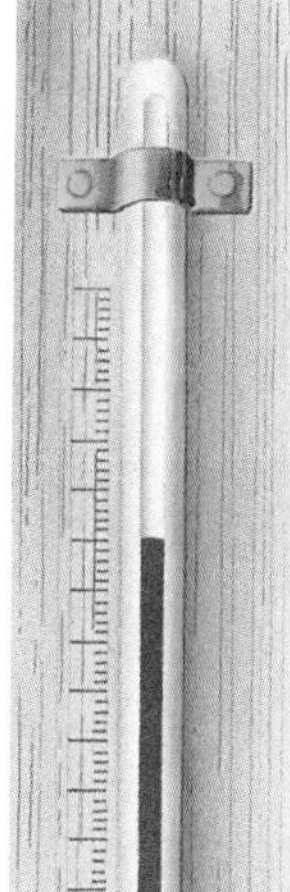

It is very useful to hang a thermometer in the greenhouse.

thermal *adjective* relating to heat, using heat. *Thermal energy.*

thermometer *noun* an instrument for measuring temperature in degrees Celsius or Fahrenheit.

thermostat *noun* a device that automatically switches off radiators, irons etc. when the temperature is hot enough.

thesaurus (thesauruses) *noun* a book that lists together words with similar meanings. In my thesaurus the words 'glow', 'gleam', 'glitter', 'sparkle' and 'flash' are listed under the headword 'shine'.

thick *adjective* 1 measuring a long way between two sides. Wide, not thin or slender. 2 measuring a certain amount between two sides. *The wood block is 5 cm thick.* 3 dense and closely packed. *Thick, blond hair.* 4 fatty and not flowing freely. *Thick cream.* 5 (slang) stupid. **thickness** *noun*. **thicken** *verb*. The opposite of thick is thin.

T

thief (thieves) *noun* a person who steals things. *The thief ran off with my money.*

thigh *noun* (rhymes with high) the top part of your leg above your knee.

thimble *noun* a small metal or plastic covering for the tip of your finger to prevent you pricking it when sewing.

Thimphu *noun* the capital of Bhutan.

thin (thinner, thinnest) *adjective* 1 measuring a short distance between two sides. Narrow, not thick. The opposite is thick. 2 having very little fat on your body, slender. The opposite is fat.

thing *noun* 1 an unnamed object that you see or touch. 2 **things** belongings. *Have you packed your things for our holiday?* **it's a good thing** it's lucky. *It's a good thing you arrived on time.*

think (thinks, thinking, thought) *verb* 1 to use your mind. 2 to believe, to have an opinion or idea. 3 to remember. 4 to plan or intend. *We're thinking of learning karate.* 5 to admire. *I think a lot of you.* **think up** to invent. **think twice about something** to consider very carefully whether to do something or not.

third *adjective* the next after the second. *You're the third person to ask me that.* **third** *noun* one of three equal parts that make up a whole. **third rate** *adjective* of poor quality. **third world** the poorer countries of the world that are slowly developing, many of them in Asia and Africa.

thirst *noun* 1 feeling the need to drink. 2 a strong wish for something. *a thirst for adventure.* **thirsty** *adjective.*

thistle *noun* a prickly wild plant with purple flowers.

thorax *noun* 1 the middle section of an insect's body, carrying the wings and legs. 2 the chest of a human.

thorn *noun* a sharp point on the stem of a plant such as a rose.

Thorax

Abdomen

Sting

All insects have a thorax and an abdomen.

thorough *adjective* (say **thur**-uh) 1 done well and carefully. *A thorough search.* 2 complete. *A thorough shambles.* **thoroughness** *noun. He was famed for his thoroughness.*

AMAZING FACT

Some people believe that we can communicate by thought alone. This is called 'telepathy'.

DID YOU KNOW

You can avoid ambiguity by the correct placing of a hyphen. Where would you put a hyphen in these sentences? 'There are 20 odd pupils in the class.' 'She has nine inch long feet'.

thoroughfare *noun* a main road or street.

thought past tense of think. **thought** *noun* an idea, something that you think. *Have you any thoughts about what we should do?*

thoughtful *adjective* 1 thinking quietly and carefully. 2 considerate and thinking about others. *It was very thoughtful of you to buy me flowers.*

thoughtless *adjective* inconsiderate and not thinking about other people's feelings.

thread *noun* a long thin piece of twisted cotton, silk etc. used for sewing or weaving. **thread** *verb* to put thread through a hole (eye) of needle to sew.

She matched the thread with the colour of her dress.

threadbare *adjective* (of clothes) worn thin.

threat *noun* 1 a warning that something unpleasant may happen. 2 a possible cause of future harm, a danger. *A threat of drought hung over the country.*

threaten *verb* to warn that you may do something unpleasant or harm somebody. *Mat threatened to hit me.*

three-dimensional *adjective* having depth as well as height and width, solid.

thresh *verb* to beat grain from stalks of corn. *We threshed the grain at harvest.*

threw past tense of throw.

thrifty (thriftier, thriftiest) *adjective* not wasteful, careful about spending money etc. **thrift** *noun.*

thrill *noun* a feeling of great excitement and enjoyment. **thrill** *verb. She was thrilled to be chosen.*

They all screamed because the rollercoaster ride was such a thrill.

T

thriller *noun* a book, play or film with an exciting story about crime and detection.

thrilling *adjective* very exciting.

thrive *verb* to be healthy and successful. *A thriving business.*

throat *noun* the front part of your neck. The tube from inside your mouth that takes food and drink to your stomach and air to your lungs. *He has a sore throat.*

throb (throbs, throbbing, throbbed) *verb* to beat strongly and rapidly. *My heart throbbed with terror.*

throne *noun* a special seat for a king or queen. *The king sat on the throne.*

through *preposition, adverb* (say throo) 1 from one side to the other. *The train went through the tunnel.* 2 among or between. *We walked through the crowd.* 3 by means of, because of. *We bought it through the catalogue, but it's not very nice.*

throughout *preposition* 1 in all parts. *Throughout the world.* 2 from the beginning to the end, during. *Throughout the night.*

throw (throws, throwing, threw, thrown) *verb* to make something go through the air, to hurl or fling. Tracy threw the ball. **throw away** to get rid of something you do not want. **throw together** to put something together quickly. **throw up** (slang) to be sick, to vomit.

thrush *noun* a small brown bird with a speckled breast that sings beautifully.

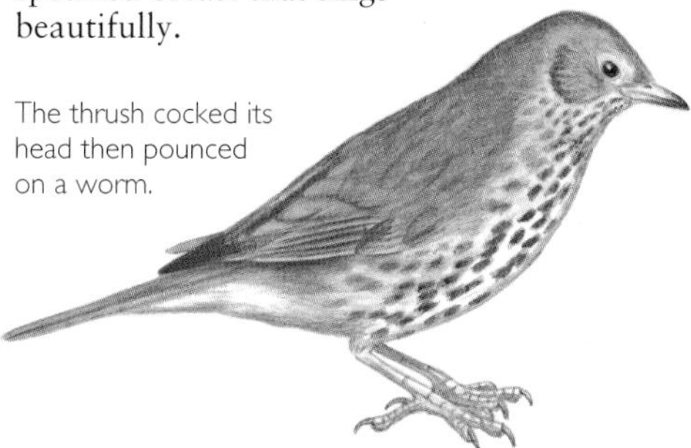

The thrush cocked its head then pounced on a worm.

thrust *verb* to push suddenly and with force, to shove. *Doug thrust the clothes into the bag.* **thrust** *noun.*

thud *noun* a low, dull sound made, for example, by something heavy hitting the ground. **thud** *verb.*

thumb *noun* the short, thick finger at the side of your hand. **thumb a lift** to hitch-hike. **thumbs down** showing that you do not approve. **thumbs up** showing that you approve. *Our plan got the thumbs up.*

thump *noun* the dull heavy sound made by punching somebody.

thunder *noun* the rumbling noise you hear after a flash of lightning. **thunder** *verb* to make the dull, continuous noise of thunder.

AMAZING FACT

In the tropics thunderstorms may occur on as many as 200 days a year.

DID YOU KNOW

The word 'tide' originally meant 'time'. The meaning of the modern word came about because of the rising and falling of the sea at regular times of the day.

thunderstorm *noun* a storm with thunder, lightning and heavy rain.

thunderstruck *adjective* amazed.

thwart *verb* to hinder somebody doing what they planned. *He thwarted my plan.*

thyme *noun* a herb, a plant whose leaves are used for flavouring food.

tiara *noun* a small, jewelled crown worn by women. *A golden tiara.*

The princess wore her most beautiful tiara to the ball.

tick *noun* 1 a small mark (✓) used to show that something is correct or to mark in a list. 2 a small, regular sound. *The tick of a clock.* 3 a very short time. *I'll be back in a tick.* **tick** *verb. She ticked off the names on her list as the pupils entered the class.*

ticket *noun* a small printed piece of paper that shows that you have paid for something such as a train or bus fare or for a seat in a cinema or theatre etc. Traffic wardens give a ticket to a driver who has committed a parking offence.

tickle *verb* to touch somebody very lightly in a place that makes them laugh or giggle. *He tickled the baby's tummy.* **tickle** *noun.*

ticklish *adjective* easily tickled.

tidal wave *noun* an exceptionally huge wave caused by an earthquake.

A tidal wave is sometimes called a tsunami. It can cause enormous damage and great loss of life.

tide *noun* the regular rising and falling movement of the sea as it comes into the land and goes away from the land. Tides are caused by the pull of the Moon and Sun on the Earth. **tidal** *adjective.*

tidy (tidier, tidiest) *adjective* 1 neat and with everything in its proper place. 2 (slang) quite big. *A tidy sum of money.* **tidy** *verb.* **tidiness** *noun. Tidiness is a great virtue.*

T

tie *noun* a narrow piece of cloth that is worn around the neck under a shirt collar and knotted at the throat.

tie (ties, tying, tied) *verb* 1 to fasten something with rope, string etc. *She tied her shoelaces.* 2 to score an equal number of points in a contest. *They tied for second place.* **tie** *noun. The score was a tie.*

tier (rhymes with near) *noun* two or more layers, two or more raised rows of seats etc. one above the other.

tiger *noun* a large wild cat from Asia that has an orange coat with black stripes.

tight *adjective* 1 very closely fitting. *These jeans are too tight.* 2 firmly fixed so that it will not move. *The lid is so tight I can't open the jar.* 3 fully and firmly stretched. *Tight violin strings.* 4 having little room to spare. *A tight timetable is very hard to work to.*

tightrope *noun* a tightly stretched rope along which acrobats walk.

tights *plural noun* a piece of clothing made of very thin material that fits tightly over your feet, legs and hips and worn mainly by women. *Linda wears purple striped tights.*

tile *noun* a flat piece of hard material used for covering floors, roofs and walls. **tile** *verb. Dad tiled the bathroom.*

Tiles can be used to decorate many rooms in the house.

till *conjunction, preposition* until, up to a certain time. *Wait till I get home.*

till *noun* a box or container for money in a shop. *Sam stole money from the till.*

till *verb* to plough and cultivate land.

tilt *verb* to slope or lean so that one side is higher than the other.

SPELLING NOTE

'Tinsel' comes from a French word, 'étinceller', which means sparkle.

The pattern of stripes on a tiger's skin is unique. No two tigers have quite the same pattern.

SPELLING NOTE

Both 'till' and 'until' are interchangeable, meaning 'up to the time that' or 'as far as'. For example: 'I will stay until you get back.' And: 'Go straight ahead till you come to a roundabout.'

timber *noun* wood ready for building or making furniture etc.

time *noun* 1 the passing of years, months, weeks, days, hours etc. 2 a particular moment. *What time does the train go?* 3 how long something takes or a period in which you do something. **time** *verb* to measure how long something takes. **from time to time** occasionally. **in time** in step with the music. **once upon a time** some time long ago. **on time** not late.

times *preposition* multiplied by. *Four times four are 16.*

timetable *noun* a list showing the times of classes at school or the times when trains, planes etc. depart and arrive.

timid *adjective* lacking courage and easily frightened, shy. **timidity** *noun.*

tin *noun* 1 a soft, silvery-white metal. usually mixed with other metals or forming a coat on other metals. 2 a tin-coated metal container for storing food etc., a can.

It's best to open a tin of paint by levering off the lid with a screwdriver.

tinge *noun* a slight colouring. *White paint with a tinge of blue.*

tingle *verb* to have a slight stinging or tickling feeling. **tingle** *noun.*

tinker *verb* to fiddle with or make small changes to something with the idea of repairing or improving it.

tinkle *noun* a ringing sound like a small bell. **tinkle** *verb.*

tinsel *noun* strips of glittering material used for decorations.

tint *noun* a light, delicate shade of a colour. **tinted** *adjective. Tinted glasses.*

tiny (tinier, tiniest) *adjective* very small. *A tiny insect fell into his beer.*

tip *noun* 1 the end of something long and thin. *The tip of your nose.* 2 a small gift of money you give, for example, to a waiter or taxi driver. 3 a place for dumping rubbish. 4 a useful piece of advice. *He gave me a few tips on how to draw faces.*

tip (tips, tipping, tipped) *verb* 1 to knock over something so that the contents spill out, to empty. *He tipped over the milk bottle.* 2 to give somebody a small gift of money for helping you.

T

tipsy *adjective* very slightly drunk.

tiptoe *verb* to walk on your toes so that you make very little noise.

Simon walked on tiptoe so as not to wake his parents.

Tirana *noun* the capital of Albania.

tire *verb* to become tired or to make somebody tired and weary. 2 to become bored with something. **tired** *adjective*.

tiresome *adjective* irritating, annoying.

tissue *noun* 1 the cells that make up a particular part of an animal or plant. *Leaf tissue.* 2 **tissue paper** very soft, thin paper used for wiping, wrapping etc. Paper handkerchiefs are often called tissues.

tit *noun* any of a variety of small European birds. *The tits were nesting in an old kettle.*

titbit *noun* a small piece of particularly tasty food (US tidbid).

title *noun* 1 the name of a book, film, piece of music etc. 2 a word like Dr, Mrs, Sir put before a person's name to show rank etc.

titter *verb* to laugh in a silly, nervous way, to giggle. **titter** *noun*.

toad *noun* an amphibian like a frog with a rough, warty skin. Toads live mainly on land.

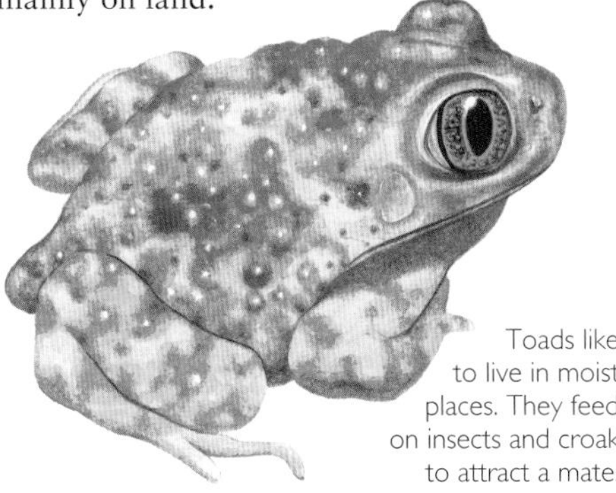

Toads like to live in moist places. They feed on insects and croak to attract a mate.

toadstool *noun* an umbrella-shaped fungus similar to a mushroom, but nearly always poisonous. *The fairy under the toadstool.*

toast *noun* a slice of bread that has been heated under a grill until it has turned crisp and brown. *Toast and marmalade.*

toast *verb* to hold up your glass and wish for the success or happiness of somebody. **toast** *noun*. *We drank a toast to the bride.*

AMAZING FACT

Tokyo is one of the biggest cities in the world. Many people work there, but most of them live outside of the city. Some people have to spend over 4 hours a day travelling to and from work.

WORD HISTORY

'Tyre' (or 'tire' in the old or US spelling) comes from the word 'attire' (clothing), because it was thought of as the clothing of a wheel. And the fitting of tyres to wheels was once known as shoeing.

tobacco *noun* the cut and dried leaves of the tobacco plant which people smoke as cigars and cigarettes or in pipes.

toboggan *noun* a small sledge without runners. **toboggan** *verb*.

today *adverb, noun* 1 this very day. 2 the present time, nowadays. *People travel more by plane today than they used to.*

toddler *noun* a child who is just learning to walk. *Toddlers are a real handful.*

toe *noun* 1 one of the five parts at the end of your foot. 2 the front part of a shoe, sock etc. that fits over your toes. **on your toes** ready and alert. **toe the line** to do as you are told. *Imran expected his staff to toe the line.*

toffee *noun* a sticky sweet made from sugar and butter. *Toffee and pear crumble.*

toga *noun* a loose flowing garment worn by men in ancient Rome.

together *adverb* 1 with another. *She stuck the two pieces together.* 2 at the same time as another. *They arrived home together.*

Togo *noun* a country in Africa.

The flag of Togo has a ground of yellow and green stripes and a white star on a red square.

toilet *noun* a room with a bowl called a toilet for getting rid of waste from the body.

token *noun* 1 a piece of printed plastic or paper that can be used instead of money for buying things. *A book token.* 2 a small sign or symbol of something. *A token of love.*

Tokyo *noun* the capital of Japan.

told past tense of tell.

tolerate *verb* to put up with or allow something to happen, to endure. *How can you tolerate living in such a mess!* **tolerable** *adjective*. **tolerance** *noun*. **tolerant** *adjective*.

tomahawk *noun* a war hatchet once used by Native Americans.

tomato (tomatoes) *noun* a round, sweet fruit eaten raw in salads and much used in cooking. *Tomato ketchup.*

tomb *noun* a place where a body is buried. A grave. **tombstone** a stone with writing on it marking where a person is buried.

tomorrow *adverb, noun* 1 the day after today. 2 the future. *Tomorrow's children.*

ton *noun* a unit of weight equal to 1,016 kg. *This dictionary weighs a ton!*

tone *noun* 1 the quality of a sound or the way something is said. *The piano has a mellow tone.* 2 a shade of colour. 3 muscle tone. **tone** *verb*.

Tonga *noun* a country of many islands in the Pacific Ocean.

tongue *noun* the long, soft pink thing that moves about inside your mouth and that helps you taste things and talk. **tongue-twister** something that is difficult to say.

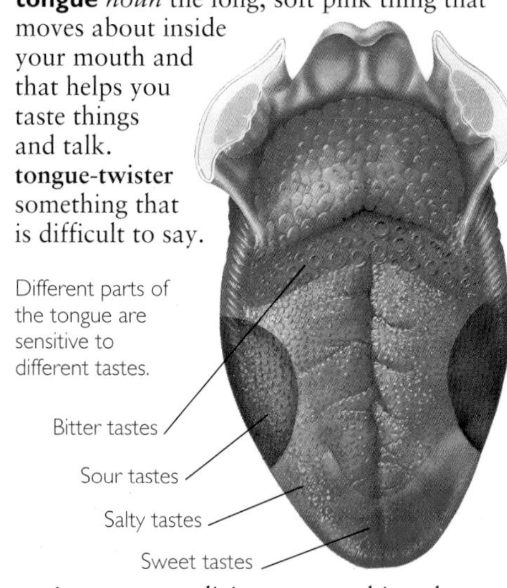

Different parts of the tongue are sensitive to different tastes.

tonic *noun* a medicine or something else that makes you feel better or stronger.

tonight *adverb*, *noun* this night of this day.

tonne *noun* a unit of weight equal to 1,000 kg. *Tonnes of cargo.*

tonsils *plural noun* two soft lumps of flesh at the back of your throat. They may swell and become sore in an illness called tonsilitis.

too *adverb* 1 as well, also. *I can sing too.* 2 more than enough or than is needed. *There are too many knives in this drawer.*

took past tense of take.

tool *noun* a hand-held instrument or implement such as a hammer or drill that you use to do a particular job.

tooth (teeth) *noun* 1 one of the hard white bony parts inside your mouth that you use for biting and chewing. 2 one of the pointed parts of a comb or saw.

A tooth is coated in enamel. Inside it are blood vessels and nerves.

toothache *noun* severe pain in a tooth.

toothbrush *noun* a brush for cleaning teeth.

top *noun* 1 the highest part of something; the summit. *The top of the mountain.* 2 a covering, a lid. *Put the top back on the toothpaste.* 3 a piece of clothing that a woman or a girl wears on the upper part of her body. 4 a cone-shaped toy that spins on a point. **top** *adjective* the highest or best. *A top football player.* The opposite of top is bottom. **top** (tops, topping, topped) *verb*. **top dog** *noun* a leader or winner. **top heavy** *adjective* heavier at the top than at the bottom and so likely to topple over. **top secret** information that is very secret.

TONGUE TWISTER

A tutor who tooted the flute
Tried to tutor two tooters to flute
Said the two to the tutor:
Is it harder to toot, or
To tutor two tooters to toot?

SPELLING NOTE

Try not to confuse 'to', 'too', and 'two'. 'Two days is too long to wait. Do you think so too?'

AMAZING FACT

Tornados or 'twisters' can reach speeds of up to 300 miles per hour.

topaz *noun* a semi-precious stone of varying colours.

topic *noun* a subject to talk about or write about. *A fascinating topic.*

topical *adjective* relating to important or interesting things happening now.

topography *noun* the study and description of the landscape's features such as the position of its mountains, roads, towns etc.

topple *verb* to overbalance and fall because it is too heavy at the top.

topsy-turvy *adjective* upside-down and in a state of confusion.

Torah *noun* a scroll used in synagogues on which are written the first five books of the Old Testament – Genesis, Exodus, Leviticus, Numbers and Deuteronomy known as the Pentateuch.

torch *noun* 1 a light with an electric battery that you can carry around with you (US flashlight). 2 a pole with burning material at one end that gives light.

tore past tense of tear.

torment *verb* (say tor-**ment**) to tease and be deliberately cruel to somebody or an animal. **torment** *noun* (say **tor**-ment).

tornado (tornadoes) *noun* a violent storm with strong winds that spin at high speeds causing great damage.

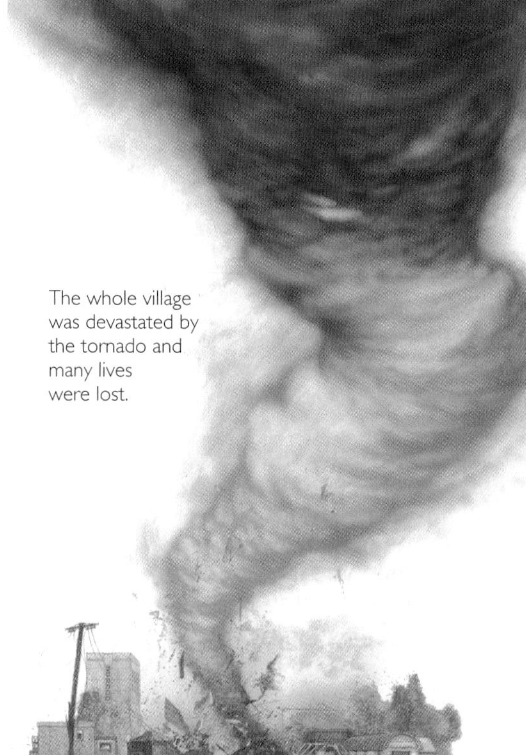

The whole village was devastated by the tornado and many lives were lost.

torrent *noun* 1 a violent rushing stream. 2 a flood or heavy downpour of rain. **torrential** *adjective*. *Torrential rain.*

torso (torsos) *noun* the main part of a body but excluding the head and limbs.

tortoise *noun* (say **tor**-tuss) a slow-moving land reptile with a hard shell.

The tortoise lost its race against the hare.

torture *verb* to make somebody suffer extremely cruel physical or mental pain, often to force them to confess something. **torture** *noun*. *He was cruelly tortured.*

toss *verb* 1 to throw something carelessly into the air. 2 to move up and down and from side to side. *The boat tossed on the sea.* 3 to spin a coin to see whether heads or tails faces upwards.

total *noun* the amount when everything is added together. **total** *adjective* complete. *A total success.*

totem pole *noun* a large pole carved or painted with traditional symbols of Native American families.

Magical creatures are carved on this totem pole. It was made by skilled craftsmen in Northwest America (present-day Canada).

totter *verb* to walk in an unsteady way.

toucan *noun* a brightly coloured South American bird with a huge beak.

touch *verb* 1 to feel something with your hand or with some other part of your body. 2 to come into contact and be so close to something that there is no space in between. 3 to move the feelings. *I was touched by your kind letter.* **touch** *noun* one of the five senses, the ability to feel. **in touch** in communication. **out of touch** not in communication.

touching *adjective* causing a deep feeling of pity, sorrow etc. *A touching love story.*

touchline *noun* the line around the edge of a football pitch etc.

touchy *adjective* easily offended or annoyed. *Beth seemed very touchy.*

WORD HISTORY

'Toupee' comes from the French word 'toupe', meaning a tuft of hair.

DID YOU KNOW

American spelling was simplified by the lexicographer Noah Webster. One of his reforms was to drop the 's' in words like backward(s), westward(s) and toward(s). Words that may be spelled '–ize' or '–ise' are always '–ize' in American English.

tough *adjective* (say tuff) 1 strong and very hard to damage or break. 2 able to put up with hardships or difficulties. *Arctic explorers need to be tough.* 3 difficult. *A tough exam.* 4 hard to chew. *Tough meat.* 5 strict. *The government is tough on crime.* **toughen** *verb*. **toughness** *noun*.

toupee *noun* a false piece of hair worn to cover a bald part of the head.

tour *noun* 1 a journey on which you visit many different places. 2 a short trip around one place. **tour** *verb*.

tourist *noun* a person who visits different places for pleasure.

tournament *noun* a sports competition or contest in which the skills of the players are tested.

tousled *adjective* (of hair) untidy.

tow *verb* to pull or drag something behind. *The tractor towed the car out of the mud.*

towards *preposition* 1 in the direction of *Towards the beach.* 2 regarding. *My feelings towards you.* 3 as a contribution. *Everyone gave £2 towards the cost.*

towel *noun* a piece of thick, absorbent cloth or paper for drying things.

tower *noun* a tall, narrow building or part of building. **tower** *verb* to rise very high. *The chimney towered over the factory.* **towering** *adjective*.

Paris's most famous landmark is the tower designed by Gustave Eiffel.

town *noun* a place with a lot of houses and other buildings such as schools, shops, factories and offices.

towpath *noun* a path along the side of canal. *Let's walk along the towpath.*

toxic *adjective* poisonous. *Toxic waste.*

toy *noun* a thing for a child to play with. **toy** *verb* to play with or consider something not too seriously. *Ted toyed with the idea of becoming a policeman.*

trace *verb* 1 to copy a design etc. by placing a thin piece of half-transparent paper over it and drawing over the lines of the design etc. 2 to search and find where somebody is. *The police traced her to a hotel in Crewe.* **trace** *noun* a small mark or amount.

T

track *noun* 1 a series of marks left on the ground by an animal, person or vehicle. 2 a path. 3 a railway line. 4 a course for horses, runners, cars etc. 5 one of the pieces of music on a CD or tape recording. **off the beaten track** remote and not near a made-up road. **keep (or lose) track of** to know where somebody is, what is going on etc.

tract *noun* 1 a wide area of land. *Huge tracts of desert.* 2 a leaflet.

tractor *noun* a strong vehicle used on farms to pull ploughs and other machinery.

Tractor cabs are air-conditioned for comfort in the heat of the summer.

trade *noun* 1 the business of buying and selling goods. 2 an occupation or job that requires a special skill, a craft. *Paul's a farrier by trade.* **trade** *verb* to buy and sell, to exchange.

trade union *noun* a group of workers in the same job who join together to represent common interests on such things as working conditions and wages to their employers.

tradition *noun* customs, beliefs and habits that people hand down from one generation to another. **traditional** *adjective. A very traditional folk song.*

traffic *noun* vehicles travelling along the road at the same time.

traffic jam *noun* a long queue of traffic that has come to a standstill.

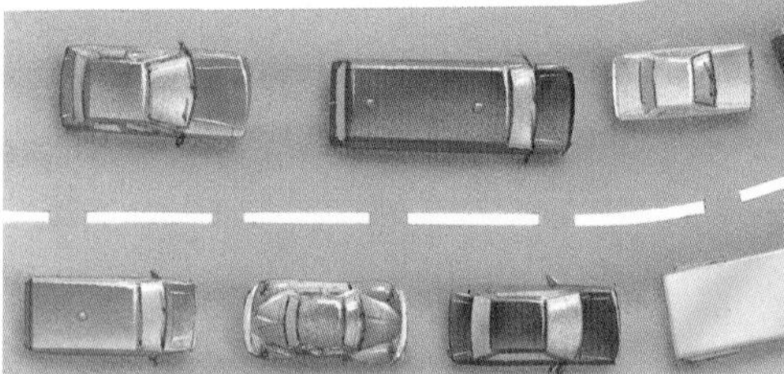

It is very frustrating to get stuck in a traffic jam behind a broken-down lorry.

traffic warden *noun* a person whose main job is to control where cars are parked.

tragedy *noun* 1 a very sad event, a terrible disaster. 2 a play about sad events and with an unhappy ending. **tragic** *adjective. Two children were killed in the tragic accident.*

trail *noun* 1 marks left behind by a person or animal as they move through a place. *A trail of footprints in the snow.* 2 a track or narrow path through the countryside.

WORD HISTORY

A tram was originally a sledge or truck that was pulled along. The word was then used for the wooden or iron track along which the tram was pulled. The later passenger vehicles were called tramcars – 'trams' for short.

trail *verb* 1 to follow a trail of somebody or something. *I am on your trail.* 2 to drag or be dragged along the ground.

trailer *noun* 1 a vehicle for carrying things that is towed by a car or lorry. *The car pulled a yacht on a trailer.* 2 an advertisement for a film that shows short extracts from it.

train *noun* 1 a railway engine with a set of carriages or trucks. 2 a series of ideas or events. *You broke my train of thought.*

train *verb* 1 to learn the skills you need to do something. 2 to teach an animal or person how to do something. 3 to practise and exercise for a sport.

trainer *noun* a person who trains or teaches somebody or an animal to compete in a sport. *A horse trainer.*

trainers *plural noun* shoes with soft, thick soles worn by runners and other sports people. *Trainers are really expensive.*

traitor *noun* a person who is disloyal and betrays friends or country.

tram *noun* a large vehicle like a bus but which runs on rails in the road and is driven by electricity (US streetcar).

tramp *verb* to walk a long way slowly and steadily. **tramp** *noun* a person without a home who travels from place to place on foot.

trample *verb* to walk heavily on something and crush it.

tranquil *adjective* (say **tran**-kwill) calm and quiet. **tranquillity** *noun. The tranquillity of a monastery.*

tranquilizer *noun* a medicine that is given to somebody to make them feel calm and peaceful. **tranquilize** *verb.*

trans- *prefix* across or beyond. *Transatlantic telephone calls.*

transfer (transfers, transferring, transferred) *verb* (say tranz-**fur**) to move somebody or something from one place to another. *She transferred her affection to another man.*

transfer *noun* (say **tranz**-fur) 1 the act of moving a person or thing from one place to another. 2 a design or picture on a small piece of paper that can be transferred and stuck to another surface by rubbing or heating. *A transfer of a teddy bear.*

T

transform *verb* to make a complete change in form or nature. *We transformed the shed into a bathroom.* **transformation** *noun.*

transfusion *noun* injecting blood into a person who has lost a lot of blood in an accident. *He needed a blood transfusion.*

transistor *noun* 1 an electronic device that controls the flow of electricity in radios and television sets. 2 a small portable radio that uses a transistor.

translate *verb* to change words from one language into another. **translator** *noun.* **translation** *noun.*

transmit (transmits, transmitting, transmitted) *verb* 1 to pass something on from one place or person to another. *How are diseases transmitted?* 2 to send out a radio or television programme over the air. **transmission** *noun.*

transparency *noun* a photograph that lets light through so that you can project it on to a screen.

transparent *adjective* able to be seen through. *Clear water is transparent.*

The cocktail glass is transparent, and so is the drink. You can see the olive on the stick inside it.

transplant *verb* 1 to move a plant growing in one place to another place. 2 to perform a surgical operation to put a part of one person's body into the body of another person. **transplant** *noun. A heart transplant.*

transport *noun* cars, buses, trains and planes or any other way of travelling.

transport *verb* to carry people or goods from one place to another.

trap *noun* a device for catching birds and animals. **trap** *verb* 1 to catch an animal using a trap. 2 to catch a person by a trick. *They trapped her into admitting guilt.*

trapeze *noun* a bar hanging from two ropes used by acrobats and gymnasts to swing from and perform skilful movements.

trash *noun* anything to be thrown away.

DID YOU KNOW

'Treble' and 'triple' are interchangeable in the sense of 'three times as much'. But 'treble' is usually preferred when meaning 'three times as great', as in 'treble the amount', and 'triple' is preferred when meaning 'consisting of three parts', as in 'triple bypass'.

The treasure Sally found in the attic consisted of beautiful jewels and valuable gold coins.

AMAZING FACT

The first successful human heart transplant operation was performed in South Africa by Dr Cristiaan Barnard in 1967.

travel (travels, travelling, travelled) *verb* to journey or move from one place to another. *Sound travels fast.* **travel** *noun. Air travel.*

traveller *noun* 1 a person who travels regularly. 2 a person who travels from place to place in a mobile home or van.

trawl *verb* to fish with a wide net called a trawl. *Rod trawled the deep ocean for fish.*

trawler *noun* a fishing boat that pulls a large net called a trawl behind it.

tray *noun* a flat object with a rim around the edge for carrying things such as food and drinks.

treachery *noun* disloyalty, the betrayal of people who trust you. **treacherous** *adjective* 1 disloyal. 2 dangerous. *Treacherous rocks.*

treacle *noun* a thick, sticky syrup made from syrup. *Treacle tart.*

tread (treading, trod, trodden) *verb* to walk or to put your foot down on something, to trample. *She trod on the cat's tail!* **tread** *noun* 1 the top part of a ladder or stairs you put your foot on. 2 the raised pattern of ridges on a car tyre or on the sole of a shoe.

treason *noun* the betrayal of your country, especially by giving away secrets to the enemy in wartime. **treasonable** *adjective. A treasonable crime.*

treasure *noun* 1 a store of gold, jewels and other precious things. 2 a precious object such as a painting. **treasure** *verb* to value something very much or to look after something because it is important to you.

treasurer *noun* a person who looks after the money of a club etc.

treat *verb* 1 to behave towards somebody in a particular way. *She treats me like a servant.* 2 to give medical care to a person or animal. *The doctor is treating her for eczema.* **treatment** *noun.* **treat** *noun* a special gift such as an outing or a meal.

treaty *noun* a formal agreement between two or more countries. *An arms treaty.*

treble *adjective, adverb* three times as much, as many or as big. **treble** *verb. He has trebled his income.*

treble *noun* a boy with a high singing voice.

tree *noun* a tall plant that has a long, thick wooden stem called a trunk and branches and leaves. *Many trees in the forest.*

Trees are the lungs of the world, as they take in carbon dioxide and give out oxygen.

AMAZING FACT

Trees are the largest of all plants. Some grow to over 100 metres high.

trek *noun* a long journey, usually on foot and in a remote area. **trek** *verb.*

trellis *noun* a fence or framework of wooden strips for plants to climb up.

tremble *verb* to shake all over because you are frightened, cold or excited.

tremendous *adjective* 1 very big. *A tremendous crowd.* 2 very good. *We had a tremendous time.*

trench *noun* a long, thin ditch or channel dug in the earth. *Trench warfare.*

trend *noun* the general direction in which things seem to be changing and becoming different. *A trend for smaller families.* **set a trend** to start a fashion.

trespass *verb* to go on somebody's land without their permission. **tresspasser** *noun.*

tri- *prefix* meaning three or three times. *Tricycle, triangle, trilogy, tripod, tripartite.*

trial *noun* 1 the period of time when a prisoner is in a law court and when the lawyers, jury and judge try to decide whether or not he or she has done wrong and is guilty. 2 a test of something to see how well it works.

triangle *noun* 1 a flat shape with three straight sides and three corners. 2 a triangular musical instrument that makes a bell-like sound when you hit it. **triangular** *adjective.*

A triangle has three sides.

DID YOU KNOW

English spelling does not allow triples of the same letter, so where a compound word contains three of the same letters consecutively a hyphen is inserted, as in bell-like, cross-section, Inverness-shire.

tribe *noun* a group of families descended from the same ancestors who live together and who have the same traditions, language etc. **tribal** *adjective. Tribal chief.*

The Masai people of Kenya are a tribe of cattle herders. They wear bright cloth and beaded collars.

tributary *noun* a stream that flows into a river or another stream.

trick *noun* 1 something you do to cheat somebody or to make a fool of somebody. 2 some clever or skilful thing that you have learned to do to entertain people. *Card tricks.* 3 a practical joke. **trick** *verb* to deceive or make a fool of somebody.

trickle *verb* to flow slowly like a very small stream. *Tears trickled down his cheeks.* **trickle** *noun. A trickle of water.*

tricky *adjective* difficult to deal with. *A tricky situation.*

tricolour *noun* a flag with three bands of different colours such as the French and Irish flags.

tricycle *noun* a cycle with three wheels.

tried past tense of try.

trifle *noun* 1 a sweet made of sponge cake and fruit covered in jelly, custard and cream. 2 something that is of no importance. **trifling** *adjective.*

trigger *noun* the small lever you pull with a finger to fire a gun.

trilogy *noun* a group of three novels, plays, operas etc. that go together and make a related series by having the same people or themes in common.

trim (trims, trimming, trimmed) *verb* 1 to cut the edges or ends off something to make it neat, to clip. *He trimmed her hair.* 2 to decorate a piece of clothing. *She trimmed the hat with flowers.* **trim** *adjective* having a good shape. *He has a trim figure.*

Trinidad and Tobago *noun* a country in the West Indies.

The flag of Trinidad and Tobago has a diagonal black and white stripe on a red ground.

trinity *noun* 1 a group of three. 2 the Trinity in Christianity, the Father, the Son and the Holy Spirit as one God.

trio *noun* a group of three singers or players, a piece of music written for three musicians. *A string trio.*

trip (trips, tripping, tripped) *verb* 1 to catch your foot in something and stumble or fall over. 2 to move with quick, light steps. *She tripped along the path as happy as could be.* **trip up** to make a mistake.

trip *noun* 1 a short return journey or visit. *A trip to Paris.* 2 (slang) a dream-like experience caused by drugs.

tripe *noun* 1 the stomach lining of such animals as cows and pigs which is cooked and eaten. 2 worthless nonsense. *Don't talk such tripe.*

triple *adjective* three times as great or many. 2 consisting of three parts. **triple** *verb. The tree has tripled in height in one month.*

triplet *noun* one of three babies born at the same time to the same mother.

tripod *noun* (say **try**-pod) a three-legged support for a camera etc.

Tripoli *noun* the capital of Libya.

triumph *noun* (say **try**-umf) a great success or achievement, a victory. **triumph** *verb. He triumphed over evil.* **triumphant** *adjective.*

trivial *adjective* of very little importance. *A trivial problem.*

troll *noun* an ugly, mischievous creature in fairy tales from Scandinavia.

Trolls are favourite storybook creatures for children in Norway, Sweden and Denmark.

trolley *noun* a small cart or a large basket on wheels for carrying things. *A supermarket trolley.*

trombone *noun* a large, brass musical instrument that you blow through and move a slide to change the note.

This tropical rainforest can be found in the equatorial region of South America.

WORD HISTORY

'Truant' once meant a beggar. In the 16th century it took on the meaning of a pupil absent without leave from school. It originally comes from a Welsh word 'truan', meaning 'wretched'.

AMAZING FACT

Trinidad and Tobago is one country made up of two islands in the West Indies.

troops *plural noun* a group of soldiers. **troop** *verb* to move together as a crowd. *The fans trooped into the stadium.*

trophy *noun* (say **trow**-fee) an award or prize such as a silver cup given to somebody who wins a game or competition.

tropic *noun* 1 one of the two lines of latitude running around the Earth at about 23 degrees north and south of the equator and known as the Tropic of Cancer and the Tropic of Capricorn. 2 **tropics** *plural noun* the very warm regions between the Tropic of Cancer and the Tropic of Capricorn. **tropical** *noun. Tropical rain forests.*

trot *noun* one of the four paces of a horse, between a walk and a canter. **trot** (trots, trotting, trotted) *verb* 1 of a horse, to run but not to canter or to gallop. 2 of humans, to move quickly. *Trot along now.*

trouble *noun* a difficult, unpleasant or worrying situation, a problem. **trouble** *verb* 1 to cause worry, concern or distress. 2 to make an effort to do something, to bother. *She didn't trouble to ask if she could help.*

troublesome *adjective* causing problems or worries, annoying. *A troublesome wasp.*

trough *noun* 1 a long, narrow container for food and water for animals. 2 in weather forecasting, an area of low pressure between areas of high pressure.

trousers *plural noun* a piece of clothing covering your body from your waist to your ankles with a separate part for each leg.

trout (trout) *noun* a silvery-brown freshwater fish of the salmon family that can be eaten. *Trout with almonds.*

trowel *noun* 1 a small spade-like hand tool with a short handle used for garden work. 2 a flat hand tool used by builders to spread plaster etc. *Lay it on with a trowel.*

truant *noun* a pupil who stays away from school without permission or a good excuse.

truce *noun* a short period when two sides in a war etc. agree to stop fighting.

truck *noun* a motor vehicle that can carry heavy loads, a lorry. An open railway wagon. *A truck full of coal.*

trudge *verb* to walk slowly with tired, heavy steps. **trudge** *noun.*

true *noun* 1 what really happened. 2 not invented or guessed at but real and accurate. 3 loyal and trustworthy. *A true friend.*

trumpet *noun* a brass musical instrument that makes high sounds when you blow into it.

T

trunk *noun* 1 the long stem of a tree from which the branches grow. 2 a large container with a hinged lid and a handle for carrying or storing things such as clothes. 3 the main part of your body but not including your limbs, neck and head, the torso. 4 an elephant's long nose. 5 (US) the boot of a car.

trunks *plural noun* shorts worn by men and boys for swimming.

The best event at the village fete was the tug o' war.

trust *verb* to believe that somebody is honest, reliable and truthful and that they will do nothing to harm you, to depend on. **trustworthy** *adjective*. **trustworthiness** *noun*.

truth *noun* what is real, accurate and correct, what has actually happened. *Are you telling me the truth?* **truthful** *adjective*. **truthfulness** *noun*.

try (tries, trying, tried) *verb* 1 to attempt to do something. *I don't think I can do it but I'll try.* 2 to test something by using it to see what it is like. *Try this ice-cream and see if you like it.* 3 to judge somebody in a court of law. **try** *noun* 1 an attempt. 2 in rugby, a way of scoring by putting the ball down on the ground over the opponents' goal line. **trying** *adjective* exhausting and irritating. *A trying child.*

tsar *noun* (say zar) in former times, a Russian king or emperor. His wife was called a tsarina. Also spelt czar, czarina.

T-shirt a kind of shirt or vest with short sleeves and no collar.

tub *noun* a round, wide and usually open container.

tuba *noun* a large brass musical instrument that makes deep sounds when you blow into it.

tubby *adjective* short, round and rather fat.

tube *noun* 1 a long, hollow metal, plastic or rubber cylinder, a pipe. 2 a long container. *A tube of toothpaste.* 3 London's underground railway. **tubular** *adjective*.

My dad played oom-pah music on the tuba.

tuber *noun* the roundish swollen part of the underground stem of some plants. Potatoes are tubers.

tuck *verb* to fold under or push the loose end of something into a place to make it look tidy. *He tucked his shirt into his trousers.* **tuck in** *verb* to eat with great enjoyment. *Bunter tucked into the cake.*

tuft *noun* a bunch or clump of hair, feathers, grass etc.

WORD HISTORY

'Tsar' is sometimes spelled 'Czar'. It is a Russian word derived from the Latin, 'Caesar'. The German equivalent is 'kaiser'.

WORD HISTORY

'Turban' comes from the Portuguese 'turbante', which in turn comes from a Persian word for this headdress.

tug or tugboat *noun* a small powerful boat that tows ships in and out of port.

tug o' war *noun* a contest between two teams who pull on opposite ends of a long rope to test their strength.

tulip *noun* a plant with brightly coloured flowers that grows from a bulb in the spring. *The tulips of Amsterdam.*

tumble *verb* to fall down suddenly or to fall and roll over. *Tim tumbled down the stairs.*

tumbler *noun* a drinking glass.

tummy *noun* (slang) the stomach.

tumour *noun* a lump or growth on the body made of diseased or abnormal cells.

tuna *noun* a large sea fish, used for food.

tundra *noun* the vast treeless plains of the Arctic that remain frozen all year.

tune *noun* a sequence of musical notes in a pattern that is pleasant to listen to and often easy to remember. **tune** *verb* 1 to adjust a musical instrument so that it plays the correct notes. 2 to adjust a radio so that it receives the programme you want. **tuneful** *adjective*. **change your tune** to change the way you think.

tunic *noun* 1 a tight-fitting jacket, often worn as part of a uniform. 2 a loose, sleeveless garment without a collar.

Tunis *noun* the capital of Tunisia.

Tunisia *noun* a country in Africa.

Tunisian *noun* a person who comes from Tunisia. **Tunisian** *adjective*. *The Tunisian coast is extremely beautiful.*

tunnel *noun* a long underground passage for a railway etc. **tunnel** (tunnels, tunnelling, tunnelled) *verb* to dig a tunnel.

turban *noun* a headdress worn by Muslim and Sikh men consisting of a long piece of cloth wound around the head.

turbine *noun* an engine that works by water, steam, or hot air etc. pushing round the curved blades on a wheel.

Wind turbines produce a clean, renewable source of electricity.

turbojet *noun* an aircraft driven by a turbine.

turf *noun* 1 short, thick grass. 2 a piece of earth with grass growing from it, cut from the ground.

turkey *noun* a large bird that is reared for its meat.

Turkey *noun* a country partly in Europe and mostly in Asia.

Turkish *noun* 1 a person who comes from Turkey. 2 the language of Turkey. **Turkish** *adjective. Turkish architecture.*

Turkmenistan *noun* a country in West Asia.

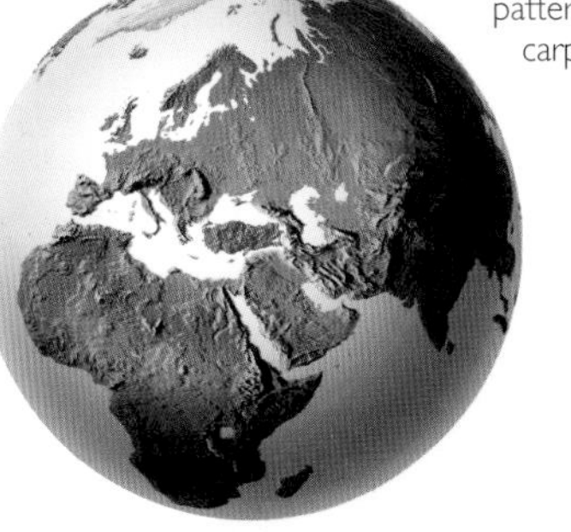

Turkey is famous for its richly patterned carpets.

turmoil *noun* a state of great confusion and unrest.

turn *verb* 1 to go around or move around a central point, to revolve or twist. *Turn the handle.* 2 to move and change direction. *He turned to look at me.* 3 to move so as to make the topside become the bottom side. *He turned the mattress.* 4 to change or to become different. *The frog turned into a prince.* 5 to adjust a switch, tap etc. *Turn the lights off.* **turn** *noun.* **do somebody a good turn** to help somebody. **turn down** 1 to refuse. 2 to make quieter. **turn up** 1 to arrive. 2 to make louder. *Please turn up the sound.*

turnip *noun* a round, white root vegetable.

turnstile *noun* a revolving gate that lets people walk through one at a time.

turquoise *noun* a greenish-blue semi-precious stone. The colour of the stone.

turret *noun* a small tower on a castle or the side of a building.

turtle *noun* a large reptile covered with a shell like a tortoise that lives in the sea.

Turtles swim ashore to lay their eggs in the sand on the beach.

tusk *noun* one of a pair of long, curved, pointed teeth that sticks out of the mouth of elephants, walruses and wild boar.

tutor *noun* a teacher who gives classes to one person at a time or to very small groups of people. *My maths tutor is very clever.*

tutu *noun* the very short, stiff skirt worn by female ballet dancers.

Tuvalu *noun* a country of islands in the Pacific Ocean.

TV *abbreviation* television.

DID YOU KNOW

Many of our clichés rely on twinning words as in 'leaps and bounds', 'fast and furious', 'pick and choose', 'slow but sure' and 'nice and easy'.

Sabon

'Sabon' is the name of the type used in this book.

AMAZING FACT

The female turtle buries her eggs in the sand. When the eggs of the turtle hatch, the hatchlings have to dig their way up to the surface.

tweed *noun* a strong woollen cloth, often made of several colours.

tweezers *plural noun* a small tool with two prongs for lifting things or for pulling out hairs etc., pincers.

twice *adverb* two times.

twiddle *verb* to turn something round and round in a purposeless way. *He kept twiddling with the radio knobs.* **twiddle your thumbs** to have nothing to do.

twig *noun* a thin, tiny branch of a tree.

twilight *noun* the time of day when it is getting dark, between sunset and night.

twin *noun* one of two babies born at the same time to the same mother.

twine *noun* very strong string made by twisting threads together.

twinge *noun* a sudden, short pain. *A twinge of rheumatism.*

twinkle *verb* to sparkle with little unsteady flashes of light. *Stars twinkle in the sky.* **twinkle** *noun. He has a twinkle in his eye!*

twirl *verb* to turn or spin something quickly round and round.

twist *verb* 1 to turn. *To open the box you must twist the knob.* 2 wind something around something else. *She twisted her hair around her finger.* 4 to bend and turn in different directions. *The road twisted around the mountain.* 4 to bend something so as to damage it. *She twisted her wrist.* **twist** *noun.* **round the twist** mad.

tycoon *noun* a rich, powerful business person or industrialist. *A newspaper tycoon.*

type *noun* 1 the different designs of letters used in printing. 2 a kind or sort. *Apples and pears are two types of fruit.*

type *verb* to write something by pressing the keys of a typewriter or computer.

typewriter *noun* a machine with keys that you press to print letters and figures on a piece of paper.

typhoid *noun* (say **tie**-foid) a very dangerous infectious disease in which the intestines become inflamed.

typhoon *noun* (say tie-**foon**) a tropical storm with violent winds.

typical *adjective* 1 the most usual or characteristic of its kind. *A typical Tudor house.* 2 what you would expect. *It's typical of you to be late, I'm afraid.*

tyrant *noun* a cruel, unjust and unkind ruler. **tyranny** *noun.* **tyrannical** *adjective. A tyrannical dictator.*

tyre *noun* the thick ring of rubber usually filled with air around the wheel of a vehicle.

Uu

udder *noun* the bag-like part of a cow, sheep etc. that hangs down between its back legs and from which milk is taken.

UFO *abbreviation* unidentified flying object. *Ted likes films about UFOs.*

Uganda *noun* a country in Africa.

Ugandan *noun* a person who comes from Uganda. **Ugandan** *adjective. Ugandan exports include avocado pears.*

ugly (uglier, ugliest) *adjective* unattractive and not beautiful to look at. **ugliness** *noun.*

UHF *abbreviation* ultra high frequency.

Ukraine *noun* a country in eastern Europe.

Ukrainian *noun* a person who comes from the Ukraine. **Ukrainian** *adjective. Ukrainian wheat is an important export.*

Ulan Bator *noun* the capital of Mongolia.

ulcer *noun* (say **ull**-sur) an open sore on the body usually with a flow of pus.

ultimate *adjective* final, last. *Our ultimate wish is to win.*

ultimatum *noun* a final offer or warning.

ultra- *prefix* beyond. *Ultra high frequency.*

ultraviolet light *noun* light that is beyond the visible spectrum at its violet end and which causes your skin to tan.

umbilical cord *noun* the tube that connects the body of a mother and child until the child is born.

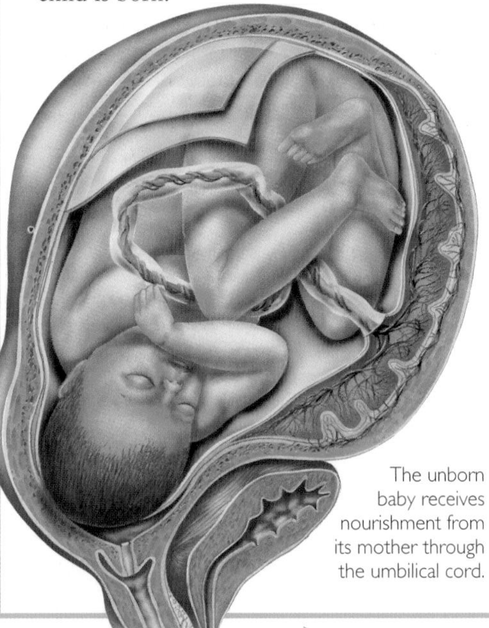

The unborn baby receives nourishment from its mother through the umbilical cord.

DID YOU KNOW

The shape of the letters U, V and W comes from a Semitic letter called 'waw', which was symbolised as a tenthook. The Romans used V for both U and V sounds. In the Middle Ages scholars began using U for the vowel sound and V for the consonant sound.

WORD BUILDER

Here are some words with the 'un–' prefix. You can easily work out the meaning if you look up the root word: 'unable', 'unaffected', 'unaided', 'unarmed', 'unbearable'.

umbrella *noun* something that you hold over your head to keep you dry when it rains. The umbrella's frame is covered with a round piece of material and joined to a long handle. An umbrella folds up when you are not using it.

umpire *noun* a person who watches a game and makes sure that the rules are followed.

UN *abbreviation* United Nations.

The flag of the United Nations is a symbol of world peace and harmony.

un- *prefix* 1 not, opposite. *Uncomfortable.* 2 the opposite of an action. *Unfasten.*

unaccustomed *adjective* not used to doing something. *He is unaccustomed to work.*

unanimous *adjective* (say you-**nan**-im-us) of the same opinion, agreed by everybody. *A unanimous decision.* **unanimity** *noun.*

unassuming *adjective* modest and not showing off. *An unassuming young man.*

unaware *adjective* not knowing that something exists or is happening.

unbalanced *adjective* 1 lacking balance, unfair. *An unbalanced account of what happened.* 2 slightly mad. *She became rather unbalanced after the accident.*

unbecoming *adjective* not suitable.

unbiased *adjective* not favouring one side or the other, fair. *An unbiased opinion.*

uncanny *adjective* strange, weird and unnatural. *An uncanny silence.*

uncle *noun* the brother of your mother or your father or the husband of your aunt.

unconscious *adjective* 1 not conscious, in a kind of sleep and not knowing what is happening. 2 not being aware of something. *I was unconscious of the difficulties you were in until yesterday.*

uncooperative *adjective* making no attempt to help or do things for others.

uncouth *adjective* coarse and rough in behaviour and speech, rude.

undaunted *adjective* not discouraged or put off doing something despite setbacks and difficulties. *Her grandmother's criticism left her undaunted.*

U

undeniable *adjective* so certainly true that you cannot disagree.

under- *prefix* 1 below, beneath. *Underground.* 2 less than or not enough. *Underdeveloped.* 3 lower in rank. *Undersecretary, understudy.*

undercarriage *noun* the landing gear of an aircraft, including the wheels.

undercover *adjective* secret. *Undercover activities were common during the war.*

underdog *noun* in a game or contest, an unfortunate person or team that is unlikely to win. *I always want the underdog to win.*

undergo (undergoes, undergoing, underwent, undergone) *verb* to experience, endure or suffer something. *The town has undergone many changes in recent years.*

undergraduate *noun* a person studying for a first degree at a university.

underground *adjective* 1 beneath the ground or surface of the Earth. *Underground passages.* 2 acting in secret. *An underground group.* **underground** *noun* a railway that runs through tunnels under the ground (US subway).

WORD BUILDER

Here are some words with the 'under–' prefix. You can easily work out what they mean: 'underclothes', 'undercook', 'underemployed', 'underfeed'.

understanding *noun* 1 having a knowledge of something and knowing what it means or how it works, intelligence. *He has no understanding of machinery.* 2 sympathy and knowledge of a person. *There's a deep understanding between them.* 3 an agreement. *Perhaps we could come to an understanding about who does what.* **understanding** *adjective* tolerant and kind.

understudy *noun* an actor who learns the lines of the actor who usually plays a part and who takes over that part in an emergency. *The understudy was a great hit.*

undertake (undertakes, undertaking, undertook, undertaken) *verb* to agree or promise to do something and to be responsible for it. **undertaking** *noun.*

undertaker *noun* a person whose job it is to prepare dead bodies for burial or cremation and arrange funerals.

underwear *noun* clothes that you wear under your other clothes next to your skin. Knickers and vests are underwear.

underworld *noun* 1 all the criminals and their activities in a city. 2 the place in myths where the spirits of dead people go.

Moles spend most of their time underground. Because they are used to living in the darkness, their eyesight is very poor.

undergrowth *noun* bushes and plants that grow near the ground under trees in woods and forests. *He hid in the undergrowth.*

underhand *adjective* secret and dishonest, deceitful. *An underhand plot.*

underline *verb* 1 to draw a line under words to make them stand out. 2 to stress the importance of something *The accident underlines the need to be more careful.*

undermine *verb* to weaken or slowly destroy something. *The cold, damp climate is undermining her health.*

understand (understands, understanding, understood) *verb* 1 to know what something means, how it works or why it happens. 2 to know somebody or something well. *I quite understand what you feel.* 3 to believe something to be true because you have been told. *I understand that you got married in secret.*

undo (undoes, undoing, undid, undone) *verb* 1 to unfasten, untie, unwrap something that was fixed or tied. *She undid her shoelaces.* 2 to do away with or reverse something that has been done. *Try to undo the damage your remarks have done.*

Marcus undid his shoelaces, took off his shoes and put on his slippers.

undoubted *adjective* accepted as true, certain. *An undoubted success.*

undress *verb* to take your clothes off.

undue *adjective* excessive, more than necessary. *Undue noise.*

undying *adjective* never dying or fading. *They swore undying love.*

unearth *verb* to dig up or find something after searching for it, to discover. *He unearthed some old photos in a trunk.*

unearthly *adjective* 1 strange and terrifying, like nothing on Earth. *An unearthly sound of howling.* 2 absurdly unreasonable. *She telephoned at some unearthly hour.*

uneasy *adjective* anxious, not settled. *I feel uneasy around dogs.* **uneasiness** *noun.*

uneven *adjective.* 1 not smooth or flat. 2 not equally matched, one-sided. *An uneven contest.* 3 (of a number) odd and leaving a remainder of one when divided by two. Five is an uneven number.

The track through the hills was very uneven, making our journey uncomfortable.

unfailing *adjective* never failing or weakening, continuous, endless. *You have my unfailing sympathy.*

unfeeling *adjective* severe and hard-hearted.

unfit *adjective* 1 unhealthy, in poor physical condition. 2 unsuitable and not good enough. *This food is unfit to eat.*

unfold *verb* 1 to spread out by opening. *He unfolded the blanket.* 2 to reveal or gradually to make something clear. *The story unfolded gradually.*

unfurl *verb* to unroll, spread out and display something that has been wrapped up. *The soldier unfurled the flag.*

unforeseen *adjective* not expected. *Due to unforeseen circumstances, I cannot come.*

unfounded *adjective* not based on fact. *Unfounded rumours.*

ungainly *adjective* clumsy and ungraceful.

unicorn *noun* an animal in stories that looks like a white horse with a long, spiralled horn on its forehead.

Legend says that if a maiden falls asleep with the head of a unicorn in her lap, she will dream of the man she is to marry.

SPELLING NOTE

Try not to confuse 'uninterested' meaning 'not interested' with 'disinterested' meaning 'not favouring one side and being fair to both'.

GRAMMAR NOTE

You cannot say something is 'very unique' or 'rather unique' because 'unique' means 'the only one, so either it's unique or it's not!

uniform *noun* special distinctive clothes worn by members of a particular group or organization. Nurses, firefighters and soldiers wear uniforms. **uniform** *adjective* not changing, always the same. *The concrete blocks are of uniform size and colour.*

unify *verb* to make several things come together to form a whole to share a common purpose. *The various Italian states unified to make modern Italy.*

unintelligible *adjective* very difficult to understand. *Your writing is unintelligible.*

uninterested *adjective* showing no interest or enthusiasm. *I told him about the match but he seemed quite uninterested.*

union *noun* 1 A trade union is an organized group of workers who discuss with managers any problems affecting all the workers. 2 the act of joining things together, something united.

unique *adjective* (say yoo-**neek**) 1 being the only one of its kind and different from anybody or anything else. *His style of painting is unique.* 2 very unusual. **uniqueness** *noun.*

unisex *adjective* designed for or capable of being used by both men and women. *A unisex hairdresser.*

unison *noun* **in unison** all together.

unit *noun* 1 a single, complete thing that is part of a whole. 2 a group working together. *The physiotherapy unit.* 3 an amount that is used as a standard weight or measurement. *A litre is a unit of liquid measurement.*

unite *verb* to join together to form one thing or to do something together, to combine. **unity** *noun.*

United Arab Emirates *noun* a country in Southwest Asia.

United Kingdom *noun* a country in Northwest Europe, made up of England, Scotland, Wales and Northern Ireland.

United States of America *noun* a country in North America.

Alaska (top left on the map) belongs to the United States of America.

universal *adjective* relating to and including everybody and everything.

universe *noun* (say **yoo**-ni-verse) the whole of everything that exists, including the Earth, Sun, Moon, planets and all the stars in space. *The end of the universe.*

university *noun* a place of higher education where people go after they have left school to study for a degree or do research.

unkempt *adjective* untidy and not well looked after. *An unkempt beard.*

unleaded *adjective* (of petrol) containing no lead. *This car runs on unleaded petrol.*

unless *conjunction* if not. Except when. *I will go unless you stop talking.*

unlucky *adjective* 1 having bad luck and with bad things happening to you. 2 causing bad luck. *Some people believe it is unlucky to walk under ladders.*

unmistakable *adjective* distinct and not possible to be mistaken for somebody or something else. His handwriting is quite unmistakable. *An unmistakable style.*

UNO *abbreviation* United Nations Organization.

unravel (unravels, unravelling, unravelled) *verb* to undo knots or untie woven, knitted or tangled threads. 2 to solve a mystery or difficult problem.

The cat unravelled my knitting. I had to roll the wool back up into a ball.

unreasonable *adjective* 1 not sensible. *An unreasonable fear of spiders.* 2 too much, excessive. *Unreasonable demands.*

unreliable *adjective* not to be trusted or depended on. *Dad's old car is unreliable.*

unrest *noun* 1 discontent. 2 restlessness. Disturbance and riots. *There was great unrest among the workers.*

unruly *adjective* badly behaved, hard to control or rule. *An unruly child.*

unscathed *adjective* not harmed or damaged. *The horses escaped the stable fire unscathed and lived to see another day.*

unscrupulous *adjective* not caring whether something is right or wrong, having no principles. *An unscrupulous employer.*

unseemly *adjective* not suitable for the time and place. *Her laughter at the funeral was really quite unseemly.*

unsettle *verb* to make or become unstable and anxious, to disturb. *Thunder unsettles our dogs and cats.*

AMAZING FACT

The United Nations, or UN, was founded in 1945 after the Second World War to encourage world peace.

Shelby left her bedroom in an untidy mess.

GRAMMAR NOTE

We use 'an' instead of 'a' before words that start with a vowel **sound.** *So say and write 'a uniform' or 'a used car' but say or write 'an unusual vase' or 'an umbrella'.*

unsightly *adjective* unpleasant to look at, ugly. *An unsightly building blocks the view.*

unsound *adjective* 1 not in a good condition, unhealthy. *The upstairs floors are unsound.* 2 not based on fact. *I thought her theory was very unsound.*

unstable *adjective* 1 liable to change suddenly. *She's very moody and unstable.* 2 not steady, wobbly. *The table is unsteady.*

unsuitable *adjective* not right or fitting for a particular purpose. *Slippers are unsuitable for playing football.*

untidy (untidier, untidiest) *adjective* messy and with nothing in its proper place. *Adrian's office is always untidy!*

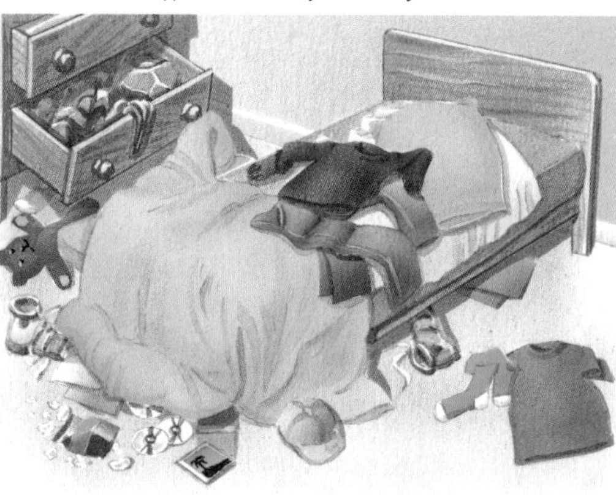

untie (unties, untying, untied) *verb* to undo or loosen the knots of something that was tied. *She untied the bows in her hair.*

until *conjunction, preposition* up to the time of or when. *She stayed up until long past midnight to welcome in the New Year.*

untold *adjective* too much or too many to calculate. *Locusts do untold damage to some crops.*

unusual *adjective* strange, rare and unexpected. *An unusual necklace.*

This very unusual vase will create lots of interest at the antiques fair.

unwelcome *adjective* not wanted. *An unwelcome visitor.*

unwieldy *noun* bulky, clumsy and difficult to hold, manage or move.

U

unwitting *adjective* 1 not knowing and not intended. *An unwitting error.*

unworthy *adjective* not deserving. *Such a ridiculous story is unworthy of attention.* 2 out of character and below standards expected. *It's unworthy of you to tell lies.*

unwrap (unwraps, unwrapping, unwrapped) *verb* to remove the covering or wrapping off something such as a parcel, to

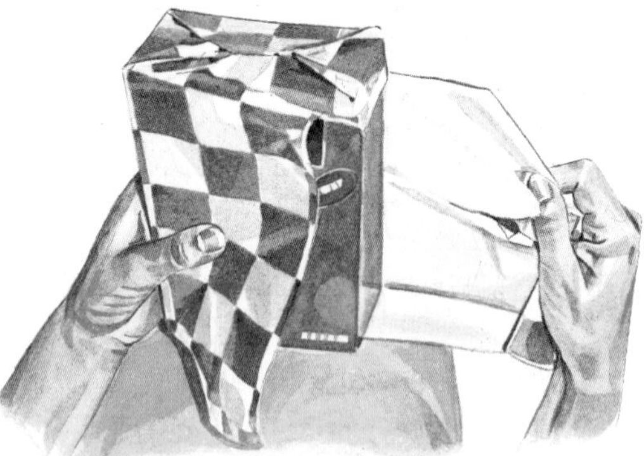

Simon unwrapped the parcel and was astonished to find a box of pasta inside.

up *adverb, preposition* 1 to a higher level, amount etc. *Jack went up the hill.* 2 to a sitting or standing position. *Please stand up.* 3 completely, so that it is finished. *She ate up her crusts.* 4 out of bed. *She gets up early.* 5 along. *I was walking up the road.* 6 into pieces. *He tore up the letter.* **ups and downs** good times and bad times. **up and coming** on the way to being successful.

upbeat *adjective* happy and ever hopeful.

upbringing *noun* the way that a child is brought up and told how to behave.

update *verb* to add all the latest information and make more modern. *The files are constantly updated.*

upheaval *noun* a great change causing a lot of worry. *Moving is a huge upheaval.*

uphill *adverb* going up a slope or hill. *We walked uphill.* The opposite is downhill. **uphill** *adjective* difficult and needing a lot of effort. *An uphill struggle to survive.*

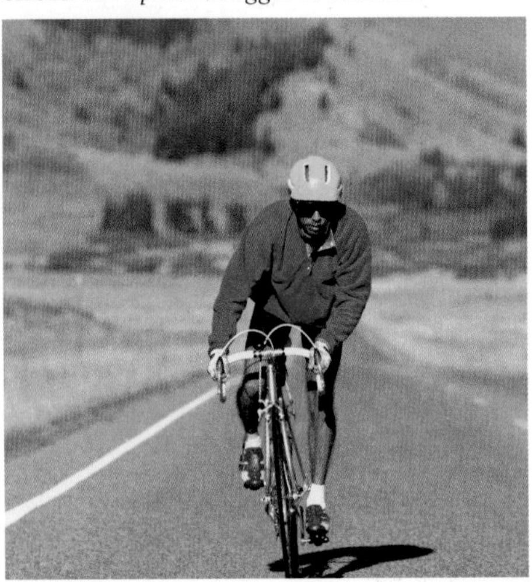

Adam cycled slowly uphill, thinking of the chocolate he would eat when he reached the top.

GRAMMAR NOTE

'Upon' and 'on' are synonymous and interchangeable. 'He threw himself upon the bed.' 'She walked on a tightrope.' 'Upon' is slightly more formal, and in speaking 'on' is usually preferred.

AMAZING FACT

The word 'urchin' comes from an ancient word meaning hedgehog.

uphold (upholds, upholding, upheld) *verb* to give support to or defend an action or cause. *The umpire upheld the referee's decision, and was booed.*

upholstery *noun* the springs, padding, covering and cushions of chairs and sofas. *Leather upholstery.* **upholster** *verb.*

upkeep *noun* the cost of keeping something in a good condition. *What's the upkeep of your car?*

upon *preposition* on, on top of.

upper *adjective* above, in a higher position. the upper part of your body.

upright *adjective, adverb* 1 in a vertical position. *Upright posts.* 2 good and honest. *An upright person.*

uprising *noun* a rebellion or revolt against people in authority.

uproar *noun* noisy and angry or excited confusion, a disturbance.

uproot *verb* to pull a plant out of the ground by its roots.

upset (upsets, upsetting, upset) *verb* 1 to overturn or knock something over by accident. *The cat upset the milk jug.* 2 to make somebody feel worried or unhappy. *You've upset your mother by being so rude.* **upset** *noun* 1 a minor illness. *A tummy upset.* 2 a sudden change. *The bad weather has caused an upset to our plans.*

upside-down *adjective* 1 with the top facing down and the bottom facing up. 2 utter disorder. *She turned the house upside-down looking for her watch.*

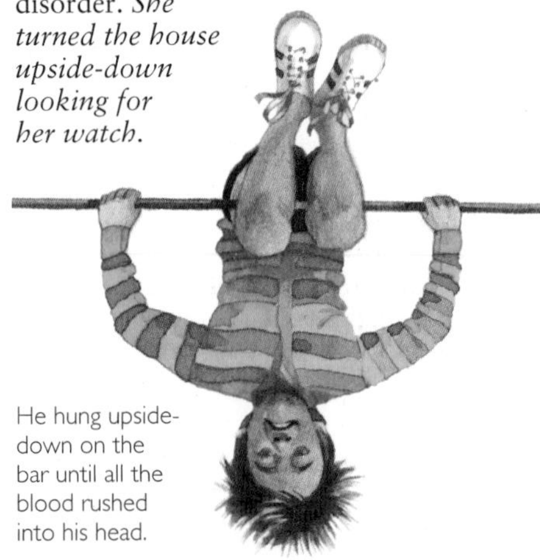

He hung upside-down on the bar until all the blood rushed into his head.

upstairs *adjective, adverb* situated on or going to a higher floor. *He walked upstairs.* The opposite is downstairs.

uptight *adjective* 1 (slang) nervous, angry, irritated. 2 (US) prim and conventional.

up-to-date *adjective* modern, containing all the very latest information etc. *An up-to-date map.* The opposite is out-of-date.

urchin *noun* a poor, shabbily dressed, mischievous child.

Urdu *noun* one of the official languages of Pakistan, also widely spoken in India.

urge *verb* to encourage and try to make somebody do something, to plead. *He urged her to try a little harder.* **urge** *noun* a strong desire to do something, an impulse. *She had a sudden urge to go for a walk.*

urgent *adjective* very important and needing to be dealt with at once. *An urgent phone call.* **urgency** *noun.*

urine *noun* the clear, yellowish fluid waste passed from the bodies of animals and humans from the bladder. **urinate** *verb* to pass urine from the body.

urn *noun* 1 an ornamental vase or a container for a dead person's ashes. 2 a large container for holding hot drinks. *A tea urn.*

Uruguay *noun* a country in South America.

Uruguay is famous for its pampas grasslands, its fine herds of beef cattle and the cowboys called gauchos.

Uruguayan *noun* a person from Uruguay. **Uruguayan** *adjective. Uruguayan pasturelands.*

USA *abbreviation* United States of America.

usage *noun* 1 a way of using, treatment. *The video has been damaged through rough usage.* 2 the usual or customary way of doing or saying things. *American usage is to say 'hood' for 'bonnet', 'billfold' for 'wallet', and 'windshield' for' windscreen'.*

use *verb* (say **yoo-zz**) 1 to make something do a job. *She used scissors to cut the cloth.* 2 to consume or take. *Don't use all the hot water.* **use** *noun* (rhymes with juice) 1 the act of using or being in use. *The photocopier is in constant use.* 2 the purpose for using something. *This tool has many uses.*

used *adjective* not new, already owned by somebody. *It is sometimes possible to find a real bargain at used car sales, especially if you understand engines and can repair them.*

Roy did not trust the used car salesman.

AMAZING FACT

When the United States of America was formed, a vote was taken to decide what the official language of the US would be. English won, but only by one vote. Otherwise, the US would have been a German-speaking country.

"These whisks are my favourite cooking utensils," cried Mary.

WORD HISTORY

'Utopia' comes from a Latin word for 'no place' and was the title of a book by Sir Thomas More (1477–1536) describing an ideal land where everything is shared by everyone and where everyone is educated.

used to *verb* 1 accustomed to. *He isn't used to so much exercise.* 2 something that once happened often or that was once true. *We used to swim every afternoon.*

useful *adjective* helpful, having a purpose. *Useful tips on removing stains.* **usefulness** *noun. Gary's usefulness was very limited.*

useless *adjective* 1 of little or no help, having no effect. *It's useless asking him the way* . 2 (slang) very bad. *I'm useless at maths.* **uselessness** *noun.*

user *noun* a person who uses something. *A rehabilitation centre for drug users.*

user-friendly *adjective* designed to be easy to use and understand. *A user-friendly video-recorder.*

usual *adjective* happening often or most of the time, normal and everyday. *She arrived home at her usual time.* **usually** *adverb. We usually go shopping on Friday.*

utensil *noun* a tool or container, especially one used everyday in the home. *Cooking utensils.*

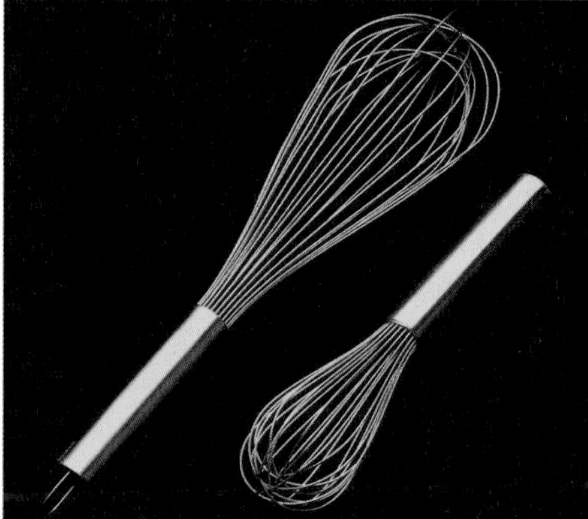

uterus *noun* the womb in which a baby develops. *The uterus was our first home.*

utmost *adjective* 1 the greatest possible. *It's a matter of the utmost importance.* 2 farthest. *The utmost ends of the Earth.*

utopia *noun* an imaginary place where everything is perfect, a paradise. **utopian** *adjective. Sarah leads a utopian existence.*

utter *verb* to speak or make a sound with your mouth. *He uttered a squeal of delight.*

utterly *adverb* completely. *An utterly stupid thing to do.* **utter** *adjective. An utter idiot.*

U-turn *noun* 1 a U-shaped turn that a vehicle makes to go back the way it came. 2 a reversal of plans.

Uzbekistan *noun* a country in West Asia.

Uzbekistan was a member of the Soviet Union. It became independent in 1991.

V

Vv

vacant *adjective* empty, unoccupied and not in use. *The bathroom is vacant.* **vacancy** *noun* a job that is available. *Are there any vacancies in the factory?* **vacate** *verb. The room should be vacated by 11 a.m.*

vacation *noun* 1 a holiday between terms at college or university. 2 (US) a holiday.

vaccinate *verb* (say **vak**-sin-ate) to inject somebody to protect them from a disease such as measles. **vaccination** *noun.*

vaccine *noun* (say **vak**-seen) a medicine made from the germs of a disease injected into people to protect them from the disease.

vacuum *noun* space that is quite empty with all gases removed. **vacuum** *verb* to clean with a vacuum-cleaner.

vacuum-cleaner *noun* an electrical machine that sucks up dust from carpets etc.

The first ever vacuum-cleaner was designed to blow the dust away rather than to suck it up.

Vaduz *noun* the capital of Liechtenstein.

vagina *noun* a passage in a woman's body that leads to the womb.

vague *noun* (say vayg) not clear or definite. *I could just see a vague shape in the twilight, but I couldn't identify who it was.*

vain *adjective* 1 too interested in your appearance or what you can do, too proud. 2 useless or unsuccessful, meaningless. *A vain attempt.* **in vain** without success.

valentine *noun* 1 a card you send to somebody you love on 14 February – Saint Valentine's Day. 2 the person to whom you send the card. *You are my valentine.*

valiant *adjective* brave.

valid *adjective* acceptable, legally acceptable. *A valid ticket.* **validity** *noun.*

WORD HISTORY

The shape of the letter V – as well as U and W – comes from a Semitic letter called 'waw', which was symbolized as a tenthook. The Romans used V for both V and U sounds. In the Middle Ages scholars began using U for the vowel sound and V for the consonant sound.

WORD HISTORY

Vandals were Germanic people who invaded Gaul, Spain and Rome in the fourth and fifth centuries, destroying beautiful cities, churches and palaces as they went. Any destructive people became known as vandals after the word was first used during the French Revolution.

Valletta *noun* the capital of Malta.

valley (valleys) *noun* low land between hills, usually with a river flowing through it.

valuable *adjective* 1 precious and worth a lot of money. **valuables** *plural noun.* 2 useful, helpful. *Valuable advice.*

value *noun* 1 the amount of money that something is worth or that it can be sold for, price. *What is the value of this diamond?* 2 the importance or usefulness of somebody or something. **value** *verb. I greatly value your friendship.*

valve *noun* a device on a tube, pipe etc. that controls the flow of a gas or liquid. You pump air into a tyre through a valve.

vampire *noun* in stories, a corpse that leaves its grave at night to suck people's blood.

The best way to protect yourself against a vampire is to carry a cross or some garlic.

van *noun* a small enclosed lorry for carrying goods. *The van delivered the new sofa.*

vandal *noun* a person who deliberately and for no good reason smashes and ruins things. **vandalize** *verb.* **vandalism** *noun.*

vane *noun* **weather vane** a pointer that moves with the direction of the wind and so shows which way the wind is blowing.

vanilla *noun* a sweet flavouring for ice cream, cakes etc. made from the pod of a tropical kind of orchid.

vanish *verb* to disappear, to become invisible. *The bus vanished into the mist.*

vanity *noun* being too proud of what you look like or of what you can do. Conceit.

Vanuatu *noun* a country of islands in the Pacific Ocean.

Eighty islands make up the Pacific nation of Vanuatu. Some are coral islands with reefs and brilliant blue lagoons.

vapour *noun* a gas produced by heating a liquid or solid form of the substance. Steam is water vapour.

variable *adjective* changing or varying a lot, not stable. *The weather has been variable.*

variation *noun* 1 varying. 2 something that has changed. 3 differences.

varied *adjective* different kinds of.

variety *noun* a collection or number of different things or kinds. *There are many varieties of sheep.*

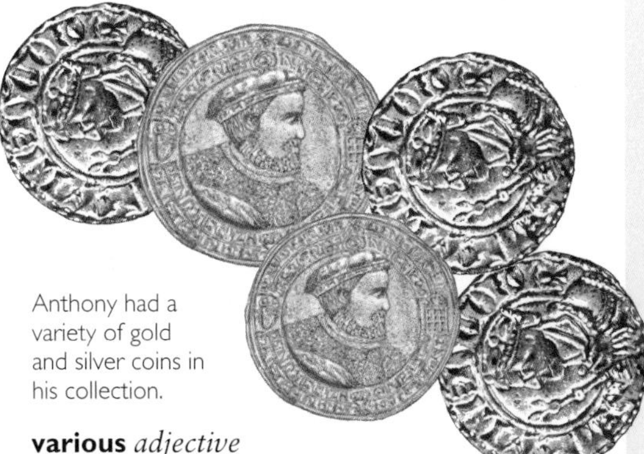

Anthony had a variety of gold and silver coins in his collection.

various *adjective* of different sorts, several. *Victor had various jobs after he left school.*

varnish *noun* a shiny, transparent liquid that you paint on to wood to protect it and to make it look glossy.

vary (varies, varying, varied) *verb* 1 to alter, to change constantly. *The weather varies from day to day.* 2 to make different. *I try to vary the menu from one day to the next.*

vase *noun* an ornamental container or jar for flowers.

vast *adjective* very wide, immense. *The vast rainforests of the Amazon.*

VAT *abbreviation* value-added tax.

vat *noun* a large container or tub for storing liquid. *A vat of wine.*

Vatican City *noun* an independent city and state within the city of Rome, Italy.

vault *noun* 1 a room below a church. A strong underground room in which to store valuable things. 2 an arched roof.

Down in the vaults the air was very cold and damp.

vault *verb* to jump over something using a pole. **vault** *noun*.

DID YOU KNOW

The word 'veal' comes from the French word for calf, 'veau'. After the Norman Conquest (1066) the French word for some animals was used for the name of the meat, so we get beef (from the French 'boeuf'), pork (from 'porc'), mutton (from 'mouton') and veal.

AMAZING FACT

Vatican City is the world's smallest independent country. It is tiny, about the size of a small farm, and stands on a hill in northwest Rome. Only about 750 people live there, yet it has its own flag, railroad and radio station and issues its own stamps.

VCR *abbreviation* video cassette recorder.

VDU *abbreviation* visual display unit.

veal *noun* the meat of a calf used as food.

veer *verb* to turn suddenly and change direction, to swerve.

vegan *noun* a vegetarian who does not use or eat any animal products.

vegetable *noun* a plant that is grown to be eaten. Carrots and peas are vegetables. **vegetable** *adjective. Vegetable curry.*

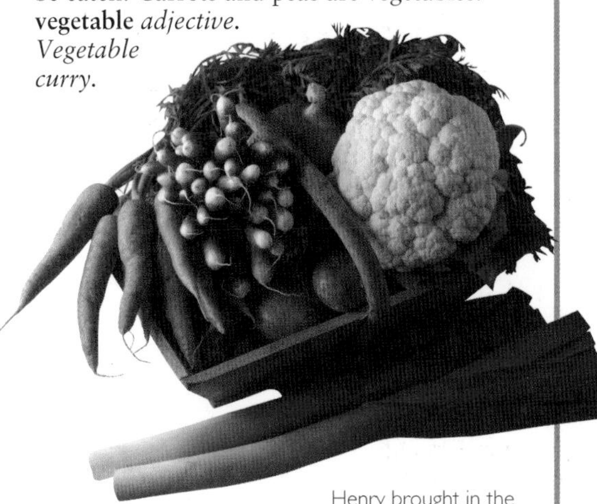

Henry brought in the vegetables that he had grown in his allotment.

vegetarian *noun* somebody who does not eat meat, only vegetables and sometimes dairy foods and fish.

vegetation *noun* plant life. *Rainforests have lush vegetation.*

vehicle *noun* a machine such as a car, bus or lorry that transports people and goods from one place to another on land.

veil *noun* a very fine piece of material worn by some women to cover their face or head.

vein *noun* (rhymes with pain) 1 one of the tubes inside your body through which blood flows back to your heart. 2 one of the fine lines on a leaf or insect wing.

velocity *noun* speed, particularly speed at which something travels in one direction.

velvet *noun* a material with a soft thick pile. *The cat sat on a velvet cushion.*

Venezuela *noun* a country in South America.

Venezuelan *noun* a person who comes from Venezuela. **Venezuelan** *adjective. Venezuelan oil wells.*

venison *noun* the meat from deer, used as food. *Vension was served at the banquet.*

venom *noun* poison produced by some snakes and spiders. **venomous** *adjective*.

ventilate *verb* to let fresh air move freely through a place. *A well-ventilated bathroom.* **ventilation** *noun*.

V

ventriloquist *noun* a person who entertains by making their voice seem to come not from their mouth but from a dummy or from another place.

venture *verb* to risk doing something. *'Nothing ventured, nothing gained.'* **venture** *noun. A risky business venture.*

verandah *noun* a platform around the outside of a house, usually with a roof.

verb *noun* a word or words in a sentence that describes what somebody or something is doing etc. In the sentence 'The dog is eating its bone,' 'is eating' is the verb.

verbose *adjective* using too many words. 'At this point in time' is a verbose way of saying 'now'.

verdict *noun* the decision of the judge and jury at the end of a trial in a law court saying whether the accused is guilty or not guilty. *The jury returned a verdict of guilty.*

verge *noun* the grassy strip of ground along the edge of a road or path. **verge** *verb. His behaviour verges on rudeness.*

verify (verifies, verifying, verified) *verb* to prove by showing the truth of something.

vermin *noun* any animal, bird or insect that can transmit a disease or that damages food crops. Pests.

The old house was infested with vermin.

verse *noun* 1 a part of a poem consisting of a group of lines. 2 poetry and having rhythm and sometimes rhyme.

version *noun* 1 one form or a changed type of something. *A new version of the Bible.* 2 one person's description. *Mary gave her version of the accident.*

versus *preposition* a Latin word meaning against, often shortened to v. *Swansea versus Cardiff. Sheffield v. Nottingham.*

vertebra (vertebrae) *noun* any one of the bones that make up the spine.

vertebrate *noun* any animal with a backbone. *Humans are vertebrates.*

vertical *adjective* upright, straight up. *The telegraph posts should be vertical.* The opposite is horizontal.

vessel *noun* 1 a ship or boat. 2 a container for liquids. *A drinking vessel.*

WORD HISTORY

The ancient Greeks believed that ventriloquism was the work of demons and thought the voice came from the abdomen. The word comes from the Latin 'venter' (belly) and 'loqui' meaning 'to speak'.

The train travelled across the viaduct.

WORD HISTORY

'Vermin' comes from a Latin word meaning 'worm'. It was later used to describe any unwanted animals.

Paul had a new vice clamped to his work bench.

AMAZING FACT

There are seven main groups of vertebrates: mammals, birds, reptiles, amphibians, fish, sharks, skates and, the simplest group, lampreys.

vet or **veterinary surgeon** *noun* a person who is trained to treat sick animals, an animal doctor.

veto *noun* the ability not to allow something to happen. **veto** *verb. The general vetoed the decision.*

vex (vexes, vexing, vexed) *verb* to annoy or worry somebody.

via *preposition* (say **vye**-ah) by way of. *We fly to Tehran via Rome.*

viable *adjective* likely to be successful, workable. *Building a bridge across the Atlantic is simply not viable.*

viaduct *noun* (say **vye**-a-dukt) a long, arched bridge that carries a road or railway across a valley.

vibrate *verb* to shake to and fro rapidly. *The windows vibrate when lorries whizz past.* **vibration** *noun.*

vicar *noun* a clergyman in charge of a parish in the Anglican Church.

vicarage *noun* the house where a vicar lives.

vice *noun* very bad, immoral or criminal behaviour. A bad habit.

vice *noun* a device that grips things firmly while you are working on them.

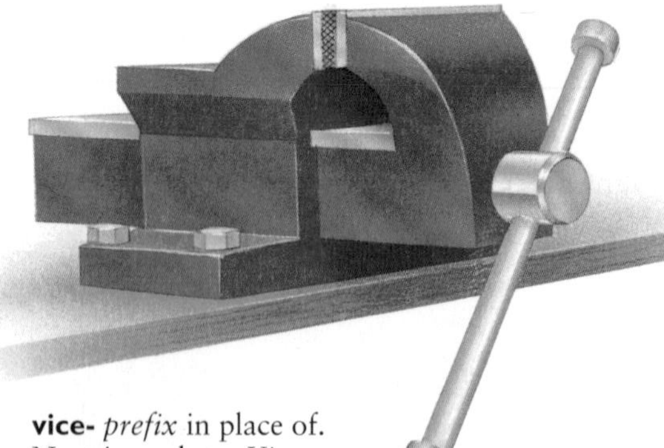

vice- *prefix* in place of. Next in rank to. *Vice-president.*

vice-versa *adverb* the same is true either way or the other way round. *When he wants to eat, she doesn't want to eat and vice versa.*

vicinity *noun* (say viss-**in**-it-ee) the surrounding or nearby area.

vicious *adjective* violent, cruel.

victim *noun* a person who has been attacked, injured, robbed or killed.

victimize *verb* to deliberately choose somebody to treat unfairly or cruelly.

victor *noun* the winner in a competition, battle etc. *The victor was given a medal.*

Victoria *noun* the capital of Seychelles.

victory *noun* success in a battle, contest etc. A win. **victorious** *adjective.*

video *noun* 1 a machine (video cassette recorder) that records television programmes so that you can watch them at another time. 2 a tape (videotape contained within a videocassette) used to record a television programme.

vie (vies, vying, vied) *verb* to compete.

Vienna *noun* the capital of Austria.

Vientiane *noun* the capital of Laos.

Vietnam *noun* a country in Southeast Asia.

Vietnamese *noun* a person who comes from Vietnam. **Vietnamese** *adjective. Vietnamese ricefields.*

vigorous *adjective* physically energetic, enthusiastic, strong. *A vigorous walk in the Black Forest.* **vigour** *noun.*

Vikings *plural noun* seafarers from Scandinavia who invaded many parts of Europe between the 8th and 11th centuries. **Viking** *adjective. Viking hordes.*

SPELLING NOTE

'Vigorous' is often misspelled. Notice how the 'u' of 'vigour' is dropped before the suffix '–ous' in vigorous. Also take care not to spell 'villain' as 'villian'.

vile *adjective* disgusting and very unpleasant, horrible. *A vile smell.*

villa *noun* a detached house with a garden in the suburbs. In Roman times a villa was a country house.

village *noun* a small group of houses, often with a church, school, shop and pub.

villain *noun* 1 a person who breaks the law on purpose. 2 a wicked person, especially in a film, novel etc. *The villain of the story was a cruel king.* **villainy** *noun.*

Vilnius *noun* the capital of Lithuania.

vine *noun* a climbing plant on which grapes grow. *A vine clambered up the terrace.*

vinegar *noun* a sharp-tasting liquid made from wine or malt and used to flavour food.

vineyard *noun* (say **vin**-yard) a place where grapes are grown for making wine.

We drank a full-bodied red wine that came from the south end of the vineyard.

vintage *adjective* (of wine) 1 a very good example of a particular year. 2 (of cars) made between 1919 and 1930. 3 of high and enduring quality.

The Vikings sailed for thousands of kilometres across the icy northern oceans in small wooden boats that were completely open to the elements. They leaped from their boats and rushed up the beach to make a surprise attack.

V

viola *noun* a stringed musical instrument that is slightly larger than a violin and with a lower sound. *The beautiful mellow sound of the viola reached my ears.*

Rachel played the viola in the youth orchestra.

violent *adjective* 1 using a lot of physical force to frighten, hurt or even kill. 2 sudden, strong and rough. *A violent storm blew up over the dark Sargasso Sea.* **violence** *noun. I don't like violence on television or in films.*

violet *noun* 1 a small plant with purplish flowers and a sweet smell. *Come, buy my lovely violets!* 2 the purplish colour of a violet. **violet** *adjective*.

violin *noun* a musical instrument with four strings stretched across a wooden frame. *Hilary was learning to play the violin.*

viper *noun* a European poisonous snake, an adder. *Ian was bitten by a viper.*

virgin *noun* a person who has never had sexual intercourse. *Queen Elizabeth I remained a virgin.* **virginity** *noun.*

virtual *adjective* 1 in practice, but not in name. *His wife was the virtual prime minister.* 2 almost but not completely; not actually said. *The virtual collapse of law and order.* **virtual reality** an impression of a real environment in which you can interact, created by a computer.

virtue *noun* a particular good quality, goodness. Kindness and honesty are virtues.

virus *noun* 1 a microscopically tiny organism or living thing, smaller than bacteria, that can carry or cause disease. *A flu virus.* 2 a computer program that can damage or destroy data in a computer.

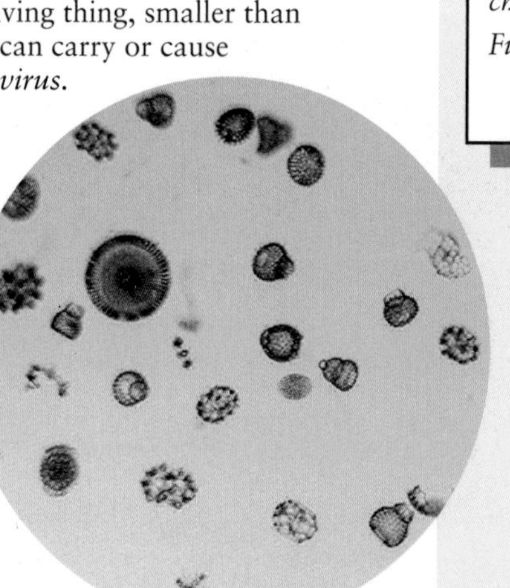

We looked at the virus under the microscope.

AMAZING FACT

New computer viruses are developed every day. A virus might send just a harmless joke or a cryptic message to your screen – or it could do serious damage.

WORD HISTORY

The word 'vitamin' is taken from the Latin word 'vita' meaning 'life' and the chemical 'amine'. The word was invented by the chemist Casimir Funk in 1913.

viscount *noun* (say **vie**-count) the title of a nobleman. *We invited the viscount and the viscountess to luncheon, but unfortunately, they had a prior engagement.*

viscountess *noun* (say **vie**-count-ess) the wife of a viscount. *The viscountess wore blue at her sister's wedding.*

visible *adjective* capable of being seen. *From the top of a bus the whole street is visible.* **visibility** *noun* how clearly you can see. *On foggy days visibility is poor.*

vision *noun* 1 sight, your ability to see. 2 what you can see or imagine in a dream. 3 great power of imagination and ability to plan. *His vision is that everybody should own their own home.*

visit *verb* 1 to go to see somebody or a place. 2 to stay somewhere for a short time. **visit** *noun.* **visitor** *noun.*

visual *adjective* relating to seeing and sight. *Computers display information on a visual display unit.*

visualize *verb* to form a picture in your mind, to imagine. *Can you visualize the awful situation Jane put me into?*

vital *adjective* essential to life, very important. *Air and water are vital to all living creatures.*

vitality *adjective* full of life and energy.

vitamin *noun* any one of several substances in food that we need to stay healthy. *Terry takes a vitamin supplement with her morning coffee.*

vivid *adjective* bright and clear. *Vivid colours are the ones I like best.*

vivisection *noun* the use of living animals in scientific experiments.

vixen *noun* a female fox. The male is called a dog. The young are called cubs.

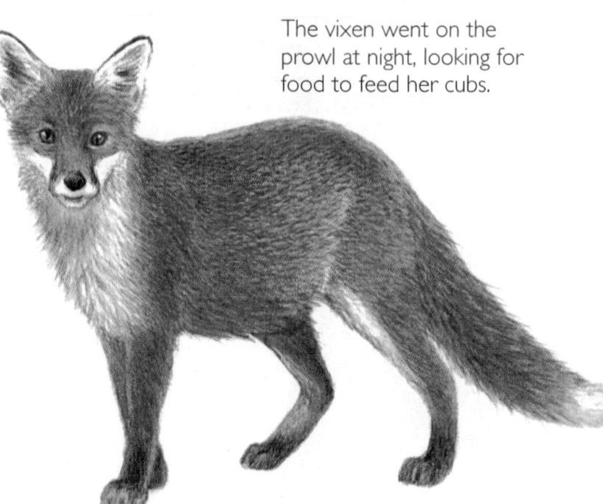

The vixen went on the prowl at night, looking for food to feed her cubs.

viz *adverb* namely.

vocabulary *noun* all the words somebody knows in a language. *His vocabulary in Spanish is about 1,000 words.*

vocal *adjective* 1 relating to the voice. *Vocal cords.* 2 speaking out freely and loudly. *He is very vocal about his beliefs.*

vocation *noun* a calling or very strong feeling that you want to do a particular job. *Dan had a vocation to become a priest.* 2 a profession or occupation, a career.

vodka *noun* a colourless, strong alcoholic drink. *Penny likes vodka and tomato juice.*

vogue *noun* a fashion.

voice *noun* the sound produced by your vocal cords when you speak or sing, the power to speak.

void *noun* emptiness, a huge space with nothing in it. **void** *adjective* having no legal effect. *Null and void.*

volcano (volcanoes) *noun* a mountain with a crater (hole) on top through which molten lava from below the Earth's crust erupts from time to time. **volcanic** *adjective.*

WORD HISTORY

'Vodka' is a Russian word meaning 'little water'. Other Russian words that have come into the English language include 'steppe', 'tundra' and 'samovar'.

AMAZING FACT

Volcanoes have caused enormous damage throughout history. One of the most famous of volcanoes, Vesuvius, destroyed the city of Pompeii in AD 79.

volume *noun* 1 the amount of space that something takes up or contains. *The volume of water in the lake.* 2 one of a set of books. *A 20-volume encyclopedia.* 3 the loudness of sound. *Turn up the volume so I can hear.*

voluntary *adjective* done willingly and not because you have been forced. *She made a voluntary statement.* 2 done without payment. *She does voluntary work for charity.* **volunteer** *noun.*

vomit *verb* to bring food back from your stomach through your mouth, to be sick.

vote *verb* to choose from a group the person or thing you prefer by raising your hand or marking a piece of paper. **vote** *noun. Each candidate got three votes.*

vow *verb* to make a very serious promise, to pledge. *He vowed to improve conditions for all the householders in the street.* **vow** *noun.*

vowel *noun* a letter that is not a consonant – a,e,i,o and u and sometimes y.

voyage *noun* a long sea journey.

vulgar *adjective* rude, offensive, coarse. **vulgarity** *noun. The teacher put a stop to vulgarity in the playground.*

vulnerable *adjective* easily harmed because unprotected, weak. *Old people are particularly vulnerable during the cold winter months.* **vulnerability** *noun.*

vulture *noun* a large bird of prey that feeds mostly on carrion (dead animals). *The vulture swooped out of the sky and landed on the sheep's carcass.*

When a volcano erupts, igneous rocks are formed from magma, which may solidify beneath or on the Earth's surface. Magma reaches the surface through vents, which are holes in the ground.

wad *noun* a thick lump of soft material, a tight bundle or pile of paper. *A wad of banknotes was thrust into my hand.*

waddle *verb* to walk in a clumsy way with short steps like a duck.

wade *verb* to walk through water or mud. To move slowly and with difficulty.

wafer *noun* a very thin crisp biscuit.

waffle *noun* a light crisp cake made of batter with a pattern of little squares on it. Waffles are very popular in North America.

waffle *verb* to speak or write eloquently and at great length without saying anything important. **waffle** *noun. What a lot of waffle you talk!*

wag (wags, wagging, wagged) *verb* to move quickly from side to side or up and down. *The cat wagged its tail in anger.*

wage (wages, waging, waged) *verb* to begin and carry on something for a period of time. *The police are waging war on car theft.*

wages *plural noun* the money you earn for the work you do.

wagon *noun* 1 a four-wheeled cart pulled by a horse. 2 an open railway truck for carrying freight. *Twenty wagons carrying coal.*

The wagons rolled westwards across America. The weary people were in search of a dream.

wail *noun* a long, sad cry. **wail** *verb. The wind wailed in the trees.*

waist *noun* the narrow, middle part of your body above your hips.

waistcoat *noun* a close-fitting jacket without sleeves, usually worn under another jacket (US vest).

wait *verb* to stay where you are until something happens or someone arrives, to pause. *We waited 15 minutes for the bus.*

DID YOU KNOW

The shape of the letter W – as well as U and V - developed from a Semitic letter called 'waw' which was symbolized as a tenthook. The Romans used V for both V and U sounds. In the Middle Ages scholars began using U for the vowel sound and they doubled the U to make W and called the new letter double U.

waiter *noun* a man or a woman (also waitress) who brings food and drinks to you in a restaurant.

wake (waking, woke, woken) *verb* 1 to stop being asleep. 2 to rouse somebody from sleep. **wake** *noun* (especially in Ireland) a group of people who stay with a dead body to mourn on the night before it is buried.

Wales *noun* a country that is part of the United Kingdom.

walk *verb* to move along on your feet. **walk** *noun. A walk in the hills.* **walker** *noun.* **walk off with** to take something without asking. **walk-over** an easy victory in a competition.

wall *noun* a structure made of bricks or stones surrounding a piece of land. The side of a building or room. **walled** *adjective. A walled garden.* **up the wall** crazy. *The noise is sending me up the wall.*

wallaby *noun* a small kind of kangaroo.

Wallabies are marsupials. The female wallaby carries her baby in a pouch.

wallet *noun* a small, folding case or purse for keeping money and credit cards.

wallflower *noun* 1 a sweet-smelling plant with red or orange flowers. 2 somebody who nobody ever seems to want to dance with.

wallow *verb* 1 to roll and splash about in water or mud. 2 to enjoy something to excess. *She wallowed in everybody's praise.*

walnut *noun* the edible nut of the walnut tree. Walnut wood is used for furniture.

walrus *noun* a large sea animal similar to a seal with two long tusks.

waltz *noun* a graceful dance for two people with three beats to a bar.

wan *adjective* pale and tired-looking.

wand *noun* a stick that magicians and fairies use to perform magic.

wander *verb* to move slowly from one place to another without going in any particular direction, to roam. **wanderer** *noun.*

wane *verb* to become smaller, to lose power. *The Moon is waning tonight.* The opposite is to wax.

want *verb* 1 to desire something or to wish to do something. *I want to go home.* 2 to need. *The dogs want feeding.*

war *noun* 1 armed fighting between countries or groups of people. A long period of fighting. 2 a struggle or campaign. *The war against poverty.*

Shortly after the tanks landed on the beach, the soldiers charged ahead to fight the war.

ward *noun* 1 a room in a hospital with beds where patients are treated. 2 a ward of court is a child who is under the protection of a court or an adult guardian. 3 a part into which a town is divided for voting.

-ward, -wards *suffix* in the particular direction of. *Homewards, southward.*

warden *noun* somebody who is in charge of a college, hostel etc., a guard. *Tom wants to be a traffic warden when he grows up.*

warder *noun* a prison guard.

wardrobe *noun* a cupboard in which to hang your clothes.

warehouse *noun* a building for storing goods that are to be sold.

The farmer used his barn as a warehouse for the fertilizers he was selling.

warfare *noun* the state of fighting wars.

warlike *adjective* hostile and prepared for war. *The soldiers had a warlike manner.*

warm *adjective* 1 slightly hot but not too hot. 2 friendly and enthusiastic. *A warm smile.* **warm** *verb. Can you warm the plates?* **warmth** *noun. The warmth of the Sun is doing my old bones a lot of good.*

warn *verb* 1 to tell somebody about a possible danger in the future. 2 to advise. *He warned me to go carefully.* **warning** *noun* a notice or statement that warns.

DID YOU KNOW

The 'DC' in Washington DC stands for District of Columbia. The city of Washington covers the entire District. The site was chosen by George Washington in 1790 and planned by the French engineer Pierre L'Enfant.

warp *verb* to become twisted or misshapen through damp or heat. *The heat of the fire has warped the table.*

warren *noun* a network of underground burrows or passages in which rabbits live.

warrior *noun* a great fighting soldier.

Warsaw *noun* the capital of Poland.

warship *noun* a ship armed with guns for use in war.

wart *noun* a hard lump on your skin. **warty** *adjective. He has warty hands.*

was past tense of be.

wash *verb* 1 to clean with water, soap etc. *Wash your hands.* 2 to flow over or against something. 3 to carry away by flowing water. *The rain washed the mud away.*

washing *noun* clothes that need washing or that have been washed.

The washing blew madly on the line and was dry in no time in the warm sunshine.

washing-machine *noun* a machine that washes clothes.

washing-up *noun* the plates, knives and forks etc. that you wash after a meal. **wash up** *verb. I'll wash up, you dry.*

Washington DC *noun* the capital of the United States of America.

wasp *noun* a yellow and black striped insect that can sting.

waste *noun* 1 things that you throw away because they are broken, worn or you do not need them any more, rubbish. 2 not using things in a careful way. *It's a waste to throw away food.* **waste** *verb* to use more of something than you need or to throw something away that could be used. **waste** *adjective. Waste paper.*

wasteful *adjective* extravagant, using more than is needed. **wastefulness** *noun.*

wastepaper basket *noun* a basket or container for paper rubbish.

watch *verb* 1 to look at for some time. *Watch how I do this.* 2 to notice and be careful about something. *Watch how you cross the road.* 3 to keep guard or take care of somebody or something. *Watch the soup doesn't boil over.* **watchdog** *noun* a dog that guards property **watch out!** be careful.

W

watch *noun* a small clock that you usually wear on your wrist.

watchful *adjective* always noticing what is happening, alert. **watchfulness** *noun.*

water *noun* a clear liquid that falls as rain and that all living things drink to survive. Water is found in oceans, rivers and lakes. Water is made of two gases – oxygen and hydrogen. **water** *verb* 1 to pour water on. 2 to produce tears in the eyes or saliva in the mouth. 3 to dilute.

watercolour *noun* a painting done with watercolours, paints you mix with water.

waterfall *noun* water from a stream or river flowing down over a cliff or big rock to the ground below.

water-lily *noun* a plant with flat, floating leaves that grows in water.

watermill *noun* a mill – a tall building for grinding grain – with machinery powered by water. *The watermill on the River Floss.*

The wheel on the mill is turned by the running water. The energy is used to turn stones inside the mill to grind corn into flour.

water-polo *noun* a ball game played in a swimming pool by two teams of seven players. *Water-polo is a sport of the rich.*

waterproof *adjective* not letting water through. *A waterproof coat.*

water-skiing *noun* a sport of skimming over the water on skis, towed by a rope attached to a motorboat.

watertight *adjective* closed so tightly that water cannot get through.

watery *adjective* full of water or containing too much water. *Watery soup.*

watt *noun* a unit of electricity.

wave *noun* 1 a moving curved line or ridge on the surface of water, especially the sea. 2 a curl or curved piece of hair. 3 the vibrating way in which energy such as heat, light, sound and radio travels. 4 the act of moving your hand up and down to attract attention, say goodbye etc.

wave *verb* 1 to move your hand up and down to say 'hello' or 'goodbye'. 2 to move something quickly to and fro, to flutter. *The flag waves in the wind.*

All the different colours of light have different wavelengths. The longest waves we can see are red.

HANDY HINT

Remember the order of the colours of the spectrum – red, orange, yellow, green, blue, indigo, violet – by using a mnemonic (a word or sentence made up of the first letter of each word.)

'Richard of York gave battle in vain.' or 'Roy G. Biv'.

WORD HISTORY

Watt, the unit of electricity, is named after James Watt, a Scottish inventor who developed the steam engine.

HANDY HINT

Be careful when you write words that sound the same, like 'wear' and 'where'.

wavelength *noun* 1 the size of a radio wave to transmit a programme. 2 the distance between electrical, radio or sound waves.

wax *noun* 1 a solid substance made from fat or oil that becomes soft and sticky when you heat it. Wax is used to make things like candles and furniture polish. 2 a similar substance produced by bees (beeswax). 3 a wax-like substance found in your ears.

wax *verb* to grow bigger. *The Moon waxes and then it wanes (grows smaller).*

way (ways) *noun* 1 an opening, a passage. *Don't block the way.* 2 a road or path that you should follow, a route. *Is this the way home?* 3 a direction. *Look the other way.* 4 a distance that you travel. *It's a long way to your aunty Lou's.* 5 a state or condition. *He's in a bad way.* 6 means or method of doing something. *Is this the right way to mix paints?* 7 manner. *In a clumsy way.* 8 **ways** customs. The typical behaviour of somebody. **by the way** incidentally. **in the way** blocking the place you want to go.

-ways *suffix* in the direction of. *Widthways.*

weak *adjective* having little strength or power, easily broken. **weakness** *noun.*

weaken *verb* to make or become weak.

wealth *noun* 1 a lot of money and possessions, great riches. 2 a large amount. *A wealth of detail.* **wealthy** *adjective* rich.

weapon *noun* some device such as a gun, dagger or sword with which to fight.

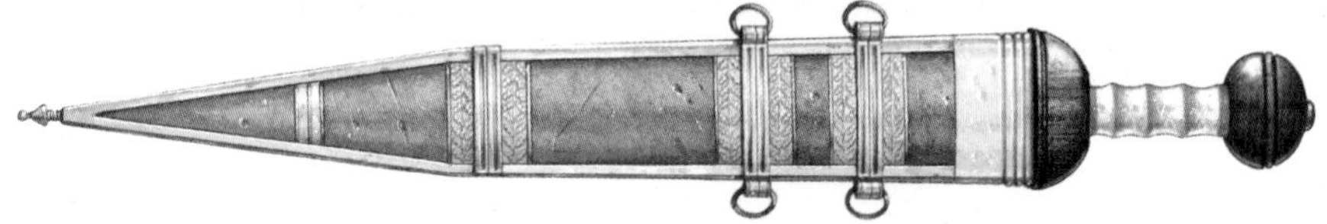

The magnificent dagger in its scabbard was one of the prize weapons in the museum's collection.

wear (wears, wearing, wore, worn) *verb* 1 to be dressed in, to have on your body. *Do you wear glasses?* 2 to become damaged through use. *I wore a hole in the knee.* **wear** *noun. Men's wear.* **wear down** to weaken a person's resistance. *She wore him down with her nagging.* **wear off** to fade away or to become less. *The pain is wearing off.* **wear out** 1 to become damaged and useless. 2 to feel tired.

wearing *adjective* tiring, exhausting.

weary (wearier, weariest) *adjective* very tired. *You must be weary after your long journey.* **weariness** *noun.*

weather *noun* the condition of the atmosphere at a particular time or place. Whether it is warm, cold, windy or rainy.

weathercock *noun* a weathervane shaped like a cockerel.

weather forecast *noun* a report on what the weather is expected to be like in the near future. *The weather forecast is good.*

weathervane *noun* a pointer that moves with the wind and so shows which way the wind is blowing.

weave (weaves, weaving, woven, woven) *verb* 1 to make cloth by using a machine called a loom that passes threads over and under other threads. 2 to make baskets etc. by plaiting cane etc. 3 (past tense weaved) to move in and out between people or things. *He weaved through the traffic on his bike.*

web *noun* **cobweb** a fine sticky net of threads spun by a spider to catch insects.

webbed *adjective* having the toes joined by pieces of skin. *Ducks and geese have webbed feet to help them swim better.*

Dewdrops glistened on the spider's web that morning.

wedding *noun* the marriage service.

we'd *abbreviation* we had.

wedge *noun* 1 a piece of wood that is thick at one end and thin and pointed at the other, used to stop things such as doors from moving. 2 something in the shape of a wedge. *A wedge of cheese.* **wedge** *verb. She wedged the door open.*

wee *adjective* very small.

weed *noun* a wild plant that grows where it is not wanted. **weed** *verb* to remove weeds.

weedy *adjective* 1 full of weeds. 2 weak and thin. *A weedy person.*

week *noun* a period of time from Monday to the following Sunday. There are seven days in a week and 52 weeks in a year. **weekly** *noun. A weekly magazine.*

weekend *noun* Saturday and Sunday.

weep (weeps, weeping, wept) *verb* to cry. *She wept when she read the sad story.*

SPELLING NOTE

Avoid misspelling these words, which sound similar: 'weather' and 'whether'; 'weave' and 'we've'; 'we'd' and 'weed'; 'week' and 'weak'; 'weigh' and 'way'; 'weight' and 'wait'.

WORD BUILDING

Here are some words with the prefix 'well–': 'well-advised'; 'well-balanced'; 'well-behaved'; 'well-bred'; 'well-built'; 'well-earned'; 'well-educated'; 'well-fed'; 'well-groomed'; 'well-informed' and 'well-intentioned'.

weigh *verb* 1 to place something on scales to find out how heavy it is. 2 to have a certain weight. *Dave weighs more than he used to.*

weight *noun* 1 how heavy somebody or something is. 2 a unit of weight or a piece of metal of a certain weight.

There were two sets of weights, one to weigh cooking ingredients, the other for heavier things.

weird *adjective* very strange, unusual.

welcome *verb* to greet somebody in a way that shows that you are very pleased to see them. **welcome** *noun, interjection. Welcome home!* **welcoming** *adjective.*

weld *verb* to join two pieces of metal together by melting the ends and pressing and hammering them together. **welder** *noun.*

welfare *noun* 1 A person's welfare is their general wellbeing, health, happiness and prosperity. 2 money or help a person in need gets from the state.

well *noun* a very deep hole in the ground from which you can get water or oil from far beneath the Earth.

well *adjective* in good health, in good order. *I'm very well thank you.* **well** *adverb* 1 in a good or correct way. *Wendy plays tennis well.* 2 thoroughly. *I washed the car very well.* 3 also. *Two packets of crisps and a bar of chocolate as well.* **well** *interjection. Well, I hope you had a nice time.*

we'll *abbreviation* we shall or we will.

Wellington *noun* the capital of New Zealand.

wellingtons or wellington boots *plural noun* rubber or plastic boots up to your knees that keep your feet and legs dry.

John kept his wellingtons by the door so he could go straight out into the farmyard in the morning.

W

well-off *adjective* wealthy. *We are well-off.*

Welsh *noun* the language of Wales. **the Welsh** the people of Wales. **Welsh** *adjective. Welsh sheep are very hardy.*

went past tense of go.

wept past tense of weep.

were past tense of be.

we're short for we are.

weren't short for were not.

werewolf *noun* in stories and folklore, a man who sometimes turns into a wolf, usually at full moon.

David gave a charming smile, and we suddenly realized that he had turned into a werewolf.

west *noun* the direction in which the Sun sets. The opposite direction is east. **west** *adjective, adverb. They travelled west.*

western *adjective* relating to the west, of the west. *Western Europe.* **western** *noun* a book or film about life in the 19th century in the western USA and involving gunfights and cowboys.

Western Samoa *noun* a country of islands in the Pacific Ocean.

West Indian *noun* a person from the West Indies. **West Indian** *adjective. A West Indian cricketer won the man of the match award.*

West Indies *plural noun* a series of islands that separate the Caribbean Sea from the Atlantic Ocean.

wet (wetter, wettest) *adjective* covered with or full of water or some other liquid. 2 rainy. *The weekend was very wet.* **wet** (wets, wetting, wet or wetted) *verb* to make something wet. The opposite is dry.

we've short for we have.

whale *noun* a very large sea mammal that looks like a fish. Whales need air to breathe.

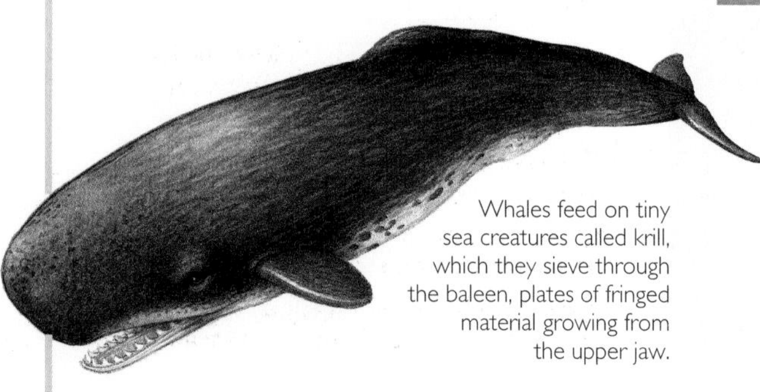

Whales feed on tiny sea creatures called krill, which they sieve through the baleen, plates of fringed material growing from the upper jaw.

AMAZING FACT

The biggest animal that has ever lived is the blue whale. It may grow to more than 30 metres in length and weighs about 160 tons when fully grown. Blue whales have been hunted by whalers over the years and are now very rare.

SPELLING NOTE

The following words sound similar and should not be confused: 'we're' and 'weir' (a small dam across a river), 'we've' and 'weave', 'whale' and 'wail' (a long, sad cry), 'wheel' and 'we'll', 'where' and 'ware', 'whine' and 'wine'.

wharf (wharfs or wharves) *noun* platform or landing place where ships dock to be loaded or unloaded.

wheat *noun* a cereal crop from whose grain flour is made.

Wheat is the world's second largest crop after rice.

wheel *noun* a circular object or disc that rotates around an axle and that is used to move a vehicle or help make machinery work. **wheel** *verb. She wheeled the trolley down the aisle.*

wheelbarrow *noun* a small handcart with one wheel at the front and two legs and two handles at the back.

wheelchair *noun* a chair with large wheels for somebody who cannot walk easily.

when *adverb, conjunction* 1 at what time. *When does the bus arrive?* 2 at the time that. *When I get home I change my clothes.*

whenever *adverb, conjunction* when, at every time, at any time. *Come whenever you like, as long as you bring me a present.*

where *adverb* 1 in what place. *Where's the dog?* 2 to what place. *Where did you go at the weekend?* 3 from what place. *Where did you find those shoes?* **where** *conjunction* at or in what place. *He went over to the window where there was more light.*

whiff *noun* a sudden, slight scent of something. *A whiff of honeysuckle.*

whim *noun* a sudden, and often silly, desire or thought. *On a sudden whim, Richard bought two tickets for Paris and gave one to the delighted Sarah.*

whimper *verb* to make a quiet, crying noise because of pain. **whimper** *noun. The puppy gave a frightened whimper.*

whine *verb* to keep moaning and complaining in a miserable, irritating voice.

whinge *verb* to grumble and complain all the time. **whinger** *noun. Steve was a real whinger, but no one took any notice of him.*

whip *noun* a strip of leather or a cord attached to a stick, used for hitting animals. **whip** (whips, whipping, whipped) *verb* 1 to hit with a whip. 2 to whisk or beat eggs etc. until they are stiff. 3 to move very quickly. *The actress whipped off her clothes.*

whirl *verb* to move round and round quickly. **whirl** *noun. A whirl of activity.*

whirlpool *noun* a current of water that turns round and round rapidly.

Janet stared mesmerised into the whirlpool, hoping she would not be sucked in.

whirlwind *noun* a strong wind that spins as it travels over land and sea.

whisk *noun* a kitchen implement made of wire for beating air into eggs, cream etc. **whisk** verb. *The chef whisked the sauce.*

whisker *noun* 1 a long, stiff hair growing around the mouth of an animal such as a cat or dog. 2 hair growing on a man's face.

whisky *noun* an alcoholic drink made from barley, rye or other grains *Whisky and water.* (Ireland and USA whiskey).

whisper *verb* to speak very quietly using only your breath without vibrating your vocal cords. **whisper** *noun.*

whistle *noun* 1 the shrill noise you can make when you blow through your lips. 2 a device you blow to make a sound like a whistle. **whistle** *verb. He whistled a happy tune.*

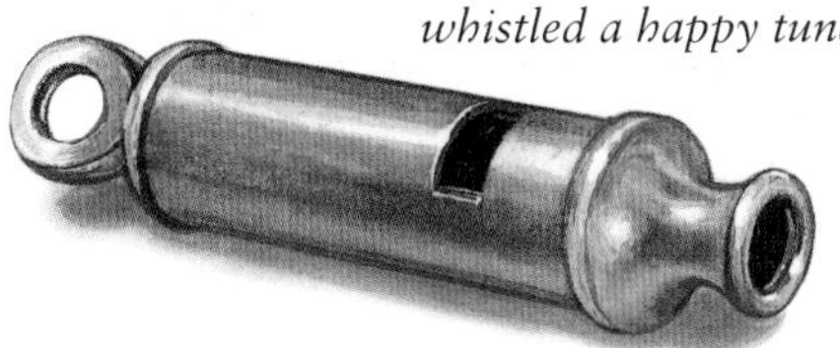

white *noun* 1 the colour of milk or new snow. 2 the liquid in an egg around the yoke. 3 (often White) a person belonging to a race with light-coloured skin. **white** *adjective.* **whiten** *verb.* **white lie** a small lie told in order to avoid hurting somebody's feelings. *It was just a little white lie.*

whizz (whizzes, whizzing, whizzed) *verb* to move very quickly with a rushing noise. *The racing cars whizzed past.*

whizz kid *noun* a very clever and successful young person. *Dean is a real whizz kid.*

WHO *abbreviation* World Health Organization.

GRAMMAR NOTE

Try not to confuse 'who's' and 'whose'. 'Who's' is an abbreviation of 'who has' or 'who is', as in 'Who's eaten all the cake?' 'Whose' means 'of whom' or 'of which', as in 'The man whose mother is a singer.' It also means 'of whom' in questions, as in 'Whose book is this?'

WORD HISTORY

'Whisky' comes from Gaelic words meaning 'water of life'. Gaelic is the original language of Scotland.

"Stop, thief!" cried Granddad, and he blew his whistle, racing after the burglar.

AMAZING FACT

Words like WHO are acronyms, words made up of the first letter of each of the words in a title. Other acronyms are NATO, North Atlantic Treaty Organization and SCUBA, self-contained underwater breathing apparatus.

whole *adjective* the complete and total amount of something. *She ate a whole box of chocolates.* **whole** *noun. Two halves make a whole.*

wholesale *noun* 1 the sale of goods in large quantities or amounts by a wholesaler to shops (retailers) who then sell to the public. 2 on a big scale. *Wholesale slaughter.*

wholesome *adjective* good for you. *Wholesome soup.*

whooping cough *noun* an infectious disease that makes you cough a lot and make a terrible noise as you breathe in.

who's short for who is.

why *adverb* for what reason.

wick *noun* the twisted thread in a candle or oil lamp which you light.

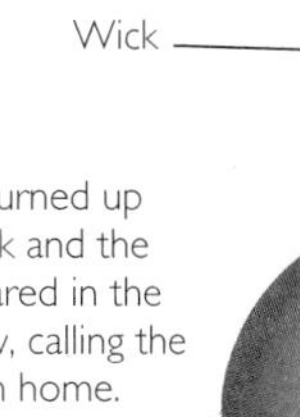

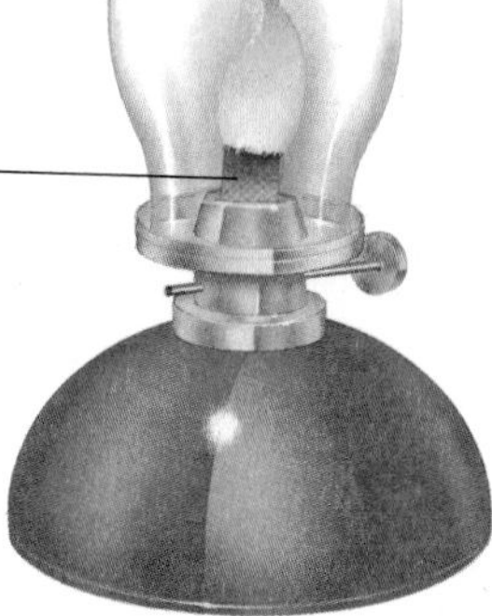

Matty turned up the wick and the lamp flared in the window, calling the children home.

wicked *noun* very bad, evil and cruel. **wickedness** *noun.*

wicket *noun* three stumps with two bails on top at which the ball is bowled in cricket.

wide *adjective* 1 measuring a long way from one side to the other, broad. *Motorways are very wide roads.* 2 measuring a certain distance. *10 m wide.* 3 including a large area or variety. *Wide experience.* The opposite of wide is narrow.

widespread *adjective* happening over a wide area or among many people. *Widespread flooding.*

widow *noun* a woman whose husband has died. *The widow sobbed beside the grave.*

widower *noun* a man whose wife has died.

width *noun* how much something measures from one side to the other. *What is the width of the door?*

wield *verb* 1 to hold and use with the hands. *He wielded an axe.* 2 to exercise power. *Dictators wield complete power.*

wife (wives) *noun* the woman that a man marries. *The sultan had 20 wives.*

wig *noun* a false covering of hair that fits on a bald head or over somebody's own hair.

wigwam *noun* a dome-shaped tent made from animal skins by Native Americans.

wild *adjective* 1 natural and not cultivated or tamed by people. *A wild flower.* 2 uncontrolled, angry. *A wild night.*

wilderness *noun* a wild, uncultivated area where nobody lives. A desert.

wildlife *noun* wild animals and plants in their natural habitats.

will *noun* 1 an ability to make firm decisions, determination. *A will to win.* 2 what somebody wants. *The will of the people.* 3 a written document listing who is to have your belongings and money after your death. *I burned my will.*

willing *adjective* happy to do whatever is needed. **willingness** *noun. Eva always shows a great willingness to help.*

willow *noun* a tree with long thin, hanging branches that grows near water.

The weeping willow is a graceful tree to plant beside a pond.

willowy *adjective* tall and graceful like a willow tree. *A willowy young girl.*

wilt *verb* to become weak and droop and shrivel like a plant without water.

wily (wilier, wiliest) *adjective* cunning and full of artful tricks.

wimp *noun* a man who is weak, feeble and lacking courage. *Poor Rob is a real wimp.*

win (wins, winning, won) *verb* 1 to come first in a contest. 2 to obtain something through luck. *He won the lottery.* **win** *noun.*

wince *verb* to jerk and make your face look twisted because of pain or fear.

winch *noun* a machine with a rope around a turning part for lifting things.

wind (winds, winding, wound) *verb* (rhymes with kind) 1 to bend and twist. 2 to roll or wrap around. 3 to tighten a clock spring. **wind up** 1 to end in a place or situation. 2 to tease. *Stop winding me up.*

wind *noun* (rhymes with pinned) 1 a strong moving current of air. **windy** *adjective. A windy day.* 2 gases in the stomach that make you feel uncomfortable.

winded *adjective* out of breath through heavy exercise.

Windhoek *noun* the capital of Namibia.

DID YOU KNOW

The American's use different words for many parts of a motor car (automobile). Besides 'windshield' (for 'windscreen') they say 'fenders' ('bumpers'), 'gear shift' ('gear lever') 'hood' ('bonnet') and 'muffler' ('silencer').

AMAZING FACT

In Greek mythology, Icarus tried to escape imprisonment by fastening wings made of wax and feathers to his shoulders. Icarus flew so close to the Sun that the wax melted and he fell to his death.

wind instrument *noun* a musical instrument that you play by blowing into it. *Clarinets, flutes and trombones are wind instruments.*

windmill *noun* a mill – a tall building for pumping water, grinding grain etc. – with machines powered by wind blowing a set of arm-like sails.

Some windmills are still working, others have been turned into museums or homes.

window *noun* a hole covered with glass in a wall or roof of a building that lets in light and air.

windpipe *noun* a tube leading from your mouth to your lungs that carries air to your lungs. *A fishbone got stuck in her windpipe.*

windscreen *noun* the window at the front of a car, lorry etc. (US windshield).

windsurf *verb* to ride over waves on a special board with a sail. **windsurfer** *noun.*

wine *noun* an alcoholic drink made from grapes or sometimes other plants.

wing *noun* 1 one of the parts of a bird, bat or insect used for flying. 2 one of the parts sticking out of the side of an aircraft that it uses for flying. 3 one of the parts covering a wheel of a car. 4 a part of a building that stands out from the main part. *The east wing.* 5 a side of a stage hidden from the audience. 6 the right or left edge of the pitch in games such as hockey, rugby and soccer.

Birds evolved the power of flight millions of years ago. Humans have tried and failed to fly, like birds, with wings.

wingspan *noun* the length across the wings of a bird, insect or aeroplane.

wink *verb* 1 to open and close one eye quickly. 2 (of light) to flash on and off. **wink** *noun. He gave me a wink to show that he was only joking.*

winner *noun* a person, animal or vehicle that wins a race, contest etc.

winning *adjective* charming. *Will has a winning smile, but he doesn't fool me!*

winnings *plural noun* money that has been won. *She frittered all her winnings away.*

winter *noun* the season of the year between autumn and spring. **wintry** *adjective.*

wipe *verb* to rub something with your hand or a cloth in order to clean or dry it. **wiper** *noun* a windscreen wiper.

wire *noun* a thin length of metal that can easily be twisted, used especially to carry electricity and for fencing. **wire** *verb* to put in wires to carry electricity. *The house was wired last year.* **wire** *adjective. Wire fencing.*

wireless *noun* an old-fashioned word for radio. *Let's listen to the wireless tonight.*

wisdom *noun* being wise and having great understanding and judgement. **wisdom tooth** *noun* a tooth that sometimes grows at the back of your jaw after the other teeth have stopped growing.

wise *adjective* sensible and having a great understanding and experience of something, knowing the right action or decision.

-wise *suffix* 1 acting like somebody or something. In the direction of. *Clockwise.* 2 with reference to something. *Health-wise, I'm fine, and so is your dear father.*

wish *verb* 1 to want or to desire something. 2 to say that you hope something will happen. *I wish you well.* **wish** *noun* a strong desire for something. *A wish to travel.*

wishbone *noun* the V-shaped bone in the breast of birds.

wit *noun* 1 common sense, the ability to think clearly. 2 skill in saying things in a clever and funny way. 3 a clever and amusing person. *He's a great wit.* **witty** *adjective. What a witty writer!* **at your wits' end** not knowing how to solve a serious and worrying problem.

-witted *suffix* having a particular kind of ability. *Quick-witted.*

witch *noun* a woman in fairy stories who can perform magic.

witchcraft *noun* magic used by witches.

The witch said a magic spell over the toad and turned it into a prince.

AMAZING FACT

Radio broadcasting, from a 'wireless' began in 1920. The system for naming radio stations, or assigning call letters, in the US is based on which side of the Mississippi River the station is based. Stations to the east of the Mississippi start with the letter 'K' like KROC, stations west of the Mississippi begin with the letter 'W'.

SPELLING NOTE

Are you a pronunciation wizard? Try these: 'bough', 'cough', 'enough', 'plough', 'hiccough', 'through', 'though', 'thought', 'thorough'.

AMAZING FACT

The Salem Witchcraft Trials took place in Salem, Massachusettes in 1692. As a result of the trials, nineteen people were hanged for witchcraft.

witchdoctor *noun* a person who is believed to have magic powers to cure illnesses.

withdraw (withdraws, withdrawing, withdrew, withdrawn) *verb* 1 to take back or take away, to remove. *She withdrew £100 from her bank account.* 2 to go away from. *After the war the troops withdrew.* **withdrawal** *noun.* **withdrawn** *adjective.* 1 remote. 2 unable to communicate. *She's unhappy and withdrawn.*

wither *verb* to dry up, droop and die, to shrivel. *Flowers wither without water.*

Sue forgot to put fresh water in the vase and the flowers began to wither.

within *preposition* inside, not beyond. *They were within a mile of home.*

withhold (withhold, withholding, withheld) *verb* to hold on to and refuse to give something, to keep back. *He withheld the evidence from the court.*

without *preposition* not having, in the absence of. *He made it without any help.*

witness *noun* a person who has seen something important happen and so can describe what happened to others, especially to the police or in a law court. **witness** *verb.*

wives the plural of wife.

wizard *noun* 1 a man in fairy stories who can perform magic. 2 an expert at something. *A computer wizard.*

wobble *verb* to move in an unsteady way from side to side, to shake a little. **wobbly** *adjective. A wobbly jelly.*

woe *noun* great sorrow, misery. **woeful** *adjective. A woeful look.*

woke past tense of wake.

wolf (wolves) *noun* a wild animal of the dog family that hunts in a packs. **wolf** *verb* to eat greedily.

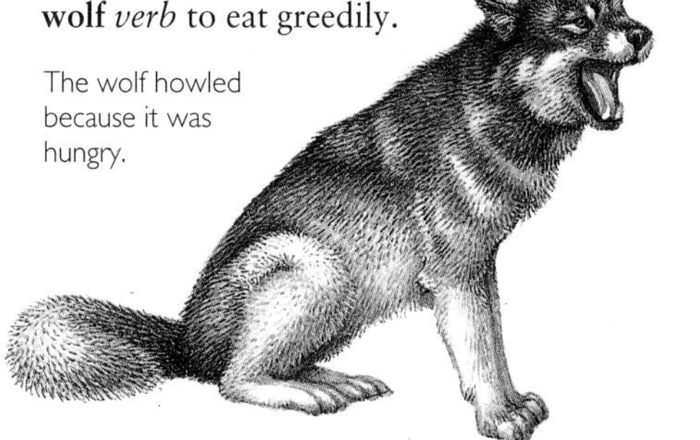

The wolf howled because it was hungry.

W

woman (women) *noun* a grown-up female human. *A truly beautiful woman.*

womb *noun* a part inside a woman or any female mammal where her young develop before being born.

wombat *noun* a small burrowing Australian marsupial related to the koala.

In Australia, there are signs by the road telling you to beware of wombats.

won past tense of win.

wonder *verb* 1 to ask yourself something, to want to know about. *I wonder what day it is.* 2 to be surprised or astounded. **wonder** *noun* 1 a feeling of surprise and amazement. 2 something so impressive that it causes a feeling of amazement.

wonderful *adjective* 1 very pleasing, excellent. *What a wonderful day.* 2 marvellous and very impressive. *Computer technology is a wonderful achievement.*

wonky *adjective* unsteady and liable to collapse. *This chair is a bit wonky.*

wood *noun* the substance that trees are made of. Furniture is usually made of wood and so is paper. 2 a place where there are a lot trees growing closely together. **woody** *adjective. Woody carrots.*

wooded *adjective* covered with trees. *A wooded mountainside.*

wooden *adjective* made of wood.

woodpecker *noun* one of a family of tree-climbing birds that have a strong pointed beak for drilling holes in trees to find insects to eat.

woodwind *noun* a group of musical instruments that you play by blowing through a mouthpiece and into a hollow tube. *The flute and clarinet are woodwind instruments.*

woodwork *noun* (the making of) things made of wood.

woodworm *noun* the larva of a beetle that makes holes in wood by feeding on it.

wool *noun* the thick hair of sheep and goats used for knitting and making cloth, the yarn made from wool.

AMAZING FACT

Wombats and other marsupials such as wallabies, opposums and kangaroos, carry their young in a pouch on their stomach where they continue their development. Australia has only marsupial mammals.

SPELLING NOTE

Try not to confuse 'wander' and 'wonder'. 'Wander' means 'to move about without trying to reach anywhere in particular'. 'Wonder' means 'something exciting, strange or marvellous'. As a verb it can also mean 'to think about' or 'to feel surprise'.

The clarinet is Helen's favourite woodwind instrument.

AMAZING FACT

Not all woodwind instruments are made of wood. Saxophones and most flutes are made of metal, while recorders are sometimes made of plastic.

woolly *adjective* made of wool. *A woolly hat keeps his head warm in winter.*

word *noun* a group of letters that mean something. We speak or write words to communicate. **give your word** to promise. **keep your word** to keep your promise. **in a word** to sum up. **word for word** each word exactly as said or written. **have words with** to quarrel.

word processor *noun* a computer with a keyboard and screen that is used to type letters, write articles, store information etc.

wore past tense of wear.

work *noun* 1 the job that somebody does to earn money. 2 the energy you use to do or make something. *Hard work.* 3 something you have made or done. *Works of art.* **work** *verb* 1 to do a job. 2 to use effort to do work. 3 to operate or make something go. *Can you work this machine?* **work out** to calculate and solve. *Work out a problem.* **have your work cut out** to have a difficult task to do.

workable *adjective* able to be done successfully. *A workable plan.*

worker *noun* somebody who works or who does a particular job. *Factory workers.*

works *plural noun* 1 the working parts of a machine. 2 a factory.

workshop *noun* a place where things are made or repaired.

world *noun* 1 the universe and space with all the stars and planets. 2 the Earth and everything on it. 3 all the things concerned with a particular subject or activity. *The world of music.* **the New World** America.

When seen from outer space, our world seems extremely fragile. On the brightly illuminated globe, we can see not only continents and oceans, but also the devastation we have caused to the world's rainforests.

worldly *adjective* interested only in money and things of the world.

worm *noun* a small, long, thin creature without legs that lives in the soil.

worn past tense of wear.

worn-out *adjective* 1 too old and no longer in a good condition. 2 exhausted. *You must be worn-out after running so far.*

worry (worries, worrying, worried) *verb* 1 to be upset and and uneasy and think something bad may happen. *She worried about leaving her dog alone all day.* 2 to trouble somebody. *Stop worrying me with your silly questions!*

worse *adjective* less good or well. More bad but not as bad as worst. *The weather was bad yesterday but it's worse today.*

worship (worships, worshipping, worshipped) *verb* 1 to pray to and give praise to God or gods, to take part in a religious ceremony. **worshipper** *noun.* 2 to love somebody very much.

worst *adjective*, *adverb* least good or well, most bad. Worst is the opposite of best.

worth *noun*, *adjective* 1 the value of something or somebody. 2 good or useful. *This job is worth doing well.*

The jewels fetched twice as much at the auction as Mary thought they were worth.

worthless *adjective* having no value, not useful. *Worthless ideas.* **worthlessness** *noun.*

worthwhile *adjective* useful and important enough to spend time on. *A worthwhile scheme is always a pleasure for the committee to consider.*

worthy *adjective* good and deserving respect. **worthiness** *noun.*

wound (rhymes with sound) past tense of wind.

wound *noun* (say **woon**-d) an injury or bad cut, especially one caused by a knife or gun etc. **wound** *verb. The soldier was badly wounded in the battle.*

wove, woven past tense and past participle of weave.

WPC *abbreviation* woman police constable.

wrap (wraps,wrapping, wrapped) *verb* to put a cover around or to fold paper, cloth etc. around. *We wrapped up Dad's present.*

wrapping *noun* paper or other material put around something to cover or protect it.

wreath *noun* flowers and leaves arranged in a circle and tied together.

wreck *verb* to destroy or ruin something completely so that it is unusable. *Vandals wrecked the bus shelter.*

AMAZING FACT

The opposite of 'worthless' is 'valuable' (meaning that it has worth) or 'priceless' (meaning so valuable that it is impossible to attach a price to it). Something may be priceless to us, not because it is worth a lot of money, but because it is something that cannot be replaced or has sentimental value.

SPELLING NOTE

Words that sound similar and should not be confused are: 'wrap' and 'rap', 'wring' and 'ring', 'write', 'right' and 'rite', and 'wrung' and 'rung'.

wreckage *noun* all the pieces that remain after something has been wrecked. *We cleared up the wreckage after the flood.*

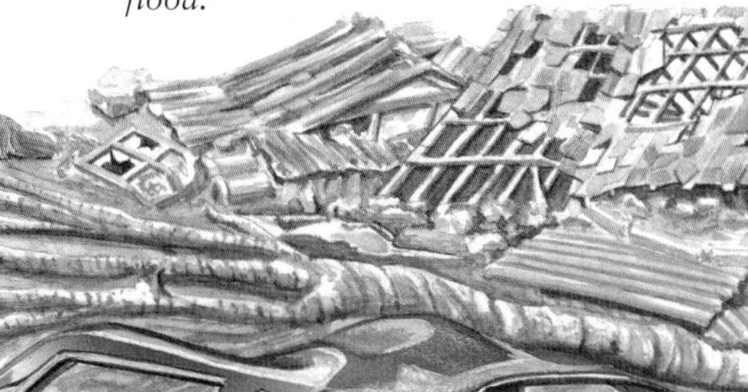

An international team of aid workers helped clear up the wreckage after the flood.

wren *noun* a very small brown bird with an upward-pointing tail.

wrench *verb* to tug or twist something with violence. *He wrenched off the lid.* **wrench** *noun* a tool used for gripping and twisting things such as nuts and bolts.

wrestle *verb* 1 to get hold of somebody and try to throw them to the ground, especially in a sport called wrestling. 2 to struggle. *I'm wrestling with my feelings.* **wrestler** *noun* somebody who wrestles as a sport.

wretched *adjective* 1 sad and very unhappy. 2 poor quality or unpleasant. *This wretched machine won't work.*

wriggle *verb* to twist and turn about. *Stop wriggling in your chair.*

wring (wrings, wringing, wrung) *verb* to force water out of a wet cloth by squeezing it. *He wrung out the wet dish cloth.*

He wrung out the flannel and laid it on the side of the bath.

wrinkle *noun* a crease or line in your skin or in cloth etc. **wrinkle** *verb.*

wrist *noun* the joint connecting your arm to your hand. *A limp wrist.*

write (writes, writing, wrote, written) *verb* 1 to form words, especially with a pen or pencil on paper. 2 to compose a book, piece of music etc. **writer** *noun* a person who writes books etc., usually to earn money.

writing *noun* 1 anything that has been written. Literature, poems etc. 2 handwriting *He has neat writing.*

wrong *adjective* 1 incorrect. The opposite is right. 2 bad and immoral. *It's wrong to lie.*

wrung past tense of wring.

wry *adjective* 1 twisted, bent. *A wry smile.* 2 slightly mocking. *A wry remark.*

WYSIWYG *abbreviation* what you see (on the screen) is what you get (when printed).

xenophobia *noun* a hatred of all foreigners.

Xmas *noun* a short informal spelling for Christmas. *Merry Xmas.*

X-ray *noun* 1 a kind of ray that can pass through solid things. 2 a photograph using x-rays of a part of the inside of your body. This enables doctors to see if anything is broken or diseased.

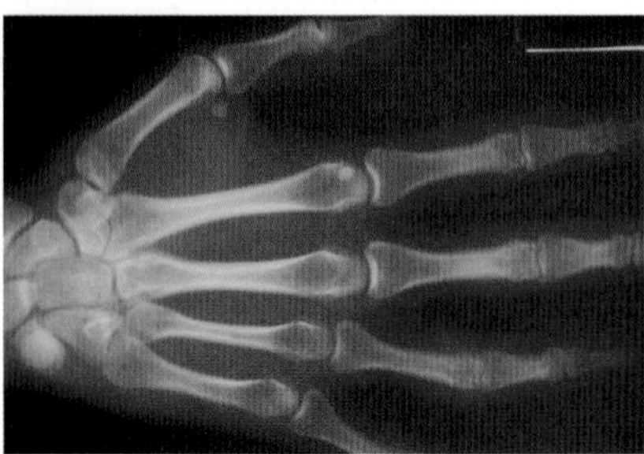

This X-ray of a human hand shows that no bones are broken.

xylophone *noun* a musical instrument with wooden bars that you hit with small hammers to make notes.

yacht *noun* a sailing boat or a small motor-driven used for cruising or for racing.

yak *noun* a long-haired ox from Tibet and the Himalayas.

yam *noun* a tropical vegetable similar to a potato. *Yams are delicious in stews.*

Yamoussoukro *noun* the capital of the Ivory Coast.

yank *verb* to pull something suddenly and violently. **yank** *noun.*

Yaoundé *noun* the capital of Cameroon.

yap *noun* the short high-pitched bark of a small dog. **yap** (yaps, yapping, yapped) *verb. Their terrier yapped at the postman.*

yard *noun* 1 a measure of length equal to 3 feet or 0.91 metres. 2 an enclosed area next to a building and sometimes used for a particular purpose. *A timber yard.* 3 (US) a garden next to a house.

WORD HISTORY

The shape of the letter X comes from an ancient Egyptian symbol for a fish. The Semites called it 'samekh', their word for a fish. The Greeks used the symbol for the sound 'ch'.

AMAZING FACT

The whole of a yeast plant is just one cell and very tiny. As a fungus, it cannot produce its own food. Instead, it lives on sugar. Yeast turns sugar into alcohol (in wine and beer making) and carbon dioxide (in bread baking). The process is called fermentation.

WORD HISTORY

The shape of the letter Y – like the letters U, V and W developed from the Semitic word 'waw', meaning 'tenthook'. The Greeks called the letter Upsilon.

yarn *noun* 1 wool or cotton spun into thread for sewing, knitting etc. 2 a long and often untrue story.

yasmak *noun* a veil worn by some Muslim women to cover all or part of their face.

Muslim women often wear a yasmak in public.

yawn *verb* to open your mouth wide and take in a deep breath because you are tired or bored. **yawn** *noun.*

year *noun* 1 the time it takes the Earth to travel once around the Sun – 365 days or 12 months or 52 weeks. 2 the period of time between 1 January and 31 December. **leap year** *noun* a year having 366 days, occurring every four years. In leap years February has 29 days.

yearly *adjective* 1 taking place once a year. 2 during or lasting a single year. *A yearly membership fee.* **yearly** *adverb.*

yeast *noun* a kind of fungus used in making bread rise and in brewing beer.

yell *noun* a loud shrill shout. **yell** *verb. He yelled above the noise of the traffic.*

yellow *noun* the colour of ripe bananas and lemons. **yellow** *adjective. Yellow roses.*

yelp *noun* a sudden, sharp sound of pain or excitement. **yelp** *verb. The dog yelped when I stood on its tail.*

Yemen *noun* a country in Southwest Asia.

The main exports of Yemen are petroleum products, cotton and fish.

yen *noun* the main Japanese unit of money.

Yerevan *noun* the capital of Armenia.

yesterday *noun, adverb* the day before today. *Today is Monday, yesterday was Sunday.*

yew *noun* an evergreen tree with dark, needle-like leaves.

yield *verb* 1 to surrender, to give up and admit defeat. *He yielded under pressure.* 2 to produce. *How much wheat does this field yield?* **yield** *noun.*

yoga *noun* an Hindu system of meditation and self-control involving exercises to exercise and relax the body and the mind.

yogurt *noun* a thick, liquid food made from soured milk. *Greek yogurt.*

yoke *noun* a bar with two pieces that fit around the necks of a pair of oxen to keep them together so they can pull a plough etc. yoke *verb.*

yolk *noun* (rhymes with oak) the yellow part in the middle of an egg.

The yolk of an egg is its most nutritious part.

Yom Kippur *noun* a Jewish holy day at the start of the Jewish New Year in mid-September. It is a time of fasting and prayer.

yonder *adjective, adverb* (old-fashioned) over there. *The bench is under yonder tree.*

young *adjective* not old, having lived or existed for only a short time. **young** *plural noun* the offspring of animals. *The young of cows are called calves.*

youngster *noun* a young person.

youth *noun* 1 the time when a person is young. *He was a gymnast in his youth.* 2 a young man. 3 young people in general.

youthful *adjective* 1 young. 2 having the qualities of being young, relating to the young. *Youthful enthusiasm.*

yo-yo *noun* a toy made of two joined discs that you make run up and down a string that you hold.

Yugoslavia *noun* a country in Europe, made up of Serbia and Montenegro.

yule *noun* Christmas.

AMAZING FACT

A zebra's stripes make them stand out in a zoo, but in their natural habitat, the grasslands of Africa, the stripes act as camouflage and help conceal them from predators.

DID YOU KNOW

The 12 signs of the zodiac are: Aries, Gemini, Taurus, Cancer, Leo, Virgo, Libra, Scorpio, Sagittarius, Capricorn, Aquarius and Pisces.

Zz

Zagreb *noun* the capital of Croatia.

Zambia *noun* a country in Africa.

Zambian *noun* a person who comes from Zambia. **Zambian** *adjective. Zambian copper mines.*

zany *adjective* funny in an odd kind of way. **zanily** *adverb.*

zap (zaps, zapping, zapped) *verb* 1 to strike or attack something suddenly in, for example, a computer game. 2 to keep changing quickly from one section of a tape, video, TV program etc.

WORD HISTORY

The shape of the letter Z developed from an ancient Egyptian symbol for an arrow. The Semites gave it the name 'zayin', their word for an arrow. The Greeks called it 'zeta'.

zeal *noun* enthusiasm, determined eagerness. *Religious zeal.*

zebra *noun* an African animal like a horse with black and white stripes on its body. **zebra crossing** a crossing place on a road marked with broad black and white stripes where traffic must stop for pedestrians.

zenith *noun* 1 the sky directly overhead. 2 the highest point, the peak or summit.

zero (zeros) *noun* nought, the name of the figure 0.

zest *noun* 1 enthusiasm, great enjoyment. *A zest for living.* 2 the outer peel of a lemon or orange.

zigzag *noun* a line that sharply bends one way then another like the letter Z. **zigzag** *verb. The path zigzagged up the hillside.*

Zimbabwe *noun* a country in Africa.

Zimbabwean *noun* a person who comes from Zimbabwe. **Zimbabwean** *adjective. Zimbabwean lakes.*

zinc *noun* a hard white metal used in alloys.

zip or zipper *noun* a long narrow fastener with two rows of teeth that can be made to lock and unlock by sliding a tab up or down. *His zip got stuck.*

zither *noun* a ancient musical instrument with strings that are plucked.

zodiac *noun* (say **zoh**-dee-ak) a band in the sky through which the Sun, Moon and planets move and which astrologers divide into twelve sections each with its own symbol or sign and name.

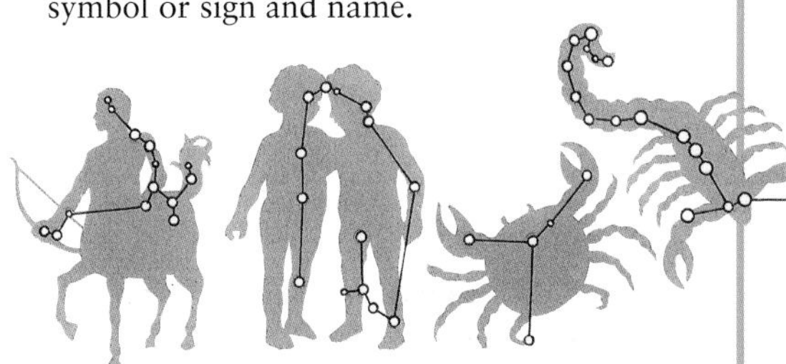

On the right are some of the signs of the zodiac as seen in the sky: Sagittarius, Gemini, Cancer and Scorpio.

zombie *noun* 1 in stories, a dead body that is brought back to life. 2 a person who does not seem to be aware of what is going on and does things without seeming to think.

zone *noun* an area that is made separate for some special purpose. *A no-parking zone.*

zoo *noun* a place where wild animals are kept for people to look at and study.

zoology *noun* (say zoo-**ol**-ogee) the scientific study of animals. **zoological** *adjective.* **zoologist** *noun.*

zoom *verb* 1 to move very quickly. 2 to focus a camera quickly from long distance to close up. **zoom lens** a camera lens that can be made to focus quickly on close-up things then far-away things.

What's wrong?

Try to correct the mistakes in these sentences.

1 Was you angry with me?

2 The cat is eating it's supper.

3 Im to busy to see you.

4 He drunk all the milk.

5 He dances good.

6 You could of said you wasn't coming.

7 Lie the book on the desk.

8 The cacti needs watering.

9 This is the widower of the late Mrs Jones.

10 Calm down and don't get so historical.

Answers 1 were 2 its 3 I'm 4 drank 5 well 6 have 7 lay 8 need 9 no late 10 hysterical.

Guess my definition

In this game you read out the definition of a word and ask your friends to say what the headword is. For example 'a soft yellow food made from cream and milk'. The answer is butter.

Matching sounds

Try to match the words that sound the same: beat him thyme cymbal steal knight meddle bear see two symbol steel beet bare time night sea medal.

Hidden words

Take a long word like 'drawing' or 'measurement' and see how many other words you can find in it. 'Drawing' contains draw, raw, win, wing, in.

Odd ones out

Which are the odd ones out in these groups:

Cod, trout, whale, herring, shark.

Car, lorry, van, aeroplane, motorbike.

Orange, apple, lamb, plum, cherry.

Backword

The word 'evil' becomes 'live' if you spell it backwards. Can you think of any other words that do this?

Code words

This code hides a simple sentence. All you have to do is read down the first column and then up the last column to find the message 'Thanks for the presents'.

TENS
HURT
AVON
NINE
KISS
SIDE
FOUR
OLOP
RISE
TOSH

In alphabetical order

Put these words in their correct alphabetical order:

Crown, cruise, crane, crow.

Live, lamb, loose, letter, likely.

Dragon, donkey, dust, dinosaur, deaf.

Sounds right

Think of a phrase or sentence using these words:

Roar, croak, neigh, bellow.

Crash, clang, bang, thud.

Kinds of

A crow is a kind of ?

A violin is a kind of ?

A beetle is a kind of ?

An apple is a kind of ?

Sets

Think of a single word for each of these sets of words:

Aluminium, brass, bronze, iron, zinc.

Plaice, cod, herring, trout.

Chair, sofa, bed, table.

Scrambled words

See if you can make new words from these words, e.g. the eyes – they see.

Angered, astronomers, evil, funeral, nameless, night, nuclear, orchestra, organ.

(Answers: enraged, moon-starers, veil, real fun, maleness/lameness, thing, unclear, groan.)

Changed

Take two words of the same length and link these two words together by putting in other words, each different from the next word by one changed letter. Here, for example, is how you could change 'head' into 'tail': HEAD HEAL TEAL TELL TALL TAIL.

Guess words

Open the dictionary at any page with a friend and read out the first and last word on that page. Your friend must try to guess other words on that page.

Chain words

A game to play with several people. Using the last two letters of the previous word make another word, e.g. reserve vest street etiquette telescope pedal alone negligent entire and so on.

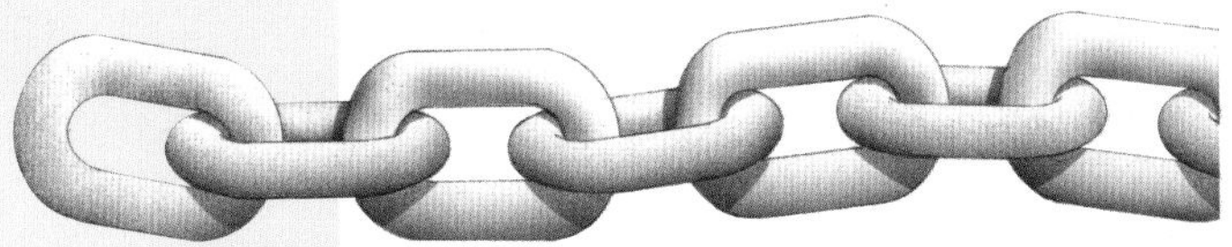

Months of the year

January was named after Janus, the Roman god of doors.

February comes from the Latin for a religious festival.

March is named after the Roman god of war. This was originally the first month of the year.

April comes from the Latin for 'to open' and refers to buds opening.

May is named after the Roman earth goddess, Maia.

June was named after Juno, the queen of the Roman gods.

July was named after Julius Caesar.

August was named after the emperor Augustus Caesar.

September was once the seventh month (after 'septem', Latin for seven).

October was the eighth month (after 'octem', Latin for eight).

November was the ninth month (after 'novem', Latin for nine).

December was the tenth month (after 'decem', Latin for ten).

Some general spelling rules

(But always remember there are lots of exceptions to most rules!)

Nouns

To make a noun plural you normally add 's' – road roads, cake cakes.

But if the noun ends in -ch, -s, -ss, -sh or -x you add -es –

Ass asses, church churches, bush bushes, bus buses, mix mixes.

Nouns ending in a consonant plus a 'y' lose the 'y' and add -ies –

Baby babies, copy copies.

Many nouns ending in 'o' generally add -es – Cargo cargoes, hero heroes.

Plurals that do not follow these rules are shown in the dictionary –

child children, mouse mice.

Some nouns that are always plural in form:

Scissors, shears, oats, clothes, pyjamas, trousers, measles, spectacles.

Some very irregular plurals:

Man men, mouse mice, woman women, goose geese, mouse mice, foot feet, tooth teeth, ox oxen.

Some nouns that are both singular and plural in form:

Fish, sheep, deer.

Adverbs

Adverbs are usually formed by adding -ly to the adjective – Odd oddly, amazing amazingly, quick quickly.

But if the adjective ends in -ll, just add -y – Dull dully.

If the adjective ends in -le, drop the -le and add -ly –

Simple simply.

If the adjective ends in -ic, add ally –

Historic historically.

(A notable exception is public publicly.)

Adverbs that do not follow these rules will be found in the dictionary.

Adjectives

To most adjectives of one syllable you normally add -er to make a comparative –

Near nearer, fast faster – Anne can run faster than her sister.

And you add -est to make a superlative –

Nearest, fastest – Andy is the fastest runner in his class.

If the adjective ends in -e just add 'r' or 'st' –

Simple simpler simplest.

With some short adjectives ending with a consonant the consonant is doubled –

Red redder reddest.

With adjectives of more than two syllables use 'more' and 'most' for the comparative and superlative –

Careful, more careful, most careful. He's the most careful person I know.

Adjectives that do not follow these rules will be shown in the dictionary, for example –

Bad worse worst, good better best.

Verbs

To make the present participle, past tense and past participle to most regular verbs you add -ing, or -ed or -d –

Talk talking talked, pray praying prayed.

If the verb ends in 'e', the 'e' is dropped and -ing, or -ed are added –

Tame taming tamed.

The final consonant is doubled when a short word ends in a consonant –

Chat chatting chatted, slam slamming slammed.

I before E

'I before e except after c' is a good general rule, but only applies if the 'ie' in the word is pronounced like an 'ee'. So it is 'ie' in words such as field, believe and siege, and 'e' in words such as ceiling and receipt.

Some exceptions are: either, neither (which can be pronounced 'ee'), seize, weird, protein, and certain names such as Keith and Neil.

Words like eight, deign, reign and neighbour are spelled with 'ei' because they are not pronounced 'ee'.

Apostrophies

The possessive form of a noun is shown by writing ''s' at the end –

The boy's book.

The children's house.

Charles's bike.

When a noun is plural with the ending 's', add an apostrophe alone –

The girls' mother.

Each other or one another

Use 'each other' for two –

The two boys helped each other.

Use 'one another' for more than two.

All the children helped one another.

Double negative

'I never said nothing' is incorrect if what you want to say is 'I never said anything'. But it is correct if what you want to say is 'At no time did I ever say nothing'.

Aa Bb Cc

Gg Hh Ii Jj

Nn Oo Pp

Uu Vv Ww

Dd Ee Ff

Kk Ll Mm

Qq Rr Ss Tt

Xx Yy Zz

Acknowledgements

The publishers would like to thank the following artists who have contributed to this book:

The Maltings Partnership
Andrew Clark
Julie Banyard
Gill Platt
Sally Launder
Wayne Ford
Guy Smith
Mike Saunders

All photographs supplied by Miles Kelly Archives.